AMERICAN DEFENSE POLICY

AMERICAN DEFENSE POLICY
Second Edition

Edited by:

MARK E. SMITH III   CLAUDE J. JOHNS, JR.
Associate Professor   *Tenure Associate Professor*

With a Foreword by:

RICHARD F. ROSSER
Professor and Head

Department of Political Science
United States Air Force Academy
Colorado

The Johns Hopkins Press, Baltimore

Dedicated to

WESLEY W. POSVAR
Soldier–Scholar–Colleague

FOREWORD: THE STUDY OF AMERICAN DEFENSE POLICY

Every citizen must be concerned with American defense policy. No subject today is ultimately more vital to the people of the United States. Never has the defense of the nation been a more urgent task, and never a more complex problem. The military power of the United States is immense, yet security of the vital interests of our nation is increasingly difficult to achieve. To see why this is so we must examine the fundamental changes in the international environment since World War II.

The first change is technological. The twilight of World War II saw the dawn of the nuclear era, and the primitive prototypes of nuclear delivery systems—jet aircraft and ballistic missiles. In the midst of the last great wartime conference at Potsdam, President Truman received a cryptic message on July 16, 1945, announcing the first atomic test at Alamogordo, New Mexico: "Operated on this morning. Diagnosis not yet complete but results seem satisfactory and already exceed expectations." In a few weeks the atomic bomb would be ready for Hiroshima. The full implications of this revolutionary weapon, however, could not be imagined. The hydrogen bomb, still to be developed, would have a hundred times the destructive force of the crude atomic device. And once perfected, the new weapons could not be forgotten no matter how horrible they proved to be. Technological change is not reversible.

One week after news of Alamogordo, Truman privately informed Stalin of the new weapon. Stalin was delighted—what a bit of luck! Churchill thought Stalin hadn't understood the significance for he failed to ask one question about the experiment. Molotov later claimed that Stalin understood this to be a "super bomb," the like of which had never been seen—but not an "atomic" bomb. Some were ready to believe Stalin was this naive, and Russia this backward. The Russians would not have their "bomb" for a hundred years, it was predicted. In reality, Stalin would soon launch a crash program to develop nuclear weapons and their delivery systems. On September 23, 1949, President Truman announced that an atomic explosion had been detected in the Soviet Union. The United States could no longer rest comfortably with its nuclear monopoly. If we soon could destroy an aggressor with one climactic stroke, the time would come when we could face the same fate.

The second great change in the international environment was wrought by more conventional weapons—and the Russian foot soldier. The distribution of power in the international political system had been radically altered. Gaping holes existed in Europe and the Far East with the defeat of the Third Reich and the Japanese empire. Britain and France, kingpins of the interwar security system, could no longer assume the burden of maintaining the peace. Although Churchill was loath to admit it, the sun was setting on the British Empire. The French nation then seemed to reside mainly in the obstinate and visionary General de Gaulle.

Perhaps the fundamental alteration in the balance of power was the appearance of a new kind of nation-state—the superpower. There were two—the United States and the Soviet Union. Before World War II, America had been isolationist, Russia had been isolated. Now their armies had met on the Elbe in the heart of Europe. Because of their new world interests, neither state could ignore the other.

America's new role, which she accepted with some hesitation, required profound changes in American defense policy. For over 150 years the United States had been a reluctant participant in world politics. Except for a brief foray abroad in the latter days of World War I "to make the world safe for democracy," Americans lived a relatively secure and tranquil life. The rape of Ethiopia and Czechoslovakia was deplorable but not our concern. Our security supposedly was not involved. Two huge oceans protected us from invasion. We tended to forget that other nations were carrying the burden of opposing aggression.

We were lucky to have England and Churchill. We also found that the Pacific was not quite the barrier we supposed on December 7, 1941.

After World War II, American national security clearly depended on American military power. Allies were helpful, but they were dependent on us for economic and military aid. More important, the tremendous cost of nuclear weaponry dictated that the ultimate military power of the Western world would come only from the United States. The primary threat to the security of the United States could come only from the other superpower—the Soviet Union. The USSR, as should all nations, worried first about its own security. But its leaders were dedicated followers of an ideology called Marxism–Leninism. This ideology predicted the inevitable transformation of country after country to communism, and the Soviet leaders had a moral duty to support such transformations. The confrontation between the two superpowers thus seemed preordained. There was a fundamental conflict of interest involved because the United States was opposed to an extension of the communist system. The Cold War resulted—and is not yet over.

Even in the darkest days of the Cold War, neither nation appeared to seriously consider a frontal attack on the other. Each soon realized the power of nuclear weapons and the probable result of a nuclear exchange on their countries. Each was concerned with perfecting its deterrent, which it hoped never to use. The primary conflict therefore would not take place between the two superpowers, but in the area now called the "Third World."

The third fundamental change in the international political system after World War II was the emergence of the Third World, composed of the so-called "developing" nations. For centuries, Europe had been the center of the world political system. European powers controlled vast empires and dominated the few independent countries of Africa and Asia. (More recently, the United States had made Latin America a special domain.)

As Western power disintegrated after World War II, colony after colony gained independence. But freedom did not usher in the land of plenty. Economically, politically, and socially the new states—they were not yet really "nations"—lived essentially as they had for centuries.

The process of political and economic development inevitably created profound strains on each society. Opportunities appeared for leftist, sometimes communist, parties to gain power under the guise of "national liberation" movements. In the West, such movements were often seen as extensions of the Soviet empire, and Soviet communism had to be "contained."

Yet in the space of twenty-five years, one fact is obvious. Change has not stopped. Indeed, the world today and in the foreseeable future is more complex, the challenges to United States national security more serious, and American defense policy more vital a subject than ever before.

To begin with, the military-technological revolution has not ceased. The primitive device dropped in 1945 bears little relation to the sophisticated intercontinental missile with its multiple, separately targetable, thermonuclear warheads. At the same time, the knowledge and technology to build the simpler nuclear weapons is widely diffused. Moreover, they can be built more cheaply than ever. It is entirely possible to soon have a world of not five nuclear powers, but twenty.

Delivery systems also have undergone drastic change. The German V–2 flew several hundred miles and sometimes hit London. Today, the intercontinental ballistic missile can travel thousands of miles and hit its target with amazing accuracy. Moreover, the present balance in favor of offensive weapons is being challenged. The United States and the Soviet Union are developing antiballistic missile systems. To counteract such systems, each nation must in turn increase the sophistication of its missile delivery systems and their warheads. The technological race seems endless. New weapons systems are obsolescent before they enter the inventory.

The political dominance of the superpowers also is in question. The so-called

Soviet empire—"monolithic" communism—no longer exists. (Even in its heyday, the bloc was never fully under Moscow's control.) Communist China is Russia's main competitor for leader of the socialist camp. But Yugoslavia has held an independent course for twenty years, and now even Czechoslovakia is giving Moscow fits.

Because the Soviets today have so little direct control, indeed little influence in some cases, over other communist states and parties, it is misleading to talk of a general "communist" threat. In addition, it is incorrect to assume that communist inspired activity in any given country is directly influenced by one communist state. Within most parties there are now Soviet and Chinese wings, and in Latin America, Castroite factions. All this does not mean, of course, that the threat of "communism" no longer exists. It is merely diffused and much more complex. In response, American policy-makers must create a defense policy to meet the constantly changing threat from the many strains of communism.

Similarly, the Western alliance is in disrepair. In effect, France has left NATO. Other NATO members question the continuing relevance of this defense organization. The threat is not as evident since the USSR appears to accept the status quo in Europe. Meanwhile, Western Europe makes steady progress toward economic, and perhaps eventually political, integration. The resulting political unit will almost certainly be a third superpower. America's defense relationship with a United Europe inevitably would differ from the present NATO system. The new superpower might acquire its own nuclear arsenal and weapons delivery systems matching the sophistication of those held by the United States and the USSR.

Finally, developments in the Third World have not always matched predictions. The Western powers and the communist states have given much economic and military aid to the developing countries. The influence of the "northern" industrialized states on the "southern" area has not been in direct proportion to this support. The developing countries are eager for aid from wherever it may come, as long as they can avoid foreign domination. They do not want to be pawns in the East-West struggle. The so-called national liberation movements, even where communist influence is significant, generally are more nationalist than communist. American defense policy must adapt to this possibility.

In summary, the threats to American security today and in the future will be diverse and of complex composition. To be successful, the defense policy of the United States must be carefully attuned to the constantly changing face of international conflict. Perhaps the greatest challenge will be the accurate determination of whether or not an international crisis directly threatens the vital interests of the United States.

Meanwhile, the ultimate hope is that all states someday will settle conflicts without the use of force, that leaders and peoples will find satisfactory and peaceful alternatives to military power in their respective national interests. The final result may not be general and complete disarmament, long the goal of those who would replace the state system with a world government. But any lowering of the level of tension will be desirable—provided peace with justice results. To this end, American policymakers must develop a defense policy which provides satisfactory national security at each progressive step in arms control negotiations.

Having set the international stage, it is now appropriate to discuss the specific field of American defense policy. For many years Americans had been writing on international politics, on foreign policy, on military strategy—but not on the unique ground where these subjects meet—American defense policy. Strategy had been treated as separate from foreign policy objectives. Once in war, America fought for victory and then worried about the political settlement. (The "unconditional surrender" formula of World War II was the most recent reminder.) In peacetime, United States policymakers had shunned the limited use of military force to achieve foreign policy objectives. This in turn reflected the inability of Americans to understand the realities of international politics and America's responsibility to fight for international peace with justice.

After World War II, it became painfully evident that much thinking was needed to devise theoretical guidance for American policymakers in their attempts to insure national security in an entirely new international environment. The old simplistic prewar (and wartime) approach to national security questions would not suffice. American defense policy, a new field of study integrating the concepts and approaches of international politics, foreign policy, and military strategy, was born. The theoreticians were scholars from the traditional disciplines generally writing in direct response to government request, or military staff officers attempting to meet the new challenges to their profession. The questions were so serious and policymakers so concerned that government could not wait for academe to discover the new field of study.

Today, political scientists are heavily represented in the field of defense policy, but the breadth and seriousness of the questions involved concern scholars from many disciplines: economics, psychology, sociology, history, physics, to name a few. And each discipline has something to contribute to the study of defense policy, given the ramifications of the subject for all phases of national and international life.

In addition to the central concerns of the new subject, interest has developed in the process by which defense policy is formulated and the institutions involved in the process. It is evident that sound policy is generally the result of careful consideration and full analysis of all alternatives. The integration of relevant organizations in the decisionmaking process therefore is a critical ingredient in the formulation of a successful defense policy. The budgetary process is of particular interest because decisions about weapons systems involve staggering cost, and the efficient allocation of scarce resources. The proper organization of the Department of Defense also is of special concern. The result of the interest in process and institutions is another facet in the study of defense policy.

The subject of American defense policy in all its ramifications is of vital interest to the military profession. Members of the armed forces wield the weapons, the ultimate sanction of military power. Yet the responsibility of the professional soldier today does not end on the battlefield. President Kennedy told the graduating class of the United States Air Force Academy on June 5, 1963:

Your major responsibilities, of course, will relate to the obligations of military command. Yet, as last October's crisis in the Caribbean so aptly demonstrated, military policy and power cannot and must not be separated from political and diplomatic decisions. . . . We needed in October—and we shall need in the future—military commanders who are conscious of the enormous stakes involved in every move they make—who are aware of the fact that there is no point where a purely political problem becomes a purely military problem—who know the difference between vital interests and peripheral interests—who can maneuver military forces with judgment and precision as well as courage and determination—and who can foresee the effects of military moves on the whole fabric of international power.

The armed services need soldiers who are also scholars. Learning can never cease because the military profession in the twentieth century is infinitely complex and the parameters of defense constantly changing.

There is tension, of course, in the character of the soldier-scholar. The soldier must function in a disciplined and highly structured organization. The scholar must constantly question the most sacred dogmas of his profession in the endless search for truth. Yet the roles can be compatible. The soldier-scholar searches for new answers to defense problems, but ultimately acquiesces in the decision of his civilian and military superiors. The role of the soldier always must prevail.

The education of the soldier-scholar in the complexities of defense policy should begin early, preferably during his undergraduate education. This requirement has been particularly obvious to leading military educators at the service academies. At the United States Military Academy, Colonel George A. Lincoln, Professor and

Head of the Department of Social Sciences, has long been a driving force in the development of the soldier-scholar concept. His work in turn was an inspiration to other military educators. Brigadier General Robert F. McDermott, the first permanent Dean of the Faculty of the United States Air Force Academy, in particular saw the potentialities of American defense policy as a new academic subject and quickly introduced it into the basic curriculum at the new Academy. The subsequent development of defense policy as a field of interest was a constant concern of Wesley W. Posvar, the first permanent professor and head of the Department of Political Science at the Air Force Academy. Until his retirement in 1967 to become Chancellor of the University of Pittsburgh, Colonel Posvar for ten years led his colleagues in a continual effort to collect the latest and best materials in defense policy, and to develop a conceptual framework for the presentation of this complex subject.

The first edition of this book, published in 1965, was the direct result of the efforts of Colonel Posvar and his colleagues to present the subject of defense policy in a logical framework. Colonel Posvar and Captain John C. Ries (now Professor of Political Science at the University of California at Los Angeles) were the editors-in-chief of the first edition. They in turn had built upon the work of earlier directors of the Academy's required course in defense policy: John J. Boyne; John W. Carley; Donald W. Galvin; William F. Lackman, Jr.; Larry J. Larsen; and Thomas C. Pinckney. Colonels William G. McDonald and Brent Scowcroft also played a vital role in the production of the first edition while serving as acting chairmen of the Department of Political Science in 1963 and 1964, respectively.

The present edition is essentially a new book. Because of the rapidly developing field of defense policy, ninety per cent of the articles were not in the first edition. Almost three fourths of these articles have been written since 1965. Moreover, the book has been expanded by some twenty per cent.

New issues and emphases are found in the second edition: a more sophisticated treatment of limited war and counterinsurgency; greater weight on the decision-making process, including theories of bargaining and compellence; arms control as a special strategy, including the antiballistic missile question; and alternatives to the use of force. Over-all, the major integrating theme is the necessity of limiting the use of force in the era of credible and invulnerable second-strike capabilities. Finally, the revised edition has a number of articles considerably more sophisticated than similar selections in the earlier work. We believe, however, that the more sophisticated materials can be understood by the contemporary undergraduate. We have tested the new articles on the junior and senior cadets in our basic defense policy course. The results have been pleasantly surprising.

The editors of the revised edition are Major Claude J. Johns, Jr., Tenure Associate Professor, and Major Mark E. Smith, III, Associate Professor, both of the Department of Political Science. They have been aided by Captains Roy W. Stafford and Charles A. May, Jr., of the Department. Valuable suggestions on the manuscript were given by Assistant Secretary of Defense Alain C. Enthoven, Professor William W. Kaufmann of the Massachusetts Institute of Technology, and Professor Raymond H. Dawson of the University of North Carolina. Invaluable editorial assistance was provided by Mrs. Jackie Bouker at the Academy and Mrs. Nancy Gallienne at The Johns Hopkins Press.

As before, we have built on the years of hard work of the long list of able soldier-scholars mentioned earlier, particularly the efforts of Wesley W. Posvar and John C. Ries. In this sense, the revised edition is a corporate product of the military profession. We hope that it will make a contribution to the field of defense policy, and will be of aid to practitioners, scholars, and students.

RICHARD F. ROSSER

April, 1968
U.S. Air Force Academy, Colorado

CONTENTS

xivCONTENTS

Davis B. Bobrow: Chinese Views on Escalation............................ 326
Charles L. M. Ailleret: Directed Defense................................. 331

Part II. American Defense Policymaking: The Management of Force.......... 337
Chapter 6.   Organization of Defense Policymaking.......................... 339
Wesley W. Posvar: Dispersion of the Strategy-making Establishment........ 340
Harry H. Ransom: Department of Defense: Unity or Confederation?........ 361
Lawrence B. Tatum: The Joint Chiefs of Staff and Defense Policy Formulation 377
Gene M. Lyons: The New Civil-Military Relations........................ 392
Jack Raymond: The "McNamara Monarchy"............................. 405

Chapter 7.   Methods of Defense Policymaking............................. 415
Burton M. Sapin: Intelligence, Planning, and Policy Analysis.............. 416
Harold Brown: Planning Our Military Forces............................ 432
Charles J. Hitch: Development and Salient Features of the Programming System 440
Wesley W. Posvar: The Easy Magic of Systems Analysis................... 455
Anatol Rapoport: The Outcomes are Partially Controlled by Another....... 467
Norman C. Dalkey: Simulation.. 482

Part III: Arms and Morality: The Paradoxical Effects of Force............... 491
Chapter 8.   The Just Use of Force: Nuclear Deterrence and Limited Inter-
        vention 493
Alain C. Enthoven: Moral Aspects.................................... 494
Hans J. Morgenthau: To Intervene or Not to Intervene................. 496

Chapter 9.   The Effects of Force: The Warfare State and American Democracy 503
Samuel P. Huntington: Civil-Military Relations in the Postwar Decade...... 504
Harry Howe Ransom: Defense and Democracy.......................... 521

Chapter 10.   Critiques of Deterrence: Alternatives to Force.................. 525
Gene Sharp: Control of Political Power and Conduct of Open Struggle...... 526
Kenneth E. Boulding: Epilogue: The Present Crisis of Conflict and Defense.. 538

Index 547

INTRODUCTION

Nation-states interact in many ways: politically, economically, and socially. As these relations became more complicated and more scholarship was devoted to them, the broad study of international relations was divided into international politics, international economics, international law, etc. As the complexities and the scholarship continued to increase, further subdivisions were developed to permit more specialization. International military affairs is one such specialty.

To further narrow the discussion, we focus on American defense policy in this book. While this makes the subject more manageable, we still find that there are some issues that must be either oversimplified or omitted. Focusing on the United States is generally acceptable because we have pioneered in nuclear and limited war strategies. However, for insurgencies this may be a disadvantage until the lessons of Vietnam are clear. For American readers the concern with American policy is obviously pragmatic.

In Chapter 1 we present the two linchpin concepts around which the remainder of the book pivots. These two concepts involve both the role of nuclear weapons and the role of the national interest.

Despite beliefs that the acquisition of the first few nuclear weapons provided the capability instantly and automatically to obliterate an enemy, we were several years into the nuclear era before the United States really had the ability to inflict upon the Soviet Union a level of destruction so devastating that reasonable men could agree that it would be unacceptable to the Soviets. And it was later still before the Soviet Union developed the same capability against the U.S. In addition, quite a different capability is required to wreak "unacceptable damage" when one is striking second after absorbing the enemy's surprise counterforce attack, than when one is striking first. The former, a second-strike capability, is called "assured destruction."

When considering nuclear strategy, a simplified model of the opposing nations may be thought of as consisting of two elements: *values*, people and property, which are mainly grouped into cities; and *forces*, the strategic capabilities that are used to protect or attack the homelands. Again in the early days of the nuclear era, it was relatively easy to destroy forces, but difficult to destroy all the values of a major nation-state. In contrast today, because of the increased numbers, dispersal, mobility, concealment, and hardening of their strategic forces, both the United States and the Soviet Union have an "assured destruction" capability against each other. That is, each can destroy an "unacceptable" amount of the other's *values*, but not enough of the other's *forces* to prevent an "unacceptable" retaliation. Thus the most startling characteristic of the Sixties is that for the first time in history there are two states mutually able to annihilate each other. Moreover, the possibility exists that this number will increase.

In this book, we refer to nations that possess an "assured destruction" capability as superpowers. An all-out nuclear war, at least between superpowers, is therefore often spoken of as "unthinkable." Indeed, the effects of the unprecedented catastrophe of thermonuclear holocaust stagger the mind. Knowing that one's society would be destroyed, what national objective could possibly justify starting such a war? Yet an all-out thermonuclear war between superpowers can occur. There is no guarantee that the "unthinkable" will be the "undo-able." There is always some possibility of accident, error, or miscalculation. In addition, lesser uses of force have continued, as the number of international conflicts since World War II clearly demonstrates. The smaller wars have involved the superpowers and there is no assurance that in the future these lower levels of conflict will not escalate into thermonuclear war.

The capabilities for mutual destruction and the possibility that those capabilities might be used is the first consideration of Chapter 1. The second consideration is the national interest.

xvi   INTRODUCTION

We recognize that defense policy is but a part of foreign policy. There are other tools—diplomacy, economic persuasion, international organizations, world opinion —for obtaining the goals of our foreign policy. Yet military force is of peculiar importance in relations between nations. The basic relationship is that foreign policy directs and shapes defense policy. In fact, foreign policy establishes the objectives for defense policy.

A major burden of our military policymakers then, is to devise strategies which promote our national interests and at the same time give the greatest assurance of avoidance of general war. Therefore, the overwhelming imperative weighing on the minds and consciences of today's strategists is the limitation of force in order to minimize the possibility of a nuclear Armageddon. We have adopted the limited employment of force as the theme of Part I: Defense Policies.

We define force as the distinguishing feature of defense policy (as some define power as the distinguishing feature of politics). The book is organized into three parts based on three facets of force: the limited employment of force, the management of force, and the paradoxical effects of force.

We examine specific defense policies regarding the employment of force in Part I. This part is subdivided into five major headings: general (central) war, arms control, limited (noncentral) war, counterinsurgency, and other nations' views. The major topics explored in the consideration of general war strategies are theories and strategies of deterrence and defense. Arms control is considered as a special strategy. In the extensive chapter on limited war, the theory of limitation and the concepts of alliances, flexible response, compellence, escalation, and counterinsurgency are presented. In the final chapter of Part I some military doctrines and strategies of the Soviets, Chinese, and French are analyzed as important "other views" on the modern employment of force.

In Part II we examine the management of force in terms of the American defense environment. The first section deals with the organization of defense decisionmaking. We see this arrangement as funnel shaped. At the broad end of the funnel are the many and dispersed organizations which are primarily involved in providing relevant data and analysis to help the decisionmaker. At the nozzle is decisionmaking, which has become increasingly centralized. The complicated activity which goes on in the entire funnel is described within the framework of civil-military relations.

In the second chapter of Part II, we review specific analytical methods such as systems analysis, cost-effectiveness, game theory, and gaming, the roles of intelligence, planning, and programming, and the decisionmakers themselves, to give some appreciation for the complex nature not only of decisionmaking, but also of modern warfare. For example, it should become apparent that it is unlikely that any President would ever plan a retaliatory response to an attack by the North Vietnamese upon United States destroyers in the Tonkin Gulf or to the seizure of the *U.S.S. Pueblo* by the North Koreans, based upon game theory. However, the utility of game theory in providing the student with some insights about reacting to attacks, ship seizures, or other crisis situations should also become apparent.

In Part III we continue the examination of force and concentrate upon its sometimes paradoxical effects. More specifically, we believe there is the ever-present danger that force in some respects destroys, or at least may destroy, that which it is created to protect and preserve, even when the force is not directly employed. Internationally, there is the question of when the use of force is just, a problem that is particularly difficult at the extremes of the spectrum of violence: nuclear deterrence and limited interventions. In the first case, it is paradoxical for the superpowers to maintain nuclear forces that are useless if used. In the second case, changes in the nature of aggression have clouded the justification of the use of force against it. In the earlier part of this century, aggression usually was clear because it involved the use of mass, uniformed armies that attacked across recognized traditional borders. Containment or counterattack was more easily justified in moral terms because it was distinctly "self-defensive." Today aggression is considerably less clear because it involves guerrillas, "wars of national liberation," and states whose legitimate boundaries may be in question. When American force is used against these forms of aggression it is interpreted by many persons as "intervention"—a form of response that is less distinctly defensive than a classic counterattack. And since these types of aggression are the most likely pattern of future aggression, the problem of "just wars" is even more significant.

These two external effects are also reflected on the internal or domestic scene in the United States. The maintenance of the forces necessary to deter or fight an attacker may lead to a warfare or garrison state in which our domestic values may be sacrificed on the altar of national security. This is the paradoxical worry: What if deterrence works? The "just war" becomes a problem of preserving national unity when the threats are the ambiguous cases of insurgency or subversion and American force is used in response.

The last chapter presents an alternative to the use of organized military force, namely civilian resistance. The final article summarizes the crises that many see in the paradoxical effects of military force.

Defense policy is a relatively new field of academics. As such there is no accepted organizing concept and there are gaps in any framework adopted. The structure we use—the employment, the management, and the effects of force—is based on some simple ideas.

One underlying belief is that two of the basic approaches to the study of political science and government should be used. One should study both the substantive issues and the process of deciding the issues. Thus, we have Part I on defense policies and Part II on the American defense environment. The problem here is: Which approach should be studied first? One can understand each subject better if he already knows the other. Logic would suggest reading the process first and then the output of the process, the policies. Certainly that is the accepted way for the well-developed field of American government. However, here at the Air Force Academy we have taught the course both ways and experience has shown that it is preferable to study the policies first. Pragmatically, students seem to follow and understand the course better and, theoretically, they are better able to judge the process if they understand the problems and policies it is dealing with. In American defense policy, in contrast to American government, the policies loom more important than the process.

To the two basic approaches we added Part III, the paradoxical effects of force. We believe that the often long-range, unintended, and nonmilitary effects of force are best considered after looking at both the policies and the process. These effects must be weighed when making the final evaluation of the earlier parts.

The editors, and the authors who are members of the Department of Political Science at the Air Force Academy, have presented their personal views in this volume. These views do not necessarily represent those of the United States Government.

M.E.S.
C.J.J.

April, 1968
U.S. Air Force Academy, Colorado

AMERICAN DEFENSE POLICY

CHAPTER 1

Nuclear Weapons and the National Interest

One of the most fundamental considerations in the formulation and execution of American defense policy is the present and potential impact of nuclear and thermonuclear weapons. The United States and some of its adversaries and allies prepare for a war that none wishes to wage. And this fact raises significant questions: Has the appearance of nuclear multi-megaton weapons, which erased the invulnerability of the United States and gave the United States and the Soviet Union the capability to destroy each other, made the use of force obsolete? Have these weapons led to a bankruptcy of force in the modern state system? Have nuclear weapons superseded the "tried and true" conventional weapons, or can the "tried and true" weapons still be used without a concomitant escalation into a nuclear conflict?

Over half a century ago, Henry Adams observed that "during a million or two of years, every generation in turn had toiled with endless agony to attain and apply power, all the while betraying the deepest alarm and horror at the power they had created." If he were living today, one wonders whether Adams' talent for expression would be equal to describing the impact of nuclear weapons upon the minds and actions of men.

The first reading by Bernard Brodie has been the primer for the understanding of the impact of nuclear weapons. The experience and strategic concepts and doctrines of World War II are examined to determine whether they provide guidance for future military operations. Nuclear weapons were, of course, integrated into existing strategic concepts without complete realization of the extent to which the concepts were inadequate to the advance in weaponry. For example, Brodie expounds and critiques Doughet's theory that command of the air should be won by bombing and that this command ensures victory. In 1959 this pioneering student of nuclear strategy felt that with "The Advent of Nuclear Weapons" Doughet's theory had been vindicated since nuclear strategic bombardment is "bound to be decisive," destroying both strategic forces, population and industrial centers. A decade later Professor Brodie would qualify these statements, but the major significance of his seminal work is the lesson that an all-out nuclear exchange between superpowers would destroy them as viable societies. Brodie invites the reader to reflect upon the altered nature of war and the kinds of military posture suited to deal with it.

The major theme of the second article by Morton Halperin, in his words, is that "force does continue to play a role despite the development of thermonuclear weapons and intercontinental ballistic missiles." He rejects the more extreme views that nuclear weapons have abolished war, that nuclear weapons have made war unthinkable, and that preventive nuclear war is the way to produce peace. At higher levels of conflict the nuclear bomb has been a powerful international stabilizer. The United States, the Soviet Union, and their allies have relied upon either nonmilitary political instruments or conventional, limited military forces to settle disputes in the postwar period. Halperin accounts for the relative stability by pointing out that vital interests of the major powers have not been challenged, which he feels produces what he calls "the central paradox of the Nuclear Age: total ideological conflict plus total means of destruction have produced a situation in which a total solution is impossible."

Since military forces continue to be used as instruments for settling disputes among the nations of the world, perhaps the most fundamental problem for American policymakers is to decide when or under what conditions U.S. force will be used. The basic rationale for the existence of American military force is that it is a deterrent, but if it is used it must be controlled and limited. It exists to protect our vital interests, our national security. What, then, are our vital interests? What is national security? These concepts are obviously abstract and obscure. Nevertheless, since any armed conflict in which the United States engages is justified only in terms of protection of its "interests" or its "security," there must be a constant attempt to translate these concepts into operational goals capable of implementation. This necessity is dramatically reflected in the war in Southeast Asia. The focus of the debate regarding U.S. involvement in the war is the question of whether or not the independence of South Vietnam is "vital to U.S. interests."

As Lincoln Bloomfield points out, "to try to identify and put into words the vital interests of the United States is as difficult as it is presumptuous." Indeed, even though any such undertaking is fraught with imprecision and even though it is doubtful that any list would gain consensus among reasonable men, the effort must be made! How else can we intelligently affect our own destiny? Bloomfield, with courage, common sense, and elegance, suggests as our paramount national objective: "to create the sort of world environment around us in which the United States can survive with its own values intact." He then suggests seven middle-range objectives for our country.

THE ADVENT OF NUCLEAR WEAPONS

BY BERNARD BRODIE

People often speak of atomic explosives as the most portentous military invention "since gunpowder." But such a comparison inflates the importance of even so epoch-making an event as the introduction of gunpowder.

Those who lived through the first military use of gunpowder, sometime in the early part of the fourteenth century, seem to have been quite unexcited about it, and actually failed to record the occasion. Not until a century later, at the siege of Orleans in 1428–1429, do we find firearms, in this case siege guns, playing a major part in battle, though still an indecisive one. In leading the final storming of that city, Joan of Arc was wounded by an arrow.

Gunpowder is often said to have established the superiority of the infantryman over the armored knight, and thus to have helped spell the death of feudalism. But the ascendancy of the infantryman, even without firearms, was in fact demonstrated effectively by English archers at Crecy (1346), Poitiers (1356), and Agincourt (1415), and during the same period by other foot soldiers elsewhere in Europe. A shrewder interpretation has held that it was not firearms but the reintroduction of discipline on the battlefield—lost since Roman times—that caused the demise of the armored, mounted knight.

When in 1605—three centuries after the introduction of firearms—Cervantes published the first part of his great novel that buried in mockery the Age of Chivalry, the flintlock had not yet been invented. Field artillery did not become important until the Seven Years War, in the middle of the eighteenth century. As late as the American Revolution, so sensible a man as Benjamin Franklin was able seriously to consider the wisdom of arming the Continental soldiers with bows and arrows rather than with the cumbersome, slow-firing, unreliable, and grossly inaccurate muskets. Not until the middle of the nineteenth century —five centuries after the first military use of gunpowder—did we enter the age of modern firearms, with the development in all arms of breech loading and rifling and, in artillery pieces, of explosive projectiles.

In short, when we speak of the revolution wrought by gunpowder, we are talking about something that required centuries to accomplish. It required also centuries of perspective to discern. Yet the gradualness of the development, with all the opportunities it permitted for doctrinal adjustment in the military arts, is still not the crux of the matter. The gun and its relatives remained from first to last strictly *tactical* weapons, gradually displacing weapons such as the battering ram, the arrow, the sword, and the lance, but only by proving superior in the same functions that those weapons had exercised on the battlefield.

At least until World War I, which for the first time produced the phenomenon of nationwide continuous lines that could not be outflanked, the study of military strategy and of the grand tactics of battles, whether of land or sea, could profitably proceed from the study of campaigns going back to antiquity. The thesis that "methods change but principles are unchanging" had much to justify it, because methods did not change very much, or at any rate not too abruptly. Certainly they were not changing very rapidly in the time of Jomini, from whom that maxim is derived. The application of lessons of the past to

Reprinted by permission from *Strategy in the Missile Age,* RAND R-355, 1959 (Princeton: Princeton University Press, 1959), pp. 147–172. Copyright 1959 by The RAND Corporation.

Mr. Brodie is Professor of Political Science and Director of the Security Studies Project at the University of California, Los Angeles. He was formerly a Senior Staff Member of the RAND Corporation, and has been a consultant to a number of government agencies. He is the author of numerous books, reports, and articles on U.S. military strategy.

current and predicted military issues always required a proper appreciation of changed technological conditions, but not until the latter half of the nineteenth century did the problem of adjustment offer any difficulties. In the twentieth century it became increasingly critical, and with the advent of nuclear weapons the entire value of past military experience as a guide to the future was called basically into question.

Even before the atomic bomb the airplane threatened to take war away from the battlefield, and Douhet and his followers proclaimed that it had done so. But because of the limitations of the high-explosive and incendiary weapons fired and dropped from aircraft in two world wars, it took time to achieve decisive results. During that time aircraft had to fight for command of the air, and land and naval campaigns unfolded in their old accustomed fashion, profoundly affected by the new arm as they had always been by each other, but nevertheless retaining their essential and distinctive characteristics.

Instead of taking war away from the battlefield, the airplane only added a new area of battle behind the fronts, and a third dimension to those already prevailing on land and at sea. The science of strategy, which had always been divisible into two parts, was now divisible into three. For the two traditional forms of war, the basic treatises had been written and needed only to be modified. Air strategy still awaited its Mahan—for Douhet's philosophy, however farsighted, had proved critically deficient —but the early appearance of the new air philosopher could be confidently expected. The air experience of World War II was sufficient in bulk and variety to provide him with the necessary materials. Then the atomic bomb came and changed everything.

Few people were unexcited or unimpressed by the first atomic weapons. That something tremendously important had happened was immediately understood by almost everyone. Interpretations of the military significance of the new weapons naturally varied greatly, but even the most

conservative saw nothing inappropriate or extravagant in such extraordinary consultations and decisions as resulted in the Truman-Atlee-King Declaration of November 15, 1945, or the Baruch Proposals before the United Nations in the following year. Then the MacMahon Act set up the Atomic Energy Commission, an autonomous government agency hedged about by all sorts of special provisions, for the manufacture and development of atomic weapons. Nothing of the sort had ever happened before; but photographs of the destruction wrought at Hiroshima and Nagasaki had been spread across the land, and few persons were unaffected by the thought that the damage had in each case been done by a single aircraft.

This was the response evoked by the explosion of two atomic bombs over Japan, plus the simultaneously released news of the test shot at Alamagordo, at a time when few additional ones were presumed to exist. We can now see that the more conservative of the opinions then expressed on the implications of atomic weapons were in the main wedded to presumptions that were soon to be disproved; for example, that the bomb was fated to remain scarce, extremely costly, bulky and therefore difficult to deliver, and limited to about the same power (20,000 tons of TNT equivalent or 20 kilotons) and spatial effectiveness as the Nagasaki bomb.[1]

In an age that had grown used to taking rapid advances in military technology for granted, how remarkable was this immediate and almost universal consensus that the atomic bomb was different and

[1] At an early date in the nuclear era, the AEC adopted the 20 kiloton (K.T.) yield as a standard, referring to it in the literature of the time as the "nominal" atomic bomb. The book prepared under the direction of the Los Alamos Laboratory entitled *The Effects of Atomic Weapons* (Government Printing Office, 1950) based all its quantitative data on the "nominal" bomb. A later version of this book, under the title *The Effects of Nuclear Weapons*, was prepared by the same editor, Dr. Samuel Glasstone, and published by the AEC in 1957. The later book contains effects calculated up to 20 megatons, or 1,000 times greater than the earlier volume.

epochal! Equally striking was the fact that the invention caused the greatest forebodings in the hearts of the people who first possessed it and benefited from it. The thought that it represented a fabulous and mostly American scientific and engineering accomplishment, that it had apparently helped to end World War II, and that the United States had for the time being a monopoly on it seemed to cause no exhilaration among Americans.

Subsequent events did not undermine the early consensus on the importance of the new weapon, nor did they qualify the misgivings. On the contrary, the first decade of the atomic age saw the collapse of the American monopoly, of the myth of inevitable scarcity, and of reasonable hopes for international atomic disarmament. It saw also the development of the thermonuclear weapon in both major camps. If at the end of that decade one looked back at the opinions expressed so voluminously at the beginning of it, one found almost none that had proved too extravagant. Only the conservative guesses had proved to be hopelessly wrong.

It is no longer possible to distinguish between the new weapons on the one hand and the "battle-tested" or "tried and true" ones on the other, because in this new world no weapons are tried and tested. The hand rifle, the field gun, and the tank, as well as the infantry division or combat team that uses them, are at least as much on trial in the age of atomic warfare as is the atomic bomb itself; indeed, they are more so.

THE THERMONUCLEAR BOMB

Since we are now well launched into the thermonuclear age, we might first ask what differences, if any, the thermonuclear or fusion or hydrogen bomb must make for our strategic predictions. We have been living with the fission bomb for more than a decade, and it may well be that the fusion type introduces nothing essentially new other than a greater economy of destruction along patterns already established. Unfortunately, that is not the case.

No doubt the strategic implications of the first atomic bombs were radical in the extreme, and it was right at the time to stress the drastic nature of the change. The effectiveness of strategic bombing as a way of war could no longer be questioned. It at once became, incontrovertibly, the dominant form of war. A strategic-bombing program could be carried through entirely with air forces existing at the outset of a war, and at a speed which, however variously estimated, would be phenomenal by any previous standard. Also, because any payload sufficient to include one atomic bomb was quite enough to justify any sortie, strategic bombing could be carried out successfully over any distance that might separate the powers involved. If the limited ranges of the aircraft made a refueling necessary, it was worthwhile. These conclusions represented change enough from the conditions of World War II. They served, among other things, to end completely American invulnerability.

Nevertheless, fission bombs were sufficiently limited in power to make it appear necessary that a substantial number would have to be used to achieve decisive and certain results. That in turn made it possible to visualize a meaningful even if not wholly satisfactory air defense, both active and passive. It was therefore still necessary to think in terms of a struggle for command of the air in the old Douhet sense, hardly shorter in duration than what he imagined. It was also still necessary to apply, though in much modified form, the lore so painfully acquired in World War II concerning target selection for a strategic-bombing campaign. Even with fission weapons numbering in the hundreds, there was still a real—and difficult—analytical problem in choosing targets that would make the campaign decisive rather than merely hurtful. It was possible also to distinguish between attacks on population and attacks on the economy. Finally, the functions of ground and naval forces, though clearly and markedly affected by the new weapons, still appeared vital.

Even these tenuous ties with the past

were threatened when it became known that thermonuclear bombs were not only feasible but apparently also inexpensive enough to justify their manufacture in substantial numbers. Possibly the feeling that the H-bomb was distinctively new and significantly different from the A-bomb argued in part an underestimation of the A-bomb. But when one has to confront a basic change in circumstances, it helps if it is unequivocal.

The "Mike" shot of the Operation IVY series, set off on November 7, 1952, caused the complete disappearance of the small island of Elugelab on which the thermonuclear device was placed. In its place was left an underwater crater over one mile across and about 175 feet deep at the center, or, as was later publicly stated, large enough to hold fourteen buildings the size of the Pentagon. It was announced that the amount of energy released was over five million tons (or five "megatons") of TNT equivalent, and the fireball itself was about three and one-half miles across, compared to about one-sixth of a mile for a "nominal" 20 K.T. bomb.

At the time this information was released, almost a year-and-a-half after the event, at least one other American thermonuclear explosion had taken place (the "Bravo" shot in the CASTLE series on March 1, 1954), and it was reported to have been several times more powerful than "Mike." Small wonder that the AEC Chairman, Rear Admiral Lewis L. Strauss, stated on that occasion that the H-bombs that the United States could build and deliver would be individually capable of wiping out any city in the world! Later the world learned that the March 1954 shot had also produced an unexpectedly large amount of radioactive debris, which was deposited as "fallout" of dangerous and even lethal intensity over thousands of square miles and up to distances of 200 miles or more downwind from the explosion.

One immediate result of the new development was the realization that questions inherited from World War II concerning appropriate selection among industrial target-systems were now irrelevant. Only a few industries tend to have important manufacturing facilities outside cities, these being notably in steel and oil production. Since a large thermonuclear bomb exploded over a city would as a rule effectively eliminate all its industrial activities, there is hardly much point in asking which industries should be hit and in what order, or which particular facilities within any industry. New and important kinds of discrimination are still possible—for example, between disarming the enemy and destroying him —but henceforward attacking his industrial economy is practically indistinguishable from hitting his cities, with obvious consequences for populations. Cities are in any case the easiest targets to find and hit. Of course the enemy's strategic retaliatory force must be the first priority target in time, and possibly also in weight of bombs, but destroying that force, if it can be done, is essentially a disarming move which seems to await some kind of sequential action.

There is nothing in logic to require such a sequence. It is likely, however, in view of traditional attitudes, to be considered a practical necessity. The attacker may feel he cannot count with high confidence on fully eliminating the enemy air force, even if he strikes first. He might, therefore, feel obliged to begin the counter-economy competition before he knew the results of the counter-air-force strike. At any rate, decisions of the sort we are implying would have to be made well before hostilities began. The plan which goes into effect at the beginning of a war, insofar as circumstances permit its going into effect, is the emergency war plan, which is prepared in peacetime and periodically revised. As a matter of practical strategic planning, one would expect that even where a counter-air-force attack was given top priority in such a war plan, a counter-economy attack would to some degree be integrated with it.

There could indeed be a significant difference in ultimate results between a strategy aimed primarily at the enemy air force and one aimed chiefly at population, even if a lot of people were killed in both. However, it must be remembered that in striking at an enemy strategic air force, an attacker will normally feel obliged to hit many more airfields than those indicated to be major strategic air bases, because he must assume in advance that some dispersion of enemy aircraft will have taken place as a result either of warning or of routine operating procedures. In striking at airfields near cities, he might, especially if he entertained conventional attitudes about maximizing effects, choose to use some quite large thermonuclear weapons.

Thus the distinction in priority could turn out to be an academic one. It is idle to talk about our strategies being counter-force strategies, as distinct from counter-economy or counter-population strategies, *unless* planners were actually to take deliberate restrictive measures to refrain from injuring cities. They would have to conclude that it is desirable to avoid such damage, which would be a reversal of the traditional attitude that damage done to enemy installations or populations in the vicinity of the primary target is a "bonus." Otherwise it can hardly matter much to the populations involved whether the destruction of cities is a byproduct of the destruction of airfields or vice versa.

The number of cities that account for the so-called economic war potential of either the U.S. or the U.S.S.R. is small: possibly fifty or less, and certainly not over two hundred. The range in these figures is the result of the varying weight that can be given to certain tangible but difficult-to-measure factors, such as interdependence. The leading fifty-four American "metropolitan areas" (as defined by the Census Bureau) contain over 60 per cent of the nation's industrial capital, and a population of over 80,000,000 including a disproportionate number of the people whose special skills are associated with large-scale production. Altogether the Census Bureau lists 170 metropolitan areas in the United States, which together contain over 75 per cent of industrial capital and 55 per cent of the nation's population. We must note that far the greater portion of these cities are concentrated in the eastern and especially the northeastern part of the United States, where most of the non-urban population is also gathered, and where urban and non-urban populations alike may be subject to over-lapping patterns of radioactive fallout. The concentration of industry in Russian cities, and the concentration of cities and populations in the western part of their national area, make of the Soviet Union a target area roughly comparable to the United States, which has similar concentrations in its eastern parts.

The great Hamburg raids of July 1943, which were so tremendous a shock to the whole German nation, caused the destruction of about 50 per cent of the city's housing and resulted in casualties amounting to about three per cent of its population. A single H-bomb of anything above one megaton yield bursting within the confines of a city such as Hamburg would cause a degree of housing destruction much higher than 50 per cent; and unless the city had been evacuated in advance the proportion of casualties to housing destroyed would certainly be far greater than it was at Hamburg.

The latter fact underlines one of the distinctive features of nuclear weapons. There are at least four reasons why casualty rates with nuclear weapons are likely to be far greater in relation to property destroyed than was true of nonatomic bombing: (1) warning time is likely to be less, or non-existent, unless the attacker deliberately offers it before attacking; (2) the *duration* of an attack at any one place will be literally a single instant, in contrast to the several hours' duration of a World War II attack; (3) shelters capable of furnishing good protection against high-explosive bombs might be of no use at all within the fireball radius of a large ground-burst nuclear weapon, or within the oxygen-consuming fire-storm that such a detonation would cause; and (4) nuclear weapons have the distinctive effect of producing radioactivity, which can be lingering as well as instantaneous, and which causes casualties but not property injury.[2]

There are a few very large metropolitan centers in the United States and in other countries which are wide enough in area to be able to escape complete destruction by a single large thermonuclear weapon. For such areas, two or three such weapons, or half a dozen, can easily be made available. The difference in cost between large and small warheads will not be great enough to be the critical factor in determining the choice between them for distant targets.[3] The weight factor will matter, especially in missiles, but even ICBMs can carry multi-megaton weapons. What all this means is that "overkilling"

will be cheap and therefore, according to the military considerations normally brought to bear, no longer to be shunned.

The problem of getting nuclear weapons delivered to some scores or hundreds of widely spaced points may not, especially with aircraft, look simple to those who have to plan the operation. Enemy strategic airfields and missile launching sites must be hit within minutes of each other. On the other hand, we should be clear that with missiles there is nothing intrinsically impossible about getting hundreds of bombs to detonate on their targets more or less simultaneously. In any case, after the enemy retaliatory force is accounted for, the number of bombs that have to be dropped on other targets in order to put any nation out of business as a producing or even functioning organism is, when measured against the standards of World War II, absurdly small.

THE THEORY OF "BROKEN-BACKED" WAR

The British in their 1954 *Defence White Paper* used the expressive phrase "broken-backed war" to describe what presumably would happen after the first huge exchange of thermonuclear weapons, assuming the exchange itself failed to be decisive.[4] Various Americans have adhered to the same conception without necessarily using the phrase.[5] The essential feature of the

---

[2] The direct gamma radiation of any nuclear detonation is of extremely brief duration, and its lethal radius depends roughly on the size of the explosion and on the amount of shielding people in the target area have. Since air itself provides shielding, the limit of direct radiation effects is likely to be a very few miles in radius (probably under five) even for the larger thermonuclear bombs. On the other hand, the radioactive products of the nuclear reaction, if deposited on the earth's surface, remain as a lingering though decaying hazard. The amount created varies not only in direct proportion to the bomb yield, but also according to the physical constitution of the bomb. The significance of whether the bomb is air- or ground-burst is that in the latter the soil and rock particles carried into the air in huge volume capture the condensed fission products and deposit them within a matter of hours over an area of ground which in size and shape is governed by the winds aloft as well as by the spreading force of the explosion itself. This constitutes the "fallout" effect. An air-burst bomb, on the other hand, quickly sends its volatilized fission products to extremely high altitudes, beyond the reach of rain and without the larger particles necessary to bring them down quickly. This eliminates the hazard of the short-lived radioactive products and spreads out the distribution of the longer-lived ones which ultimately drift down, though the latter will include the extremely noxious strontium 90.

[3] We are of course using the cost index as a gage of availability, with the knowledge that doing so presupposes some reasonably intelligent planning decisions in the past. Once the shooting begins the dollar cost of a weapon in the stockpile is in itself an absolutely irrelevant historical datum so far as the use of that weapon is concerned.

[4] "In this event [global war], it seems likely that such a war would begin with a period of intense atomic attacks lasting a relatively short time but inflicting great destruction and damage. If no decisive result were reached in this opening phase, hostilities would decline in intensity, though perhaps less so at sea than elsewhere, and a period of broken-backed warfare would follow, during which the opposing sides would seek to recover their strength, carrying on the struggle in the meantime as best they might." *Statement on Defence, Presented by the Minister of Defence to Parliament . . . February, 1954,* Command Paper #9075. Her Majesty's Stationery Office, London, p. 5.

[5] "Presumably massive blows would continue as long as either side retained the capability. . . . With the passing of that initial phase, and if the issue is still unresolved, tough people would carry on across the radioactive ashes and water, with what weapons are left. Sea control will be an ele-

idea is the insistence, usually implicit, that war resources, human and mechanical, will continue to be drawn from the national "mobilization base" and that the margin of advantage that one side or the other enjoys in this respect is what will prove decisive in the end. Although the conception of "broken-backed war" appeared to be entirely abandoned in the *Defence White Paper* for 1955, which tended instead to rest everything on "deterrence," it has nevertheless continued to underlie and to confuse the basic structure of American and Allied defense planning.

One can easily conceive of conditions in both contending camps so chaotic, following the opening reciprocal onslaughts, that the war issue will not be immediately resolved and hostilities not formally concluded. One can also picture surviving military units, including some possessing thermonuclear weapons and the means of delivering them, continuing to hurl blows at the enemy to the utmost of their remaining though fast-ebbing capacity. But it is difficult to imagine such intensive continuing support from the home front as would enable "conventional" military operations to be conducted on a large scale and over a long enough time to effect any such large and positive purpose as "imposing the national will on the enemy," or, to use the words of our own former Army Chief of Staff, General Matthew B. Ridgway, "carrying the fight to the enemy and defeating him." [6]

The major premise of the "broken-backed war" conception was that the result of the initial mutual nuclear violence would be something like a draw. Otherwise it could hardly fail to be decisive. Moreover, the nuclear phase would have to end cleanly, or diminish to a trivial magnitude, early in the hostilities and at about the same time for both sides! The second and related premise was that the level of damage on both sides following the strategic nuclear bombing phase would be limited enough to permit each to equip and sustain air, ground, and naval forces sufficiently large to carry on noteworthy military operations. These would, for one side or the other, be conducted at some distance from home, and would therefore require facilities such as ports and associated railway terminals which are generally found only in those larger coastal cities certain to be among the first targets hit in the nuclear phase! Surely these are dubious assumptions.

Another more practical reason for questioning the "broken-backed war" conception is that no one seems to know how to plan for such a war. At least, no one seems willing to do so. There are special psychological reasons why official war planners have always in times past found it impossibly difficult to predicate a war plan on the assumption of national disaster at the outset. In this case, even if the spirit were willing, the data and the imagination would be much too weak.

There are, of course, numerous examples in recent history of magnificent improvisation following upon disaster, or rather upon what used to be called disaster. In each of those cases the means of making war, including such vital intangibles as established governmental authority operating through accustomed channels of communication, remained intact. A few battle-

mental consideration in accomplishing either the follow-through phase of atomic war or the better appreciated chores of a prolonged non-atomic war." Admiral Robert B. Carney, then U.S. Chief of Naval Operations, in a Cincinnati speech of February 21, 1955, as reported in the *Washington Post and Times Herald* for the following day.

[6] In his speech before the National Press Club in Washington, D.C., March 19, 1954. This speech was reproduced in full in the *Congressional Record, Appendix*, March 24, 1954, pp. A2254–6 (under "Extension of Remarks of Hon. Dewey Short"). It is noteworthy that at this time General Ridgway still found himself able to conceive of a future war in which we would "reduce the other side's industrial potential and military bases" but would nevertheless succeed in carrying out on our own side "not

merely the mobilization and training of men but also the conversion of industry to full war production." In other words, General Ridgway was imagining not so much a "broken-backed" war as a war marked by an essentially one-way strategic air attack. One might well question, under such premises, the necessity for a full mobilization of the national resources!

ships sunk, a few armies defeated and lost, even large territories yielded, do not spell the kind of over-all disaster we have to think about for the future. There are limits to the burden that can be placed on improvisation. The improvisation which the survivors of thermonuclear attack may find it within their capacities to carry out will have to be largely occupied with restoring the bare means of life.

No one who has studied the German military, economic, and even social performance under World War II strategic bombing can fail to be impressed by it. But the German capacity to absorb the blows and to take compensatory measures for the damage received depended, among other things, on their having both the time and the incentive to organize those measures. When the main weight of our strategic bombing descended upon them in the spring of 1944, they had had at least three years of serious attacks, including the terrible warning of the Hamburg raids of July 1943. Even so, the campaign waxed only gradually to its climax, and never, even when the British-American strategic bombing forces were at the height of their power, were they able to inflict in six months or even a year of bombing the scale of destruction that would lie easily within the capability of the United States or the Soviet long-range bombing forces on Day One or even Hour One of a new war. The differences in circumstance that prevailed between the French resistance in 1914 and the collapse in 1940 were trivial compared with the differences between pre-atomic and present-day strategic bombing.

No one can specify how many nuclear bombs it would take to "knock out" (by which we presumably mean "render helpless") a country as large as the Soviet Union or the United States, since analytical studies of the problem can do little more than suggest broad limits to the reasonable range of figures. Such studies must depend on what are little more than educated guesses for various critical planning factors, including even those pertaining to the physical effects of bomb explosions. They

must work with quite wide ranges of assumptions concerning such things as the size and the positioning of bombs delivered, the length of warning time, and so on. They cannot even touch the imponderables, such as popular panic and administrative disorganization, which might easily govern the end result. The people who do such analyses are as a rule interested in the results from the offensive or targeting point of view, and they therefore consider it a virtue to be conservative in their estimates of damage. One of the ways to be conservative is to dismiss imponderables as unmeasurable.

At the other end of the scale, methodologically speaking, is a judgment such as the following one by Marshal of the Royal Air Force Sir John Slessor:

I have the perhaps somewhat unenviable advantage of an experience, which fortunately has been denied to most people, of being in a city which was literally wiped out, with most of its inhabitants, in fifty-five seconds by the great earthquake in Baluchistan in 1935, a far more effective blitz than anything laid on by either side in the late war, except Hiroshima and Nagasaki. When people talk light-heartedly about that sort of thing on a widespread scale not being decisive, I have to tell them with respect that they do not know what they are talking about. No country could survive a month of Quetta earthquakes on all its main centres of population and remain capable of organized resistance.[7]

Sir John's conviction, which accords with the average layman's judgment, reflects a tacit assumption concerning defenses. In general, the assumption is that the prospects for the radical improvement of both active and passive defenses against nuclear weapons are not bright. We shall consider this question in detail in the following chapter, but when we recall the fantastic degree to which the coming of the A-bomb gave a lead to the offense over the defense, and consider also that subsequent

[7] Sir John Slessor, *Strategy for the West*, William Morrow, New York, 1954, p. 111.

developments in nuclear weapons have tended to further that advantage, the assumption referred to looks fairly invulnerable.

THE DECISIVENESS OF STRATEGIC BOMBARDMENT

From all this one would seem justified in drawing the following conclusion: barring revolutionary and presently unforeseen advances in air defense, including extensive hardening of targets, an unrestricted strategic air campaign in a war in which the United States is engaged is bound to be decisive. It does not matter greatly whether the number of bombs-on-target required to guarantee decisiveness is a few score or several hundred, because we remain in realms of figures well within the capabilities of the United States and probably also the Soviet Union, the critical factor being delivery capability rather than size of the nuclear stockpile. If this capability is not in the hands of the Soviet Union at the particular date of this writing, it will be soon enough thereafter.

It is barely conceivable that an enemy would have a capability only sufficient to destroy our Strategic Air Command (SAC), which it would then proceed to do by a sudden missile or bomber attack, but not enough to destroy or threaten our economy, especially if critical segments of the latter were hardened. In such a case strategic nuclear bombing could fail to be decisive. But this and various other conceivable contingencies tending to a like result are in the aggregate too improbable to be taken seriously.

When we say that strategic bombing will be decisive, we mean that if it occurs on the grand scale that existing forces make possible, other kinds of military operations are likely to prove both unfeasible and superfluous. The Red Army, if poised to spring, could perhaps have a certain brief career as an autonomous force even if its homeland were laid entirely waste behind it, though in such a case it would itself also be the target of nuclear weapons of all sizes. Anyway, such a career would be possible only for the Red Army, since it has the advantage, denied to the ground forces of Britain and the United States, of having its main potential spheres of operation in areas contiguous to its homeland.

If these views are rejected, the burden of proof rests on those who would show us how modern armies and navies can operate effectively and to a useful purpose when their home territories, and certainly the larger towns thereof, including all naval bases and ports, are masses of rubble and radioactive dust. Discussions in military journals of the operations of armies and navies, and even air forces, in a major war of the future almost always tacitly assume an intact home front, or at least one where the damage is so small as to be irrelevant to offensive plans.

From a sober appreciation of the possibilities in this field of dismal speculation, it seems safe to assume that the number of people and the kind and quantity of capital that may survive strategic attack will be important far more for determining the character and degree of national recovery *following* the hostilities than for controlling the subsequent course of those hostilities. The *minimum* destruction and disorganization that one should expect from an unrestricted thermonuclear attack in the future is likely to be too high to permit further meaningful mobilization of war-making capabilities over the short term.

We should also recognize once and for all that when it comes to predicting human casualties, we are talking about a catastrophe for which it is impossible to set upper limits appreciably short of the entire population of a nation. It is not only those in cities and in towns who will be exposed to risk, but, in view of the fallout effect, practically all. It is not true that the fallout effect, where the attacker is determined to amplify and exploit it, is something that is easily met and contained. The attacker, incidentally, has the option not only of selecting ground rather than air bursts but also, within wide limits, of altering the components of his bombs to get the kind of fallout he wants. Although the

uninjured survivors of attack may indeed
be many, it is all too easily conceivable
that they may be relatively few. The latter contingency is the more likely one in the
absence of large-scale protective measures, involving shelters, such as we have
not yet shown ourselves prepared to take.
But whether the survivors be many or few,
in the midst of a land scarred and ruined
beyond all present comprehension they
should not be expected to show much concern for the further pursuit of political-military objectives.

The reader who was prepared to accept
as obvious at the outset the conclusion we
have labored these many pages to establish will wonder why all the bother. The
answer is that in these respects there is
a monumental ambiguity in public policy,
which reflects in part the ambiguity in the
public pronouncements of relevant officials
of the highest rank. Even those who forecast catastrophic paralyzation following
nuclear strategic bombing seem to find it
impossibly difficult to grasp the full significance of what they predict. Sir John
Slessor, whose trenchant comment on what
to expect from nuclear strategic bombing
we have already quoted, has furnished an
outstanding example. A former Chief of
Staff of the Royal Air Force, Sir John
can also be abundantly quoted on the other
side of the "decisiveness" question from
the very same book, a book that has had
a special importance as the most lucid
and comprehensive presentation of the
"massive retaliation" doctrine to be found
in print.

Sir John urged, to be sure, that "it is
very seldom wise to carry things to their
logical conclusions, and the airmen can no
doubt rely upon their comrades of the older
services to assist them in resisting that
temptation." [8] Nevertheless, this distinguished airman, who regarded it as "almost inconceivable" that a major war of
the future fought with weapons of mass
destruction (which he insisted *must* be
used) could last "for any length of time," [9]

[8] *Ibid.*, p. 76.
[9] *Ibid.*, pp. 107, 114.

still considered it very important that navies be able to carry out their traditional
functions of convoy protection,[10] which are
defenses against attrition warfare and
therefore strategically meaningful only
over a considerable span of time. One
wonders also why he considered it necessary
even in 1954 to profess disbelief in the
thought "that air power by itself can defeat a first-class enemy." [11]

No doubt an answer is to be found in the
only place in the book where Sir John por-
trayed his conception of the United Kingdom under nuclear attack:

When things are really bad the people's
morale is greatly sustained by the knowledge that we are giving back as good as
we are getting, and this engenders a sort
of combatant pride, like that of the char-
lady in a government office who was asked
during the London blitz where her hus-
band was—"he's in the Middle East, the
bloody coward!" We must ensure that defence, as adequate as we can reasonably
make it, is afforded to those areas or installations which are really vital to our survival at the outset of a war, or to our
ability to nourish our essential fighting
strength. Much-Binding-in-the-Marsh and
Littleville, Pa., are not in that category
unless they happen to contain some utterly
indispensable installation, and the inhabitants must steel themselves to risks and
take what may come to them, knowing that
thereby they are playing as essential a part
in the country's defence as the pilot in the
fighter or the man behind the gun.[12]

There is only one thing to be said about
such language and imagery: it fits World
War II, but it has nothing to do with thermonuclear bombs. Certainly it has no
pertinence for the United Kingdom, which
is both small in area and geographically
close to the most likely enemy. One does

[10] *Ibid.*, pp. 92, 99, 101. See also Field Marshal
The Viscount Bernard Montgomery, "A Look
Through a Window at World War III," *Journal of
the Royal United Service Institution,* XCIX (November 1954), 507ff.
[11] Slessor, *op. cit.,* p. 106.
[12] *Ibid.*, p. 120.

not have to think in terms of modern missiles but only in terms of the V–1, the
V–2, and the jet bomber to see Britain a
shambles at the end of the first hour of
nuclear attack.

For countries such as the United States
or the Soviet Union it might take a little
longer. There was, however, no justification in 1954 for the kind of optimism expressed in the following sentence: "But
when it is suggested . . . that the United
States could be knocked out as the arsenal
of the North Atlantic Alliance, then writing
as one who has been concerned for a good
many years with air bombardment planning, I beg leave to say that it is nonsense." [13]

It remains to be added that in an article
published two years after the book in which
he made these remarks, Sir John Slessor
was seeing things in a quite different
light.[14] Among the events that had intervened between the two publications was
the release of a good deal of information
about thermonuclear weapons and their
effects, but one must also give the credit
to Sir John for a flexibility of mind that is
among his special distinctions. Perhaps
there is also something about the experience of being the author of a book that
brings one intimately into the rough-and-
tumble of the marketplace so far as ideas
are concerned. Anyway, the kind of drastic conversion in some of his fundamental
beliefs that Sir John underwent within two
years is not a common occurrence among
his professional colleagues. As Sir John
observes in the aforementioned article:
"Not many people, even in the fighting
services themselves, have really grasped
the full tactical implications of an age in
which nuclear power is the dominant strategic factor in war. There is a tendency
almost subconsciously to shy away from
those implications, which should not be

[13] Ibid., p. 34.
[14] See his "The Great Deterrent and its Limitations," Bulletin of the Atomic Scientists, XII (May
1956), 140–146. It is the emphasis on the limitations
of "the great deterrent," and the policy implications
of those limitations, that mainly distinguishes this
article from his earlier book.

ascribed merely to the influence of vested
interest."

The tendency to "shy away" to which
Sir John refers is, to be sure, often overcome by the force of events. Such events
are often not foreseen when they should be,
but it is much harder to deny developments
when they become present realities than
it is when they are merely predictions.
Even the acceptance of present realities
may be reluctant enough to result in grave
distortions, but it may nevertheless represent an ideological change of some consequence. In that connection, we should
remember that Soviet ideas about the tactical and strategic consequences of nuclear
weapons have also undergone some change.
When the Soviets did not have the bombs
they felt impelled (1) to acquire them as
fast as they could, and (2) to depreciate
their importance. Now that they have
had them for more than a decade and had
ample opportunity to test them and to reflect on what they imply, Soviet ideas on
what can be accomplished, for example by
surprise nuclear attack, seem to be developing along lines familiar in the United
States.

The sense of Emerson's remark about
consistency being "the hobgoblin of little
minds" has on the whole enjoyed remarkable verification in military history. Historical examples of prejudiced rejection
of the novel need not detain us, except possibly to note that the catalog is long. More
interesting for our purposes are the instances where eager acceptance of the new
is coupled, not only within the same organizations but often within the same persons,
with stubborn insistence upon retaining
also much of the old. Such people have
usually come off well when the scores were
in. Their very inconsistency often provided
them with a hedge against wrong predictions.

The intensely conservative among the
military are always proved wrong, because changes in armaments over the
past century have been altogether too rapid
and drastic to offer any cover to those who
will not adjust. But, as we saw in our

chapter on Douhet, the occasional brilliant seers who possess the analytical skill to recognize and expose inconsistency when they see it have often been tripped up by one or more critical assumptions which turned out to be in error. In such a case their consistency worked only to make their whole logical construction dangerously wrong.

No doubt a proper intuitive feeling for the hazards of prediction and for the terrible forfeits involved, in the military sphere, in finding oneself overcommitted to a wrong guess, is one of the reasons why military men as a group tend to put a rather modest value on analytical brilliance as an alternative to mature military judgment. Nevertheless, there is a limit to the amount of inconsistency that is reasonable, especially since in the world of nuclear armaments it may become, to say the least, exceedingly expensive. The kind of inconsistency which will permit some of our leaders to place a nearly exclusive dependence on thermonuclear weapons for the security of the country, and at the same time reject the most obvious consequences of the use of such weapons against us, is clearly beyond the limits that Emerson desired to indulge.

THE ROLE OF FORCE IN THE NUCLEAR AGE

BY MORTON H. HALPERIN

This book examines from the perspective of the major powers the role of force in international politics in the age of the nuclear missile. It is based on the assumption, which will be examined briefly in this chapter, that force does continue to play a role despite the development of thermonuclear weapons and intercontinental ballistic missiles. The approach taken here to the role of force in the Nuclear Age may be contrasted with several absolute views about the nature of war in the current period. Holders of the first of these views argue that nuclear weapons have abolished war: that war has become unthinkable and impossible. Their line of thinking is that because nuclear weapons now exist, all war would be total war; therefore, war will not take place. The events of the postwar period, however, make it clear that the invention of atomic weapons has not made war impossible. In fact, while major world war has been avoided, the amount of violence in the world—however it is measured—has not been appreciably reduced. Nuclear weapons, then, have not abolished war; war very much remains a thinkable and possible instrument of policy.

A second view suggests that while nuclear weapons have not yet made war impossible, war must be abolished if mankind is to survive. Those who adhere to this theory argue that unless all war is abolished, we will eventually have a nuclear war that will destroy most, if not all, of civilization. But this approach does not suggest how one can go about abolishing war. Nor does it demonstrate that nuclear war is inevitable unless all violence is eliminated.

Supporters of a third, somewhat less extreme, approach contend that while war may continue, *nuclear* war has now become "unthinkable"; either a nuclear war will never occur or nuclear war must be prevented if mankind is to survive. Some who hold this opinion would argue that nuclear war should not be studied, for to study nuclear war is to allow that such a war is thinkable and acceptable, and therefore more likely. A counter view—the view maintained throughout this book—holds that since nuclear war may occur, despite our best efforts to avoid it, it is necessary to try to understand what a nuclear war might be like. In any case, the threat of nuclear war and of the use of nuclear weapons plays a significant role in international politics. Even if, as appears likely, there never is a nuclear war, the invention of nuclear weapons will have had a profound effect on the course of international politics and, indeed, on the course of human history.

A fourth, more extreme approach advocates preventive nuclear war to produce peace. This approach suggests that a nuclear war is in the long run inevitable; therefore, the sooner the better. Implicit in this theory, then, is the belief that human violence can be ended but that preventive war, not international disarmament, is the means to this utopia.

Each of the approaches discussed above prescribes how nations should act, and each proposes substantial changes. This book will adopt a more descriptive technique by examining the changes in the behavior of nations in the Nuclear Age. In addition, marginal changes, which might improve the military situation, will be suggested.

Reprinted by permission from *Contemporary Military Strategy* (Boston: Little, Brown and Company, Inc., 1967), pp. 3–12. Copyright © 1967, by Little, Brown and Company (Inc.)

Mr. Halperin is Director of the Policy Planning Staff in the Office of the Assistant Secretary of Defence, International Security Affairs. He was formally an Assistant Professor of Government at Harvard University and a Research Associate at the Harvard Center for International Affairs. He is the author of a number of books on U.S. defense policy, including *Limited War in the Nuclear Age* (1963), and Chinese nuclear policy.

Does force, both in its employment and the threat of its employment, affect the behavior of nations and of individuals? The answer seems clearly to be yes, despite the development of nuclear weapons. Therefore, one must consider how, in fact, force does affect behavior in the current period, in contrast to the pre-Nuclear Age.

Through the ages, the evolution of technology for warfare has been marked by a search for, as well as a fear of, the absolute weapon. At various times men have thought the crossbow, the machine gun, and the airplane the absolute weapon, which, depending upon one's point of view, would either enable one state to dominate the world or would force all men to live in peace. The destruction of Hiroshima and Nagasaki led some people to describe the atomic bomb as "the absolute weapon." It has since become clear that the atomic bomb alone is not the ultimate weapon, and the search has gone on for this weapon in the form of intercontinental missiles, submarine-launched missiles, and others. While recognizing that we are never likely to obtain anything that can really be called an absolute weapon, it is important to have some understanding of the changes in weapon technology that have occurred with the development of the atomic, and then the hydrogen, bomb; namely, the destructive power of weapons and the ability to deliver them.

The destructive power of weapons should be thought of in terms of its yield to weight ratio; that is, how much destruction is caused for each given pound of explosive material. The base taken for comparison in describing the destructive power of nuclear weapons is the weight of a TNT bomb that would cause the same destruction. The yield of an atomic bomb is expressed in the equivalent of one thousand pounds of TNT (kilotons) or one million pounds of TNT (megatons) ; that is, a two-megaton bomb has the equivalent destructive power of two million tons of TNT.

The destructive power of weapons has increased enormously twice during the Atomic Age. The first atomic weapons, the so-called fission bombs, had a destructive power a thousand times greater per pound than traditional TNT or other high explosive weapons. The hydrogen, or fusion, bomb was again a thousand times more powerful per pound than fission weapons. Thus, the two revolutions in fire power have produced a millionfold increase in power for a given weight.

Another way to indicate this changed magnitude of destruction is to say that one American bomber now carries more than the total destructive power of all the weapons dropped in all the wars in human history. The largest bombs of World War II were the equivalent of approximately *five* tons of TNT, and the Hiroshima bomb was equal to approximately *twenty thousand* tons of TNT. Current American nuclear weapons have yields from tenths of a kiloton to *one million* tons on the warhead of the Minuteman intercontinental missile and *twenty million* tons in America's large intercontinental bombers.

The fantastic increase in the destructive power of weapons has almost been matched by improvements in the ability to deliver these weapons. ICBM's possessed by the Soviet Union and by the United States can reach any point on the globe from any other point within thirty to forty minutes with incredible accuracy. This accuracy is expressed in terms of a *CEP* (circular error probability). The number identified as the CEP is the radius of a circle within which half of all the fired weapons land. For example, if four missiles with a CEP of two miles were fired at a target, two of the missiles would land within two miles of the target. In these terms, American and Soviet missiles appear to have a CEP of considerably less than two miles. Superpowers thus can fire missiles five thousand miles or more and have half of their missiles land within two miles of their target.

The development and deployment of ballistic-missile defenses (BMD) by the United States and the Soviet Union would affect the number of missiles that can reach their targets but would not alter the basic facts: both of the superpowers have thermonuclear weapons a million times more powerful than World War II weapons and both can deliver these weapons with intercontinental missiles in about thirty minutes.

In trying to understand the impact of thermonuclear weapons on international politics, it is important to keep in mind these two very general quantitative developments.

In the postwar period these changes in technology have been accompanied by an essential bipolarity of power centered around the United States and the Soviet Union. Some countries, most recently France and China, have challenged the policies of the superpowers. However, the two leading countries still dominate, at least in part because they are the only powers possessing substantial nuclear capability. The postwar period has also been marked by intense ideological conflict between colonial and ex-colonial powers and between the Communist and non-Communist world.

THE MILITARY BALANCE

While analysts have argued about whether or not military force still has a role to play, governments have been under no illusion about the consequences of not having adequate military capability. Both the United States and the Soviet Union have spent very large sums of money, perhaps exceeding the combined total of one hundred billion dollars, for the development of nuclear forces and their delivery systems. To assess the role of nuclear weapons, it is important to have some understanding of the nuclear and conventional forces existing on both sides. These will be considered in terms of strategic nuclear forces, tactical nuclear forces, and conventional forces.

STRATEGIC NUCLEAR FORCES

Through the 1960's the American strategic nuclear force will consist of a very large missile force and a moderate number of intercontinental bombers in addition to shorter-range, fighter-bomber aircraft and missiles in Europe and perhaps elsewhere. When the present program is completed, the missile force will consist of 1,000 Minuteman intercontinental ballistic missiles—kept in well-protected underground silos in the United States and capable of reaching all of the Soviet Union—and 656 Polaris missiles. The yield of these weapons is approximately one megaton. The United

States also has some older Titan II missiles that can carry a much larger warhead, perhaps as high as eight to ten megatons, but that burn a liquid fuel and consequently can be fired neither as quickly nor as efficiently as the Minuteman or Polaris, nor can they be as well protected.

There has been much controversy about the role that manned bombers can play in a period in which intercontinental missiles have dominated the strategic scene. While the importance of bombers has declined, it seems clear that both the United States and the Soviet Union will maintain some bomber fleets through the rest of the decade and into the 1970's. The American bomber force, some of which is on airborne alert and much of which is on ground alert, has been declining in size in the 1960's; but a fleet of at least two hundred bombers will be kept in service into the 1970's. Bombers can carry either several bombs of twenty megatons or more, or a number of smaller bombs, perhaps fired from air-to-surface missiles.

The major addition to the American capability for attacking targets in the Soviet Union will be the F-111. While designed primarily to attack military targets on the battlefield, the F-111, particularly in a special bomber version, will be able to carry a significant nuclear payload—that is, a number of bombs—over desired targets. The United States will be producing more than one thousand of these bombers, and as many as two hundred might be modified for the strategic bombing role.

The Soviet strategic nuclear force (discussed in Chapter Five) appears to be much smaller and much less sophisticated than the American force. From all reports, the Soviets have less than half the number of intercontinental missiles the United States has. These missiles burn liquid fuel and react more slowly than the American Minuteman but carry a much larger payload. The Soviets also have a small bomber force that can reach the United States. The bulk of the Soviet strategic nuclear capability is concentrated in approximately one thousand medium-range and intermediate-range missiles (MRBM's and IRBM's)—that is, missiles that go a distance of fifteen hundred miles or less—stationed in the western part of the Soviet Union and targeted on Western Europe, with the capability of destroying any desired targets in Western Europe.

TACTICAL NUCLEAR FORCES

Since the mid-1950's the United States has built up an impressive array of so-called tactical nuclear weapons; that is, nuclear weapons designed to support land forces, particularly in Europe. Developments in this area have given the United States a capability in the form of nuclear weapons from extremely low yields—below that of the largest conventional weapons—to a kiloton, and larger weapons for attacking air bases and other large targets. American stockpiles of tactical nuclear weapons in Europe have grown steadily during the first half of the 1960's to a force of weapons numbering in the thousands; these weapons are carried by a variety of delivery systems. The Soviets are reported to have a much smaller and less varied arsenal of tactical nuclear weapons consisting mainly of short-range rockets with warheads in the kiloton range.

CONVENTIONAL FORCES

It is important to recognize that despite the growth of nuclear power and the increasing sophistication of the arsenals of the two superpowers, both the United States and the Soviet Union, as well as their allies, have maintained large conventional ground forces. While it is true that these forces might be employed along with tactical nuclear weapons, they also have the capability to fight alone. The United States and its NATO allies have put less emphasis than the Soviet Union and China have on spending for conventional ground forces, although the United States substantially increased its spending for these forces in the 1960's. Whatever the relative emphasis, it is important to realize that all of the major powers spend more than half of their military budgets on conventional forces, much of it on salaries. Thus, along with their nuclear capabilities, the superpowers have a very real ability to fight conventionally.

THE ROLE OF MILITARY FORCE

We can consider the role of existing military power in terms of its effect on peacetime diplomacy, crises, conventional wars, and nuclear conflict.

PEACETIME DIPLOMACY

The great expense involved in developing large, sophisticated thermonuclear capabilities has been one of the prime reasons for the maintenance of bipolarity. Only the United States and the Soviet Union have been able to afford such weapons. The United States, for example, spends on defense approximately three times the total United Kingdom budget and six times the British defense budget. Similar, perhaps greater, disparities exist between the Chinese and the American and Russian budgets. Thus, while France, Britain, and China have begun to develop nuclear capabilities, the Soviet Union and the United States are—and are likely to remain for quite awhile—the two giant and dominant superpowers.

The existence of thermonuclear weapons has forced the two superpowers to take a new view of their relations. Under a classic balance of power we would expect the two main powers to be in total conflict with each other and to seek support from various other countries in an effort to tip the balance. However, particularly in the last several years, the two superpowers have come to see that while there are many things that separate them, they are joined by a common desire to avoid thermonuclear war. This insight has led to pressure for *détente* in both the United States and the Soviet Union. The search for disarmament and arms-control agreements has changed in focus and emphasis from the attempt of idealists to create a world of total peace to an attempt by realists to improve the nature of the military balance and to reduce the likelihood of general nuclear war. Thus, in a world situation in which conflict between the superpowers remains great, we have had the partial test ban treaty and other measures, including the "hot line" agreement linking the United States and the Soviet Union with a high-speed, reliable communication system. The greater emphasis on agreement between the two superpowers, particularly in the arms-control area, must be attributed almost entirely to their destructive potentialities. As former Soviet Premier Nikita Khrushchev put it, "The atom bomb recognizes no class differences."

The fear of thermonuclear war has led the superpowers to try to avoid situations of intense international political crisis. Both sides have refrained from pressing political advantages that might upset the military balance. There has also been extreme caution in the use of conventional military forces. Thus, the Soviet Union has never actually employed its conventional capabilities to seize Berlin; and the United States has, in the end, refrained from an effective invasion of Cuba. While other restraints have been operative in both cases, the fear of setting in motion a chain of events that might lead to general nuclear war has been a dominant factor.

The same pressures have compelled the superpowers to become more directly involved in local conflicts throughout the world. The Soviet Union and the United States believe that any conflict runs the risk of precipitating general nuclear war. There has been a tendency, particularly on the part of the United States, to intervene quickly at the first sign of local conflict in order to isolate the conflict and to halt the fighting before it spreads to general war.

CRISES

Caution has marked the approach of the superpowers to crises as well as to peacetime diplomacy. Both sides have sought to contain quickly any spontaneous crisis, such as the Hungarian uprising of 1956. Even in crises induced by one of the two superpowers—for example, the Cuban missile crisis in 1962—both sides have acted in a cautious way designed to reduce the likelihood of general war and to end the conflict as quickly as possible. This is not to say that the superpowers and their allies have not sought to get political advantage from a crisis. It is simply to note that their willingness to maneuver and to seek advantage has been severely limited by the nature of the overall military balance. In fact, the history of postwar crises suggests that the probability of nuclear war has—if anything—been exaggerated and has tended to dominate the thinking of decision-makers during a crisis. One has only to recall Mr. Khrushchev's statements about the world being close to thermonuclear war during the Cuban missile crisis or to read memoirs of American leaders at that time to realize the extent to which top leaders will allow this problem to influence their views. Because of the fear of a general nuclear war and the desire to end the conflict quickly, local conventional military power, which could be brought to bear quickly, has tended to be critical in crises such as those in Hungary and in Cuba.

CONVENTIONAL WAR

The existence of thermonuclear weapons has made extremely unlikely another very large-scale military conflict of the order of World War I or World War II. While neither of the superpowers has ruled out such a conflict in developing its military capabilities, neither seems to attach high priority to the probability of such a war. Nor if such a war were to occur, would it likely remain conventional and limited. Further, with the improbability of worldwide, general war, has come an increase in local conventional wars—both international and, more frequently, civil—for example, in Vietnam, Laos, Greece, and Korea. Such wars have all been fought under the shadow of the nuclear deterrent capability of the two superpowers; that is, the actions of the superpowers in these conflicts have been influenced by their belief that local conflicts could explode into general nuclear war. Though this phenomenon has led to the exercise of restraint on the part of the superpowers in the exploitation of success in local conflict, it has nevertheless been the case that local conventional military forces and local political factors have tended to dominate and determine the outcome of any particular military clash. Limited local wars, including guerrilla wars, have been an instrument of international political change and have become, to a large extent, the ultimate arbitrator of political conflict because nobody wants to use the real, ultimate weapons—the nuclear weapons.

NUCLEAR WAR

The United States and the Soviet Union have been willing to allow conventional and local political factors to determine the outcome of much conflict in the postwar period precisely because this conflict does not threaten the vital interests of the superpowers. However, it is clear that nuclear weapons would remain the final arbiter when and if the vital interests of the superpowers were challenged. This produces what many observers have pointed to as the central paradox of the Nuclear Age: total

ideological conflict plus total means of destruction have produced a situation in which a total solution is impossible. The major powers compete with each other in non-military ways and in the use of conventional military force but with no hope of total military victory. Whatever we may choose to call it, we are doomed to peaceful coexistence with our enemies because we live in a world in which war cannot be abolished, because there is no other means to settle issues that men feel are worth fighting for. But war—at least war in the sense of general nuclear war—can only lead to such complete destruction that in the final analysis, the war could not have been worth fighting. It is this central paradox which provides the challenge and the setting for discussion of the role of military strategy in the current era.

VITAL SECURITY INTERESTS AND OBJECTIVES OF THE UNITED STATES

BY LINCOLN P. BLOOMFIELD

To try to identify and put into words the vital interests of the United States is as difficult as it is presumptuous. One difficulty is describing what one means by the United States. As an English anthropologist, who was quite anti-American, put it: "It is not at all clear whether the United States is a territorial state on the old European pattern or a political organ dedicated like the Soviet Union to an idea." The conviction that this country represents some kind of unique, metaphysical idea has a very long and very honorable history in our tradition. John Adams, for example, said: "Our pure, virtuous, public-spirited republic will last forever, govern the globe and introduce the perfection of man." There are some who feel that we are well

on the way to governing the globe, although we have not perfected man. But John Adams wrote that a very long time ago, and it does not sound to me like a description of, let us say, Andorra from *The Statesman's Year Book*. It is a unique kind of conception of what a country is. Woodrow Wilson said: "The idea of America is to serve humanity," which I think persists in much of what we do and represents a part of our spiritual confusion about Vietnam.

This theme of the purpose of the United States is in terms of a transcendent mission; it is a powerful counterpoint to the sorts of hardheaded, precise geopolitical calculations which one is accustomed to making in basic national security planning papers or

This paper is based on an address delivered to the National War College, Washington, D.C., August 22, 1967.

Mr. Bloomfield is Professor of Political Science at M.I.T. and Director of the Arms Control project at the Center for International Studies there. He is consultant to various government agencies and other organizations, and author of books and articles on foreign policy.

Air Force doctrine and objectives papers. And it is a counterpoint which has to be kept sight of because otherwise there is no music; there are just words; and this is an orchestrated kind of national strategy that we operate.

I had occasion to look over some of the recent efforts to put into words the national interests and the national objectives of the United States. These seemed to me very disappointing. In about the middle 1950s there was a sense of great spiritual malaise in the United States, with a lot of soul-searching and navel contemplating. There were half a dozen efforts, sponsored by *Life* magazine, the President's Commission on National Goals, the *New York Times*, the Senate Foreign Relations Committee, and so on, to formulate our national purpose: Who are we? Where are we heading? What is our identity? We sounded almost like an adolescent having an identity crisis.

The results of this were somehow less than electrifying. They seemed to me, on reading them then and again on reading them now, to be trite, full of platitudes, and not really saying anything new. They sounded like sermons, and they did not seem to bear any relationship to the kind of policy the United States in fact operated around the world. The strange thing was that in the decade prior to that spasm of identity-searching, our national goals were made brilliantly explicit in the great national programs that had been developed, in the commitments that the United States made in the late 1940s and the early 1950s, and in the grand strategies that were formulated by the political process in this country—the President with the Congress, and the consensus that followed. These together made up the postwar American response to the situation. I would have thought it was there that one would look for the national strategies of the United States, and from those one could deduce the kinds of objectives we were pursuing. From that one could synthesize American national interests, rather than in the abstract formulations which inevitably took a very lofty moral tone and had trouble descending to the plane where the action really was.

One reason for trying to do this anyway is that it is a good idea to try consistently and perpetually to formulate objectives. I think civilian planning is still very weak by contrast with military type planning. I do not mean in content so much as in acceptability—its place in the system, and the kind of tangible material with which it works.

I think we still, even today, fall into the trap we have dug for ourselves where so-called pure military objectives are supposed to take precedence over political objectives. I thought we had learned that lesson in World War II and certainly in Korea. I do not think the Communists very often make this kind of blunder; I hope we do not in places like Vietnam. Of course, the uses of military power have become complicated beyond recognition. My own view is that deterrence of general war remains the highest use of military power; arms control is perhaps the second most important thing one can say about military power. These are two vital strategic uses of hardware. Both of them depend upon the establishment of political objectives and on the design of certain kinds of military systems just as much as they depend upon nonmilitary instruments. I will come back to these in a more orderly way.

But now science and technology, where the curve of change is almost exponential, pose a new danger to the planning process —like the danger of trying to juxtapose military and civilian purposes. Once again, particularly at a place like M.I.T., we hear all kinds of misleading advice about not sullying the pure principles of science with politics. It seems to me this attitude was not good enough when it was applied to the fighting of wars, and it is not good enough when it is applied to the waging of peace.

One final prefatory note before I get specific is about time spans. I myself have lived in several different worlds in recent years where the lenses were ground quite differently. Policymakers, bureaucrats, diplomats, and soldiers have to face short-term deadlines. That is, they tend to be hospitable to things that will be helpful in the near future, and not to be very hospitable to much that goes beyond the fiscal year, the next session of Congress, the next NATO council meeting, or the next UN General Assembly in September. They live with a series of close-in targets, when the black book has to be ready with all the papers in it, and therefore policy formulated.

On the other hand, scholars, of whom I see little these days, like to breathe the more rarified pure air of the long range. My own feeling is that the most imperative need of planning is between the two, in the middle range—let us say five to nine years—where planning can be done with some sense of attachment to current realities but is a little bit free to escape from the sort of dense gravitational field of present policy commitments.

I think it was Bismarck who once said, "Political decisions should not be concerned with periods of more than three years." This was very poor advice, certainly as far as we are concerned. The lead time of a new weapon system or space system is about seven or eight years, from the first idea until there is deployed operational hardware in the form of a system. The gestation period for a new industrial power is about one generation. So everything argues for better planning, and everything argues for having a clearer picture of where we want to go, as well as predictions about where we are being taken.

I am always struck by the fact that the papers of the sort I described before begin with a definition of the threat. Then policy is formulated on the basis of the threat. I think this contributes to a constant sense of a reactive policy that is racing to keep up with events that others are creating. Of course, this is true; this is why we have a State Department and a military establishment. But it is not enough, which I think is the theme of today's lecture.

In exercises such as this it is customary to start out with primordial values of national security and survival. I would like to have it taken as given, so we do not spend very much time on it.

The first charge on American leadership is, of course, national survival in a form that maximizes our national values. This of course makes security a prime yardstick, but it does something else; it means that policies that are pressed on the political center by the extremes simply cannot be contemplated by responsible leadership— and I mean the President. For example, by this reasoning it is not in the national interest to launch a surprise nuclear attack in order to crush our enemies preemptively, an attack which is likely to take tens of millions of lives at a minimum. This simply does not conform to the definition of survival in a form that is consistent with values that individuals as well as the nation as a whole cherish.

It also means to me that a President cannot indulge in acts of extreme self-renunciation such as unilateral disarmament, because this too does not comply with his basic charge. I think one takes it as given as the primordial national purpose. To sum up this country's external purposes in an overall way would go something like this; it sounds like what Dean Rusk, Walt Rostow, and other members of this and previous Administrations said: "To create the sort of world environment around us in which the United States can survive with its own values intact." Here is perhaps where I deviate from the others, by adding "but can also enjoy its survival."

If you do not have any fun, if life is as bleak as some of our statements of national purpose suggest, I am not sure it is worth it, so I would add to this statement of the environment we are trying to create, "one in which we not only survive but can enjoy our values as well as talk about them."

Having said these things, I would like to abandon all clichés now and forever, or at least until I give another speech on this subject, and become as precise as possible by looking into this middle range of time and trying to identify what seem to me the most important of what you would call "specific national objectives," of American foreign policy and strategy. By "strategy" I do not mean purely military; I mean an orchestration of policies which may include military, economic, political, psychological, and others.

It seems to me these are objectives which a present President of the United States or a future President might legitimately see as what he is aiming to achieve, fitted into a hierarchy of national values, national purpose, national strategies, national policies, national tactics. When I do this as just one lonely scholar I come up with seven paramount, vital, middle-range, specific national objectives of this country in the world around it. You may disagree with this; you may think there are three or five or twenty. These are my seven. (Some of these have subgoals.) And this is generally the order in which I see the United States pursuing its interests in the form of pursuing specific national objectives.

The first one, in my view, is *prevention of a general thermonuclear war*. If this is not attained, all other goals, including "winning over communism"—whatever that means in your own minds—become relatively meaningless. I think President Kennedy gave the best, succinct relationship of this to the overall American interest when he told an off-the-record group once, "Our major problem overall is the survival of our country, the protection of its vital interests without the beginning of the third and perhaps the last war." This is the decade we live in.

Here is where the peaceniks and I part company; this objective does not, as some people assert, automatically imply that military power is either irrelevant or obsolete. It does not imply that chances for world peace would necessarily improve by dismantling our military establishment. Besides being essential in the pursuit of other national objectives which I will talk about, military power (as I said at the very outset) serves our highest interests at the highest level as the deterrent of the war no one wants, and, I think, has succeeded in doing so. I think that maybe instead of fighting World War III we will go straight to World War IV, which will be somewhere in the southern half of Africa. I will come back to that.

For two decades the Cold War has been waged without a thermonuclear war. I think it is probably the presence of nuclear weapons which has done this. The Cuban Crisis of 1962 was a powerful convincer to me, at least, of the truth missed by many

who are genuinely dedicated to peace, that such peace as we have is presently served by our occasional willingness to risk nuclear war. This, of course, sums up the fundamental paradox of the age.

Deterrent capability means above all a well protected or mobile or invisible or unreachable, and well controlled second strike nuclear capability. Here I am at odds with some of my friends in and out of government, but I must say that this kind of philosophy or this kind of apparatus would still be necessary under almost any conceivable kind of arms control and even disarmament agreements.

Under this category of security, then, I would put as the first subobjective: *To maintain a military capability that deters major aggression.* Having accepted that, we are caught in the fantastic dilemma that to actually use this apparatus would be, if not suicidal, close to fatal.

The second subgoal is this: There is an increasing questioning in this country about how automatic American intervention ought to be in local conflicts around the world. Some vital interests of the United States make the outcome of some of these conflicts of extreme importance to the United States and make it imperative for the United States to manipulate the conflict in order to insure an outcome consistent with U.S. security interests. But the question is: Are there other local conflicts in the developing areas where it is not in the United States' interest to intervene, where there are no vital U.S. interests, where we should not have an automatic response to insurgency or to local wars, where we should not feel that we have to choose sides?

I think the objective here is *a strategy of local conflict control alongside our strategy of intervention.* Achieving such an objective would mean caring less about certain pieces of real estate in the world. It means being less dogmatic about an automatic danger of communism in any insurgency; over half the insurgencies since World War II have had no Communist elements of any significance. It means using multilateral peacekeeping and peacemaking agencies as substitutes for U.S. intervention, but always with great power deterrence in the background.

I think it was Herman Kahn who pioneered the notion that before you design a new weapons system you should always ask the question of how it specifically will affect the arms race, or such arms race as may take place. This is now commonplace. I think it was not a decade ago. So, the third subgoal of American security policy in the middle range, to me, would run something like this: *To moderate the arms race, preferably to reverse the trend of quantitative and qualitative acceleration in the building of weapons of great destructive power and to create new arrangements for political and military security which conform to the realities.*

My best authority here would be Secretary McNamara, who said: "We view arms control as a major component of our efforts to achieve security, and the day when Americans will no longer regard arms control and deterrents as enemies will be the day of great sophistication and great promise for American policy." I think that is a fine statement. To me this does not mean anything as frankly nonsensical as general and complete disarmament, particularly in four years, which was the bad joke advanced by Mr. Khrushchev in New York in 1959. It means to me regulation, limitation, balanced reductions of armaments, and a wide variety of measures, many of which we are taking or have taken to stimulate reciprocal action. So far as the spread of nuclear weapons is concerned, this belongs in the same subcategory. If the achievement of our strategic goal does call for limiting the spread of nuclear weapons—and I think it does—we may have to pay some higher costs than we are now prepared to pay, such as enforcing agreements that are reached on countries that go ahead and build nuclear weapons anyway, giving guarantees where we do not want to give guarantees, or finding agencies to act as umbrellas or fig leaves for American and Soviet power. I am speaking about the United Nations.

The second great middle-range objective of the United States, I would say, is *to find a better basis for U.S.–Soviet relations.* If the U.S. is unable or unwilling to crush the physical power of the Soviet Union, there is, of course, no rational alternative but to work out arrangements for living with them, arrangements which are more advantageous to both. This means a number of specific things—encouraging the process of change in the Communist world, while being quite certain not to offer new opportunities they cannot resist. I think this is one of the crucial things about détente that is not often enough said.

I remember when President-elect Kennedy sent Walt Rostow and Jerry Weisner to a Pugwash meeting in the Soviet Union in 1960 as a kind of cover to conduct some conversations with Soviet leaders. They came back with a very strong conviction that the Soviet leadership had been on the verge of seeing things in a way that we would consider more acceptable, except for one thing that had happened, and that was Cuba. It was just too tempting a plum. No good Marxist could go home and face his mother if he had foregone an opportunity like this, which, of course, is fundamental to Marxism—the seizing of opportunities. The Cuban opportunity was overwhelming. So to achieve our objective here, we have to make certain that these sorts of openings are minimized.

General De Gaulle, whose perhaps most irritating quality is that of occasionally being right, sees the future of Russia as an essentially European power, purged of its messianic drives. But I do not think this prophecy is necessarily self-fulfilling, so it seems to me in the U.S. interest to bring Russia out of Asia and into Europe, particularly as the Chinese supply the momentum with a kick from the rear. It seems to me a vivid image of what is happening in the 1960s.

As far as China is concerned—and here we move to two more objectives—there is no indication that the Chinese comrades are ready yet for this kind of *embourgeoisement,* the Fiat factory, superhighways, and "Let's not have a war in the Middle East," although in practice China operates a very cautious policy.

One of the fascinating questions to put to Kremlinologists is this: "Where on the

Soviet timetable is China?" You get some fascinating answers, ranging from 1922 and the NEP all the way to about 1950. The answer may be, "There is no comparability. There is no one-to-one relationship."

But even given our profound ignorance about China, I would advance two more specific American objectives—three and four, if you will—and I would like to list them together. The first is *to contain and civilize Communist China.* The other is *to avert a worldwide racial conflict.* You will notice I state these together, and I am sure the reasons are obvious. So far as China is concerned, my military friends rate mainland China as of only moderate concern for the next decade or so in terms of efficient nuclear delivery systems of at least intermediate range, in terms of sophisticated warheads, economic yield-to-weight ratios, invulnerable launching platforms, advanced early warning systems, and all the paraphernalia of superpower military command and control and power.

The thing that interests me here is China in two other roles. The first is China as an unsettling force on the Asian periphery. I do not necessarily say "expansive," although there are Chinese maps which show you where China presumably would expand to if she could—former Chinese territories in many cases. The second (and this is why I have related these objectives three and four) is China as a catalyst for something which I think we should be more afraid of than China lobbing nuclear weapons into San Francisco, and that is China as a catalyst for a fundamental conflict between the races. I do not think this should need any spelling out for students of the American scene today or of the world scene. I do not propose to spell it out except to say that Peking has tried occasionally and very seriously to act on her belief that conflict along racial lines is a sort of polarity that is useful to manipulate and to exacerbate. The awakening of nonwhite races around the world to all of the implications of power and affluence which have long been the monopoly of white Western European man is an enormously potent force in the world, which China has frequently seemed to view as a level by which, through some kind of

political judo, she will convert great weakness to get strength.

In Africa the Chinese have said: "The Russians are your enemies, too; they are white." The time may not be ripe for this, and the Chinese have played it down for the last couple of years, but I think that is purely tactical, and one should not write it off.

This great fourth strategic objective of the United States should be to see that the crystallization of latent racial antagonisms, this mobilization along blood lines, continent against continent, never takes place. Of course, this means a number of things. It means above all resolving our racial problems at home. It also means the related problem of racism and colonialism in the southern half of Africa.

Southern Africa (not just South Africa) has, I think, two meanings to American strategy; one is as a kind of time bomb which is ticking very slowly, very slowly, but someday could open the way to chaos and perhaps to communism; the Communists are about the only effective opposition force left in South Africa. And it could someday also be the trigger for this larger racial cannon, or tidal wave, if I can change the metaphor, on which Chinese Communist leaders apparently fancy themselves riders of the crest.

I think myself that vital U.S. interests are going to be served by detailed policy goals that aim at these two problems: China and the racial problem. To me they are inextricably linked.

George Kennan's prescription for containment sounds pretty good here, although perhaps not completely applicable. But China's capacity to inflame racist passions into a kind of holy war also must be reduced, and it is very late for this. Having visited Africa, I am even more depressed about the possibility. As someone put it: "The sleeping princess that was China, has been awakened by the wrong kiss." It is a beautiful metaphor; I do not really know what to do with it, but I wanted to use it.

The American policy of "containment without isolation" seems to be the catch word of the times. This probably means deliberate American moves to demonstrate to Peking that normally acceptable behavior will be a passport to tolerable relations with the U.S., but without demanding total surrender of the Chinese Communist regime. There is a role in the UN for the Chinese Communists. We saw them almost get in last year, but they did not. Arms talks do not make too much sense without the Chinese Communists. I think we are just beginning to see the beginning of this strategy of exposure, containment, and efforts to bring China into the established order.

As far as South Africa is concerned, there is a powder train there, starting with Rhodesia, running through Angola down to Mozambique, through Southwest Africa into South Africa. I am fully aware that American investments are flourishing there, that the South African regime is strong, that they may even moderate. I am aware that you can get, I think, 27 percent return on your investments in South Africa; it is that secure in the eyes of investment bankers. But if you look ahead and follow this powder train, I just do not want to see the United States posed at the end of it with a kind of impossible choice, with a do-or-die stand by the white man in Southern Africa as the only alternative. I think our country is going to find itself asked to make some very difficult choices, and I do not want to see us forced into that corner. So I think the objective of policy under this heading is to see that it never comes to that, which means working out our own preferred alternative for solutions. I do not see the alternatives coming from either extreme as of any value, and I do not think there is much choice but to develop something which will appeal to moderate white men and indeed to all reasonable men. Perhaps we will come back to all of these.

I will move on to the fifth middle-range objective. I would call this *winning the battle of modernization in the developing countries.* Here is one place where I would suggest we can win over communism; it has one of the few tangible meanings you can get a hold on; it is very hard to measure and very hard to get a box score, but there is a "war" going on which is creative and constructive. I think the United States is

doing rather badly in it. If the present Senate bill on foreign aid is passed, we will be not only sixth among the countries of the world in the proportion of our participation in the development process, but we will be contributing something like one-third of one percent of our gross national product to this process, which seems to me a very paltry investment given the vital interests of ours involved in it.

The one thing I would like to say about this is that our objective had better not be to try to manipulate or control or even have particularly good relationships with these countries as they are passing through the most acute phases of modernization. I think that has proven to be an unworkable and an unrealistic objective. I think our objective is to lay the foundation for good relations with these countries *after* they have passed through the first rude stages of transition, and you can find all the documentations for that you want in the history of the United States during its first forty years.

In passing through that stage we are going to have a sequence of disappointments and disillusionments and frustrations, and perhaps an unending series of Dominican Republics and trying to buy off the head man in Singapore (which bounced back on us badly), even Cubas. But to give just two other examples—Indonesia and Ghana—the investments we have made when people were sticking their fingers in our eyes, but we still put a little money and a bit of confidence on the line for them, have paid off dramatically. So I would say we seek in the long run societies that will be friendly to us and preferably democratic in their complexion. But this does require an investment of resources, a commitment to people, and a willingness to encourage peaceful revolution without any real assurance about the outcome.

The next basic, vital, specific U.S. national objective that I can find expressed as a middle-range objective I will state rather generally and become more specific. It is *to make progress towards a longer-term goal, which is that of transforming international society into something representing a little more true community.* I make the distinction between "society" and "community." This does not to me necessarily mean world government. It does not even mean what was popular in our policy community for some years: amalgamating countries into ever larger units.

This age is one of neo-nationalism and does not look like a very fertile soil for drastic supranationalism. As far as world government is concerned, I do not think the advocates have ever really thought through the implications of tyranny on a global scale. I do not think I like world government, but I do like this kind of process of transformation into community from society. It means establishing reasonable and preferably exciting goals of community-building. That is where one recognizes the growing web of interconnectedness between national societies in which everyone in this world is bound up and where creative political substitutes can be found. They can be found for historically disruptive nationalism of the virulent and exclusive type, always remembering that the vices of extreme nationalism are mirror images of its virtues, that for example, in Eastern Europe are beginning to create a newer and a freer pattern for those people.

So we are talking about a society of independent states (I think the catchword in Washington for some years has been "interdependent") that on some issues will have agreed in advance to submit to the will of some qualified majority but with some form of national veto when *in extremis*. This seems to me the realistic goal in the realm of building order and building community.

Universal collective security remains an ideal. Dean Rusk will go down in history, I imagine, as the man who desperately clung to the lessons of the 1930s, particularly the lesson of collective security. He is so deeply committed to this in the context of world order that whether he is right or wrong about his views on Vietnam he deserves respect.

The creation of consensus—and I do not mean necessarily in any partisan American sense—to me as a political scientist is so fundamental that when I hear people talking about the goal of world law, world order, and international armies to do the

will of the United Nations, and so on, it seems to me that any high school student should know (but very few orators at conferences of international law seem to know) that before you can have law you must have some kind of community, and before you can have some kind of community you have to have some kind of consensus about certain basic values or about certain basic tasks. Fear of being annihilated just is not enough of a common interest to work with, although it is a beginning.

To build these fragments of communities, to encourage the formation of functional cooperation, of institutions, regional and global, within this context, is an American goal. I could spell this out, but I do not think I will take the time except to say with respect to Europe that it is no news to anyone that regarding U.S. policy in Europe we are still a decade behind the way the Europeans see Europe, and I do not think we have caught up. I think we are still prisoners of the '40s and '50s in our policies and even in our rhetoric. They go along with us when they come to the ranch, but they do not go along with us in their own chancellories, parliaments, and newspapers. The subgoal here would certainly be *to develop a kind of relationship with Europe that conforms to the changed realities*—realities not just as seen from the basement of the White House or the seventh floor of the State Department, but from Whitehall, the Quai d'Orsay, and a dozen other places.

The final middle-range objective I phrased as *capturing the technological revolution before it captures us*. As I suggested at the outset, I feel the time is overripe when one must question this unbalanced worship of science for science's sake, technology for technology's sake, because this is a cult that could end by annihilating us. Just as military actions are meaningless without political purposes, so I believe scientific actions may end up having no real meaning apart from the values they have for the individual and for the community. This may seem a very political view of science. I suppose it is, but I just do not think we have been well served by this mystique which you have heard over and over again that insists on the right to make vital national choices for us but at the same time scorns "politics" as a dirty word, diplomacy as some kind of obsolete activity, and military power as an evil. I think this is what we are up against in our dialog with our fellow scientists.

It seems to me there are areas of action here where applied science conforms to all the purposes of American policy that I have stated. The obvious ones are population, food supply, power and water for the arid zones, massive technical and scientific solutions to urban blight, and the tremendously unfulfilled need for housing around the world. These are tangible, concrete, vital problems. To include these in strategic national goals and national doctrine would, I think, generate pressures on technology which would adapt to socially valuable purposes.

I do not want to be understood as advocating Lysenkoism and the totalitarian disease of controlling science—not a bit. Science must remain free. But government in this country is virtually supporting science, and without a better thought-through linkage between their respective values and purposes, I am gripped by the fear that statesmen, soldiers, diplomats, and all of us the world over are going to continue to be confronted and threatened with the products of politically mindless choices that were made on some drawing board or in some laboratory ten years ago.

I do not think I could conclude this brief, superficial and doubtless unsatisfactory summary of how I see this problem any better than quoting from the redoubtable Reinhold Niebuhr on the relationship of national interests to the wider community of men when he said this:

Every nation must come to terms with the fact that though the force of collective self-interest is so great that national policy must be based on it, yet also the sensitive conscience recognizes that the moral obligation of the individual transcends his particular community. Loyalty to the community is therefore morally tolerable only if it includes values wider than those of the community.

PART I

DEFENSE POLICIES: THE LIMITED EMPLOYMENT OF FORCE

This first major part of the book is concerned with American defense policies—the substantive issues of strategy. These are complex and varied policies covering such subjects as deterrence, alliances, compellence, and civic action. They are grouped into chapters and within each chapter various categories of war are discussed. Alternate strategies are examined within each category. Generally, within the chapters the earlier articles are more theoretical, wheras the latter articles deal with more specific issues. Hopefully, these readings provide information concerning both actual defense policies and the nature of war.

Superpowers are nations which have an "assured destruction" capability, that is, an invulnerable second-strike force which can inflict "unacceptable damage." Chapter 1 presents the idea that is the linchpin of modern defense policy: the recognition that an all-out thermonuclear exchange between superpowers would be an unprecedented and unmitigated disaster. While seemingly an obvious fact, it is difficult to keep constantly in mind, both because the results would be so horrible and also because there is a psychological tendency on the part of the individual to reject the idea that he and his society can be destroyed. And that is exactly what this linchpin concept means—that in narrow terms of military capabilities there is nothing we can do to prevent the Soviet Union from destroying the United States if she is determined to do so. Robert McNamara indicated the psychological difficulties involved in accepting this idea when, at the end of his seven years in office, he stated that his greatest achievement as Secretary of Defense was to educate the American people "that there can be no victory in strategic nuclear war."

Nevertheless, as history has shown, force still plays a role in the nuclear age. But the important lesson is that the rational role of force must be a limited role. In precise terms, by "limited" we mean something less than an all-out thermonuclear exchange between superpowers. In addition, even lesser uses of force must themselves be limited in order to decrease the probability of escalation to that cataclysm. This means that the range of rational uses of force is still very wide, but because of the threat of escalation, uncertainly wide.

Limitation is the central theme for modern defense policy and the central theme of Part I. Since all of the policies discussed are limited policies, the critical question is how well are they limited? The dilemma here, of course, is to limit them enough to avoid igniting the all-out exchange and yet to keep them large enough to be effective.

One can study this limitation by dividing the spectrum of war into three categories, categories which are themselves based upon increasing limitations on the use of force.

The first category is normally referred to as general war. Unfortunately, the names for these categories are not universally accepted. McNamara, in the quote above, refers to this category as "strategic nuclear war." For teaching purposes, we believe the title "central war" is most useful, and so include it, in parentheses, in the heading for Chapter 2 which deals with the subject. Central war is primarily defined in geographic terms. It is a war involving strikes on the homelands of superpowers (at this writing, the United States and the Soviet Union). It is generally assumed that nuclear weapons would be used, because the nuclear threshold is likely to be crossed before reaching the central sanctuary threshold. Even in this chapter on general war, the theme of limitation is apparent. The chapter's dual topics of deterrence and defense are both limitations, one by avoidance, the other mainly by damage limitation. A third type of limitation that is most closely related to central war is Arms Control, discussed in Chapter 3 which follows.

Chapter 4 clearly indicates the theme of Part I in its title "limited war." However, the subject matter of limited war falls naturally into two divisions that we call noncentral war and counterinsurgency. These two divisions, plus the one earlier discussed, comprise the three categories of war: central war, noncentral war, and counterinsurgency.

The literature which deals with the second category of war, noncentral war, again reflects the lack of consensus on the names for these categories. What we refer to as noncentral war is often called local war or even more simply, limited war. We prefer noncentral as it emphasizes that the geographic locale is other than the superpowers' homelands and as it avoids the inference that general (central) wars are unlimited.

The third category of war, counterinsurgency, also has produced a profusion of names. It is variously called sub-limited war, guerrilla war, revolutionary war, wars of national liberation, and insurgencies. Writing on American defense policy, we choose "counterinsurgency." A greater difficulty is that this category is logically a subspecies of our second category, which more precisely would be, "noncentral war except counterinsurgency." This relationship is indicated by including the last two categories in the same chapter, Chapter 4.

Finally, Chapter 5 presents the views of some other nuclear nations to provide further basis for understanding and evaluating American defense policies.

CHAPTER 2

General (Central) War: Alternate Strategies

In this chapter we begin the discussion of actual American defense policies, the substantive issues of vital significance to our country. The introduction to Part I divides these policies into three categories of war: general war, noncentral war, and counterinsurgency. This chapter deals with the category highest on the spectrum of violence—general war.

Instead of the term "general war," we have stated our preference for "central war," a title which reflects the primary characteristic of these wars—strikes on the homelands of the superpowers. The assumption is that nuclear weapons probably would be used in these strikes. Nuclear strikes on the homelands of the superpowers brings us frightfully close to an all-out thermonuclear exchange, the unprecedented and unmitigated disaster which we established as our linchpin concept of modern defense policy.

Since nations must try to avoid a cataclysmic all-out thermonuclear exchange, the strategies, even for general war, reflect the theme of limitation whenever there is rational "thinking about the unthinkable."

In general war there are two primary strategies to limit the use of force. One strategy is deterrence, which utilizes the threat of our retaliation to limit both the enemy's use of force and damage to ourselves. If successful, both the enemy's use of force and our damage are limited completely—they are avoided, or deterred. Deterrence essentially works on an enemy's *intentions* during peacetime (although the concept has been extended to intrawar deterrence, the discouraging of movement to higher levels of action during a war).

The second strategy of limitation is defense, which Glenn Snyder initially defines as a "denial [of occupation of territory]

capability plus capacity to alleviate war damage." Defense reduces the enemy's *capabilities* to damage or deprive us during wartime.

Glenn Snyder's work on deterrence and defense and the tradeoffs between them is a brilliant theoretical introduction to these two strategies. Perhaps the most important lesson in his article is the idea that deterrence deals with intentions, measured as *probabilities*; and defense deals with capabilities to reduce damage, measured in terms of *values*. Both probabilities and values have always been important, but in the past there has been a tendency to ignore the latter. However, in the nuclear era when every military action not only can gain or lose some value, but also can change the probability of an all-out thermonuclear exchange, both factors must be made explicit. Thus, even the most simplified "risk calculus" for actions must include both values and probabilities.

This division into two strategies, deterrence and defense, is continued in the two articles by Herman Kahn. The first article is an examination of possible postures for deterrence. His Table I depicts eight deterrent postures, listed in order of increasing numbers of weapons required. Four postures are selected as especially realistic: Finite Deterrence, Counterforce as Insurance, Preattack Mobilization Base, and Credible First Strike Capability.

Kahn's second article is concerned with the period in which defense occurs: wartime. Here he goes beyond deterrence to consider how, even with the existing deterrent forces, war might begin. He groups the ways general war might start into four rough categories: inadvertent war, war as a result of a miscalculation, calculated war, and catalytic war. Then he lists the ways general war might be fought in terms of five different types of targeting objectives. Here again the theme of limitation appears as the different attacks are listed in order of increasing "possibilities of limiting destruction and death."

The dual topics of deterrence and defense are central to Robert McNamara's statement to Congress. He discusses these concepts in terms of capabilities. Deterrence requires a capability for "assured destruction," the ability "to inflict unacceptable damage on an attacker, even were that attacker to strike first." The capability for defense is called "damage limitation," since that is the function it performs for us. The Secretary of Defense makes an annual defense "posture statement" to Congress. We selected the 1966 fiscal year statement because we consider it the best basic exposition of the general nuclear war problem. More recent posture statements contain more specific up-to-date information.

Finally, Thomas Schelling's reading on what is today generally called "limited strategic retaliation" demonstrates the extent to which the theme of limitation has become accepted, even within the realm of general war. Limited strategic retaliation is a central war—a war involving strikes on the homelands of the superpowers—but it is a war in which very few weapons are exploded on the initial strikes.

In the form of city exchanges (for example, trading New York for Moscow) it seems especially bizarre on first glance. However, it is the nuclear world that is bizarre; the strategy is rational within that fantastic world. Certainly compared to an all-out thermonuclear exchange, limited strategic retaliation is more sane. Perhaps the logic of limited strategic retaliation can be seen if compared with the logic of a union strike in industry. A union strike is illogical in that both workers and management are hurt by and during the strike. However, the union strike is a competition in resolve, and the two sides may be able to come to an agreement that they could not have reached without the "irrational" mutual punishment of the strike. General nuclear war may be analogous, and certainly the damage resulting from, say the loss of New York, however huge and horrible, is preferable to the apocalyptic destruction of our entire society. Of course, the frightful and unanswerable questions are: Could such a strategy be controlled and could the process be stopped? Limited strategic retaliation is a grim reminder of the horrors of the thermonuclear era.

DETERRENCE AND DEFENSE:
A THEORETICAL INTRODUCTION

BY GLENN H. SNYDER

National security still remains an "ambiguous symbol," as one scholar described it almost a decade ago.[1] Certainly it has grown more ambiguous as a result of the startling advances since then in nuclear and weapons technology, and the advent of nuclear parity between the United States and the Soviet Union. Besides such technological complications, doctrine and thought about

[1] Arnold Wolfers, " 'National Security' as an Ambiguous Symbol," *Political Science Quarterly*, Vol. LXVII, No. 4 (December 1952), pp. 481ff.

Reprinted by permission from *Deterrence and Defense: Toward A Theory of National Security* (Princeton: Princeton University Press, 1961), pp. 3–51. Copyright 1961 by Princeton University Press.

Mr. Snyder is Professor of Political Science at the State University of New York, Buffalo. He was formerly associated with the Princeton University Center for International Studies, and is the author of *Stockpiling of Strategic Materials* (1966), and other works.

the role of force in international politics have introduced additional complexities. We now have, at least in embryonic form, theories of limited war, of deterrence, of "tactical" vs. "strategic" uses of nuclear weapons, of "retaliatory" vs. "counterforce" strategies in all-out war, of "limited retaliation," of the mechanics of threat and commitment-making, of "internal war," "protracted conflict," and the like. Above all, the idea of the "balance of terror" has begun to mature, but its relation to the older concept of the "balance of power" is still not clear. We have had a great intellectual ferment in the strategic realm, which of course is all to the good. What urgently remains to be done is to tie together all of these concepts into a coherent framework of theory so that the end-goal of national security may become less ambiguous, and so that the military means available for pursuance of this goal may be accumulated, organized, and used more efficiently. This book can claim to make only a start in this direction.

The central theoretical problem in the field of national security policy is to clarify and distinguish between the two central concepts of *deterrence* and *defense*. Essentially, deterrence means discouraging the enemy from taking military action by posing for him a prospect of cost and risk outweighing his prospective gain. Defense means reducing our own prospective costs and risks in the event that deterrence fails. Deterrence works on the enemy's *intentions;* the *deterrent value* of military forces is their effect in reducing the likelihood of enemy military moves. Defense reduces the enemy's *capability* to damage or deprive us; the *defense value* of military forces is their effect in mitigating the adverse consequences for us of possible enemy moves, whether such consequences are counted as losses of territory or war damage. The concept of "defense value," therefore, is broader than the mere capacity to hold territory, which might be called "denial capability." Defense value is denial capability plus capacity to alleviate war damage.

It is a commonplace, of course, to say that the primary objectives of national security policy are to deter enemy attacks and to defend successfully, at minimum cost, against those attacks which occur. It is less widely recognized that different types of military force contribute in differing proportions to these two objectives. Deterrence does not vary directly with our capacity for fighting wars effectively and cheaply; a particular set of forces might produce strong deterrent effects and not provide a very effective denial and damage-alleviating capability. Conversely, forces effective for defense might be less potent deterrents than other forces which were less efficient for holding territory and which might involve extremely high war costs if used.

One reason why the periodic "great debates" about national security policy have been so inconclusive is that the participants often argue from different premises—one side from the point of view of deterrence, and the other side from the point of view of defense. For instance, in the famous "massive retaliation" debate of 1954, the late Secretary of State Dulles and his supporters argued mainly that a capacity for massive retaliation would deter potential Communist mischief, but they tended to ignore the consequences should deterrence fail. The critics, on the other hand, stressed the dire consequences should the threat of massive retaliation fail to deter and tended to ignore the possibility that it might work. The opposing arguments never really made contact because no one explicitly recognized that considerations of reducing the probability of war and mitigating its consequences must be evaluated simultaneously, that the possible consequences of a failure of deterrence are more or less important depending on the presumed likelihood of deterrence. Many other examples could be cited.

Perhaps the crucial difference between deterrence and defense is that deterrence is primarily a peacetime objective, while defense is a wartime value. Deterrent value and defense value are directly enjoyed in different time periods. We enjoy the deterrent value of our military forces prior to the enemy's aggressive move; we enjoy defense value after the enemy move has already been made, although we indirectly profit from defense capabilities in advance of war through our knowledge that if the enemy attack occurs we have the means of mitigating its consequences. The crucial point is that *after* the enemy's attack takes place, our military forces perform different functions and yield wholly different values than they did as deterrents prior to the attack. As deterrents they engaged in a psychological battle—dissuading the enemy from attacking by attempting to confront him with a prospect of costs greater than his prospective gain. After the enemy begins his attack, while the psychological or deterrent aspect does not entirely disappear, it is partly supplanted by another purpose: to resist the enemy's onslaught in order to minimize *our* losses or perhaps maximize *our* gains, not only with regard to the future balance of power, but also in terms of intrinsic or non-power values. That combination of forces which appeared to be the optimum one from the point of view of deterrence might turn out to be far inferior to some other combination from the point of view of defense should deterrence fail. In short, maximizing the enemy's cost expectancy may not always be consistent with minimizing our own. Thus we must measure the value of our military forces on two yardsticks, and we must find some way of combining their value on *both* yardsticks, in order accurately to gauge their aggregate worth or "utility" and to make intelligent choices among the various types of forces available.

Before launching into a theoretical analysis of the concepts of deterrence and defense, it may be useful to present a sampling of policy issues involving a need to choose between deterrence and defense; the examples will be treated in more detail in subsequent chapters.

A. EXAMPLES OF CHOICES AND CONFLICTS BETWEEN DETERRENCE AND DEFENSE

A strategic retaliatory air force sufficient only to wreak minimum "unacceptable" damage on Soviet cities—to destroy, say, 20 cities—after this force had been decimated by a surprise Soviet nuclear attack, would have great value for deterring such a surprise attack and might be an adequate deterrent against that contingency. But if deterrence were to fail and the Soviet attack took place, it would then not be rational to *use* such a minimum force in massive retaliation against Soviet cities, since this would only stimulate the Soviets to inflict further damage upon us and would contribute nothing to our "winning the war." If we are interested in defense—i.e., in winning the war and in minimizing the damage to us—as well as in deterrence, we may wish to have (if technically feasible) a much larger force and probably one of different composition—a force which can strike effectively at the enemy's remaining forces (thus reducing our own costs) and, further, either by actual attacks or the threat of attacks, force the enemy to surrender or at least to give up his territorial gains.

The threat of massive nuclear retaliation against a Soviet major ground attack in Western Europe may continue to provide considerable deterrence against such an attack, even if actually to carry out the threat would be irrational because of the enormous costs we would suffer from Soviet counter-retaliation. Strategic nuclear weapons do not provide a rational means of defense in Western Europe unless they not only can stop the Russian ground advance but also, by "counterforce" strikes, can reduce to an acceptable level the damage we would suffer in return. We may not have this capability now and it may become altogether infeasible as the Soviets develop their missile technology. For a means of rational defense, therefore, NATO may need enough ground forces to hold Europe against a full-scale attack by Soviet ground forces. This does not mean, however, that we necessarily must maintain ground forces of this size. If we think the probability of attack is low enough, we may decide to continue relying on nuclear deterrence primarily, even though it does not provide a rational means of defense. In other words, we might count on the Soviet uncertainties about whether or not nuclear retaliation is rational for us, and about how rational we are, to inhibit the Soviets from attacking in the face of the terrible damage they *know* they would suffer if they guessed wrong.

An attempt to build an effective counter-force capability, in order to have both a rational nuclear defense and a more credible nuclear deterrent against ground attack in Europe, might work against the *deterrence* of direct nuclear attack on the United States. Since such a force, by definition, would be able to eliminate all but a small fraction of the Soviet strategic nuclear forces if it struck first, the Soviets might, in some circumstances, fear a surprise attack and be led to strike first themselves in order to forestall it.

Tactical nuclear weapons in the hands of NATO forces in Europe have considerable deterrent value because they increase the enemy's cost expectation beyond what it would be if these forces were equipped only with conventional weapons. This is true not only because the tactical weapons themselves can inflict high costs on the enemy's forces, but also because their use (or an enemy "pre-emptive" strike against them would sharply raise the probability that the war would spiral to all-out dimensions. But the defense value of tactical nuclear weapons against conventional attack is comparatively low against an enemy who also possesses them, because their use presumably would be offset by the enemy's use of them against our forces, and because in using such weapons we would be incurring much greater costs and risks than if we had responded conventionally.

For deterrence, it might be desirable to render automatic a response which the enemy recognizes as being costly for us, and communicate the fact of such automation to the enemy, thus reducing his doubts that we would actually choose to make this response when the occasion for it arose. For example, a tactical nuclear response to conventional aggression in Europe may be made semi-automatic by thoroughly orienting NATO plans, organization, and strategy around this response, thus increasing the difficulty of following a non-nuclear strategy in case of a Soviet challenge. But such automation would not be desirable for defense, which would require flexibility and freedom to choose the least costly action

in the light of circumstances at the time of the attack.

The Continental European attitude toward NATO strategy is generally ambivalent on the question of deterrence vs. defense; there is fear that with the Soviet acquisition of a substantial nuclear and missile capability, the willingness of the United States to invoke massive retaliation is declining, and that therefore the deterrent to aggression has weakened. Yet the Europeans do not embrace the logical consequence of this fear: the need to build up an adequate capacity to defend Europe on the ground. A more favored alternative, at least in France, is the acquisition of an independent strategic nuclear capability. But when European governments project their imaginations forward to the day when the enemy's divisions cross their borders, do they really envisage themselves shooting off their few missiles against an enemy who would surely obliterate them in return? One doubts that they do, but this is not to say that it is irrational for them to acquire such weapons; they might be successful as a deterrent because of Soviet uncertainty as to whether they would be used, and Soviet unwillingness to incur the risk of their being used.

Further examples easily come to mind. For the sake of deterrence in Europe, we might wish to deploy the forces there as if they intended to respond to an attack with nuclear weapons; but this might not be the optimum deployment for defense once the attack has occurred, if the least-cost defense is a conventional one. For deterrence of limited aggressions in Asia, it might be best to deploy troops on the spot as a "plate-glass window." But for the most efficient and flexible defense against such contingencies, troops might better be concentrated in a central reserve, with transport facilities for moving them quickly to a threatened area.

As Bernard Brodie has written,[2] if the object of our strategic air forces is only deterrence, there is little point in developing "clean" bombs; since deterrence is to be effected by the threat of dire punishment, the dirtier the better. But if we also wish

[2] Bernard Brodie, *Strategy in the Missile Age,* Princeton: Princeton University Press, 1959, p. 205.

to minimize our own costs once the war has begun, we might wish to use bombs producing minimum fall-out, to encourage similar restraint in the enemy.

For deterrence, it might be desirable to disperse elements of the Strategic Air Command to civilian airfields, thus increasing the number of targets which the enemy must hit if he is to achieve the necessary attrition of our retaliatory power by his first strike. However, this expedient might greatly increase the population damage we would suffer in the enemy's first strike, since most civilian airfields are located near large cities, assuming that the enemy would otherwise avoid hitting cities.[3]

B. THE TECHNOLOGICAL REVOLUTION

The need to *choose* between deterrence and defense is largely the result of the development of nuclear and thermonuclear weapons and long-range airpower. Prior to these developments, the three primary functions of military force—to *punish* the enemy, to *deny* him territory (or to take it from him), and to *mitigate damage* to oneself—were embodied, more or less, in the same weapons. Deterrence was accomplished (to the extent that military capabilities were the instruments of deterrence) either by convincing the prospective aggressor that his territorial aim was likely to be frustrated, or by posing for him a prospect of intolerable costs, or both, but both of these deterrent functions were performed by the *same* forces. Moreover, these same forces were also the instruments of defense if deterrence failed.

Long-range airpower partially separated the function of punishment from the function of contesting the control of territory, by making possible the assault of targets far to the rear whose relation to the land battle might be quite tenuous. Nuclear weapons vastly increased the relative importance of prospective *cost* in deterring the enemy and reduced (relatively) the importance of frus-

trating his aggressive enterprise. It is still true, of course, that a capacity to deny territory to the enemy, or otherwise to block his aims, may be a very efficient deterrent. And such denial *may* be accomplished by strategic nuclear means, though at high cost to the defender. But it is now conceivable that a prospective aggressor may be deterred, in some circumstances at least, solely or primarily by threatening and possessing the capability to inflict extreme punishment on his homeland assets and population, even though he may be superior in capabilities for contesting the control of territory. Nuclear powers must, therefore, exercise a conscious choice between the objectives of deterrence and defense, since the relative proportion of "punishment capacity" to "denial capacity" in their military establishments has become a matter of choice.

This is the most striking difference between nuclear and pre-nuclear strategy: the partial separation of the functions of pre-attack deterrence and post-attack defense, and the possibility that deterrence may now be accomplished by weapons which might have no rational use for defense should deterrence fail.

C. DETERRENCE[4]

Deterrence, in one sense, is simply the negative aspect of political power; it is the power to dissuade as opposed to the power

---

[3] This particular choice between deterrence and war costs has been analyzed by Thomas C. Shelling in an unpublished paper which I have been privileged to read.

[4] Other treatments of the theory of deterrence include Bernard Brodie, "The Anatomy of Deterrence," *World Politics*, Vol. XI, No. 2 (January 1959), pp. 173–92; Morton A. Kaplan, "The Calculus of Deterrence," *World Politics*, Vol. XI, No. 1 (October 1958), pp. 20–44; William W. Kaufmann, "The Requirements of Deterrence," in W. W. Kaufmann (ed.), *Military Policy and National Security*, Princeton: Princeton University Press, 1956; Thomas W. Milburn, "What Constitutes Effective Deterrence?" *Conflict Resolution*, Vol. III, No. 2 (June 1959), pp. 138–46; Glenn H. Snyder, "Deterrence by Denial and Punishment," Research Monograph No. 1, Center of International Studies, Princeton University, January 2, 1959; and Glenn H. Snyder, "Deterrence and Power," *Conflict Resolution*, Vol. IV, No. 2 (June 1960), pp. 163–79. Robert E. Osgood has allowed me to read several of his manuscripts on the subject which were unpublished at this writing.

to coerce or compel. One deters another party from doing something by the implicit or explicit threat of applying some sanction if the forbidden act is performed, or by the promise of a reward if the act is not performed. Thus conceived, deterrence does not have to depend on military force. We might speak of deterrence by the threat of trade restrictions, for example. The promise of economic aid might deter a country from military action (or any action) contrary to one's own interests. Or we might speak of the deterrence of allies and neutrals as well as potential enemies—as Italy, for example, was deterred from fighting on the side of the Dual Alliance in World War I by the promise of substantial territorial gains. In short, deterrence may follow, first, from any form of control which one has over an opponent's present in prospective "value inventory"; secondly, from the communication of a credible threat or promise to decrease or increase that inventory; and, thirdly, from the opponent's degree of confidence that one intends to fulfill the threat or promise.

In an even broader sense, however, deterrence is a function of the *total* cost-gain expectations of the party to be deterred, and these may be affected by factors other than the apparent capability and intention of the deterrer to apply punishments or confer rewards. For example, an incipient aggressor may be inhibited by his own conscience, or, more likely, by the prospect of losing moral standing, and hence political standing, with uncommitted countries. Or, in the specific case of the Soviet Union, he may fear that war will encourage unrest in, and possibly dissolution of, his satellite empire, and perhaps disaffection among his own population. He may anticipate that his aggression would bring about a tighter welding of the Western alliance or stimulate a degree of mobilization in the West which would either reduce his own security or greatly increase the cost of maintaining his position in the arms race. It is also worth noting that the benchmark or starting point for the potential aggressor's calculation of costs and gains from military action is not his *existing* value inventory, but the extent to which he expects that inventory

to be changed if he refrains from initiating military action. Hence, the common observation that the Russians are unlikely to undertake overt military aggression because their chances are so good for making gains by "indirect" peaceful means. Conceivably the Soviets might attack the United States, even though they foresaw greater costs than gains, if the alternative of not attacking seemed to carry within it a strong possibility that the United States would strike them first and, in doing so, inflict greater costs on the Soviet Union than it could by means of retaliation after the Soviets had struck first. In a (very abstract) nutshell, the potential aggressor presumably is deterred from a military move not simply when his expected cost exceeds his expected gain, but when the net gain is less or the net loss is more than he can expect if he refrains from the move. But this formulation must be qualified by the simple fact of inertia: deliberately to shift from a condition of peace to a condition of war is an extremely momentous decision, involving incalculable consequences, and a government is not likely to make this decision unless it foresees a very large advantage in doing so. The great importance of *uncertainty* in this context will be discussed below.

In a broad sense, deterrence operates during war as well as prior to war. It could be defined as a process of influencing the enemy's *intentions*, whatever the circumstances violent or non-violent. Typically, the outcome of wars has not depended simply on the clash of physical capabilities. The losing side usually accepts defeat somewhat before it has lost its physical ability to continue fighting. It is deterred from continuing the war by a realization that continued fighting can only generate additional costs without hope of compensating gains, this expectation being largely the consequence of the previous application of force by the dominant side.[5] In past wars, such deterrence usually has been characteristic of the terminal stages. However, in the modern concept of limited war, the intentions fac-

[5] For an excellent extended discussion of this point, with case studies, see Paul Kecskemeti, *Strategic Surrender*, Stanford: Stanford University Press, 1959.

tor is more prominent and pervasive; force may be threatened and used partly, or even primarily, as a bargaining instrument to persuade the opponent to accept terms of settlement or to observe certain limitations.[6] Deterrence in war is most sharply illustrated in proposals for a strategy of limited retaliation,[7] in which initial strikes, in effect, would be *threats* of further strikes to come, designed to deter the enemy from further fighting. In warfare limited to conventional weapons or tactical nuclear weapons, the strategic nuclear forces held in reserve by either side may constitute a deterrent against the other side's expanding the intensity of its war effort. Also, limited wars may be fought in part with an eye to deterring future enemy attacks by convincing the enemy of one's general willingness to fight.

The above observations were intended to suggest the broad scope of the concept of deterrence, its non-limitation to military factors, and its fundamental affinity to the idea of political power. In the discussion following, we shall use the term in a narrower sense, to mean the discouragement of the *initiation* of military aggression by the threat (implicit or explicit) of applying military force in response to the aggression. We shall assume that when deterrence fails and war begins, the attacked party is no longer "deterring" but rather "defending." Deterrence in war and deterrence, by military action, of subsequent aggressions will be considered as aspects of defense and will be treated later in this chapter.

1. THE LOGIC OF DETERRENCE

The object of military deterrence is to reduce the probability of enemy military attacks, by posing for the enemy a sufficiently likely prospect that he will suffer a net loss as a result of the attack, or at least a higher net loss or lower net gain than would follow from his not attacking. If we postulate two contending states, an "aggressor" (meaning potential aggressor) and a "de-

terrer," with other states which are objects of conflict between these two, the probability of any particular attack by the aggressor is the resultant of essentially four factors which exist in his "mind." All four taken together might be termed the aggressor's "risk calculus." They are (1) his valuation of his war objectives; (2) the cost which he expects to suffer as a result of various possible responses by the deterrer; (3) the probability of various responses, including "no response"; and (4) the probability of winning the objectives with each possible response. We shall assume, for simplicity's sake, that the deterrer's "response" refers to the deterrer's entire strategy of action throughout the war precipitated by the aggressor's move—i.e., not only the response to the initial aggressive move, but also to all subsequent moves by the aggressor. Thus the aggressor's estimate of costs and gains is a "whole war" estimate, depending on his image of the deterrer's entire sequence of moves up to the termination of the war, as well as on his own strategic plans for conducting the war, plans which may be contingent on what moves are made by the deterrer during the war.[8]

Obviously, we are dealing here with factors which are highly subjective and uncertain, not subject to exact measurement, and not commensurate except in an intuitive way. Nevertheless, these are the basic factors which the potential aggressor must

---

[6] See Thomas C. Schelling, *The Strategy of Conflict*, Cambridge: Harvard University Press, 1960, chap. 3.

[7] This strategy will be discussed in Chapter 3.

[8] By way of example, NATO capabilities might raise the prospect of the following possible reactions to a Soviet attack on West Germany: massive retaliation, limited retaliation with nuclear weapons on the Soviet homeland, a tactical nuclear response confined to the local theater of battle, a conventional response, or no response at all. Theoretically, the Soviets would assign a probability and a net cost or gain for themselves to each possible response (the net cost or gain representing the summation of their territorial gains, other gains, and war costs as a consequence of the entire war following the initial response), calculate an expected value for each response by multiplying the probability times the assumed net cost or gain, and determine an expected value for the aggression by summing the expected values for all possible responses. If the expected value were negative, or positive but less than the positive expected value of non-military alternatives, the Soviets would be deterred.

weigh in determining the probable costs and gains of his contemplated venture.

Certain generalizations can be made about the relationship among these factors. Factor 3 in the aggressor's calculus represents the "credibility" of various possible responses by the deterrer. But credibility is only one factor: it should not be equated with the deterrent *effectiveness* of a possible or threatened response, which is a function of all four factors—i.e., the net cost or gain which a response promises, discounted by the probability (credibility) of its being applied. An available response which is very low in credibility might be sufficient to deter if it poses a very severe sanction (e.g., massive retaliation) or if the aggressor's prospective gain carries very little value for him. Or a threatened response that carries a rather high credibility but poses only moderate costs for the aggressor—e.g., a conventional response, or nuclear retaliation after the aggressor has had the advantage of the first strategic strike—may not deter if the aggressor places a high value on his objective and anticipates a good chance of attaining it.

The credibility factor deserves special attention because it is in terms of this component that the risk calculus of the aggressor "interlocks" with that of the deterrer. The deterrer's risk calculus is similar to that of the aggressor. If the deterrer is rational, his response to aggression will be determined (within the limits, of course, of the military forces he disposes) largely by four factors: (1) his valuation of the territorial objective and of the other intangible gains (e.g., moral satisfaction) which he associates with a given response; (2) the estimated costs of fighting; (3) the probability of successfully holding the territorial objective and other values at stake; and (4) the change in the probability of future enemy attacks on other objectives which would follow from various responses. Variations on, and marginal additions to, these factors may be imagined, but these four are the essential ones. The deterrer will select the response which minimizes his expectation of cost or maximizes his expectation of gain. (As in the case of the aggressor's calculus, we assume that the deterrer's estimates of cost and gain are "whole war" estimates—i.e., the aggregate effects not only of the deterrer's initial response, but also of all the aggressor's countermoves, combined with the deterrer's counter-countermoves, over the entire progress of the war.) The credibility of various possible responses by the deterrer depends on the aggressor's image of the deterrer's risk calculus—i.e., of the latter's net costs and gains from each response—as well as on the aggressor's assessment of the deterrer's capacity to act rationally.

The aggressor, of course, is not omniscient with respect to the deterrer's estimates of cost and gain. Even the deterrer will be unable to predict in advance of the attack how he will visualize his cost-gain prospects and, hence, exactly what response he will choose once the aggression is under way. (Witness the United States response to the North Korean attack in 1950, which was motivated by values which apparently did not become clear to the decision-makers until the actual crisis was upon them.) Nor can the aggressor be sure the deterrer will act rationally according to his own cost-gain predictions. Because of these uncertainties, the aggressor's estimate of credibility cannot be precise. More than one response will be possible, and the best the aggressor can do is attempt to guess how the deterrer will visualize his gains and losses consequent upon each response, and from this guess arrive at a judgment about the likelihood or probability of each possible response.

The deterrer evaluates the *effectiveness* of his deterrent posture by attempting to guess the values of the four factors in the aggressor's risk calculus. In estimating the credibility factor, he attempts to guess how the aggressor is estimating the factors in *his* (the deterrer's) calculus. He arrives at some judgment as to whether the aggressor is likely to expect a net cost or net gain from the aggressive move and, using this judgment and his degree of confidence in it as a basis, he determines the probability of aggression. Happily, the spiral of "guesses about the other's guesses" seems to stop here. In other words, the aggressor's decision whether or not to attack is not in turn affected by his image of the deterrer's estimate of the likelihood of attack. He knows that once the attack is launched the deterrer will select the response which promises him the least cost or greatest gain—at that point, the deterrer's previous calculations about "deterrence" of that attack become irrelevant.

2. DENIAL VS. PUNISHMENT

It is useful to distinguish between deterrence which results from capacity to deny territorial gains to the enemy, and deterrence by the threat and capacity to inflict nuclear punishment.[9] Denial capabilities—typically, conventional ground, sea, and tactical air forces—deter chiefly by their effect on the fourth factor in the aggressor's calculus: his estimate of the probability of gaining his objective. Punishment capabilities—typically, strategic nuclear power for either massive or limited retaliation—act primarily on the second factor, the aggressor's estimate of possible costs, and may have little effect on his chances for territorial gain. Of course, this distinction is not sharp or absolute: a "denial" response, especially if it involves the use of nuclear weapons tactically, can mean high direct costs, plus the risk that the war may get out of hand and ultimately involve severe nuclear punishment for both sides. This prospect of cost and risk may exert a significant deterring effect. A "punishment" response, if powerful enough, may foreclose territorial gains, and limited reprisals may be able to force a settlement short of complete conquest of the territorial objective. However, there are some differences worth noting between these two types or strategies of deterrence.

Apart from their differential impact on the cost and gain elements of the aggressor's calculations, the two types of response are likely to differ also in their credibility or probability of application. As a response to all-out nuclear attack on the deterrer, the application of punishment will be highly

credible. But for lesser challenges, such as a conventional attack on an ally, a threat to inflict nuclear punishment normally will be less credible than a threat to fight a "denial" action—assuming, of course, that denial capabilities are available. While the making of a *threat* of nuclear punishment may be desirable and rational, its *fulfillment* is likely to seem irrational after the aggressor has committed his forces, since punishment alone may not be able to hold the territorial objective and will stimulate the aggressor to make counterreprisals. The deterrer therefore has a strong incentive to renege on his threat. Realizing this in advance, the aggressor may not think the threat a very credible one. A threat of denial action will seem more credible on two counts: it is less costly for the deterrer and it may be effective in frustrating the aggressor's aims, or at least in reducing his gains. A denial response is more likely than reprisal action to promise a rational means of *defense* in case deterrence fails; this consideration supports its credibility as a deterrent.

A related difference is that the threat of denial action is likely to be appraised by the aggressor in terms of the deterrer's *capabilities*; threats of nuclear punishment require primarily a judgment of *intent*. It is fairly certain that the deterrer will fight a threatened denial action if he has appropriate forces;[10] the essential question for the aggressor, therefore, is whether these forces are strong enough to prevent him from making gains. In the case of nuclear reprisals, however, the capability to inflict unacceptable punishment is likely to be unquestioned, at least for large nuclear powers; here the aggressor must attempt to look into the mind of the deterrer and guess whether the will to apply punishment exists. Thus a denial threat is much more calculable for the aggressor than a reprisal threat—assuming that a comparison of military capabilities is easier than mind-reading.

[9] This distinction is discussed by Robert E. Osgood in "A Theory of Deterrence," mimeographed, 1960, and in my own "Deterrence by Denial and Punishment," *op. cit.*

[10] It is possible that the aggressor may be able to deter "denial" resistance by threatening to take punitive action if resistance occurs. This is perhaps most feasible with respect to allies of the country attacked whose troops are not deployed on the territory of the victim.

This may make a denial strategy the more powerful deterrent of the two if the deterrer has strong denial forces; but if he obviously does not have enough ground and tactical forces to block conquest, the threat may be weaker than a nuclear reprisal threat. Even if there is doubt in the aggressor's mind that the reprisals will be carried out, these doubts may be offset by the possible severity of his punishment if he miscalculates and the threat is fulfilled.

3. A Mathematical Illustration

It is possible to express some of these relationships mathematically. The illustrations which follow are based on the assumptions that each side is able to translate and combine all of its own relevant values into a single numerical utility, that each can and does estimate probabilities for the other's moves, and that each acts rationally according to the principle of "mathematical expectation."[11] This principle states that the "expected value" of any decision or act is the sum of the expected values of all possible outcomes, the expected value of each outcome being determined by multiplying its value to the decision-making unit times the probability that it will occur. To act "rationally," according to this criterion, means simply to choose from among the available courses of action the one which promises to maximize expected value (or minimize expected cost) over the long run.

[11] The numerical illustrations are intended simply to set out as starkly as possible the essential logic of deterrence; there is no intent to light a torch for the "quantifiability" of the factors involved, which are, of course, highly intangible, unpredictable, unmeasurable, and incommensurable except in an intuitive way. It is worth keeping in mind, however, that decision-makers do have to predict, to measure, and, in some sense, to make incommensurable factors commensurate if they are to reach wise decisions. Although, in practice, the factors cannot be given precise numbers, it is legitimate, for theoretical purposes, to pretend that they can be in order to clarify the logic or method by which they should be weighed and compared. The logic is just as applicable to imprecise quantities as to precise ones; to express it in mathematical terms can provide a useful check on intuitive judgment and may bring to light factors and relationships which judgment would miss.

Imagine a world of four states: A, B, C, and D. By a happy alphabetical coincidence, we can say that A is the "aggressor" and D the "deterrer." (Those who prefer not to think in abstractions may think of A as the Soviet Union, D as the United States, B as Western Europe, and C as non-Communist Asia.) Both A and D are thermonuclear powers. They are in a condition of "nuclear stalemate"—that is, neither, by striking first at the other, can prevent the other from striking back with an effect outweighing any possible gains. We assume, therefore, that surprise attack on D is not a rational move for A, since D is practically certain to retaliate. The model deals with "secondary deterrence"—i.e., deterrence of enemy attack not against oneself, but against a third party.[12]

In the first illustration (Figures 1 and 2), which we might call the "massive retaliation" model, A has substantial conventional ground forces, but D has none. B and C are the objects of contention between A and D, and they are allied to D. B and C have neither nuclear nor conventional forces. We assume that both A and D are rational but that they are not certain of each other's rationality.

To simplify, we postulate that A has only two possible moves: to attack B with full conventional strength or not to attack at all. Similarly, D has only two available responses: to "retaliate massively" or to do nothing—i.e., to acquiesce in the loss of its ally. The cost of all-out war for both sides is 100 and the value of B to A and D is 20. We assume, for simplicity, that an all-out response will preserve the independence of B.

Figure 1 represents A's cost-gain estimates ("payoffs") and the probabilities he associates with each of D's possible responses to an attack. Figure 2 represents

[12] For the preparation of this section, I am indebted to Daniel Ellsberg for permitting me to read his unpublished manuscript on "The Theory and Practice of Blackmail." This paper, which contains a mathematical model similar to the one I am presenting here, was delivered as part of the Lowell Lectures, "The Art of Coercion: A Study of Threats in Economic Conflict and War," Boston, March 1959.

A's CALCULUS

UNITED STATES	SOVIET UNION	
	Attack	Not attack
Retaliate .10	—100	0
Not retaliate .90	+ 20	0
Expected value	+ 8	0

Figure 1.

D's CALCULUS

UNITED STATES	SOVIET UNION	
	Attack .60	Not attack .40
Retaliate	—100	0
Not retaliate	— 20	0
Expected value	— 12	0

Figure 2.

D's payoffs and his estimate of the probability of attack. For convenience, we have made their valuations and losses symmetrical.

A estimates the probability of retaliation by D by attempting to guess D's payoffs and D's capacity to act rationally in accordance with them. This probability, in theory, is determined by the size and direction of the "gap" between D's two payoffs, as estimated by A.[13] If A were to estimate D's payoffs to be roughly equal, and if he assumed that D would act rationally, logically he would assign a probability of about .5 to "retaliation." It would be a "toss-up," in A's calculations, whether D would retaliate or not. In the example, however, A suspects (correctly) that the gap is large and that retaliation is irrational for D. But he

is not sure, because he is not privy to D's estimate of the consequences of war and of D's valuation of those consequences, and of D's valuation of the continued independence of B. Moreover, he is not sure that D will act rationally. Therefore, he believes the chances of retaliation are small but not zero—in the diagram, one chance out of 10. This risk is not sufficient to deter him because his expected value from attacking is greater than the expected value from not attacking. A calculates the expected value for attack as follows:

.10 (—100) plus .90 (20) equals 8.

If D were able to divine A's calculations, he would expect an attack with certainty. But on the best evidence available to him about A's payoffs and probability estimates (the latter depending on how he thinks A visualizes his own [D's] payoffs), the most he can say is that A's "expected value" is probably positive and small. This leads him to consider an attack more likely than not, but not much more. Therefore he assigns a probability of .60 to the attack. This is D's measure of the effectiveness of his deterrent posture. D's "expected value" of minus 12 (probability of A's attack times D's losses with his best response) is a rough measure of D's degree of insecurity.

It is useful to note that the probability of retaliation at which A will be indifferent between attacking or not (at which his expected value for "attack" is 0) is approximately .17.[14] From D's point of view, this is the "required credibility" of his threat—i.e., the minimum credibility necessary to make it an effective deterrent.[15] Required credibility depends on A's payoffs; credibility depends on A's image of D's payoffs and his appraisal of D's rationality. Obviously, D wishes at all times to keep "credibility" higher than "required credibility." If it is lower, as in Figure 1, his opponent is like-

---

[13] Strictly speaking, not only the absolute size of the gap, but also the ratio between the size of the gap and the size of the payoffs, would have to be considered.

[14] Since the probabilities must sum to 1.00, the probability of "no retaliation" is .83 when the probability of retaliation is .17.

[15] Daniel Ellsberg has shown that when a deterrent threat is expressed in a 2 x 2 matrix, a "critical risk" for the potential aggressor can be calculated. The aggressor's critical risk is identical with the deterrer's "required credibility." See Ellsberg, op. cit.

ly not to be deterred. *D* can attempt to bring credibility over the required threshold either by lowering the threshold, which involves changing *A*'s payoffs, or by increasing credibility, which requires shifting his own payoffs or, more accurately, changing *A*'s image of them. He can also try to increase *A*'s doubts about his (*D*'s) capacity to act rationally.

Let us consider first how *D* may affect *A*'s payoffs and thus influence required credibility. Obviously, he can increase his nuclear striking power and thus increase the costs which he can inflict on *A* in retaliation. If his capabilities are already at the level where they can completely destroy *A*'s society and productive economy, such a move would have little effect on *A*'s calculations. But let us assume they are not. Then an increase might conceivably raise *A*'s all-out war costs to 200, as shown in Figure 3.

This change (assuming that *A*'s capabilities do not change) makes *D*'s nuclear deterrent effective by reducing required credibility to .09. Or, to put it another way, it makes *A*'s expected value negative. Of course, if *A* increases his own retaliatory capability, too, the *actual* credibility of *D*'s threat of retaliation may also decline. But there is no inherent reason why, with similar increases in armament on both sides, these effects should exactly offset each other. They are more likely to do so if both parties are symmetrical in their estimates of the consequences of all-out war or, more exactly, if the aggressor believes such symmetry exists. But if *A* thinks *D* is less concerned than himself

A's CALCULUS

	D Attack	A Not attack
Retaliate .10	—200	0
Not retaliate .90	+20	0
Expected value	— 2	0

Figure 3.

about increases in potential damage in all-out war—perhaps because *D* has a much better civil defense program—a rise in the nuclear striking power on both sides would be likely, on balance, to increase *D*'s deterrent power. Required credibility, in other words, would fall more than credibility. Such a relationship is illustrated in Figure 4. The intersection of the lines represents the point at which *D*'s deterrent power just begins to be effective; reciprocal increases in striking power beyond this point will increase *D*'s deterrent effectiveness, since credibility exceeds the credibility requirement by a greater and greater margin. Of course, if the position of the lines is reversed, so that the solid line intersects the dotted line from above, *D* will reduce his deterrent influence by an increase in capability which *A* matches.

If the forces that *D* adds are suitable for "counterforce" action—e.g., very accurate missiles, piloted bombers, and facilities for accurate reconnaissance of enemy airbases and missile launching sites—the effect

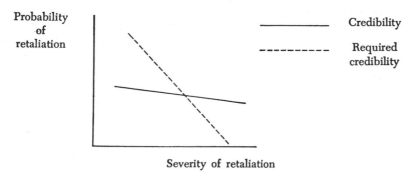

Probability of retaliation

———————— Credibility

------------ Required credibility

Severity of retaliation

Figure 4.

would be to reduce his own costs in all-out war and thus to increase the credibility of his massive retaliation threat, and perhaps also to increase total war costs for A and hence reduce required credibility. D would also increase the credibility of his threat if he were to increase substantially his civil defense and air defense capabilities.

Suppose, as an alternative, that D were to build up a sizable army—though not one strong enough to defeat A's ground forces—and deploy it on B's boundary with A. Also, suppose that both D's and A's ground forces have tactical atomic weapons. The situation might then change, as shown in Figures 5 and 6.

This change in D's capabilities forces A to consider three possible initial responses: massive retaliation, tactical nuclear warfare, and a conventional surface response. "No response" is ruled out because D's ground forces are practically certain to fight if they are attacked. A expects net costs of 40 in the event of a tactical nuclear response, which he calculates by considering two possible outcomes and their probabilities: a tactical nuclear war which stays at that level, and an initial tactical nuclear response which spirals to all-out war.[16] The fact that D has created an alternative to all-out war leads A to reduce the probability of an initial all-out response to .05. A ascribes a much higher probability to a conventional response than to a tactical nuclear one because he believes D fears the consequences of tactical nuclear warfare. Figure 6, which shows D's payoffs, indicates that A is correct in this assumption. A estimates a net gain of 12 if D responds conventionally. This figure also is calculated from a "cluster" of "sub-outcomes" and their probabilities, including the possibility that the conventional response will stay limited, that it will grow to tactical nuclear war and

[16] If A's cost of all-out war is 100, if his cost of fighting a tactical nuclear war is 40, if he expects to conquer B in a tactical nuclear war which stays at that level but not in one that spirals to all-out war, if the destruction of B's assets in a tactical nuclear war is of no consequence to A, and if he thinks there is a .25 chance that a war which starts at the tactical nuclear level will eventually become all-out, A's calculation is .25 (—100) plus .75 (20 — 40) equals — 40.

stay at that level, or that it will eventually spiral to all-out war. A's entire calculation yields him an expected value of about minus 9—which, of course, deters him.

The chief point to be noted about this last example is that over-all deterrent effectiveness can be increased by the provision of ground forces which, although they cannot hold the objective and they depreciate the credibility of an *immediate* massive retaliation, do insure *some* violent response and pose risks of still greater eventual violence, risks which the aggressor is unable to accept.

By holding constant the probability of any one of the three initial responses, a "required credibility" can be calculated for either one of the other two. For example, if the probability of massive retaliation is held at .05, the probability of a tactical nuclear defense must be at least as high as .13 for effective deterrence.

If we introduce the assumption that A is uncertain whether he can "win"—i.e., conquer B—in a tactical nuclear war, he must discount the value of his possible territorial gain (20) by the probability that he will be unsuccessful. This raises the over-all expected cost of the tactical nuclear response for A because he has less potential gain to set off against his estimate of potential loss and risk.

We might also note that A's valuation of the objective affects required credibility, as A's estimate of D's valuation affects credibility. For example, if the object of contention is C rather than B, and C is valued at only 10 by both sides, required credibility in the massive retaliation model (Figures 1 and 2) is only .09, rather than .17 as it is when B is the object. But since A recognizes that C carries also a lower value for D, he will attach less credibility to the massive retaliation threat. If the comparative valuations of B and C are symmetrical for both sides, there is a *prima facie* case for believing that the relation between required and actual credibility—and hence the deterrence effectiveness of the threat—is roughly the same for both objects. This offends common sense, which seems to indicate that very violent threats—such as that of massive retaliation—have lower ef-

A's CALCULUS

A		
	Attack	Not attack
Massive retaliation .05	—100	0
Tactical nuclear retaliation .30	— 40	0
Conventional response .65	12	0
Expected value	— 9.2	0

Figure 5.

D's CALCULUS

A		
	Attack .40	Not attack .60
Massive retaliation .05	—100	0
Tactical nuclear retaliation .30	— 70	0
Conventional response .65	— 24	0
Expected value	— 9.6	0

Figure 6.

fectiveness as well as lower credibility when the prize is small than when it is large. This intuitive appreciation rests on the assumption—a plausible one—that the potential aggressor ignores very small probabilities; that probabilities of retaliation as low as, say, one chance out of 50, are considered equivalent to zero in his calculus.

If the ratio of the value of the objective to the anticipated cost of the war is higher for the deterrer than for the aggressor—if, for example, C is valued at 30 by D and at 10 by A when both anticipate war costs of 100—then (assuming that both sides are aware of this asymmetry in valuations) required credibility is lower and actual credibility is higher than when the ratios are symmetrical.[17]

An entire later chapter will be devoted to the deterrent usages of diplomatic declarations and threats.[18] However, some preliminary observations are appropriate here. Threats by the deterrer may serve to impress

upon the aggressor that a certain objective is valued highly by the deterrer. Threats may also *change* the deterrer's payoffs and consequently enhance the credibility of the threatened action. They do so by increasing the cost of *not* responding in the threatened way, by implicating additional values beyond the bare value of the territorial objective, values which would be lost if the threat were not carried out. For example, in our massive retaliation model (Figures 1 and 2), if D were to pledge his honor and prestige in an unambiguous threat to retaliate, the cost of failure to retaliate might be raised from 20 to 30 or 40. Retaliation would still be irrational for D, but A would be less certain of this than he was before. Fearing that in making the threat D *might* have increased his cost of not retaliating above his cost of retaliating, A would assign a somewhat greater probability than .10 to the retaliation outcome.

In addition to the intrinsic losses in failing to carry out a threat, there may also be deterrent and political losses in the form of reduced credibility of other threats and a reduced capacity to attract allies. In making a threat, in other words, the deterrer places in hostage not only his own honor and moral self-respect but also certain aspects of his future deterrent power. In doing so, he makes it rationally more difficult to fail to make the response, and the aggressor, recognizing this, expects a response with greater probability.

The credibility of an irrational response

---

[17] Note that this generalization does not depend on "interpersonal comparability of utilities," but rather on the comparability of different forms of utility in the value scale of each *side*. Thus the appropriate intercountry comparison is that between the *ratios* of value-of-the-prize to anticipated war costs on each side. To say that one side "values" an objective higher than the other has meaning only when "higher" means "in relation to the expected costs of fighting for the objective."

[18] For a lucid discussion of threats, commitments, and bargaining, see Thomas C. Schelling, *op. cit.*, esp. chaps. 2 and 5. See also Daniel Ellsberg, *op. cit.*

may be increased if the deterrer can appear to commit himself to this response by some device which removes or reduces his freedom of choice. Such "automation" is itself rational—even though, paradoxically, the response is not—if the aggressor can be expected to believe with high confidence that the commitment is irrevocable and is thereby deterred. Automation differs from threat-making in that it does not change the underlying payoffs, but rather inhibits the choice of all responses except the one which is being relied on for deterrence. Complete mechanical automation is probably impossible in military affairs, but it can be approached in various ways. The use of ground troops as a "trip-wire" for nuclear retaliation is a kind of automating device. A military commander may be given conspicuous advance authority to order retaliation as soon as he sees that an attack is under way. Or military organization and planning may become oriented around a particular response to such a degree that the inertia in its favor is very difficult to overcome in a sudden crisis. The integration of tactical atomic weapons into NATO forces, and the plans to use them in case of major aggression against Western Europe, are a clear case in point. The commitment to massive retaliation may also be subject in some degree to such administrative automation.

The enemy does not have to believe that automation is complete—that freedom of choice has been entirely relinquished—in order for deterrent effects to accrue. Even if the deterrer can only commit himself partially to an irrational response—i.e., restrict his freedom of choice but not eliminate it—doubts may arise in the aggressor's mind as to whether the deterrer has retained enough flexibility to be able to overcome the built-in bias in favor of this response. One might say that the commitment of the United States to resist aggression in the Middle East—contained in the "Eisenhower Doctrine"—is at least partially automatic by virtue of the Doctrine's provision that U.S. intervention will take place at the request of the country attacked.

The deterrer may increase the credibility of a seemingly irrational response by creating the general impression that he is prone to act irrationally. It is certainly paradoxical, even bizarre, to say that a certain amount of "irrationality" can be an aspect of "rationality." Yet this follows logically if deterrence is to depend on a threat which it would be madness to carry out.

"Rationality" may be defined as choosing to act in the manner which gives best promise of maximizing one's value position, on the basis of a sober calculation of potential gains and losses, and probabilities of enemy actions. This definition is broad enough to allow the inclusion of such "emotional" values as honor, prestige, and revenge as legitimate ends of policy. It may be perfectly rational, in other words, to be willing to accept some costs solely to satisfy such emotions, but of course if the emotions inhibit a clear-eyed view of the consequences of an act, they may lead to irrational behavior. It would be irrational, however, to satisfy a momentary passion if sober judgment revealed that the satisfaction obtained would not in the long run be worth the cost.

Irrationality may take the form either of failing to act in accordance with one's best estimate of costs, gains, and probabilities, or of faulty calculation of these factors in the light of the evidence available. Irrationality of the latter kind may stem from such sources as commitment to a dogma or theory which is inapplicable to the situation or which shuts out relevant data; education, training, and experience which prevents attainment of the "whole view"; or limited or distorted perspectives resulting from bureaucratic parochialism.

Irrationality may work in the direction either of recklessness or of timidity; in most cases, for deterrence, one wishes to project an image of excessive boldness rather than of excessive caution. But is it possible for a government to *appear* irrational and *be* rational? This would mean appearing to be willing to act contrary to one's payoffs, or appearing to have miscalculated them, when in fact one has calculated, and intends to act, rationally. A democratic government may not be able to practice credibly this kind of sophisticated deceit. In the United States it is difficult enough to achieve consensus about what is rational; to attempt to go further and practice "calculated lunacy," while secretly intending to act sanely, may be infeasible, if only because of the risk of being found out in the pretense. Perhaps the only way a democratic government can appear irrational is actually to *be* irrational. If this is true, it leads to some interesting thoughts.

For example, even if I, as an individual, believe it would be irrational for the United States deliberately to initiate nuclear war in any circumstances, I may not be inconsistent if I also believe that it is rational for the President not only to threaten, but actually to intend, to undertake such a war in defense of West Berlin. I may not wish to argue against this intent if I think the deterrent effect is great enough. Or I may think it would be irrational for the United States to retaliate all-out against Russian cities after a surprise attack which reduced SAC by three-fourths and left the Soviet Union with an enormous preponderance in striking power, but for the sake of deterrence I might not want the government to think so, if I believed the Soviets were sensitive to our government's apparent intentions.

On the other hand, the United States government has demonstrated a considerable ability to keep secrets when it is not under serious domestic political pressure to reveal them. Even if the enemy suspects that our proclaimed intentions are not our real ones, it may be possible to prevent him from getting enough information to confirm this suspicion. It may be possible deliberately to create enough doubts about our capacity to calculate and act rationally to deter a moderately conservative enemy by a threat which we know and he knows it would be irrational to fulfill.

One should not underestimate the capacity of democratic governments to practice self-deceit or uncalculated irrationality. For example, it would not be too much of an exaggeration to say that U.S. military budgets between 1954 and 1961 were based on the premise that the resources available for military use were limited, that the limited resources should be allocated so as to produce the maximum firepower, that

maximum firepower could be obtained by concentration on nuclear weapons, and that nuclear weapons were therefore the most efficient means of fighting wars of any size larger than a mere incident or "brushfire." This syllogism, and the fervor with which the basic premise of limited resources was believed, forced the government to stress the efficacy of nuclear deterrence in a wide range of contingencies, in order to appease domestic and allied opinion, as well as to justify its own predilections. There is impressive evidence that the government committed itself so thoroughly to the nuclear deterrent thesis that by a certain process of psychological repression it failed to consider thoroughly the consequences of having to carry out the deterrent threat. If this habit of thinking continues, the government may not be able in time to disengage itself from its own preconceptions and act rationally when the *casus retaliati* arises. This kind of self-deceit may not, on balance, be desirable, especially if the enemy fails to recognize it. But if the Soviets do recognize it, deterrence should be enhanced.

Of course, the deterrer must consider not only the usages of apparent irrationality in his own policy, but also the degree of irrationality of the potential aggressor. A certain minimum degree of rationality in the latter is required for the communication of threats, and to enable the aggressor to understand their import and risk for himself. Ideology and doctrine which distort the aggressor's image of the deterrer's values and emotional propensities may work against deterrence. Before World War II, the judgment of the Japanese and German leaders that the Western democracies were weak-willed and soft, unwilling to continue fighting after early defeats, or unable to stand up for long under the horrors of warfare, were examples of the kind of irrationality which tends to inhibit deterrence. Certain aspects of Soviet ideology and doctrine may also reduce the efficacy of deterrent threats and capabilities. For example, the Soviets' obsessive fears about the intention of "capitalist" nations to "encircle" them and eventually to attack them probably contribute to the current prominence of "pre-emptive war" in Soviet military doctrine and may reduce our capacity to deter them from an all-out surprise attack.[19] However, there may be other aspects, such as the injunctions against "adventurism," which tend to promote caution and careful weighing of risks and which therefore support deterrence.

The potential aggressor's irrationality may affect his appreciation of the deterrer's possible irrationality. For example, if the Soviets really believe their ideological tenet that the "capitalist" elites are cool, calculating, and highly rational,[20] any image of irrationality which we project, whether contrived or not, may be fruitless.

4. UNCERTAINTY

I have assumed that the aggressor will have sufficient evidence bearing on the deterrer's payoffs to be able to assign precise probabilities to the responses open to the deterrer. He does have some evidence, of course—chiefly, the record of the deterrer's past reactions to aggression, the existing size, composition, and deployment of his military establishment, and his policy declarations, including expressions of articulate public opinion in the deterring country and its allies. Supplementing these sources, the aggressor could turn to what evidence is available concerning the "national character" or "psychology" of the deterrer as it pertains to foreign and military policy. For example, in judging the probability of American nuclear retaliation after an attack in Western Europe, the Soviets would be wise to take note of certain American attitudes: our deep emotional involvement with Western Europe, and our strong sense of honor, which might lead us to fulfill a commitment at whatever cost.

After making use of all these sources of evidence, the potential aggressor would still have only a set of very general inferences about the deterrer's probable behavior— not certain predictions, or even statements of precise probability. The hypothetical

stimulus—i.e., the contemplated aggression —is likely to be unique in many important respects; therefore there is not likely to be any similar situation in the deterrer's action record. Observance of the deterrer's preparedness of course will indicate fairly clearly what the deterrer *can* or *cannot* do. But within the range of what is possible, preparedness is not a reliable indicator of intent, chiefly because of the various capabilities that will be available and because some forces may be designed to deter rather than to provide a capability for action. Nor are threats a reliable indication of intent, for they may be uttered for deterrent purposes only—that is, they may be bluffs and, moreover, they are likely to be vague.

The aggressor faces uncertainty at two levels concerning the deterrer's payoffs: first, in his estimate of the opponent's estimate of the consequences of his response; and, secondly, in his estimate of the opponent's valuation of the consequences. The Soviets, for example, cannot know what consequences the U.S. leaders see arising from the initiation of tactical nuclear war in Europe. Do we believe that the first bombs dropped would influence the Soviets to call off the war in fear of suffering further costs? Or do we believe that tactical nuclear war in Europe would inevitably spiral into all-out war? Many other possible expectations lying between these two extremes might be imagined. But beyond that, even if the Soviets *knew* how the United States estimated the consequences, they could not know how we valued them. They might well doubt, even if we did foresee a high probability that a limited nuclear war would not stay limited, that we had fully realized ourselves how much we valued the things that would be lost to us in an all-out war.

All of these considerations tend to raise the question whether it is valid at all to introduce "probabilities" into the analysis of deterrence. Everything depends, of course, on whether the enemy thinks in probability terms. If the Soviets simply come to a flat decision as to whether massive retaliation (or whatever response they are appraising) will occur or will not occur, then the analysis of deterrence would be considera-

[19] See Herbert S. Dinerstein, *War and the Soviet Union,* New York: Frederick A. Praeger, 1959.

[20] See Nathan Leites, *The Operational Code of the Politburo,* New York: McGraw-Hill, 1951, pp. 18, 23.

bly different and rather simpler than we have presented it. The problem for the deterrer then would be to make sure that his military posture and threats posed greater costs than gains for the aggressor, and make sure that his threat was believed. There would be no need then to speak either of "levels of credibility" or of "expected value." Threats would be either credible or not credible. Of course, the deterrer would still face the problem of estimating how much evidence supporting the threatened intent (or absence of contrary evidence) would be necessary to achieve credibility.

I am inclined to believe, however, that decision-makers, Russians included, do implicitly think in rough probabilities. The phrase "calculated risk" connotes more precision than is probably actually practiced, but it does suggest at least an awareness of the relevance of probabilities and even some sort of rough-and-ready expected value calculation. Of course, the probabilities cannot be "objective" ones, such as one calculates in estimating the chances that a certain face will turn up when a die is thrown, or in projecting a "frequency distribution" from a large number of identical cases. But potential aggressor and deterrer do have some information bearing on each other's intent, enough to establish at least rough orders of subjective "likelihood." Such subjective "feelings" of likelihood may become more precise in the actual crucible of decision than their verbal statement would suggest. If the Soviets consider a massive response to ground attack in Europe to be "unlikely" in the abstract, they will be driven to make some judgment of "how unlikely" when they actually sit down around a table to decide whether to order such an attack. If the judgment then becomes "possible, but highly improbable," this will carry a meaning for the participants which is close enough to a mathematical statement of probability to allow them to make some rough judgment concerning the "expected cost" of the venture—i.e., some combination of "likelihood" and "value" (or cost) of different possible outcomes. If pressed, the decision-makers probably would be able to choose the probability figure which seemed to them

the most plausible, even if they were careful also to assign a wide margin of error to their choice. At least they would be able to specify a range of probabilities which seemed to be more plausible than any others and equally plausible. Such a statement would take the form: "Less than 10 per cent, but not more than 50 per cent."

If we assume that the aggressor will see enough evidence in the deterrer's behavior to justify the assignment of a range of "most plausible" probabilities to possible responses, or if his subjective feelings of likelihood or uncertainty (whether or not based on evidence) in effect take the form of such a range, the next question to ask is: what use does the aggressor make of this estimate? If he is to calculate an "expected cost" for his venture, he needs, for working purposes at least, a precise probability, not a range of plausible ones. Does he "split the difference" between the extremes of the range? Or does he, more conservatively, choose to base his decision on the most unfavorable probability within the range of the plausible? Or, even more conservatively, does he base it on the most unfavorable probability which is at least conceivable, though not as plausible as some others? The answer would seem to depend on the risk-taking propensities of the aggressor.

Since it is the aggressor who takes the initiative, it is he who must bear most of the burden of weighing the uncertainties. In the nuclear age, when the eventual outcome of even the smallest border skirmish *might* be utter devastation, the aggressor's uncertainty is an important deterring factor. This does not mean, however, that it is uniformly desirable to "keep the enemy guessing." To increase the aggressor's uncertainty *is* desirable with respect to deterrent threats—such as massive retaliation—which he probably is inclined to disbelieve in the first place. To increase his uncertainty forces him to attach a somewhat higher working probability to the outcome "all-out war" in order to cover himself against miscalculation. But of course it would be better to increase his *certainty* that the threatened response would be carried out. And if the aggressor is thought to be already fairly certain that aggression will produce costs for him greater than his gains, it obviously does not pay to reduce his certainty.

D. DEFENSE[21]

The deterrer, in choosing his optimum military and threat posture in advance of war, must estimate not only the effectiveness of that posture for deterrence, but also the consequences for himself should deterrence fail. In short, he is interested in defense as well as in deterrence; his security is a function of both of these elements. Capabilities and threats which produce a high level of deterrence may not yield a high degree of security because they promise very high costs and losses for the deterrer should war occur. We turn now to a discussion of the factors which go into the deterrer's estimate of the consequences of the failure of deterrence and into his evaluation of the defense effectiveness of his military forces. In other words, we will now talk about how military forces influence the "numbers in the boxes" in the deterrer-defender's matrices given in the preceding section.

1. THE COMPONENTS OF DEFENSE VALUE

As already pointed out, military forces affect not only the probabilities of various enemy moves, but also the potential costs which the defender would suffer should the enemy undertake aggressive moves. We will asssume, for simplicity, that the consequences of aggression are always net costs to the defender. This does not mean, of course, that aggression should not be resisted, for much greater losses might be entailed in not resisting. The extent to which given military forces potentially can mitigate the defender's costs and losses of all kinds is the measure of the "defense

21 The reader is reminded that I am using the word "defense" in a rather special sense, which is narrower than one ordinary usage of the term and broader than another. Obviously it is narrower than the usage which makes "defense" synonymous with all military preparedness. It is broader, however, than "capacity to hold territory in case of attack," which I would prefer to call "denial capability."

value" of those forces in various contingencies. It is assumed that, to all possible enemy moves, the most rational response will be made—i.e., the response which the defender thinks will minimize his aggregate loss during, and as a result of, the ensuing war.

The potential costs of enemy moves—followed by one's own optimum responses—are counted in two categories of value: intrinsic value and power value.

Intrinsic values are "end values"; they are valued for their own sake rather than for what they contribute to the power relations between the protagonists. They include such things as the value we place upon our own independence (including all the subsidiary values which flow from this independence), the value we attach to the independence (or non-Communization) of other countries with which we feel a cultural or psychic affinity (apart from what their independence contributes to our own security), the economic values which we find in trading with other free countries (to the extent that these values would be lost should these countries fall under Communist control), and moral values such as self-respect, honor, and prestige. Some of these intrinsic values obviously attach to the continued independence either of our own country or of other countries, others are inherent in the response or lack of response rather than in the political entity or territory attacked. Other intrinsic values are the material assets and lives (again as valued for their own sake rather than for their contribution to the power equation) which would be lost in the act of resisting aggression.

Power values are "instrumental values," not end values. That is, they are valued not for their own sake but for what they contribute to the security of intrinsic values. It might be more precise to say that the "assets" at stake in international conflict are valued on two scales—a power scale and an intrinsic scale—and that the aggregate value of any given asset is the sum of its valuation on both scales. "Assets" of course may be either tangible, like raw materials and productive resources, or intangible, like prestige or a set of enemy expectations concerning one's willingness to fight in future contingencies. The "defense value" of given military forces includes both the power values and the intrinsic values which can be preserved by using the forces in various contingencies.

Power values are of three major kinds: strategic value, deterrent value, and political value. Strategic value is the potential contribution of the territorial prize to the military capabilities of either side: it includes such familiar elements of power as population, industrial capital, natural resources, and strategic location, valued as war potential. More precisely, the strategic value of any country or territory is the probable effect of its loss in increasing the chances that the aggressor would be able to take other areas, or in increasing the costs to the defender of holding other areas.

While strategic value is entirely a function of the war-making potential inherent in the contested territory, deterrent value is an attribute primarily of the *act of responding* to aggression. Deterrent value may be described as the effect of a response in reducing the probability of enemy attacks against other areas in the future—i.e., reducing it below what it would be if no resistance were offered to the immediate aggression. The enemy may be discouraged from making future attacks either if (1) his territorial gains from his present move are limited or denied entirely, or if (2) the costs we inflict upon him by our response are greater than he had expected. In the main, deterrent value stems from the evidence which our response provides to the enemy concerning our future intentions.

Political value is the effect of a response, and of its direct consequences, on the alignment or attitudes of third countries. Although we have classified political value under the rubric of "power values," it is really a mixture of intrinsic and power effects. In its power dimension, political value may be subsumed under either strategic value or deterrent value. That is, the political loss of an ally to the other side may increase the enemy's capability to make future conquests, or reduce our own capabil-

ity to prevent such conquests. It may also increase the enemy's inclination to attempt future aggression and reduce our own capacity to deter it. It may reduce the cohesion of our own alliances. All of these are power effects. However, we also place an intrinsic value on "having friends" abroad, on keeping democratic countries out of the Communist sphere of influence, on economic relations which might be disrupted by a transfer of political allegiance or the adoption of a "neutralist" stance. Political value is the sum of all such considerations.

A net loss in power value means an increase in the probability, and/or the potential adverse consequences, of *future* aggressive enemy moves, after completion of the "first" enemy move, and the ensuing war (if the move is resisted). A strategic loss is an increase in the potential estimated loss as a result of such future attacks. A deterrent loss is an increase in the probability of future enemy moves. A political loss may affect either the probabilities or the costs of future attacks (or both).

Power values, especially strategic value, may be lost as a result of losses of lives and attrition of military capabilities and future war potential in the process of fighting. More subtle strategic forms of war cost might include such things as a weakening of the population's willingness to sacrifice in future wars or willingness to stand up to enemy threats in future political crises. This, in other words, along with the intrinsic value of the lives and economic assets sacrificed in the war, is an offset to the power and intrinsic values which may be gained or saved by fighting.

In summary, the total value of a response (and the defense value of the military forces available for making the response) is the sum of the power values and intrinsic values which can be saved or gained by the response, minus the power values and intrinsic values lost as the result of war casualties and damage.

2. STRATEGIC VALUE AND DETERRENT VALUE

Much of the inconclusiveness of the recurring "great debates" about military policy might be avoided if the concept of "strategic value" could be clarified and clearly separated from the deterrent effects of military action. The strategic value of a particular piece of territory is the effect which its loss would have on increasing the enemy's *capability* to make various future moves, and on decreasing our own capacity to resist further attacks. The deterrent value of defending or attempting to defend that piece of territory is the effect of the defense on the enemy's *intention* to make future moves. The failure to recognize this distinction contributed to the apparent about-face in United States policy toward South Korea, when we decided to intervene after the North Korean attack in June 1950. Earlier, the Joint Chiefs of Staff had declared that South Korea had no strategic value—apparently meaning that its loss would have no significant effect on the U.S. capacity to fight a general war with the Soviet Union. This determination was thought to justify —or at least was used as a rationalization for—the withdrawal of U.S. combat forces from the Korean peninsula in 1948 and 1949. Secretary of State Dean Acheson strengthened the impression that "no strategic value" meant "no value" when, in a speech early in 1950, he outlined a U.S. "defense perimeter" in the Far East which excluded Korea. Then when the North Koreans, perhaps encouraged by these high-level U.S. statements, attacked in June 1950, the United States government suddenly discovered that it had a deterrent interest, as well as strong political and intrinsic interests, in coming to the rescue of South Korea. The dominant theme in the discussions leading up to the decision to intervene was that if the Communists were "appeased" this time, they would be encouraged to make further attacks on other areas.[22] The chief motive behind the intervention was to prevent such encouragement from taking place, and positively to deter similar attempts in the future.

Another case in point was the debate about the desirability of a United States commitment to defend the Chinese offshore islands of Quemoy and Matsu. Those who took the negative in this debate stressed that these two small islands held no "strategic value" for the United States, that they were not "vital" to the defense of Formosa, etc. Former Secretary of State Dean Acheson declared that the islands were not worth a single American life.[23] Administration spokesmen, on the other hand, emphasized the political and deterrent value of defending Quemoy and Matsu. President Eisenhower, for example, said that this country's allies "would be appalled if the United States were spinelessly to retreat before the threat of Sino-Soviet armed aggression."[24] Secretary of States Dulles asserted that the stakes were not "just some square miles of real estate," but the preservation of con-

---

[22] As former President Truman has stated: "Our allies and friends abroad were informed through our diplomatic representatives that it was our feeling that it was essential to the maintenance of peace that this armed aggression against a free nation be met firmly. We let it be known that we considered the Korean situation vital as a symbol of the strength and determination of the West. Firmness now would be the only way to deter new actions in other portions of the world. Not only in Asia but in Europe, the Middle East, and else-

where the confidence of peoples in countries adjacent to the Soviet Union would be very adversely affected, in our judgment, if we failed to take action to protect a country established under our auspices and confirmed in its freedom by action of the United Nations. If, however, the threat to South Korea was met firmly and successfully, it would add to our successes in Iran, Berlin and Greece a fourth success in opposition to the aggressive moves of the Communists. And each success, we suggested to our allies, was likely to add to the caution of the Soviets in undertaking new efforts of this kind. Thus the safety and prospects for peace of the free world would be increased." Harry S. Truman, *Years of Trial and Hope*, New York: Doubleday and Co., 1956, pp. 339–40.

The primary political value of the intervention, as U.S. decision-makers saw it, was that it would give other free nations confidence that they could count on U.S. aid in resisting aggression. The most salient intrinsic values were moral value in opposing the aggressive use of force, support for the "rule of law" in international affairs, support for the collective security system embodied in the United Nations Charter, and the special responsibility the United States felt for the Republic of Korea, whose government it had played a major role in establishing. "Support for the collective security system" of course had deterrent and political as well as moral overtones.

[23] *New York Times*, October 3, 1958, p. 3.

[24] *Ibid.*, October 5, 1958, p. 1.

fidence in other countries—both allies and enemies—that the United States would resist aggression. It was better to meet the challenge at the beginning, Mr. Dulles said, than after "our friends become disheartened and out enemies over-confident and miscalculating."[25]

Power values are sometimes discussed in terms of the "falling domino" theory. According to this reasoning, if one objective is lost to the enemy, other areas contiguous to the first one inevitably will be lost as well, then still additional areas contiguous to these, etc., as a whole row of dominoes will fall when the first one is knocked over.[26] In its extreme form, the domino thesis would value any objective, no matter how small, as dearly as the value which the United States placed on the continued independence of all other non-Communist countries. Thus we should be as willing to fight for one place as another, since a failure to resist once inevitably means future losses. The important thing is to "draw a line" and resist violations of the line, whatever their dimensions and wherever and whenever they may occur.

The domino theory tends to overstate power values: since the enemy may have limited aims and may be satisfied with a small gain, his increase in capability from a single small conquest may not significantly shift the balance of capabilities in his favor, and the loss of single small areas may not have adverse political effects among neutrals and allies.[27] Nevertheless,

the domino image does highlight an important truth: the strategic and intrinsic value of the immediate territorial prize is not a sufficient criterion for evaluating the wisdom of resisting aggression, or for estimating the forces necessary for successful resistance. The enemy's possible ultimate objective must also be considered, as well as the effect of resistance in discouraging him from attempting further progress toward that objective, and in forestalling political changes among other countries which would tend to further that ultimate objective.

There is a relationship between the strategic, political, and intrinsic value which the enemy believes one attaches to a given objective, and the deterrent value which can be realized by responding to an attack on that objective. For example, a failure to resist effectively a Communist attack on the offshore islands of Quemoy and Matsu might not increase perceptibly the chances of Chinese Communist attacks on other non-Communist countries in Asia, if the Communists did not believe we placed a high intrinsic and strategic value on these islands. On the other hand, it could be argued that a determined and costly response to an attack on an objective which the enemy thinks means little to us in strategic and intrinsic terms is likely to give him greater pause with respect to his future aggressive intentions. Thus, if the objective is to "draw a line" to deter future aggression, perhaps the best place to draw it is precisely at places like Quemoy and Matsu. The enemy would reason that if the United States were willing to fight for a place of such trivial intrinsic and strategic value to itself, it must surely be willing to fight for other places of greater value. Thus, the deterrent value of defending any objective varies inversely with the enemy's perception of its value to us on other accounts. There is a further consideration: if it is thought necessary to fight a certain amount of war, or risk a certain amount of war, to convince the other side of our willingness to fight generally, what better place to do it

[25] *Ibid.*, September 26, 1958, p. 1.

[26] Apparently the domino theory was first given public expression by President Eisenhower on April 7, 1954, when he said, in reply to a request that he explain the strategic value of Indo-China to the United States: "You had a row of dominoes set up, and you knocked over the first one, and what would happen to the last one was the certainty that it would go over very quickly. So you could have a beginning of a disintegration that would have the most profound influences." The President then referred to "the possible sequence of events, the loss of Indo-China, of Burma, of Thailand, of the peninsula, and Indonesia following." *Ibid.*, April 8, 1954, p. 18.

[27] It is hard to believe, for example, that a Communist Chinese conquest of Quemoy and Matsu would have reduced the confidence of the European allies in the willingness of the United States to

defend Europe. The solidarity of NATO might have been weakened by a U.S. attempt to defend the islands.

than at places like Quemoy and Matsu, where it is least likely that the war will spiral to all-out dimensions?

Mutually shared expectations are extremely important in determining the deterrent value of military actions. The United States did not lose much in deterrent utility by failing to intervene in Hungary in 1956, because both sides regarded Hungary as part of the Communist camp. But a failure to defend Berlin would severely undermine the U.S. capability to deter future Communist incursions in Europe or elsewhere.

The consequences of enemy moves, and the defense value of forces for resisting them, are subject to modification by policy declarations. Threats and commitments may involve one's honor and prestige in a particular area or objective, and this involvement increases the deterrent, political, and intrinsic value of defending such places and the value of forces which are able to defend. Thus the adverse consequences of an unresisted Communist attack on Quemoy and Matsu were increased by the various official statements, including the Formosa Resolution passed by Congress, to the effect that these offshore islands were "related" to the defense of Formosa. But these consequences were not increased as much as they might have been, had the United States made an unequivocal commitment to defend the islands.

Of course, losses of power values through the loss of an ally or neutral to the enemy may be offset by increased mobilization of domestic resources. The cost of the additional mobilization required might be taken as a measure of the power value of the territory in question. Thus the defending power might ask itself: "If I let this piece of territory or this ally be taken over by the enemy, how many additional resources will I have to spend for military weapons to have the same degree of security I have been enjoying?"

Once war is entered into, consideration of deterrent possibilities may call for a different strategy than would be the case if we were interested only in the strategic and intrinsic values of the particular area attacked. If the latter were our only interest,

our war aims might be limited to restoration of the *status quo ante*; deterrence of future aggressions, however, might dictate more ambitious aims. In the Korean War, for example, it is possible that if closer consideration had been given to deterrent benefits, the U.N. armies might have pushed on farther than they did—if not to the Yalu, then perhaps at least to the "narrow neck" of the Korean peninsula. The opportunity was not taken to show the Communists that their aggressions were likely to result in losses not only of manpower but also of territory; that in future limited wars they could not hope to end up at least where they started.

In general, we will be willing to suffer higher costs in fighting a limited war if deterrence is an objective than if it is not. In other words, it may be desirable to fight on longer and in the face of a higher cost expectancy if an important objective is to assure the enemy of our willingness to suffer costs in future contingencies.

The objective of deterrence may call for the use of different weapons than would the simple objective of blocking enemy conquest of an area at least cost. Our use of nuclear weapons probably would support the Communist estimate of our willingness to use them in the future; and, conversely, to refrain from using them when such use would be militarily advantageous would weaken that estimate. However, as in the decision whether or not to fight at all, the strategic and intrinsic value of the immediate objective is relevant to the deterrent effects: the use of nuclear weapons to defend highly valued objectives might support but little the probability that they would be used to meet lesser challenges;[28] the failure to use them when the prize was small would not necessarily signal a reluctance to do so when the object of the conflict was vital.

Finally, for deterrent reasons it might be desirable to *attempt* resistance against

---

[28] On the other hand, any use of nuclear weapons would set a precedent. The symbolic or psychological barrier to their use which had rested on their previous non-use would be eroded. The Russians might believe, after they had been used once, that the probability of their use in *any* future conflict had increased.

a particular limited enemy attack even though we knew in advance that our resistance would fail. The purpose would be to inform the enemy, for future reference, that although he could expect to make gains from limited aggression in the future, these gains could be had only at a price which (we hoped) the enemy would not want to pay. Proposals for limited nuclear retaliation against one or a few enemy cities in response to limited ground aggression may draw on this kind of reasoning.

Of course, the concept of "deterrence by action" has no relevance in determining the appropriate response to a direct thermonuclear attack on the United States, or in valuing the forces for the response. In that event there would be no future contingencies which would seem worth deterring or worrying about at all, compared with the magnitude of the catastrophe which had already taken place. The primary values would be intrinsic values associated with reducing war damage, perhaps limiting the enemy's territorial gains in Eurasia, and preserving the independence of the United States itself.[29]

Power values lost by the defender represent power values gained by the attacker, although the values may not be equally important to each side. For example, the Middle East has strategic value for the United States because its geographic location and resources add significantly to the West's capacity to fight limited war in Europe and elsewhere, and because the area, in the hands of the Soviets, would increase the Soviets' capacity to fight such wars—because of its position athwart vital transportation routes if not because of its oil resources. Our strategic loss if the Middle East should fall under Communist control would be the sum of the deprivation of the West's future military capabilities and the increment to the Soviet capabilities. Simi-

larly, the strategic gain to the Soviets would be the sum of their own direct gain in military resources plus the losses for the West.

It is less obvious that deterrent values also have this reciprocal character. When, by fighting in Korea, we demonstrated our willingness to defend free institutions in Asia, not only did we gain "deterrent value" with respect to other possible Communist moves in Asia; the Communists lost something analogous to it in their own value system. Presumably they became less confident that overt aggression could be attempted again without U.S. intervention. Their "expected value" from future aggressive moves declined perhaps below what it was before Korea, and certainly below what it would have been if the North Korean aggression had been unopposed by the United States.

When an aggressor state successfully completes a conquest, or has its demands satisfied short of war, its willingness in the future to make war, or to make demands at the risk of war, presumably is strengthened by the reduction of expected cost or risk which perceives in such future moves. This reduction in the perceived chances of being opposed in the future we might label "expectational value," to differentiate it from "deterrent value," which is peculiarly associated with *status quo* powers. Deterrent and expectational values are in obverse relationship—i.e., when the defender loses deterrent value by failing to fight or to carry out a threat, the aggressor gains expectational value, and vice versa—although again the gain or loss may have a stronger psychological impact on one side than on the other, since the value in question is highly subjective.

This distinction is similar to Thomas Schelling's distinction between "compellent" and "deterrent" threats.[30] A compellent threat is used in an aggressive way; it is designed to persuade the opponent to give up some value. A deterrent threat, on the other hand, is intended to dissuade the opponent from initiating some positive action. A successful conquest would increase an aggressor's compellent power with respect to

---

[29] We might, of course, attempt to "deter" the enemy from continuing his attacks, thus reducing our war costs and perhaps preserving our independence and the essential fabric of our society, by a discriminating use of the weapons we had left after absorbing a surprise attack, accompanied by appropriate bargaining tactics. Possibilities along this line will be explored in the next chapter.

[30] Thomas C. Schelling, *op. cit.*, pp. 195–96.

other possible victims, especially if the fighting had included the use of nuclear weapons; other countries would lose deterrent power, since their psychological capacity to resist demands would be weakened by the aggressor's demonstration of willingness to risk or to undertake nuclear war.

Strategic gains by the Soviets might appear in their risk calculus as an increased probability that future attacks on other areas would be successful, or perhaps as a decreased expectation of cost in making future conquests. Gains in expectational value would appear as a decreased probability of resistance to future attacks, or perhaps as a reduced probability of a high-cost response by the defender or its allies. The aggregate of strategic gains and expectational gains produces an increase in "expected value" to be gained from future moves (or a reduction in "expected cost").

This might not always be the case if the consequence of a successful aggression were to stimulate an increased level of military mobilization by the United States and its allies and/or an increased determination to resist future attacks. Thus a successful limited attack might backfire and *reduce* the Soviets' strategic position as well as their expectational value, although of course they would retain whatever intrinsic values they had gained by their conquest.

E. THE NEW BALANCE
OF POWER[31]

The separation of the functions of punishment and denial, and especially the enormous magnification of the capability to inflict punishment, have profoundly affected the traditional concept of "balance of power." In effect, nuclear weapons, long-range aircraft, and missiles have superimposed a new balance upon the old. These weapons have not simply added higher levels of potential destructiveness to the traditional balancing process; they have changed the very nature and meaning of "balance." Two balancing systems—the

strategic balance of terror and a truncated tactical balance of power—now operate simultaneously, each according to different criteria, but interacting in various ways which are not yet thoroughly understood.

The "power" that was balanced in the pre-nuclear balancing process was essentially the military power to take or hold territory. Moreover, territory, and the human and material resources on it, were the predominant source of power. The motive for engaging in the balancing process was to prevent any single state or bloc from becoming so powerful that it could make territorial conquests with impunity and eventually achieve hegemony over the other states in the system. The objectives were, first, to *deter* the potential disturber from initiating war by forming alliances and building up armaments sufficient to defeat him; and, second, if deterrence failed, to *defend* or restore the balance by engaging in war. Whether a balance existed or not depended essentially on whether the states interested in preserving the *status quo* were able to *deny* territorial gains to the expansion-minded state or states.

The balance of terror centers on a different form of power—not the power to contest the control of territory directly, but the power to inflict severe punishment, to prevent the enemy from inflicting punishment on oneself, and to deter by the threat of punishment. In its pure deterrent form, a balance of terror exists between two nuclear powers when neither can strike first at the other without receiving a completely intolerable retaliatory blow in return. A balance does not exist when one power, in striking first, can eliminate all but a tolerable portion of the opponent's capacity to strike back.

At present, three states participate in the balance of terror. (France can hardly be considered a full-fledged participant as yet.) Of the three, two—the United States and Great Britain—are so closely allied, politically and culturally, that for all intents and purposes they are one unit. Thus the balance of terror is essentially a bipolar system, tending to heighten, sharpen, and preserve the bipolarity which has existed in the non-nuclear balance since World War

[31] This section essentially is a condensation of my article, "Balance of Power in the Missile Age," *Journal of International Affairs*, Vol. XIV, No. 1 (1960), pp. 21–35.

II and which is now beginning to break down with the emergence of China as a great military power and the increase in the economic strength of the Western European countries. There is good reason to believe that other states eventually will become nuclear or thermonuclear powers, thus possibly creating a multipolar balance of terror system.

1. DIFFERENCES BETWEEN THE BALANCE OF TERROR AND THE BALANCE OF POWER

The traditional balancing process continues to operate as a balance between conventional forces (and the potential for building such forces) in all situations in which there is no significant possibility that nuclear weapons will be used. Hereafter, we shall refer to this balance as the "tactical" balance of power, differentiating it both from the strategic balance of terror and from an over-all balance of power involving interactions between the strategic balance and the tactical balance. Some significant differences between these two balancing systems in their "pure" form are worth noting.[32]

One difference is that, in the strategic balance, quantitatively matching the enemy's capabilities is virtually irrelevant as a criterion for balance. A balance of terror exists when neither side can eliminate enough of the other's forces in striking first to avoid an unacceptable retaliatory blow. Depending chiefly on technological conditions, especially the degree of vulnerability of the opposing forces, a potential attacker may be balanced with a force only a fraction of the size of the attacker's forces; or balance may require having more forces than the potential attacker. The proper criterion is to be able to inflict unacceptable retaliatory damage.

[32] The term "tactical balance of power" refers chiefly to the balance of conventional capabilities; "strategic balance of terror" to the balance of long-range nuclear air and missiles forces. Tactical nuclear weapons fall somewhere in between, but I am inclined to consider them principally as components of the balance of terror. Presently, I shall discuss the "mixed" balance—i.e., the over-all balance of power when the strategic and tactical balances interact.

By contrast, in the modern tactical balance centering on conventional ground forces, as in the traditional balancing process, simply equaling the strength of the enemy's forces is still the most plausible balancing criterion, although of course a sophisticated calculation would require that it be modified to take account of factors such as a possible advantage of the defense over the offense, possibilities for post-attack mobilization, geography, asymmetries in supply capabilities, etc.

The balance of terror is primarily a *deterrent* balance rather than a *defensive* balance. That is, a "balance" is said to exist when a potential aggressor faces the prospect of retaliatory damage sufficient to deter him, not when he faces the prospect of defeat or frustration of his aims. Conceivably, a balance of terror could exist in the defensive sense, if the forces on both sides were so invulnerable that the side which absorbed the first blow could still retaliate with sufficient force to destroy or prostrate the attacker. But the forces required for winning the war after being attacked would be considerably larger in number and probably different in kind than the forces required to deter the attack.

The tactical balance of power, on the other hand, centers primarily on the function of defense. A balance of power exists when the defending side has enough forces to defeat the attacker or at least to prevent him from making territorial conquests. Deterrence is the consequence of this defensive capability, not of a capacity to inflict unacceptable costs. In the tactical balance, the requirements for deterrence and for effectively fighting a war more or less coincide; this is not the case in the balance of terror.

Another difference concerns the strategic value of territory and of territorial boundaries. In the tactical balance, the strategic value of territory and of the human and material assets associated with territory continues to be high. The traditional elements of national power, such as manpower, natural resources, industrial strength, space, geographic separation, command of the seas, and so on, remain the primary sources of power and they are important criteria for determining the existence or non-existence of a tactical balance.

These territorially based elements are also a source of power in the balance of terror, but their significance is less and considerably different than in the tactical balance. Strategic nuclear weapons have re-reduced the importance of geographical separation of the opponents in the balance of terror, since ICBM's can reach from continent to continent. However, distance still retains some significance in the strategic balance of terror. An aggressor can reduce the required range and hence increase the accuracy and possible payload of his missiles by obtaining control of territory between himself and his prospective nuclear opponent. He may also increase the points of the compass from which he can attack, thus complicating the opponent's warning and air defense problem. He may increase the space available for dispersal of his striking forces, and he may obtain useful staging bases and post-attack landing points for his long-range aircraft.

The acquisition of industrial and resource assets by conquest may increase a nuclear power's capability to produce additional strategic weapons. While "raw" manpower is not a significant source of power in the balance of terror, an aggressor may turn to his own uses the scientific brainpower of a conquered nation. On balance, however, the strategic value of territory and its associated assets is probably smaller in the balance of terror than in the tactical balance.

Overconcentration on the strategic balance and the contingency of all-out war has caused us, in recent years, to downgrade excessively the importance of industrial potential for war. War potential continues to be a source of power in the tactical balance not only prior to war but also after the war has begun. Stockpiles of raw materials, stand-by war production plants, and the like can be translated into actual military power during the progress of a limited war, provided of course that the forces ready in advance of the attack can hold off the enemy until the additional power can be mobilized. However, in the balance of terror, industrial potential provides only

pre-attack power, not post-attack power. Once the war has started, if such potential were not destroyed, its usefulness probably would be limited to survival and reconstruction. Even in a very restrained war, involving only counterforce attacks on military installations, with minimum damage to economic assets, a decision probably would be reached before industrial potential could be brought into play.

In the tactical balance, alliances are useful for both deterrence and defense, in roughly equal proportions; the costs of war are low enough and the incentives to prevent the conquest of an ally are high enough that allies are likely to see a net advantage in coming to each other's aid. The conquest of an ally means a very serious erosion of one's own power and security position, and such erosion may be prevented at bearable intrinsic costs, if the necessary forces are available. Since the potential aggressor is aware of this, the credibility of alliance obligations tends to be high.

In a world of many nuclear powers—i.e., in a "multipolar" balance of terror—alliances are likely to have less utility and credibility for protection against nuclear attack. Obviously, a country which could mount a completely unacceptable retaliation to a nuclear attack on itself would not need allies for security against this contingency. (It might, of course, enter into an alliance for security against non-nuclear attack.) Countries which doubted their individual capacity to deter a nuclear attack might feel they could gain security by combining. In combination, they might be able to muster enough retaliatory power to deter either an attack on the whole alliance simultaneously or an attack on a single member.

The alliance's capacity to deter attack on a single member would depend critically on the amount of his forces which the aggressor would have to use up in attacking the first victim. It is conceivable that the attacker would so deplete his own forces that the other members of the alliance could strike without fear of serious retaliation; at least the prospect of this would limit the amount of force which the attacker could use against the initial victim and might deter the attack. But if the aggressor could retain substantial and invulnerable forces while successfully attacking a single member, the supporting allies would feel powerful incentives to renege. Fulfilling the alliance obligation would mean accepting severe destruction. These costs might be suffered in vain, for there would be little chance of saving the attacked ally by nuclear retaliation. And, in retaliating, the supporting allies would be using up forces which they would need for their own future protection. Thus the alliance pledge may not seem very credible to a prospective nuclear aggressor.

Nevertheless, alliances might have some deterrent value in a multipolar balance of terror, because of the aggressor's uncertainties, because an alliance would limit the amount of force which an aggressor would be free to apply against a single victim, and because deterrence does not depend on absolute credibility. A nuclear attack on a single country would be a very momentous act which might stimulate enough emotional reaction and irrationality among the victim's allies to trigger retaliation on their part. The aggressor would have to realize that the *possible* damage he might suffer at the hands of the whole alliance would be very much higher than the value he placed on conquest of a single member. The magnitude of the possible retaliatory damage might very well offset in his mind the low credibility of an alliance response.

2. INTERACTION BETWEEN THE BALANCE OF TERROR AND THE BALANCE OF POWER

The strategic and tactical balancing processes do not function independently, but impinge on each other in various ways. In its pure form, the balance of terror operates only to deter an all-out nuclear attack by the Soviet Union against the United States and Great Britain, or by the latter countries against the Soviet Union. The traditional or tactical balancing process operates independently only in conflict situations which involve no possibility of the use of nuclear weapons. Thus it operates between non-nuclear countries and blocs with respect to issues in which the nuclear

powers are not significantly interested, and in minor conflicts between nuclear powers. But between the two balancing processes in their pure forms is a wide range of situations in which they are interdependent.

For example, since the end of World War II, the United States has used its dominant position in the balance of terror to deter a considerably wider range of contingencies than a direct nuclear attack on itself. The *means* of the balance of terror—the threat and capability to inflict punishment—have been applied to the furtherance of certain *ends* in the tactical balance of power, notably the deterrence of a large-scale Soviet ground attack in Western Europe. Consequently, in U.S. and Western policy, the scope of the tactical balancing process has shrunk to the deterrence and defense of limited aggression, primarily outside Western Europe. The validity of this concept became increasingly questionable after 1953 and 1954, when the Russians exploded a hydrogen bomb and then demonstrated that they had a modern, long-range delivery capability. These and further Russian advances in missilry since 1957 have tended to reduce the plausible scope of our threat of a "first strike" and to increase the scope of the tactical balancing process.

However, it is not likely that the scope of the balance of terror will narrow to its pure form or that the tactical balance will widen to its pre-nuclear dimensions. In other words, some form of nuclear response remains a possibility whenever the interests of one of the superpowers are challenged militarily—especially if challenged directly by the other superpower. In some circumstances, and with appropriate capabilites, the threat of massive retaliation may retain some significant credibility. Even if a nuclear response takes only a limited form, there is always the chance—and a conservative aggressor must consider it a good chance—that the war will escalate to severe levels of destruction, perhaps to all-out war. Thus the modern balance of power takes a "mixed" form: any conventional military attack by one nuclear power (or its adherent) against the interests of another nuclear power creates a risk of nuclear reprisal of some kind; whether a balance exists with respect to *that act* depends not only on the defender's "denial" forces but also on the attacker's appreciation of the risk that punishment will be imposed and the possible severity of that punishment. The greater the severity of the provocation, the greater the relative importance of the punishment component.

The idea of a mixed balance can be extended and elaborated in terms of a "spectrum of violence." The pole of least violence would be "peaceful competition"—the use of economic aid, propaganda, infiltration of subversive agents, and the like—to affect the internal political complexion of a country. Such competition shades into lower-keyed forms of violence like sabotage and the fomenting of rebellion. The next higher stage would be military (matériel) aid to rebellious or potentially rebellious groups or to the established government for use against such groups. Successively higher stages would be covert assistance in manpower to either side in a civil war—e.g., by military missions, advisers, and "volunteers"—then limited interstate conventional conflict, then limited or tactical nuclear warfare, then limited strategic warfare involving the territories of the superpowers, and finally all-out nuclear warfare. The word "spectrum" is appropriate because it suggests a gradual shading or progression from one intensity to another and gets away from a common tendency to think of the dimensions of warfare as sharply defined categories, such as "limited war" and "all-out war." One suspects that such sharp delineation does not correspond to the realities of human behavior.

At each shading of the spectrum—i.e., for each possible aggressive act—an over-all balance of power either does or does not exist, depending on the potential aggressor's image of the defender's capabilities and intentions. A balance of capabilities would exist at any level if the defender had sufficient forces to deny gains to the aggressor or could impose such high costs as to offset any possible gains. But true balance requires an additional condition: that the aggressor recognizes a will or intent on the part of the defender to use his capabilities. This might be recognized only as a "likeli-hood" or "probability," rather than with certainty, and still present a prospect of defeat, or high costs, sufficiently serious to deter attack.

A potential aggressor is "balanced" at each level of violence if his objectives can be denied him at that level, if his costs of fighting at that level would be higher than his expectation of gain, or if, by attacking at that level, he would exceed a certain critical threshold of risk that the defender would "up the ante" to a higher level at which either the aggressor's aims would be frustrated or he would suffer unacceptable costs. A balance exists at any level in both a deterrent and a defensive sense when the aggressor knows he would not be able to make gains in attacking at that level. A balance exists only in a deterrent sense when the aggressor can make territorial gains but foresees too great a risk of suffering war costs incommensurate with the gains. For example, should the Russians attack conventionally in Europe, they would be balanced or deterred either if the NATO "shield" could contain their attack, or if, in attacking with sufficient force to break through the shield, they incurred too serious a risk that NATO would respond with tactical nuclear weapons or make some other nuclear response which would either frustrate the Soviets' objectives or produce excessive costs for them.

An over-all balance of power depends on the existence of a balance at all possible levels of violence, in the sense described above. The potential disturber would not be balanced in an over-all sense if there were one or more weak links—i.e., levels of conflict at which he could achieve his goal at tolerable cost and risk. The defender or *status quo* power can achieve a balance at some levels by having forces which can frustrate the enemy's aims; at other levels, by threatening to impose unacceptable costs on the aggressor.

There are feedbacks between the various levels. For example, if we were to use nuclear weapons in response to a North Vietnamese attack on South Vietnam, we might alienate other Asian countries to the extent that our position in the balance of "peaceful competition" would be grievously weakened. Consideration of this might deter us from using nuclear weapons; also, if the North Vietnamese were to discover or suspect strongly that we would not use nuclear weapons for this reason, they would be less likely to be deterred. For some years, the Soviets have been making gains in the balance of peaceful competition more or less as a by-product of their strengthening position in the balance of terror. Also, the Russians have attempted to use their new missile strength to strengthen their position in the tactical balance by making threats of rocket attacks on various NATO members that are clearly intended to weaken the cohesion of the alliance.

As the above discussion has implied, nuclear technology has increased the importance of *intentions*, relative to *capabilities*, in the balancing process. Intentions have always been important, of course. In the pre-nuclear balance, the balancing process was set in motion by the perception of the disturber's aggressive intent, as well as by his military capabilities and war potential. And the adequacy of the balance as a deterrent rested in part on the aggressor's being clear about the intentions of the states which would eventually oppose him. But both sides could be fairly sure that, once the conflict was joined, all states which did participate would do so to the full extent of their military power. An important calculation for each side, therefore, concerned the balance of total capabilities.

The relation between total capabilities is still important at the level of the balance of terror—i.e., in the deterrence and fighting of all-out war. But for conflicts beginning at lower levels, the balance between over-all capabilities is less important, and a new dimension has been added to the factor of intentions—namely, each side's assessment of the other's intent regarding what portion of its destructive power will be used. Each knows that the other can inflict costs far outweighing the value of any political objective if it cares to do so. Total capabilities establish the bounds of what is possible, but what is probable depends on a reciprocal assessment of wills, which in turn depends on each side's appraisal of the opponent's values at stake in each

particular issue, his gambling propensities, his tendencies toward irrationality, his ideological or organizational commitments to certain responses, and his image of one's own characteristics in these respects.

Such estimates are of course highly subjective and uncertain, and the pervasive uncertainty adds an important element of stability to the over-all balance of power. Each side is driven to think in terms of probabilities, and when even the smallest military action *may* eventuate in nuclear war and totally unacceptable costs, small probabilities are likely to be important. Consequently, there is considerable deterrent value in making threats which the threatener knows, and the threatened party suspects, it would be irrational to carry out; if the threat increases the probability of unacceptable costs to the other side by only a few percentage points, it may be sufficient to deter.

This is to say that the existence of a balance of power, or the capabilities requirements for balancing, can hardly be determined without attempting to look into the "mind" of the enemy. One might say that a subjective "balance of intentions" has become at least as important as the more objectively calculable "balance of capabilities."

A corollary of the increased relative importance of intentions is that methods of communicating intent have become more important *means* in the balancing process than they have been in the past. First, nations are becoming more sensitive to what they say to each other about their intentions; the psychological importance of threats and other declarations is on the increase. Secondly, the function of military forces themselves may be shifting in the direction of a demonstrative role: the signaling of future intentions to use force in order to influence the enemy's intentions, as opposed to being ready to use, or using, force simply as a physical means of conquest or denial. Hence the enhanced importance of *deterrence* in the modern balance of power as compared with *defense*. We are likely to see more imaginative and subtle uses of "force demonstration" in time of peace—the Russians have given the lead with such acts as the U-2 incident, test-firing of missiles in the Pacific near U.S. territory, and the shooting-down of the U.S. RB-47 in the summer of 1960. Warfare itself may in the future become less a raw physical collision of military forces and more a contest of wills, or a bargaining process, with military force being used largely to demonstrate one's willingness to raise the intensity of fighting, with the object of inducing the enemy to accept one's terms of settlement. While direct conflict or competition is going on at a low level of the spectrum of violence, selective force demonstrations using means appropriate to higher levels may take place as threats to "up the ante."

ALTERNATIVE NATIONAL STRATEGIES

BY HERMAN KAHN

INTRODUCTION

On July 16, 1960 the world entered the sixteenth year of the nuclear era. Yet we are increasingly aware that after living with nuclear bombs for fifteen years we still have a great deal to learn about the possible effects of a nuclear war. We have even more to learn about conducting international relations in a world in which force tends to be both increasingly more available and increasingly more dangerous to use, and therefore in practice increasingly

Reprinted by permission from *On Thermonuclear War* (Princeton: Princeton University Press, 1961), pp. 3–39. Copyright 1961 by Princeton University Press.

Mr. Kahn is the Director of the Hudson Institute, a nonprofit research organization which specializes in problems of national security and international order. He was formerly an analyst with the RAND Corporation and has authored a number of books on U.S. defense policy. Most recently, he co-authored *Can We Win in Vietnam?* (1968).

unusable. As a result of this continuous secular change in the basic structure of the international situation, foreign and defense policies formulated early in the nuclear era badly need review and reformulation.

In considering these basic foreign and defense policies it is desirable to distinguish many different military postures and the corresponding possible strategies for both the United States and the Soviet Union. This treatment of thermonuclear warfare will mostly concern itself with four typical possible postures, which I will call Finite Deterrence, Counterforce as Insurance, Preattack Mobilization Base, and Credible First Strike Capability respectively. I will discuss the possibilities and implications of these postures from the point of view of the Soviet Union and the United States. While there is no reason why the two most powerful nations should have similar views, I will not initially dwell on possible asymmetries, deferring discussion of the separate national problems. A number of typical basic postures (important concepts italicized for emphasis) are listed in Table 1, roughly in order of increasing ability to wage general war.

Probably the most valuable thing that the Executive Office could do to improve over-all defense planning would be to select one of these postures and the corresponding strategies, or possibly some clearly defined alternative not on the list, and let the Office of Civil and Defense Mobilization, the Department of Defense, and the Department of State know its decision. The decision could then be debated at the proper level, and it would not be necessary to conduct a philosophical debate at the staff level, on what business the Department of Defense should be in every time somebody brought up a technical question on Air Defense, Command and Control, and so on. National debates should be conducted at the national level where feasibility, desirability, and possible consequences can be discussed responsibly and from proper points of view. It is not possible to do this even at the level of a senior but technical advisory group attached to Departments or even to the Executive Office, much less at lower staff levels. Advisory groups and agency and departmental staffs should be mainly concerned with implementing the general policy and reporting back to their superiors on cost, performance, and feasibility. In actual practice the great national debate on what business the Department of Defense should be in often occurs at the advisory group or relatively low staff levels, and important projects whose approval or disapproval may set crucial constraints on over-all policy are approved or rejected on the basis of some very narrow and parochial views of what this over-all national policy ought to be; sometimes the effects on over-all national policy are not even examined. All of this could be eliminated if the big decisions were consciously formulated, debated, and then decided at the proper level rather than treated as a number of fragmented issues to be treated on an ad hoc basis.

TABLE I
ALTERNATIVE NATIONAL POSTURES *

1. Internal Police Force plus "World Government"
2. *Minimum Deterrence* plus *Limited War* plus *Arms Control*
3. Add insurance to the *Minimum Deterrent:*
   (a) for reliability (*Finite Deterrence*)
   (b) against unreliability (*Counterforce as Insurance*)
   (c) against a change in policy (*Preattack Mobilization Base*)
4. Add *Credible First Strike Capability*
5. "Splendid" First Strike and no Limited War Capability
6. Dreams

* I am indebted to Richard B. Foster of Stanford Research Institute for the suggestion to make a list of this sort. He has used a somewhat different breakdown in some unpublished investigations on the actual strategic views held by U.S. decision makers.

*   *   *   *

1. INTERNAL POLICE FORCE PLUS "WORLD GOVERNMENT"

There seems to be little point in discussing the view that finds a solution in a totally disarmed world. Neither our own emotional desires nor the fact that there are many earnest proponents for this policy should sway us toward a position that ignores some of the basic realities. It has probably always been impractical to imagine a completely disarmed world, and the introduction of the thermonuclear bomb has added a special dimension to this impracticality. Given the large nuclear stockpiles in the Soviet Union, the United States, and the British Isles, it would be child's play for one of these nations to hide completely hundreds of these bombs. Even if some caches were found, one could not be sure that these were not decoys to allay suspicions, and yet there would be a great loathness to cancel the agreement just because "a few malcontents had conspired against the peace." The violator would then have an incredible advantage if the agreement ever broke down and the arms race started again. This surely means that even if all nations should one day agree to total nuclear disarmament, we must presume that there would be the hiding of some nuclear weapons or components as a hedge against the other side doing so. An international arrangement for banishing war through disarmament will not call for total disarmament but will almost undoubtedly include provisions for enforcement that cannot be successfully overturned by a small, hidden force. Otherwise, it would be hopelessly unstable. Even if the problem of what we may call the "clandestine cache" were solvable, the writer still is of the belief that one could not disarm the world totally and expect it to remain disarmed. But the problem of the clandestine nuclear cache in itself makes total disarmament especially infeasible.

While total disarmament can be ruled out as an immediate possibility, one can conceive of some sort of international authority which might have a monopoly of war-making capability. Such a postulated international authority would have to have enough power to be able to overwhelm any nation that had reserved hidden destructive potential. An international agency with a near-monopoly of force might come from any of the following possibilities (listed in order of apparent probability rather than desirability): (1) a Soviet or U.S. dominated world arising most likely out of war; (2) some other kind of postwar organization; (3) an S.U.-U.S. combination which is in effect a world government, though it may not openly be called that; (4) some of the NATO nations and China added to the above combination as influential, if not equal partners; (5) the Haves against the Have Nots, most likely without exploitation, but with stringent arms control in which authority and responsibility are roughly proportioned to military and economic development and, perhaps, with aid to underdeveloped nations; (6) a sort of World Federal state where power is proportioned to sovereignty and population as in the U.S. Congress. However, it is most doubtful in the absence of a crisis or war that a world government can be set up in the next decade. There are to date no serious proposals along such lines.[1] Certainly the official suggestions occasionally put out

[1] The most serious recent attempt to describe a possible world government is given in the book, *World Peace Through World Law* (Harvard University Press, Cambridge, 1958), by Grenville Clark and Louis B. Sohn. One problem with proposals such as those in the Clark-Sohn book is the same problem that many of the white colonists in Africa have in trying to deal with African independence movements. If independence is granted, they are not sufficiently protected from the new government; if only limited sovereignty is granted the nonwhite population gets to be very unhappy at the attempt to maintain the unsatisfactory *status quo*. It is worth noting in this connection that it is easier to be a hero than a saint. It really would not be difficult to find thousands of Westerners willing to give up their lives for a world government of a satisfactory sort but one would find very few willing to accept Chinese or Indian standards of living, or any appreciable risk of this occurring, for either themselves or their families. Similarly, the underdeveloped nations are going to resent any real or fancied hindrances to their working out their salvation.

by the Soviet and U.S. governments are not to be taken seriously as possible solutions.

While it may seem high time to spell out practical proposals for world government, no such attempt will be made in this book. While I believe that even a poor world government might be preferable to an uncontrolled arms race, I also believe that the practical difficulties are so large that it is a digression to dwell on such possibilities as a possible solution for the problems of the sixties. And the problems of the sixties are important! About the only way "world government" and other long-run considerations affect the kind of analysis done here is the avoidance of otherwise desirable short-term measures that might seriously hinder or foreclose desirable long-term possibilities. Even this modest ambition toward shaping the seventies is difficult to realize because there are controversies over where we want to be, as well as how to get there. However, there seems to be some consensus on what we are trying to avoid even if we cannot agree on what we are for. This book will concentrate on the problem of avoiding disaster and buying time, without specifying the use of this time. This seeming unconcern for long-term objectives will distress some readers, but some of our immediate problems must be understood more clearly than in the past if we are to control the direction in which we are going. It is the hallmark of the amateur and dilettante that he has almost no interest in how to get to his particular utopia. Perhaps this is because the practical job of finding a path may be more difficult than the job of designing the goal.[2] Let us consider, then,

some of the practical military alternatives that we face in the 1960–1975 time period. [See chapters 37 and 38 for further discussion of Arms Control.]

2. Minimum Deterrence Plus Limited War Plus Arms Control

This view, or the modest variant of it called Finite Deterrence, is probably the most widely held view in the West of what is a desirable and feasible strategic posture. Among the adherents to this position can be found most intellectuals interested in military affairs, staff people in the federal government, civilians who seek to qualify as "military experts" (including scientists and technicians), many military planners in the three services, and the vast majority of foreign and domestic lay analysts. What, then, is meant by Minimum Deterrence?

The notion is dramatic: It is that no nation whose decision makers are sane would attack another nation which was armed with a sufficiently large number of thermonuclear bombs. Thus all a nation that is so armed has to worry about is insanity, irresponsibility, accident, and miscalculation. Even such a sober expert as General Maxwell Taylor expressed this view as follows:

The avoidance of deliberate general atomic war should not be too difficult since its unremunerative character must be clear to the potential adversaries. Although actual stockpile sizes are closely guarded secrets, a nation need only feel reasonably sure that an opponent has some high-yield weapons, no matter how indefinite their exact number, to be impressed with the possible consequences of attacking him.[3]

The above was written in 1956 but is quoted in a book he published in 1959. It

---

[2] One of my amateur friends has pointed out that "It is the hallmark of the expert professional that he doesn't care where he is going as long as he proceeds competently." This seems to be a reasonable charge against this book, but I still believe that the limited focus of this book is valuable. Of those readers who are most interested in long-term goals, very few will have ever seen much discussion of the military problem as a "military problem" or the interactions of military calculations, or the lack of them, with policy. Some of these

readers will deny the existence of such interactions. Just as it would do the "militarists" some good to be exposed to utopian thinking, it will do the "utopians" even more good to be exposed to some military thinking.

[3] Maxwell D. Taylor, *The Uncertain Trumpet*, Harper & Brothers, New York, 1959, p. 184.

is only fair to add that General Taylor's views have changed and, as expressed in the book, now show much more concern with the problem of deterring general war than this quotation would indicate. He also mentions that it was very difficult for him to change his views and take the problem of deterrence seriously. It is even more difficult for laymen who do not have access to the same information to achieve this feat.

In general, the believers in Minimum Deterrence seem to view the deterrence of a rational enemy as almost a simple philosophical consequence of the *existence* of thermonuclear bombs. They argue that the decision to initiate thermonuclear war is such a momentous one—the risks are so great—that it is unlikely that such a decision will be affected by the relatively minor details of each side's military posture. One is tempted to call this "the layman's view," since people holding it show only the slightest interest in such matters as the status of the alert forces, holes in the warning networks, the range of the bombers, reliability of missiles, the degree of protection offered by current arrangements for hardening, dispersal, and concealment, and the multitude of other questions that bother sober students of the probem of retaliation. Nevertheless, the Minimum Deterrence view is held by such a surprisingly large number of experts that it may be gratuitously insulting to call it a layman's view.

An extreme form of the Minimum Deterrence theory is the view that the current strategic forces of the United States and the Soviet Union, if used, will automatically result in world annihilation or at least mutual homicide. In 1955, fifty-two Nobel laureates signed a statement (the Mainau Declaration) which included the following: "*All* nations must come to the decision to renounce force as a final resort of policy. If they are not prepared to do this they will *cease to exist*." There is a beautiful simplicity about this statement. It does not differentiate between attacker and defender, belligerent and neutral, Northern

and Southern Hemisphere, but simply says *all* nations. It does not talk about degree of damage but simply says *cease to exist*.

Everybody recognizes that statements such as the above are sometimes no more than rhetoric. If this were all there is to it one would not worry. But belief follows language as much as the other way round. Contemporary phrases, used by both experts and laymen in describing war, expressions like "balance of terror," "thermonuclear stalemate," "suicidal war," "mutual annihilation," "inescapable end of civilization," "destruction of all life," "end of history," "live together or die together," and "nobody wins a suicide pact," indicate a widespread inclination to believe that thermonuclear war would eventuate in mutual annihilation as the result of almost any plausible turn of military events. The view of the phrasemakers is reinforced by the use of deterrence analogies, such as two people on a single keg of dynamite—each with a button, two scorpions in a bottle, two heads on a single chopping block, or the bee that dies when it stings.

*   *   *   *   *

The automatic mutual annihilation view is not unique to the West. . . . Malenkov publicly introduced it to the Soviet Union several years ago, apparently arguing in the now-classical fashion that with nuclear war entailing the end of civilization, the capitalists would not attack; the Soviet Union, he said, could afford to reduce investment in heavy industry and military products and concentrate on consumer goods. A different view seems to have been held by Khrushchev and the Soviet military. They agreed that war would be horrible, but at the same time they argued that this was no reason for the Soviet Union to drop its guard; given sufficient preparations only the capitalists would be destroyed. With some important modifications their views seem to have prevailed.

Why do reasonably sober and knowledgeable people hold some version of this view of automatic mutual annihilation? In this first lecture, I will try to describe some of the data and calculations that have given

if we could not buy phonographs.) In fact, if we make allowances for current unutilized resources, the country should be somewhat better off than in World War II. Such spending would undoubtedly leave a very unpleasant post-crisis legacy of debt, economic dislocation, some inflation, and so on. But if it ever came to a serious question of choosing between such spending and a high risk of national defeat, I think there is no question that the United States would choose to spend between $200 and $300 billion annually on national security—rather than face the alternative. We are actually spending today about one-fifth of this potential. Clearly there is an enormous amount of fat which could be converted into muscle if we felt that circumstances warranted this step. The problem is, could we move fast enough? Whether we could would depend not only on how critical the military situation was, but also on our stop-gap military preparations, on our ability to recognize that circumstances have changed, on our resolve, and on the preparations already made for such an expansion. It would be most important that the actual physical plant and equipment of the Department of Defense (including installations) be such that it could be used as an existing base for a higher capability.

4. CREDIBLE FIRST STRIKE CAPABILITY

The next position on Table 1, that there are circumstances in which a nation may wish to have a Credible First Strike Capability, may seem to many Americans like a possibility for the Soviets—but not for us. One sees many statements to the effect that "We will never strike first." In the context in which the remark is usually made (a "dastardly" surprise attack out of the blue against an unprepared enemy), this position is undoubtedly correct. Such a capability would not be worth much to the U.S. However, we have many treaties and other obligations. There is the obligation to come to the aid of NATO nations if they are attacked. It is generally supposed that this aid includes the use of our

SAC against the Soviet heartland, even if the Soviets attack Europe *but not the United States.* From a technical point of view this means that in this instance *we* would strike *first!* The agonizing decision to start an all-out thermonuclear war would be ours. Surely there is a serious question whether we would live up to our treaty obligations under such circumstances.

That this doubt is plausible can be seen in the response of Christian Herter to a question by Senator Morse on the occasion of the hearings on his nomination: "I cannot conceive of any President involving us in an all-out nuclear war unless the facts showed clearly we are in danger of all-out devastation ourselves, *or that actual moves have been made toward devastating ourselves.*" [10] [See chapter 27.]

A thermonuclear balance of terror is equivalent to the signing of a non-aggression treaty which states that neither the Soviets nor the Americans will initiate an all-out attack, no matter how provoking the other side may become. Sometimes people do not understand the full implications of this figurative nonaggression treaty. Let me illustrate what it can mean if we accept absolutely the notion that there is no provocation that would cause us to strike the Soviets other than an immediately impending or an actual Soviet attack on the United States. Imagine that the Soviets have taken a very drastic action against our allies in Europe. Let the action be as extreme or shocking as the reader's imagination permits. Suppose, for example,

[10] *Hearings on the Nomination of Christian A. Herter to be Secretary of State, Committee on Foreign Relations,* U.S. Senate, 86th Congress, 1st Session, pp. 9–10 (italics mine). Whether he means it or not, Khrushchev speaks a different language. On January 14, 1960, in a speech to the Supreme Soviet, he said: "I am emphasizing once more that we already possess so many nuclear weapons, both atomic and hydrogen, and the necessary rockets for sending these weapons to the territory of a potential aggressor, that should any madman launch an attack on our state *or on other Socialist states* we would be able literally to wipe the country or countries which attack us off the face of the earth" (italics mine). *New York Times,* January 15, 1960.

of war. They regard programs other than their own as foolish or sinister and designed to cause people discomfort by making it sound plausible that there really is a national security problem toward the relief of which considerable amounts of money, energy, and intelligence need to be allocated.

Among those who take the view that Minimum Deterrence is a desirable, feasible, or the only possible strategic goal are many who nevertheless seek to add a Limited War capability. They recognize that *even if the United States and the Soviet Union cannot wage all-out war against each other this does not mean that the role of force will be entirely eliminated.* There may still be many disputes between the two nations—disputes which may tempt one side to use force on a small scale. If the only counter the other nation has is to commit suicide by starting a thermonuclear war, that nation most likely will not act. Therefore, one needs Limited War capabilities to meet limited provocations. Those who adhere to the Minimum Deterrence theory often feel that the "non-aggression treaty" of mutual deterrence is so binding and so stable it is impossible to provoke the other side to violate it by anything less than an all-out attack. Seen in this perspective, cannot one safely use the most extreme forms of violence in a limited war?

We must expand on this point. Some of those who feel strongly that it is easy to make deterrence reliable suggest using the threat of limited or controlled nuclear retaliation to "regulate" Soviet behavior. An extreme form of this notion might go as follows: If the Soviets threaten to take over Berlin, the U.S. could threaten to blow up a major Soviet City in retaliation, perhaps after warning the inhabitants to evacuate it. In their anger and distress the Soviets would then blow up one U.S. city in exchange. We would be enraged in turn, but because we would want to stop the tit-for-tat exchange, we would call a halt after warning the Soviets that any similar aggressions in the future would also result in

a city exchange. However angry both of us would be, we would not start an all-out war, according to this argument, because suicide is not a rational way of expressing one's anger. It would be in the interests of both to stop the exchange at this point. By then, from the Soviet point of view, the taking of Berlin would seem unprofitable, since the loss of the Soviet city would appear more costly than the value of Berlin plus the destruction of a U.S. city. We have gained through making it clear to the Soviets that similar future actions would be equally unprofitable. On the other hand, by destroying a U.S. city, the Soviets have made it clear that we should not lightly use controlled thermonuclear retaliation as a tactic. While the whole idea sounds bizarre, concepts like this are bound to be a logical consequence of a world in which all-out war has been made to seem *rationally infeasible,* but one in which we feel it is necessary to punish or limit the other side's provocations. The timid or *sober* may feel that Minimum Deterrence might be strained to the breaking point by such acts; for them there must be caution on the types and levels of violence to accompany limited war or limited provocations.

3. Three Kinds of Insurance

The next view of what could result in a satisfactory strategic capability adds several kinds of "insurance" to the simple Minimum Deterrence position.[4] There are at least three kinds of insurance which a survival-conscious person might wish to add, the first being *Insurance for Reliability.* We will label the view that *worries about the details* of obtaining a "punishing" retaliation, but does not want any more strategic capability than this, the *Finite Deterrence* strategy.[5] In many

[4] The addition is meant in terms of the capability of the force that is being procured; the entire force may be redesigned to get some appropriately modified version of the original capability (possibly at a reduced level) and the new insurance one.

[5] Originally, Minimum Deterrence and Finite Deterrence meant the same thing. The word

ways, and with some inconsistencies, this is the official U.S. view. The believers in Finite Deterrence do not quite accept the idea that reliable deterrence can be obtained simply by stocking thermonuclear bombs and having a weapon system which could deliver these bombs in peacetime. They notice that when the problem of retaliation is studied, rather than asserted, it is difficult to retaliate effectively, since the enemy can do many things to prevent, hinder, or negate retaliation. Evaluation of the effectiveness of retaliation must bear in mind that the Russians can strike *at a time and with tactics of their choosing.* We will strike back, no doubt, but with a *damaged and not fully coordinated* force which must conduct its operations in the *postattack environment.* The Soviets use *blackmail threats to intimidate our postattack tactics.* Under these conditions, the Russian defense system is likely to be *alerted.* Indeed, if the strike has been preceded by a tense period, their active defense forces would long since have been *augmented,* and their cities may be at least partially *evacuated.*

Any of the considerations referred to by italicized words can change the effectiveness of a retaliatory strike by an order of magnitude. Yet almost all of them are ignored in most discussions of the effectiveness of our deterrent force. Sometimes they are even relegated to the position of unimportant "technical details." They are far more than this. . . . I only want to mention here that the believer in Finite Deterrence is somewhat aware of these problems; he wants to have ready more than the bare minimum force that *might* be able to retaliate effectively (the Minimum Deterrence position). The advocate of Finite Deterrence wants enough forces to cover

"Minimum" was coined by some Polaris enthusiasts who argued we needed very little to deter the Soviets. Because the word "Minimum" carried a connotation of gambling with the nation's security for budgetary reasons, it was changed to "Finite" (which had the connotation of wanting enough and no more and also suggested that the opponents wanted an infinite or at least an unreasonable amount).

all contingencies. He may even want mixed forces, considering that it may be possible for a clever enemy to discover an unexpected countermeasure against a single kind of force no matter how large. Thus he may well want different types of missiles, bombers, strategic submarines, aircraft carriers, and so forth. In addition, sober advocates of Finite Deterrence wish to have the various weapons systems so deployed and operated that they will have a guaranteed capability, even in a crisis in which the enemy has taken extraordinary measures to negate the capability. They want these forces dispersed, protected, and alert; the arrangements for command, control, and communications must be able to withstand degradation by both peacetime and wartime tactics of the enemy. These sober believers in Finite Deterrence tend to insist on an objective capability as opposed to one that is only "psychological." And even those believers in Finite Deterrence who would be satisfied with a facade yearn for an impressive-looking facade. One might characterize the Finite Deterrence position as an expert version of the Minimum Deterrence position, held by an expert who wants to look good to other experts.

The notion of Finite Deterrence is therefore not as dramatic as the notion of Minimum Deterrence. The believer in Finite Deterrence is willing to concede that it takes some effort to guarantee Mutual Homicide, that it is not automatic. However, the notion of Finite Deterrence is still dramatic, since most followers of this doctrine believe that *the advent of thermonuclear bombs has changed the character of an all-out war in such a way that if both opponents are prepared the old-fashioned distinctions between victory, stalemate, and defeat no longer have much meaning.* It was once believed that if one country had forces twice as large as those of another country, the first country was the stronger. Those who believe in Finite Deterrence challenge this view. Sometimes they rest their case on this idea: the only purpose of strategic forces is to deter rather than to fight; once one has the ability to damage seriously, say, 10 or 20 enemy cities, this is enough force to deter, and therefore enough force. More often, backers of Finite Deterrence take a more extreme position. They argue that you can do no more than kill somebody once, to overkill by a factor of ten is no more desirable than overkilling by a factor of two—it is simply a waste of effort. They also usually argue that with some thought it should be easy to design strategic systems that can overkill, even in retaliation. Once we procure the limited (i.e., finite) forces required to do this job we have enough strategic forces and do not need any more—no matter what the enemy does.

In the year 1960 I believe that even adherents to an extreme Minimum Deterrence position tended to agree, under pressure, that the nation should buy whatever insurance is needed to make retaliation at least "look" potentially reliable and effective. In this sense, the orthodox Minimum Deterrence School is no longer as respectable as might once have been inferred from the remarks of the most enthusiastic proponents of a defense built solely around small Minuteman and Polaris systems. Most of the more sober analysts have come to talk about *Finite* Deterrence, by which they mean having a generous adequacy for deterrence, but that is all they want for the general war. Specifically, they often tend to be against any counter-force capability. (The word "counterforce" includes not only an active counterforce that can destroy or damage the enemy's force on the ground, but also other methods of countering the opponent's force, such as Active and Passive Defense.) [6]

Some believers in Finite Deterrence are against counterforce as a useless diversion of forces; others would not even be interested in having any counterforce even if it were free, because they consider it destabilizing. They notice at least one circumstance in which an enemy is likely to attack even if he is worried about the retaliatory destruction that he will suffer. This circumstance occurs when he believes his attack is pre-emptive, that by striking first he is only forestalling an attack being launched on him. Most believers in Finite Deterrence are so convinced of the efficacy of their deterrence that they believe such an idea could only arise as a result of miscalculation, since no rational man could order an attack against an enemy who has made at least moderate preparations to ward it off. However, they recognize that if both forces are in a condition of super alert it may be easy to have such a misunderstanding. Or equally likely, there is the problem that Thomas Schelling of Harvard (and RAND) has called "the reciprocal fear of surprise attack," where each side imputes to the other aggressive intentions and misreads purely defensive preparations as being offensive. There are unfortunately many postures possible in which a disastrous train of self-confirming actions and counteractions could be set into motion. In order to prevent this from occurring, some believers in Finite Deterrence think it is important for us to disabuse ourselves of the idea that there can be any circumstance in which it makes sense to attack the Soviet Union, and they want us to adopt a posture which makes it clear to the Soviets that we are so disabused. As part of this posture we should make as few preparations as possible to alleviate the effects of the war or protect ourselves from a Soviet

---

[6] The word "counterforce" is usually used to apply to an ability to destroy the enemy on the ground. It is true that the best *counter* against an unprotected SAC base is a bomb on the base. But the best counter against a hidden missile may be a shelter; the best counter against a bomber carrying many bombs may be active defense; the best counter against the enemy destroying our cities may be the use of retaliatory threats; the best counter against fallout-type attacks is shelters plus anti-contamination. I will use the term counterforce to cover all of the above—to include anything which might counter the use or effectiveness of the enemy's force. While many of my colleagues object to my generalizing the definition in this manner, the new definition has the important virtue of discouraging parochial attitudes. It emphasizes that any method of countering the enemy's force may be useful, and that the allocation between the different methods should be made by objective considerations and not by slogans or outworn doctrine.

retaliatory strike. This will convince the Soviets that we do not intend to attack them except in retaliation; they will then be able to relax and not be trigger-happy. As one (partial) adherent to Finite Deterrence, Oskar Morgenstern, explained: "In order to preserve a nuclear stalemate under conditions of nuclear plenty it is necessary for *both* sides to possess invulnerable retaliatory forces. . . . it is in the interest of the United States for Russia to have an invulnerable retaliatory force and vice versa [i.e., one may wish to strengthen the enemy and weaken oneself]." [7]

Many who accept the Finite Deterrence view have another reason for not defending or protecting anything but the retaliatory capability; they see no need for programs to protect people and property, because they think it is not feasible to protect either people or property. These people often argue that it does not matter whether one dies immediately from blast, heat, or radiation, or dies later from the effects of radioactivity, disease, or starvation—as long as one is going to die. And they go on to assert that modern war is so horrible that everyone or almost everyone will be killed immediately—or will eventually be destroyed by one of the after-effects.

A surprisingly large number of official military experts and planners seem to hold views, at least unconsciously, which are really a variation of the Finite Deterrence view that the only purpose of the strategic forces is to deter. . . .

* * * * *

. . . If one were to deduce the beliefs of some policy makers from the decisions they make, he would find that in a rather high percentage of cases the planners seem to care less about what happens after the buttons are pressed than they do about looking "presentable" before the event. They show slight interest in maintaining an appreciable operational capability on the second day of the war; if deterrence

[7] *The Question of National Defense*, New York, Random House, 1959, pp. 74, 76.

should fail, they, as well as many scientists, could not be less interested in the details of what happens—so long as the retaliatory strike is launched.

It is my contention that failure to launch an effective retaliatory attack is only the first of many possible failures. Even if one retaliates successfully, there can ensue significant and meaningful failures. These will occur one after another if the attitude exemplified in the above quotation becomes too universal in either the making or execution of policy. And even Deterrence Only advocates should realize that there are subtle but important differences between a posture which is to be a facade to impress the enemy and one which is supposed to have an objective capability.

Insurance Against Unreliability. Some of the proponents of Finite Deterrence do not have an antipathy toward all forms of counterforce. They are willing to insure against unreliability. That is, even though deterrence has been made as reliable as they think it can be made, they realize that it may still fail; for example, from accident, human irrationality, miscalculation, or unauthorized behavior. Given this nonzero probability of a war, they find it difficult not to go through the motions of doing "something" to mitigate its effects. Even totally convinced "mutual annihilation" decision makers may be unwilling to admit openly that there are no preparations to alleviate the consequences of a war. It is difficult for any government to look at its people and say in effect, "We can no longer protect you in a war. We have no answer to blackmail except a counterblackmail threat, and we have no preparations to deal with accidental war except trying to make it so dreadful that everybody will be careful in advance."

A facade of being able to alleviate may also be useful in international relations. It reassures one's allies about one's resolve and induces uncertainty and (hopefully) fear in the enemy. Even if it were true that both sides in the cold war conflict were unwilling to risk a thermonuclear war over any issue that could arise between them, it would weaken their diplomatic strength to admit this openly since the admitting power would be conceding that the other power could always get its way by staking a little more.

Some decision makers who accept the Finite Deterrence view are willing to pay for insurance against unreliability for more than political or psychological reasons. Even those who hold that war means mutual annihilation are sometimes willing for us to act beyond their beliefs—or fears. While this is inconsistent, it is not necessarily irrational. They understand that paper calculations can be wrong and are willing to hedge against this possibility. Sometimes these decision makers are making a distinction that (rather surprisingly) is not usually made. They may distinguish, for example, between 100 million dead and 50 million dead, and argue that the latter state is better than the former. They may distinguish between war damage which sets the economy of a country back fifty years or only ten years. *Actually, when one examines the possible effects of thermonuclear war carefully, one notices that there are indeed many postwar states that should be distinguished.* If most people do not or cannot distinguish among these states it is because the gradations occur as a result of a totally bizarre circumstance —a thermonuclear war. The mind recoils from thinking hard about that; one prefers to believe it will never happen. If asked, "How does a country look on the day of the war?" the only answer a reasonable person can give is "awful." It takes an act of iron will or an unpleasant degree of detachment or callousness to go about the task of distinguishing among the possible degrees of awfulness.

But surely one can ask a more specific question. For example, *"How does a country look five or ten years after the close of war, as a function of three variables: (1) the preparations made before the war, (2) the way the war started, and (3) the course of military events?"* Both very sensitive and very callous individuals

should be able to distinguish (and choose, perhaps) between a country which survives a war with, say, 150 million people and a gross national product (GNP) of $300 billion a year, and a nation which emerges with only 50 million people and a GNP of $10 billion. The former would be the richest and the fourth largest nation in the world, and one which would be able to restore a reasonable facsimile of the prewar society; the latter would be a pitiful remnant that would contain few traces of the prewar way of life. When one asks this kind of question and examines the circumstances and possible outcomes of a future war in some detail, it appears that it is useful and necessary to make many distinctions among the results of thermonuclear war. The figures in Table 2 illustrate some simple distinctions which one may wish to make at the outset of his deliberations in this field.

TABLE 2

TRAGIC BUT
DISTINGUISHABLE
POSTWAR STATES

Dead	Economic Recuperation
2,000,000	1 year
5,000,000	2 years
10,000,000	5 years
20,000,000	10 years
40,000,000	20 years
80,000,000	50 years
160,000,000	100 years

Will the survivors envy the dead?

Here I have tried to make the point that if we have a posture which might result in 40 million dead in a general war, and as a result of poor planning, apathy, or other causes, our posture deteriorates and a war occurs with 80 million dead, we have suffered an additional disaster, an *unnecessary* additional disaster that is almost as bad as the original disaster. If on the contrary, by spending a few billion dollars, or by being more competent or lucky, we can cut the number of dead from 40 to 20 million, we have done something vastly worth doing: The survivors will not dance in the streets or congratulate each other if there have been 20 million men, women, and children killed; yet it would have been a worthwhile achievement to limit casualties to this number. It is very difficult to get this point across to laymen or experts with enough intensity to move them to action. The average citizen has a dour attitude toward planners who say that if we do thus and so it will not be 40 million dead—it will be 20 million dead. Somehow the impression is left that the planner said that there will be *only* 20 million dead. To him is often attributed the idea that this will be a tolerable or even, astonishingly enough, a desirable state!

The rate of economic recuperation, like the number of lives saved, is also of extreme importance. Very few Americans can get interested in spending money or energy on preparations which, even if they worked, would result in preindustrial living standards for the survivors of a war. As will be explained later, our analysis indicates that if a country is moderately well prepared to use the assets which survive there is unlikely to be a critical level of damage to production. A properly prepared country is not "killed" by the destruction of even a major fraction of its wealth; it is more likely to be set back a given number of years in its economic growth. While recuperation times may range all the way from one to a hundred years, even the latter is far different from the "end of history."

Perhaps the most important item on the table of distinguishable states is not the numbers of dead or the number of years it takes for economic recuperation; rather, it is the question at the bottom: "Will the survivors envy the dead?" It is in some sense true that one may never recuperate from a thermonuclear war. The world may be permanently (i.e., for perhaps 10,000 years) more hostile to human life as a result of such a war. Therefore, if the question, "Can we restore the prewar conditions of

life?" is asked, the answer must be "No!" But there are other relevant questions to be asked. For example: "How much more hostile will the environment be? Will it be so hostile that we or our descendants would prefer being dead than alive?" Perhaps even more pertinent is this question, "How happy or normal a life can the survivors and their descendants hope to have?" *Despite a widespread belief to the contrary, objective studies indicate that even though the amount of human tragedy would be greatly increased in the postwar world, the increase would not preclude normal and happy lives for the majority of survivors and their descendants.*

My colleagues and I came to this conclusion reluctantly; not because we did not *want* to believe it, but because it is so *hard* to believe. Thermonuclear bombs are so destructive, and destructive in so many ways, that it is difficult to imagine that there would be anything left after their large-scale use. One of my tasks with The RAND Corporation was to serve as project leader for a study of the possibilities for alleviating the consequences of a thermonuclear war. That study was made as quantitatively and objectively as we could make it with the resources, information, and intellectual tools available to us. We concluded that for at least the next decade or so, any picture of total world annihilation appears to be wrong, irrespective of the military course of events.[8] Equally important, the picture of total disaster is likely to be wrong even for the two antagonists. Barring an extraordinary course for the war, or that most of the technical uncertainties turn out to lie at the disastrous end of the spectrum, one and maybe both of the antagonists should be able to restore a reasonable semblance of prewar conditions quite rapidly. Typical estimates run between one and ten years for a reasonably successful and well-prepared attacker and somewhat longer for the defender, depending mainly on the tac-

[8] *Report on a Study of Non-Military Defense,* The RAND Corporation, Report R–322–RC, July 1, 1958.

tics of the attacker and the preparations of the defender. In the RAND study we tried to avoid using optimistic assumptions. With the exceptions to be noted, we used what were in our judgment the best values available, or we used slightly pessimistic ones. We believe that the situation is likely to be better than we indicate, rather than worse, though the latter possibility cannot be ruled out.

Exactly what is it that one must believe if he is to be convinced that it is worth while to buy Counterforce as Insurance? Listed below are eight phases of a thermonuclear war. If our decision makers are to justify the expense (and possible risk of strategic destabilization) that would be incurred in trying to acquire a capability for alleviating the consequences of a war, they must believe thay can successfully negotiate each and every one of these phases, or that there is a reasonable chance that they can negotiate each of these phases.

TABLE 3

A COMPLETE DESCRIPTION OF A THERMONUCLEAR WAR

Includes the Analysis of:

1. Various time-phased programs for deterrence and defense and their possible impact on us, our allies, and others.
2. Wartime performance with different preattack and attack conditions.
3. Acute fallout problems.
4. Survival and patch-up.
5. Maintenance of economic momentum.
6. Long-term recuperation.
7. Postwar medical problems.
8. Genetic problems.

I repeat: To survive a war it is necessary to negotiate *all eight* stages. If there is a catastrophic failure in any one of them, there will be little value in being able to cope with the other seven. Differences among exponents of the different strategic views can often be traced to the different estimates they make on the difficulty of negotiating one or more of these eight

stages. While all of them present difficulties, most civilian military experts seem to consider the *last six* the critical ones. Nevertheless, most discussions among "classical" military experts concentrate on the *first two*. To get a sober and balanced view of the problem, one must examine all *eight*.

* * * * *

. . . The only point to be made now is that those waging a modern war are going to be as much concerned with bone cancer, leukemia, and genetic malformations as they are with the range of a B–52 or the accuracy of an Atlas missile. Senior military advisors in particular will increasingly be forced to deal with what would once have been called "nonmilitary" problems. They will need to be armed with documented studies rather than opinions.

Once one accepts the idea that deterrence is not absolutely reliable and that it would be possible to survive a war, then he may be willing to buy insurance—to spend money on preparations to decrease the number of fatalities and injuries, limit damage, facilitate recuperation, and to get the best military result possible—at least "to prevail" [9] in some meaningful sense if you cannot win.

Insurance Against a Change in Policy. . . [T]*he military problem really is complicated and it is impossible for fallible human beings to predict ahead of time exactly what capabilities they will wish or need.* This does not mean, of course, that one has to buy everything. Resources may not be as limited as some of the more budget-mind-

[9] The word "prevail" is much used in official statements. It is a carefully chosen word that shows that the user is trying to do the best he can even though he is aware that many deny the old-fashioned distinctions between victory and defeat. Because its use is ambiguous, the reader does not know whether the author is serious about his goal or is just making a meaningless concession to old-fashioned thinking; it probably does more harm than good to set it up as a goal. It would be better to use the old-fashioned concept of victory, as denoting the one who writes the peace treaty, while at the same time making explicit that victory can be costly.

ed people think, but they are still quite limited. However, it does mean that whenever it is *cheap* to do so (and sometimes when it is moderately expensive), we should be willing to hedge against changes in our desires. The fact that it is expensive to buy and maintain a complete spectrum of military capabilities in being does not mean that we should not have what might be called "mobilization bases" for a complete spectrum of adequate military capabilities. The government, relying on current doctrine, current military capabilities, its estimates of the political situation, might be satisfied with current allocations for national defense. But it should still be willing to hedge against the possibility that circumstances may so change that the reluctance to spend money will also change, either increasing or decreasing. This hedging can be accomplished by spending a relatively small amount on advance planning and physical preparations. We will then be in a position where we can make the most rapid and effective use of larger funds if they become available, or we will be able to get the most value out of a smaller military budget if it seems desirable to cut back on expenditures.

There are many different kinds of programs that come under the heading "Hedging Against a Change in Policy." It is obvious that there is need for very broad research and development programs. While research is not cheap, it is far from true that research is so expensive that it can be afforded only on clearly needful items. The opposite is true. The penalty for not having researched on an item that turns out to be useful is so great that we must have an extremely broad program to be certain that all the things that could conceivably be useful will in fact be investigated. Development is somewhat more expensive than research. As a result, we cannot afford to have quite as broad a menu. But even here we should *develop* many more items than we actually procure. We may also *procure* some systems in part, even if we do not feel they are ab-

solutely needful. Requirements can change.

* * * * *

There is a special type of mobilization base which I will call a "Preattack Mobilization Base." This can be extremely important. It is a capability for being able to improve rapidly our ability to fight or to threaten to fight either a limited or a general war. It includes preparations for putting in *adequate civil defense programs.* It also includes the procurement of very long *lead time* items for our strategic air defense and air offense, so that by just spending money rapidly we could bring all of these capabilities up to an adequate level. There is a very broad spectrum of preparations possible here. One kind of preparation would be useful only if a situation occurred in which substantial tactical warning (hours) was available; another set of preparations would be most useful in situations in which we had strategic warning—days, weeks, or even months. And still another set of preparations could be made to improve our ability to compensate for a possible deterioration in the international situation or an increase in our standards for an acceptable level of defense. . . . I will only make here the obvious point that what might be called the Finite Deterrence function of the strategic force is too important to depend on warning. There should always be an adequate capability *in-being* to deter a surprise attack.

There are large resources available for defense if it becomes necessary to use them. Many economists have estimated that the United States could allocate between 40 and 50 per cent of its gross national product to military purposes for some years without subjecting individual citizens to any appreciable physical hardships. (Postattack living standards would be adequate by almost any reasonable standard. The situation would be much like World War II where we spent, at peak, about 43 per cent of our GNP on military products, and we could still buy phonograph records even

rise to these cataclysmic expectations and explain why the situation is not, at least for the immediate future, as they describe it.

A thermonuclear war is quite likely to be an *unprecedented catastrophe* for the defender. Depending on the military course of events, it may or may not be an unprecedented catastrophe for the attacker, and for some neutrals as well. But an "unprecedented" catastrophe can be a far cry from an "unlimited" one. Most important of all, sober study shows that *the limits on the magnitude of the catastrophe seem to be closely dependent on what kinds of preparations have been made, and on how the war is started and fought.*

While the notions in the above paragraph may strike some readers as being obvious, I must repeat that they are by no means so. The very existence of the irreconcilable group predicting total catastrophe is proof. One can divide military thinkers into two classes: those who believe that any war would result in no less than mutual annihilation, and those who feel this is not necessarily so or even that it is in all likelihood wrong. The latter group is probably correct, at least for the military capabilities that are likely to be available in the next decade or so. Yet on the whole they have not done very much "homework" to prove their point. The total disaster group has done a great deal of homework. This could mean that the first group is likely for a time to win many an argument on this question.

This concept of mutual homicide, sure and certain, has in many ways been peculiarly comforting to those holding it. It makes plausible the conviction that when governments are informed of the terrible consequences of a nuclear war they will realize there could be no victors. There would be no sense to such a war. Would a sane leader ever start such a cataclysm? Of course not. The expected violence of war would deter him. Those who hold this comforting concept may even get angry at anyone who ventures to assay estimates of the precise degree of risk which a "successful" attacker might actually face.

The mutual homicide theory yields other comforts. If one grants that each side will utterly destroy the other, one must also grant that expensive preparations to reduce casualties, lessen damage, and facilitate postwar recuperation are useless. Can we not spare ourselves the financial burden of such preparations? The "logic" has sometimes been carried further, some arguing that modern weapons are so enormously destructive that only a few are needed to deter the enemy. Therefore, the argument goes, war can be deterred with much smaller forces than in the past; in any case we certainly do not need more.

The view from this plateau is attractive to many groups who are determined on disarmament and certain types of arms control. For them, the Minimum Deterrence notion implies a certain kind of automatic stability which makes it safe to be casual about both agreements and possible violations. One must concede that the very concept of Minimum Deterrence implies that the two nations involved have in effect signed a reliable non-aggression treaty with their populations as hostages to insure adherence to this treaty; the only strategic problem that seems to be left is an accidental or unauthorized violation of this nonaggression "treaty." It is such possibilities that are the subject of arms control negotiations.

The mutual annihilation view is also comforting to many idealistic individuals, particularly to those who have an intrinsic abhorrence of any use of force. The bizarreness of a war in which both sides expect to get annihilated confirms their intuition that this whole business of military preparations is silly: a stupid and dangerous game which we ought to discourage nations—our own country, at least—from playing. At the same time these idealists can afford to scoff at attempts to reduce casualties from, say, 100 million to 50 million Americans, reflecting that the situation is hopeless anyway and that the only Respectable Cause is the total elimination

that the Soviets have dropped bombs on London, Berlin, Rome, Paris, and Bonn *but have made no detectable preparations for attacking the United States, and our retaliatory force looks good enough to deter them from such an attack.* As far as we can tell they have done this horrible deed simply to demonstrate their strength and resolve. Suppose also that there is a device which restrains the President of the United States from acting for about twenty-four hours. It is probably true that if the President were not restrained he would order an attack on the S.U. (even if he had previously bought either the Minimum Deterrence or Finite Deterrence positions that no sane decision maker initiates a thermonuclear war against an enemy who can retaliate). However, we have assumed the existence of a 24-hour device which forces him to stop and think and make his decision in cold blood. The President would presumably call together his advisors during this time. Most of the advisors would probably urge strongly that the U.S. fulfill its obligations by striking the Soviet Union. Now let us further suppose that the President is also told by his advisors that even though we will kill almost every Russian *civilian,* we will not be able to destroy all of the Soviet strategic forces, and that these surviving Soviet forces will (by radiation or strontium–90 or something else) kill every American in their retaliatory blow—all 180 million of us.

Is it not difficult to believe that under these hypothetical circumstances any President of the United States would initiate a thermonuclear war by all-out retaliation against the Soviets with the Strategic Air Command? Few would contend that there is any plausible public policy which would justify ending life for everyone. It should be clear that our retaliation would not restore Europe; we could only succeed in further destroying it either as a by-product of our actions or because the surviving Soviet forces would subsequently destroy Europe as well as the United States. I am not saying that the United States would stand idly by. We would clearly declare

war on the Soviets. We would make all kinds of *limited* military moves. We would go into a crash mobilization on at least the hundred-billion-dollars-a-year level. But there is one thing that we almost certainly would not do: We would not launch an all-out attack on Soviet cities.

There were two important caveats in the situation described: 180 million Americans would be killed, and the President would have twenty-four hours to think about his response. Let us consider these in turn. If 180 million dead is too high a price to pay for punishing the Soviets for their aggression, what price would we be willing to pay? This is a hard and unpleasant question. I have discussed this question with many Americans, and after about fifteen minutes of discussion their estimates of an acceptable price generally fall between 10 and 60 million, clustering toward the upper number. (There first reaction, incidentally, is usually that the U.S. would *never* be deterred from living up to its obligations by fear of a Soviet counterblow—an attitude that invariably disappears after some minutes of reflection.) The way one seems to arrive at the upper limit of 60 million is rather interesting. He takes one-third of a country's population, in other words somewhat less than half. No American that I have spoken to who was at all serious about the matter believed that any U.S. action, limited or unlimited, would be justified—no matter what our commitments were—if more than half of our population would be killed in retaliation.

The 24-hour delay is a more subtle device. It is the equivalent of asking, "Can the Soviets force the President to act in cold blood and full knowledge, rather than in the immediate anger of the moment?" This depends not only on the time he has to learn and ponder the effects that would flow from his actions (and I will describe many circumstances in which this time for reflection would occur), but also on how deeply and seriously the President and his advisors have thought about the problem in advance. This latter, in turn, would depend on whether there had been any tense situations or crises which forced the President and the people to face the concept that war is something which can happen, rather than something that is reliably deterred by some declaratory policy that never need be acted upon. (The effects of the war are usually considered irrelevant to one's declaratory policy, since it is assumed that the declarations will deter the war.)

* * * * *

. . . It is most important that we be able to convince our continental allies that the U.S. posture is such that the Soviets really would find it too dangerous to give such an ultimatum, and that if they did the U.S. would be able to take some corrective action that would not result in most of the Northern Hemisphere being wiped out or in a situation such as de Gaulle described in his press conference. . . .

It should now be clear what I mean by a Credible First Strike Capability. Crediblity does not involve the question "Do we or the Soviets have the capability to hurt the other side on a first strike?" It is well known that this capability exists and in all likelihood will continue to exist. Credibility depends on being willing to accept the other side's retaliatory blow. It depends on the harm *he* can do not on the harm *we* can do. It depends as much on *air defense* and *civil defense* as on *air offense*. It depends on *will* as well as *capability*. It depends on the *provocation* and on the *state of our mind* when the provocation occurs. One should also note that being able to use a Credible First Strike Capability to influence Soviet or European behavior depends not only on our will, but also on Soviet and European estimates of our will. Serious problems may be created for us if either of them does not believe in our willingness to attack under certain kinds of provocation.

Let us consider some European estimates first. I have discussed with many Europeans the question of how many casualties an American decision maker or planner would be willing to envisage and still be willing to see this country live up to its obligations. Their estimates, perhaps not surprisingly, range much lower than the estimates of Americans, that is, roughly 2 to 20 million (clustering toward the lower numbers). In fact, one distinguished European expert thought that the U.S. would be deterred from retaliating with SAC against a major Soviet aggression in Europe by a Soviet threat to destroy five or ten empty U.S. cities.[11]

Will the Soviets find the threat of U.S. retaliation credible? I have not asked any Soviet citizens, so I lack the advantage of any introspection by Russians. But we do know that their formal writings strongly emphasize that decision makers should be able to control their emotions. The Soviets do not believe in cutting off their noses to spite their faces; they write and seem to believe that one should not be provoked into self-destructive behavior. They probably would assume that we do likewise. One would not think that the Soviets could believe that the U.S. would willingly commit suicide. In fact, I would conjecture that they would feel fairly certain about this matter. They could readily underestimate our *resolve*. We might easily be irrationally determined to resist the Soviets. We have no tradition in the United States of controlling our emotions. We have tended to emphasize the opposite notion (e.g., "Give me liberty or give me death"). A Soviet underestimation of U.S. resolve could create the worst of all situations— one in which we had not made preparations for the failure of deterrence because we knew we had enough resolve, but the Soviets did not believe it so they went ahead and provoked us and we were forced to initiate a war in retaliation, a war in which we were not prepared to do

---

[11] After observing, in passing, that the case for more civil defense was "perhaps best put eighteen months ago in a study by The RAND Corporation," the London *Times* of January 4, 1960 editorialized, "No amount of money or concrete could guarantee to prevent the deaths of some millions of city-dwellers from blast and heat, and it is just as difficult to imagine an American President willing to risk deaths of five million Americans as of fifty million."

anything more than kill Russians.[12] But it seems likely that unless we institute remedial measures, the Soviets may estimate that we will be deterred, and they will be right in their estimate. It should be realized that a very low additional probability of war might not deter the Soviets. It is not as if there were no probability at all of war and their action had created this probability. It would be much more reasonable to say that just the existence of the U.S.—S.U. rivalry means that somehow there is always a probability of war of, say, one in fifty every year, and that if the Soviet action increased this by, in any one year, 50 per cent—from the assumed .02 to .03—that this might not be, for many reasons, as deterring as raising the probability of war .01. As the engineer would put it, the increased probability of war must dominate "the noise level" to be deterring. This is particularly true if the Soviets believe that their action would either decrease the long-run probability of war or increase markedly their chance of coming out of such a war very much better than if they had not improved their position. In addition, if the Soviets were not to risk all by a single attempt but tested our resolve more gradually by instigating a series of crises, then without running excessive risks they could probably find out experimentally a great deal about our reactions to extreme provocations. No matter what our *declared policy* might be, our *actual policy* could be probed. Most important of all, it is difficult to believe, in the absence of adequate measure for air defense and civil defense, that the Europeans will have faith in our declared policy when it is strained. The Soviets may be able to make their gains more easily by working on the will and resolve of the Europeans than by working

on ours. We must convince the Europeans as well as the Russians of our resolve if we are to prevent appeasement or an undue degree of accommodation.

* * * * *

As has already been explained, one does not have to be trying to achieve a Credible First Strike Capability to be interested in trying to cope with the eight phases of a thermonuclear war. Even if one believes in mutual annihilation, he may still be willing to endorse Counterforce as Insurance Capability (the insurance against unreliability discussed in the previous section). This is because a reasonable person generally knows that his beliefs can be wrong. Many will agree, therefore, that some portion of the defense budget should be allocated to Counterforce as Insurance and to other measures designed to alleviate the consequences of a war. Because paper calculations can be misleading, it is rational to have even an inconsistent program which hedges against this possibility.

There is, however, a difference between Counterforce as Insurance and Credible First Strike Capabilities. In the case of the latter we do not say that there is a *modest* probability that the mutual annihilation theory is wrong; instead, we require that there be a *very high* probability that it is wrong. In short, *the time has come when we must believe that our programs are very likely to be successful under wartime and postwar conditions.*

When this has been said, it is still important to know (abstractly, we hope) that a war in which the U.S. made the first strike would result in more favorable conditions for us than would the wars that are generally considered. And even here we are more interested in *deterrence* than in *striking first!* We are more deeply interested in what the Soviets will conclude when they ask themselves, "If we try this very provoking act, will the United States strike us?" than in speculating on what could happen to us if we should actually strike them. It is quite possible that the Soviets may conclude when contemplating action that

---

[12] Nathan Leites points out to me that a convinced Communist might be perfectly willing to believe that the cold-hearted capitalist ruling class would be willing to lose 60 million or so of the "lower" classes; but even this ideological estimator would probably feel safe from an attack if a Soviet retaliation could kill many more than 60 million Americans.

their risks are too high (even though the fact may be that we have already concluded that we would not actually dare to initiate the war). It is for such reasons that even a facade may be invaluable. Everyone knows that there is an enormous difference between a probability and a certainty.

5. "Splendid" First Strike and No Limited War Capability

It is difficult for most people to believe that any nation would initiate a thermonuclear war against an opponent capable of retaliation no matter what capabilities it had and no matter how much it was provoked; nevertheless, there are many military planners who oppose having limited war capabilities to handle modest provocations. They say this is a diversion of our resources from more important and essential central war capabilities. They seem to feel that our strategic force can be so effective in Soviet eyes that they would not dare to provoke us in even a minor way. They also believe that if the Soviets did provoke us we should then hit them at "a time and place of our choosing," thereby punishing the Soviets for their provocation. This is, roughly speaking, the massive retaliation theory as enunciated by former Secretary of State John Foster Dulles. [See chapter 27.] While a Credible First Strike Capability to correct or avenge a limited but major aggression also involves massive retaliation, the distinction is that it is massive retaliation over *major* issues, not minor ones. It should also be clear that if the terror in the "balance of terror" intensifies, the line between major and minor issues will shift so that the level of provocation we will accept without triggering SAC will increase.

Anyone who studies even superficially the likely effects of thermonuclear war will inevitably reach certain conclusions. Chief among these is the idea that *even if one could launch a very successful first strike, the net damage, if only from the backlash (i.e., the fallout on the U.S. and the world from the bombs dropped on Russia, not to speak of the Russian people who would be killed), would make it unreasonable to make such a strike on a minor issue.* Is it not true that if we were to launch such a war it would not be over the minor issue bothering us but really because we had decided to engage in a form of preventive war? In the real world we would have to worry about far more than just the backlash from our blow; we would have to worry about Soviet retaliatory action. For such *practical* reasons alone, not to speak of vitally important moral and political ones, the notion of having a "Splendid" First Strike Capability seems fanciful.

6. Dreams

If a "Splendid" First Strike Capability seems in the light of facts and reason to be fanciful, it is no less strange than many of the ideas which make the rounds in Washington or in European capitals. In such places one finds consideration given to very implausible notions. One of these is a conflict in which a thermonuclear blow is followed by a three-year war of production accompanied by the kind of mobilization we had in World War II. Another is the notion that the enemy can go ahead and strike us first, but that our defenses would keep us essentially untouched, and that we in turn can strike back and then survey the situation. There is the fervid belief in the possibility of a "leakproof" active defense system. There is the concept of a long drawn-out conflict, a "broken backed war," waged with conventional weapons because both sides have simultaneously used up all their nuclear weapons. There is the claim that in a thermonuclear war it is important to keep the sea lanes open. And there is the quaint idea that the main purpose of civil defense is to support a thermonuclear war effort with men and materials. Or the equally quaint notion that after a massive interchange of thermonuclear bombs the major objective of the U.S. Army forces in the United States will not be civilian recuperation but to move to a (destroyed) port of embarkation for movement overseas. While all of these views are most implausible, they can be found in various types of official and semi-official statements.

Where do such ideas come from? They generally result, it can be assumed, from doctrinal lags or from position papers which primarily reflect a very narrow departmental interest or which are the result of log-rolling compromises between several partisan departments of the government. We are fortunate that on the whole these views are no longer taken seriously even by many of the decision makers who sign the papers. Unfortunately, this does not prevent the papers themselves from influencing public opinion and policy to an important extent.

It should be noted that those who are convinced of the efficacy of Minimum or Finite Deterrence tend to believe that the Counterforce as Insurance, the Credible First Strike Capability, and the "Splendid" First Strike Capability views are as fanciful as the dream capabilities mentioned above. If anything, they find them more dangerously fanciful because so many people take them seriously. In this book only the following strategic positions will be considered seriously: Finite Deterrence, Counterforce as Insurance, Preattack Mobilization Base, and Credible First Strike Capability—*all* with varying degrees of Arms Control and Limited War Capability . . . . Our national policy at this writing seems to be drifting (mostly as a result of decisions evaded or decided for relatively

minor technical reasons) toward accepting a strategy between Finite Deterrence and Counterforce as Insurance. *It is one of my main arguments that at least for the immediate future we should be somewhere between the Preattack Mobilization Base and the Credible First Strike Capability.* This posture would have, at least, enough capability to launch a first strike in the kind of tense situation that would result from an outrageous Soviet provocation, so as to induce uncertainty in the enemy as to whether it would not be safer to attack us directly rather than provoke us. The posture should have enough of a retaliatory capability to make this direct attack unattractive. It should have enough of a Preattack Mobilization Base to enable us to increase our first strike and retaliatory capabilities rapidly enough so that, if international relations deteriorate seriously, we will be able to acquire sufficient power in time to control or influence events. There should be enough Counterforce as Insurance so that if a war occurs anyway —perhaps as a result of accident or miscalculation—the nation will continue and unnecessary death and destruction will not occur. And lastly, the posture should include enough Arms Control and Limited War Capability to deter and correct "minor" conflicts and to make the day to day course of international relations livable until more permanent and stable arrangements are set up.

SOME POSSIBLE SIZES AND SHAPES OF THERMONUCLEAR WAR

BY HERMAN KAHN

It was the main thesis of Chapter One* that even if one were to consider thermonuclear war unthinkable, that would not make it impossible. It is the thesis of this chapter that failure to think may even

make it more probable that the lethal equipment which indubitably exists might be used, and, if used, be used more destructively than necessary. In this chapter, therefore, I would like to consider both the

---

*Reprinted by permission from *Thinking About the Unthinkable* (New York: Horizon Press Publishers, 1962), pp. 39–69. Copyright 1962 by Horizon Press Publishers.

possibility and character of thermonuclear war.

It is well to note at the outset a recurring tendency to underestimate the likelihood of war. Ever since the catastrophic and disillusioning experience of 1914–18, war has been unthinkable to most people in the West. Many illogically have tended to assume it was consequently also unlikely or even impossible. In December, 1938, only three months after Munich, Lloyd's of London gave odds of 32 to 1 that there would be no war in 1939. On August 7, 1939, *The London Daily Express* reported the results of a poll of its European reporters. Ten out of twelve said, "No war this year." Hitler invaded Poland three weeks later. It seems fair to suspect that a great deal of wishful thinking influenced these predictions.

HOW WAR MIGHT COME

There are many ways in which a war might start today. In semitechnical jargon, these can be put into four rough categories: (1) Inadvertent War; (2) War as a Result of Miscalculation; (3) Calculated War; and (4) Catalytic War. These categories doubtless do not exhaust the ways in which a war might start, nor do they represent mutually exclusive possibilities. Our weapons systems are so new, and their impact upon each other and upon international relations are so little known, it would not be too surprising if a war started in some unanticipated manner.

1. *Inadvertent War.* At the top of the list I have put the unpremeditated war, the fearful possibility that war might occur almost unintentionally as a result of mechanical or human error, false alarm, self-fulfilling prophecy, or unauthorized behavior. I believe the current probability of inadvertent war is low. It is at the top of the list for two reasons: First, because I believe that the other ways in which a war might occur today are even less probable; and, second, because I believe that inadvertent war might well become a much more dangerous possibility in the not too distant future, partly as a result of the growing number of buttons that can be pressed acci-

dentally, but chiefly as a result of the proliferation of independent nuclear capabilities in other countries, each with its own standards of safety and stability.

In a complex industrial society people generally have had enough experience with broken vacuum cleaners and wrong telephone numbers, not to mention serious public disasters, to comprehend the possibility of a catastrophic accident through mechanical failure or human error. There is a widespread concern that an electrical circuit might short, a relay stick, a switch fail, or that a button might be pressed accidently, a message misunderstood, an aurora borealis, meteor, or flock of geese be mistaken for an attack, and so on. Such things have happened and may happen again.[1]

Notwithstanding the possibility of mechanical or human error, it is most unlikely that any single mechanical or human error would trigger an attack unless one side or the other is foolish enough to buy and install a quick-reacting, nonrecallable strategic weapons system. It is just because radars do occasionally give false alarms, accidents do happen, and people do make mistakes that it is essential for both sides to install weapons systems that have either "fail safe" or "positive control"[2] features

---

[1] Since the Marxist view of history might incline Soviet planners away from the view that a defective switch could influence history, the Soviets may not be as concerned about this type of problem as the West has been. On the other hand the Soviets seem even more concerned than we with the dangers of unauthorized behavior by high officials or junior officers and thus may take the same precautions we do.

[2] "Fail safe" is a term borrowed from engineering and used to describe a system whereby bombers can be launched on ambiguous warning, fly to a point of no return, and then turn back unless they receive additional positive orders to fly on. In this way the central authorities have additional time to confirm or deny the validity of the original warning. Such a system introduces an additional vulnerability in the mechanism of retaliation; if the enemy can prevent the second communication, he will not be attacked. "Positive control" properly refers to systems which are, at all times, under the control of the central authorities. There is some tendency today for the latter terminology to replace the former, because it is believed that the

built into them, or are large enough and well enough protected that they need not be "trigger-happy" to survive.

The question of vulnerability influences the probability of accidental war in an important way. If a strategic weapons system can accept the enemy's attack and still hit back effectively, the decisionmaker has time to evaluate and decide—time to be careful. He is not under overwhelming pressure to launch a strike simply because he thinks he is about to be struck and must launch a forestalling or spoiling attack before his forces are destroyed. When the owners of "safe" systems receive an ambiguous warning, their decisionmaker can and would most reasonably react in some less drastic fashion. He might, for example, act to reduce vulnerability to enemy attack, or to provide a better posture from which to hit back. The decisionmaker can then wait further confirmation. Similarly, if the command and control system is not vulnerable, then subordinate commanders can confidently wait for their legal orders before making irrevocable commitments.

Probably the major protection against inadvertent war is the widespread belief among almost all decisionmakers that only an insane man would go to war and that the other side is not insane. Therefore the cautious decisionmaker will discount any signals or events that might be construed as warning of an attack. (It should be noted that, as such, "caution" makes inadvertent war less probable; it makes a Pearl Harbor more feasible.) The degree of such caution may vary from time to time. A considerable degree of tension, or some of the temporizing measures which may be instituted upon an ambiguous warning, will tend to remove certain psychological, legal, and physical safeguards. A greater load is then thrown on the remaining safeguards. For this reason several accidents in sequence, or a simple accident during a period of considerable tension, could be dangerous.

---

term "fail safe" may arouse anxiety among laymen (who ask, "You mean it can fail?"). However, the new term is likely to arouse anxiety among experts (they ask, "You mean it has to work to work?").

This type of situation might also set in motion a disastrous "self-fulfilling prophecy," in much the same way that hostility often breeds hostility. That is, one side's defensive action may be observed by the other which, misinterpreting it as aggressive, may therefore make some defensive move. This, if misread in turn by the opposite side, confirms the original suspicions. Reactions and signals may thus be set into motion until a point of no return is reached. This is one reason why it is necessary for each side not only to be cautious and responsible, but also to make sure that the other understands what is happening. If a temporizing measure involves doing things which raise apprehensions on the other side, it is important to allay those apprehensions. If either side fears that a surprise attack on its military forces could result in unacceptable damage then, unless there is some degree of cooperation between them, there is an ever-present possibility of a false preemption—a possibility that the apprehensive side may launch an attack simply because it fears one from the other side and thinks that only by preempting can its forces survive.

The Soviets are aware of the danger of the "self-fulfilling prophecy." In a United Nations Security Council debate on April 21, 1958, Arkady S. Sobolev said:

American generals refer to the fact that up to the present time the American planes have taken off on their flights and returned to their bases as soon as it became clear that it was a case of false alarm. But what would happen if American military personnel observing their radar screens are not able in time to determine that a flying meteor is not a guided missile and that a flight of geese is not a flight of bombers? Then the American planes will continue their flight and will approach the borders of the Soviet Union.

But in such a case the need to insure the security of the Soviet people would require the USSR to make immediate retaliatory measures to eliminate the oncoming threat. The Soviet Government would like to hope that matters will not go so far.

In order to get a clearer idea of the extremely dangerous character of acts of the United States [that are] dangerous to peace, it is enough to ask the question what would happen if the military Air Force of the Soviet Union began to act in the same way as the American Air Force is now acting? After all, Soviet radar screens also show from time to time blips which are caused by the flight of meteors or electronic interference. If in such cases Soviet aircraft also flew out carrying atom and hydrogen bombs in the direction of the United States and its bases in other states, what situation would arise?

The air fleets of both sides, having discerned each other somewhere over the Arctic wastes or in some other place, apparently would draw the conclusion natural under those circumstances, that a real enemy attack was taking place. Then the world would inevitably be plunged into the hurricane of atomic war.[3]

Despite their awareness of this danger the Soviets have emphasized disarmament almost to the exclusion of other aspects of arms control, such as preventing the self-fulfilling prophecy they describe. At the 1958 Surprise Attack Conference, they stressed large political issues and refused to discuss narrow technical issues. Our own position may have been excessively narrow; but it is dangerous to wait for a settlement of the political issues before considering this problem. While it takes two to make an agreement, even informal implicit agreements or, in some cases, unilateral concessions or practices may be helpful.

It is also conceivable that some pathological or irresponsible person might deliberately try to start a war. The Soviets have made much of the possibility that a deranged or irresponsible American pilot on airborne alert might take it into his head to attack Russia alone. Not only are there many safeguards against this, but it is most unlikely that a single-plane attack would touch off a war. A more ominous possibility is illustrated in the novel *Red Alert*.[4] A determined SAC general, who, unknown to his superiors, is sick with an incurable ailment (and whose judgment and sense of discipline are thus affected), personally decides to end the Soviet problem once and for all. The clever way he gets around the elaborate system set up to prevent exactly

this kind of behavior suggests that no system is proof against everything.

I have already made clear my belief that the current probability of inadvertent war is low. Moreover, many methods recommended to reduce the probability of war by accident might result in increasing the likelihood of war from one of the other causes. On the other hand, I must also emphasize that nobody can realistically estimate the probability of inadvertent, or any other war. It would be hard to convince me that the probability of this type of war is higher than, say, one in ten a year. But if it were that high, the situation would be entirely unsatisfactory. Even if it were as low as one in fifty a year, the annual risk would be too high. (A constant annual probability of one in fifty of a war would mean about an even chance that there would be a war before the year 2000.)

2. *War by Miscalculation.* Nearly as worrisome as the possibility of inadvertent war is the more or less premeditated war which might result from a decisionmaker's miscalculation, misunderstanding, or failure to think adequately through the consequences of his actions. I would include in this category wars resulting from a committal strategy, escalation, or overconfidence.

Many people believe that war by miscalculation is most likely to arise through the use or misuse of a committal strategy. For example, one side may believe that if it makes it clear it is going to stand firm in some crisis then, "since neither side wants war," the other side will back down. It then makes whatever announcements and takes whatever actions may be necessary or appropriate to give the appearance, and perhaps the reality, of having committed itself irrevocably. If, then, the other side does not back down, war can result. A graphic if somewhat oversimplified example of such a situation is given by Bertrand Russell:[5]

This sport is called "Chicken!" It is played by choosing a long straight road with a white line down the middle and starting two very fast cars towards each other from opposite ends.

---

[3] *New York Times*, April 22, 1958, p. 10.

[4] Peter Bryant, *Red Alert* (New York: Ace Books, 1958).

[5] Bertrand Russell, *Common Sense and Nuclear Warfare* (New York: Simon and Schuster, 1959), p. 30.

Each car is expected to keep the wheels of one side on the white line. As they approach each other mutual destruction becomes more and more imminent. If one of them swerves from the white line before the other, the other, as he passes, shouts "Chicken!" and the one who has swerved becomes an object of contempt.

To win this game one must try to convince the opponent that it is not worthwhile for him to be so reckless. One can do this by convincing him that one is totally reckless, oblivious to the danger, or out of control. These objectives can probably be met best by getting into the car dead drunk, wearing very dark glasses, and conspicuously throwing the steering wheel out of the window as soon as the car has gotten up to speed. If the opponent is watching, he will feel under some pressure to get out of the way. However, if the opponent refuses to back down after the "irrevocable" commitment has been made, it would be irrational to carry out this rationally made commitment. Since both sides may use the same strategy, it is obvious the game may end in disaster.

The game of chicken is an extreme example of the use of "rationality of irrationality" strategies, but it illustrates clearly a situation in which each side can demonstrate logically that by using a committal strategy it can force the other side to back down. Yet an observer might correctly conclude that neither side or both sides, will back down. "Rationality of irrationality" strategies can be important in almost any bargaining situation. It can make sense to commit oneself irrevocably to do something in a particular eventuality, and at the same time it may not make sense to carry out the commitment if the eventuality occurs. For this reason, the success of such a strategy may well depend upon the taking of some action which in appearance to the other side, and perhaps in fact, removes the power to revoke the commitment. The success of such a strategy may also depend upon using it before the other side does.

According to Bertrand Russell, the game of chicken is played by youthful degenerates and by nations. Actually, it is played at one time or another by everyone (even in the raising of children), if in less potentially disastrous form. The analogy of the game of chicken to diplomacy is useful to illustrate a valid point but, as in the case of all analogies, it can be misleading if one ignores the significant differences between the game as played with cars by youthful degenerates and the game as played by diplomats. Most bargaining situations involve potential gains and losses for both sides. The central issue is usually the division of these gains and losses and not the humiliation of one side or the other; a major purpose of diplomacy is to prevent a crisis which can only be settled by the total and humiliating defeat of one side or the other.

Nonetheless, the dangerous game of chicken can occur at the international level. Barring enforceable alternatives, the less one is willing to play, the more likely it is that one may have to end up playing the most dangerous form. Whether we like it or not, our life, liberty, and security may depend on being willing to play. As Russell states:

Practical politicians may admit all this, but they argue that there is no alternative. If one side is unwilling to risk global war, while the other side is willing to risk it, the side which is willing to run the risk will be victorious in all negotiations and will ultimately reduce the other side to complete impotence. "Perhaps"— so the practical politician will argue—"it might be ideally wise for the sane party to yield to the insane party in view of the dreadful nature of the alternative, but, whether wise or not, no proud nation will long acquiesce in such an ignominious role. We are, therefore, faced, quite inevitably, with the choice between brinkmanship and surrender.[6]

The Soviets seem to fully appreciate the advantages of a greater willingness to risk war. For example, the reader should consider Stalin's remark to our then ambassador, Walter Bedell Smith:

We do not want war any more than the West does, but we are less interested in peace than the West, and therein, lies the strength of our position.[7]

Krushchev's flexible-inflexible time limits for the signing of an East German peace treaty also suggest that the Soviets, includ-

[6] *Ibid*, pp. 30–31.
[7] *Time*, June 13, 1949, quoting a statement made by Ambassador Smith after his final return from Moscow.

ing the "peaceful coexistence" bloc now in power, fully appreciate both the desirability of appearing committed and the danger of actual irrevocability.

The possibility of war as a result of playing chicken once too often could go up. Of course, if international bargaining is carried on with skill, and if both sides are cautious, the bargaining will tend to take on the aspects of a normal commercial transaction in which both sides gain and both sides lose, the exact division of the gains and losses depending in large part on their relative skill and stubbornness. However, in any long period of peace, there is a tendency for governments to become more intransigent as the thought of war becomes unreal, particularly if there is a background of experiences in which those who stand firm do well, while those who are reasonable seem to do less well. After a while the averted war may look less real than the tangible gains and prestige that are being won and lost. It is often only when peace fails that governments can learn it is not feasible to stand firm on incompatible positions. Today there is reason to hope that we can lessen the dangers of the game of chicken by careful consideration of how wars might start and be fought. However, unless workable arrangements are made for effective arbitration, somebody may play the international analogue of this game once too often.

War by miscalculation might also result from the process generally called "escalation." A limited move may appear safe, but set into motion a disastrous sequence of decisions and actions. One may readily imagine some intensifying crisis in which neither side really believes the issue is big enough to end in war, but in which both sides are willing to accept some small risk of war. Escalation might develop as a result of other parties becoming involved, as a consequence of the issues taking on new significance, or as a result of accident, miscalculation, unauthorized behavior, or other inadvertent cause. Escalation can also be deliberate—as in the game of chicken.

The possibility of escalation may be useful in deterring certain kinds of crises or limited wars. For example, the nuclear weapons systems we and the British have in Europe are fairly vulnerable to Soviet attack. Even though they have little second-strike capability, the Soviets might be afraid to destroy them in a limited European attack, for such an attack could easily escalate into all-out war. On the other hand, if the Soviets attacked Western Europe without destroying these weapons, the Europeans might take them over—with or without our permission—and use them in retaliation. Thus all forms of military attack might be deterred. A similar argument is sometimes used in favor of national nuclear deterrents.

Deterrence by fear of escalation might also operate if we decide to open a route to Berlin by force should the Soviets or East Germans try to close it. As of 1962, the Soviets have the capacity to apply all the counterforce they need to stop any such limited action. The purpose of our limited action would not be to overwhelm Soviet countermeasures, but to make it clear that the stakes are large and that we are willing to take a small but appreciable risk of an all-out war. Our action might be effective precisely because it would be so dangerous. On the other hand, if the Soviets or the East Germans were to try to close our access to Berlin, they might be banking on our fear of escalation to deter our military action. They have already deterred the military destruction of the Berlin wall, at least in part, by relying on our fear of escalation.

Perhaps it would not be overly suspicious to suppose that this sort of thinking underlies, in some measure, the Soviet statement on its decision to resume nuclear testing. This statement explicitly disclaims any possibility of a limited military response without immediate escalation into some form of all-out war:

Those who are preparing a new world holocaust are sowing illusions that a new war, if unleashed, would allegedly be waged without thermonuclear weapons. But this is a deceit of the peoples.
The experience of history teaches that it has never been possible to keep the fire of war within predetermined limits. Wars have inexorable severe laws of their own. An aggressor starts a war to bring his victim to its knees and to impose his will on it. But even the

aggressor is aware that in case of defeat the fate that he was preparing for his victim will befall him. Therefore each state that takes part in the war, regardless of the fact whether it attacks or defends, will stop at nothing for attaining victory and will not accept defeat without having used and spent all means in its possession for waging war. Under these conditions any armed conflict, even insignificant at first, would inevitably grow into a universal rocket and nuclear war should the nuclear powers have been drawn into it.

The fact that the threat of escalation is used, perhaps effectively, to deter limited action presents a serious problem for arms controllers. To the extent that various types of arms control measures would reduce the possibility of escalation, to that extent an important deterrent upon limited actions might also be decreased. Although I feel that this is not sufficient reason for refusing to adopt arms control measures, many Europeans are antagonistic to any reliable limits upon the use of nuclear weapons precisely because such limitations may indeed make it safer for the Soviets to use or threaten lesser kinds of violence.[8] It may be that before arms control measures can or should be adopted, effective substitute deterrents, less violent in effect, will have to be devised. For this reason, a strengthened conventional force might be necessary were we to reach a nuclear arms control agreement.

A war by miscalculation might also result from simple overconfidence. Overconfidence, of course, can take many forms— ranging from ignorance, stupidity, and negligence, through a failure to realize that even the most closely calculated paper plans are still only paper plans with possibly no more than a tenuous relationship to the real world and the actual course of events. Overconfidence can be based on a mystical

belief in the manifest destiny of the West or the historical imperative of ultimate victory for the East. It can consist of a mistaken belief by one side that its force and war plans are such that it can win without serious damage to itself if it initiates an attack. Lastly, war through overconfidence can come about because of a mistaken belief by one side that it has a sufficient preponderance of force or such clever war plans that the other side would not dare initiate an attack, no matter what the provocation.

It is almost impossible to imagine a Western government initiating an attack on the basis of optimistic calculations unless the decisionmakers have had their judgment affected by desperation. I am less confident of the possible effect of underestimation, overestimation, ignorance, or recklessness in the Communist bloc. The Chinese clearly underestimate the effects of nuclear war. Hopefully, it will be some time before they have a significant nuclear capability, and time may bring them greater wisdom. The Soviet estimates seem plausible ones. It is hard to tell whether these estimates are the result of more or less sophistication than the West has. They talk of the possibility of great destruction and suffering, but they also talk of survival and recovery by the "victor." They do not seem to be triggerhappy or reckless. They may underestimate the need for collaboration in controlling technological development and dissemination of modern weapons. This might make them unwilling to compromise to arrive at arms control programs that are acceptable to both sides. If the Soviets go to war, however, it is as likely to be the result of calculation as of miscalculation.

3. War by Calculation. It is commonly believed that war could arise only as a result of inadvertence or miscalculation— a belief based partly on the view that war would automatically result in mutual annihilation, and partly on the assumption that no decisionmaker who is calculating correctly would ever knowingly take action that entailed an appreciable probability of war. The first view is demonstrably incorrect, at least today. The second assumption is not borne out by past or current

---

[8] These Europeans sometimes argue that if we make conventional aggression or other limited action safer, we should not be surprised if the Soviets are tempted or pressured into such actions. Once violence has occured the possibility of escalation into the use of nuclear weapons is created. As a result, in our attempt to make the use of nuclear weapons less probable, by arranging for other responses to non-nuclear provocation, we may increase the probability of the eventual use of nuclear weapons.

history. After due study, a nation might decide that going to war would be the least undesirable of its choices, and it might be right in its calculation; we must therefore include this unpleasant prospect as one of the possible ways in which wars could start. The common statement, "There is no alternative to peace," may not look as convincing when it appears as—"No alternative to any kind of peace," or "Peace at any price."

To mention one often-used example: 15 to 30 million Soviet citizens were killed in World War II; in addition the Soviet Union lost about one-third of its wealth. It is sometimes pointed out that this was not the result of calculation, and that no alternatives were ever really offered to the Soviets. However, given the nature of the Nazis and their program, I believe that even the average Soviet citizen (not to mention the government), if presented with a choice, would have been willing to accept the cost of World War II in order to achieve the position they have since won, as an alternative to Nazi domination. They might feel themselves presented with a similar choice someday. Only now both the risks and the prize would be greater. It is also conceivable that the West, or the United States alone, could believe itself faced with a choice between domination and occupation by the Soviets or China, on the one hand, and substantial casualties and property damage, but survival and possibly even "victory," on the other. Faced with such a choice it is not inconceivable that we might choose to go to war.

One type of war resulting at least partly from deliberate calculation could occur in the process of escalation. For example, suppose the Soviets attacked Europe, relying upon our fear of their reprisal to deter strategic attack by us; we might be deterred enough to pause, but we might evacuate our cities during this pause in the hope we could thereby convince the Soviets we meant business. If the Soviets did not back down, but continued their attack upon Europe, we might decide that we would be less badly off if we proceeded to attack the Soviet Union. The damage we would receive in return would then be considerably reduced compared with what we would have suffered

had we not evacuated. We might well decide at such a time that we would be better off to attack the Soviets and accept a retaliatory blow at our dispersed population rather than let Europe be occupied and so be forced to accept the penalty of living in the hostile and dangerous world that would follow. This would be especially likely if it appeared to be only a matter of time before we were next.

The so-called "preventive war" furnishes another example of possible war by calculation. A preventive war might be in the nature of a preemptive strike, or it might simply be an unprovoked attack, depending more upon the motivations of those initiating it than anything else. The so-called false preemption has already been included in the category of inadvertent wars. It can occur where the possessor of a weapons system which cannot survive an enemy attack might feel it necessary to react with a forestalling or spoiling attack even in the event of a false alarm. There is also the possibility of a more deliberate and calculated preemption. Almost all authorities agree that at present the advantages of striking first are so great that, should there seem to be a high probability that the other side is actually attacking, it might be better to risk the certainty of a relatively small retaliatory strike, rather than the high probability of a much more destructive first blow. Calculated preemption is not unlikely in the event of a reciprocal fear of surprise attack,[9] a situation very similar to the self-fulfilling prophecy. Situations could arise in which each side felt there was a more or less symmetrical fear of attack by the other side. In such a situation each side may feel itself under pressure to preempt because it knows the other side is under similar pressure. Reciprocal fear itself may make it rational, indeed almost imperative, to strike, even though the fear may be based on a mutual misunderstanding. The danger of such a situation increases directly with the advantage to be gained by striking first, and with each side's estimate of the likelihood that the other will strike first. The

[9] Thomas C. Schelling, *The Strategy of Conflict* (Cambridge, Mass.: Harvard University Press), pp. 207–29.

advantage to an enemy of striking us first will depend on the difference between our striking power before and after he attacks, that is, on the vulnerability of our forces. Moreover, his estimate of the likelihood of our striking him will be influenced by the vulnerability of his forces to our first strike.[10] As described, a preemptive strike resulting from reciprocal fear of surprise attack is not a case of miscalculation. It is a case of correct calculation; though each side has nothing to fear but fear, the knowledge that the other side is afraid fully justifies that fear.

Many things could create a real reciprocal fear of surprise attack. For example, suppose that one of our Polaris submarines accidently launched some missiles at our own country. Even if the submarine commander succeeded in informing us of what happened before the missiles landed, the accident could cause a war. The Soviets might observe these missiles exploding; if they did not know where the missiles came from, they might decide it would be too dangerous to wait to find out whether one of theirs had gone off accidentally. Even if the Soviets knew that the missiles had not

accidentally come from a Soviet source, they might not believe we would wait to find that out. Indeed, we would ourselves be under some pressure to attack, even if we conjectured that the Soviets knew nothing about the incident, because we would not be sure. Even if we felt they knew, it might conceivably appear safer to preempt than to let precious minutes slip away while we tried to persuade the Soviets that we knew they were innocent.

I have put preemption relatively low on the list of possible causes of war because I believe that, so long as decisionmakers are consciously in control of events, they are more likely to draw back from pressing buttons and accepting the resulting risks, than of doing something which would make war inevitable—particularly at a time and under circumstances not of their choosing. Nevertheless, the possibilities of trouble are many. It would be wise to reinforce the natural caution of decisionmakers with explicit measures, both unilateral and multilateral, to facilitate communication and persuasion so as to make waiting a safer and more reasonable course.

A preventive war need not be a preemption. It might be a deliberate and calculated attack made without regard to the immediate likelihood of an attack by the other side, or even the likelihood that the other side is planning to attack eventually. One side has only to feel that a war is inevitable—or so likely that it might as well get the disaster over with as soon as it attains a sufficient lead, or before more destructive weapons are constructed. One side has only to believe it safer, either for itself or for the world, to seize the opportunity than to wait.

A preventive war might result from a technological or other change to which one side has not reacted adequately. It might also occur if an arms control agreement broke down with the result that one side had a considerable lead, because of its previous success in undetected violations or greater ability to rearm. The side with a commanding lead might well feel that, rather than see the world subjected again to all the dangers of an arms race, it would be accomplishing an essential public service by

---

[10] The requirement that both sides be relatively invulnerable has led some analysts to recommend that we deliberately weaken our ability to attack an enemy's strategic forces and to survive his counterattack. The other side can then feel safe that we will not preempt. It is indeed true that if we eliminated all capabilities for Type II Deterrence or Improved War outcome we would have made clear our peaceful intentions. We would also have made, at least for a short run, a real contribution to slowing down the arms race. In addition, the resulting posture would be a good basis for many types of arms control negotiations. Surrender or unilateral disarmament would also fulfill all of the above requirements. I mention this because the pure city-busting deterrent force advocated above amounts to a dangerous kind of unilateral disarmament, dangerous both from the viewpoint of the competition between the Soviet Union and the United States and dangerous because a war can still occur, even though there have been no precautions taken for surviving that war.

We must realize that the stability we want in a system is more than just stability against accidental war or even against an attack by the enemy. We also want stability against extreme provocation. (See OTW, pp. 141–44, for discussion of Multistable Deterrence.)

stopping the race from starting anew. This could best be done by stopping the cause of the race—the government of its opponent. A nation might be willing to start the war soon after an arms control agreement ended because the risks of such a war, even if things went awry, would not be so great as they might have been before the agreement had lowered the level of the balance of terror.

The likelihood of war breaking out soon after a renewed arms race, but before both sides have fully rearmed, is often ignored. Most writers focus their attention on the time of the breakdown, when the posture is more likely to be determined by the agreement, and on feasible violations of the agreement, and do not consider adequately the possible situation some months or a year or two later. A more dangerous situation, neglected by many unilateral disarmers, is what happens after a substantial degree of unilateral disarmament if we should change our minds or even if the Soviets or Chinese should fear that we were about to change our minds.

Even bilateral disarmament to the point where the weapons systems would not present such awful potentialities might itself enhance the possibility of preventive war. By reducing the balance of terror to the point where an aggressor fears only conventional defeat, and not an unprecedented catastrophe if his plans go awry, disarmament can reduce the sanctions against, and create greater pressures toward, preventive war. Where the consequences of a military disaster are reliably and sufficiently reduced it will no longer be true that, "Even if the probability of success were 90%, war would still be preposterous." Nine out of ten chances are pretty good odds, in a situation where war has become only immoral and not unthinkable. Moreover, a simple computation can show that the more missile forces are reduced the more a relatively slight numerical superiority can offer the attacker freedom from retaliation—thus adding another temptation toward preventive war.

Finally, we must also consider the more remote possibility that one side or the other might deliberately go to war simply to achieve world domination. Most people (the author included) believe the risks involved in going to war are so great today that no matter how promising an attack might look on paper, the "imponderables" and other uncertainties are so large that not even a moderately irresponsible decisionmaker would go to war for positive gains, though one like Hitler might.

Though decisionmakers may be unwilling to go to war for positive gains, they may go to war if they conclude that it is less risky to attack than not to do so. There are many situations in which this could occur. For example, an internal or external crisis getting out of hand, especially one deliberately aggravated by the opponent, or perhaps merely by his very existence. One might then be tempted to go to war, not because it would be inviting, but because it would seem the least undesirable alternative.

I believe that the probability of war by calculation is low because I think this is the place where deterrence is most likely to work and—perhaps optimistically—that we are going to be competent about deterrence. If we weaken our deterrent prematurely, however, the possibility of war by calculation may move to the top of the list.

Many people interested in disarmament or arms control *at any cost* (not to speak of many professional planners) refuse to take seriously the potential effect of disarmament upon deterrence. There are, and in spite of anything we do there will remain, great pressures toward war. While the arms controllers are going to try to balance these effects by making the peaceful alternatives to war more attractive, there are practical limits to what they can accomplish, at least for some time. The pressures toward war are likely to be restrained effectively only if the fear of punishment is not diminished to the vanishing point.

These cautions as to arms control do not mean that arms control should not be pursued with vigor. The uncontrolled arms race also involves fearful risks. They do mean that an insistence on reasonable and workable arrangements is essential to prevent an even more unstable situation than we have today. A bad arms control agreement may be vastly worse than none at all.

4. *Catalytic War.* This last category is based on the notion that some third party nation might for its own reasons deliberately start a war between the two major powers. There is a wide range of possible motivations and means for such an attempt. For example, some third, fourth, or fifth power in the international hierarchy might wish to improve its relative position by arranging for the two top nations to destroy each other. It might attack the United States under circumstances which would suggest a Soviet attack, counting on our retaliation to precipitate a full scale war. Some people fear the dissemination of nuclear weapons among "ambitious" powers because they feel that such weapons provide a particularly handy and dangerous means by which to precipitate the mutual destruction of the Soviet Union and the United States.

This, however, would not be the greatest danger that would result from the dissemination of nuclear weapons and delivery systems. Above all else, the risks of destruction would be so great for the triggering power, if discovered, that it is difficult to believe any nation would take such a chance. Moreover, by the time nuclear capability spreads much further, the United States and the Soviet Union will probably put into effect more slowly reacting systems with a greater number of stops in them before a decision for all-out war can be reached. This would make it much harder (though still not impossible) for an interloper to start a war. Most important, however, there are less dangerous and more likely ways in which a third nation's actions can start a war between two other powers. For example, a nation might use diplomacy to embroil larger nations or increase the scope of an existing conflict. World War I was a catalytic war, set off by Serbia and Austria.[11]

The present alliance systems of the respective major powers are a likely area for the operation of other powers as catalytic agents. However, there may be less need today for either major power to give an ally a blank check, similar to that which Germany wrote for Austria in 1914. Nevertheless, the existence of allies on both sides enormously complicates the problem of catalytic war and contributes to its possibility. As an example, let us imagine a situation in which the Chinese felt hard pressed, possibly over Formosa, and told the Russians, "We are going to strike the United States tomorrow, and you might as well come along with us, for they will undoubtedly strike you, even if you do not join our attack." Indeed a catalytic war seems much more likely to be touched off by a desperate or vengeful power than an ambitious one.

HOW A WAR MIGHT BE FOUGHT

If we believe a war to be possible (not probable—possible), then we must for several reasons consider how a war might be fought. In the first place if there are more and less destructive ways of fighting a war, humanitarian considerations alone require that we make some investigation of the possibilities of limiting destruction and death. The morality of refusing to think seriously about the unthinkable is for this reason alone at least open to question. Second, careful consideration of the ways in which a war might be fought sheds additional light on the possible ways in which a war might start. We must learn all we can about this, both to help us avoid starting a war inadvertently or by miscalculation, and to allow us to contribute to preventing a war being started by others. Third, the more thought one gives to these problems the more possible it becomes to mitigate some of the disastrous effects of thermonuclear war and to protect our values, both from the holocaust and from the more subtle politico-military forces in the world. And, last, it might prove essential to the preservation of these values, whether we like it

---

[11] World War I also had overtones of "reciprocal fear of surprise attack" and "self-fulfilling prophecy," because the side which mobilized first was likely to win. It meant that even a defensive mobilization (by the Russians) touched off a defensive-offensive mobilization (by the Germans), in much the same way, some believe, that a badly designed, quick-reacting force can be touched off by defensive moves by the other side. This example is probably typical in that the actual cause of war is likely to be a mixture of the four basic types described.

or not, to be able to "fight, survive and win" a thermonuclear war.

The usual image of war today held by many experts as well as most laymen can be summed up in the phrase "orgiastic spasm of destruction," or, "spasm war." Many believe that if one single button is pressed all the buttons will be pressed, and that some 30 minutes or so later missiles will rain enough destruction to terminate the defender's existence as a nation; subsequently, some minutes or hours later, a similar rain of death and destruction will annihilate the attacking nation. Within perhaps an hour or two the war will be effectively over—both combatants having received death blows—with only one question left: "How bad will the radioactivity be for the rest of the world?"

This is fanciful in 1962; missile forces are still small and limited, and the main striking power of both countries still lies in their bombers which, under most circumstances, also have a limited capability with respect to total annihilation. The image of total mutual homicide as a possible consequence of a war may become reasonable in the near future—say the mid- or late sixties. However, even if the offensive forces grow quite large, and counterbalancing active and passive defenses are not procured, it is by no means inevitable that quick mutual annihilation will actually result from the use of thermonuclear weapons.

To orient the reader as to the possible outcomes of a war today, I shall first consider the possible targeting objectives a warring nation might choose, and comment briefly upon the strategic implications of each attack. I shall then describe and analyze several special situations in which an ability to fight, survive, and terminate a war would be especially feasible or especially necessary to us or to the Soviet Union.

TARGETING OBJECTIVES

There are at least five different possible types of attack, each with different targeting objectives:

1. Countervalue   (Population-property damage)

2. Counterforce + Countervalue (Population-property-military)
3. Straight Counterforce (Narrow military considerations only)
4. Counterforce + Bonus   (Population and property as a bonus)
5. Counterforce + Avoidance   (Population and property actively spared)

1. *The Countervalue Attack.* The attacker may try to destroy those things which the defender prizes most highly regardless of whether such destruction helps the attacker to achieve an immediate or essential military objective. Presumably, nations prize people and property most highly.[12] Therefore, the most likely Countervalue attack would be made against the cities which contain the greatest concentrations of people and property in a manner designed to cause the greatest possible number of deaths and injuries and handicaps to recuperation. For example, an attacker might deliberately attempt to achieve massive blast and thermal effects with missiles and warheads of the highest megatonnage available.

Attacks concentrated upon people and property are likely to be based only upon a Countervalue motivation. Massive destruction of people and property is not likely to achieve any immediate or essential military objective. It would be more important militarily, for example, for an attacker to try to destroy forces which can hurt him in immediate retaliation. Most experts agree that, unlike World Wars I and II, any future wars are likely to be short and fought only by military forces in being. If this be true, populations and production lines are of doubtful value at best as a military mobilization base. Moreover, since the number of usable delivery vehicles—bombers and missiles—may be limited, any vehicles "wasted" on cities will be unavailable for their primary mission of destroying the defender's retaliatory forces.

It is generally easy for laymen to believe that a city-busting attack would be the

---

[12] It is possible, of course, that a particular nation might value military power more highly than people and property. Some observers believe that such a priority of values is plausible in the case of the Soviet Union and China.

most likely beginning to a thermonuclear war. Visualizing themselves as the defenders, they naturally think of the attacker as vindictive or malevolent, and interested primarily in hurting them. But it is irrational for an attacker to ignore his own priority of interests in order to hurt the defender. The attacker is usually not nearly so interested in hurting the defender as he is in the dual objects of achieving his military objective and escaping destruction himself. If later he decides that the defender must be completely eradicated, he will be in a much better position to achieve it after the defender has been disarmed or badly weakened by the loss of the war. Hence, most experts now doubt that a surprise attack is likely to involve an all-out concentration on people and cities.

However, an exclusively Countervalue attack could occur, as a result of doctrinal lag or irrationality. In the early sixties the Soviets might be able, by devoting all their striking power to such an attack, to inflict as many as 50 to 100 million casualties upon the United States. If we do not acquire elaborate and expensive systems of active and passive defense, it will no doubt be technically and economically feasible for them to kill between 75 to 100 per cent of our population by the mid- or late sixties; even if we develop and install elaborate and expensive systems of defense there would be considerable uncertainty as to the effectiveness of such systems if the Soviets are vigorous in developing offensive techniques and systems. Many experts believe that by the mid- or late sixties there will be no practicable defensive measures which would enable us to save most of our population in the event of an all-out attack solely upon it, other than a permanent and disciplined alert status for all—civilians and military —and even more elaborate and expensive physical preparations.

Fortunately, an all-out attack in which all resources are devoted to Countervalue targets would be so irrational that, barring an incredible lack of sophistication or actual insanity among Soviet decisionmakers, such an attack is highly unlikely. Small Countervalue attacks, initiated by us or by the Soviets, are not as highly unlikely, how-

ever, as moves in the international game of chicken, or as desperate alternatives to all-out thermonuclear war.

Consider as an example the following extremely hypothetical situation: Imagine that both sides had achieved such an enormous potential that it was actually possible for each, using only one per cent of its strategic forces, to destroy totally the other's civilians and its economy (but not its strategic forces). Then, if either side used all of its forces in a Countervalue attack, it could totally destroy its opponent's society 100 times over. Imagine also that the forces on both sides were invulnerable enough so that an attack directed at the opponent's strategic forces could at most destroy 50 per cent of such strategic forces. This means that the opponent who had been struck would still be able to "overkill" his attacker. In fact, he would have the ability to destroy his attacker's society fifty times over. If, therefore, the attack on the defender's strategic forces touched off an all-out Countervalue retaliation it would not have accomplished anything except national suicide, although it had destroyed 50 per cent of the defender's strategic force. An all-out attack on the defender's cities would also be senseless, since it too could only cause the opponent to retaliate with an all-out destructive attack. In these circumstances, there should be a firm balance of terror between the two nations.[13]

In order to understand some of the possible impacts of this firm balance of terror upon policy in the real world, it is well to consider an extreme situation. Suppose for a moment that the Soviets were to drop nuclear bombs on several West European cities and were to couple this action with a demand for the European nations to surrender. The Soviets could then, of course, point out quite persuasively that no American action would result in the protection of Europe. Even if we were to launch an all-out Counterforce attack on

[13] In terms of this balance of terror each side does not have a factor of safety of 100 but only of 2. If either side reduced its deterrent by 50 per cent that deterrent could, by hypothesis, be destroyed completely by the opponent's attack.

the Soviets, they would still have more than enough weapons surviving the attack to destroy both the United States and Europe in retaliation. The Soviet argument would, under these hypothetical assumptions, be correct. The all-out attack would be senseless.

This does not mean there would be no checks upon Soviet action. Aside from the ever-present fear that calculations, however rationally made, might prove wrong, there would remain another deterrent. We might take a leaf from the Soviet book and destroy some Soviet cities, coupling this with a demand that the Soviets desist from further violence. The Soviets could retaliate by destroying some of our cities, pointing out that since they had the greater resolve they were unlikely to back down first, and we had therefore better acquiesce in the surrender of Europe. At this point both nations would be engaging in a super-destructive game of chicken.

As stupid and bizarre as this game of chicken may seem, under the assumptions of mutual Countervalue over-kill, it would be less stupid and bizarre than initiating an all-out Countervalue exchange. Obviously, the "controlled" city exchange might escalate into an all-out spasm war as a result of anger or miscalculation or some other event. Such drastic action is obviously inappropriate for minor provocations. It is, in fact, hard to imagine a "controlled" city exchange or similar limited Countervalue attack being used more than once in two generations. If used once, the shock might be sufficient to cause drastic and irreversible changes in the international order which would make repetitions unlikely. At the least it would provide a powerful impetus toward a satisfactory arms control plan.

I will refer to the limited Countervalue attack as a Controlled Reprisal or a nuclear show of force, depending on whether the nation using the operation is defending or attacking. In a Controlled Reprisal or nuclear show of force one would be trying not so much to destroy the enemy's military capability or people or property as to force one's will on him by threatening destruction of Countervalue targets. The operations would be chosen so as to demonstrate resolve, commitment, and/or recklessness,

and to frighten and harass the enemy, but not to destroy him or provoke him to suicidal desperation. A Controlled Reprisal or nuclear show of force need not be designed to kill many people. It could even be a spectacular fireworks display (such as exploding a megaton bomb at 200,000 feet over Moscow or Washington), or it could involve the destruction of such targets as isolated military bases, dams, factories, and so on. Such targets would not result in the severe human casualties or psychological aftermath of an attack on major cities.

Many experts (notably Kaplan, Schelling, and Szilard) have advocated that we replace our policy of deterring extreme provocation by the threat of massive retaliation with some variation of a policy of Controlled Reprisal. These experts point out that the threat of a Controlled Reprisal is more credible than the threat of mutual annihilation, and that it may therefore be more deterring though less potentially destructive. Most of the experts who have advocated the use of Controlled Reprisal as a punishment for some provocation assume that if we initiate a Controlled Reprisal to punish the Soviets for some act we will have to allow them to do a certain amount of damage to ourselves in return. While the damage that the Soviets do to us will not compensate them for the cities or other valuable things they have lost, allowing them to return the blow in a tit-for-tat fashion introduces an element of stability into the situation by giving the exchange an appearance of "equity" and by making it clear that no principle or custom has been established that would lead to the expectation that we would lightly initiate a Controlled Reprisal. The side using a type of Controlled Reprisal requiring the sacrifice of whole cities of its own will no doubt experience enormous political problems at home and among the uncommitted countries, most of which prefer any "peaceful" resolution of East-West difficulties to the use of nuclear force. Moreover the "controlled" city exchange is a device that the Soviets or Chinese, both of which have control of internal information and fewer problems with public opinion, must be able to use far more effectively than we could.

I have mentioned only a few of the many serious difficulties with the idea of Controlled Reprisal. There will also be serious difficulties in any other policy that tries to restrain an aggressor in a world in which there is a firm balance of terror based on a reliable mutual over-kill capability and no effective rule of law, reason, or ritual to substitute for the threat or use of force.

2. *Counterforce-Plus-Countervalue.* The next kind of attack to be examined is a mixed attack against both our strategic forces and the things we value most highly. The objects of such an attack might be divided approximately 50–50, or possibly less symmetrically. This type of attack corresponds to the picture most experts had of war until quite recently. This was not because historically most wars have been fought this way (historically they have not), but because World War I and World War II were fought this way. The possibility of such an attack must not be discounted. If either side refuses to "think about the unthinkable," "old fashioned" ideas may prevail. In the previously described hypothetical situation in which each side can over-kill by a factor of 100, the mixed attack is as senseless as the all-out Countervalue attack. It seems to make sense to some planners only because it is more in accord with intuitions gained from the irrelevant experience in World Wars I and II.

As we have previously pointed out, unless the attacker has an over-kill capability as to the defender's strategic forces, the mixed attack is likely to be a great mistake. If the attacker lacks the capability to destroy totally the other side's strategic forces, he should not waste resources attacking his opponent's cities. If, on the other hand, he wishes only to punish the other side, there is probably no reason for hitting the other side's military forces in addition to his cities unless such destruction of forces contributes in some desirable way to the peace negotiations, the state of the postwar world, or some other useful objective.

3. *Straight Counterforce.* In the third kind of attack, the attacker ignores the things which the defenders particularly value, and concentrates on those targets which may be used to hurt him most im-

mediately in retaliation. Reverting to fundamental and historical military principles, and reversing the trend of the most recent years, the "modern" attacker should realize that destroying the defenders' cities, factories, and population cannot help his war effort or do much harm to that of the defenders. Unlike World Wars I and II, and in a war lasting between a few hours and a month, the defenders today are not going to manufacture anything of importance, or draft any soldiers, or even hold elections. Moreover, the potential fallout which would force the surviving civilian population to seek shelter in any event, makes it more unlikely that problems of civilian morale would worry the defenders during the war. Lastly, and probably most important, the surviving civilian population may be valuable hostages in deterring retaliation and in achieving political objectives, including the enforcement of peace terms without further mass violence. If fewer cities were destroyed more hostages would be available for this purpose, and the likelihood of irrational and self-destructive responses caused by anger and a desire for revenge would be diminished.

Adding all this up, why should an attacker waste bombs on cities, particularly in the initial attack? A Straight Counterforce attack is a reasonable tactic and quite likely to be chosen if the planning is determined by narrow military considerations. There are also strong political considerations in its favor. Whoever launches a surprise nuclear attack will have to justify it to his own people and to future generations. Since the probable justification would be that they had to beat the other side to the punch, a relatively humane attack might help to reinforce the argument. In the early sixties a Straight Counterforce attack by the Soviets might well result in 1 to 20 million dead, with a vigorous civil defense program; or 5 to 30 million dead, if we had even a modest civil defense program; or perhaps 10 to 50 million if we had no program at all. In the middle and late sixties, if the Soviets increase their force and we disperse hard missile bases throughout the country these estimates might be multiplied by as much as five.

4. *Counterforce and Bonus.* In the fourth kind of attack the attacker has basically the same attitude toward the military importance of cities that he had in the third; however, he feels it desirable to destroy as much of the other side's civilian population and property as he can, though not at the cost of decreasing significantly the military efficiency of an attack concentrated upon the defender's strategic forces. An attacker might want to obtain a "bonus" to foreclose any possibility of a long war, to prevent or lessen postwar competition, to be revenged, or simply to be malevolent. He might also have an obsolete doctrine, or even some reasons which he could not articulate, but which might still seem sufficient to make him accept a modest decrease in military efficiency over the Straight Counterforce attack. To obtain a "bonus" the attacker could move the designated ground zeros slightly, use the largest workable weapons, and in other ways greatly increase bonus damage to civilians and property without materially decreasing the efficiency of the Counterforce operation. This attack can be combined with "postattack coercion" by deliberately sparing some, but not all, of the hostages.

Such an attack would result in quite different casualties and damage from that of the straightforward Counterforce attack, though the primary targets would be much the same. Depending upon the details of the capabilities and tactics used in pursuing a Counterforce-Plus-Bonus attack over that of a Straight Counterforce attack, the casualties might be increased by factors of 5 to 10 in the lower ranges (1–10), and by factors of 2 to 5 in the higher ranges (10–50).

5. *Counterforce-Plus-Avoidance.* In this last type of attack the attacker's attitude and objectives with respect to Countervalue targets are the opposite of his objectives in the Counterforce-Plus-Bonus attack. The attacker actively wishes to avoid destroying the defender's population. He may be motivated by moral or political reasons, because he wishes to hold hostage as many as possible, or because he wishes to avoid unnecessary provocation. If an avoidance objective

is pursued vigorously, an attacker might accept some relatively large potential military disadvantages. For example, should there be a SAC base near a major U.S. city, then, rather than drop a 20 megaton bomb on it, he might avoid the base completely or he might compromise and drop only 100 kilotons. (In most circumstances 100 kilotons are likely to be almost as effective in destroying the SAC base as a 20 megaton bomb and far less damaging to the nearby city.) It has been estimated that a Counterforce-Plus-Avoidance attack on the United States in the early sixties might result in as "few" as one million casualties. It would certainly be less than five million so long as the attacker is careful, no weapons go disastrously astray, and we have a modest civil-defense capability.

In an actual war, which of these five types of attacks might we most reasonably expect? I have no idea. There is nothing in law or logic that says we or an enemy have to be reasonable. However, for the side which strikes first, only the third and fifth attacks—the Straight Counterforce and the Counterforce-Plus-Avoidance—seem to me to make sense, and in most cases the last is to be preferred. The other three types of attacks involve either a waste of resources or an unnecessary and likely self-defeating brutality. The side which strikes second (the side presumably trying to deter the war), might in fact wish to appear committed to an all-out Countervalue response. It might best deter the attack by this *appearance* of irrationally inexorable commitment. If deterrence fails, however, it would then be irrational to carry through the commitment. In most people's value system, revenge will have a lower priority than survival. One would wish, if one could, to revoke the commitment after the first attack, and use whatever force has survived the aggressor's strike to prevent further strikes and to terminate the war on the best terms possible. This implies that the defender should rationally concentrate his attack on Counterforce targets, perhaps withholding some forces to increase his future negotiating strength. Alternatively, he might attack Countervalue targets according to the previously outlined principles of Controlled Reprisal.[14]

There is also some advantage in not using too extreme a "rationality of irrationality" strategy. If the enemy suspects that one may not reply with an all-out Countervalue retaliation, the original attack might be made carefully (counterforce-Plus-Avoidance) and combined with a reasonable peace offer. Such care would not cost the attacker

[14] See pp. 178–87 of OTW for a discussion on possible objectives of the defender.

much, and might buy him a great deal if it were to induce the defender also to be careful. This knowledge or expectation, even if weak or uncertain, might motivate the attacker to adhere to a Counterforce and Avoidance objective. While this expectation on the part of the attacker might weaken the defender's deterrence, it might not weaken it much. It is unlikely that an attacker would be so willing to rely on these expectations as to be induced, in normal circumstances, to attack.

GENERAL NUCLEAR WAR: ASSURED DESTRUCTION AND DAMAGE LIMITATION

BY ROBERT S. McNAMARA

NATURE OF THE GENERAL NUCLEAR WAR PROBLEM

A general nuclear war would be one in which the U.S. or its allies had been attacked by an aggressor in such a manner as to require the use of U.S. strategic nuclear forces in retaliation. We are dealing here with an exceedingly complex problem, and in order to hold it within manageable bounds for the purposes of this presentation, I will limit my discussion primarily to situations involving strategic exchanges between the United States and the Soviet Union alone. It should be possible in this way to illustrate the types of considerations that, fitted into the broader context of the overall problem, form the basis for the Strategic Offensive and Defensive programs proposed for the fiscal years 1966–70 period.

In the event of general nuclear war, attacks might be directed against military targets only, against cities only, or against both types of targets, either simultaneously or with a delay. They might be selective in terms of specific targets or they might be general. In this regard, it is important to bear in mind that the types of situations I shall be discussing are illustrative. They reflect the way we go about determining our requirements. They do not necessarily reflect all the ways in which a general nuclear war might be fought.

In such a war, the following types of U.S. strategic forces would be involved:

1. Strategic Offensive Forces

   Manned bombers, strategic reconnaissance aircraft, intercontinental ballistic missiles and submarine-launched missiles, and their associated sup-

This article is composed of excerpts from the statement of Secretary of Defense Robert S. McNamara before the Committee on Armed Services, U.S. House of Representatives, 89th Cong., 1st Sess., February and March, 1965. *Hearings on Military Posture and H. R. 4016*, pp. 172–74, 188–91, 201–6, and 208–9. The statement was read by Deputy Secretary of Defense Cyrus R. Vance because of the illness of Secretary McNamara. The editors have made deletions and added emphases wherever they judged appropriate.

Mr. McNamara is now President of the World Bank, an office he assumed after serving as Secretary of Defense from 1961 to 1968. He is the public official most responsible for the revolutionary changes which have taken place during this decade in U.S. strategy and methods of defense decision-making. He is the author of a soon-to-be published book on U.S. defense policy.

port forces and command and control systems.

2. Strategic Defensive Forces

Anti-aircraft defenses: manned interceptors; surface-to-air missiles; and their associated warning and control systems (including a capability against air-breathing missiles).

Anti-ballistic missile defenses: anti-missile missiles together with the associated sensing, data processing and communciations systems; and the anti-submarine warfare forces directed against enemy missile launching submarines, together with the associated sound surveillance systems.

Anti-satellite defenses: Interceptor missiles and the space detection and tracking systems.

3. Civil Defense Programs

Fallout shelters, warning, etc.

The strategic objectives of our general nuclear war forces are:

to deter a deliberate nuclear attack upon the United States and its allies by maintaining a clear and convincing capability to inflict unacceptable damage on an attacker, even were that attacker to strike first; in the event such a war should nevertheless occur, to limit damage to our populations and industrial capacities.

The first of these capabilities (required to deter potential aggressors) we call "Assured Destruction," i.e., the capability to destroy the aggressor as a viable society, even after a well planned and executed surprise attack on our forces. The second capability we call "Damage Limitation," i.e., the capability to reduce the weight of the enemy attack by both offensive and defensive measures and to provide a degree of protection for the population against the effects of nuclear detonations.

While, for the most part, I will be discussing general nuclear war from the point of view of the United States, it is important to note that we are actually dealing here with a two-sided problem. Assuming that both sides have the same general strategic objectives, which I believe to be the case,

our Assured Destruction problem is the other side's Damage Limiting problem, and our Damage Limiting problem is their Assured Destruction problem. The significance of this point will become more apparent when we discuss the possible interactions between the U.S. and the Soviet offensive-defensive programs later in this section.

Viewed in this light, our Assured Destruction forces would include *a portion* of the ICBM's, the submarine-launched ballistic missiles (SLBM's) and the manned bombers. The Damage Limiting forces would include the remainder of the strategic offensive forces (ICBM's, SLBM's and manned bombers), as well as area defense forces (manned interceptors and anti-submarine warfare forces), terminal defense forces (anti-bomber surface-to-air missiles and anti-ballistic missile missiles), and passive defenses (fallout shelters, warning, etc.). The *strategic offensive* forces can contribute to the Damage Limiting objective by attacking enemy delivery vehicles on their bases of launch sites, provided that our forces can reach them before the vehicles are launched at our cities. *Area defense* forces can destroy enemy vehicles enroute to their targets before they reach the target areas. *Terminal defenses* can destroy enemy weapons or delivery vehicles within the target areas before they impact. *Passive defense measures* can reduce the vulnerability of our population to the weapons that do impact.

It is generally agreed that a vital first objective, to be met in full by our strategic nuclear forces, is the capability for Assured Destruction. Such a capability would, with a high degree of confidence, ensure that we could deter under all foreseeable conditions a calculated, deliberate nuclear attack upon the United States. What kinds and amounts of destruction we would have to be able to inflict in order to provide this assurance cannot be answered precisely. But, it seems reasonable to assume that the destruction of, say, one-quarter to one-third of its population and about two-thirds of its industrial capability would mean the elimination of the aggressor as a major power for many years. Such a level of destruction would certainly represent intolerable punishment to any industrialized nation and thus should serve as an effective deterrent.

Once high confidence of an Assured Destruction capability has been provided, any further increase in the strategic offensive forces must be justified on the basis of its contribution to the Damage Limiting objective. Here, certain basic principles should be noted.

First, against the forces we expect the Soviets to have during the next decade, it would be virtually impossible for us to be able to provide anything approaching perfect protection for our population no matter how large the general nuclear war forces we were to provide, including even the hypothetical possibility of striking first. Of course, the number of fatalities would depend on the size and character of the attack as well as on our own forces. But the Soviets have it within their technical and economic capacity to prevent us from achieving a posture that would keep our immediate fatalities below some level. They can do this, for example, by offsetting any increases in our defenses by increases in their missile forces. In other words, if we were to try to assure survival of a very high percent of our population, and if the Soviets were to choose to frustrate this attempt because they viewed it as a threat to their Assured Destruction capability, the extra cost to them would appear to be substantially less than the extra cost to us.

Second, since each of the three types of Soviet strategic offensive systems (land-based missiles, submarine-launched missiles and manned bombers) could, by itself, inflict severe damage on the United States, even a "very good" defense against bombers, for example, could be outflanked by targeting missiles against those areas defended solely by anti-bomber systems. This is the principal reason why, in the absence of an effective defense against missiles, the large outlays for manned bomber defenses made during the 1950s now contribute disproportionately little to our Damage Limiting capabilities. A meaningful capability to limit the damage of a determined enemy attack, therefore, requires an integrated, balanced combination of strategic offensive forces, area defense forces, terminal defense forces and passive defenses. Such a structure would provide a "defense in depth," with each type of force taking its toll of the incoming weapons, operating like a series of filters or sieves, progressively reducing the destructive potential of the attack.

Third, for any given level of enemy offensive capability, successive additions to each of our various systems have diminishing marginal value. While it is true that in general the more forces we have, the better we can do, beyond a certain point each increment added to the existing forces results in less and less additional effectiveness. Thus, we should not expand one element of our Damage Limiting forces to a point at which the extra survivors it yields per billion dollars spent are fewer than for other elements. Rather, any given amount of resources we apply to the Damage Limiting objective should be allocated among the various elements of our defense forces in such a way as to maximize the population surviving an enemy attack. This is what we mean by a "balanced" Damage Limiting force structure.

The same principle holds for the Damage Limiting force as a whole; as additional forces are added, the incremental gain in effectiveness diminishes. When related to our other national needs, both military and non-military, this tendency for diminishing marginal returns sets a practical limit on how much we should spend for Damage Limiting programs. Accordingly, the question of how much we should spend on Damage Limiting programs can be decided only by carefully weighing the costs against expected benefits.

Pervading the entire Damage Limiting problem is the factor of uncertainty of which there are at least three major types—technical, operational and strategic. *Technical uncertainties stem from* the question of whether a given system can be developed with the performance characteristics specified. *Operational uncertainties stem from* the question of whether a given system will actually perform as planned in the operational environment.

The third type, *strategic uncertainty, is perhaps the most troublesome* since it stems from the question of what our opponent or opponents will actually do—what kind of force they will actually build, what kind of attack they will actually launch, and how effective their weapons will actually be. What may be an optimum defense against one kind of attack may not be an optimum defense against a different kind of attack. For example, within a given budget, a Nike X defense optimized for an attack by ICBM's with simple penetration aids would include fewer high cost radars than one optimized against an attack by ICBM's with more advanced penetration aids. Thus, for a given cost, the efficiency of our defenses depends upon the correctness of the assumptions we make during the design of these defenses about the size and character of enemy attacks.

In the same way, the effectiveness of our strategic offensive forces in the Damage Limiting role would be critically dependent on the timing of an enemy attack on U.S. urban targets. Our missile forces would be most effective against the enemy bombers and ICBM's if the attack on our urban centers were withheld for an hour or more after an attack on U.S. military targets—an unlikely contingency. Our manned bomber forces would be effective in the Damage Limiting role only if the enemy attack on our urban centers were withheld for several hours.

To reduce the technical uncertainties, we rely on painstaking studies and research and development tests; and to hedge against the risks of technical failure, we support parallel development approaches. We try to cope with the operational uncertainties by repeated testing in a simulated operational environment. We hedge against the strategic uncertainties by accepting a less than optimum defense against any one form of attack in order to provide some defense against several forms of attack, and by purchasing "insurance," i.e., keeping open various options—to develop and deploy, for example, a new bomber, a new interceptor, or an anti-missile defense system. . . .

CAPABILITIES OF THE PROGRAMMED FORCES FOR ASSURED DESTRUCTION

In order to assess the capabilities of our general nuclear war forces over the next several years, we must take into account the size and character of the forces the potential aggressors are likely to have during the same period. . . . Certain development and deployment patterns which have already become apparent make it possible to identify likely future trends, at least in their broad outline.

1. The Potential Aggressors' Strategic Offensive-Defensive Forces

By and large, the current estimates of potential aggressors' strategic forces projected through mid-1970 are of the same order of magnitude as the projections through mid-1969 which I discussed here last year. . . . With these long range projections of the potential aggressors' forces as background, I would now like to discuss the adequacy of the Strategic Offensive-Defensive Forces we propose to build and maintain through fiscal year 1970.

2. Adequacy of our Strategic Offensive Forces for Assured Destruction

In evaluating the adequacy of our forces from the standpoint of convincing others that the initiation of general nuclear war would inevitably bring about their own destruction, it is helpful to recall that in all industrialized (or industrializing) societies, population and industry tend to be clustered in a relatively limited number of urban areas. The degree of concentration, of course, varies from country to country. Thus, for example, if we look ahead to the 1970s, we find that the concentration of population in the United States will continue to be greater than that in the Soviet Union. However, in both countries, about three-fourths of the industrial capacity will be concentrated in the 200 largest urban areas. Parenthetically, I might note that although much of Communist China's large population is distributed outside of major urban areas, Communist China remains vulnerable since most of its industrial capacity, its key governmental, technical, and managerial personnel, and its skilled workers are concentrated in far fewer urban areas than is the case with the United States and the Soviet Union.

Beyond the 200 largest urban areas, the amount of population and industrial capacity located in each additional increment of 200 cities falls off at a rapidly declining rate, and smaller and smaller percentages of the total population and industrial capacity would be destroyed in the event that such areas were subjected to attack. It is apparent, then, that a point of diminishing returns is soon encountered, insofar as requirements for Assured Destruction forces are concerned. The ability to destroy smaller and smaller urban areas would add little to our ability to deter attack.

Based on the projected threat for the early 1970s and the most likely planning factors for that time period, our calculations show that even after absorbing a first strike, our already authorized strategic missile force, if it were directed against the aggressor's urban areas, could cause more than 100 million fatalities and destroy about 80 percent of his industrial capacity. If our manned bombers were then to mount a follow-on attack against urban areas, fatalities would be increased by 10 to 15 million and industrial destruction by another percent or two.

I believe it is clear that only a portion of our total programmed ICBM and Polaris force and none of the strategic bombers would be required to inflict on an aggressor unacceptably high levels of destruction. *The remaining elements of the strategic offensive forces are being procured because it is believed they, along with air defense forces, will limit damage in the event deterrence fails.*

The fact that the programmed missile force alone should provide a more than adequate deterrent capability *does not, in and of itself, mean that the Assured Destruction job might not be done more efficiently by bombers alone or with higher assurance by a mix of bombers and missiles.* To test the first possibility, i.e., using bombers alone, we have examined the comparative cost and effectiveness of four alternative strategic offensive systems which could be avail-

able by the early 1970s—Minuteman, Polaris, B-52/SRAM and AMSA/SRAM (SRAM is a new short-range air-to-ground missile; AMSA* is the new bomber proposed by the Air Force). Each system was examined in terms of its effectiveness against a given urban/industrial complex. Using the operational factors expected for the early 1970s, any one of the four forces alone could, with a high degree of confidence, destroy this complex even after absorbing a surprise attack.

However, a comparison of the approximate incremental costs of the four alternative forces makes it clear that AMSA would be the most expensive way of accomplishing this particular task. Indeed, against improved defenses, which might be available by the 1970s, the cost of AMSA would be roughly four times the cost of Minuteman, the least expensive of the four systems examined.

This leaves the second question to be answered—*would a mixed force of bombers and missiles provide greater confidence that we could achieve our Assured Destruction objective?* There are two principal arguments usually advanced to support the case for a mixed missile and bomber force.

a. Complicating the Enemy's Defensive Problem—It is clear that *as long as we have strategic aircraft the enemy cannot effectively defend himself against ballistic missiles without concurrently defending himself against the aircraft and their air-to-surface missiles* (ASM). Conversely, defense against aircraft without concurrent defense against ballistic missiles also leaves him vulnerable. In the absence of a bomber threat, a potential enemy could reallocate his resources to strategic offensive forces, or to anti-missile defenses or some other military program.

This fact, however, does not necessarily argue for a large bomber force. Most of the major elements of cost in an anti-aircraft defense system (e.g., the ground environment and part of the interceptor force) are quite insensitive to the size of the opposing bomber force. The requirement for air de-

* *Editor's Note*: Acronym for Advanced Manned Strategic Aircraft.

fense is more a function of the number of targets to be defended than of the number of attacking bombers. Since the enemy would not know in advance which targets our bombers would attack, he would have to continue to defend all of the targets. Accordingly, his expenditures for air defense are likely to be about the same regardless of whether we have a relatively small bomber force or a large one.

b. Hedging Uncertainties in the Dependability of Our Strategic Offensive Forces—The percentage of the "Unit Equipment" of a particular system which can be depended upon to penetrate to the target is termed the System Dependability Rate. There are four major factors which determine this rate: readiness, survivability, reliability and penetration. *The readiness (alert) rate* is the proportion of the operational force which can immediately respond to an execution order; *the prelaunch survival rate* is the proportion of the alert operational force which is expected to survive an enemy attack in operating condition; *the reliability rate* is the probability that the surviving "alert" missiles or aircraft will operate successfully, exclusive of enemy defensive action; *the penetration rate* is the probability that a reliable system will survive enemy defenses to detonate its warhead.

The readiness and reliability rates of Minuteman and Polaris, which constitute the bulk of our missile forces, are excellent. We are providing substantial amounts of money for extensive testing programs. There can be no reasonable doubt that, for the time period in question, the readiness and reliability of these systems will be fully satisfactory.

With regard to survival, it is highly unlikely that an enemy, even by the early 1970s, would be able to destroy any significant number of Polaris submarines at sea. Since the enemy's intercontinental missile force will face over 1,000 hardened and dispersed U.S. ICBM's, I believe that our land-based missiles also have high survival potential. I am not as confident of the survival potential of our aircraft. If, for any of a number of reasons, they are not airborne within the BMEW's warning time, they

could be caught on their home bases by an enemy ICBM or SLBM attack.

With regard to penetration, if and when the enemy deploys anti-ballistic missile defenses, our penetration aids and other measures should keep the "entry price" of missile attacks against the defended targets within tolerable limits. ("Price" is defined as the number of missiles that must be placed over the defended target area to ensure that the target is destroyed.)

Aircraft also will face penetration difficulties. Our studies have shown that an effective anti-bomber defense is a necessary complement to an anti-missile defense and that the two should have an "interlocked" deployment to avoid obvious vulnerabilities. The cost of an effective anti-bomber defense appears to be much less than the cost of a comparably effective anti-missile defense.

In summary, I see little merit to the argument that bombers are needed in the Assured Destruction role because our missiles are not dependable. *But I do recognize that presently unforeseeable changes in the situation may occur against which a bomber force might possibly provide a hedge. Therefore, as will be discussed later, I propose to retain the option to maintain indefinitely bomber units in our Strategic Offensive Forces.*

CAPABILITIES OF THE PROGRAMMED FORCES FOR DAMAGE LIMITATION

The ultimate deterrent to a deliberate nuclear attack on the United States and its Allies is our clear and unmistakable ability to destroy an aggressor as a viable society, even after our forces have been attacked. But *if deterrence fails, whether by accident or miscalculation, it is essential that forces be available to limit the damage of such an attack to ourselves and our Allies.*

The utility of the Strategic Offensive Forces in the Damage Limiting role is critically dependent on the timing of the enemy attack on U.S. urban targets. For example, if an enemy missile attack on U.S. cities were to be sufficiently delayed after an attack on U.S. military targets (an unlikely contingency), our strategic missiles (which can reach their targets in less than one hour) could significantly reduce the weight of that attack by destroying, prior to launch, a large part of the enemy's forces withheld for use against our cities.

If the urban attack were delayed still longer, our bomber force could also contribute to the Damage Limiting objective. However, if the enemy were to launch his attack against our urban areas at the beginning of a general nuclear war, our Strategic Offensive Forces—both missiles and bombers—would have a greatly reduced value in the Damage Limiting role. Their contribution in that case would be limited to the destruction of enemy residual forces—unlaunched strategic missiles and bombers, re-fire missiles, and any other strategic forces the enemy might withhold for subsequent strikes.

Since we have no way of knowing how the enemy would execute a nuclear attack upon the United States, we must also intensively explore alternative "defensive" systems as means of limiting damage to ourselves. *The problem here is to achieve an optimum balance among all the elements of the general nuclear war forces, particularly in their Damage Limiting role. This is what we mean by "balanced" defenses.*

Although a deliberate nuclear attack upon the United States may seem a highly unlikely contingency in view of our unmistakable Assured Destruction capability, it must receive our urgent attention because of the enormous consequences it would have. In this regard, I should make two points clear. First, in order to preclude any possibility of miscalculation by others, I want to reiterate that although the U.S. would itself suffer severely in the event of a general nuclear war, we are fully committed to the defense of our allies. Second, *we do not view Damage Limitation as a question of concern only to the U.S.* Our offensive forces cover strategic enemy capabilities to inflict damage on our allies in Europe just as they cover enemy threats to the continental United States.

To appreciate fully the implications of an attack on our cities, *it is useful to examine the Assured Destruction objective from the attacker's point of view*, since our Damage Limiting problem is, in effect, his Assured Destruction problem.

Several points are evident from our analysis of this problem. First, it is clear that with limited fallout protection, an enemy attack on our urban areas *would cause great loss of life*, chiefly because of the heavy concentration of population in our large cities which I noted earlier. Second, the analysis clearly demonstrates the *distinct utility of a nationwide fallout shelter program* in reducing fatalities, at all levels of attack. Third, the analysis shows that *the attack would destroy a large percentage of our industrial capacity*. Each successive doubling of the number of delivered warheads would increase the destruction of our population and industrial capacity by proportionately smaller amounts, since smaller and smaller cities would have to be attacked.

In order to assess the potentials of various Damage Limiting programs we have examined a number of "balanced" defense postures at different budget levels. These postures are designed to defend against the assumed threat in the early 1970s. To illustrate the critical nature of the timing of the attack, we used two limiting cases. *First,* we assumed that the enemy would initiate nuclear war with a simultaneous attack against our cities and military targets. *Second,* we assumed that the attack against our cities would be delayed long enough for us to retaliate against the aggressor's military targets with our missiles. In both cases, we assumed that all new systems will perform essentially as estimated since our main purpose here was to gain an insight into the overall problem of limiting damage.

Estimated Effect on U.S. Fatalities of Additions to the Approved Damage Limiting Program
(Based on 1970 population of 210 million)

Additional investment	Millions of U.S. fatalities	
	Early urban attack	Delayed urban attack
$ 0 billion	149	122
5 billion	120	90
15 billion	96	59
25 billlion	78	41

The $5 billion of additional investment (of which about $2 billion would come from non-Federal sources) would provide a full fallout shelter program for the entire population. The $15 billion level would add about $8½ billion for a limited deployment of a low cost configuration of a missile defense system, plus about $1½ billion for new manned bomber defenses. The $25 billion level would provide an additional $8½ billion for anti-missile defenses (for a total of about $17 billion) and another $1½ billion for improved manned bomber defenses (for a total of $3 billion) . . . .

The high utility of a full nationwide fallout shelter program in the Damage Limiting role is apparent from the foregoing table—it would reduce fatalities by about 30 million compared with the present level of fallout protection.

Estimated Effect of Fallout Protection on
U.S. Fatality Levels for Several Damage
Limiting Programs
(Based on 1970 total population of
210 million)

| | Millions of U.S. fatalities | | | |
| | Early urban attack | | Delayed urban attack | |
Additional investment	Partial protection	Full protection	Partial protection	Full protection
$ 0 billion	149	149	122	122
5 billion	145	120	107	90
15 billion	121	96	79	59
25 billion	107	78	59	41

The figures indicate that in the case of an early attack on our urban centers, for the same level of survivors, any Damage Limiting program which excludes a complete fallout shelter system would cost at least twice as much as a program which includes such a system—even under the favorable assumption that the enemy would not exploit our lack of fallout protection by surface bursting his weapons upwind of the fallout areas. In addition, *fallout shelters should have the highest priority of any defensive system because they decrease the vulnerability of the population to nuclear contamination under all types of attack.* Since at the $15 and $25 billion budget

levels, the bulk of the additional funds would go to missile defense, a high confidence in the potential effectiveness of the system would have to be assured before commitment to such large expenditures would be justified. Furthermore, at these budget levels, *missile defenses would also have to be interlocked with either local or area bomber defenses in order to avoid having one type of threat undercut a defense against the other.*

Although missiles clearly have a better chance than bombers of destroying residual enemy offensive forces because they can reach them much sooner, we also examined the effectiveness of bombers in the Damage Limiting role. In one such analysis we compared a strategic aircraft—the AMSA—and two strategic missiles—Minuteman II and an improved missile for the 1970s. (This improved missile could be developed and deployed within the same time frame as the AMSA.) Although there are many uncertainties with regard to both the assumptions and the planning factors used in this comparison, it did demonstrate clearly one important point, namely, that there are less costly ways of destroying residual enemy missiles and aircraft than by developing and deploying a new AMSA—even ignoring the fact that enemy missile silos and bomber fields are far more likely to be empty by the time the bombers pass over than when the missiles arrive.

There is also the possibility in the 1970s of a small nuclear attack on the United States by a nation possessing only a primitive nuclear force. Accordingly, we have undertaken a number of studies in this area. Our preliminary conclusion is that a small, *balanced* defense program could, indeed, significantly reduce fatalities from such an attack. However, the lead time for additional nations to develop and deploy an effective ballistic missile system capable of reaching the United States is greater than we require to deploy the defense.

In summary, *several tentative conclusions* may be drawn from our examination of the Damage Limiting problem:

1. With no new U.S. defenses against nuclear attack in the early 1970s, the

strategic offensive forces likely to confront us could inflict a very high level of fatalities on the United States.

2. A nationwide civil defense program costing about $5 billion could reduce fatalities by about 30 million.

3. If active defense systems operate as estimated, a large, balanced Damage Limiting program for an additional $20 billion could reduce fatalities associated with an early urban attack by another 40 million.

4. There is no defense program within this general range of expenditures which would reduce fatalities to a level much below 80 million unless the enemy delayed his attack on our cities long enough for our missile forces to play a major damage limiting role.

Moreover, we have thus far not taken into account a factor which I touched on at the beginning of this discussion, and that is possible reactions of potential aggressors which could serve to offset our Damage Limiting initiatives. Let me illustrate this point with the following example. Suppose we had already spent an additional $15 billion for a balanced, Damage Limiting posture of the type I described earlier, expecting that it would limit fatalities to, say, 95 million in the event of a first strike against our cities. We then decide to spend another $10 billion to reduce the fatalities to about 75 million. If the enemy chooses to offset this increase in survivors, he should be able in the 1970s to do so by spending about $6 billion more on his offensive forces, or 60 percent of our cost.

At each successively higher level of U.S. expenditures, the ratio of our costs for Damage Limitation to the potential aggressor's costs for Assured Destruction becomes less and less favorable for us. Indeed, at the level of spending required to limit fatalities to about 40 million in a large first strike against our cities, we would have to spend on Damage Limiting programs about four times what the potential aggressor would have to spend on damage creating forces, i.e., *his* Assured Destruction forces.

This argument is not conclusive against our undertaking a major new Damage Limiting program. The resources available to the Soviets are more limited than our own and they may not actually react to our initiatives as we have assumed. But it does underscore the fact that beyond a certain level of defense, the cost advantage lies increasingly with the offense, and this fact must be taken into account in any decision to commit ourselves to large outlays for additional defensive measures.

* * * * *

In the light of the foregoing analysis, it seems to me that there are six major issues involved in our fiscal years 1966–70 general nuclear war programs. These issues concern:

1. The development and deployment of a new manned bomber (estimated five-year systems cost—$8.9 to $11.5 billion).

2. The size of the strategic missile force (estimated five-year cost for an additional 200 Minuteman II missiles—$1.3 billion).

3. The overall level of the anti-bomber defense program (estimated five-year cost if units proposed for phase out are retained in the forces—$300 to $350 million) .

4. The production and deployment of a new manned interceptor (estimated five-year cost—$4 billion).

5. The production and deployment of the Nike X anti-missile system (estimated five-year cost—$24 billion).

6. The construction of fallout shelters for the entire population (estimated cost to individuals, state, local and Federal Government—$5 billion).

The first two issues are related to the Strategic Offensive Forces, the next three to the Strategic Defensive Forces and the last to the Civil Defense Program.

LIMITED STRATEGIC RETALIATION

BY THOMAS C. SCHELLING

There used to be, back in the 1950's, a neat distinction between "general war" and "limited war." The several chapters of this book have done their best to confound that distinction. And properly so; the only question is whether they have gone far enough. There is a tendency, when a traditional dichotomy begins to fail, to identify the original categories as end points on a single scale (or "spectrum," as current language would have it). But it is not evident that the other varieties of potential warfare, or of military strategies, necessarily lie somewhere between two such end points.

Limited war and general war have been polarized concepts—each characterized by a cluster of attributes that seemed logically, or perhaps only historically, to go together. Limited war has been viewed as a local conflict, voluntarily limited in the military resources committed to it, not involving the homelands of the major powers, not involving long-range "strategic" weapons, not involving avowedly punitive damage, characterized by maintenance of civilian political control, the continuation of diplomacy and of negotiation (explicit or tacit) between the major powers, restrained and inhibited by some background of strategic deterrence, and terminating in only an incremental change in the *status quo*. General war has been thought of as unlimited in the military resources committed, epitomized by long-range nuclear weapons directed by the major powers against each other's homeland, including or even emphasizing sheer punitive damage, with diplomacy and civilian political control in abeyance, "deterrence" having given way to action, ending with only one major military power surviving at best.

If we imagine a hypothetical questionnaire asking whether homelands are involved, whether diplomacy continues, whether there is to be punitive action, whether the expenditure of military resources is voluntarily limited, and so forth, the two new categories of warfare corresponded to two types of responses—those that answered "yes" to every question, and those that answered "no" to every one. The authors in this book are suggesting that a census of possible wars, or of strategies for conducting war, might turn up a more variegated population.

Some look like freaks. A war, say, in Southeast Asia, that looked like the Korean War, except that on alternate days the Russians and the Americans scared the wits out of people by detonating large nuclear weapons high in the air over selected cities in each other's countries, or gave each other twenty-four hours to clear out and then converted floor space into piles of rubble, is surely strange and unreal to contemplate, either as a possible phenomenon or as a prescribed mode of conduct. What we have to keep reminding ourselves is that any large nuclear war is strange and unreal to contemplate. "Unfamiliar" is what we have to call these novel conceptions; the concepts of all-out war, massive retaliation, or limited nuclear war are not more real, natural, logical, or necessarily more likely. Even limited conventional war in the modern era is, when you come to think of it, a strange idea. That massively armed nuclear powers would clank swords in a remote jungle in something called "war" and never use their expensive, potent, "quality" weapons is an idea that takes some getting used to. The only one that takes more is the op-

Reprinted by permission from *Limited Strategic War,* edited by Klaus Knorr and Thornton Read (New York: Frederick A. Praeger, 1962), Chap. VIII, "Comment," pp. 241–58. Copyright 1962 by the Center of International Studies, Princeton University.

Mr. Schelling is Professor of Economics at Harvard University and a former director of its Center for International Affairs. He has written extensively on economics, game theory, and arms policy, and is the author of *The Strategy of Conflict* (1960) and *Arms and Influence* (1966).

posite—that they would actually loose all that fury.

But strangeness provides no immunity; we live in an era of strange power relations, and nothing can be judged implausible just because we have never thought of it before or because it appears to contradict what used to be called common sense. The human foot would seem wildly improbable to a creature that had never seen one.

We must judge the concepts and strategies discussed in this book in that fashion— not according to whether they are strange, but according to whether in the strange world of modern weaponry and international relationships they are much more implausible than the conceptions of war and the strategies that we daily discuss.

AN ANCIENT STYLE OF WARFARE

The idea that war can take the form of measured punitive forays into the enemy's homeland, aimed at civil damage, fright, and confusion rather than tactical military objectives, is not particularly new; this is probably the oldest form of warfare. Recently it has characterized the struggle in Algeria; earlier it characterized Arab-Israeli cold-war relationships; and it is present in a greater or lesser degree in strategies of intimidation that range from lynchings to strategic bombing. In early days, wealthy San Franciscans, it is said, conducted their "duels" by throwing gold coins one by one into the Bay until one or the other called it quits.

But actual violence is rarely as pure in its character and purpose as our theoretical formulations might suggest. The beginnings in World War II of what became known as "strategic bombing" involved an important element of "limited reprisal." The first British bombing attacks on Berlin were in direct response to the German bombing of London in August, 1940.[1] The

initial German attacks were not so much "reprisal" as an initiative to intimidate the British population and British leaders. The massive bombings in later years were aimed at retarding military mobilization, at degrading civil organization and morale, and undoubtedly also at impressing on the German leadership and population the destructive consequences of continuing the war. The bombs at Hiroshima and Nagasaki were avowedly intended to intimidate the Japanese into submission; but so, to some extent, were the fire bombings.

It is hard to sort out the motives, because motives are bound to be combined and confused. Analytically, though, it is worthwhile to identify some of the different effects and possible purposes of purely destructive exchanges, even though there are limits to how well a strategy could be tailored to an intention.

One purpose is to intimidate governments or heads of governments, or to impress them with one's own resolve and one's own refusal to be intimidated. The punitive blow (a) hurts the enemy, (b) implies that more will come unless he desists, and (c) displays resolve or daring in the face of his possible countermeasures. Already this is complex. One can display resolve by hurting oneself, not just by hurting the opponent; and the punitive act can be either an initiative or a response. If a response, it can be conceived and communicated as a "normal" mode of response—just a substitute for tactical military activity elsewhere—or as an "extraordinary" response to enemy action that is beyond the bounds of warfare.

The destructive blow can also be aimed

---

[1] "The sporadic raiding of London towards the end of August was promptly answered by us in a retaliatory attack on Berlin. Because of the distance we had to travel, this could only be on a very small scale compared with attacks on London from nearby French and Belgian airfields. The War Cabinet were much in the mood to hit back,

to raise the stakes, and to defy the enemy. I was sure they were right, and believed that nothing impressed or disturbed Hitler so much as his realisation of British wrath and will-power. In his heart he was one of our admirers. He took, of course, full advantage of our reprisal on Berlin, and publicly announced the previously settled German policy of reducing London and other British cities to chaos and ruin. 'If they attack our cities,' he declared on September 4, 'we will simply rub out theirs.' He tried his best." (Winston S. Churchill, *Their Finest Hour* [Boston, Mass.: Little, Brown and Company, 1949], p. 342.)

at intimidating populations and affecting governments indirectly rather than directly. Populations may be frightened into bringing pressures on their governments to yield or desist; they may be disorganized in a way that hampers their government; they may be led to bypass, or to revolt against, their own government to make accommodation with the attacker.

Ordinary terrorism usually appears to be aimed mainly at intimidating populations and perhaps separating them from their governments. But national leaders can be directly influenced by the prospect of continued pain and destruction, particularly if they are at all responsive to, and part of, the population affected. The British Government was affected directly as well as indirectly by the prospect of continued violence in Palestine and Cyprus; the Japanese Government, in 1945, was directly affected by what was happening to their national power if not to civilian welfare.

The idea of limited retaliation or reprisal is therefore not new; but as a type of war that might involve the United States it has been little discussed for nearly a decade. The idea of selective nuclear bombing of, perhaps, China, if not the U.S.S.R., was certainly implicit in some of the nuclear-retaliation discussions of the late 1940's and early 1950's—the period before the prospects of massive nuclear counter-retaliation made escalation into general war seem so inevitable that a slow-motion beginning would be dangerous and inefficient.

In recent years, two mutually opposing views have tended to concert in keeping limited retaliation off the agenda of discussion. One is that, to deter Soviet advances, we must make the retaliatory consequences appear unlimited in scope. Any suggestion of a limited response, according to this view, would be a sign of hesitancy, a possible assurance of "bearable" pain to the aggressor, and a weakening of our resolve. The other is that "all-out" war is so awful that no national leader, particularly no American government, would consider initiating it except in extremity; but if nuclear retaliation were available in small sizes, it might become tempting. It might

take just enough terror out of the balance of terror to induce adventurism or a limited step that might get out of hand. In effect, one of these views is that the middle ground must be eschewed else the Soviets not be deterred; the other is that the same middle ground must be eschewed else the West itself not be deterred.

But while Americans have not openly discussed the possibility of limited nuclear reprisal as a substitute for more conventional "limited war," or as an adjunct to it, the concept has nevertheless been with us. Not only was something of the sort explicitly adverted to by the Soviets in relation to U-2 bases in 1960; more important, the populations of many countries, especially in Europe, have been quite sensitive to the fact that to be "protected" by a tactical nuclear campaign, or to be "liberated" by one, might hurt. In this country we may have thought of local nuclear warfare, whether in Europe or in Asia, as essentially a tactical military campaign. The populations of the areas likely to be involved are undoubtedly susceptible to intimidation by the process of nuclear destruction, and probably so are their leaders. In the event of such a tactical nuclear campaign, the outcome might be at least as much affected by the incidental or deliberate civil damage as by the tactical military results of nuclear use. Thus the consequences might be those of nuclear reprisal, even though the weapons were delivered for a purely tactical purpose.

In other words, the availability of a strategy of limited nuclear reprisal, and the likelihood of the phenomena associated in war with such a strategy, have been with us all along; what is new is acknowledging it, considering it for what it is, and perhaps explicitly incorporating it into our military doctrine.

Incidentally, words like "reprisal" and "retaliation" embody a peculiarly American or Western attitude toward the initiation of such a mode of warfare. My dictionary gives these terms the meaning of "requital," or something "given in return," of returning evil for evil. A strategy of measured nuclear punitive attacks may, if it commends itself to us at all, commend itself as a mode of *response* to aggression and mischief initiated by the enemy. But Soviet use of the tactic may not always look to us like requital; it may look like a bold intimidating initiative. If we are to understand the strategy, we had better look at it from the Soviet as well as the American point of view and recognize that, if the phenomenon occurs, it will not necessarily be at our choice. Limited nuclear *intimidation*, as well as *reprisal*, may be involved.

AN EXAGGERATED CONTRAST

Any limited military conflict impinges on enemy decisions in a number of ways. As suggested earlier, it may be difficult, if not impossible, to design a campaign of pure limited reprisal; it may also be difficult, if not impossible, to design a campaign that contains no element of intimidation through civil damage and the promise of more. The papers in this book have focused on this one particular element of strategy in the belief that it has been substantially overlooked; once it has been identified, however, we need to put it in perspective. One reason that limited nuclear reprisal seems to contrast so sharply with the prevailing notion of "limited war" is that the latter, too, has been artificially purified in discussion during the last several years.

The idea that limited war is a purely local, tactical operation, won or lost on the battlefield, confinable only if the objectives are limited and both sides are concerned to prevent any break of the limits, is a rather narrow idea that has been somewhat prompted by the need to prove that limited war is a meaningful phenomenon and not a contradiction in terms.

A helpful result of examining concepts like nuclear reprisal is that, whatever their merits or deficiencies, they remind us that a limited war in which we and the Soviets are interested is strategic and global in its motives, objectives, and consequences, no matter how localized the violence may be geographically. The principal motive, however localized the violence, is likely to be to impress on the adversary an appreciation of one's own intentions, resolves, capabilities, and modes of reaction. Also important is

to impress the same on the rest of the world (and even, perhaps, on oneself). The main consequences of any limited conflict are in the expectations that they create in the minds of national leaders about how other nations will behave.

There is thus a large element of demonstration—of dare and challenge, of learning and teaching; and while the battleground gained or lost matters, the main struggle is the continuing one between the major powers. The switch from a local tactical campaign to a strategy of limited nuclear reprisal is therefore not so much of a change in the locus of conflict as it might seem. It is more of a change in tactics than a change in participants and issues.

Any limited campaign involves several consequences that deserve sorting out. First, of course, there is the gain or loss of ground, casualties and prisoners, control of airspace, loss or protection of supply lines, build-up of firepower, and local occupation —in other words, the tactical campaign.

Second, there is civil damage and the fear of more. The civil damage may be incidental or deliberate; if deliberate, it may be an avowed objective or may result from military actions that are cloaked with the pretense of pursuing military objectives. A countryside can be panicked, or a city destroyed, in the bombing of an airfield; the airfield may have been picked as a target either in spite of what would happen to the local population or *because* of what would happen to it.

Third, there is always the risk of general war; this is a risk that undoubtedly increases in crisis, particularly during warfare, and probably increases more, the greater the violence or the greater the surprise and novelty in the conduct of the war. To introduce nuclear weapons will raise the sensed danger of general war, not only among the public but among national leaders; to breach a national boundary, to engage in a daring or provocative act or to commit new resources to the war must tend to raise further the appreciated risk of general war.

This being so, it is an important strategic consequence of the local campaign and of decisions on how to conduct it and how to enlarge it. Raising the risk of general war is part of a strategy of conducting limited war. There is an element of Russian roulette in any war we engage in, whether purely localized or involving nuclear reprisal or anything else; to ignore it is to ignore a dimension of the conflict.

Limited war has local political consequences, too. Laos, it seems to be predicted, will never be the same after the recent warfare. Fighting in Berlin, or along the East-West German frontier, could cause political upheavals in East Germany, and perhaps other satellites, important enough to count as one of the main consequences of the fighting. Even a modest military campaign, aimed only at stirring things up a little, coming to nought in military terms, might thus have local political consequences sufficient to rank as a major mischievous objective. And, evidently, the recognition of this is one of the reasons for reluctance about defending areas that, once subjected to a campaign of military defense, might not be politically defensible.

Most or all of these factors are likely to be present to some degree in any kind of campaign. And if one follows even the rather stylized prescriptions of some of the papers in this book, and (whether he is Soviet or American) lobs a lone nuclear weapon into the territory of the other, it is no simple matter to describe just what the intent is, whether the intent is being communicated, how it is being perceived by the recipient, and what the consequences are.

THE AMBIGUOUS INFLUENCE OF "STABILITY"

That is why the relation of a "nuclear-reprisal" strategy to the prevailing degree of strategic stability is ambiguous. "Stability" here refers to the unlikelihood that the deterrent balance would be upset by provocative acts, sudden surprises, political and technological events, or a changed appreciation of the imminence of general war. Stability usually refers to the advantage, in case of war, of striking first and the advantage, in case war is already launched against one, of reacting quickly. The less there is to be gained by initiating war, and the less there is to be lost by waiting a little, the less is the likelihood that a small war would escalate into general war or that an untoward act would trigger it.

If the main East-West adversaries acquire weapons of such character that either can substantially destroy the other on any time schedule he pleases, with or without the advantage of surprise, with or without being hit first, with or without quick reaction, so that there is never any great incentive to do quickly what might be done slowly, or to jump to conclusions, limited nuclear reprisals become a good deal less immediately dangerous. The main inhibition on a nuclear foray into the other country—"But that would mean general war"—might substantially disappear. It would not mean general war unless at least one side wanted general war; and it is hard to see why either would elect it under the circumstances. Extreme strategic stability may thus seem to invite this kind of war endurance.

But extreme instability can also invite it. Crudely speaking, the greater the instability, the less violent the act required to create the risk and apprehension of general war. Whatever the degree of instability, one can choose a small enough act of mischief, pain, or intrusion to keep the risk within limits. If the purpose of the act were to create pain and damage, the smaller acts would accomplish less and might become too trivial to matter. But if the purpose is to subject the adversary to a fear of war and to demonstrate a willingness to incur continued risks, then nothing is necessarily lost by scaling down the provocative act in accordance with the degree of instability.

Take "Condition A," moderately stable: Somebody considers destroying a city in the enemy homeland. Take "Condition B," much less stable: Somebody proposes hitting an air base within the country. Take "Condition C," still more unstable: Somebody proposes detonating a weapon high overhead, or on the surface of a desert within the country. What for? To intimidate—to rock the boat, to display boldness or even wildness, to make the other side apprehensive, to test them out, to humiliate them.

Nobody is killed in condition C, and

losses are incidental in condition B; if the object is to create unbearable civilian pain, conditions B and C preclude the tactic. But it is far from evident that the purpose behind limited reprisal, if it ever were undertaken, would be mainly the civilian pain and damage. Since civilian pain and damage would not necessarily be the main consequence, they would not necessarily provide the main motivation.

Viewed this way, limited reprisal is essentially a war of nerve, of resolve, of risk-taking, of intimidation. And that kind of war is not confined to nuclear weapons. A ton of high explosives sent halfway around the world to explode in the center of Red Square or Lafayette Park would somewhat serve the purpose. So would various hostile and mischievous acts—on the high seas, by way of electronic devices, or through any other form of harassment.

It is not an attractive prospect. Not only is it unattractive as a way of conducting war between the United States and the U.S.S.R.; it may lend itself peculiarly well to "poor man's warfare." The Chinese or the Cubans would have acute difficulty in putting up much of a strategic show against the United States, or even in combatting us with conventional ground troops in areas where they would have no great logistic advantage. But nuclear explosives sufficient in yield to cause painful casualties in the United States are surely going to be available before many years to countries that are far from being able to afford fancy delivery systems. The one kind of target that will always be the easiest to hit with nuclear weapons will be conglomerations of people. Cities cannot be hardened, dispersed, kept mobile, hidden, or made immune to explosions. When a fishing boat tied to the dock in Baltimore has become an adequate means of delivery for a weapon of nuclear reprisal, the United States may have lost a good deal of its military supremacy. We and the Russians may be wise to try, between us, to maintain rules against cheap warfare. We can hope to keep a monopoly for some time of great bomber fleets, flotillas of nuclear submarines, and intercontinental missiles; the weapons of nuclear reprisal, or even bacteriological re-

prisal, may unfortunately be not expensive enough.

A RICHER MENU OF CONTINGENCIES AND STRATEGIES

In thinking about limited nuclear punishment, or limited nuclear exchanges, two mistakes should be avoided. One has recently been called "set-piece warfare" by Sir Solly Zuckerman.[2] It consists of thinking about strategies and situations as though they were predictable, artificially pure and simple, could be relied on to go off as expected, and recognizable at the time for what they were—without the fog of war; the passions and the uncertainties; the snafus, misunderstandings, missed cues, and compromises; and the inevitable lack of any detailed plan for the actual situation that arises.

It can be extremely useful to reflect on a strategy of giving twenty-four hours' warning, for the purpose of evacuation, and sending a missile with a nuclear warhead to flatten all the buildings in a designated city at the end of that time, awaiting the enemy's response to see whether a larger or a smaller city is struck in return. It is useful to reflect on it, because it is not quite as silly as it may seem at first sight, relative to other modes of conducting warfare in a nuclear age. For coming to grips intellectually with the bizarre principles of violence in the nuclear age, a number of special cases, artificially purified, are worth examining. But the almost ritualistic character of some of these conjectural situations should not then be carried in mind as the epitome of limited nuclear-reprisal warfare, or as representing the way the strategy would actually appeal to anyone who might be induced to take it seriously.

Some of the papers in this book may err in that fashion. I am struck with how customary it is to propose that advance warning be given to cities that are to be destroyed, so that the people can evacuate. That is going to extremes. It involves not only pursuing a strategy of limited nuclear

[2] Sir Solly Zuckerman, "Judgment and Control in Nuclear Warfare," *Foreign Affairs*, XL (January, 1962), 196–212.

destruction, but doing so consciously, avow-edly, publicly, dramatically, with announce-ments, with an almost incredible deliber-ateness, patience, and self-confidence, and on a time schedule that is not only nerve-wracking in suspense but imprudent in its relinquishment of initiative. It seems to re-flect a peculiar American penchant for warning rather than doing, for postponing decision, for anesthetizing the victim be-fore striking the blow, for risking wealth rather than people, and for doing grand things that do not hurt rather than small things that do. It seems to me much more likely that any realization of such a strategy would be less clearly differentiated, more in the guise of "military tactics," more im-petuous, more mixed and confused in its purposes and effects. The purified extreme case—as typified by Leo Szilard's provoca-tive suggestions—should be accepted as theoretical exploration, not as pictures of how the phenomenon would actually appear if it occurred.

This leads to the second mistake that one may be seduced into: that is, thinking that to conduct war in the measured ca-dence of limited reprisal somehow rescues the whole business of war from impetuos-ity and gives it rational qualities that it would otherwise lack. True, there is a sense in which anything done coolly, deliberate-ly, on schedule, by plan, upon reflection, in accordance with rules and formulas, and pursuant to a calculus is "rational." But it is a very limited sense. It helps if we slow down a war, induce reflection, and provide national leaders with a consciousness that they are still responsible, still in control, and still capable of affecting the course of events. But this is different from saying that there is some logical way to conduct a war of limited reprisal, or that good sense will prevail, or that a decisive intellect can pro-vide guidance on what to do next.

Even if this kind of warfare were irra-tional, it could still enjoy the benefits of slowness, of deliberateness, and of self-con-trol. The situation is fundamentally inde-terminate as far as logic goes. There is no logical reason why two adversaries will not bleed each other to death, drop by drop, each continually feeling that if he can only hold out a little longer, the other is bound to give in. There is no assurance that both sides will not come to feel that everything is at stake in this critical test of endurance, that to yield is to acknowledge uncondi-tional submissiveness. It may take great luck as well as skill to taper off together in a manner that leaves neither side a loser in a final showdown of resolve.

Nor is there any guarantee—or even a moderate presumption—that the more ra-tional of the two adversaries will come off the better. There is in fact likely to be great advantage in appearing to be on the verge of flying off the handle. However "rational" the adversaries, they may compete to ap-pear the more irrational, impetuous, and stubborn.

This is not to deprecate the value of cool, measured, deliberate action in con-trast to spasmodic violence. It is simply to remind us that there is no way to convert war between major adversaries into a ra-tional process that both sides will find satisfying. There are bound to be limits to the safety and security that can be achieved in any style of limited war. The reason is simple: Limited war is to a large extent a competition in risk-taking.

Whatever the merits of the particular ideas put forth in this book, it serves a pur-pose to explore them. Theorists will never anticipate with accuracy the situations that national leaders will confront; detailed pre-scriptions will never be of use. Analysts can never determine much in advance the deci-sions that might be taken in a crisis; their conclusions will never be quite persuasive and their predictions will never be fully credible.

There are two things the theorists can do. First, they can awaken planners to cer-tain contingencies that might not other-wise have been taken seriously and acquaint decisionmakers in advance with some of the options that may be available to them and with situations that may arise. This is a matter of widening the range of contin-gencies foreseen, making plausible contin-gencies that might not have been taken seriously, focusing attention on the prere-quisites for certain decisions that might need to be taken, and raising the likelihood that the right decisions will occur to the decisionmakers when the time comes.

Theorists may also clutter things up with too many contingencies, too many options, too rich a menu of advance preparations. This we have *not* been doing. Strategic thinking in the nuclear era has not been characterized by an undisciplined imaginativeness, by hypercreativity, by a tendency to overdo the permutations and to engage in flights of fancy or science fiction. Instead, students of war and strategy have been guilty of oversimplifying, of narrowing the focus, of lacking imagination.

My own belief is that the concept of limited nuclear reprisal is something that a national decisionmaker can invent or discover in five minutes, once he is in a situation in which general war is an appalling prospect, a local tactical campaign is ineffectual, and inactivity and withdrawal are intolerable. It takes an act of intellect to *exclude* this kind of strategy from consideration; the analyst, bent on emphasizing certain arguments, seems capable of suppressing certain possibilities. Responsible decisionmakers, when motivated to seek alternatives to a narrow array of unpromising options, may discover in a flash what we painstakingly try to make plausible. The ideas that have been explored, perhaps clumsily, in this book may not represent a great intellectual achievement. It is just an embarrassing gap that is tardily being filled.

The other thing that theorists can try to do is to see that physical and organizational preparations do not become too inflexible. One of the revolutionary characteristics of modern strategy is that decisions are "canned" in advance much more than they were for earlier wars. There is not much time for adaptation, new indoctrination, ironing out misunderstandings, and changing plans. The options that have been anticipated are programmed into the weapons systems; those that have not been anticipated may be physically unavailable.

Decisions that depend on unexpected information, and that have to be made quickly, just cannot be made if the required information cannot be obtained. Decisions that require coordination and planning cannot be made if the procedures and organization have not been designed in advance, if some plans have not been drawn up, communicated, and embodied in operational procedures.

To identify possible situations and strategies in advance not only helps with respect to those situations and those strategies; it also helps in emphasizing the need for flexibility, for adaptability, for communication systems and planning systems and weapon systems that can meet unexpected situations, can improvise, and can react to surprise.

If the present book does nothing else, it may add some variety where variety is needed and stimulate imagination where imagination is needed. If it seems exploratory rather than definitive, that is all right.

CHAPTER 3

Arms Control: A Special Strategy

The great paradox of the Nuclear Age is that the United States and the Soviet Union have both acquired the capability to unleash unlimited force in armed conflict, yet neither can use unlimited force without running the risk of national suicide. Therefore, force, if it is used, must be limited. In more precise terms, both superpowers possess invulnerable second strike nuclear forces. This means that neither can launch a nuclear attack against the other without also being destroyed. As former Secretary of Defense McNamara points out, "it is precisely this mutual capability that provides us both with the strongest possible motive to avoid nuclear war."

The acquisition of invulnerable retaliatory capabilities has been, of course, a deliberate strategy of both superpowers. This is a strategy of nuclear deterrence. Yet, deterrence is not foolproof. And arms obviously do not guarantee the security they are supposedly designed to provide. In fact, arms themselves are considered partially a source of tension and insecurity and their existence may be a stimulus to additional production of armaments. There is also the increased possibility of a war starting through accident, miscalculation, desperation, or folly. And there is the added concern over the incredibly high economic costs of modern armaments.

All of the above considerations have pressed policymakers and scholars to attempt to design arms control techniques in order to provide greater national security. There is common agreement, largely a product of the 1960's, that national security must not be considered solely as a state of armed readiness. Armed readiness is not an end in itself; it is simply one method of protecting our national security. Similarly, arms control is another method of obtaining the same objectives. Arms and arms control are not opposing methods as frequently believed. Both serve the same end. Under certain circumstances, one method may be superior to the other in the attainment of national objectives. This realization reflects an increased level of sophistication in the formulation of American defense policy in the 1960's by public officials as well as members of the intellectual community who are concerned with questions of strategy.

President Johnson has suggested that "arms control is the most urgent business of our time," and that arms control allows the nations of the world to join together in their "quest for freedom from nuclear terror." Arms control, then, is a special strategy to reduce worldwide insecurity. It is a positive attempt to avoid nuclear war. It is a strategy to limit the use of force. It is another method of maintaining the strategic balance. It is an attempt to provide for our national security and the security of other nations.

With the United States and the Soviet Union providing the major impetus, many nations have indeed mutually pledged to attempt to combine their efforts for arms control measures. There are numerous examples of accomplishment: (1) the Hot Line between Washington and Moscow; (2) the United Nations Resolution 1884 (unanimously adopted) calling upon states to refrain from orbiting nuclear bombs and other weapons of mass destruction; (3) the Limited Nuclear Test Ban Treaty which prohibits testing nuclear weapons anywhere but underground; (4) the Treaty on Outer Space providing for peaceful exploration and use; (5) the 1968 draft Nonproliferation of Nuclear Weapons Treaty agreed to by the United States and the Soviet Union. Hopefully, other measures will follow. The existence of organizations such as the 17-nation disarmament conference, the International Atomic Energy Agency, the six-nation European Atomic Energy Community (Euratom), the United States Disarmament and

Arms Control Agency, etc., are all further evidence of national and international concern for seeking methods of arms control. They are symbolic of a sincere desire of many nations to limit violence.

Thomas Schelling and Morton Halperin, in the first selection, consider arms control as "an enlargement of the scope of our military strategy" and provide an operational definition of arms control as a strategic concept. Secretary McNamara explains why the United States decided to deploy a limited antiballistic missile system while also expressing the hope for a future agreement between the United States and the Soviet Union to limit and actually reduce their offensive and defensive strategic nuclear forces. Richard Rosecrance and James Schlesinger deal with various aspects of the problem of nuclear proliferation, particularly the implication for international stability and peace.

STRATEGY AND ARMS CONTROL

BY THOMAS C. SCHELLING AND MORTON H. HALPERIN

INTRODUCTION

This study is an attempt to identify the meaning of arms control in the era of modern weapons, and its role in the pursuit of national and international security. It is not an advertisement for arms control; it is as concerned with problems and difficulties, qualifications and limitations, as it is with opportunities and promises. It is an effort to fit arms control into our foreign and military policy, and to demonstrate how naturally it fits rather than how novel it is.

This is, however, a sympathetic exploration of arms control. We believe that arms control is a promising, but still only dimly perceived, enlargement of the scope of our military strategy. It rests essentially on the recognition that our military relation with potential enemies is not one of pure conflict and opposition, but involves strong elements of mutual interest in the avoidance of a war that neither side wants, in minimizing the costs and risks of the arms competition, and in curtailing the scope and violence of war in the event it occurs.

Particularly in the modern era, the purpose of military force is not simply to win wars. It is the responsibility of military force to deter aggression, while avoiding the kind of threat that may provoke desperate, preventive, or irrational military action on the part of other countries. It is the responsibility of military policies and postures to avoid the false alarms and misunderstandings that might lead to a war that both sides would deplore.

In short, while a nation's military force opposes the military force of potentially hostile nations, it also must collaborate, implicitly if not explicitly, in avoiding the kinds of crises in which withdrawal is intolerable for both sides, in avoiding false alarms and mistaken intentions, and in providing—along with its deterrent threat of resistance or retaliation in the event of unacceptable challenges—reassurance that restraint on the part of potential enemies will be matched by restraint on our own. It is the responsibility of military policy to recognize that, just as our own military establishment is largely a response to the military force that confronts us, foreign military establishments are to some extent a response to our own, and there can be a mutual interest in inducing and reciprocating arms restraint.

We use the term "arms control" rather than "disarmament." Our intention is simply to broaden the term. We mean to include all the forms of military cooperation between potential enemies in the interest of reducing the likelihood of war, its scope and violence if it occurs, and the political and economic costs of being prepared for it. The essential feature of arms control is the recognition of the common interest, of the possibility of reciprocation and coopera-tion even between potential enemies with respect to their military establishments. Whether the most promising areas of arms control involve reductions in certain kinds of military force, increases in certain kinds of military force, qualitative changes in weaponry, different modes of deployment, or arrangements superimposed on existing military systems, we prefer to treat as an open question.

If both sides can profit from improved military communications, from more expensive military forces that are less prone to accident, from expensive redeployments that minimize the danger of misinterpreta-tion and false alarm, arms control may cost more not less. It may by some criteria seem to involve more armament not less. If we succeed in reducing the danger of certain kinds of war, and reciprocally deny our-selves certain apparent military advantages (of the kind that cancel out for the most part if both sides take advantage of them), and if in so doing we increase our military requirements for other dangers of warfare, the matter must be judged on its merits and not simply according to whether the sizes of armies go up or down. If it appears that the danger of accidental war can be re-duced by improved intelligence about each other's military doctrines and modes of de-ployment, or by the provision of superior communication between governments in the event of military crisis, these may have value independently of whether military forces increase, decrease, or are unaffected.

This approach is not in opposition to "disarmament" in the more literal sense, in-volving the straightforward notion of simple reductions in military manpower, military budgets, aggregate explosive power, and so forth. It is intended rather to include such disarmament in a broader concept. We do not, however, share the notion, implicit in many pleas for disarmament, that a reduc-tion in the level of military forces is neces-sarily desirable if only it is "inspectable" and that it necessarily makes war less like-ly. The reader will find that most of the present study is concerned less with reduc-ing national *capabilities* for destruction in the event of war than in reducing the *in-centives* that may lead to war or that may cause war to be more destructive in the event it occurs. We are particularly con-cerned with those incentives that arise from the character of modern weapons and the expectations they create.

An important premise underlying the point of view of this study is that a main determinant of the likelihood of war is the nature of present military technology and present military expectations. We and the Soviets are to some extent trapped by our military technology. Weapon develop-ments of the last fifteen years, especially of the last seven or eight, have themselves been responsible for some of the most alarming aspects of the present strategic situation. They have enhanced the ad-vantage, in the event war should come, of being the one to start it, or of responding instantly and vigorously to the evidence that war may have started. They have in-humanly compressed the time available to make the most terrible decisions. They have almost eliminated the expectation that a general war either could be or should be limited in scope or brought to a close by any process other than the sheer exhaus-tion of weapons on both sides. They have greatly reduced the confidence of either side that it can predict the weapons its enemy has or will have in the future. In these and other ways the evolution of mili-tary technology has exacerbated whatever propensities towards war are inherent in the political conflict between us and our potential enemies. And the greatly increased destructive power of weapons, while it may make both sides more cautious, may make the failure to control these propensities ex-tremely costly.

Arms control can be thought of as an effort, by some kind of reciprocity or cooperation with our potential enemies, to minimize, to offset, to compensate or to deflate some of these characteristics of modern weapons and military expectations. In addition to what we can do unilaterally to improve our warning, to maintain close control over our forces, to make our forces more secure against attack, to avoid the need for precipitant decisions, to avoid accidents or the mistaken decisions that they might cause and to contain conflict once it starts, there may be opportunities to exchange facilities or understandings with our enemies, or to design and deploy our forces differently by agreement with our enemies who do likewise, in a way that enhances those aspects of technology that we like and that helps to nullify those that we do not.

We say this to anticipate the objection that armaments are only a reflection of existing conflicts and not a cause of them. It is true that modern armaments and military plans are a response to basic international conflicts. It is also true that the size and character of military forces are an important determinant of national fears and anxieties, and of the military incentives of our potential enemies. There is a feedback between our military forces and the conflicts that they simultaneously reflect and influence. We have no expectation that by working on weaponry alone, or military deployments or expectations, we can eliminate the political, economic and ideological differences that genuinely underlie present international antagonisms. We do believe that much can be done through careful design of our military strategy, our weaponry, our military deployments and doctrines, to reduce the military danger of those hostilities to our security. We believe that, in addition to what can be accomplished unilaterally in this regard, there are actions and restraints for which the inducements are greater on each side if the other side reciprocates or leads the way. And we believe that something in the way of rules, traditions, and clearer expectations about each other's reactions and modes of behavior may reduce the likelihood of military action based on mistake or misunderstanding.

What is striking is not how novel the methods and purposes of arms control are, and how different from the methods and purposes of national military policy; what is striking is how much overlap there is. There is hardly an objective of arms control to be described in this study that is not equally a continuing urgent objective of national military strategy—of our unilateral military plans and policies. What this study tries to do is to suggest those points at which these unilateral actions can be extended or supplemented through joint understandings with our potential enemies. In some cases the scope for such reciprocal action seems substantial, in other cases very modest; but in all cases it seems worth taking into consideration. Since this dimension of military policy has traditionally been so little appreciated, we have felt it worth while to indicate many areas in which arms control may possibly prove helpful, even if we cannot yet perceive just where the promise lies.

We have also considered arms control to include the less formal, less institutionalized, less "negotiated" understandings and agreements. Some may object that there is no "control" when both sides simply abstain from an action which, if done by one party, yields an advantage but if done by both parties cancels out the advantages and raises risks all around. Our resolution of this semantic problem is to interpret "control" to mean induced or reciprocated "self-control," whether the inducements include negotiated treaties or just informal understandings and reciprocated restraints.

In surveying the possible areas in which arms control may play a role, we have tried to err on the generous side, doubting whether we can yet perceive all of the forms that arms control may take and the areas in which it may occur. In our discussion of the negotiation and administration of concrete agreements, we have been concerned to identify the difficulties, in the belief that these must be anticipated if experiments at arms control are to avoid unnecessary disappointment or disaster.

We have not stated what we believe to be the "ultimate goal" of arms control—

whether it would be disarmed, a world policed by a single benevolent force or a world in which some military "balance of prudence" has taken the fear out of the "balance of fear." We should, however, acknowledge that we do not believe the problems of war and peace and international conflict are susceptible of any once-for-all solution. Something like eternal vigilance and determination would be required to keep peace in the world at any state of disarmament, even total disarmament. International conflict, and the military forces that are their reflection, are not in our judgment simply unnatural growths in human society which, once removed, need never recur. Conflict of interest is a social phenomenon unlikely to disappear, and potential recourse to violence and damage will always suggest itself if the conflict gets out of hand. Man's capability for self-destruction cannot be eradicated—he knows too much! Keeping that capability under control—providing incentives to minimize recourse to violence—is the eternal challenge.

This is the objective of responsible military policy. And a conscious adjustment of our military forces and policies to take account of those of our potential enemies, in the common interest of restraining violence, is what we mean by arms control.

In the study that follows we are concerned mainly with the direct relation of arms control to the military environment. Arms control can also affect, for good or ill, our political relations with allies, neutrals and potential enemies. It can reduce tension or hostilities; it can reduce vigilance. It can strengthen alliances, collapse them, or make them unnecessary. It can create confidence and trust or create suspicion and irritation. It can lead to greater world organization and the rule of law or discredit them. And it evidently lends itself to the short-run competition in propaganda.

In focusing this book on the military environment we have not meant to depreciate the more purely political and psychological consequences. We have just not covered the whole subject. We do, however, incline to the view that the political and psychological benefits that may stem from arms control will be the more genuine, the more genuine is their direct contribution to international security. We doubt therefore whether the approach of this book is wholly inconsistent with an approach that emphasizes the political environment more and the military environment less.

In Part I we explore the potential contributions of arms control to the military environment. "Potential" needs emphasis. It is easy to see, under most of the headings in Part I, that some kind of formal or informal arms control could in theory help in the solution of our security problems. It is quite another matter to identify important, feasible applications of the principle. We have included illustrative suggestions, but have no comprehensive scheme to propose.

And we particularly emphasize that there may be more, much more, to be accomplished under many of the headings of Part I by unilateral improvements in our military policies and posture than through the medium of arms control. It is not true that an improvement in our military posture is necessarily a disadvantage to a potential enemy. The right kind of "improvement" can reduce the danger that a potential enemy will become an active one, and can lay the groundwork for deflating the enmity itself.

Part I is concerned with potential benefits. Problems and difficulties, risks and uncertainties, receive attention in Parts II and III.

ARMS CONTROL AND GENERAL WAR

The most mischievous character of today's strategic weapons is that they may provide an enormous advantage, in the event that war occurs, to the side that starts it. Both Russian and American strategic doctrines reflect preoccupation with the urgency of attacking in the event of evidence that the other is about to. The urgency is in the vulnerability of strategic weapons themselves, and of the communication and other facilities they depend on; the side that attacks first can hope to blunt the other's retaliation. Closely related is the advantage, in the event the other is already attacking, of responding quickly and vigorously—or being a close second if not first.

By itself this urgency would pose the danger of unintended war, a war provoked by ambiguous evidence of attack. The greater the urgency with which the decision must be made in the event of alarm, the greater the likelihood of converting a false alarm into war itself. These dangers compound themselves: each side must be alert not only to the other's premeditated attack, but to the other's incentive to reach quick decisions in an emergency.

Hardly any other characteristic of weapons dramatizes so well that some of the danger of war resides in the very character of modern weapons.

Hardly anything would be as tragically ironic as a war that both sides started, each in the belief that the other was about to, each compelled by its expectations to confirm the other's belief that attack was imminent.

This danger does not depend on the belief that by striking quickly one may come off with a clean win. The comparison is not between initiating war and no war at all, but between initiating war and waiting for the other to initiate it. It may not be optimism that provides the dangerous incentive, but pessimism about the loss from failing to act in time. It is essentially "preventive war," improvised at a moment when war is considered imminent. *Preemptive* war is the term now in use for the case of war initiated in the expectation that attack is imminent.

At no time before in modern history did military technology make it so likely that the first moments of general war might determine its outcome. Whatever the Japanese expected from Pearl Harbor, it would have been a mistake to believe that they could foreclose an American victory by anything they might accomplish that one morning. In World War I, when nations were caught in the ponderous grip of mobilization procedures that provided advantage to the side that first started to mobilize, there may have been a slow-motion equivalent to nuclear attack. But in 1914 the difference between mobilizing half a day before the enemy and half a day behind was on a different scale of importance.[1]

THE INCENTIVE TO PRE-EMPT

There are several ways that arms control might possibly help. One is to alter the character of the weapons themselves, especially their vulnerability to each other—their potency in foreclosing return attack. Whatever reduces the ability of weapons to achieve advantage by going quickly, and to suffer a great disadvantage by responding slowly, may reduce the likelihood of war.

A second approach is oriented towards the events that might precipitate pre-emptive decisions. Essentially, the urge to pre-empt is an *aggravating* factor: it converts a possibility of war into an anticipation of war, precipitating war. The pre-emptive advantage makes a suspicion of war a cause of war. If the actions, false alarms, accidental events, mischief or other occurrences that bring the pre-emptive urge into play can be minimized and damped, by cooperative arrangements or arms limitations, the danger of pre-emptive war may be reduced.

Third, arms control may possibly address itself to the decision process, and particularly to the expectations of each side about the other's actions or intentions on the brink of war. If cooperative arrangements can improve each side's intelligence about the other's preparatory actions, this may (but also may not) stabilize expectations.

[1] For a discussion of vulnerability in relation to the strategic balance see Bernard Brodie, *Strategy in the Missile Age* (Princeton: Princeton University Press, 1959); Herman Kahn, *On Thermonuclear War* (Princeton: Princeton University Press, 1960); Washington Center for Foreign Policy Research, *Developments in Military Technology and Their Impact on United States Strategy and Foreign Policy*, Study No. 8, December 1959, prepared for the Senate Committee on Foreign Relations, 86th Congress, 2d Session (Washington: U.S. Government Printing Office, 1959); Albert Wohlstetter, "The Delicate Balance of Terror," *Foreign Affairs* XXXVII (January 1959), 211–34, and his forthcoming book. For an analysis of the problem in the arms-control context see Thomas C. Schelling, "Surprise Attack and Disarmament," in *The Strategy of Conflict* (Cambridge: Harvard University Press, 1960), pp. 230–54.

If each is able to reassure the other that it is not misinterpreting certain events as signaling the onset of war, dangerously compounding expectations may be averted. If each can avoid, in responding to the enhanced danger of war, actions, and deployments that appear as preparations for attack, and can enhance the other's ability to perceive this, the interacting decisions that might explode into war may be dampened.

Finally, it is likely that any forms of arms control that reduce the general expectation of war would reduce the urgency to pre-empt and the fear of each other's obsession with pre-emption.

THE INCENTIVE FOR PREMEDITATED ATTACK

As far as major war is concerned, the incentive to initiate a premeditated attack is akin to the incentive towards pre-emptive attack. The reason is that with thermonuclear weapons on both sides, there might be little inducement in either case if it were not for the possibility of achieving, by taking the initiative, a substantial reduction in the other's ability or willingness to retaliate.

What creates the principal danger of premeditated attack is the same as with pre-emptive attack: the vulnerability of either side's retaliatory forces to an attack by the other. With a technology that permits an enormously potent weapon to arrive on an enemy target in a matter of minutes, the possibility is open that a well-coordinated surprise attack on the other side's own strategic forces might greatly reduce the size of these forces. By disrupting communications and disorganizing the victim's forces, the attacker can reduce the efficiency even of the weapons surviving; and they would have to be used against an attacker whose own defenses had the advantage of alertness and preparation. There is also the possibility that an attacker might hope to disarm the victim sufficiently to make retaliation appear futile.

Thus premeditated strategic attack by one major power against the other is largely a matter of the advantage of initiative and surprise. Collaborative measures to re-duce this advantage, and to reduce thereby the incentive that either might have towards premeditated attack, might be an important supplement to the measures that we undertake unilaterally to assure our strategic forces against attack.

First there may be measures that, taken jointly, would reduce the likelihood that the attacker could achieve *surprise*. Exchange of warning and intelligence facilities would be an example; and the original "open-skies" idea was oriented this way. In addition to warning arrangements, there might be limitations on weapons themselves, or on their use and deployment, designed to reduce their *capability for achieving surprise*. Limitations on the basing of weapons, or a requirement that they show up and be counted, might be of this sort. In other words, cooperative measures to improve intelligence and warning facilities, or cooperative measures with respect to weapons themselves designed to facilitate warning, might be considered.

Second, measures might be considered that would make weapons *less vulnerable even in the event of surprise*. Agreement to develop and to acquire weapons of a character relatively better for retaliation than for achieving surprise (as might have been the case if it had been possible to limit the accuracy of missiles) might reduce the incentives on both sides for initiating general war. Alternatively, since the advantage in striking first is largely in reducing or precluding a punitive return attack, measures to defend the homeland against incoming punitive weapons are complementary to offensive weapons of surprise attack. Thus abstention from active defense of cities (or, conceivably, from civil defense preparations) might increase the potency of each side's retaliatory forces in a manner analogous to the protection of the retaliatory forces themselves.

It has to be asked whether there is not some logical contradiction in both sides' wishing to eliminate the advantages that go with premeditated attack. Either one side is in fact interested in carrying out a well-coordinated attack on the other's strategic forces, or else not. If not, the measures appear superfluous. If so, there is at least one partner who is against the purpose of the agreement, and who either would not enter it or would do so only if he were certain that he could subvert it. Can there be a mutual interest in measures to frustrate premeditated attack?

For several reasons the answer can be "yes." It may be that neither side intends to attack but is uneasy about the other's intentions. It is thus obliged to develop military forces and to deploy them in a way that assumes the other side *may* attack; and it is obliged to react to ambiguous events as though the other side would indeed attack. If, then, neither in fact intends deliberate attack, there could be a good deal to gain by creating for both sides the reassurance that may accompany measures jointly taken to reduce the likelihood that either side, if it attacked, would succeed. In other words, since estimates of each other's *intentions* will necessarily be uncertain, measures reciprocally to reduce *capabilities* for preclusive attack may help both.

Second, even though neither side presently considers it wise or necessary to initiate general war, political events or technological change may alter the situation. But it may change either way: *either* we *or* the Russians may be the victim or beneficiary of technological break-through, of moments of military weakness, or of political incentives that override the fear of general war. Each of us may well be willing to relinquish capabilities in future contingencies on condition that the other side do likewise. (If a flip of a coin might give either of us the capability for successful attack it could look like a bad bet to both of us.)

Third, a main incentive—perhaps the overwhelmingly important motivation—towards premeditated attack on the other side's strategic forces would be a belief that war, sooner or later, is fairly likely, and that the *conservative* course would be to initiate it on the best possible terms. So-called "preventive war" considerations may be uppermost. This, in effect, is the "preemptive" urge in slow motion. The preemptive motive is the incentive to attack in the belief that the other is already attacking or is about to; the "preventive urge" has the same forestalling motives, but with respect to a war that is not yet imminent.

But the "preventive" and the "pre-emptive" urges can interact dangerously. The greater the "preventive urge" that either imputes to the other, the more probable it must expect an attack to be. The more alert it must itself then be to the need for a preemptive decision.

Furthermore, the preventive urges on both sides compound with each other. A powerful reason why one side might decide that a planned "preventive" attack was the only prudent action would be a belief that the other would sooner or later reach the same conclusion. The danger might be substantially deflated by measures that reduced the likely success of attack, by reducing both sides' *expectations* of attack.

THE DANGER OF ACCIDENTAL WAR

In current usage "accidental war" refers to a war that, in some sense, neither side intended, expected or deliberately prepared for. It includes war that might result from errors in warning systems or misinterpretations of tactical evidence. It includes the notion that a literal accident, such as the inadvertent detonation of a nuclear weapon, might precipitate war through misinterpretation, through expectation of the enemy's misinterpretation or through some sequence of automatic or semiautomatic responses and decisions. It includes the possibility of unauthorized provocative action by a pilot or bomber or missile commander; sabotage that inadvertently goes beyond its limited objectives; and plain mischief with or without the intended consequences of war.

And it has come to include what is sometimes called "catalytic war"—a deliberate plot by some third country or countries, perhaps with nuclear weapons, to precipitate a war between the major powers (or just to precipitate a crisis, but with the consequences of war).[2]

"Accidental war" is sometimes used also

[2] For a discussion of accidental war see Thomas C. Schelling, "Meteors, Mischief, and War," *Bulletin of the Atomic Scientists* XVI (September, 1960), 292–97; John B. Phelps *et al., Accidental War: Some Dangers in the 1960's*, RP-6, The Mershon National Security Program, The Ohio State University, June 29, 1960.

to refer to mistakes in "brinkmanship," failure to foresee the consequences of military actions, or the accumulation of irreversible threats in the heat of a crisis. And it may refer to the particular occurrences or misunderstandings by which limited war explodes into general war.

The essential character of accidental war is that of a war initiated in the belief that war has already started or become inevitable. In most of the hypothetical cases of "accidental war," evidence is misread by one or both sides. (There is an important qualification: if both sides jump to the conclusion that instant war is inevitable, both sides may immediately make this conclusion "correct.")

It would not be accidents themselves, ambiguous spots on a radarscope, the mischief of a deranged bomber pilot, the sabotage, or the catalytic actions of third parties, that would *directly* bring about war. These occurrences provoke *decisions* that bring about war. The problem, therefore, is not solely one of preventing the "accidents"; it is equally, or more, one of forestalling the kinds of *decisions* that might lead to war as a result of accident, false alarm or mischief.

This idea of "accidental war" rests largely on the same premise that underlies preemptive war—that there is an enormous advantage, in the event war occurs, in starting it (or enormous advantage, in the event it seems to have started, in responding instantly) and that each side will be not only conscious of this but conscious of the other's preoccupation with it. It seems quite unlikely that war would be brought about by an electronic false alarm, by a mechanical accident, by the mischief of someone in a message center or on an airbase or by the provocative action of a third party, if there were not some urgency of responding before the evidence is in. The essence of a false alarm is that, if one fails to act upon it, it is seen to have been a false alarm. An accident is almost certain to be recognized as an accident, if war has not intervened meanwhile. And among all those who may have it in their power to bring about a provocative event that might precipitate the decisions that bring about war, very few, if any, would have the pow-

er to wage a persuasive imitation of war if the consequences of their actions could be assessed and analyzed for even a brief period of time. Thus "accidental war" is war that may be initiated on misinformation, incomplete evidence or misunderstanding, of a kind that could likely be cleared up were it not that the time to clear it up might seem a disastrous delay to a government confronted with the possibility that war has already started. "Accidental war" is, for the most part, pre-emptive war sparked by some occurrence that was unpredictable, outside the control of the main participants and unintended by them.

There are several ways that arms control might possibly help to reduce the danger of accidental war. An important one has been mentioned: reducing the urgency of quick action at the outset of general war. Cooperative or unilateral measures to improve the ability of each side's strategic forces to survive an attack, *and to remain under good command and control under attack*, might slow down the tempo of decisions. Slowing down decisions on the brink of war not only means that either side, if it wishes to, can take more time to clear up whether or not the war has already started; it also means that each can impute less impetuous action to the other, and reduce thereby the need for its own quick reaction.

Measures to reduce the incidence of false alarm could be helpful. Exchange of warning facilities, of facilities for last-minute tactical intelligence, might reduce the incidence of false alarms by increasing the reliability of the warning system and improving the flow of evidence to each side. (Increased warning facilities might also increase the false-alarm rate; and some superficially attractive schemes for mutual warning probably could not communicate rapidly enough to be of use within the relevant span of time.) Agreements to limit the kinds of activities and deployments that might create misunderstandings or false alarms could also be helpful; even arrangements or activities that just improved each side's understanding of the other's behavior, facilitating discrimination between normal and abnormal traffic, might help.

And because the essence of this accidental-war problem is misunderstanding on one side or both, it is not out of the question that communications and other arrangements might be set up to facilitate direct contact between governments, of a sort that could clear up misunderstandings and provide certain assurances in an emergency. (The possibility that such arrangements could be abused is discussed later. Here—as emphasized—we are exploring the potential advantages of arms arrangements; the qualifications and disadvantages will appear in Parts II and III.)

Finally, to the extent that arms control helps to limit local war, or can reduce American and Soviet expectations of general war, the less likely it is that accidental occurrences will be construed as evidence of war.

CAPABILITIES FOR DESTRUCTION

Arms limitations might reduce the capability for destruction so that, in the event of a thermonuclear American-Soviet exchange, no matter how the war gets out of hand, the damage is less than it would have been otherwise. The main form such an agreement might take is to reduce existing nuclear stockpiles or the capability for delivering them. No agreement can erase the knowledge of how to produce nuclear weapons and long-range missiles; an agreement could, however, aim at reducing the amount of fissionable material or the vehicles for their delivery. The capability for instantaneous destruction might thus be lowered, and the likelihood increased that war would come to an end within the time it would take to increase nuclear stockpiles or delivery systems. Acceptance of reduced nuclear stockpiles and vehicles would imply acceptance of the notion that something less than unlimited supplies of nuclear weapons and missiles may be adequate to deter attack. It could also reflect a belief that retaliatory forces might not be much degraded, if at all, if both they *and* the attacking force were comparably diminished. Also, since small nuclear weapons can fairly easily and quickly be converted into large weapons, any agreement to reduce substantially the nuclear stock-

pile, and hence the capability for destruction in general war, might require some willingness on both sides to reduce their dependence on nuclear weapons in limited warfare. (A missile agreement in itself might not be very effective in reducing over-all capability for destruction—in contrast to capability for, e.g., surprise attack—because bombers can carry much greater loads than contemporary missiles.)

Any agreement that reduced the capability for destruction in general war might make war more likely, in that the costs and risks in initiating it would not appear as great.

It should be noted that since both the Soviet Union and the United States now produce large quantities of nuclear weapons, and presumably will continue in the absence of any agreement to cut off production, such an agreement could have some effect of reducing future capability for destruction in general war, whether or not there was an agreement to reduce previously existing stockpiles.

A most important possibility is that the over-all level of potential destruction might be substantially reduced by arms arrangements that did not focus on numbers and sizes of weapons *per se*. If both Soviet and American forces should succeed, through cooperative measures or unilaterally, in developing reasonably invulnerable retaliatory systems, so that neither could disarm the other in a sudden attack and neither needed to be obsessed with the imminence of attack, a large reduction in numbers might come naturally. Certainly, nothing like the nuclear energy delivery capability of our present bomber force would be needed if the entire force were reasonably secure against attack and if Soviet forces were similarly secure against our attack. Insurance in *numbers* against enemy surprise attack would be less needed if security were achieved qualitatively. Furthermore, the kinds of forces that would maximize *retaliatory* capability, in contrast to preemptive capability, and that would permit the most deliberate and controlled response to alarms and accidents, could prove to be quite expensive in relation to explosive energy. A weapon system, or mix of weapons, that maximizes the explosive power it could deliver to targets *after* being attacked is likely to involve a much smaller aggregate warhead yield (per dollar expended on it) than a force designed to profit from a pre-emptive attack.

Thus an appreciable quantitative "disarmament" may result as a natural by-product of qualitative changes in strategic armaments.

COLLATERAL DAMAGE

It seems to be widely thought that a war between the U.S. and the U.S.S.R. would necessarily be an "all-out" affair, motivated towards maximum destruction of each other. In contrast to so-called "limited war," general war is seen as a wholly indiscriminate and unrestrained orgy of punitive action. To some extent, this belief is cultivated by a deterrent strategy that feels obliged to make the threat of war as awful as possible (or by a strategy of intimidation that aims at the same thing). Both American and Soviet expressed doctrine has often implied that "limited war" is local war and occupies some range at the lower end of the scale, while "general war" must be total.

It is not evident that this would be the case. Whatever the tragedy and damage that one should anticipate in the event of war, it is not at all clear that a strategic war between the U.S. and the U.S.S.R. would necessarily be motivated towards maximum destruction. Particularly as we consider an "accidental" or pre-emptively motivated war, one that the initiator himself deplores, one that is "self-defensive," or one that results from the piling up of threatening commitments on both sides from which no retreat seems possible, we have to consider a war that would be aimed less at punitive destruction and more at the survival of each country and its further military security. Furthermore, even if a nation tries to deter or to intimidate the other with a threat that any war, once it passes some threshold, will know no bounds, the government's actual motivation if war occurs would not—if any rationality at all remains and if command arrangements are adequately designed—be towards fulfilling

a threat that had failed. It would instead be motivated towards maximizing the nation's security and other interests.

If this is so, there are at least two considerations suggesting that general war might be less destructive than is generally thought. One is that the highest priority targets would be retaliatory forces, not populations and economic assets. A cold-blooded war plan might have antipopulation measures low on its list of objectives.

The second consideration is that an attacker might deliberately abstain from destroying population centers, if those population centers did not contain high priority strategic targets, in the hope of deterring the all-out destruction of his own cities and bringing the war to a close. "General war" might also be "limited war." The attacker might consider it in his interest to avoid cities because alive they represent hostages with which he can bargain. He could use the *threat* of further destruction in bargaining for a termination of the war, perhaps a termination that included subsequent arms control. The attacked country might be similarly alert to the possibility of defending cities not through active measures but through coercion, through preserving the *threat* of destroying the attacker's cities. Whether one or both sides abstain altogether from population targets, or engage in limited "negotiatory" blows at population centers, there is at least some reason to suppose that the deliberate military action would be somewhat confined to urgent military targets.

If this is a possibility—if the attacker either cannot afford to waste weapons on population strikes, or prefers to exploit the *threat* of further destruction rather than to destroy potential hostages at the outset—there remains the important question whether it is physically possible. Might cities and populations be destroyed as a by-product of a war that, in so far as deliberate military action is concerned, is aimed at "military" targets? Might arms limitations, or reciprocal modifications in arms programs, or *understandings about the conduct of war*, reduce the collateral damage (by-product damage) of a war confined as far as possible to military engagements?

The issue of clean and dirty bombs comes immediately to mind. Similarly important is the location of strategic weapons; if they are located away from cities, and if strategic communications are independent of city communications, there may be little blast damage to major population centers, at least from weapons that do not go astray. If weapons and related facilities (i.e., if the prime targets) can be isolated from population centers, the fallout can be reduced and its arrival retarded.

Efforts along these lines would likely be unilateral rather than collaborative. Nevertheless, any comprehensive understanding that specifies the *kinds* of strategic weapons that each side should have ought to take into consideration the desirability of weapons that need not destroy cities and populations unless deliberately aimed at them, or that do not, by their location, make urgent targets out of population centers.

There is admittedly a dilemma. An important objective of arms control may be to permit each side a reasonably potent retaliatory force—a force that could do acute punitive damage to the other side's population and other values. If so, it might seem a contradiction of purpose to "sanitize" a weapon system in such a way as to remove its retaliatory potential. Indeed this would be true of measures designed to make retaliatory weapons *incapable* of retaliation. What is being suggested here is much more modest—the possibility of leaving an *option* to the possessor of the weapons, so that while he has a capability for retaliation he need not create enormous destruction as a by-product of a pre-emptive or an "accidental" war initiated by one side or the other in a manner designed to minimize damage. True, the threat of retaliation may be deflated by anything that leaves the deterrent force the option of restraining itself. Nevertheless, there is a possibility here that deserves consideration even though the arguments go both ways. (To the extent that damage to third areas —noncombatants in the war—would be affected, the retaliatory dilemma does not arise.)

It is interesting that *types* of weapons often involve *locational* questions. A main difference between Polaris submarines and the fixed-base ICBM's is that the former spend most of their time away from population centers, while the latter tend to be within national boundaries and, depending on geographical considerations, perhaps quite close to populations. Thus an important issue in the question whether arms control should promote or suppress, say, ballistic-missile submarines, is the implication for collateral damage in a preemptively motivated war.

And here it is clear that there may be a difference between a retaliatory system that achieves invulnerability by requiring a large number of attacking weapons to destroy it, and one that achieves invulnerability by providing no useful target to the enemy. In the event a military duel should get started, digging up each other's missiles by exploding large warheads on each other's territory creates enormous amounts of fallout; *searching* for hidden or mobile missiles does not. Blanketing an area known to contain weapons whose exact location is not known, on the other hand, can involve large amounts of fallout. And so on. Collateral damage to earthbound population and structures may even depend on whether the violent attempts to destroy each other's retaliatory forces are out in space.

THE INCENTIVE FOR DESTRUCTION

We have just discussed the possibility that arms control might help to limit damage in general war in the event both sides wish to limit damage. It may also concern itself with reducing the incentive for destruction in case of war.

One possibility is to create *expectations* that even a major strategic war might be susceptible of limitation. The main motivation for restraint would be to induce reciprocation; the likelihood of its being reciprocated depends on the other side's being alert to the possibility of restraint, being able to recognize restraint if it occurs, and having some capability for responding to it. Creating a shared expectation of the possibility may therefore be a prerequisite to restraint; and any understandings, even tacit ones, that can be reached, however informal they are, deserve to be considered.

Being able to observe and to respond to restraint depends on more, however. The nature of the restraint must be recognizable; it must form some kind of pattern that the other side can recognize and respond to. There must also be some sensation of appropriateness about the restraints observed. Limits are more likely to be stable, to be appreciated by both sides as a common expectation, if they meet certain psychological and legalistic requirements, and have some rationality. A certain amount of communication, even inadvertent communication and communication of a quite informal sort, may prepare the ground for some common notion of what restraints it would be sensible to observe in the course of war. If the two sides' anticipations differ too greatly, it may be impossible to strike a "bargain" in the process of war.

Each side must furthermore have some reconnaissance and intelligence capability for knowing what is going on in the course of war—knowing a good deal more than would be required just to fight a war of extermination and exhaustion. In fighting an "all-out" war, a war of sheer destructive fury, it may make little difference to the conduct of one's offensive efforts whether particular cities of his own have yet been hit by the enemy or not; but in fighting a restrained war, in knowing whether one's own abstention has been reciprocated, and in knowing what limits the enemy is proposing by his conspicuous observance of them, one must know enough of what the enemy is doing to appreciate what his expectations are.

It may be worth considering whether direct communication between enemies in the course of war would help in arriving at restraints. It is by no means obvious that direct communication helps rather than hinders even where there is a will to use it and a desire to observe restraints; but the possibility is an important one and needs to be considered. Certainly the preparation of facilities and procedures for communication, if communication is deemed desirable, may require some overt cooperative preparation between enemies.

It is interesting that cooperation between potential enemies in reaching agreed limits and restraints in case of war may be less dependent on any "outcome" of negotiations than simply on the negotiations themselves. "Negotiations" may be too strong a word here, since the pertinent communications need not be formalized, institutionalized, or even recognized as negotiation. In reaching some expectation shared with the enemy about conduct in wartime it is the *understanding* that matters, not the instrument (if any) in which the understanding is expressed. For that reason, one side alone, or even a third party, might influence each side's anticipation about the conduct of war; power of *suggestion* is an important part of the process. The problem is one of creating an awareness of certain possibilities, and an understanding of how to take advantage of them in the event of war.

THE TERMINATION OF WAR

Terminating a war through anything other than just the exhaustion of weapons requires some form of arms control. Even surrender of one side to the other would require something analogous to arms control for policing the terms imposed by the victor and any conditions exacted by the surrendering side. Actually, surrender may be a poor term for the termination of thermonuclear war: anywhere between the two extremes of unconditional surrender by one side or another, the truce or other arrangements for bringing the war to a close would almost certainly require some direct communication between governments, and understanding about the disposition of weapons, and some capability for monitoring the agreement reached—the latter likely involving a substantial exchange of facilities subject to various safeguards. Each may have to police the other with vehicles that are themselves sufficiently under surveillance to preclude double cross.

Studies of arms control rarely consider the case that war has already started. Nevertheless, the kind of arms control required for terminating a war will depend on an awareness of the problem and some exploration of its implications *beforehand*; and it will require communications, reconnaissance, and command responsibilities that differ from those required for prosecuting unconditional total war. Prospects for success may be improved by any coordinated understanding reached between enemies beforehand.

This and the preceding section may seem a little unrealistic. It is not obvious that the necessary sophistication, self-control, control over the military forces, intelligence, reconnaissance, and imaginative thinking and bargaining, will be available. However, bargaining and communication between enemies might be plausible under some circumstances of general war. A war resulting from some military crisis, whether triggered by an "accidental" event or just by an irresistible urge to pre-empt, or arising out of a limited war, is likely to be one in which the opposing governments are already in communication. If the war itself is preceded by ultimata and other last minute threats and proposals, bargaining in general war might be a continuation of bargaining already in process.

This depends, of course, on the existence of facilities for wartime communication, and may depend on each side's decision not to destroy the other's communication facilities. But at least there is some reason to suppose that communication between enemies under the circumstances of general war might be a continuation of a brink-of-war state, not a complete innovation.

A LIMITED ABM DEPLOYMENT

BY ROBERT S. McNAMARA

I want to discuss with you this afternoon the gravest problem that an American Secretary of Defense must face: the planning, preparation, and policy governing the possibility of thermonuclear war.

It is a prospect most of mankind would prefer not to contemplate.

That is understandable. For technology has now circumscribed us all with a conceivable horizon of horror that could dwarf any catastrophe that has befallen man in his more than a million years on earth.

Man has lived now for more than twenty years in what we have come to call the Atomic Age.

What we sometimes overlook is that every future age of man will be an atomic age.

If, then, man is to have a future at all, it will have to be a future over-shadowed with the permanent possibility of thermonuclear holocaust.

About that fact, we are no longer free.

Our freedom in this question consists rather in facing the matter rationally and realistically and discussing actions to minimize the danger.

No sane citizen; no sane political leader; no sane nation wants thermonuclear war.

But merely not wanting it is not enough.

We must understand the difference between actions which increase its risk, those which reduce it, and those which, while costly, have little influence one way or another.

Now this whole subject matter tends to be psychologically unpleasant. But there is an even greater difficulty standing in the

Reprinted by permission from *The New York Times*, September 19, 1967. Copyright © 1967 by The New York Times Company.

This address was given by Secretary of Defense McNamara to editors of United Press International in San Francisco, September 18, 1967.

way of constructive and profitable debate over the issues.

And that is that nuclear strategy is exceptionally complex in its technical aspects. Unless these complexities are well understood, rational discussion and decision making are simply not possible.

What I want to do this afternoon is deal with these complexities and clarify them with as much precision and detail as time and security permit.

DEFINITION OF TERMS

One must begin with precise definitions.

The cornerstone of our strategic policy continues to be to deter deliberate nuclear attack upon the United States, or its allies, by maintaining a highly reliable ability to inflict an unacceptable degree of damage upon any single aggressor, or combination of aggressors, at any time during the course of a strategic nuclear exchange—even after our absorbing a surprise first strike.

This can be defined as our "assured destruction capability."

Now it is imperative to understand that assured destruction is the very essence of the whole deterrence concept.

We must possess an actual assured destruction capability. And that actual assured destruction capability must also be credible. Conceivably, our assured destruction capability could be actual, without being credible—in which case, it might fail to deter an aggressor.

The point is that a potential aggressor must himself believe that our assured destruction capability is in fact actual, and that our will to use it in retaliation to an attack is in fact unwavering.

The conclusion, then, is clear: If the United States is to deter a nuclear attack on itself or on our allies, it must possess an actual and a credible assured destruction capability.

When calculating the force we require, we must be "conservative" in all our estimates of both a potential aggressor's capabilities, and his intentions. Security depends upon taking a "worst plausible case" —and having the ability to cope with that eventuality.

In that eventuality, we must be able to absorb the total weight of nuclear attack on our country—on our strike-back forces; on our command and control apparatus; and our industrial capacity; on our cities; and on our population—and still be fully capable of destroying the aggressor to the point that his society is simply no longer viable in any meaningful, twentieth century sense.

That is what deterrence to nuclear aggression means. It means the certainty of suicide to the aggressor—not merely to his military forces, but to his society as a whole.

Now let us consider another term: "First-strike capability." This, in itself, is an ambiguous term, since it could mean simply the ability of one nation to attack another nation with nuclear forces first. But as it is normally used, it connotes much more: the substantial elimination of the attacked nation's retaliatory second-strike forces.

KEY STRATEGIC CONCEPT

Now, clearly, such a first-strike capability is an important strategic concept. The United States cannot—and will not—ever permit itself to get into the position in which another nation, or combination of nations, would possess such a first-strike capability, which could be effectively used against it.

To get into such a position vis-à-vis any other nation or nations would not only constitute an intolerable threat to our security, but it would obviously remove our ability to deter nuclear aggression—both against ourselves and against our allies.

Now, we are not in that position today— and there is no foreseeable danger of our ever getting into that position.

Our strategic offensive forces are immense: 1,000 Minuteman missile launchers, carefully protected below ground; 41 Polaris submarines, carrying 656 missile launchers—with the majority of these hidden beneath the seas at all times; and about 600 long-range bombers, approximately 40 per cent of which are kept always in a high state of alert.

Our alert forces alone carry more than 2,200 weapons, averaging more than one megaton each. A mere 400 one-megaton weapons, if delivered on the Soviet Union, would be sufficient to destroy over one-third of her population, and one-half of her industry.

And all of these flexible and highly reliable forces are equipped with devices that insure their penetration of Soviet defenses.

Now what about the Soviet Union?

Does it today possess a powerful nuclear arsenal?

The answer is that it does.

Does it possess a first-strike capability against the United States?

The answer is that it does not.

Can the Soviet Union, in the foreseeable future, acquire such a first-strike capability against the United States?

The answer is that it cannot.

It cannot because we are determined to remain fully alert, and we will never permit our own assured destruction capability to be at a point where a Soviet first-strike capability is even remotely feasible.

Is the Soviet Union seriously attempting to acquire a first-strike capability against the United States?

Although this is a question we cannot answer with absolute certainty, we believe the answer is no. In any event, the question itself is—in a sense—irrelevant. It is irrelevant since the United States will so continue to maintain—and where necessary strengthen—our retaliatory forces, that whatever the Soviet Union's intentions or actions, we will continue to have an assured destruction capability vis-à-vis their society in which we are completely confident.

A STAND-OFF ON RETALIATION

But there is another question that is more relevant.

And that is, do we—the United States—possess a first-strike capability against the Soviet Union?

The answer is that we do not.

And we do not, not because we have neglected our nuclear strength. On the contrary, we have increased it to the point that we possess a clear superiority over the Soviet Union.

We do not possess first-strike capability against the Soviet Union for precisely the same reason that they do not possess it against us.

And that is that we have both built up our "second-strike capability" to the point that a first-strike capability on either side has become unattainable. (A "second-strike capability" is the capability to absorb a surprise nuclear attack and survive with sufficient power to inflict unacceptable damage on the aggressor.)

There is, of course, no way in which the United States could have prevented the Soviet Union from acquiring its present second-strike capability—short of a massive pre-emptive first strike on the Soviet Union in the 1950s.

The blunt fact is, then, that neither the Soviet Union nor the United States can attack the other without being destroyed in retaliation; nor can either of us attain a first-strike capability in the foreseeable future.

The further fact is that both the Soviet Union and the United States presently possess an actual and credible second-strike capability against one another—and it is precisely this mutual capability that provides us both with the strongest possible motive to avoid a nuclear war.

The more frequent question that arises in this connection is whether or not the United States possesses nuclear superiority over the Soviet Union.

The answer is that we do.

But the answer is—like everything else in this matter—technically complex.

The complexity arises in part out of what measurement of superiority is most meaningful and realistic.

Many commentators on the matter tend to define nuclear superiority in terms of gross megatonnage, or in terms of the number of missile launchers available.

Now, by both these two standards of measurement, the United States does have a substantial superiority over the Soviet Union in the weapons targeted against each other.

But it is precisely these two standards of measurement that are themselves misleading.

For the most meaningful and realistic measurement of nuclear capability is neither gross megatonnage, nor the number of available missile launchers; but rather the number of separate warheads that are capable of being *delivered* with accuracy on individual high-priority targets with sufficient power to destroy them.

Gross megatonnage in itself is an inadequate indicator of assured destruction capability, since it is unrelated to survivability, accuracy, or penetrability, and poorly related to effective elimination of multiple high-priority targets. There is manifestly no advantage in over-destroying one target, at the expense of leaving undamaged other targets of equal importance.

Further, the number of missile launchers available is also an inadequate indicator of assured destruction capability, since the fact is that many of our launchers will carry multiple warheads.

But by using the realistic measurement of the number of warheads available, capable of being reliably delivered with accuracy and effectiveness on the appropriate targets in the United States or Soviet Union, I can tell you that the United States currently possesses a superiority over the Soviet Union of at least three or four to one.

Furthermore, we will maintain a superiority—by these same realistic criteria—over the Soviet Union for as far ahead in the future as we can realistically plan.

GREATER THAN PLANNED

I want, however, to make one point patently clear: our current numerical superiority over the Soviet Union in reliable, accurate, and effective warheads is both greater than we had originally planned, and is in fact more than we require.

Moreover, in the larger equation of security, our "superiority" is of limited significance—since even with our current superiority, or indeed with any numerical superiority realistically attainable, the blunt, inescapable fact remains that the Soviet Union could still—with its present forces—effectively destroy the United States, even after absorbing the full weight of an American first strike.

I have noted that our present superiority is greater than we had planned. Let me explain to you how this came about, for I think it is a significant illustration of the intrinsic dynamics of the nuclear arms race.

In 1961, when I became Secretary of Defense, the Soviet Union possessed a very small operational arsenal of intercontinental missiles. However, they did possess the technological and industrial capacity to enlarge that arsenal very substantially over the succeeding several years.

Now, we had no evidence that the Soviets did in fact plan to fully use that capability.

But as I have pointed out, a strategic planner must be "conservative" in his calculations; that is, he must prepare for the worst plausible case and not be content to hope and prepare merely for the most probable.

Since we could not be certain of Soviet intentions—since we could not be sure that they would not undertake a massive build-up—we had to insure against such an eventuality by undertaking ourselves a major buildup of the Minuteman and Polaris forces.

Thus, in the course of hedging against what was then only a theoretically possible Soviet buildup, we took decisions which have resulted in our current superiority in numbers of warheads and deliverable megatons.

But the blunt fact remains that if we had had more accurate information about planned Soviet strategic forces, we simply would not have needed to build as large a nuclear arsenal as we have today.

Now let me be absolutely clear. I am not saying that our decision in 1961 was unjustified. I am simply saying that it was necessitated by a lack of accurate information.

Furthermore, that decision in itself—as justified as it was—in the end, could not possibly have left unaffected the Soviet Union's future nuclear plans.

What is essential to understand here is that the Soviet Union and the United States mutually influence one another's strategic plans.

Whatever be their intentions, whatever be our intentions, actions—or even realistically potential actions—on either side relating to the buildup of nuclear forces, be they either offensive or defensive weapons, necessarily trigger reactions on the other side.

It is precisely this action-reaction phenomenon that fuels an arms race.

Now, in strategic nuclear weaponry, the arms race involves a particular irony. Unlike any other era in military history, today a substantial numerical superiority of weapons does not effectively translate into political control, or diplomatic leverage.

ALL-POWERFUL, INADEQUATE

While thermonuclear power is almost inconceivably awesome, and represents virtually unlimited potential destructiveness, it has proven to be a limited diplomatic instrument. Its uniqueness lies in the fact that it is at one and the same, an all-powerful weapon—and a very inadequate weapon.

The fact that the Soviet Union and the United States can mutually destroy one another—regardless of who strikes first—narrows the range of Soviet aggression which our nuclear forces can effectively deter.

Even with our nuclear monopoly in the early postwar period, we were unable to deter the Soviet pressures against Berlin, or their support of aggression in Korea.

Today, our nuclear superiority does not deter all forms of Soviet support of Communist insurgency in Southeast Asia.

What all of this has meant is that we, and our allies as well, require substantial non-nuclear forces in order to cope with levels of aggression that massive strategic forces do not in fact deter.

This has been a difficult lesson both for us and for our allies to accept, since there is a strong psychological tendency to regard superior nuclear forces as a simple and unfailing solution to security, and an assurance of victory under any set of circumstances.

What is important to understand is that our nuclear strategic forces play a vital and absolutely necessary role in our security and that of our allies, but it is an intrinsically limited role.

Thus, we and our allies must maintain substantial conventional forces, fully capable of dealing with a wide spectrum of lesser forms of political and military aggression—a level of aggression against which the use of strategic nuclear forces would not be to our advantage, and thus a level of aggression which these strategic nuclear forces by themselves cannot effectively deter. One cannot fashion a credible deterrent out of an incredible action. Therefore security for the United States and its allies can only arise from the possession of a whole range of graduated deterrents, each of them fully credible in its own context.

Now I have pointed out that in strategic nuclear matters, the Soviet Union and the United States mutually influence one another's plans.

In recent years the Soviets have substantially increased their offensive forces. We have, of course, been watching and evaluating this very carefully.

Clearly, the Soviet buildup is in part a reaction to our own buildup since the beginning of this decade.

Soviet strategic planners undoubtedly reasoned that if our buildup were to continue at its accelerated pace, we might conceivably reach, in time, a credible first-strike capability against the Soviet Union.

That was not in fact our intention. Our intention was to assure that they—with their theoretical capacity to reach such a first-strike capability—would not in fact out-distance us.

But they could not read our intentions with any greater accuracy than we could read theirs. And thus the result has been that we have both built up our forces to a point that far exceeds a credible second-strike capability against the forces we each started with.

REALITIES OF SITUATION

In doing so, neither of us has reached a first-strike capability. And the realities of the situation being what they are—whatever we believe their intentions to be, and whatever they believe our intentions to be —each of us can deny the other a first-strike capability in the foreseeable future.

Now, how can we be so confident that this is the case?

How can we be so certain that the Soviets cannot gradually out-distance us—either by some dramatic technological break-through, or simply through our imperceptively lagging behind, for whatever reason: reluctance to spend the requisite funds; distraction with military problems elsewhere; faulty intelligence; or simple negligence and naiveté?

All of these reasons—and others—have been suggested by some commentators in this country, who fear that we are in fact falling behind to a dangerous degree.

The answer to all of this is simple and straightforward.

We are not going to permit the Soviets to out-distance us, because to do so would be to jeopardize our very viability as a nation.

No President, no Secretary of Defense, no Congress of the United States—of whatever political party and of whatever political persuasion is going to permit this nation to take that risk.

We do not want a nuclear arms race with the Soviet Union—primarily because the action-reaction phenomenon makes it foolish and futile. But if the only way to prevent the Soviet Union from obtaining first-strike capability over us is to engage in such a race, the United States possesses in ample abundance the resources, the technology, and the will to run faster in that race for whatever distance is required.

But what we would much prefer to do is to come to a realistic and reasonably riskless agreement with the Soviet Union, which would effectively prevent such an arms race. We both have strategic nuclear arsenals greatly in excess of a credible assured destruction capability. These arsenals have reached that point of excess in each case for precisely the same reason: we each have reacted to the other's buildup with very conservative calculations. We have, that is, each built a greater arsenal than either of us needed for a second-strike capability, simply because we each wanted to

be able to cope with the "worst plausible case."

PACT WOULD BENEFIT BOTH

But since we now each possess a deterrent in excess of our individual needs, both of our nations would benefit from a properly safe-guarded agreement first to limit, and later to reduce, both our offensive and defensive strategic nuclear forces.

We may, or we may not, be able to achieve such an agreement. We hope we can. And we believe such an agreement is fully feasible, since it is clearly in both our nations' interests.

But reach the formal agreement or not, we can be sure that neither the Soviets nor we are going to risk the other's obtaining a first-strike capability.

On the contrary, we can be sure that we are both going to maintain a maximum effort to preserve an assured destruction capability.

It would not be sensible for either side to launch a maximum effort to achieve a first-strike capability. It would not be sensible because the intelligence-gathering capability of each side being what it is, and the realities of lead-time from technological breakthrough to operational readiness being what they are, neither of us would be able to acquire a first-strike capability in secret.

Now, let me take a specific case in point.

The Soviets are now deploying an anti-ballistic missile system. If we react to this deployment intelligently, we have no reason for alarm.

The system does not impose any threat to our ability to penetrate and inflict massive and unacceptable damage on the Soviet Union. In other words, it does not presently affect in any significant manner our assured destruction capability.

It does not impose such a threat because we have already taken the steps necessary to assure that our landbased Minuteman missiles, our nuclear submarine-launched new Poseidon missiles, and our strategic bomber forces have the requisite penetration aids—and in the sum, constitute a force of such magnitude, that they guarantee us a force strong enough to survive a Soviet attack and penetrate the Soviet ABM deployment.

Now let me come to the issue that has received so much attention recently: The question of whether or not we should deploy an ABM system against the Soviet nuclear threat.

To begin with, this is not in any sense a new issue. We have had both the technical possibility and the strategic desirability of an American ABM deployment under constant review since the late 1950s.

While we have substantially improved our technology in the field, it is important to understand that none of the systems at the present or foreseeable state of the art would provide an impenetrable shield over the United States. Were such a shield possible, we would certainly want it—and we would certainly build it.

And at this point, let me dispose of an objection that is totally irrelevant to this issue.

It has been alleged that we are opposed to deploying a large-scale ABM system because it would carry the heavy price tag of $40 billion.

Let me make very clear that the $40 billion is not the issue.

FLAW OF SYSTEM

If we could build and deploy a genuinely impenetrable shield over the United States, we would be willing to spend not $40 billion, but any reasonable multiple of that amount that was necessary.

The money in itself is not the problem: The penetrability of the proposed shield is the problem.

There is clearly no point, however, in spending $40 billion if it is not going to buy us a significant improvement in our security. If it is not, then we should use the substantial resources it represents on something that will.

Every ABM system that is now feasible involves firing defensive missiles at incoming offensive warheads in an effort to destroy them. But what many commentators on this issue overlook is that any such system can rather obviously be defeated by an enemy simply sending more offensive war-

heads, or dummy warheads, than there are defensive missiles capable of disposing of them.

And this is the whole crux of the nuclear action-reaction phenomenon.

Were we to deploy a heavy ABM system throughout the United States, the Soviets would clearly be strongly motivated to so increase their offensive capability as to cancel out our defensive advantage.

It is futile for each of us to spend $4 billion, $40 billion, or $400 billion—and at the end of all the spending, and at the end of all the deployment, and at the end of all the effort, to be relatively at the same point of balance on the security scale that we are now.

In point of fact, we have already initiated offensive weapons programs costing several billions in order to offset the small present Soviet ABM deployment, and the possibly more extensive future Soviet ABM deployments.

That is money well spent; and it is necessary.

But we should bear in mind that it is money spent because of the action-reaction phenomenon.

If we in turn hope for heavy ABM deployment—at whatever price—we can be certain that the Soviets will react to offset the advantage we would hope to gain.

It is precisely because of this certainty of a corresponding Soviet reaction that the four prominent scientists—men who have served with distinction as the science advisers to Presidents Eisenhower, Kennedy and Johnson, and the three outstanding men who have served as directors of research and engineering to three Secretaries of Defense—have unanimously recommended against the deployment of an ABM system designed to protect our population against Soviet attack.

These men are Doctors Killian, Kistiakowsky, Wiesner, Horning, York, Brown, and Foster.

The plain fact of the matter is that we are now facing a situation analogous to the one we faced in 1961: we are uncertain of the Soviets' intentions.

At that time we were concerned about their potential offensive capabilities; now we are concerned about their potential defensive capabilities.

But the dynamics of the concern are the same.

We must continue to be cautious and conservative in our estimates—leaving no room in our calculations for unnecessary talk. And at the same time, we must measure our own response in such a manner that it does not trigger a senseless spiral upward of nuclear arms.

Now, as I have emphasized, we have already taken the necessary steps to guarantee that our offensive strategic weapons will be able to penetrate future, more advanced, Soviet defenses.

Keeping in mind the careful clockwork of lead-time, we will be forced to continue that effort over the next few years if the evidence is that the Soviets intend to turn what is now a light and modest ABM deployment into a massive one.

Should they elect to do so, we have both the lead-time and the technology available to so increase both the quality and quantity of our offensive strategic forces—with particular attention to highly reliable penetration aids—that their expensive defensive efforts will give them no edge in the nuclear balance whatever.

But we would prefer not to have to do that. For it is a profitless waste of resources, provided we and the Soviets can come to a realistic strategic arms-limitation agreement.

As you know, we have proposed U.S.-Soviet talks on this matter. Should these talks fail, we are fully prepared to take the appropriate measures that such a failure would make necessary.

REALISTIC RESPONSE

The point for us to keep in mind is that should the talks fail—and the Soviets decide to expand their present modest ABM deployment into a massive one—our response must be realistic. There is no point whatever in our responding by going to a massive ABM deployment to protect our population, when such a system would be ineffective against a sophisticated Soviet offense.

Instead, realism dictates that if the Soviets elect to deploy a heavy ABM system, we must further expand our sophisticated offensive forces, and thus preserve our overwhelming assured destruction capability.

But the intractable fact is that should the talks fail, both the Soviets and ourselves would be forced to continue on a foolish and feckless course.

It would be foolish and feckless because —in the end—it would provide neither the Soviets nor us with any greater relative nuclear capability.

The time has come for us both to realize that, and to act reasonably. It is clearly in our own mutual interest to do so.

Having said that, it is important to distinguish between an ABM system designed to protect against a Soviet attack on our cities, and ABM systems which have other objectives.

One of the other uses of an ABM system which we should seriously consider is the greater protection of our strategic offensive forces.

Another is in relation to the emerging nuclear capability of Communist China.

There is evidence that the Chinese are devoting very substantial resources to the development of both nuclear warheads and missile delivery systems. As I stated last January, indications are that they will have medium-range ballistic missiles within a year or so, an initial intercontinental ballistic missile capacity in the early 1970s, and a modest force in the mid-70s.

Up to now, the lead-time factor has allowed us to postpone a decision on whether or not a light ABM deployment might be advantageous as a countermeasure to Communist China's nuclear development.

But the time will shortly be right for us to initiate production if we desire such a system.

China at the moment is caught up in internal strifes, but it seems likely that her basic motivation in developing a strategic nuclear capability is an attempt to provide a basis for threatening her neighbors, and to clothe herself with the dubious prestige that the world pays to nuclear weaponry.

We deplore her development of these weapons, just as we deplore it in other countries. We oppose nuclear proliferation because we believe that in the end it only increases the risk of a common and cataclysmic holocaust.

President Johnson has made it clear that the United States will oppose any efforts of China to employ nuclear blackmail against her neighbors.

We possess now, and will continue to possess for as far ahead as we can foresee, an overwhelming first-strike capability with respect to China. And despite the shrill and raucous propaganda directed at her own people that "the atomic bomb is a paper tiger," there is ample evidence that China well appreciates the destructive power of nuclear weapons.

China has been cautious to avoid any action that might end in a nuclear clash with the United States—however wild her words—and understandably so. We have the power not only to destroy completely her entire nuclear offensive forces, but to devastate her society as well.

Is there any possibility, then, that by the mid-1970s China might become so incautious as to attempt a nuclear attack on the United States or our allies?

It would be insane and suicidal for her to do so, but one can conceive conditions under which China might miscalculate. We wish to reduce such possibilities to a minimum.

And since, as I have noted, our strategic planning must always be conservative, and take into consideration even the possible irrational behavior of potential adversaries, there are marginal grounds for concluding that a light deployment of U.S. ABMs against this possibility is prudent.

The system would be relatively inexpensive—preliminary estimates place the cost at about $5 billion—and would have a much higher degree of reliability against a Chinese attack than the much more massive and complicated system that some have recommended against a possible Soviet attack.

OTHER ADVANTAGES

Moreover, such an ABM deployment designed against a possible Chinese attack would have a number of other advan-
tages. It would provide an additional indication to Asians that we intend to deter China from nuclear blackmail, and thus would contribute toward our goal of discouraging nuclear weapon proliferation among the present non-nuclear countries.

Further, the Chinese-oriented ABM deployment would enable us to add—as a concurrent benefit—a further defense of our Minuteman sites against Soviet attack, which means that at modest cost we would in fact be adding even greater effectiveness to our offensive missile force and avoiding a much more costly expansion of that force.

Finally, such a reasonably reliable ABM system would add protection of our population against the improbable but possible accidental launch of an intercontinental missile by any of the nuclear powers.

After a detailed review of all these considerations, we have decided to go forward with this Chinese-oriented ABM deployment, and we will begin actual production of such a system at the end of this year.

In reaching this decision, I want to emphasize that it contains two possible dangers—and we should guard carefully against each.

The first danger is that we may psychologically lapse into the old over-simplification about the adequacy of nuclear power. The simple truth is that nuclear weapons can serve to deter only a narrow range of threats. This ABM deployment will strengthen our defensive posture—and will enhance the effectiveness of our land-based ICBM offensive forces. But the independent nations of Asia must realize that these benefits are no substitute for their maintaining and, where necessary, strengthening their own conventional forces in order to deal with more likely threats to the security of the region.

A MAD MOMENTUM

The second danger is also psychological. There is a kind of mad momentum intrinsic to the development of all new nuclear weaponry. If a weapon system works —and works well—there is strong pressure from many directions to produce and deploy the weapon out of all proportion to the prudent level required.

The danger in deploying this relatively light and reliable Chinese-oriented ABM system is going to be that pressures will develop to expand it into a heavy Soviet-oriented ABM system.

We must resist that temptation firmly—not because we can for a moment afford to relax our vigilance against a possible Soviet first-strike—but precisely because our greatest deterrent against such a strike is not a massive, costly, but highly penetrable ABM shield, but rather a fully credible offensive assured destruction capability.

The so-called heavy ABM shield—at the present state of technology—would in effect be no adequate shield at all against a Soviet attack, but rather a strong inducement for the Soviets to vastly increase their own offensive forces. That, as I have pointed out would make it necessary for us to respond in turn—and so the arms race would rush hopelessly on to no sensible purpose on either side.

Let me emphasize—and I cannot do so too strongly—that our decision to go ahead with *limited* ABM deployment in no way indicates that we feel an agreement with the Soviet Union on the limitation of strategic nuclear offensive and defensive forces is any the less urgent or desirable.

ROAD FROM AX TO ICBM

The road leading from the stone ax to the ICBM—though it may have been more than a million years in the building—seems to have run in a single direction.

If one is inclined to be cynical, one might conclude that man's history seems to be characterized not so much by consistent periods of peace, occasionally punctuated by warfare; but rather by persistent outbreaks of warfare, wearily put aside from time to time by periods of exhaustion and recovery—that parade under the name of peace.

I do not view man's history with that degree of cynicism, but I do believe that man's wisdom in avoiding war is often surpassed by his folly in promoting it.

However foolish unlimited war may have been in the past, it is now no longer merely foolish, but suicidal as well.

It is said that nothing can prevent a man from suicide, if he is sufficiently determined to commit it.

The question is what is our determination in an era when unlimited war will mean the death of hundreds of millions—and the possible genetic impairment of a million generations to follow?

Man is clearly a compound of folly and wisdom—and history is clearly a consequence of the admixture of those two contradictory traits.

History has placed our particular lives in an area when the consequences of human folly are waxing more and more catastrophic in the matters of war and peace.

In the end, the root of man's security does not lie in his weaponry.

In the end, the root of man's security lies in his mind.

What the world requires in its twenty-second year of the Atomic Age is not a new race towards armament.

What the world requires in its twenty-second year of the Atomic Age is a new race towards reasonableness.

We had better all run that race.

Not merely we the administrators. But we the people.

INTERNATIONAL STABILITY AND NUCLEAR DIFFUSION

BY RICHARD N. ROSECRANCE

The spread of nuclear weapons may well represent a serious problem of future international relations. But that possibility is not an immutable feature of the coming world environment; it can be shaped and even altered by national and international decisions. The Nth country phenomenon has to undergo a series of metamorphoses before it can be transformed into the Nth country problem. Nuclear diffusion has an unstabilizing impact upon world politics only under a concatenation of circumstances. First, there must be dissemination of the ability to build or acquire nuclear bombs; second, a capability of creating or obtaining a delivery, command, and control system must be present; third, there must be a resolute national will to create a nuclear weapons capability; fourth, possible counteraction by major powers must not be permitted to nullify the advantages of nuclear status; fifth, and finally, the nuclear system developed must actually be used in such a fashion as to endanger local or international peace. Failure to pass through each of the five stages means that nuclear diffusion does not attain to international significance; it does not pose an independent problem to world stability and peace.

THE BOMB

The first (and easiest) requirement which diffusion must meet is that of a concrete capability of producing or acquiring nuclear bombs. In the first instance bomb construction depends upon knowledge of nuclear and weapons technology, much of which is widespread. Experience with power reactors is undifferentiable from experience with production reactors. The accumulation of weapons-grade material can be commenced even with research reactors. Detonation mechanisms for a bomb are somewhat less well understood, but the United States has released considerable data on both implosion and gun-type methods in its histories of atomic energy work during World War II. International conferences have provided information on criticality magnitudes for plutonium. The necessity of nuclear testing has been substantially reduced by the wealth of scientific results available. Information, then, does not constitute a serious obstacle to a nuclear weapons program.

Reactor capabilities are multiplying rapidly in many areas of the globe. Exclusive of the four nuclear countries, national reactor capacity is partly under bilateral control. The United States, for instance, insists on fuel cycle and other controls on the nuclear materials it provides to other countries under the Atoms for Peace program, and the large number of reactors it has sent overseas are also subject to bilateral control. The Soviet Union, on the other hand, claims it does not oversee the reactors or fuels it offers to other countries. Bilateral arrangements, however, are not the only means of acquiring nuclear technology. As of 1962 at least eighteen countries were engaged in building nuclear power reactors for their own use.[1] Toll enrichment facilities available in the United Kingdom and perhaps in other countries may alter the reactor and associated programs of incipient Nth countries. If fuels may be en-

[1] Christoph Hohenemser, "The Nth Country Problem Today," in Seymour Melman, ed., *Disarmament: Its Politics and Economics* (Boston, 1962), p. 252.

Reprinted by permission from *The Dispersion of Nuclear Weapons* edited by Richard N. Rosecrance (New York: Columbia University Press, 1964), pp. 294–314.

Mr. Rosecrance, Professor of Political Science, is on leave from the University of California, Berkeley, to serve as a member of the Policy Planning Council of the Department of State. He was formerly an Associate Professor of Political Science and Director of the Security Studies Project at the University of California, Los Angeles.

riched to any degree of purity through arrangement with a third state, gaseous diffusion plants may not be necessary, and different types of uranium reactors may be built. Since a gaseous diffusion establishment is a very costly undertaking, toll enrichment may possibly permit omission of one of the normal stages of a nuclear weapons program and vastly reduce costs. As yet there is no information on the control (if any) which will be levied by the servicing nation of the enriched fuels which it returns to the client. Chemical separation plants to remove weapons grade plutonium from irradiated fuel also are necessary to complete a bomb program.

Physical capabilities depend not only upon knowledge and the state of nuclear plant and equipment, they are also importantly affected by costs. A substantial nuclear production program involving say 1,000 kilograms of plutonium per year, would be beyond the reach of many industrial nations. Initial costs would be of the order of $700 million to $1.4 billion. Operating costs would be approximately $50 million per year.[2] A much smaller program could be funded for an initial investment of about $80 million, with yearly operating and maintenance costs at the level of $20–25 million.[3] This minimal program would produce the nuclear material for about ten fission bombs per year.[4]

Shortages of skilled technological personnel would be more likely to impede a low level production program than the costs involved.

It must be expected that numerical shortages of the necessary skilled people will make it impossible for some countries wishing to do so to mount even the smallest nuclear power programme for military purposes. It is not merely that all the new countries of Africa, most of those in South America, and—with the exception of Israel—all of the countries of the Middle East would be unable to find enough of the right people to make nuclear explosives; even countries like Spain, Portugal, and Greece, in which advanced technologies are largely undeveloped, would find the problems of getting the men to make nuclear weapons insurmountable.[5]

This could be true even where other nations gave significant assistance in the construction of plutonium reactors.

The cost and complexity of a nuclear weapons program will also be affected by technological breakthroughs. A pure fusion bomb which did not require a fission "trigger" might have certain advantages over the typical fission-fusion combination of contemporary hydrogen bombs. A very abundant neutron source, provided for example by the harnessing of thermonuclear power, could facilitate the pure fusion process and make bombs of any composition relatively cheap and inexpensive. Whether the thermonuclear reactor would be cheap or exorbitantly costly, however, cannot presently be determined.

Finally, the diffusion of atomic bombs will depend upon what the Great Powers do to facilitate access. Except in the case of very important nuclear assistance to the British after 1958, the core nuclear states apparently have been hesitant to build up nuclear weapons capacity in other nations. The limited test-ban agreement recently signed by the United States, Britain, and the Soviet Union precludes assistance to other countries' nuclear test programs[6] and there is little indication that it is in the current interest of any of the three powers to develop nuclear capacity elsewhere on a national basis. The USSR apparently substantially curtailed the Chinese effort for a bomb by withdrawing her technicians three years ago; the United States, reconsidering the impact of the Nassau Agreement, seems now to be even more opposed to the proliferation of nuclear weapons.

The physical acquisition of nuclear bombs is likely to be the easiest stage in the evolution of an Nth country problem. Knowledge is available and minimal bomb programs can be financed at relatively

---

[2] Leonard Beaton and John Maddox, *The Spread of Nuclear Weapons* (London, 1962), p. 22.
[3] *Ibid.*, pp. 21–22.
[4] *Ibid.*, p. 5.

[5] *Ibid.*, pp. 23–24. The existence of toll enrichment facilities in other countries, however, could considerably ease the problem of shortage of scientific manpower.
[6] Partial Nuclear Test Ban Treaty, Art. I, par. 2. New York *Times* (Western ed.), July 26, 1963, p. 2.

slight cost. Though dissemination of weapons by the core nuclear states seems unlikely at present, the provision of reactor technology, even under control, contributes to the understanding necessary for a weapons program. The shortage of skilled scientific manpower is likely to represent the greatest limitation upon a nuclear weapons course, though this can and is being overcome with the passage of time. Atomic bombs themselves, will not be difficult to obtain.

DELIVERY AND COMMAND CAPABILITY

The physical ability to build a delivery, command and control system is presumably less widespread than the ability to manufacture a limited number of atomic bombs. As always, the requirements for an effective delivery capability are set by the preparations of the antagonist. Against non-nuclear states with rudimentary defense systems, subsonic bombers could provide a satisfactory delivery force. Boeing 707s or Douglas DC-8s are available to quite a number of countries, and even certain jet fighters might be re-equipped to carry nuclear weapons. At least eleven countries are capable of producing reasonably advanced jet fighter aircraft and others might obtain the obsolescent models of the major Powers.[7] The most significant constraint may be the absence of trained crews to man the airborne delivery system.

Supersonic bombers, on the other hand, would be likely to be more expensive and to entail a very substantial production effort. Subject to political criteria, such vehicles may be purchased for national use on the international market, but they are not likely to be pressed on enterprising claimants by the major nuclear states. Exclusive of the atomic energy establishment itself, Britain spent about $3 billion between 1948 and 1963 on the development of its deterrent, largely consisting of the V-bombers.[8] Total costs were probably more than half

again as much. Yet the subsonic V-bombers are vulnerable to Russian air defense. Supersonic delivery systems are likely to cost even more, as the French are now apparently discovering. Further, where the enemy is a developed nuclear foe, even supersonic aircraft do not assure reliable delivery on target.

Hypersonic ballistic missiles and associated systems are likely to be even more costly. Assuming a stabilization of the arms competition between East and West, one might expect unit costs of a standardized missile like the Minuteman to fall.[9] They would be likely to be reduced only for the Great Powers, however, where substantial economies of scale could be realized. If the arms race continues at its current pace, on the other hand, any individual missile system will have to be adjusted to avoid feasible enemy countermeasures. Under such conditions, the cost of strike or retaliatory systems will be likely to go up, not down. The marked rise in expenditure on nuclear vehicles which Albert Wohlstetter has noted for the recent past will probably be projected into the future.[10] As anti-ballistic missile systems become more sophisticated, moreover, even ICBMs may become vulnerable. Developments in anti-submarine warfare may conceivably reduce the utility of such concealed and mobile systems as the Polaris. The state of the art does not remain fixed while tyro or apprentice seek to master it. At the present moment it does not seem probable that lesser nuclear states could attain a position of stable deterrence as measured against either the systems of the United States or the Soviet Union. This is not to say, of course, that considerably more potent capabilities might not be developed against either ingénue nuclear or conventional powers.

Command and control arrangements

---

[7] Hohenemser, pp. 260–61.

[8] Statement by Defense Minister Peter Thorneycroft, *House of Commons Debates*, Jan. 30, 1963, col. 913.

[9] Cf. Herman Kahn, "The Arms Race and World Order," in Morton A. Kaplan, ed., *The Revolution in World Politics* (New York, 1962), pp. 335–36.

[10] Wohlstetter observed: "The cost of the first 100 B-58s, Atlas, or submarine-launched Polaris—including development and all other fixed and variable expenses needed for five years of peacetime operations—will be from three to five times greater than the costs of the first 100 B-47s."

pose additional obstacles. Even a quite ir-responsible state will wish to avoid un-authorized attacks upon other powers, and to ensure the success of a deliberate attack when it decides to mount it. Communica-tion with nuclear forces, and positive con-trol over nuclear devices, would be mini-mal requirements on both counts. Under nuclear or even large-scale conventional attack from an enemy, a nation will need protected command and control systems, first, to ensure retaliation, second, to devise an appropriate response. Without such sys-tems, a nuclear striking force might be beheaded and retaliation rendered ineffec-tive or impossible. Warning systems would be imperative to avoid a knockout blow. If a doctrine of controlled response is devel-oped, both command and control and coun-terforce capabilities would be necessary. Avoidance of spasm retaliation and the pro-tection of cities would involve preservation of intrawar deterrence. This in turn would depend upon complex nuclear control and guidance systems and upon the ability to withhold a portion of an attack force. Since small nations may be just as hesitant to com-mit suicide on behalf of a city-retaliatory strategy as larger states, a corresponding sophistication of weapon and control sys-tems may also be required. There is no cheap or easy way to a defense mechanism which is not prone to accident and yet may be flexibly used for diverse purposes once war is underway.

While obsolescent bomber and fighter aircraft have been available to smaller powers through purchase or gift from the core nuclear states, there is little indication that advanced delivery technologies will be provided to sustain a variety of indepen-dent "deterrents." Under the Nassau Pact the United States offered to allow Britain to buy Polaris submarine systems; the same overture was made to the French, and re-fused by General de Gaulle. The United States has now apparently changed its posi-tion and wishes to avoid further prolifera-tion either of atomic weapons or delivery systems. There is no indication that the So-viet Union has been more willing to enhance the military power of its allies or of neutral nations by granting them a very significant

nuclear delivery capability.[11] Such grants of technology seem even less likely now that a limited nuclear test ban pact with stric-tures on further atomic proliferation has been signed by the United States, the Unit-ed Kingdom, and Russia.

The military system into which nuclear weapons would be fitted would vary in ex-pense and elaboration with the countervail-ing measures of the enemy. A non-nuclear foe, lacking an adequate air defense, would be vulnerable to a rudimentary nuclear at-tack. If enemy retaliation were impossible, even a botched assault would not portend serious dangers, and liquidation of the core of enemy strength could be accomplished at leisure. Delivery and command systems would be neither complicated nor expen-sive. If, conversely, a foe's retaliatory pow-er were both flexible and substantial, op-posing systems would have to attain a corresponding subtlety. Military costs would rise in proportion. Against the omi-nous power of the two thermonuclear giants, no national "deterrent" in process of crea-tion or contemplation would be likely to do effective service. It is not sufficient to plan to possess by 1970 a truncated deterrent force which is the product of 1963 technol-ogy. Delivery, command, and control sys-tems do not constitute an insurmountable hurdle for the Nth country problem. But they do ensure that nuclear dilettantes will be unlikely to make the leap.

THE WILL TO GO NUCLEAR

Physical and economic capacity to pro-duce or procure atomic and associated de-livery and command systems does not guar-antee their acquisition. A nation may have the ability to do something which it con-sciously abjures. Not only capability, but also will is necessary. At this point impon-derables of psychology enter the scene, and prediction is chimerical. Yet, there are some guideposts on this otherwise perilous route. Leonard Beaton and John Maddox pointed out that it is not true that "no coun-try has resisted the temptation to make its

[11] Indonesia probably does not constitute an ex-ception to this statement.

own atomic weapons once it has acquired the physical ability to do so."[12] Canada and India have not taken up their options on a bomb, though they might do so at any time. Japan, a nation clearly capable of building a nuclear force, is determinedly hostile to nuclear weapons and has acceded to the partial test-ban accord. Sweden and Switzerland could both make the bomb in the not too distant future, but are extremely unlikely to do so.[13] Some states are aiming for an option on a bomb, not the bomb itself; others are apparently not even creating an option. Weapons are not spreading as ineluctably as the instruments of modern industrialism.[14]

In actuality incentives and disincentives to acquire nuclear weapons are not wholly disproportionate. And it is probably true that substance has been lent to the disadvantages of nuclear capacity in recent months. Reflex nuclear decisions of the past may be forced to yield to well-calculated balancings of costs and returns. Various historic incentives have been associated with the desire for nuclear weapons. In the British case, the desire to find a weapon to defeat Nazi Germany was the original precipitating cause of British weapons research, and the British program was set in train during World War II. After the war, Britain decided to continue the program though there was no immediate antagonist, accelerating it with the development of the cold war. Notions of sovereignty, nationalism, and Great Power status, however, were bound up with the postwar British effort on the bomb. Attlee himself claiming that the United Kingdom had to hold up its end against the United States. In certain respects perhaps, the British postwar decision was an almost unconsidered prolongation of wartime work. Britain was a Great Power; the United States had the bomb; why should Britain not possess it? Even intrawar discussions reveal nascent British

intentions to proceed with atomic weapons programs after the war.

In the French case national independence and prestige motivations figured importantly. A nation which had to depend for its defense upon another state was in some sense not fully sovereign. French grandeur was an objective of General de Gaulle, and this could not be acquired apart from nuclear weapons. In the French instance, also, the decision to build a nuclear weapon was apparently taken in the aftermath of the resounding defeat in Indo-China and the beginning of the Algerian war. Nuclear weapons might in some measure compensate for past defeats and help to prevent future ones. At the time the United States itself was relying on nuclear forces for the great burden of military tasks. Later on, General Gallois developed a rationale stressing the weakness of the American guarantee. From this point of view a national nuclear force was seen as a trigger on the force of a core power ally, ensuring all-out war at the instance of the national nuclear state. Little consideration was apparently given to the impact of such plans upon the firmness of the U.S. nuclear commitment to Europe. Attempts at ironclad and automatic guarantees on French terms would be likely to reduce the U.S. obligation and disrupt unified strategic planning. In any event the French *force de frappe ou disuasion* is not the reaction to a declining American commitment in Europe; it is the product of prior nationalism for which declining U.S. involvement is given as justification.

In the Chinese example, the incentives for nuclear capability are somewhat different. Neither China nor France nor Britain are likely to have a significant impact upon their immediate military environment. None of the three countries will probably be able to undertake military ventures in their own regions which they could not sustain without nuclear weapons. In the presence of great opposing force in all three cases, important military advances could not be hoped for. Unlike the British and French, however, the Chinese may hope for signal political gains in their theater. The Eastern European nations are not likely to

[12] Statement by Denis Healey quoted in Beaton and Maddox, p. 98n. Recently, moreover, there have been press reports of a future Swiss atomic capability.

[13] See *Ibid.*, chaps. 5, 8, 9, 10, and p. 189.

[14] *Ibid.*, p. 210.

be cowed into submission by the French "deterrent"; uncertain Asian nations may conceivably be awed by a Chinese nuclear capability. While in certain states a Chinese bomb will produce a positive and firm response, in others neutralism will be accentuated, and there will be pressures on the United States to follow a more "tractable" policy. Political vulnerabilities may well increase in certain regions. China's capability, thus, does not have to be measured against formidable Western forces, but rather against the sensitivities of Asian states already sharpened to a fine point by inordinate fears of nuclear war. In the Chinese instance, nuclear capability may produce dividends not found in other contexts.

If there are important incentives to attain nuclear status, there also are significant inhibiting factors. Largely unforeseen at the time Britain began its nuclear program, the costs of a viable nuclear capability may be very high indeed. If the objective is a realistic capability against the core powers, costs may be prohibitive. The advances in penetration systems previously attained by the two nuclear giants will probably be accompanied by advances in defensive systems in the next few years. Imitation of existing penetration weapons will not necessarily ensure deterrence for smaller nuclear powers. In this instance costs will intrude upon prior incentives. How much are prestige and status values worth? How much should be spent to further the rationale of American unreliability? Does a "deterrent" against Russia conflict with the assumption that a Russian attack is wholly improbable? The British are giving different answers to these questions than are the French.

Where the prospective enemy is a lesser state, nuclear expense may be more tolerable. Still, there are certain largely irreducible costs if one wishes to get over the nuclear threshold. Various plants must be built, even if a few bombs are to be produced. Costly research and development will have to be carried on, even if procurement of delivery systems is strictly limited. As Albert Wohlstetter points out: "There are huge 'entrance fees' for getting even one's first strategic missile and the communications and other elements to go with it. The costs of a small force are disproportionately high." Even costs of a demonstration capability will not be negligible.

This is not to say that relatively imposing nuclear capabilities cannot be acquired by other powers. But the expenses compared with the rewards are not so favorable as they once seemed. Nuclear weapons themselves do not automatically elevate a nation to Great Power status. At this writing major capabilities have been attained only by the United States and the Soviet Union; no other state has been able to match them. Potential nuclear states must now decide whether they will gain important national objectives through costly atomic weapons programs or whether their efforts will be vain. Cost-effectiveness calculations are even more relevant for potential Nth countries than they are for the United States.

Financial costs are not the only strictures a budding Nth power must contemplate. Moral and psychological debits may also be involved. If a nation has rested its international political prestige upon nuclear abstention and appeals for disarmament, it may find it difficult to embrace a nuclear course. At the present moment India shows no disposition to make nuclear weapons on her own, though she was not the first to declare her willingness to adhere to the partial test-ban treaty.[15] She may rely on the United States and Britain to protect her against China, and even perhaps on the Soviet Union.[16] In such an eventuality indigenous nuclear bombs would perhaps not be necessary even against a Chinese nuclear adversary. And they would enormously tarnish the escutcheon of Indian moralism in world politics. Neutralist moral supremacy could no longer be asserted to counterbalance Western and Soviet material power.

Psychological readjustments might also be involved in a decision for nuclear weap-

[15] See Michael Michaud, "India as a Nuclear Power," National Security Studies Program Paper (U.C.L.A., June 1963).

[16] The USSR was reported to have offered missiles to India in Aug., 1963. New York *Times* (Western ed.), Aug. 2, 1963, pp. 1 and 3.

ons. Just as it was true that nations with claims to a Great Power status often proceeded automatically and resolutely down the nuclear route, so it might follow that nations with no such pretensions would abjure a nuclear course. If nuclear weapons are attributes solely of major powers, small or middle powers may not consider them appropriate to their status. Canada might have become the second or third possessor of nuclear weapons, but elected not to do so. Her status in world affairs was apparently not deemed consonant with independent construction of nuclear bombs.[17]

External political costs may also accompany independent pursuit of nuclear weapons. In the context of the major alliance systems an "independent" nuclear power may find itself excluded from crucial decisionmaking processes and access to rewards. France and China have undoubtedly gained greater autonomy in national decisions, but they have lost correspondingly in participation in international decisions. Within NATO France probably exerts less influence than was once the case, and she no longer is the leader of the movement for European integration. In both military and political fields West Germany will probably emerge as the ultimate beneficiary of French nuclear intransigence. General de Gaulle's "independent" position has not merely served to raise his bargaining position within Western and alliance councils; it has raised the question whether France is a full and participating member of either group. In both French and Chinese cases alliance bonds have been attenuated, and it is no longer certain that alliances fulfill original purposes. Persistent assertion that an alliance cannot be relied on for nuclear defense may ultimately be a perverse form of self-fulfilling prophecy. An unwanted "independence" may eventually be obtained.

Nuclear capacity may also have the untoward impact of adding to a state's strategic vulnerability. It is by no means true that nuclear weapons are a net increment

to defensive power. Under certain circumstances a state may be more redoubtable without nuclear weapons than with them. Nuclear weapons add to both risks and strengths, and at certain stages the first may more than counterbalance the second. A vulnerable strategic capacity, for instance, which could be fired only on a first strike might be highly provocative without providing defensive reassurance. It would be added to an enemy's target list, but would not deter an attack. Those who desire to acquire nuclear bombs must first compile a catalogue of probable foes. While nuclear weapons may provide an advantage against certain weak non-nuclear states (a potentially cancelable gain) they may only serve as lodestone for attack against more powerful enemies. If anonymous delivery capabilities are ever attained, they will raise hazards for all nuclear countries. The criterion of anonymity for any one state is the ascription of "authorship" to others.

Finally, nuclear status may involve internal political costs. The "ban the bomb" movement is already widespread in Western countries, and it may effect others. It would, of course, be in error to assume that the diffusion of unilateralism will proceed coterminously with the diffusion of nuclear weapons. France manifests no such phenomenon, and in the Chinese case it would be unthinkable in every context but that of a radical transformation of the Communist regime. Japan and Denmark have no bombs, but a powerful unilateralist groundswell exists. It is unlikely that unilateralism will be a major feature of internal politics in the underdeveloped, nationalist countries in the near future. There are other political, social, and economic issues to preoccupy the electorate. If, on the other hand, the development of a nuclear weapons capability violated explicit political mandates articulated at the internal level, it could affect patterns of domestic support. In any event, the countries enjoying the most substantial economic, scientific, and industrial base for a weapons program would be those most prone to political revulsion directed against the bomb. With the signing of the limited test-ban treaty, and accession

[17] See Beaton and Maddox, chap. 5, and John Mueller, "Canada as a Non-Nuclear Power," National Security Studies Program Paper (U.C.L.A., June, 1963).

by more than 100 states, internal pressures against a nuclear course may mount. In the net, incentives and disincentives to nuclear capability are in rough approximation. The prestige and status arguments are offset by economic costs; the increment to defense positions by enhanced vulnerability; and the attempt to gain a foolproof trigger on an ally's force may have the impact of diluting the alliance bond. In some cases special political gains may flow from even a demonstration nuclear capacity, and in others the threatened or actual acquisition by an enemy of nuclear bombs may be a potent incentive to a national capability. Where diffusion is both rapid and asymmetrical, it may have unsettling international consequences.[18] Even in these instances, though, rapid and uneven diffusion will be affected by what the two core nuclear powers do. Diffusion in the non-bloc environment can be forced to meet standards of central block confrontation, if the two major powers intervene. The barriers to a viable independent nuclear capability can be raised.

GREAT POWER COUNTERACTION

National capacity and determination to make nuclear bombs still does not give rise to the full-blown Nth country problem. National capabilities may be subject to counteraction by the major powers. The measures the core nuclear states themselves take will affect the dimensions of national nuclear disruption. Capacity to delay re[s]ponse, protected command and control mechanisms, positive control devices of all sorts, and the "hot line" to the Kremlin will facilitate management of the problem. Catalytic and accidental war will be less likely to occur when "spoofing" or detonation can be fully investigated prior to action. The catalyst, moreover, will find it difficult to avoid involvement in the nuclear reaction. The smaller the number of countries possessing the bomb and appropriate delivery and command systems, the easier it will be to unmask the

[18] See Robert W. Tucker, *Stability and the Nth Country Problem*, I. D. A. Study Memorandum No. 5 (Washington, D.C., Nov. 8, 1961).

catalytic aggressor. Air defense systems will also make overt attack a rather unfruitful enterprise. A nuclear "catalyst" would have to possess systems roughly similar to those of the United States and the USSR to be sure of escaping detection, but if this requirement were met the instigator would be easy to identify. Only a very few states (if any) could attain capabilities comparable to those of the United States and the Soviet Union. The greater the approximation to invulnerability in any military-technological generation, the less likely it would be that the nuclear forces of the two major protagonists could be triggered inadvertently.

Great Power countermeasures, however, are not limited to intra-war defense or interdiction. There is much that may be done before the onset of conflict to prevent its occurrence. Political tactics include the isolation of the potential Nth power from rewards and the provision of benefits for those who renounce nuclear capacity. Alliance members can be disciplined by core nuclear powers where the threat or actuality of independent development is concerned. Insofar as the alliance serves the interests of the potential nuclear recalcitrant, exclusion from some of its benefits or protections may be of no little significance. Even outside the major alliance systems, pressure may be exerted upon potential non-bloc states. Neutralist states which had traditionally favored test-ban or other disarmament arrangements would be particularly vulnerable to this kind of influence. To the degree that suasion was exerted by both the United States and the Soviet Union, it would be even more difficult to resist, politically and internationally. Economic aid considerations would be of some moment. The U.S. Congress would be unlikely to support a fledging nuclear capability by loans or grants; Soviet decision-makers could well adopt the same attitudes. While France and China would still remain as sources of nuclear material and technology, it would not be in their interest to create capabilities elsewhere; the reverse would be more likely to be true. Even an Nth country worries about the state which will be N + 1.

The limited nuclear test-ban treaty will probably have a retarding influence upon the spread of nuclear capabilities. Under Article I, paragraph 2 of the pact, the three signatories (the United States, Britain, and Russia) undertook "to refrain from causing, encouraging, or in any way participating in, the carrying out of any nuclear weapon test explosion or any other nuclear explosion anywhere"[19] which would take place in the forbidden environments. As President Kennedy observed later, this obligated the three powers not to assist "other nations to test" in such realms.[20] While the test-ban treaty was no more than "an opening wedge" in the campaign to prevent proliferation of nuclear weapons, it seemed likely to have an important impact upon the nuclear spread. The pact placed a moral imprimatur upon the renunciation of weapons tests, and thereby asked nations to stand up and be counted on the nuclear issue. Those which had avoided commitment in the past had to declare themselves as accessions snowballed. Nuclear weapons, of course, can be made without a testing program, and there is no known instance of a nuclear test which failed in the sense that the bomb did not detonate. Precise weapons effects, however, are difficult to ascertain in the absence of tests. In addition a prohibition on atmospheric testing was likely to raise political as well as scientific obstacles to the pursuit of a nuclear weapons capability. In many countries accession to the treaty will be taken as political *bona fides* of the intention to remain a non-nuclear power.

The test-ban, moreover, may pave the way for "further limitations on the spread of nuclear weapons."[21] Restrictions on the export of highly sophisticated and/or long-range delivery systems, upon information relating to warhead design or reentry techniques could conceivably follow. In certain continents where nuclear weapons have not penetrated, like Africa or Latin America, it might be possible to agree to nuclear-free zones. Such accords could represent pilot nuclear disarmament schemes, and provide a laboratory for experimentation with inspection and verification techniques.

If political measures failed to stem the spread of weapons, more drastic tactics might be employed. It would be possible for the two major nuclear states to provide defensive surface-to-air missiles for protection against nuclear attack. Radar warning nets might be extended to smaller nations potentially threatened by nuclear attack from a newly emergent Nth power. More substantial defense commitments might be extended from the major nations to states imperiled by the sudden development or introduction of nuclear weapons into new regions. At minimum this would pose risks for the aggressor more formidable than those raised by the defender; at maximum the aggressor might have to contemplate a full-scale confrontation with one of the nuclear giants. In this way the threshold of an effective nuclear capability could be raised to prohibitive levels by the involvement of superpowers. If none of these techniques succeeded in dissuading an aggressive Nth country, coercive disarmament might be essayed. Such intervention would be a tactic of last resort, but it might be effective where a state had flouted the interests of its neighbors on myriad occasions and was about to wage aggressive nuclear war. International political sentiment might support intervention for disarmament purposes where all other alternatives had failed.

The Nth country problem, in short, does not attain to significance merely because one or more nations have both the capacity and the will to make a nuclear capability. That determination must be sustained in the face of counteraction by major powers and by the non-nuclear sector of the world. The measures the major powers take to reduce the vulnerability of their own forces to inadvertent or miscalculated firing will lower the probability of central war. The diplomatic tactics employed to prevent the spread of weapons or to neutralize them militarily where they exist will lower the probability of local war. Counteraction will not only affect the unstabilizing impact of weapons diffusion,

[19] New York *Times* (Western ed.), July 26, 1963, p. 3.
[20] New York *Times*, July 27, 1963, p. 2.
[21] Kennedy Speech, New York *Times*, July 27, 1963, p. 2.

it will also reduce the incentives for further diffusion. If nuclear weapons do not reassert a bygone independence or make possible military or political action that was impossible to sustain by conventional capabilities they add little but expense to national position and prestige.

NUCLEAR IRRESPONSIBILITY

Even if all aforementioned hurdles are o'erleaped, however, the Nth country phenomenon is not necessarily transmuted into the Nth country problem. For the international environment to be drastically altered by the diffusion of weapons, a state's nuclear capacity, resolution, and evasion of counter-measures must be capped by reckless action. The Nth country problem does not thrive on the capability to disrupt the international system; it rests on concrete disruption. Unless the capacities that are acquired are used for destabilizing purposes, the international system remains intact.

Opportunities for reckless activity vary with international context. A nation in one of the major alliance system[s] enjoys one set of options; a state in the non-bloc area possesses another. The Nth power ally may engage in separate nuclear planning and even separate nuclear action. But the possible consequences are not reassuring. The nuclear alliance with the core power may give way to nuclear dissociation in an extreme moment of peril. It is a fine line of policy that the nuclear ally must follow: he must evade the direction of the core power in alliance affairs, political and strategic; but he must not jeopardize his ultimate nuclear support. His "independence" should be used for the purpose of acquiring greater control of his major ally's strategic force, not of losing control altogether. Intrinsically then, direction and dissociation are linked on a continuum. Reckless action to avert the former may ensure the latter. Hence, highly provocative nuclear action runs the greatest risks and concretely jeopardizes the alliance. A higher integration of all nuclear forces might be an ultimate solution, but if attained, it would preclude national nuclear disruption and so bypass the Nth country problem.

In the non-bloc area reckless action might be less dangerous to the general international peace and thus more permissible. Even in this realm, however, constraints apply. As India discovered belatedly, lack of defensive preparations may force a neutralist state into a de facto alliance with one of the major powers. Indeed, many neutralists presume such de facto alliances in perilous contingencies. President Nasser relied upon such connections in the Suez affair and came out unscathed. Such informal bonds, however, would be unlikely to survive a nuclear strike by a non-bloc power on a helpless victim. More plausibly, the Nth power might have to confront the operation of such a de facto alliance on behalf of his opponent. It is impossible to have it both ways: either states have informal major power support, or they are free to impose and accept risks on their own. It takes egregious confidence, however, to plan on support for aggression and disinterest in self-defense. If the major states are involved at all, they will be likely to affect decisively the outcome of a nuclear encounter. Even non-bloc nations, then, may hazard their national substance in an aggressive nuclear attack. President Kennedy noted that as nuclear weapons were diffused there would be "an increased necessity for the great powers to involve themselves in otherwise local conflicts."[22] This presumption should serve as warning to those nationalist powers who believe that their nuclear wars will not be of interest to the major states.

The disruptive impact of the Nth country phenomenon depends not only on reckless action of new nuclear states, it is determined by how many such actions are initiated. The magnitude of disruption rises roughly as a multiple of the number of disruptors. If only a very few states clamber over the hurdles of nuclear and delivery capacity, counteraction and concrete disruption, the impact on the international system may be held within bounds. In any international environment there will be a few lunatics; possessing nuclear weapons and ancillary capacity, they could cause trouble and they could kill thousands of

[22] *Ibid.*

people. If only a few disturbers exist, however, they will be far easier to deal with than if they are in abundant supply. The source of a nuclear aggression may be located; anonymity or pseudonymity is much less likely. The destabilizing impact on the central balance is slight. Moreover, the disadvantages of reckless nuclear action in such a context will be obvious. Even brandishing nuclear weapons, all new nuclear states are not going to "shoot the moon." Some will be cowed, not inspired.

And others, significantly, will have learned responsibility in the employment of weapons. A slow rate of diffusion, as Samuel Huntington points out, "will permit both governments acquiring the weapons and other governments affected by the acquisition time to adjust their politics and diplomacy to the new situation." The United States and the Soviet Union learned responsibility over time and in the absence of prior models of nuclear decorum. Now such models exist, and they may exert some influence for the newly enfranchised nuclear power. It no longer seems necessary for nuclear states to proceed tediously and laboriously through the three stages outlined by Henry Kissinger; there is knowledge aforethought.

Even for those states which evade the barriers to a functioning nuclear capability, there are still obstacles to concrete disruption. Allies may hesitate to press their radical policies too far for fear of endangering the strategic guarantee. Non-allies may jeopardize de facto support or become the object of powerful nuclear countermeasures. The few states who are able and willing to offend may be readily identifiable, and thus incapable of action. Others may avoid disruption and behave responsibly. The diffusion of weapons may be as phenomenological as problematic.

CONCLUSION

This does not mean that there can be no such thing as the "Nth country problem." But fundamental disturbance of the present international system will not automatically occur upon the manufacture of nuclear bombs by other countries. There is much that can be done to retard the spread in the first instance and to ameliorate its consequences in the second. It is possible that "independent" nuclear capabilities will lose attraction for those states which are willing to calculate costs and benefits.

There is a suppressed inconsistency in many of the arguments about the Nth country problem. On the one hand it is claimed that nuclear weapons serve no purpose for Nth countries; on the other that the diffusion of weapons will seriously disrupt or disable the international environment. National nuclear capabilities are not valuable to their owners because they cannot inflict great destruction upon enemies or commit allies to all-out war. National nuclear capabilities are dangerous to the major states because they may raise the likelihood or level of destruction and raise the probability of central nuclear war. Both contentions are unlikely to be true simultaneously. National capabilities are either significant or insignificant: if they are significant, they are an advantage to their possessor and a disadvantage to the system; if they are insignificant, they are of no use to their owners and of no concern to the system.

The inconsistency is real, but misleading. The thresholds of significance in the two cases are different. A national nuclear power demands substantial advantages to justify embarking on a costly program of independent nuclear development. His questions are: "Can deterrence be achieved?" "Will I be able to trigger the force of my ally?" "Can I attain the special prestige of a Great Power in world politics?" Relatively formidable capabilities are necessary to ensure favorable answers. If they cannot be attained, incentives are no longer fully operative. But a capacity which is too small to be helpful to an Nth power may yet be significant for purposes of the system. The system is concerned not with what one capability will accomplish, but with the impact of serial accumulation of national capabilities. Each incremental capacity raises slightly the probability of accidental or deliberate war, though it may not enhance the position of its holder.

It is in this sense that the Nth country phenomenon is linked with the Nth country problem. It may be possible to neutralize the additional dangers to the system th[r]ough countervailing political or military measures. But the balance is not automatically redressed; it can be redressed only by concrete action. The Great Powers must protect their own forces against inadvertent firing, discourage diffusion by political means, and dissuade action by diplomatic or in last resort by military means. The international system is not self-adjusting; it must be equilibrated by individual or multilateral action. In the absence of such balancing activity the Nth country phenomenon is the Nth country problem. The diffusion of weapons then, may not in the last resort unsettle the system, but it does enjoin resolute action to ensure stability.

The consequences of the dispersion of nuclear weapons cannot yet be foreseen. At one extreme there is the completely bipolar world, parceled into two gigantic nuclear camps; at the other is a largely multi-polar system and a considerable retraction and reduction of Great Power influence. Various forms of these situations are imaginable. The most dangerous outcome would be a tight bipolar system, where any conflict of lesser states entailed a probability of central war. The United States and the Soviet Union would be far more involved in political outcomes all over the globe than is now the case, and they would be involved on diametrically opposite sides. A second outcome could be large-scale dissociation. The Soviets and the United States would reduce their commitments on an area or nation, rather than be drawn into its nuclear conflicts. A third solution could be joint Western-Soviet activity to reduce the impact of the Nth country phenomenon. This would undoubtedly mean greater involvement of both powers in the affairs of third countries, but it would not be intervention on opposite sides. In such nuclear matters unipolar solutions might be imposed. Outcomes would vary from case to case; in some instances involvement might succeed in reducing the destabilizing consequences of diffusion or in preventing it from happening; in others outside influence might fail, and dissociation would be required. The

final balance would be partially neutralized bipolarity with multi-polar facets.

Insofar as Great Power involvement characterized the situation the probability of local war would decline. Insofar as the major states were involved on the same side, the probability of central war would also fall. Where dissociation was the order of the day, local war would be more likely, but the probability of central war need not rise. Nuclear dispersion may possibly be managed.

This collective study has rehearsed the past and present implications of the nuclear spread. To mid-1963 the diffusion of weapons had gone rather slowly, but its portents were not bright. Britain and France were partially spurred to obtain weapons to vindicate a departed eminence. Nationalist assertion was present in both cases. The Chinese may use nuclear weapons symbolically to further their political penetration of Asia and to enhance overall international status. Within NATO the nuclear issue has been vexed: the alliance hesitated to accept continued American direction of strategic affairs; yet could not agree on a multilateral compromise. Neither the French national solution, nor a European integrationist solution seemed both acceptable and feasible. The future of technology remained uncertain, and equal cases could be made for redemption as for Doomsday.

A preliminary assessment would stress the possibilities of political and diplomatic intervention in a technological process. Nuclear information is very widely diffused; but nuclear capabilities need not spread implacably. Many have written of the Nth country problem as if it were a fact of nature to which, perforce, mankind would simply have to adjust. But nuclear military forces are the results of human decision based on evaluation. The incentives which spurred nuclear development in the past need not accelerate it in the future. Nationalism may militate against nuclear force as well as for it. Not only are physical capabilities not diffusing rapidly, there are powerful means of dealing with them as they spread. The dispersion of weapons is not purely technological; it is eminently a problem in strategy and politics.

THE STRATEGIC CONSEQUENCES OF
NUCLEAR PROLIFERATION

BY JAMES R. SCHLESINGER

The impression has grown that dire consequences will inevitably flow from failure to prevent the further spread of nuclear weapons. In part, this apprehension reflects the argumentation and propaganda put forth in the endless sessions of the Seventeen Nations Disarmament Conference at Geneva. The slow pace of those deliberations suggests that in practice the several governments feel something less than their well-advertised sense of urgency. Nonetheless there is widespread public concern, to which political leaders quite naturally respond.

Much of the public discussion of the issue seems to be predicated on the conviction that proliferation poses a single, dominating threat to the continued existence of mankind. Senator Robert Kennedy has asserted, rather melodramatically, that without an anti-proliferation treaty "the chances of the survival of mankind on this planet beyond the twentieth century would become remote." At a more parochial level, it is argued that continuing proliferation would call into question the survival of the United States.

Contrary to the usual view, the most weighty reasons for apprehension are political rather than strategic. The spread of weapons may generate fear, and when publics or governments become fearful, they are likely to adopt unfriendly and divisive policies. Borders may be more rigorously policed, internal security tightened, and the tolerance of dissent diminished. Even on the strategic level, proliferation would bring certain untoward consequences, if only by increasing the number of uncertainties affecting international tensions and thus adding to the problems of managing the world. The truth is, however, that without substantial U.S. or Soviet assistance, the strategic capabilities that other nations can achieve out of their own resources would be too limited to alter the power balance.

Consider the exaggerations regarding the threat to the United States. By adopting measures that would reduce the damage that limited nuclear forces could inflict and by adjusting its policies, the United States can reduce the risks to itself to very low levels. Such steps would maintain the already enormous gap between U.S. military capabilities and those possessed by the lesser powers. The effects would be that (1) the ability to inflict damage on the United States would be kept low; (2) the United States, if it so desired, would remain in a position to deter attack by lesser nuclear powers against third countries; and (3) the incentives to acquire nuclear capabilities would be weakened—and hopefully reduced toward the vanishing point. This ability to demonstrate that acquisition of nuclear weapons cannot significantly alter the strategic balance provides in the long run the best hope of controlling proliferation and its consequences.

If proliferation does take place we may continue to complain about it, but we shall live with it. And leaders who now assert that nonproliferation is indispensable to our security will presumably find other subjects to dramatize.

The fact that existence will continue to be quite tolerable is not, however, the only reason for allaying public anxiety over proliferation. An attitude of despair regarding the spread of nuclear weapons can be more than misleading; it can seriously

Reprinted by permission from *The Reporter*, Vol. 35, No. 6, October 20, 1966. Copyright 1966 by The Reporter Magazine Company.

Mr. Schlesinger is Director of Strategic Studies at the RAND Corporation and the project leader of a RAND study on nuclear proliferation. Before joining RAND in 1965, Mr. Schlesinger was a Professor of Economics at the University of Virginia.

reduce the chances for establishing effective control. By understating the difficulties of acquiring a serious nuclear capability and by exaggeratiig its advantages, we may strengthen the incentives for acquisition. The danger inherent in exaggerated chatter about the damage that additional nuclear forces can achieve is that it encourages the false notion of nuclear weapons as "the great equalizer" in international conflict. IIopefully, most nations will perceive the fallacy. Others, however, may be lured into believing that nuclear weapons will provide adequate protection, or alternatively an effective instrument of blackmail.

To indicate the way in which such illusions can be fostered, Senator Kennedy has misappropriated these words of his brother the late President: "Every man, woman, and child lives under a nuclear sword of Damocles hanging by the slenderest of threads, capable of being cut at any moment by accident or miscalculation or by madness." The "sword" in President Kennedy's United Nations address obviously referred to American and Soviet capabilities. The Senator's point, however, is that each additional nuclear capability, no matter how slight, automatically creates an additional Damoclean threat. This is simply not true, for the damage potential of such nuclear forces is sure to be strictly limited. It is essential to recognize that the danger of nuclear spread is above all a quantitative problem subject to fairly exact calculation. In the public excitement over the threat of proliferation, failure to perceive this point generates needless anxiety and fosters the illusion of nuclear weapons as equalizers.

DIMENSIONS AND MEASUREMENTS

Any serious attempt to assess the dimensions of the proliferation threat should begin with some calculations of the varying levels of investment involved. The range of possible nuclear capabilities is tremendous, and the distinctions to be drawn among them in relation to size and vulnerability are of prime importance. Consider the existing array of nuclear capabilities. The United States, which has invested most heavily, possesses a nuclear force that not only is a solid deterrent but also is not incredible in terms of a carefully controlled counter-military initial strike. The Soviet Union, which has invested less, has an impressive second-strike force, which is an effective deterrent. Britain possesses a much more limited and declining force, presently dependent for delivery on obsolescent aircraft. The French *force de frappe* is even more limited in terms of damage potential against the Soviet Union, though it is scheduled to exploit more advanced delivery systems produced in France. Finally, the Chinese capability—presently drawing the lion's share of attention—is barely past the embryonic stage.

The degree to which a nuclear force is strategically useful and credible is determined by its size and sophistication and by the vulnerability of the society it is designed to protect. Strategic posture in turn ultimately depends upon the ability to inflict and to limit damage. All these are roughly correlated with the volume of resources that the society has invested or is able to invest in nuclear arms and delivery systems. The cost of developing a nuclear force that could seriously disturb the two superpowers is staggering. A nation must be prepared to spend anywhere from $3 to $5 billion annually—and these expenditures would continue for a decade and longer. Such sums run well beyond what most nations have been prepared to spend —including some that are now members of the nuclear club. Additional resources are required not only for delivery systems and compatible weapons but also for such indispensable items as reconnaissance and intelligence. Any nation contemplating a confrontation with a superpower had better learn something about the location and capabilities of its opponent's air and missile defense systems.

To indicate the size of the outlays involved, take the matter of weapons development and stockpiling. Up to now the United States has invested on the order of $8 billion merely on the *development* of nuclear weapons. On AEC operations generally, including provision of the weapons stockpile, it has now appropriated close to

$40 billion. These are substantial sums. How many nations are in a position to spend even twenty or twenty-five per cent of these amounts?

The cost of a modern system is in itself very substantial, conditioned as it is by the requirements of highly sophisticated weapons. To develop a warhead for an early-generation missile with limited thrust and size (the initial goal of a program for an aspiring nuclear power), there must be heavy investment in weapons testing in order to get yield-to-weight ratios to a point where a weapon adequate for target destruction can successfully be delivered in the vehicle. Major investment in guidance technology is required simply to ensure that missiles will be accurate enough to place weapons near the point targeted—whether military bases or cities. In this respect, it is vital to recognize the intertwining relationship between weapon size and weapon accuracy. With large-yield weapons, considerable inaccuracy may be tolerated. However, with the very low-yield weapons of the sort that can be developed with small amounts of money and yet be delivered with limited-payload vehicles, the accuracy requirements become very severe.

It follows that no nation is going to be in a position to develop a strategic capability that is both sophisticated and cheap. In the absence of major investments or extraordinary outside assistance, the only option open to most nuclear aspirants is the aerial delivery of rather crude nuclear weapons. Though such capabilities can, of course, dramatically transform a regional balance of power (if the superpowers remain aloof), the superpowers themselves will remain more or less immune to such limited nuclear threats. For the foreseeable future, only the Soviet Union will be able to deliver the requisite megatonnage to threaten major devastation in the United States. Threats from elsewhere may be faced down.

The two superpowers therefore will remain in a position in which they can dominate any nuclear confrontation. Only a superpower—and in this connection the term applies particularly to the United States —will be able to intervene in such confrontations in third areas. If the United States is willing to pay the costs and to run the risks, other nations—including the present three minor members of the nuclear club—will continually be deterred. Furthermore, their capabilities will remain vulnerable to a disarming first strike—unless they are given protection by an associated superpower. In any showdown with a superpower, a minor nuclear power relying on its own resources will simultaneously be deterred and be subject to disarming.

The likelihood that the first nuclear war, if it comes, will originate in and be confined to the underdeveloped world should play a prominent role in any assessment of proliferation's consequences. The penalties for proliferation would be paid, not by the United States or the Soviet Union, but by third countries. Much of the public discussion to date has led some in the underdeveloped countries to conclude, on the contrary, that the major powers would be the chief beneficiaries of curtailing the spread. If nuclear spread is to be effectively opposed, it should be made crystal clear just whose security is placed at risk.

COUNTERMEASURES

The effort to dissuade additional states from acquiring nuclear capabilities, while good in itself, is not likely to be wholly successful. We should recognize realistically that the long-run problem is how to live with the spread with minimal risk. This implies that any effective controls will require continuing effort over a considerable time. If we take the position that any increase in the number of nations claiming nuclear-weapons status spells failure, then the second-stage opportunities for control will be lost.

What are these additional opportunities? First, if new weapons programs are launched, we may hope to keep them as limited as possible. Second, we can take steps to reduce the risk that these weapons will actually be employed. Moreover, such measures may also serve to weaken the motives for acquiring weapons.

The means at our disposal to limit the

effectiveness of budding nuclear forces are mainly indirect. The primary element here is to keep at a high level the cost of all components and materials essential to nuclear capabilities. Through rigorous controls we can hope to limit indirect assistance on the part of American or other commercial suppliers. Above all, we should make every effort to see that the support of peaceful nuclear programs from whatever quarter is not diverted to support of military programs. To be sure, the mechanisms for control are imperfect. Costs alone will not necessarily prevent other nations from seeking nuclear capabilities. And our ability to influence the decisions of other sovereign states is obviously limited. Nonetheless, something can be accomplished.

Certain steps can be taken to reduce the risk that new capabilities, once achieved, will be actually employed or, if they are employed, to limit the potential damage they may cause. One would be to buttress the air-defense capabilities of threatened states. A more controversial possibility would be the deployment of new systems that would sharply reduce the damage that Nth countries, including China, could eventually inflict on the major nuclear powers. An ABM (anti-ballistic missile) system of the kind long debated as a further protection against major nuclear attack provides a current example. Such a system, enormously costly to be sure, would involve complex calculations on arms control, strategy, and cost effectiveness, but one of its by-products would be additional insurance against the harmful consequences that could flow from proliferation. Through such measures, the American ability to prevent the misuse of nuclear capabilities would be strengthened. The strongest deterrent to threats by a lesser nuclear power is the possibility that a major nuclear power will enter the lists against it.

Given the existing preponderance of U.S. power, the deployment of major new systems may not be essential. Less costly measures, however, are both feasible and desirable. For example, assuming a world in which there was an increasing number of uncontrolled nuclear powers, we should invest considerable effort in developing methods for identifying the debris of nuclear weapons and their supporting intelligence systems that in a crisis would enable us quickly to ascribe responsiblity for any detonation that occurs. We would then be in a position to mete out punishment, if it served our policies, for any such irresponsible act.

An approach of this sort, which relies on superpower preponderance, is not one that is universally and automatically appealing. It dramatizes the strategic gap, whereas some would argue that muting the differences in power provides a better means for obtaining arms stability. Certain comments seem needed regarding this point of view.

First, the gap in military nuclear power between the superpowers and other nations is enormous and will continue to be so. It is, in fact, more likely to increase than diminish. What is really important is to recognize that. the gap permits the superpowers to exert a stabilizing influence on the restless third areas of the world and on the ambitions of lesser nuclear powers. It would be unwise to ignore or neglect this potential stabilizing function merely in order to maintain a spurious myth of equality among sovereign nations.

Second, nuclear capabilities in third areas will be unsophisticated and vulnerable. This being the case, the likelihood of nuclear aggression through a hair-trigger response seems obvious. Most persons who seek a more peaceful world should welcome the ability of the superpowers to forestall the initial use of such capabilities.

Third, many nations, even when they strongly disapprove of specific aspects of U.S. policy, want the United States to stand ready to counter nuclear threats against nations lacking the means of self-protection. If the United States is expected to play the role of a nuclear Galahad, risking retaliation and loss of population in behalf of others, it does not seem unreasonable for the United States to possess protective measures of a type not universally available in order to hold the potential losses to a minimum.

THE OUTLOOK

The strategic importance of proliferation has tended to be exaggerated because the problem has been viewed in terms of the number of nations that might acquire a small capability rather than in terms of the destructive potential of any given capability that might be achieved. As far as we can see into the future, the strategic environment will continue to be dominated by the preponderant military power of the United States and the Soviet Union. The willingness of either one or both to use power independently in regions of less than vital concern could be inhibited by the spread of weapons, but the degree of inhibition would depend on the level of risk deemed acceptable. It is difficult to envisage conflicts in third areas escalating into direct nuclear exchanges between the major powers. Therefore, the risk involved in the spread of nuclear weapons is imposed primarily on other nations. The superpowers will continue to be relatively immune; the threat to them will continue to come primarily from each other. Once clearly recognized, this asymmetrical distribution of the risks could become an effective curb on the nuclear ambitions of lesser powers.

While nuclear spread is basically destabilizing, its strategic consequences can be contained. Limited nuclear capabilities cannot play the role of "equalizers" in international conflict. The strategic position that the United States and the Soviet Union currently enjoy is so unassailable that even continuing action by third parties is unlikely to upset the central strategic balance for the next twenty years. Properly exploited, this central strategic balance could continue to provide some stability in regional conflicts—even in the face of nuclear spread.

CHAPTER 4

Limited War: The Strategies for Today

Having studied the category of general war and the closely related issue of arms control, the next category on the spectrum of conflict is that of limited war. Our basic premise established in Chapter 1 is that an all-out thermonuclear exchange between superpowers would not be a rational use of force. But because general war can occur, we concentrate on ways to deter it. And, if general war should occur, we hope to be able to limit it and its damage.

A second premise is that because of the high risks and costs of general war and the superpowers' recognition of those risks and costs, limited war is the level of conflict more likely to occur. That is, limited war is more likely to involve the actual use of force than general war. Thus, limited war strategies are the action strategies for today.

Recognizing that there is no consensus regarding "categories" of limited wars, we have divided our discussion of the topic into (A) Noncentral War and (B) Counterinsurgency. Since we define central war as war involving strikes on the homelands of two opposed superpowers (today the United States and the Soviet Union), all other wars are noncentral wars. Accordingly, counterinsurgencies become subspecies of both limited wars and noncentral wars. What we refer to as noncentral war is often called either local war or simply, limited war. We prefer the title noncentral because it emphasizes that the geographic locale is other than the superpowers' homelands and because it also avoids the inference that general wars are unlimited.

A. NONCENTRAL WAR

The previous chapter dealt with the limitations of arms themselves, not their direct use. Robert Osgood, the first author in this chapter, states that "As long as the necessary international political conditions for the limitation of armaments do not exist, the best assurance that armaments will not destroy civilization lies in the limitation of their use." Osgood then develops a rationale for limitations. The second author, Morton Halperin, sketches the evolution of American strategy, an evolution which is characterized by an increasing emphasis on limitation. The increased emphasis is seen both in general war where the shift has been from the unlimited strategy of massive retaliation to the limited strategies of controlled response and counterforce and in a shift in emphasis from concern with general war to a concern with limited war.

One basic strategy for noncentral war is a policy of alliances. Henry Kissinger examines the theory of coalitions in the nuclear age. Bernard Brodie's critique of NATO, the major example of our alliance structure today, illustrates the complexity of modern alliance policies. Flexible response, the strategy which emphasizes the use of conventional forces, is presented by its most noted proponent, Maxwell Taylor.

Traditionally, flexible response focuses on battle by attrition. In contrast, Thomas Schelling views war as essentially a bargaining process in which opponents trade "hurts" or punishments. This is the strategy of conflict called "compellence," in which messages can be communicated by combatant actions on the field of battle. Schelling is perhaps the most fascinating author writing on defense policy today. He unveils new ideas such as "tacit bargaining," a process which provides insights as to how opponents can coordinate their expectations; and also the idea of the importance of the "art of commitment." Increasing compellence over time can be considered as a definition of escalation, a strategy for which Herman Kahn's escalation ladder serves as a framework.

Views on the possible use of nuclear

weapons in noncentral wars have changed over the years. Fifteen years ago a discussion on that subject would have focused on a conflict in Europe which would have involved large numbers of small-yield nuclear weapons—"Tactical Nuclear War." The intervening wars have forced us to consider the possibilities of conflict in Asia and the increasing sophistication of our strategic thought has led us toward a greater concern with limitation. Therefore, a discussion on the possible use of nuclear weapons in noncentral wars today would include the consideration of possible Asian conflicts and would focus upon the use of very few nuclear weapons—"The Nuclear Option."

The major effect of using nuclear weapons in a noncentral war today would not be its effect on the tactical situation, but its indication of determination and its establishment of a bold new precedent concerning the future use of nuclear weapons. Thus, if the United States exploded one nuclear weapon in the defense of a besieged position (like Khe Sanh in Vietnam in the winter of 1968), its major effect would not be the destruction of hundreds of North Vietnamese or the saving of the U.S. position, but the signal of our resolve and the creation of a new precedent regarding the role of nuclear weapons. In the final two articles on noncentral wars, Bernard Brodie and Thomas Schelling argue the pro and con of "the nuclear option."

B. COUNTERINSURGENCY

The first two authors on counterinsurgency are perhaps the most experienced and knowledgeable experts on that subject: Sir Robert Thompson and the late Bernard Fall. Both discuss the principles involved in counterinsurgency and both focus on the same point: that while counterinsurgency involves a mixture of the military and political, it is the political which is in the long run decisive. As Fall puts it, "When a country is being subverted it is not being outfought; it is being outadministered. Subversion is literally administration with a minus sign in front."

The final article, by Paul Kecskemeti, examines three major causes of insurgency: nationalism, populism (land and economic reform), and communism.

THE THEORY OF LIMITED WAR

BY ROBERT E. OSGOOD

THE PRINCIPLE OF POLITICAL PRIMACY

In practice, the limitation of war is morally and emotionally repugnant to the American people. Yet it is in accord with America's own best principles. The explanation of this paradox lies partly in the fact that Americans have not understood the relation between military force and national policy, and so they have misconceived the real moral and practical implications of national conduct. Therefore,

Reprinted by permission from *Limited War: The Challenge to American Strategy* (Chicago: The University of Chicago Press, 1957), pp. 13–27 and 236–51. Copyright 1957 by The University of Chicago Press.

Mr. Osgood is Director of the Washington Center of Foreign Policy Research and Professor of Political Science at the Johns Hopkins University School of Advanced International Studies. He has published several books and many articles on U.S. foreign and military policy. His most recent work is, with Robert W. Tucker, *Force, Order and Justice* (1967).

it is imperative at the beginning of this study to develop a sound conception of the relation between force and policy as the first step in examining the requirements of an American strategy of limited war.

The justification of limited war arises, in the most fundamental sense, from the principle that military power should be subordinate to national policy, that the only legitimate purpose of military force is to serve the nation's political objectives. This principle of political primacy is basic to all forms and all uses of military power, whether employed overtly, covertly, or only tacitly. It is as applicable to the formulation of military policies and military strategy as to the actual waging of war. In this principle morality and expediency are joined.

The principle of political primacy is essential to the nation's self-interest because military power is of no practical use as a thing in itself but is useful only insofar as it serves some national purpose. It is useful because it is a prerequisite of national security and because upon security all other national goals depend. Coercion is an indispensable feature of all human relations in which basic security and order cannot be guaranteed by the innate sympathy, reasonableness, and morality of men. The essential role of coercion is especially large in international relations, where institutional organization is anarchical or rudimentary and the bonds of law, custom, and sentiment are relatively impotent as against the intense ties of loyalty binding men to their separate and sovereign national groups.

The practical necessity of military power is obvious to Americans today, but it is not always so obvious that military power does not automatically translate itself into national security. Military power may actually be translated into national insecurity when it is employed without a proper regard for its non-military objectives and consequences. Without intelligent and vigilant political control even the most ef-

fective use of military force, by purely military standards, will not necessarily bring comparably satisfactory political results. A capricious, impulsive, or irresponsible use of military power cannot be expedient; for when military policy and strategy lack the guideposts of limited and attainable objectives and become, in effect, ends in themselves, they cease to be controllable and predictable instruments of national policy.

The individual soldier, even the commander of a battle, may sometimes promote the national interest by the kind of boldness that does not calculate the results of military action too closely, but it would be a dangerous error to apply to the whole complex problem of harmonizing military policy with national policy in accordance with an over-all strategic plan the far simpler imperatives of the battlefield. In the field of national strategy, uncalculating heroism is mere self-indulgence at the expense of national survival.

In order that military power may serve as a controllable and predictable instrument of national policy, it must be subjected to an exacting political discipline. This discipline depends upon the existence of controlling political objectives that bear a practical and discernible relation to specific policy goals. These kinds of objectives are, pre-eminently, those that envision specific configurations of power supporting the nation's security. A treaty recognizing specific international relationships; the control or protection of a certain geographical area; the establishment, recognition, or security of a particular regime; access to certain material resources—these are the kinds of objectives that must form the hard core of politically disciplined power.

One must add, because the rule is so frequently violated in practice, that the controlling political objectives in the use of military power must be not merely desirable but also attainable. Otherwise, there will be no practical and discernible relationship between ends and means. Of course, there are an indefinite number of possible objectives toward which nations may direct military power. One can easily establish a whole hierarchy of interdependent objectives, leading from the most insignificant to the most desirable objective imaginable. However, only a very limited number of these objectives will ever be closely enough related to available national power to serve as a controlling political discipline. Unless the nation's objectives pertain to specific and attainable situations of fact, they will remain in the realm of aspiration, not in the realm of policy; and, consequently, the essential condition for the primacy of politics over force will not exist. Therefore, one can describe the principle of political primacy in terms of the following rule: In the nation's utilization of military power, military means should be subordinated to the ends of national policy through an objective calculation of the most effective methods of attaining concrete, limited, and attainable security objectives.

The principle of political primacy described in this rule is as cogent on moral grounds as on grounds of national self-interest. At the outset, before examining the moral basis of the principle, one must recognize that the primacy of policy over power can be moral only if the political ends toward which military power is directed are themselves moral—or, at least, as consistent with universal principles as the ambiguities of international relations permit. But even if one assumes that this is the case (as I shall for the purposes of this book), one can hardly judge the moral validity of either political ends or military means aside from their interrelationship. The following discussion focuses upon this interrelationship, which is only one aspect of the broader problem of reconciling national policy with liberal, humane ideals that transcend purely national purposes. The principle of political primacy does not embrace all the moral problems that arise in the use of military power. It does not, for example, deal with the question

of when or under what circumstances a nation should employ force. However, it is of vital relevance to the question of how and for what purpose a nation should employ force.

The moral basis of political primacy is also its practical basis: the principle that armed force ought to be treated as a means and not an end. Force gains moral justification only by virtue of its relation to some valid purpose beyond its own immediate effect. Furthermore, even when it is a means to a worthy end, armed force must be morally suspect—not only because it is inhumane but because, like all forms of coercion, it is subject to the corruption that accompanies man's exercise of power over man. In Lord Acton's words, "Among all the causes which degrade and demoralize man, power is the most constant and the most active." Certainly, the exercise of military power holds extraordinary opportunities for the degradation of its user and the abuse of those against whom it is used.

But the problem of force is not so easily dismissed. Once we admit that it is morally suspect, we are involved in a moral dilemma. On the one hand, in an ideal world men would dispense with all forms of coercion and settle their conflicts by impartial reference to reason and morality; or, at least, they would channel coercion in social directions by legal controls, which receive the consent of the community. Yet, on the other hand, we know that in the real world men are not sufficiently unselfish or rational to make this ideal practicable. The abolition of force in society would lead either to the anarchy of unrestrained egoism or else to the tyranny of unrestrained despotism. Because of the imperfection of man, force is a moral necessity, an indispensable instrument of justice. Therefore, men are confronted with the fact that their own imperfection makes both force and restraint of force equally imperative from a moral standpoint. There is no way to escape this dilemma. Men can only mitigate its effects. The aim should be, not to abolish force in society, but to moderate it and control it so as to promote social purposes in a manner most compatible with ideal standards of human conduct. How can we translate this principle into the use of military power?

We commonly assume that force is least objectionable morally, as well as most effective practically, when it is exercised with a minimum of violence—preferably, as in the case of police power, when it is implied rather than directly exercised and when it is exercised legitimately, that is, in accordance with the general consent and approval of society. This assumption suffices for the conduct of everyday affairs within the national community, because the conditions which make it practicable are present—primarily, the conditions that permit force to be exercised in accordance with the orderly procedures of law and government. These legitimate restraints not only moderate force and channel it in social directions; they also provide the individual members of a nation with the basic security they need in order to feel safe in voluntarily subordinating their self-interest to the general welfare.

However, the same procedures for moderating, controlling, and channeling force in socially sanctioned directions do not exist among nations, where the bonds of law, custom, and sympathy are frail and rudimentary. In this age national egoism has such a compelling hold over men's minds that each nation must look to its own independent exercise of power merely in order to survive. The exercise of military power among nations is subject to few of the formal and informal restraints that permit altruism to operate among individuals and groups within nations.

This situation makes a vast difference between what is justifiable in the exercise of force in national society and what is justifiable in international society. It means that among nations military force becomes an indispensable means for promoting national self-interest but a thoroughly ineffective means for attaining the great universal moral goals that transcend national self-interest. This is true, in the first place, because every exercise of military power must be tainted with self-interest and, secondly, because the imperatives of national power and security do not closely conform to the dictates of universal morality.

But military force is not only ineffective as an instrument for attaining transcendent moral goals; it is morally dangerous as well. It is dangerous because the exercise of force for such grandiose goals tends to become an end in itself, subject neither to moral nor practical restraints but only to the intoxication of abstract ideals. The explanation for this tendency lies in the nature of supranational goals. Aside from the powerful tendency of national egoism to corrupt idealistic pretensions, supranational goals are too remote and too nebulous to discipline a nation's use of force. When the determining objective of force is an ideological goal, there is no way of knowing precisely when force has achieved its purpose, since the tangible results of force have no clear relation to the intangible tests by which the attainment of such goals must be measured. When a conflict of wills is put to the test of force, the final restraint and control of force must be the resolution of the conflict by accommodation, unless it is to continue until one party obtains complete acquiescence or both parties become impotent. But differences of principle, unlike conflicts of interests, by their very nature resist accommodation. Rather, they tend to arouse passions that can be satisfied only by the unconditional surrender of the adversary. Therefore, in effect, the great idealistic goals, once put to the test of force, become the rationalization of purely military objectives, governed only by the blind impulse of destruction.

That is not to say that moral principles are unjustifiable or irrelevant in a nation's use of military power or that the exercise of force, either overtly or tacitly, cannot indirectly promote ideal ends. The point is simply that universal principles must be translated into practical courses of action, directed toward achieving specific situations of fact appropriate to the nature of force, in order to constitute truly moral and rational guides for the exercise of military power. Only if the realization of these principles is conceived as a by-product of attaining concrete limited objectives can they exert a civilizing influence upon national egoism. The great idealistic goals that have traditionally provided the dynamism and inspiration of American foreign policy, insofar as they can be attained at all by military means, must be attained through a series of moderate steps toward intermediate objectives, defined in terms of national power and interest.

An important corollary of the principle of political primacy may be called the economy of force. It prescribes that in the use of armed force as an instrument of national policy no greater force should be employed than is necessary to achieve the objectives toward which it is directed; or, stated another way, the dimensions of military force should be proportionate to the value of the objectives at stake.

Clearly, this is an expedient rule; for unless a nation has a large surplus of available military power in relation to its policy objectives, one can hardly conceive of the effective use of power without the efficient use as well. Moreover, as an examination of the interaction between military means and political ends will show, the proportionate use of force is a necessary condition for the limitation and effective control of war.

The moral implications of an economy of force are no less significant. For, as we have acknowledged, the violence and destruction that accompany the use of force are an obvious, though sometimes necessary, evil. Therefore, it is morally incumbent to use force deliberately and scrupulously and as sparingly as is consistent with the attainment of the national objective at stake.

In applying the principle of political primacy we must make allowances for the legitimate claims of military considerations

upon national policy as well as the other way around. The relationship between military means and political ends should be understood as a two-way relationship, such that the ends are kept within range of the means as well as the means made adequate to attain the ends. Common sense tells us that a nation must decide what it ought to do in light of what it is able to do; that it should establish policy objectives in the light of military capabilities. Otherwise, military power will be no more effective or politically responsible than if it were employed as an end in itself.

Moreover, we must recognize the fact that, however scrupulously we may seek to impose political discipline upon military power, military power will remain an imperfect instrument of politics. To a disturbing extent it bears its own unpredictable effects, which create, alter, or preclude the objectives for which it can feasibly be employed.

However, this does not obviate the necessity of determining the claims of military means upon political ends—so far as conscious control permits—within the general framework of national strategy; for in the absence of such a framework there can be no clear criterion for judging the validity of any claims. In other words, if military power is to serve as a rational instrument of policy, the entire process of balancing ends and means, co-ordinating military with non-military means, must be subordinated to the controlling purpose of pursuing national policy objectives.

WAR AS AN INSTRUMENT OF NATIONAL POLICY

The principles of political primacy and the economy of force apply to the whole spectrum of military power in its various uses, not just to its active use in warfare; but this book is concerned primarily with their application to war itself. There is a good reason for stressing this aspect of military power: In all uses of military power, whether overt, covert, or tacit; in all accumulation, allocation, and distribution of military power; and in all military planning there is at least an implicit assumption that the basic measure of a nation's power is its ability to wage war in defense of its interests. In the struggle for power among nations, the ability to wage war has something of the status of a common currency by which nations can roughly measure their capacity to achieve certain basic needs and desires—ultimately, if necessary, by violence.

However, the ability to wage war cannot be measured in purely quantitative terms of military power. A nation can be adequately prepared to wage one kind of war under one set of circumstances and inadequately prepared to wage another kind of war under a different set of circumstances. The utility of a nation's military power, either in diplomacy or in war itself, will depend not merely upon the size and firepower of the military establishment but also upon its suitability for countering the specific kinds of military threats impinging upon the nation's interests and objectives. Thus the effectiveness of military power depends upon the nature of the military threat, the nation's estimate of that threat, and its ability to fight the kind of war that will successfully meet the threat. It depends, equally, upon the nation's will to wage war; the way in which it combines force with diplomacy; how it enters war, how it terminates war, and how it conducts policy after a war. In other words, the effectiveness of military power depends not only upon a nation's physical and technical command of the means of warfare but, just as much, upon its whole conception of war—especially, the relation of war to international politics. And this conception of war is reflected throughout the whole spectrum of military power—in defense policies and the formulation of military strategy as well as in the actual conduct of war. Therefore, since a nation's military power depends upon its conception of war, it behooves us to act upon a conception of war that is compatible with

the use of military power as a rational instrument of national policy. That conception must be based upon the principle of political primacy.

But, first, let us be clear what we mean by "war." War can be defined most simply as an organized clash of arms between sovereign states seeking to assert their wills against one another. However, it would be a mistake to regard war as a single, simple, uniform entity or as an independent thing in itself, to which one applies a wholly different set of rules and considerations than properly apply to other forms of international conflict. It is more realistic in the light of the complex and multifarious nature of international conflict to regard war as the upper extremity of a whole scale of international conflict of ascending intensity and scope. All along this scale one may think of sovereign nations asserting their wills in conflict with other nations by a variety of military and non-military means of coercion, but no definition can determine precisely at what point on the scale conflict becomes "war." In this sense, war is a matter of degree, which itself contains different degrees of intensity and scope.

Accepting this description of war, we must see how the principle of political primacy applies to the conduct of war. The primacy of politics in war means, simply, that military operations should be conducted so as to achieve concrete, limited, and attainable security objectives, in order that war's destruction and violence may be rationally directed toward legitimate ends of national policy.

On the face of it, the validity of this principle seems clear enough; and yet in its practical implications it does not meet with ready or universal acceptance. In fact, quite contrary principles of war have commonly received the applause of democratic peoples. For example, in the Kellogg-Briand Pact of 1928 the United States and fourteen other nations promised to "renounce war as an instrument of national policy in their relations with one another," thereby expressing in treaty form a wide-spread conviction that is still congenial to the American outlook. The principle is valid, of course, if it is interpreted merely as a proscription against unprovoked aggression; but insofar as it implies the divorce of war from the ends of national interest, it is valid neither practically nor ideally. In this sense, nations might better renounce the use of war as an instrument of *anything but* national policy.

Karl von Clausewitz, the famous German military theorist of the nineteenth century, expounded the principle of political primacy with an unsurpassed cogency. In his famous work *On War* he concluded his comprehensive analysis of the mass of factors comprising war by singling out their unifying characteristic. This, he believed, was the essential basis for apprehending all war's complexities and contradictions from a single standpoint, without which one could not form consistent judgments. He described that characteristic in the following words:

Now this unity is the conception that war is only a part of political intercourse, therefore by no means an independent thing in itself. We know, of course, that war is only caused through the political intercourse of governments and nations; but in general it is supposed that such intercourse is broken off by war, and that a totally different state of things ensues, subject to no laws but its own. We maintain, on the contrary, that war is nothing but a continuation of political intercourse with an admixture of other means . . . . Accordingly, war can never be separated from political intercourse, and if, in the consideration of the matter, this occurs anywhere, all the threads of the different relations are, in a certain sense, broken, and we have before us a senseless thing without an object.

As a description of the actual nature of war, Clausewitz' dictum that war continues political intercourse is by no means universally true; but as a statement of what war should be, it is the only view in accord with universal moral principles and national self-interest, for it is the only view

consistent with the use of force as a means rather than an end. If we find this view as repugnant as the sentiment of the Kellogg-Briand Pact is congenial, then we have not fully grasped the practical and moral necessity of disciplining mass violence. On the other hand, many who can agree with Clausewitz' dictum in the abstract find it difficult in practice to accept the corollary that victory is not an end in itself. Nevertheless, the corollary is logically inseparable from the principle of political primacy. For if war is not an end in itself, but only a means to some political objective, then military victory cannot rightly be a self-sufficient end. If war is a continuation of political intercourse, then success in war can be properly measured only in political terms and not purely in terms of crushing the enemy. To be sure, a measure of military success is the necessary condition for achieving the political objectives of war; but the most effective military measures for overcoming the enemy's resistance are not necessarily the most effective measures for securing the continuing ends of national policy in the aftermath of war.

Therefore, one of the most important practical implications of the principle of political primacy is this: The whole conduct of warfare—its strategy, its tactics, its termination—must be governed by the nature of a nation's political objectives and not by independent standards of military success or glory. Statesmen, far from suspending diplomacy during war, must make every effort to keep diplomacy alive throughout the hostilities, to the end that war may be as nearly a continuation of political intercourse as possible rather than "a senseless thing without an object."

THE DIMENSIONS OF WAR

The practical requirements of maintaining the primacy of politics in the conduct of war are not so clear as the general principle, for the general principle must be qualified in the light of the actual conditions of war. The most serious qualification results from the difficulty of controlling the consequences of war as the dimensions of violence and destruction increase. This difficulty emphasizes the importance of striving for an economy of force.

Despite the theoretical validity of the principle of political primacy, in practice we must recognize that war is not a delicate instrument for achieving precise political ends. It is a crude instrument of coercion and persuasion. The violence and destruction of war set off a chain of consequences that can be neither perfectly controlled nor perfectly anticipated and that may, therefore, contravene the best laid plans for achieving specific configurations of power and particular political relations among nations.

At the same time, the legitimate claims of military means upon political ends are particularly strong when national conflict reaches the extremity of war. The sheer physical circumstances of the military struggle may narrowly restrict the choice of military means that nations can safely employ. To subordinate military operations to political considerations might mean sacrificing the military success indispensable for the attainment of any worthwhile national purpose at all. Therefore, in practice, military necessities and the fortunes of war may determine the nature of the feasible political choices, and the subordination of certain political considerations to military requirements may be the necessary condition for avoiding defeat.

However, the need for compromising political objectives in the light of immediate military necessities only qualifies, it does not negate, the applicability of the principle of political primacy; because the wisdom of such compromises must still be judged by their relation to some superior political objective if purely military objectives are not to become ends in themselves. Clausewitz acknowledged this very qualification and reconciled it with his view of war as a continuation of political intercourse in words that are compelling today. While recognizing that the political object of war could not regulate every aspect of

war, he nevertheless maintained that war would be sheer uncontrolled violence without this unifying factor:

Now if we reflect that war has its origin in a political object, we see that this first motive, which called it into existence, naturally remains the first and highest consideration to be regarded in its conduct. But the political object is not on that account a despotic lawgiver; it must adapt itself to the nature of the means at its disposal and is often thereby completely changed, but it must always be the first thing to be considered. Policy, therefore, will permeate the whole action of war and exercise a continual influence upon it, so far as the nature of the explosive forces in it allow . . . What now still remains peculiar to war relates merely to the peculiar character of the means it uses. The art of war in general and the commander in each particular case can demand that the tendencies and designs of policy shall be not incompatible with these means, and the claim is certainly no trifling one. But however powerfully it may react on political designs in particular cases, still it must always be regarded only as a modification of them; for the political design is the object, while war is the means, and the means can never be thought of apart from the object.

If, then, the principle of political primacy holds good despite the considerable claims of military necessity, the task of statesmen is to minimize the difficulties and maximize the potentialities of political control. There are three closely related rules of general application that would greatly facilitate this purpose:

1. Statesmen should scrupulously limit the controlling political objectives of war and clearly communicate the limited nature of these objectives to the enemy. The reason for this is that nations tend to observe a rough proportion between the scope of their objectives and the scale of their military effort; that is, they tend to exert a degree of force proportionate to the value they ascribe to the objectives at stake. Therefore, the more ambitious the objectives of one belligerent, the more im-

portant it is to the other belligerent to deny those objectives and the greater the scale of force both belligerents will undertake in order to gain their own objectives and frustrate the enemy's. In this manner a spiral of expanding objectives and mounting force may drive warfare beyond the bounds of political control.

2. Statesmen should make every effort to maintain an active diplomatic intercourse toward the end of terminating the war by a negotiated settlement on the basis of limited objectives. This rule rests on the following considerations. War is a contest between national wills. The final resolution of this contest must be some sort of political settlement, or war will lack any object except the purely military object of overcoming the enemy. To the extent that statesmen keep political intercourse active during hostilities, war becomes a political contest rather than a purely military contest. The immediate object of political intercourse must be a negotiated settlement, but a negotiated settlement is impossible among belligerents of roughly equal power unless their political objectives are limited. This consideration becomes especially important in the light of the fact that even a small nation that possessed an arsenal of nuclear weapons might, in desperation, inflict devastating destruction upon a larger power rather than accept humiliating terms.

3. Statesmen should try to restrict the physical dimensions of war as stringently as compatible with the attainment of the objectives at stake, since the opportunities for the political control of war—especially under the conditions of modern war, with its tremendous potentialities of destruction —tend to decrease as the dimensions of war increase and tend to increase as the dimensions of war decrease. This proportion between the dimensions of war and its susceptibility to political control is neither universally true nor mathematically exact; but as a rough generalization it finds important verification in the history of war. Three underlying reasons for this fact are especially germane to the war-

fare of this century:

a) The greater the scale and scope of war, the more likely the war will result in extreme changes in the configurations of national power. These extreme changes are not amenable to control; they result more from the internal logic of the military operations than from the designs of statesmen. At the same time, they tend to create vast new political problems which confound the expectations and plans of the victor and the vanquished alike. Moreover, modern war can change the configurations of power not only through the massive destruction of material and human resources but also by disrupting the whole social, economic, and political fabric of existence. On the other hand, when the destructiveness and the resulting disturbance of the configurations of power are moderate, the chances of anticipating and controlling its political effects are proportionately greater; and the whole character of warfare, in proportion as it is removed from the domination of military events, becomes more nearly a continuation of political intercourse.

b) The magnitude of a war's threat to national survival is likely to be proportionate to the scale and the scope of hostilities. But in proportion as the belligerents' very survival is threatened, they must logically place a higher priority upon immediate military considerations as compared to political considerations. For when war reaches extremities, a belligerent must calculate that even the slightest interference with the destruction of the enemy in the most effective manner possible for the sake of some uncertain political maneuver will involve an exorbitant risk of the enemy destroying that belligerent first. Military victory, no matter how it comes about, at least provides a nation with the opportunity to solve its political problems later; whereas the dubious attempt to manipulate the vast and unpredictable forces of war in precise political ways may end by placing this postwar opportunity at the disposal of the enemy. When immediate military considerations are at such a premium, political control must obviously suffer accordingly; but, by the same reasoning, when the scale and scope of a war impose no such immediate threat of total defeat, the primacy of politics can more readily be asserted.

c) As the dimensions of violence and destruction increase, war tends to arouse passionate fears and hatreds, which, regardless of the dictates of cold reason, become the determining motives in the conduct of war. These passions find their outlet in the blind, unreasoning destruction of the enemy. They are antithetical to the political control of war, because political control would restrict the use of force. Thus the greater the scale of violence, the greater the suffering and sacrifice; and the greater the suffering and sacrifice, the less the inclination either to fight or to make peace for limited, prosaic ends. Instead nations will seek compensation in extreme demands upon the enemy or in elevating the war into an ideological crusade. Unlimited aims will, in turn, demand unlimited force. Thus, in effect, the scale of war and the passions of war, interacting, will create a purely military phenomenon beyond effective political guidance.

In the light of this proportion between the dimensions of warfare and its susceptibility to political control, the importance of preserving an economy of force is apparent. For if modern warfare tends to exceed the bounds of political control as it increases in magnitude, then it is essential to limit force to a scale that is no greater than necessary to achieve the objectives at stake. By the same token, if war becomes more susceptible to political control in proportion as its dimensions are moderated, then the economy of force is an essential condition of the primacy of politics in war.

THE RATIONALE OF LIMITED WAR

If this analysis is sound, the principal justification of limited war lies in the fact that it maximizes the opportunities for the effective use of military force as a rational instrument of national policy. In accordance with this rationale, limited war would be equally desirable if nuclear weapons had never been invented. However, the existence of these and other weapons of mass destruction clearly adds great urgency to limitation. Before nations possessed nuclear weapons, they might gain worthwhile objectives consonant with the sacrifices of war even in a war fought with their total resources. But now the stupendous destruction accompanying all-out nuclear war makes it hard to conceive of such a war serving any rational purpose except the continued existence of the nation as a political unit—and, perhaps, the salvage of the remnants of civilization—in the midst of the wreckage. Only by carefully limiting the dimensions of warfare can nations minimize the risk of war becoming an intolerable disaster.

Beyond this general reason for limiting war, which applies to all nations equally, there are special reasons why democratic nations should prefer limited war. Obviously, limited war is more compatible with a respect for human life and an aversion to violence. But apart from humanitarian considerations, we should recognize that liberal institutions and values do not thrive amid the social, economic, and political dislocations that inevitably follow in the wake of unlimited war. The liberal and humane spirit needs an environment conducive to compromise and moderation. Only tyranny is likely to profit from the festering hatreds and resentments that accompany sudden and violent upheavals in the relations among governments and peoples. The aftermath of the two total wars of this century amply demonstrates this fact.

The external interests of democratic powers are not necessarily identified with the status quo in all respects, nor do they require that the rest of the world be democratic. Clearly, neither condition is feasible. However, they do require that the inevitable adjustments and accommodations among governments and peoples should be sufficiently moderate and gradual to permit orderly change. Long-run interests as well as immediate interests of democratic nations lie in preserving an external environment conducive to relative stability and security in the world.

The mitigation of sudden and violent change becomes all the more important in a period like the present, when the most resourceful tyranny in the modern world strives to capture an indigenous revolution among colonial and formerly colonial peoples who yearn to acquire the Western blessings of national independence and economic power but who are fearfully impatient with the evolutionary processes by which the West acquired them. In these areas peace may be too much to expect, but we can anticipate revolutionary chaos or Communist domination if the world is seized by the convulsions of unlimited war.

Finally, we must add to these considerations one of even broader significance. As long as the necessary international political conditions for the limitation of armaments do not exist, the best assurance that armaments will not destroy civilization lies in the limitation of their use.

* * * * *

Assuming that the United States maintains an adequate capacity for total war and that the Communists continue to conduct a rational and cautious foreign policy, designed to gain their ends by indirection and limited ventures rather than by massive military assault, the chief function of our capacity for total war will be to keep war limited and to strengthen our diplomacy against the blackmail that a strong and unscrupulous power can wield. However, the fulfilment of this function will not be sufficient for the purposes of containment unless it is accompanied by a ready capacity to resist lesser aggressions by limited war. Otherwise the Communists can confront us with the choice between total war, nonresistance, and ineffective resistance; and the results of that situation would probably be piecemeal Communist expansion, the paralysis of Western diplomacy,

and the further disaffection of uncommitted peoples.

Therefore, preparation for limited war is as vital to American security as preparation for total war. It is a matter for thorough and systematic planning, not for improvisation. After all, in developing our capacity for total war we are preparing for the least likely contingency; its principal justification lies in the fact that it may never be used. But in developing a capacity for limited war we would be preparing to meet the most likely contingency; we woud be maintaining the only credible military deterrent to Communist advances in the most vulnerable areas of the world.

THE LIMITATION OF POLITICAL OBJECTIVES

The specific requirements of a strategy that will enable the United States and its allies to deter and fight limited wars must be determined in the light of the many forms such wars can assume and the great variety of circumstances under which they may occur. These wars may vary in character from guerrilla actions to a massive clash of modern arms. They may result from clandestine Communist support of an indigenous revolution, from the intervention of Communist "volunteers" in a war between smaller powers, or from a direct invasion across a well-defined boundary. As an increasing number of smaller powers acquire the will and strength to act according to their independent designs, the United States may have to consider intervention in wars that do not directly involve Communist powers at all. One can readily imagine the different means by which limited wars might have to be fought in the Formosa Straits, the jungles and swamps of Southeast Asia, the mountains of Afghanistan, or the deserts of the Middle East.

The detailed military plans to meet these varied requirements are beyond the scope of this study; but we can properly formulate the essential guidelines for these plans. These guidelines extend from the framework of the two general prerequisites of limited war: the limitation of political objectives and the limitation of military means. What do these prerequisites mean in terms of a strategy of limited war under contemporary military and political conditions? Let us examine the question of limited objectives first.

Clearly, the over-all strategic objective of containment requires that the specific political objectives for which the United States must be prepared to fight limited wars will not entail radical changes in the status quo. The very fact that a war remains limited although the belligerents are physically capable of imposing a much greater scale of destruction assumes that neither of the belligerents' objectives constitute such a serious challenge to the status quo as to warrant expanding the war greatly or taking large risks of precipitating total war. However, this does not mean that we must necessarily confine our war objectives to the exact territorial boundaries and the other political conditions that existed prior to aggression. This kind of mechanical requirement, making no allowance for the dynamic, unpredictable elements of war, would impose rigid political constraints, unrelated to the actual balance of military power and the enemy's response. Moreover, if potential aggressors could count upon ending a war in at least no worse position than they began it, they might come to regard this situation as an irresistible invitation to launch a series of limited incursions at a minimal risk in proportion to the possible gain.

In the final analysis the precise objectives of a war can be determined only in the light of the specific circumstances in which it occurs. However, this does not mean that the objectives should be left entirely to improvisation. They should be derived from a pre-existing framework of concrete political aims, expressing the particular power interests of the United States throughout the various strategic areas of the world. This is a matter of balancing power and commitments, of combining force with policy, in advance of crises, so

that when crises occur, the government will not be forced to formulate under the pressure of the moment the kind of basic judgments of strategic priority and enemy intent that are essential to the rational conduct of war.

The Korean War illustrates the dangers of ignoring this rule. Although we did manage to improvise limited objectives once the war broke out, these objectives had no clear relation to our strategic planning before the war. Throughout the war the government gave the unfortunate impression of being in doubt about its own aims, as well as the aims of the adversary. Our objectives during the war suffered unnecessary ambiguity because they seemed to be more the product of intuition and changing military fortunes than of firm military and political policies formulated in the light of an over-all national strategy. Clearly, our general commitment to the Truman Doctrine and the principle of collective security was no substitute for strategic forethought; in fact, our reliance upon these generalities tended to obscure rather than to clarify the determining objectives of the war.

This is not to say that wartime political objectives should or can be formulated with the precision of legal documents prescribing binding rules in perpetuity. What is necessary is that the government establish concrete, feasible objectives, sufficiently well defined yet flexible enough to provide a rational guide for the conduct of military operations, and that it communicate the general import of these objectives —above all, the fact that they are limited —to the enemy. The importance of this requirement is evident in view of the fact that one of the essential elements of limited war is the operation of some kind of system of mutual self-restraint based upon the belligerents' observance of a reasonable proportion between the dimensions of war and the value of the objectives at stake.

Political objectives need not be made explicit at all times in order to serve their proper function of limiting and controlling war. The method of conducting military operations, especially the particular military restraints observed, may convey the nature of determining political objectives more effectively than explicit announcements. But since the political character of limited war is all-important, diplomacy— the public statement of positions, the private exchange of official views, the bargaining over terms—is an indispensable instrument of limitation, not only for communicating objectives but for terminating hostilities on the basis of accommodation. However, diplomacy is not something that nations can readily turn on and off. It operates best when it is in continual use. Diplomacy is not apt to serve its moderating function during war unless there exists in advance of war an expectation that neither side will push things too far without recourse to political accommodation.

Admittedly, there are grave difficulties in conducting useful diplomatic relations with Communist powers. The Communists do not regard diplomacy as a means of ironing out conflicting positions among nations sharing a fundamental harmony of interests. They regard it, rather, as a device and a tactic for pursuing an inevitable conflict of interests. Nevertheless, there is nothing to indicate that they are unwilling to strike bargains of mutual advantage. They neither make nor accept concessions as a tender of good will, but we should not on that account exclude compromises that advance our interests as well as theirs. They understand better than we that diplomacy, like force, cannot properly be divorced from power; rather it is a function of power. If we were to comprehend the function of diplomacy as an instrument for attaining limited political objectives in conjunction with military force, rather than as an alternative to force, we would be in a better position to cultivate useful channels of communication for keeping the present struggle for power cold and limited.

When one considers the general requirement of the formulation and communication of limited objectives, one must also take into account the method of promulgating strategic objectives. For the impression of its objectives that the government seeks to convey through diplomacy can be undone by the way in which it publicly announces its strategy. The essential requirement here is that the government announce its strategy in such a way as to make credible its limitation of objectives and its ability to back them up with proportionate force. This is not a matter of giving fuller publicity to the details of American strategy but rather of publicizing strategy in words that correspond with capabilities and intentions and that avoid raising false expectations. It would be foolish to try to relieve potential aggressors of all their doubts about our intentions under every conceivable circumstance, even if we could know those intentions ourselves. But it would be dangerous to leave them with the impression that our conduct is reckless, capricious, and unrelated to our words. And the point is equally applicable to the impression we convey to allied and uncommitted nations.

Unfortunately, much of the hyperbole we use to convince ourselves that we are conducting our strategy in the American way convinces others that we are incurably aggressive. Foreign states are peculiarly sensitive to our emphasis upon military considerations and the ideological aspects of the cold war. The bold phrases which, presumably, give us courage make our allies shiver. It is ridiculous that we should be the ones to bear the onus of militarism and imperialism when it is the Communists who have the huge armies and who have been the determined expansionists while we have had to be begged and frightened into making the minimum effort necessary to defend even the positions essential to our security. But if our bellicose talk is the obverse of our pacific inclinations, we cannot expect other nations to appreciate that paradox. Sometimes we even fool ourselves into taking this talk at face value. Perhaps if we were clear in our own minds about the limited nature of our strategic objectives, we would be in a better position to clarify the thoughts of others. And then we could place the onus of militarism and imperialism where it belongs.

THE LIMITATION OF MILITARY MEANS

The problem of limiting the political objectives of war and national strategy is inseparable from the problem of devising limited military means. Unless we have military policies, weapons, techniques, and tactics capable of supporting limited objectives, we cannot have an effective strategy of limited war; for containment depends less upon what we say than upon what we are ready to do. An effective strategy requires more than the mere formulation of objectives; it requires a balance between objectives and means, such that the objectives are within range of the means and the means are commensurate with the objectives. Otherwise, we shall have to intrust our security to bluff, improvisation, and sheer luck.

One great difficulty in developing a military establishment and a military strategy and tactics capable of meeting the threat of limited war lies in the fact that the requirements for limiting war do not necessarily correspond with the requirements of fighting limited wars effectively; and yet the fulfilment of one requirement is incomplete without the other. Therefore, nations must be ready to weigh the risk of expanding wars against the need for military success. In balancing these two factors the importance of the political stakes must be the crucial determinant.

At the same time, the requirements of both military limitation and effectiveness are, in themselves, complicated by the great variety of circumstances under which limited wars might have to be fought. The kind of measures that would be effective in fighting a limited war in the Formosa Straits might be ineffective in Thailand or incompatible with limited war in Iran. Moreover, both the limitation and the effectiveness of military operations embrace a number of separate but related criteria, which are not susceptible to precise measurement. The scale of war, for example, can be limited in area, weapons, targets, manpower, the number of belligerents, the duration of war, or its intensity. And military effectiveness must be measured not only by physical capabilities on the battlefield but also by the political and psychological consequences of various measures and the relation of these measures to the general resources of the United States and its allies, especially manpower and economic potential.

The proper blending and balancing of all these considerations in a coherent strategy assumes an accurate anticipation of the response of potential adversaries to a wide range of measures and circumstances. Such an anticipation will depend upon calculating the value that the potential adversaries attach to various objectives and the proportionate effort they are willing to expend upon achieving them or upon preventing us from jeopardizing them. And this sort of calculation must rest upon a sound appraisal of their intentions, strategy, and general international behavior.

Moreover, we must anticipate the response to our policies and actions in terms of a two-way interaction, calculating that the adversary will respond on the basis of his own anticipation of our counter-response. In other words, the course of action—the means of resistance and deterrence—upon which we plan to rely under different circumstances must be determined in the light of the same kind of complex calculation of response and counter-response that chess players or boxers must make. Therefore, it is too simple to operate on the principle that successful deterrence depends merely upon letting potential aggressors know that they will suffer damage outweighing any possible gains from aggression; for the same measure might also cause the potential aggressor to respond in a way that would impose intolerable penalties upon our own interests. Calculating the deterrent effect of this risk upon our own actions, the aggressor might well conclude that he could safely ignore our threat. The Chinese Communists seem to have done this very thing in supporting the Viet Minh seizure of Dien Bien Phu.

Thus the first requirement of deterrence is that it be credible to the potential aggressor; and credibility, in turn, requires that the means of deterrence be proportionate to the objective at stake. This commensurability may be difficult to achieve in practice, but the underlying principle is simple enough: it is the principle of economy of force, without which the reciprocal self-restraints essential to limited war cannot exist.

Even this elementary outline of the general considerations concerning the limitation of military means should leave no doubt that the different factors involved and the complexity of their relationship to one another confront American strategists with a perplexing problem of military planning. Nevertheless, if we are at least aware of the various elements that enter into the military equation, it should not be beyond our ingenuity to devise means of preparing the nation for the most serious contingencies of limited war. After all, there are only a limited number of areas in which such wars might occur, and there are only a limited number of circumstances, or kinds of circumstances, from which they are likely to arise.

The history of American strategy since 1947 strongly suggests that we have excluded from our military planning some of the central elements in the equation of limitation, that we have obscured them with handy but misleading generalizations, simply because our aversion to the very idea of limited war has inhibited us from approaching the problem objectively and systematically. One might almost say that the things we have failed to consider in the realm of military preparation have been less of a handicap than the things we have taken for granted; for it is the major unexamined premises of our approach to force and policy that have established the pattern and focus of our strategic thinking.

GEOGRAPHICAL LIMITATION

Under the military and political conditions of the foreseeable future the decisive limitations upon military operations that are within the power of belligerents to control would seem to be limitations upon the area of combat, upon weapons, and upon targets. Without these three kinds of limitations, it is difficult to imagine a war remaining limited. With them, the other limitations would probably follow, and wars might remain limited even if they did not follow. Therefore the heart of the problem of developing a strategy of limited war lies in devising methods of conducting military operations that are compatible with these three limitations and yet militarily effective in terms of supporting America's security objectives.

The importance of geographical limitation is obvious. Without the localization of war, hostilities involving the United States and the Communist bloc, directly or indirectly, would almost certainly exceed the scale of practicable limitation, given the existing military potentials of major powers. For a war not fought within well-defined geographical limits would probably pose such a massive threat to American and Russian security that both powers would feel compelled to strike at the center of opposition. The same thing can be said of the simultaneous occurrence of several local wars, for both the Soviet Union and the United States would probably regard such wars as the sign of a general contest that it could not afford to counter on a local and piecemeal basis. Geographical limitation is all the more important because it is the easiest, most practical limitation to establish, to observe, and to communicate.

However, like any other limitation designed to control the dynamics of warfare, limitation of the area of combat must not be construed in an absolute sense. Thus it need not under all circumstances preclude naval action or tactical air retaliation beyond the immediate area of attack. Whether the extension of a war by air and sea action is warranted must be judged in the light of the danger of enlarging the scope of war beyond the bounds of control, balanced against the political urgency and the military efficacy of the measures involved. For example, if important political objectives are at stake in a peripheral contest supported by Communist China, and if they can only be attained by bombing Chinese bases and supply lines supporting the aggression, then this measure might be worth the additional risk of enlarging the scale of war that it would entail. However, if the military efficacy of such a measure is dubious, if bombing Chinese bases would probably lead to retaliation by counter-measures that would nullify the anticipated military advantage or that would entail a risk of total war disproportionate to the importance of the objective at stake, then the least objectionable course might be to adhere to existing limitations and make the best of them.

Ideally, we should like to be able to contain every possible Communist aggression on a strictly local basis, for then we could avoid the choice between undertaking ineffective resistance and risking total war or, at least, war on a scale beyond our ability to sustain at a tolerable cost—a dilemma that would probably result in nonresistance unless aggression occurred in the most vital strategic area. However, we must recognize that in some highly industrialized and economically integrated areas—certainly the core of the NATO area—even limited military incursions would constitute such a serious threat to our security interests (and would be so difficult to check on a purely local basis) that we could not afford to confine our resistance to the immediate combat area. This might be true even if the topography, the industrial and transport linkages, and other physical features made restriction theoretically feasible. Therefore, in these areas, except in cases of insurrection and minor military coups, we shall have to continue to rely primarily upon our capability to strike at the center of aggression to deter Communist advances.

But the American government, especially under the Eisenhower administration, has frequently argued another reason for the unfeasibility of relying upon purely local defense, a reason with much less claim to validity. It has argued that because of the Communists' central geographical position and their numerical superiority in manpower the free world cannot afford the expenditure of men and money necessary to resist aggression locally at every possible point along the Sino-Soviet periphery. American strategists have been frightened by this theoretical situation ever since the inauguration of containment. What they have envisioned is the Russians and Chinese, secure in the heartland of Eurasia and enjoying the advantages of inexhaustible manpower and interior lines of communication, striking out at will at a series of soft spots along the periphery, remote from the center of our own strength, while the American coalition dissipates its precious manpower and resources in endless futile efforts to hold a kind of Maginot Line against assaults initiated by the Communists at places and with weapons of their own choosing. The prospect is, indeed, a disturbing one; but how realistic is it?

In the first place, the image of trying to hold every point on a 20,000-mile Maginot Line is, to say the least, exaggerated. It is true that in the European sector of such a line we would certainly operate at an irrevocable disadvantage in trying to contain Communist assaults on a local basis, since the West suffers such substantial numerical inferiority in mobilizable manpower.[1] But, as we have observed, the defense of the part of the Communist perimeter that adjoins the NATO area does not

[1] Thomas R. Phillips has pointed out that on the basis of UN statistics the 15 NATO nations have a population of 436,060,000, whereas Russia and her European satellites have only 278,125,000 (*St. Louis Post-Dispatch*, November 21, 1954, p. 3 C). However, because of foreign policies and domestic economic and political considerations, the free world clearly suffers a great numerical disadvantage in terms of the troops it is willing to mobilize and maintain.

depend primarily upon local resistance. Furthermore, other sectors of the perimeter are less vulnerable than a simple line drawn on a map suggests. India and Pakistan are protected by a formidable mountain barrier. Political considerations may protect other segments equally effectively. For example, India's close interest in Burma and the reluctance of Communist China to turn India from a neutral power into a dangerous competitor in Southeast Asia may deter an attack on Burma—and, perhaps, on Laos, Cambodia, and Thailand too—far more effectively than a large local garrison, providing that these nations have a minimum capacity to police their territories.

The Middle Eastern and Asian rimlands are undoubtedly vulnerable but not so vulnerable as the purely spatial relation between the heartlands and the rimlands implies. We shall deal with the methods of defending these rimlands when we examine the specific problem of applying containment to the gray areas; but it can be noted now that the image of Sino-Soviet interior lines of communication facilitating the rapid transfer of great masses of troops from one peripheral point to another is not supported by the logistical realities of the situation. The tremendous length of those lines, their distance from major supplies, their sparseness, and the poor transportation facilities refute any analogy with our own elaborate and highly developed network of communications. And as for transferring troops rapidly from one peripheral point to another, the Communists are in no better position to do that then we are; for the Asian rimland is not a continuous open field but actually a series of terrain compartments, between which communication is far easier by sea and air than by land. In a contest with the Sino-Soviet heartland for this Asian rimland we and our allies have the tremendous advantage of easy access to the sea and control of the sea, as well as a large number of naval and air bases encircling Eurasia and the technical capability of transporting great quantities of men and equipment to various points on the Sino-Soviet periphery. The Korean War was an impressive illustration of this fact.

As for a number of more or less simultaneous attacks on the periphery of Communist power, there is no reason to think that the Communists are in a better position to fight more than one local war at a time than we, providing that we take full advantage of our superior mobility, our geographical position, and our logistical advantages. Moreover, assuming that the Communists continue to conduct a strategy of caution and limited risk, they will realize that a series of small wars could constitute such a serious threat to our prestige and security as to incur an inordinate risk of precipitating a full-scale war; for their simultaneous attacks would be a signal to us that they had deliberately accepted the grave risk of a general war, and we would have to accept the same risks. If we could not contain these attacks locally, we probably could not afford to confine our resistance to the combat area; nor would the American people tolerate piecemeal defeat under this circumstance. Presumably, the Communists would know this.

Therefore, with the exceptions and qualifications noted above, it seems both feasible and essential that the United States develop its strategy around the conception of local defense that has been implicit in containment from the first. Of course, the particular geographical restrictions upon a war must be determined in the light of such factors as the direction and scope of the aggression and the geographical features of the area. Clearly, island and peninsular wars will be easier to localize than wars in areas with no clear physical demarcations; and small-scale attacks directed at well-defined territorial objectives will be easier to localize than large-scale assaults or general insurrectionary activity unaccompanied by clear indications of military and political intent.

However, we must also recognize that alliances may inject a complicating factor into geographical limitation of warfare; by creating an obligation for many nations to come to the aid of one, they also create the danger that an attack on one country will result in spreading the war to several. Thus we might find it difficult to resist the demands of an ally under attack that other allies share the burden of the war in their own territories. We must remember that such an ally will not feel the same restraints as we. For the war which we strive to confine geographically may, in effect, be unlimited from the standpoint of the ally whose country happens to be the scene of battle. He may already have reached that stage of desperation that we are trying to avoid. This situation will afford him considerable bargaining power, especially if the adversary offers him conditional surrender. If this hard-pressed ally should also have a nuclear capacity, he could increase his bargaining power that much more by threatening to expand the war on his own.

* * * * *

WEAPONS AND TARGETS LIMITATION

Before the momentous economic and technological expansion of the Industrial Revolution, the severely restricted physical capacity for war which states could draw upon made limited war virtually an automatic by-product of limited objectives. But, with the tremendous capacity for destruction available to modern nations, the limitation of war demands a deliberate restriction not only of the area of combat but also of weapons and targets. For it is doubtful that any war could be controlled for limited political purposes, no matter how narrowly and precisely a belligerent might try to define his objectives, if all the present means of destruction were employed indiscriminately, even though they were employed initially within a narrowly circumscribed area.

At the same time, it would be a mistake to assume that there is a mathematical correlation between the destructiveness or firepower of weapons and the scale and scope of warfare. The effect that use of a certain weapon exerts on the dimensions of warfare depends largely upon the seriousness with which the enemy regards the resulting threat to national values. The careful limitation and clarification of objectives can go far to keep that threat ordinate, even when the most powerful weapons are employed. Therefore, nothing inherent in a wide range of atomic weapons renders them incompatible with limited war, apart from the targets toward which they are directed and the political context in which they are employed. For this reason it is a serious mistake to equate nuclear warfare with total warfare and oppose them both to "conventional" warfare. Of course, we must reckon with the fact that weapons as destructive as the multi-megaton nuclear bombs are preeminently instruments for obliterating large centers of population. Consequently, the employment of these weapons under almost any conceivable circumstance would be a signal that a general war upon strategic targets had begun. But there is a vast difference between the multi-megaton bomb and the variety of "low-yield" kiloton weapons—a much greater difference than between the most powerful World War II "block-busters" and conventional artillery shells. A two-kiloton bomb has a maximum damage radius of several hundred yards; its radioactive fallout is negligible. A twenty-megaton H-bomb, by no means the largest available, would virtually obliterate everything within a radius of ten miles and dust a downwind area with deadly or harmful fallout for hundreds of miles (unless it were exploded at a great height). Since the enemy's exact response to the use of certain weapons against certain targets under particular circumstances is difficult to anticipate, it would be dangerous not to allow for a considerable margin of error in planning our weapons system and our military strategy and tactics; but it would be equally dangerous to assume that the powerful new weapons that have recently become available are necessarily and under all circumstances less compatible with limited war than the conventional weapons of World War II.

The essential requirement in adapting weapons to a strategy of limited war is that we have a flexible weapons system and flexible military strategies and tactics capable of supporting limited objectives under a wide variety of conditions. Clearly, all the weapons and measures that are suitable for total war are not suitable for limited war. For example, it is almost inconceivable that any war in which airpower was employed against major strategic targets would remain limited; nor would the indiscriminate employment of air power necessarily promote local defense even if the war did remain limited. The special techological requirements of limited war are particularly marked in the realm of mobile, airborne troops capable of employing low-yield nuclear weapons and the most advanced conventional weapons with precision against military targets. Therefore, we cannot simply devise our military policies to meet the threat of major aggression and total war and expect to deter and repel lesser aggressions by improvising resistance with whatever can be spared from the total-war arsenal. Precisely because the requirements of reconciling the limitation of war with military effectiveness are so varied and complex, we cannot afford to rely too heavily upon any single weapon or any single tactic. We need to have a weapons-and-delivery system as flexible as the probable military contingencies are varied, lest the range of measures from which we can select our response in the event of an attack be so narrow as to deprive us of an intermediate response between total war and nonresistance. For, even though the Communists may never force us to choose between nuclear suicide and acquiescence, we shall have to act as though they might; and our diplomatic position will profit or suffer in proportion as we are prepared or unprepared to avoid the dilemma. By the same token, in proportion as our range of military capabilities increases, the flexibility of our diplomacy will be enhanced; and as the flexibility of our diplomacy is enhanced, we shall

increase our bargaining power with Communist nations and improve our relations with other nations.

GROUND TROOPS

Under existing technological conditions, one essential requirement of a flexible military establishment is sufficient numbers of ready combat troops to check Communist aggression locally. If we cannot check aggression locally, we shall be compelled to run larger risks of total war by striking at targets beyond the area of combat that support the aggression, unless, of course, we choose to acquiesce in defeat. It follows that the greater our capacity for local military containment, the better we shall be able to minimize the risk of total war. Some advocates of tactical air power notwithstanding, there is little military support for the view that "mobile striking power" can provide this capacity in the absence of substantial ground strength—except, perhaps, in a very few island and peninsular positions, such as the Formosa Straits, with naval support. The Korean War is only the latest war to demonstrate this fact.

However, if we recognize the desirability of possessing ground strength capable of checking aggression locally, we must also recognize that we cannot realistically expect to achieve this condition of limitation in all areas of potential aggression, since we cannot count on the free world mobilizing sufficient manpower for the purpose. However, this drawback is rendered somewhat less significant by the fact that western Europe, the area in which local ground defense is least likely to be feasible, is of such great strategic importance and so uncongenial to limitation on other grounds that we shall have to rely primarily upon the deterrent of massive retaliation for its defense anyway.[2]

At the same time, we need not conclude that our relative numerical deficiency in

[2] The possibilities of local ground defense are assessed in greater detail in the discussion of the application of a strategy of limited war to the NATO area and to the gray areas on pp. 259–73 (not included in this volume).

ready, mobilized manpower precludes successful local ground defense in all areas. That would be true only if we had to match the Communists man for man. But the experience in Korea confirmed the lesson of other wars that troops with superior firepower, technical skill, and logistical support can hold forces several times as numerous. Throughout the gray areas our superior mobility and our superior ability to train, equip, and supply troops can go a long way toward compensating for numerical inferiority. Indeed, in the light of this superiority, considered in conjunction with the growth of Communist air power, some students of military strategy have suggested that we may actually enjoy our greatest potential advantage in ground warfare.[3]

[3] See, for example, the observations of Roger Hilsman and William W. Kaufmann in Kaufmann (ed.), *Military Policy and National Security* (Princeton: Princeton University Press, 1956), pp. 182, 250.

THE EVOLUTION OF AMERICAN MILITARY STRATEGY

BY MORTON H. HALPERIN

American military strategy has evolved continuously over the postwar period in response to changes in technology as well as increased sophistication in the understanding of strategic questions. This chapter will trace the evolution of American policy as well as the evolution of the analysis of strategic questions. The role of technology in shaping these evolutions will be considered.

THE EARLY POSTWAR PERIOD

During the early postwar period the United States gradually came to accept the need for a policy designed to halt the spread of Soviet communism, which threatened to engulf all of Europe. The Truman Administration accepted the containment doctrine, which argued that if Soviet expansion could be stopped, the Soviet Union would gradually lose its urge to expand. The doctrine developed from an analysis of Soviet society, and the implications of this doctrine were viewed largely in political and economic terms. The military implications of an attempt to stop Russian expansion and, consequently, the kind of military forces which might be needed over the next ten years were not given much attention.

Defense strategy in the early postwar period focused on the problem of general war, which was defined at this time as the danger of large-scale Soviet aggression in Europe. The possibility of limited local aggression, either in Europe or outside of it, was not taken seriously in war planning or force development. Very early in this period the concept of deterrence—that is, *preventing* a Soviet attack in Europe—became important. The main emphasis here was on a political commitment by the United States to defend Europe; this commitment culminated in the signing of the NATO Defense Treaty in 1949. There was a widespread belief that the Second (and even the First) World War had come about because aggressors had assumed that the United States would remain aloof and would permit them to dominate Europe. Thus, it was argued that a firm commitment in the form of the North Atlantic Treaty would be a major step toward effectively deterring a Soviet attack. Although it was recognized that the atomic bomb might potentially change all military strategy, this bomb was viewed in the post-war period simply as a somewhat bigger bomb to be used in the same way other bombs had been used at the end of the Second World War. The United States had a very small stockpile of atomic weapons, and there was no strong drive to increase to any great extent the size of the stockpile. Conventional forces were even smaller. The United States' defense budget stood at approximately fifteen billion dollars a year, and there was a popular notion in Washington that any sum larger than that would bankrupt the economy.

NSC 68 (1950)

By 1950 a number of pressures made a reevaluation of American defense policy in the Atomic Age a necessity. It had become clear that since the Cold War would last for a long time, the United States would continue to have defense commitments, which should be reevaluated in light of the growing American atomic stockpiles.

First, the Soviet Union had become a nuclear power much more quickly than anybody had expected; and the United States had decided to proceed on a top priority basis with the development of the hydrogen (fusion), or "super," bomb. This decision, made by President Truman, was one of the three immediate pressures that led to a review of American defense strategy. The second pressure came from the growing American military assistance program and the efforts of the State Department to coordinate defense and foreign policy. The tradition of separating foreign policy from military strategy made it difficult to devise an effective military assistance program; officials in the State Department, particularly Paul Nitze of the Policy Planning Staff, became aware of the need to coordinate defense and foreign policy. Finally, President Truman called on the National Security Council to take a more active role in coordinating security policy and asked the National Security Council for an appraisal of the United States' strategic situation.

These pressures led to the creation of a joint State-Defense Department committee, which was instructed to reexamine American security policy without considering either budgetary or political constraints. The committee, with the strong support of Secretary of State Dean Acheson and the active guiding role of Nitze, met for several months during 1950 and finally reported to the National Security Council in April. The report, which was endorsed by both the State Department and the Defense Department, called for a very substantial increase in the American defense effort and warned of the danger of local wars. President Truman indicated his intention to accept the report but asked for cost estimates. These were being prepared when the Korean War broke out; and the report of the committee, NSC 68, served as a blueprint for actual rearmament.

THE KOREAN WAR

The Korean War was accompanied by a vast increase in American defense spending. The defense budget went up very rapidly and then leveled off at approximately forty billion dollars a year—almost three times the fifteen billion dollar ceiling that had been reaffirmed shortly before the war. Despite the attack in the Far East and the fighting in the Korean Peninsula, the emphasis remained on Europe. It was believed that the Korean War might even be a feint on the part of the Communists to draw American power into Asia while preparing for a Soviet move in Central Europe. Thus, while the Korean War was going on, the American forces in NATO were built up very substantially. The decision was made to create the post of Supreme Allied Commander for Europe, and General Eisenhower was appointed to the position. In 1952 the NATO Council met in Lisbon and established goals for the buildup of NATO ground forces to a total of about seventy-five active and reserve divisions on the central front. The United States rapidly expanded its own nuclear and airpower capabilities. In defense planning during the Korean War, the United States adopted the notion of a "crisis year": that several years in the future there would be a peak period of danger for the United States; in order to prepare for war in that crisis year, excessive American defense expenditures were currently required.

THE NEW LOOK

The Eisenhower Administration came into office in 1953 committed not only to ending the Korean War but also to taking a "new look" at American military strategy. We can identify at least three major sources of the new approach of the Administration.

The first of these was an affinity for air-power, which strangely enough influenced both President Eisenhower—a former Army general—and Admiral Arthur William Radford, who was to become Eisenhower's first Chairman of the Joint Chiefs. The belief that airpower could be the backbone of the American military establishment stemmed from a notion that technology could somehow substitute for manpower. The United States, being short on manpower but highly advanced technologically, could be expected—it was argued—to find a solution to its military problems by relying on its strengths and deemphasizing its weaknesses. In addition, the emphasis on airpower reflected the search for a single solution to a complex problem, which characterizes the American approach to many situations.

Of perhaps equal importance in the search for a new strategy was the notion of the great equation: the belief that the security of the United States depended as much on the health of the American economy as it did on the actual weapons used in warfare and that this health resulted from keeping expenditures down. For this reason it was felt that a lower defense budget would, in the long run, contribute more to military security than a higher budget would.

Finally, an important technological innovation of the new strategy in the United States was the development of the so-called tactical nuclear weapons—nuclear weapons of low yield which might be employed on the battlefield. Breakthroughs in technology and vast increases in the American stockpile of nuclear weapons made it possible to talk about such a use of nuclear weapons.

What, then, were the characteristics of this New Look? First of all, the notion of a crisis year was discarded and was replaced by the "long haul" concept. The crisis-year notion had been used by the Truman Administration to justify very large expenditures on the grounds that they would level off and be reduced after the United States had passed the year of great crisis; the new long haul concept, on the other hand, justified reduced expenditures on the grounds that they would be continued indefinitely. In addition, nuclear deterrence was given more attention than it had been given before. As was noted, even under the Truman Administration prior to, and during, the Korean War the greatest threat was believed to be in Europe; it was felt that this threat was best deterred by political commitments and by nuclear power. With the advent of the New Look, the dominant role of the Air Force in American strategy was also formalized. From this followed a deemphasis on ground forces—particularly on the possibility and desirability of a conventional defense. By 1954 the NATO Council had formally committed NATO to the use of tactical nuclear weapons in the event of large-scale fighting on the central front, and NATO force requirements were reduced in the belief that tactical nuclear weapons could substitute for manpower.

In comparing the New Look policy with the pre-Korean War policy of the Truman Administration, both innovations and similarities become apparent. In both periods, the need to keep the defense budget low in order to permit the growth and health of the economy was emphasized; deterrence was largely to come from the use of atomic or nuclear weapons. Nevertheless, articulation of the military doctrines inherent in United States' policy since the Second World War resulted in a major critique of this policy, leading ultimately to its drastic revision.

CRITICISM OF MASSIVE RETALIATION

In January, 1954, Secretary of State John Foster Dulles made a speech, which later was reprinted in the *Department of State Bulletin*, to the Council on Foreign Relations in New York. The speech was an attempt on Dulles' part to explain and to justify the New Look policy of the Administration—particularly the Administration's reluctance to engage in renewed ground combat in Asia. In his talk, Dulles declared that no local defense could contain the manpower of the Communist world; therefore, he said, local defense must be reinforced by the threatened deterrent of massive retaliatory power. The United States, then, could deter local aggression by maintaining a great capacity to retaliate instantly "by means and in places of our own choosing." Dulles' formal statement of what, in reality, had long been the policy of the Administration provoked a storm of criticism, not only from leading Democrats, but also from a number of students of national security policy. These critics, who included Chester Bowles and Dean Acheson, as well as such academics as William Kaufmann and Henry Kissinger, argued that the doctrine of massive retaliation would not be effective in deterring local, more ambiguous Communist moves. They contended that massive retaliation could not be the action policy of the United States because to implement a doctrine of massive retaliation would be suicidal. Therefore, they concluded, a local-war strategy for the defense of those areas outside of Europe was needed. At least at this stage most critics of the massive-retaliation doctrine did not question its validity in Europe; only in the late 1950's and early 1960's was it felt that a direct defense strategy was essential for Europe also.

As has already been indicated, Dulles' statement was not a major change in policy, certainly not from earlier formulations of the New Look, and not even from the policy of the Truman Administration. Neither was it clear that the policy should be interpreted—as its critics suggested—as one which warned that the United States would bomb Moscow in the event of an attack by Communist forces anywhere in the world. On the contrary, the doctrine might well be interpreted as a form of limited retaliation: that the United States would not necessarily meet ground action where it occurred but might respond—with or without nuclear weapons—with attacks on strategic targets, perhaps in the Soviet Union, perhaps only in Communist China and other Communist states. There seems to be little doubt that the option of limited-retaliation, and even massive-retaliation, strategy is desirable in that it contributes to general deterrence. Even more specifically, it is now believed that Dulles' threats did enhance American deterrence of Chinese action in the Far East.

Moreover, the assumption implicit in most of the criticism was that there was inherently a stable nuclear balance between the United States and the Soviet Union: that nuclear war was very unlikely and was deterred simply by each side's having nuclear weapons. There was little regard for the vulnerability of these weapons to an enemy attack; rather, it was believed that nuclear war would consist primarily of attacks on cities. It was this image that enabled Dulles' critics to say that if he was threatening Moscow, he had to accept in return the threat of New York's destruction. In fact, in 1954 and for several years after, both the United States and the Soviet Union could have destroyed, in a strategic first strike, much of their enemy's capacity to retaliate. It was not until several years later that critics outside the government began to warn that the Administration was not only overlooking the need for large ground forces but also the need for well-protected strategic forces.

Finally, it should be noted that at least some of the issues between Dulles and his critics were quantitative ones that had been expressed qualitatively. Dulles recognized and accepted the need for local-war forces; he argued, however, that by themselves they would never be large enough to contain communism and therefore had to be supplemented by nuclear power. His critics presumably were contending that larger forces could—and should—be supplied and that these forces might at least in some circumstances be sufficient to deter or defeat a Communist attack. The real issue, then, was the size of the American ground forces, not what they should be used for.

In the long run, the critics of the massive-retaliation doctrine made their impact on the intellectual climate and defense thinking in the United States. This influence culminated in 1961, when a number of these critics were brought into power with the Kennedy Administration. The effect on policy during the remaining years of the Eisenhower Administration, however, was to be much less dramatic. The criticisms did slowly bring about a few changes, though. The need for larger ground forces—at least for tactical nuclear ground defense—was accepted. Finally, the need for a limited-war strategy—albeit a nuclear one—was acknowledged in 1957, when the trend of thinking was suddenly reversed by events in the latter part of that year.

SPUTNIK AND THE GAITHER COMMITTEE

In October, 1957 the first artificial earth satellite—the Soviet Sputnik—was launched into the sky, creating the impression of Soviet superiority, not only in technology, but also in military capability. This event dramatically turned attention to the Soviet nuclear threat to the United States and, consequently, turned it away from the more remote threat of local war. It generated a climate in which increases in the American defense budget were possible; but the increases were to be for counteracting the impending Soviet ICBM capability, which threatened the United States with destruction.

If Sputnik provided the emotional impetus for a fresh appraisal of the direct defense of the United States, the Gaither Committee provided the intellectual support.

The Gaither Committee was appointed by President Eisenhower early in 1957 to consider a proposal for an extensive fallout-shelter program in the United States. The Committee was comprised of private citizens, many of whom had served under President Truman and were later to serve during the Kennedy and Johnson Administrations. They included William C. Foster, who was to become Director of the Arms Control and Disarmament Agency, and Jerome Wiesner, who later served as science advisor to President Kennedy. This group, like the committee which drew up NSC 68, was bound neither by current strategy nor by a budget ceiling. In its report, which was presented to the President and the National Security Council shortly after the launching of Sputnik, the Committee warned, for the first time, of the danger of a "missile gap." It stated that unless the United States stepped up its program of intercontinental strategic force, the Soviet Union would have a larger strategic force and, moreover, would have the capability in a first strike of destroying all of the American strategic capability. The Committee thus urged a substantial increase in the defense budget, aimed primarily at improving the American strategic posture. The report of the Committee, which has never been formally released, made recommendations very similar to those of an unclassified study that was part of the Rockefeller Brothers Fund report on the United States at mid-century. These recommendations, coupled with the impact of Sputnik, led to a slight increase in the defense budget; the shift to a greater emphasis on local defense forces was never realized. Perhaps most important, the Gaither episode demonstrated the inability of any group, either in opposition to the President or comprised mainly of private citizens (or, as in this case, both), to influence military strategy. However, the Committee—largely because many of its findings were leaked to the press—did provoke the missile-gap debate.

The reports of both the Gaither Committee and the Rockefeller Brothers Fund were influenced by a revolution that was taking place in strategic analysis in the United States. The assumption of previous thinking had been that the strategic balance was in some way inherently stable. An image of the nuclear powers as scorpions in a bottle who could sting each other to death but only at the price of being stung to death in return, prevailed. Most of the intellectual basis for revising this image was taken from the work of Albert Wohlstetter, of the RAND Corporation. The most systematic public statement of the position was made by Wohlstetter in an article entitled "The Delicate Balance of Terror," in the January, 1959 issue of *Foreign Affairs*. Wohlstetter said that by attacking its enemy's strategic forces, a country could disarm the other "scorpion" and not be stung back. This position stressed the importance of second-strike forces; that is, forces which could survive a first strike and could retaliate. It maintained that a country should assess the vulnerability of its forces to a counterforce first strike and then should develop well-protected second-strike forces, using such techniques as hardening, dispersal, and airborne or ground alert. This view, which has not been generally accepted within the defense community, implied that there was no inherent stable balance, but rather that a country had to spend a good deal of money—including resources for research, development, communications, and control systems—to build up a credible deterrent against a determined opponent with an efficient first-strike capability. This position, in suggesting that even for the long run a significant portion of American spending would have to be on strategic forces, had important implications for the allocation of defense resources.

1960 ELECTION

Defense issues played an important part in the 1960 presidential campaign between John F. Kennedy and Richard Nixon. Nixon, while feeling obliged to defend the Administration, did suggest that larger spending would be necessary. Kennedy launched a full-scale attack on the Administration's defense posture, criticizing its effort both in the strategic field and in the field of conventional forces. He warned of the danger of a missile gap, which would permit the Soviets to have a larger strategic force—one perhaps capable of destroying the American force in a coordinated first strike—than the United States. Although this charge was clearly made in good faith, there apparently never was any real danger of a missile gap or a deterrence gap. Kennedy also suggested—more accurately—that the United States had seriously neglected conventional forces and an air- and sea-lift capability for them. He expressed the need for having the option to fight without the use of nuclear weapons.

THE McNAMARA PENTAGON

Secretary of Defense Robert S. McNamara has been responsible for very significant changes in both the substance and the method of formulating American defense policy. Three basic sources of the changes brought about by McNamara, with the support of President Kennedy and later President Johnson, can be identified. The first of these was an intellectual one. During the 1950's a growing discontent with the massive-retaliation policy of the Eisenhower Administration was perceptible. Much work was being done in the universities, in private research corporations such as RAND, and by the Democratic party through the Democratic Advisory Committee, on alternative approaches to both the content and the method of formulating defense policy. In addition, because defense had become one of the campaign issues Kennedy used to challenge the Eisenhower Administration, sweeping changes were needed to justify the use of this issue. Of great importance was the attitude of the new Administration toward economic questions. Kennedy's economic advisers believed that the threat to the American economy—and what, in fact, explained its sluggish growth rate during the 1950's—was the Administration's reluctance to spend money. They felt that the economy could afford, and would be stimulated by, increases in defense spending. Thus, while some attention was given to reduction of governmental expenditures, there was no strong pressure to keep the defense budget down in order to keep the economy strong. The removal of this constraint made it possible to realize substantial increases in the defense budget.

Breakthroughs in technology were also important in shaping the new defense strategy. Improvements in missiles made it possible for the United States to manufacture, in large numbers, sophisticated missile systems with great accuracy and low megatonnage, such as the Minuteman and Polaris submarine-launched strategic systems. In addition, the reconnaissance capability of the United States, mainly comprised of orbiting satellites, made possible the development of a strategy with much more reliable information about Soviet capability. Finally, the growing Soviet strategic capability, mainly against Europe, but also against the United States, made it necessary to rethink American defense policy.

Perhaps the most important and enduring change was in the structure of the Pentagon and in the decision-making processes. Mr. McNamara relied more on his civilian advisers than on the armed services and employed the techniques of systems analysis and cost-effectiveness analysis. The Administration also introduced program budgeting; that is, organizing the budget around functions. For example, budget headings such as Strategic Offensive and Defensive Forces, and General Purposes (local war) Forces were used rather than such administrative headings as Personnel, Maintenance, and Construction. In addition to the procedural changes, there were important alterations in the areas of counterinsurgency, conventional forces, and general war doctrine.

Counterinsurgency—that is, actions to defeat guerrilla operations—received much more attention than it had in the past. Apparently President Kennedy came into office with a deep personal interest in problems of counterinsurgency; this interest was reinforced by the developing crises in Laos and Vietnam. A special school was set up for training military officers in aspects of counterinsurgency; and, at the high policy levels of the government, more study was given to the problem. However, in

this area, the Administration did not have a large amount of intellectual capital to draw on; and only limited headway was made.

In the area of conventional forces, much work had been done. President Kennedy, as a senator, had been concerned with shortages in American conventional capability. Shortly after Mr. McNamara took over the Pentagon, programs that increased the size of the Army from twelve to sixteen combat divisions and stressed procurement, research, and development for conventional capability were initiated. This was the first noteworthy effort in this direction since the Second World War. The United States also began to urge its NATO allies to engage in a conventional buildup. Although the United States did develop an improved capability to fight conventionally, its action and communication policies on the relative role of conventional and nuclear forces continued to be ambiguous. It was evident, though, that the focus of statements did shift toward a greater emphasis on conventional forces. The President and the Secretary of Defense continued to stress the need for options and the need to develop a conventional capability; but they refused to be drawn into any specific discussion of when nuclear weapons would be used, except to assert that they would be used "if necessary." In the early 1960's the United States developed an increased capability to fight without the use of nuclear weapons and began to use some of that capability in Vietnam. But what the action policy would be in other parts of the world remained uncertain.

Judging by his statements during the campaign, Mr. Kennedy expected to come into office confronted with Soviet superiority in strategic weapons. Instead, he found that the United States still possessed an overwhelming strategic advantage. The Administration asserted the political value of this superiority: that it gave the United States greater freedom of political maneuver on international questions. At the same time, an increase in American strategic forces, with well-protected, accurate strategic systems and good command and control, was ordered. The United States began to develop forces that could survive a nuclear attack and sought ways to limit a general nuclear war. This led to the enunciation of the controlled-response strategy and later to the development of the assured-destruction for (deterrence) and damage-limiting (should war occur) strategies. At the same time, the Administration be-

gan to talk about allied joint nuclear planning.

By the mid-1960's the McNamara revolution in the Pentagon was in a sense complete. Defense decisionmaking was relying more and more on quantitative techniques of analysis. A series of options for meeting a wide variety of military threats had been developed.

COALITION DIPLOMACY IN A NUCLEAR AGE

BY HENRY A. KISSINGER

For several years now disputes have rent the Atlantic Alliance. They have focused on such issues as nuclear strategy and control, the organization of Europe and the nature of an Atlantic Community. However, the most fundamental issue in Atlantic relationships is raised by two questions not unlike those which each Western society has had to deal with in its domestic affairs: How much unity do we want? How much pluralism can we stand? Too formalistic a conception of unity risks destroying the political will of the members of the Community. Too absolute an insistence on national particularity must lead to a fragmentation of the common effort.

One does not have to agree with the methods or policies of President de Gaulle to recognize that he has posed an important question which the West has yet to answer. There is merit in his contention that before a political unit can mean something to others, it must first mean something to itself. Though de Gaulle has often acted as if he achieved identity by opposing our

purposes, our definition of unity has occasionally carried overtones of tutelage.

There is no question that the abrupt tactics of the French President have severely strained the pattern of allied relationships which emerged after the war. But no one man could have disrupted the Alliance by himself. Fundamental changes have been taking place in the nature of alliances, in the character of strategy and in the relative weights of Europe and the United States. A new conception of allied relationships would have been necessary no matter who governed in Paris or in Washington. The impact of particular statesmen aside, a farsighted policy will gear itself to dealing with these underlying forces. It will inquire into the degree to which objectives are common and where they diverge. It will face frankly the fact that different national perspectives—and not necessarily ignorance—can produce differing strategic views. It will examine the scope and limits of consultation. If this is done in a new spirit on both sides of

Reprinted by permission from *Foreign Affairs*, July, 1964, pp. 525–45. Copyright by the Council on Foreign Relations, Inc., New York.

Mr. Kissinger is Professor of Government at Harvard University and a member of the Harvard Center for International Affairs. He has served as an advisor to the National Security Council and to the U.S. Arms Control and Disarmament Agency. He is the author of many books on U.S. foreign policy and defense policy including *Nuclear Weapons and Foreign Policy* (1958), *The Necessity for Choice* (1962), and editor of *Problems of National Strategy* (1965).

the Atlantic, a more vital relationship can take the place of the previous U.S. hegemony.

THE CHANGE IN THE NATURE OF ALLIANCES

Since the end of World War II an important change has taken place in the nature of alliances. In the past, alliances have been created for three basic reasons. (1) To provide an accretion of power. According to the doctrine of collective security, the wider the alliance, the greater its power to resist aggression. (2) To leave no doubt about the alignment of forces. It has often been argued that had Germany known at the beginning of both World Wars that the United States—or even England—would join the Allies, war would have been averted. (3) To provide an incentive for mutual assistance beyond that already supplied by an estimate of the national interest.

To be sure, even before the advent of nuclear weapons, there was some inconsistency among these requirements. The attempt to combine the maximum number of states for joint action occasionally conflicted with the desire to leave no doubt about the collective motivation. The wider the system of collective security, the more various were the motives animating it and the more difficult the task of obtaining common action proved to be. The more embracing the alliance, the more intense and direct must be the threat which would produce joint action.

This traditional difficulty has been compounded in the nuclear age. The requirements for tight command and control of nuclear weapons are to some degree inconsistent with a coalition of sovereign states. The enormous risks of nuclear warfare affect the credibility of traditional pledges of mutual assistance.

As a result, most of the theories of nuclear control now current within the Western Alliance have a tendency either to turn NATO into a unilateral U.S. guarantee or to call into question the utility of the Alliance altogether. American strategic thought verges on the first extreme; some

French theorists have hinted at the second.

As for the United States, official spokesmen have consistently emphasized that the European contribution to the over-all nuclear strength of the Alliance is negligible. European nuclear forces have been described as "provocative," "prone to obsolescence" and "weak." For a considerable period after the advent of the Kennedy Administration, some high officials held the view that on nuclear matters the President might serve as the Executive Agent of the Alliance. Since then the United States has made various proposals for nuclear sharing, the common feature of which has been the retention of our veto over the nuclear weapons of the Alliance.

However sensible such schemes may appear from the point of view of the division of labor, they all would perpetuate our hegemony in nuclear matters within the Alliance. Allies are considered necessary not so much to add to over-all strength as to provide the possibility for applying power discriminately. In these terms, it is not surprising that some allies have considered their conventional contribution as actually weakening the over-all strength by raising doubts about the *nuclear* commitment of the United States.

According to the contrary view, alliances have lost their significance altogether. The French theorist, General Gallois, has argued, for example, that nuclear weapons have made alliances obsolete. Faced with the risk of total destruction, no nation will jeopardize its survival for another. Hence, he maintains, each country must have its own nuclear arsenal to defend itself against direct attack, while leaving all other countries to their fate.

This formula would mark the end of collective security and would be likely to lead to international chaos. Under conditions of growing nuclear power on both sides, it would be idle to deny that the threat of nuclear retaliation has lost some of its credibility. The Gallois theory would, however, transform a degree of uncertainty into a guarantee that the United States would *not* come to the assistance of its allies, thus greatly simplifying the aggressor's calculation. Moreover, in order to protect itself in this new situation, each country would need to develop not only a nuclear arsenal of its own but also fool-proof procedures for assuring the Soviets that a given nuclear blow did not originate from its territory. If Gallois is right, and each country is unwilling to risk nuclear devastation for an ally, it will also want to prevent itself from being triggered into nuclear war by a neighbor. Thus each country will have a high incentive to devise methods to protect itself from a counter-attack based on a misapprehension. The Gallois theory would lead to a multiplication of national nuclear forces side-by-side with the development of methods of surrender or guarantees of non-involvement.

When views such as these carry influence on both sides of the Atlantic, it is no accident that much of the debate on nuclear matters within NATO turns on the question of confidence. We tend to ask those of our allies possessing nuclear arsenals of their own: If you trust us, why do you require nuclear weapons? Our nuclear allies reply: If you trust us, why are you concerned about our possession of nuclear weapons? Since the answer must inevitably emphasize contingencies where either the goals or the strategy would be incompatible, the debate on nuclear control within NATO has been inherently divisive.

The concentration of nuclear power in the hands of one country poses one set of problems; the range of modern weapons raises another. In the past, a threatened country had the choice either of resisting or surrendering. If it resisted, it had to be prepared to accept the consequences in terms of physical damage or loss of life. A distant ally could be effective only if it was able to bring its strength to bear in the area of conflict.

Modern weapons have changed this. What each member country wants from the Alliance is the assurance that an attack on it will be considered a *casus belli*. It strives for deterrence by adding the strength of a distant ally to its own power. But, equally, each state has an incentive to reduce damage to itself to a minimum should deterrence fail. The range of modern weapons provides an opportunity in in this respect for the first time. In 1914 Belgium could not base its defense on a strategy which transferred to Britain the primary risks of devastation. In the age of intercontinental rockets this technical possibility exists.

Part of the strategic dispute within the Alliance, therefore, involves jockeying to determine which geographic area will be the theater of war if deterrence fails (though this obviously cannot be made explicit). A conventional war confined to Europe may appear relatively tolerable to us. To Europeans, with their memory of conventional wars, this prospect is not particularly inviting. They may find a nuclear exchange which spares their territory a more attractive strategy and the threat of nuclear retaliation a more effective deterrent. The interests of the Alliance may be indivisible in an ultimate sense. But this does not guarantee the absence of sharp conflicts on methods to reach these objectives.

In short, the destructiveness and range of modern weapons have a tendency to produce both extreme nationalism and neutralism. A wise alliance policy must take care that in dealing with one of these dangers it does not produce the other.

The nature of alliances has changed in yet another way. In the past, one of the reasons for joining an alliance was to impose an additional obligation for assistance in time of need. Were each country's national interests completely unambiguous, it would know precisely on whom it could count; a formal commitment would be unnecessary. Both the aggressor and the defender would understand what they would confront and could act accordingly. Wars could not be caused by a misunderstanding of intentions. They would occur only if the protagonists calculated the existing power relationships differently.

Traditionally, however, the national interest has not been unambiguous. Often the aggressor did not know which countries would ultimately be lined up against it; Germany in 1914 was genuinely surprised by the British reaction to the invasion of Belgium. Occasionally the defenders could not be certain of the extent of their potential support—as was the case with the Allies in both wars regarding U.S. participation. Historically, the existence of an understanding on this point, tacit or expicit, has often been the determining factor in the decision to go to war. In the decade prior to World War I, the staff talks between Britain and France, which led to the transfer of the French fleet to the Mediterranean, were one of the key factors in Britain's decision to go to war in August 1914. (Thus the talks achieved one objective of traditional alliances: to commit Britain to the defense of France. They failed in another: to make the opposing alignment clear to the potential aggressor.)

One of the distinguishing features of the nuclear period is that the national interest of the major powers has become less ambiguous. In a bipolar world, a relative gain for one side represents an absolute weakening of the other. Neither of the major nuclear countries can permit a major advance by its opponent regardless of whether the area in which it occurs is formally protected by an alliance or not. Neutral India was no less assured of American assistance when the Chinese attacked than allied Pakistan would have been in similar circumstances. In these conditions, the distinction between allies and neutrals is likely to diminish. A country gains little from being allied and risks little by being neutral.

This inevitably results in the weakening of allied cohesion, producing what some have described as polycentrism. But polycentrism does not reflect so much the emergence of new centers of actual power as the attempt by allies to establish new centers of decision. Polycentrism is virulent not because the world has ceased to be bipolar, but because it essentially remains so. Far from doubting America's military commitment to Europe, President de Gaulle is so certain of it that he does not consider *political* independence a risk. He thus adds American power to his own in pursuit of his policies.

No matter how troublesome a major ally may be, it cannot be allowed to suffer defeat. France's policy is made possible by our nuclear umbrella—a fact which adds to the irony of the situation and the annoyance of some of our policy-makers. Our frequent insistence that in the nuclear age an isolated strategy is no longer possible misses the central point: for this precise reason allies have unprecedented scope for the pursuit of their own objectives. And the more the détente—real or imaginary—proceeds, the more momentum these tendencies will gather. We live in a curious world where neutrals enjoy most of the protection of allies and allies aspire to have the same freedom of action as do neutrals.

These conditions turn coalition diplomacy into an extraordinarily delicate undertaking. Appeals which were effective in the past either work no longer or turn counterproductive. Thus the warning that certain European actions might lead the United States to withdraw is bound to have consequences contrary to those intended. If believed at all, it demonstrates that there are at least *some* contingencies in which the United States might abandon its allies, thus magnifying pressures for European autonomy.

The scope for real Third Force policies is vastly overestimated. Realism forces close association between Europe and the United States whatever the vagaries of individual statesmen. But it has happened often enough in Western history that an underlying community of interests was submerged by subsidiary rivalries. Ancient Greece foundered on this discord. Western Europe nearly tore itself apart before it submerged its rivalries. And now the Atlantic area faces the challenge of how to combine common action with a respect for diverse approaches to the central problem.

THE ABSTRACTNESS AND NOVELTY OF MODERN POWER

The destructiveness of modern weapons gives the strategic debate unprecedented urgency. The speed with which they can be delivered complicates the problem of command and control in a way unimaginable even a decade and half ago. Doctrinal and technical disputes occur within each government. It is not surprising, then, that they should rend the Alliance as well.

The novelty of modern weapons systems gives the disputes a metaphysical, almost theological, cast. Never before in history has so much depended on weapons so new, so untested, so "abstract." No nuclear weapons have been exploded in wartime except on Japan, which did not possess means of retaliation. No one knows how governments or people will react to a nuclear explosion under conditions where both sides possess vast arsenals.

Moreover, modern weapons systems are relatively untested. During the debate in this country over the nuclear test-ban treaty, a great deal of attention was focused on the adequacy of our warheads. In fact, the other components of our weapons systems contain many more factors of uncertainty. The estimated "hardness" of Minuteman silos depends entirely on theoretical studies. Of the thousands of missiles in our arsenal, relatively few of each category have been thoroughly tested. There is little experience with salvo firing. Air-defense systems are designed without any definite knowledge of the nature of the offense. A high proportion of the phenomena discovered in nuclear testing have been "unexpected."

The situation is further complicated by the fact that the purpose of modern weapons is deterrence: to prevent—by a particular threat—a certain course of action. But deterrence is primarily a psychological problem. It depends on the aggressor's assessment of risks, not the defender's. A threat meant as a bluff but taken seriously is more useful for purposes of deterrence than a "genuine" threat interpreted as a bluff. Moreover, if deterrence is successful, aggression does *not* take place. But it is impossible to demonstrate why something has not occurred. It can never be proved whether peace has been maintained because NATO pursues an optimum strategy or a marginally effective one. Finally, the longer deterrence lasts the more color will be lent to the argument that pehaps the Communists never intended to attack in the first place. An effective NATO deterrent strategy may thus have the paradoxical consequence of strengthening the arguments of the quasi-neutralists.

Even if there is agreement about the correct weapons system, there may be disagreement about how it can best be coupled with diplomacy to produce deterrence. How does one threaten with solid-fuel missiles? As these are always in an extreme state of readiness, how then does one demonstrate an increase in preparedness such as historically served as a warning? From a technical point of view it is highly probable that missiles can perform most of the functions heretofore assigned to airplanes. The shift to missiles and the elimination of airplanes envisaged by the former Deputy Secretary of Defense Roswell Gilpatric[1] makes a great deal of sense technically. But has adequate attention been given to the kind of diplomacy which results—particularly in crisis situations—when the retaliatory threat depends on solid-fuel missiles in underground silos? During the Cuban missile crisis, dispersing SAC planes to civilian airports proved an effective warning. What will be an equivalent move when our strategic forces are composed entirely of missiles?

These questions do not permit clear-cut answers. Yet they are at the heart of many of the disputes within NATO. The United States has held the view that deterrence was best achieved by posing a credible threat. And it has related credibility to whether the risks, if deterrence failed, were tolerable. The Europeans for a variety of reasons have generally been of a different opinion. They have maintained that deterrence depended on posing the most extreme risks. They have been prepared to sacrifice a measure of credibility in favor of enhancing the magnitude of the threat. This debate has been inconclusive because it ultimately depends on a psychological, not a technical, judgment.

The controversy originated in an attempt by the United States in 1961 to change the relative weight to be given to conventional and nuclear weapons in NATO doctrine. The method of effecting this change was not new—though it was urged with new insistence. NATO had been presented many times before with American blueprints and had seen its consultative role

[1] "Our Defense Needs: The Long View," *Foreign Affairs*, April 1964.

limited to discussing the technical implementation of an American conception. What gave the dispute its particular urgency was that the advent of a new, highly analytical American Administration coincided with the growing strength and self-confidence of Europe and the deliberate policy of President de Gaulle to assert a more independent role.

In the process, many of the issues that had been obscured in the previous decade by the curious, somewhat one-sided nature of the transatlantic dialogue came for the first time into sharper focus. This highlighted a difference in perspective between the American and the European conception of NATO which had existed since its begining.

When the Korean War raised the spectre of Soviet military aggression, both sides of the Atlantic made a serious effort to turn NATO into a more effective military instrument. However, given the enormous disparity in military and economic strength between the United States and Europe, the primary concern of the European countries was to commit the United States to their defense. They saw in NATO above all a means to obtain American protection, by which was meant American nuclear protection.

However, the Europeans had too much experience with the tenuousness of formal commitments not to strive for more tangible guarantees. This led to pressures for the stationing of American troops in Europe. European reasoning was similar to that ascribed to a French marshal in 1912 when he was asked how many British troops he wanted for the outbreak of a European war. He is reported to have replied: "We need only one, who we will make sure is killed on the first day of the war." In the nuclear age, the price of a guarantee has risen to something like five divisions.

With so many American troops permanently stationed in Europe, it was only sensible to try to give them some meaningful military mission. Even during the period of the doctrine of massive retaliation, NATO forces were larger than the prevailing strategic concept seemed to demand. Indeed, the number was somewhat inconsistent with it. Despite our commit-

ment to a retaliatory strategy, we constantly pressed for a European contribution of ground forces. The Europeans, though they agreed to a succession of NATO force goals, never really believed in the doctrines used to rationalize them. Rather they saw in their military contribution a form of fee paid for United States nuclear protection. The Europeans agreed to our requests. But they tried to see to it that their actual contributions would be large enough to induce us to keep a substantial military establishment in Europe, yet not so high as to provide a real alternative to nuclear retaliation. They were opposed to giving the conventional forces a central military mission; but they also resisted any hint of American withdrawal.

This ambivalence was brought into the open by the shift in United States strategic doctrine in 1961. The American attempt to strengthen the forces for local defense had the paradoxical consequence of bringing to the fore the issue of nuclear control which for many Europeans had always been the crux of the matter. For the first time, U.S. strategic views were publicly challenged, at first hesitantly, then ever more explicitly. Europe had now gained sufficient strength and confidence so that the mere enunciation of an American policy no longer guaranteed its acceptance. The peremptory way in which the United States proceeded only sharpened the controversy. And France added fuel to the flames by giving European misgivings their most extreme formulation.

But if French policy has deliberately sharpened conflicts, the United States tendency to turn an essentially psychological issue into a technical one has unintentionally exacerbated disagreements beyond their intrinsic significance. Our spokesmen often leave the impression that disagreement is due to the ignorance of our allies, and that it is destined to yield ultimately before extensive briefings and insistent reiteration. Faced with opposition, we are less given to asking whether there may be some merit in the arguments of our allies than to overwhelming them with floods of emissaries preaching the latest version of our doctrine.

But the real problem is not that the Europeans fail to understand our quest for multiple options. They simply reject it for themselves. When the issue is Asia or Latin America, Europeans favor an even more flexible response than we do; with respect to the defense of Europe, their attitude is more rigid. As long as the United States retains ultimate control over nuclear weapons, the European incentive is bound to be exactly the opposite of ours. Rather than permit a "pause" for "appreciating the wider risks involved," Europeans prefer to force us to make our response as automatic as possible.

This problem has little to do with whether the United States could afford to give up Europe. It is rooted in the nature of sovereignty and made more acute by the destructiveness of nuclear weapons. Robert Bowie, one of the most eloquent spokesmen of the dominant school of U.S. thought, criticized British nuclear policy before the Assembly of the Western European Union as follows: "Britain has retained its national command structure and the right to withdraw them at its option. This means that they *certainly* could not be counted on by any of the others to be available in case of need."[2] [Italics supplied.] If this concern is real regarding British nuclear forces, which are, after all, assigned to NATO, it must be even stronger regarding U.S. strategic forces which remain under exclusive American control.

The problem can then be summed up as follows: Exclusive U.S. control of nuclear strategy is politically and psychologically incompatible with a strategy of multiple choices or flexible response. The European refusal to assign a meaningful military mission to conventional forces in Europe is incompatible with the indefinite retention of large U.S. forces there. If the United States prizes a conventional response sufficiently, it will have to concede Europe autonomy in nuclear control. If the Europeans want to insist on an automatic nuclear response, a reconsideration of our conventional deployment on the Continent will become inevitable. Refusal to face these facts will guarantee a perpetuation of present dis-

[2] Proceedings of Western European Union Assembly. Ninth Ordinary Session, December 3, 1963.

putes and increasing disarray within NATO.

The United States-European dialogue on strategy is confused further by the nature of the intra-European debate. Many of those who applaud our views do so for reasons which may not prove very comforting in the long run. We must be careful not to take every agreement with us at face value. Acquiescence in our opinion can have two meanings: It can represent either a sincere commitment to Atlantic partnership or disguise a neutralist wish to abdicate responsibility. For the American nuclear umbrella, now sometimes exploited by President de Gaulle for his own purposes, can also be used—and more dangerously for the West—to support policies amounting to neutralism. In many countries it is the leaders and groups traditionally most committed to national defense who have developed views on strategy which challenge American concepts; while some of those most ready to accept U.S. strategic hegemony have in the past been the least interested in making a serious defense effort. We may therefore have to choose between our theories of nuclear control and Atlantic cohesion, between the technical and the political sides of Atlantic policy.

DIFFERENCES IN HISTORICAL PERSPECTIVE

Some of the strains in Atlantic relationships have resulted from factors outside anybody's control. Many reflect the growth in Europe of the very strength and self-confidence which American policy has striven to promote since the end of World War II. Others have been caused by the tactics of President de Gaulle, whose style of diplomacy is not really compatible with the requirements of coalition. We share the responsibility through too much insistence on technical solutions and too little allowance for the intangibles of political judgment and will.

But perhaps the deepest cause of transatlantic misunderstandings is a difference in historical perspective. Americans live in an environment uniquely suited to an engineering approach to policy-making. As a result, our society has been characterized by a conviction that any problem will yield if subjected to a sufficient dose of expertise. With such an approach, problems tend to appear as discrete issues without any inner relationship. It is thought that they can be solved "on their merits" as they arise. It is rarely understood that a "solution" to a problem may mortgage the future—especially as there is sufficient optimism to assume that even should this prove to be the case, it will still be possible to deal with the new problem when it materializes.

But Europeans live on a continent covered with ruins testifying to the fallibility of human foresight. In European history, the recognition of a problem has often defined a dilemma rather than pointed to an answer. The margin of survival of European countries has been more precarious than ours. European reasoning is likely to be more complicated and less confident than ours. This explains some of the strains in Atlantic relationships. Americans tend to be impatient with what seems to them Europe's almost morbid obsession with the past, while Europeans sometimes complain about a lack of sensitivity and compassion on the part of Americans.

In the fall of 1963, our newspapers were filled with derisory comments about French manœuvres then taking place. The scenario of these manœuvres supposed that an aggressor force was attacking France through Germany. France's allies had surrendered. As the aggressor's armies were approaching her borders, France resorted to her nuclear weapons. It is, of course, easy to ridicule this scenario by contrasting the small size of the French bomber force with the magnitude of the disaster envisaged. But the crucial issue is not technical. It arises from the fact that France has undergone shattering historical experiences with which Americans find it difficult to identify. The scenario of the French manœuvres recalled importantly—perhaps too rigidly—France's traumatic experience of 1940, when foreign armies attacked all along the Western front and France's allies collapsed. The British Fighter Command remained in England; the fact that this

critical decision was wise does not affect the basic psychological point. Moreover, the French disaster came at the end of two decades in which France almost single-handedly shouldered the responsibility for the defense of Europe while her erstwhile allies withdrew into isolation or offered strictures about France's obsession with security. The nightmare that some day France might again stand alone goes far deeper than the obstinate ill-will of a single individual.

A comparable problem exists in Germany. Washington has at times shown signs of impatience toward the German leaders and their constant need for reassurance. Secretary Rusk has been reported more than once to be restless with what he has called the "pledging sessions" which the Germans seem so often to demand. However, insecurity is endemic in the German situation. A divided country with frontiers that correspond to no historical experience, a society which has lived through two disastrous defeats and four domestic upheavals in forty years, cannot know inward stability. The need to belong to something, to rescue some predictability out of chaos, is overwhelming. The memories of our allies should be factors as real in the discussions of our policymakers as the analysis of weapons systems.

The importance of this difference in historical perspective is compounded by the continuing disparity in strength between the two sides of the Atlantic. While it has become fashionable to speak of Europe's new-found equality, it is important not to take it too literally. Europe *has* gained in strength over the past decade and a half. It can and should play an increasingly responsible role. But for the foreseeable future we are likely to be by far the stronger partner.

It is important to be clear about this because it requires us to show unusual tact and steadiness. Many of our allies have been guilty of unilateral actions far more flagrant than ours. But when we act unilaterally, disarray in the Alliance is almost inevitable. Drastic changes in U.S. strategic doctrine or action without adequate consultation—such as the removal of

IRBMs from Italy and Turkey or the withdrawal of troops from Germany—create
either a sense of European impotence or
increase the pressure for more autonomy.
Bilateral dealings with the Soviets, from
which our allies are excluded, or about
which they are informed only at the last
moment, are bound to magnify Third Force
tendencies. When our allies resist such U.S.
policies and practices, it is not necessarily
because they disagree with our view but
because they are afraid of creating a precedent for unilateral changes in other policies. (Even statements of substantive disagreement may be a smoke-screen for
deeper concerns.) Moreover, many allied
leaders who have staked their prestige on
certain U.S. policies can suffer serious domestic consequences if we change them
drastically.

Thus the voice of Europe reaches us in
extremely distorted form. President de
Gaulle sharpens all disputes and even
creates them in pursuit of his policy of independence. But some other leaders do not
give full expression to their disquiet because they do not want to undermine
further the solidarity on which their security is thought to depend. Whereas France
exaggerates her disagreements, some other
countries obscure theirs. Thus the dialogue
with Europe is often conducted on false
issues, while real issues—like the future of
Germany, or arms control, or the role of
tactical nuclear weapons—are swept under
the rug in order not to magnify the existing discord.

We, in turn, are faced with the problem
that technology and political conditions are
changing so rapidly that no policy can be
maintained over an indefinite period of
time. How to shape policies that are responsive to change while maintaining the
confidence of our allies? The future vitality
of the Western Alliance depends on understanding the possibilities and limits of the
consultative process.

THE LIMITS AND PURPOSES
OF CONSULTATION

The always difficult problem of coalition
diplomacy is magnified by three factors:
  (1) The fact that the two superpowers

are committed to the existing balance provides their European allies with wide
scope for purely national actions.

(2) The internal workings of modern
government are so complex that they create
a variety of obstacles to meaningful consultation. Nations sometimes find it so
difficult to achieve a domestic consensus
that they are reluctant to jeopardize it afterwards in international forums. The tendency of the United States to confine consultation to elaborating its own blueprint reflects
less a quest for hegemony—as some of our
European critics occasionally assert—than
a desire to avoid complicating still further
its own decisionmaking process.

(3) As governments have found in their
domestic experience, access to the same
technical data does not guarantee unanimity of understanding. In an alliance of
states very unequal in size and strength,
and with widely varying histories, differences are almost inevitable. And they are
likely to be made all the more intractable
by a technology of unprecedented destructiveness and novelty.

Thus consultation is far from being a
magic cure-all. It will not necessarily remove real differences of geography, perspective or interest. Nevertheless, an improvement in the consultative process
should be one of the chief concerns of the
Alliance.

The dominant American view has been
that consultation would be most effective
if there were a division of labor within
the Alliance according to which the United
States retained control over nuclear weapons while Europe specialized in conventional forces. Similarly, it has been suggested in Great Britain that the independent British nuclear deterrent could be
given up in return for a greater voice in
American policy.[3] The proposed NATO
Multilateral Force on which the United
States increasingly stakes its prestige is
basically a device to make its nuclear hegemony acceptable.[4]

[3] See "The Labor Party's Defense and Foreign
Policy," by Patrick Gordon Walker, *Foreign Affairs*,
April 1964, pp. 391–98.
[4] For the author's view on the NATO Multi-
lateral Force see "NATO's Nuclear Dilemma," *The
Reporter*, March 28, 1963.

In other words, the thrust of our policy is to create a structure which makes it physically impossible for any of the allies (except the United States) to act autonomously. This raises the following problems: (a) How effective will consultation based on such premises be? (b) Is such a system as useful for the long-term political vitality of the Alliance as it is for the conduct of a general nuclear war?

With regard to the first of these, any process of consultation must be responsive to the following three questions: Who has a right to be consulted? Whose voice carries weight? Who has enough competence?

These three levels are not necessarily identical. Many agencies in our own government have a right to express their views, but not all carry the same weight. When some of Britain's Labor leaders suggest that they want a greater voice in our decisions in return for giving up British nuclear weapons, the answer has to be: Like whose voice? Like that of the Arms Control and Disarmament Agency? Or the Joint Chiefs of Staff? Or the State Department? Or the Commerce Department? In our interdepartmental disputes, clearly, the outcome often depends on the constituency which the agency or department represents. The weight given to advice is inevitably related to the competence that it reflects.

If the United States retains indefinitely an effective monopoly of nuclear power, we would probably find in time that Europe simply does not have sufficient technical competence for its views to carry weight. And this in turn is likely to breed irresponsibility on both sides of the Atlantic. A right of consultation without ability to make a serious judgment may, in fact, be the worst possible system. Over a period of time it is bound to reduce Europe's voice in Washington; while in Europe it must produce a sense of impotence or extreme nationalism. Indeed, it may enable neutralists to focus all Europe's anti-nuclear sentiment against the United States. Some European autonomy on nuclear matters—preferably growing out of existing programs—seems therefore desirable.

The emphasis placed on a unitary strategic system for the Alliance has reversed the proper priorities. The real challenge to the consultative process is less in the field of strategy than in diplomacy. The ability to fight a centrally controlled general war is useful; but the ability to devise common policies in the face of a whole spectrum of eventualities is much more important.

If the Alliance cannot develop procedures for a common diplomacy—or at least an agreed range of divergence—it seems contradictory to insist on a system of unitary strategic control. When NATO has proved unable to develop even a common trade policy toward the Communist world, it is not surprising that countries are reluctant to entrust their survival to a NATO ally, however close. Policies on a whole range of issues such as Suez, the Congo, negotiating tactics over Berlin or the defense of Southern Arabia have been unilateral or divergent. The United States is now in the curious situation of staking a great deal of its prestige on establishing the NATO Multilateral Force and a system of unitary strategic control while East-West negotiations or the war in Southeast Asia or arms control are dealt with more or less unilaterally.

In re-assessing these priorities, it may be important to ask how unitary a system of control for strategy and diplomacy is in fact desirable. What kind of structure is more vital in the long run: An Atlantic system that automatically involves all partners? Or one that permits some autonomy? On many issues—particularly East-West relations—united action is essential. With respect to others, some degree of flexibility may be desirable. Over the next decades the United States is likely to find itself increasingly engaged in the Far East, in Southeast Asia and in Latin America. Our European allies will probably not consider their vital interest at stake in these areas. President de Gaulle's views on this subject are far from unique in Europe, even if his methods are.

If the Atlantic system is absolutely centralized, policy may be reduced to the lowest common denominator. The Soviets may use our involvements elsewhere to blackmail Europe. This, combined with the lack of interest among Europeans in the issues involved, may strain the Alliance beyond the breaking point. On the other hand, if Europe is accorded some capacity for autonomous action—military and political —its concern would be no greater, but the temptation for Soviet adventures might be reduced. Put positively, a structure which permits a variety of coordinated approaches toward the new nations could enhance the vigor of our policies, the self-confidence of our allies and the long-term vitality of the Alliance. Paradoxically, the unity of the Atlantic area may well be furthered by a structure which grants the possibility of autonomous action while reducing the desire for it.

WHAT STRUCTURE FOR THE ATLANTIC AREA?

The most delicate problem faced by the United States in its Atlantic policy, then, is to promote cohesion without undermining the self-confidence and the political will of its allies. Formal structures can help in this effort. But when they become ends in themselves they may cause us to beg the key question by the very terms in which we state it.

Some of the current theories of Atlantic partnership run precisely this risk. According to the dominant U.S. view, shared by such wise Europeans as Jean Monnet, there is only *one* reliable concept of Atlantic partnership—that described by the image of "twin pillars" or a "dumbbell," composed of the United States and a united Europe organized on federal lines with supra-national institutions. This is, of course, one form of Atlantic partnership. But is it wise to stake everything on a single approach? History is rarely such a linear and simple process.

Every European state is the product of some process of integration at some time over the past four centuries; and Germany and Italy achieved unity less than one hundred years ago. European history suggests that there is more than one way to achieve integration. In Italy, it came by way of plebiscite and annexation abolishing the individual states. In Germany, unification occurred under the aegis of one state but as the act of sovereign govern-

ments which remained in existence after unity was achieved. The resulting structure clearly did not lack cohesiveness.

Moreover, how valid is a concept of European integration which is rejected by *both* France and Great Britain? In the outrage over Britain's exclusion from the Common Market, it has not always been noted that Britain's view (shared by both major parties) of the organization of Europe is almost identical with that of France. Both countries would find it difficult, if not impossible, to commit themselves now to a federal structure and a common parliament. It only adds to the irony of the situation that many of the most ardent advocates of Britain's entry into the Common Market both here and in Europe are also dedicated proponents of a federal Europe. How do they propose to reconcile these two objectives?

There may be various roads to European cooperation. The one traced by the Fouchet Plan—calling for institutionalized meetings of foreign ministers and sub-cabinet officials—is not the least plausible, and indeed it is the one most consistent with British participation. It has the advantage of producing some immediate progress without foreclosing the future. It would also permit a more flexible arrangement of Atlantic relations than the "twin pillar" concept now in vogue.

While the United States should welcome any European structure that reflects the desires of the Europeans, it would be unwise to stake everything on one particular formula. A very rigid conception of Atlantic partnership can easily fail to do justice to the richness and variety of relationships possible within the Atlantic context. Is it really possible or useful to lump the countries of Europe together on all issues? Are they always inherently closer to one another than any of them is to the United States? Do the Dutch inevitably feel a greater sense of identification with the French, or the British with the Germans, than either does with the United States? If we separate the question into political, military or economic components, is the answer always uniform and does it always point in the same direction? Would it not be wiser to retain some flexibility? There is a grave risk that too doctrinaire an approach will produce either a collapse of political will, or more likely, a new and virulent form of nationalism, perhaps even more intense than the nationalism of the *patries*. A Europe largely constucted on theoretical models might be forced into an anti-American mold because its only sense of identity will be what distinguishes it from America. Our bent for structural remedies sometimes blinds us to the fact that institutions produce their own momentum and that this cannot be foreseen from the proclamations of their founders.

In assessing our own Atlantic policy, we must cut through slogans to such questions as: Is it wise to insist that the only road to European unity is by institutions unacceptable to both France and Britain? Is the best way to solve the strategic problem by staking our prestige on a device—the Multilateral Force—which compels us to oppose the existing nuclear programs in Europe while bringing a host of presently non-nuclear countries (among them Germany, Italy, Greece and Turkey) into the nuclear business, occasionally with only their reluctant assent? Can it be in the interest of NATO, of the Federal Republic, or of the United States, to make Germany the senior European nuclear partner in the Multilateral Force and to create an institution which can rally all anti-U.S., anti-German and anti-nuclear sentiments against us?

European history teaches that stability is unattainable except through the coöperation of Britain, France and Germany. Care should be taken not to resurrect old national rivalries in the name of Atlanticism. The United States should not choose a special partner among its European allies. The attempt to woo one, or to force European countries to choose between us and France—a tendency which despite all disavowals is real—must magnify the European nationalism which French policy has already done so much to foster.

Our concern thus returns to the somewhat out-of-scale figure of President de Gaulle. A sense of frustration resulting from his policies, and even more from his style, has caused many to see him as individually responsible for the failure to realize many deeply felt objectives. This is not the place to attempt an assessment of his character. Conceivably he is as petty, as animated by remembered slights, as some of our commentators suggest. It is also possible that a man so conscious of his historic role has larger purposes. At any rate, we will not know until we have had a real dialogue with him. In a period of détente with Soviet Russia, is it impossible to conduct a serious conversation with a traditional ally? President de Gaulle has repeatedly expressed his willingness to coördinate strategy rather than to integrate it. We should make new efforts to explore what he means. His 1958 proposal of a Directory is not acceptable when confined to Britain, France and the United States. Do we know his attitude toward a wider forum?

Irritation with de Gaulle's tactics does not change the fact that in his proposals of 1958 for a Directory he puts his finger on perhaps the key problem of NATO. In the absence of a common foreign policy—or at least an agreed range of divergence—the attempt to devise a common strategy is likely to prove futile. Lord Avon and Dean Acheson have come to the same conclusion. The time seems ripe to create a political body at the highest level—composed perhaps of the United States, the United Kingdom, France, the Federal Republic and Italy—for concerting the policies of the nations bordering the North Atlantic. Such a body should discuss how to implement common Atlantic purposes and define the scope of autonomous action where interests diverge. It should also be charged with developing a common strategic doctrine.

Conceivably this could end the sterile scholastic debate over the relative benefits of integration as against coördination. It might heal a rift which if continued is bound to hazard everything that has been painfully built up over fifteen years. Both the United States and France are able to thwart each other's purposes. Neither can create an alternative structure—France even less than we. As in a Greek tragedy, each chief actor, following a course that seems quite reasonable, is producing consequences quite different from what he intends.

This should not happen. The problems will become insuperable only if technique is exalted above purpose and if interest is too narrowly conceived. The West does itself an injustice by comparing its disagreements to the rifts in the Communist bloc. In the Communist world, schisms are inevitable and unbridgeable. Western societies have been more fortunate. Their evolution has been richer; they have forged unity by drawing strength from diversity. Free from the shackles of a doctrine of historical inevitability, the nations of the West can render a great service by demonstrating that if history has a meaning it is up to us today to give it that meaning.

HOW NOT TO LEAD AN ALLIANCE

BY BERNARD BRODIE

The North Atlantic Treaty Organization has now lost one of its two major continental powers, and is clearly diminished by more than that very substantial loss. It is presently moving its most meaningful organ, SHAPE (Supreme Headquarters Allied Powers Europe), from the Western outskirts of Paris to a corner of Belgium called Casteau, references to which are usually amplified with the information that it is "near Mons," which some of us last heard of as a place the British Army retreated from in the early days of the First World War. The North Atlantic Council, never really important but symbolic of something important, is moving from the large edifice built for it at the Porte Dauphine in Paris to Brussels.

All this has proceeded in large part from a commonly shared conviction, which even the United States government has begun openly to accept, that the Soviet Union does not really threaten a direct attack in Europe. Even so, the obvious illness of what is left of the Organization stems also from other causes. Although one hesitates to call an international body dead to which many good and some quite able people are still devoting considerable energies, we know from long experience that organizations may go through the motions of being alive while being in fact spent. NATO seems to be in or approaching that condition. Is this decay our fault, or is it due mostly to the disdainful blows of the French President? Inasmuch as the United States has been the acknowledged leader of NATO, we really have to ask, first, how much did our actions contribute to or provoke de Gaulle's behavior, and second, what did we do independently to supplement or amplify the negative consequences of his actions?

THE TURNING POINT

Among people who should know, European as well as American, many believe that nothing the United States could reasonably have done could have altered substantially the relevant policies of de Gaulle. On the other hand, if we accept the somewhat old-fashioned (or at least lately neglected) axiom that the national interests are likely to be best served through taking into account the conceptions, aspirations, and sensibilities of those with whom we must deal, and certainly not less of those whose collaboration we seek than of those whom we must regard as basically hostile,

Reprinted by permission from *The Reporter*, March 9, 1967. Copyright 1967 by the Reporter Magazine. The editors made slight deletions in this reprint at the request of the author.

then the list of American sins of omission or commission against one of its most important allies is long and grievous.

The key U.S. decision in this respect—"key" because it symbolizes and in a sense contains all the others—was the rejection of de Gaulle's proposal to President Eisenhower in the autumn of 1958 that a sort of directorate be formed comprising France, Britain, and the United States to run the affairs of NATO and to co-ordinate international policy on the highest diplomatic as well as strategic levels. The United States dismissed this proposal apparently with no show of interest in seeking a compromise alternative, allegedly on the grounds that it would be inequitable to other members of NATO. No doubt among the real reasons was that the United States did not wish the intrusion of French advice concerning its foreign policies, especially in areas outside Europe, such as Africa—or Vietnam.

Anyway, far from reasserting the equality in principle of all the members of NATO, the United States by this rejection asserted its unwillingness to water down or share its extraordinarily dominant role in the Organization. In French eyes it was seeking to keep France on a level with Luxembourg. The subsequent conduct of France toward the Organization would have had to be basically different if we had accepted something like its 1958 proposal and lived up to it in good faith, which, of course, would have meant giving an appropriate hearing thereafter to French views.

After the inauguration of the Kennedy administration at the beginning of 1961, our relations with France were markedly worsened by, among other things, the hortatory and scornful public comments that Secretary of Defense Robert S. McNamara directed toward the French nuclear program, which we wanted to see abandoned in its military aspects. This was incredibly clumsy diplomacy on our part, because it should have been obvious that de Gaulle would not in the slightest degree be deflected from his course by our castigations. We were, however, bemused by the domestic opposition within France to the nuclear program, and were no doubt expecting to hasten by our policy the po-

litical demise of de Gaulle. Even so, we should not have expected Frenchmen to appreciate the reasons for our overtly differentiating between the British nuclear effort, which we regretted but found excusable, and the French effort, which we condemned.

The irritations we thereby inflicted on our ally were probably secondary in importance to the support our remarks gave to some already deeply embedded French and German suspicions. These were that American insistence on maintaining monopoly control within the alliance of its nuclear power reflected a diminishing reliability of that power. This apprehension was strongly enhanced by our concurrent pressure upon our allies to build up their conventional forces for a strictly conventional role. Our repeated insistence that the United States was absolutely to be trusted in these vital nuclear matters, and that American views concerning them were not at all subject to change into the indefinite future, could of course not be taken seriously by any reasonable European with some sense for history—least of all a Frenchman, who has a tradition of skepticism about political morality and who should hardly be asked to attribute to the United States a sharply higher degree of morality and fidelity than he can possibly accord his own country. Must we ask him to believe that Frenchmen and Britons but not Americans are capable of a Munich-type sellout? And especially in a nuclear age?

An American military commitment to Europe, which is what the North Atlantic Treaty originally represented, is basically a good thing for our interests as well as for those of Europe. However, that does not mean that the highly complex structure that developed on the basis of the treaty and the immobilism that long ago set in concerning NATO staff planning were in anybody's interest. The drastic shake-up that NATO has received during the past year, and the readjustments that it must in any case undergo, offer an opportunity for the inception of a new system for safeguarding the security of Western Europe. Real rejuvenation of the old system is out of the question, but the required new departures are also out of the question unless we try to understand where our NATO policy was going awry.

SWITCHING SIGNALS

Since its beginning, American officials having anything to do with NATO have usually been sure that they understood far better that the Europeans the problems of European defense and their solution, and they did little or nothing to avoid projecting that conviction. Most Europeans long accepted this claim as probably correct, partly because of the American near-monopoly of nuclear weapons but more especially because of the initially impressive and peculiarly American efflorescence of strategic thinking and writing, especially on the part of highly intellectual civilians. We had institutions like the RAND Corporation, which attracted to themselves not merely respect but mystique, and out of these institutions came such esoteric new phenomena as "cost-effectiveness" analysis, with which the brilliant Mr. McNamara was known to be enamored, and various gaming techniques reputed, with much exaggeration, to depend heavily on the use of computers. The Europeans had nothing at all like this, and both they and we were impressed.

In recent years, however, the Europeans have become increasingly disenchanted. For one thing, there have been sudden and drastic changes in American strategic doctrine—as for example between the Radford Plan submitted to NATO in 1957, which placed reliance for the defense of Europe primarily on tactical as well as strategic nuclear weapons, and the McNamara conception embodied in the latter's Athens speech to NATO representatives in 1962 and some weeks later in his public Ann Arbor speech. The McNamara conception was a complete reversal of the Radford Plan.

Five years may seem like a long enough time to warrant a basic change in thinking, but each strategy was supposed to look indefinitely into the future. Besides, international bureaucracies are not as flexible as all that. Also, the later developments in American strategic thinking, especially the McNamara emphasis on conventional weapons even in the event of large-scale war, seemed to suggest to most Europeans that the ingenuity reflected in those conceptions was not necessarily combined with wisdom, political or strategic. More recently the problem has been a refusal of the McNamara school to change its position despite its complete failure to secure any of the preconditions for it.

Henry A. Kissinger has put it well: "American policy-makers often act as if disagreement with their views is due to ignorance which must be overcome by extensive briefings and insistent reiteration. They are less inclined to inquire whether there may be some merit in an opposing view than in overwhelming it with floods of emissaries, official and semi-official. As a result, the United States and Europe have too often conducted their dialogue over the technical implementation of a blueprint manufactured in America."

THE PUSHY AMERICANS

To get the flavor of this, one need only talk with American officials and see them in action at the frequent international conferences, small and large, quasi-private and semi-public, within the Atlantic Community. At such conferences, where officials may participate with persons of no official status, one sees that while American public servants may be individually as modest and engaging as those of any other nationality, in their roles as representatives of the United States they often become quite different people.

Ambassador Harlan Cleveland, for example, our senior representative to the North Atlantic Council, is clearly a very nice man, dedicated but unassuming. Yet in one thirty-minute statement before an international gathering at Oxford University last September, he said approximately the following: (a) Up to now the Europeans have had no opportunity of knowing anything about nuclear weapons, so their views on how to use them could be of little value. However, the United States is now giving its allies the requisite data, and they can therefore be expected in a year or two to have opinions that will warrant respect. (b) The problem of France has been solved so far as NATO is concerned, and no other serious problems remain.

What the ambassador seemed to mean on the latter issue was that the problem of adjusting to France's clearly unreasonable desires had disappeared by its exit from the Organization, and that the problems created by that exit were minimal. These remarks were less characteristic of American attitudes than those on nuclear weapons, and probably reflected only Cleveland's special brand of personal optimism.

On nuclear weapons, however, he was repeating only what American officials had been saying all along, though not usually so sharply etched. His audience was largely comprised of Europeans, most of them fairly senior officers in the NATO military forces, and there was even the novelty of a Soviet reporter present from the London office of Moscow Radio and TV.

Conversations with senior officials in European defense ministries or NATO delegations have tended increasingly in the last few years to expose complaints of American "doctrinalism" and "pushing," to use the words of one of them. From being a highly respected figure, Secretary McNamara has for many, especially in Germany but by no means exclusively there, turned into the personification of all that is wrong with American leadership in NATO.

THE CLICHÉ OF CLICHÉS

Indeed, it is difficult to understand the extraordinary insensitivity of those highly intellectual Americans who characterized the New Frontier approach to NATO affairs—an insensitivity concerning not only European touchiness about status, to which at least lip service was paid, but also concerning the possible merit of European ideas. It has not been due to any lack of diplomatic contact: members of our embassies do talk to the local people. One would not be concerned about their often disagreeing with and dismissing the views of their hosts—it is not a diplomatist's

job, after all, to be in accord with the views of his hosts—except that the dissent seems to take the form of reiterating the clichés one has so often heard back in Washington. In Bonn, for example, one hears again that the Germans don't understand nuclear weapons, and anyway they don't contribute enough to their own defense. Besides, why don't they come through with the offset agreements necessary to ease the strain on the American balance of payments caused by the residence within Germany of so many American military personnel and their dependents?

The word "clichés" is itself a cliché word. It is easy enough to damn as cliché any view which is expressed more than once and with which one does not agree. However, in a bureaucratic environment where a great many people of all ranks embrace ardently and repeat to their opposite numbers abroad conceptions which they certainly did not originate and which they only partially understand themselves, clichéism is apt to flourish. How many Americans have explained the merits of the conventional buildup or the Multilateral Force to European civilians and military officers of far greater relevant experience than themselves! It does not require much experience with members of the State Department to be made aware of the fact that there is very definitely a "party line."

What we have suggested about the State Department naturally also goes for the Department of Defense, except that there are always a number of civil wars going in the latter much more ample establishment—wars between the military and the civilians and also between the several services. However, so far as the projection of our policies in NATO is concerned, the Secretary of Defense and his own band of civilian aides, including those in the Division of International Security Affairs, have been a united and powerful influence, usually in support of or supported by the State Department. The ardor of the partnership would normally be commendable, but it does matter what kind of policy is being promoted.

The great cliché of them all is "integration," for which Americans seem to have a special penchant. Did not America become great from the fact that the states united? Is not the American economy great because it has a vast internal market untrammeled by barriers to trade other than distance? Do not American industries, already the greatest in the world individually, seek irresistibly to reduce their vulnerabilities through mergers? One of the things we have therefore been most in favor of for Europe is integration. Difficult as it is for most Europeans to believe, our interest in their integration is basically altruistic and is only rationalized for their benefit and ours as being in our own self-interest. We are, for example, in favor of the Common Market—which is certainly contrary to our earlier concern with "most favored nation" treatment. We even went so far as to intervene diplomatically at the last minute in January, 1963, in an attempt to prevent de Gaulle's veto of British admission to the Common Market. What a help that was!

Integration is what NATO is all about. The Organization stands for integration of forces and of planning. Integrated war planning has been going on at SHAPE since its beginning. Integration of forces is a good deal of what concerns SACEUR (Supreme Allied Commander Europe). The highest aspirations of the principle were embodied in the so-called Stikker Exercise, designed to bring the armed forces of our NATO partners to a higher state of individual efficiency and also into a closer harmony.

One of the things most wrong with "integration" is that we don't practice it ourselves. By far the greatest single force in the NATO arsenal is the American strategic bombing force, which is decidedly not integrated. The Multilateral Force (MLF) idea, which was going to bring integration down to the manning of individual ships, was designed from the outset with a built-in American veto. This might possibly disappear with time, but only might. European ground forces were to be integrated with American ones by redesigning themselves in large part after the American image. American participation in any stra-

tegic dialogue has hardly been one of give-and-take. Naturally, no end of lip service is paid to the idea of accommodation to the views of our partners, but how could we really accommodate when we knew the problems, had the answers, and were covering three-quarters of the cost?

In SHAPE, the integration of planning has been accomplished only by a process of ossification around views that almost everyone now agrees are completely out of date. SHAPE planning has always been, and probably continues to be, for a war that will never be—a war that begins with a massive Soviet nuclear attack to which we reply in kind, and where the ground forces play only the role of stopping the Red Army. When some "contingency planning" for the defense of Berlin was prompted by the Berlin crisis of 1961, the planning had to be done outside of SHAPE. What good is integrated planning that is necessarily bad planning?

It was with his usual hauteur, but alas also with his frequent accuracy, that President de Gaulle originally announced his departure from NATO in the following terms:

"Thus . . . our country will remain the ally of her allies but, upon the expiration of the commitments formerly taken—that is, in 1969 by the latest—the subordination known as 'integration' which is provided for by NATO and which hands our fate over to foreign authority shall cease, as far as we are concerned."

From the beginning, SACEUR has been an American, and few Europeans have challenged the necessity for this arrangement. The orginal SACEUR was General Eisenhower, whose tremendous prestige helped give viability to the new organization. Subsequent SACEURs were bound to have less prestige, but have been very able. Until the replacement of General Lauris Norstad in 1963, the fiction had been that SACEUR was not an American but an allied commander, subordinate equally to all the governments whose forces were under his command. The fact that he was also EUCOM (European Commander) of American forces could be glossed over with the observation that he wore two hats. However, President Kennedy dismissed Norstad without consulting the NATO allies. The man who fires is clearly the man who controls. Moreover, Norstad was known to have been dismissed because of his unreadiness to accept some of those McNamara doctrines which the Europeans themselves did not like. Inasmuch as his replacement, General Lyman Lemnitzer, is three years older than Norstad, it was not easy to use the kind of excuses that might normally have been advanced for the retirement of a general.

General Lemnitzer also came into his present post with a kind of stigma that could do him no good in his new position. He had been Chairman of the Joint Chiefs of Staff at the time of the Bay of Pigs, and had added his consent to that dismal and still incredible operation. The dispatch of Lemnitzer to SHAPE could only inspire speculations throughout Europe, and perhaps more than speculations, that the President had sent him to this new post simply to get him out of Washington.

In recent years there has also been a mounting irritation on the part of European governments over the admonitions and requirements that SACEUR has considered it his duty to make known to them. Part of this has to do with the feeling by some governments that SACEUR is being used by their own commanders to obtain equipment which they feel unable to acquire by their own request. How handy to have a desire for more vehicles fed into a SACEUR "requirement" to one's own government! These charges may be greatly exaggerated, and even if valid are hardly nefarious. The fact that they are even repeated probably shows only the general weariness with "integration" and American leadership.

BOWIE'S BRAINCHILD

In a conversation with this writer last autumn, a high official of the secretariat to the North Atlantic Council referred to the MLF as a "near disaster." The "near" was added simply as a thankful acknowledgment that the scheme had not been adopted. The origin of the idea has its roots in the

need to respond to a proposal of SACEUR (at that time Norstad), who wished land-based IRBMs installed in Europe under his command. His object seemed to be the control of missiles that he could direct against those the Soviets had aimed at targets in Europe. There were several reasons why the SACEUR proposal was not palatable in Washington. A State Department study group headed by Harvard Professor Robert R. Bowie (who had previously been director of the Policy Planning Council of the State Department, and who has now returned to the department as counselor) proposed in turn that a preferred alternative to the Norstad proposal was to put a force of Polaris submarines off the coasts of Europe. These vessels were to be financed and jointly operated by the participants, each of which was to have a veto on the firing of their missiles.

Later, ostensibly because the "mixed manning" was going to be applied to individual vessels, and was supposed to make for special hazards on submarines, the plan was changed to allow for a force of twenty-five surface ships armed with Polaris missiles. The surface ships happened also to be a good deal cheaper than submarines, and this is important because it put the United States in the position of recommending for adoption as a joint venture something decidedly inferior to the kind of seagoing Polaris force it maintained for itself. If it was not inferior, why was the United States paying all that extra money for high-performance submarines?

Actually, the original basic idea seems to have been thought up by two scholars on Professor Bowie's team. The scheme was submitted to the North Atlantic Council by Secretary of State Christian Herter in December, 1960, but simply for study. The Kennedy administration came into office a month later, and its first expressed attitudes toward the MLF were lukewarm to negative. President Kennedy himself openly stated the view that it was quite unnecessary.

What happened subsequently provides us with an exemplary lesson in how zeal, combined with shrewdness in bureaucratic infighting, on the part of a few officials in key positions can cause the adoption of a major initiative in United States foreign policy. To Professor Bowie the idea was both a kind of brainchild, even if by adoption, and also a means of achieving the greatest of his heart's desires concerning NATO—integration.

Professor Bowie can write very persuasive memos, and so can another man whom he early enlisted in this cause and who soon displayed equal ardor in pursuit of the objective—Henry Owen, then deputy to Walt W. Rostow as head of the State Department Policy Planning Council and now officially holding the latter position (the Council, incidentally, never meets as a corporate body and seems to have no function except to lend prestige to its director). Bowie and Owen brought Under Secretary George W. Ball into their alliance. Secretary of State Dean Rusk simply went along. By March, 1963, Ambassador Livingston Merchant had been called from retirement to carry out the negotiations that were to convert the MLF from a dream to a reality. The bureaucratic hierarchy was not slow in catching on. As the year wore on, the intensity and urgency of American pressure upon our allies to adopt this idea steadily increased.

Many things have been said for and against the MLF, but the strongest argument against it is simply that the allies did not want it. This scheme that was supposed to further integration was inherently divisive. When British participants in a semi-private meeting with Americans held in England in the autumn of 1963 to discuss NATO problems made some telling arguments against the MLF and expressed their doubts concerning the genuineness of German interest in the project, J. Robert Schaetzel, now our ambassador to the European Communities, asserted that "We can argue until doomsday why the Germans want the MLF, the fact is they want it." He was wrong on both points. It was easy enough to discover why they had agreed to it. All one needed to do was ask the appropriate persons and listen to the replies, but that sort of experience was rare to those who might have been

asked. Candor among allies is not difficult to achieve; it is, however, rarely sought by those who are trying to put a point across and who listen only as salesmen listen to resistive arguments—with the intention not of learning but of scoring.

This writer, in various conversations at about that time with officials in the German Foreign and Defense Ministries, failed to detect any real enthusiasm for the MLF. In some instances, quite the contrary was expressed. The Germans seemed to be going along with the idea because they knew that the Americans wanted it very much; and because de Gualle was behaving so badly, somebody had to be doing something to please America.

My suspicion was confirmed last fall in a conversation with a top German Foreign Service official who had been present in the room when Chancellor Adenauer, while discussing the MLF proposal with his colleagues, received the message informing him that de Gaulle had just vetoed British admission to the Common Market. Adenauer, in announcing the content of the message, added that this settled the matter of German adherence to the MLF. Later Germany began to project an attitude that seemed to reflect almost as much enthusiasm for the idea as the United States. For a while in 1964 it looked as though the United States and Germany, with the participation "in principle" of Italy, Turkey, and Greece, would go ahead with this project even if other members of NATO abstained.

Then suddenly President Johnson, no doubt disturbed by the now obvious divisiveness of the proposal, took another hard look at it himself and ordered that the U.S. pressures for the adoption of the project be relaxed. The effect of this relaxation was naturally to let quick death overtake it. The sigh of relief in the Atlantic Alliance was general, though the Germans now had reason to resent being left exposed by the sudden abandonment of a scheme to which they had committed themselves. They and other Europeans, incidentally, must have been other than amused when they read Under Secretary Ball's testimony before the Senate Foreign Relations Committee on July 13, 1966, where he said concerning the MLF and our NATO allies: ". . . we have been very careful not try to bring any pressure on them and not to try to insist upon this particular solution." Later he added, "We certainly are not doctrinaire about any particular kind of solution, and we think whatever solution is found should be one which the Europeans themselves play a large part in developing." Senator Frank Church (D., Idaho) later wrote concerning this statement of Ball's: "If we are so unaware of the resentment our tactics produced, our antennae are in need of major repair."

One of the reasons why Professor Bowie so strongly advocated the idea, as he explained at an international conference at Dedham, Massachusetts, in the spring of 1963, was that he considered German aspirations to gain a nuclear capability "inevitable" and he believed the MLF to be the way of anticipating and deflecting those aspirations. The answer to such a remark is twofold: (1) the inevitability of the German demand—for any reasonable time span in the future—was simply one man's view; and (2) if Germany really wanted a nuclear capability, the MLF with its multilateral and especially American veto was hardly the device to beguile it from that desire.

The MLF has stood out, along with the "conventional buildup" which we shall next describe, as the apotheosis of American "doctrinalism" and "pushing." The conception concerned a gadget. Whether or not it could have worked technically— and mixed manning of ships probably presents no great difficulties—the special force conceived of involved expense, it might additionally provoke the Soviet Union to comparable replies, and there was simply no need for it.

THE CONVENTIONAL BUILDUP

We must now take up the item that has perhaps caused more trouble in NATO and more disenchantment with American leadership than all the others put together—U.S. insistence on revising the strategy for the defense of Europe to avoid reliance not only on strategical nuclear weapons but on tactical nuclear weapons as well, even in the event of large-scale war. The ramifications of this idea have pervaded every aspect of our NATO relations, including the offset-purchase agreements with Germany, against which the latter country has finally rebelled in the series of actions that began with the fall of Chancellor Erhard and the subsequent elections.

Let us first be clear that no sane person wants to see nuclear weapons exploding in anger either strategically or even tactically, especially in densely populated Europe. Moreover, no one wants to see any kind of serious war breaking out in Europe, whether nuclear or non-nuclear. But the Europeans would rather see war avoided by the threat of using nuclear weapons than take the risks which might stem from letting that threat become ambiguous. They also want to avoid the great added costs of the proposed conventional buildup for a war they consider almost impossible. Washington, on the other hand, has continued to insist that we must think not only about deterring war but about keeping it non-nuclear if it comes.

Let us also be clear that we are talking not about skirmishes resulting from "pinpricks" but about real war, usually conceived of as resulting from a massive, deliberate, but somehow non-nuclear attack by the Soviet Union. No one questions the need for suitable conventional forces to deal with accidental outbreaks of violence along the frontiers or the Berlin autobahns. But one does not have to *build up* for these purposes.

President Kennedy came to office determined, as one of his assistants put it, to put "the nuclear genie back in the bottle." In his Secretary of Defense the new President found a servant willing to oblige in any case, and also sharing the same preoccupations for somewhat independent reasons. New administrations want to make a show of changing things over from predecessor administrations, especially of the opposite party, and the New Frontier wanted to change everything connected with the "New Look," the Radford Plan, and the Dulles doctrine of massive retaliation. Considering the extremes reached under those conceptions, some change was surely in order.

It is hard for a layman to understand the lengths to which the new doctrine proceeded. Not only did the United States begin, with the McNamara speeches of Athens and Ann Arbor in 1962, to press our allies to build up their conventional forces, but stemming from this pressure were a host of other pressures that had the same negative political effect. For some time there was a good deal of haggling on how much conventional ammunition and other supplies should be held ready for combat, the United States at one time holding out for a ninety-day combat supply at a large and intense level of fighting.

The American denunciation over a period of years of the French nuclear effort was also directly tied in large part to the same conception. All our copious advice to the European countries about how they should arm themselves has stressed the importance of their preparing themselves for conventional combat. The offset agreements with West Germany, which have become increasingly burdensome and irritating to that country, have stressed the purchase in the United States of costly war material suitable only for conventional combat.

When Under Secretary Ball observed on April 10, 1966, that the French withdrawal from NATO might force the West to use nuclear weapons earlier than we might otherwise do in a world conflict, such an outcome being conceivable because "we are removing a part of a defense in depth which is useful," he could not have had in mind how the Germans might respond to such a remark. For it means simply that West Germany could be considered expendable before nuclear weapons were used.

There was even a proposal by some Americans connected with a prominent research organization to build a new Maginot Line of fixed fortifications across the line dividing East and West Germany. Although this proposal was fortunately not adopted by the United States government, the idea was expounded abroad and became well enough known to become a subject of comment in the European press. Characteristically, it was admitted by the authors that such a line would be utterly useless against nuclear weapons, and of course it would be needless in small outbreaks, so that one might say it would be effective only against attacks exquisitely tailored to make it so.

AS EUROPE SEES IT

From the European point of view, the objections to the American anti-nuclear doctrine may be summed up under two points—apart from the obvious one that the Russians could always match in kind a western conventional buildup.

(1) The deterrence of large-scale war has been at least as important as attempting to avoid the use of nuclear weapons in such a war, the more so as deterrence appeared nearly certain of accomplishment.

(2) The European leaders felt, in common with many of our own specialists in Kremlinology, that the conventional-war arguments completely distorted the image of the opponent. It would in fact take an extraordinarily bold enemy to possess what the advocates of the doctrine imputed to him: not only a readiness to commit large-scale military aggression against the West, but a readiness to assault our nuclear-armed forces with conventional arms alone! The doctrine thus asserted that the Russians could be willing to enter a duel to the death while leaving to us the choice of weapons.

The recently growing movement among the Germans to turn to de Gaulle even at the risk of blighting their relationship with the United States is an acknowledgment that although de Gaulle's nuclear power is only a fraction that of the American, he at least knows how to use the advantage that power gives him. Meanwhile, his nuclear power is growing and in time will be respectable. Besides, the French are not constantly demanding offset purchases of materials that the Germans do not want.

Finally, there may be some point in the opinion of one experienced British official that an alliance is more likely to hold together when all the other members feel they have to sit on the nuclear power's coattails to keep him from doing something rash—the attitude that prevailed until the end of 1961—than when they feel his nuclear power simply cannot be counted upon

We should not close without at least mentioning the American involvement in Vietnam, concerning which the Europeans were not consulted and in which the United States appears to have become increasingly absorbed to the growing exclusion of other concerns. Practically every European official or leader of opinion interviewed by this writer last fall expressed dismay at and inability to comprehend that involvement. To de Gaulle, filled with the sense of France's historic role in that area until only yesterday, a role which in fact continues in the French air patrolling of the Demilitarized Zone under its Geneva commitments, the absence of consultation was especially rankling. He has not missed his chance to make public statements about Vietnam calculated to cause us maximum embarrassment. No doubt we have a right to resent this, but where did the provocation begin? His 1958 proposal apparently asked for this kind of consultation, and in view of the situation we have got ourselves into in Vietnam, hindsight tells us we could have done worse than consult with him beforehand.

WHAT NOW?

Before we can consider what we should do now, we ought to ask what our officialdom has learned from its experience in Europe. On the surface at least, not much. On March 30, 1966, Senator Wayne Morse asked Secretary McNamara whether his Ann Arbor speech of four years earlier still held and McNamara answered thus:

"I think that that speech, plus others that have been made by military and civilian officials of the Department, and other government representatives over the years, is gradually introducing some sense of realism in the thinking about nuclear forces.

"More and more Frenchmen are beginning to realize that the *force de frappe* is not a true deterrent force in any sense of the word. It is a myth as far as deterrent force is concerned."

If this kind of immobilism really reflects the views of the Secretary and his colleagues in the government, then the future of our efforts in Europe is not promising.

What the French seem to fear most is that we will seek a détente with the Soviet Union in which they are left out. They are far from being opposed to such a détente, but they are determined to be partners in it, and partners of the first rank. The British seem not to have the same fears of betrayal by us, and they still cherish their special relationship with the United States. But their eyes are turning increasingly toward Europe. They have long sought improved relations with the Soviet Union, and in this respect their policy seems to bear a close kinship to that of France—as well as to that of West Germany, whose new leaders appear to have concluded that the only hope for eventual reunification is by opening doors to the East. For all of them, the North Atlantic Treaty is an important backstop that can enable them to pursue openings to the East with steady eyes and without fear.

In all this, SHAPE and SACEUR and all the other accoutrements of the old Organization seem to have little place. We can no doubt insist on their continuation, if that is the price of our continued commitment to the treaty and to Europe. But that would make the price very high, not only for the Europeans but for ourselves. It is time we let things loosen up, and doing so would win a new kind of respect for our leadership, which ought as much as possible to acknowledge the role of partnership. Such respect will certainly not be gained by our continuing to insist that nothing fundamental has changed.

FLEXIBLE RESPONSE—A NEW NATIONAL MILITARY PROGRAM

BY MAXWELL D. TAYLOR

At the outset of this reappraisal, we should recognize and accept the limitations of our atomic retaliatory forces. Under the conditions which we must anticipate in the coming years, it is incredible to ourselves, to our allies, and to our enemies that we would use such forces for any purpose other than to assure our national survival. When would our survival be at stake? Two clear cases would be an atomic attack on the Continental United States or the discovery of indisputable evidence that such an attack was about to take place. A third possible case would be a major attack upon Western Europe, since the loss of that area to Communism would ultimately endanger our national survival. These seem the only situations imaginable in which our atomic retaliatory forces might be deliberately used. Hence, they are the only situations to which their deterrence applies.

Having recognized the limitations of our atomic deterrent forces, we should, in consistence, redefine general war as being synonymous with a nuclear exchange between the United States and the USSR. Limited war would then be left to cover all other forms of military operations. The question of using atomic weapons in limited wars would be met by accepting the fact that primary dependence must be placed on conventional weapons while retaining readiness to use tactical atomic weapons in the comparatively rare cases where their use would be to our national interest.

The National Military Program of Flexible Response should contain at the outset an unqualified renunciation of reliance on the strategy of Massive Retaliation. It should be made clear that the United States will prepare itself to respond any-where, any time, with weapons and forces appropriate to the situation. Thus, we would restore to warfare its historic justification as a means to create a better world upon the successful conclusion of hostilities.

These broad, fundamental decisions as to the objectives and nature of our strategy, the use of atomic weapons, and the definitions which indicate the kinds of war which we must prepare to fight should be taken by the President on the recommendation of the National Security Council. When approved, they would serve as the basis for action by the Joint Chiefs of Staff in determining the type, size, and priority of the military forces required to execute the approved strategy.

In a field where costs are staggering, it is essential that our new Military Program put first things first and know why the priority is right. In my judgment, the first priority of our Military Program is a double-barreled extension of our "quick fixes"—to modernize and protect the atomic deterrent force and to build up our limited-war, counterattrition forces to offset the present preponderant Soviet forces on the ground. Thereafter, I would make carefully selective provision for continental air defense, for the requirements of full mobilization, and for survival measures to hedge against the failures of deterrence. Our money will go fast in these latter areas and it will not be clear how much we can do until the over-all program is costed in some detail.

Assuming that the Secretary of Defense approves this priority of effort in concept, the JCS would then be ready to get down to the brass tacks of determining the kinds

Reprinted by permission from *The Uncertain Trumpet* (New York: Harper & Row Publishers, 1960), pp. 130–64. Copyright 1959, 1960 by Maxwell D. Taylor.

General Taylor is President of the Institute for Defense Analyses. He has been Chief of Staff of the U.S. Army, Chairman of the Joint Chiefs of Staff, Ambassador to South Vietnam, and has served as a Special Assistant to Presidents Kennedy and Johnson.

and sizes of specific forces required and the way to use them—in the jargon of the Pentagon, to determine the criteria of sufficiency, the force tabs, and the strategic concept.

The statement of the strategic concept as it might be written into our Military Program would indicate how the United States expects to employ its military forces under conditions of cold, limited, and general atomic war. It would indicate broadly where the weight of our effort would lie and would assign general tasks to our forces at home and abroad in anticipation of various military contingencies.

A listing without regard to priorities of the kinds of forces necessary to implement this strategic concept would include: first, the atomic deterrent forces, both their offensive and defensive components; second, the continental air defense forces in the United States; third, our overseas deployments; fourth, strategic reserve forces in the United States; fifth, the air and sea forces necessary to give strategic mobility to the U.S. reserves and to maintain the air and sea lines of communications. There will be no difficulty getting agreement among the Chiefs that we need some of all of these types. But the question of how much of each is a hard one, upon which we can expect them to divide. But if we are consistent with the priority effort which we adopted above, a solution should be possible, at least in qualitative terms.

There is no argument over a top priority for the modernization and protection of the atomic deterrent forces. We must provide for a striking force which is clearly capable of surviving a surprise attack and of inflicting unacceptable losses on the USSR. This means there must be an offensive and a defensive component. The size of the offensive part can be determined fairly accurately, figuring back from the enemy targets which, if destroyed, will represent the loss of his war-making capacity. These targets amount only to a few score, at the most to a few hundred. After due allowance has been made for aborts, enemy action, and failures both human and mechanical, the number of atomic vehicles needed to destroy this target system can be determined by simple arithmetic. Even after adding a heavy factor of safety to cover imponderables, the size of the required atomic retaliatory force will be found to be much smaller than the bombers and missiles of our present force.

The size of the force is only one part of the problem—the quality is even more important. Our Military Program must inject new life into the long-range missile program—not the Atlas, Titan, Redstone, and Regulus, but their successors, the Minuteman of the Air Force, the Pershing of the Army and the Polaris of the Navy. For protection, all will need mobility, dispersion, and concealment, as well as early warning.

In addition to these passive, protective measures, the deterrent force must have an active, defensive component based largely on the Nike-Zeus antiballistic-missile missile. We need a crash program to make up for the time lost by past indecision. It is the only weapon in sight for the job and we cannot afford to be without it. Also we shall continue to need some bomber defense against both high- and low-flying bombers. The Zeus, though capable of coping with incoming missiles, is not designed to shoot down aircraft. The Nike-Hercules and Hawk will have this role to play for some years to come.

So much for the size, composition, and modernization of the atomic deterrent force. In equal priority is the need to improve what we have called limited-war or counterattrition forces. It is perhaps a mistake to label them limited-war forces because all of them have an important use in case of general war. These counterattrition forces have a dual capability for either limited or general war, whereas the strictly general-war forces do not have this flexibility. A B-52 bomber, an ICBM missile, or a Polaris submarine are good for use in general war and for little else. An Army division or a tactical air squadron has a use in any kind of war.

Under the National Military Program of Flexible Response, the JCS will need to increase significantly the attention paid heretofore to the counterattrition forces. Their required size can be determined by studies and war games of hypothetical military situations assumed to arise in various sensitive areas. These studies will show the rate at which our forces will need to arrive, the total number needed to restore peace, and the length of time required to do the job. These figures will then determine the size of the regular and reserve forces to be maintained in the U.S., and the quantities of supplies to be accumulated in war reserve. Such studies will indicate, I believe, the need for an extensive program to improve our capability for waging limited war.

In emphasizing this need, I would not suggest that we are without current assets for this purpose. If one regards the force structure of our three services, one finds that nearly all of the Army and of the Marine Corps, much of the Tactical Air Force, some of the Navy's carriers, and large parts of our strategic air and sea lift may be accounted limited-war forces and available in an emergency. While this statement is accurate as far as it goes, it does not take into account our lack of planning and organization to make the most of these assets. For this reason, as Chief of Staff of the Army, I proposed a five-point program to improve the limited-war capability of all the services. It included the improvement in planning, training, and air movement previously included in the "quick fixes." In addition, this program called for the modernization of the organization and equipment of the limited-war forces of all three services. This modernization would give consideration to the characteristics of the geographical areas in which limited war is likely to occur, as well as the armaments of potential enemies and the military capabilities of indigenous allies. Bearing in mind that limited wars are not necessarily either small or short wars, the modernization program would take into account the needs of the first six months of war—both our own and those of our possible allies. With regard to atomic weapons, it would provide our forces with small tactical atomic weapons but they would remain prepared to fight entirely without them. Reversing the current emphasis, these forces would place main, but not sole, reliance upon conventional weapons. This

change of attitude would have an important effect upon the design of future tactical bombers and aircraft carriers as well as upon the plans for supporting logistic systems on land. In the design of tactical atomic weapons, emphasis should be placed upon developing those of very low yield, which offer no hazards of fall-out nor serious danger to friendly troops and allied populations.

Another point in the program concerned itself with improving the strategic mobility of limited-war forces. Staff studies and war games of hypothetical, limited-war situations always develop logistic limitations and bottlenecks affecting adversely the movement of our forces. The size of our landing in Lebanon in July, 1958, was controlled by the capacity of the single airfield and port at Beirut. Similarly, military movements to other parts of the world will inevitably encounter limitations which can only be removed by prior identification and elimination. The prompt projection of naval power about the world is possible today only because the British and U.S. navies long ago determined the needs for harbors, port facilities, and fuel supplies at strategic world points and provided for the need in advance. A similar analysis of the future requirements for the mobility of limited-war forces is necessary on the part of the joint staffs of the United States and its allies. Improved mobility will also come from the modernization program, which should produce better ships and planes for strategic movement. The Army likes very much the roll-on-roll-off type of ship with which the Navy has been experimenting. New jet cargo land and sea planes offer great advantages for fast air movement. Our National Military Program must be prepared to make an annual allotment of funds for these measures for improved mobility.

If these two long-term projects, the modernization of counterattrition forces and the improvement of their mobility, are carried out along with the planned "quick fixes," we will then be prepared to proceed to the final point. By that time we will not merely talk a good game in terms of our limited-war capability, we will be prepared to play a good game as well. Under these conditions, it will be important to display our peacetime readiness to move limited-war forces anywhere about the globe. Periodic demonstrations of this sort would have a great political effect in that they would show our friends that we are capable of responding militarily with something other than a heavy atomic weapon. By the same token, we would show our enemies that we are prepared to resist attrition quickly and effectively. In conjunction with our atomic deterrent forces, we would have counterattrition forces capable of extending the scope of our potential military reaction across the entire spectrum of possible challenge in accordance with a strategy of Flexible Response.

Two categories of forces which fall into this double-barreled, first priority of effort deserve special attention. The first are our overseas deployments in Europe and the Far East. They have an important part to play both in deterring and in fighting general and limited war. In general war, they must cover the vital ground areas in which they are deployed and hold the enemy at arm's length while we punish him with our heavy weapons of great destruction. Thereafter they must have the residual strength to occupy his lands and claim whatever may be called the victory. For limited war, they must be strong enough to turn back infiltrations, raids, and border forays and gain the necessary time to make sure of an enemy's intentions. They should be able, if needed, to detach forces to adjacent areas in the way that our forces in Europe provided elements for the Lebanon landing.

Apart from their strictly military requirement, these overseas deployments have a very important psychological role to play. They exemplify to our allies the willingness of the United States to share with them the hazards of living under the Communist guns. There is no substitute for the personal sharing of the danger. I was in Berlin in 1950 at the time that our troops were sent into Korea to stop the Communist invasion. Interested in the German reaction. I asked a leading Socialist of Berlin what he thought of our action. For a man of his pacifistic and antimilitary leanings, I was surprise to find him highly in favor of the U.S. decision to act. When I asked why, he replied, "We Germans have always known you Americans are generous and kindhearted. Look at what the Marshall aid has done for Berlin. But we never were sure how you really stood until you offered Korea the lives of your sons and *pfannkuchen* [pancakes]."

Even the dependents accompanying our soldiers play a part in establishing the earnestness of our intentions. Again in Berlin, at a time when the Soviets were putting heavy political pressure on the town, I asked a citizen why the city remained so calm. "It will be time to worry when your family leaves," he replied.

So the National Military Program must continue to provide for overseas deployments certainly at no lower strength than at present. Actually, we have trimmed their personnel so often in recent years that a moderate increase is needed to balance the internal composition of these forces.

The other point needing special comment is the requirement in the top priority for a back-up of military strength in the form of strategic reserves in the U.S. This point has been touched on before but it needs to be emphasized. We must have a large bloc of mobile forces ready for quick intervention either to put out a brush fire, to reinforce our overseas garrisons, or to effect a prompt strengthening of our general military posture in a time of tension. Regular forces in being must be available for the immediate tasks in the first few months of an emergency, but thereafter we can call upon selected civilian reserve units which have been given particular attention in time of peace. These forces must have all the equipment, supplies, and munitions necessary for at least six months of combat. Thereafter expanded war production will begin to take over the burden. But this early back-up is so vital that it must be paid for in the first priority of our efforts.

Passing to second priority forces and activities, we must consider the scope to give to continental air defense beyond that proposed above to defend our retaliatory forces. This question is likely to remain as difficult a problem under the new Military Program as it has been in the past. It is hard to be sure of the right course of action because of the great cost of air-defense weapons and installations, their untested effectiveness in war, and the fact that they will never be used if our general-war deterrent succeeds. Nonetheless, it is apparent that some level of air defense is necessary, if only to maintain the morale of our citizens and to inject the greatest possible factor of doubt into the war plans of the Soviet General Staff. Such a defense should give preponderant attention to the growing ballistic missile threat, but for some time to come cannot ignore the dangers of high- and low-level bomber attack.

The quantity of air defense required is susceptible to a mathematical analysis, which is more or less the converse of the problem of determining the size of our atomic deterrent forces. It is possible to assume that the protection of certain percentages of our population and industrial capacity is necessary to assure survival in the case of general atomic war, then to site air-defense weapons and installations capable of giving a high mathematical probability of attaining that level of protection. However, the result will be no better than the initial assumption, which is exposed to a high degree of uncertainty since no one can really conceive of the effects of a massive atomic attack upon a modern nation. Nonetheless, no better way has occurred to anyone for establishing some scientific basis for air-defense sufficiency. The cost of any such program is likely to make it unfeasible at the optimum level, so that the task would be divided into two parts, that for protecting a limited number of vital areas and the remainder required for a fairly complete defense of our homeland. The first part should be supported in second priority behind the deterrent and counterrattrition forces, the second at the end of our list among the hedges against the failure of deterrence.

Having determined the size and the quality of the atomic deterrent forces, the counterattrition forces, and the most important forms of continental air defense, the artisans of the new Military Program will reach the grab-bag category of forces needed to hedge against the failure of deterrence of general atomic war or of protracted conventional war. There will be a competition for resources among the requirements of a total conventional mobilization, a higher level of continental air defense, more anti-submarine warfare forces, civil defense beyond the "quick fix" fall-out shelter program, stockpiling to offset bomb damage, and other expensive programs. Fiscal availability and common sense will be the only guidelines for the military planners. However, they will be consoled in the knowledge that up to this point our preparations have had a rational basis and that there is justified confidence in their over-all deterrent effect. With justified faith in deterrence, there will be less need for concern about hedges against its failure.

Thus far in the discussion of priorities and forces we have said little about anti-submarine warfare forces and where they fit in. They have always been difficult to classify with finality because many of the ships and airplanes involved in antisubmarine warfare are capable of other missions as well. An antisubmarine warfare aircraft carrier, for example, may provide air support to Army forces in limited war, as was often the case in Korea.

However, considering these forces only in their antisubmarine role, where do they fall in the priorities established under the National Military Program of Flexible Response? Naval forces engaged in the surveillance of the USSR submarine fleet and in protecting the shores of the United States from enemy missile-firing submarines would apparently fall into the first priority, as would those naval elements necessary to assure the freedom of the sea lanes for the movement of counterattrition forces. The remainder of the antisubmarine warfare forces, however, would fall largely in the third category, of hedges against the failure of the deterrence of general war. Only in the latter event will the Soviet submarines swarm out to sea and present a serious menace to the sea lanes. Incidentally, considering the size of the Russian U-boat fleet, their leaders are apparently not counting on the next war being a short one.

Another observation with regard to our

antisubmarine warfare forces is that they are less likely to encounter obstacles in the use of atomic weapons than our ground and air forces. Since their objectives are identifiable military targets found in areas generally removed from civilian populations where the fall-out hazards are minimal, it would appear reasonable to count on the use of atomic weapons with fewer restrictions than ashore. This assurance is increased by the fact that action against enemy submarines is likely to occur only in the context of general war with the USSR.

To tabulate the conclusions of the foregoing discussion, the new Military Program should provide for the following forces and resources in the indicated order of priority.

PRIORITY I

Kind	Size and Composition
1. Atomic deterrent forces	
a. Offensive retaliatory	A few hundred reliable and accurate missiles, supplemented by a decreasing number of bombers capable of destroying a sufficient number of vital Soviet targets to assure destruction of enemy warmaking capability. To be mobile, concealed, and dispersed.
b. Active defensive	Enough Nike-Zeus, Nike-Hercules, and Hawk missile batteries to protect the offensive retaliatory forces. Sophisticated early-warning service capable of timely reporting of incoming missiles.
2. Counterattrition	Size to be based on studies of hypothetical limited wars. Modernized in weapons, equipment, air and sea lift. To carry very-small-yield atomic weapons but be prepared to fight with conventional weapons alone.
3. Overseas deployments	Generally, same unit composition as now, but modernized like the other counterattrition forces and moderately increased in numerical size to achieve better internal balance.
4. Mobile reserve forces and supplies	A partial mobilization to assure a back-up of units, trained individuals, supplies, and equipment necessary to support at least the first six months of combat.
5. Air and sea lift to move and support the foregoing categories of forces	Progressively modernized through introduction of cargo jet land and sea planes and roll-on-roll-off shipping.
6. Antisubmarine warfare forces	Those necessary for surveillance of USSR submarine fleet and for defense of the atomic retaliatory force against missile-launching submarines.

PRIORITY II

1. Continental air defense	Emphasis on defense against missiles. Weapons comprise principally Nike-Zeus, Nike-Hercules, and Hawk missiles. Size sufficient to give ___ per cent probability of protection to ___ per cent of U.S. population and industry. (JCS to determine percentages from specific studies.)
2. Antisubmarine warfare forces	Those necessary to protect foregoing U.S. targets from attack by submarine-launched missiles, especially civilian targets (if there is a requirement beyond forces in Priority 1-6 above).

PRIORITY III

1. Hedges against the failure of deterrence	Size and character of these programs indeterminable. Depends largely on resources left over for these purposes after meeting requirements in higher priorities.
a. Requirements of general mobilization	
b. Remaining needs of air defense	
c. Civil defense	
d. Remaining needs for antisubmarine warfare	
e. Stockpiling against bomb damage	

We have now said enough about the kinds and quantities of military forces required to support a National Military Program of Flexible Response. It is now time to consider how the defense budget should be constructed to assure that our defense dollars are spent in consistence with the foregoing priorities. Here are the steps, as I see them, which should be taken to build a budget on horizontal principles in support of the functional categories of forces above.

It is assumed that by this point in building our new program the Joint Chiefs of Staff have produced a strategic concept based on a strategy of Flexible Response and have agreed on the priorities of forces tabulated above. They have submitted this preliminary work to the Secretary of Defense, who has given it his approval. The Joint Chiefs of Staff should now determine the specific forces, in terms of units of the Army, Navy, Marines, and Air Force, which are necessary to fill out the approved functional categories according to the priorities. In so doing, they would first call upon the unified commanders overseas to submit their estimates of the kinds and quantities of forces which they require to perform their missions. The unscreened total of these overseas requirements will probably be excessive and the Joint Chiefs of Staff will have to amalgamate and modify them, taking into account overlaps and duplications unknown to the individual commanders. They would then present the refined force structure to the Secretary of Defense for his approval.

The Secretary of Defense will always be concerned about defense costs, as he will inevitably have been the recipient of Administration guidance from the Bureau of the Budget. Hence, he would now refer the recommended force structure to the Defense Comptroller and the military services for rough costing estimates. The Comptroller would supervise this work and would return the results to the Joint Chiefs of Staff, who by this time would have received from the Secretary of Defense an indication of the approximate over-all dollar ceiling for the defense budget.

The Chiefs would now have the difficult task of compressing the desired force structure within a dollar ceiling, which we hope would be a reasonable one, related in size to the enemy threat. To do this compression, they would need to consult repeatedly the overseas commanders as well as the military services. It would be most useful if they could present to the Secretary of Defense two or more force structures, corresponding to as many levels of fiscal availability. This device would permit the Secretary of Defense to see clearly the implications of fiscal limitations on the Armed Forces.

In the end, the Secretary of Defense must discharge his grave responsibility of making the decision—following discussions with the President—which will determine the military posture of the United States for the next three or four years. No one else can do it for him; it is an essential part of the job. But whatever his decision, if a procedure such as the one outlined herein has been followed, he will have successfully linked together military missions, force structure, and the budget, an accomplishment that has never yet been achieved.

COMPELLENCE

BY THOMAS C. SCHELLING

THE DISTINCTION BETWEEN DETERRENCE AND "COMPELLENCE"

Blockade illustrates the typical difference between a threat intended to make an adversary do something and a threat intended to keep him from starting something. The distinction is in the timing and in the initiative, in who has to make the first move, in whose initiative is put to the test. To deter an enemy's advance it may be enough to burn the escape bridges behind me, or to rig a trip-wire between us that automatically blows us both up when he advances. To *compel* an enemy's retreat, though, by some threat of engagement, I have to be committed to *move*. (This requires setting fire to the grass behind me as I face the enemy, with the wind blowing toward the enemy.) I can block your car by placing mine in the way; my *deterrent* threat is passive, the decision to collide unless I move, you enjoy no such advantage; the decision to collide is still yours, and I still enjoy deterrence. You have to arrange to *have* to collide unless I move, and that is a degree more complicated. You have to get up so much speed that you cannot stop in time and that only I can avert the collision; this may not be easy. If it takes more time to start a car than to stop one, you may be unable to give me the "last clear chance" to avoid collision by vacating the street.

The threat that compels rather than deters often requires that the punishment be administered *until* the other acts, rather than *if* he acts. This means, though, that the action initiated has to be tolerable to the initiator, and tolerable over whatever period of time is required for the pressure to work on the other side. For deterrence, the trip-wire can threaten to blow things up out of all proportion to what is being protected, because if the threat works the thing never goes off. But to hold a large bomb and threaten to throw it unless somebody moves cannot work so well; the threat is not believable until the bomb is actually thrown and by then the damage is done.[1]

There is, then, a difference between *deterrence* and what we might, for want of a better word, call *compellence*. The dictionary's definition of "deter" corresponds to contemporary usage: to turn aside or discourage through fear; hence, to prevent from action by fear of consequences. A difficulty with our being an unaggressive nation, one whose announced aim has usually been to contain rather than to roll back, is that we have not settled on any conventional terminology for the more active kind of threat. We have come to use "defense" as a euphemism for "military," and have a Defense Department, a defense budget, a defense program, and a defense establishment; if we need the other word, though, the English language provides it easily. It is "offense." We have no such obvious counterpart to "deterrence." "Coercion" covers the meaning but unfortunately includes "deterrent" as well as "compellent" intentions. "Intimidation" is insufficiently focused on the particular behavior desired. "Compulsion" is all right but its adjective is "compulsive," and that has come

---

[1] A nice illustration occurs in the movie version of *A High Wind in Jamaica*. The pirate captain, Chavez, wants his captive to tell where the money is hidden and puts his knife to the man's throat to make him talk. After a moment or two, during which the victim keeps his mouth shut, the mate laughs. "If you cut his throat he can't tell you. He knows it. And he knows you know it." Chavez puts his knife away and tries something else. [Footnotes renumbered]

---

to carry quite a different meaning. "Compellence" is the best I can do.[2]

Deterrence and compellence differ in a number of respects, most of them corresponding to something like the difference between statics and dynamics. Deterrence involves setting the stage—by announcement, by rigging the trip-wire, by incurring the obligation—and *waiting*. The overt act is up to the opponent. The stage-setting can often be nonintrusive, nonhostile, nonprovocative. The act that is intrusive, hostile, or provocative is usually the one to be deterred; the deterrent threat only changes the consequences if the act in question—the one to be deterred—is then taken. Compellence, in contrast, usually involves *initiating an action* (or an irrevocable commitment to action) that can cease, or become harmless, only if the opponent responds. The overt act, the first step, is up to the side that makes the compellent threat. To deter, one digs in, or lays a minefield, and waits—in the interest of inaction. To compel, one gets up enough momentum (figuratively, but sometimes literally) to make the other *act* to avoid collision.

Deterrence tends to be indefinite in its timing. "If you cross the line we shoot in self-defense, or the mines explode." When? Whenever you cross the line—preferably never, but the timing is up to you. If *you*

cross it, *then* is when the threat is fulfilled, either automatically, if we've rigged it so, or by obligation that immediately becomes due. But we can wait—preferably forever; that's our purpose.

Compellence has to be definite: We move, and you must get out of the way. By when? There has to be a deadline, otherwise tomorrow never comes. If the action carries no deadline it is only a posture, or a ceremony with no consequences. If the compellent advance is like Zeno's tortoise that takes infinitely long to reach the border by traversing, with infinite patience, the infinitely small remaining distances that separate him from collision, it creates no inducement to vacate the border. Compellence, to be effective, can't wait forever. Still, it has to wait a little; collision can't be instantaneous. The compellent threat has to be put in motion to be credible, and *then* the victim must yield. Too little time, and compliance becomes impossible; too much time, and compliance becomes unnecessary. Thus compellence involves timing in a way that deterrence typically does not.

In addition to the question of "when," compellence usually involves questions of where, what, and how much. "Do nothing" is simple, "Do something" ambiguous. "Stop where you are" is simple; "Go back" leads to "How far?" "Leave me alone" is simple; "Cooperate" is inexact and open-ended. A deterrent position—a status quo, in territory or in more figurative terms—can often be surveyed and noted; a compellent advance has to be *projected* as to destination, and the destination can be unclear in intent as well as in momentum and braking power. In a deterrent threat, the objective is often communicated by the very preparations that make the threat credible; the trip-wire often demarcates the forbidden territory. There is usually an inherent connection between *what* is threatened and what it is threatened *about*. Compellent threats tend to communicate only the general direction of compliance, and are less likely to be self-limiting, less likely to communicate in the very design of the threat just what, or how much, is demanded. The garrison in West

---

[2] J. David Singer, has used a nice pair of nouns, "persuasion," and "dissuasion," to make the same distinction. It is the adjectives that cause trouble; "persuasive" is bound to suggest the adequacy or credibility of a threat, not the character of its objective. Furthermore, "deterrent" is here to stay, at least in the English language. Singer's breakdown goes beyond these two words and is a useful one; he distinguishes whether the subject is desired to *act* or *abstain*, whether or not he is *presently* acting or abstaining, and whether he is likely (in the absence of threats and offers) to *go on* acting or abstaining. (If he is behaving, and is likely—but not certain—to go on behaving, there can still be reason to "reinforce" his motivation to behave.) Singer distinguishes also "rewards" and "penalties" as well as threats and offers; while the rewards and penalties can be the *consequences* of threats and offers, they can also be *gratuitous*, helping to communicate persuasively some new and continuing threat or offer. See his article "Inter-Nation Influence: A Formal Model," *American Political Science Review*, 17 (1963), 420–30.

Berlin can hardly be misunderstood about what it is committed to resist; if it ever intruded into East Berlin, though, to induce Soviet or German Democratic Republic forces to give way, there would be no such obvious interpretation of where and how much to give way unless the adventure could be invested with some unmistakable goal or limitation—a possibility not easily realized.

The Quemoy escapade is again a good example: Chiang's troops, once on the island, especially if evacuation under fire appeared infeasible, had the static clarity that goes with commitment to an indefinite status quo, while the commitment just to *send* troops to defend it (or air and naval support) according to whether a Communist attack there was or was not prelude to an attack on Formosa, lacked that persuasive quality, reminding us that though deterrent threats tend to have the advantages mentioned above they do not always achieve them. (The ambiguous case of Quemoy actually displays the compellent ambiguity, seen in reverse: a "compellent" Communist move against Quemoy was to be accommodated, as long as its extent could be reliably projected to a terminus short of Formosa, if the Communists thought we meant it, it was up to them to design an action that visibly embodied that limitation.) An American or NATO action to relieve Budapest in 1956—without major engagement but in the hope the Soviets would give way rather than fight—would have had the dynamic quality of "compellence" in contrast to Berlin: the stopping point would have been a variable, not a constant. Even "Budapest" would have needed a definition, and might have become all of Hungary—and after Hungary, what?—if the Soviets initially gave way. The enterprise might have been designed to embody its specific intent, but it would have taken a lot of designing backed up by verbal assurances.

Actually, any coercive threat requires corresponding *assurances*; the object of a threat is to give somebody a choice. To say, "One more step and I shoot," can be a deterrent threat only if accompanied by the implicit assurance, "And if you stop I won't." Giving notice of *unconditional* intent to shoot gives him no choice (unless by behaving as we wish him to behave the opponent puts himself out of range, in which case the effective threat is, "Come closer and my fire will kill you, stay back and it won't"). What was said above about deterrent threats being typically less ambiguous in intent can be restated: the corresponding assurances—the ones that, together with the threatened response, define the opponent's choice—are clearer than those that can usually be embodied in a compellent action. (Ordinary blackmailers, not just nuclear, find the "assurances" troublesome when their threats are compellent.)[3]

They are, furthermore, confirmed and demonstrated over time; as long as he stays back, and we don't shoot, we fulfill the assurances and confirm them. The assurances that accompany a compellent action —move back a mile and I won't shoot (otherwise I shall) and I won't then try again for a second mile—are harder to demonstrate in advance, unless it be through a long past record of abiding by one's own verbal assurances.

Because in the West we deal mainly in deterrence, not compellence, and deterrent threats tend to convey their assurances implicity, we often forget that *both* sides of the choice, the threatened penalty and the proffered avoidance or reward, need to be credible. The need for assurances—not just verbal but fully credible—emerges clearly as part of "deterrence" in discussions of surprise attack and "preemptive war." An

[3] The critical role of "assurances," in completing the structure of a threat, in making the threatened consequences persuasively *conditional* on behavior so that the victim is offered a choice, shows up in the offers of amnesty, safe passage, or forgiveness that must often be made credible in inducing the surrender of rebels or the capitulation of strikers or protesters. Even libraries and internal revenue agencies depend on parallel offers of forgiveness when they embark on campaigns to coerce the return of books or payment of back taxes. In personal life I have sometimes relied, like King Lear, on the vague threat that my wrath will be aroused (with who knows what awful consequences) if good behavior is not forthcoming, making a tentative impression on one child, only to have the threat utterly nullified by another's pointing out that "Daddy's mad already."

enemy belief that we are about to attack anyway, not after he does but possibly before, merely raises his incentive to do what we wanted to deter and to do it even more quickly. When we do engage in compellence, as in the Cuban crisis or in punitive attacks on North Vietnam that are intended to make the North Vietnamese government act affirmatively, the assurances are a critical part of the definition of the compellent threat.

One may deliberately choose to be unclear and to keep the enemy guessing either to keep his defenses less prepared or to enhance his anxiety. But if one wants not to leave him in doubt about what will satisfy us, we have to find credible ways of communicating, and communicating both what we want and what we do not want. There is a tendency to emphasize the communication of what we shall *do* if he misbehaves and to give too little emphasis to communicating *what* behavior will satisfy us. Again, this is natural when deterrence is our business, because the prohibited misbehavior is often approximately defined in the threatened response; but when we must start something that then has to be stopped, as in compellent actions, it is both harder and more important to know our aims and to communicate. It is particularly hard because the mere initiation of an energetic coercive campaign, designed for compellence, disturbs the situation, leads to surprises, and provides opportunity and temptation to reexamine our aims and change them in mid course. Deterrence, if wholly successful, can often afford to concentrate on the initiating events—what happens *next* if he misbehaves. Compellence, to be successful, involves an action that must be brought to successful closure. The payoff comes at the end, as does the disaster if the project fails.

The compellent action will have a time schedule of its own, and unless it is carefully chosen it may not be reconcilable with the demands that are attached to it. We cannot usefully threaten to bomb Cuba next Thursday unless the Russians are out by next month, or conduct a six weeks' bombing campaign in North Vietnam and stop it when the Vietcong have been quies-

cent for six months. There will be limits, probably, to how long the compellent action can be sustained without costing or risking too much, or exhausting itself or the opponent so that he has nothing left to lose. If it cannot induce compliance within that time—and this depends on whether compliance is physically or administratively feasible within that time—it cannot accomplish anything (unless the objective was only an excuse for some act of conquest or punishment). The compellent action has to be one that can be stopped or reversed when the enemy complies, or else there is no inducement.

If the opponent's compliance necessarily takes time—if it is sustained good behavior, cessation of an activity that he must not resume, evacuation of a place he must not reenter, payment of tribute over an extended period, or some constructive activity that takes time to accomplish—the compellent threat requires some commitment, pledge, or guarantee, or some hostage or else must be susceptible of being resumed or repeated itself. Particularly in a crisis, a Cuban crisis or a Vietnamese crisis, there is strong incentive to get compliance quickly to limit the risk or damage. Just finding conditions that can be met on the demanding time schedule of a dangerous crisis is not easy. The ultimate demands, the objectives that the compellent threat is really aimed at, may have to be achieved indirectly, by taking pledges or hostages that can be used to coerce compliance after the pressure has been relieved.[4] Of course, if some kind of surrender statement or acknowledgment of submission, some symbolic knuckling under, will itself achieve the object, verbal compliance may be enough. It is inherent in an intense crisis

[4] Lord Portal's account of the coercive bombing of the villages of recalcitrant Arab tribesmen (after warning to permit evacuation) includes the terms that were demanded. Among them were hostages—literal hostages, people—as well as a fine; otherwise the demand was essentially cessation of the raids or other misbehavior that had brought on the bombing. The hostages were apparently partly to permit subsequent enforcement without repeated bombing, partly to symbolize, together with the fine, the tribe's intent to comply. See Portal, "Air Force Cooperation in Policing the Empire," pp. 343–58.

that the conditions for bringing it to a close have to be of a kind that can be met quickly; that is what we mean by an "intense crisis," one that compresses risk, pain, or cost into a short span of time or that involves actions that cannot be sustained indefinitely. If we change our compellent threat from slow pressure to intense, we have to change our demands to make them fit the urgent timing of a crisis.

Notice that to deter *continuance* of something the opponent is already doing —harassment, overflight, blockade, occupation of some island or territory, electronic disturbance, subversive activity, holding prisoners, or whatever it may be—has some of the character of a compellent threat. This is especially so of the timing, of who has to take the initiative. In the more static case we want him to go on *not* doing something; in this more dynamic case we want him to *change* his behavior. The "when" problem arises in compelling him to stop, and the compellent action may have to be initiated, not held in waiting like the deterrent threat. The problems of "how much" may not arise if it is some discrete, well-defined activity. "At all" may be the obvious answer. For U-2 flights or fishing within a twelve-mile limit, that may be the case; for subversive activity or support to insurgents, "at all" may itself be ambiguous because the activity is complex, ill defined, and hard to observe or attribute.

Blockade, harassment, and "salami tactics" can be interpreted as ways of evading the dangers and difficulties of compellence. Blockade in a cold war sets up a tactical "status quo" that is damaging in the long run but momentarily safe for both sides unless the victim tries to run the blockade. President Kennedy's overt act of sending the fleet to sea, in "quarantine" of Cuba in October 1962, had some of the quality of deterrent "state setting"; the Soviet government then had about forty-eight hours to instruct its steamers whether or not to seek collision. Low-level intrusion, as discussed earlier, can be a way of letting the opponent turn his head and yield a little, or it can be a way of starting a compellent action in low gear, without the conviction

that goes with greater momentum but also without the greater risk. Instead of speeding out of control toward our car that blocks his way, risking our inability to see him and get our engines started in time to clear his path, he approaches slowly and nudges fenders, crushing a few lights and cracking some paint. If we yield he can keep it up, if not he can cut his losses. And if he makes it look accidental, or can blame it on an impetuous chauffeur, he may not even lose countenance in the unsuccessful try.

DEFENSE AND DETERRENCE, OFFENSE AND COMPELLENCE

The observation that deterrent threats are often passive, while compellent threats often have to be active, should not be pressed too far. Sometimes a deterrent threat cannot be made credible in advance, and the threat has to be made lively when the prohibited action is undertaken. This is where *defense* and *deterrence* may merge, forcible defense being undertaken in the hope, perhaps with the main purpose, of demonstrating by resistance that the conquest will be costly, even if successful, too costly to be worth while. The idea of "graduated deterrence" and much of the argument for a conventional warfare capability in Europe are based on the notion that if passive deterrence initially fails, the more active kind may yet work. If the enemy act to be deterred is a once-for-all action, incapable of withdrawal, rather than progressive over time, any failure of deterrence is complete and final; there is no second chance. But if the aggressive move takes time, if the adversary did not believe he would meet resistance or did not appreciate how costly it would be, one can still hope to demonstrate that the threat is in force, after he begins. If he expected no opposition, encountering some may cause him to change his mind.

There is still a distinction here between forcible defense and defensive action intended to deter. If the object, and the only hope, is to resist successfully, so that the enemy cannot succeed even if he tries, we can call it pure defense. If the object is to *induce* him not to proceed, by making his encroachment painful or costly, we can call it a "coercive" or "deterrent" defense. The language is clumsy but the distinction is valid. Resistance that might otherwise seem futile can be worthwhile if, though incapable of blocking aggression, it can nevertheless threaten to make the cost too high. This is "active" or "dynamic" deterrence, deterrence in which the threat is communicated by progressive fulfillment. At the other extreme is forcible defense with good prospect of blocking the opponent but little promise of hurting; this would be purely defensive.

Defensive action may even be undertaken with no serious hope of repelling or deterring enemy action but with a view to making a "successful" conquest costly enough to deter repetition by the same opponent or anyone else. This is of course the rationale for reprisals after the fact; they cannot undo the deed but can make the books show a net loss and reduce the incentive next time. Defense can sometimes get the same point across, as the Swiss demonstrated in the fifteenth century by the manner in which they lost battles as well as by the way they sometimes won them. "The [Swiss] Confederates were able to reckon their reputation for obstinate and invincible courage as one of the chief causes which gave them political importance. . . . It was no light matter to engage with an enemy who would not retire before any superiority in numbers, who was always ready for a fight, who would neither give nor take quarter."[5] The Finns demonstrated five hundred years later that the principle still works. The value of local resistance is not measured solely by local success. This idea of what we might call "punitive resistance" could have been part of the rationale for the American commitment of forces in Vietnam.[6]

"Compellence" is more like "offense."

Forcible offense is taking something, occupying a place, or disarming an enemy or a territory, by some direct action that the enemy is unable to block. "Compellence" is *inducing* his withdrawal, or his acquiescence, or his collaboration by an action that threatens to hurt, often one that could not forcibly accomplish its aim but that, nevertheless, can hurt enough to induce compliance. The forcible and the coercive are both present in a campaign that could reach its goal against resistance, and would be worth the cost, but whose cost is nevertheless high enough so that one hopes to induce compliance, or to deter resistance, by making evident the intent to proceed. Forcible action is limited to what can be accomplished without enemy collaboration; compellent threats can try to induce more affirmative action, including the exercise of authority by an enemy to bring about the desired results.

War itself, then, can have deterrent or compellent intent, just as it can have defensive or offensive aims. A war in which both sides can hurt each other but neither can forcibly accomplish its purpose could be compellent on one side, deterrent on the other. Once an engagement starts, though, the difference between deterrence and compellence, like the difference between defense and offense, may disappear. There can be legal and moral reasons, as well as historical reasons, for recalling the status quo ante; but if territory is in dispute, the strategies for taking it, holding it, or recovering it may not much differ as between the side that originally possessed it and the side that coveted it, once the situation has become fluid. (In a local tactical sense, American forces were often on the "defensive" in North Korea and on the "offensive" in South Korea.) The coercive aspect of warfare may be equally compellent on both sides, the only difference perhaps being that the demands of the defender, the one who originally possessed what is in dispute, may be clearly defined by the original boundaries, whereas the aggressor's demands may have no such obvious definition.

The Cuban crisis is a good illustration of the fluidity that sets in once passive de-

5 C. W. C. Oman, *The Art of War in the Middle Ages*, (Ithaca: Cornell University Press, 1953), p. 96.

6 An alternative, but not inconsistent, treatment of some of these distinctions is in Glenn H. Snyder, *Deterrence and Defense* (Princeton: Princeton University Press, 1961), pp. 5–7, 9–16, 24–40.

terrence has failed. The United States made verbal threats against the installation of weapons in Cuba but apparently some part of the threat was unclear or lacked credibility and it was transgressed. The threat lacked the automaticity that would make it fully credible, and without some automaticity it may not be clear to either side just where the threshold is. Nor was it physically easy to begin moderate resistance after the Russians had crossed the line, and to increase the resistance progressively to show that the United States meant it. By the time the President determined to resist, he was no longer in a deterrent position and had to embark on the more complicated business of compellence. The Russian missiles could sit waiting, and so could Cuban defense forces; the next overt act was up to the President. The problem was to prove to the Russians that a potentially dangerous action was forthcoming, without any confidence that verbal threats would be persuasive and without any desire to initiate some irreversible process just to prove, to everybody's grief, that the United States meant what it said.

The problem was to find some action that would communicate the threat, an action that would promise damage if the Russians did not comply but minimum damage if they complied quickly enough, and an action that involved enough momentum or commitment to put the next move clearly up to the Russians. Any overt act against a well-defended island would be abrupt and dramatic; various alternatives were apparently considered, and in the end an action was devised that had many of the virtues of static deterrence. A blockade was thrown around the island, a blockade that by itself could not make the missiles go away. The blockade did, however, threaten a minor military confrontation with major diplomatic stakes—an encounter between American naval vessels and Soviet merchant ships bound for Cuba. Once in place, the Navy was in a position to wait; it was up to the Russians to decide whether to continue. If Soviet ships had been beyond recall, the blockade would have been a preparation for inevitable engagement; with modern communications the ships were not beyond recall, and the Russians were given the last clear chance to turn aside. Physically the Navy could have avoided an encounter; diplomatically, the declaration of quarantine and the dispatch of the Navy meant that American evasion of the encounter was virtually out of the question. For the Russians, the diplomatic cost of turning freighters around, or even letting one be examined, proved not to be prohibitive.

Thus an initial deterrent threat failed, a compellent threat was called for, and by good fortune one could be found that had some of the static qualities of a deterrent threat.[7]

There is another characteristic of compellent threats, arising in the need for affirmative action, that often distinguishes them from deterrent threats. It is that the very act of compliance—of doing what is demanded—is more conspicuously compliant, more recognizable as submission under duress, than when an act is merely withheld in the face of a deterrent threat. Compliance is likely to be less casual, less capable of being rationalized as something that one was going to do anyhow. The Chinese did not need to acknowledge that they shied away from Quemoy or Formosa because of American threats, and the Russians need not have agreed that it was NATO that deterred them from conquering Western Europe, and no one can be sure. Indeed, if a deterrent threat is created before the proscribed act is even contem-

[7] Arnold Horelick agrees with this description. "As an initial response the quarantine was considerably less than a direct application of violence, but considerably more than a mere protest or verbal threat. The U.S. Navy placed itself physically between Cuba and Soviet ships bound for Cuban ports. Technically, it might still have been necessary for the United States to fire the first shot had Khrushchev chosen to defy the quarantine though other means of preventing Soviet penetration might have been employed. But once the quarantine was effectively established—which was done with great speed—it was Khrushchev who had to make the next key decision: whether or not to risk releasing the trip-wire." "The Cuban Missile Crisis," *World Politics*, 16 (1964), 385. This article and the Adelphi Paper of Albert and Roberta Wohlstetter mentioned in an earlier note are the best strategic evaluations of the Cuban affair that I have discovered.

plated, there need never be an explicit decision *not* to transgress, just an absence of any temptation *to* do the thing prohibited. The Chinese still say they will take Quemoy in their own good time; and the Russians go on saying that their intentions against Western Europe were never aggressive.

The Russians cannot, though, claim that they were on the point of removing their missiles from Cuba anyway, and that the President's television broadcast, the naval quarantine and threats of more violent action, had no effect.[8]

If the North Vietnamese dramatically issue a call to the Vietcong to cease activity and to evacuate South Vietnam, it is a conspicuous act of submission. If the Americans had evacuated Guantanamo when Castro turned off the water, it would have been a conspicuous act of submission. If an earthquake or change in the weather had caused the water supply to dry up at Guantanamo, and if the Americans had found it wholly uneconomical to supply the base by tanker, they might have quit the place without seeming to submit to Castro's cleverness or seeming afraid to take reprisals against their ungracious host. Similarly, the mere act of bombing North Vietnam changed the status of any steps that the North Vietnamese might take to comply with American wishes. It can increase their desire, if the tactic is successful, to reduce support for the Vietcong; but it also increases the cost of doing so. Secretary Dulles used to say that while we had no vital interest in Quemoy we could not afford to evacuate under duress: intensified Chinese pressure always led to intensified determination to resist it.[9]

If the object is actually to impose humiliation, to force a showdown and to get an acknowledgment of submission, then the "challenge" that is often embodied in an active compellent threat is something to be exploited. President Kennedy undoubtedly wanted some conspicuous compliance by the Soviet Union during the Cuban missile crisis, if only to make clear to the Russians themselves that there were risks in testing how much the American Government would absorb such ventures. In Vietnam the problem appeared the opposite; what was most urgently desired was to reduce the support for the Vietcong from the North, and any tendency for the compellent pressure of bombing to produce a corresponding resistance would have been deprecated. But it cannot always be avoided, and if it cannot, the compellent threat defeats itself.

Skill is required to devise a compellent action that does not have this self-defeating quality. There is an argument here for sometimes not being too explicit or too open about precisely what is demanded, if the demands can be communicated more privately and noncommittally. President Johnson was widely criticized in the press, shortly after the bombing attacks began in early 1965, for not having made his objectives entirely clear. How could the North Vietnamese comply if they did not know exactly what was wanted?

Whatever the reason for the American Administration's being somewhat inexplicit —whether it chose to be inexplicit, did not know how to be explicit, or in fact was explicit but only privately—an important possibility is that vague demands, though hard to understand, can be less embarrassing to comply with. If the President had to be so explicit that any European journalist knew exactly what he demanded, and if the demands were concrete enough to make compliance recognizable when it occurred, any compliance by the North Vietnamese regime would necessarily have been fully public, perhaps quite embarrassingly

---

[8] The tendency for affirmative action to appear compliant is vividly illustrated by the widespread suspicion—one that could not be effectively dispelled—that the U.S. missiles removed from Turkey in the wake of the Cuban crisis were part of a bargain, tacit if not explicit.

[9] Almost everyone in America, surely including the President and the Secretary of State, would have been relieved in the late 1950s if an earthquake or volcanic action had caused Quemoy to sink slowly beneath the surface of the sea. Evacua-

---

tion would then not have been retreat, and an unsought commitment that had proved peculiarly susceptible to Communist China's manipulation would have been disposed of. Such is the intrinsic value of some territories that have to be defended!

so. The action could not be hidden nor the motive so well disguised as if the demands were more privately communicated or left to inference by the North Vietnamese.

Another serious possibility is suggested by the North Vietnamese case: that the initiator of a compellent campaign is not himself altogether sure of what action he wants, or how the result that he wants can be brought about. In the Cuban missile case it was perfectly clear what the United States government wanted, clear that the Soviets had the ability to comply, fairly clear how quickly it could be done, and reasonably clear how compliance might be monitored and verified, though in the end there might be some dispute about whether the Russians had left behind things they were supposed to remove. In the Vietnamese case, we can suppose that the United States government did not know in detail just how much control or influence the North Vietnamese regime had over the Vietcong; and we can even suppose that the North Vietnamese regime itself might not have been altogether sure how much influence it would have in commanding a withdrawal or in sabotaging the movement that had received its moral and material support. The United States government may not have been altogether clear on which kinds of North Vietnamese help—logistical help, training facilities, sanctuary for the wounded, sanctuary for intelligence and planning activities, communications relay facilities, technical assistance, advisors and combat leaders in the field, political and doctrinal assistance, propaganda, moral support or anything else—were most effective and essential, or most able to be withdrawn on short notice with decisive effects. And possibly the North Vietnamese did not know. The American government may have been in the position of demanding *results* not specific *actions*, leaving it to the North Vietnamese through overt acts, or merely through reduced support and enthusiasm, to weaken the Vietcong or to let it lose strength. Not enough is known publicly to permit us to judge this Vietnamese instance; but it points up the important possibility that a compellent threat may have to be focused on results rather than contributory deeds, like the father's demand that his son's school grades be improved, or the extortionist's demand, "Get me money. I don't care how you get it, just get it." A difficulty, of course, is that results are more a matter of interpretations than deeds usually are. Whenever a recipient of foreign aid, for example, is told that it must eliminate domestic corruption, improve its balance of payments, or raise the quality of its civil service, the results tend to be uncertain, protracted, and hard to attribute. The country may try to comply and fail; with luck it may succeed without trying; it may have indifferent success that is hard to judge; in any case compliance is usually arguable and often visible only in retrospect.

Even more than deterrence, compellence requires that we recognize the difference between an individual and a government. To coerce an individual it may be enough to persuade him to change his mind; to coerce a government it may not be necessary, but it also may not be sufficient, to cause individuals to change their minds. What may be required is some change in the complexion of the government itself, in the authority, prestige, or bargaining power of particular individuals or factions or parties, some shift in executive or legislative leadership. The Japanese surrender of 1945 was marked as much by changes in the structure of authority and influence within the government as by changes in attitude on the part of individuals. The victims of coercion, or the individuals most sensitive to coercive threats, may not be directly in authority; or they may be hopelessly committed to non-compliant policies. They may have to bring bureaucratic skill or political pressure to bear on individuals who do exercise authority, or go through processes that shift authority or blame to others. In the extreme case governing authorities may be wholly unsusceptible to coercion—may, as a party or as individuals, have everything to lose and little to save by yielding to coercive threats —and actual revolt may be essential to the process of compliance, or sabotage or assassination. Hitler was uncoercible; some of his generals were not, but they lacked organization and skill and failed in their plot. For working out the incentive structure of a threat, its communication requirements and its mechanism, analogies with individuals are helpful; but they are counterproductive if they make us forget that a government does not reach a decision in the same way as an individual in a government. Collective decision depends on the internal politics and bureaucracy of government, on the chain of command and on lines of communication, on party structures and pressure groups, as well as on individual values and careers. This affects the speed of decision, too.

"CONNECTEDNESS" IN COMPELLENT THREATS

As mentioned earlier, a deterrent threat usually enjoys some *connectedness* between the proscribed action and the threatened response. The connection is sometimes a physical one, as when troops are put in Berlin to defend Berlin. Compellent actions often have a less well-defined connectedness; and the question arises whether they ought to be connected at all. If the object is to harass, to blockade, to scare or to inflict pain or damage until an adversary complies, why cannot the connection be made verbally? If the Russians want Pan-American Airways to stop using the air corridor to Berlin, why can they not harass the airline on its Pacific routes, announcing that harassment will continue until the airline stops flying to Berlin? When the Russians put missiles in Cuba, why cannot the President quarantine Vladivostok, stopping Soviet ships outside, say, a twelve-mile limit, or perhaps denying them access to the Suez or Panama Canal? And if the Russians had wanted to counter the Presi-

dent's quarantine of Cuba, why could they not blockade Norway?[10]

A hasty answer may be that it just is not done, or is not "justified," as though connectedness implied justice, or as though justice were required for effectiveness. Surely that is part of the answer; there is a legalistic or diplomatic, perhaps a casuistic, propensity to keep things connected, to keep the threat and the demand in the same currency, to do what seems reasonable. But why be reasonable, if results are what one wants? Habit, tradition, or some psychological compulsion may explain this connectedness, but it has to be asked whether they make it wise.

There are undoubtedly some good reasons for designing a compellent campaign that is connected with the compliance desired. One is that it helps to communicate the threat itself; it creates less uncertainty about what is demanded, what pressure will be kept up until the demands are complied with and then relaxed once they are. Actions not only speak louder than words on many occasions, but like words they can speak clearly or confusingly. To the extent that actions speak, it helps if they reinforce the message rather than confuse it.

Second, if the object is to induce compliance and not to start a spiral of reprisals and counteractions, it is helpful to show the limits to what one is demanding,

---

[10] It has often been said that American tactical superiority and ease of access in the Caribbean (coupled with superiority in strategic weaponry) account for the success in inducing evacuation of the Soviet missiles. Surely that was crucial; but equally significant was the universal tendency—a psychological phenomenon, a tradition or convention shared by Russians and Americans—to *define*

the conflict in Caribbean terms, not as a contest, say, in the blockade of each other's island allies, not as a counterpart of their position in Berlin, not as a war of harassment against strategic weapons outside national borders. The countermeasures and counterpressures available to the Russians might have looked very different to the "Russian" side if this had been a game on an abstract board rather than an event in historical time in a particular part of the real world. The Russians tried (as did some unhelpful Americans) to find a connection between Soviet missiles in Cuba and American missiles in Turkey, but the connection was evidently not persuasive enough for the Russians to be confident that, if the dispute led to military action or pressure against Turkey, *that* definition would hold and things would go no further. The Caribbean definition had more coherence or integrity than a Cuban-Turkish definition would have had, or, in terms of reciprocal blockade, a Cuban-United Kingdom definition would have had. The risk of further metastasis must have inhibited any urge to let the crisis break out of its original Caribbean definition.

and this can often be best shown by designing a campaign that distinguishes what is demanded from all the other objectives that one might have been seeking but is not. To harass aircraft in the Berlin air corridor communicates that polar flights are not at issue; to harass polar flights while saying that it is punishment for flying in the Berlin corridor does not so persuasively communicate that the harassment stops when the Berlin flights stop, or that the Russians will not think of a few other favors they would like from the airline before they call off their campaign. Most of the problems of defining the threat and the demands that go with it, of offering assurance about what is not demanded and of promising cessation once compliance is forthcoming, are aggravated if there is no connection between the compellent action (or the threat of it) and the issue being bargained over.

The same question can arise with deterrent threats; sometimes they lack connectedness. To threaten the Chinese mainland in the event of an overland attack on India has a minimum of connectedness. If the threatened response is massive enough, though, it may seem to comprise or to include the local area and not merely to depart from it. But it often lacks some of the credibility, through automatic involvement, that can be achieved by connecting the response physically to the provocation itself. Contingent actions—not actions *initiated* to induce compliance, but actions *threatened* against potential provocation— often need the credibility that connectedness can give them.

Connectedness in fact provides something of a scheme for classifying compellent threats and actions. The ideal compellent action would be one that, once initiated, causes minimal harm if compliance is forthcoming and great harm if compliance is not forthcoming, is consistent with the time schedule of feasible compliance, is beyond recall once initiated, and cannot be stopped by the party that started it but *automatically* stops upon compliance, with all this fully understood by the adversary. Only *he* can avert the consequences; he can do it only by complying; and compliance automatically precludes them. His is then the "last clear chance" to avert the harm or catastrophe; and it would not even matter which of the two most feared the consequences as long as the adversary knew that only he, by complying, could avert them. (Of course, whatever is demanded of him must be less unattractive to him than the threatened consequences, and the manner of threatened compliance must not entail costs in prestige, reputation, or self-respect that outweigh the threat.)

It is hard to find significant international events that have this perfectionist quality. There are situations, among cars on highways or in bureaucratic bargaining or domestic politics, where one comes across such ideal compellent threats; but they usually involve physical constraints or legal arrangements that tie the hand of the initiator in a way that is usually not possible in international relations. Still, if we include actions that the initiator can physically recall but not without intolerable cost, so that it is evident he would not go back even if it is equally clear that he could, we can find some instances. An armed convoy on a Berlin Autobahn may sometimes come close to having this quality.

A degree less satisfactory is the compellent action of which the consequences can be averted by *either* side, by the initiator's changing his mind just in time or by his adversary's compliance. Because he can stop before the consequences mount up, this type of compellent action may be less risky for the party that starts it; there is a means of escape, though it may become a test of nerves, or a test of endurance, each side hoping the other will back down, both sides possibly waiting too long. The escape hatch is an asset if one discovers along the way that the compellent attempt was a mistake after all—one misjudged the adversary, or formulated an impossible demand, or failed to communicate what he was doing and what he was after. The escape hatch is an embarrassment, though, if the adversary knows it is there; he can suppose, or hope, that the initiator will turn aside before the risk or pain mounts up.

Still another type is the action that,

though beyond recall by the initiator, does not automatically stop upon the victim's compliance. Compliance is a *necessary* condition for stopping the damage but not *sufficient*, and if the damage falls mainly on the adversary, he has to consider what other demands will attach to the same compellent action once he has complied with the initial demands. The initiator may have to promise persuasively that he will stop in compliance, but stoppage is not automatic. Once the missiles are gone from Cuba we may have afterthoughts about antiaircraft batteries and want them removed too before we call off the quarantine or stop the flights.

Finally, there is the action that only the initiator can stop, but can stop any time with or without compliance, a quite "unconnected" action.

In all of these cases the facts may be misperceived by one party or both, with the danger that each may think the other can in fact avert the consequences, or one may fail to do so in the mistaken belief that the other has the last clear chance to avert collision. These different compellent mechanisms, which of course are more blurred and complex in any actual case, usually depend on what the connection is between the threat and the demand—a connection that can be physical, territorial, legal, symbolic, electronic, political, or psychological.

COMPELLENCE AND BRINKMANSHIP

Another important distinction is between compellent actions that inflict steady pressure over time, with cumulative pain or damage to the adversary (and perhaps to oneself), and actions that impose risk rather than damage. Turning off the water supply at Guantanamo creates a finite rate of privation over time. Buzzing an airplane in the Berlin corridor does no harm unless the planes collide; they probably will not collide but they *may* and if they do the result is sudden, dramatic, irreversible, and grave enough to make even a small probability a serious one.

The creation of risk—usually a shared risk—is the technique of compellence that probably best deserves the name of "brinkmanship." It is a competition in risk-taking. It involves setting afoot an activity that may get out of hand, initiating a process that carries some risk of unintended disaster. This risk is intended, but not the disaster. One cannot initiate *certain* disaster as a profitable way of putting compellent pressure on someone, but one can initiate a moderate *risk* of mutual disaster if the other party's compliance is feasible within a short enough period to keep the cumulative risk within tolerable bounds. "Rocking the boat" is a good example. If I say, "Row, or I'll tip the boat over and drown us both," you'll not believe me. I cannot actually tip the boat over to make you row. But if I start rocking the boat so that it *may* tip over—not because I want it to but because I do not completely control things once I start rocking the boat—you'll be more impressed. I have to be willing to take the risk; then I still have to win the war of nerves, unless I can arrange it so that only you can steady the boat by rowing where I want you to. But it does lend itself to compellence, because one may be able to create a coercive risk of grave consequences where he could not profitably take a deliberate step to bring about these consequences, or even credibly threaten that he would.

ESCALATION AS A STRATEGY

BY HERMAN KAHN

Escalation is a relatively new word in the English language. Though it is becoming more common in newspaper headlines, especially in connection with Vietnam, the dictionaries have yet to define it in a military sense. To many people, escalation connotes an automatic rise in the scale of warfare from the level of an incident to the level of catastrophic nuclear exchange. But to more and more students of military strategy and tactics, it has also come to describe the kind of calculated risk taking that is an established factor of limited conflict in the nuclear age.

Strategies that emphasize the possibility of escalation are associated with the term "brinkmanship." Under modern circumstances no nation wishes to play at brinkmanship recklessly. But to the extent that any nuclear nation is serious in any incipient conflict—or to the extent that it *pretends* to be serious—it will have to face the consequences of being on the escalation ladder. However, a strategy of escalation, carefully carried out, can actually reduce the dangers of insensate, spasmodic nuclear destruction.

Events in Vietnam provide a case in point. Our opponent in Vietnam can function with great success in one dimension of warfare: guerrilla combat and subversion. The U.S., in turn, has an immense superiority in air and naval power and, beyond that, in nuclear power. Behind the North Vietnamese are the Russians, with their nuclear forces, and the Chinese, with their major but ponderous land armies. But how close the ties may be, and how willing North Vietnam and its allies might be to involve themselves against the U.S., remains uncertain. In this complex situation, the U.S. has been attempting to use its areas of advantage to counter the special strengths of the opponents, to "esclate" the war in a calculated way, all the time trying to make it clear that it intends to abide by certain limitations—unless further provoked. In Vietnam, the U.S. is clearly a nation practicing the new dimensions of escalation, reflecting its new understanding of the reasoned and restrained, yet determined, use of limited force in a world of political challenge and nuclear danger.

To make this study concrete, I have devised a ladder—a metaphorical ladder—that provides a convenient list of some of the more important options facing the strategist. This ladder indicates that there are many continuous paths between a low-level crisis and an all-out war, none of which are necessarily or inexorably to be followed. My ladder provides a useful framework for the systematic study of a crisis. There is no attempt here to recommend any courses of action. What is attempted is to describe the way stations of ascending conflict so that the elements can be recognized, and the distance from all-out war estimated. There are, of course, those who think a study of escalation is dangerous and perhaps immoral; I believe that it is dangerous and perhaps immoral *not* to understand how nations might act under the pressures of successive crises. Hence this study of the rungs and thresholds is the best contribution I know how to make to the avoidance of recklessness or panic.

RUNG 1: OSTENSIBLE CRISIS. In this stage, one or both sides asserts, more or less openly and explicitly, that unless a given dispute is resolved in the immediate future, the rungs of the escalation ladder will be climbed. These threats are made credible by various hints as to how important the government considers the issues. There may be

Reprinted by permission from *On Escalation: Metaphors and Scenarios* (New York: Frederick A. Praeger, Publishers, 1965); as condensed in *Problems of National Strategy: A Book of Readings,* edited by Henry A. Kissinger (New York: Frederick A. Praeger, Publishers, 1965), pp. 17–33. Copyright 1965 by Frederick A. Praeger, Inc.

officially inspired newspaper stories to the effect that the chief of state takes a serious view of the matter. There may be explicit announcements or speeches by other important officials—but none of them of the bridge-burning variety, none deliberately designed to make it really difficult for these same officials to back down later.

RUNG 2: POLITICAL, ECONOMIC, AND DIPLOMATIC GESTURES. Legal but unfair, unfriendly, inequitable, or threatening acts are carried out against the opponent to punish or put pressure on him.

RUNG 3: SOLEMN AND FORMAL DECLARATIONS. Such declarations go much further than Rung 2 in demonstrating resolve and commitment, but they need not be deliberately hostile. They may provide merely an executive declaration to the other states of a nation's policy in a certain area, perhaps deliberately avoiding a precise statement of the policy's applicability and limitations. An example of such ambiguity is the Congressional Resolution of August, 1964, passed at President Johnson's request as a result of the escalation in the Gulf of Tonkin. Congress resolved that "the United States is, therefore, prepared, as the President determines, to take all necessary steps including the use of armed force, to assist any member or protocol state of the Southeast Asia Collective Defense Treaty requesting assistance in defense of its freedom."

Such a proclamation is usually a warning to a potential opponent not to climb farther up the escalation ladder, at least in the area covered by the announcement. The declaration may be thought of as pre-emptive or preventive escalation, which tries to forestall further escalation by the opponent. It also marks the limit to which either side can go without dangerously rocking the boat.

RUNG 4: HARDENING OF POSITIONS. As soon as negotiations take on much more of a coercive than a contractual character, I would argue that we have passed the "don't-rock-the-boat" stage and reached Rung 4. Certainly this is true if either or both of the antagonists attempt to increase the credibility of their resolve and committal by irretrievable acts. Such an act might be an announcement by the Soviet Union

that it has signed a peace treaty with East Germany and no longer has any direct control over the access routes to Berlin.

In such confrontations, either side could point out vividly to the other side's population or to its allies the totally destructive character of thermonuclear war, and state that there is thus no alternative to peace—with the clear implication that, unless the madmen on the other side come to their senses, all will be lost. Alternately, one can reassure one's own side by pointing out that the other side is not mad and will therefore back down.

RUNG 5: SHOW OF FORCE. As the crisis intensifies, one side or the other may draw attention to the fact that it does have the capability to use force if need be. There are various ways of showing such force—direct or indirect, silent or noisy. In a direct show of force, one or the other nation might move naval or air units, mobilize reserves, conduct provocative military exercises or maneuvers (particularly in sensitive areas), or even order "routine" deployment of naval and military units in such areas—all with widespread publicity. In an indirect show of force, one could test missiles in a provocative way, conduct normal maneuvers but with possibly abnormal publicity, publicize the use of military equipment in "normal" but special maneuvers that simulate an element in the current crisis—e.g., the use of tanks to break roadblocks.

RUNG 6: SIGNIFICANT MOBILIZATION. A show of force can be accompanied by a modest mobilization that not only increases one's strength but also indicates a readiness to call on more force or to accelerate the arms race. An example of this was President Kennedy's call-up of reserves in the Berlin crisis of 1962. As always, private communications, either direct or indirect, through principals or intermediaries, or through the use of more or less deliberately arranged leaks, can all play an important role.

RUNG 7: "LEGAL" HARASSMENT. One may harass the opponent's prestige, property, or people legally. That is to say, one may act in a very hostile and provocative manner but within the limits of international law.

RUNG 8: HARASSING ACTS OF VIOLENCE. If the

crisis is still not resolved, one side or the other may move on to illegal acts, such as acts of violence, or harassments intended to confuse, exhaust, frighten, and otherwise harm, weaken, or demoralize the opponent or its allies. Bombs may be exploded by unauthorized or anonymous means. Enemy nationals within one's borders may be badly mistreated or killed. An "aroused" citizenry may stone or raid the other nation's embassy. Frontier guards may be shot. There may be the limited covert use of guerilla warfare, piracy, sabotage, or terrorization. Both sides could step up reconnaissance probing operations or other intelligence activities. One side or the other may launch overflights or other invasions of sovereignty.

If the acts are carried out clandestinely or covertly—under the guise of being individually motivated—the escalation is relatively low. As the size, scale, and degree of organization of these acts are increased and their official character made plain, the escalation is increased, until finally we reach a level at which uniformed personnel, obviously under the orders of their government, are carrying through the actions.

RUNG 9: DRAMATIC MILITARY CONFRONTATIONS. The existing permanent alert of U.S. and Soviet strategic-bomber and missile forces is an almost continual global confrontation. Under the circumstances of prolonged cold war, this may be regarded as pre-escalation. However, the situation changes if there is a dramatic local confrontation of land or sea forces (as, for example, at the Brandenburg Gate). Such confrontations are direct tests of nerve, resolve, and recklessness. They are also dramatic enough to make everyone take note of what has happened. Because it seems obvious that these confrontations can blow up, and because in the past such incidents have often caused wars, many people think of them as being closer to the brink of all-out war than in fact they usually are. But despite contemporary conditions of a relatively firm balance of terror, they do indeed indicate that large acts of violence are possible, and that the unthinkable all-out war is becoming "thinkable."

Thus we cross the "nuclear-war-is-unthinkable" threshold. It was to this threshold that we came during the Cuban missile crisis of October, 1962 at the climax of a case of abrupt escalation. President Kennedy's dramatic television address to the nation on October 22 explicitly told the Soviet Union where it had been unbearably provocative. Both the U.S.S.R. and the U.S., he said, had recognized the need for tacit rules in the postwar world and accordingly had "deployed strategic nuclear weapons with great care, never upsetting the precarious status quo which insured that these weapons would not be used in the absence of some vital challenges." He indicated that while the Americans had always been careful, the Russians had now broken the rules in "this secret, swift, extraordinary build-up of Communist missiles in an area well known to have a special and historical relation to the United States. . . . This sudden clandestine decision to station strategic weapons for the first time outside of Soviet soil is a deliberately provocative and unjustified change in the status quo, which cannot be accepted by this country if our courage and our commitments are ever to be trusted again by either friend or foe."

He went on to describe the detailed measures that the U.S. was taking (mobilization, blockade, air alerts) and issued the famous warning: "it shall be the policy of this nation to regard any nuclear missile launched from Cuba against any nation in the Western Hemisphere as an attack by the Soviet Union on the United States, requiring a full retaliatory response upon the Soviet Union." (Of course, anyone familiar with current U.S. policy would note that the phrase "full retaliatory response" does not specify the form of the attack.)

Then, and possibly most important of all, Mr. Kennedy issued the following warning: "Any hostile move anywhere in the world against the safety and freedom of peoples to whom we are committed, including in particular the brave people of West Berlin, will be met by whatever action is needed." Some students of the subject have questioned whether the President was wise to call the Russians' attention to the option of

Berlin. In fact, it is quite important to show that one is willing to face the possibility of such counter-escalations.

RUNG 10: PROVOCATIVE DIPLOMATIC BREAK. This act would be intended to communicate to the opponent that one's reliance on the traditional peaceful measures of persuasion or coercion is at an end and that acts of force may now be resorted to.

RUNG 11: SUPER-READY STATUS. Strategic forces may be dispersed, leaves canceled, preventive and routine maintenance halted, training deferred, every possible piece of equipment and unit put in a ready status and limited-war forces deployed. Because of the relative invulnerability and alertness under normal peacetime conditions of the U.S. Minuteman and Polaris forces (and to some extent of the SAC bombers on alert), such actions may make a greater difference and thus mean more to the Soviet Union than to the U.S.

RUNG 12: LARGE CONVENTIONAL WAR. The stage has now been set for some kind of organized military violence. It may be undeclared war or border fighting such as occurred between the Japanese and the Russians in 1939 (involving thousands of soldiers), a Trieste-type occupation of disputed territory, or a major "police action," as in Korea. If such a war is fought with any intensity, both sides suffer casualties in large numbers but neither will use its most "efficient" or "quality" weapons—the nuclear, bacteriological, or chemical weapons. Paradoxically, the more "useful" these weapons are in the narrow military sense, the less likely they are to be used. In any case, there would be many casualties at this rung and, at least in the initial stages of the action, a significant deepening of the crisis.

RUNG 13: LARGE COMPOUND ESCALATION. One way to achieve a high over-all level of escalation and still keep each separate act as an act relatively low on the ladder is to retaliate or escalate in a completely different theater from that in which the primary conflict is being waged. This may be especially escalatory if the second theater is sensitive or potentially vital: such a situation might have arisen, for example, if the

Soviet Union had moved against Berlin during the Cuban crisis.

It is interesting to note that, except for rather small-scale exceptions, this obvious technique has not been used since World War II, even though there has been much concern about the possibility. Nearly everyone has instinctively recognized the danger of compound escalation. The sheer audacity of starting a new crisis when another is at full force is very provocative, yet in the paradoxical world of escalation, this might be the very reason it would be judged in certain circumstances to be an effective measure.

RUNG 14: DECLARATION OF LIMITED CONVENTIONAL WAR. This would be an attempt to achieve one or both of the following objectives: (1) a clear-cut, unilateral announcement of "no nuclear first use"; (2) a setting of the limits to a conventional war, geographically or otherwise, in a manner considered favorable or stable by the side making the declaration. Such a declaration would have grave symbolic, political, and moral effects upon one's own country and the opponent.

RUNG 15: BARELY NUCLEAR WAR. It may occur during a conventional warlike act (Rung 12) or the super-ready status (Rung 11) that a nuclear weapon is used unintentionally (accidentally or without authorization). Or one of the antagonists may make military or political use of nuclear weapon and try to give the impression that its use was unintentional.

RUNG 16: NUCLEAR "ULTIMATUMS." One side or the other seriously considers the possibility of a central war and communicates this fact convincingly to its opponent. People begin leaving cities; in fact, one might define an intense crisis as that point when 10 per cent of the population of New York City or Moscow has left out of fear of attack.

RUNG 17: LIMITED EVACUATION (ABOUT 20 PERCENT). This would most likely be at least a quasi-official move ordered by a government either for bargaining or prudential reasons, or both. The difficulties, and possible public and political reactions, make such an evacuation a momentous decision.

RUNG 18: SPECTACULAR SHOW OF FORCE. A spectacular show or demonstration of force would involve using major weapons in a way that does no obvious damage but appears determined, menacing, or reckless. An example would be the explosion of a weapon at a high altitude over enemy territory. This would intensify the fear of war in the hope of frightening the enemy into backing down.

RUNG 19: "JUSTIFIABLE" COUNTER-FORCE AT-TACK. A "justifiable" attack would be sufficiently specialized and limited to seem a reasonable response to provocation, and yet it might significantly, or even decisively, degrade the military capability, prestige, or morale of the opponent. An example would be the destruction of a submarine on the claim that it had carried out threatening maneuvers: here, a high degree of escalation could easily be involved, particularly if the casualty were a strategic-weapons submarine. A nation could invent an excuse for such an act by manufacturing an incident—perhaps by fabricating a limited nuclear attack and blaming the submarine.

RUNG 20: "PEACEFUL" WORLD-WIDE EMBAR-GO OR BLOCKADE. Worldwide embargo would be an extreme measure of non-violent coercion brought to bear against an opponent.

Once war has started, no other line of demarcation is at once so clear, so easily defined, and so easily understood as the line between not using and using nuclear weapons. There are, of course, criticisms of this point of view. Some of them take as their point of departure a fact of physics and engineering—that it is possible to have an extremely low-yield nuclear weapon that is no more powerful than a chemical explosive. True, the distinction between very small nuclear weapons and large chemical explosives does tend to narrow under analysis. But any argument designed to refute the nuclear prohibition on purely technical energy-release grounds misses the point: even though the distinction between nuclear and non-nuclear war may have defects from some technical points of view,

the distinction possesses a functional meaning or utility that transcends any purely technical question.

We should support and encourage this distinction because, for a variety of reasons that cannot be detailed in this space, it works to the advantage of both the U.S. and the world as a whole. But it is equally important to understand that once the threshold has been crossed—by an enemy, by accident, or by us—we do not stand automatically in the balance of the unthinkable war. The first use of nuclear weapons, even if against military targets, is likely to be less for the purpose of destroying the other side's military forces or to handicap its operations than for redress, bargaining, or deterrence purposes.

RUNG 21: LOCAL NUCLEAR WAR—EXEMPLARY. One side can drop a nuclear bomb or two in order to show the other side that, unless it backs down or accepts a reasonable compromise, more bombs are likely to follow. As this would be the first unmistakably deliberate use of these weapons since World War II, it would be a profoundly consequential act.

RUNG 22: DECLARATION OF LIMITED NUCLEAR WAR. A nation could use a formal declaration to set relatively exact limits to the types of nuclear action that it intends to initiate—and to indicate the type of retaliation it is prepared to countenance from the enemy without escalating further himself. In this way, eruption to all-out war might be made less likely, and the escalation itself made more explicit—which might increase the pressure to compromise. The declaration could also include a formal announcement of the conditions under which the declarer would be prepared to de-escalate.

RUNG 23: LOCAL NUCLEAR WAR. Past NATO planning has envisaged the immediate use of hundreds of nuclear weapons in reply to even a conventional attack in Europe by the U.S.S.R. As opposed to the exemplary purposes of Rung 21, NATO planned to use nuclear weapons for traditional military purposes—for defense, destruction of the opponent's local capability, etc.—and the scale of the action and the targeting

were to be dictated by these military considerations. The increasing actual or potential availability of a varied inventory of
small, inexpensive, nuclear weapons (including such esoteric devices as the Davy
Crockett missile and the neutron bomb) is
likely to renew discussion of this possibility.* It is, and will likely continue to be, an
important objective of U.S. military forces
to be able to wage such a war—at least in
Europe, even if a "no-bomb-use policy" is
explicitly adopted by all nations.

RUNG 24: UNUSUAL, PROVOCATIVE, AND SIGNIF-
ICANT COUNTER-MEASURES. One side might
carry out re-deployments or maneuvers
that have the effect of increasing an opponent's vulnerability to attack or otherwise
degrading its capability, morale, or will.

RUNG 25: EVACUATION OF CITIES (ABOUT 70
PERCENT). At this point, the situation may
be very close to large-scale war. It might
now seem advisable to evacuate a large
number of people from cities. The total
would probably amount to between two-
thirds and three-fourths of the population
—women and children and those men who
are not essential to the functioning of the
cities. I would judge that all important industries, communications, transportation
facilities, etc., could be operated by about
a quarter of the population or less.

*Attacks so far have avoided the enemy's
zone of interior and have thus observed a
salient threshold. The line between the external world and the nation may even be
stronger as a firebreak than the threshold
between conventional and nuclear war,
since it is an older distinction, invested
with far more emotion and prestige. Under
current conditions, it is reasonably clear
that, in the next decade, the likelihood that
a nation (including the U.S. and the Soviet
Union) would invite certain annihilation
for the sake of its allies is going to tend to
diminish to the vanishing point, however
repugnant or dishonorable this development may now seem. But the likelihood of
a nation risking the kind of restrained attacks discussed below may or may not diminish so sharply, depending in part on the*

---

*EDITOR'S NOTE: The Davy Crockett missiles were,
in late 1965, in the process of being withdrawn
from Europe.

*decision-makers' expectations of the "rules"
being observed.*

RUNG 26: DEMONSTRATION ATTACK ON ZONE
OF INTERIOR. An attack could be made, perhaps on an isolated mountain top or empty
desert, which does dramatic and unmistakable physical damage, if only to the
topography.

RUNG 27: EXEMPLARY ATTACK ON MILITARY
TARGETS. One side might begin destroying
portions of the other side's weapons systems, but in a careful way, so as not to
cause much collateral damage. These attacks could be launched primarily to reduce the defender's military capability
significantly by finding leverage targets.

RUNG 28: EXEMPLARY ATTACKS AGAINST PROP-
ERTY. The next step would increase the
level of these limited, nuclear, strategic
attacks. One possibility would be attacks
on such installations as bridges, dams, or
gaseous-diffusion plants. More damaging
and dangerous would be limited attacks on
cities, presumably after warning had been
delivered and the cities evacuated. The
purpose would be to destroy property, not
people.

RUNG 29: EXEMPLARY ATTACKS ON POPULA-
TION. In any crisis of the mid-1960's, this
attack would probably be much higher on
the ladder than I put it here. But if the balance of terror becomes sufficiently stable,
and governments are believed to be under
intense and graduated mutual deterrents,
even this attack could occur without an
eruption to spasm or other central wars.

RUNG 30: COMPLETE EVACUATION (ABOUT 95
PER CENT). At this point, large-scale warfare has begun. If at all possible, each side
is likely to evacuate its cities almost completely, leaving 5 to 10 per cent of the population behind for essential activities.

RUNG 31: RECIPROCAL REPRISALS. This is a
war with more or less continual exchanges.
Many strategists believe that reciprocal-re-
prisal wars might be a standard tactic of
the future when the balance of terror is
judged—whether correctly or not—to be
almost absolute.

*Thermonuclear wars are likely to be
short—lasting a few hours to a couple of
months at most. In such a war it is unlikely
that cities would in themselves be targets*

of any great military consequence. But it is perfectly possible that a nation might attack cities simply without thinking it through. In Defense Secretary Robert McNamara's speech at Ann Arbor on June 16, 1962, the U.S. more or less formally enunciated a "no cities except in reprisal" strategy, but the strategy is neither clearly understood nor firmly held even here. Soviet strategists and political leaders, for their part, have declared that Soviet forces would not recognize any such "artificial" distinctions in a nuclear war. This position could be an accurate reflection of current Soviet strategic doctrine, but it is most likely that it is a very unreliable indicator of actual Soviet behavior in a "moment of truth"—or of Soviet beliefs about U.S. conduct at such a time.

Let us assume, for the moment, that a threshold between central military targets and central civilian targets (i.e., cities) can be maintained in an actual war. Thus we can consider the possibility of waging a very large, "all-out," but very closely controlled, central war, in which there is a deliberate attempt to avoid civilians and their property.

RUNG 32: DECLARATION OF "GENERAL" WAR. The formal declaration of war could indicate that the side issuing the declaration had no immediate intention of attacking (since if it had such an intention, there would be strong reasons to ignore pre-nuclear convention and simply attack). Such a declaration certainly would remove some inhibitions against the use of force and coercion, put pressures on allies and some neutrals to cooperate, and mobilize a nation's facilities for defense and tend to suppress internal opposition. It would force the other side to recognize explicitly that a formal peace treaty would have to be written before the issue is settled; delaying tactics would not settle the matter. But while tending to prevent de-escalation and to threaten future (eventual) escalation, it nonetheless might *look like* temporizing and provide an opening for bargaining.

RUNG 33: SLOW MOTION COUNTER-"PROPERTY" WAR. In this attack, each side destroys the other's property, still attempting to force the other side to back down.

RUNG 34: SLOW-MOTION COUNTER-FORCE WAR. This is a campaign in which each side attempts attrition of the other side's weapons systems over a period of time. One can conceive of a slow-motion counter-force war lasting for weeks or months during which, for example, submarines are hunted down.

RUNG 35: CONSTRAINED FORCE REDUCTION SALVO. The attacker here attempts to destroy a significant but small portion of the defender's force in a single strike while avoiding undesired collateral damage. It is especially likely to be used against weak links or high-leverage targets at the outbreak of a war.

RUNG 36: CONSTRAINED DISARMING ATTACK. The attacker tries to destroy a significant portion of the defender's first-strike nuclear forces and even some of his second-strike weapons, such as missiles in silos. But the attacks would avoid, as much as possible, civilian targets. This would make it disadvantageous for the defender to launch a counter-strike, since the defender's damaged forces might be able to do only a limited amount of damage even with a counterstrike on cities. The defender is also under pressure to negotiate since it is now probable that the attacker could threaten another attack, this one an all-out strike.

RUNG 37: "COUNTER-FORCE WITH AVOIDANCE" ATTACK. This attack differs from a constrained disarming attack by being less scrupulous about avoiding collateral damage to cities and by not deliberately sparing much if any of the enemy's second-strike weaponry. In the case of a Soviet strike against the U.S., such an attack might include hitting Tucson (a city with a population of 265,000, completely ringed with Titans) but would probably avoid the Norfolk Navy Yard and the Pentagon. If it did hit these targets or the SAC bases near very large cities, Russia might use 20-kiloton weapons rather than 20 megatons, in order to limit the collateral destruction. After such an attack, one must assume a counter-attack, but one might still try to use threats of further escalation to limit the defender's response.

RUNG 38: UNMODIFIED COUNTER-FORCE ATTACK. Although the targets would still be enemy weapons systems, the military plans would be formulated and the operation carried out with general disregard as to whether enemy civilians are killed or non-military property destroyed (though there might be disadvantages accepted, in order to avoid fallout or other dangers to allies or neutrals). No attempt would be made either to lessen or to increase collateral damage to the enemy. This attack might be described as the classical form of all-out or total war.

At this point, the warring nations are at the threshold of civilian central wars. Under current U.S. "controlled response" doctrine, not only does the U.S. intend to observe the city threshold, but an enormous incentive is given to the U.S.S.R. to do so as well and to avoid attacking U.S. cities in the first wave—whether this wave is the first or second strike of the war. But even if population is not the target of the first wave, it could be the target of the second or later waves. In any case, it would always be threatened. The residual vulnerability of the civilian hostages and cities could then affect, to a great extent, the kind of peace treaty that the U.S.S.R. could force on us or that we could force on the U.S.S.R. For this reason, it makes sense to try to protect people from being threatened by second- and later-wave attacks, even though they may not have been adequately protected on the first wave.

It seems to me that the U.S. should, at the minimum, undertake a civil-defense program that is compatible with what the controlled-response doctrine foresees in a time of war. Part of such a program would be fallout protection for the entire population and blast protection for the 5 million to 10 million people who live within approximately ten miles of priority strategic targets. Such a program might require $5 billion to $10 billion spread over five years or so. In a very large range of types of wars these measures could save the lives of 30 million to 50 million people, and in addition make it more likely that a war, if it came, would in fact be a war of "controlled response."

RUNG 39: SLOW-MOTION COUNTER-CITY WAR. This takes the ultimate form—"city trad-

ing." This is, of course, the most bizarre of all the options that are discussed in modern strategic analysis. The possibility of trading cities arises because of today's unprecedented situation, in which both sides have almost invulnerable forces while both sides' civilians may be completely and irrevocably vulnerable to these forces. There has never before been such a situation in the history of mankind. This kind of war would be the extreme and ultimate form of deliberate, selective, and controlled response—but one not necessarily or even likely to be beyond the phychological capabilities of decision-makers, if the only alternatives were total destruction or complete capitulation.

RUNG 40: COUNTER-VALUE SALVO. It is always possible—in fighting a slow-motion counterforce, or slow-motion counter-*value* war—that one side will fire a large number of missiles at civilian targets, either in inadvertent or deliberate eruption.

RUNG 41: AUGMENTED DISARMING ATTACK. This would be an attack on military targets deliberately modified to obtain as much collateral counter-city damage as a "bonus" as feasible.

RUNG 42: CIVILIAN DEVASTATION ATTACK. This attack corresponds to the usual popular picture of nuclear war, in which there is a deliberate effort to destroy or greatly damage the enemy's society. It is distinguished from "spasm" or insesate war only by having some element of calculation and by the fact that there may be some withholding or control.

RUNG 43: SOME OTHER KIND OF CONTROLLED GENERAL WAR. It is possible to have many kinds of "all-out" but controlled as well as "all-out" but uncontrolled wars. In a "rational," "all-out," but controlled war, military action would be accompanied by threats and promises, and military operations themselves would be restricted to those that contributed to attaining victory—an acceptable or desirable peace treaty.

RUNG 44: SPASM OR INSENSATE WAR. The figurative word "spasm" is chosen because it describes the usual image of central war in which there is only a "go-ahead" order, all the buttons are pressed. A spasm war, of course, may occur, but to the extent that there is any art of war possible in the thermonuclear age, the attempt must be made to prevent it.

DOWN THE LADDER

In the same way, the study of de-escalation and its limits and of crisis termination —how to climb down and off the ladder— is vital to the management of crises and escalation. De-escalation is even more sensitive to accurate communication and shared understandings than escalation is. The opponent may have a different conception of escalation and still understand well enough the pressures being applied to him; but, typically, in order to coordinate de-escalation moves by easing pressure, both sides must have a shared understanding of what is happening. They may not have a sufficient shared understanding if one side's paradigm of the world differs in important ways from the other's.

Because of the need for shared understanding in de-escalation, unilateral initiatives are often mentioned in connection with de-escalation. Unilateral initiatives may be quite helpful. They may relax tension to a point where it is easier to settle a dispute, or to leave it unresolved but less dangerous. Even small concessions can be significant as turning points in the escalation process. Thus, even if a move is more symbolic than meaningful in itself, its de-escalatory value may be large. A serious concern, however, may be to maintain the appearance of resolve while making conciliatory moves. For this reason, the side which is doing better may find that it should take the burden of the initial de-escalatory step.

Typical de-escalation gestures take many forms. They can include the reversal of a previous escalation move, the settling of an extraneous dispute, the freeing of prisoners, conciliatory statements, the replacement of a "hard" key official by a "softer" or more flexible individual, or simply waiting for time to have its cooling effect. Concessions need not be made explicitly. Nor need the matter under dispute be settled, as long as tension is decreased to the point where the dispute is no longer so high on the escalation ladder as it once was.

Escalation is a "competition in resolve," and resolve is often measured by a willingness to pay costs in pursuit of certain objectives. One side or the other may decide to de-escalate simply because it feels it has suffered enough. It is sometimes difficult for dedicated and resolute military leaders to accept this notion. The World War I theory of the "last fifteen minutes" (in which it was asserted that that side which could hold out fifteen minutes longer would win) is still very widespread. But this theory of conflict is often completely inappropriate for a high-level escalation and may not be the most relevant aspect of a low-level conflict. In low-level conflicts, both sides typically have virtually unlimited resources that can be deployed. Both sides thus can, and usually will, insist on a compromise solution.

Escalation is also referred to as a "competition in risk-taking." One side or the other may decide that it no longer is willing to endure these risks. In the nuclear age, this is likely to be the greatest factor in de-escalation.

Most people will accept without argument that there will always be conflict. But conflicts need not inevitably lead to the kinds of crises and escalations that lie on the rungs of the ladder I have discussed. Any crisis that reaches the upper rungs of the escalation ladder is likely to be regarded by both participants as a potential—and mutual—disaster. As both sides learn that the gains of these conflicts are small compared to the dangers and other costs, they are likely to be cautious about either starting or intensifying such conflicts. Arms control has its place in this scheme of things: it should be a major objective of arms control to prevent the kinds of crises in which the options on the escalation ladder become important, and to lessen the damage and risk if these crises arise. But our first and most important need is to escape the inertia that tends to hold us captive to obsolete notions and the desire for simplistic solutions, which can only lead to disastrous capitulation or eruption—to paraphrase President Kennedy, we need wider choices than holocaust or surrender.

FIGURE 3*
AN ESCALATION LADDER
A Generalized (or Abstract) Scenario

AFTERMATHS

CIVILIAN
CENTRAL
WARS
- 44. Spasm or Insensate War
- 43. Some Other Kinds of Controlled General War
- 42. Civilian Devastation Attack
- 41. Augmented Disarming Attack
- 40. Countervalue Salvo
- 39. Slow-Motion Countercity War

(CITY TARGETING THRESHOLD)

MILITARY
CENTRAL
WARS
- 38. Unmodified Counterforce Attack
- 37. Counterforce-with-Avoidance Attack
- 36. Constrained Disarming Attack
- 35. Constrained Force-Reduction Salvo
- 34. Slow-Motion Counterforce War
- 33. Slow-Motion Counter-"Property" War
- 32. Formal Declaration of "General" War

(CENTRAL WAR THRESHOLD)

EXEMPLARY
CENTRAL
ATTACKS
- 31. Reciprocal Reprisals
- 30. Complete Evacuation (Approximately 95 per cent)
- 29. Exemplary Attacks on Population
- 28. Exemplary Attacks Against Property
- 27. Exemplary Attack on Military
- 26. Demonstration Attack on Zone of Interior

(CENTRAL SANCTUARY THRESHOLD)

BIZARRE
CRISES
- 25. Evacuation (Approximately 70 per cent)
- 24. Unusual, Provocative, and Significant Countermeasures
- 23. Local Nuclear War—Military
- 22. Declaration of Limited Nuclear War
- 21. Local Nuclear War—Exemplary

(NO NUCLEAR USE THRESHOLD)

INTENSE
CRISES
- 20. "Peaceful" World-Wide Embargo or Blockade
- 19. "Justifiable" Counterforce Attack
- 18. Spectacular Show or Demonstration of Force
- 17. Limited Evacuation (Approximately 20 per cent)
- 16. Nuclear "Ultimatums"
- 15. Barely Nuclear War
- 14. Declaration of Limited Conventional War
- 13. Large Compound Escalation
- 12. Large Conventional War (or Actions)
- 11. Super-Ready Status
- 10. Provocative Breaking Off of Diplomatic Relations

(NUCLEAR WAR IS UNTHINKABLE THRESHOLD)

TRADITIONAL
CRISES
- 9. Dramatic Military Confrontations
- 8. Harassing Acts of Violence
- 7. "Legal" Harassment—Retortions
- 6. Significant Mobilization
- 5. Show of Force
- 4. Hardening of Positions—Confrontation of Wills

(DON'T ROCK THE BOAT THRESHOLD)

SUBCRISIS
MANEUVERING
- 3. Solemn and Formal Declarations
- 2. Political, Economic, and Diplomatic Gestures
- 1. Ostensible Crisis

DISAGREEMENT—COLD WAR

*Figure 3 is reprinted by permission from *On Escalation: Metaphors and Scenarios* (New York: Frederick A. Praeger, Inc., 1965), p. 39. Copyright © 1965 by Hudson Institute.

BARGAINING, COMMUNICATION, AND LIMITED WAR

BY THOMAS C. SCHELLING

Limited war requires limits; so do strategic maneuvers if they are to be stabilized short of war. But limits require agreement or at least some kind of mutual recognition and acquiescence. And agreement on limits is difficult to reach, not only because of the uncertainties and the acute divergence of interests but because negotiation is severely inhibited both during war and before it begins and because communication becomes difficult between adversaries in time of war. Furthermore, it may seem to the advantage of one side to avoid agreement on limits, in order to enhance the other's fear of war; or one side or both may fear that even a show of willingness to negotiate will be interpreted as excessive eagerness.

The study of tacit bargaining—bargaining in which communication is incomplete or impossible—assumes importance, therefore, in connection with limited war, or, for that matter, with limited competition, jurisdictional maneuvers, jockeying in a traffic jam, or getting along with a neighbor that one does not speak to. The problem is to develop a modus vivendi when one or both parties either cannot or will not negotiate explicitly or when neither would trust the other with respect to any agreement explicitly reached. The present chapter will examine some of the concepts and principles that seem to underlie tacit bargaining and will attempt to draw a few illustrative conclusions about the problem of limited war or analogous situations. It will also suggest that these same principles may often provide a powerful clue to understanding even the logically dissimilar case of explicit bargaining with full communication and enforcement.

The most interesting situations and the most important are those in which there is a conflict of interest between the parties involved. But it is instructive to begin with the special simplified case in which two or more parties have identical interests and face the problem not of reconciling interests but only of coordinating their actions for their mutual benefit, when communication is impossible. This special case brings out clearly the principle that will then serve to solve the problem of tacit "bargaining" over conflicting preferences.

TACIT COORDINATION (COMMON INTERESTS)

When a man loses his wife in a department store without any prior understanding on where to meet if they get separated, the chances are good that they will find each other. It is likely that each will think of some obvious place to meet, so obvious that each will be sure that the other is sure that it is "obvious" to both of them. One does not simply predict where the other will go, since the other will go where he predicts the first to go, which is wherever the first predicts the second to predict the first to go, and so ad infinitum. Not "What would I do if I were she?" But "What would I do if I were she wondering what she would do if she were I wondering what I would do if I were she . . . ?" What is necessary is to coordinate predictions, to read the same message in the common situation, to identify the one course of action that their expectations of each other can converge on. They must "mutually recognize" some unique signal that coordinates their expectations of each other. We cannot be sure they will meet, nor would all couples read the same signal; but the chances are certainly a great deal better than if they pursued a random course of search.

The reader may try the problem himself with the adjoining map (Fig. 1). Two people parachute unexpectedly into the area

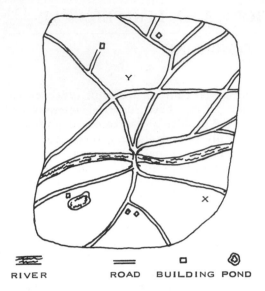

RIVER   ROAD   BUILDING POND

Figure 1.

shown, each with a map and knowing the other has one, but neither knowing where the other has dropped nor able to communicate directly. They must get together quickly to be rescued. Can they study their maps and "coordinate" their behavior? Does the map suggest some particular meeting place so unambiguously that each will be confident that the other reads the same suggestion with confidence?

The writer has tried this and other analogous problems on an unscientific sample of respondents; and the conclusion is that people often can coordinate. The following abstract puzzles are typical of those that can be "solved" by a substantial proportion of those who try. The solutions are, of course, arbitrary to this extent: any solution is "correct" if enough people think so. The reader may wish to confirm his ability to concert in the following problems with those whose scores are given in a footnote.[1]

1. Name "heads" or "tails." If you and your partner name the same, you both win a prize.

2. Circle one of the numbers listed in the line below. You win if you all succeed in circling the same number.

7   100   13   261   99   555

3. Put a check mark in one of the sixteen squares. You win if you all succeed in checking the same square.

☐ ☐ ☐ ☐
☐ ☐ ☐ ☐
☐ ☐ ☐ ☐
☐ ☐ ☐ ☐

4. You are to meet somebody in New York City. You have not been instructed where to meet; you have no prior understanding with the person on where to meet; and you cannot communicate with each other. You are simply told that you will have to guess where to meet and that he is being told the same thing and that you will just have to try to make your guesses concide.

---

[1] In the writer's sample, 36 persons concerted on "heads" in problem 1, and only 6 chose "tails." In problem 2, the first three numbers were given 37 votes out of a total of 41; the number 7 led 100 by a slight margin, with 13 in third place. The upper left corner in problem 3 received 24 votes out of a total of 41, and all but 3 of the remainder were distributed in the same diagonal line. Problem 4, which may reflect the location of the sample in New Haven, Connecticut, showed an absolute majority managing to get together at Grand Central Station (information booth), and virtually all of them succeeded in meeting at 12 noon. Problem 6 showed a variety of answers, but two-fifths of all persons succeeded in concerting on the number 1; and in problem 7, out of 41 people, 12 got together on $1,000,000, and only 3 entries consisted of numbers that were not a power of 10; of those 3, 2 were $64 and, in the more up-to-date version, $64,000! Problem 8 caused no difficulty to 36 out of 41, who split the total fifty-fifty. Problem 9 secured a majority of 20 out of 22 for Robinson. An alternative formulation of it, in which Jones and Robinson were tied on the first ballot at 28 votes each, was intended by the author to demonstrate the difficulty of concerting in case of tie; but the respondents surmounted the difficulty and gave Jones 16 out of 18 votes (apparently on the basis of Jones's earlier position on the list), proving the main point but overwhelming the subsidiary point in the process. In the map most nearly like the one reproduced here (Fig. 1), 7 out of 8 respondents managed to meet at the bridge.

5. You were told the date but not the hour of the meeting in No. 4; the two of you must guess the exact minute of the day for meeting. At what time will you appear at the meeting place that you elected in No. 4?

6. Write some positive number. If you all write the same number, you win.

7. Name an amount of money. If you all name the same amount, you can have as much as you named.

8. You are to divide $100 into two piles, labeled A and B. Your partner is to divide another $100 into two piles labeled A and B. If you allot the same amounts to A and B, respectively, that your partner does, each of you gets $100; if your amounts differ from his, neither of you gets anything.

9. On the first ballot, candidates polled as follows:

Smith 19   Robinson 29
Jones 28   White 9
Brown 15

The second ballot is about to be taken. You have no interest in the outcome, except that you will be rewarded if someone gets a majority on the second ballot and you vote for the one who does. Similarly, all voters are interested only in voting with the majority, and everybody knows that this is everybody's interest. For whom do you vote on the second ballot?

These problems are artificial, but they illustrate the point. People *can* often concert their intentions or expectations with others if each knows that the other is trying to do the same. Most situations—perhaps every situation for people who are practiced at this kind of game—provide some clue for coordinating behavior, some focal point for each person's expectation of what the other expects him to expect to be expected to do. Finding the key, or rather finding *a* key— any key that is mutually recognized as the key becomes *the* key—may depend on imagination more than on logic; it may depend on analogy, precedent, accidental arrangement, symmetry, aesthetic or geometric configuration, casuistic reasoning, and who the parties are and what they know about each other. Whimsy may send the man and his wife to the "lost and found"; or logic

may lead each to reflect and to expect the other to reflect on where they would have agreed to meet if they had had a prior agreement to cover the contingency. It is not being asserted that they will always find an obvious answer to the question; but the chances of their doing so are ever so much greater than the bare logic of abstract random probabilities would ever suggest.

A prime characteristic of most of these "solutions" to the problems, that is, of the clues or coordinators or focal points, is some kind of prominence or conspicuousness. But it is a prominence that depends on time and place and who the people are. Ordinary folk lost on a plane circular area may naturally go to the center to meet each other; but only one versed in mathematics would "naturally" expect to meet his partner at the center of gravity of an irregularly shaped area. Equally essential is some kind of uniqueness; the man and his wife cannot meet at the "lost and found" if the store has several. The writer's experiments with alternative maps indicated clearly that a map with many houses and a single crossroads sends people to the crossroads, while one with many crossroads and a single house sends most of them to the house. Partly this may reflect only that uniqueness conveys prominence; but it may be more important that uniqueness avoids ambiguousness. Houses may be intrinsically more prominent than anything else on the map; but if there are three of them, none more prominent than the others, there is but one chance in three of meeting at a house, and the recognition of this fact may lead to the rejection of houses as the "clue."[2]

But in the final analysis we are dealing with imagination as much as with logic; and the logic itself is of a fairly casuistic kind. Poets may do better than logicians at this game, which is perhaps more like "puns and anagrams" than like chess. Logic

[2] That this would be "correct" reasoning, incidentally, is suggested by one of the author's map experiments. On a map with a single house and many crossroads, the eleven people who chose the house all met, while the four who chose crossroads all chose different crossroads and did not even meet one another.

helps—the large plurality accorded to the number 1 in problem 6 seems to rest on logic—but usually not until imagination has selected some clue to work on from among the concrete details of the situation.

TACIT BARGAINING
(DIVERGENT INTERESTS)

A conflict of interest enters our problem if the parachutists dislike walking. With communication, which is not allowed in our problem, they would have argued or bargained over where to meet each favoring a spot close to himself or a resting place particularly to his liking. In the absence of communication, their overriding interest is to concert ideas; and if a particular spot commands attention as the "obvious" place to meet, the winner of the bargain is simply the one who happens to be closer to it. Even if the one who is farthest from the focal point knows that he is, he cannot withhold his acquiescence and argue for a fairer division of the walking; the "proposal" for the bargain that is provided by the map itself—if, in fact, it provides one—is the only extant offer; and without communication, there is no counterproposal that can be made. The conflict gets reconciled—or perhaps we should say ignored—as a by-product of the dominant need for coordination.

"Win" and "lose" may not be quite accurate, since both may lose by comparison with what they could have agreed on through communication. If the two are actually close together and far from the lone house on the map, they might have eliminated the long walk to the house if they could have identified their locations and concerted explicitly on a place to meet between them. Or it may be that one "wins" while the other loses more than the first wins: if both are on the same side of the house and walk to it, they walk together a greater distance than they needed to, but the closer one may still have come off better than if he had had to argue it out with the other.

This last case illustrates that it may be to the advantage of one to be unable to communicate. There is room here for a motive to destroy communication or to refuse to collaborate in advance on a method of meeting if one is aware of his advantage and confident of the "solution" he foresees. In one variant of the writer's test, A knew where B was, but B had no idea where A was (and each knew how much the other knew). Most of the recipients of the B-type questionnaire smugly sat tight, enjoying their ignorance, while virtually all the A-questionnaire respondents grimly acknowledged the inevitable and walked all the way to B. Better still may be to have the power to send but not to receive messages: if one can announce his position and state that his transmitter works but not his receiver, saying that he will wait where he is until the other arrives, the latter has no choice. He can make no effective counteroffer, since no counteroffer could be heard.[3]

The writer has tried a sample of conflicting-interest games on a number of people, including games that are biased in favor of one party or the other; and on the whole, the outcome suggests the same conclusion that was reached in the purely cooperative games. All these games require coordination; they also, however, provide several alternative choices over which the two parties' interests differ. Yet, among all the available options, some particular one usually seems to be the focal point for coordinated choice, and the party to whom it is a relatively unfavorable choice quite often takes it simply because he knows that the other will expect him to. The choices that cannot coordinate expectations are not really "available" without communication. The odd characteristic of all these games is that neither rival can gain by outsmarting the other. Each loses unless he does exactly what the other expects him to do. Each party is the prisoner or the beneficiary of their mutual expectations; no one can disavow his own expectation of what the other will expect him to expect to be expected to do. The need for agreement overrules the potential disagreement, and each must concert with the other or lose altogether. Some of these games are

[3] This is an instance of the general paradox, that what is impotence by ordinary standards may, in bargaining, be a source of "strength."

arrived at by slightly changing the problems given earlier, as we did for the map problem by supposing that walking is onerous.

1. A and B are to choose "heads" or "tails" without communicating. If both choose "heads," A gets $3 and B gets $2; if both choose "tails," A gets $2 and B gets $3. If they choose differently, neither gets anything. You are A (or B); which do you choose? (Note that if both choose at random, there is only a 50-50 chance of successful coincidence and an expected value of $1.25 apiece—less than either $3 or $2.)

2. You and your two partners (or rivals) each have one of the letters A, B, and C. Each of you is to write these three letters, A, B, and C, in any order. If the order is the same on all three of your lists, you get prizes totaling $6, of which $3 goes to the one whose letter is first on all three lists, $2 to the one whose letter is second, and $1 to the person whose letter is third. If the letters are not in identical order on all three lists, none of you gets anything. Your letter is A (or B, or C); write here the three letters in the order you choose:

———, ———, ———.

3. You and your partner (rival) are each given a piece of paper, one blank and the other with an "X" written on it. The one who gets the "X" has the choice of leaving it alone or erasing it; the one who gets the blank sheet has the choice of leaving it blank or writing an "X" on it. If, when you have made your choices without communicating, there is an "X" on only one of the sheets, the holder of the "X" gets $3 and the holder of the blank sheet gets $2. If both sheets have "X's" or both sheets are blank, neither gets anything. Your sheet of paper has the original "X" on it; do you leave it alone or erase it? (*Alternate*: your sheet of paper is the blank one; do you leave it blank or write an "X"?)

4. You and your partner (rival) are to be given $100 if you can agree on how to divide it without communicating. Each of you is to write the amount of his claim on a sheet of paper; and if the two claims add to no more than $100, each gets exactly what he claimed. If the two claims exceed $100, neither of you gets anything. How much do you claim? $———.

5. You and your partner are each to pick one of the five letters, K, G, W, L, or R. If you pick the same letter, you get prizes; if you pick different letters, you get nothing. The prizes you get depend on the letter you both pick; but the prizes are not the same for each of you, and the letter that would yield you the highest prize may or may not be his most profitable letter. For you the prizes would be as follows:

K	. . . .	$4	L	. . . .	$2
G	. . . .	$3	R	. . . .	$5
W	. . . .	$1			

You have no idea what his schedule of prizes looks like. You begin by proposing to him the letter R, that being your best letter. Before he can reply, the master-of-ceremonies intervenes to say that you were not supposed to be allowed to communicate and that any further communication will disqualify you both. You must simply write down one of the letters, hoping that the other chooses the same letter. Which letter do you choose? (Alternate formulation for the second half of the sample shows schedule of K–$3, G–$1, W–$4, L–$5, R–$2, and has the "other" party make the initial proposal of the letter R before communication is cut off.)

6. Two opposing forces are at the points marked X and Y in a map similar to the one in Fig. 1. The commander of each force wishes to occupy as much of the area as he can and knows the other does too. But each commander wishes to avoid an armed clash and knows the other does too. Each must send forth his troops with orders to take up a designated line and to fight if opposed. Once the troops are dispatched, the outcome depends only on the lines that the two commanders have ordered their troops to occupy. If the lines overlap, the troops will be assumed to meet and fight, to the disadvantage of both sides. If the troops take up positions that leave any appreciable space unoccupied between them, the situation will be assumed "unstable" and a clash inevitable. Only if the troops are ordered to occupy identical lines or lines that leave virtually no unoccupied

space between them will a clash be avoided. In that case, each side obtains successfully the area it occupies, the advantage going to the side that has the most valuable area in terms of land and facilities. You command the forces located at the point marked X (Y). Draw on the map the line that you send your troops to occupy.

7. A and B have incomes of $100 and $150 per year, respectively. They are notified of each other's income and told that they must begin paying taxes totaling $25 per year. If they can reach agreement on shares of this total, they may share the annual tax bill in whatever manner they agree on. But they must reach agreement without communication; each is to write down the share he proposes to pay, and if the shares total $25 or more, each will pay exactly what he proposed. If the proposed shares fail to add up to $25, however, each will individually be required to pay the full $25, and the tax collectors will keep the surplus. You are A (B); how much do you propose to pay? $————.

8. A loses some money, and B finds it. Under the house rules, A cannot have his money back until he agrees with the finder on a suitable reward, and B cannot keep any except what A agrees to. If no agreement is reached, the money goes to the house. The amount is $16, and A offers $2 as a reward. B refuses, demanding half the money for himself. An argument ensues, and the house intervenes, insisting that each write his claim, once and for all, without further communication. If the claims are consistent with the $16 total, each will receive exactly what he claims; but if together they claim more than $16, the funds will be confiscated by the house. As they sit pondering what claims to write, a well-known and respected mediator enters and offers to help. He cannot, he says, participate in any bargaining, but he can make a "fair" proposal. He approaches A and says, "I think a reasonable division under the circumstances would be a 2-1 split, the original owner getting two-thirds and the finder one-third, perhaps rounded off to $11 and $5, respectively. I shall make the same suggestion to him." Without waiting for any response, he approaches the finder,

makes the same suggestion, and says that he made the same suggestion to the original owner. Again without waiting for any response, he departs. You are A (B); what claim do you write?

The outcomes in the writer's informal sample are given in the footnote.[4] In those problems where there is some asymmetry between "you" and "him," that is, between A and B, the A formulations were matched with the B formulations in deriving the "outcome." The general conclusion, as given in more detail in the footnote, is that the participants can "solve" their problem in a substantial proportion of the cases; they certainly do conspicuously better than any chance methods would have permitted, and even the disadvantaged party in the biased games permits himself to be disciplined by the message that the game provides for their coordination.

The "clues" in these games are diverse. Heads apparently beat tails through some kind of conventional priority, similar to

[4] In the first problem, 16 out of 22 A's and 15 out of 22 B's chose heads. Given what the A's did, heads was the best answer for B; given what the B's did, heads was the best answer for A. Together they did substantially better than at random; and, of course, if each had tried to win $3, they would all have scored a perfect zero. Problem 2, however, which is logically similar to 1 but with a more compelling structure, showed 9 out of 12 A's, 10 out of 12 B's, and 14 out of 16 C's, successfully co-ordinating on ABC. (Of the remaining 7, incidentally, 5 discriminated against themselves in departing from alphabetical order, all to no avail.) Problem 3, which is structurally analogous to 1, showed 18 out of 22 A's concerting successfully with 14 out of 19 B's, giving A the $3 prize. In problem 4, 36 out of 40 chose $50. (Two of the remainder were $49 and $49.99.) In problem 5 the letter R won 5 out of 8 votes from those who had proposed it, and 8 out of 9 votes from those who were on the other side. In problem 6, 14 of 22 X's and 14 of 23 Y's drew their boundaries exactly along the river. The "correctness" of this solution is emphatically shown by the fact that the other 15, who eschewed the river, produced 14 different lines. Of 8 x 7 possible pairs among them, there were 55 failures and 1 success. Problem 7 showed 5 out of 6 of those with incomes of $150 and 7 out of 10 of those with incomes of $100 concerting on a 15–10 division of the tax. In problem 8 both those who lost money and those who found it, 8 and 7 persons respectively, unanimously concerted on the mediator's suggestion of an even $5 reward.

the convention that dictates A, B, C, though not nearly so strong. The original X beats the blank sheet, apparently because the "status quo" is more obvious than change. The letter R wins because there is nothing to contradict the first offer. Roads might seem, in principle, as plausible as rivers, especially since their variety permits a less arbitrary choice. But, precisely because of their variety, the map cannot say *which* road; so roads must be discarded in favor of the unique and unambiguous river. (Perhaps in a symmetrical map of uniform terrain, the outcome would be more akin to the 50-50 split in the $100 example—a diagonal division in half, perhaps—but the irregularity of the map rather precludes a geometrical solution.)

The tax problem illustrates a strong power of suggestion in the income figures. The abstract logic of this problem is identical with that of the $100 division; in fact, it could be reworded as follows: each party pays $25 in taxes, and a refund of $25 is available to be divided among the two parties if they can agree on how to divide it. This formulation is logically equivalent to the one in problem 7, and, as such, it differs from problem 4 only in the amount of $25 instead of $100. Yet the inclusion of income figures, just by *suggesting* their relevance and making them prominent in the problem, shifts the focal point substantially to a 10-15 split rather than 12.5-12.5. And why, if incomes are relevant, is a perfectly *proportional* tax so obvious, when perhaps there are grounds for graduated rates? The answer must be that no *particular* graduation of rates is so obvious as to go without saying; and if speech is impossible, by default the uniquely simple and recognizable principle of proportionality has to be adopted. First the income figures take the initial plausibility away from a 50-50 split; then the simplicity of proportionality makes 10-15 the only one that could possibly be considered capable of tacit recognition. The same principle is displayed by an experiment in which question 7 was deliberately cluttered up with *additional* data—on family size, spending habits, and so on. Here the unique attraction of the income-proportionate split apparently be-

came so diluted that the preponderant reply from both the high-income and the low-income respondents was a simple 50-50 division of the tax. The refined signal for the income proportionate split was drowned out by "noise," and the cruder signal for equality was all that came through.

Finally, problem 8 is again logically the same as problem 4, the amount being $16 available for two people if they can write claims that do not exceed the amount. But the institutional arrangement is discriminatory; finder and loser do not have a compelling equality in any moralistic or legalistic sense, so the 50-50 split seems not quite obvious. The suggestion of the mediator provides the only other signal that is visible; its potency as a coordinator is seen even in the rounding to $11 and $5, which was universally accepted.

In each of these situations the outcome is determined by something that is fairly arbitrary. It is not a particularly "fair" outcome, from either an observer's point of view or the points of view of the participants. Even the 50-50 split is arbitrary in its reliance on a kind of recognizable mathematical purity; and if it is "fair," it is so only because we have no concrete data by which to judge its unfairness, such as the source of the funds, the relative need of the rival claimants, or any potential basis for moral or legal claims. Splitting the difference in an argument over kidnap ransom is not particularly "fair," but it has the mathematical qualities of problem 4.

If we ask what determines the outcome in these cases, the answer again is in the coordination problem. Each of these problems requires coordination for a common gain, even though there is rivalry among alternative lines of common action. But, among the various choices, there is usually one or only a few that can serve as coordinator. Take the case of the first offer in problem 5. The strongest argument in favor of R is the rhetorical question, "If not R, what then?" There is no answer so obvious as to give more than a random chance of concerting, even if both parties wanted to eschew the letter R after the first offer was made. To illustrate the force of this point, suppose that the master-of-ceremonies in that problem considered the first offer already to have spoiled the game and thought he might confuse the players by announcing the reversal of their prize schedules. A will get whatever prize B would have gotten, and B will get the prizes shown in A's schedule in problem 5. Does the original offerer of R have any reason to change his choice? Or suppose that the master-of-cermonies announced that the prizes would be the same, no matter what letter were chosen, so long as they both picked the same letter. They will still rally to R as the only indicated means of coordinating choices. If we revert to the beginning of this game and suppose that the original proposal of R never got made, we might imagine a sign on the wall saying, "In case of doubt always choose R; this sign is visible to all players and constitutes a means of coordinating choices." Here we are back at the man and his wife in the department store, whose problems are over when they see a conspicuous sign that says, "The management suggests that all persons who become separated meet each other at the information booth in the center of the ground floor." Beggars cannot be choosers about the source of their signal, or about its attractiveness compared with others that they can only wish were as conspicuous.

The irony would be complete if, in game 5, your rival knew your prize schedule and you did not know his (as was the case in a variant of question 5 used in some questionnaires). Since you have no basis for guessing his preference and could not even do him a favor or make a "fair" compromise if you wished to, the only basis for concerting is to see what message you can both read in your schedule. Your own preferred letter seems the indicated choice; it is hard to see why to pick any other or which other to pick, since you have no basis for knowing what other letter is better for him than R itself. His knowledge of your preference, combined with your ignorance of his and the lack of any alternative basis for coordination, puts on him the responsibility of simply choosing in your favor. (This, in fact, was the preponderant result among the small sample tested.) It is

the same situation as when only one parachutist knew where the other was.[5]

EXPLICIT BARGAINING

The concept of "coordination" that has been developed here for tacit bargaining does not seem directly applicable to explicit bargaining. There is no apparent need for intuitive rapport when speech can be used; and the adventitious clues that coordinated thoughts and influenced the outcome in the tacit case revert to the status of incidental details.

Yet there is abundant evidence that some such influence is powerfully present even in explicit bargaining. In bargains that involve numerical magnitudes, for example, there seems to be a strong magnetism in mathematical simplicity. A trivial illustration is the tendency for the outcomes to be expressed in "round numbers"; the salesman who works out the arithmetic for his "rock-bottom" price on the automobile at $2,507.63 is fairly pleading to be relieved of $7.63. The frequency with which final agreement is precipitated by an offer to "split the difference" illustrates the same point, and the difference that is split is by no means always trivial. More impressive, perhaps, is the remarkable frequency with which long negotiations over complicated quantitative formulas or *ad hoc* shares in some costs or benefits converge ultimately on something as crudely simple as equal shares, shares proportionate to some common magnitude (gross national product, population, foreign-exchange deficit, and so forth), or the shares agreed on in some previous but logically irrelevant negotiation.[6]

Precedent seems to exercise an influence

[5] And it is another example of the power that resides in "weakness," which was commented on in an earlier footnote.

[6] From a great variety of formulas proposed for the contributions to UNRRA, the winner that emerged was a straight 1 per cent of gross national product—the simplest conceivable formula and the roundest conceivable number. This formula was, to be sure, the preferred position of the United States during the discussion; but that fact perhaps adds as much to the example as it detracts from it.

that greatly exceeds its logical importance or legal force. A strike settlement or an international debt settlement often sets a "pattern" that is followed almost by default in subsequent negotiations. Sometimes, to be sure, there is a reason for a measure of uniformity, and sometimes there is enough similarity in the circumstances to explain similar outcomes; but more often it seems that there is simply no heart left in the bargaining when it takes place under the shadow of some dramatic and conspicuous precedent.[7] In similar fashion, mediators often display a power to precipitate agreement and a power to determine the terms of agreement; their proposals often seem to be accepted less by reason of their inherent fairness or reasonableness than by a kind of resignation of both participants. "Fact-finding" reports may also tend to draw expectations to a focus, by providing a suggestion to fill the vacuum of indeterminacy that otherwise exists: it is not the facts themselves, but the creation of a specific suggestion, that seems to exercise the influence.

There is, in a similar vein, a strong attraction to the *status quo ante* as well as to natural boundaries. Even parallels of latitude have recently exhibited their longevity as focal points for agreement. Certainly there are reasons of convenience in using rivers as the agreed stopping place for troops or using old boundaries, whatever their current relevance; but often these features of the landscape seem less important for their practical convenience than for their power to crystallize agreement.

These observations would be trivial if they meant only that bargaining results were *expressed* in simple and qualitative terms or that minor accommodations were made to round off the last few cents or miles or people. But it often looks as though the ultimate focus for agreement did not just reflect the balance of bargaining powers but provided bargaining power to one side or the other. It often seems that a cynic could have predicted the outcome on the basis of some "obvious" focus for agreement, some strong suggestion contained in the situation itself, without much regard to the merits of the case, the arguments to be made, or the pressures to be applied during the bargaining. The "obvious" place to compromise frequently seems to win by some kind of default, as though there is simply no rationale for settling anywhere else. Or, if the "natural" outcome is taken to reflect the relative skills of the parties to the bargain, it may be important to identify that skill as the ability to set the stage in such a way as to give prominence to some particular outcome that would be favorable. The outcome may not be so much conspicuously fair or conspicuously in balance with estimated bargaining powers as just plain "conspicuous."

This conclusion may seem to reduce the scope for bargaining skill, if the outcome is already determined by the configuration of the problem itself and where the focal point lies. But perhaps what it does is shift the locus where skill is effective. The "obvious" outcome depends greatly on how the problem is formulated, on what analogies or precedents the definition of the bargaining issue calls to mind, on the kinds of data that may be available to bear on the question in dispute. When the committee begins to argue over how to divide the costs, it is already constrained by whether the terms of reference refer to the "dues" to be shared or the "taxes" to be paid, by whether a servicing committee is preparing national-income figures or balance-of-payments figures for their use, by whether the personnel of the committee brings certain precedents into prominence by having participated personally in earlier negotiations, by whether the inclusion of two separate issues on the same agenda will give special prominence and relevance to those particular features that they have in common. Much of the skill has already been applied when the formal negotiations begin.[8]

[7] This and the preceding paragraph are illustrated by the speed with which a number of Middle Eastern oil-royalty arrangements converged on the 50–50 formula a few years after World War II.

[8] Perhaps another role for skill is contained in this general approach. If one is unsuccessful in

If all this is correct, as it seems frequently to the author to be, our analysis of tacit bargaining may help to provide an understanding of the influence at work; and perhaps the logic of tacit bargaining even provides a basis for believing it to be correct. The fundamental problem in tacit bargaining is that of *coordination*; we should inquire, then, what has to be coordinated in explicit bargaining. The answer may be that explicit bargaining requires, for an ultimate agreement, some coordination of the participants' expectations. The proposition might be as follows.

Most bargaining situations ultimately involve some range of possible outcomes within which each party would rather make a concession than fail to reach agreement at all. In such a situation any potential outcome is one from which at least one of the parties, and probably both, would have been willing to retreat for the sake of agreement, and very often the other party knows it. Any potential outcome is therefore one that either party could have improved by insisting; yet he may have no basis for insisting, since the other knows or suspects that he would rather concede than do without agreement. Each party's strategy is guided mainly by what he expects the other to accept or insist on; yet each knows that the other is guided by reciprocal thoughts. The final outcome must be a point from which neither expects the other to retreat; yet the main ingredient of this expectation is what one thinks the other expects the first to expect, and so on. Somehow, out of this fluid and indeterminate situation that seemingly provides no logical reason for anybody to expect anything except what he expects to be expected to expect, a decision is reached. These infinitely reflexive expectations must somehow converge on a single point, at which each expects the other not to expect to be expected to retreat.

If we then ask what it is that can bring their expectations into convergence and bring the negotiation to a close, we might propose that it is the intrinsic magnetism of particular outcomes, especially those that enjoy prominence, uniqueness, simplicity, precedent, or some rationale that makes them qualitatively differentiable from the continuum of possible alternatives. We could argue that expectations tend not to converge on outcomes that differ only by degree from alternative outcomes but that people have to dig in their heels at a groove in order to make any show of determination. One has to have a reason for standing firmly on a position; and along the continuum of qualitatively undifferentiable positions one finds no rationale. The rationale may not be strong at the arbitrary "focal point," but at least it can defend itself with the argument "If not here, where?"

There is perhaps a little more to this need for a mutually identifiable resting place. If one is about to make a concession, he needs to control his adversary's expectations; he needs a recognizable limit to his own retreat. If one is to make a finite concession that is not to be interpreted as capitulation, he needs an obvious place to stop. A mediator's suggestion may provide it; or any other element that qualitatively distinguishes the new position from surrounding positions. If one has been demanding 60 per cent and recedes to 50 per cent, he can get his heels in; if he recedes to 49 per cent, the other will assume that he has hit the skids and will keep sliding.

If some troops have retreated to the river in our map, they will expect to be expected to make a stand. This is the one spot to which they can retreat without necessarily being expected to retreat further, while, if they yield any further, there is no place left where they can be expected to make a determined stand. Similarly, the advancing party can expect to force the other to retreat to the river without having his advance interpreted as an insatiable demand for unlimited retreat. There is stability at the river—and perhaps nowhere else.

---

getting the problem so formulated that the "obvious" outcome is near his own preferred position, he can proceed to confuse the issue. Find multiple definitions for all the terms and add "noise" to drown out the strong signal contained in the original formulation. The technique may not succeed, but in the variant of our income-tax problem mentioned above it certainly did.

This proposition may seem intuitively plausible; it does to the writer, and in any event some kind of explanation is needed for the tendency to settle at focal points. But the proposition would remain vague and somewhat mystical if it were not for the somewhat more tangible logic of tacit bargaining. The latter provides not only an analogy but the demonstration that the necessary psychic phenomenon—tacit coordination of expectations is a real possibility and in some contexts a remarkably reliable one. The "coordination" of expectations is analogous to the "coordination" of behavior when communication is cut off; and, in fact, they both involve nothing more nor less than intuitively perceived mutual expectations. Thus the empirically verifiable results of some of the tacit-bargaining games, as well as the more logical role of coordinated expectations in that case, prove that expectations can be coordinated and that some of the objective details of the situation can exercise a controlling influence when the coordination of expectations is essential. *Something* is perceived by both parties when communication is absent; it must still be perceptible, though undoubtedly of lesser force, when communication is possible. The possibility of communication does not make 50-50 less symmetrical or the river less unique or A B C a less natural order for those letters.

If all we had to reason from were the logic of tacit bargaining, it would be only a guess and perhaps a wild one that the same kind of psychic attraction worked in explicit bargaining; and if all we had to generalize from were the observation of peculiarly "plausible" outcomes in actual bargains, we might be unwilling to admit the force of adventitious details. But the two lines of evidence so strongly reinforce each other that the analogy between tacit and explicit bargaining seems a potent one.

To illustrate with the problem of agreeing explicitly on how to divide $100: 50-50 seems a plausible division, but it may seem so for too many reasons. It may seem "fair"; it may seem to balance bargaining powers; or it may, as suggested in this paper, simply have the power to communicate its own inevitability to the two parties in such fashion that each appreciates that they both appreciate it. What our analysis of tacit bargaining provides is evidence for the latter view. The evidence is simply that *if* they had to divide the $100 without communicating, they could concert on 50-50. Instead of relying on intuition, then, we can point to the fact that in a slightly different context—the tacit-bargaining context—our argument has an objectively demonstrable interpretation.

To illustrate again: the ability of the two commanders in one of our problems to recognize the stabilizing power of the river —or, rather, their inability not to recognize it—is substantiated by the evidence that if their survival depended on some agreement about where to stabilize their lines *and communication were not allowed*, they probably could perceive and appreciate the qualities of the river as a focus for their tacit agreement. So the tacit analogy at least demonstrates that the idea of "coordinating expectations" is meaningful rather than mystical.

Perhaps we could push the argument further still. Even in those cases in which the only distinguishing characteristic of a bargaining result is its evident "fairness," by standards that the participants are known to appreciate, we might argue that the moral force of fairness is greatly reinforced by the power of a "fair" result to focus attention, if it fills the vacuum of indeterminacy that would otherwise exist. Similarly, when the pressure of public opinion seems to force the participants to the obviously "fair" or "reasonable" solution, we may exaggerate the "pressure" or at least misunderstand the way it works on the participants unless we give credit to its power to coordinate the participants' expectations. It may, to put it differently, be the power of *suggestion*, working through the mechanism described in this paper, that makes public opinion or precedent or ethical standards so effective. Again, as evidence for this view, we need only to suppose that the participants had to reach ultimate agreement without communicating and visualize public opinion or some prominent ethical standard as providing a strong suggestion analogous to the suggestions contained in our earlier examples. The mediator in problem 7 is a close analogy. Finally, even if it is truly the force of moral responsibility or sensitivity to public opinion that constrains the participants, and not the "signal" they get, we must still look to the source of the public's own opinion; and there, the writer suggests, the need for a simple, qualitative rationale often reflects the mechanism discussed in this paper.

But, if this general line of reasoning is valid, any analysis of explicit bargaining must pay attention to what we might call the "communication" that is inherent in the bargaining situations, the signals that the participants read in the inanimate details of the case. And it means that tacit and explicit bargaining are not thoroughly separate concepts but that the various gradations from tacit bargaining up through types of incompleteness or faulty or limited communication to full communication all show some dependence on the need to coordinate expectations. Hence all show some degree of dependence of the participants themselves on their common inability to keep their eyes off certain outcomes.

This is not necessarily an argument for expecting explicit outcomes as a rule to lean toward exactly those that would have emerged if communication had been impossible; the focal points may certainly be different when speech is allowed, except in some of the artificial cases we have used in our illustrations. But what may be the *main* principle in tacit bargaining apparently may be at least *one* of the important principles in the analysis of explicit bargaining. And, since even much so-called "explicit" bargaining includes maneuver, indirect communication, jockeying for position, or speaking to be overheard, or is confused by a multitude of participants and divergent interests, the need for convergent expectations and the role of signals that have the power to coordinate expectations may be powerful.

Perhaps many kinds of social stability and the formation of interest groups reflect the same dependence on such coordinators as the terrain and the circumstances can provide: the band wagon at political con-

ventions that often converts the slightest sign of plurality into an overwhelming majority; the power of constitutional legitimacy to command popular support in times of anarchy or political vacuum; the legendary power of an old gang leader to bring order into the underworld, simply because obedience depends on the expectation that others will be obedient in punishing disobedience. The often expressed idea of a "rallying point" in social action seems to reflect the same concept. In economics the phenomena of price leadership, various kinds of nonprice competition, and perhaps even price stability itself appear amenable to an analysis that stresses the importance of tacit communication and its dependence on qualitatively identifiable and fairly unambiguous signals that can be read in the situation itself. "Spontaneous" revolt may reflect similar principles: when leaders can easily be destroyed, people require some signal for their coordination, a signal so unmistakably comprehensible and so potent in its suggestion for action that everyone can be sure that everyone else reads the same signal with enough confidence to act on it, thus providing one another with the immunity that goes with action in large numbers. (There is even the possibility that such a signal might be provided from outside, even by an agent whose only claim to leadership was its capacity to signal the instructions required for concerted action.)

TACIT NEGOTIATION AND LIMITED WAR

What useful insight does this line of analysis provide into the practical problems of tacit bargaining that usually confront us, particularly the problems of strategic maneuver and limited war? It certainly suggests that it is *possible* to find limits to war—real war, jurisdictional war, or whatever—without overt negotiation. But it gives us no new strong sense of *probability*. War was limited in Korea, and gas was not used in World War II; on the possibility of limited war these two facts are more persuasive than all the suggestions contained in the foregoing discussion. If the analysis provides anything, then, it is not a judgment of the probability of successfully reaching tacit agreement but a better understanding of where to look for the terms of agreement.

If there are important conclusions to be drawn, they are probably these: (1) tacit agreements or agreements arrived at through partial or haphazard negotiation require terms that are qualitatively distinguishable from the alternatives and cannot simply be a matter of degree; (2) when agreement must be reached with incomplete communication, the participants must be ready to allow the situation itself to exercise substantial constraint over the outcome; specifically, a solution that discriminates against one party or the other or even involves "unnecessary" nuisance to both of them may be the only one on which their expectations can be coordinated.

Gas was not used in World War II. The agreement, though not without antecedents, was largely a tacit one. It is interesting to speculate on whether any alternative agreement concerning poison gas could have been arrived at without formal communication (or even, for that matter, with communication). "Some gas" raises complicated questions of how much, where, under what circumstances: "No gas" is simple and unambiguous. Gas only on military personnel; gas used only by defending forces; gas only when carried by vehicle or projectile; no gas without warning—a variety of limits is conceivable; some may make sense, and many might have been more impartial to the outcome of the war. But there is a simplicity to "no gas" that makes it almost uniquely a focus for agreement when each side can only conjecture at what rules the other side would propose and when failure at coordination on the first try may spoil the chances for acquiescence in any limits at all.

The physical configuration of Korea must have helped in defining the limits to war and in making geographical limits possible. The area was surrounded by water, and the principal northern political boundary was marked dramatically and unmistakably by a river. The thirty-eighth parallel seems to have been a powerful focus for a stalemate; and the main alternative, the "waist," was a strong candidate not just because it provided a shorter defense line but because it would have been clear to both sides that an advance to the waist did not necessarily signal a determination to advance farther and that a retreat to the waist did not telegraph any intention to retreat farther.

The Formosan Straits made it possible to stabilize a line between the Communist and National government forces of China, not solely because water favored the defender and inhibited attack, but because an island is an integral unit and water is a conspicuous boundary. The sacrifice of any part of the island would have made the resulting line unstable; the retention of any part of the mainland would have been similarly unstable. Except at the water's edge, all movement is a matter of degree; an attack across water is a declaration that the "agreement" has been terminated.

In Korea, weapons were limited by the qualitative distinction between atomic and all other; it would surely have been much more difficult to stabilize a tacit acceptance of any limit on size of atomic weapons or selection of targets. No definition of size or target is so obvious and natural that it goes without saying, except for "no size, on any target." American assistance to the French forces in Indochina was persuasively limited to material, not people; and it was appreciated that an enlargement to include, say, air participation could be recognized as limited to air, while it would not be possible to establish a limited *amount* of air or ground participation. One's intentions to abstain from ground intervention can be conveyed by the complete withholding of ground forces; one cannot nearly so easily commit *some* forces and communicate a persuasive limit to the *amount* that one intends to commit.

The strategy of retaliation is affected by the need to communicate or coordinate on limits. Local aggression defines a place; with luck and natural boundaries, there may be tacit acceptance of geographical limits or limits on types of targets. One side or both may be willing to accept limited defeat rather than take the initiative in breaching the rules, and to act in a manner that reassures the other of such willingness. The "rules" may be respected because, if they are once broken, there is no assurance that any new ones can be found and jointly recognized in time to check the widening of the conflict. But if retaliation is left to the method and place of the retaliator's own choosing, it may be much more difficult to convey to the victim what the proposed limits are, so that he has a chance to accept them in his counter-retaliation. In fact, the initial departure of retaliation from the locality that provokes it may be a kind of declaration of independence that is not conducive to the creation of stable mutual expectations. Thus the problem of finding mutually recognized limits on war is doubly difficult if the definition implicit in the aggressor's own act is not tolerable.

In sum, the problem of limiting warfare involves not a continuous range of possibilities from most favorable to least favorable for either side; it is a lumpy, discrete world that is better able to recognize qualitative than quantitative differences, that is embarrassed by the multiplicity of choices, and that forces both sides to accept some dictation from the elements themselves. The writer suggests that the same is true of restrained competition in every field in which it occurs.

PRIOR ARRANGEMENTS

While the main burden of this paper has been that tacit bargaining is possible and is susceptible of systematic analysis, there is no assurance that it will succeed in any particular case or that, when it succeeds, it will yield to either party a particularly favorable outcome compared with alternatives that might have been available if full communication had been allowed. There is no assurance that the next war, if it comes, will find mutually observed limits in time and of a sort to afford protection, unless explicit negotiation can take place. There is reason, therefore, to consider what steps can be taken before the time for tacit bargaining occurs, to enhance the likelihood of a successful outcome.

Keeping communication channels open seems to be one obvious point. (At a minimum, this might mean assuring that a surrender offer could be heard and responded to by either side.) The technical side of this principle would be identification of who would send and receive messages, upon what authority, over what facilities, using what intermediaries if intermediaries were used, and who stood in line to do the job in what fashion if the indicated parties and facilities were destroyed. In the event of an effort to fight a restrained nuclear war, there may be only a brief and busy instant in which each side must decide whether limited war is in full swing or full war has just begun; and twelve hours' confusion over how to make contact might spoil some of the chances for stabilizing the action within limits.

Thought should be given to the possible usefulness of mediators or referees. To settle on influential mediators usually requires some prior understanding, or at least a precedent or a tradition or a sign of welcome. Even if we rule out overt arrangements for the contingency, evidences by each side of an appreciation of the role of referees and mediators, even a little practice in their use, might help to prepare an instrument of the most extreme value in an awful contingency.

But all such efforts may suffer from the unwillingness of an adversary to engage in any preparatory steps. Not only may an adversary balk at giving signs of eagerness to come to agreement; it is even possible that one side in a potential war may have a tactical interest in keeping that war unrestrained and aggravating the likelihood of mutual destruction in case it comes. Why? Because of the strategy of threats, bluffs, and deterrents. The willingness to start a war or take steps that may lead to war, whether aggression or retaliation to aggression, may depend on the confidence with which a nation's leaders think a war could be kept within limits. To be specific, the willingness of America to retaliate against local aggression with atomic attack depends—and the Russians know that it depends—on how likely we consider it that such retaliation could itself remain limited. That is, it depends on how likely it is in our judgment that we and the Russians, when we both desperately need to recognize limits within which either of us is willing to lose the war without enlarging those limits, will find such limits and come to mutually recognized acquiescence in them. If, then, Russian refusal to engage in any activity that might lead to the possibility of limited war deters our own resolution to act, they might risk forgoing such limits for the sake of reducing the threat of American action. One parachutist in our example may know that the other will be careless with the plane if he is sure they can meet and save themselves; so if the first abstains from discussing the contingency, the other will have to ride quietly for fear of precipitating a fatal separation in the terrain below.

Whether this consideration or just the usual inhibitions on serious negotiation make prior discussion impossible, there is still a useful idea that emerges from one of our earlier games. It is that negotiation or communication for the purpose of co-ordinating expectations need not be reciprocal: unilateral negotiation may provide the coordination that will save both parties. Furthermore, even an unwilling member cannot necessarily make himself un-available for the receipt of messages. Recall the man who proposed the letter R in one of the bargaining games: as long as the partner heard—and it is obvious that he heard—the letter R is the only extant proposal, and, being unchallenged, it may coordinate in default of any counterproposal nearly as well as if it had been explicitly accepted. (Even *denial* of it by the other party might not manage to dislodge its claim to prominence but rather simply prove his awareness of it, as long as no rival claim was made that created ambiguousness.) If one of our parachutists, just before the plane failed and while neither of them dreamed of having to jump, idly said, "If I ever had to meet somebody down there, I'd just head for the highest hill in sight," the other would probably recall and know that the first would be sure he recalled and would go there, even though it had been on the tip of his tongue to say, "How stupid," or "Not me, climbing hurts my legs," when the plane failed. When some signal is desperately needed by *both* parties and both parties know it, even a poor signal and a discriminatory one may command recognition, in default of any other. Once the contingency is upon them, their interests, which originally diverged in the play of threats and deterrents, substantially coincide in the desperate need for a focus of agreement.

PREDICTING THE PROBABILITIES OF ESCALATION: SOME SAMPLE CASES

BY BERNARD BRODIE

We must now consider the implications of the foregoing observations for our central subject: the problem of predicting the probabilities of uncontrolled escalation—or the dangers attending deliberate escalation—in the event of the outbreak of hostilities between either of the major Communist powers and the United States. We shall continue, however, to consider mainly the special case of Europe.

If the foregoing analysis is in essence reasonably correct, it should be clear that

Reprinted by permission from *Escalation and the Nuclear Option*, RAND Memorandum RM-4544-PR, 1965, pp. 71–88. The RAND Corporation.

at least in Europe, wherever deterrence-of-war objectives diverge from either war-fighting or anti-escalation objectives, as they inevitably do in important ways, it would be seriously wrong to sell the former short. The appreciation that Europe is in all the important relevant respects entirely different from pre-1914 Europe, an appreciation which seems much rarer in the United States than among historically-minded Europeans, justifies a kind of "going for broke" on deterrence that would have been irresponsible in an earlier age.

Actually, that is exactly the aim which the United States is pursuing on the strategic level. We have gone to great expense to build up a powerful and low-vulnerability strategic bombing system, the success of which will be measured chiefly by whether or not it is ever challenged. The dominant persuasion today among defense specialists is that it faces little danger, at least in the near-term, of being challenged.

Nevertheless, it is possible to imagine deterrence failing in Europe, and we therefore have to consider what to do militarily if it does. The first point to make, and to stress, is that it is impossible to consider intelligently what to do if deterrence fails without at the same time considering how and under what circumstances it will have failed. This must be done in terms not so much of the physical events themselves as of the context of desires, aspirations, fears, and threats between the parties. It should be obvious that Soviet behavior with respect to escalation will be affected one way if the Soviet Union is reacting to a military initiative on our part, especially one that it considers a dangerous threat to its very life, and quite another way if it sees us responding forcefully to its own aggressive moves at relatively detached places like Berlin or Cuba.

To be sure, even in the latter case the aggressor may, in theory at least, be willing to take substantial risks to accomplish his ends. To be capable of some disturbing act, some infringement on the status quo, means at least to be other than wholly wedded to the bliss of peace and quiet. This attitude may already sharply distinguish the aggressor from his opponent.

However, it is also possible that the initiator of the disturbance may have calculated that he faces no real risk of harm or loss, in which case the only real courage he is demonstrating by his act is the courage of a conviction that denies the existence of danger. He may expect the opponent to yield, or to compromise, or at the very minimum to go to some lengths to leave him an easy out. He may in fact be so firm in his conviction of the softness of the opponent that an initial act of resistance will not be enough to shake him; he will ascribe it to bluff. Nevertheless, such an aggressor is clearly not prepared to go very far in pursuing his object. The conviction that he can have something for nothing is inherently brittle and bound (or at least *very* likely) to collapse quickly in the face of real determination.

Let us now imagine, as an example, the Russians firing at an American convoy which, after having been halted on the Berlin autobahn, has been ordered by its commander (acting upon higher orders) to continue on its way without awaiting permission. Or one could picture a similar case where the Russians put up a road-block on the autobahn that American forces then proceed to destroy or to push out of their way.[1]

If we assume—as we are bound to for most comparable cases in view of our present knowledge of the Soviet leaders—that they are anxious to avoid any war with us and certainly don't want one over Berlin, we can understand the Russians being most unwilling to let this situation escalate. For this assumption carries also the corollary assumption that they will be not merely unwilling to persist but positively anxious to retreat if their probe provokes a suitably hostile response from us.

Let us now make the added assumption

[1] There have indeed been incidents where Soviet guards went as far as uncovering their guns when American convoy commanders announced they were going to proceed despite withheld permission, but when the declared deadline arrived the Soviet commander in fact waved through the convoy. One such incident, of October 10, 1963, is described in Horst Mendershausen, *A View of U.S.–European Relations in 1964*, The RAND Corporation, RM-4334-PR, November, 1964, pp. 7f.

that the issue over which the Soviets have stopped our convoy was an important one in which they feel themselves to be clearly in the right (e.g., we have made a specific agreement with them over access rights which they feel we are now violating; or, more likely, we have previously let some of our prerogatives go to the Russians by default, but we are now trying to recapture some of them), and let us assume also that we have a considerably more stubborn and more confident man (concerning Soviet chances of prevailing) in control in the Soviet Union than either Khrushchev or his successors have thus far proved to be. Now we have a stickier situation to consider. The Soviet leaders are still anxious to avoid any real war with us, but they are not necessarily willing to retreat from their position the very moment some shots are exchanged. Let us assume further that both sides rush in such reinforcements as are locally available. Now we have a representative initiation of the so-called "inadvertent war," the kind nobody wants but which nevertheless breaks out.

But what *has* broken out and how far has it gone? Both sides, we can imagine further, have remained in diplomatic contact (perhaps with "hot line" intact) or, if conceivably we must think of diplomatic relations having been ruptured before the circumstances above described, some substitute communications have been quickly developed. For the United States it would make a great deal of difference whether the Soviet action seemed to be designed to push us out of West Berlin or had a considerably lesser objective. The former issue is not negotiable, but others might be. If it remains our basic assumption that the Russians will not accept war over Berlin, we must make the corollary assumption that they are not ready to push us out. However, our leaders may not know that. One of the questions we should be prepared to examine is: How much can U.S. political leaders be in doubt or in gross error about Soviet basic intentions? One merit of negotiations, incidentally, is that while they often fail to bring about a satisfactory agreement, they do sometimes help to clarify for each party what the other

really wants—though it is often possible to know that quite well without negotiations.

The main question we are concerned with is the following: What are the circumstances that can really make such a situation as the one described above go out of control? It would seem that these circumstances boil down basically to two categories of factors, with various conceivable permutations and combinations among them. One of these is the prevalence of rigid mechanisms of military response, such as do tend to pervade war-initiation concepts and also to get written into war plans. The other embraces that bundle of psychological factors summed up by (a) concern with loss of face and (b) tendencies to yield to feelings of hatred and rage.

The "rigid mechanisms" category is reflected in various common expressions about "pushing the button" or "the balloon going up." An interesting and possibly alarming aspect of the Cuban crisis of 1962 was the degree to which the crisis stimulated even among American administration leaders a tendency to think or at least to talk in such simplistic but absolute terms, despite the sophistication they had presumably been accumulating in the preceding months concerning the appropriateness of flexible response and the feasibility of limited operations. One has to be ready, it appears, for a kind of crisis-induced regression to older patterns of thinking about war and peace.

However, several things must be said on the other side. First, the fear of precisely such semi-automatic escalatory reactions on the part of the opponent acts as a powerful deterrent to both sides. Perhaps the degree of fear will be somewhat asymmetrical (which is *not* to say that it will likely be greater on our side). However, the present intensity of such fears among all the major powers suggests that the asymmetries are likely to be marginal and to be dominated by the circumstances of the occasion.

We are here dealing again with one of the ways in which the world, and especially that part of it which is Europe, is today strikingly different from what it was before 1914 or even 1939. We have been moving towards much higher levels of tolerance for types of behavior that previously would have been considered impossibly offensive, including limited acts of violence, which we are much readier to distinguish from acts of war. Also, all sorts of precautions and devices are being ground into the relevant systems—certainly on our side, and there is little doubt on the Soviet side as well—to keep military reactions from escalating spontaneously. It is a fair surmise, therefore, that the fears to which we have referred are counterescalatory at lower levels of violence, and that the levels at which automatic or spontaneous escalation may tend to take over are being pushed critically higher.

The other group of factors that we have referred to as possibly tending to stimulate uncontrolled escalation are the psychological ones, which, as we have seen, break down into two main sub-categories: (a) concern with saving face and (b) yielding to emotions like rage or fear.

An imputed preoccupation with saving face is probably the greatest single reason why most people so readily assume that resort to nuclear weapons must make for spontaneous escalation. We are all familiar with the normal human tendency to resist or rebel against letting the other fellow "get away with it," where "it" involves any deliberate blow or damage to our position or self-esteem. Also, among nations as among people but usually more so, the word "prestige" covers a number of considerations ranging from mere vainglory to values of serious political moment. Damage to a nation's prestige can be a real injury in the sense that such damage may impose a cost on that nation—conceivably heavy and payable at some future time. This is especially true of military prestige, in which is bound up the image that other nations may have of one's willingness as well as ability to fight, and one's resolution to fight effectively, in various appropriate circumstances. One could easily give numerous examples of the reality of this consideration, historical and contemporary, but it should be hardly necessary to do so.

However, this is not the whole story. Nations are loath to suffer blows to their military prestige; yet they will at times suffer

them in preference to suffering something worse. It is a question of imminent danger, pain, or penalty weighed (though not necessarily, or even usually, with cool and detached calculation) against possible future costs. The Soviet Union backed down in Cuba in October, 1962, and the United States to a considerable degree backed down in Korea in 1951–52, when it quite clearly modified its objectives as a result of Chinese intervention.

One of the most often repeated but nevertheless inane and historically unwarranted axioms about the behavior of nations in wartime is the familiar one that begins: "When one side finds itself losing, [etc.] . . . ." The idea is that then all stops are pulled—*nothing* is worse than defeat. The axiom used to be used to explain why war could not be kept limited under any circumstances, more recently to explain why it was hopeless to expect a nation to refrain from using nuclear weapons in its possession when under extreme pressure on the battlefield. Well, one instance does not tell very much, but the United States refrained from using nuclear weapons while undergoing at the Yalu one of the worst defeats in its history, and that at a time when it enjoyed for all practical purposes a monopoly on such weapons.

Concern with saving face is what each side tends primarily to attribute to the other. As Leites first pointed out a dozen years ago, Communists have strongly inculcated themselves to be ready to retreat when necessary without worrying about humiliation, except where the pretense of being greatly concerned is a useful tactical maneuver to impress the other side. Naturally, this precept, like most other precepts, is not likely to prevail in full or to remain unchanged—we are dealing after all with human beings—but one of the amazing demonstrations of the Cuban crisis was the degree to which Khrushchev seemed to be following the classic Bolshevik precept that if one has to retreat one must reject any concern with a notion so puerile and so unworthy a professional revolutionary as humiliation. Khrushchev could probably have done much to conceal or minimize his humiliation—President Kennedy seemed quite ready to assist him in doing so—but the Soviet leader appeared to be little if at all interested in that objective; at least he seemed unwilling to take any risks at all in order to pursue it.

We can also say of humiliation what we can say of reactions of rage—that governments, even Communist dictatorships, tend today to be corporate entities in which the emotional feelings of individuals, regardless of how highly placed, are likely to be moderated and contained by the counsels of their advisers. The Hitler regime was different and exceptional in this respect, though even Hitler, despite being much given to rages, seems rarely if ever to have made a really important political or strategic decision under the influence predominantly of that emotion. Where his decisions were irrational, they were so for reasons other than his fits of temper or rage.

Let us now imagine that a conflict has broken out involving American access to Berlin, and, with neither side willing to yield to the other, reinforcements have been run in by both sides and local fighting has intensified. We should notice again the point that we have already alluded to—that one of the great drawbacks of following the so-called firebreak theory is that the more that confidence is built up in the firebreak, the less is each side restrained from committing larger and larger conventional forces within the limits of its capabilities. In other words, the effect is to stimulate escalation on the conventional side of the barrier, though fortunately, the location of that barrier is bound to be ill-defined.

Let us make now the quite realistic assumption that the above-described fighting takes place in a context in which the NATO partners have not succeeded in building up their conventional forces on the European central front to parity with the Russians. The Americans and their NATO allies now find themselves outnumbered on the ground, and the Russians, whose initiation of the action was probably without any clear desire to expel us from Berlin, now begin to feel that it has perhaps become possible for them to do so. The Americans, sensing this, decide to threaten the use of nuclear weapons. Perhaps the threat is, or promises to be, ineffective, and the U.S. government decides to use two or three substantial weapons as a demonstration of resolve—though with the understanding that the best way to demonstrate resolve is to use any nuclear bombs detonated with the highest possible degree of military effectiveness. What is the likely Soviet response?

The common tendency in referring glibly to the "escalatory effect of nuclear weapons" is to assume that "Red" reacts to "Blue's" move by making the same kind of demonstrations, only with larger weapons and more of them. In the real world, however, we should have to ask with what misgivings and in fact utter dismay would the Russians now be contemplating such an act. To repeat, we are trying to describe a situation in which both sides have been anxious to avoid hostilities and both certainly fear nuclear war. The Soviet Union is conscious that the existing dangerous situation has resulted from its own initiative, but it has been willing to barge ahead so long as (a) the fighting was still limited to conventional arms, in which it was not likely to suffer great damage, and (b) it could retreat from excessive danger in good time. How does it now resolve the question of how to respond to the opponent's resort to nuclear weapons?

We have in the present example deliberately left unclear the issue of responsibility for the outbreak of the fighting, but the Soviet Union nevertheless remains aware that it is over an issue having to do with allied access to Berlin, and not with something that deeply threatens her. Still, let us imagine that the Soviet leaders persist.

Perhaps they do feel it imperative for prestige reasons to make some semblance of a reply in kind, but if they decide to do so it will very likely be mostly because they still expect that the NATO powers will back down. Anyway, such a decision is immeasurably more likely to be the result of deliberate calculation, perhaps based on clear perception and good information, and perhaps not, than of a compulsive urge to save face or vent their spleen. In any case, unless the Russians have what they must consider incontestable indication that we will yield first, they are acting with a kind of recklessness that they have not hitherto displayed in real life. Perhaps we too are acting with a courage unusual for us, but the question we are putting to ourselves is: What happens if we do so act?

It remains to be observed also that the situation above described has not by any means reached a cataclysmic stage, where everything goes up if the Russians decide to test us a little further. On the other hand, the whole situation now appears markedly incompatible with our initial surmise (or stipulation)—that the Russians do not wish to be engaged in real fighting for the sake of getting us out of Berlin.

Let us therefore now alter our basic assumption and assert that the Russians might be willing to accept a limited war in Europe, even if there is risk or actual use of some nuclear weapons, for the sake of achieving its political objectives, because (a really necessary proviso) it is *quite confident* that we will not push the issue to general war. This is a bold assertion, but we are now describing a kind of situation that is actually implied or posited when one talks about a possible large Russian attack against the NATO line on the central front. The questions we must ask at this point are: (a) Is it *possible* for us to keep the ensuing fighting conventional? and (b) Is it *desirable* for us to do so or to attempt to do so? We are assuming the Russians are bent on aggression, and can bring themselves to accept the detonation of a score of nuclear weapons, perhaps even considerably more.

We should notice that if we are to be at all consistent with our previous assumptions, we have to assume also a good chance that even if we do not use nuclear weapons but somehow manage to resist effectively, the Russians will themselves introduce nuclear weapons. Our basic assumption, after all, *is that they have accepted the risks entailed in large-scale aggression,* which must include in their minds the risk that *we* will use nuclear weapons. How can they exclude that risk? If, nevertheless, with battle joined, they

now see us signalling by our restraint our desperate desire to avoid the use of such weapons, they are open to some new ideas. From this demonstration they might well deduce that we must be markedly less prepared than they to withstand nuclear weapons.

Perhaps they will not make that deduction; but how can we then assume that they will be more willing to accept defeat in a battle that has remained conventional than in one that has gone nuclear? Is it not a compelling surmise that it must be just the other way around? Thus it would seem that under the admittedly unrealistic premises we have set for ourselves (in terms of Russian readiness for nuclear risk-taking) the best way, perhaps the only way, for us to avert not only defeat but unnecessary escalation is to demonstrate that our readiness to take risks is not less than theirs. How can we do that except by using the weapons rather more abruptly than the Russians seem to have bargained for?

Another and final notion that we will here consider, not because it makes a great deal of sense but because it is frequently encountered, is that the Russians might launch a deliberate large-scale aggression against us without planning to use nuclear weapons or wishing to do so but prepared to retaliate in kind and to at least comparable degree if we use them. This idea thus assumes that the Russians will, according to the old code of the duel, blithely leave to us the "choice of weapons" while remaining committed to fighting either way! However, we do permit the assumption that they strongly expect that we will not use them.

Certainly under any circumstances remotely like those existing today, this example assumes "adventurism" of really fantastic proportions, totally out of line with any behavior of theirs that we have witnessed in the past. Nevertheless, let us try to think the situation through a little further. How do we cope in advance with the conceivability of such an attack?

One answer often heard is that we must anticipate it by building up our conventional forces, thus deterring the enemy from starting his fight. But the premise is *essential* to this argument that the opponent is either (a) prepared to fight even with nuclear weapons or (b) is utterly convinced that we will not under any circumstances use them. Otherwise, he will certainly not let himself be provoked into attacking our forces with their large nuclear capabilities. Now if he is prepared to fight with nuclear weapons, but observes from our costly efforts to build up to con ventional parity with him in Europe that we are deeply unwilling to see them used, his cue, as we have already noted, is to threaten their use or actually to introduce a few. But if one insists that he will not do so, in other words that the portion (a) of the premise above does not apply, why should we permit or even encourage the conviction described under the portion (b)? What has our conventional buildup bought us except the encouragement of that conviction?

We have to remind ourselves once more that we have in these speculations deliberately bestowed upon the Soviet leaders a far, far greater capacity for aggression than they have yet shown evidence of. We have also left completely open the question whether our own leaders could marshal the necessary psychological resources to introduce the use of nuclear weapons and to outbid any Soviet use. Perhaps that will not be true in the real world in the future. But it is one thing to say we could not, and quite another to say we should not. Nor should we confuse the issue by arguing that we should not *because* we could not. It would at this stage in time be a hazardous assertion indeed to say that in *the event of major Soviet aggression against our forces in Europe* we could not bring ourselves to use tactical nuclear weapons.

Anyway, if we could not, we would be in a bad way for defending Europe against Soviet aggression (*if* the Soviet Union were really that aggressive). We certainly could not solve the problem by securing from our allies and contributing ourselves to a buildup to conventional parity with the Russians. To build up conventional forces because we feel we dare not use nuclear

forces even against a major attack is only to underline and to signal our weakness. True, they may not be alert to that signal because of their own deep and abiding fear of nuclear weapons. If so, good; then they will not attack. One simply has to have it one way or another. We cannot go on assuming a Soviet Union bent on major aggression but afraid of using nuclears!

Our brief speculations have encompassed only cases in which a relatively small number of nuclear weapons are used more or less in demonstrations. Is this a grave weakness of these speculations? Not within the assumptions or hypotheses suggested, which state simply that both sides share a common determination to avoid going into an exchange that is many, many times more costly than any imaginable political goal could justify. Drop those assumptions and we are inevitably back in the world of massive retaliation.

If we turn now to the Far East we see that the situation is different in certain vital respects. For one thing, we have fought a fairly large war on the Korean peninsula without once using nuclear weapons that were in our possession. We have set a pattern for enemy expectations, as well as for our own. Secretary Dulles's verbal effort to change those expectations never had much strength and is by now largely dissipated.

The Chinese Communists obviously have little nuclear capability now, and will not have any substantial one for a long time to come. In this situation, where the risk of unwanted escalation hardly exists for us, we would likely stay conventional just because the enemy would be quite willing to let us do so. Or perhaps the lands and the peoples there mean less to us in terms of cultural affiliation than do those of Europe, and for this and other reasons we may feel that there is less prestige or other value to be lost from forced retreat in that part of the world than from one in Europe. Perhaps even some romantic (i.e., morbid) spirit of fair play might prevent us from dropping nuclear bombs upon an enemy who does not have many and who therefore *must* leave the decision for going nuclear entirely up to us. Also, we are restrained by the firebreak idea, which permits few if any distinctions between regions of the world. What undermines it in one place admittedly undermines it everywhere.

It is therefore quite possible that we could fight another war in the Far East as large as the Korean War without using nuclear weapons, assuming the American people permitted the government to engage again in such a war. Probably we would even prevail on that basis, as we did militarily in the previous Korean War (only to discard our advantages upon entering negotiations by halting the then ongoing offensive that was succeeding so brilliantly and that was our major leverage upon the opponent).[2] But surely it would be going about the job in the hard way, especially since timely indication of readiness to use nuclear weapons is *bound* to have an enormous even if not utterly guaranteed deterrent power.

It would probably also have repercussions for the future that would in the net not be to our liking. If the Chinese should manage to fight two wars with us during the first three or four decades of the nuclear age without suffering exposure to a single nuclear weapon, we will have fixed for them a pattern which they have every further incentive to exploit.

The gigantic nuclear capabilities of the United States have already been appreciably cut down in their effectiveness for deterring aggression by what might be called established world opinion opposed to their use. To a large extent this has been inevitable and, because it was right to dis-

sociate ourselves from the "just another weapon" philosophy, even desirable. Perhaps too it is a necessary part of the price we pay for attempting to restrain nuclear proliferation. But it behooves us to examine much more carefully than we have thus far some of the main propositions and arguments commonly made in support of our own drive to advance even further toward what is in effect the psychological self-neutralization of our nuclear capabilities.

We have in the above exercise examined particularly those arguments which attach great weight to the alleged escalatory potential of any and all uses or threats of use of nuclear weapons. Although our speculations have been as yet too lean and circumscribed to serve in themselves as a basis for major policy recommendations, they have perhaps registered the fact that some of the arguments upon which major policy recommendations have previously been based are extraordinarily vulnerable to systematic analysis. They may also have helped to point out the directions in which it is both feasible and desirable to pursue additional relevant knowledge.

If it be charged that we have not really faced up to the awful risks inherent in miscalculation, or in the tendency to madness that sometimes seems to go with resort to violence, the answer can only be that risks are something we have to measure as best we can. The above essay is an effort to contribute to such measurement. We cannot forfeit the task simply by allowing in advance such gross exaggeration of the risks as to "play it safe." A second look quickly tells us that we do not really add to our safety by doing so.

2 See my R–335, *op. cit.*, p. 318.

NUCLEAR WEAPONS AND LIMITED WAR

BY THOMAS C. SCHELLING

With the development of small-size, small-yield nuclear weapons suitable for local use by ground troops with modest equipment, and with the development of nuclear depth charges and nuclear rockets for air-to-air combat, the technical characteristics of nuclear weapons have ceased to provide much basis, if any, for treating nuclear weapons as peculiarly different from other weapons in the conduct of limited war. It has, of course, been argued that there are political disadvantages in our using nuclear weapons in limited war, particularly in our using them first. Even those who consider a nuclear fireball as moral as napalm for burning a man to death must recognize as a political fact a worldwide revulsion against nuclear weapons.

This Appendix is about another basis for distinguishing between nuclear and other weapons. It involves our relations with the enemy in the process of limiting war. In the interest of limiting war or of understanding limited war, it may be necessary to recognize that a distinction can exist between nuclear and other weapons even though the distinction is not physical but is psychic, perceptual, legalistic, or symbolic. That small-yield nuclears delivered with "pinpoint" accuracy are just a form of artillery, and consequently do not prejudice the issue of limits in war, is an argument based exclusively on an analysis of weapons effects, not on an analysis of the limiting process—of where limits originate in limited war, what makes them stable or unstable, what gives them authority, and what circumstances and modes of behavior are conducive to the finding and mutual recognition of limits. The premise of the "just-another-weapon" argument is that, if there is no compelling weapon-effects basis for a distinction between nuclears and other weapons, there is no basis at all that is pertinent to the limiting process.

Is not the same point involved in discriminating among the users of weapons? There is no more difference between Russians and Chinese than there is between nuclear and other weapons; similarly for the difference between Chinese and North Koreans, or between Americans and Nationalist Chinese, British and Jordanians, Egyptians and Algerians. Yet nationality has been an important distinction in the process of limiting war or destroying its limits. Similarly, there is little difference between the terrain a hundred miles north of the Soviet-Iranian border and the terrain a hundred miles south, or what lies above the Yalu and below it, or the two sides of the Greek-Yugoslav border. Yet boundaries like these play an important role in the limiting process, quite aside from any physical difficulty in the crossing of rivers or the scaling of mountains that happen to coincide with them.

One could reply that these are "legal" distinctions and that legal distinctions are real ones while those between nuclear and other weapons are fictitious. But they are not really legal; they are "legalistic." There is no legal authority that forces the participants in limited war to recognize political boundaries or nationalities; the Russians are not legally obligated to treat a modest penetration of their border as a qualitative change in the war—as a dramatic act discontinuous with action up to their border. The Chinese were not legally obliged to retaliate (rather than just to resist) if we deliberately crossed the Yalu River; they did not lose any legal right to deny trespass by admitting occasional thoroughfare. We are not legally obliged to take cognizance of Russian pilots if they participate in a limited war, or Russian "vol-

Reprinted by permission of the publishers from *The Strategy of Conflict* (Cambridge, Mass.: Harvard University Press, 1960), Appendix A, pp. 257–66. Copyright © 1960 by the President and Fellows of Harvard College.

unteers" in a Near Eastern ground army fighting against our side. The inhibition on the penetration of a border, or on the introduction of a new nationality into the conflict, is like that on the introduction of a nuclear weapon; it is the risk of enemy response. And an important determinant of enemy response is his appreciation of what he has tacitly acquiesced in if he fails to respond, or makes only an incremental response, to our symbolically discontinuous act.

What makes the Soviet or Chinese border a pertinent or compelling place to draw a line in the event of war in that area is principally that there is usually no other plausible line to draw. For Western troops to cross the Russian border is to challenge —not physically but symbolically—the territorial integrity of the USSR, and to demonstrate or at least to imply an intention to proceed. Unless one can find some "obvious" limit inside that border, such that it would be clear to the Russians where we intended to stop in the event that we cross the border, and such that it would be obvious to us that there was a limit to how far the Russians would let us advance if we did cross it and that the Russians knew that we knew it, there is just no other stopping place that can be tacitly acknowledged by both sides. Under the circumstances, for the USSR to accept the penetration of that border without a dramatic retaliation of some sort would be to admit that Soviet territory is fair game for a gradually expanding war. The political boundary is therefore *useful* as a stopping place, not legally mandatory; it is useful to *both* sides in default of any plainly recognizable alternative, since both sides have an interest in finding some limit. The border has a *uniqueness* that makes it a plausible limit. It is one of the few lines—perhaps the only line, but certainly one of the few —that one could draw in the region that could be tacitly recognized by both sides as the "obvious" geographical limit that both sides might observe. It has a compelling *power of suggestion*, a claim to attention, the denial of which might seem—in default of any plainly recognizable alternative—to be a denial of any limitation.

But, if political-boundary and nationality considerations still seem to be legal, and therefore real, consider some other distinctions that are significant in the limiting process. We provided much equipment but no manpower to the war in Indochina; we provided equipment, leadership, and advice to the Greek troops during the guerrilla war but no combat troops. We provide direct naval support to the Nationalist Chinese in the Straits of Formosa. It has been thought that we might have given air support to the French and Vietnamese in Indochina, without appearing to the Chinese and Russians to be as "involved" as if we had put ground forces in.

An economist can argue—with the same persuasiveness as those who argue that "pinpoint"-delivered small-yield weapons are just another form of artillery—that equipment and manpower are fungible resources in a military campaign, that air intervention is not "really" different from ground intervention, that military intellect is as important as leg muscle for troops that lack leadership and planning skill. The controversy about redefinition of service functions in the light of modern weapons, and about the usefulness of defining military-service functions in terms of the means of locomotion, suggests that an air-ground distinction or a naval-ground distinction rests on nothing but tradition. But the point of all this is that, in limiting war, tradition matters.

In fact, what we are dealing with in the analysis of limited war is tradition. We are dealing with precedent, convention, and the force of suggestion. We are dealing with the theory of unwritten law—with conventions whose sanction in the aggregate is the need for mutual forbearance to avoid mutual destruction, and whose sanction in each individual case is the risk that to breach a rule may collapse it and that to collapse it may lead to a jointly less favorable limit or to none at all, and may further weaken the yet unbroken rules by providing evidence that their "authority" cannot be taken for granted.

What makes atomic weapons different is a powerful tradition that they *are* different. The reason—in answer to the usual rhetorical question—why we do not ban bows and arrows on the grounds that they too, like nuclear weapons, kill and maim people, is that there is a tradition for the use of bows and arrows, a jointly recognized expectation that they will be used if it is expedient to use them. There is no such tradition for the use of atomic weapons. There is instead a tradition for their non-use—a jointly recognized expectation that they may not be used in spite of declarations of readiness to use them, even in spite of tactical advantages in their use.

Traditions or conventions are not simply an analogy for limits in war, or a curious aspect of them; tradition or precedent or convention is the essence of the limits. The fundamental characteristic of a limit in a limited war is the psychic, intellectual, or social characteristic of being mutually recognized by both sides as having some kind of authority, the authority deriving mainly from the sheer perception of mutual acknowledgement, of a "tacit bargain." And a particular limit gains in authority from the lack of confidence that either side may have in what alternative limits may be found if the limit is not adhered to. The rationale behind the limit is legalistic and casuistic, not legal, moral, or physical. The limits may correspond to legal and physical differences or to moral distinctions; indeed, they usually have to correspond to something that gives them a unique and qualitative character and that provides some focus for expectations to converge on. But the authority is in the expectations themselves, and not in the thing that expectations have attached themselves to.

Whether limits on the use of atomic weapons, other than the particular limit of no use at all, can be defined in a plausible way is made more dubious, not less so, by the increasingly versatile character of atomic weapons. It is now widely recognized that there is a rather continuous gradation in the possible sizes of atomic-weapon effects, a rather continuous variation in the forms in which they can be used, in the means of conveyance, in the targets they can be used on, and so forth. There seems consequently to be no "natural" break be-

tween certain limited uses and others. If we ask, then, where we might draw a line if we wished to limit somehow the size of the weapons, the means of conveyance, the situations in which or the targets on which they can be used, the answer is that we are—in a purely technical sense—free to draw a line anywhere we please. There is no cogent reason for drawing it at any one particular gradation rather than another. But that is precisely why it is hard to find a rationale for any particular line. There is no degree of use, or size of weapon, or number of miles, that is so much more plausible than other degrees, sizes, or distances that it provides a focal point for both sides' expectations. Legalistic limits have to be qualitative and discrete, rather than quantitative and continuous. This is not just a matter of making violations easy to recognize, or of making adherence easy to enforce on one's own commanders; it concerns the need of any stable limit to have an evident symbolic character, such that to breach it is an overt and dramatic act that exposes both sides to the danger that alternative limits will not easily be found.

The need for qualitatively distinguishable limits that enjoy some kind of uniqueness is especially enhanced by the fact that limits are generally found by a process of tacit maneuver and negotiation. They are jockeyed for, rather than negotiated explicitly. But if the two sides must strike a "bargain" without explicit communication, the particular limit has to have some quality that distinguishes it from the continuum of possible alternatives; otherwise there is little basis for the confidence of each side that the other acknowledges the same limit. Even a parallel of latitude, or an international date line, or the north pole, may have this quality when no other natural, plausible, "obvious" point or line is available for expectations to converge on.

A test of this point with respect to atomic weapons might be to pose the following problem. Let any of us try to cooperate for a prize: we are to sit down right now, separately and without any prior arrangements, and write out a proposed limitation on the use of nuclear weapons, in as little or as great detail as we please, allowing ourselves limitations of any description that appeals to us—size of weapons, use of weapons, who gets to use them, what rate or frequency of use, clean versus dirty, offensive versus defensive use, tactical versus strategic, on or not on cities, with or without warning—to see whether we can all write the *same* specification of limit. If we are in perfect agreement on the limits we specify, we get a prize; if our limits are different, we get no prize. We are doing this only for the sake of the prize, to see whether we can in fact agree tacitly on a statement of limits, and to see—for those of us who do manage to coordinate our proposals tacitly—what kinds of limits appear to be susceptible of tacit joint recognition. We are permitted the extremes of no limits at all on the one hand, or no atomic weapons at all on the other, and any gradation or variation defined in any way we please.

My argument is that there are particular limits—simple, discrete, qualitative, "obvious" limits—that are conducive to a concerted choice; those who specify other kinds of limits, I predict, can find few partners or none at all whose limits coincide with theirs. (Since our object is to agree, we are to take no consolation in the other virtues of our proposed limits; in this exercise the main consideration in choosing any particular limits is the likelihood that if we chose those limits in an effort to coincide exactly with the limits of the others, knowing that they were trying to coordinate theirs with ours, we would succeed.)

I do not allege that this exercise proves what kinds of limits are capable of possessing stability and authority. It does demonstrate that certain characteristics of limits, particularly their simplicity, uniqueness, discreteness, susceptibility of qualitative definition, and so forth, can be given an objective meaning, one that is at least pertinent to the process of tacit negotiation. It suggests that certain kinds of limits are capable of being jointly expected by both sides, of focusing expectations and being recognized as qualitatively distinct from the continuum of possible alternatives.

The first conclusion to be drawn from this line of argument is that there is a distinction between nuclear and nonnuclear weapons, a distinction relevant to the process of limiting war. It is a distinction that to some extent we can strengthen or weaken, clarify or blur. We can strengthen the tradition, and enhance the symbolic significance of this distinction, by talking and acting in a way that is dramatically consistent with it; we can erode the distinction—but not readily destroy it—by acting as though we do not believe in it, by emphasizing the "just-another-weapon" argument and by making it evident that we in fact have little compunction about using nuclears. Which policy we should follow depends on whether we consider the distinction between nuclear and other weapons to be an asset that we share with the USSR, a useful distinction, a tradition that helps to minimize violence—or instead a nuisance, a propaganda liability, a diplomatic obstruction, and an inhibition to our decisive action and delegation of authority. Those who believe that atomic weapons ought to be used at the earliest convenience, or whenever military expedience demands, should nevertheless recognize the distinction that exists so that we can take action to erode the distinction during the interim.

This is not just a matter of what the Asian neutrals or our European allies feel about the distinction. It concerns a relation between us and the Russians—an understanding that may exist between us whether we like it or not. It has to do with whether the Russians think we share with them a tacit expectation that there is a limit against the use of nuclear weapons. In the interest of limiting war, we should want the Russians or the Chinese not to believe that our initial use of atomic weapons in a local war was a challenge to the whole idea of limitations, a declaration that we would not be bound by any kinds of limits. We should want them to interpret our use of nuclear weapons as consistent with the concept of limited war and consistent with our willingness to collaborate tacitly in the discovery and recognition of limits; we should want our use of atomic weapons not to be charged with excessive symbolic content. So, if I am right that a distinction does exist in the sense pertinent to the limiting of war, and if nevertheless we want maximum freedom to use atomic weapons, we ought in the interest of limiting war to destroy or to erode the distinction as best we can. (For example, a deliberate program for early and extensive use of "nuclear dynamite" in earth-moving projects, especially in underdeveloped countries, might help to erode the distinction; the same might be true of a program for training friendly troops in underdeveloped countries in how to survive nuclear weapons explosions, using some actual weapons for the purpose in their own country.) If on the contrary we wish to enhance the tacit understanding we have with our enemies that nuclears are a class apart and subject to certain reservations, agreement on nuclear test suspension (or even just extensive discussion of such an agreement) will probably contribute to the purpose.[1]

A second conclusion is that the principal inhibition on the use of atomic weapons in limited war may disappear with their first use. It is difficult to imagine that the tacit agreement that nuclear weapons are different would be as powerfully present on the occasion of the *next* limited war after they had already been used in one. We can probably not, therefore, ignore the distinction and use nuclears in a particular war where their use might be of advantage to us and *subsequently* rely on the distinction in the hope that we and the enemy might both abstain. One potential limitation of war will be substantially discredited for all time if we shatter the tradition and create a contrary precedent. (There may also be some limits or sanctuary concepts that we take for granted that should be reexamined to see whether they were originally by-products of the assumed nuclear ban and might disappear with it. We may want to look again at the role of naval vessels, for example, partly to anticipate enemy treatment of them, partly to avoid misinterpret-

ing enemy intentions if he treats them differently after nuclears are brought into play.)

A third conclusion is that on the occasion of their first use we should perhaps be at least as concerned with the patterns and precedents that we establish, and with the "nuclear role" that we adopt, as with the original objectives of the limited war. For example, if nuclear weapons were used in defense of Quemoy, we probably ought to be much less concerned about the outcome on Quemoy than about the character of the nuclear exchange, the precedents that it establishes, the role we manage to assume for ourselves, and the role the enemy assumes in the process. We shall be not only using them *ad hoc* for the little war in question, but importantly shaping the limited nuclear wars to come. (When a boy pulls a switch-blade knife on his teacher, the teacher is likely to feel, whatever the point at issue originally was, that the overriding policy question now is his behavior in the face of a switch-blade challenge.)

Fourth, we should recognize that—at least on the first occasion when nuclear weapons are used in limited war—the enemy too will really be engaged in at least two different kinds of limited-war activity at the same time. One will be the limited struggle over the original objectives; the second will be the tacit negotiation or gamesmanship over the role of nuclear weapons themselves. To illustrate, we might in connection with Quemoy decide to use nuclear weapons; ordinarily it would be supposed that we should do this only if it were quite necessary to the defense of Quemoy, and that we should use them in a manner that achieves our Quemoy objectives. But, in considering whether the Chinese or Russians would use them in return, we should perhaps not worry mainly about what they think their use of nuclear weapons would do for the invasion of Quemoy. Much more important to them, it seems, would be the nature of their "response" to our nuclear initiative. They would be interested in not assuming a submissive role, but in demanding a kind of "parity" if not dominance in their own nuclear role. And, unless we are ready for some kind of deci-

[1] On the symbolic significance of a test agreement, see Henry A. Kissinger, "Nuclear Testing and the Problem of Peace," *Foreign Affairs,* 37:1–18 (Oct. 1958), especially pp. 12–13.

sive showdown in which we either win all or lose all, we must be as willing to "negotiate" (by our actions) for limited objectives in terms of nuclear dominance, traditions and precedents of nuclear use, and the "rules" we jointly create for future wars, as for any other types of objectives in limited war.

BASIC PRINCIPLES AND OPERATIONAL CONCEPTS OF COUNTERINSURGENCY

BY SIR ROBERT G. K. THOMPSON

BASIC PRINCIPLES OF COUNTERINSURGENCY

I have endeavoured in the first three chapters to give a general idea of some of the problems which face a government during the three main phases of an insurgency. Two obvious points emerge from this. The first is that any sensible government should attempt to defeat an insurgent movement during the subversive build-up phase before it enters the guerilla phase, and if that is not possible owing to circumstances perhaps outside the government's control, then the movement must be defeated as early as possible during the guerilla phase. Unfortunately, during the build-up phase, the signs are not always recognized, and the existence of a subversive movement may even be ignored or denied for short-sighted political reasons. It is not easy for a government to alert its people to the danger. If restrictive measures are successfully taken, there will be little evidence of subversion, and the government runs the risk of being accused of repression. If, on the other hand, subversion leads to insurgency, there will then be plenty of evidence, but the government has a war on its hands.

The second point is that anyone having any responsibility for dealing with an insurgent movement must know his enemy and what that enemy is attempting to do at all stages. This does not mean that those responsible should be solely concerned with countering the enemy's moves. I dislike for this reason the very term "counterinsurgency." It implies that the insurgents have the initiative, and that it is the government's role merely to react and counter that initiative.

Accepting, therefore, that prevention is better than cure, and that the government must be positive in its approach, I suggest that there are five basic principles which must be followed and within which all government measures must fall.

First principle. The government must have a clear political aim: to establish and maintain a free, independent and united country which is politically and economically stable and viable.

It may be contended that this is rather too broad, if desirable, an aim; but in newly independent or underdeveloped territories it is essential to recognize that an insurgent movement is only one of the problems with which such governments are faced. The insurgency may demand priority, but it cannot be treated in isolation. For example, in most Asian territories there is an explosive population problem, with

Reprinted with permission from *Defeating Communist Insurgency: The Lessons of Malaya and Vietnam* (New York: Frederick A. Praeger, Inc., 1966), pp. 50–62 and 111–20. Copyright 1966 by Frederick A. Praeger, Inc.

Sir Robert Thompson spent twelve years in Malaya during the period of insurgency there known as the Emergency. From 1961 to 1965 he headed the British Advisory Mission in Saigon. He serves as a consultant to the RAND Corporation and is a member of the Institute for Strategic Studies.

an annual growth rate of over 3 per cent. The development of the country to meet this problem can be just as vital as the defeat of the insurgent movement. It would be futile to succeed in defeating the insurgency, especially by military means alone during its guerilla phase, if the end result is a country which is not politically and economically viable, and which might therefore fall to the communists at any moment in the future, perhaps without a shot being fired.

An insurgent movement is a war for the people. It stands to reason that government measures must be directed to restoring government authority and law and order throughout the country, so that control over the population can be regained and its support won. This cannot be done unless a high priority is given to the administrative structure of government itself, to its institutions and to the training of its personnel. Without a reasonably efficient government machine, no programmes or projects, in the context of counterinsurgency, will produce the desired results.

I have already stressed the great advantage which the Communists derive from weaknesses in the government and seeds of conflict within the community—what they term the "contradictions." By nibbling away and maintaining pressure, they can use these as a powerful lever for toppling the government. Corruption, for example, was an important factor in the downfall of Nationalist China. The correction of these weaknesses is as much a part of counterinsurgency as any military operation. In fact, it is far more important because unless the cracks in the government structure are mended, military operations and emergency measures, apart from being ineffectual, may themselves widen the cracks and be turned to the enemy's advantage.

Unless the long-term aim is constantly borne in mind, there will be a tendency to adopt short-term *ad hoc* measures merely as reactions to insurgent initiative or with the limited aim of attempting to defeat the insurgents militarily in the guerilla phase. A good example in Vietnam was the proliferation of provinces; these were increased from thirty-seven in 1956 to forty-five in 1964. The new provinces were created solely for military and security reasons as sector commands, and completely lacked the administrative backing necessary to enable them to function as provinces. In circumstances in which there is a shortage of trained staff but in which modern means of communication are available, the fewer the centres of authority outside the capital, the easier it is for the central government ministries to control and supervise the execution of policy. In South Vietnam, thirty provinces would have been enough and twenty-five better.

Another example was the establishment of a multitude of forces to meet special counterinsurgency tasks, resulting in an indiscriminate issue of arms. When asked towards the end of 1962 what was the total distribution of American weapons to the Vietnamese, an American general informed me that it was equivalent to fifty-one divisions. When I then asked what were the plans for recovering these after victory, he shrewdly replied: "That is a problem which will worry neither you nor me!"

Second principle. The government must function in accordance with law.

There is a very strong temptation in dealing both with terrorism and with guerilla actions for government forces to act outside the law, the excuses being that the processes of law are too cumbersome, that the normal safeguards in the law for the individual are not designed for an insurgency and that a terrorist deserves to be treated as an outlaw anyway. Not only is this morally wrong, but, over a period, it will create more practical difficulties for a government than it solves. A government which does not act in accordance with the law forfeits the right to be called a government and cannot then expect its people to obey the law. Functioning in accordance with the law is a very small price to pay in return for the advantage of being the government.

Action in accordance with the law was a vital factor during the Huk insurgency in the Philippines, where Magsaysay made a reality of the constitution, and in Malaya, where the civil courts functioned normally throughout the Emergency. Statute law can be modified by emergency law, and laws of procedure and evidence can be simplified. There is nothing to prevent a government enacting very tough laws to cope with the situation, but the golden rule should be that each new law must be effective and must be fairly applied. It is no good enacting laws which cannot be enforced, thereby bringing the government into disrepute, or which fall unfairly on particular groups in the population.

Some very tough laws were enacted in Malaya. One enabled the government to seize and deport all Chinese found in a declared bad area. Another allowed the government to impose a collective fine on all the inhabitants of an area where the people were unco-operative. Both these laws were dropped after being used only two or three times because they were unfair to innocent members of the population. On the other hand, laws imposing strict curfews, a mandatory death penalty for carrying arms, life imprisonment for providing supplies or other support to terrorists, restricted residence or detention for suspected terrorist supporters and so on were introduced and effectively used. The main point about them was that they were seen by the population to be effective and were applied equally to all. The population knew what the law was, and because the government itself functioned in accordance with law and could be held responsible in the courts for its actions, the population could be required to fulfil its own obligation to obey the laws.

Detention is perhaps one of the most controversial powers which a government may exercise. If the power to arrest and detain is clearly laid down within certain limits and the individual is given a full opportunity to appear, represented by counsel, before a tribunal presided over by a judge which advises the government whether or not the case against the detainee is adequate, then there are sufficient safeguards to prevent the power being used for purely arbitrary arrests. It should be recognized that it is the aim of detention to prevent suspected persons from carrying out hostile acts. It is a power that most western governments have taken in time of war, and it cannot be denied to govern-

ments which face a national emergency caused by terrorism and insurgency.

As a corollary of preventive detention, it should be the firm policy of the government to bring all persons who have committed an actual offence to public trial. This has the great advantage not only of showing that justice is being done, but of spotlighting the brutality of terrorist crimes and the whole nature of the insurgent conspiracy, including any direction and assistance received from outside the country. The evidence is there for all to hear, and it automatically receives the fullest publicity at home and abroad. If the due processes of the law are followed, no justifying statements by the government are required. Trials in camera, martial law and military tribunals can never be satisfactorily justified. They are in themselves a tacit admission that responsible government has broken down. In the long term, adherence to the law is a great advantage to the government. It helps to make all officers and civilian officials responsible and accountable for their actions. It puts torture and the shooting of captured terrorists in their proper place: however great the provocation, both are crimes and the latter is murder. It puts the government in a position in which it is represented as a protector of those who are innocent, and it puts the terrorists in the position of criminals. This creates the proper psychological attitude in the country as a whole, with the government as the "cops" and the terrorists as the "robbers."

If the government does not adhere to the law, then it loses respect and fails to fulfil its contractual obligation to the people as a government. This leads to the situation in which officers and officials cease to be responsible for their actions, with the result that, instead of an insurgency, there is to all intents and purposes a civil war within the country in which neither side can claim to be the government. In such circumstances there is so little difference between the two sides that the people have no reason for choosing to support the government.

I remember saying to General Khanh, then Prime Minister in Vietnam, that when I heard of a case of a peasant suing the government for a buffalo killed by the army during operations and being paid compensation, we would be winning the war. A police constable stopping a general's car and summoning him for a traffic offence would have been too much to hope for.

Third principle. The government must have an overall plan.

This plan must cover not just the security measures and military operations. It must include all political, social, economic, administrative, police and other measures which have a bearing on the insurgency. Above all it must clearly define roles and responsibilities to avoid duplication of effort and to ensure that there are no gaps in the government's field of action.

It is essential, too, that there should be a proper balance between the military and the civil effort, with complete co-ordination in all fields. Otherwise a situation will arise in which military operations produce no lasting results because they are unsupported by civil follow-up action. Similarly, civilian measures, particularly in areas disputed with the insurgents, are a waste of time and money if they are unsupported by military operations to provide the necessary protection.

Because a government's resources, notably in trained manpower, are limited, the plan must also lay down priorities both in the measures to be taken and in the

areas to be dealt with first. If the insurgency is country-wide, it is impossible to tackle it offensively in every area. It must be accepted that in certain areas only a holding operation can be conducted.

The plan must be positive, forcing the insurgents to react to government measures, but flexible enough to take advantage of success. Only in this way can the initiative be held. If there is no plan or if the plan is not followed consistently, then gradually but perceptibly the government will find itself in the position of merely reacting to insurgent initiative. From this position it is not easy to recover.

Fourth principle. The government must give priority to defeating the political subversion, not the guerillas.

This is obviously the case in the build-up phase before the insurgency has started, but it holds equally good during the insurgency. Unless the Communist subversive political organization in the towns and villages is broken and eliminated, the insurgent guerilla units will not be defeated. If the guerillas can be isolated from the population, i.e. the "little fishes" removed from "the water," then their eventual destruction becomes automatic.

This can be made clear by repeating the earlier diagram, again at district level, and drawing through it a heavy line to indicate where all government attention should be focussed. If the subversive political organi-

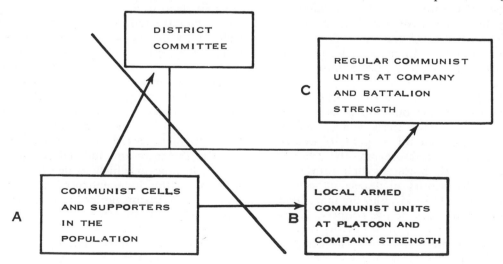

Note: C may or may not be stationed in every district, but is moved in to reinforce B for specific operations.

zation at A can be eliminated, then the guerilla units at B and C, being short of supplies, recruits and intelligence, will be steadily reduced by a process of attrition until their members are either killed or surrender.

In the process of eliminating the political organization, the attention of the intelligence organization should also be directed to identifying, and eliminating if possible, all members of the insurgent organization who for one reason or another have to cross this heavy line between the insurgent units and the population. This should then be followed up by civilian measures and military operations designed to break the contact between the guerilla units and the subversive political organization. As this process develops, the guerilla units will themselves be forced to cross the line in an attempt to make contact with, and support, their political organization and to secure their sources of supply. The area of the heavy line is turned into a sort of barrier, and will become the killing ground because the guerillas will be forced to fight the government where it is ready for them and at its greatest strength. If the guerilla units fail to pierce the barrier and to regain contact with the subversive political organization and with the population on which they depend for support, they will be forced to retire to the jungles and swamps and to disperse into smaller and smaller units in order to maintain their day-to-day existence. The mopping-up period can then begin.

Fifth principle. In the guerilla phase of an insurgency, a government must secure its base areas first.

This principle should to a large extent be reversed in the build-up phase, before the open insurgency starts, when considerable attention should be paid to security and economic measures in the remoter rural areas. If, however, such preventive action fails, priority in respect of security measures should be given to the more highly developed areas of the country. These contain the greatest number of the population and are more vital to the government from the point of view of its communications and the economy of the country. This

may mean accepting that the insurgent movement gains control over certain remoter areas and that there will be a degree of infiltration across inaccessible borders (which cannot be prevented anyway at this stage). Such infiltration will initially be limited in any case by the absorptive capacity of the areas under insurgent control. But if the area under the insurgents' control expands and the base of their support broadens, the absorptive capacity will increase. It must therefore be one of the government's aims to limit that capacity by securing its own base areas and working methodically outwards from them.

There is a second advantage in this approach: the more highly developed areas of the country are easier to secure and control, and the government will therefore start the campaign with some successes. This instils confidence, which is quite the most important ingredient for further success. A thoroughly methodical approach to the problem, which may appear rather slow, encourages a steam-roller outlook which provides the people with faith in ultimate victory. By preparing for a long haul, the government may achieve victory quicker than expected. By seeking quick military victories in insurgent controlled areas, it will certainly get a long haul for which neither it nor the people may be prepared.

*   *   *   *   *

Partly as a result of a sound administrative structure and a strong independent judiciary, which made the second principle sacred, these principles gradually emerged in Malaya by a process of trial and error rather than conscious decision. They were helped by an imaginative approach to the political problem and by a strictly methodical approach to the practical problems. South Vietnam lacked the necessary administrative structure and judicial system and had little time in which to develop them. Moreover, after independence, it was saddled with a major policy decision which either offended, or caused an inevitable breach of, all the principles. This was the creation of a large conventional army.

This decision stemmed from the lessons of Korea, not those of the Philippines and

Malaya, and resulted from a wrong assessment of the threat, which at that time was considered to be direct aggression by the armed forces of Communist North Vietnam. A large conventional South Vietnamese army, numbering eventually over 200,000, was established as a deterrent to this threat.

The inevitable effect of creating such a large army was that political power in the country rested entirely with control of the army. President Diem was forced to devote much of his time and energy to manipulating the army commands in order to retain control and maintain his position. All efforts to encourage him to broaden the base of his government and attract more popular support were meaningless in a situation in which the reality of political power lay not with the people but with the army. That he lasted for nine years through several attempted coups was a great tribute both to his own political sagacity and to that of his brother Ngo Dinh Nhu. His successors after the *coup d'état* of November 1, 1963, were not so adroit. One of the illuminating remarks which President Diem made in 1962 was that any successor, if he wished to maintain an effective government, would have to be twice as repressive as he himself had been. He also said to me more than a year before the final coup: "Après moi le déluge!" How right he was.

In this respect, the fact that the army was conventionally organized with corps and divisional commands created a warlord outlook in the senior commanders and fired their ambitions. In a long dissertation one afternoon on the ancient history and administration of Vietnam, President Diem told me that successful generals were always retired. He had recourse to this step himself on occasion, but few of the present generals made their mark as senior commanders, and all owed what little success they had to the presence and support of President Diem behind them. On their own they lacked the experience or ability to command much more than a regiment, let alone run a country. They also lacked the modesty to comprehend this.

In addition to political instability, the large army also created major economic problems. To pay the recurrent expenditure on the armed forces, the South Vietnamese government was committed to accepting indefinite American aid on a large scale, including the import of subsidized consumer goods in order to generate local piastre funds to pay the army wage bill. For a young independent country to be so completely dependent on foreign aid is both politically and psychologically a misfortune. Similarly, the American commitment to the army was not one that could easily be terminated. It put both sides firmly on the hook and allowed for no flexibility in the provision of aid.

On the civilian side it had further effects. A powerful army naturally attracted all the best young men into its officer ranks. With the army getting the cream, the remaining government services had to make do with skimmed milk. When the insurgency broke out, it soon became apparent that the standard of officials to carry out the civil functions of government, particularly in the provinces, was too low, and army officers were transferred to take their places. By the end of 1964, out of nearly three hundred province and district chiefs, there was hardly a civilian left.

A large army requires a lot of supporting specialized services, including engineers and hospitals. In a country where there were insufficient trained personnel to staff a civilian service, there was now a requirement to support two such services. This would not have been so bad during the insurgency if, for example, the military hospitals had been prepared to treat other than military personnel. However, not even wounded Civil Guard or Self-Defence Corps casualties were admitted, let alone any civilians. In other fields such as information, radio and psychological warfare, the army also usurped civilian functions and tried to make amends by promoting what was called "civic action." What in effect was happening was that the army, organized on conventional lines to defeat a foreign invader and to occupy and administer a foreign country, was attempting to do almost exactly that in its own country. This created a completely wrong attitude and led to operations and actions which might just have been excusable as acts of war if carried out in enemy territory. The one vital aspect of civic action which the army failed to develop was good, strict, disciplined behaviour towards its own population. Without that, all assistance or other good works in the rural areas which the army can so admirably provide for the population, and which would contribute generally to better relationships, are so much eyewash.

The conventional organization of the army led naturally to operations of a conventional type. This was not helped by the constant changes amongst the corps and divisional commanders, all of whom wished to make their name with a quick, spectacular military victory. Unless there is a strong overriding authority directing the war, a young inexperienced officer appointed to a division thinks immediately in terms of divisional operations. Time and time again the following type of report would appear in the newspapers: "A two-day operation involving some 1,200 Vietnamese troops against a Viet Cong stronghold twenty-five miles north of Saigon ended early Wednesday with practically no results. Military sources said one Viet Cong woman was captured and one friendly soldier was killed by sniper fire in the operation." Not all reports were quite so frank.

A British General in Malaya, commanding an area equivalent to a division, was once asked what he considered the role of a divisional commander to be. He replied: "As far as I can see, the only thing a divisional commander has to do in this sort of war is to go round seeing that the troops have got their beer!" He had got it right.

The conventional command structure also led to a lack of initiative in the junior ranks. An insurgency is a junior commander's war, especially in its early stages, but no junior commander would dare to take action without superior orders, preferably written. I often put the question to Vietnamese officers: "If you were ordered to take an infantry company from A to B and passed a Civil Guard post being attacked by the Viet Cong, would you go to their assistance or would you continue to B?" The answer was invariably: "Continue to B." After all, if the junior officer's action had

saved the post, the senior commanders would have taken the credit; but if anything had gone wrong, the junior officer would have got the blame. The principle of "carrying the can," under which the senior officer gets the blame and the junior officer the credit, was unknown.

The existence of corps and divisional commands extending over a number of provinces, which in turn were commanded by junior military officers, led to constant problems over the control of operations and of intelligence. The province chief as commander of his sector was subservient to the divisional commander, but as province chief he was responsible to the Ministry of the Interior and, in President Diem's day, to the President himself. The sector command had control over the para-military forces within the province, and the dual system of command made combined operations and the co-ordination of civil and military measures an almost insoluble problem.

A further side-effect of a conventionally equipped army is that weapons designed for conventional war and not suitable for anti-guerilla operations are carried into action. A number of these weapons, such as recoilless rifles, are quite useless against insurgents, but are absolute murder to the government side if they are lost and fall into insurgent hands.

I have dealt with this problem of a large army at some length because I believe that the balance of forces within a country is one of the most vital issues both for the political stability of the country and for ensuring the full co-ordination of civilian measures and military operations in an insurgency. The requirement is for a small, elite, highly disciplined, lightly equipped and aggressive army, with a supporting air force and navy of sufficient capability to make the army highly mobile, so that it can fulfil its proper military role in support of the civil government and in accordance with the five basic principles laid down in this chapter.

BASIC OPERATIONAL CONCEPTS

I have dealt with the government, its organization and the type of forces required to deal with the threat of communist subversion which develops into an insurgency. It is now necessary to consider the measures and tactics required to defeat that insurgency.

As already stated in the basic principles, the government must have an overall plan to coordinate all military and civil effort and to lay down priorities. The plan must also take into account the fourth and fifth principles that the main emphasis should be given to defeating subversion, not the guerillas, and that the government must secure its base areas first. When applying this to action and operations on the ground, there will be four definite stages which can be summed up as clearing, holding, winning, and won.

The first stage of clearing may not be necessary in the initial priority areas if they are reasonably secure, but, in order to maintain the sequence, it will be assumed that we are dealing with areas containing insurgent units which must be cleared before the next three stages can follow. For "clear" operations the military tactics will vary according to the terrain and the size and composition of the insurgent units. The area itself should be selected as an extension of an area already securely held, and should first be subjected to an intense intelligence effort before any operations start. It helps if there are natural boundaries with a good central communciation access. Having selected the area, and prepared the plan, the first essential is to saturate it with joint military and police forces. This will force the insurgent units either to disperse within the area or possibly to withdraw to neighbouring areas still under their control or disputed. The government's forces should then be so deployed as to make it impossible for the insurgent forces to reconcentrate within the area or to re-infiltrate from outside. Clear operations will, however, be a waste of time unless the government is ready to follow them up immediately with "hold" operations. If there is no follow-up, then the clear operation will develop into no more than a general sweep through the area, which, when the government forces withdraw, will revert to its original state. This does positive harm to the government's cause (for reasons already explained)

and psychologically suggests to the people that the guerilla mosquito is proof against the government sledgehammer. Sweep operations are only justified when carried out in neighbouring areas in conjunction with a nearby clear operation in order to prevent insurgent reinforcements entering the area of the clear operation, and to keep the insurgents off balance while the clear and subsequent hold operations are being carried out.

The measures required in "hold" operations will vary according to whether the area was originally comparatively secure, with a minimum of clearing therefore required, or whether it was disputed territory subject first to a clear operation. The objects of a hold operation are to restore government authority in the area and to establish a firm security framework. This involves the creation of strategic hamlets, the formation of hamlet militia and the imposition of various control measures on the movement of both people and resources, all of which are designed to isolate the guerilla forces from the population, to provide protection for the people themselves and to eliminate the insurgent underground subversive organization in the villages. This hold period of operations inevitably takes a considerable time and requires a methodical approach and a great attention to detail. It never really ends, and it certainly overlaps into the following stage of "winning" the population over to positive support of the government.

"Winning" the population can tritely be summed up as good government in all its aspects. From the point of view of the immediate impact, there are many minor social benefits which can easily and fairly inexpensively be provided, such as improved health measures and clinics (it is a fact that no population suffering from debilitating diseases will ever take positive action either on behalf of the government or even on its own behalf); new schools (education for their children is probably the priority demand in most rural communities); and improved livelihood and standard of living. This last point covers every aspect of increased agricultural production, including better seeds, livestock and poultry, and the provision of fruit trees and other suitable cash crops. More desirable than outright gifts are schemes which are self-perpetuating or encourage a chain reaction. For example, building plans should stimulate the production of local building material. Improved communications are particularly important in the remoter areas, and this calls for a major programme for the repair of rural roads, canals and bridges. All this helps to give the impression not only that the government is operating for the benefit of the people but that it is carrying out programmes of a permanent nature and therefore intends to stay in the area. This gives the people a stake in stability and hope for the future, which in turn encourages them to take the necessary positive action to prevent insurgent reinfiltration and to provide the intelligence necessary to eradicate any insurgent cells which remain.

When normal conditions have been restored, and the people have demonstrated by their positive action that they are on the side of the government, then, as soon as the government advance has been extended well beyond the area so that the threat of insurgent reinfiltration is removed, the area can be declared "white." The government has "won." All restrictions can be removed, and greater attention can be given to the government's long-term aim of creating a politically and economically stable and viable community. The seeds of democracy planted during the winning stage can now begin to sprout. Economically this is the time when more ambitious self-help projects become feasible, and, in the urban areas, secondary industry will begin to grow and flourish of its own accord. It is a great mistake to imagine that either democracy or economic progress can be forced in unstable conditions. They will achieve a far more dynamic growth when normal conditions are restored and the population's energies, relieved from the strain of war, can be released for constructive purposes.

These four phases are simple enough to understand in the areas where government operations can be started and to which its limited resources can be applied. The really difficult problem lies in the non-priority areas, where the government must hold out and prevent the insurgents from gaining full control. A very careful assessment is required of the insurgent potential in these areas as compared with the remaining resources available to the government. Depending on this, the government must then decide whether to let a few outlying areas go and to ignore them until such time as the whole programme has advanced sufficiently for further resources to be made available. This is a difficult decision for a government to take, and there is always a risk that such areas, however unimportant, may be declared "liberated" by the insurgents. This may have to be accepted, provided that the government, by using its reserve forces during a period of lull in the priority areas, can undertake operations in such areas with the object of showing the flag. This type of operation requires very careful handling indeed; under no circumstances must it be carried out as a punitive raid into enemy territory. Its purpose is psychological rather than military, and it is designed to show the population still living there that the government has not forgotten them and that it will return as soon as it is in a position to do so. The intention of the operation is to encourage the people to welcome the future return of the government, not, as was so frequently the case in Vietnam, to make them hope that the government forces never show their faces in the area again.

Apart from these areas, which become to all intents and purposes insurgent-controlled, there will be a considerable area of disputed territory in provinces which are of a low priority. Here the aim of the government must be to keep its flag flying in the main centres of population, such as the province capitals and district towns, and to accept that, outside these, what the government controls by day may be controlled by the insurgents by night. In these circumstances no effort should be made to involve the inhabitants on the side of the government: it is merely asking them to commit suicide. No attempts should be made to conduct clear operations by forces operating through the villages and hamlets of such areas when there is no prospect of holding any area which may be cleared. The main purposes of operations and patrols are to keep insurgent forces on the move, to lay ambushes at likely points and to obtain tactical information, i.e., to keep the areas disputed and to prevent them from falling fully under insurgent control.

It must be recognized that the insurgents require control only for limited purposes: to obtain supplies, recruits and intelligence and to prevent the inhabitants of the area giving the government any positive support. They are not at this stage attempting to establish an elaborate rival administration or government, though they may carry out some land redistribution and will certainly collect taxes. It is therefore important to keep offensive operations going in the disputed areas to thwart the insurgents' purpose—for example, with the aim of buying up all surplus rice stocks. If possible, such operations should be combined with a very limited strategic hamlet programme in the immediate vicinity of district towns and province capitals. This will provide experience and a firmer base from which "clear-and-hold" operations can be started when the area is accorded a greater priority. The offensive spirit must be maintained, and any tendency just to fall back on the static defence of district towns and other vital points must be avoided. This situation requires the best officers and the most disciplined troops because it is the hardest task of all to play a waiting game.

* * * * *

As for the more military aspect of operations, a number of books have already been written on tactics and personal experience in guerilla warfare, and there have been further developments in Vietnam which are bound to be the subject of more books. I have only one general point to make, which I call the "Same-Element Theory of Guerilla Warfare."

It is the secret of guerilla forces that, to be successful, they must hold the initiative, attack selected targets at a time of their own choosing and avoid battle when the odds are against them. If they can maintain their offensive in this way, both their strength and their morale automatically increase until victory is won. As a corol-lary, it must be the aim of counter-guerilla forces to compel guerilla forces to go on the defensive so that they lose the initiative, become dispersed and expend their energy on mere existence. Their condition then changes from one of automatic expansion to one of certain contraction, as a result of which both their strength and their morale steadily decline.

The aim of the government's forces must therefore be to force the insurgent to go on the defensive. In order to achieve this, in addition to maintaining a high rate of operations and continually improving the contact rate, the basic principle which should govern military strategy and tactics must be to engage the guerilla forces in their own element. There are three such elements: the populated areas, including the popular bases of the insurgents, from which they draw their main support; the unpopulated areas or war zones, which provide sanctuary and training areas for their main forces; and their communications, particularly those between the popular bases and the war zones.

The battle in the populated areas represents a straight fight between the government and the insurgents for the control of the rural population. The main method required to restore government authority and control is the strategic hamlet programme, supported by "clear-and-hold" operations. The purpose of the programme, supported by these operations, is not just to kill insurgents in the populated areas but to destroy the insurgent subversive organization and infrastructure there. The mere killing of insurgents, without the simultaneous destruction of their infrastructure, is a waste of effort because their subversive organization will continue to spread and all casualties will be made good by new recruits.

The strategic hamlet programme, properly implemented and supported by clear-and-hold operations, will gradually destroy the insurgent infrastructure. This has two simultaneous effects: first, it forces the insurgent units to fight to preserve their infrastructure at the point at which government forces are at their most concentrated and strongest, thereby automatically increasing the contact-and-kill rate; and, second, it reduces their sources of supplies and new recruits. The reason for the success which will be gained from this type of operation is that the government forces are fighting in the same element and for the same purpose (control of the population) as the insurgent forces to which they are opposed.

The chief emphasis, therefore, must be on "clear-and-hold" operations as opposed to "search-and-clear" operations (or sweeps). Search-and-clear operations, however aggressive, do not achieve the dual purpose of killing insurgents and destroying their infrastructure. The ratio of contacts and the number of insurgents killed are very limited and depend greatly on chance. Moreover, this type of operation often requires the most tremendous effort by large-scale air and ground forces, which is wasteful. The reason for its lack of success is that it does not put the government forces into the same element as the insurgent forces opposed to them. As a result, it does not force insurgent units to fight in defence of their organization and infrastructure, because it does not threaten these at all.

The unpopulated areas are the war zones of the insurgents, where their main forces can be trained and grouped for offensive operations in support of their own programme for gaining control of the populated areas of the country. The principle here is exactly the same as in the populated areas. The government forces must operate in these areas under similar conditions to the insurgent. This requires that regular military units, not only companies of the Ranger type, must be trained for long-term deep penetration operations, particularly in mountain and jungle. Short-term raids into the war zones, no matter how offensive or large their scale, achieve no lasting results. Some insurgents may be killed, some dumps may be found, but within a short time all such losses are made good.

The secret of the insurgents' strength in these areas is their freedom of movement, allowing them to concentrate or disperse their forces at will. The type of operation required is one in which government forces are inserted into the area as covertly as possible and maintained there for a long period, by air supply if necessary (there are a number of techniques whereby air supply need not give away their position). Units should be confined to comparatively restricted areas so that their own movement, which makes them vulnerable, is limited, and so that they can maintain almost permanent ambushes on tracks which the insurgents must use. Not only will this inflict casualties on the insurgents, but it will deny them freedom of movement and gradually break down their essential communication and supply systems. This in turn causes their units to disperse into small parties and forces them to seek food and other supplies on the perimeter of the populated areas, where they are even more vulnerable to small ambushes. Again it will be seen that the more government forces can operate in exactly the same element as the insurgent, the greater will be their success.

The type of operations just described will also be effective against insurgent communications within their war zones in the mountain and jungle areas of the country. Similar operations on a smaller scale and for shorter periods, carried out both by military and by para-military forces on the perimeter of the populated areas (within one to five hours patrolling time), will, by using ambushes as a main tactic, disrupt the insurgent communications between the populated areas and their war zones.

It is not often realized that in guerilla warfare guerilla forces are just as vulnerable to ambushes as are government forces. One reads so often of government convoys being ambushed on main roads, or of government forces being ambushed on their way to give relief to a post under attack (a favourite Viet Cong tactic in Vietnam). The insurgent is just as vulnerable, particularly to small-scale ambushes. There is constant insurgent movement of forces, supplies, couriers, agents and the like. The pattern of this movement on the ground is like a spider's web, and if the intelligence effort is directed on it, many possible targets can be selected which will disrupt the insurgent supply organization and deny continued freedom of movement. Many of the most successful ambushes in Malaya were carried out by small parties of two to five men at night, on small tracks which the terrorists were known to be using. The fire power of a small party with modern weapons is such that it can safely take on a larger insurgent unit, inflict heavy casualties and then, if necessary, fade away.

In the Mekong Delta in Vietnam much greater control needed to be established over the waterways. These were the main Viet Cong communications in the Delta, as contrasted to the government's dependence on air and road. In order to get into the same element as the Viet Cong, the government itself should have made greater use of the waterways for its own requirements and, at the same time, controlled the movement of other traffic on the waterways. Control points, curfews and registration of boats were some of the measures required to give effect to this.

All this does not mean that there should be no other types of operations. When good intelligence is limited, sweep-and-clear operations in insurgent-controlled territory may be necessary to keep the insurgent forces stirred up and off balance. Such operations can have only the limited aim of killing insurgents contacted, and trying to prevent them concentrating for their own offensive operations. When intelligence improves (or as a result of another operation or insurgent attack) and an insurgent unit can be definitely located,

then "fix-and-destroy" operations are required. It must be borne in mind, however, that these operations serve only the limited purpose of killing insurgents. They do not destroy their organization or infrastructure. They must, therefore, be regarded as secondary to those operations which are achieving the primary aim.

The basic military strategy, therefore, must be to insert as many as possible of the government forces, both military and paramilitary, into the same element as the insurgent forces to which they are opposed. If they are not so engaged, then they are being wasted. The main military tactic should be the ambush (in the populated areas, particularly at night), and the units carrying out this tactic should restrict their movements in order to avoid being ambushed themselves—like Jim Corbett with the man-eaters.

Getting government forces into the same element as the insurgent is rather like trying to deal with a tomcat in an alley. It is no good inserting a large, fierce dog. The dog may not find the tomcat; if he does, the tomcat will escape up a tree; the dog will then chase the female cats in the alley. The answer is to put in a fiercer tomcat. The two cannot fail to meet because they are both in exactly the same element and have exactly the same purpose in life. The weaker will be eliminated.

THE THEORY AND PRACTICE OF INSURGENCY AND COUNTERINSURGENCY

BY BERNARD B. FALL

THE CENTURY OF SMALL WARS

If we look at the twentieth century alone we are now in Viet-Nam faced with the forty-eighth small war. Let me just cite a few: Algeria, Angola, Arabia, Burma, Cameroons, China, Colombia, Cuba, East Germany, France, Haiti, Hungary, Indochina, Indonesia, Kashmir, Laos, Morocco, Mongolia, Nagaland, Palestine, Yemen, Poland,

Reprinted with permission from the *Naval War College Review*, April, 1965.

Mr. Fall was killed in February of 1967 while accompanying U.S. Marines in Viet-Nam. Before his death, he was Professor of International Relations at Howard University and had become America's most generally esteemed Viet-Nam authority. He was the author of numerous articles and books on Viet-Nam, including *Street Without Joy* (1961), *Hell in a Very Small Place* (1966), and *The Two Viet Nams* (1967).

South Africa, South Tyrol, Tibet, Yugoslavia, Venezuela, West Irian, etc. This, in itself, is quite fantastic. In fact, if a survey were made of the number of people involved, or killed, in those forty-eight small wars it would be found that these wars, *in toto*, involved as many people as either one of the two world wars, and caused as many casualties. Who speaks of "insurgency" in Colombia? It is mere banditry, apparently. Yet it has killed 200,000 people so far and there is no end to it. The new Viet-Nam war, the "Second Indochina War" that began in 1956–57 and is still going on, is now going to reach in 1965, according to my calculations, somewhere around the 200,000-dead mark. Officially, 79,000 dead are acknowledged, but this is far too low. These may be small wars as far as expended ordnance is concerned. But they certainly are not "small wars" in terms of territory or population, since such countries as China or Algeria were involved. These wars are certainly not small for the people who fight in them, or who have to suffer from them. Nor are they small, in many cases, for the counterinsurgency operator.

One of the problems one immediately faces is that of terminology. Obviously "sublimited warfare" is meaningless, and "insurgency" or "counterinsurgency" hardly define the problem. But the definition that I think will fit the subject is "revolutionary warfare" (RW).

Let me state this definition: RW=G+P, or, "revolutionary warfare equals guerrilla warfare plus political action." This formula for revolutionary warfare is the result of the application of guerrilla methods to the furtherance of an ideology or a political system. This is the *real* difference between partisan warfare, guerrilla warfare, and everything else. Guerrilla simply means "small war" to which the correct Army answer is (and that applies to *all* Western armies) that everybody knows how to fight small wars; no second lieutenant of the infantry ever learns anything else but how to fight small wars. Political action, however, is the difference. The Communists, or shall we say, any sound revolutionary warfare operator (the French underground, the Norwegian underground, or any other

European anti-Nazi underground) most of the time used small-war tactics, not to destroy the German Army, of which they were thoroughly incapable; but to establish a competitive system of control over the population. Of course, in order to do this, here and there they had to kill some of the occupying forces and attack some of the military targets. But above all they had to kill their own people who collaborated with the enemy.

But the "kill" aspect, the military aspect, definitely always remained the minor aspect. The political, administrative, ideological aspect is the primary aspect. Everybody, of course, by definition, will seek a military solution to the insurgency problem, whereas by its very nature, the insurgency problem is militarily only in a secondary sense, and politically, ideologically, and administratively in a primary sense. Once we understand this, we will understand more of what is actually going on in Viet-Nam or in some of the other places affected by RW.

RECENT AND NOT-SO-RECENT CASES

The next point is that this concept of revolutionary war can be applied by anyone anywhere. One doesn't have to be white to be defeated. One doesn't have to be European or American. Colonel Nasser's recent experience in Yemen is instructive. He fought with 40,000 troops, Russian tanks, and Russian jets, in Yemen against a few thousand barefoot Yemenite guerrillas. The tanks lost. After three years of inconclusive fighting the Egyptian-backed Yemen regime barely holds the major cities, and Nasser is reported to be on the lookout for a face-saving withdrawal.

Look at the great Indian Army's stalemate by the Nagas. And who are the Nagas? They are a backward people of 500,000 on the northeastern frontier of India. After ten years of fighting, the Indian Army and government are now negotiating with the Nagas. They have, for all practical purposes, lost their counterinsurgency operations. In other words, (this is perhaps reassuring), losing an insurgency can happen to almost anybody. This is very important because one more or less comes to accept as "fact" that to lose counterinsurgency operations happens only to the West.

Very briefly, then, let me run through the real differences between, let us say, a revolutionary war and any other kind of uprising. A revolutionary war is usually fought in support of a doctrine, but a doctrine may be of a most variegated kind. It could be a peasant rebellion or it could be religion. For example, in Europe between the 1300s and 1600s, as the feudal system evolved and then disappeared and was replaced by the early stages of the capitalist system, there were many peasant rebellions. Those peasant rebellions were fought, even though the people did not know it, for economic and social doctrines. The peasants were sick and tired of being serfs and slaves working for a feudal lord. Those peasant rebellions were in line with later socio-economic movements. This is why the Communists, of course, retroactively lay claim to the European peasant rebellions.

There were, of course, the religious wars in Europe—Protestant versus Catholic. Their doctrinal (ideological) character was self-explanatory. As soon as we run into that kind of war, not all the rich and not all the poor will stick together with their own kind. Doctrine somehow will cut across all social lines. This is often misunderstood. We look, for example, at the Viet-Cong insurgency in Viet-Nam, and expect that all the Viet Cong are "communists" of low class. Then we find out that there are intellectuals in the Viet Cong. There are Buddhist priests, Catholic priests, and minority people. Hence, this very oversimplified view of the enemy falls by the wayside; we are now faced with something which is much more complicated and multifaceted, and the enemy, of course, thanks to doctrine, cuts across all classes. Pham Van Dong, the Prime Minister of Communist North Viet-Nam, is a high-ranking Vietnamese nobleman whose father was Chief of Cabinet to one of the late Vietnamese emperors. One of his colleagues at school was Ngo Dinh Diem, a high-ranking nobleman whose father also had been Chief of Cabinet to one of the Vietnamese emperors. Ho Chi Minh was not exactly born on the wrong side of the tracks. His father had a master's degree in the mandarin administration. This is very important.

In a doctrinal conflict there are people on both sides who probably embrace the whole social spectrum. Although Communists will always claim that all the peasants and workers are on their side, they find out to their surprise that not all the peasants or workers are on their side. On the other hand, neither are all the élites on our side.

Finally, we have the French Revolutionary War and the American Revolutionary War. There is a difference between the two. The American Revolutionary War was literally a "national liberation war." It did not advocate the upsetting of the existing socio-economic structure in this new country called the United States. But the American Revolutionary War brought something into this whole field which nobody really studied, and that is the difference in certain types of foreign aid that the United States received during its liberation war. What basically made the difference between, say, Lafayette and Rochambeau? Lafayette was an integrated military adviser, but Rochambeau commanded a separate military force. He commanded French forces fighting alongside the United States forces, whereas Kosciusko, Von Steuben, and Lafayette were actually the allied parts of the army that were sandwiched in (the new word for this in Washington is "interlarded") with the United States forces.

What would happen if American officers actually were put into the Vietnamese command channels—not as advisers, but as operators; or if a Vietnamese officer were to serve in the American Army like the Korean troops in the U.S. Army in Korea? Perhaps this is one approach to the problem of "advisermanship." There was a whole group of foreign officers in the American Revolutionary War army. Were they "mercenaries," and if so, who paid them? I don't know. Were they Rochambeau's men or not? Or, what was the difference between Lafayette and the mercenaries of the Congo? I don't quite know. It would be interesting to find out.

The American Revolutionary War was a national liberation war in present-day terms. The French Revolution was, again, a social, economic, doctrinal war—a doctrinal revolution. In fact, it is amazing how well the doctrine worked. The French had developed three simple words: *Liberté! Égalité! Fraternité!* And that piece of propaganda held an enormous sway. For ten years after the French Revolution was dead and gone, French imperialism in the form of Napoleon marched through Europe taking over pieces of territories in the name of liberty, equality, and fraternity. Millions of people throughout Europe turned on their own natural or home-grown leaders believing that this French concept of liberty, equality, and fraternity was carried around at the point of French bayonets.

To be sure, in many cases, Napoleon left behind a legacy of orderly administration, of such things as the Napoleonic Code, but certainly Napoleon did not bring independence any more than the Communists bring independence. He did bring a kind of Western order which was highly acceptable. To this day there are slight remnants of Napoleon's administration in the Polish Code. The streets are lined with poplar trees in Austria because Napoleon lined such streets 167 years ago.

One thing that Napoleon also brought with him was French occupation and the first true, modern guerrilla wars against his troops. For example, the word *guerrilla,* as we know it, comes from the Spanish uprising against the French. There were similar wars, for example, in Tyrol. The Tyrolians rose up under Andreas Hofer against the French. There were such uprisings in Russia also, although they were in support of an organized military force, the Russian army. In that case we speak of partisan warfare. We also had such things in Germany, the *Tugend-Bund,* the Virtue-League. This was sort of a Pan-Germanic underground which got its people into the various German states to work for the liberation of the country from French occupation.

Very interestingly we see the difference between Napoleon and some of the other leaders in the field of counterinsurgency. Napoleon tended to make his family members and his cronies kings of those newly created French satellite states. One of his brothers, Joseph, got Spain, and Jerome got Westphalia, a French puppet state cut out in the Rhine area. The population of Westphalia rose up against Jerome. He sent a message to his brother saying, "I'm in trouble." The answer returned was typically Napoleonic. It said, "By God, brother, use your bayonets." (Signed) Bonaparte. A historic message came back from Jerome to his brother saying: "Brother, you can do anything with bayonets—except sit on them." In other words: One can do almost anything with brute force except salvage an unpopular government. Jerome Bonaparte had the right idea, for *both* the right or wrong ideas about insurgency are just about as old as the ages. We have always found somebody who understood them.

What then, did communism add to all this? Really very little. Communism has not added a thing that participants in other doctrinal wars (the French Revolution or the religious wars) did not know just as well. But communism did develop a more adaptable doctrine. The merit of communism has been to recognize precisely the usefulness of the social, economic, and political doctrines in this field for the purpose of diminishing as much as possible the element of risk inherent in the military effort. But if one prepares his terrain politically and organizes such things as a Fifth Column, one may reduce such risks by a great deal.

INSURGENCY INDICATORS

The important thing is to know how to discover the symptoms of insurgency. This is where I feel that we are woefully lagging in Viet-Nam. I will show you how badly mistaken one can be in this particular field. For example, I have a Vietnamese briefing sheet in English which the Vietnamese Government used to hand out. It is dated 1957 and is called *The Fight Against Communist Subversive Activities.* At the end of the last page it says: "From this we can see that the Vietminh authorities have disintegrated and been rendered powerless." Famous last words!

Here is a communication by Professor Wesley Fishel, who was the American public police adviser in Viet-Nam in the late 1950s. He said in August, 1958, "Indeed, Viet-Nam can be classed as about the most stable and peaceful country in all of Asia today." I would underline the fact that in 1958 the Vietnamese were losing something like three village chiefs a day. But village chiefs were not considered a military target. They were not considered part of our calculations with regard to what makes a war. For example, the *Infantry Journal* of August, 1960, stated:

The Communist objectives, for the most part, have been thwarted by South Vietnamese military strength. Threats and actual attacks have been made on American advisers through their armed forces. The fact that these attacks have been made is a good indication that the American aid is effective.

What this seems to mean is that if American advisers get killed in Viet-Nam we are doing fine. *The Air Force and Space Digest* of June, 1962, stated:

There are a few things about the insurgent warfare that favor the use of air power and one of them is that the jungle rebels are not equipped with antiaircraft, so that air superiority is practically assured.

That would be good news to the helicopter pilots who represent the bulk of our casualties. In another *Air Force and Space Digest* article of August, 1964, the following statement is made:

The figures of 1963 in the Vietnamese theater indicate that the cost/effectiveness of the air effort is high. It is estimated that the Viet-Nam Air Force uses less than 3% of the total military personnel. . . . These planes account for more than a third of the total Viet Cong killed in action; that is 7,400 out of 20,600.

The joke, of course, if you can see the point, is that if 3% of the Vietnamese personnel effects 33% of the casualties, a simple tripling of that 3% of Air Force personnel would effect 100% of the casualties. There-

fore, we need not send anybody else. But no one has considered that in all likelihood, of the 23,500 killed, a large part are noncombatant civilians. It is pretty hard to tell a Viet Cong flying at 250 knots and from 500 feet up, or more. This leads to the completely incongruous reasoning that if there are 100,000 Viet Cong in South Nam and the A.R.V.N.[1] kill 23,500 a year and maim perhaps another 25,000, and if we divided 100,000 Viet Cong by 50,000 a year the war should be over in two years. This meaningless equation probably accounted for 1963 estimates of victory by 1965. This is precisely where cost/effectiveness has its limitations.

Such reports point to a phenomenon which seems to conform to a pattern. Allow me to cite a report on the subject:

There was little or no realism in the sense of appreciating facts and conditions as they really were or were going to be, instead of what was imagined or wanted to be. The cause was fundamental, consisting of an academic bureaucratic outlook, based on little realistic practice and formed in an environment utterly different to what we experienced in the war. In the case of the staff this environment was in the cool of an office or the comfort of the road, scarcely ever the rubber jungle with its storms and claustrophobic oppressiveness. All seemed good in a good world. There was no inducement to look below the surface or to change our appreciations.

The document is declassified now. It is a report of a British colonel whose regiment was destroyed in Malaya by the Japanese in 1941. This document is twenty-three years old. Yet it sounds like a U.S. adviser from yesterday. Then as now everybody likes to fight the war that he knows best; this is very obvious. But in Viet-Nam we fight a war that we don't know best. The sooner this is realized the better it is going to be.

When I first arrived in Indochina in 1953, the French were mainly fighting in the Red River Delta. This was the key French area in North Viet-Nam. The French headquarters city was Hanoi. When I arrived I checked in with the French

[1] Army of the Republic of Viet-Nam.

briefing officer and asked what the situation was in the delta. He said:

Well, we hold pretty much of it; there is the French fortified line around the Delta which we call the Marshal de Lattre Line—about 2,200 bunkers forming 900 forts. We are going to deny the communists access to the 8 million people in this Delta and the 3 million tons of rice it produces. We will eventually starve them out and deny them access to the population.

In other words, this was the strategic hamlet complex seen five thousand times bigger. There were about 8,000 villages inside that line. This fortified line also protected the rice fields then, whereas now the individual strategic hamlets do not protect the same fields. "Well," I said, "do the communists hold anything inside the delta?" The answer was, "Yes, they hold those five black blotches." But at the University of Hanoi, which was under national Vietnamese control, my fellow Vietnamese students just laughed. They said that their home villages inside the Delta were Communist-controlled and had Communist village chiefs, and just about everybody else said the same thing; that both the French and the Vietnamese Army simply did not know what was going on.

Most of these villages were, in fact, controlled by the Communists and I decided to attempt to document that control. It was actually very simple: To the last breath a government will try to collect taxes. So I used a working hypothesis; I went to the Vietnamese tax collection office in Hanoi to look at the village tax rolls. They immediately indicated that the bulk of the Delta was no longer paying taxes. As a cross-check on my theory I used the village teachers.

The school teachers in Viet-Nam were centrally assigned by the Government. Hence, where there were school teachers the Government could be assumed to have control. Where there were none, there was no Government control. The resulting difference between military "control" and what the Communists controlled *administratively* was 70% of the delta inside the French battlelines! This was *one year before the Battle of Dien Bien Phu*, in May,

1954. In fact, the military situation was complete fiction and had absolutely no bearing on the *real* situation inside the Delta. Of course, when regular Communist divisions became available to attack the Delta in June, 1954, the whole illusion collapsed. The area was solidly Communist-infiltrated and, of course, collapsed overnight. That is revolutionary warfare.

"RW" IN SOUTH VIET-NAM

When I returned to Viet-Nam in 1957, after the Indochina War had been over for two years, everybody was telling me that the situation was fine. However, I noticed in the South Vietnamese press, obituaries of village chiefs, and I was bothered. I thought there were just too many obituaries—about one a day—allegedly killed not by Communists, but by "unknown elements," and by "bandits." I decided to plot out a year's worth of dead village officials. The result was that I counted about 452 dead village chiefs to my knowledge at that time. Then I also saw in the press, and here and there in Viet-Nam heard discussions about "bandit attacks." These attacks were not made at random, but in certain areas. That too worried me, so I decided to plot the attacks. I immediately noted in both cases a very strange pattern. The attacks and the village chiefs were "clustered" in certain areas.

I went to see the Vietnamese Minister of the Interior, Nguyen Huu Chau, who then was, incidentally, the brother-in-law of Madame Nhu, and I said to him: "Your Excellency, there is something I'm worried about. You know that I was in the North when the French were losing and I noticed the village chiefs disappearing and I think you now have the same problem here." He said, "What do you mean?" So I just showed him the map. He said, "Well, since you found that out all by yourself, let me show you *my* map." And he pulled out a map which showed not only the village chiefs but also the Communist cells operating in South Viet-Nam in 1957–58 when Viet-Nam was at peace and there was supposedly nothing going on. It was wonderful. We all congratulated each other. Yet, very obviously, to use a somewhat unscientific term, the whole Mekong Delta was going "to hell in a basket," and much of South Viet-Nam with it.[2]

The insurgency cross-check was unexpectedly provided to me by the International Control Commission. They get reports from the Communists as well as from our side, but in this case what interested me was the alleged incidents inside South Viet-Nam. The Communists would report from Hanoi, through the ICC, that Americans or Vietnamese were doing certain things out in the villages which Hanoi alleged were "violations" of the cease-fire agreement. I said to myself, "If I plot out all the Communist reports about alleged violations on a map, and if they match high-incident areas, there may be a logical connection between the guerrilla operators and the intelligence operators who provide the basis for the ICC reports." Sure enough the same areas with the high incidents also had high reports. As of early 1958, I knew we were in deep trouble in Viet-Nam and I kept saying so.

In 1959 the Southeast Asia Treaty Organization gave me a research grant to do a study on Communist infiltration in the area. The results of the study showed that Saigon was deliberately *encircled* and *cutoff* from the hinterland with a "wall" of dead village chiefs. President Kennedy, in his second State of the Union Message on May 25, 1961, stated that during the past year (meaning April 1960–61) the Communists killed 4,000 *small officials* in Viet-Nam! This was one year before the Taylor Report which got the whole American major effort going. In other words, in 1960 and 1961 the Communists killed 11 *village officials a day*. By the time we woke up and learned that we had a problem, the Communists had killed about 10,000 village chiefs in a country that has about 16,000 hamlets. This, gentleman, is "control"— not the military illusion of it.

From then on, it was open and shut. One year later, in 1963, somebody discovered that my system of judging insurgent control from tax returns was applicable to

South Viet-Nam also. A study produced by AID (The U.S. Agency for International Development) showed the extent of tax collection in South Viet-Nam. It reflected the situation for March-May 1963, six months before Diem was overthrown, and four months before the Buddhist outbreaks.

To make a long story short, there were only three provinces out of forty-five which reported no Communist tax collections.

THE ERRONEOUS CRITERIA OF "SUCCESS"

I have emphasized that the straight military aspects, or the conventional military aspects of insurgency, are not the most important. Tax collections have nothing to do with helicopters. Village chiefs have nothing to do with M-133's except in the most remote sense, nor with the aerial bombardment of North Viet-Nam. What we are faced with precisely is a Communist, military-backed operation to take over a country under our feet. I would like to put it in even a simpler way: *When a country is being subverted it is not being outfought; it is being outadministered.* Subversion is literally administration with a minus sign in front. This is what I feel has to be clearly understood. Whether it is the Congo, Viet-Nam or Venezuela, is totally irrelevant. Whether we have the "body count," the "kill count," the "structure count," or the "weapons count"—these are almost meaningless considerations in an insurgency situation. We can lose weapons and still win the insurgency. On the other hand, we can win the war and lose the country.

We always hang on for dear life to the Malayan example, which, of course, is totally unworkable. The only thing that Viet-Nam has which resembles Malaya, is the climate. We don't give the Communists credit for making mistakes, yet Malaya was one of their big mistakes. They actually decided to take on the British in a straight-forward military operation and, predictably, failed.

If revolutionary war simply were jungle war, every regular force could win it. Americans know how to fight jungle wars. One can fight a revolutionary war in Norway,

[2] Cf. Fall, "South Viet Nam's Internal Problems," *Pacific Affairs*, September, 1958.

or fight a revolutionary war in France. It doesn't take a jungle to fight a revolutionary war. One can take over villages not only in the highlands of Viet-Nam, but in the lowlands of Belgium the same way. This is, of course, the key point. Remember that the British fought in Cyprus, and Cyprus seemingly had everything in her favor. It is an island half the size of New Jersey. The Royal Navy, which can be trusted to do its job, sealed off the island from the outside. There were 40,000 British troops on Cyprus under Field Marshal Sir John Harding and his opponent, Colonel Grivas, had 300 Greeks in the EOKA. The ratio between regular troops and guerrillas were 110-to-1 in favor of the British! After five years the British preferred to come to terms with the rebels.

The French in Algeria learned every lesson from the French in Viet-Nam. The troop ratio there was a comfortable 11-to-1; the French had 760,000 men; the Algerians had 65,000. The French very effectively sealed off the Algerian-Tunisian border, and by 1962 had whittled down the guerrillas from 65,000 to 7,000. But the French were winning at the expense of being the second-most-hated country in the world, after South Africa, in the United Nations. They were giving the whole Western Alliance a black name.[3] At what price were the French winning? Well, 760,000 men out of about 1 million men of the French armed forces were tied down in Algeria. It cost $3 million a day for *eight years*, or $12 billion in French money. No American aid was involved. The price also included two mutinies of the French Army and one overthrow of the civilian government. At that price the French were winning the war in Algeria, *militarily*. The fact was that the military victory was totally meaningless. This is where the word grandeur applies to President de Gaulle: He was capable of seeing through the trees of military victory to a forest of political de-

feat and he chose to settle the Algerian insurgency by other means.

Some of these wars, of course, *can* be won, as in the Philippines, for example. The war was won there *not* through military action (there wasn't a single special rifle invented for the Philippines, let alone more sophisticated ordnance) but through an extremely well-conceived Civic Action program and, of course, a good leader—Magsaysay.

Civic action is not the construction of privies or the distribution of antimalaria sprays. One can't fight an ideology; one can't fight a militant doctrine with better privies. Yet this is done constantly. One side says, "Land reform," and the other side says, "Better culverts." One side says, "We are going to kill all those nasty village chiefs and landlords." The other side says, "Yes, but look, we want to give you prize pigs to improve your strain." These arguments just do not match. Simple but adequate appeals will have to be found sooner or later.

CONCLUSION

What, then, can be done in a war like Viet-Nam? Does the West have to lose such wars automatically? I said at the beginning that even the non-Westerners can lose those wars. But, either way, one must attempt to preserve the essentials. The question in my mind is this: Can we in Viet-Nam, or anywhere else, save (or improve) the administrative or governmental structure? The answer is obvious, and there is no other effort really worth doing. We have tried this with the strategic hamlets and that literally failed. Out of 8,500 strategic hamlets, about 1,400 survived the effort. Some people have spoken of what is called the Oil-slick Principle which has been described as the holding of one particular area, one central area, and working one's way out of the center. That was fine when the French developed the concept for the Sahara, because in the Sahara there are obligatory watering points. If they have all the oases, those outside have to come in and get water. But Viet-Nam doesn't happen to be the Sahara or an oasis. Thus,

---

[3] For example, when the French effected a reprisal raid on rebel bases in Tunisia on February 8, 1958, several senior U.S. leaders expressed shock and demanded the return to U.S. control of American-made aircraft used by the French.

the oil-slick method succeeds mostly in pushing the Viet Cong units into the next province. Of course, it looks good, at least, because for one week there will be a cleared province. For the time being this is considered adequate until something more imaginative is discovered.

The actual thing that can be done, and is also being done, is what the French call gridding.[4] One doesn't start from the center of something and work one's way out, but he starts from the periphery and works his way in. The chances are that if it is done right, and if it is done in enough places at once, some Communist units will

[4] Quadrillage.

finally get fixed (as the army says) and caught. This may yet work, but this requires a high degree of manpower saturation not available in Viet-Nam.

There are no easy shortcuts to solving the problems of revolutionary war. In fact, I would like to close with one last thought which applies, of course, to everything that is done in the Armed Forces, but particularly to revolutionary war: *If it works, it is obsolete.* In Viet-Nam and in many other similar situations we have worked too often with well-working but routine procedures and ideas. It is about time that new approaches and—above all—ideas be tried; since, obviously, the other ones have been unequal to the task.

INSURGENCY AS A STRATEGIC PROBLEM

BY PAUL KECSKEMETI

COUNTERINSURGENCY VS. PREVENTION OF INSURGENCY

In the early stages of the Vietnam conflict, counterinsurgent warfare was viewed as fulfilling a specific strategic function.

The paramount strategic problem, to be sure, was possible attack by Soviet nuclear forces, but the American strategic deterrent had "solved" this problem. If the enemy did attack, it was argued, our retaliatory strike would destroy him; but since he knows this, he will not move. So far, so good, but an approach was still needed to deal with those forms of attack that were not considered to be reliably deterred by our strategic posture. In the early nineteen-sixties, insurgency emerged as the principal form in which Communist aggression seemed likely to materialize. As President Ken-

nedy put it in June 1961, after his meeting with Khrushchev in Vienna:[1]

In the nineteen-forties and early fifties the great danger was from Communist armies marching across free borders, which we saw in Korea. Our nuclear monopoly helped to prevent this in other areas. Now we face a new and different threat. We no longer have a nuclear monopoly. Their missiles, they believe, will hold off our missiles, and their troops can match our troops should we intervene in these so-called wars of liberation.

Thus the local conflict they support can turn in their favor through guerrillas or insurgents or subversion. A small group of disciplined Communists could exploit discontent and misery in a country where the average income may be $60 or $70 a year and seize control, therefore, of an entire country without Communist troops ever crossing any international frontier.

[1] *The New York Times*, June 7, 1961.

Reprinted by permission from *Insurgency as a Strategic Problem*, RAND Memorandum RM-5160-PR, February, 1967. The RAND Corporation.

Mr. Kecskemeti is a member of the Social Science Division of the RAND Corporation. He has been a Senior Fellow of the Research Institute on Communist Affairs of Columbia University and a Visiting Professor in the Department of Public Law and Government there. He is the author of *Strategic Surrender: The Politics of Victory and Defeat* (1964).

Thus "counterinsurgency" suggested itself as the American war-fighting strategy *par excellence*, for it filled a major gap left open by the strategy of nuclear retaliation.

The key condition for successful deterrence is credibility, that is, a high degree of certainty, shared by the deterring power and the recipient of the threat, that the former would *actually* carry out its threat if it were challenged. While conditional threats must be "realistically" credible if they are to have a deterrent effect, credibility alone is not sufficient for deterrence, since a credible threat that is *taken in stride* is not a *deterrent* threat. Conditional threats are deterrent threats only if, besides being credible, they are of a kind which the potential opponent, having calculated the probable damage to his forces or society, wants to prevent being carried out. In order to be successful, a deterrent strategy need neither be based upon any decisive disparity of forces nor promise an "asymmetrical" outcome. Deterrent strategies can work under conditions of reciprocity. But this does not hold for war-fighting strategies. These stand under the constraint of asymmetry. That is, if in a potential conflict situation I have serious doubts either about the credibility or about the unacceptable nature of my threatened countermove to the enemy's attack, the central question for me will be whether, and how, I can achieve an asymmetrical outcome, one that will give me dominant bargaining power based upon a superior position of strength at the end of the conflict. This asymmetry implies, in particular, that the costs and losses incurred will not leave me exhausted or seriously weakened.[2]

Now counterinsurgency was deemed eminently suitable as a war-fighting strategy, because it would cope with the very type of attack that could not be deterred and that therefore might occur at any time when the asymmetry condition appeared satisfied. The counterinsurgent objective could be attained at relatively low cost, it was assumed, if the right mixture of military, political, socio-economic, and psychological moves were employed.

This confidence in the asymmetrical nature of counterinsurgency as a strategy may appear odd in view of the many successful insurgencies on record and in particular in view of the notoriously heavy toll that guerrillas can levy upon regular military and security forces. The disproportionate costs and manpower requirements of antiguerrilla warfare were familiar to American military experts: They noted that in recent instances one guerrilla could tie down ten regular soldiers, that the fatality ratio could be fifteen to one as between regular and irregular forces, that in Malaya a numerical ratio of thirty to one was needed to put down the insurgency, and so on.[3] According to the counterinsurgency doctrine developed in the early sixties, however, these disproportionate manpower requirements could be reduced if the local government gained the confidence of the population by suitable socio-economic policies and mastered the specialized military techniques of antiguerrilla warfare developed in earlier parallel cases. The United States could provide threatened local regimes with the needed military and economic means, as well as with instruction

[2] If the would-be attacker knows that the defender has an asymmetrical, winning strategy, this will in itself be sufficient to deter him, if he is rational. But it does not follow that the defender can always use his possession of an asymmetrical strategy to achieve deterrence. In order to threaten credibly, he must communicate his winning strategy to the attacker, but the result then may be that, far from being deterred, the attacker will develop an effective counterstrategy removing the asymmetry. A visible, obvious, asymmetrical posture necessarily has a deterrent effect. It may be said in this sense that the best (most reliable) deterrent posture also

is a potentially winning posture. But some winning postures can work only if they are not conveyed to the opponent in the form of a deterrent threat, while some deterrent postures can work under conditions of reciprocity.

[3] See Bernard Fall, "Revolutionary Warfare in Southeast Asia," in *Readings in Guerrilla Warfare* (Fort Bragg, North Carolina: U.S. Army Special Warfare School, 1960), p. 156, and William H. Hessler, "Guerrilla Warfare is Different," *U.S. Naval Institute Proceedings*, April, 1962, cited in John S. Pustay, Major, USAF, U.S. Air Force Academy, *Counterinsurgency Warfare* (New York: Free Press, 1965), pp. 86f.

and advice in counterinsurgency tactics, without having to assume heavy war costs and losses. The major manpower needs, in particular, would be supplied by the local government.

Secretary of Defense McNamara outlined this approach in 1962 in the following terms:

But we shall have to deal with the problems of "wars of liberation." These wars are often not wars at all. In these conflicts, the force of world Communism operates in the twilight zone between political subversion and quasi-military action. Their military tactics are those of the sniper, the ambush, and the raid. Their political tactics are terror, extortion, and assassination. We must help the people of threatened nations to resist these tactics by appropriate means. You cannot carry out a land reform program if the local peasant leaders are being systematically murdered.

To deal with the Communist guerrilla threat requires some shift in our military thinking. We have been used to developing big weapons and mounting large forces. Here we must work with companies and squads, and individual soldiers, rather than with battle groups and divisions. In all three services we are training fighters who can, in turn, teach the people of free nations how to fight for their freedom. . . . *Combating guerrilla warfare demands more in ingenuity than in money or manpower.*[4]

The escalation of the Vietnam war since 1964, however, has changed the outlook. When it turned out that American forces had to be committed *en masse*, the possible recurrence of insurgency became an extremely forbidding prospect. Counterinsurgency could no longer be considered a universally applicable war-fighting strategy.

An analogous problem had already arisen in connection with the Korean War. Limited, undeterred aggression at that time took the form, not of insurgency, but invasion by regular military units. The attack was turned back, but there was general consensus that the United States would never again become involved in limited conflicts of the Korean type. Should this happen, it was said, it could only lead to our being "nibbled to death."

[4] Address before the Fellows of the American Bar Association, Chicago, February 17, 1962. (Author's emphasis.)

The question then became: How does one prevent such limited peripheral attacks? The answer was found in deterrence. "Massive retaliation" emerged as the counter to limited, "nibbling-to-death" aggression, and the United States seemed to be saying that it could invest local attacks with deterrability by putting them in the front rank of threats to U.S. interests along with all-out nuclear attack. Secretary of States Dulles formulated the doctrine of "massive retaliation" six months after the conclusion of the Korean armistice. He pointed out that forces sufficient to meet local attacks could not be stationed everywhere. The basic decision was

to depend primarily upon a great capacity to retaliate, by means and at places of our own choosing. Now the Department of Defense and the Joint Chiefs of Staff can shape our military establishment to fit what is our policy, instead of having to try to be ready to meet the enemy's many choices. That permits a selection of military means instead of a multiplication of means. As a result, it is now possible to get, and share, more basic security at less cost.[5]

Bernard Brodie stressed the close connection between the Korean experience and the "massive retaliation" doctrine. Secretary Dulles's speech, he noted, "was a rejection, on tactical and strategic grounds, of our entire strategy in that war. . . . The Secretary fairly condemned the scope and methods of Korea as intolerably wasteful and unsatisfactory."[6] In the present author's opinion, however, the "rejection" of the Korean strategy was not meant in the sense (as Brodie seems to imply) that we ought to have waged the war differently by extending the scope of our action beyond the local theater; it only amounted to proposing that *in the future* the United States ought publicly to rule out localized warfare, in order to deter local attacks.[7]

[5] Speech before the Council on Foreign Relations, February 12, 1954. For a discussion, See Bernard Brodie, *Strategy in the Missile Age*, The RAND Corporation, R-335, January, 1959, pp. 248ff.

[6] *Ibid.*, pp. 250f.

[7] The "massive retaliation" doctrine was widely criticized on various grounds. Many critics took this as a prescription for war-fighting, that is, as a strategy for coping with a recurrence of local attacks of the Korean type, an eventuality with

Although American force planning in the nineteen-fifties and sixties actually stressed massive second-strike retaliatory power and thus reflected a deterrent orientation, strategic *thinking* in the military establishment was much concerned with the possibility of the failure of deterrence and hence with war-fighting problems.[8] Yet the practical difficulties in the way of evolving an asymmetrical formula turned out to be formidable. Insofar as strategic forces are concerned, we still have to rely on their deterrent function. The only asymmetries that have emerged are those related to minimal use of force in the creation of political *faits accomplis*. The Communist regimes, as well as various local Communist parties, have exerted considerable effort in this field, with varying success. The counterinsurgency doctrine developed in the United States also belonged to this general problem area, but it turned out not to provide enough asymmetry. Hence the need to transform large-scale insurgency into a preventable activity. This is the strategic problem raised by recent developments in Vietnam. The solution, however, cannot be sought in the direction of deterrence. Since the objective in counterinsurgent

warfare is not just to penalize or defeat an enemy, but to bring a disaffected population back to the government's allegiance, threats of massive retaliation or unlimited escalation cannot be credible. Is some other strategy available to prevent insurgency?

THE DETERRENT EFFECT OF THE OUTCOME

The outcome of the Vietnam conflict, it is widely believed, will in itself have a decisive effect upon the future recurrence or nonrecurrence of insurgency. This belief was reflected, for example, in the following statement by President Johnson:

What happens in South Vietnam will determine—yes, it will determine—whether ambitious and aggressive nations can use guerrilla warfare to conquer their weaker neighbors.
It will determine whether might makes right. Now, I do not know of a single more important reason for our presence than this. . . . The American purpose is to convince North Vietnam that this kind of aggression is too costly, that this kind of power cannot succeed![9]

In other words, besides solving the immediate problem, our intervention in Vietnam will also achieve a deterrent effect by inhibiting the recurrence of aggression.

Deterrence, however, rests upon the credibility of the deterrent threat. The defender's success in a past encounter will discourage future attack only if the prospective attackers are convinced that the defender's response would be the same and achieve the same result. The successful outcome of the Vietnam conflict, however, would not establish a convincing precedent for similar intervention in analogous situations. In fact, the strategic problem raised by escalation in the Vietnam conflict is precisely how to prevent the recurrence of insurgency *without* relying on escalatory threats. The outcome in Vietnam cannot solve this problem, whatever other political advantages it may achieve.

The "war to end war" argument (if we win this one, we need not worry about having to fight any more) is congenial to

---

which we had to reckon at any time. On this interpretation, the doctrine clearly was untenable, inasmuch as the Soviets had developed a matching —or, according to some, superior—overall nuclear capability. In these circumstances, "massive retaliation" as a deterrent strategy would have been a cure worse than the disease, since it lacked asymmetry.

Another criticism was that the threat of "massive retaliation" represented a poor deterrent strategy, since it lacked credibility. To be credible, retaliatory threats had to be "graduated," made proportionate to the offense. (On "graduated deterrence," see Morton H. Halperin, *Limited War in the Nuclear Age* (New York and London: Wiley & Sons, 1963), pp. 61ff.

Dulles himself abandoned "massive retaliation" in favor of the use of tactical nuclear weapons in case of local attacks ("Challenge and Response in United States Policy," *Foreign Affairs*, October, 1957), but this idea, as he developed it, also seems to have been conceived essentially along deterrent lines.

[8] On the problem of "flexible response," see William W. Kaufmann, *The McNamara Strategy* (New York, Evanston, and London: Harper & Row, 1964), Chapter II, esp. pp. 51f.

[9] Omaha speech, *The New York Times*, July 1, 1966.

the American temper, but repeated tests have cast considerable doubt upon its validity. Even complete defeat inflicted upon the aggressors in the so-called "total" wars of the twentieth century did not eliminate the possibility of aggression once and for all. This result is still less to be expected from the defeat of limited acts of Communist aggression, which differ in kind from the aggressive acts of the thirties and forties, and in any case take place in a political and technological environment different from that of the period preceding the Second World War.

In the East-West cold war confrontation, both sides are determined to avoid all-out conflict. Armed clashes indeed have occurred only over limited, peripheral issues, which have been handled on a local basis. Intervention policy has not been governed by any immutable principle. The United States has intervened in some cases and abstained from intervention in others, depending on the value of the objective and on such contingent matters as the capabilities available and the prospective risks and costs.

The record indicates that whenever the United States has decided to intervene it has tended to persevere until the minimum objective of preserving or restoring the status quo was achieved and the aggrandizement of the opponent's side prevented or reversed. Presumably the Communist powers view the United States' "operational code" for dealing with local attack as providing for two main alternative responses —nonintervention, or intervention to restore the status quo ante. The pursuit of such a minimum objective, however, limits *both* sides' costs and risks. Defensive success achieved in these circumstances can "prove" only that aggression, if opposed by the United States, cannot lead to aggrandizement. It does not "prove" that aggression as such is a high-risk proposition. Thus the precedent of a defensive success need not deter further aggressive probing. Whenever it appears doubtful that the United States will intervene, or that it has enough time to intervene with effect before a *fait accompli* is secured, Communist powers can afford to experiment with local

probing moves, in view of the fact that their existing holdings are secure.

The point of this argument is not that a defensive success in Vietnam (the preservation of the Saigon regime) would be irrelevant to deterring future Communist aggression, but only that its deterrent effect would be conditional and incomplete. It would only extend to those cases in which successful intervention would be credible on grounds of feasibility, cost, and risk. This would leave us in a bleak position if Vietnam-type (large-scale, Communist-led) insurgency were to become a global phenomenon. As we shall argue later, however, such a pessimistic assumption is not warranted.

In any case, forestalling insurgency is not necessarily a matter of deterrence. The problem may be tackled from a different angle.

CRISIS PREVENTION

An alternative approach to the wider strategic problem of preventing insurgency consists in attacking its root causes, the conditions that give rise to it. This preventive concept has been authoritatively described by General Maxwell D. Taylor:

We should give priority to the prevention of subversive insurgency and emphasize what should be done to improve preventive measures including the early detection of symptoms. The next question is, where do you look for symptoms of subversive insurgency? The answer is that they are found in virtually every emerging country in the world. Subversive insurgency is encouraged and fomented by conditions of poverty, of poor government, of lack of education, all of which are conditions one finds in most of the 90-odd emerging countries.[10]

The preventive strategy called upon to obviate "subversive insurgency," General Taylor went on, required an organization that would, to begin with, "observe and evaluate continuously the conditions in some 90 countries in the world." But this would not

[10] Speech to the American Foreign Service Association luncheon, March 31, 1966, in *Foreign Service Journal*, May, 1966, p. 35.

be sufficient. Crises could occur elsewhere than in the newly independent countries, suggesting that the study of potential crisis situations also had to include the other countries of the world within its purview; "the basic organizational requirement is really crisis anticipation and crisis management wherever found." According to this concept, "crisis management" on a global basis, using general indices of social, political, cultural, and economic deficiencies as predictive indicators, provided the answer to the strategic problem raised by the escalation of the Vietnam conflict.

Now there can be no doubt that grave social ills go together with political instability, radicalization, and potential violence. A global program designed to mitigate social ills is well warranted from the point of view of promoting political stability, besides being desirable on general humanitarian, social, and moral grounds. In the strategic setting with which we are concerned here, however, "subversive insurgency" arises as a specific problem, affecting the world political balance. What we are interested in predicting and forestalling is civil war affecting the interests of great powers, and possibly provoking their intervention.

Can indices of general socio-economic and related deficiencies serve as predictive indicators of "subversive insurgency" in this sense? In other words, if studies focused upon poverty, bad government, lack of education, etc., had been made in the past, would they have alerted us beforehand to the massive "subversive insurgency" of the civil war type that did in fact occur? Let us consider briefly the most important recent instances of "subversive insurgency." If these coincide with a clustering of the lowest socio-economic indices, we shall have prima facie evidence in favor of this sort of indicator. If not, then perhaps some more fitting indicator will suggest itself.

TYPES OF INSURGENCY

"Subversive insurgency," which the Communists call "people's liberation war," is not just any social disturbance that may be provoked by poverty or bad government. It is a form of warfare, characterized by guerrilla or terrorist tactics, sometimes combined with the use of regular units, sustained through time, and engulfing extended areas.[11] The scale of this phenomenon must first be taken into account if we wish to understand it. Why do such large segments of the population of entire regions or countries become and long remain involved in combatant or auxiliary activities? Can their behavior be explained in terms of particularly bad social conditions capitalized upon by counter-elites, notably the Communists?

This would be a satisfactory explanation if a correlation were found to exist between the incidence of "insurgency" and the gravity of socio-economic, cultural, and related ills. The actual instances of "insurgency" observed in our time, however, fail to reveal such a correlation.

In our time, more or less protracted and extensive warfare of the "insurgency" type has been observed, to mention only the most salient cases, in China, Yugoslavia, Greece, the Philippines, Malaya, Vietnam, Indonesia, Palestine, Algeria, Cyprus, and Cuba. These are all relatively poor countries. Taken as a group, however, they are not set apart by a particularly low standard of living or educational level. What does seem to distinguish them from other poor countries not affected by "insurgency" is their experience of either alien (colonial) rule that was not given up voluntarily, or invasion by a foreign power. All the populations in question experienced either the denial of their aspirations to national independence or an extreme threat to their national existence and integrity. Nationalist motivations, then, seem intimately connected with the phenomenon of "subversive insurgency," although the role they have played has varied from one case to another.

In anticolonial insurgency, the impulse was given by a colonial or mandate power's refusal to relinquish authority (Algeria, Indonesia, the first Vietnam war,

11 On the doctrine and strategy of insurgent warfare, see Pustay, *Counterinsurgency Warfare*, with extensive references. Also Peter Paret and John W. Shy, *Guerrillas in the 1960's*, Princeton Studies in World Politics, No. 1, published for the Princeton Center of International Studies, Praeger, New York, 1962.

Palestine, Cyprus). This type of insurgent warfare shows a relatively simple structure. The insurgent activists resorted to guerrilla warfare and acts of terrorism to paralyze the control and security machinery of the colonial power, and also to force as large a part of the population as possible to cooperate with them. In addition to this, regular combat units were committed where available. Anti-invasion partisan warfare, however, as exemplified in our list by China, Yugoslavia, and Greece, was a more complex matter.

The anti-invasion (partisan) forces employed techniques similar to those used by the anti-colonial insurgents, but partisan warfare itself made up only a segment of a wider war effort. In combating the invader, the partisans operated separately from national and allied forces, and also from rival resistance or partisan networks, where these existed. All these war activities were more or less loosely coordinated, but leadership was typically fragmented. (We are not speaking here of the Soviet Union in World War II, where Communist partisan forces were controlled by a Communist national regime. In the three examples cited above, the national regimes were strongly anti-Communist; before the war, the Communists had engaged in extreme, extra-legal opposition. The resulting internal conflicts were more or less precariously suspended or soft-pedalled during the war, but the Communist forces maintained their organizational and operational autonomy.)

When the invader was defeated by the wider war effort, the separately operating partisan armies became civil war forces. Those under Communist control moved to subvert or destroy the national regimes (as well as the rival partisan units, if any), and to install a Communist one-party regime. In China, this meant overt civil war in which subversive political methods played a large role, but military activities as such were predominantly carried out by regular rather than guerrilla units. In Yugoslavia, there was latent civil war with no encounter between regular units, but massive application of police terror. In Greece, the Communist partisans organized insurgency against the national government in rural areas. (It may be noted that this change of front by the wartime partisans was not the result of a globally directed, central Communist strategy. Stalin, the supreme leader of the Communist movement, opposed it. Only partisan forces not sufficiently controlled by Moscow started civil wars. The French and Italian Communist resistance forces, over which Moscow had effective organizational and political control, did not. Here, of course, the presence of American forces was a weighty inhibiting factor.)

In the post-liberation civil wars or insurgencies, the wartime partisans, although now fighting domestic rather than foreign opponents, still made the national mystique serve them. The momentum of the wartime impulse to combat a foreign enemy carried over into domestic civil war. The Communists' objective was to establish themselves as the standard-bearers of genuine national unity, sovereignty, and freedom, and to discredit the old regimes as not truly national, but rather neocolonial puppets.

Some of the cases included in our list cannot be classified either as anticolonial or as anti-invasion (partisan-type) insurgencies. Thus, in the Philippines and Malaya, the achievement of national independence was not an issue; in both countries postwar insurgency had ethnic as well as social overtones. In the Philippines, the existence of a legitimate sovereign domestic government made it possible to isolate the insurgent hard core and to pacify the area of insurgency without great difficulty. In Malaya, pacification was achieved by heavy commitment of regular forces.

In Cuba, the target of the insurgency was domestic rather than alien authority. But the Batista regime's national legitimacy was impugned, and the insurgency had a strong element of nationalist, anti-imperialist fervor. American influence and economic penetration acted as a potent irritant.[12]

Finally, in the second Vietnam war,

12 On Cuba and Castro see Theodore Draper, *Castro's Revolution: Myths and Realities* (New York: Praeger, 1962); *Castroism: Theory and Practice* (New York-Washington-London: Praeger, 1965). For a pro-Castro view, see J. P. Murray, ed., *Cuba and Communism* (New York: Monthly Review Press, 1961).

which also belongs neither to the purely anticolonial nor to the purely anti-invasion or post-invasion type, the defective national legitimacy of the Saigon regime is an important political factor. One of the political weaknesses of the South Vietnam regime in relation to that of North Vietnam, for example, is the lack of a platform of national unification; another is the presence of the American supporting force.[13] These enable the Viet Cong and Hanoi to denounce the Saigon regime as a colonial puppet.

We may say, then, that frustrated national-ethnic aspirations provided mobilizing slogans, not only in anticolonial and anti-invasion insurgency, but also in the other instances observed.

NATIONALISM, POPULISM, AND COMMUNISM

National goals (the achievement of independence, the liberation of the national territory did not provide the sole impulse, the sole motivation for sustained, organized violence in subversive insurgencies. It was only in Palestine and Cyprus that insurgency had a purely nationalist character. Elsewhere, social and economic grievances were a potent factor in radicalizing broad strata of society and stimulating insurgent activity. In typical "subversive insurgency," we find nationalism merged with various socio-political revolutionary or reforming ideologies.[14] The role of populism, the anti-landlord ideology of landless peasants and poor tenant farmers, is particularly significant. In some colonial areas, the pre-emption of land by European settlers acted at once as a national and social irritant. In radicalized urban groups, democratic, libertarian, socialist, and Communist ideologies provided strong combat motivations. But each of these socio-economic ideologies appealed to a distinct social stratum; thus

they all had a potentially divisive and fragmenting effect. Nationalism, by contrast, offered an integrating platform on which all radicalized groups could unite. Also, in our age, nationalism is that ideology which has the greatest efficacy in mobilizing people for sustained combat. In this it is far superior to revolutionary class ideologies and even to populism, which in poor agricultural countries pervades a large part of the society.

Although nationalism was the principal recruiting slogan and mobilizing ideology in all insurgencies, whether of the anticolonial, partisan, or some other type, the largest share of political power and influence did not uniformly belong to nationalist-populist leaderships. Who had political control depended on special circumstances. In the anti-invasion insurgencies, for example, the Communists generally had political and organizational ascendancy; and this was also true of one anticolonial campaign, Vietnam I. In the other anticolonial insurgencies, political and military control positions were held, wholly or in part, by nationalist-populist elements organizationally independent of the Communists (though often harboring strong political sympathies for the Communist movement).

In Cuba, Castro personally enjoyed complete ascendancy by virtue of his political charisma. As long as he acted as a populist-nationalist leader, the Cuban revolution had a predominantly populist-nationalist character. When he identified himself with Marxism–Leninism and gave his personal apparatus a Communist orientation, Cuba passed into the Communist orbit.[15] It is

[13] Pustay, *Counterinsurgency Warfare*, pp. 109f, points out that foreign assistance exposes the local regime to the charge of being a "foreign puppet regime."

[14] For China, see Chalmers A. Johnson, *Peasant Nationalism and Communist Power* (Stanford University Press, 1962).

[15] In his books on the Cuban revolution referred to in fn. 12, Theodore Draper goes extensively into the question of the class background of the Cuban revolution. In *Castro's Revolution*, he emphasized middle-class leadership and peasant rank-and-file participation. In *Castroism: Theory and Practice*, he arrives at the following conclusion:

Castroism is not a peasant movement or a proletarian movement any more than it was a middle-class movement. The déclassé revolutionaries who determined Cuba's fate have used one class or another, or a combination of classes, for different purposes at different times. Their leader functions above classes, cuts across classes, or maneuvers be-

noteworthy that the Cuban Communist Party, even where it was in organizational and military control, relied on the mobilizing efficacy of nationalism and populism, rather than of Marxism–Leninism as such, to attract combatants. It was by presenting themselves as the most authentic spokesmen of popular aspirations that the Communists gained access to broad, varied, radicalized strata of the population.

In no insurgency could the rank and file be considered as predominantly Communist in their composition. In fact, to insist upon belief in Marxist–Leninist doctrine as a pre-condition for admission to the ranks would have been suicidal; politically knowledgeable Communist leaderships always avoided this in spite of their own strong ideological attachment. Marxist–Leninist orthodoxy was a criterion only for filling leading political and military positions.

The acquisition and consolidation of exclusive political power by the CP was a different matter. This was in every case an operation separate from the mobilization for insurgency and the conduct of insurgent (partisan) operations. The latter required emphasis upon general, undif-

---

tween them. He belongs to a leadership type, not unprecedented in this century, which establishes a direct, personal, almost mystical relationship with the masses that frees him from dependence on classes (p. 133).

The present writer believes that, in any case, political power cannot be understood as the projection of class power. It belongs in a different dimension. In stable stratified societies, class membership is associated with differences in "power" in the sense of access to sources of income and wealth, educational advantages, chances of entering the decision-making elite, and so on. But the distribution of political power as such is subject to a mechanism of its own; political elite positions are not obtained by virtue of class membership or class support. Likewise, in societies caught up in a process of revolutionary transformation, the acquisition of political power is not predicated upon class membership or class support but upon the effective use of specifically political instruments of power. Ability to mobilize radicalized elements of *various* classes is essential to this, but in any case the final constitution of a political elite presupposes a power struggle among contenders *not* differentiated in terms of class membership or class support.

ferentiated, national or societal (populist) objectives rather than specifically party ones. The establishment of the one-party state, on the other hand, was predicated upon the subversion or forcible breaking up of national forces, rival insurgent groups, and those elements in the insurgency itself who were not ideologically indoctrinated and organizationally controlled by the party.

This second operation apparently could succeed only where the Communists monopolized military command positions. Post-liberation regimes possessing a military establishment not fully controlled by the party could not be subverted (as in Algeria and Indonesia).

Sometimes the Communists achieved a monopoly of military strength by destroying those forces that had participated in the liberation struggle and had been organized under non-Communist (in fact, anti-Communist) auspices. This pattern may be seen, notably, in China and Yugoslavia. In the first Vietnam war, an anticolonial struggle, the liberation army as a whole had been created under Communist auspices. When the campaign ended, military command monopoly was achieved automatically. The "second operation," the setting up of the party state in North Vietnam, only called for the purge of the alien elements in the party who had been active in the insurgency. Vietnam II, the present conflict, on the other hand, is not an anticolonial struggle, but in part a civil war between two indigenous armed forces, both of which have an anti-French colonial record and tradition. Here the Communist (Viet Cong and North Vietnamese) objective is to eliminate (destroy or subvert) the South Vietnamese army, thus gaining military command monopoly; this struggle, however, is deadlocked as a result of American intervention.

The Vietnamese civil war, then, cannot be viewed as a prototype or paradigm of Communist aggression and expansion. It is the outgrowth of an anticolonial insurgency in which forces under Communist control gained a decisive victory but failed to occupy the entire colonial territory when the French forces withdrew. On the basis of the indicators emerging from this discussion—nationalism, populism, Communist organizational and military strength—both the first and the second round in Vietnam could have been predicted. But, by the same token, one would have to expect Communist seizure of power via "subversive insurgency" only where analogous conditions prevailed—alien rule, populist-nationalist ferment, and a heavily armed Communist movement capable of posing both as the standard-bearer of national independence in the past and as the champion of national unification in the future.

This specific constellation of circumstances exists in Vietnam but not elsewhere. It cannot be used to define the problem of limited Communist aggression that the United States may actually have to face, or avert, by "crisis prevention" methods. Vietnam must be viewed as the last reverberation of a cycle of anti-invasion and anti-colonial struggles into which the Communists were able to inject massive organizational and military strength owing to specific historical circumstances. It is not the pattern for widespread outbreaks of limited Communist aggression.

POTENTIAL CRISIS AREAS TODAY: AFRICA

Nationalist and populist uprisings and disturbances are indicators of possible "subversive insurgency" in parts of sub-equatorial Africa: the Portuguese colonies, Rhodesia, and the South African Union. While only the Portuguese colonies represent "alien rule" of the classic type, Rhodesia and the Union of South Africa also may be placed in the same general category, inasmuch as their nonwhite populations are disfranchised and subject to civic and economic discrimination.

Whether "subversive insurgency" will actually materialize in these countries is contingent upon the armed strength of the potentially insurgent groups in relation to that of the incumbent colonial or racial-minority regimes. At present, the ascendancy of the latter does not seem to be in immediate danger, but a crisis may break out sooner or later.

In any case, possible insurgency in sub-equatorial Africa is not directly related to the strategic problem raised by "subversive insurgency" in Vietnam. Should a violent crisis erupt, the advent of radical nationalist-populist rather than Communist regimes would seem to be the most likely outcome. But the problem goes beyond considerations of advantage in the cold war. Protracted civil war in South Africa would have extremely damaging consequences, not only locally, but for the Western economy as a whole. The importance of preventing a disastrous crisis of this sort can hardly be exaggerated. Yet American policy cannot undertake to preserve the status quo by every means in its power. The traditional American approach to preventing crises of this sort consists in encouraging *evolutionary* change. It is problematic, however, whether this approach would work in South Africa. American policy is caught between pressures for coercive measures and sanctions on the one hand, and pressures to keep revolutionary forces under control on the other. While for this reason it is difficult to develop a coherent American policy toward South Africa, active involvement in the forcible maintenance of colonial or racial-minority rule seems out of the question. "Counter-insurgency" does not appear to be an appropriate or feasible response, and the prospects for "crisis management" are uncertain.

POTENTIAL CRISIS AREAS TODAY: LATIN AMERICA

Nationalist resentment directed at the United States is a pervasive element in the political life of the Latin American countries. The overwhelming power of the United States, American economic penetration, and the American presence act as chronic irritants. Memories of numerous interventions add up to a hateful image of "dollar imperialism" which was not blotted out by Roosevelt's "good neighbor policy" in the nineteen-thirties.[16] The following is

16 Bryce Wood, *The Making of the Good Neighbor Policy* (New York: Columbia University Press, 1963).

a characteristic expression of the typical position taken by Latin American intellectuals:

Whatever the dominant beliefs in Washington concerning the nature of economic imperialism, in Latin America opinion is practically unanimous that this phenomenon is one of the primary causes, if not the primary source of such striking evils as the low standard of living of the masses and the resurgence and strength of despotic governments engendered by small privileged groups and based on the pretorianism of the so-called national armies. It is for this reason that attitudes toward imperialism are, among Latin Americans, the touchstone of political and moral positions and an unavoidable aspect of any discussion of political and social matters.[17]

Here frustrated nationalism, the sense of being crushed by alien power, is clearly the primary "crisis indicator." Thus Latin America must be reckoned among potential crisis areas, although it offers no terrain for the major pure type of "subversive insurgency," anticolonial warfare. There is no alien power apparatus or alien ethnic ruling minority to be combated or overthrown by the national forces; where colonial rule has not been liquidated or is not in the process of liquidation, it is not felt to be oppressive. Thus "subversive insurgency" could materialize only in the form of domestic civil war.

Now certain phenomena related to civil war and revolution are endemic to Latin America. *Coups d'état* and sudden changes of regime are frequent, and there is a historic pattern of desultory guerrilla activity. It should be noted, however, that there have been few sustained civil wars of the "subversive insurgency" type, involving a large part of the population in an active or supporting capacity and recently familiar to us from events elsewhere. Revolutionary action tends either to achieve quick

success or to lose momentum. But political instability is chronic, and there is a constant pattern of radicalization, involving potential coalescence of nationalist, populist, libertarian, and Communist action groups. In Cuba, this combination has produced a successful insurgency, eventually resulting in a Communist takeover. But, as suggested above, this outcome was due to a unique set of circumstances. Castroism cannot be regarded as a paradigm readily transferable to the other Latin republics. Here, as in Vietnam, the observed pattern of insurgency fails to represent a strategic prototype.

Because of the chronic instability of Latin American politics, one must always reckon with more or less radical political upheavals. This is necessarily a matter of deep concern for the United States, not so much because immediate or delayed (Castro-type) takeover is particularly likely, but because shifts in the direction of more radical nationalism and populism, possibly of a "popular front" character, can widen the gulf between the United States and Latin America.

Exploiting nationalist as well as populist and other economic grievances is a prime objective of the Communist movement in Latin America. Here, as elsewhere, it is by championing general societal causes that the Communists expect to gain access to politically and numerically important groups of potential supporters, sympathizers, and allies. The most significant dimension of Communist political activity is neither "direct action" nor ideological propaganda and recruitment, but the establishment of connections with other political forces. This policy is a source of division within the Communist movement: The most radical sector (sometimes identified with the "Chinese" tendency) is inclined to advocate direct action and to reject cooperation with more moderate elements. It can be isolated and has little chance of organizing large-scale insurgency. The less militant type of Communist political action, oriented toward political combinations of the "popular front" type, presents more urgent problems for American policy.

[17] Gonzalo Barrios, "Seguridad Politica e Imperialismo en la America Latina," *Humanismo*, No. 25, November, 1954, p. 63, quoted in Luigi Roberto Einaudi, "Marxism in Latin America," unpublished dissertation, 1966, p. 138.

THE STRATEGIC FRAMEWORK OF "CRISIS MANAGEMENT"

The objective of "crisis management" is to forestall the outbreak and snowballing of "subversive insurgency" by removing its causes. This raises a fundamental question about the dynamic requirements of "crisis management." What kind of power is needed to accomplish the objective in areas of potential insurgency? This question will be answered according to how one views the dynamic factors involved in "subversive insurgency" itself.

According to a widespread theory, which may be called the "manipulative" one, the chief dynamic element in insurgency is the organizational and agitational activity of a small, closely knit, professional revolutionary vanguard of the Leninist type, operating at the core of insurgent activity. The extreme version of the manipulative theory holds that such a vanguard can bring about a civil war situation in *any* society, regardless of what social, political, economic, or other conditions prevail. In the West, it is often argued that the examples of Russia, China, and Cuba have demonstrated what a handful of revolutionaries can achieve by the sheer application of conspiratorial techniques. On this theory, police methods alone can effectively deal with problems of subversive insurgency. The danger can be averted only by the relentless hunting down of all Communist conspiratorial centers.

The main tradition of Communist revolutionary doctrine, while stressing the importance of the revolutionary "vanguard," is rather hostile to the manipulative view in its extreme form. The accepted, orthodox thesis is that revolutionary action can be successful only where an objective "revolutionary situation" exists. Disregarding this all-important caveat is "adventurism," a grievous deviation. In practice, however, there are widely divergent views in the Communist movement about whether a given situation does or does not have a "revolutionary" character. Some Communists tend to apply stringent, restrictive criteria, thus steering clear of any highly manipulative concept of revolution. For the most radical ones, on the other hand, the general conditions in society are so unspeakably bad as to amount to a chronic "revolutionary situation," leaving no doubt that action is called for. Among Communist writers dealing with revolutionary warfare, Che Guevara comes closest to the manipulative view, as far as Latin America is concerned:

Given suitable operating terrain, land hunger, enemy injustices, etc., a hard core of thirty to fifty men is, in my opinion, enough to initiate armed revolution in any Latin American country.[18]

Through Guevara here acknowledges the causal role played by broad objective conditions, manipulative activity emerges as the main independent variable. Elsewhere he has suggested that the insurrectionist center could *create* revolutionary conditions, but he has also referred to certain minimum conditions that have to be satisfied to render this possible.[19] He cannot be taken to hold the purely manipulative view, in spite of the emphasis he puts upon the potentialities of conspiratorial activity.

American policymakers on the whole seem to lean toward a qualified manipulative theory, as reflected in President Kennedy's statement quoted above (p. 279). It is this view, according to which Communist conspiratorial activity can set off insurgency wherever living conditions are poor, that underlies the "crisis management" approach outlined by General Taylor (p. 283). The observations presented above, however, argue not only against the extreme manipulative theory, but also against specifying poor living conditions as the "root cause" of insurgency, that factor which lies behind general turbulence and its exploitation by conspiratorial and manipulative Communist activity. The crucial factors on which the likelihood of insurgency in general, and of its resulting in a Communist takeover in particular, seems to depend in the first place are, as we have found, *political*: alien or illegitimate rule,

[18] Ernesto "Chi" Guevara, *On Guerrilla Warfare* (New York: Praeger, 1961), p. 3; quoted in Pustay, *Counterinsurgency Warfare*, p. 46.
[19] Theodore Draper, *Castroism*, p. 65.

external aggression, coalescence among various radicalized elements, control over administrative and military command positions, and so on.

Emphasis upon these political variables by no means implies belittling the causal role played by Communist political manipulation. On the contrary, the latter clearly has the potential to shape history. Only there is more to it than agitation harping upon economic discontent, or the recruitment by a conspiratorial center of adherents to be trained in methods of sabotage and terror. It is not by these micro-techniques in themselves that Communist core groups can change the course of history, but by complex strategies designed to tap large reservoirs of human energy built up outside the movement under the impact of climactic historical and political developments. Civil wars, whether conducted under populist-nationalist or Communist auspices, belong in the realm of what may be called political "macro-dynamics," where a large part of the human energies stored up in the society becomes released to generate society-wide patterns of violence that tend to break up the existing political authority structure.

Accordingly, such an objective as the elimination of the root causes of insurgency also must be approached from the "macro-dynamic" point of view. Where a potential insurgency situation exists, micro-techniques such as propaganda or piecemeal police action cannot cope with it. Only political measures affecting the entire society and its general political structure can be effective.

A strong repressive apparatus can "deter" insurgency, but this is not the same thing as eliminating its causes, which is the specific objective of "crisis management." Repression can preserve the *status quo* but in doing so it may intensify the macro-dynamic ferment and prepare the ground for a violent explosion. "Crisis management" in the sense of removing the political root causes of insurgency, on the other hand, calls for changing rather than freezing the *status quo*. It boils down to replacing an alien and illegitimate central authority with an indigenous and legiti-

mate one. This, however, is enormously difficult, except perhaps in the special case of colonial rule: Colonial powers can forestall insurgency by relinquishing authority. This will remove the main irritant, alien rule, but even so the second part of the problem, the establishment of legitimate indigenous rule, will still remain to be solved. The arduousness of this task is clearly shown by the situation prevailing in many newly independent countries.

But the liquidation of colonial rule is just the *easiest* macro-dynamic "crisis management" problem. It is much more difficult, in a sovereign country, to forestall revolution by constitutional reform and to transform illegitimate into legitimate rule. For one thing, entrenched illegitimate and unpopular regimes, in order to stay in power, often prefer massive repression to voluntary concessions. For another, voluntary concessions, far from removing the irritant, may stimulate radical opposition and turbulence. For example, the relaxation of police terror after Stalin's death had serious destabilizing effects in some of the Communist bloc countries (although it did contribute to the normalization of the situation in the Soviet Union itself).[20]

In any case, macro-dynamic "crisis management" on a worldwide scale is clearly beyond the capabilities of any organization set up within the policy apparatus of a single power, even one wielding worldwide influence. The liquidation of the colonial system, it is true, was an instance of global "crisis management," but it was largely carried out under the auspices of the interested powers themselves. American policy could only make a minor contribution. The limitations upon the American role in managing macro-dynamic *domestic* political crises are even more stringent. Even within its own sphere of influence, the United States cannot remove illegitimate and unpopular governments and replace them with legitimate ones. In fact, where the irritant is the government's lack of a generally recognized, *national* repre-

[20] On the destabilizing effects of "decompression" after Stalin's death, see the papers in *Annals of the American Academy of Political and Social Science*, Vol. 317, May, 1958.

sentative function, remedying the deficiency under the guidance and control of a foreign power is a contradition in terms.

We must conclude that effective "crisis management" techniques, by which Communist armed aggression in a macro-dynamic societal setting could be prevented are not available to the United States. Economic aid and the like may lower the level of discontent and thereby help prevent the outbreak of economically motivated disturbances. But where major *political* irritants are present, economic measures will not remove them. Insurgency (under populist, nationalist, or Communist auspices) can then be prevented either by repression (as long as it works) or by "crisis management" (reform), but in either case effective action belongs essentially in the domain of the exercise of *local* governmental power. This applies in particular to the "crisis management" approach, that is, the removal of *political* irritants. No political machinery operating from the outside can undertake this. The case of repression is somewhat different: The United States can encourage or finance it, but this is inadvisable because underwriting the political *status quo* when it is under severe pressure is a precarious and possibly self-defeating policy. In any case, opportunities for doing so are limited.[21]

The course of macro-dynamic political crises is essentially determined by the interaction of local social and political forces. The United States cannot direct or "manage" this process; it can only take a position in relation to it, counteract risks, and seize its opportunities.

This would be a gloomy conclusion if the macro-dynamics of the political process unfolding in the outside world (notably in "Asia, Africa, and Latin America," to use the stock formula of Communist propaganda) actually favored insurgency issuing in a Communist takeover. What we have found instead, however, is a trend toward nationalism and populism. This trend involves considerable political liabilities for the West. The advance of radical, anti-imperialist, nationalist currents means both the diminution of Western influence and increased political leverage for the Communist movement. But this problem cannot be handled in terms of protecting political freedom against Communist totalitarian encroachment.

In all newly independent regimes, there is likely to be both political affinity and latent tension between the nationalist-populist and Communist elements. Western policy might be able to take advantage of the tension, but it cannot ignore the affinity. In other words, we cannot expect the nationalist-populist regimes and their rank and file to equate "Communism" with "aggression" and "denial of freedom." Political strategies based upon this equation are bound to be sterile in the "third world." *A priori*, anti-imperialist populists and nationalists are prone to see imperialism rather than Communism as the prime menace to freedom. This calls for Western policies that allow latent tensions between nationalism-populism and Communism to work themselves out in indigenous terms. Even where nationalist-populist regimes are threatened by Communist subversion and move to protect themselves against it, we cannot expect them to adopt *our* cold-war attitude toward Communism *in general*.

The key strategic and political problems facing the United States in the contemporary world cannot be sliced into two segments—"all-out aggression" which is to be deterred, and "insurgency" which is to be "managed"—so that both will be prevented. To be sure, "deterrence" still is the basic strategy, as far as all-out attack is concerned. But in dealing with "insurgency," prevention cannot be our sole objective. For one thing, we have to reckon with insurgencies, notably of the nationalist-populist kind, that cannot be prevented. For another, there is no need to consider massive intervention with counterinsurgency warfare as the only alternative open to us if insurgency is not prevented. While insurgencies that may break out in

---

[21] Intervention after insurgency has broken out is a problem *sui generis*. In such cases there are fewer inherent limitations, but the question with which we are concerned in this study is not how to deal with overt insurgency but how to prevent it.

the areas of interest to us are bound to pose challenges, the chances are that it will be possible to come to terms with them without opening the road to Communist expansion. Keeping macro-dynamic pressures under a lid forever cannot be the sum and substance of American policy.

We must recognize that the world political constellation is no longer bi-polar either in the grouping of states or in ideology. We are no longer faced with Communist expansion as the sole alternative to freezing the *status quo*. Nationalism has entered the picture as a factor cementing or breaking up coalitions, reinforcing or diluting Communism and other ideological motivations.

No sound "crisis anticipation" is possible without taking the nationalist factor into account. Not much would be gained, however, if one were to deal with nationalist currents only to the extent that they may be conjoined with anti-Western populism and Communism. The real problem is a wider one. In fact, our major "insurgency" indicator, nationalist opposition to foreign rule appears outside areas at present or formerly subject to Western imperialist control or ascendancy. It represents a substantial threat to the cohesion of the Communist empires and of the Communist camp. "Crisis anticipation" must take this point into account.

Nationalism in Communist states has nothing to do with the cold-war concept of "rolling back" Communism. American policy is essentially *status-quo*-oriented; the breaking up of the Communist empires is not one of its working objectives. But centrifugal tendencies do manifest themselves within the Communist world, and American policy cannot avoid involvement in them, whether they appear in the form of insurgency, or some other kind of armed conflict, or—what of course seems most likely—on the level of nonviolent political conflict. (That a major indicator of insurgency is present does not mean that actual insurgency is inevitable or even very likely. Military weakness may inhibit resort to arms on the nationalist side. Many countries do not offer a favorable terrain for insurgency.)

It is conceivable that even in the absence of armed resistance or insurgency the Soviets may resort to armed force to prevent the further disintegration of their empire. In other areas, too, invasion or intervention by the regular (conventional) forces of Communist powers must be reckoned a possible concomitant of political struggles. Thus, limited conflict may well continue to arise as a strategic problem. Here we see a serious gap in our planning, since the problem of "asymmetry" in a nuclear environment is still unsolved. The solution is being sought in the direction of controlled escalation, but it is uncertain whether and how escalation in limited war can be controlled. In any case, "insurgency" (and its prevention by "crisis management" or other methods) covers only a small segment of the questions affecting our security that are left open by our major deterrent posture.

CHAPTER 5

Other Views: Soviet, Chinese, and French Strategies

The military doctrines and strategic concepts of potential adversaries as well as allies have been a major concern of every nation's political decisionmakers and their military establishments since the beginning of organized warfare. This information has been thought necessary to protect vital interests of nation-states, whether individual states were interested in avoiding war, or whether they were preparing to wage war. Traditionally, the decision of a nation consciously to initiate hostile military operations resulted from the considered judgment that its forces were superior to those of the enemy—that its national objectives could be pursued and accomplished with the total "cost" held within acceptable limits.

Today, however, the possession of thermonuclear weapons by nation-states with grave conflicts of political interest and purpose, has added important dimensions to the functions and significance of the military doctrines of sister states. The mutually catastrophic results of a large-scale thermonuclear exchange and the threatening possibility that lesser conflicts might expand into such a holocaust obviously mean that total "cost" may not be held within acceptable limits. The possibility of complete destruction of a state and its people, indeed, has become a reality. There is, then, the grave burden of states in the nuclear era, not only to communicate their individual intentions but to interpret correctly the intentions of their friends and their potential enemies. Hopefully, nuclear war can be deterred.

Official pronouncements, national budgets and force structures, and scholarly writings comprise a nation's open declaratory doctrine; they are the means for communicating probable patterns of action and reaction in cases of potential or actual conflict. Among nuclear weapons possessors, while relative military capabilities remain a major concern, the emphasis has shifted to an increased concern for *limitation* in the application of military means. This is especially true with nuclear superpowers—particularly the United States, and to a somewhat lesser degree, the Soviet Union. As time passes, it is apparently realized that if a confrontation occurs between the nuclear nations, only the practice of reciprocal restraint, whether tacitly or explicitly agreed upon, would appear capable of averting ultimate catastrophe. For this reason, the declaratory policies of other nations serve not only as a source of information for guiding one's own doctrines, but also represent a primary communications medium by which every nation can transmit its conception of possible spheres and means of mutual restraint. While declaratory policies of certain states may be purposely unclear and even misleading, it appears that all nuclear nations have an interest in wanting nuclear deterrence to work.

A nation's concern with the necessity for limitation in the use of force seems to develop proportionally to its level of sophistication of technology and its superiority in nuclear weaponry; the concern increases (changes) over time as the level of technology increases. The United States, as the prime example, possesses a nuclear force which is virtually unlimited in destructive capacity. And it is the United States which increasingly expresses the most concern for the necessity to limit the use of force. The U.S. doctrine of controlled or flexible response—a broadened range of military options—reflects this concern. In contrast, the Soviets have failed to advocate a similar doctrine; in fact, they still speak of the probable use of nuclear weapons in a world war, and even the strong possibility of escalation of local wars into nuclear conflict. The vociferous Communist Chinese deprecation of America's "paper tiger" nuclear arsenal and her own threats to use whatever weapons she has at her disposal both reflect a less responsible attitude regarding nuclear weapons. It is felt that China's attitude will continue until she reaches the status of a nuclear superpower. France, too, is racing toward attaining full membership in the nuclear superpower club.

The purpose of this chapter is to present the approaches of different nations—the Soviet Union, Communist China, and France—to key questions such as deterrence, defense, escalation, and the viability of independent nuclear forces. These divergent views will provide the student with an insight into contemporary problems of international security in general, and with American national security in particular.

Richard Rosser views the understanding of Soviet national objectives as the key to understanding Soviet defense policy. Edward Warner traces the changes in Soviet strategic doctrine which have occurred in the 1960s. One of his most important observations is that the Soviets, while openly expressing rejection of the possibility of limiting the use of force in a world war and while continuing to emphasize the inevitability of escalation of local wars, are nonetheless broadening their range of military options—obviously reflecting a concern for the need for limiting force.

Sin Ming Chiu writes about China's crash nuclear weapons program which is being pursued at the expense of improving her conventional forces. She simply cannot afford to do both. In Chiu's opinion, China's military doctrine will remain primarily "defensive" until she has become a full-fledged nuclear power. Davis Bobrow presents China's view of escalation as a unique, major challenge to American defense policy. China's "asymmetrical" escalation doctrine, by which is meant that China will not (in a conflict involving the United States and China or their proxies) reciprocate United States military escalation and will, instead, rely primarily on political and psychological escalation. This latter, separate sphere of escalation indicates that China, by failing to reciprocate U.S. escalation, will be able to hold any conflict to the level of sublimited war—a level at which they are most likely to excel.

General Ailleret of the French Army provides an elegant defense of the *force de frappe*. It is evident that his defense may be the basic rationale for the development of other independent nuclear forces. The article by Ailleret is somewhat mistitled. Instead of "Directed Defense," the author insists that the French nuclear force is a "system of defense not directed against anyone, but worldwide and at 'every point of the compass.'" The implications of an impressive nuclear capability of France for world peace are, of course, uncertain at this time.

SOVIET NATIONAL OBJECTIVES: THE KEY TO SOVIET DEFENSE POLICY

BY RICHARD F. ROSSER

Soviet defense policy, perhaps more than the defense policy of any other nation, is directly and continually subordinated to Soviet political objectives. The authors of *Soviet Military Strategy* cite Lenin as the source of this requirement: war is considered "part of a whole and that whole is politics."[1]

Struggle, according to Marxist–Leninist theory, is the normal condition of life. The traditional Western view of periods of peace interspersed with war is wrong. Every society—except a lucky society progressing toward "socialism"—is wracked with conflict between exploiting and exploited classes. This is the basic "contradiction" discovered by Karl Marx. Lenin and later Soviet leaders also saw contradictions in international politics: the conflict among capitalist states; between the capitalists and their colonies and dependent countries—what we presently term the developing areas; and now between the two great "world systems"—the capitalist and socialist. The current program of the Soviet Communist party states:

Our epoch, whose main content is the transition from capitalism to socialism, is an epoch of struggle between the two opposing social systems, an epoch of socialist and national-liberation revolutions, of the breakdown of imperialism and the abolition of the colonial system, an epoch of the transition of more and more peoples to the socialist path, of the triumph of socialism and communism on a world-wide scale. The central factor of the present epoch is the international working class and its main creation, the world socialist system.[2]

"American imperialism," Soviet leaders assert, "today plays the role of world gendarme, opposing democratic and revolutionary changes and launching aggression against peoples fighting for independence." West German "imperialism," with the aid of the American "monopolists" and their English and French allies, represents "a dangerous breeding ground for war and for new aggressive forces" that menace peace in the heart of Europe. In the Far East, the United States is reviving Japanese militarism. However, the most likely areas where the imperialists will incite "aggressive" wars are in the Middle East, in Korea, in Taiwan ("occupied" by the United States), and, of course, in Vietnam. Wars between the imperialist powers on the pattern of World Wars I and II also cannot be ruled out. Finally, there always is the possibility for a decisive and climactic clash between the two opposing camps of socialism and imperialism.[3]

The critical question is what policy the Soviet leaders might pursue in the various kinds of conflicts described above. Will they intervene whenever and wherever the interests of the international Communist movement are threatened? Do they have other objectives besides the furtherance of

[1] V. D. Sokolovskii, *Soviet Military Strategy* (Santa Monica: The RAND Corp., 1963), p. 270. This work is the fundamental contemporary source on Soviet defense policy.

[2] Jan F. Triska, ed., *Soviet Communism: Programs and Rules* (San Francisco: Chandler, 1962), p. 25.

[3] Sokolovskii, *op. cit.*, p. 279. This typology of war and its impact on Soviet defense policy is discussed in more detail in the following article by Captain Warner.

The article is printed here for the first time.

Colonel Richard Rosser is Professor and Head of the Department of Political Science at the United States Air Force Academy. He is the author of articles and a forthcoming textbook on Soviet foreign policy. The views expressed in this article are the author's own and do not necessarily represent those of the United States Government.

world communism? Unfortunately, there is no definitive answer to such questions. Even if we had access to minutes of the Soviet Politburo, it is doubtful whether we could find precise commitments in advance. The *formal* statement of the obligations of the Soviet Union toward the international proletarian movement moreover is not a very good guide. If their word is accepted at face value, the Soviets always appear to be the most steadfast supporters of proletarian internationalism. The USSR is supposedly the bulwark of the world socialist movement and the altruistic big brother of Communist states and parties around the world. According to the 1961 Program of the Communist Party of the Soviet Union:

The C.P.S.U. and the Soviet people as a whole will continue to oppose all wars of conquest, including wars between capitalist countries, and local wars aimed at strangling people's emancipation movements, and consider it their duty to support the sacred struggle of the oppressed peoples and their just anti-imperialist wars of liberation.[4]

Our problem is to cut through the Marxist–Leninist jargon. We must indicate the basic goals of Soviet foreign policy, which contrast rather sharply with *formal* international commitments. These goals in turn dictate Soviet defense policy. We will begin with a concept which the Soviets rarely talk about—the Soviet "national interest."[5]

THE SOVIET NATIONAL INTEREST

Every state has a national interest, even though it may be difficult to define. And every state's national interest must be served, even by Soviet rulers formally committed to an ideology transcending national concerns.[6]

From the first, the Bolsheviks could not avoid concern for "Russia." They personally might despise the masses, but they couldn't ignore them—and the traditional interests of the country. In Leninist terms, Russia was the base for all future revolutions. The desires and needs of the people and the country had to be served to preserve this base.

Early in their regime, the Soviet leaders began to rationalize any apparent conflict between the goals of world communism and the national interest. This, of course, had not always been the case. At the very beginning of the new Soviet state, Lenin, basically an "internationalist," claimed:

We defend, not a Great-power status; there is nothing left of Russia except for Great-Russia; we do not defend national interest. We declare that the interests of socialism, the interests of world socialism, are superior to national interests of states.[7]

Yet even Lenin showed traces of an emotional attachment to the motherland. Apparently it was difficult for the most hardened revolutionary to be unsentimental about Russia. Lenin wrote in 1915: "Is the feeling of national pride foreign to us, the Great-Russian, class-conscious proletarians? Of course not! We love our language and our country."[8] Stalin was just as patriotic. He proclaimed at the end of World War II: "I raise a toast, first of all, to the Russian people because it is the

---

[4] Triska, *op. cit.*, p. 67.

[5] One of the rare instances when the use of the national interest concept crept into Soviet jargon occurred in the speeches of Soviet admirals on Navy Day, July 30, 1967. The mission of the Soviet Navy was stated to be the defense of Soviet "state interests" anywhere in the world as well as the defense of the "members of the commonwealth" (other socialist countries).

[6] George Kennan has written: "Anyone who has

looked reasonably closely at political history will have had many occasions to observe that the very experience of holding and exercising supreme power in a country saddles any ruler, whatever his own ideological motives, with most of the traditional concerns of government in that country, subjects him to the customary compulsions of statesmanship within that framework, makes him the protagonist of the traditional interests and the guardian against the traditional dangers. . . . However despotic he may be, and however far his original ideas may have departed from the interests of the people over whom he rules, his position of power gives him, as Gibbon once pointed out, a certain identity of interest with those who are ruled." *Russia and the West under Lenin and Stalin* (Boston: Little, Brown, 1961), p. 392.

[7] Quoted in W. W. Kulski, *Peaceful Coexistence* (Chicago: Regnery, 1959), p. 38.

[8] *Ibid.*, p. 39.

most outstanding nation among all the nations forming together the Soviet Union ... because it has a clear mind, a reliable character, and the power of resistance."[9]

Lenin, Stalin, Khrushchev, and the present Soviet leaders have never forgotten Russia. But this attachment has been more than simple Russian nationalism. The devotion of the Soviet leaders to "Russian" interests is bound up with commitments to the Marxist-Leninist ideology. And the protection of the national interest is naturally necessary for the preservation of their personal power, also an important motivation behind Soviet foreign policy.

The Soviets *publicly* see no basic conflict between Soviet national and Communist interests. In their view, anything advancing the interests of the USSR advances the interests of world communism. Many non-Soviet Communists appeared to believe this—at least through the 1930s. It was logical to give first priority, for example, to the defense of the Soviet Union. This base was indispensable for future revolutions. Moreover, the USSR controlled the international Communist movement, making it wise policy to accept the Soviet line.

But even in this period some non-Russian Communists began to see a divergence between what they considered best for world communism, and what the Soviets claimed to be best. The dramatic signing of the Nazi-Soviet Non-Aggression Pact in 1939, and the subsequent orders for all communists to embrace the Germans and hate the Western capitalists, made certain party members outside the USSR believe the whole communist movement was being sacrificed (as it was) for the security of the USSR.

The differences today between the Soviet national interest and the interests of world communism are vividly illuminated by the split within the communist bloc and the attendant charges of "great power chauvinism" and "narrow nationalism." The conflict within the bloc in turn seems largely based on the Soviet *national* interest, versus the *Chinese* national interest, versus the Rumanian *national* interest, and

so on. However, this begs the question. We still must define the Soviet national interest—a rather complex task.

The Soviets will not give us our solution. They imply that no difference exists between the Soviet national interest and that of world communism. Perhaps we can look for certain "interests" which would be pursued by *any* government controlling what is now the USSR. There may be certain immutable goals which any "Russian" regime must strive for.

The basic goal of any leader of Russia concerned with the national interest, it can be argued, must be national survival. This is the *minimum* objective—a certain degree of security.[10] Another question then arises. What do you need to provide Russian security? One clue comes from Russian history. Cyril Black, for example, has suggested that Russian leaders traditionally have pursued security through four general categories of objectives: (1) the stabilization of frontiers to protect the motherland by defeating neighboring powers, extending Russian control over relatively uninhabited territories, or relying on existing natural barriers; (2) the attempt to establish favorable conditions for economic growth, long recognized by Russian statesmen as important for national security and one of the motivations behind the desire for ice-free ports; (3) the unification of territories considered Russian by virtue of dynastic, religious, or national claims if they could add to Russian strength and provide defense in depth; (4) participation in alliances, both short- and long-term, and in international organizations designed to promote international security.[11]

From the peace settlement of 1921 to that of 1947, Black believed, the immediate objectives of Soviet foreign policy were

---

[9] *Ibid.*, p. 42.

[10] The national interest could, of course, be directed primarily toward the promotion of a higher standard of living for the populace, toward world peace, etc. But today the term generally refers to the promotion of national security, and it will be used in this manner. However, the possible existence of other, *higher* Soviet national interests are noted at the end of this section.

[11] "The Pattern of Soviet Objectives," in *Russian Foreign Policy* (New Haven: Yale University Press, 1962), ed. by Ivo J. Lederer, pp. 3–38.

determined primarily by security needs. This was evident in Soviet pursuit of the same four general categories of objectives. However, only the furthering of ecomomic interests through the provision of ice-free ports had been relatively unaffected by the peace settlement. Soviet achievement of the other three categories of objectives had been drastically restricted. The Soviet Union's western frontier was, by traditional standards, very unstable. Many Ukrainians and white Russians now were under foreign rule. Finally, Soviet ability to form alliances or participate in international organizations to protect Russian security had been hampered by the Russian Revolution.

The problem with any such analysis is that a Western scholar, not the Soviet leaders, is defining the Soviet national interest. And the Soviets, as noted previously, formally deny any difference between this interest and that of world communism. The primary concern of a Russian leader serving the national interest must be to achieve a certain degree of national security. But security for a Soviet leader steeped in Marxism–Leninism is quite different from security for a Tsarist official. Marxism–Leninism predicts the Soviets will be in perpetual conflict with hostile imperialist states until the world is communized. This extends the requirements for the *complete* satisfaction of their national interest far beyond those Professor Black lists.

Yet there surely are *degrees* of security for the Soviets. Certainly domination of Eastern Europe makes them feel much more secure than the possession of some island chain in the Indian Ocean. There also probably exist certain minimum requirements the Soviets leaders consider absolutely necessary for national security— for which they would fight. We cannot list these requirements. Even the Soviets probably would hesitate to do this, assuming they could. Too much depends on the circumstances, Soviet motivations, and Soviet capability. In 1918 the new Soviet government, largely because of Lenin's forceful leadership, agreed to a drastic butchering of European Russia with the

Treaty of Brest–Litovsk. It is doubtful whether the USSR today, with its present capability, would agree to a similar ultimatum. The contemporary Soviet "Brest–Litovsk"—an area which the Soviets want, but do not consider necessary for survival— probably lies geographically far to the west of the heart of Russia. (The more a nation has, the more it tends to consider vital.) In 1962, Cuba apparently was a contemporary "Brest–Litovsk." In the next decade, Berlin may qualify.

These *minimum* Soviet security requirements probably correspond roughly to the national interest which would be pursued by any "Russian" government. The problem we face, however, is that the Soviet government is not just any "Russian" government. The Soviet regime is run by men professing adherence to Marxism–Leninism. And this ideology does have an impact on their foreign and defense policies. It would be a grave mistake for Western policy-makers to assume that the USSR is merely a great power protecting the traditional interests of a great power. It would be equally disastrous to assume that the primary interest of the USSR is furthering world communism. Soviet foreign policy— and the defense policy which derives from it—is a complex amalgam of national interest tempered by Marxist–Leninist ideology. Let us now look in more detail at the impact of the ideology on Soviet foreign policy.

THE NATURE OF THE IDEOLOGICAL IMPACT

The Marxist–Leninist ideology, particularly its strategy and tactics, deals primarily with national and international conflict among economic classes. The thrust of the ideology is clearly revolutionary, predicting and requiring communist promotion of change through class conflict until world communism is achieved. Soviet foreign policy reflects this revolutionary thrust. Even the primary motivation of furthering the Soviet national interest is expressed in revolutionary terms and rationalized by the ideology. Soviet leaders naturally try to be good "bourgeois" diplomats when the occasion demands, arguing for "legitimate" Soviet national interests or world peace. But they cannot escape their revolutionary conditioning. Khrushchev's outburst at a Kremlin reception on November 26, 1956, hardly contributed to the theme of peaceful coexistence: "Whether you like it or not, history is on our side. We will bury you!"[12]

The ideology, in effect, permeates all Soviet activity in international politics. It is an integral part of the mental environment in which Soviet decisionmakers think and work. To be specific, the ideology gives the Soviet leaders: (1) certain long-range goals for Soviet foreign policy; (2) a system of knowledge with which to view the world; (3) a method of analysis; and (4) strategy and tactics.

The Long-Range Goals. The vision of the utopian "never-never land" of Marx and Engels still exists. Lenin, Stalin, Khrushchev, and the present regime may have junked or radically altered the Marxian road to utopia where circumstances have required, but the essence of the Marxian dream remains. Khrushchev boasted in 1957 during an interview with a Japanese news correspondent: "We are convinced that sooner or later capitalism will perish, just as feudalism perished earlier. The socialist nations are advancing towards communism. All the world will come to communism. History does not ask whether you want it or not."

The Communist belief may appear childlike, naive and ridiculous. The continuing force of the vision, however, does not depend on its rationality. Certain fundamental elements of any philosophical system, including the so-called "science" of Marxism–Leninism, must be taken on faith. And for Communists, faith continues to exist. Milovan Djilas, a leading member of the Yugoslavian Communist Party until his

imprisonment, knew Stalin and his cohorts well. Djilas writes:

Every revolution, and even every war, creates illusions and is conducted in the name of unrealizable ideals. During the struggle the ideals seem real enough for the combatants; by the end they often cease to exist. Not so in the case of Communist revolution. Those who carry out the Communist revolution as well as those among the lower echelons persist in their illusions long after the armed struggle. Despite oppression, despotism, unconcealed confiscations, and privileges of the ruling echelons, some of the people—and especially the Communists—retain the illusions contained in their slogans.[13]

Djilas is noting the increasing gap between reality and ideals in the internal development of Communist societies. But there also are problems for Communist theory in external developments. The robust health of modern capitalism furnishes an illustration. Improverished workers and exploited peasants obviously are not driving the millions of automobiles clogging American highways.

History has disproved much of Marxian theory. But what appears faulty logic in Marxism–Leninism to Western observers does not seem to bother most Communists. They find, for instance, "new" contradictions in capitalism—or simply ignore embarrassing developments.

In any case, the long-range theoretical predictions and the utopian goals of the ideology generally do not distort daily decisions in Soviet foreign policy. Soviet leaders no longer expect an immediate "socialist" millennium. They do not retire every evening hoping for signs of world revolution when they awake. But they believe world communism will be achieved *someday.* And this faith performs three important functions for them: (1) it justifies their continuance in power, both to themselves and theoretically to the populace; (2) it is the foundation on which they rationalize all of their actions; (3) it sets the general *direction* of Soviet policy, both foreign and domestic. These policies, assuming the leaderships avowed faith in com-

[12] Khrushchev clarified his comment to Los Angeles civic authorities during his tour of the United States in 1959: "The words 'We will bury capitalism' should not be taken literally as indicating what is done by ordinary gravediggers who carry a spade and dig graves and bury the dead. What I had in mind was the outlook for the development of human society. Socialism will inevitably succeed capitalism."

[13] *The New Class* (New York: Praeger, 1957), p. 30.

munism is sincere, must reflect an attempt to move toward internal and international communism. Foreign observers, and even other Communists, may argue *particular* policies are destructive of these long-range goals. But this is irrelevant for our study. It is important only that Soviet leaders believe they are advancing the cause. The final goals also may be vague. But this does not mean they are nonexistent. Few Americans, for example, would question the United States commitment to promote "freedom" in the world. On the other hand, few Americans probably could agree on exactly what this concept means.

A System of Knowledge. The system of knowledge the ideology gives the Soviet leadership probably has a more important impact on Soviet foreign policy, particularly on day-to-day decisions, than the long-range goals of the ideology. This system determines the leadership's view of the world. It provides the "red-colored" glasses through which they view current happenings. The peculiar *tone* or *style* of Soviet foreign policy results.

Several aspects of this world view particularly affect Soviet behavior in world politics. First, the Soviets believe each nation, as well as the international society, is wracked with conflict. The only exceptions are future communist societies in the socialist stage of development, and the USSR, now building communism. No antagonistic classes exist; therefore, conflict does not exist—except that caused by individuals with lingering "bourgeois" tendencies. Second, conflict, and with conflict *change*, is the natural order of things. The *status quo* indeed *is* change. In Marxist–Leninist terminology, the material world is constantly being altered through the clash of antagonistic contradictions. There is no innate tendency toward harmony of classes or interest in either domestic or international societies.[14] Third, national and international conflict finally will be resolved through struggle, not compromise. The communists, since they are on the side of

the progressive forces, will win this struggle. On the nation-state level, particularly in the relations between the socialist and capitalist states, armed struggle may be ruled out. The strength of the peaceful socialist states restricts warlike moves by the imperialists, and the existence of nuclear weapons makes total war useless. But such periods of formal international calm do not stop change. The conflict merely is transferred to a different plane. In the present time period, conflict develops on the ideological and economic levels, as well as through revolutions and wars of "national liberation."

A Method of Analysis. The ideology provides the Soviet leaders with certain guidelines for analyzing problems in international politics. The science of Marxism–Leninism tells them how to evaluate any situation to get the "big picture," after which the correct strategy and tactics can be selected.

A Communist might go through the following analytical process when examining a problem in foreign policy. (He probably would not consciously recognize it as a process, would not necessarily ask the questions in the order given below, and would assume the more basic "facts.") First, the historical era must be defined. In our time, it is the epoch of transition to the next formation, the Communist formation, the first phase of which is called "socialism." Imperialism, "parasitic or decaying capitalism," is on the way out. (Certain backward countries still may be in earlier economic stages such as feudalism.) Second, a Communist analyzes the productive relations of the particular country or countries he is dealing with—specifically, who owns the means of production. This tells him who really controls policymaking in a given country. In an imperialist nation such as the United States the monopoly capitalists are in charge. American foreign policy inevitably reflects their interests. Carrying through this analysis for all states reveals enemies, friends, and potential allies. The antagonistic contradictions subsequently become apparent, the forces making for change through the dialectical process in each country and the world at large. For

---

[14] See Arthur Schlesinger, Jr., *A Thousand Days* (Boston: Houghton Mifflin, 1965), pp. 358–74, for an excellent summary of Khrushchev's view on the *status quo*.

example, the Soviets believe the conflict is obvious between the monopoly capitalists and the masses in an imperialist nation, and between the imperialist nations as a whole and the underdeveloped countries.

The above "facts" are fundamental generalizations. The crucial, daily questions facing Soviet decisionmakers center around current alterations in these basic relationships. Is *revolution* in the air? Is the tide within a country's strategic period ebbing or flowing? Are the class forces both within the particular country and the world at large in favor of the Communists?

These, of course, are the really sticky questions to which Marxism–Leninism provides no clear answer. But the important point to remember is that the ideology conditions Soviet decisionmakers to ask such questions. Debates on foreign policy, in turn, arise from differing answers to them.

Strategy and Tactics. Once the situation is analyzed, Soviet policymakers select the appropriate strategy and tactics. A change in the general strategy for a particular country is not necessary unless a major revolutionary change is imminent. The usual decision thus involves a choice of tactics, which come from the vast "storehouse of Marxism–Leninism." Tactics include the united front from above, the united front from below, the contemporary "national liberation front," and so on. New variations, of course, are constantly appearing because the world of the present regime is considerably different from that of Lenin. Such changes on occasion may be attacked as non-Marxist—their initiator, as a deviationist or a revisionist. But in each case, the initiator defends his new tactic as being in the basic spirit of the doctrine. And generally this is true. The "storehouse" permits the policymaker great latitude. Any ally, for example, can be used if he aids the advance of communism, regardless if he is "temporary, vacillating, unstable, unreliable, and conditional."

THE ATTITUDES IMPARTED BY THE IDEOLOGY

Because of the impact of the ideology on the whole decisionmaking process in foreign policy, Soviet leaders have certain peculiar attitudes toward international politics. These attitudes are apparent in the way the Soviets talk and act. They are: (1) certainty of success; (2) a sense of righteousness; (3) patience; and (4) expansionist tendencies.

Certainty of Success. The Soviets feel sure of the eventual success of communism, and thus of their foreign policies. Bertram D. Wolfe vividly describes the origin of the optimism:

What reason does a man looking with Khrushchev's eyes have for abandoning the view that "capitalist-imperialism" is decadent when it is losing all its colonies, did not show the resolution to protect Hungary's freedom or complete the unification of Korea, failed to make the military moves to prepare its sort of peace during World War II, thereby letting maimed and bleeding Russia pick up all of Eastern Europe, half of Germany, win powerful allies and partners in Asia, expand the "camp of Communism" from one-sixth of the earth to one-fourth, with one-third of the earth's population? We may offer our explanations of all this. None of them would seem to him to refute his simple explanation of "decadence" and "progress."[15]

There is no doubt or uncertainty for the Soviet communist leaders. They are on the side of the fundamental forces making for progress through the operation of the dialectic. Soviet foreign policy, state Soviet scholars, consequently must be successful:

The decisive source of the strength or weakness of a foreign policy, of its historical prospects or lack of prospects, is the correlation of that policy and social progress: its conformity or non-conformity to the laws of social development, to the objective course of the historical process. The victory-bringing strength of Socialist foreign policy lies in it being *an advanced and progressive policy, correctly reflecting the urgent requirements of the development of society's material life, the objective laws of contemporary international development, and in its making use of them in the interests of society, for the good of the working people.*[16]

The "victory-bringing strength" of So-

[15] "Communist Ideology and Soviet Foreign Policy," *Foreign Affairs* (October, 1962).
[16] M. Airapetyan and G. Deborin, "Foreign Policy and Social Progress," *International Affairs* (Moscow), February, 1959. Italics in the original.

viet foreign policy naturally comes from the Soviet leadership's use of the science of Marxism–Leninism:

The fact that Soviet foreign policy is based on science is the most important source of its strength and successes. Profound knowledge of the objective laws of international development and the scientific analysis of the world relation of forces enable the Communist Party of the Soviet Union and the Soviet Government to take the right course in the complicated international situation, to foresee the course of events, to discover in time and disrupt the perfidious designs of the warmongers, to determine and carry out whatever steps are necessary in foreign policy to defend with credit the interests of our country and of Socialism and to uphold peace throughout the world.[17]

There may, of course, be temporary setbacks. In some cases, the USSR may suffer unforeseen defeat. Naturally the ideology is not at fault. Certain party members simply have failed to apply the precepts of Marxism–Leninism.

A Sense of Righteousness. He who advances communism is acting *morally.* He who opposes communism is acting *immorally.* The science of Marxism–Leninism— and no one can question science—proves beyond doubt that communism will triumph. What is scientifically proven is true. What is *true*, is *good*, and therefore, *moral*.

Communist self-righteousness also is reflected, Bertram Wolfe argues, in "the unresponsiveness to argument, the stubbornness and repetitiveness of Communist negotiators, the lack of communication in dialogues which are only ostensible dialogues. How can there be genuine dialogue without some consensus? How can there be give-and-take between that which is self-evidently and totally right, and that which is self-evidently wrong, both scientifically and morally?"[18]

Patience. Certainty of success tends to breed patience in a Communist. For him the world is marching inexorably toward communism. His own actions can be extremely important in aiding or retarding this progress, but they are not critical. It is

never a question of now or never. True, the inevitable may seem further and further in the future for some Communists. But this is no reason for Soviet leaders to undertake risky international ventures in the name of communism. No specific timetable must be met. Neither Marx, Lenin, Stalin, Khrushchev, nor the present leaders have predicted when the world will be communized. In the meantime, the Soviets are actually poor practitioners of Marxism–Leninism if they consciously jeopardize the existence of that great power base for the extension of communism—the Soviet Union (Khrushchev's successors obviously thought he was a poor practitioner. They criticized him for "hare-brained scheming," as well as "immature conclusions and hasty decisions and actions divorced from reality, boasting, and empty phrase mongering." One example given was his precipitation of the Cuban Missile Crisis in 1962, the most serious threat to Soviet security since World War II.)

On the other hand, patience does not mean inaction. If the Soviets must avoid total war, they also must avoid total peace. When the balance of forces is in their favor, they must act. Conflict and change until the millennium are the natural order of things. But *men* actually bring about conflict and change: ". . . historical laws themselves, without people, do not make history. They determine the course of history only through the actions, the struggle and the consciously directed efforts of millions of people."[19]

Expansionist Tendencies. The world's inevitable march toward communism, and the requirement for communists to aid this movement, make Soviet foreign policy inherently "internationalist," or, as it appears to the West, expansionist. Soviet internationalism comes from the continuing assertion that the common interests of similar economic *classes* in different states are much more fundamental and binding than those interests shared by different classes in the same nation-state: "Whoever has mastered the Marxist doctrine and under-

[17] *Ibid.*

[18] "Communist Ideology and Soviet Foreign Policy," *op. cit.*

[19] *Fundamentals of Marxism–Leninism*, 2nd ed. (Moscow: Foreign Languages Publishing House, 1963), p. 135.

stands the historic mission of the proletariat that Marx discovered is bound to be an internationalist, to strive consciously for the unity and cooperation of the working people of all nations, and to place the common interests of the international working class above partial, local and narrow national interests."[20] The clarion call of the Communist Manifesto of 1848 remains: "Working men of all countries, unite!"

The Soviets have a moral *right* and a *duty* to aid the unification of the world proletariat for their interests and those of the world's oppressed are one. This obligation inevitably became a vital cornerstone of Soviet foreign policy. Workers of the world, however, found a reciprocal obligation to defend the Soviet Union—even if this meant sacrificing their own hopes of revolution. And while Stalin was alive, this obligation was much more pressing than the Soviet duty to the spread of communism in other countries.

With the founding of other "socialist" states after World War II, foreign communists again questioned the asserted identity of Soviet foreign policy with the interests of the world proletariat. The Soviets had the duty to support the peoples of the communist bloc. (The "rich" USSR certainly was able to aid the development of fraternal states.) Instead, the Soviets lavished economic aid on India, a capitalist country, and cut off help to Communist China.

We now need to set the ideological commitment of the Soviet leaders to promote world communism in perspective with the need to promote the national interest of the USSR. As the history of Soviet foreign policy since 1917 demonstrates, the protection of the national interest takes precedence over all other state goals—in particular, over the furthering of world communism. When Soviet *minimum* security needs as described earlier in this paper are in jeopardy, the Soviet leaders present world communism in muted form. When the Soviets seem to feel relatively secure, the pursuit of world communism is more energetic.

CONCLUSION

I have argued that world communism is the publicly stated, long-range maximum goal of the Soviet leaders. This goal, however, is always second in priority to the minimum goal—minimum national security. If we accept such a proposition, certain assumptions regarding Soviet defense policy inevitably follow. First, priority is always given in Soviet thinking to the defense of the USSR and its vital interests. Second, Soviet military power will be used to further communism in other areas as long as the security of the USSR is not endangered. Above all, the Soviets sincerely hope to avoid general nuclear war. Their diligence and their sacrifices in building a powerful nation-state would come to naught if a climactic clash were to occur. And there is no reason for the Soviet Union to precipitate such a war. The Marxist–Leninist ideology predicts the inevitable triumph of communism. Only patience is necessary.

[20] *Ibid.*, p. 305.

THE DEVELOPMENT OF SOVIET MILITARY DOCTRINE AND CAPABILITIES IN THE 1960's

BY EDWARD L. WARNER III

Since 1960, the Soviet military establishment has been caught up in two simultaneous and interrelated revolutions. On one hand, it has actively promoted and been gravely affected in turn by the continuing military-technical revolution, which has radically altered the international military capabilities environment within which the Soviet state must operate. At the same time, Soviet military thinking has undergone a strategic doctrinal revolution, in which it has been forced to adapt its major tenets of strategic thought to the new realities of the world of modern missile and space delivery systems and thermonuclear weapons. These transformations have produced a turbulent and intensely contentious atmosphere within the Soviet polity. The period also has been marked by conflict between identifiable groupings within the political system, including strains between the political leadership and the powerful military establishment, as well as perceptible conflict between rival groupings within the military itself.

Visible signs of the prolonged doctrinal debate have been evident within a voluminous body of Soviet literature on military affairs[1] and in the major policy pronouncements of leading political and military figures. This dialogue has included both an internal and external aspect. Internally, it represents the attempts by various individuals and groups to promote the official acceptance of their own conceptions of the proper Soviet reaction to the new challenges of strategy and policy. As such, it is a highly important internal debate, whose outcome has important repercussions in terms of the allocation of roles in possible conflict situations and, more important, the receipt of adequate budgetary resources to sustain such roles. Externally, the composite Soviet position has become a part of an ongoing dialogue between the Soviets and other national actors, in particular, their own self-proclaimed "chief adversary" within the capitalist camp, the United States. There appears to exist a mutually keen awareness of the doctrinal development of one another and in some cases, the exchange of specific criticism, commentary, and even "corrective messages" concerning the interpretations of one another's positions.

Just as the discussion of problems of contemporary military policy in the West has produced a rather standardized typology of possible types of warfare to help guide discussion, a similar classification scheme has arisen in the course of Soviet debate. The most prevalent Soviet typology was first definitively set forth by then Premier and Party leader, Nikita S. Khrushchev, in January, 1961.[2] This speech set forth a three-fold classification of possible military conflicts, based on considerations of the questions of the scope and destructiveness of the wars, as well as ideological judgments concerning the socio-political nature of possible conflicts. He established three

[1] Articles dealing with Soviet defense policy may be found in such Soviet publications as *Red Star*, *Communist of the Armed Forces*, *Military-Historical Journal*, *Kommunist*, *Pravda*, *Izvestia*, *International Affairs*, and the many books and pamphlets published by the Military Publishing House in Moscow.

[2] N. S. Khrushchev, "For New Victories of the World Communist Movement," *Kommunist*, No. 1, Jan., 1961.

The article is printed here for the first time.
Captain Warner is an Instructor in the Department of Political Science at the United States Air Force Academy. He attended the U.S. Naval Academy and Princeton University where he specialized in Soviet Studies. The views expressed in this article are the author's own and do not necessarily represent those of the United States Government.

major types of war: general-world war, lo-cal/limited war, and wars of national liber-ation. These categories provide the frame-work for the discussion of Soviet doctrinal and capabilities developments in this article.

WORLD WAR

Soviet military writings depict world war as a titanic, life and death struggle between the two fundamentally opposite systems of political, economic, and social order—capi-talism and socialism. World war is to be marked by global geographic scope, enor-mous destructiveness (primarily due to the inevitable employment of weapons of mass destruction) and the hostile involvement of the two contemporary superpowers, the Soviet Union and the United States. As such, this category partially coincides with that type of conflict defined in Western discussion as "general," "central," or "stra-tegic" war. However, whereas Western analysts have subdivided this category in accordance with various limitations in war-waging, thus creating subtypes of so-called "limited strategic war," the Soviets have steadfastly refused to acknowledge any such possibilities of limitation in their "de-claratory" pronouncements concerning world war.

Doctrinal Challenge and Response

At the dawn of the 1960's, the Soviet doctrinal depiction of world war was fun-damentally a conservative continuation of concepts developed during the course of World War II. Although in the latter 50's, Soviet military thinking had successfully escaped from the stultifying and constrain-ing mold of Stalinist military thought, which had virtually prohibited serious con-sideration of the impact of nuclear weap-ons on modern war, it had not fully acknowledged the revolutionary effects of these weapons and the newly emerging missile systems of delivery. These weapons systems were merely assimilated within a basic World War II strategic framework which envisioned possible world wars as protracted conflicts, characterized by large-scale theater of operations, aimed at the invasion and occupation of the enemy's territory. Soviet doctrine included the war-time initiation of large-scale mobilization, and required the combined operations of all combat arms and branches of the Soviet Armed Forces, the so-called "combined arms concept," as the prerequisites for "victory." In this general war scenario, the employment of nuclear weapons in either strategic strikes at the rear of the enemy or in support of immediate battlefield oper-ations, merely represented an additional factor to be reckoned with and adapted to, but one that did not overturn the fun-damental assumptions concerning the basic outline for the waging of the war or the prerequisites for victory. Additionally, So-viet strategic thought specifically rejected the possible decisiveness of any single type of weapon in modern warfare, stressing in contrast the need for "balanced" forces, both offensive and defensive systems and considerable diversity within these two categories.[3]

This planning scenario for world war was strongly challenged by Nikita Khrush-chev in January, 1960. In a major policy address before the Supreme Soviet, Khrush-chev fired the first salvo of a determined personal campaign to shift the basic strate-gic stance of the Soviet Armed Forces to a posture of finite deterrence.[4] Boldly asserting the superiority of Soviet missile forces, Khrushchev declared his intention to rely upon these forces as the backbone of Soviet deterrence and, should deterrence fail, he accorded them the decisive role in the waging of world war. Correspondingly, Khrushchev asserted that manned aircraft, naval surface forces and large standing armies had become obsolete, thus relegat-ing these elements to minor strategic roles. On this basis, he proposed a major reduc-tion in the manpower of the traditionally dominant Soviet land forces, a move de-signed to cut the total manpower of the

[3] See R. L. Garthoff's *Soviet Strategy in the Nu-clear Age* (New York: Praeger, 1958), and *The Soviet Image of Future War* (Washington, D.C.: Public Affairs Press, 1959).

[4] *Pravda*, 15 Jan. 1960.

armed forces from 3.6 to 2.4 million men over a two-year period.

Khrushchev's strategic initiative blatantly violated the "balanced forces" principle by declaring a Soviet shift to the previously proscribed reliance upon a single weapons system, the nuclear-armed missile. More significantly, he did so at the expense of the long-established and dominant theater ground forces. Similarly, he noticeably refrained from the previously mandatory homage to the time-honored axiom that the combined operations of all branches of the armed forces were required for victory. Instead, he referred only to the importance of massive strategic nuclear exchanges striking all strategic areas deep in the rear of the enemy, in the first minutes of the war, thus inferring that these would be adequate for military victory.

This sally by Khrushchev into the field of strategic doctrine marked the beginning of a prolonged conflict with various elements within the military establishment over a number of questions. This challenge helped provoke the emergence of significantly differing factions within the military itself. Western analyst Thomas Wolfe has identified three major groupings within the Soviet military: the "traditionalists," the "modernists" and a compromise, "centerist" group which managed to keep a foot in both of the other camps.[5] All three of these groupings appeared to accept the basic fact that the nuclear armed missile had wrought important changes on the military environment. Yet key differences were apparent in the widely varying viewpoints concerning just *how* drastically these products of the military-technical revolution had transformed the nature of a general war.

The modernists were prepared to follow Khrushchev's lead in claiming an enormous and decisive significance for these new weapons and the newly formed Strategic Rocket Forces which had been established as an independent service branch in December, 1959, even at the expense of the traditional forces. These thinkers stress-

ed the role of nuclear rocket forces in the deterrent confrontation with U.S. and, if deterrence failed, massive nuclear strikes in the initial period of war as the decisive elements in the waging of a world war. The traditionalists, in contrast, were compelled to acknowledge the existence and even significant importance of the new weapons systems but cautioned against the abrupt abandonment of previous doctrines and experience, preferring to defend the validity of the older concepts of continued reliance on a balanced force posture, the combined arms concept, and the need for multimillion-man ground armies for large-scale offensive theater operations. The centerists, whose views were in fact to gain official acceptance and are discussed below, chose to endorse a rather contradictory compromise solution, one marked by the acceptance of the arguments of both conflicting schools.

The resistance of the military in general to the radically modernist minimum deterrence solutions of Khrushchev and his few supporters within the military itself became evident in a number of newspaper and journal articles and military policy pronouncements. In all cases, the dialogue was waged by indirection, in the form of oblique criticisms conveyed via significant shifts in emphasis and the reassertion of the validity of some of the basic traditionalist arguments noted above. A particularly prominent example was the speech of Defense Minister Marshal Rodion Ya. Malinovsky before the Twenty-second Party Congress in October, 1961.[6]

Malinovsky, whose general line over the years was that of the centerist school, took this prestigious occasion to establish a position which varied significantly from the Khrushchev position. After paying his respects to his "Supreme Commander and Chief" Khrushchev, he proceeded to depict a considerably more dangerous international political and military environment for the Soviet state than that of Khrushchev, thus casting doubt on Khrushchev's optimistic "sufficient deterrent." While acknowledging the point that any

[5] T. W. Wolfe, *Soviet Strategy at the Crossroads* (Cambridge, Mass.: Harvard Univ. Press, 1964), pp. 6–7.

[6] *Pravda*, 25 Oct. 1961.

future world war would inevitably assume a nuclear rocket character, Malinovsky returned to the tried and true assertion that only the "combined action of all arms and services" could produce "final victory." The general tenor of his presentation was a classic example of dutiful homage to some of the ideas of the modernist school, while at the same time reintroducing some of the very issues Khrushchev had previously disposed of.

The final compromise doctrinal solutions to the Khrushchev-military interactions on deterrence and the nature of world war were evident in the two editions of the highly important work, *Military Strategy*. This jointly written volume on the entire gamut of military questions, edited by former Chief of the General Staff Marshal V. D. Sokolovsky, was first published in the summer of 1962 and revised and republished just thirteen months later.[7]

The hallmark of both editions is the inclusion of many ambiguous and contradictory statements that deal with the major issues of dispute. While some of this ambiguity might be explained as the natural product of a collectively written work, a more plausible explanation is that it accurately reflects the series of uneasy compromise solutions which were produced by the clash of opposing doctrinal perspectives. In regard to the basic outline of a possible world war, however, the depiction presented in the revised second edition of *Military Strategy* has remained fundamentally unaltered within subsequent declaratory pronouncements and writings. Although Soviet strategic capabilities, both offensive and defensive, have changed greatly in recent years, as will be discussed below, by the fall of 1963, a year prior to the fall of Khrushchev, the period of intense doctrinal dispute and transforma-

tion concerning the issues of basic deterrence and world war was largely completed.

Contemporary Soviet military writing depicts a possible world war as a decisive clash on a global scale between two opposing social and political systems, the imperialist and socialist camps. The war is to be marked by unprecedented destructiveness, directly attributed to the impact of thermonuclear weaponry delivered by various missile systems, which will inevitably be used.

The crucial considerations of the impact of these new nuclear rocket weapons upon such questions as the importance of surprise and the probable duration of such a war continue to produce accounts which display varying "modernist" or "traditionalist" emphases. Yet the composite picture in *Military Strategy* and subsequent writings is the centerist compromise of paying homage to both schools. In accordance with the modernist view, great emphasis is placed on the dangers of surprise attack and the potentially decisive results that might be gained from such a move. Since ideological propaganda constraints forbid even the declaratory consideration of a surprise first strike by the "peaceloving" Soviets, such intentions to unleash war in this manner are always attributed to the imperialists. The "solutions" to this threat have included the following repeated claims: a high level of vigilance and combat readiness of all Soviet forces; the survivability of Soviet forces due to the "damage limitation" combination of active defenses, antiaircraft and antimissile; the passive measures of missile launch site hardening, dispersal, camouflage and mobility; and a series of ambiguous assertions of the capability of the Strategic Rocket Forces to respond "in time" in order to "repulse" and "frustrate" the enemy by dealing them a "crushing retaliatory blow." (The latter claims appear to border on the endorsement of a preemptive Soviet strike.)

The contemporary world war scenario further reflects the modernist line by depicting the opening stages, measured in hours and perhaps even minutes, as a period dominated by the exchange of strategic

[7] This significant work produced a number of English translations of the first edition. The two most important of these are *Soviet Military Strategy*, with Analytical Introduction and Annotations by H. S. Dinerstein, L. Gouré, and T. W. Wolfe of the RAND Corporation (Englewood Cliffs, N.J.: Prentice-Hall, 1963), and *Military Strategy: Soviet Doctrines and Concepts*, with an Introduction by R. L. Garthoff (New York: Praeger, 1963).

nuclear rocket missile salvos. The volleys, at least for the Soviet's part, will be aimed at *all* strategic centers in the rear of the enemy, including both military (counterforce) and social, political, and economic (countervalue) centers, as well as the theater area force deployments of the enemy. The execution of these strikes is entrusted to the Strategic Rocket Forces with their missiles of varying range, to submarine launched ballistic and cruise missiles, and to some units of the Long Range Aviation Fleet, some of which will utilize "stand-off" air-to-surface missiles. During this same period, the extensive Soviet air defense (PVO) system will exert its efforts to repel the aircraft and missile attacks of the enemy.

In keeping with the "modernist" view, much is often said of the "decisive" significance of this initial period and the possibility that it might "predetermine" the entire outcome of the war. This might lead to the conclusion that a short war dominated by a single type of weapon had won full acceptance. Yet in the very next paragraph, most writings go on to resurrect the familiar "combined operations" dogma, insisting that "final victory" will require the annihilation of opposing ground forces and the occupation of the territory of the enemy as a result of massive frontal ground offensives.

The descriptions of these theater operations are reminiscent of the Soviet scenarios produced in the late fifties. Although the current versions include greater attention to the need for widely dispersed, rapidly advancing, largely armored, open frontal offensive formations in response to the predicted nuclear environment, as well as openly proclaiming the theater applications of operational-tactical nuclear weapons, this remains basically the classic combined arms offensive of yesteryear. Mention is also made of the important roles of airborne landings, at key political and military control points, the close air support of the tactical air armies, the importance of theater air defense, and the possible employment of amphibious operations on the seaward flanks. All of these elements supplement the operations of the deeply penetrating frontal armies, as they boldly seize the initiative and overrun the imperialist forces in areas contiguous to the Soviet Union.

In the noncontiguous zones, in addition to the massive nuclear rocket strikes on the enemy's homeland, operations consist of naval operations (surface, submarine, and land-based naval air), against the naval attack forces, carrier and missile launching submarines, and maritime logistic efforts of the enemy. A notable omission in these discussions is consideration of the problems of any large-scale invasion operations against noncontiguous opponents. This spotlights a Soviet doctrinal dilemma in that her main opponent, the United States, is such a noncontiguous country, and the Soviets' own repeated assertions preclude a "final victory" without the achievement of territorial occupation.

This secondary phase of a world war clearly indicates the successful resistance of the traditionalists and centerists within the military to Khrushchev's attempt at imposing a thoroughgoing strategic revolution. While admitting the supposed "decisiveness" of the initial period of nuclear rocket strikes of the Strategic Rocket Forces, they have maintained sizable and even "indispensable" roles for all of the other branches of the armed forces. In this effort they have even managed to establish grounds for considerable efforts and expenditures for continual force modernization, so that they might accomplish their assigned tasks in a difficult nuclear environment.

This rather lengthy depiction of simultaneous military operations on the largest possible scale represents the standard contemporary "line" on general war. It is important to note that the Soviets have never openly discussed the possibility of limitation in such a world war. Thus, they have failed to develop a doctrinal position of "controlled response" either in the terms of targeting discrimination for large-scale salvos or in the form of highly controlled "bargaining" or demonstrative strikes on single targets as discussed in the West un-

der the label of "limited strategic retaliation" or "controlled reprisal."[8]

Soviet spokesmen have gone to considerable length to attack specifically the city-
avoidance, counterforce approach espoused
by the U.S. Defense Department. Former
Defense Secretary McNamara's declaratory "proposal" of this approach at Ann
Arbor in June, 1962, elicited a direct response from the prestigious Marshal V. D.
Sokolovsky.[9] His critique and other subsequent discussions, including a rather detailed analysis of this strategic posture and
the requirements for its successful implementation which appeared in the revised
edition of *Military Strategy*, tend to emphasize a series of similar points. The concept is characterized as an attempt by the
U.S. to "legalize" the intentional resort to
nuclear war and designed to conceal a series
of concrete preparatory measures prior
to the unleashing of preventive war. In
addition, the Soviet commentators deny
the actual possibility of implementing such
a strategy in the face of the co-location of
strategic military forces and population
centers in both the Soviet Union and the
United States, as well as the enormous destructive radius of nuclear weapons, especially radioactive fallout. Finally, the
Soviets have declared their own intentions
to devastate not only military but also
economic, political, and population centers
in the rear of the enemy, and justified
these measures on the basis of the necessity
to eliminate the war-making capabilities
of the enemy and break his will to continue to fight. This, in fact, appears to
represent their only escape from the theoretical necessity of successful territorial occupation as the prerequisite for final victory
over the United States.

From an analytical standpoint, the Soviet declaratory insistence on a "counter-
center"[10] strategic posture appears quite

logical. Throughout the contemporary era,
despite various claims of capability superiority, the Soviets have remained strategically inferior to the military might of the
United States. In this position, as in the
case of the "independent" *force de frappe*
French deterrent, to maximize the deterrent value of its strategic forces, the inferior state will logically seek to communicate a maximum punishment image to its
adversary. Declaratory doctrinal insistence
upon such a posture helps communicate
this threat. In addition, Soviet writing
pointedly does *not* avoid the targeting of
counterforce targets, but rather refuses to
avoid the "countervalue" targets. It should
be remembered, however, first, that a concealed "operative" doctrine may, in fact,
include the option to go strictly "counterforce," a strategy which they have clearly
analyzed in some detail, should deterrence
fail. Additionally, in light of the enormous
qualitative and quantitative improvements
in Soviet offensive forces in recent years,
one might note that the possibility of some
future declaratory adoption of the counterforce strategy is not to be precluded.

WORLD WAR CAPABILITIES

General Purpose Forces. Since the post-
World War II outbreak of the Cold War,
a major factor in the Soviet deterrent threat
to the West has been its strong ground
force formations in Eastern Europe and the
western USSR and their menace to Western Europe. A major revision of unofficial
Western estimates of the actual magnitude
of this threat opened the 1960s. Previous estimates which had placed Soviet ground
force strength as high as 175 fully manned
divisions, the majority poised for European
operations, were replaced by new estimates
which pegged the total strength of the Soviet Army at 160 divisions, of which only
approximately one-half were maintained
in full combat-ready status.[11] Of these full

[8] See K. Knorr and T. Read, *Limited Strategic War* (New York: Praeger, 1962).

[9] Marshal V. D. Sokolovsky, "A Suicidal Strategy," *Red Star*, July 19, 1962.

[10] J. R. Thomas, "The Role of Missile Defense
in Soviet Strategy and Foreign Policy" in J. Erickson, ed., *The Military-Technical Revolution* (New
York: Praeger, 1966), p. 198.

[11] *The Military Balance, 1960–1961* (London:
The Institute of Strategic Studies, 1960). These
figures and all subsequent force level figures will
be drawn from this annual publication of the Institute of Strategic Studies unless specifically foot-
noted otherwise.

strength divisions only twenty-six were in Eastern Europe (20 in East Germany, 4 in Hungary, 2 in Poland) and forty in all of European Russia, west of the Urals. Subsequent studies of Soviet ground capabilities have even further reduced estimates to the point that one recent study[12] places the overall strength of the Soviet ground forces at 140 divisions, of which only 65 were rated at full combat-ready status, the remaining divisions being either in Category II, capable of being fully manned in a short period (40 divisions), or Category III, having only a cadre organization and thus requiring major reinforcement (35 divisions). It appears that the troop cuts initiated by Khrushchev were only successful in cutting overall strength in the armed forces to approximately 3.0 million men rather than his proposed 2.4 million mark. These reductions were primarily felt in the second line infantry formations in the Soviet interior, thus resulting in the maintenance of a sizeable number of divisions in non-combat-ready status.

According to unofficial estimates, the full strength components of the Soviet ground forces are organized into either 10,500-man motorized rifle divisions or 9,000-man tank divisions, both of which are endowed with exceptional mobility and high firepower, including tactical nuclear missiles, organic to the massive frontal formations. These theater forces are supported by large tactical air armies and integrated elements for air defense.

In the European theater, the Soviet forces, 26 divisions in Eastern Europe and 30 full strength divisions in European Russia, are supplemented by largely modernized and well-equipped divisions of the Warsaw Pact allies. The sixties have witnessed a concerted Soviet-led drive to radically improve the combined capabilities of the Warsaw Pact. Measures in this direction have included massive infusions of the most modern Soviet equipment, increased efforts at integrated planning and operations, and a number of large-scale combined field training exercises.

Strategic Offensive Forces. The backbone

of the strategic offensive forces in recent years, however, has become the nuclear armed ballistic missile of either the medium or intercontinental range. By 1962, the present order of battle, of 700–750 medium and intermediate range ballistic missiles with ranges of 1100 and 2100 miles respectively, predominantly covering targets in Western Europe, was emplaced in the Western USSR. The deployment of the ICBMs has been considerably more dynamic. From a small force of some 50 liquid fueled, first generation missiles in "soft," above-ground sites in the fall of 1961, the Soviet Strategic Rocket Troops have grown both qualitatively and quantitatively to a force variously estimated at either 450–475[13] or as high as 720.[14] The force includes approximately 140 of the more vulnerable first generation models, the remainder are the highly improved second and third generation types, protected by dispersion, camouflage and hardening measures. This tremendous buildup did not proceed at an even pace. After a somewhat restrained deployment rate in the 1960 to 1963 period, it appears decisions were made in the last Khrushchev year to greatly accelerate the development and deployment of the second and third generation systems. It was not until some time in the 1964–65 period that the Soviets achieved a posture which included a survivable, second strike capability, thus making the long-proclaimed condition of mutual deterrence a reality.

Soviet strategic offensive force capabilities also include components from the Long Range Air Force and the submarine fleet of the Soviet Navy. The airborne capabilities have remained fairly constant in the '60s and are concentrated in the form of a modest long-range bomber force, composed of some 200 "Bison" and "Bear" aircraft. These bombers have displayed stand off, air-to-surface missiles since 1961. Of the 200, approximately 50 are configured for a mid-air refueling role, which in conjunc-

12 *Ibid.*, 1967–68 (Sept., 1967), p. 6.

13 *Ibid.*, p. 5.
14 *Statement of Secretary of Defense Robert S. McNamara Before Senate Armed Services Committee on Fiscal Year 1969 Program and Budget* (Department of Defense, Washington, D.C., 22 Feb. 68), p. 55.

tion with provisions for staging and dispersal in the Arctic area, helps provide sufficient range to threaten targets throughout the U.S.

The sub-launched missile (SLM) force includes both ballistic and cruise missiles. Current estimates credit the Soviets with 40 ballistic missile carriers, carrying an average of three missiles/submarine. These subs include 10 nuclear powered boats and a few of these are assumed to have limited sub-surface launch capability, utilizing the 650 and 1500 mile range "Serb" missiles. This ballistic missile force is supplemented by cruise missile carriers, of which there are some 44, carrying an average of four missiles per submarine.[15] These subs have only a surface launch capability and a range of approximately 450 miles.

A final area of known offensive development has been Soviet attention to space delivery systems. Recent U.S. disclosures credit the Soviets with tests of a "Fractional Orbital Bombardment System" (FOBS), designed to utilize a low trajectory system in a partial earth's orbit for the delivery of nuclear warheads. Used either in a southern polar approach or over the north pole in a "tunnel" beneath the coverage of current U.S. warning systems, this weapons system might offer additional surprise by circumventing present warning arrangements. As such, this weapons system could be an additional threat to such "soft" vulnerable targets as air bases.

Strategic Defensive Forces. The Soviets have also exerted consistent and sizeable efforts to improve their strategic defensive capability. These developments have often been attributed solely to a traditional Russian fixation upon the defense of the Mother Russia. While this consideration, particularly in the light of the disastrous effects of the Nazi invasion during World War II, must be taken into account, a number of other factors appear to be important as well. First and foremost is the fact that the Soviets have found themselves faced with an adversary whose capability efforts and doctrine have concentrated on strate-

gic air attack as the primary means of deterring and waging war. In this situation, the first priority consideration throughout the fifties and sixties placed on developing and deploying air defense systems appears to have been a rational reaction to a very tangible U.S. threat. Additionally, the Soviet commitment to "balanced forces," with its specific denial of the efficacy of a single type of weapons system, favors the simultaneous development of offensive and defensive measures. Finally, the Marxist ideological perspective is grounded upon the dialectical process, which emphasizes an action-reaction, thesis-antithesis pattern of development, thus reinforcing the conviction that any offensive delivery system will inevitably call into being a countering method of defense.

The basic framework of the extensive and well-developed Soviet antiaircraft defenses was largely completed by the end of the fifties. Recent years have produced continual efforts at modernization including the development and deployment of new all-weather fighters and advanced surface-to-air missile (SAM) systems. The primary and most controversial development in this area, however, has been the Soviet efforts in the field of anti-ballistic missile (ABM) defense systems.

The Soviet ABM exertions have included three identifiably different systems. In the early 1960s, a defense system was deployed around Leningrad, employing a new aerodynamic SAM, the "GRIFFON," which was exhibited in the 7 November parade, in 1963. This deployment was apparently halted in 1965 when only partially completed. Recent evaluations have suggested that its effectiveness was restricted to supersonic aircraft, air-to-surface missiles and the possibility of a marginal capability against MRBM's such as the Thor, Jupiter or A-1 Polaris.[16]

A second system to which has sometimes been attributed an ABM capability is the so-called Tallinn Line system, so named because its major deployment is located in

---

[15] For somewhat different figures see Capt H. B. Sweitzer (USN) "Sovereignty and the SLBM," *U.S. Naval Institute Proceedings*, Sept., 1966.

[16] J. M. Mackintosh, quoted in *The Soviet Military Technological Challenge* (Washington, D.C.: Center for Strategic Studies, Georgetown University, 1967), p. 61.

the northwestern USSR, in an arc anchored in the west at the Baltic city of Tallinn. There have been other unconfirmed reports that Tallinn configuration sites have been spotted in the southern European USSR and in Central Asia, facing China.[17] Recent Western publicized evaluations have increasingly identified this as a new SAM system with strictly antiaircraft capabilities.[18]

The system which Western observers unanimously herald as an ABM deployment is located near Moscow. It has been slowly deployed over the last four to five years and after repeated, unconfirmed stories in the press in 1965 and 1966, it was formally acknowledged by Defense Secretary McNamara in November, 1966. The scanty, open-source material on it describes the system as one built around the "GALOSH" missile, a solid-propellant vehicle capable of high acceleration and high altitude intercept which was publicly displaced in the 7 November parade in 1964. Much has been written of its probable employment of the electro-magnetic pulse (EMP) or "zapp" effect in exoatmospheric interception of attacking vehicles. This "zapp" utilizes the extremely hot x-rays produced by the explosion of a nuclear warhead in space in order to either incinerate or degrade the effectiveness of incoming warheads.[19] The pace of deployment has been alternately described as continuous, gradual and restrained.

The Soviets have thus far failed to show serious interest in a reciprocal moratorium on ABM deployment.[20] The only major open press discussion of the question stressed the "specifically defensive form" of the weapon, thus ignoring the provocative and potentially offensive role of such measures in an era of mutual deterrence. It noted as well the Soviet desire to rely on active defense measures for their own defense should the "aggressive imperialists" initiate a nuclear war, thus providing for their own security and not relying on the "good will" of the other side as they charge a purely deterrent confrontation does.[21] The Soviets have insisted that any move toward a deployment moratorium must be part of a larger disarmament measure including reductions in both offensive and defensive systems.[22]

LOCAL WAR

The second major category of military confrontation offered by Khrushchev is a rather ambiguous one labelled "local war." In the original presentation of the typology, Khrushchev indicated these wars were wars among states and depicted them as small, limited and localized conflicts. The only example given was a short discussion of the brief British, French and Israeli conflict with Egypt in the fall of 1956. This was cited as a typical, unjust local war, unleashed by the imperialists in an attempt to maintain their ebbing prestige in the face of the decline of imperialism. Thus local wars were characterized as intergovernmental, involving limited territorial scope and being of an unjust socio-political character since they were initiated by the aggressive forces of imperialism.

However, a bit of confusion has been added in subsequent discussions due to the fact that any intergovernmental war of non-global nature falls within the "local" category. As a result, this category becomes extremely inclusive, even including the Soviet-predicted eventuality of a war between the members of the capitalist camp.

[17] H. Baldwin, *The New York Times*, Feb. 5, 1967, p. 1; *The Military Balance, 1967–1968*, p. 6.
[18] *McNamara Posture Statement, op. cit.,* p. 55.
[19] *The Soviet Military-Technological Challenge, op. cit.,* pp. 63–67; Rex Pay "Technical Implications of BMD," *Survival,* July, 1967, pp. 219–22.
[20] Ed. note: [In July, 1968, the U.S. and USSR agreed to discuss limitation of strategic offensive and defensive forces.]

[21] Marshal N. Talensky, "Antimissile Systems and Disarmament," *International Affairs,* January, 1965.
[22] Recent months have produced a number of articles, pamphlets, and books which focus upon Soviet strategic force capabilities. Three such studies are: The American Security Council's *The Changing Strategic Military Balance* (Washington, D.C.: U.S. Government Printing Office, 1967); W. Kintner, *Peace and the Strategy Conflict* (esp. the Appendix) (New York: Praeger, 1967); The Center for Strategic Studies (Georgetown University), *The Soviet Military Technological Challenge* (Washington, D.C.), Sept., 1967.

The broad nature of this classification has occasionally elicited criticism within Soviet discussion, in most cases involving the problem of the primary emphasis within the definition.[23] Should it stress the "unjust" and aggressive nature of these conflicts or the limitations in geographic scope as the determining factors?

LOCAL WAR DOCTRINE

In any case, the important questions are not so much those of emphasis in definition, but instead concern the Soviet doctrinal positions on the proper Soviet actions in the event of localized conflicts. In the early sixties, Soviet declaratory pronouncements were primarily directed at stressing the dangers of such warfare. They continually dwelled upon the danger of escalation into the destructive realm of nuclear world war, creating an image of near automaticity of such escalation, particularly should the superpowers, the U.S. and the USSR, both become involved. This "inevitability of escalation" formula appeared in both editions of *Military Strategy* in the following form:

One must emphasize that the present international system and the present state of military technology will cause any armed conflict to develop, inevitably, into a general war if the nuclear powers are drawn into it.[24]

Two other qualifications in addition to superpower involvement were repeatedly cited as influencing the escalation potential of a local conflict. Strong assertions of automaticity were included in the case of a localized conflict in Europe, particularly if any tactical nuclear weapons were used. Thus even in the days of strong stress on escalation automaticity, a differential hierarchy of dangerous local situations could be found within the Soviet defense literature.

Analysts have identified this escalation formula as a Soviet attempt to impress the

West with the dangers inherent in limited, local conflict. This so-called secondary or "counterdeterrent"[25] effort is designed to discourage any Western counterefforts in the face of Communist subversion or insurgency in peripheral areas. However, the key weakness in this approach has been the fact that such a threat of escalation is applied only should *both* superpowers become involved. As such, if the West, particularly the U.S., is the first to involve themselves in a local confrontation such as Viet Nam, the Soviets find that their own declaratory formulation inhibits their own counterinvolvement, in that the "last clear chance"[26] to avoid a nuclear conflagration belongs to them!

It is noteworthy that even in the early sixties when the general line in Soviet policy strongly stressed escalation dangers, Soviet military commentators often sounded a somewhat contradictory note by calling for military doctrinal consideration and the capabilities for waging the supposedly implausible local wars. As stated in the first edition of *Military Strategy*:

The armed forces of the socialist countries must be ready for small scale local wars which the imperialists might ignite. . . . Soviet military strategy must study the methods of waging such wars too, in order to prevent their expansion into a world war and in order to achieve a rapid victory over the enemy.[27]

In recent years there has been a rather muted but nevertheless steady and significant shift in Soviet doctrinal position on local war. The stress on escalation inevitability and automaticity has gradually diminished. During the same period, an increasing number of writings have referred to the need for the Soviet armed forces to prepare themselves for all types of military encounter short of world war. This trend toward the serious consideration of military conflict of a limited/local nature became evident as early as 1963 and has con-

[23] See for example Col.-Gen. N. A. Lomov, *Soviet Military Doctrine* (Moscow: Military Publishing House, 1963), p. 21; or Col. I. Sidelnikov, *Red Star*, September 22, 1965.

[24] V. D. Sokolovsky, ed., *Soviet Military Strategy* (Prentice-Hall edition), *op. cit.*, p. 299.

[25] R. L. Garthoff, *Soviet Military Policy* (New York: Praeger, 1966), Chapter 6.

[26] T. C. Schelling, *Strategy of Conflict* (New York: Oxford U. Press, 1960), p. 37.

[27] V. D. Sokolovsky (ed.), *op. cit.*, p. 288.

SOVIET MILITARY DOCTRINE AND CAPABILITIES

tinued until the present.[28] It should be noted, however, that despite the increasing frequency of references to the need for a Soviet local war doctrine and capability, emphasis on the danger of escalation in local conflicts continues. Thus the contemporary Soviet position on the question of local war, like that on general war, is in the last analysis, a rather ambiguous one. It includes both assertions of escalation dangers and conflicting claims of the capability for fighting and winning such local encounters.

LOCAL WAR CAPABILITIES

In the capabilities area, two basic categories of military forces are relevant to local conflict questions. On one hand, capabilities for the possible waging of localized conflicts in areas contiguous to the Soviet homeland are important. Secondly, developments in the sphere of the Soviet capability to project their military presence to noncontiguous points on the globe must be considered.

Contiguous Capabilities. Soviet "contiguous capabilities" are linked directly to the nature and organization of the massive Soviet theater forces which were discussed previously during the examination of Soviet world war forces. These modern and well-equipped forces are clearly of a "general purpose" nature and could be employed in a variety of configurations and environments. It should be noted that their firepower includes both conventional and tactical nuclear elements.

[28] See T. W. Wolfe, "Trends in Soviet Thinking of Theater Warfare Conventional Operations and Limited War," in J. Erickson (ed.), *op. cit.* Some relevant Soviet quotations on the necessity to maintain both nuclear and conventional capabilities include: Marshal V. Sokolovsky and Maj. Gen. M. Cheredichenko, "The Revolution in Military Affairs," *Red Star,* 25 Aug. 1964 and 28 Aug. 1964; Marshal R. Malinovsky, "The Soldier in Modern Warfare," Radio Volga Broadcast 8 Sept. 1964, cited in T. Wolfe, *The Soviet Military Scene,* RM-4913-PR (RAND, Santa Monica, Calif., June, 1966), p. 82; Col. Gen. S. Shtemenko, *Nedelya,* 31 Jan.–6 Feb. 1965; Col. Gen. N. Lomov, "The Influence of Soviet Military Doctrine on the Development of Military Art," *Communist of the Armed Forces,* November, 1965; Marshal I. I. Yakobovsky, "Ground Forces," *Red Star,* 21 July 1967.

It is noteworthy that the survival of these theater forces in the face of Khrushchev's "minimum deterrence" challenge of the early 60s was based not on the possibility of a "flexible response," local war employment, but rather on their continuing role in the waging of world war. Nevertheless, with the emerging doctrinal shift toward a modified Soviet version of flexible response, these forces now find themselves with an additional mission responsibility which they might employ as a powerful argument in their internal lobbying for budgetary support within the defense establishment.

Noncontiguous Capabilities. It is in the area of longer range, limited war capabilities that the Soviets have recently made especially significant gains. Most of these forces with potential global applications, like those of the forces suited for contiguous limited engagement, are also accorded roles in a world war. As noted, Soviet general war doctrine includes theater support roles for seaward flank amphibious operations as well as airborne operations. Thus it is impossible to say that such general purpose forces have been developed strictly as a result of a major Soviet policy decision to "go global." Nevertheless, the traditional capability constraints which had previously inhibited Soviet involvement in noncontiguous areas now appear to be at least signally breached.

Some of the primary developments of this nature have occurred in the Soviet Navy. In addition to a large-scale naval construction program which has produced a steady increase in Russian transport tonnage, the Soviets have made a number of advances in the area of marine-amphibious operational capabilities. The Naval Infantry, the Soviet version of the U.S. Marine Corps, which had been disbanded in the early 1950s, was resuscitated in 1964. Although its numerical strength remains quite small (it is estimated at approximately 10,000 men), its black-bereted personnel provide an elite cadre which might be used to establish a highly visible Soviet presence in far-flung areas. In addition, supporting transport capability in the form of newly constructed amphibious support ships and landing vessels, as well as the three helicopter carriers now either operational or under construction,[29] provide the Soviet Navy with a nominal capability for projecting Soviet power into coastal areas throughout the globe. This projective capability is further enhanced by the increasingly global scope of Soviet naval operations. This was demonstrated by the movement of a sizeable Soviet naval task force in the Mediterranean following the June War of 1967[30] and smaller oceanic operations in the Far East since the mid-sixties.

Another area of capabilities development with possible noncontiguous, local war applications is recent Soviet improvement in various air power techniques. The Soviet acquisition of the AN–22, a monstrous turboprop cargo aircraft, provides the Soviets with a workhorse vehicle for quick reaction, long-range, air logistic operations. The utilization of this plane as part of an impressive vertical envelopment demonstration which included a portion of the Soviets' considerable helicopter capability, other transport aircraft, and airborne troops at the July 1967 Air Show at Domodedovo, near Moscow, provided visible proof of Soviet interest in and mastery of this modern technique of force employment.[31]

Finally, in addition to hardware factors, Soviet military operations in the support of foreign military assistance programs and foreign policy commitments in the last decade have provided valuable experience for the personnel of the Soviet Armed Forces. Their involvement in both logistic support and advisor roles in such places as Indonesia, Algeria, Cuba, North Vietnam, and the Middle East has provided a firsthand acquaintance with the manifold problems of planning, supplying and conducting military operations in varied environments at great distances from the Soviet homeland.[32]

WARS OF NATIONAL LIBERATION

The third category of the Khrushchev typology, "wars of national liberation," is one heavily influenced by the Marxist–Leninist perspective. In contrast to the so-called unjust, aggressive local wars that are pictured as the product of evil imperialist machinations, these struggles are described as those which inevitably mark the rising of subjugated colonial peoples in their fight to cast off the yoke of imperialism. As such, these conflicts, which are forecast to continue to flare up as long as the imperialist system exists, are just struggles and thus deserve the support and encouragement of the leading nation in the Socialist Camp, the Soviet Union.

However, proceeding further into Soviet treatment of this category, a considerable amount of confusion is encountered. In Khrushchev's initial exposition of the classification scheme, he specifically sought to differentiate wars of liberation from local wars, on the grounds that only local wars were intergovernmental, i.e., "among states." Yet the struggle between an insurgent, native organization and a metropolitan, colonial ruler, whether in Kenya, Indochina, or Algeria, is, in fact, one between opposing national groups and in this sense, quite similar to an intergovernmental, local war. Similarly, such struggles appear to be simultaneously just wars of liberation for the insurgent forces and unjust, local wars of suppression for the colonial power. Thus the British conflict with the Mau-Mau in Kenya or the French efforts during the Algerian conflict, appear to fall equally well within both of the supposedly separate classification types.

Moving past this classification weakness, by stressing the supposedly internal nature of wars of national liberation, the Soviets have constructed for themselves a definitional trap which proscribes active Soviet participation in such liberation struggles. For should the Soviets become active com-

[29]W. Beecher, "Third Soviet Carrier Believed on the Ways," *New York Times*, 13 Feb. 1968, p. 10.

[30] C. Sterling, "The Soviet Fleet in the Mediterranean," *Reporter*, 14 Dec. 1967, pp. 14–18.

[31] "Soviets Demonstrate Vertical Envelopment Capability with the AN-22," *Aviation Week and Space Technology*, August 14, 1967, pp. 52–53.

[32] See T. W. Wolfe, *The Soviet Quest for More*

Globally Mobile Military Power, RM-5554-PR (Santa Monica, Calif.: RAND Corporation, Dec., 1967).

batants, such an action would immediately transform the conflict from a national liberation struggle into a local war, that is, a war between states.

Soviet doctrinal discussion consistently pledges the Soviet Union to all possible means of support for wars of national liberation. Yet such discussions consistently leave the exact nature of this promised support in vague terms. In consonance with the definitional trap noted above, if the struggle is to maintain its liberation character, the primary fighting forces themselves must be indigenous to the area being liberated. This very fact narrows the range of possible Soviet support obligations to efforts of material and political support. If troops are to be proffered, without transforming the liberation war into a local conflict, this must be done under the guise of "volunteers," a method which seeks to maintain the fiction of non-governmental involvement.

The Soviet doctrinal positions and actions in support of liberation struggles have been most studiously examined and criticized, not by members of the adversary imperialist camp but rather by elements within the Marxist–Leninist camp itself— in particular, the Chinese Communists. One of the most severe bones of contention between the two major Communist powers has been the degree of emphasis to be placed on the fomenting and support of revolutionary liberation struggles. While both leadership groups stress the inevitability of such conflicts and pledge their respective support, the Chinese demand an aggressive posture which calls for a maximally offensive stance, including the manipulation of Soviet military might in an effort to hasten the decline of imperialism.[33]

The actual Soviet performance in the support of wars of national liberation has been nominal. Although Soviet leaders were eager to claim important roles in the successful liberation struggles of the Algerian FLN, Castro's Cuban rebels, and the Viet Minh, in none of these cases was Soviet military support essential to the victory of the insurgents. Soviet behavior in fact appears to somewhat justify the basic thrust of Chinese charges of timidity, in that Soviet concern to avoid risky confrontation with the West appears to have played an important role in restricting Soviet support efforts.

A prominent example of Soviet behavior relative to national liberation struggles is found in the examination of Soviet actions in reacting to the evolving crisis in Viet Nam. On the definitional side, the Soviets clearly perceive the struggle of the Viet Cong and its National Liberation Front for control of South Viet Nam as a national liberation struggle aimed against the current regime in South Viet Nam and their imperialist American sponsor. Yet this war produced rather limited Soviet political and military support until the sizable buildup of U.S. forces had begun to transform the struggle into a quasi-local war.

The major change in the level of Soviet participation came after U.S. air attacks on North Viet Nam transformed the entire conflict by adding a full-fledged intergovernmental local war in the North to the continuing liberation struggle in the South. Nevertheless, Soviet moves since then have remained confined to large-scale support activities, ranging from the provision of a vast and sophisticated air defense system, including the dispatch of limited numbers of Soviet military personnel to operate these components and train native operators, to the supply of various rocket and armor components for transfer to the South.[34] Even when faced by a blatant attack on a fellow Socialist state, the closest the Soviets have come publicly to threatening any national involvement in the military struggle has been a couple of pointed references to the possibility of sending "volunteers" to aid in the struggles in South East Asia.[35]

---

[33] R. L. Garthoff, *Soviet Military Policy,* Chapter 11.

[34] A. Parry, "Soviet Aid to Viet Nam," *The Reporter,* 12 Jan. 1967.

[35] Soviet suggestions of the possibility of sending of "volunteers," if requested by North Viet Nam, include a comment by L. Brezhnev (*Pravda,* March 24, 1965) and participation in a joint Warsaw Pact communiqué which proffered a similar offer in July, 1966.

Soviet capabilities for national liberation support or participation are clearly
the same ones discussed previously in the
context of noncontiguous local wars.
Growing Soviet maritime transport, airlift, and amphibious capabilities are all
potentially applicable for Soviet commitment in the support of liberation struggles.
Thus, as in the case of local war, these capabilities now give the Soviets an increased
potential for global involvement. However,
a major foreign policy reversal, which
would include a marked dimunition of
Soviet apprehension over the dangers of
escalation and thus the conviction that
support of revolutionary liberation wars
would not endanger the security of the
Soviet Union itself, would be necessary for
any drastic departure from the conservative pattern of support that has been evident to date.

CONCLUSION

The sixties have undoubtedly produced
significant change on the Soviet military
scene. As their military writings continuously repeat, the Soviets claim to be
fully aware of the ongoing "revolution in
military affairs" wrought by the appearance of thermonuclear armed weapons
systems and the dynamic changes produced
by continuing technological innovation
and discovery. However, their basic declaratory military doctrine accepted these new
developments without fully abandoning the
precepts of the past. Instead, the doctrine
includes the confusing coexistence of such
modern concepts as deterrence and escalation along with the traditional consideration of large-scale battlefield operations
designed to defeat the enemy in the classical theater clash of massive land armies.
The final doctrinal product, with its compound of modern and traditional factors,
provides a sufficiently ambiguous series of
authoritative assertions to allow rather flexible interpretation by political or military
spokesmen.

In the capabilities area, the last decade
has been marked by a significant buildup in
Soviet military power. Although subject to
varying development rates within the time
period, the most recent years have seen
increases in Soviet capabilities in strategic
and conventional weapons systems.

These force buildups have unquestionably absorbed sizeable expenditures of
limited Soviet resources. Thus, the decisions
to undertake and continue such costly
programs represent major policy commitments by the Kremlin leadership. However, the fundamental implications of
these capabilities improvements for future
Soviet foreign policy moves are not easily
deciphered.

At a conservative minimum, the current
Soviet military posture provides the Kremlin leadership with an impressive storehouse of military power. This supply includes emerging capabilities for a wide
variety of contingency applications ranging from impressive nuclear rocket might
to global projective forces. As a result, the
Soviets have broadened their range of military options, providing themselves with
the potential for many alternative courses
of action in their own escalation spectrum.

The actual decisions to apply military
means aggressively on the international
scene are not directly derivable from capabilities analysis. Clearly, the decisional
matrix underlying future Soviet patterns of
policy and force employment will include a
myriad of factors including Soviet perceptions and evaluations of opportunities,
possible and probable Western responses,
as well as the international balance of
military capabilities.[36] Conservative concern with the security of the Soviet state
itself will most certainly be weighed
against great power and ideological aspirations for expanded political influence in the
world. From the perspective of the study
of contemporary Soviet military doctrine
and capabilities, one may merely conclude
that Soviet decisionmakers are being provided with an expanded catalogue of military options which add considerable flexibility to Soviet policy choices.

---

[36] For some conflicting interpretations of possible
Soviet foreign policy postures with varying project-
ed military capabilities see T. W. Wolfe, *The
Soviet Military Scene*, Part VII; Wm. Kintner, *op.
cit.*, Chapter 5; or R. L. Garthoff, *Soviet Military
Policy*, Chapters 6 and 10.

CHINA'S MILITARY POSTURE

BY SIN MING CHIU

The paroxysms of the past year gave every indication that the entire fabric of Chinese society was seriously disrupted and that the economic gains Peking had made since 1949 had been nullified. Yet on June 17, 1967, a hydrogen bomb was exploded at least a month ahead of schedule, touching off anxious speculation that Peking might test an intercontinental ballistic missile before the end of the year. This seeming paradox has made estimates of China's military capabilities extremely hazardous.

It is generally agreed that the People's Liberation Army (P.L.A.) is the largest conventional force in the world.[1] In the past ten years, the force level has remained at about 2.3 million men, excluding the half million men in the public security forces whose functions are best described as those of a national police. This force is backed up by tens of millions in the partially-armed militia.

Since 1949, the P.L.A. has undergone at least two significant organizational and doctrinal changes. First, during and after the Korean War, it was completely reequipped and its table of organization was revised with Soviet assistance. This modernization process was largely completed by 1956. Then, shortly thereafter, the trend was reversed because of internal problems arising from the professionalization of the officer corps, the subsequent withdrawal of Soviet aid, the priorities given to nuclear development, and the costly updating of conventional weapons. In 1960, the military committee of the Central Committee (C.C.) decided to revive the revolutionary traditions of the P.L.A. instead of continuing to modernize it. The Guideline for National Defense Construction for 1961 adopted by the committee made it clear that the weapons then in use "would not be replaced until they are worn beyond repair."[2]

There is no evidence that the conventional-technical level of the P.L.A. has since been raised significantly. In fact, though Peking is reportedly self-sufficient in standard weapons, including light artillery, it is doubtful that it is prepared to expend any effort to raise the physical quality of its infantry until its industries can manufacture heavy and complex equipment or until the nuclear program is sufficiently developed to permit the diversion of funds for conventional armament.

The Chinese Communist air force is the third largest in the world, boasting about 2,500 planes. It is believed that most of them are obsolescent MIG–15's and MIG–17's. However, as early as 1957, P'eng Te-huai, then defense minister, hinted that China was producing her own jet fighters that were superior to the MIG–17's.[3] It is reasonable to assume that her engineers and technicians are capable of copying the latest Soviet types. MIG–21's have been sighted by American and Nationalist Chinese pilots over the China coast. At the present time, the air force is still severely handicapped by the shortage of fuel, and the consequent inadequacy of pilot training has been repeatedly demonstrated by

[1] See Ralph L. Powell, "Peking Army Ruled From Party HQ," *The Christian Science Monitor*, May 25, 1966; and Samuel B. Griffith, *The Chinese People's Liberation Army* (New York: McGraw-Hill, 1967), Ch. 13.

[2] General Political Department, Chinese People's Liberation Army, *Kung Tso Tung Hsün* (news release) No. 7, Feb. 1, 1961, p. 7.

[3] *Chinese World* (San Francisco), July 30, 1957.

Reprinted by permission from *Current History*, September, 1967.

Mr. Chiu, a research associate at Princeton University in 1960–1961, has taught at the University of Utah, the University of Delaware, and the University of Southern California. The author of articles for professional journals and monographs, he is editor of "Topics on Communist China" (Salt Lake City: University of Utah Institute of International Studies, 1962).

the kill-ratio of better than ten to one in favor of the Nationalists in skirmishes over the Taiwan Straits. The bomber force is believed to be mostly of World War II vintage and has limited operational capabilities.

Although the People's Republic of China has a young but capable shipbuilding industry, the navy is still essentially a coastal defense force, with about 200 craft of different sizes. The flagship is a 5,400-ton light cruiser which defected from the Nationalists in 1949. The cost in building a seagoing navy will remain prohibitive for the regime in the years ahead, and it can be expected at this point that Peking will concentrate instead on less expensive submarines of which there are reportedly 40, some equipped to fire short-range missiles above water. The navy also has an air arm, of unknown quantity.

NUCLEAR DEVELOPMENT

The most significant development—the one that causes the greatest anxiety—is the rapid advance made by China in nuclear weapons. In less than three years, six tests have been conducted, including a nuclear-tipped short-range missile and a hydrogen bomb—all this by a country that only a few years ago was believed to lack all the requirements for such accomplishments. This success can be attributed to the regime's organizational skills, the high priorities given to the program, and a core of brilliant scientists. It has been said that progress in the nuclear field could be made only at the expense of the economy, which was already threadbare. However, it should be remembered that: (1) China is not a typical underdeveloped country, as Professor John Lindbeck has pointed out,[4] because although her per capita income is low her total productivity places her among the top ten industrial powers; (2) the nature of her state organization permits great flexibility and a wide range of options in regard to the concentration or allocation of resources without restraints imposed by

either public opinion or higher priorities; and (3) Chinese scientists have benefitted from the experience (including the mistakes) of other nuclear powers and therefore could cut corners. China has consistently claimed that she would never be the first to use nuclear weapons and has pressed for destruction of all stockpiles. This is a natural position for a fledgling nuclear power especially when its delivery system is at best still primitive. United States defense authorities estimate that China will not be a threat to the United States until the mid-1970s. Whether Peking will acquire a greater sense of responsibility as it achieves full nuclear status is a question of consuming importance.

The most unique feature of the P.L.A. is its political control system.[5] Since its inception in 1927, the army has been an arm of the party; and through a hierarchy of political officers parallel to the professional staff all officers and men have been subjected to intensive indoctrination in the party's ideology, through organized discussions and more often through what appeared to be cultural and recreational activities. Despite the difficulties inherent in the system—such as the inevitable conflict between the political and professional staffs— it has been an important contributory factor to the army's high morale.

In the years after Lin Piao replaced P'eng Te-huai as defense minister, the political control system was strengthened for various reasons. First, it is in the nature of communist dialectics that the P.L.A., like other institutions in the country, should reflect the economic system. By 1959, the economy had moved from the cooperatives to a "higher form" of collectivization—the communes. Not only did the P.L.A. need education to accept this change, but it had to reflect the new social relationships that inevitably resulted from the change in the means of production. Lin Piao observed in 1959 that "quite a number of comrades lack a high degree of socialist consciousness, though they have certain aspirations

[4] John M. H. Lindbeck, "Chinese Science: It's Not a Paper Atom," *The New York Times Magazine*, January 8, 1967, p. 38.

[5] See S. M. Chiu, "Political Control in the Chinese Communist Army," *Military Review*, August, 1961.

for socialism."[6] He added that the country was entering the stage of socialist construction, but that many people remained in the period of bourgeois democratic revolution.

Second, the professionalization of the officer corps in the preceding period had produced certain manifestations inimical to the interests of the party. If uncorrected, these tendencies, including what the communists called a "purely military point of view," might eventually divest the army of its "party character."

Third, as mentioned above, at about this time the military committee of the party decided to "freeze" the development of conventional arms in favor of a policy of selective development. Therefore, the army had to be "revolutionized" through political education in the invincible traditions of the P.L.A.

DISCONTENT IN THE P.L.A.

Finally, from 1960 to 1962, China suffered heavily from natural disasters and from the consequences of the Great Leap. Discontent was widespread among the soldiers, particularly those whose families were in afflicted areas.

To cope with all these problems, Lin Piao launched a campaign in 1960 to produce so-called Four Good Companies throughout the P.L.A. Ostensibly to strengthen the basic units in the army, the aim of the campaign was to tighten the party's control, and to encourage retrenchment. At the end of the year, 5,000 companies were said to have earned the distinction of Four Good Companies, and the campaign was adjudged so successful that it has been renewed every year up to the present time. One outgrowth of the campaign has been the organized army-wide "creative study and application of the writings of Chairman Mao," which, by 1966, had become "the highest instruction for all work in the army."

To insure the success of the political control system, political attitude was made

the sole criterion for promotion in 1964 in an effort to cultivate a generation of "successors to the revolution." In the celebrated ninth company of a certain unit, 21 soldiers were said to have been promoted to cadres by the end of 1966 on the basis of their achievements in studying and applying Mao's writings.[7]

CULTURAL REVOLUTION

There is no doubt that Mao effectively controls the P.L.A., and his control was the decisive factor in the latest and most serious upheaval in China, the Cultural Revolution.[8] Starting as a seemingly harmless and routine campaign against nonproletarian ideas in art and literature in late 1965, the revolution erupted into a multi-faceted movement engulfing the entire party and army by the second half of 1966. The nature of this implosion is outside the scope of this article, but it may be pointed out that its roots can be traced to the incipient disagreement between Chairman Mao and a group headed by President Liu Shao-chi over economic policies in 1958–1959 when Mao was allegedly forced to relinquish his position as chief of state. For the next three years, it now appears, the party was directed by Liu with the support of Teng Hsiao-p'ing, the general secretary of the party. When Mao returned to more active duties in 1964 he found that the party, particularly in economic matters, had been impregnated with "bourgeois ideas and practices," and the city of Peking itself was completely dominated by its mayor, P'eng Chen, another ally of Liu, making it prudent on Mao's part to leave for Shanghai in the middle of 1965.

What Mao did in Shanghai is not known, but it is a strange coincidence that the first salvo of the Cultural Revolution was fired in Shanghai in November, 1965, against

6 Lin Piao, *March Ahead Under the Red Flag of the Party's General Line and Mao Tse-tung's Military Thinking* (Peking: Foreign Languages Press, 1959), p. 5.

7 Chen Chin-yuan, *"Pa Lien Tui Chien She Cheng Mao Tse Tung Ssu Hsiang Ti Hao Hsueh Hsiao"* ("Turn the companies into good schools for Mao Tse-tung's thought"), in *Hung Ch'i*, No. 13, October 1, 1966, p. 22.

8 For a complete survey of the Cultural Revolution, see Gene T. Hsiao, "The Background and Development of 'The Proletarian Cultural Revolution,'" in *Asian Survey*, June, 1967, pp. 389–404.

Wu Han, historian and playwright. Soon after the attack on Wu Han, Lo Jui-ch'ing, chief of the P.L.A. general staff, quietly disappeared from the public scene.[9] It was known that at least since 1959 Lo had been a supporter of Liu Shao-chi; and although he had also long been associated with Lin Piao he was nevertheless opposed to Lin's military line of "putting politics in command" to the detriment of professionalism. A Red Guard poster later charged him with the "crime" of having sponsored an All-P.L.A. Military Tournament in 1963 which emphasized technical skills at the expense of politics. Again, in May, 1965, he had obliquely suggested in a speech commemorating the defeat of Nazi Germany that in the interest of the revolution it was not impossible to negotiate with the imperialists. This speech brought upon him the indefensible charge of revisionism and the stigma of being anti-party and anti-Mao. It has even been suggested that Lo was an accomplice in a plot directed by Liu, Teng, and P'eng to stage a Hungarian-type *coup* against Mao in February, 1966.[10]

At any rate, P.L.A. involvement in the Cultural Revolution began with the army newspaper (*Chieh Fang Chun Pao*) editorial on April 18, 1966, which pledged the P.L.A.'s support of the revolution and enjoined the entire army to take an active part "to raise still higher the banner of Mao's thought." It is not certain what happened in the several months prior to the eleventh plenum of the Eighth Central Committee held in the first part of August, 1966. According to a Yugoslav source, Liu and his friends were busy conspiring to convene the meeting on July 21 with the intention of impeaching Mao, who was still in Shanghai.[11] As Liu's power lay in his control of the party bureaucracy, he could have mustered enough members to do so.

As the delegates began to arrive in Peking in mid-July, Lin Piao sent his troops into the city to take over the mass media and force the reorganization of the Peking party committee headed by P'eng Chen. According to the same source, Liu responded by asking Lo Jui-ch'ing to order Commander of the Sinkiang military district General Wang En-mao to send his units to the capital. Sensing the seriousness of the situation, Lin reinforced the Peking garrison and dispatched other units to intercept General Wang.

With the plot thus foiled, Mao flew back to Peking on July 18. The party meeting was rescheduled for August 1. Supported by the P.L.A. and Lin Piao, Mao personally led the criticism of Liu and Teng at the meeting which then adopted a 16-point resolution to serve as the guideline for the further development of the Cultural Revolution.[12] This was clearly a victory for Mao. After the meeting Mao could pursue the revolution in the name of the party and the reorganized Politburo and military committee.

SHIFTS IN COMMAND

The party plenum also reshuffled military personnel on three levels. On the highest level—the military committee—Lo Jui-ch'ing and Ho Lung were dropped as secretary-general and second vice-chairman respectively. Added to the committee were three former marshals of the P.L.A. long inactive because of age or disfavor: Yeh Chien-ying, Hsu Hsiang-ch'ien and Liu Po-ch'eng. The first two were also elevated to membership in the Politburo. On the second level, two vice ministers and the director of the administrative office of the ministry of national defense were removed, as were the chief of operations of the general staff, two deputy directors of the general political administration, the director of rear services, the commissar of the navy, and two deputy commanders of the air force. On the third level—the regional commands—the "purges" were effected by the "revolutionary masses" under

9 Chiang Chih-nan, *"Chung Kung Chung Ti 'Ke Ming Tsao Fan' Hsing Shih"* ("The situation of seizure of power in the Chinese communist army") in *Studies on Chinese Communism*, Vol. 1, No. 2, February, 1967, p. 15.

10 *Ibid.*, p. 16.

11 Cited by Cheng Chi, *"Wen Hua Ta Ke Ming Ti Ling Yi Mien Kuan"* ("Another view of the Great Cultural Revolution"), in *Jen Wu Ping Lun* (Vancouver), No. 90, March 15, 1967, pp. 8–9.

12 Resolution in *Hung Ch'i*, No. 10, August, 1966.

each command by criticism, mass rallies and posters in the manner of the Red Guards. Those who were ousted included the commanders of the Chengtu, Lanchow, Sinkiang, Honan, Inner Mongolia and Chekiang military districts.

It is interesting to note that almost all the purged military leaders were long associated with Deputy Premier Ho Lung, some from the days of guerrilla warfare in the late 1920s. Probably many of them rose to high positions in the army through the influence and patronage of Ho. Over the years, these men, like Wang En-mao, had been stationed in remote and uninviting areas and it is not inconceivable that they had become disenchanted and responsive to conspiratorial suggestions. Since 1949, Ho Lung himself has not held any position of real consequence. He was assailed by the Red Guards in Peking as a bandit chieftain, which he was before he joined the communists. By the same token, while Ho's henchmen were being purged, Mao and Lin felt constrained to rehabilitate or bring out of retirement such erstwhile heroes as Hsu Hsiang-ch'ien and Lui Po-ch'eng, possibly to appease their own followers. How long they will stay in the limelight remains to be seen. All these developments suggest that factionalism could very well have been involved in the purges.

ANTI-MAO FORCES

Until the end of 1966, a reconciliation between Mao and Liu still seemed possible inasmuch as Liu had confessed his errors at a party meeting called by Mao in October. By December, however, anti-Mao forces had re-emerged and mounted a furious counterattack, organizing their own version of the Red Guards and putting up their own posters and using Maoist slogans. Even some P.L.A. units, notably in Canton, discovered some anti-Maoist elements within their own ranks. Clashes were reported in wide areas and economic activities were disrupted by sabotage. Surprisingly restrained up to this point, Mao ordered the "suppression of and seizure of power from those in authority following

the capitalist road" in the early days of January, 1967.

ROLE OF THE P.L.A.

Apparently, Mao had hoped that the P.L.A. would be kept out of the revolution, which he wanted to be a revolution from below. Also, as Professor Franz Schurmann has pointed out,[13] by using the P.L.A., violence would escalate and the chances for compromise would diminish. After Mao's call to seize power, "rebel" groups mushroomed in all provinces and cities, all economic enterprises and educational insitutions that were supposedly controlled by those "taking the capitalist road."

Those P.L.A. units which were stationed in the areas were alerted by their political departments, and political officers were sent to establish liaison with the "rebel" groups. In most instances, Maoist "rebel" groups seized power from "those in authority following the capitalist road" without the direct support of the P.L.A., but always in the presence of fully-armed P.L.A. patrols. In a few cities, such as Kweichow and Heilungkiang, where the "reactionaries" put up stubborn resistance, the P.L.A. took more direct action.[14] After power passed to the hands of the "rebels," a new provisional organ of power—the revolutionary committee—was established, based on an alliance of revolutionary leading cadres (meaning the pro-Mao elements among those in authority), members of the revolutionary masses and the P.L.A.

It is still early to speculate on the true significance of the Proletarian Cultural Revolution. Past patterns suggest that as the turmoil subsides, radical economic changes or new forms of political power reflecting the dominance of the proletariat may emerge (perhaps something like the urban communes). Regardless of the outcome, the P.L.A., which played a key role, will perhaps emerge more powerful than ever.

[13] *The New York Review*, October 20, 1966, pp. 18–25.
[14] See *Survey of the China Mainland Press* (Hong Kong: U.S. Consulate), No. 3924, April 24, 1967, pp. 13–18; No. 3926, April 12, 1967, pp. 8–12.

ARMY AND PARTY

For the P.L.A., should Mao and Lin succeed in the Cultural Revolution, it will mean the perpetuation of the "proletarian line of army building." The army will remain under the control of the party and serve it as an instrument of proletarian power. Moreover, it will be guided by Mao's military thought, which emphasizes man rather than weapons, and political consciousness rather than technical skill. On the basis of recent developments, the following major trends may be noted:

1. In the relentless "politicization" of the P.L.A. after 1958, an evolving doctrine was apparent. If Peking was determined to become a nuclear power, it had few options in military policy. China could choose between a simultaneous development of both nuclear and conventional arms, or she could opt for a crash nuclear program while improvising a defense doctrine based on the use of existing conventional power to maximum advantage. From the commune movement to the Proletarian Cultural Revolution, with their military implications, it is evident that China chose the latter course, and any opposition was removed in the recent purges of top political and military leadership. While the nuclear program, carefully shielded from day-to-day political activities, has moved ahead rapidly, increasing attention has been given to "people's war" fought by regular armies with the support of a massive militia, in the manner in which the Chinese Communist armies of the past fought the Japanese and the Nationalists. China cannot afford to risk destruction of her nuclear installations, but in case of an invasion the Chinese maintain that the invader would be "drowned in the human sea of 700 million." This appears to be Peking's doctrine in the present transitional period until its nuclear weapons system is operational.

2. If the above is valid, then Peking's military posture is defensive, for the kind of War that Mao's concepts envisage can hardly be waged effectively in aggressive action. However, in Mao's view, this is strategic defense, analogous to the first phase of China's war against Japan, in which guerrillas were constantly engaged in *offensive* action against the enemy in tactical situations. By extension, wars of national liberation may be regarded as tactical offensives which, according to Lin Piao,[15] must be fought and won by the indigenous people themselves just as the guerrillas had to rely on their own resources.

3. Until China becomes a full-fledged nuclear power her leaders will continue to deprecate the atom bomb. The very nature of "people's war," according to the Communists, precludes the use of weapons of mass destruction. However, such derogation of nuclear weapons should not obscure Mao's injunction that "in guerrilla warfare the guerrillas do not remain as such permanently but become gradually regularized as the war progresses." Again he has said: "We fight with whatever weapons we have; the type of war we fight depends on the type of weapons at our disposal."[16] It is clear that the current level of Peking's technology determines its doctrine, and its current doctrine reflects the current stage of its weapons development.

[15] Lin Piao, "Long Live the Victory of People's War," in *Hung Ch'i*, No. 10, September, 1965, pp. 1–28.
[16] Mao Tse-Tung, *"Lun Ch'ih Chiu Chan"* ("On Protracted War"), *Selected Works of Mao Tse-tung*, I (Peking: People's Publishing House, 1951), 440.

CHINESE VIEWS ON ESCALATION

BY DAVIS B. BOBROW

A focus of the Chinese régime's views as expressed in their own publications enables us to see two important differences between Chinese and Western attitudes on escalation. Peking spokesmen place much greater emphasis on psychological and political operations as forms of escalation and as instruments to manage escalation. Their statements also differ in their positive evaluation of asymmetrical forms of escalation, that is, of wars where military escalation by China's enemy is not matched either by the People's Republic of China or her proxies.[1]

Escalation is here used in a broad sense to include expansion of war in geographical, formally military (troops and weapons), and political ways. When views are attributed to "Chinese," I mean views expressed as being "correct" in China mainland publications. No assumption is made that these are common to all Chinese officials.

LEADERSHIP MODEL

The Chinese leadership assesses the desirability and feasibility of particular forms of escalation in terms of their general policy objective and the intermediate ends which they believe that this entails. Simply, the Peking régime wants to become the leader of the developing countries at the expense of the United States and the Soviet Union. The leadership model which the Chinese hope to implement is that of suzerainty, used by Imperial China, rather than that of the "baggage train" governments, used by the USSR in Eastern Europe after World War II. We can note that this model does not neces-

[1] Unless otherwise indicated, all references to China in this article are to Communist China—the People's Republic of China.

sarily imply that the Chinese have to escalate foreign wars to the point of occupying contested territory.

THREE IMAGES

To attain its foreign policy goal, the Peking régime simultaneously seeks to discredit and exclude other foreign influences—whether Washington, Moscow, or New Delhi—from target societies, and to persuade key groups in these societies to admire Chinese policies and accomplishments. Accordingly, Chinese Communist Party leaders try to communicate three complicated images to the developing nations.

The first is that China's opponents are both militarily weak and dangerous. The Chinese expect this image to suggest that the United States can be expelled from Southeast Asia, but that Chinese militancy and support are needed to cope with the United States.

The second image is that China's opponents are both politically domineering and devious. To the extent that this image is accepted, leaders of the developing nations will feel the need to minimize involvement with these enemies and to reject their offers of protection and assistance.

The third image, and perhaps the most complicated, is that of the People's Republic of China. The Chinese want their own and foreign populations to perceive the mainland as both backward and weak, and modern and strong. The first pair of attributes is meant to suggest that many developing nations have problems similar to those of China, and that China starts at a disadvantage relative to the superpowers. The second pair is meant to suggest that China has and will continue to manage these problems and disadvantages impres-

Reprinted by permission from *Military Review,* January, 1966.

Mr. Bobrow is a member of the Director's Division of the Oak Ridge National Laboratory in Tennessee, and the author of many articles on Chinese military affairs.

sively. The morals which the régime wants its own people to draw are the need for abstinence and effort and the inevitability of domestic improvement and international stature. The morals which the régime wants its foreign audience to draw are the helpful relevance of the Chinese experience to national development and the ability of the Peking régime to hurt those who oppose Chinese policy.

CAPABILITY ESTIMATES

Chinese perceptions of their capability provide some insight into how and why they believe they can manage escalation and its consequences. The Chinese base their capability estimates on three maxims:

1. Political and psychological assets are inseparable from military capabilities. Accordingly, the ability of the People's Republic of China to maintain the level of escalation its officials prefer cannot be established without considering political and psychological factors.

2. Capability estimates tend to be overly optimistic.

3. Professional officers tend to escalate and to prefer the total use of their troops and weapons.

The last two maxims suggest that Chinese leaders tend to downgrade the capability estimates of their defence establishment.

Peking officials are acutely aware of the limited Chinese nuclear and conventional war capabilities. They recognize that only massive growth in their industrial base can produce nuclear warheads, delivery systems, and equipment for mechanized land warfare. However, Chinese leaders do not imply that they cannot deter escalation to nuclear and conventional levels, or that they cannot cope with an opponent who escalates to these levels.

The Chinese maintain their fledgling nuclear capability and their ordinary aircraft can convince Asian leaders that their cities are hostage against US nuclear attack on China, and that, indirectly, this should restrain the United States from bombing the mainland. Even if they cannot use threats of reprisal to deter the United States from nuclear escalation, the Chinese leaders believe that they can reduce the gains which our officials expect from nuclear attack.

Accordingly, increases in Sino-American tension are accompanied by increased emphasis on the dispersed locations of Chinese counter-value targets, the self-sustaining, cellular nature of rural Chinese society, and the capabilities of the militia for broken-back war. The Chinese expect these capabilities to enable them to build a significant nuclear deterrent force and, in the meantime, to deter the United States from a nuclear attack on the People's Republic of China.

The Chinese also believe that they may be able to deter, and can cope with, a war which their opponent escalates to the conventional level of the Korean War, for example. They expect to deter the opponent by arousing fears of becoming bogged down, of being outnumbered, of domestic public resentment, and of foreign condemnation. Should the escalation occur, Peking analysts expect to cope with it not by reciprocal escalation, but with the military guile expounded in Mao Tse-tung's writings.

With regard to conventional war, the Chinese do not dismiss tanks and mobile artillery as unimportant, but they do dismiss them as insufficient for victory. However, the Chinese do not seem to believe that they or their proxies can cope with enemy escalation to conventional war except when certain requirements are met. The Chinese proxy must have competent leadership, effective political organization, a seasoned army, and popularity with the general population. If Chinese troops are needed, the theatre of war must border the Chinese mainland.

"NATIONAL LIBERATION" WARS

In contrast, the Chinese seek to bring conflicts to the level of "national liberation" wars, and believe that they can both manage and win wars at that level. Because the Chinese initiate such wars, they can pick targets which are particularly vulnerable. Because this was the route by which the Chinese Communist Party took power, the

Chinese are expert in such wars, unlike conventional and nuclear combat. Finally, the Chinese estimate that their ability to manipulate political and psychological factors determines the outcome of "national liberation" wars more than the outcome of nuclear and conventional wars.

However, it would be incorrect to assume that the Chinese believe that they and their proxies universally have the capability to escalate to the guerrilla war level. Peking analysts realize that such escalation is futile until their proxies have developed a political and military strategy appropriate to their environment, developed committed cadres, and organized a reliable army. Premature escalation may eliminate a promising proxy.

WASHINGTON SEEN FROM PEKING

A major set of perceptions which shape the Chinese position on escalation is their estimate of the obstacles which the United States and her associates pose for Peking's objectives.

Chinese spokesmen describe US capabilities as powerful, but unequal to the ambitions and commitments of Washington leaders; America cannot increase her military commitments on one front without seriously weakening her posture on another; and the effectiveness of US military and economic resources is significantly curtailed by political and psychological limitations.

The Peking régime recognizes that what Secretary Robert S. McNamara calls our "assured destruction" forces can inflict immense damage and act as a potent instrument of deterrence and persuasion. However, it also seems to the Chinese that we are unlikely to escalate to the use of these weapons because our leaders fear nuclear reprisals, and hesitate to destroy the possible economic spoils of a war. Chinese analysts also believe that US threats of nuclear escalation can be made costly to our Government. With judicious propaganda these threats can create boomerang

effects in terms of the trust of US citizens in their leaders, of US allies in Washington officials, and of neutrals in US goodwill.

Our conventional war capabilities are perceived as our one great strength which Washington officials are likely to commit to war. The Chinese perceive that conventional war is particularly compatible with our economic base and the interest of our economic and military élites. The Chinese do not doubt that we can confront them with a conventional war effort—they do doubt that we can sustain it and achieve conclusive victory in the field.

Peking analysts reason that our ground troops are too few, soft, and politically uninvolved for us to attrite the Chinese proxy. Accordingly, the United States will rely heavily on more complicated weapons, such as napalm bombs, which the Chinese feel play into their hands by inflicting casualties on the local population and alienating them from us and our local associates.

The Chinese expect three developments to produce pressure from the US voters and Washington's allies to de-escalate and end the war: civilian casualties in the theatre of war; the loss of US troops without visible military success; and the possibility of further escalation by US reliance on airpower.

The Chinese also believe that the United States has only a token capability for sub-limited war, and if we use it, that it will boomerang in ways similar to a conventional war effort. In contrast to conventional war, Peking analysts do not expect Washington officials to initiate sublimited war.

DIFFERENT LEVELS OF ESCALATION

Chinese experts conclude from their analyses that the capabilities available to Washington and Peking are the reverse of each other. They believe that the leaders of the People's Republic of China and the United States prefer different levels of escalation. Given the Chinese perception that the mainland would be at a disadvantage in the wars which US leaders would like to fight, the challenge to Chinese policy is how to inhibit the United States from implementing her escalation preferences.

The Chinese leadership believes that the objective of our policy is the elimination of Chinese Communism. Further, they believe that US élites intend to pursue this goal in a series of steps which subdue surrounding territories first and culminate in an attack on the Chinese mainland. These beliefs imply to the Chinese that there must be escalation at least to the level of sublimited war. They also imply that the Chinese need not greatly fear a sudden US nuclear strike against the mainland.

Between these points on the escalation ladder, the Chinese believe that they can manipulate US policy by affecting the cost-gain expectations of US officials. So long as Washington policymakers believe that nuclear war will on balance produce negative results, they will opt for limited wars. However, they will do so on the basis of an unrealistically optimistic estimate of the capabilities of the two sides. Peking analysts predict that the resultant tendency will be that unexpected costly wars will become a liability to the US Government which will seek some face-saving escape from the "consequences of an extended war."

The Chinese believe that the highly differentiated conflict spectrum used in our military planning makes Peking's attempts to manipulate our expectations both safe and feasible. These attempts are safe, they say, because Washington will escalate gradually, for example, from bombing raids in Vietnam south of the 18th parallel to strikes north of the 20th parallel. They are feasible because the slow pace of US escalation provides sufficient time for the Chinese proxy to develop militarily, for our domestic opinion to oppose continued military sacrifice, and for fears of escalation in the United States, the theatre of war, and allied capitals to inhibit Washington officials.

LIMITED RESPONSE

Peking analysts point out that the United States has, in fact, not escalated to nuclear war or even to prolonged conventional war in response to crises involving Laos, Hungary, Cuba, Korea, the Suez Canal, and West Irian. They argue that our military behaviour record since World War II supports their view that escalation can be successfully managed by Communist and nationalist movements. Of course, these spokesmen are careful to point out that inhibiting US use of nuclear weapons is difficult if Washington officials feel immediately threatened with nuclear attack—for example, our reaction to Nikita Khrushchev's location of missiles in Cuba.

To the extent that they can restrict American escalation while producing some US military response, the Chinese expect to benefit. Each time we either restrict or downgrade our escalation, the Chinese expect revolutionaries to be less deterred by our military guarantees. Each time we escalate to the point of sending US troops to developing nations, the Chinese expect the "imperialist" image of the United States and the "nationalist" image of Peking's proxy to be reinforced.

In addition, each time US weapons kill civilians and damage property in the theatre of war, the Chinese expect the involved population and residents of foreign countries to resent our leadership. Each time we escalate to the sublimited or conventional war levels without achieving decisive victory, the Chinese expect the foreign leaders associated with Washington to lose some faith in the usefulness of an American military shield.

EIGHT MAIN POLICIES

The goals, beliefs, and estimates which have been summarized lead Chinese officials, I believe, to eight conclusions about escalation:

1. Chinese leaders plan to communicate to all their audiences—at home, in the developing countries, and in the United States—that Washington officials will es-

calate unless deterred. Peking analysts expect acceptance of this communication to undermine US pursuit of a "flexible response" strategy. Our military actions will be seen as a prelude to massive escalation rather than as a limited response to insurgency. If they can establish this perception, Chinese leaders expect to gain, whatever the United States does. If we do not escalate, Peking can claim the credit for the remaining seven policies. If we do escalate, Peking can claim that the fault lies with other governments which did not accept the Chinese interpretation of US intentions.

2. Chinese leaders plan to communicate to US officials that the People's Republic of China has the will and the ability to survive and to respond to any form of US escalation. This policy is a logical companion to the one just presented. Peking must practice deterrence to balance our predisposition to exploit US military technology and industrial war potential.

3. Chinese leaders plan to advocate unilateral escalation of civil discontent to "national liberation" war in the developing states. It seems to them that this is their most cost-effective policy option to increase China's international stature and prevent US escalation harmful to Peking.

4. Chinese leaders plan to avoid initiating above the level of sublimited war. This unilateral restraint ranges from "no first use" of nuclear weapons to, in many cases, "no second use" of airpower and modern tactical weapons. Of course, this Chinese policy reflects a limited arsenal. However, it also reflects predictions about the efficacy of US escalation and the extent to which we will climb higher on the escalation ladder than our pro-Chinese opponents. Apparently, Peking analysts believe that if China and her proxies do not reciprocate US escalation, it will halt at a level they can handle. They believe that the next three policies will confirm their predictions.

5. Chinese leaders plan to respond to US military escalation with political and psychological escalation. In the theatre of war, this Chinese policy takes the form of psychological warfare designed to create dissension among their opponents. For example, they have associated the recent assassinations of captured Americans with the execution of Viet Cong captives by the South Vietnamese Government. Outside the theatre of war, the Chinese try to persuade others that the United States has escalated the war to a point extremely dangerous for world peace, and also attempt to generate vocal and violent condemnation of US policies.

6. Chinese leaders plan to respond to US military escalation in a particular war with "national liberation" wars and diversionary military appearances in other places. The Chinese reason that escalation in geography, but not in weapons or troop commitments, does not provoke further US military escalation. They expect it to inhibit US conventional war moves by thinning out scarce US ground troops. As we are made to "rush about from one part of the world to another," the Chinese expect Washington officials to feel a need to restrict the number of troops sent to any one conflict site. Accordingly, the Chinese ability to cope with US conventional war escalation increases. Peking analysts also expect the initiation of sublimited wars in several other locations to influence the governments of the developing countries. The Chinese reason that these governments care more for their own fate than for that of the society we have escalated to defend. In an attempt to avoid revolution in their country, leaders of these governments may pressure Washington officials to de-escalate.

7. Chinese leaders intend to respond militarily in the same theatre of war when US escalation reaches their borders. Given the Chinese image of US intentions, Peking officials perceive that otherwise the next step will be an attack on the mainland. Even in this case, which most conforms to a Chinese policy of imitative escalation, the Chinese probably intend to escalate to a notch below the level of the US commitment. For example, Peking will probably employ "volunteers" rather than official personnel of the People's Liberation Army.

8. Chinese leaders intend to acquire, with "deliberate speed," the technology for credible threats of nuclear escalation. They contend that if China does not develop the

ability to move to the nuclear rung on the conflict ladder, the policy objectives of the People's Republic of China would have to be sharply modified and the United States and the Soviet Union appeased.

For the immediate future we can expect that Chinese leaders will not significantly escalate wars. They will attempt first to deter and then to stabilize US escalation. We can also expect Chinese views on escalation to change if and when Peking analysts find that they have mistakenly believed that China can benefit from a conflict, even though we escalate to conventional war.

To bring Chinese policy to this point of major review, the United States and her associates will have to demonstrate to Chi-

nese officials that we can and will maintain conventional war commitments capable of immobilizing "national liberation" movements without destroying the social fabric and political autonomy of our associate.

We will have also to demonstrate that the Chinese Communists and their proxies cannot credibly present our accomplishment as a *de facto* Communist victory—for example, the industrialized United States stalemated by the military establishment of a small and under-developed country. Only if we succeed with these demonstrations can we confront Chinese leaders with an unpleasant choice between trying to match our escalation or withdrawing support for "national liberation" wars.

DIRECTED DEFENSE

BY CHARLES L. M. AILLERET

For a long time now, we in France have been accustomed to having a favourite possible enemy, and sometimes even such a favorite as to be, in fact, the only one. Having been England for many years, this enemy was more recently the German Reich.

Thus in 1912 and 1913, when General Joffre was Chief of the General Staff and Commander in Chief designate of our forces, there was for him only one main enemy against whom he had to prepare: Germany. Although she might be assisted by Austria–Hungary, Joffre knew that it was against Germany that he would have to conduct operations with our forces. In the 1930s, too, it was still the same for the unfortunate General Gamelin, who knew that if he had to fight against anybody, it would be the armies of Hitler.

In these circumstances, with the passage of time it had become a sort of necessity for us to have a single, well-defined, possible enemy, against and in terms of whom it was expedient to prepare our plans and our forces. After World War II our main former enemy, Germany, had disappeared. That country, crushed and occupied, would need a long time to repair the extensive destruction which it had brought down upon itself as well as upon others. For the moment at least, it was no longer the dangerous enemy which it had been.

But exactly at that time another, equally dangerous, threat seemed to appear on the horizon, to the East of Europe, with the rise of Stalin's imperialism. Having already swallowed up half of the continent, it seemed ready to conquer the rest, and it certainly had the means to do so, even with

Reprinted with permission. Général d'Armée Ailleret, "Directed Defence," as translated in *Survival*, February, 1968, London, Institute for Strategic Studies. Originally published under the title " 'Défense dirigée' ou 'Défense tous azimuts', " in *Revue de Défense Nationale,* December, 1967.

General Ailleret was Chief of the French General Staff from 1962 until his death in 1968. He directed France's first atomic project.

conventional armaments only. Faced with this visible danger, our country again found one of those favorite enemies, of a special kind, against whom her defenses had to be organized.

This was done; and, as was only natural in view of the disproportion between our forces and those of the possible aggressor, it was done within the framework of an alliance of a certain number of countries all concerned about the same threat: the Atlantic Alliance.

But since in those days the only threat to its members seemed to be that of the Soviet bloc, this alliance soon came to endow itself with a military organization whose aim was to concentrate all the defense efforts of the member countries in a single system, adapted to that threat; and it seemed reasonable to assume that the maximum output and efficiency would be obtained from the resources of the various allied countries.

A chain of integrated allied operational commands was formed in peacetime, and a common infrastructure, jointly financed and spread over the territory of the various members, was launched. In these circumstances, it was not illogical from the point of view of the Alliance to wish to determine the amounts and types of forces which each country should put at the disposal of the Alliance in the event of a crisis, in terms of the single criterion of the output which it was possible to obtain from the global resources of the Alliance. NATO was continually trying to fix the possible national contributions. Since the United States' atomic "umbrella" furnished the destructive power with intercontinental range—which was also an effective deterrent—the other countries would be obliged to supply certain quantities of conventional forces, whose modern armaments would as far as possible, and preferably, be manufactured in the United States of America, "the arsenal of democracies."

According to this conception, it would have been quite useless, and even regrettable, that France should make the effort to manufacture her own nuclear armament, since there already was one in the USA, and since the effort would use up resources which, in the opinion of NATO, would be better employed in creating conventional units capable of reinforcing the famous "shield," to use the terminology of that time.

Even in the case of a single danger in the present and in the future, that of Soviet aggression, this system would have had the serious disadvantage for us of basing our safety strictly on our membership in the Alliance, of making it depend entirely on the Alliance and in fact on the United States, since nuclear arms would henceforth be playing the vital role in world strategy.

The defense of France would therefore have been entrusted entirely to the United States of America, and French forces would, if the necessity arose, have been engaged by the decisions of American generals and not of French leaders acting upon the instructions of our Government. Our forces would thus have become a species of French sharpshooters in the American armies, integrated into a system of which we would have formed one of the primitive parts; the sophisticated parts, powerful by nature and consequently considered noble, being American. France would thus have lost, together with her autonomy in defense, her actual independence.

There would, of course, have been the fiction of the collective management of the Alliance in which our country would have had a voice. But what could that one voice have been, compared with that of the most powerful (and by how much) member of the Alliance. France would only have been able, at the cost of much energy and thanks to the system of unanimity required for any "decision" to be adopted, to block the publication of certain "papers" without being in the least able to modify or even bend the policy of the predominant member. French forces and our whole country could thus have become engaged in a strategy which would have had the approval neither of our Government nor of our Command.

Thus, in the case of a threat of Soviet aggression, which was assumed to be the only threat now and for the future, France would no longer have had any role to play in her own defense, within the NATO system, except that of providing the Alliance's military organization with conventional facilities which would be at the disposal of an integrated command, i.e., in practice, of an American Command.

The operations in Algeria were soon to show one of the dangers of shutting oneself up in a system with a single purpose. It became essential to remove many units which were in theory assigned to NATO Commands in order to meet military requirements in Algeria at that time.

Yet another danger seemed, during the 1950s, to reduce the menace of Soviet aggression: the integrated military organization which was essentially defensive should it need to face external aggression, necessarily involved a mixture of the military systems of the member countries. There were many bases functioning on our territory. And, starting from those bases—especially air bases—which in theory had no other purpose than to meet aggression, our allies could operate freely with their resources, to support their policies of the time, which, unless we became protectorates, could be different from ours, or could even be opposed to ours.

Moreover, the dispositions of our forces, as well as our support organizations, were closely enmeshed with those of the allied forces. If then one of our allies came to be involved in a war which was not a result of Soviet aggression, and therefore in a situation which did not conform to the basic presumption of the Treaty, it was possible, if not probable, that he might or might not operate from bases situated on our territory, that these bases might be attacked by his enemy, which would involve our territory being attacked, and that his forces might also be attacked wherever they were, and consequently our forces, which were integrated with his, would also be attacked.

We thus ran the risk of being involved, without being able to decide upon our attitude, in a conflict which might not concern France. NATO thus presented a great danger for us in that it could draw our forces into military operations for the sole reason that certain of our allies, and in particular the leading allies, were involved in them.

But an even greater danger would have been that of continuing the French military effort in one direction only, namely against the threat which the Atlantic Alliance was designed to meet. For unrestricted participation in NATO would necessarily lead us to that situation. Already dependent upon the United States for our defense against a hypothetical Soviet attack, we should also have been dependent upon her in any other danger, whatever it was, which might threaten us. But could we then be certain that the Alliance, or its most powerful member, would always agree to defend us, especially in a situation which did not conform to the presumption of the Treaty?

This risk had not escaped those in our armies who from 1950 onwards, while proving that it was feasible, had begun to urge that France should form her own atomic armament, which would enable her to meet those threats not covered by NATO and, consequently, to recover a certain amount of national independence.

However, at the time when Stalin's imperialism was reaching its apogee and also had the nuclear weapon, one could reasonably have asked whether, apart from a few decolonization military operations, France would have to face any serious threats other than that of the possible Soviet aggression anticipated by the Atlantic Alliance.

Today an analysis of the world situation shows that we should not allow ourselves to be obsessed by the contemplation of this one danger. First, that danger, in its original form, seems to be considerably reduced. The Soviets appear at the moment to have no wish to launch a war. Busy as they are in rapidly developing their economy, in striving to raise the people's standard of living, they realize that to do this they need peace and also a certain amount of technical co-operation with the West. Moreover, the balance of terror between the Soviet and the American thermonuclear forces inevitably leads both parties to renounce war—at least large-scale war, if not war in its disguised, localized and proxy forms—in order to promote their policies.

On the whole, it does not seem that the great fear of Soviet aggression, so logical and explicable a few years after World War II, is justified today. Although the hypothesis of such aggression is still clearly a theoretical hypothesis which cannot be completely excluded for an indefinite future, it is certainly not to be considered the only or even the primary hypothesis.

The world situation offers us, on the contrary, a spectacle of such disorder, such agitation, such development, that while it is hardly possible to identify anywhere precisely the potential threats to our country, it is also impossible to rely on the present balances of power in order to forecast the future. These balances of power are, more often than not, so unstable that they may be replaced at any moment by completely different situations.

It should be noted here that one does not produce a defense and the means of defense (which are both, especially armies, their armaments and their doctrines, the result of a long process of continuous creation) shortly after setting to work. They are organized at the same time for the immediate future and for a more distant future; this gives rise to particularly difficult problems of selection when the world is developing as fast as it is today. If we plan the setting up of a defense today, it will not be completed for twenty years. What will the world situation be at that time? Who can say?

What will have become of the world rivalry between the Soviet and the American empires which reached the height of their power following World War II and their nuclear and space achievements? Where will their armaments race, and the conquest of space, have led to? Will one have outstripped the other technically to the extent of dominating the other militarily, or will there be a *status quo* in the balance of terror such as to prevent any risk of total war?

What, too, will have become of those empires which, however monolithic they seem with their allies and satellites, show today undeniable centrifugal tendencies?

Will the United States have succeeded in eliminating their internal racial tensions, or will these handicap them in the exercise of their power?

We might also ask what will have become of Asia, that continent plunged into a veritable turmoil, resulting from the collapse of the old worm-eaten structures and the social and political troubles caused by acute overpopulation which spreads and perpetuates underdevelopment and poverty.

We might ask what will have become of China, where the establishment of a brutal and authoritarian Communist regime enables a centralization and organization of activities which, in their turn, lead to a rapid development of power—though at the cost of an intensive effort by the population and the maintenance of a very low level of its standard of living. If this enormous country with its hundreds of millions of inhabitants succeeds in overcoming its internal difficulties, what progress will it have made? If it has, or has not, been able to manufacture its own nuclear armament and operational intercontinental missiles, what will then be its power, and to what extent will that power enable it to sustain its present or limited ambitions?

We cannot know what the situation in Southeast Asia will be, nor how the American intervention in this strategic sector of the world, where fighting has been going on ceaselessly for the last twenty-five years, will finally be liquidated. It is, therefore, impossible to predict with any chance of success anything concerning the vast continent of Asia.

And although Europe may appear almost calm—despite its problems, such as that of Germany—Africa in all its elements does not offer a prospect much more stable than Asia, since the painful development of certain countries forming part of Africa is being complicated by the intermingling of external influences which are spreading there.

As for the political instability of certain countries of South America and the explosive condition of the Middle East, how can one say whether they are likely to calm down more or less quickly, or on the contrary to cause disturbances in the balance of power which, in their turn, could bring or facilitate other disturbances and give rise to new instabilities.

Finally, how can one know to what extent there will be worldwide dissemination of nuclear weapons, which the great atomic powers could slow down at the start, but could not completely halt once the application of nuclear techniques and the corresponding industries become wide spread.

Thus, instead of the relatively stable picture of the world shown at the beginning of the century to a Europe which was itself the seat of serious tension, we now have the appearance of fairly general instability. Moreover, if the Europe of today gives an impression of calm, this is due to the fact that the internal tensions which still exist there have temporarily crystallized by virtue of a tacit common consent. There is no reason for thinking that this will always be so.

In the centre of such a world plunged into a turmoil whose effects can hardly be foreseen, it is justifiable to fear that almost anywhere, in the future, large-scale wars may break out which would probably tend to spread very quickly and take in the greater part of our planet.

Those who went to war would soon be compelled, the rhythm of modern war being what it is, to fight their battles over all continents and seas. The range of present-day ballistic missiles—without considering the space missiles of tomorrow—which allow us to strike from one point of the globe at any other, removes the obstacle which distances once constituted in the geographical spread of wars of contact. The almost instantaneous action of these missiles, as well as the speed of the massive air transports now in service, has removed the delays which, in the time of shipping and railways, were involved in carrying invasion operations from one part of the world to another. Finally, the terrifying destructive power of the nuclear and thermonuclear missiles enables the greatest organizations on the human scale to be destroyed in a few seconds, "lightning" operations of destruction being substituted for

the lengthy operations-conquest or bombardment of the conventional periods.

For all these reasons, a major war of the future, other than those phoney wars which are the present-day local and limited conflicts, could henceforth originate anywhere and could immediately, or at least very quickly, set the whole world ablaze.

Our country, although it is utterly peaceful and has no intention of attacking anyone or interfering in the affairs of anyone, could thus be involved in a conflict of unforeseen origin, whether we were attacked by one of the adversaries who wanted to use our territory or our facilities in his struggle, or whether we were attacked or destroyed from a distance by one of the belligerents who wanted to prevent his enemy from using our land or our resources.

How can our country escape this threat since it would no longer be protected by distance or time? An *a priori* alliance could not give us a general guarantee of safety, since it is almost impossible to foresee what could one day be the cause of a serious conflict, and what would be the distribution of the powers between the various sides, or what hold, even unauthorized, any power would have over the territory of any other power.

It seems that, in order to be able to meet such situations, our country must have the maximum possible capacity to dissuade, by its possible actions, those who might be induced to seize our territory or destroy it with bombs. Our country must, therefore, be as strong as possible by itself, with due regard to its resources and the philosophy of life of its people. Now, in the arsenal of modern armaments, those which have the best output, that is the most efficiency for a given cost, are, by a long way, nuclear armaments. These are, moreover, those weapons which are capable, by their long-distance action, by the threat of their terrible effects, of dissuading possible attacks by making them quite disproportionate to the benefits to be obtained.

If France wishes to escape the dangers which could threaten her, she must, therefore, possess a significant quantity—which does not need to be large by reason of their unit power—of megaton ballistic missiles, with a worldwide range, whose action could deter those who, from whatever part of the world they might be operating, might wish to exploit or destroy us in order to achieve their war aims.

To be as strong as possible, autonomously and individually, and to possess our own very long-range armament with very great power, capable of dissuading any aggressor, whatever his starting point, is clearly a completely different formula from that which would consist of forming, for the same expenditure, a force supplementary to that of the main member of an *a priori* alliance.

Moreover, where dissuasion was not enough to keep us out of a war, this formula would not prevent us joining an alliance suited to the danger to be repulsed; it would even enable us to join it under the best conditions, as a member who, in the last resort, would be fully responsible for his own actions within the common framework of the alliance.

Our independent force, intrinsically as powerful as possible, should also—since we cannot anticipate from which part of the world the threat to future generations will come—not be oriented in only one direction, that of the *a priori* enemy, but be capable of intervening everywhere, or as we say in our military jargon, at every point of the compass.

This basic conception would be realized, first, by developing our present strategic nuclear force to become a thermonuclear force with a world-wide range, under technical conditions which would subsequently enable it to expand further, when this becomes necessary and possible, into a spatial force in an age when the military use of space will have become a reality; second, by developing our existing air, ground and naval "battle forces" so as to correspond to the operational conditions of the atomic age, battle forces which must necessarily be equipped with nuclear weapons and possess the required capabilities for acting offensively, even beyond

our frontiers, the moment we are attacked; and, finally, as a last resort, by increasing the effort already undertaken to form our territorial defense, which would at all times give close protection to our other forces and which—in the event of our country being, in spite of all our precautions and endeavors, temporarily invaded by enemy forces—would enable us to continue to resist on our own ground, at least in the regions where this was possible.

But whatever the detailed arrangements required to organize, compose and equip our various forces, we must not deceive ourselves; in the age in which we live and for a country such as ours, where its safety is concerned there is only one choice:

—Either to integrate itself with an *a priori* system and rely entirely on an alliance, that is to say on the most important member (or members) of this alliance, with the following results: the quick, definitive atrophy of the nation's independent means of defense; the impossibility of keeping out of a major war, whatever the causes, in which its protectors might become engaged; the possibility in certain cases of not being defended, as was the case at Munich for Czechoslovakia in 1938; and finally the steady but definitive loss of national independence.

—Or to endeavor to constitute, with its own resources, a system of defense not directed against anyone, but worldwide and at "every point of the compass," which would wield the maximum power afforded by its national resources and which, handled with as much sangfroid as determination, should enable it, by dissuasion, to avoid certain major wars and, if it cannot, then to take part in them under the best conditions; in short, a system which, during future crises that may rock the world, would place France in a position where she could freely determine her own destiny.

Only this second solution appears to me to be in the best interest of our country, whose name for two centuries has stood for liberty.

PART II

AMERICAN DEFENSE POLICY-MAKING: THE MANAGEMENT OF FORCE

This second major part of the book is concerned with the processes that are involved in developing the policies which were discussed in Part I. These processes are significant because they critically influence the policies which emanate from them. In fact, the best way to ensure good defense policies over the long run is to have effective and wise policymaking. As a corollary, the most pragmatic test of the process is the success of its policies. We dealt with the issues before the process so that such an evaluation now can be made.

The management of defense is certainly a matter of administration. Moreover, since the contributions of Herbert Simon, administrative theory includes a focus on decisionmaking. We are using the same focus, except that we have chosen the term "policymaking" because it permits us to make a useful distinction. In defense management, one can speak of analysis—the development of alternatives and recommendations, and decision—the choosing of an alternative. Thus, policymaking consists of analysis plus decision.

We examine only the American defense establishment since it is the largest and most advanced, and also to keep the size of this work within limits. The American Department of Defense manages unquestionably the largest, most complicated, most expensive business in the world. Today it spends over $80 billion annually and employs over 4½ million people. But dwarf-

ing the physical dimensions of its tasks is its control over the means of the immediate death of hundreds of millions of people. Because of these awesome responsibilities, some of our best and most inventive minds have been devoted to American defense policymaking—both inside and outside government. Many of the newest management and decisionmaking techniques have been developed in the national security field rather than in industry.

The immense costs and the intricate technologies involved in defense affairs require unified direction. The key problem of interservice rivalry, which sometimes led to either gaps in our national security forces or to duplication of effort, cannot run unbridled. We cannot afford either to neglect airlift or to produce both the similar Thor and Jupiter missiles.

The necessary unified direction can come either from more centralized organization or from more unified methods of management. The two chapters of this part examine these two alternatives. Chapter 6 deals with the "Organization of Defense Policymaking" along the central theme of centralization of decisionmaking, but including the elements of decentralization in the analysis and support functions. Chapter 7, "Methods of Defense Policymaking," treats of management tools—especially the programming system and systems analysis —that permit more unified control of the Department of Defense.

CHAPTER 6

Organization of Defense Policymaking

In discussing the management of violence, we begin by examining the organizations involved in defense policymaking. Many institutions influence American defense policy. We focus on the organizations that are involved in the basic formulation of defense policy, such as research institutes and the Department of Defense. We omit those, like the President, the Congress, and the State Department, which make the over-riding national decisions, because the narrower focus is more in keeping with our one-volume collection. The other institutions are covered more appropriately in books on American government or American foreign policy. The next chapter, however, does touch upon the impact of these other institutions.

Two questions are fundamental to the discussion of the organization of defense policymaking: where is policy formulated and who formulates it?

The location question is central to all organizational theory. In simplest terms, policymaking is either centralized or decentralized. However, we think the question is best answered by considering the formulation as a two-step, funnel-shaped process. The first step is analysis, the broad part of the funnel, which Wesley Posvar describes in his article on "Dispersion of the Strategy-making Establishment." The number of agencies which analyze defense policy has increased and includes not only the military services, but also research institutions working under government contract (RAND, RAC, IDA, etc.), academic institutions (Harvard, MIT, Stanford, etc.), and independent institutions (Carnegie, Brookings, Council on Foreign Relations, etc.). Alain Enthoven has pointed out that this pluralism, plus the separation of powers in our government which permits Congressmen to probe and speak independently, has led to an American defense policy environment which is unique in the amount of public debate, both informed and uninformed, surrounding it. The second step is decisionmaking, which has become extremely centralized, and therefore is the nozzle portion of the funnel. It is described by Harry Ransom. Since the analysis step significantly influences the final decision, one must consider both steps in attempting to understand policymaking today.

In addition to the split referred to between analysis and decision, there is another division between support and operations. Ransom's article, "Department of Defense: Unity or Confederation?" also discusses this. In his analogy the military services are similar to the American states. He traces the evolution of defense organization from a "confederacy" when the services were sovereign or as one commentator put it, prior to World War II, the only thing they were agreed upon was that in the next war they would all fight on the American side. Today, the arrangement is more "federal," with the services primarily responsible for support (training, equipping, and administration) with the unified (multiple-service) commands responsible for actual operations. If the split between analysis and decision is seen as a vertical concept, the division between support and operations is a horizontal concept which separates different kinds, rather than levels, of decisions.

Thus, we answer the location question by saying that decisionmaking itself has become more centralized, but that there are still many elements of decentralization in the policymaking process.

We consider the second question—Who formulates defense policy?—by asking whether civilians or military officers make policy? Theoretically, the newly centralized decisionmakers could be either. Obviously, the American answer is influenced by the constitutional principle of civilian supremacy, our belief that "war is too important to be left to the generals," and our fear of a "general staff" system. However, as Lawrence Tatum's article points out, the military has abdicated to a large extent the central authority by providing compromise, rather than decisive advice. Tatum maintains that the staff action procedures of the military Joint Chiefs of Staff have ensured "compromise at the lowest common denominator," which have been "low-quality" solutions to defense problems. Therefore, civilians had to, and did, step into the vacuum. However, Gene Lyons's thesis is that the concept of civilian control of the military is too simple for the "new civil-military relations." The character of leadership in defense affairs has

changed with civilians becoming more "militarized" and the military more "civilianized." His essay examines these changes and their significance.

Not only is the collective character of leadership often as important as the more basic organizational structure; so, often, is the personality of some specific leader. While Secretary of Defense from 1961 to 1968, Robert McNamara was such a man. Because of his profound influence on the role of "Sec Def" (as it is referred to in Pentagonese jargon), he can almost be called the "John Marshall" of the Department of Defense. The controversy which resulted from his dramatic leadership is reflected in the title and thesis of Jack Raymond's article, "The McNamara Monarchy."

DISPERSION OF THE STRATEGY-MAKING ESTABLISHMENT

BY WESLEY W. POSVAR

In the years since its inception and early development, strategy expertise has continued to burgeon into many new institutions and kinds of activities. One can say that the function of formulating national security policies and programs in the United States—strategy-making—has become "dispersed."

Don K. Price of Harvard University observes that the device of large-scale contracting for the services of science and industry has become a new kind of federalism.[1] Thus the applications of nuclear

energy, the advancement of medical research, the placement of communication satellites in orbit, not to mention the whole field of development and maintenance of military hardware represent billion-dollar functions that the United States govern-

[1] "The Scientific Establishment," *The George Washington Law Review*, Washington, D.C., April, 1963, Vol. 31, No. 4, pp. 713–31. [Some of the

problems in the new kind of federalism are reflected in "Project Themis," begun in January, 1967, by Secretary of Defense McNamara, which is an attempt to allocate more equitably public funds for federally sponsored research programs in American universities. It is a response of the Johnson Administration to the frequent criticism that most of the contracts have been awarded to too few institutions. See John I. Brook, "Centers of Excellence," *The Virginia Pilot*, July 16, 1967.]

Reprinted by permission of The Viking Press, Inc. The article is a chapter from a book manuscript to be published by The Viking Press, Inc.

Colonel Posvar (Ret.) is Chancellor of the University of Pittsburgh. He is a U.S. Military Academy graduate, Rhodes Scholar, and former graduate fellow at Harvard University and M.I.T. Prior to his appointment at Pittsburgh, Chancellor Posvar was Professor and Head of the Department of Political Science and Chairman of the Division of Social Sciences at the United States Air Force Academy. He is co-editor of the first edition of American Defense Policy (1963).

ment has decentralized and delegated mostly to the private sector of its society. The alternative would have been for government to accrue these functions to itself and thereby augment an already monolithic bureaucracy.

The dispersal of the strategy-making process is one version of "federalism by contract." It is a tiny segment of the whole in terms of monetary expenditure upon the salaries and activities of the strategists themselves, but its weighty policy implications make it unique and important in its own right.

The financial support of strategy expertise outside of government comes mainly from that category of governmental expenditure devoted to research and development. But here again, strategy-making represents only a small portion of the whole. It is a portion difficult to isolate, because of the interlocking interests and activities of strategists and their more numerous colleagues engaged in all types of scientific research and development. Overall governmental expenditures on research and development do provide, however, a rough index of the magnitude of the task of strategy expertise. Total annual outlays by the United States government for research and development were about $100 million prior to World War II. By 1950, they had risen to over $1 billion, and by 1963 to well over $10 billion.[2] The bulk of these expenditures are now directed to programs that are either military or have potential military applications, such as the space programs of the National Aeronautics and Space Administration. The bulk of the expenditures are also "federal," that is, contracted out to industry. This geometric rate of increase of tenfold each decade for research and development staggers the imagination. It also demonstrates the fantastic importance and complexity of long-range strategic planning. Admittedly, this rate is certain to taper off in the face of

other sectors of the economy that must retain their own share of national resources. Yet it is obvious that the strategic posture of the United States becomes increasingly dependent upon the weapons environment that is shaped, long in advance, by the colossal research and development effort of the U.S. government.

Although the gross magnitude of the strategic task looms hugely over everyone concerned, there is great difficulty in mapping the dispersion of the strategy-making process, or in conducting a census of strategy experts. They are scattered throughout government offices and the professional staffs of the hundreds of non-profit research organizations, aircraft, electronics, and space corporations, and quasi-academic research institutes that lend their efforts to spending these billions. However, despite the difficulty, it is useful to attempt a crude census. This can be done by identifying experts in strategy as "generalists" in respect to their relatively undistracted concern with all facets of national security policy, attentive to the "big picture" of the strategic posture of the United States. The remainder of the professional research staffs, then, consist mostly of "specialists," such as the scientists, technologists, and staff officers who work on particular elements of the defense posture without primary regard for the whole, or those who are interested in collateral fields of study.

According to this criterion, concentrations of strategy expertise may be identified in certain government offices, research corporations, and academic institutions. To conduct the census, then, it is necessary to survey the more prominent of these organizations, compare their scope and affiliations, and assess their population of strategic "generalists." The survey will provide some insight of the reasons for dispersion, and enable a discussion, in the next chapter, of the strengths and weaknesses of this uniquely American policy-making establishment with its sprawling configuration.

The organizations are grouped in the following paragraphs according to their "degree of dispersion," from the government outward. First, at the center, are govern-

[2] U.S. Congress, Senate, Committee on Government Operations, *Report to the President on Government Contracting for Research and Development*, prepared by the Bureau of the Budget and referred to the Committee, 87th Congress, 2d Session, 1962, p. 1.

ment agencies that are involved directly in strategy formulation. Next are a half dozen nonprofit research organizations that work directly for the government, including the early postwar establishments of the armed services, like RAND. Along with these are classed certain profit-making defense corporations that are similarly concerned with strategy because the government is their principal customer. Beyond this category lies the academic locale, where scholarly research centers such as those at M.I.T., Harvard, and Princeton operate more independently but usually with the benefit of government contracts. Finally, on the periphery are to be found certain unaffiliated institutions and foundations that share in the widespread concern for problems of national security, and therefore also support research activities that should be counted as part of the nation's strategy expertise. Of the combined professional staffs of all these organizations numbering in the thousands, it will be found that only a total of several hundred can be judged to be strategy experts, "generalists" at the national policy level.

IN-HOUSE STRATEGY EXPERTISE

In mapping the dispersion of the strategy-making process, the Pentagon Building naturally springs first to mind. It is the hub of strategic planning in the United States, the focal point toward which the efforts and arguments of strategy experts are aimed. It is also the dreary seat of bureaucratic impediments and frustrations—the centrifugal forces that have helped cause the dispersion of strategy expertise.

The building itself presents a grim physical aspect. It is a huge warren of plasterboard partitions and cubicles strung along five concentric "rings," each about a mile in circumference and each with five flat sides and five floors deep. Direction signs within the building are pentagon-shaped. The possible psychological imprint of this pentagonal emphasis upon the building's occupants is an intriguing subject for speculation. Why not five unified commands, operating in five theaters, and guided by five essential principles of war? The U.S. Army

has already invented (and later rejected) a pentagonal organization for its divisions.

Inside the Pentagon, permanent crews work at the continuous task of moving walls and doors to accommodate changes in organization and status of some thirty thousand staff officers, senior civil servants, and clerical employees. Some of the most able professional officers of the armed services and the civil service spend half their careers in this structure, enduring 60-hour work weeks and the hazards of hypertension, advancing job by job closer to the ultimate mark of success—an office on "E" ring with an outside window and a reserved parking space nearby.

Most of the persons who work in the Pentagon, as well as many others employed in the State Department and other executive agencies, contribute directly and indirectly to the design, maintenance, and control of the massive security establishment of the United States. There are certain offices, however, that are especially concerned with the broad kind of security problems that can be characterized as strategy. Within each of the military departments is to be found a special planning staff of several hundred officers, much of whose attention is directed at "crystal ball" type questions: How many and what kind of divisions, air wings, and aircraft carriers are needed five, ten, and fifteen years in the future? What changes are indicated in concepts of deployment and base requirements overseas? These officers examine, through war games, the strengths and deficiencies of programmed forces. Relative to the more immediate future, they review in detail the operational plans of American military commands in overseas theaters, and they help evaluate the military alliances and military assistance programs of the United States.

In the Army this work is done by the Directorate of Strategic Plans and Policy, under the Deputy Chief of Staff for Military Operations; in the Navy it is the Strategic Plans Division, under the Deputy Chief of Naval Operations for Plans and Policy; and in the Air Force the Directorate of Plans, under the Deputy Chief of Staff for Plans and Operations.

Of course, there are a great many other

military activities whose efforts overlap with or are related to the work of these three principal planning offices. There are other tremendous staffs, also in the Pentagon, concerned with research, procurement, budget formulation, construction, and personnel for each of the armed services. Each such staff has its own special branches devoted to the correlation of its own long-range planning with more general strategic plans and programs. Overseas, the "unified" American military commands in Europe, the Pacific, and elsewhere, as well as the headquarters of the Strategic Air Command in Omaha, the North American Air Defense Command in Colorado Springs, and the Strike Command in Tampa all perform their own planning as a counterpart to that done in the Pentagon.

It should be obvious that the output of all these military staffs, inside and outside the Pentagon, is colored by their own organizational viewpoints. Much of their effort must go into preparing their "positions" to be advocated at higher echelons of authority, often in competition with the other services or commands.

Within the higher echelons, the planning staffs are somewhat smaller and a little more generalized in their perspectives. In the Joint Staff, the Directorate of Plans and Policy, or J-5, is composed of military officers of all services. They strive to reach agreement on the kinds of questions that are treated separately by the planning agencies of the individual services. The process of reaching agreement has proved to be tedious, and, so far, has left little room for the sort of initiative in strategic thought that would seem desirable.

On the other hand, considerable initiative does reside in the staff of the Assistant Secretary of Defense for International Security Affairs (ISA), which is a mixture of civilians and officers. That staff, however, has its own limitations. It works under the severest pressures and consequently has little time for considering the long-term goals and implications of U.S. policy. ISA must respond to the daily and hourly needs of the Secretary of Defense for data and advice for the actual prosecution of war and for the Secretary's dealings with

other executive agencies. The staff of the Assistant Secretary of Defense for Systems Analysis is under a little less pressure, but its role is cast mainly in terms of controlling physical resources, playing the part of reviewer, critic, and arbitrator of the analytical studies of new weapons systems prepared within subordinate staffs.

In the State Department, the Policy Planning Council attempts to devote itself to the broad and long-range view of national strategy, but with only about sixteen members. Finally, in the White House itself are a number of overworked individuals, including the staff of the National Security Council, who are concerned with matters of defense and foreign policy. They are sympathetic and keenly attentive to all these lower-level planning endeavors, even though their own time for contemplative thought is virtually nonexistent.

It is evident, then, that the overall function of strategic planning in the United States government is by no means a neat procedure, to be clearly demarcated on charts of organization. It is a pervasive activity, interconnected in all its aspects. And the process of reaching decisions in this maze of agencies is a political process, more than a scientific or analytical one, for it consists of dialogue, persuasion and compromise.

These official strategic planning agencies, therefore, should not be pictured as tranquil centers of objective contemplation of fundamental issues, as the wishful and uninitiated citizen might be tempted to believe. On the contrary, their members are harried by the pressures of time and the political implications of their tasks. Their workloads are often overwhelming, and the atmosphere in which they work is sometimes frantic. Any government official, however, is unavoidably constrained by the administrative bounds and procedural aspects of his duties—by red tape. In addition, the scope of view of military officers and career civil servants is often limited by their technical specialties, whether they be logistics, electronics, or a particular brand of ground, naval, or air tactics.

There have been repeated attempts to establish special offices within the headquarters planning staffs that would be insulated against daily pressures and granted the freedom to contemplate and to originate novel programs and doctrines. However, these "crystal ball" shops, or "think groups," seem to have had a consistently unfortunate history. It is one which really ought to be thoroughly documented and analyzed as a fascinating topic in the field of public administration.

In the above absence of such a thorough study, the typical historical cycle of those groups can be summarized. First, a high-ranking officer, a Director of Plans or sometimes a Chief of Staff, becomes aware of the need to augment his personal judgment. Forced as he is to make twenty or thirty important decisions a day, he recognizes that some of these require more time than he has available. Further, he realizes that the ideas that filter up to him through many layers of authority are diluted, reduced to a common denominator that was found acceptable in all those layers. So he hits upon a solution. He appoints a small committee, perhaps three or four highly selected and precocious planning officers, to perform the needed creative, critical thinking in his behalf, and to do so in response to his personal direction.

Next, this group produces a series of studies and reports that are of dramatically high quality. The ideas of the group are translated into recommendations for actual programs, which are promptly approved. The programs now require implementation. Representatives from other staff agencies besiege the group members with requests for detailed interpretations of what the original recommendations intended. And while all this is going on, the high officer himself, increasingly impressed by the talent at his immediate disposal, has found it desirable to seek the assistance of his group on many of the detailed matters that press him daily. The reflective "crystal ball" group thus becomes converted into a frantic "fire brigade."

Finally, when the senior officer moves up to another job, his successor (egged on, perhaps, by a few disgruntled rivals of the special group), quickly discovers that the small "fire brigade" is performing the very same functions that large established staff agencies are meant to do. There is no excuse for such duplication. The special committee is abolished.

A year or so later, under the pressure of making twenty or thirty important decisions a day. . . .

At another level, there was once reason to expect that the advanced service schools, particularly the war colleges, would serve to produce strategic theory, with the military professionals in tranquil setting inventing the strategic doctrine of tomorrow. Regrettably, the early hopes for these war colleges were not fulfilled. The war colleges after the Second World War emphasized remedial gap-filling in the general college education of their students, and their faculties were understandably not inspired by their task. Much attention has recently been directed at the need for upgrading the curricula of the war colleges, and some of the suggested changes are being made. Whether these changes will ultimately provide a better climate for creative work remains to be seen.

As a result of these factors, bibliographies on the subject of strategy reveal a very small percentage of authors who are career officers. This is in contrast to the situation in this country before the war and in contrast to the situation in other countries—the Soviet Union, for example, where the current definitive work (limited as it is) is a collection of articles by military officers, and edited by Marshal Sokolovskii.[3]

This lack of creativity is not, however, merely a deficiency of the American military profession. Similar evidence is mutely provided by certain civilian members of the strategy community, the "Whiz Kids" and others, who have moved into key jobs in the Department of Defense. They were former prolific scholars, but their output of theoretical writing has dropped to zero, as they wrestle with Vietnam, Berlin, Cuba, and the budget. To be sure, they continue to make strategy in an applied, direct manner, and their influence is thus more decisive than ever; but the reflective, abstract mode of study and analysis is no longer theirs to employ. They have experienced on

[3] V. D. Sokolovskii (ed.), *Soviet Military Strategy* (Englewood Cliffs, New Jersey, 1963).

their own higher level the fate of many aspiring authors in the military services who have found that headquarters duty does not allow the time (if not the inspiration) for professional writing.

At worst, then, government strategic planners are unfortunate captives of bureaucracy. At best, if they hold high positions, they must work with such intensity that they are denied opportunity for profound, creative reflection about policy issues. Their role is likely limited to a cursory review and selection from alternative courses of action presented to them by their subordinates. The strict definition of strategic "generalist" employed in the present context, therefore, is applicable to relatively few of them. One might guess that there are a dozen such persons in each agency mentioned above—but, admittedly, this is to pick numbers out of the air. All in all, perhaps one or two hundred persons in government planning agencies are permitted the time and freedom, and that sometimes by accident, to enable them to operate as true "strategy experts."

This brief description of "in-house" strategy expertise thus provides in itself an explanation of the dispersion of the strategy-making process, in terms of the needs for greater freedom, continuity, and objectivity of study. Various ways of meeting those needs will be revealed in the following survey of strategists employed in nongovernmental institutions. The strategy-making establishment, as will be shown, is not divisible into two simple parts, the "in-house" with its handicaps and the remainder, outside government, with its virtues. "Out-house expertise" (the pun is irresistible) takes a variety of forms, each with its peculiar strengths and weaknesses.

REASEARCH CORPORATIONS WORKING DIRECTLY FOR THE GOVERNMENT[4]

Looking, then, outside of government, the most highly organized strategy expertise is found to be concentrated in a half dozen nonprofit research corporations that

[4] Factual material for this section is obtained from *Report to the President on Government Contracting for Research and Development, op. cit.*;

work directly for the government. Three of these are the descendants of the postwar establishments created by the armed services: RAND still works mostly for the Air Force. The Research Analysis Corporation (RAC), successor to the Operations Research Organization (ORO), primarily serves the Army. The Center of Naval Analyses (organized as a division of the Franklin Institute) includes the original Operations Evaluation Group (OEG) and works entirely for the Navy. Another three are variations of the nonprofit research formula: the Institute for Defense Analyses (IDA) works directly for the Office of the Secretary of Defense and several of its components. The Hudson Institute, while serving various government agencies, attempts as a guiding principle to avoid close affiliation with any of them. It is the smallest of the half dozen. The Stanford Research Institute (SRI), which is the largest, works for industry as well as government.

Of their combined professional staffs numbering over two thousand, perhaps only a few hundred can be labeled as "generalists" at the national policy level. The greatest number of generalists are undoubtedly at RAND, where there are estimated to be 75 to 100 bona fide strategy experts, plus that many more who come close to meeting the definition. The percentage of generalists in these six organizations ranges from one extreme at the Hudson Institute, where all of the two dozen professionals are concerned with broad policy matters, to the other extreme at the SRI, where only a few of the one thousand staff researchers are interested in nontechnical questions.

RAND.—Of the corporations that are aimed directly at meeting the government's needs, RAND is the prototype. It has not

Lyons and Morton, *op. cit.*, chap. 11; Archie M. Palmer (ed.), *Research Centers Directory*, Second Edition (Detroit: Gale Research Co., 1965); and brochures and annual reports of corporations mentioned. The judgments as to the scope and purpose of these corporations are based upon personal observations of the author and are his own responsibility.

changed its fundamental purpose or initial organizational concept as established with the agreement of the Air Force in 1948. RAND now occupies a sprawling complex of modern quadrangles that were added in successive states of growth. They stand in Santa Monica, just across the street from the Pacific Ocean—significantly, about as far removed from Washington as possible while remaining on American soil. Within these buildings stretch several miles of interconnected hallways, faced by long rows of small offices, each lined with books, stacks of pamphlets, a well-marked blackboard, and each occupied by a mathematician, an historian, a physicist, an engineer, or an economist who would be welcome on almost any college faculty or highly paid industrial staff. In all, there are about five hundred of these experts at RAND, including, as mentioned, some 100 strategists. When one observes this rare collection of scholars meditating like dons in their private cells, and also notes their informal Southern Californian garb, the characterization occurs that RAND is like an Oxford University in bright sport shirts. This is not an unfair commentary on both the extraordinary intellectual abilities of the RAND staff and the historic novelty of their direct intervention as scholars into practical affairs.

That intervention has been on a formidable scale. On its fifteenth anniversary in 1963, RAND, with understandable pride, declared that it had produced about 7,000 research reports, memoranda, and technical papers, and had distributed over a million copies of these. More than seventy books, most of them on public and some of them on famous issues, had been written at RAND and issued by commercial publishers and university presses.[5]

The nature of strategy expertise cannot be fully understood without reference to the organization and unique *modus operandi* of RAND. Various intellectual disciplines are represented at RAND in the divisions of aircraft, economics, electronics, mathematics, missiles, nuclear physics, and

social sciences. For particular projects, study teams are drawn up with representatives from these divisions, and an interdisciplinary flavor is thus acquired. This flavor is also informal. A recent RAND visitor, enroute to Southeast Asia to study problems of political and economic assistance, found that his inquiries in one afternoon took him to economists, who were especially interested in the political aspect, to political scientists, concerned with the sociological aspect, and to electronics engineers, who were deeply preoccupied with quite non-electronic tactics of ground patrolling and visual reconnaissance in Vietnam.

An important value at RAND, and one imperfectly obtained in other research corporations, is an intellectual freedom which serves as a counterpart to the academic freedom of universities. While its strength derives from its collectivity, that collectivity in turn depends upon unimpeded intellectual intercourse and the individuality and autonomy of its analysts. As one observer put it, "In semi-cloistered cubicles, they pursue elusive tangents in an atmosphere as rare as that of the Institute for Advanced Study."[6]

This freedom is effective in two dimensions. First, externally RAND enjoys a high degree of autonomy under its principal contractor, the United States Air Force. RAND exercises its own initiative regarding the choice of study projects, and is under no compulsion to pursue any project against its will.* Some of RAND's most valuable studies have served to further the

---

[5] *The RAND Corporation, The First Fifteen Years,* op. cit., p. 32.

[6] Bill Becker, "RAND Corporation Furnishes Brain Power for the Air Force," *New York Times,* May 22, 1960.

* [In contrast, Analytic Services Inc. (ANSER), Consultant to the USAF Air Staff's Directorate of Operational Requirements and Development Plans, is physically located near the Pentagon, and works only on short-term problems which have been assigned by the Air Staff. The President of ANSER is said to contrast his organization with RAND by suggesting that RAND studies what RAND thinks the Air Force needs to have looked at, while ANSER studies what the Air Force wants studied. See William Jeavitt, "ANSER: USAF's 'Short Order' Think Tank," *Air Force/Space Digest,* August, 1967.]

particular interests of other military services, perhaps to the detriment of the Air Force—for example, those studies in the area of limited war. But no really effective barrier was raised against this kind of freedom. RAND analysts, practically speaking, have nearly total access to classified data and resources available within the Air Force.

Second, internally RAND functions with great flexibility and grants considerable independence to its individual analysts and offices. Much like a university, RAND organization cannot be characterized so much as a hierarchy as an amalgamation, in which discipline and authority are oriented more toward goals of study than toward corporate success. RAND analysts do not admit to working "under" one another, and there is no chain of command of the usual kind, but rather procedures for widening dialogue, incorporating suggestions, and responding to criticism.

Persons who are closely involved in the system will react to these statements by pointing out some important exceptions and contradictions. Externally, there have been instances of attempted control or even censorship of RAND thinking. Internally, there is evidence that RAND is experiencing Parkinsonian tendencies toward growth and the acquisition of a corporate consciousness which does not always serve the pure aim of objectivity. And one vigorous critic of all strategic thinkers says "The RAND Corporation is financed mainly by the United States Air Force, so that its studies must be accepted with the same kind of reserve that, shall we say, we might greet a study of the Reformation by Jesuits based on unpublished and secret documents in the Vatican; there is the same combination of honesty in the value system and bias in the commitment."[7]

Nevertheless, it seems clear that through RAND's method of operation the cause of objectivity is effectively preserved. A thorough Congressional study extols the not-for-profit research corporation as a source of objective advice which in some ways functions better than could an organization within government.[8] Further, as will be shown, systems analysis, with its extra dividends, is made possible. The unhampered flow of ideas is essential to systems analysis. It can even be posited that the value of the output of a research corporation is a function of its intellectual freedom, both external and internal. This dual freedom, then, has fostered research methods at RAND with a whole new order of effectiveness.

The other two research corporations initially founded under armed service patronage developed with similarly high intellectual standards. They were affected differently, however, by their proximity to Washington, which not only ruled out sports shirts but also introduced additional elements of patronal pressure. Moreover, their organizational concepts underwent considerable change.

RAC.—In 1961 the Operations Research Office, after thirteen years of operation, was liquidated by mutual agreement between the Army and the parent institution, Johns Hopkins University. Evidently the need for structuring research in order to meet the needs of a government sponsor, modest as that need may have been, was felt by both parties to be incompatible with the autonomy desired by a university. The ORO was immediately transformed into the Research Analysis Corporation, which retained most of the staff and the quarters of the ORO, located just outside Washington. RAC, like RAND, was set up as a private, non-profit corporation, authorized to work for clients other than the Army, such as the Advanced Research Projects Agency (ARPA), a part of the Office of the Secretary of Defense (OSD). RAC employs about 250 professionals including technical specialists and some strategists, and is thus about half the size of RAND.

CNA.—The Navy found it desirable to expand the scope of its research interests from basic operations analysis, performed since the war by the Operations Evaluation Group, to include questions of high policy.

---

[7] Kenneth E. Boulding, *op. cit.*, p. 332.

[8] U.S. Congress, Senate, Committee on Government Operations, *Report to the President on Government Contracting for Research and Development, loc. cit.*

To this end it established an Institute of Naval Studies, involving civilian researchers under naval direction, and placed it in the academic milieu of Cambridge, Massachusetts. The Navy also saw the need to move in the direction of extra-governmental organization for research. The Franklin Institute of Philadelphia was the medium finally chosen. The Institute in 1962 assumed contractual responsibility for the management of both the OEG and the new Institute of Naval Studies, and both were organized together as the Center of Naval Analyses with headquarters in Washington. The locales of both components were unchanged, however, the OEG continuing to work directly with the Naval staff in Washington, and the Institute of Naval Studies remaining in the detached environment of Cambridge. The overall scale of this naval research is about the same as that of the Army's RAC.

OSD SPONSORSHIP: IDA

The Institute for Defense Analyses (IDA) is sponsored by agencies of the Office of the Secretary of Defense. IDA differs significantly from other non-profit research organizations because it is a unique amalgam of the external and the internal (government) analytical apparatus.

The making of the amalgam was a long and trying process. It began in 1948, when the newly established Office of the Secretary of Defense and the Joint Chiefs of Staff determined that they too needed a special research organization to conduct studies and to give advice on their own military problems. The Weapons Systems Evaluation Group (WSEG) was established for this purpose. It was located within the Pentagon and staffed entirely by military officers and civil service employees. Thus the official status of this group, as well as its initially narrow technical scope, were comparable to the operations analysis staffs that were continued by the armed services after the war.

WSEG, however, was expected to cope with more far-reaching questions than wartime operations analysis, questions such

as the choice between complete, new alternative bomber systems. Serious staffing difficulties and the bureaucratic handicaps of the Pentagon were soon encountered. The quality of WSEG work was not impressive when highlighted against the product of institutions like RAND and ORO, able as they were to attract the most competent civilian analysts to their freer and more attractive settings.

It seemed natural, then, to seek a new institutional formula outside of government. University sponsorship was decided upon. In 1955 the Massachusetts Institute of Technology took over WSEG's functions and became the employer of its civilian staff. Soon the sponsorship was expanded to a consortium of five, later eleven schools, including M.I.T., the California Institute of Technology, Stanford, Chicago, Columbia, and Michigan. Their new, non-profit progeny was named the Institute for Defense Analyses. It too is about half as big as RAND, and employs nearly three hundred research professionals, including its own small concentration of strategy experts.

IDA, while nominally sheltered under the aegis of its academic patrons, is now ensconced in a new high-rise building adjacent to the Pentagon. And IDA maintains a direct presence within Pentagon staff agencies. The WSEG staff itself is a division of IDA. Similar services are now provided, by other divisions of IDA, to other parts of the Office of the Secretary of Defense. One of these is the Advanced Research Projects Agency, which is devoted to such tasks as inventing methods for nuclear test detection. Another client is the Director of Defense Research and Engineering himself (DDR&E), under whom WSEG and ARPA are assigned. In behalf of DDR&E, IDA seeks answers to basic technical questions, such as the design limitations of future supersonic vehicles according to the metallurgical "state of the art." An International Studies Division of IDA is concerned more with the strategic aspect, and performs contract studies, for example on arms control and the prospects for international military (police) forces for offices like the Assistant Secretary of Defense for International Security Affairs and the Department of State.

Therefore, among all the non-profit research organizations, IDA is an institutional anomaly. Despite its numerous university connections, its projects are so closely linked to the needs and prescriptions of its Pentagon clients that IDA operates in less an academic atmosphere than the others.

This may not be obvious, in view of the continuing identification of RAND with the Air Force, RAC with the Army, and OEG (as part of the new Center for Naval Analyses) with the Navy. The three armed services are institutions of tradition (even the Air Force, whose ancestry goes back at least as far as the Flying Corps and the Cavalry). To be identified with one of the services therefore invokes the strong appearance of commitment to its values—a bias, in other words, unsuited to objective analysis. Committed to their sponsors these three research organizations may be, but the commitment is somewhat more apparent than real. Their organizational structures show that they do operate at least partly on the principle that detachment from the Pentagon is conducive to better research. IDA does not. (The true autonomy of RAND will later be explained as one of its main strengths.)

In contrast to the three armed services, the offices that surround the Secretary of Defense and that are served by IDA are relatively new embellishments of the military establishment. Their very newness, their diversity, and their consequent lack of dogma may give the impression that they are inherently and permanently blessed with the "objective" view. Time will provide the answer, but it is conceivable that these agencies of the Office of the Secretary of Defense will one day develop their own brand of vested interest and doctrinal inertia. If they do, one might expect the Institute for Defense Analyses, because its staffs interlock so closely with these agencies, to contract the same bureaucratic disabilities.

VARIATIONS IN FORM

Hudson Institute.—An important variation in the form of the non-profit research organization is the Hudson Institute. In respect to direct government affiliation, it occupies the opposite end of the scale from the Institute for Defense Analyses. Indeed, one of the reasons for the formation of Hudson in 1961 was to improve upon the degree of autonomy already enjoyed by RAND, which itself stood out among all the non-profit research institutions in that respect.

The Hudson Institute can be understood only in relation to RAND. In truth Hudson is RAND's offspring. Hudson displays toward RAND the natural filial tendencies to emulate and admire, mixed with the impulse to criticize and improve upon the parent. Some of RAND's best genes were transmitted to the Hudson Institute in the person of Herman Kahn, one of the most brilliant and versatile of RAND analysts, and the founder of Hudson. Kahn says,

The difference between Rand and Hudson is that Rand is the loyal opposition, and Hudson is not necessarily even loyal. We will have people with security clearance, without it, people who don't want it and people who couldn't get clearance if they tried.[9]

Like RAND, Hudson is located near the coast, close enough to many centers of scholarship, and yet far enough away from Washington. Like RAND, Hudson operates in a semicloistered atmosphere, in which researchers enjoy both intellectual freedom and immediate access to one another. But, interestingly, the Hudson coast is the opposite coast, the Hudson architecture is traditional rather than modern. The premises, in fact, are a rambling set of Tudor-style buildings that previously served as a mental institution. (The present occupants sometimes assert in good humor that "nothing has changed.")

A more important difference is that Hudson claims smallness as a virtue, and limits its professional staff to about twenty-five

[9] *Newsweek,* Oct. 9, 1961, p. 93.

persons, all of whom are interested in questions of strategy. The size of RAND, on the other hand, has gradually climbed to about five hundred professionals, and not without misgivings on the part of the RAND administration. As pointed out earlier, Hudson deliberately spreads its affiliation around various government agencies. And to insure its nonpartisanship, Hudson is governed by an unusual management principle. "Membership" in the Institute is provided to a select group composed of one-third public figures, such as industrial executives; one-third scholars representing widely disparate views about national security, from pacifists to advocates of stiff anticommunism; and one-third Hudson's own staff. These Institute members elect trustees and hold these trustees and the officers of Hudson responsible for the performance of its mission.

The official statement of that mission reveals the most significant feature of the Hudson Institute. According to its brochure:

The primary function of the Institute is to conduct and support studies designed to produce thorough, objective, and informed analyses of problems relating to national security and international order. The phrase "international order" is intended to include not only issues of peace and war, but also questions of freedom and international justice, and the relationship to these of economic, social, and political development.

"We must study all strategies," according to Herman Kahn. "You cannot have a sense of awe about the realities of the nuclear age. You must be detached. We will make a better case for unilateral disarmament and for preventive war than has ever been made before."[10]

In contrast, the other nonprofit research corporations, even RAND, place greatest emphasis upon the technological kind of question, using "hard" data. They perform a relatively small admixture of "soft" studies at the general policy level. This more common approach to research is not merely an attempt to concentrate on the

easy objective problems and avoid the difficult, abstract ones. The approach is vested in an important analytical principle called "suboptimization," which will occupy a major place in a later discussion. In brief, suboptimization means that the more a problem is subdivided into manageable components for which empirical data are readily available, the more valid the results of the study should be entered into with caution. It should be based upon a foundation of experience gained in the more elementary, component studies.

Thus the RAND investigations of major issues like the utility of civil defense, or the relation of SAC vulnerability to a policy of deterrence, are meant to be built upon the information and judgment obtained in analysis of more concrete and "suboptimal" subjects like the performance characteristics of bomber systems, penetration aids, interceptor missiles, and so forth. While this kind of suboptimization is the *modus operandi* at RAND, RAC, IDA, and other research organizations, the Hudson Institute, as its charter says, is committed to the consideration of general values like "freedom and international justice." This is to start at the top and work down, to exclude suboptimization at the outset as a working principle. The difference between the two approaches will have an important bearing on the examination, in later passages, of the potentialities and the limitations of strategy expertise in dealing with matters of national policy.

Stanford Research Institute.—This Institute stands at the fringe of the system of strategy expertise. It is included in this list of strategy-oriented research corporations partly because of the worthy contributions of its own generalists, who are a tiny fraction of the SRI staff, and partly because it is representative of a host of other corporations that also employ a sprinkling of researchers interested in national policy questions.

The SRI was established in 1946 by the trustees of Stanford University and a group of business leaders. The intent was, and is, to make available to industrial firms the benefits of the new postwar "enlightenment" of uninhibited and interdisciplinary

10 *Ibid.*

technical research. SRI research is performed in a large plant of offices and laboratories at Menlo Park, near the University. The best customer—expectedly—turned out to be the United States government. But, still, one-third of SRI's work is for private clients; the initial aim of aiding private industrial development remains in clear focus.

Most of the SRI work that can be classed as strategic is performed in its Operational Technology Division. This division emphasizes the use of operations analysis techniques. A few general studies are performed on subjects like civil defense; articles of some strategic importance appear in the quarterly *SRI Journal*. However, the bulk of the effort is linked to the development of new weapons and associated tactical doctrine for the Army and the Navy.

Arthur D. Little, Inc.—An organization with objectives similar to those of the SRI is Arthur D. Little, Inc., of Boston. It was organized in order to work on management and engineering problems for private firms, but it has added a number of study contracts for the government in the military sphere. To look further afield, many of the major defense corporations contain small groupings of strategy expertise. The Raytheon Corporation in Massachusetts, for example, employs several analysts attempting to design a computer model of international politics. Boeing, Douglas, North American, Bendix, and General Electric employ staffs that are expected to peer into the future strategic environment.

Understandably, the basic concern of corporation employees tends to be the welfare of the corporation; the future strategic environment is likely to be perceived by corporation analysts as a marketplace for weapons. But not invariably. General Electric has a staff of long-range thinkers known as the "Tempo" Division at Santa Barbara, which performs independent policy contract studies for the government. GE also produces its own *Defense Quarterly* with some attention to strategic issues. Bendix employs a division at Ann Arbor that devotes itself to the analysis of problems related to arms control.

New Corporations.—There are many small, new research corporations beginning to blossom on the periphery. United Research, Inc., is composed of a group from the Harvard Business School. Operations and Policy Research, Inc., of Washington, farms out its government-sponsored studies to consultants under contract. A bizarre newcomer is the Historical Evaluation and Research Organization, Inc. (HERO), which is founded on the appealing assumption that some answers to the questions of the nuclear age might be found by reexamining the lessons of military history. Another newcomer is Abt Associates, Inc., of Cambridge, where a group of young graduate scholars from the MIT-Harvard-Fletcher School complex are applying their talents to the design of games and mathematical models that are intended to reveal the character of such kinds of conflict as counterinsurgency and political revolution.

KINDS OF AFFILIATION

It was shown above that there are different formulae for affiliation of the research corporations with government clients. The RAND Corporation is a model of how to stay relatively independent while being supported almost entirely by federal funds. This independence is made possible by the geographical and intellectual detachment of RAND from Washington. It is a value believed in and supported by key administrators, both in RAND and in the Pentagon, who protect RAND's right of access to sensitive data in all quarters and RAND's right of initiative in setting its own study objectives. The Institute of Defense Analyses, in contrast, lacks such independence. It is so closely interlocked with government agencies, that it seems virtually an annex to the Pentagon with somewhat better salaries, parking, lighting, ventilation, and—of course—architecture.

There is another aspect to the matter of affiliation, however. What about the number of clients? What is the difference between research corporations sponsored mainly by a single government agency, like RAC, RAND, and the Center for Naval

Analyses, and those that spread their efforts among various clients, like IDA, The Stanford Research Institute, and the Hudson Institute? It will be recalled that Hudson's management deliberately eschews a single affiliation, and intends thereby to avoid being captive, to "play the field" and thus to enhance its independence.

Apart from IDA, for reasons stated, it would seem that playing the field should definitely produce a more impartial approach to research on the part of organizations like SRI and Hudson. As Kahn says, Hudson is able to hire people both with and without security clearances. Hudson is able to study the widest possible range of questions, to think not only about the "unthinkable," thermonuclear war, but also to accept a contract, as it has, to examine the merits of unilateral disarmament for the Society of Friends.

To develop the "captive" argument further, it seems that in the organizations serving a single client there would be an unavoidable tendency toward the development of a single style. While adhering as best they can to objective standards, analysts in those organizations, so the criticism goes, are unconsciously lured into line. Their standards are subtly but inevitably shaped to conform to the environment and the attitudes of the Air Force, or the Navy, or the Director of Defense Research and Engineering, as the case may be. Studies unfavorable to the client's interests tend not to be initiated, because the analyst is not inclined toward them anyhow. If he were not emotionally involved in his line of work, he would not likely have taken his job in the first place. And if he finds himself in general disagreement with his associates, he will probably select himself out of the organization.

There can be no denying that this criticism has some validity. A certain homogeneity of outlook within the research corporation seems obvious: There are few skeptics about the utility of naval power at the Center for Naval Analyses. One is not likely, on a visit to IDA, to get persuaded that the United States ought to pull out of Southeast Asia. But, curiously, there is another side to this matter of spreading the

affiliation of a research organization among a diversity of clients.

While it is true that the single-affiliation organization like RAND is liable to be client-oriented, the multi-affiliated organization like Hudson may suffer from another malady, that of being *contract-oriented*. First of all, the firm with many individual study contracts must produce results on each one of them, for the simple reason that delivery is required in the terms of the contract. And if performance is not satisfactory in any instance, there is a risk of alienating that client for the future. And what does "satisfactory" mean? It means, in individual contracts like these, fulfilling the expectations not of a vague entity like the Navy or the Army at large but the expectations of the particular office that originated or sponsored the contract, such as a Marine Corps branch studying the requirements for seaborne transport or an Army directorate investigating the need for more helicopters. In each case there will be a persistent colonel, with ideas of his own, monitoring the outcome.

So the multi-affiliated organization, while serving many clients, finds that each one of those clients can be a demanding taskmaster. The working agenda of such an organization is less likely to permit placid, detached contemplation than to require intensive concentration, first on one study and then the next, with the analytical staff marshalled and the focus shifted so as to perform as well as possible on each. And the result, at least a good part of the time, must be a product, good or bad, that does not disappoint the customer. Even if the research corporation is nonprofit, the directors do have a natural inclination to stay in business.

The RAND Corporation, as it happens, has an easier time getting along with its single, principal sponsor and also, consequently, getting along with its studies. Since most of its revenue comes from one blanket Air Force contract, RAND has much greater freedom to cancel an uninteresting project and to reject a bad report. It is possible for RAND analysts to devote their time to a project that is justified only by the fact that it seems worthwhile, not solicited nor supported by the Air Force. It is obvious that a good share of ideas that are really creative must come from such a free source as this. Another useful by-product of the single-client research environment is the liberty of analysts to specialize, to continue to work in their chosen field simply because they want to. A much-sought-after Soviet expert recently took employment at RAND, rather than IDA, because at IDA he expected to be pulled frequently out of his own work when the staff was mobilized to participate in short-term, high-priority projects.

Finally, in reviewing the whole field of government-supported strategic research corporations, large and small, sponsored and independent, one concludes that the particular question of whether they are nonprofit or profit-making is of less importance than might be expected. The research corporations do not fall into two distinct classes according to the lack or presence of corporate financial incentives. For all of them, success is measured immediately by their standing with their client, who almost invariably is some agency of the United States government. Ultimately, their true success is determined by the degree of their beneficial impact upon military decisions in particular and national security policy in general. And that true success, as will be explained, depends largely upon the permissiveness of the environment in which their policy analysts are permitted to work.

THE ACADEMIC LOCALE

Academic research centers are also an important part of the strategic community. They differ in organization and purpose from the research corporations, and make a different kind of contribution to the strategy formulation process. If the mainstream of strategic thought can be said to flow from the research corporations into the decision-making centers of government, then some of the most important sources of strategic thought rise on or near university campuses in a number of their affiliated research centers.

The dispersion of strategy expertise throughout the academic realm is just as widespread as its dispersion throughout the industrial world. One directory listed over 1600 academic research centers in the United States in 1965, ranging from the Princeton Plasma Physics Laboratory to the Purdue Public Opinion Panel.[11] However, just as six research corporations were identified as noteworthy for their concentration of strategy expertise, so it is possible to examine certain academic research centers, representative of the whole group, that contain scholars interested in strategic questions. These centers are generally clustered in the East, sponsored by such institutions as MIT, Harvard, Johns Hopkins, Princeton, Columbia, Chicago, and Pennsylvania.

Other strategic thinkers are found in institutions like Brookings and the Council on Foreign Relations that are education-oriented but unconnected with any university. The size of these scholarly organizations is usually quite small, numbering typically a handful of professionals and seldom more than a dozen or two. Within them, moreover, as in the research corporations, the strategists are generally outnumbered by their colleagues.

Although in the academic locale, the distinction between "generalist" and "specialist" is not really suitable, the strategists there are also distinguishable from their colleagues. The latter work in diverse nonmilitary fields like electoral behavior, fiscal policy, political communication, economic development, or public administration. Like the technologists in the research corporations, the work of these colleagues may have an important bearing upon national security, but they are not interested in strategy as a study in itself; indeed, many scholars working in traditional academic disciplines purposely disdain any contact with military affairs. Taking ac-

[11] *Research Centers Directors, op. cit.* Data as to size and activities of academic research centers throughout this section are obtained, in part, from this reference volume. The judgments as to scope and purpose of these centers are based upon personal observations of the author and are his own responsibility.

count of these factors, then, a fair assessment of the combined number of strategy experts in all scholarly research centers is between fifty and one hundred.

CHARACTER OF ACADEMIC RESEARCH CENTERS

Although there are important differences in the style and purpose of the particular research centers, which will be pointed out, they have certain characteristics in common that may be described first.

To begin with the physical characteristic, the centers usually occupy their own quarters in the midst of the academic bustle of the host campus. The actual facilities, however, range from the ultramodern, concrete box resembling a battlement that encloses the MIT Center for International Studies to the dreary Semitic Museum, just a few miles away in Cambridge, housing the Harvard Center for International Affairs together with certain archeological relics. These ancient stone figures gaze sternly upon the enigmatic haste of the professors, international research fellows, and typists who have set up shop among them.

The academic locale of these centers is appropriate and necessary, for the typical staff member performs both as researcher and teacher, often with regular academic rank and tenure. However, the centers receive part of all of their funds from outside sources, such as proceeds from government contracts and foundation grants. The Ford Foundation, for example, has lent vital support to both the MIT and Harvard Centers. A common formula for compensating a staff member calls for a half-time teaching and a half-time research workload, with the salary paid jointly by the university and the research center. Administratively, then, the centers represent overlapping jurisdictions, in which individuals possess dual status as members of the center and as members of academic departments. Most professionals in the research centers are economists and political scientists, with a few historians, sociologists, basic scientists and engineers blended in. According to Max F. Millikan, Director of the Center for

International Studies at the Massachusetts Institute of Technology, "the most rewarding aspect of the Center's development over the past dozen years has been its increasingly close identification with the growth of social science education at the Institute . . . with virtually every member of the Center's senior staff contributing to the Institute's undergraduate and graduate program in economics and political science. The contribution in economics has been primarily in the development field. In political science, the doctoral program emerged largely from the research enterprises of the Center and has remained strongly oriented toward the fields of comparative development, international communication, and foreign and defense policies."[12]

The output of scholarly works in the academic centers and its importance to society are at least as great as in the research corporations previously described. The MIT Center alone has produced over eighty volumes in the past fifteen years.[13] Much of the effort, however, is applied to nonmilitary subjects. At MIT, these include the examination in depth of the political, social, and economic structures of particular underdeveloped countries, such as India, Indonesia, Burma, and Venezuela, and behavioral-oriented investigations of matters like the attitudes of Europeans toward unification and the impact of educational TV in the U.S.

The studies accomplished at these centers are interdisciplinary. However, they represent combinations or refinements of conventional academic categories like comparative government, foreign relations, and international economics. The intimate connection with military technology, as found in the research corporations, and which requires the utmost in the "interdisciplinary approach," is not present. Methods of collective analysis, the use of intricate devices like gaming and mathematical models of conflict, are far less frequently employed.

[12] *12th Annual Report*, Center for International Studies, Massachusetts Institute of Technology, 1963, pp. 3, 4.
[13] *Ibid.*, pp. 49 ff.

The main difference between the university research centers and the research corporations is that in the academic locale staff members are more likely to work singly than as part of groups or teams, and they typically employ orthodox methods of scholarly investigation such as library research, travel, and interviews. The product, then, takes more the form of commercially published books and articles than speculative papers and theoretical memoranda.

Nevertheless, in these centers are found some of the most prominent strategic theorists who serve as key advisors to the government. That they are able to do so is due in part to their maintenance of contact with their counterparts in places like IDA and RAND, often much closer contact than with their own faculty associates who work in other fields. They are part of a strategic community whose members are very mobile and maintain a common dialogue with one another.*

Differences among Academic Research Centers

Along with their similarities, there are variations among the more prominent academic research centers that ought to be mentioned. In order to aid in appreciating their differences, the centers are grouped here, again somewhat arbitrarily, into several categories.

Centers Closely Involved in Policy.—In the first category are included the MIT Center for International Studies, the Harvard Center for International Affairs, and the Washington Center of Foreign Policy Research (affiliated with Johns Hopkins). These three centers are distinctive because of their intimate connection with the current formulation of national security policy through the writings and the consulting activities of their staff members.

* [Since 1961 the Air Force has assigned for one-year tours a small number of highly competent senior officers to several of the civilian research centers. The major purpose of the "Air Force Research Associate" program is to keep open the channels of communication between the Air Force and the civilian strategy community. Improved rapport between Air Force planners and civilian defense scholars is the continuing goal.]

The MIT Center for International Studies is the largest, most organized, and probably most productive of this group. Headed by Max Millikan, it contains over thirty professionals including professors of political science interested in military affairs like Lincoln Bloomfield, Lucian Pye, Ithiel Pool, and William Griffith, as well as William Kaufmann.[14] Its most distinguished alumnus is economist Walt W. Rostow, who left MIT to become Chairman of the Policy Planning Council of the Department of State.

The Harvard Center for International Affairs is much smaller and its members are more fully committed to academic activities. One of these is a fellowship program for about a dozen senior foreign service and military officers from the U.S. and other countries. Another academic activity is the Defense Policy Seminar, a pioneering venture in teaching about military affairs, established in 1954 by W. Barton Leach, Professor of Law, and which has now become a fixture of the graduate program in public administration. A similar Harvard program, though not connected with the Center, is the Science and Public Policy Seminar, under the direction of Don K. Price, Professor of Government and Dean of the Graduate School of Public Administration.

In respect to the Harvard Center's output of strategic thought, the place should really be characterized less as a center, with the coordination of effort that the term implies, than as a cohabitation of its noted and highly individualistic professors. Those who are particularly interested in military matters are Robert R. Bowie, Director of the Center, and Henry Kissinger, Samuel P. Huntington, and Morton Halperin, all political scientists, and Thomas C. Schelling, a professor of economics. With its other members who specialize in the fields of European politics and economic development of new nations, the Harvard Center contains over a dozen professionals.[15]

The MIT and Harvard Centers, despite

[14] *Ibid.*
[15] Center for International Affairs, *Seventh Annual Report 1964–1965*, Harvard University.

their organizational differences, are really made up of a single group of close associates in Cambridge. The main medium of their association is the Harvard-MIT Joint Arms Control Seminar, which has been meeting regularly for over five years. The participants include not only Harvard and MIT professors but also regular visitors from the research corporations, other universities, and the government. The topic of arms control seems to have been exhausted (or proved too exhausting) in the first two or three years, and the agenda was expanded to consider such varied topics as the utility of nuclear submarines, the impact of Chinese nuclear weapons on world politics, the psychological elements of deterrence, and the "limiting process" in local war.

Of this first group of centers, the Washington Center of Foreign Policy Research can be characterized as bringing its sophisticated intellectual talent most closely to bear upon immediate problems of national policy. Under the guidance of its initial director, Arnold Wolfers, and his successor, Robert E. Osgood, the Washington Center has capitalized upon the availability in the national capital of such men as Paul Nitze, Roger Hilsman, James E. King, and Charles B. Marshall, who have alternated between performing research at the Center and filling high government offices or advisory positions. The Center has prepared influential reports for government agencies on foreign aid, the impact of military technology on U.S. strategy, and other topics. Despite its proximity to the government, the Washington Center has managed to maintain its scholarly detachment. It is colocated with the School of Advanced International Studies of The Johns Hopkins University. The Washington Center contains about twenty professionals, plus a number of visiting scholars, and has produced a variety of published volumes and articles on foreign affairs, besides its government work.

Traditional Centers.—A second category of research centers includes those that originated before World War II and whose activities are somewhat more closely allied with traditional, independent scholar-

ship. They are the Princeton Center of International Studies, the Columbia Institute of War and Peace Studies, and the Chicago Center for the Study of American Foreign and Military Policy.[16] These centers are generally smaller than those in the first category, and are more detached from participation in government decision-making. While they are therefore less influential upon current policy, their detachment is undoubtedly held by their staff members to be an asset in the free pursuit of their studies.

The largest of these three is the Princeton Center of International Studies, which is nearly as large as the MIT Center, and contains about two dozen professionals. The Princeton Center is the direct descendant of the great Center for International Studies at Yale, which moved to Princeton in 1951 along with most of its talent when its director, Frederick S. Dunn, had a disagreement with the Yale authorities. Under its present director, Klaus Knorr, the Princeton Center may be considered to follow a more theoretical bent in its approach to military affairs than most others, and treats such bizarre topics as "limited strategic war" (a kind of war that would involve a carefully limited number of nuclear strikes directly on an enemy homeland). The quarterly *World Politics,* published by the Center, is one of the most valuable journals dealing with international affairs.

At Columbia and Chicago the centers are quite small, containing five to ten persons, and are oriented less to the attainment of any coherent research goals than to the support of individual professors of international relations in their pursuit of their normal scholarly interests. Although both schools contain large, powerful faculties, both centers are strongly identified with their directors, William T. R. Fox, of the Institute of War and Peace Studies at Columbia, and Hans Morgenthau, of the Center for the Study of Foreign and Military Policy at Chicago.

Specialized Centers.—A third category includes those centers that are committed

16 Lyons and Morton, *op. cit.,* chap. 6.

to their own distinctive assumptions about the nature of the international security problem.[17] One is the Foreign Policy Research Institute at the University of Pennsylvania. At the Institute, the basic security need is seen as countering worldwide Communist aggression, which is viewed as relentless Communist pursuit of world dominion through "protracted conflict" at all levels. This assumption represents the position of the Institute's director, Robert Strausz Hupé, and is shared by its scholars, including William R. Kintner.[18] The Institute employs about a dozen professionals and publishes *Orbis*, a high-quality quarterly journal of world affairs that features many articles dealing with the military aspects of national policy. Two similar organizations share the Foreign Policy Research Institute's main concern with the ideological menace of Communism. These are the Center for Strategic Studies, at Georgetown University, directed by Admiral Arleigh Burke, and the Hoover Institution on War, Revolution, and Peace, at Stanford, where Stefan T. Possony is Director of International Political Studies.

At the University of Michigan, the Center for Research on Conflict Resolution takes a quite different approach. At the Michigan Center the basic international problem is seen as man's propensity for conflict under existing world social and political conditions. The objective of the Center for Research on Conflict Resolution, then, is to examine the nature of conflict in order to discover ways to bring it under control. In following this objective, the Center produces more work of a truly abstract, theoretical nature than any of the other academic research centers described. Some of the topics are quite unconventional, such as economist Kenneth Boulding's attempts to perceive parallels between the behavior of economic units in competition and political units in conflict, or

mathematician Anatol Rapoport's analysis of *Fights, Games and Debates* as kinds of human activities in his book of that title. Articles of a similar theoretical vein appear in the Center's *Journal of Conflict Resolution*. Many critics argue that speculations such as are propounded at the Michigan Center are far-fetched and quite impractical. The reply, however, is that the danger of war in the nuclear age is so grave as to require the most unusual approaches to discovering ways to eliminate that danger.

Teaching Institutions.—Besides the academic research centers represented in these brief descriptions, there are conventional educational institutions that make direct and indirect contributions to strategy expertise. These are schools with programs for the teaching of international relations with special emphasis upon national security, often with a particular course identified as "defense policy."[19]

Such emphasis can be found at Ohio State, UCLA, Stanford, Wisconsin, Duke, North Carolina, Illinois, and the United States Military and Air Force Academies. At these schools, research and writing on military-related subjects is often an important by-product of teaching. Some of these schools, notably Ohio State and UCLA, are moving beyond the educational function to expand their direct scholarly contributions to the field of strategy. At Ohio State, a large endowment gives impetus to extensive plans for research in matters of national security, in a program now under the direction of Edgar G. Furniss, Jr. At UCLA the Institute of International and Foreign Studies, under Robert G. Neumann, has inaugurated a series of cooperative seminars in defense policy employing staff members from the nearby RAND Corporation as visiting faculty.

UNAFFILIATED RESEARCH ORGANIZATIONS

The dispersion of strategy expertise extends to another sector on the verge of the academic world. That sector is occupied by a

---

[17] Lyons and Morton, *op. cit.*, pp. 185–192.

[18] See Robert Strausz-Hupé, William Kintner, Alvin J. Cottrell, James E. Dougherty, *Protracted Conflict* (New York: Harper & Brothers, 1959); and Robert Strausz-Hupé, William Kintner and Stefan T. Possony, *A Forward Strategy for America* (New York: Harper & Brothers, 1961).

[19] See Wesley W. Posvar, "Introduction" to *American Defense Policy*, edited by Associates in Political Science, USAF Academy (Baltimore: Johns Hopkins, 1964).

number of prominent institutions that are, like the academic research centers, aimed at performing both education and research regarding various aspects of public policy and foreign affairs.[20] Unlike the centers, however, these organizations were established, some of them long before the war, as autonomous institutions free of any university affiliation. Among the most venerable of these organizations are the Carnegie Endowment for International Peace, the Council on Foreign Relations and the Brookings Institution. To the extent that these unaffiliated organizations have an educational mission, that mission is performed outside the university environment and is directed not at students but at the national intellectual elite. Whatever research they conduct in the area of national security often results from a redirection of their earlier missions, as originally prescribed by their founders, to face the new policy imperative of the nuclear age.

The Carnegie Endowment for International Peace.—This organization was established by Andrew Carnegie in 1910 with the lofty objective of fostering teaching and research that would aid in abolishing war. In subsequent years, when it became obvious that the millennium was not to be readily attained, the Carnegie Endowment entered actively into the sponsorship of many books, case studies, and research projects that contribute to better understanding of contemporary foreign policy, particularly as it is affected by international organization. Andrew Carnegie also founded the Church Peace Union, recently renamed the Council on Religion and International Affairs, which is devoted to the investigation of the ethical content of issues of national security and foreign policy. By no means a pacifist organization, it attempts to direct the attention of important citizens, foreign policy analysts, and theologians to the harsh physical requirements for survival in the nuclear era, and the moral dilemmas involved in the necessary maintenance of preparations for war. It performs this task by sponsoring a series

of seminars and through the publication of scholarly books and pamphlets.

Council on Foreign Relations.—Just after World War I the Council on Foreign Relations was organized by a group of citizens in New York City to discuss and evaluate the desired role of the United States in world affairs. The Council now contains about 1500 selected members, high government officials, educators, industrial executives, and intellectuals who meet regularly in specially organized groups to examine particular problems of foreign and military policy. A number of important books, such as Henry Kissinger's *Nuclear Weapons and Foreign Policy,* have resulted from the participation of scholars in these organized groups. Perhaps the Council's most important service, however, is the publication of *Foreign Affairs,* the highly influential quarterly which serves as a medium of communication for many of the policy-interested intellectuals in the United States.

The Brookings Institution.—Brookings directs its energies to a broader range of interests than either the Carnegie Endowment or the Council on Foreign Relations. Founded in the late twenties, Brookings for some years maintained a program of graduate education leading to the award of academic degrees in the fields of economics and public administration. Only after World War II did Brookings devote attention to foreign policy through the establishment of the Foreign Policy Studies Program under the late Leo Pasvolsky. That program has continued to expand and has involved the sponsorship of a number of published books and articles, the conduct of regional seminars and, more recently, formal studies of such problems as civil defense, defense organization, and the effects of defense contracting on the national economy.

Twentieth Century Fund.—There are also a number of somewhat newer organizations with specialized interests that impinge on strategy. The Twentieth Century Fund, which has devoted tremendous resources to a wide variety of domestic as well as foreign policy questions, in recent

[20] Lyons and Morton, *op. cit.,* chap. 12.

years concentrated attention on studies of civil-military relations in the United States government. The Fund also helped launch the great new wave of interest in arms control by supporting a special summer study group at MIT in 1960. As a result of the stimulus of that meeting, several important books on arms control were written and the personal associations were developed that led to the establishment of the joint Harvard MIT Arms Control Seminar. The National Planning Association is another institution that was initially concerned only with domestic policy. The NPA has taken a special interest in arms control, producing reports that were instrumental in the establishment of the Arms Control and Disarmament Agency in 1961.

The Institute for International Order.— Established since the war, the Institute concentrates upon the prospect of developing better international institutions. Among the volumes which it has supported is Grenville Clark and Louis Sohn's *World Peace through World Law*, which spells out in detail a constitutional system and the composition of an international police force designed to enforce world peace.

Institute for Strategic Studies.—Special mention is deserved by this Institute with headquarters in London. Although most of the unaffiliated organizations mentioned here are devoted to the explicit goal of peace, to which foreign policy considerations are corollary, the ISS is designed more as a direct counterpart to the active American strategic community. It was formed a few years ago in order to attract the attention of intellectual Britons and Western Europeans to the kinds of strategic issues that were already receiving intensive professional study in the United States: "the influence of modern and nuclear weapons and methods of warfare upon the problems of strategy, defense, disarmament, and international relations."[21] This purpose has been successfully fulfilled, and the organization is now both a pro-

ducer of at least one important volume a year in the field of strategy and a clearinghouse of ideas for all its membership. Its director is the British journalist Alastair Buchan, and its members include about 150 Americans, representing a high percentage of those who can be classed as strategy experts in the U.S.

Foundations.—At the furthest end of the strategy establishment, most distant from official control, a word should be said about the great foundations. They are not operating research organizations in themselves, but several of them support research in areas related to strategy by grants to the nonprofit research corporations, academic centers, and institutes. The most important of these foundations, in order of size, are the Ford Foundation, with assets over three billion dollars, the Rockefeller Foundation, worth about a half a billion, the Carnegie Corporation of New York (yet another of Andrew Carnegie's creations), with a quarter billion, and the Rockefeller Brothers Fund, which controls nearly two hundred million dollars.[22]

The overwhelming bulk of their philanthropic activities are in areas of public education, medical research, cultural development, and the like. However, they have also played vital roles in helping to establish academic research centers, as already noted. The Ford Foundation even provided the initial funds that brought the RAND Corporation and the Institute for Strategic Studies into being. Thus the foundations, while completely autonomous from government, and though dwarfed by the high scale of government research and development enterprises, have performed a tremendous service to the government of the United States. They have done so by providing a spur for the development of strategy expertise in its predominantly nonprofit and extra-official form. Without the foundations as financial catalysts, many of the impressive intellectual resources that now aid government in the strategy-for-

[21] *Memorandum and Articles of Association of The Institute for Strategic Studies, Ltd.*, London, 1958.

[22] *The Foundation Directory*, Edition 2, published by the Russell Sage Foundation, New York, 1964.

mulation process would not have come into being.

SUMMARY

The dispersion of strategy-making activities in the United States has been sketched in the preceding pages, beginning with the government, then the nonprofit research corporations working closely with government agencies, such as RAND, RAC, and IDA, next the profit-making defense corporations, then the academic research centers more remote from government, like those at Harvard, MIT, and Princeton, and finally the unaffiliated organizations just described.

The picture is one of disparity. As indicated earlier, this scattered strategy-making establishment is a typically American institution, catering to the popular distrust for big government and centralized military authority, and also indulging the special esteem that this country holds for the expert, the man addressed as "doctor" whose advice carries with it a special mystique of its own.

The difficulties of making objective, far-sighted judgments or of developing original concepts within the tense, labored environs of government bureaucracy have been pointed out. The difficulties are not all remedied, however, simply by moving outside the Pentagon. The very diversity of organization of strategy expertise should demonstrate that there is no simple formula for making good strategy, as the next chapter will explain further.

Along with the diversity of the strategy establishment, one should also be impressed by the relatively small share of resources devoted to it. This share is minuscule in comparison to the scale of government-operated and government-financed research and development activity. It was shown that only a few hundred real strategists, generalists in respect to national security policy, are spread through all these organizations. "Within the universities," complains Thomas C. Schelling of Harvard, "military strategy in this country has been the preoccupation of a small number of historians and political scientists, sup-

ported on a scale that suggests that deterring the Russians from a conquest of Europe is about as important as enforcing the antitrust laws."[23]

To consider again the budgetary aspect, the total annual expenditures of those research organizations concerned with strategy, both corporate and academic, plus other smaller ones with similar objectives, are estimated at less than one per cent of the total federal R&D budget. Narrow the focus further to include only the strategic generalists in these organizations, add in the salaries of government officials and the salaries and research funds of individual university professors who work on strategic problems outside of these organizations, and it is a reasonable estimate that the direct cost of all strategy expertise is not more than twenty-five million dollars per year. This is about one five-hundredth of federal R&D funds expended on national security programs.

Finally, in appraising the dispersion of the strategy-making establishment, there is a subtle danger. This is the temptation to regard the dispersion, ranging from the innermost government office to the outermost academic sanctuary, as a spectrum of competence.

Nothing that has been said about the handicaps of bureaucracy at the one extreme and the advantages of intellectual detachment at the other should be construed as meaning the "outside" strategy experts as a group have greater ability. The typical Pentagon staff officer is handpicked for his superior military record and his mental agility. Frequently, he has a graduate-level education and sometimes is a scholar and author in his own right. Many of his civilian associates were themselves formerly strategy experts, analysts at RAND or professors at MIT or Harvard. Their problems do not pertain to personal qualifications, but rather to their environment and the pressures of their responsibilities.

So the dispersion of the strategy establishment should not be interpreted as a

[23] Thomas C. Schelling, *The Strategy of Conflict* (Cambridge, Mass.: Harvard University Press, 1960), pp. 8ff.

reproach against professional military officers and career civil servants. There are many who do regard it as such, or worse, who consider the efforts of civilian strategists as an unwarranted intrusion upon the domain of the military. They are just as wrong in their judgment as those who insist that civilian intellectual capacities are naturally superior, the salvation of the Defense Department.

The difficult aim of the chapters that follow is to appraise strategy expertise objectively, to dispel any military and any civilian biases about its utility. This valuable intellectual development that is contributing so much to this country is shared in by both military and civilian, within and without government. They are a single community, all clothed in the same invisible uniform of dedication to meeting the needs of national security in the nuclear age.

DEPARTMENT OF DEFENSE:
UNITY OR CONFEDERATION?

BY HARRY H. RANSOM

I

To create and manage the military power required in pursuit of the objectives set by the President and the National Security Council is the particular responsibility of one NSC member—the Secretary of Defense. From General Pershing's massive walnut desk in the Pentagon, the Defense Secretary presides over an establishment employing 3,750,000 military and civilian persons situated all around the globe and spending each year an amount greater than the total national budgets of England, France, West Germany, and Italy combined.[1] He "presides over" but does not

[1] More than $350 billion in taxpayers' money spent by the Pentagon from 1954 to 1962. The 1963 bill adds up to more than $50 billion.

Selections from *Can American Democracy Survive Cold War?* by Harry Howe Ransom. Copyright © 1963, 1964 by Harry Howe Ransom. Reprinted by permission of Doubleday & Company, Inc.

Mr. Ransom is Professor of Political Science at Vanderbilt University. He is the author and editor of books including *Central Intelligence and National Security* (1958) and *An American Foreign Policy Reader* (1965), and articles on national security policy and U.S. foreign policy.

fully control this vast enterprise. Here, in the largest and by far the most expensive sector of American government, we are face to face with the issue of centralization versus decentralization—an issue of far-reaching impact on the problem of defense and democracy.

American armed services are engaged in world-wide activities, from the operation of diaper services overseas to radio broadcasting networks in foreign lands. At the end of 1962, more than one million American servicemen were on duty in forty-one foreign nations around the globe. Defense Department exchange-of-foreign-military-persons programs—in which foreign military personnel are exchanged with similar Americans for limited periods of training—are more extensive than those of civilian agencies. Pentagon officials, civilian and military, make many more speeches and write several times as many articles on foreign policy subjects as officials of the Department of State. And, as one observer has commented, through its nation-wide links with battalions of individuals and organizations (such as veterans' groups, large industrial complexes, mayors and other officials of towns adjoining military establishments), the Defense Department has "a built-in system of communication with the American people unequaled in scale by anything available to other Federal agencies." [2]

In his farewell address to the nation as President, Dwight D. Eisenhower voiced concern about the impact upon American democracy of such "an immense military establishment and a large arms industry . . . new in American experience," adding that "the total influence—economic, political, even spiritual—is felt in every city, every State house, every office of the Federal government." He recognized the "imperative need" for a mighty defense establishment, but noted its "grave implications" for the "very structure of our society." [3] Our concern in this chapter is not primarily with the structure of American society, but with the structure and procedures of the Department of Defense as the focal point for significant decisions about national defense requirements.

Pentagon organization does not present a simple picture. Edwin Weisl, a New York lawyer working as a special counsel for a Senate subcommittee investigating the defense program in 1958, aptly referred to the defense establishment as "this complex and difficult and sometimes ununderstandable organization . . . this tremendous chart of bureau on top of bureau, committee on top of committee, office on top of office . . . the most complicated jigsaw puzzle that ever was invented." [4]

The Pentagon Building, like the organizational chart of the Department of Defense, is massive and complex though deceptively simple in basic design. It contains about 160,000 miles of telephone cable and has housed as many as 32,000 persons, from the Secretary of Defense down to the clerk in its jewelry shop. This city of workers is both the heart of a partially "unified" defense establishment and the world's largest business enterprise, spending more than $50 billion a year and with physical assets estimated in 1962 at $158 billion.

In theory, this military colossus serves as an instrument of national policy, which in turn, according to the American ideal, is based upon the consent of the governed. The armed forces, their organization and weapons systems, are, ideally, instruments of government to be used in pursuit of national purpose as defined in the consensus achieved through the political process. This basic idea underlies modern-day concepts of "civilian control" of the military: armed forces must always remain instruments of national policy.

As we have seen, modern technology and the geopolitical facts of life tend to dim

---

[2] Waldemar A. Neilsen, "Huge, Hidden Impact of the Pentagon," *The New York Times Magazine*, June 25, 1961, p. 9.

[3] Address to the Nation, January 17, 1961.
[4] Edwin Weisl, Chief Special Counsel, Senate Preparedness Investigating Subcommittee, quoted by John Osborne, "The Man and the Plan," *Life*, April 21, 1958, p. 118.

the distinction between "purely military" and "purely political" factors in national policy making. But the meaning of civilian control need not be blurred, even in an age of radical changes in the nature of military professionalism. The guiding concept of civilian supremacy was once succinctly stated by a professional military officer turned President: "Basic decisions related to the military forces must be made by politically accountable civilian officials," said Eisenhower.[5] President Kennedy, reaffirming this principle, more recently declared: "Our arms must be subject to ultimate civilian control and command at all times, in war as well as peace." [6] Whether this condition has prevailed in the period since World War II— and grave doubts exist that it has—has been heavily influenced by the organization for military defense, which in turn is conditioned by the American constitutional system.

The most significant and controversial features of defense organization in the United States are: (1) the existence of four huge military institutions, each with a distinct tradition, a sense of service identification, and public following and friends in powerful sections of the industrial community and on Capitol Hill; (2) the revolution in technology that is not only changing the nature of military professionalism but is believed by many to be erasing the traditional organizational rationale for separating armed services according to mode of transport—land, sea, and air (in which traditional service, for example, does the long-range missile belong?); (3) the widespread belief that changes in the existing administrative structure are needed to accommodate the new technology; (4) the strong differences of opinion as to how best to alter the existing organization in order to promote simultaneously efficient fighting forces with the requisite *esprit de corps* and logical and purposeful

allocation of resources and effective democratic decision making; and (5) the fact that while the President as Commander in Chief of the armed forces and Chief Executive has the initiative and final say in defense decisions, his authority and power are shared with Congress.

The question to be explored here is whether the organizational arrangements in the Department of Defense foster or impede the coherent resolution of the issues of purpose, strategy, and organization, and are in keeping with the pursuit of the ideals of security and democratic government. If not—that is, if politically responsible leaders cannot in reality make the decisions about military forces that rationally accommodate both the implications of technology and the requirements of self-government—this is indeed a serious indictment of the organizational structure. A corollary question is whether power, authority, and responsibility within the defense establishment are properly allocated, defined, and identifiable, or whether the defense establishment, reflecting the American distrust of concentration of government power relevant in an earlier age, is characterized by fragmented authority and ill-defined responsibility.

Hoping to "provide for the common defense," Pentagon activities proceed under a deliberately ambiguous working concept and structure. In 1947 Congress enacted legislation that partially "unified" the separate armed forces under the Secretary of Defense, and since then, as one veteran observer commented, "There have been only two modes of life in the Pentagon: preparation for the next reorganization and recovery from the last one." [7]

II

The concept of a highly centralized or "unified" defense establishment had the support in 1945–47 of President Truman, the War Department, and the many supporters of air power; and its promise of economy and efficiency had wide public appeal. Yet Congress blocked the enact-

[5] Message to Congress, Reorganization Plan No. 6 of 1953, April 30, 1953.

[6] Special message to Congress on the defense budget, March 28, 1961.

[7] Col. William E. Depuy, *Army*, April 1961, p. 30.

ment of proposals for a highly centralized defense system, fearing a loss of power by Congressional units—although it had itself "unified" naval and military affairs committees in the House and Senate in the Legislative Reorganization Act of 1946. The upshot was compromise legislation, strongly influenced by a carefully worked out plan commissioned by Secretary of the Navy Forrestal and developed under the aegis of Ferdinand Eberstadt, a civilian consultant.

The term "unification" was itself variously defined, as a summary of three of the most important organizational issues of 1944–47 and their resolution in the National Security Act of 1947 shows:

1. A *single war department versus three separate departments.* The Army advocated a single department, the Navy insisted upon confederation with the Defense Secretary as a relatively powerless coordinator, and the Air Force put its existence as a separate department first and a unified Department of Defense second. The final outcome was a National Military Establishment and three separate departments. The office of Defense Secretary was created but with ambiguous powers.[8] These powers, over the years, have gradually increased, at the expense of the separate armed forces departments and the Congress. But the authority of the Defense Secretary *vis-à-vis* the separate services, the Joint Chiefs of Staff, and the Congress remains the most basic and controversial issue of defense organization.

2. A *single chief of staff.* The Army supported a single chief assisted by a general staff; the Navy opposed this as dangerous centralization and risky separation

[8] In addition various coordinating devices were established: a National Security Council, a Central Intelligence Agency, and a National Security Resources Board. In general the new structure followed the lines suggested by the Navy's Eberstadt Committee Report. A good, if somewhat pro-Navy account is found in Robert G. Albion and Robert H. Connery, *Forrestal and the Navy*, Columbia University Press, 1962, Ch. 11; the most complete general account is Hammond, *Organizing for Defense;* also useful is Stanley, *American Defense and National Security.*

of authority and responsibility. The Navy argued, with powerful bipartisan support on Capitol Hill, that to separate the JCS planning role from the active leadership of the armed services would produce unrealistic plans and pose the threat of cutting off the final decision makers, such as the Secretary of Defense, the NSC, and the President, from important dissenting views and alternative choices. The Navy won the day when the concept was adopted of Joint (confederated) Chiefs of Staff, with a *joint* staff, both organized on the basis of equal representation of the Army, Air Force, and Navy (including the Marines). Each service chief wears two hats —that of head of his service and that of JCS member.

3. *Roles and missions of the Army and Air Force versus the Navy and Marine Corps.* The Army had hoped that in the postwar shaping of the military structure the Marine Corps would be strictly limited in size and function, and the corps' missions restricted virtually to the shore line. The Army lost this battle; the Marines were accorded full divisional strength and full participation in amphibious operations. The Air Force, for its part, had hoped to take over from the Navy important aspects of anti-submarine warfare and the control of land-based aircraft, to protect shipping and for reconnaissance. The Air Force lost. The assignment of basic service functions has remained to date virtually unaltered since the 1947 Act, despite the incompatibility of traditionally assigned missions and new weapons. Attempts to re-evaluate the situation in keeping with modern technology continue to run into the active opposition of the supporters of the separate services, notably in Congress.

Much "unification" history and most of the basic organizational concepts are contained in the words—and between the lines —of the often-overlooked "Declaration of Policy," which is, in effect, the "Preamble" to the National Security Act of 1947.[9] This part of the statute expresses the "In-

[9] Public Law 253, 80th Congress, July 27, 1947, 61 *Stat.* 495.

tent of Congress," with deliberate and significant ambiguity as follows:

In enacting this legislation, it is the intent of Congress to provide a comprehensive program for the future security of the
United States; to provide for the establishment of integrated policies and procedures
for the departments, agencies, and functions of the Government relating to the
national security; to provide three military
departments, separately administered, for
the operation and administration of the
Army, the Navy (including naval aviation
and the United States Marine Corps), and
the Air Force, with their assigned combat
and service components; to provide for
their authoritative coordination and unified direction under civilian control of the
Secretary of Defense but not to merge
them; to provide for the effective strategic
direction of the armed forces and for their
operation under unified control and for
their integration into an efficient team of
land, naval, and air forces but not to establish a single Chief of Staff over the armed
forces nor an armed forces general staff
(but this is not to be interpreted as applying to the Joint Chiefs of Staff or Joint
Staff).[10]

Here we have a document that calls simultaneously for "integration" *and* "separation"; for "unified direction" *but not*
merger; strategic "integration" but *not* a
unified staff by which this can be accomplished. This hodgepodge emerged from
sharply varying approaches to defense
organization, the Presidency, the National
Security Council, the Cabinet, the Secretary of Defense, and the place of military
advice in decision making, and from the
aggressive attitude of Congress toward its
role in defense policy making.

The 1947 Act was a compromise between
those, like President Truman, Secretary
of War Robert Patterson, General Marshall, General Eisenhower, and most
Army and Air leaders, who, initially at
least, had favored a centralized civil and

military setup and those, like Navy Secretary Forrestal, his adviser Ferdinand
Eberstadt, most Navy leaders, and some
influential members of Congress—notably
Democratic Rep. Carl Vinson, Georgia,
and Senator David Walsh, Massachusetts
—who feared a "monolithic" organization
that would not only merge, but submerge
the Navy—particularly naval aviation
and possibly the Marine Corps, and chip
away at Congressional influence. The
Navy raised the further objection that a
centralized structure would be unwieldy
and inefficient.

Walt W. Rostow observes of the 1944–
47 unification controversy: "It was a struggle of bureaucratic politics and of men—
not of military ideas." [11] Underlying the
organizational debate was a major strategic issue of the time: What can airpower do? But though there were some
discussions of the potentialities and limitations of strategic airpower, little attention was given to the main issues: national purpose, strategic doctrine and military requirements of the postwar decade.
More often the debate centered on the
issues of which service was to perform
which function with how much money.
One fundamental issue was summarized
by Admiral Richmond Kelly Turner, testifying before the Senate Naval Affairs
Committee in 1946:

Frankly, I believe the Navy as a whole
objects to the so-called unification because
under any system the Navy will be a numerical minority and the Army, and the
Air Force, a military majority . . . [which]
will always be in a better political position
than the Navy. Because the Navy has had
and should retain in the future its position
as the first line of military security for the
United States, I believe the Navy will never
willingly agree to a consolidation of national military forces in any manner that
will silence the Navy's voice in military

---

[10] National Security Act of 1947, as amended.

[11] *The United States in the World Arena,* New
York, Harper, 1960, p. 175.

affairs or materially restrict its present responsibilities.

In sum, the 1947 unification compromise was characterized by administrative federalism, distrust of effective concentration of power, a busy Congressional hand in details of defense requirements and organization, and a general disregard for an accelerating technology and for questions of national purpose and the reality of possible enemies who might have to be engaged or, at best, deterred.

James V. Forrestal, who effectively fought the proposals to establish a strong Secretary of Defense, became the first Secretary of Defense. He was not long in office before he realized that his authority was much too limited to allow him to function effectively as administrator of a sprawling defense establishment in which the main elements were competing fiercely for a larger share of limited resources. His first annual report called for a strengthening of his authority and much greater centralization than he had been willing, as Secretary of the Navy, to admit was advisable. Upon retiring as Defense Secretary, Forrestal wrote to the chairman of the Senate Armed Services Committee, Millard Tydings, pointing to weaknesses in the unification statute that he had not foreseen. "I am . . . convinced that a failure to endow [the Secretary] with sufficient authority to control effectively the conduct of our military affairs will force upon us far greater security risks than will be the case if singleness of control and responsibility are achieved." [12] Forrestal's recommendations, along with those of the (Hoover) Commission on Organization of the Executive Branch of Government—and its 1948 force report—prompted a further defense reorganization in 1949.

III

Since 1947 the trend of defense organi-

[12] Quoted in Murray Green, "Today's First Line of Defense," *Air Force and Space Digest,* July 1961, p. 60.

zation, on both the civil and military sides (OSD and JCS), has continued toward greater centralization. The 1949 and 1953 amendments produced some thirty-odd "Mr. Secretaries" and a huge secretariat which has numbered as high as twenty-five hundred persons in the Pentagon superstructure. The importance and power of the Chairman of the JCS have also increased. But the "states' rights" of the separate services have remained, as has their power of "interposition" in the strategic planning process.

In the 1949 amendments the Army-Navy-Air Force Departments lost their cabinet rank and became "military" departments with the Secretary of Defense speaking for all three in the National Security Council. At the same time the word "general" was omitted from the phrase giving the Secretary of Defense "direction, authority and control" over the Service Departments; and the "reserved powers" clause for the separate Departments, limiting the power of the Defense Secretary to specified authority, was eliminated. But transfer, reassignment, abolition, or consolidation of combat functions (roles and missions) was prohibited, and Congress had to be kept fully informed of any other consolidation of functions.

Two further legislative enactments of importance occurred in 1952. One created a Director of Installations and a Defense Supply Management Agency within the Department of Defense. The Director was charged with coordinating military public works planning and construction; the Agency, with developing a single catalog system and programs of interservice supply standardization. The other established a floor under the authorized personnel strength of the Marine Corps, and provided for the participation of the Marine Commandant in meetings of the Joint Chiefs of Staff when matters of concern to the Marine Corps were to be discussed.

The next major change came in 1953, following the Korean War and the 1952 Presidential election. There was considerable dissatisfaction in many quarters about the defense-organization performance during the Korean War. A rapid turnover in the Secretaryship had occurred during this period, with Louis Johnson succeeded by General George C. Marshall who was in turn followed by Robert A. Lovett. After the election of 1952 the outgoing Mr. Lovett submitted to President Truman a detailed letter criticizing Pentagon organization and recommending more authority for the Secretary and improvements in the strategic planning process. Experience had convinced him that the existing defense structure "would require drastic reorganization to fight a war." Among other things, Lovett had found it "extremely difficult for the Joint Chiefs of Staff to maintain a broad non-service point of view. Since they wear two hats . . . it is difficult for them to detach themselves from the hopes and ambitions of their own service. . . ." [13]

General Eisenhower was an early advocate of defense centralization and unification. As President he appointed a seven-man committee, headed by Nelson A. Rockefeller, to study defense organization and to make recommendations. The Rockefeller Committee's Report, submitted in April 1953, resulted in transmittal to Congress of Reorganization Plan No. 6. Some of the proposed changes were described to Congress as "terrifying" by Ferdinand Eberstadt, and organizations such as the Navy League continued to warn of the dangers to our form of government of increasing centralization within the defense establishment. Concepts of federalism, free enterprise, and competitive capitalism were equated with the organizational requirements of the military establishment. Congress made an unsuccessful attempt to reject the plan, but it went into effect on June 30, 1953.

Under the 1953 reorganization, service autonomy was reduced still further by making the Chairman of the Joint Chiefs of Staff responsible for managing the

[13] Letter, Lovett to Truman, November 18, 1952.

Joint Staff and selecting its membership; eliminating various boards and agencies with equal service representation; and tripling the number of Assistant Secretaries,[14] bringing the total to ten, including the General Counsel. Assistant Secretaries of Defense soon became "staff executives" in charge of major functions: legislative and public affairs, international security affairs, manpower, research and development, financial management, supply and logistics, properties and installation, health and medical services, applications engineering and General Counsel.[15]

Between 1953 and 1958 the controversy was nurtured and sustained by accelerating technological developments, which continued to challenge existing defense concepts and to aggravate both the normal competition among the services for defense dollars and the conflict over assignment of "missions." Proposals for further centralization of authority in the Office of the Secretary of Defense and for a more unified strategic planning system remained at the heart of the problem, entwined with the debate over the kinds and levels of forces needed for deterrence of general war and for limited war. Critics of the defense structure as reorganized in 1953, including Senator Stuart Symington, many Air Force generals, some Army leaders and a number of academic observers, continued to decry the loose federalism that they claimed still characterized the relationship of the Defense Secretary to the armed services and of the services to one another.

In late 1957 and 1958 the rising cost of weapons systems, and public shock at the discovery of Russian progress in technological development, particularly Russian exploits in space, intensified the criti-

[14] The main effect in most cases was to change the title of existing statutory positions. For example the Chairman, Research and Development Board became Assistant Secretary, Research and Development.

[15] The legislative and public affairs functions were separated into two secretariats in 1957, and research and development and applications engineering were combined into "Research and Engineering."

cisms.[16] Simultaneously interservice rivalries were aggravated by inflation and by ceilings on the total defense funds available.

IV

Following a White House-Pentagon study,[17] President Eisenhower early in 1958 moved on three fronts: he ordered important organizational changes that did not require legislation; he submitted to Congress personally drafted legislation for Pentagon reorganization; and he issued statements, including personal letters to several hundred influential friends around the country, designed to engender support for his proposals and to counter expected opposition to his reform measures, particularly on Capitol Hill and in naval circles.

In brief outline, the Administration's 1958 reorganization program called for increasing the authority of the Secretary of Defense in strategic planning, in administration of the defense establishment, and in military operation; for greater military

[16] In addition to the continuing advocacy of Department of Defense reorganization by such groups as the Air Force Association, a number of influential studies and reports were published in the wake of Russian sputniks which sharply criticized existing defense organization. These included: Rockefeller Brothers Fund, *International Security, The Military Aspect,* Special Studies Report 2, Garden City, New York, Doubleday Headline Books, January 1958; Kintner and associates, *Forging a New Sword;* and, presumably, the secret report of the Gaither Committee in late 1957. Henry A. Kissinger's *Nuclear Weapons and Foreign Policy,* New York, Harper, 1957, was also highly critical of existing defense organization. Important ideas circulating within the RAND Corporation during this period can be found in A. C. Enthoven and H. S. Rowen, "Analysis of Defense Organization," RAND Paper P–1640, 1959.

[17] Instructed by President Eisenhower to reorganize the Pentagon, as one of his first major tasks as new Secretary of Defense, Secretary Neil H. McElroy appointed a Special Assistant for this purpose. The assistant was Charles A. Coolidge, Boston lawyer and former Assistant Secretary of Defense. Consultants used were JCS Chairman Nathan Twining; former JCS Chairmen General Omar Bradley and Admiral Arthur Radford; William C. Foster, former Deputy Secretary of Defense; Nelson Rockefeller, then Chairman of President's Advisory Committee on Government Organization; and General Alfred M. Gruenther.

unification of strategic and tactical planning; and for using the unified field commands as operational instruments for implementing President Eisenhower's oft-stated view that "separate ground, sea and air warfare is gone forever."

The Administration-drafted legislative proposals submitted to Congress were quickly answered by the counterproposals contained in a Congressionally drafted bill introduced by a bipartisan group of opponents of centralization. Some parts of the "opposition" bill are patently tongue-in-cheek proposals designed for bargaining purposes, to deter the Administration from insisting on what many influential Congressmen regarded as too much centralization in the Pentagon. The Congressional bill, in part, called for the return of the Secretaries of Army, Navy, and Air Force to membership on the National Security Council; limited the number of Assistant Secretaries of Defense to four; placed a ceiling of six hundred on the number of civilians employed in the Office of the Secretary of Defense, reducing the existing number by two-thirds; and curtailed drastically the authority of the Assistant Secretary of Defense, Comptroller, limiting sharply his supervision over the programs and requirements of the separate armed services. These proposals, submitted in the names of veteran Representatives Carl Vinson, Democrat, Georgia, and Paul Kilday, Democrat, Texas, were apparently designed to scare the Pentagon bureaucracy away from any scheme that either significantly reduced Congressional influence in military affairs or seriously impaired the independence of the separate services.

The "opposition" bill reflected a set of principles in sharp contrast to those espoused by the White House. Many influential legislators believed that defense decisions should be an amalgam of the divergent views of the several military departments and not the doctrine of one service or individual. They also felt that the President and Congress should share responsibility for defense.

As in 1947, the case was settled "out of court," by compromise. Significant steps, nonetheless, were taken in direction of unification. The 1958 reforms in their long-range effect represented the greatest advance toward unification since 1947. The changes may be grouped in the following categories: Authority of the Secretary of Defense; Joint Chiefs of Staff and Joint Staff; Roles and Missions of the separate Armed Service Departments; and Lines of Command. Note, however, that there is an inter-relationship among them. If the Secretary of Defense gains greater authority, it is likely to be at the expense of the separate services and the Congress.

The Secretary of Defense. Secretarial authority was appreciably strengthened by the 1958 reform, although the Presidential desire to give the Secretary "greater flexibility in money matters" ran into a stone wall on Capitol Hill. The Departments of Army, Navy, and Air Force were no longer required by law to be "separately administered" but simply "separately organized," and, after the 1958 legislation, came under the clearly stated "direction, authority, and control" of the Defense Secretary.

The service Secretaries became responsible to the Secretary of Defense for the "efficient operation" of their departments. Orders to the departments would be issued through the service Secretaries or the Defense Secretary's various deputies—including Assistant Secretaries of Defense—but their authority in this regard had to be, at Congressional insistence, specifically delegated in writing by the Secretary of Defense.

The Secretary could propose to reassign, transfer, consolidate or abolish major combat functions—in effect, service roles and missions—subject, through specified procedure, to Congressional veto. And he could reassign at this discretion non-combat functions, such as supply.

The Joint Chiefs of Staff, as a corporate body, became "directly responsible" to the Secretary of Defense; and it was to be the Secretary who made the nomina-

tions to the President for the promotion of all officers above the rank of Brigadier General, with "suggestions" from the service Secretaries and "advice" from the Joint Chiefs of Staff. The President let it be known that such promotions would be based in part upon the officers' ability to cooperate with the other services.

The Director of Defense Research and Engineering was by statute designated the Defense Secretary's principal adviser on scientific and technical matters. He was to supervise all research and engineering in the Department of Defense and to control, assign or reassign any research and engineering activities the Secretary thought required central management. The Secretary in turn could assign a new weapons system, regardless of which service might have developed it, to any of the three armed services for production, procurement, and operational control.

The Joint Chiefs of Staff. The maximum size of the Joint Staff, a strategic planning group serving the JCS and composed of officers on assignment from the Army, Navy, Air Force, and Marine Corps, was raised from 210 to 400. And the Chairman of the Joint Chiefs of Staff, instead of the JCS as a group, was to select the Director of the Joint Staff, in consultation with the JCS and with the approval of the Secretary of Defense.

The enlarged Joint Staff was also reorganized. A "J-Staff" system replaced the old interservice committees, the "J" implying more truly integrated thinking. Of most significance was the creation of J-3, which became a new, integrated operations division of the Joint Staff and an essential addition now that the JCS assumed strategic direction of the unified field commands for the Defense Secretary, replacing the designated service departments that had been previously responsible for the Army in Europe, the Navy in the Far East, etc.

Other J-Staff directorates, containing integrated units with roughly equal representation from the three services and the Marine Corps were: Personnel (J-1); Intelligence (J-2); Logistics (J-4); Plans and Policy (J-5); and Communications-Electronic (J-6). Additional functional units established were a Joint Military Assistance Affairs Directorate, a Joint Program Office, and a Joint Advanced Study Group. The new operational concept required these units to produce "agreed" rather than "split" position papers for the Joint Chiefs of Staff.

On the negative side, Congress stipulated that the new Joint Staff "shall not operate or be organized as an over-all Armed Forces General Staff and shall have no [independent] executive authority," and placed a three-year limit on Joint Staff service.

With the approval of the Service Secretary and with the understanding that responsibility was not being delegated, the Chiefs of the armed services were authorized by statute to turn over to their Vice-chiefs such duties as were deemed necessary to permit the Chiefs to give primary attention to their JCS role.

Roles and Missions of the Service Departments. The 1958 statute specifically provided for the continued existence of separate Departments of the Army, Air Force, and Navy, the latter explicitly "including naval aviation and the United States Marine Corps." Although the authority of the Secretary of Defense in the "unified direction" of the departments was increased, Congress reiterated its intention "not to merge these departments and services." The Departments were to remain "separately organized," and the authority of the Secretary to reassign major combat functions was, as noted above, subject to veto by Congress. Assignment of roles and missions remained as ambiguous as ever, except for the effect of a strengthened unified command system—explained below—on the independence and command functions of the service Chiefs.

Two additional provisions of the 1958 legislation might be noted. One was the right of the service Secretaries and service Chiefs to make recommendations on their own initiative to Congress. President Eisenhower voiced strong objections to this, which, he said, "endorses the idea of disunity" and suggests "that Congress hopes for disobedience and interservice rivalries." [18] Congress nonetheless insisted. Congress also granted, over Presidential objection, statutory existence to the National Guard Bureau and its Chief, eliminating the possibility of any transfer, consolidation, reassignment, or abolition of the Guard's functions, which are strongly supported in Congress on behalf of state and local constituencies.

Lines of Command. Prior to 1958, the establishment of unified commands had been authorized, but the reality of the commander's control over elements on assignment from the several armed services within his domain remained in doubt. In the 1958 reorganization, commanders of unified (e.g., Pacific Command) and specified (e.g., Strategic Air Command) commands were given the authority to exercise "full operational control" over all forces assigned to them, and the possibility that a service chief might withdraw assigned forces or portions thereof was removed.

Lines of command were also clarified. They were to run from the Commander in Chief (the President) through the Secretary of Defense—via the JCS—to the unified or specified commanders. The service Secretaries and service Chiefs were removed from the chain of command except insofar as the latter, in their role as JCS members rather than as service Chiefs, were involved in issuing strategic directives in the name of the Secretary of Defense. For example, the Secretary and the Chief of Staff of the Air Force were no longer the "bosses" of the Air Force general in charge of the Strategic Air Command; only the Secretary of Defense was. But since the individual services retained the authority to organize, train, and

[18] Text of President's statement in *The New York Times,* May 29, 1958, p. 8. For pro and con comments, see *Air Force,* May 1958, p. 39, and *Navy,* October 1958, p. 46. For Congressional reaction, see House *Report* No. 1765, 85th Congress, 2d Session, May 22, 1958.

equip forces for the operational unified commands and to administer and support the forces so assigned, considerable ambiguity was left.

The 1958 reform necessitated numerous adjustments in the procedures and inter-agency relationships of a huge bureaucracy. Extensive procedural changes were required in the command structure, the staffing and operation of the Joint Staff, the roles of the military departments, the JCS and Research and Engineering Secretariat, and the staff role of the Assistant Secretaries of Defense, to name but a few. Thomas S. Gates, Jr., a former Secretary of the Navy who succeeded Neil McElroy as Defense Secretary late in 1959, instituted a number of important operational changes. In December he began to sit regularly with the Joint Chiefs of Staff so that each service view could be presented and debated in his presence and he could resolve basic differences among the chiefs on strategy and force levels. The practice has been continued in the Kennedy Administration by Gates' successor, Robert S. McNamara. Secretary Gates also took an important step toward unification by establishing a Joint Strategic Target Agency, which had become particularly urgent as the Navy entered the strategic bombing field with its Polaris nuclear submarines. A Joint Strategic Targets List was established in August 1960 as part of a Single Integrated Operational Plan, and a Joint Navy-Air Force planning staff was created—a somewhat make-shift arrangement designed to mitigate, in the event of major warfare, the absence of true unification in the defense system.

V

The platform of the victorious Democratic Party in the 1960 Presidential election contained a commitment to a "complete examination of the organization of our armed forces." On September 14, 1960, Senator John F. Kennedy commissioned a special committee to survey the problems of defense organization and to recommend to

him "what changes should be made in the organization and administration of our defense agencies to eliminate or at least to diminish the present crippling effect of these problems upon our defense power." [19] Senator Stuart Symington was appointed to head this committee. Among other members were Clark M. Clifford, Thomas K. Finletter, and Roswell L. Gilpatric, all of whom, like Symington, had extensive experience with defense organizational problems.

The Symington Committee reported to the President-elect in December 1960. Its concise report was based upon the premise that the existing Pentagon organization was "patterned primarily on a design conceived in the light of lessons learned in World War II, which are now largely obsolete." The report argued that no really fundamental change had occurred in defense organization after 1947, while, "the whole state of the art in military science has been revolutionized."

The prime objective in the recommendations made by the Symington Committee was "the clarification and strengthening of the authority of the Secretary of Defense over the entire U. S. military establishment." Additional objectives were to shorten the time required to bring new weapons from conception to utilization, to improve the strategic planning process so that strategy and plans are not merely positions compromised among the several services, and to realign the defense organization in keeping with contemporary military functions to be performed. "No longer can this nation afford the luxury of letting each service strive to develop in itself the capability of fighting any future war by itself," stated the report.

Among the report's specific proposals were these: eliminate the existing department structure of the Army, Navy, and Air Force, while preserving the military services as separate organic units; do away with the service Secretaries, while vesting directly in the Secretary of De-

[19] Press release by Senator Kennedy, St. Louis, Missouri, September 14, 1960.

fense the administration of the services; create two new Under Secretaries of Defense, one for Weapons Systems and one for Administration, and consolidate under them the existing functions performed by Assistant Secretaries of Defense and the Departmental secretariats; reconstitute the JCS, making the Chairman the principal military adviser to the President and the Secretary of Defense and transforming the JCS into a Joint Staff under a single chief; establish three major unified commands—Strategic Command, Tactical Command, and Defense Command—and various minor commands; establish a unified budget process within the Office of the Secretary of Defense, to whom Congress would appropriate all defense funds, some of which (e.g., for research and development) would be placed on a multi-year basis.

No attempt was made during the first two years of the Kennedy Administration to implement these recommendations by major new legislation. Opposition to the most fundamental changes were quickly made known on Capitol Hill by influential legislators, who kept a watchful and suspicious eye upon a new Secretary of Defense who seemed determined to force greater unification upon the Pentagon, if not by requests to Congress for statutory changes, then by vigor in exercising the considerable administrative power already at his disposal. There was a widespread impression that many of the objectives of the Symington report could be accomplished by Executive Order and administrative action, but to do this the Defense Secretary would have to surmount or circumvent the opposition of many powerful skeptics on Capitol Hill and many seasoned in-fighters within his own Pentagon domain.

Secretary McNamara set about to make full use of existing authority. First he assembled an unusually sophisticated team of deputies. As Deputy Secretary, he chose Roswell L. Gilpatric, a former Air Force Under Secretary, who himself had been seriously considered by President Kennedy for appointment as Defense Sec-

retary. An able New York lawyer, he had helped to prepare the Rockefeller Report of 1958, as well as serving on the Symington task force. Among McNamara's Assistant Secretaries were Paul H. Nitze (as head of International Security Affairs, known as the Pentagon's "little State Department"), a widely respected expert on strategy and foreign policy with extensive State Department experience; Charles J. Hitch (as Comptroller), a leading economist, member of the RAND Corporation and one of the foremost scholars of defense budgeting and the economics of national defense; and Harold Brown (Director of Research and Engineering), a first-line physicist from the Livermore Laboratory of the University of California.

Each of these deputies, in turn, assembled his own team of brilliant and knowledgeable specialists in strategy and foreign policy. Perhaps never before had so much civilian talent, sophisticated in military strategy, been assembled under a Defense Secretary, himself known for exceptional intellect combined with the ability to make difficult decisions with dispatch. If knowledge and analytical ability convey power, then the new Secretary was prepared to consolidate his position as chief of the vast and complex Pentagon.

Secretary McNamara, bolstered by the information contained in scores of task force reports and studies he had commissioned, used existing statutory authority to institute the following changes in 1961–62: (1) merger of the Army's various technical services, like ordnance, signal, finance, quartermaster, into a Materiel and Logistics Command; (2) a speed-up of the consolidated handling of all-service common use goods, like purchases of food, gasoline, spare parts, blankets, in a unified Defense Supply Agency; (3) creation of a Defense Intelligence Agency, combining in large measure the formerly separate intelligence units in Washington but not in the field commands of each of the armed services; (4) tightening of the Defense Secretary's control over the press releases and public speeches in the armed services; and (5) the strengthening of the Secretary's line of authority to the major military commands, bringing North American Air Defense, Strategic Air Command, and others under his effective control.

In addition, McNamara unified the Strategic Army Corps and the Tactical Air Forces into an operational Strike Command; placed the conception of all new weapons systems under the jurisdiction of the Director of Research and Engineering, thereby consolidating the control once held by separate services; assigned to the Air Force prime responsibility for the military aspects of outer space; and—of major long-range importance—began to revise the entire budgetary approach within the Pentagon. (The budgetary reforms will be discussed in greater detail in Chapers IV and V.)

Vigorous new assertion of civilian authority caused considerable apprehension among, and some friction with, military professionals. Early in 1962, for example, Hanson W. Baldwin, *The New York Times* military analyst, noted "the uneasiness that many military men have felt increasingly in the last year since . . . McNamara started a quiet revolution in the Pentagon's organization and methods." Later a similar fear of "creeping unification" was stated more bluntly on Capitol Hill. In August 1960, the Chairman of the House Armed Services Committee, Carl Vinson, endorsed a subcommittee report accusing McNamara of overcentralizing military authority in his own office and of jeopardizing the independence of the Army, Navy, Air Force, and Marine Corps. In Vinson's view, this could lead to "disastrous" erosion of military responsibility and readiness.[20]

Main points in a broader criticism voiced by the military journals but gener-

ally muffled by the widespread praise accorded McNamara were these: that the Secretary was thinking too much in terms of machines and mathematical calculations rather than of men; that he was relying too heavily upon academic theorists and their techniques of abstract calculations of probabilities rather than upon human judgment based upon "common sense" and experience; that inadequate attention was paid to the advice of military professionals and too much to the ideas of brilliant young slide-rule analysts; and that an inordinate centralization of the decision-making process was taking place in the offices of the Defense Secretary and his band of bright young brain trusters. On this latter point, Secretary of the Army Elvis T. Stahr, Jr., retiring after eighteen months of service with McNamara, added that "more and more, the decisions once made by the service Secretaries and the military chiefs, as individuals, are made by the Secretary of Defense and his staff." He said, in a *New York Times* interview published July 8, 1962, that the Defense Department is far too big to be run by a few people at the top and suggested that Secretary McNamara's techniques constituted "overreaching" in personal control. Essentially the complaints added up to an allegation that Secretary McNamara was imposing a kind of backdoor unification, without advice and consent from Congress or from the professional military leaders representing the separate armed services.

VI

But with all the changes, evidence supports the argument that the defense organization existing in 1962 was predicated on popular and Congressional distrust of the concentration of decision-making power. In the years since World War II the existing defense organization has produced a formidable array of military power. But its adequacy in terms of foreign policy objectives and commitments has remained in question. This may be because the armed services have been preoccupied with or-

[20] For Baldwin's comment, see "An Uneasy Military-I," *The New York Times,* January 18, 1962; the Armed Services subcommittee's views and Vinson's endorsement of them are found in House, Committee on Armed Services, *Report* No. 69 of Special Subcommittee on Defense Agencies, 87th Congress, 2d Session, August 13, 1962.

ganizational and jurisdictional issues, at the expense of meeting the true requirements for the common defense. An off-hand comment made in 1956 by the Air Force Chief of Staff is suggestive. Said General Nathan Twining: ". . . the Navy and Army are watching me like a hawk. Every time I make a move, they are making sure what I am doing and vice versa." General Twining conceded that there are advantages to this: "no one can really get off the beam," and he acknowledged the danger of a "real bad mistake" if a single military dynasty were created. Apparently as an afterthought he added, "But that [competition] can . . . lead to lack of development, too, and that is dangerous for the country." [21]

Since World War II, interservice rivalry has been the prime characteristic of the defense establishment. More time and energy has probably been expended at the policy-making levels of the three armed services on who's going to do what with how much money than on appraising the external threat to the nation. The familiar interservice controversies of the 1950s were often irrelevant to the central question of the principal military functions to be performed, i.e.: strategic deterrence, deterrence of less than all-out aggression, control of the seas, continental defense.

The organizational atmosphere in which the military system operates has been so fraught with debate that during his term as Secretary of Defense Charles E. Wilson ruefully commented that "in the [armed] services we at least ought to treat each other like allies." With all of the reorganizations since World War II, and with all of the administrative vigor and decisiveness exercised by an exceptionally able new Secretary in 1961–62, the defense structure continues to resemble an alliance of semi-independent, sovereign units, often engaged in bitter jurisdictional warfare.

A fact of recent history should be noted here: Every major investigation and re-

port on Department of Defense organization since World War II has recommended a more unified structure and greater concentration of authority in the Office of the Secretary of Defense.[22] Even the important Eberstadt Report in 1945, which opposed the degree of centralization advocated by many persons, recommended greater unification. Yet opponents of unification continue to make their voices heard.

Serious problems remain in the defense structure. In proposing or implementing further defense reform, extreme care must be taken not to sacrifice any required capability for deterrence and defense. Effective armed forces are those capable of deterring war or applying military force with discretion at any moment. This inevitably places limits on how rapidly any radical reorganization scheme can be put into effect. It also underlines the need for long-range organizational planning and the importance of laying the foundation *now* for what is likely to be needed *later*.

To postpone needed reorganization is to permit the Department of Defense to lag behind technology at great future peril to national security. Concern about "lead-time" in weapons—that is, the time between the drawing board and the production line—has overshadowed the equally serious problem of organizational "lead-time." There is urgent need to identify remaining defects in the defense organization structure, to study remedies, and to plan for smooth transition to the inevitable next step. Above all, attention must be given to the education, training, and indoctrination of the junior members of the

[21] Senate Armed Services Subcommittee on the Air Force, *Hearings*, "Study of Airpower," 1956, p. 1505.

[22] A vast literature exists on defense organization and reorganization proposals. Very useful bibliographies are those printed by the Senate Committee on Government Operations (Jackson Subcommittee): "Organizing for National Security—A Bibliography," December 15, 1959; and "Administration of National Security," December 28, 1962. See also "Recent Writing in Military Politics—Foci and Corpora," in *Changing Patterns of Military Politics*, ed. Samuel P. Huntington, New York, The Free Press of Glencoe, 1962, pp. 235–66.

defense establishment—civilian and military—who will assume posts of leadership in the future, to make them aware of the nature of the technological revolution under way. And finally, serious attention must be given to the solution of the chronic problem of the short-term service of civilians in the upper levels of the Defense Secretariat.

Some identifiable risks are inherent in complete defense unification, because of the massive size and extensive scope of the Defense Department. Logical rearrangements of decision-making and leadership roles at the top will not guarantee effective operational units at the lower echelons. Three basic operational prerequisites for any defense organization can be listed: First, unification must be compatible with the efficiency value of decentralization. A central technique, perhaps a basic prerequisite, of democratic government is to guarantee competition among ideas and interests. Our system of government and our way of decision making is distinct from that of totalitarianism largely in this regard, and the system is not likely to endure in the absence of opportunities for responsible dissent in policy making, which will come about only through a degree of decentralization of authority. But the danger of too much administrative pluralism is paralysis or stalemate as we enter an era in which proper decisions made *in time* may spell the difference between survival or surrender. Morale and *esprit de corps,* too, must not be the victims of overcentralization, for they are vital ingredients of military strength.

Second, greater unification must try to avoid, in former Secretary of Defense Wilson's blunt phrase, the risk of "concentration of stupidity." Greater unification must not stifle the expression of diverse opinions or of alternate recommendations for national security.

Third, in concentrating responsibility at the top, the risk of generating irresponsibility at the lower operating levels must be avoided. Given these prerequisites, where

is further reform needed? What direction should further changes take?

The Joint Chiefs of Staff. Given the complex nature of strategic planning and the enormous size of the armed services, the dual role of service Chief of Staff and membership on the JCS seems impossible to fulfill effectively. A service Chief now is authorized to delegate duties to his Vice Chief. But, in practice, Congressional committees, Service Secretaries, and various public groups want to see and hear the Chief; to deal with the No. 1 man. The Service Chief as a member of the JCS is inevitably torn between the loyalty expected by his service and the objective, unified outlook required by the national interest.

An example of how this works has been given by General Thomas D. White, who as Air Force Chief of Staff was a member of the JCS for the four years ending in June 1961. Each service chief annually certifies to his department Secretary and the Defense Secretary that the budget he submits represents the minimum required for his service to perform its mission. Shortly thereafter the Defense Secretary refers the budgets of all the armed services to the JCS for their recommendations. At this stage each service chief must judge his own budget in the context of all other service requirements and against an overall dollar-target ceiling. "Since the combined service requirements always exceed the tentative dollar limitations," writes General White, each service chief faces a dilemma as he "must either renounce as false or padded his earlier declaration, or lose face with his own Secretary, his staff, and his service as a whole. . . ." [23]

One authoritative critic of this system stated that "at the Joint Chiefs of Staff level, we have probably the least effective military organization to haunt the United States since the fiasco of the Civil War. . . . This means, in effect, that our present military operations are governed by a committee with widely divergent views.

[23] "The Impossible Role of the Joint Chiefs," *Newsweek,* June 11, 1962, p. 28.

There is no example in history of military command being successfully exercised under those circumstances." [24]

To remedy this, the role of member of the JCS should be separated from that of chief of service. Membership on a reconstituted JCS, perhaps limited to four years, might normally follow the tour as service Chief of Staff. But while serving on the JCS, the officer would not be identified with or return to his service.

Unified Commands. Unified commanders are said under the system of 1962 to have "full operational control" of forces assigned to them. Yet the selection, basic training, equipment and supply of these forces continues to be administered by the existing departments, which maintain firm control over the development of service doctrine and personnel administration. Unified commanders have responsibility for *joint* training of assigned forces, but the system is beset by an artificial separation of policy and administration that promises serious trouble. Perhaps these problems cannot be solved without a radical redesignation of military forces and missions on something other than the present largely *geographical* basis for existing commands.

A long-range goal might be a gradual transition into a functional rearrangement of forces, based upon the principal missions to be performed. Meanwhile there should be a speed-up of the integration of the technical forms and procedures among the military services, including nomenclature, stock numbers and specifications for all standard items such as food, clothing, and transportation. Procurement, supply, and service of common-use items should be completely integrated. Uniform systems of paper work should be developed. And the question should be asked whether the present arrangement of three separate undergraduate service acad-

[24] Major General John B. Medaris, *Countdown for Decision,* New York, Putnam, 1960, pp. 58–59.

emies, which perpetuate outmoded concepts and instill interservice rivalry, represent the best undergraduate educational base for future leaders of "unified" armed forces. Perhaps long-range planning for a radical revision of military education and realignment of educational institutions for the military functions of the future—strategic striking power, limited war, sea communications, air defense, logistics, reserves, and civil defense—should begin at once.

Defense Secretariat. The eventual establishment of regrouped military specialists will have to coincide with a rearrangement of the civilian hierarchy of the defense establishment. A principal goal must be to provide the Defense Secretary with full authority and with objective information and advice about defense requirements, particularly about the major military functions to be performed. The separate Service Departments and their Secretariats will have to be abolished, and Deputy Secretaries of Defense for each of the major military missions created in their place. And, ideally, the career civil service, its prestige and rewards, will be extended upward so that eventually only the very top positions will be filled by political appointees.

None of these changes can be effected suddenly. But, to recall the theme of this book, the greatest threat to America's defense and democracy is a failure to recognize that an accelerating technology in a totally new world environment demands the closest possible attention to organizational requirements ten, fifteen, or more years hence. History suggests that basic changes in defense structures come about either as a result of military disaster or, more rarely, imaginative leadership supported by public opinion. In the nuclear age, military disasters are no longer tolerable. This puts a premium on innovative leadership supported by an enlightened public.

THE JOINT CHIEFS OF STAFF
AND DEFENSE POLICY FORMULATION

BY LAWRENCE B. TATUM

Many prominent writers on military affairs are gravely disturbed about "the excessive influence of civilians" in the field of defense policymaking. The following statements are illustrative.

. . . the Secretary [Secretary of Defense Mc-Namara] has penetrated deep into fields once reserved for the military. He has barked shins throughout the country's polity and economy. A stream of complaints has flowed from the Armed Services and their friends and clients. Carl Vinson, the powerful chairman of the House Armed Services committee, has semipublicly "warned" the Secretary against abridging the independence of the Services and their Secretaries. Virtually the whole press has joined in criticizing McNamara for what the *Washington Post* has called "The Closed Door Policy of the Defense Department." Blue suits and brown alike have charged that, as the *Army, Navy, Air Force Journal* put it, "the professional military leadership of the nation is being short-circuited in the current decisionmaking process at the Pentagon."[1]

In structural terms, the military establishment may be one of the tripods of a "power elite," but in sociological fact the military officers feel dispossessed. . . . Since the end of World War II, the military has been involved in a number of battles to defend its elite position, beginning in 1945 with the young physicists and nuclear scientists, down to the present action against the "technipols" (the military's decisive term for technicians and political theorists whom Secretary McNamara has brought into the Department of Defense).[2]

In common with many other military men, active and retired, I am profoundly apprehensive of the pipe-smoking, tree-full-of-owls type of so-called professional defense intellectuals who have been brought into this Nation's Capital.

I don't believe a lot of these over-confident, sometimes arrogant young professors, mathematicians and other theorists have sufficient worldliness or motivation to stand up to the kind of enemy we face. . . . it seems to me the old strengths still apply. In my opinion the two that count for most in the nuclear space age, regardless of academic cerebrations, are national determination and military forces designed to achieve victory, not tailored to obtain compromise. Professional military training teaches the philosophy of victory whereas politics is based on compromise.[3]

Do civilians have inordinate power in the strategymaking field? If they do, is it because of the energetic personality and management philosophy of our present Secretary of Defense?[4]

[1] Joseph Kraft, "McNamara and His Enemies," *Harper's Magazine*, August, 1961, p. 41.

[2] Daniel Bell, "The Dispossessed—1962," *Columbia University Forum*, 5 (Fall 1962), p. 6.

[3] General Thomas D. White, "Strategy and the Defense Intellectuals," *Saturday Evening Post*, 236 (4 May 1963), pp. 10–12.

[4] Secretary McNamara has been quite explicit in stating his management philosophy:

"When I became Secretary of Defense in 1961, I felt that either of two broad philosophies of management could be followed by the man at the head of this great establishment. He could play an essentially passive role—a judicial role. In this role the secretary would make the decisions required of him by law by approving recommendations made to him. On the other hand, the Secretary of Defense could play an active role providing aggressive leadership—questioning, suggesting alternatives, proposing objectives and stimulating progress. This active role represents my own philosophy of management."—From Robert S. McNamara, "McNamara Defines His Job," *New York Times Magazine*, 26 April 1964, p. 13.

Contrast Secretary McNamara's approach with that of one of his predecessors, Secretary McElroy, as indicated by the following comment:

"The conflicting pressures on him [McElroy] from the Army and the Air Force were so great that he finally threw up his hands and asked Congress to decide which of the two services' competing and almost identical missiles—Jupiter or Thor—should be put into production."—From Julius Duscha, "Arms and the Big Money Men," *Harper's Magazine*, March 1964, p. 41.

Reprinted by permission from *Air University Review*, May–June 1966, pp. 40–45; July–August 1966, pp. 11–20.

Lieutenant Colonel Tatum is a U.S. Military Academy graduate and a Syracuse University Associate. He was formerly an Associate Professor of Political Science at the United States Air Force Academy and is a frequent contributor to military journals. He is currently listed as missing in action in Vietnam.

It is a thesis of this article that a variety of civilian groups have begun to play and—barring a large-scale war situation—will continue to play a major role in the determination of strategy and military policy.[5] Moreover, Secretary McNamara did not create the phenomenon of civilian influence.[6] At most, the Secretary's energetic implementation of an activist management philosophy has accelerated an existing trend—and exacerbated the debate over its desirability and consequences.

A subsequent and more important thesis of this article will be that civilian participation in defense policy formulation—while inevitable and to a large extent desirable—has, in recent years, tended to overwhelm the military input to strategymaking. This has happened, it will be argued, because the military, erroneously, has assumed that its advice will be ineffective unless all military suborganizations appear united behind specific policy proposals. This erroneous assumption has resulted in present Joint Chiefs of Staff organizational procedures which ensure that the military is poorly equipped to provide meaningful strategic advice. But these are matters to be dealt with later.

THE CIVILIAN'S ROLE IN DEFENSE POLICY FORMULATION

Prior to World War II, American attitudes toward war and peace were clear-cut. Normally, thought Americans, states were at peace with one another. Relations with other nations were conducted by the State Department, utilizing principally the instrument of diplomacy. War was thought to be an aberration, a temporary deviation from normality. Moreover, Americans thought war justified only when an immoral or insane aggressor compelled a state to use force in self-defense. When driven to take up arms, the total defeat of the aggressor became the only possible—and moral—objective of war.

Thus, according to American tradition, peace and war were entirely different phenomena. During peace, force or the threat of force was not a usable instrument of foreign policy; the formulation of defense policy could be of little or no concern to the nation as a whole. To whatever degree prewar planning and strategy-making were deemed essential—and that was certainly not to a great degree—they were the exclusive domain of a small group of military professionals. On the other hand, whenever war was thrust upon the United States, the goal had to be total victory. During war, military needs became paramount and "generals and admirals moved from political isolation into the seats of power."[7]

America's attitude in the era since World War II has become more sophisticated. The old traditions die hard, but slogans like "cold war," "neither war nor peace," "peaceful co-existence" have relegated more categorical descriptions of U.S. policy into the background. The principle of political primacy and its corollary, the economy of force, have become prevailing national concepts.[8] "Political primacy" asserts that the only legitimate purpose of

[5] When I refer to civilians and/or military men having an input to defense policy- or strategy-making, I imply that the input—by whomever given—involves the considerations of ends as well as means. As explained later, I believe ends and means are practically inseparable. No one should tell a military strategist that he should analyze only means and leave consideration of ends to the civilian policy-maker.

[6] As one prominent writer on military affairs says:
"Military leaders and military institutions were less powerful in the Truman administration than they were during World War II. They were less powerful under Eisenhower than they were under Truman. They are less powerful now under Kennedy than they were under Eisenhower. This constant decline in power and influence of the military profession is the single most important trend in civil-military relations during the past fifteen years."—From Samuel P. Huntington, "Power, Expertise and the Military Profession," Daedalus, Fall 1963, pp. 795–96.

[7] World War II directly reflected American attitudes toward peace and war. During the war the President and the Joint Chiefs of Staff formulated strategy. The Secretaries of State, War, and Navy played marginal roles. In 1945 Admiral Leahy declared that the Joint Chiefs were "under no civilian control whatever."—Noted in Huntington, p. 795.

[8] Robert E. Osgood, in his book Limited War (Chicago: University of Chicago Press, 1957), has brilliantly formulated these two principles and drawn what he considers to be the necessary consequences for U.S. foreign policy. The following discussion of these principles is centered on Osgood's presentation.

military force is to serve the nation's political objectives. This principle declares that force or the threat of it can be of no practical use in itself. Attainable, concrete, specific political objectives must guide the threat or the use of military power to ensure a practical and discernible relationship between ends and means.

Political primacy as a principle is especially pertinent to an age when the principal protagonists hold nuclear weapons. In addition, strategy considerations must adhere to the principle of economy of force—the use of only that amount of military force absolutely necessary to accomplish a given political objective; the more force applied, the more difficult its control and, consequently, the maintenance of political primacy.

States which follow the principles of political primacy and economy of force do not regard peace and war as entirely separate orders of existence. Given proper circumstances, force or the threat of force becomes an acceptable foreign policy instrument, whereas diplomacy and political primacy are vitally necessary throughout an actual conflagration so that force may be limited and controlled.

Wherever the principles of political primacy and economy of force prevail, the argument that the politician sets goals and the military man decides means must be regarded as outmoded. Under these twin principles, *both* the politician and the military man ought to participate in setting goals and determining means because ends and means are intimately connected—indeed, frequently inseparable. The present international situation, in which great powers are, primarily, adversaries—but still believe they cannot resort to total war to settle differences—only reinforces the conclusion that civilians must be involved in the planning of force utilization.

Of all the reasons why defense policy is no longer the exclusive domain of the military, I judge the primary one to be that American strategists are guided—and will continue to be guided—by the principles of political primacy and economy of force.[9]

There are, however, many other reasons why defense policy formulation is no longer just the military's bailiwick. I will briefly discuss some of them without belaboring the obvious. Most, if not all, the reasons discussed are permanent rather than transitory characteristics. I make this statement because some observers, though astute enough to understand why the civilian has "invaded" the strategy domain, seem to believe the present civilian "occupation" may be temporary.[10]

One reason why there is now a furor over civilian dominance of strategymaking is that a comparison with the immediate past presents a remarkable contrast. As I have already indicated, World War II military leaders had an unusual amount of influence in policy formulation. When events in the postwar era made it clear that the United States could not again shirk international responsibilities, government

---

[9] A necessary and most important concomitant idea is that the very nature of strategy is no longer—if it ever was—even primarily military. This is especially true in the absence of major war situations, as Walter Millis says:

"In the absence of major war, the problems of high command are much more organizational, technical, diplomatic—political in the larger sense of the word—than strategic. Even where 'little wars' are under way, as in Vietnam, it is coming to be realized that military strategy itself involves a much larger political factor than was once supposed."—From "Puzzle of the 'Military Mind.'" *New York Times Magazine*, 18 November 1962, p. 158.

[10] For instance, Colonel Robert N. Ginsburgh, after outlining many of the reasons why civilians are making most of the present defense policy inputs, had this to say:

"The statesman needs sound military advice; the military professional needs firm policy guidance. Each must, of course, understand the problems of the other. The military man should be aware of the political, economic, social and other factors which affect national security, but it is not his business to evaluate them. He should limit himself to a consideration of military aspects which are within his area of competence. The civilian authorities, both executive and legislative, should assist him in exercising self-restraint by not requiring his comments on nonmilitary matters. Similarly, the statesman who is concerned with a political problem must recognize that it may have important military implications but he should refrain from making military analyses. He should use the results of the analysis of the military as one of the factors bearing on his total problem."—From "The Challenge to the Military," *Foreign Affairs*, January 1964, p. 266.

Unless otherwise cited, reasons for contemporary civilian input into military affairs subsequent to this footnote are drawn either from this article by Colonel Ginsburgh, pp. 255–68, or from Huntington, pp. 793–801.

agencies were unable to find sufficient numbers of competent civilians to man important national security posts. As a result, "military officers were appointed to key State Department offices, ambassadorial posts and positions in other foreign affairs agencies."[11] Thus, throughout the late forties, military men occupied many of the prominent positions in both the foreign and defense branches of the national security policy structure.

It was inevitable that administrations would change this situation as circumstances permitted. Under Presidents Eisenhower and Kennedy the overall participation of military officers in civil office declined until very few professional military officers have been appointed to top civil governmental positions during the 1961–65 Kennedy and Johnson Administrations.[12] Even in the defense policy area itself, each political party had, by the early sixties, built up a reservoir of men knowledgeable and experienced in military affairs to man top positions in the Department of Defense.[13] The present *modus operandi* undoubtedly is more logical and relevant to the American political system than the practice followed in the immediate postwar era.

Therefore, the clamor against civilian strategists is in part due to fond memories of a yesteryear unusual in the degree of military occupancy of important national security positions. A far more significant factor, however, is that civilian influence *has* been introduced into heretofore sacrosanct military arenas.

As Professor S. P. Huntington says, three groups of civilians have "invaded" the

strategy domain. The first group is composed of the "defense intellectuals."

Most of the significant writings on strategy produced after World War II were produced by civilians. . . . Experts such as Brodie, Kaufman, Kissinger, Wohlstetter, Schelling, and Kahn took the lead in articulating theories of stabilized deterrence, limited war, tactical nuclear war, arms control and civil defense. . . . Traditionally, the professional military officer is supposed to be contemptuous of the ignorance of civilians on military problems and strategy. One striking aspect of the McNamara Pentagon, however, has been the allegation that the civilian "whiz kids" are unduly contemptuous of the military officers for *their* backwardness and ignorance.[14]

The second civilian group is comprised of the natural scientists.

In the [defense policy] debates of the late 1950's and the early 1960's concerning technology, space activities, nuclear testing, arms control, disarmament and even weapons development, the role of the scientists was as important or more important than that of the soldiers.[15]

The Department of Defense civil servants make up a final civilian group which, quite unostentatiously, has gained power and influence. Military men normally rotate through top staff positions. Many top civil servants have been with DOD since 1947. Their experience, knowledge, contacts, and power permit them to restrict and control many defense policy matters.

These three groups are, I think, permanent occupiers of the strategy domain. Given the complexity of modern strategic planning, the cost of new weapon systems, and—most important—the absolutely crucial requirement that defense policy contribute maximally to national security, then the defense intellectual, the natural scientists, and the DOD civil servant are welcome additions to the strategy team.

Another important cause of the decline of the military's input into defense policymaking is the changing nature of the political process through which strategic decisions are made. The role of Congress in determining the military budget, force

[11] Huntington, p. 797. For instance, General Marshall served alternately as Secretary of State and Secretary of Defense.

[12] *Ibid.*

[13] One author notes that, at the end of the Eisenhower Administration, "most civilian leaders in the Pentagon had spent periods of 4 to 8 years in defense work, if not in the same post."—From Gene M. Lyons, "The New Civil-Military Relations," *American Political Science Review*, 55 (March 1961), p. 57. The Kennedy and Johnson Administrations turned quite often to executives like Roswell L. Gilpatric, Deputy Secretary of Defense, 1961–64, who had held responsible DOD positions under Truman.

[14] Huntington, p. 798.

[15] *Ibid.*, p. 799.

levels, weapons, and uses of the armed forces has been practically pre-empted by the executive branch. Reflection seems to indicate that this development was inevitable and is irrevocable. Congress is not organized to formulate the strategic decisions at the heart of force-structure determination. Still, diminution of congressional influence in military affairs has removed one of the military strategists' power sources. Congress may heed plaintive cries of service advocates and appropriate additional military funds—but almost without exception the President has effectively "vetoed" the legislative action by impounding the funds.[16]

Many of the traditional, heretofore mundane, problems of military affairs are no longer handled exclusively by military professionals. Here is another area of civilian invasion of the defense policy field. For instance, choices of modern weapon systems involve extremely long lead times in planning, testing, procurement, and production. With choices now involving billions of dollars, civilian participation has become routine, especially since "unnecessary" monies spent on defense may increase the national debt, intensify the balance of payments problem, decrease amounts spent on foreign aid, poverty programs, etc. Moreover, with political primacy demanding interrelated defense and foreign policies, civilians naturally are concerned with what types of weapon systems are being planned, produced, and made operational.

Finally, because of cost and other factors such as the increasing rate of technological obsolescence, only a few weapon systems now become operational. The ideal pattern seems to be a single, long-lasting weapon system for each combat function. For example, DOD wants the Navy and the Air Force to use the same aircraft throughout the 1970's to fill their tactical fighter needs.[17]

It is evident that civilians are entering the weapon systems decision-making process quite forcefully. The argument that "we must have this particular weapon system as soon as possible"—a contention which, if accepted, maximizes military control of weapon system decisions—will carry much less weight than it has in the past. Civilian DOD leaders feel that there *is* time to make a fully staffed study before making decisions on weapon system selection and management problems—and that their participation in these decisions is not only possible but essential. Consequently, if civilians are going to participate in decisions on weapon systems, they are normally going to be involved in the strategic analysis which usually precedes the production of armaments. Ordinarily, one asks what defense policy one wishes to adopt *before* asking what kinds of technically and financially possible weapon systems are desirable.

Changes in defense organization have greatly accentuated the trend toward civilian dominance of the strategymaking process. Much water has gone over the organizational dam since the National Security Act of 1947 created the office of Secretary of Defense and vaguely instructed the Secretary "to preside" over the National Military Establishment. Through various organizational acts, the Department of Defense has been given increasing power and control over the separate services and the military professionals. Unified and specified (i.e., operational) commands have been created. Today these are directly responsible to the President and the Secretary of Defense. In regard to forces assigned to unified and specified commands, military departments are accountable only for their training, support, and administration. Functional offices at the Assistant Secretary of Defense level have been expanded in both numbers and powers. For

---

[16] One of the more recent of a growing series of "veto" instances is the Congress-Administration fight over the RS-70. At this writing, only two prototype RS-70's are contemplated, and even the Air Force has given up hope of getting the plane into operational production.

[17] The TFX (F-111) fighter airplane is DOD's

answer to the tactical fighter problem. The degree to which civilians now participate in weapon systems procurement is dramatically indicated in the history of the TFX. See Richard W. Smith, "The $7-Billion Contract that Changed the Rules," *Fortune*, March 1963, pp. 97–101, 182–88, and April 1963, pp. 110–11, 191–94, 199–200.

instance, since the office of the Director of Research and Engineering was created in 1958, the Director has supervised *all* military research and development. Defensewide agencies have been established to unite common supply and service functions and to reduce service duplication.

These defense organizational trends have unmistakably led to increased centralization and functionalism and to decreased authority of the military professionals in strategy areas. As one commentator observed:

As a result of the *expansion of the unified command concept*, the authority of the Service Chief as an individual has been supplanted by the corporate authority of the Joint Chiefs, while the authority of the Chiefs of Staff has been reduced through the creation of the elaborate superstructure for defense policy-making in Washington.[18]

Moreover, Secretary McNamara and his predecessors have acted fully within legislatively permitted limits,[19] though perhaps Congress did not intend for Defense Secretaries to *utilize* their powers as actively as they have.[20]

I have indicated why civilians now play a role in the defense policymaking process. Civilian participation in strategymaking is no transitory phenomenon. Years ago, French Premier Clemenceau said wars were too important to be left to generals. Now the same can be said for defense policy:

War is no longer a question of victory or defeat on the field of battle. With the advent of nuclear weapons and strategic delivery systems, we have reached the stage where peacetime preparedness is likely to determine the outcome of a major nuclear war. Thus not only war but also peacetime defense becomes too serious a matter to be left to the generals.[21]

If it is true that strategic decisions are, for various reasons, no longer the exclusive preserve of the military, is the converse also true? Has the military strategist gone the way of the dinosaur? Professor Samuel P. Huntington tells us that since 1950 all major revisions in overall strategy have been due to concepts and initiative supplied by civilians.[22] Must the military professional accept only an "operator" role in the force construct?

It would be dangerous for the military not to continue to be one of the important contributors to defense policy formulation. Separation of strategic policymaking and operations is artificial.

The Johnson Adminstration, like the Kennedy Administration, believes that the same people ought to be engaged in handling policy and operations problems. As McGeorge Bundy, Special Assistant to the President for National Security Affairs 1961–65, said:

We have deliberately rubbed out the distinction between planning and operation which governed the administrative structure of the NSC [National Security Council] staff in the last administration. This distinction, real enough at the extremes of the daily cable traffic and long-range assessment of future possibilities, breaks down in most of the business of decision and action. This is especially true at the level of Presidential action. Thus it seems to us best

---

[18] Ginsburgh, p. 257.

[19] The following is typical of the conclusions of experts on the Defense Secretary's organizational operating activities:
"Final approval of centralization and functionalism came in 1958—from Congress in the express words of the National Security Act amendments, not from the President or from DOD. And it came, moreover, at the behest of the Eisenhower, not of the Kennedy, Administration."—Captain Gerald Garvey, "The Changing Management Role of the Military Departments Reconsidered," *Air University Review*, XV, 3 (March–April 1964), 47.

[20] A 1962 report of Representative Carl Vinson's Special Subcommittee on Defense Agencies argues that "Congress has lost control of the organization of the Defense Department" but even it does not argue that secretarial actions have been illegal.—*Report of Special Subcommittee on Defense Agencies*, Committee on Armed Services, House of Representatives, 87th Congress, 2d Session, 13 August 1963, p. 6635. The subcommittee merely wished to amend the National Security Act so that no *additional* agency consolidation could occur without specific congressional approval.

[21] Ginsburgh, pp. 258–59.

[22] Samuel P. Huntington, "Power, Expertise, and the Military Profession," *Daedalus*, Fall 1963, p. 801. I think this is debatable. For instance, General Maxwell D. Taylor's book, *The Uncertain Trumpet* (New York: Harper and Brothers, 1959) seems to have influenced the defense philosophies of both President Kennedy and Secretary McNamara.

that the NSC staff, which is essentially a Presidential instrument, *should be composed of men who can serve equally well in the process of planning and in that of operational followup.* [Italics mine.][23]

If the distinction between planning (i.e., strategymaking) and operations is false at the national security level, it is no less so at the defense and foreign policy levels—to whatever degree these two areas can be separated and considered apart from the integrated whole. Those who know the mechanics of applying force or the threat of force ought to be involved in the making of policy calling for the use of the force instrument—if for no other reason than to give experience and operator judgments on feasibility as plans and alternatives are being considered.

There is, however, more to the argument for including the military voice in policymaking roles than the traditional reference to experience.[24] The military man spends a lifetime managing the means of warfare. He is constantly exposed to problems unique to his profession—management of personnel and matériel, mobility, mechanics of the use of force control, etc. He gains a sense (both analytic and intuitive) of what is possible and what is not possible in given situations; and—although he can be grossly wrong—he will normally have a better idea about strict operational feasibilities than will his civilian strategy teammates.[25]

[23] "Letter to Senator Henry M. Jackson from McGeorge Bundy," *Administration of National Security—Selected Papers,* Subcommittee on National Security Staffing and Operations, Committee on Government Operations, U.S. Senate, 87th Congress, 2d Session (Washington: U.S. Government Printing Office, 1962), pp. 5–8.

[24] In fact, experience, if irrelevant, may becloud analysis and make one's defense policy advice inferior. In an era of great technological change where, as Herman Kahn says, there is a revolution in weapon systems every five years, military strategists constantly must ask themselves whether their experience is relevant to contemporary doctrines concerning the use of force.

[25] I am *not* arguing that cost analysis and other analytic assistance techniques are valueless. On the contrary, the strategist needs all the assistance he can get; but even under the most imaginative utilization, many very important decisions will not be subjected to mathematical and other modular frameworks.

There is, I think, an additional reason why the military professional needs prominent inclusion in the defense policymaking process, although military men are themselves sharply divided about this one. If national security policymaking involves, as it must, the integration of all of a state's policy instruments (political, economic, psychological, and military), *who* is to be involved in the "integrating"? If we cannot separate political from military factors when we discuss strategy, either there must be a "philosopher-king" at the top of the policy pyramid who sifts out the "truths" from the arguments presented by various parochial advocates, or there must be a collection of responsible individuals representing operational organizations, and all trying to take an integrated view. Under the latter approach, with both military men and civilians officially providing defense policy advice, the military man's voice in strategy could be significant, not so much as a military man per se but as an intelligent and responsible contributor to the national security policy process. Inevitably, someone at the top of the decision-making process would have to make final decisions; but he would not be operating under the assumption that Pentagon officials give him only military inputs, or that State Department superiors offer only political advice, or that Treasury leaders comment only on economic matters, etc.

How well has the military professional been playing his role in strategymaking? Frankly, *quite inadequately.* I have tried to demonstrate that civilians are bound to make a significant input to defense policy formulation. However, it is my principal thesis that the current voice of the officer professional is dangerously weak because the military generally has assumed, incorrectly, that its effectiveness is best ensured if its advice is unanimous. The system designed to secure the unanimity believed necessity is the Joint Chiefs of Staff planning process. And, I will argue, the JCS process produces papers of such dubious substance as almost to ensure the rejection of their policy recommendations on important strategy issues.

What are the JCS empowered to do?

The Joint Chiefs of Staff are the principal military advisers to the President, the National Security Council, and the Secretary of Defense. They constitute the immediate military staff of the Secretary of Defense, serving in the chain of command that extends from the President to the Secretary of Defense, through the Joint Chiefs of Staff, to the commanders of unified and specified commands. The chain of command to the Chief or Director of Defense Atomic Support Agency, Defense Communications Agency, Defense Intelligence Agency also runs from the Secretary of Defense through the Joint Chiefs of Staff.[26]

Perhaps the functions of the JCS can be summarized as follows: (1) they do all strategic planning, and (2) they direct and supervise all military operations carried out by the principal combat commands (through a delegation of authority from the Secretary of Defense). In this article I am not concerned about the second of these responsibilities. I am concerned with the first function and what I believe to be the inability of the JCS to perform it. To put it bluntly: the military are at a distinct disadvantage regarding inputs to strategic planning because JCS planning procedure practically ensures compromise at the lowest common denominator.

Under these circumstances, the JCS can make a valuable contribution only to the extent that divisions on strategic thinking are civilian versus military. But, we are told, purely civilian-military splits are a rarity.[27] Far more frequently, defense policy issues find some military men and some civilians on contending sides. When that happens, the JCS as an organized planning entity has little impact on the final decision simply because its papers normally do *not*

---

[26] U.S. Department of Defense, *Brief of the Organization and Functions, Secretary of Defense, Deputy Secretary of Defense, Defense Staff Officers, Organization of the Joints Chiefs of Staff, Department of Defense Agencies, Joint Service Schools,* prepared by Administrative Services Division, Office of Administrative Assistant to the Secretary of Defense, April 1963, p. 13.

[27] Robert S. McNamara, "McNamara Defines His Job," *New York Times Magazine,* 26 April 1964, and Roswell L. Gilpatric, "An Expert Looks at the Joint Chiefs," *New York Times Magazine,* 29 March 1964.

reflect existing differences of opinion among military strategists. If divergencies are along service lines, the Chiefs may furnish important strategic advice through individual contact with the Secretary of Defense and the President. Far more likely, however, increased civilian dominance of the defense policy field is the result of a military planning system organized for compromise.

But this is strong medicine. Before the reader is likely to accept the contention that military consensus-seeking (as exemplified by present JCS planning procedure) is primarily responsible for diminution of the military's voice in strategymaking, it is necessary to indicate how the JCS as an agency tackles any problem (strategic planning or otherwise) assigned to it. The various channels and stages through which a JCS paper must proceed before it receives approval as an official military position are indicated by following the arrows in the accompanying chart.

Requests for JCS staff action may come from a variety of sources: the President, the Department of Defense (DOD), other executive departments through DOD, the JCS Chairman or the Chiefs as a body. However the request may have been received, the Chairman of the JCS (or the Chiefs as a body) indicates to the Director of the Joint Staff that a paper should be written on a particular problem. Because of the multitudinous demands made upon the JCS, suspense dates on papers are usually two weeks or less. Already a problem is encountered: the military strategist is not given sufficient time to turn out a quality paper, especially since so much of his effort must be devoted to the bureaucratic processes through which he must steer his "masterpiece."

The Director decides which Joint Staff directorate or agency (hereafter called agency) is principally concerned and assigns that agency primary responsibility for producing a fully staffed paper. The Director also assigns secondary responsibilities, if any, to other Joint Staff offices having an interest in the particular matter, including Defense Intelligence Agency (DIA), Defense Communications Agency (DCA), and Defense Atomic Support Agency (DAS), The primary agency appoints one of its officers as primary "action officer."[28] Throughout its "development" life the paper is *the* responsibility of the primary action officer. While this action officer has certain initiative options, the gauntlet through which he must run his paper is highly restrictive, as will be seen.

The primary action officer's first responsibility is to hold a meeting with all the Joint Staff secondary action officers to outline workload responsibilities and to agree to a Joint Staff position. Another problem arises here: an agreed Joint Staff position may be difficult to obtain if the strategy problem is important and the action officers represent different services. A need to compromise, therefore, may arise very early in the planning process. However, the problem is seldom severe at this point, since Joint Staff officers are not normally adamantly service-oriented.[29] They know, moreover, it is not their function to argue a service position. The planning process provides plenty of opportunity for others to do the arguing!

After the Joint Staff position has been decided, the primary action officer publishes a "FLIMSY." This is a draft paper which is sent to responsible agencies in each of the service staffs. Each service agency appoints an action officer for the paper, who scrutinizes the FLIMSY and all revisions to it to ensure that, to the best of his ability, the final paper reflects his service's doctrinal and budgetary positions.

The FLIMSY is the vehicle through which the planning process begins. In about two out of three cases, the initial FLIMSY remains a workable framework to modify. In the third case, however, the FLIMSY falls completely apart under attacks by service staffs and an entirely new one must be written. The FLIMSY may be a serious, thought-provoking effort by the Joint Staff, or it may be a "straw man"—an initial draft

[28] Joint Staff action officers are usually colonels or lieutenant colonels. Service staff action officers are usually majors or lieutenant colonels.

[29] In fact, a Joint Staff officer who is too active or obvious in pushing the interests of his own service may lose his job.

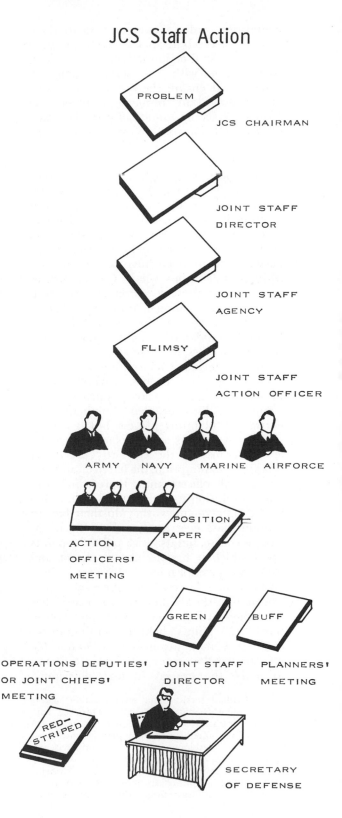

JCS Staff Action

PROBLEM

JCS CHAIRMAN

JOINT STAFF DIRECTOR

JOINT STAFF AGENCY

FLIMSY

JOINT STAFF ACTION OFFICER

ARMY   NAVY   MARINE   AIRFORCE

POSITION PAPER

ACTION OFFICERS' MEETING

GREEN   BUFF

OPERATIONS DEPUTIES' OR JOINT CHIEFS' MEETING   JOINT STAFF DIRECTOR   PLANNERS' MEETING

RED-STRIPED

SECRETARY OF DEFENSE

containing only enough information to serve as a catalyst. In the latter situation the Joint Staff action officer expects that consultation with his service staff colleagues will ensure the eventual inclusion of all important problem elements. In either case, as the Joint Staff primary action officer well knows, any resemblance between the FLIMSY and the finished approved JCS position is almost coincidental.

The next step is the action officers' meeting. The Joint Staff primary action officer indicates on the FLIMSY when this meeting is to occur. All service action officers attend, after they have decided what changes their services want reflected in the FLIMSY.[30] If the paper involves serious strategic considerations where varying service positions are present, action officers' meetings are real squabbles. Arguments abound over such matters as the use of "will" and "should" instead of "might" and "could" because changes in these small words can radically alter doctrinal content.

Here the central problem involved in the present JCS strategymaking approach is encountered. This problem dominates the entire JCS planning process, but it is most significant at the action officers' meeting level. Because of the currently prevailing unanimity assumption, the harried joint and service staff officers know there can be no mutual solution to their various approaches to the FLIMSY—unless they do their best to accommodate everyone involved. Each service, of course, has its "stick points"—points upon which it has decided it cannot and will not compromise. However, these points tend to be few in number, and action officers will do all they can to ensure that new ones are not created. The services want "stick points" held to a minimum because they have assumed that, *unless the military services agree*, civilians are bound to make the crucial strategy determina-

tions. Traditionally, military men have felt that civilians were not qualified to make such decisions.

Therefore, at the action-officer and all higher levels, the tendency is for service representatives to permit the inclusion of wordings and ideas satisfying the wishes of the other services—unless, by so doing, the interests of one's own service are damaged. On the other hand, officers representing the Joint Staff act principally as mediators, since in the final analysis the JCS does not exist apart from the services as far as the strategymaking process is concerned. Consequently, the primary requirement of those engaged in planning at both the service and joint levels becomes the attainment of a military position which does not injure the vital interests of any service.

The present JCS planning process operates to achieve unanimous military agreement. Until the present accommodation philosophy is changed, I believe the military voice in defense policy formulation will continue to be weak. If, to attain quality military advice, unity on JCS papers must be sacrificed, perhaps the sacrifice is worth making. The civilian in any case is going to play a major role in defense policy formulation. He should and he must. He is going to continue playing an inordinately large role, however, as long as achievement of consensus is the force guiding military strategists. Ironically, it seems that the military's input to strategymaking would be enhanced if it adopted the slogan, "Disunited we stand, undivided we fall."

After the hectic action officers' meeting or meetings, the primary Joint Staff action officer publishes a "BUFF" edition which becomes an official Joint Staff position. To whatever degree possible, the BUFF will reflect the views of all the services as well as those of the Joint Staff. The service action officers go over the BUFF with a fine-tooth comb. In addition, concurring initials on the BUFF must be obtained from all those intraservice agencies that previously commented on the FLIMSY. If the BUFF fails to achieve appreciable consensus, additional action officers' meetings are called so that all attainable agreement is secured before a planners' meeting is scheduled.

[30] Individual services and service action officers will handle this matter differently. However, considerable intraservice coordination *is* necessary. On most actions, intelligence, war plans, logistics, or research and development staffs are involved and must be consulted. For instance on an arms control matter involving strategic forces, the Army arms control action officer must get "concurring initials" from at least three other Army agencies.

Eventually the planners' meeting is held. Planners are designated senior officers (normally of two-star rank) from the services and the Joint Staff who represent their service chiefs and the Joint Staff agency head. They or their deputies meet to ratify action officers' activities and to improve the quality of the paper. Planners may be able to accommodate certain differences remaining in the paper because they know, better than the action officers, what their chiefs will or will not currently accept. In addition, they are more experienced in the JCS process and, therefore, more able to exercise initiative than are the action officers. Often, moreover, planners may avoid controversy because many of the points at issue have been ironed out at the action officer level.

After the planners' meeting, the primary Joint Staff action officer publishes a "GREEN," a paper fully staffed and considered by the planners to be the best paper they could produce. The GREEN, with accompanying PURPLES[31] if any, goes to the Director of the Joint Staff, who places it on the Operations Deputies' ("Ops Deps") or Joint Chiefs' calendars.[32]

During the Ops Deps' or the Chiefs' meetings, the Joint Staff action officer is present or "on call" in an anteroom adjacent to the Chiefs' room (the "tank"). He provides the Ops Deps or the Chiefs with any additional information requested during their consideration of the paper. Also, each service action officer writes a "Talking

Paper" which informally leads his Ops Dep and Chief through the entire staffing process—the background, key issues, delicate points, hearsay, personalities, politics, probable outcome, and table tactics. Action officers regard this paper as potentially the most important one they write in connection with each staff assignment. Once the Chief and Ops Deps are on their own in the "tank," their success in dealing with the paper from a service viewpoint often depends upon their advance knowledge of facts mentioned only in the Talking Paper. If any of the service controversies still remain resolved, the Chiefs often will return the paper with new guidance to the planners' level for another attempt at accommodation.

Finally, the Ops Deps or the Chiefs, as appropriate, approve the paper. A red stripe is added to the bottom of the GREEN, indicating that the paper is an official JCS position. This position is then taken from the "red-striped" GREEN and sent to the Secretary of Defense. Service PURPLES that have not been accommodated are attached. A post-briefing is held at 1400 (or fifteen minutes after the end of the Ops Deps' or Chiefs' meeting, whichever is later), at which time the Director of the Joint Staff reads final decisions to all action officers who took part in the decisionmaking process.

I believe the quest for unanimous advice —obtained through the JCS strategy-making process as I have described it—prevents the military from making a significant input into defense policy formulation. The system is organized to ensure protection of each service's short-term interests (through accommodation) rather than to project upwards the logical, fully analyzed—although probably divergent—views of military strategists.[33]

[31] Individual service disagreements to the GREEN are reflected by an accompanying paper outlining all the points of discord and indicating why that service believes wording changes should be made. This accompanying paper is called a "PURPLE." If there is any chance of removing a service's PURPLE, additional meetings (at the action officers' or planners' level, as deemed appropriate) will be called by the primary Joint Staff action officer. For easy identification, papers in the BUFF and GREEN stages actually are published in the appropriate colors.
[32] The Operations Deputies are generals and admirals of three-star rank who occupy concurrently key positions in the staff of their respective services (usually in Planning and/or Operations). They relieve the Joint Chiefs of many secondary matters and do the "preliminary spadework on major matters prior to consideration by the Chiefs." Taylor, op. cit., p. 88.

[33] I admit to "begging the question" regarding the military organizations that should be represented at the "strategist" level; perhaps the three services; perhaps the unified and specified commands; or perhaps some other arrangement considered functional. This is a complex and extremely important question. However, my aim in this article is to argue that the fully analyzed viewpoints of military strategists ought to be represented (rather than amalgamated) at the highest policy-making levels.

The obvious questions follow. Why don't those engaged in service and Joint Staff planning realize that, while the compromises to which they continually resort may initially mitigate service differences, the resultant policy proposals are so inferior that no top policy-maker is going to accept them? Do they not realize that service differences on strategy matters—if they reflect serious strategic issues—*will* be reformulated outside official military channels, either by civilians or military professionals, or both? And, finally, do service and Joint Staff planners not realize, in their short-sighted search for compromise, that ironically they bring about a result which they do not desire—the increased influence of civilians in strategy-making?

The military strategist does realize the consequences of an inferior defense policy formulation process. But, I contend, the system under which he must operate—the JCS planning process—is so restrictive that it is practically impossible for an input of value to run this gauntlet. The military strategist knows that, through gaining more knowledge and system experience, he may increase the percentage of the final JCS team effort attributable to him. But—at least subconsciously—he also knows that most of the gargantuan effort which he and his colleagues contribute to a paper will be for naught because it will not influence top national security policymakers.

I think a description of the JCS strategy-making process explains quite well why the military are not making a maximum contribution to current defense policy. However, perhaps a few comments concerning problems peculiar to the system will better explain why accommodation at the lowest common denominator is the typical result of the planning process.

First, are such decisionmaking problems inherent in large organization? Colonel William M. Jones (USAF, Ret) had extensive active duty at the service and Joint Staff action officer levels. In a recent RAND publication, Colonel Jones had this to say:

To the outsider, you may appear to be involved in a daily mass of trivia, dialogues, and meetings. From your viewpoint, however, your numerous contacts are opportunities to influence the direction of the organization effort. Within this plethora of daily interactions and decisions you are urged into certain patterns of action by your sense of your responsibilities, your responsibility to the nation, to your Service, to your immediate superior, and to the members of your own organization. Notice here the existence of opportunities for internal conflicts. Your resolution of such conflicts is a personal matter and is dependent on the situation under consideration.

Having had much experience on various military staffs, you are urged in your daily decisions toward a consistent pattern. You understand (possibly without consciously thinking about it) that your staff cannot function in support of you unless you are somewhat predictable to them. (Your superior must be consistent in his expressed views concerning things that influence your area of responsibility if he is to give you freedom, within bounds, to operate effectively.) To the outsider you may present a picture of a confirmed bureaucrat in your resistance to new and "better" ideas, but to you this resistance is the result of balancing a theoretical gain against the practical necessity of keeping your staff functioning effectively.

Another factor being urged upon you continuously is the need to "keep it simple." To insure that your staff understands your views toward certain policy matters, many subtle variations that you may well understand will have to be omitted from your formal communications. A policy statement or published plan that contain numerous "if this—then that" considerations can produce confusion at the time it is to be implemented simply because of a wide divergence in view as to what the situation really is at the time. To the outsider this can result in the appearance of stupidity or "black and white" thinking, but to you it is the only way to operate effectively.

In summary . . ., your job is one of decision-making in a management organization. The normal pattern of activities is such that your opportunities to make or influence obviously important decisions are much less frequent than your opportunities to make numerous small decisions. Most of your influence on the direction of the organization is the result of these numerous, small decisions. Consistency in the making of these decisions is, you feel, necessary for effective staff work and coordination. In addition, consistency enhances your influence on the over-all organizational decision-making since your beliefs as to what should be done are best expressed by a consistent pattern.

Your decisions, as anyone's, are based on your prediction of the consequences if they are implemented. In the making of these predictions an important factor is the effect it will have on your organization and the probable reactions of other staff elements and associated agencies. Your ability to predict, and therefore influence, the probable attitudes and activities of other staff elements and associated agencies is degraded by your lack of adequate communications with them as compared with your daily communications with your own staff. Your communications with your staff are usually at the subformal, interactive level. Your communications with other staff elements tend toward the formal level. The result is that your predictions are based on mental images that can be grossly inaccurate. Finally, and quite important, you are not conscious of many of these influences.[34]

In addition to phenomena generally associated with any large decisionmaking organization, there are obstacles more peculiar to the military. I call these "prisoner problems." There are four of these kinds of problems, and they graphically illustrate why the present JCS strategy-making system produces "waffled" papers —and why the individual caught up in the process can do so little to improve matters. Probably these problems also are common to most highly centralized organizations, but they get expressed in specific, clearly defined ways in the military planning process.

There is the great possibility that service staff officers may become prisoners of their service chief. Each service maintains a set of position papers furnishing that service's current viewpoints on any and all matters involving strategy alternatives. Naturally these position papers reflect—or, what may be more important, *are thought to reflect* — the chief's philosophy, although many staff officers may have participated in the papers' derivation.

The principal point is this: a service action officer interprets every issue raised in every paper in terms of what he believes

to be his own service's strategy position. And, one would judge, he must. He is probably intellectually committed to his service's positions. But even *if* he had doubts about certain issues, he would not be likely to raise them while working as a service action officer on a JCS paper. The action officer cannot afford to spend too much time on any single paper. If he does, work on other studies is bound to suffer. Therefore, he would want to be certain he was right and his superiors wrong before he decided to "muddy the waters." His commanders probably have told him to have ideas and to advance them boldly, but they hardly want him to generate a debate at the top level on literally hundreds of issues on every JCS paper to which he is assigned! Service strategy positions *do* change—but not because service action officers got their chiefs to agree to revisions while they were working on a particular JCS paper. [35]

Staff action officers also may become prisoners of senior staff officers. This is a problem experienced by every large bureaucracy with numerous responsibility levels. I see no necessity to discuss this issue in any detail. As far as service staffs are concerned, it will be either a slight or a grievous problem depending upon the degree to which human relations, leadership, and internal communication lines are in evidence at all command levels. However, the potential for a unique manifestation of the staff prisoner problem is found in the Joint Staff when, for instance, the Joint Staff officers involved in a paper are an Army action officer, and Air Force deputy agency head, and a Navy agency head.

Another prisoner problem that exists is one not so immediately apparent. Service action officers can make prisoners of their chiefs. General Taylor has indicated how real this problem can be:

Every Chief has to be alert to the danger of becoming a prisoner of his Indians, [action offi-

34 William M. Jones, "On Decisionmaking in Large Organizations," *RAND Memorandum RM-3986-PR*, March 1964, pp. 11–12.

35 I am not implying that the chiefs are narrow-minded. Since they undoubtedly have been action officers at one time or another, they are aware of the "prisoner" problem to which I refer. They are likely to listen when an action officer argues for doctrinal changes.

cers] who are generally able and enthusiastic young officers trained to defend their views fearlessly before their superiors. I remember a briefing of the Army Chief of Staff several years ago, when the Deputy Chief of Staff, a lieutenant general, was passed a piece of paper during the Conference. With a laugh he read it to the group. "If the Chief of Staff tries to change line 2 of page 4, oppose him at all costs. Signed Majors Miller and Mock."[36]

It is almost impossible to imagine how busy a service chief is. The tasks to which he must give some attention in his responsibility as service head are a hundredfold. Also he must devote the major portion of his time to the corporate duties which he incurs as a member of the JCS.

As former Deputy Secretary of Defense Roswell L. Gilpatric suggests, the chief's workload can be overwhelming.[37] The service chief, therefore, must rely to a heavy degree upon his staff, and especially so in those areas where his own expertise and experience do not provide an all-inclusive guide. Obviously, modern strategy-making is often one of those areas. There is a real—and, I believe, an increasing—danger that the service staff will take its chief captive. And, to complete a vicious circle, it is likely to be a service staff that is *itself* a prisoner of its chief because of the current set of position papers!

Finally, chiefs can become prisoners of the other chiefs. Sometimes a chief will have corporate responsibilities which he believes over-shadow service commitments. He may wish to take a broad view on strategic matters even if it means a short-term position loss for his own service. But is a chief likely to take such a conciliatory approach unless he is assured, somehow, that all other chiefs will act similarly? If the other chiefs do not adopt an analogous approach, the pacificatory chief soon would be reigning over a disappearing service! Therefore, the natural tendency is to wait for some *other* chief to initiate the concession process. Such a process *is* possible; I am certain the chiefs sometimes utilize it. But it is difficult to make it the normal decisionmaking pattern because of fears that

reciprocity will not prevail. Like the other prisoner problems, this one demonstrates that existent military bureaucracy mechanisms intensify those tendencies in the JCS strategic planning process leading to accommodation at the lowest common denominator.

Let me make it clear that it is not my intention to ridicule either those who devised or those who have utilized the JCS planning process. Given a belief that a single military viewpoint should be projected upward, the present system was the natural and logical resultant—especially in an environment where the individual services were not merged. There is nothing inherently "military" in the JCS planning procedure. It is quite typical of many large-scale civilian organizations where decisionmaking involves the adjustment of positions held by semiautonomous suborgans.

What can be done to increase the military's input to defense policy formulation? Manifestly, there must be significant improvement in the quality of military advice given to national security policy superiors. But how is this to be accomplished?

Many interested observers, both civilian and military, have suggested that the problem is essentially one of staffing. They believe the "whole man" approach to officer training and advancement is outmoded in this world of increasing specialization.[38] They feel that no single individual can ever accumulate enough expertise to know even the important weapon systems of his own service, especially with technology creating doctrinal and operational revolutions almost daily. Particularly outmoded, they declare, is the idea that any officer who has distinguished himself in the field for a considerable number of years is thereby qualified to do Pentagon-type work specifically in the strategymaking area. The military input to defense policy formulation will increase markedly, they aver, when the services decide to staff their strategy-pro-

[36] Taylor, *op. cit.*, p. 90.
[37] Gilpatric, *op. cit.*

[38] For instance, in 1963 the Air Force divided its officers among 40 "utilization fields," 198 air officers specialties, and 309 specialties and subspecialties. See U.S. Department of the Air Force, *Officer Classification Manual AFM 36–1*, 15 April 1963.

ducing agencies with what Professor Huntington calls "military intellectuals," military men with graduate degrees in relevant social and engineering sciences who devote the major part of their careers to intellectual endeavor applicable to defense policymaking.

Unquestionably, this argument has much merit. It is nonsense to expect an action officer to write a valuable paper in two weeks on, say, the JCS position vis à vis the Soviet-proposed NATO-Warsaw nonaggression pact when, prior to the assignment, that officer did not know the history of such proposals, the political context within which they have been suggested, or the specific positions that the U.S. and its allies have taken on past proposals of this nature. The services *are* recognizing the need to relate education and relevant experience to critical planning positions. And they are showing a willingness to dip lower in the rank structure to obtain people equipped with the proper intellectual and experience qualifications. Relatively young officers are no longer complete strangers in the Pentagon.

I believe, however, that those who see the answer to be improvement in personnel quality have, by and large, missed the essential nature of the present JCS defense planning process. Any organization can use better people, and this is certainly true of service and joint staffs, although I think present service and joint staff planners are far better than "staffing enthusiasts" have considered them.

I would argue, therefore, that even if all the services could fill their strategymaking organs with ideally qualified people the problem of a weak military voice in defense policy formulation would remain. The problem exists primarily because JCS planning procedures drastically reduce the opportunity for the military to contribute to strategymaking. If there really were a single, fully analyzed military viewpoint, the system might work.[39] However, due to

the differing environments, experiences, and operational requirements of military professionals in the many sublevel organizations involved, there is no single military position on the multitudinous defense policy issues which constantly confront strategymakers. Therefore, efforts to create such a position lead to low-quality, least-common-denominator solutions which have been the typical product of JCS planning procedures. These "solutions" will seldom, if ever, be accepted fully by top strategists, since—as I have tried to indicate—modern defense policy issues are too important.

---

[39] Between 1962 and 1964, there were indications that a new JCS planning procedure—which tried to create a single, fully analyzed military position—was utilized. The *New York Times* stated (4 February 1964) that General Maxwell Taylor (Chairman of the JCS, 1962–1964) wanted a single chief of staff, with the role of the present Joint Chiefs changed to that of "a new advisory body called provisionally the Supreme Military Council." See Taylor, *op. cit.*, pp. 126–29. However, said the *Times*, since the change General Taylor wanted requires a change in law:

". . . informed observers in the Pentagon say that General Taylor, as Chairman, has come as close to being a de facto single chief of staff as any man can be without a legal change.

"The Chairman's staff group of about 25 officers, organized on regional and functional lines, examines every paper prepared by the Joint Chiefs of Staff and freely suggests alterations intended to bring the papers into line with the views of the Chairman.

"If the revised papers are not approved by the Joint Chiefs of Staff, General Taylor nearly always wins the approval of Defense Secretary Robert S. McNamara for the versions he favors, it is said." In effect, General Taylor created a truly joint staff within the Joint Staff. Reputedly, General Taylor introduced another revolutionary idea: he assigned a paper to the Joint Staff with instructions *not* to include service action officers in the planning process. The services were allowed only to comment on the finished product.

A final technique of the present administration is the following: One of the DOD Assistant Secretary of Defense Officers (usually ASD/International Security Affairs) sometimes assigns—through the JCS chairman—a particular strategic problem to a Joint Staff agency. One study concerned the use of tactical nuclear weapons in a European limited war. The Joint Staff agency was given a *year* to do this study. The result was an excellent, thoroughly staffed piece of work including scores of war game results, etc.

While these ad hoc evolutionary arrangements probably did increase the quality of JCS papers, they gave the impression that single, fully analyzed logical military viewpoints *do* exist in defense policy areas whereas this is normally not the case. A far better arrangement, I believe, is to permit the projection upward of completely staffed papers from those military organizations which have current defense policy responsibilities—even if this means as it inevitably will that the military no longer speaks with one voice.

Ironically, until we learn that the military *cannot, will not,* and *should not* attempt to preempt defense policy formulation, advice from military men will continue to be disregarded because it will be demonstrably "waffled."

The attempt to formulate a single military point of view on strategy—through the JCS planning process—has failed. The danger is that planning—theorizing about war—may be done mostly by people having no relevant knowledge of combat or of field preparation for various modes of combat. I believe that significant inputs to strategy from the military can come only from individual officers having broad experience in operational military problems *as well as* superior understanding of all those non-military factors essential to formulation of national defense policy. These officers, while necessarily representing responsible military organizations, must be permitted to speak as *individual* members of a strategymaking team. Under the present circumstances, the military man finds it difficult even to get on the bench of that team.

Until we learn that, on most defense policy issues, a single "military" position cannot be attained without unacceptable reduction of quality, the input of a thousand modern Napoleons into the Pentagon will make very little difference, and defense policy formulation will remain the primary domain of the civilian.

Postscript

It is gratifying to note that present members of the JCS have recognized the degree to which consensus seeking can inhibit the military input to national security matters. In a 14 September 1965 letter relating to the clearance of this article, the Office of the Joint Chiefs of Staff noted:

Although there is no question that there is a strong desire for agreement, particularly at the "Indian" level, the present Chairman and Director have gone firmly on record against the very evil the author is speaking about. The record shows that their preference—to present dissenting opinions rather than "waffling" a paper into an inferior proposal—has borne fruit.

Although one happily notes this change in approach by the Joint Chiefs themselves, the *process* by which papers reach the Chiefs still has not been altered in any essential way. The process continues to emphasize compromise, and the JCS themselves remain to a degree slaves of the procedure.

L. B.T.

THE NEW CIVIL-MILITARY RELATIONS*

BY GENE M. LYONS

Historically the character of civil-military relations in the United States has been

* This article was originally prepared for the 1960 Annual Meeting of the American Political Science Association. In the preparation and in the revision I have profited from the comments of several colleagues, at Dartmouth and elsewhere, particularly my confrere, Louis Morton.

dominated by the concept of civilian control of the military. This has largely been a response to the fear of praetorianism. As recently as 1949, for example, the first Hoover Commission asserted that one of the major reasons for strengthening the "means of exercising civilian control" over the defense establishment was to "safeguard

Reprinted by permission of the copyright owner from *The American Political Science Review,* Vol. LV, No. 1, 1961, pp. 53–63. Copyright 1962 by The American Political Science Association.

Mr. Lyons is Professor of Government and Director of the Public Affairs Center at Dartmouth College. He is the author of several books, including *Military Policy and Economic Aid: the Korean Case 1950–1953* (1961) and *Schools for Strategy: Education and Research in National Security Affairs* (1965), and numerous articles on national security policy and education within the military profession.

our democratic traditions against militarism."[1] This same warning was raised in the report of the Rockefeller Committee on defense organization in 1953. While the overriding purpose of the committee's recommendations was to provide "the Nation with maximum security at minimum cost," the report made it clear that this had to be achieved "without danger to our free institutions, based on the fundamental principle of civilian control of the Military Establishment."[2] Finally, during the debate on the reorganization proposals of 1958, senators and congressmen used the theme of a "Prussianized" military staff to attempt to slow down the trend towards centralization in the military establishment.[3]

Despite this imposing support, the concept of civilian control of the military has little significance for contemporary problems of national security in the United States. In the first place, military leaders are divided among themselves, although their differences cannot be reduced to a crass contrast between dichotomous doctrines. Air Force leaders who are gravely concerned over the need to maintain a decisive nuclear retaliatory force are by now acknowledging the need to develop a limited war capability. At the same time, Army leaders are quite frank to admit that "flexible response" requires both strategic and tactical power of sizable strength, although they are particularly committed to developing a large tactical force. If these differences appear to be only differences in emphasis, they are nonetheless crucial in a political process within which priorities must be established and choices must be made. Without firm agreement on priorities, there is little reason to expect that the military can control government policy even if civilian

authorities abdicate responsibility for basic decisions. The most that can result is a compromise between different military positions. Commonly, military disagreement, if exposed, is an invitation for civilian intervention.

Secondly, the concept of civilian control of the military ignores two other factors that complicate civil-military relations. On the one hand, the military themselves accept the principle of civilian supremacy; on the other, they have been thrown into a political role in the formation of policy. The resignation of General Gavin over the budgetary restrictions of the "New Look" strategy is a case in point. The General disagreed with the judgment of his civilian superiors but, like General Ridgway before him and General Taylor after him, held his most violent fire until he was out of uniform and freed from the limits of professional restrictions.[4] His case dramatically illustrates the dilemma of the military as they move into the center of defense policymaking. Here they have to struggle between the non-partisan tenets of their creed and the requirements of effective participation in the political process. Their advice as experts is not only used by the Executive to bolster its case, but is eagerly courted by Congress and the public as a basis for testing the caliber of executive action. In one respect the political role of the military tends to dilute their own professionalism. But in another, it affords them more than one opportunity to maintain a balance between their professional code and the individual conscience. The nature of the American political system thus provides an outlet for frustration which, in other settings, has been the catalyst to set off an outburst of militarism.

In its broadest sense, the concept of civilian control of the military means military responsiveness to the policies of politically responsible government. But this too needs to be reinterpreted in the light of revolution-

[1] Commission on Organization of the Executive Branch of the Government, *The National Security Organization*, A Report to the Congress, February 1949, pp. 2–3.

[2] *Report of the Rockefeller Committee on Department of Defense Organization*, Committee Print, Senate Committee on Armed Services, 83d Cong., 1st sess. 1953, p. 1.

[3] See, *e.g.*, Rept. No. 1765, *Department of Defense Reorganization Act of 1958*, House Committee on Armed Services, 85th Cong., 2d session, esp. pp. 24–33.

[4] The views of all three Generals have been documented in books they published shortly after they retired: James M. Gavin, *War and Peace in the Space Age* (New York, 1958); Matthew Ridgway, *Soldier* (New York, 1956); and Maxwell D. Taylor, *The Uncertain Trumpet* (New York, 1959).

ary changes that have greatly complicated the formation of defense policy. Preparedness is as much the product of civilian expertise in science and engineering and of civilian decisions on the allocation of national resources as it is of military planning. At the same time, it is very often the military who put defense policy to the test of political accountability by exposing the bases for decisions to congressional and public inquiry. As a result, there is a constant reversal of traditional roles, a situation that has brought civilians and military into a new set of relationships. These relationships have been reflected only in a limited way in recent organizational changes that have strengthened the central agencies of the defense establishment. To appreciate their full significance, it is also necessary to understand changes in the character of both civilian and military leadership in defense affairs. Civilians are becoming "militarized" and the military "civilianized" and it is these changes that reflect, more clearly than organization alone, a fundamental break with tradition in the evolution of civil-military relations.[5]

I. THE EVOLUTION OF DEFENSE ORGANIZATION

Like many institutions in American political life, a highly centralized, civilian-dominated Pentagon has developed in response to changing forces and conditions. Had the Joint Chiefs of Staff been able to function as a collegial unit rather than as a divided group of service representatives, it is possible that reorganization trends might have taken different directions. Centralization, however, was probably inevitable in one form or another. Increasing defense costs made centralized budgeting and programming a necessity. The bite of military expenditures in the total federal budget makes it impossible to ignore the impact of defense on the national economy,

the government's tax program and the whole range of complex problems of resources allocation. The impact of technology has also been a centralizing factor. Indeed, work on the military applications of atomic energy had already been centralized in the Atomic Energy Commission. But work on missiles had been left in the separate services and the duplication of effort in three competitive programs brought on demands for greater coordination in propulsion programs in the late 1950s. Finally, both these areas of financial management and of research and development require skills that are "civilian," in essence, and are not yet possessed by many high ranking military officers. Thus it might be argued that "civilianization," as well as centralization, was inevitable given the nature of the problems that needed to be solved.

The growth of central civilian authority has nevertheless come in stages. The first Secretary of Defense, James Forrestal, had been opposed to the development of a large central staff even after he had come around to accept the concept of an overall defense chief. As a former Navy Secretary he was committed to the retention of strong civilian leadership in the individual services, first, to avoid a situation that might lead to the domination of a single strategic doctrine and, second, to keep civilian authority lodged at the operating levels of the military departments. He insisted that the Secretary "must be free to concentrate his efforts on the establishment of broad policy" and in so doing "must look to the secretaries of the military departments for the information and data upon which his policy is to be based and then look again to them for the execution of these policies."[6] Within these guidelines, he was reported to want only "a very small executive force for the single Secretary to consist of [a

5 For a theoretical statement of the concept of civilian control of the military, together with references to other major analyses of the subject, see Samuel P. Huntington, "Civilian Control of the Military: a Theoretical Statement," in Eulau, Eldersveld and Janowitz (ed.), Political Behavior (Glencoe, Ill., 1956), pp. 380ff.

6 See his letter to Chairman Chan Gurney of the Senate Armed Services Committee, reprinted in that Committee's Hearings, 80th Cong., 1st sess., National Defense Establishment, Pt. 1, p. 185. More generally, see Paul Y. Hammond, "The National Security Council as a Device for Interdepartmental Coordination," this REVIEW, Vol. 54 (Dec., 1960), pp. 899–910, and his forthcoming book, Organizing for Defense (Princeton University Press, 1961).

total of] 15 to 25 '$10,000-a-year men' and officers."[7]

The National Security Act of 1947, highly influenced by Forrestal's views, thus created a federation of military departments with little authority in the office of the Secretary of National Defense. In little more than a year, however, Forrestal himself recommended a number of statutory changes that mark the second step in the strengthening of centralized civilian authority. The critical problem he had faced was the absence of any military consensus upon which to develop strategic programs. He therefore sought to develop independent staff at the Defense Department level, including an Undersecretary of Defense, a Chairman for the Joint Chiefs of Staff and a larger Joint Staff. He also called for greatly clarified responsibility over the military departments to enable the Secretary to settle controversies over the roles and missions of the separate services and the allocation of the budgetary resources.[8]

Forrestal's recommendations, largely reinforced by the report of the first Hoover Commission a year later, were the basis for the National Security Act Amendments of 1949 which created a Department of Defense where only a coordinating mechanism had hitherto existed. The Secretary, however strengthened his position became, was nonetheless still forbidden, by law, to encroach upon the "combatant functions assigned to the military services." Congress deliberately used this basic prohibition to maintain the essential identity of the individual services, a tactic that has been retained in subsequent major reorganizations in 1953 and 1958. Nevertheless, this restriction has become less limiting on the authority of the Secretary of Defense as major strategic decisions have turned on problems of weapons development and financial management rather than directly on the controversy over roles and missions.

The reorganization plan of 1953 went another step in centralizing authority in the civilian leadership by creating assistant secretaries of defense with responsibilities in functional areas, such as supply and logistics, and manpower and personnel. These posts were established with the understanding that "they should not be in the direct line of administrative authority between [the Secretary] and the three military departments, but instead should assist in developing policies, prescribing standards, and bringing to the Secretary of Defense information on which he may base his decisions."[9] Under these terms, the authority of the assistant secretaries was ambiguous. Administration witnesses were always cautious to assure congressional committees that the assistant secretaries of defense had no operating authority and were exclusively advisory to the Secretary. While this was theoretically so, actual practice was often to the contrary since they were frequently in a strong position to recommend that service positions be over-ruled.[10] And the authority of the Secretary of Defense to delegate powers to his assistant secretaries was confirmed under the 1958 Act, apparently clearing away the ambiguity.

The growth of centralized civilian authority has thus been related to the decline in the authority of the service secretaries. Forrestal himself had found at an early stage that the service secretaries could not administer the individual departments and still act as his deputies in the formation and execution of overall policy. As service heads they were obliged to support major positions developed by their military chiefs or risk losing the main leverage they had to be effective in their jobs. The policy process is largely a process of bargaining and persuasion. Without the confidence of the military leaders, a civilian secretary cannot hope to persuade them to alter their views. At the same time, he has little chance to gain their confidence unless he largely supports the positions they have developed. He thus plays a dual rule, representing the Defense Department at the Service level and

---

[7] Testimony of Admiral Sherman, *ibid.*, p. 155.

[8] *First Report of the Secretary of Defense*, National Defense Establishment, 1948, pp. 2–4.

[9] *Report of the Rockefeller Committee on Department of Defense Organization, op. cit.*, p. 11.

[10] See, for example, the dialogue between Senator Symington and the Assistant Secretary of Defense (Logistics and Supply) in Hearings, Senate Committee on Armed Services, 85th Cong. 1st sess., *Nominations*, pp. 12–14.

the military department at the Defense level. Under the pressures of inter-service competition for limited resources and the development of a large secretariat in the Department of Defense, the service secretary has become more and more a spokesman for his service's position and less and less a positive instrument in the formation of policy by the Secretary of Defense.

But by far the greatest part of the increase of authority gained by the civilian leadership in the Defense Department has accrued because of the inability of the Joint Chiefs of Staff to come to agreed positions on the military requirements of national security. The far-reaching provisions of the 1958 Act were largely in direct response to the wide range of problems raised by service disagreement. Under the Act, the Secretary of Defense can exercise direct authority over unified commands, transfer weapons systems from one service to another and maintain centralized direction of all military research and development through the Director of Research and Engineering. The practical impact of these powers is to give the Secretary considerable influence over the roles and missions of the services which are still prescribed by law within the broad and flexible categories of land, air, and sea forces. The concept of unified commands and the sweeping authority over weapons development now enable the Secretary to bring about *de facto* unification of the armed services even within the framework of a three-departmental system.[11] But to accomplish this, he has a total civilian staff

[11] Almost two years after the passage of the Reorganization Act of 1958, the *Army, Navy, Air Force Journal* (May 28, 1960) summed up some of the ways Secretary of Defense Gates "is using the full powers of his office . . . to achieve increased unification within the terms of existing legislation." These included centralization of missile test ranges, centralization of toxicological research, and establishment of an All-Service Defense Communications Agency. In addition, early in 1960, Secretary Gates sent a memorandum to the Chairman of the JCS, stating: "It is requested that I be promptly informed regarding any issue on which a difference of opinion is developing within the Joint Chiefs of Staff. I intend that either the Secretary of Defense and/or the Deputy Secretary of Defense will promptly meet with the Joints Chiefs at such times as they consider the issue in question . . ." (reprinted in *Army, Navy, Air Force Journal*, January 16, 1960).

of almost 2,000—a far cry from the "15 to 25 '$10,000-a-year men' and officers" that Forrestal had wanted less than fifteen years ago.[12]

II. THE "DEPOLITICALIZATION" OF THE DEFENSE DEPARTMENT

The increasing authority of civilian leadership has not been granted without misgivings. Several aspects of this trend have been viewed with concern: the turnover of civilians in the Pentagon; the inability of civilians to come to grips with problems which have no exact parallel outside the military establishment; the tendency for the Defense Department to evolve into a fourth operating agency of the military establishment; the pre-occupation of Defense officials with budgetary matters; and delays in military programs as a result of the need to obtain clearances from a thickening layer of "functional" chiefs.[13] Indeed, Senator Henry Jackson has commented that " . . . at one time we worried about a German Gen-

[12] This contrast has risen to plague subsequent Secretaries of Defense. Secretary McElroy, facing questions on it during the reorganization hearings in 1958, offered the following: "I have heard others report to me about the expressions by Jim Forrestal about getting along with 100 people, and that kind of thing. I have also heard that after he got into the job, he found that he needed a great many more. The history is nothing that I am prepared to support because I don't know precisely what did go on there. But I honestly—while I agree with you fully that numbers are not a measure of the importance or efficiency of an organization, I mean large numbers, I wouldn't know how anybody could operate a department of this size and complexity with 100 people." Hearings, House Committee on Armed Services, 85th Cong., 2d sess., *Reorganization of the Department of Defense*, p. 6072.

[13] These misgivings are suggested by the questions raised by the staff of the Senate (Jackson) subcommittee on national policy machinery. See *Organizing for National Security*, Interim Report of the Committee on Government Operations made by its Subcommittee on National Policy Machinery, 86th Cong., 2d sess., pp. 17–19. The problem of turnover has been the subject of a proposed Senate resolution "that it is the sense of the Senate that nominees appearing before its committee shall indicate their willingness to serve so long as the President desires" (S. Res. 338), 86th Cong., 2d sess.; see also Rept. No. 1753, 86th Cong., 2d sess., *Resolution Expressing Concern of Senate over Turnover in Administrative and Policymaking Posts*.

eral Staff setup in the Pentagon. I think we are at the point of a civilian general staff. . . . " Senator Jackson was not, however, critical of the establishment of new duties in the Office of the Secretary, but rather of "a failure to exercise these functions properly."[14]

The problem of "proper" performance in top defense positions is necessarily complex. Many administrators have held top positions over long periods—longer indeed than many military officers who are subject to rotation in assignment at frequent intervals. Others have had equally long tenure although they have hedge-hopped from position to position. It has, however, been difficult to attract first-rate people into high defense posts. Charles Wilson, for example reported that, just before he took over the post of Secretary of Defense in 1953, outgoing Secretary Lovett said to him: "Charlie, do not be too critical of some of these men that are here to help you do this job, because in some cases they are the thirty-third men I propositioned to come before I could get anyone."[15] In the final analysis, the caliber of leadership in high positions will depend on the President and the kind of men he wants as advisers and his willingness to use his persuasive powers to bring them into government. It will also depend, though to a lesser degree, on the pressures the Senate puts on the Executive.

When the Eisenhower Administration took office in 1953, there was an almost complete turnover in civilian leadership (and, indeed, in military leadership as well). With the exception of the Defense Comptroller, Wilfred McNeil, all of the top Pentagon posts changed hands. This changeover was perhaps more disrupting than usual since it marked the advent of the first Republican president in twenty years. But the turnover was also very deliberate for the new Administration had almost completely divorced itself from the foreign and

military policies of the Truman Administration during the presidential campaign. The new President and his chief advisers looked for a loyalty to their leadership and policies that they felt few Truman aides could muster.[16] It is nevertheless instructive to note that by the end of the second Eisenhower Administration most civilian leaders in the Pentagon had spent periods of four to eight years in defense work, if not in the same post.[17] At the same time Thomas Gates, the last Secretary of Defense under Eisenhower, and Robert Lovett, the last Secretary under Truman, were both urging that high defense posts be protected from partisan politics and that both parties agree to maintain effective continuity in the civilian leadership of national security programs.[18]

The recommendations of Secretaries

[14] Hearings, Senate Committee on Armed Services, 84th Cong., 2d sess., *Assistant Secretaries for Research and Development*, pp. 20–22.

[15] Hearings, Senate Committee on Armed Services, 83rd Cong., 1st sess., *Nomination of Charles Wilson*, Pt. 2, pp. 110–111. For a general discussion of this problem, see John A. Perkins, "Staffing Democracy's Top Side," *Public Administration Review*, Vol. 17 (Winter, 1957), pp. 1 ff.

[16] This was also true in programs outside the field of foreign and military policy, e.g., the members of the regulatory commissions and directors of TVA. For a discussion of its impact on career executives, see Herman M. Somers, "The Federal Bureaucracy and the Change of Administration," this REVIEW, Vol. 48 (March 1954), pp. 131 ff.

[17] For example: Thomas Gates, the Secretary of Defense, had served (with one short break) since October 7, 1953, as Undersecretary and Secretary of the Navy, as well as Deputy Secretary and Secretary of Defense; James Douglas, Deputy Secretary of Defense, had served continuously since March 3, 1953, as Undersecretary and Secretary of the Air Force, as well as Deputy Secretary; Herbert York, Director of Defense Research and Engineering, came to this post (and was the first incumbent in 1958) after long experience in defense work with the Advanced Research Projects Agency, various scientific advisory committees, and non-profit institutions engaged in defense activities; Charles Finucane, the Assistant Secretary of Defense for manpower affairs, had served as Assistant Secretary and Undersecretary of the Army for almost four years when (after a short break in service) he was brought back to the post at the Defense level in 1958; similarly, the three service secretaries, Brucker in the Army, Franke in the Navy, and Sharp in the Air Force had all had almost continuous Pentagon service for at least five years.

[18] In both cases, these views were expressed in testimony before the Senate subcommittee on National Policy Machinery and were largely supported by the testimony of other witnesses, particularly James A. Perkins, John Corson, and Roger Jones. See Hearings, Subcommittee on National Policy Machinery, Senate Committee on Government Operations, 86th Cong., 2d sess., *Organizing for National Security*, Pts. II and III.

Gates and Lovett are symptomatic of the change that has slowly been developing in the character of civilian leadership in the Pentagon in spite of the sharp setback in 1953. It is marked by what might be called a "depoliticalization" of the Defense Department, that is, an emphasis on standards of competence and experience in making appointments. Appointive posts in all federal departments are, of course, subject to both political and non-political considerations. Indeed, in the areas of foreign and military policy, the motivation of national interest operates to counteract the political forces of geographic distribution, party balance and pressure groups that dominate top appointments in other departments.[19] Nonpolitical considerations regarding background and ability thus largely govern the selection process.

Most appointive posts in the Pentagon break down into three general groups.[20]

[19] Patronage proved to be a vexing problem when the Eisenhower Administration took office in 1953 after twenty years of Democratic rule. Very early in the game Secretary Dulles was reported to have made it clear that "his department could not be run on the basis of patronage," Robert J. Donovan, *Eisenhower, The Inside Story* (New York, 1956), p. 98, though this did not prevent the appointment of "fat cats," *e.g.*, to ambassadorial posts, or the wholesale purge of departmental personnel—referred to as "Stassenization"—in 1953, carried out in the name of a budget cut that Dulles did not resist. By the end of the second Eisenhower term—*i.e.*, in hindsight, a quite different vantage point—a nonpartisan policy was considered valid for the Defense Department (see reference above to testimony of Secretary of Defense Gates). For a general discussion, see Harvey C. Mansfield, "Political Parties, Patronage, and the Federal Government Service," in *The Federal Government Service: Its Character, Prestige, and Problems.* The American Assembly, 1954, pp. 81 ff.

[20] The following discussion borrows from Wallace S. Sayre, "The Political Executive in the National Government: The Constitutional and Political Setting," prepared for the Conference on the Political Executive, Woodrow Wilson School of Public and International Affairs, Princeton University, 1956, pp. 23–24 (mimeographed). The literature on executives for government is particularly pertinent to the problems discussed here. See, for example, the report of the task force on personnel and civil service of the second Hoover Commission, dated February 1955; Paul F. David and Ross Pollock, *Executives for Government*, The Brookings Institution, 1957; and Marver H. Bernstein, *The Job of the Federal Executive*, The Brookings Institution, 1958.

There is, first of all, the Secretary of Defense and his immediate staff. Here the needs and thus the will of the President himself will certainly dominate, for the prime importance of the Secretary is as a top presidential adviser. His constant occupation is to serve as a deputy to the President in the performance of his constitutional duties as commander-in-chief of the armed forces. Indeed, as the problems of national security have come to absorb so much of the President's time and energy, the Secretary of Defense has come to be one of the most prominent members of both the President's cabinet and his inner circle.

But below the Secretary and and his personal staff are a group of appointive posts at the Defense and military department levels, in which functional or "program" rather than constitutional or presidential, responsibility is emphasized. These include posts in the fields of financial management, manpower, and procurement and logistics. What is often as necessary as practical experience in the subject field itself is an ability to manage complex enterprises and a deep understanding of the political and governmental processes. Thus, experience in public service is of prime importance. Men chosen for these posts might come from several sources. They might be men who possess these qualities and are also important figures in the President's party; their appointment can thus perform two functions at once—bring a professional hand to high office and meet the party's requirement for patronage. They might also be men whose identity with one of the major political parties has been incidental but whose experience with problems of public policy has made them wise selections for office regardless of party. Finally, they might be high-ranking civil servants whose records are outstanding and who are willing to give up the security of tenure for the political risks of appointive positions. Where a choice is possible, the determining factor will be the importance with which the President and his principal advisers view the balance of interests that are involved.

Finally, there are appointive posts that require a high level of specialized expertise but cannot be included within civil service categories. This is especially true in the field of research and engineering. The incumbents will often act as policy advisers and, even within the bounds of their own professional integrity, must be in basic agreement with the political dimensions of the President's defense program. At the same time, the civil service cannot provide the high degree of expertise that is required for top direction. The background and experience which the evaluation of complex weapons systems requires can rarely be gained by working in government agencies. It is more usually found in men whose prior experience has been developed in university and industrial laboratories.

Several factors can thus be identified as vital qualifications for high Pentagon posts below the Secretary of Defense himself: the benefit of government experience; the need for expertise; and the desirability of continuity. These traits have been increasingly recognized and their recognition is operating to develop a "depoliticalization" of these posts. "Depoliticalization" nevertheless has limits. National security issues cannot (and indeed should not) be entirely taken out of politics. Top presidential advisers must be prepared to defend the choices they make before congressional and public criticism. At the same time the President needs to have the alternative of changing his close advisers if the sense of purpose and the support that he feels is necessary to his program are missing. Capable men available for such posts, no matter how broad the recruitment sources are becoming, will, moreover, continue to be few; and many of those who agree to accept political responsibilities will be under pressure to return to private life. For that matter, some turnover in the top echelons is desirable to bring a continual freshness and critical direction to government administration. Thus, no matter how far "depoliticalization" goes, political appointees will not always be able to provide the continuity and stability in government that are the principal contributions of career professionals.

"Depoliticalization" is, however, only one of the characteristics of the larger trend towards a professionalization of civilian leadership in defense affairs. Professionalization is taking other forms as well—the influence of career executives in the development of major policy decisions, innovations in administration which have brought outside experts into government through a variety of institutional devices, and a growing interest in military affairs among civilians outside government. All of these, taken together, contribute to the changing character of civilian leadership that is, in turn, influencing the character of civil-military relations.

III. THE PROFESSIONALIZATION OF CIVILIAN LEADERSHIP

The importance of continuity and stability in government is emphasized when the nature of the policy process is clearly understood; it is likelier to be appreciated more toward the end than at the beginning of any particular Administration. Policies are usually developed with a long history of conjecture, false starts and negotiation. Very often they take shape from a series of operational responses or the byplay of a number of viewpoints rather than from a single breakthrough of brilliant analysis. Within such situations, the influence of careerists, military and civilian, is enormous. It is equally impressive in moments of crisis when only professionals have the background and experience to respond quickly. The military professionals wield their greatest influence within the military departments; a large and burgeoning staff of civilian careerists exert similar powers in the Department of Defense. They perform staff work in connection with establishing budgetary and manpower priorities, supply the background material for new programs and have usually developed a network of informal contacts that make them invaluable in inter-departmental negotiations. Indeed, General Gavin recalled (perhaps with some bitterness) that " . . . the Civil Service employees . . . in the Department of Defense . . . probably have more impact on decisionmaking . . . than any other individual or group of individuals, military or civilian."[21]

The hazy line that divides policy from

[21] Gavin, *op. cit.*, p. 166.

administration and the influence of career professionals on decisionmaking are familiar themes in the literature of public administration.[22] In the Defense Department, professional influence has been increased by the tendency to seek solutions to problems at a technical level in order to minimize differences over vital matters of policy. In such cases, the guides for policy become efficiency and empirical verification rather than intuition and inspiration; and in any such atmosphere technicians and arbitrators play a critical role. Such tactics often reduce policy to a compromise between opposing positions, a practice that is often stultifying. In many cases it is nevertheless an inevitable consequence of policy-making within the democratic process, particularly in the field of national security. For within the goldfish bowl of American politics, there is a limit to the risks a political leader is willing to take in approving defense programs that can be argued in terms of national survival and for which there is no indisputable solution.

But like the "depoliticalization" of appointive posts, there are limits to the contribution that increased civil service influence can make to the professionalization of civilian leadership in the Pentagon. Some of these limits have already been suggested. For one thing, few civil servants possess the degree of specialized expertise that is required for technical staff work in fields such as research and engineering. Nor, for that matter, does the bureaucracy offer the environment in which careful study and reflection on basic problems, such as strategic policy, are encouraged and indeed rewarded. At the same time, there is little chance that the top layer of the American civil service can be transformed into an administrative class like that in Great Britain; neither the social structure nor the political system to support such a class is present.[23]

Within the special context of American governmental institutions, a series of innovating techniques have therefore been developed to bring professional competence to bear on matters of public policy where neither political nor career executives can fully meet the demands. They include *ad hoc* and standing advisory committees, contractual arrangements for consultative services, the assignment of broad investigations or actual operations to outside institutions, and government-financed independent agencies set up outside the formality of the bureaucracy.[24] These administrative techniques perform a number of functions. They bring creativity to the public service in areas where it is often discouraged by the routinization of bureaucratic procedures or the dangers of interservice and political disagreement. They offer political executives (and congressional leaders) alternative sources of expert advice to the career services, civilian and military. They permit the kind of experimentation, reflection, flexibility, and deep probing that the complex problems of national security require but that the regular federal service cannot completely accommodate because of its size, its need for standardization, and its emphasis on current operations.

The strides taken in recent years to develop new modes of government administration have largely been forced by the demands of technology. The scientific programs during the second world war and the industry-based programs of the Air Force in the postwar years established precedents for government contracting in areas that now extend beyond technological projects to projects in the social and behavioral sciences.

---

[22] See, for example, Paul H. Appleby, *Policy and Administration* (University of Alabama Press, 1949). For an earlier statement on this issue, see Carl J. Friedrich, "Public Policy and the Nature of Administrative Responsibility," *Public Policy* (1940, Cambridge, Harvard University Press), pp. 3 ff.

[23] Several of the essays in J. E. McLean (ed.), *The Public Service and University Education*

(Princeton, 1949) are concerned with this issue. See particularly Rowland Egger, "A Second View: An American Administrative Class?" pp. 205 ff.

[24] For a general discussion of the development of such innovations in government administration, see Don K. Price, "Creativity in the Public Service," *Public Policy*, Vol. IX (1959, Cambridge, Harvard University Press), pp. 3 ff. For a discussion of some of the aspects of Defense Department contracting for advisory and consultative services, see Hearings, Subcommittee of the House Committee on Appropriations, 86th Cong., 2d sess., *Department of Defense Appropriations for 1961*, Pt. 7, pp. 164–196.

Each of the services has created a "think" organization to which it can farm out problems—the RAND Corporation of the Air Force, the Operations Research Office of the Army, and the Operations Evaluation Group of the Navy. Within the Department of Defense a variety of advisory panels is available to the Secretary and his assistants —on research and development, on psychology and the social sciences and on education and manpower. In addition, the Institute of Defense Analyses has been established "to create machinery for putting a segment of the nation's intellectual resources more effectively at the disposal of the national security effort."[25] Originally established in connection with the evaluation of competing weapons systems, the scope of the Institute now encompasses broad areas of military strategy where the support for judgments on weapons evaluation is very often to be found. Indeed the close connection with strategic issues has been the link that has extended research on military operations into the far reaches of national policy.

These innovations in administration project the professionalization of civilian leadership in defense far beyond the confines of government itself. That they extend as widely as they do is, in many ways, an indication of the response of industry, science and private scholarship to the problems of national security. Like government-sponsored research, research in industry has begun to go beyond technical subjects. General Electric, for example, publishes a *Defense Quarterly* that is devoted to the broad issues of technology and foreign and military policy. It has also established a "think" group of its own, as have other corporations such as General Dynamics, IBM and many of the large aircraft companies. While most of these "in-house" divisions are set up for scientific research and development, many of them dig into military and social problems affected by technological advances. At the same, many industrial companies contract out their research activities with institutions such as the Stanford Research Institute, a

non-profit corporation which has moved into the fields of military and foreign policy in the wake of its primary interest in the frontiers of technological change.

In addition, since 1950 there has been an outpour of books and articles on national security from scholarly sources.[26] Some have actually been made possible through association with Defense Department projects or under contract with congressional groups investigating various aspects of the defense program. But a very high number of these efforts have been undertaken on private initiative, with or without foundation or university support. The subjects of these studies have ranged from the broadest issues of military strategy to more specialized problems of military organization and education. They include Kissinger's *Nuclear Weapons and Foreign Policy,* Osgood's *Limited War,* Huntington's *The Soldier and the State,* Brodie's *Strategy in the Missile Age,* the books by Walter Millis, the monographs of the Princeton Center of International Studies, the studies of the Rockefeller Brothers Fund and the volumes that have come out of the research projects conducted at the Center for International Studies at the Massachusetts Institute of Technology. In all cases, these works have plunged deeply into military problems. Indeed there are indications that some military leaders are concerned that "there has been too little solid contribution from military pens to national security policy thinking for this new age. . . . "[27]

The practical consequence of all of these activities is that professional advice, studies

25 *Annual Report II,* Institute of Defense Analyses, 1958, p. 1.

26 See Laurence I. Radway, *The Study of Military Affairs,* prepared for delivery at the 1958 Annual Meeting of the American Political Science Association (mimeographed).

27 Col. George A. Lincoln and Col. Richard G. Stilwell, "Scholars Debouch Into Strategy," *Military Review,* Vol. 40 (July 1960), p. 70. See also Captain Robert P. Beebe, "Guardians of Sea Power," United States Naval Institute *Proceedings,* Vol. 86 (June 1960), pp. 27 ff. The trend suggested here seems to contradict Bernard Brodie's thesis that "any real expansion of strategic thought . . . will . . . have to be developed largely within the military guild itself." *Strategy in the Missile Age* (Princeton, 1959), p. 9. Indeed, one might say that Brodie's own pioneering work refutes his prognosis.

and investigations on complex military issues are being made available to responsible officials from sources other than the military themselves. Civilian leaders need no longer rely entirely on the military services for the bases for policy decisions. Their own experience in service, the solid contribution of career professionals and the wide new sources of research and reflection, together with the multi-dimensional nature of defense problems, permit them to be more critical, more questioning and more constructive in their own right. Needless to say, all that has been discussed are tendencies, trends that can be perceived as we analyze the course of civil-military relations during the last ten years. Nevertheless, it seems safe to predict that these trends will continue to gain momentum—the "depoliticalization" of appointive posts, the influence of career executives, innovations in government administration and an interest in military affairs among writers, scientists and scholars. They are also bound to contribute to a growing professionalization of civilian leadership in military affairs and, in turn, this professionalization will have important repercussions on the nature of civil-military relations.

IV. THE CHANGING CHARACTER OF MILITARY LEADERSHIP

The significance of the professionalization of civilian leadership cannot be judged without some consideration of the changing character of military leadership. When General Maxwell Taylor retired in mid-1959, a veteran Washington reporter commented that this marked "the point at which the Old Army is drawing to the end of its mission—and even of its relevance." He called Taylor "the last great captain of the old hunters . . ." and his successor, General Lyman Lemnitzer, "an intellectual, a staff officer of vast experience, a kind of professor of the new kind of war."[28] The contrast is perhaps over-drawn, for it is

difficult to think of the military, without its "heroic leaders," left to the impersonal calculations of the "military managers."[29] It nevertheless catches the essence of a fundamental change in the character of military leadership.

Military leadership is changing under the impact of two forces: the revolutionary developments in weapons technology; and the close relationship between military programs and foreign and economic policies. The management of a missile program or a test range, the constabulary duties of an overseas assignment, the pseudo-diplomatic function of a military assistance advisory group, the planning involved in a Pentagon or a NATO slot—these are the tasks for which the military must prepare the officers of the future. At the same time, the threat of war, total, nuclear, limited or conventional, and the demands that open hostilities make on military leadership, are ever present. Thus the old attributes of "heroic leaders," the qualities of discipline, courage and command ability, cannot be forgotten. In this respect, the new responsibilities of military leaders have not so much altered their fundmental makeup as they have added new dimensions to their character and made them more complex human beings. This new complexity is being reflected in a number of changes in the military profession. Three of these are particularly important: the broadening base for officer recruitment; the development of higher military education; and new policies for selection and promotion to higher rank.

To a large extent, the broadening base for officer recruitment is a matter of arithmetic. In recent years the services have had to draw in more than 40,000 new officers every year, with a good percentage of these needed on a career basis. At the same time, the service academies graduate only about 1,500 new lieutenants and ensigns. As a result, the services have had to look to other sources for career officers, particularly civilian colleges and universities. This development has more than quantitative

[28]William S. White, "The End of the Old Army," *Harper's*, June 1959, pp. 82–85. The contrast might have been more apt had Lemnitzer been compared with General Ridgway who was wholly a soldier's soldier while Taylor has certain professorial features of his own.

[29] The terms in quotations are borrowed (as is much that follows) from Morris Janowitz, *The Professional Soldier* (Glencoe, Ill., 1960).

significance, however. It is also qualitative. The broadening recruitment base for young officers is bringing into the services men with new outlooks and new areas of technical competence that serve to meet the widening range of military responsibilities.[30]

The elaborate structure of higher military education is also responding to the broadening character of military responsibility. Curriculum changes in undergraduate programs at the service academies and in military programs in civilian colleges and universities are moving in two directions: first, they are incorporating new material to expose the students to the expanding technology that is making such an impact on military life; and, second, undergraduate courses are becoming less vocationalized and are taking the form of preprofessional education to lay a solid intellectual base for future career development.[31] At the post-commissioning schools—from the command and staff colleges through the service war colleges to the Industrial College of the Armed Forces and the National War College—there is an increased emphasis on the problems of international politics, the dilemmas of war and peace brought on by nuclear weapons, the impact of defense on the national economy and the complexities of life in a world of allies, international organizations and uncommitted nations. There are still weaknesses in military education: there is a tendency to be highly technical and vocational, even in dealing with social science material; service-organized programs also tend to be parochial, emphasizing the narrow views of the service itself; and the image of the world scene that is projected in military teaching is static and over-simplified. The advancements in the last fifteen years have nevertheless been striking and have taken military education far beyond the traditional emphasis on "loyalty, precedent, specific technical skill, and a gentlemanly code of conduct."[32]

Traditions, however, die hard. In the transition from one generation of military leaders to another, the qualities of the "heroic leader" continue to have primary importance and significance for those older officers who grew up in the "old Army," in the "black-shoe Navy" or even in the "propeller-driven Air Force." These are the officers, moreover, who control the machinery for selection and promotion. Here the struggle between the old and new takes place. While assignments to the war colleges and long tours of duty in technical posts seem to be good preparation for the new roles military men are undertaking, they are not always the best routes to higher rank. Loyalty, length of service and the number of tours on sea and command duty are very often the qualifications that members of a military selection board look for. A few years ago, the Secretary of the Navy, in an attempt to break down these traditional barriers to advancement, instructed the selection board to accelerate the promotions of officers who were "head and shoulders" above their colleagues. The reverberations of these orders are still shaking the Navy's high command.[33] Accelerating promotion means advancing officers in grade because of "potential" rather than actual performance. It thus involves an exercise of judgment about human behavior, as well as future military requirements, that is, at best, difficult to make. It is more difficult during a transition period when the old consensus on military qualities is breaking down and a new concept of military leadership is evolving.

More recently, the Secretary of Defense, in December 1959, issued a directive that "all officers . . . will serve a normal tour of duty with a Joint, Combined, Allied or OSD [Office of Secretary of Defense] Staff before being considered qualified for promotion to general or flag officer rank." Significantly, the directive makes an exception of Army and Air Force officers "whose proposed advancement and qualifications for

[30] Gene M. Lyons and John W. Masland, *Education and Military Leadership* (Princeton, 1959), esp. ch. I.

[31] *Ibid.*, chs. VI and VII.

[32] John W. Masland and Laurence I. Radway, *Soldiers and Scholars* (Princeton, 1957), p. 5. This work is a study of the response of military education to the widening policy role of military leadership.

[33] See Vice Admiral L. S. Sabin, "Deep Selections," United States Naval Institute *Proceedings*, Vol. 86 (March 1960), pp. 46 ff; also the large number of comments on Admiral Sabin's article in the June 1960 issue of the *Proceedings* (Vol. 86, No. 6), especially Admiral Carney's letter, pp. 104–106.

promotion are based primarily upon their scientific and technical achievement and proposed utilization in that specialty."[34] This emphasis on planning and technical experience and the deemphasis on parochial views were also underscored in the instructions of the Secretary of the Navy to the Flag Selection Board in 1960. Acknowledging the traditional concern for "a thorough sea-going background in the Line of the Navy," the Secretary brought the Board's attention to the need for "high performance on the planning level and a keen discernment of future operational requirements." He then went on, at some length, to explain that "the explosive technology of our modern weapons systems requires a high degree of concentration and knowledge in particular areas and precludes, to a great degree, the rapid rotation from job to job of many of our most outstanding officers for the purpose of qualifying them in all phases of naval warfare in the pattern of the past."[35]

Both these actions reflect the concern of civilian leaders with the new dimensions of military leadership. Nevertheless, however "civilianized" military officers may become, the profession itself will continue to be anchored in the distinct nature of its trade, the process that has so succinctly and meaningfully been called the "management of violence" by Harold Lasswell. And, in the fulfillment of their mission, the military will continue to be highly influenced by the particular tools of their craft. Indeed, without this distinction what is the meaning of the military profession as a separate group in society? And what do military leaders have to offer that physicists, engineers, diplomats and economists cannot do to meet the requirements of national security? The answer, obviously, is nothing. At the same time, within the framework of its primary and unique contribution, the military profession is dramatically changing. At the moment, it is in a state of transition from the old to the new with the dimensions of the new still unformed, still taking shape, still resembling the contours of an earlier day.

V. TOWARD A NEW CONCEPT OF CIVIL-MILITARY RELATIONS

The nature of civil-military relations is thus being changed through the strengthening of central organization in the Department of Defense, through the professionalization of civilian leadership and through the broadening character of the military profession. These trends might also be expressed as the "militarization" of civilians and the "civilianization" of the military. When extended to their logical conclusion, they suggest new relationships between civilians and military based on a more complex division of labor than has heretofore existed. These relationships, however, are responsive to the new shape of national security in which military affairs are no longer a monopoly of the military and a clean-cut division between matters of war and peace, between foreign and military policies, is a false and misleading notion.

It is nevertheless as essential as ever that defense planning be attuned to the broader perspectives of national policy. This is a problem which can no longer be met through civilian control of the military, however. We need to be concerned with the whole complex of professional direction in defense planning and the dilemma of relating the problems of security to the goals and values of national policy. In this task there are limits to what organizational techniques can accomplish. The spectrum is too broad. There is also the danger of accepting institutional devices as a solution without pressing forward along other lines as well. These include a rousing enthusiasm for public service in the leading professions in our society, developing a sense of the stakes involved in national security among the general public, encouraging the study of foreign

[34] Department of Defense Directive 1320.5, reprinted in *Army, Navy, Air Force Journal*, December 19, 1959. For a summary of the reaction of the services to this directive, see the article (p. 1) entitled "Pentagon Orders New Barriers to General and Flag Ranks," in the same issue.

[35] Dispatch from Secretary of the Navy William B. Franke to Admiral Herbert G. Hopwood, President of the Flag Selection Board, reprinted in the *Army, Navy, Air Force Journal*, July 16, 1960.

and military policy in educational programs, strengthening the civil service, urging new recruitment and educational standards for military careers and continuing innovation in government administration.

In this context the purpose of organization is not so much to control as it is to create the machinery through which to bring the full force of our intellectual resources to bear on the complex issues we have to meet.

THE "McNAMARA MONARCHY"

BY JACK RAYMOND

"The Navy, the Air Force and Army must work as a unit. If I had my way they would all be in the same uniform."
—GENERAL DWIGHT D. EISENHOWER

"I do not believe that the head of the proposed Governmental colossus . . . will ever have more than the most superficial knowledge of the Department."
—JAMES V. FORRESTAL

The first Secretary of Defense, James Forrestal, used to say that he was not so much interested in an organization chart as in the names of the men in the little boxes. It was a good point. Organizations are made of men. There is no substitute for their quality. Nevertheless, Paul Hammond correctly pointed out: "Men in Government—at least in the American Government—do not last. The things that last are the institutional arrangements which impart continuity to policy and meaning (however valid) to process, and the modes of thought which made both significant."[1] Thus regardless of who runs the building, Pentagon's organization is itself an influential factor in its performance.

[1] Paul Y. Hammond, *Organizing for Defense, the American Military Establishment in the Twentieth Century* (Princeton: Princeton University Press, 1961), p. 4.

The unification of the armed forces in 1947 has been described as the most extensive reorganization of the military establishment since George Washington assumed command of the Continental Army. It separated the Air Force from the Army and established three military departments—Army, Navy and Air Force—all within a single military establishment. The name Department of Defense came two years later. The Secretary of Defense was at first regarded merely as a coordinator with rather ill-defined powers of "general authority, direction and control" over the military departments. On the military side, the chairman of the Joint Chiefs of Staff did not command any troops, nor was he the "superior" of any of his colleagues. He was responsible mainly for the agenda of their deliberations. The JCS staff was specifically limited to one hundred officers as a protection against undue military power accruing to the chairman, whose title was intended to underscore his managerial rather than command function.

Nevertheless even this relatively mild centralization was strongly opposed, particularly by the Navy and its supporters. Secretary of the Navy Forrestal, warning that such a mammoth military element might be dangerous, once testified: "I do not believe that the head of the proposed Governmental colossus . . . will ever have

Reprinted by permission of Harper & Row, publishers, from pp. 277–293, notes, pp. 347–348, *Power at the Pentagon*. Copyright © 1964 by Jack Raymond.

Mr. Raymond is a military correspondent for *The New York Times*. He is the author of *How to Serve and Get Ahead in the Armed Forces* (1963).

more than the most superficial knowledge of the Department." As much to mollify the Navy as to assure others who worried about the new element of military authority in the Government, President Truman appointed Forrestal the first Secretary of Defense. Moving into the Pentagon, Forrestal remarked: "This office will probably be the biggest cemetery for dead cats in history." Before the year was out he sought more powers. In 1949, on his recommendation, amendments to the National Security Act removed the term "general" from the phrase "general authority, direction and control" to be exercised by the Secretary of Defense, and relieved the service Secretaries of their Cabinet status. The Joint Staff was raised from 10 to a maximum of 210. Forrestal did not live to see the Defense Department functioning under the more centralized setup. The years of government service, unceasing administrative struggles with the great problems of the postwar period, wore him down and finally broke his mind. The official Pentagon statement said his condition was "directly the result of excessive work during the war and postwar years." He took his own life May 22, 1949.

The mood of the office of the Secretary of Defense has varied according to the men who have held it. Forrestal's worried tenseness about the fate of the world communicated itself to the men around him, who worshiped him. His successor, Louis Johnson, a wily politician, held his cards closer to his chest. General Marshall was already an elder statesman when he took over; most of the job was done by Robert Lovett, his deputy, who also became his successor. Lovett generated an atmosphere of quiet wisdom. Charles E. Wilson exuded "big business." Thomas S. Gates worked quietly, effectively, unobtrusively.

Yet regardless of their individual personalities the sudden growth of American responsibilities around the world and the inevitable untidiness of the technological explosion in weaponry gave the impression that no man, just as Forrestal feared, could really get on top of the Pentagon job, as though confusion, waste and stubborn resistance to change were part of the price of maintaining the world's most powerful military-industrial complex. Somehow the hallmark of the Pentagon became indecisiveness and inaction, qualities that invite disaster on the battlefield. The grim decisions that lead to war or peace appeared to be tangled in a miasma of interservice rivalries for roles, missions and spending money. Personal feuds were dressed in the obfuscating language of high policy and military tradition.

When President Kennedy took office in 1961, he was handed a report by one of his preinauguration task forces on government that called for another sweeping reorganization of the Department of Defense —the fourth since it was created in 1947. The report said:

Throughout all proposals, past and present, to make more effective the Defense Department organization, has run one central theme—the clarification and strengthening of the authority of the Secretary of Defense over the entire United States Military Establishment. There are some who believed even prior to the 1958 amendment of the National Security Act that existing legislation provided ample basis for the Secretary's authority. Others took a contrary view. It is the conclusion of this committee that the doctrine of civilian control will be compromised as long as doubt exists on this point.[2]

Robert Strange McNamara, the new Secretary of Defense, lost no time in erasing the doubt. Within a couple of years, he was under sharp attack for exercising too much control at the Pentagon. He was accused—accurately—of forcing the armed services to "speak with one voice"; of establishing super-agencies to take over certain functions that had been handled separately by the individual military services; of downgrading, ignoring and by-passing the military chiefs; of submerging the service Secretaries as well as the uniformed chiefs beneath a hierarchy of Assistant Secretaries under his direct supervision; of overriding the voice of professional ex-

[2]Report of President-elect Kennedy's task force, headed by Senator Stuart Symington, December, 1960. Text, *New York Times*, December 5, 1960.

perience and "substituting a military party line"; of establishing what Hanson Baldwin described as "the McNamara Monarchy."[3]

Historically, the country has been alert to the dangers of military domination. But under McNamara, in the Kennedy Administration, there were widespread complaints —against a background of praise by those who favored it—of what Mark Watson, another military commentator, described as "the Pentagon's trend toward constant further depreciation of the military as essential advisors—not on political issues, but on strictly military issues." In a colorful and pertinent observation, still another military writer, Jerry Greene, described McNamara as a "civilian on horseback," who had mounted the horse from the offside while the Congress has been concerned with preventing the rise to the saddle of a General on Horseback.

Thus there developed considerable discussion whether one-man civilian rule over the military establishment was not just as dangerous to American democratic precepts as rule exercized by a man in uniform. As Baldwin put it:

The "unification" of the armed services sponsored by Secretary of Defense Robert S. McNamara poses some subtle and insidious dangers—creeping dangers that are political, military and administrative. And they could present, in their ultimate form, almost as great a threat to a secure and free nation as the attempted military coup, envisaged in the recent novel, "Seven Days in May." For the kind of "unification" being practiced and preached today has ominous overtones. It is dangerous to the nation's political system of checks and balances, dangerous to the continued development of sound military advice, dangerous to managerial and administrative efficiency.

On the other hand, others said McNamara had merely righted a military-biased tilt in what was supposed to be a civilian-controlled enterprise. Over the years, according to this view, the military chiefs had turned most of the Secretaries of Defense into "patsies." Until McNamara came along, one of his admirers said, "civilians

could be briefed, flattered, outwitted and finally absorbed by generals and admirals who systematically study all leadership patterns among men from Red Square to Wall Street. By the end of the Eisenhower Administration, control of American strategy lay not in the hands of civilian leadership, but in the hands of the uniformed chiefs of staff."[4]

This attribution of overwhelming shrewdness to generals and admirals when dealing with civilians is ludicrous. It resembles the attitude that Right Wing extremists adopt when they picture Communists outwitting supposedly naive Americans. Moreover, it flies in the face of the titanic struggles that have ensued in the Pentagon and have forced the departure of many high officers. But as a stereotype of the military, consistent with the conspiracy theory of war, it has had wide acceptance. Anyway, when McNamara took office, there was a feeling that he had come along in the nick of time to knock the rival generals' and admirals' heads together and "keep them in line."

McNamara, the man who came along, did not meet the criteria for the job laid down by the experts—although neither did most of his predecessors. Ideally, the Secretary of Defense is supposed to be policy- and strategy-minded, one who commands the admiration of the public, a man of experience, possibly having moved up from other posts in the Department of Defense or some equivalent branch of government; a man who, according to Samuel P. Huntington, probably should be concluding his career and thus not be in a position to use it as a steppingstone.[5] McNamara had virtually no experience either in the military or in government. Far from being ready to conclude his career, he had just risen, at forty-five, to the presidency of the Ford Motor Company. When he was named for the post of Secretary of Defense, it took the country by surprise. Most people in Washington had never heard of him.

McNamara was born just outside of San

[3] Hanson W. Baldwin, "The McNamara Monarchy," *Saturday Evening Post*, March 9, 1963.

[4] Theodore H. White, "Revolution in the Pentagon," *Look Magazine*, April 23, 1963.

[5] S. P. Huntington, *Soldier and the State*, pp. 452–53.

Francisco in an almost country-like community in the bay area. High school friends almost without exception recall his excruciating neatness. He was the boy in the class who wore jackets, ties and white shirts while the other kids dressed in sweaters and jeans. He was a good student and became editor of the yearbook, president of the French club, a member of the glee club and a member of the board of student control. He was popular despite his odd addiction to tidiness. He went to the University of California, where he made Phi Beta Kappa in his junior year. He shipped out on merchant vessels in the summers. He went to Harvard Business School on a partial scholarship, worked with an accounting firm for a year, married his University of California sweetheart and returned to Harvard as an instructor.

McNamara's specialty was statistical control. At the outbreak of World War II, he taught specially selected Army Air Force officers the techniques of calculating the thousands, millions and billions of people and things that went into military logistics. He joined the Air Force as a captain and rose to lieutenant colonel. He reportedly was so serious about the official order to save scarce paper that he did his calculations on the cardboard backs of writing pads. When the war was over, he and nine other "stat control" officers sold themselves as a management team to the Ford Motor Company. They were so successful that they became known as "Whiz Kids," and McNamara himself was named president of the company on November 9, 1960, one day following the election that named John F. Kennedy President of the United States.

McNamara did not fit the image of a millionaire industrialist. He was an aloof "egghead" at Ford, preferring to live in a comfortable old house in the college community at Ann Arbor rather than in the wealthy Grosse Point suburb peopled with auto executives. He was regarded as a Republican but had been known to support Democrats, including John F. Kennedy, for public office. He was an elder in the Presbyterian Church. When he arrived in Washington, he immediately sent two of his

three children to a Quaker school in the District. With his slicked-down, thinning black hair and rimless gold spectacles he gave the impression of a brash college professor.

His relations with the Joints Chiefs of Staff started abrasively as he ignored them on certain issues, sidestepped their recommendations on others and demanded speedy, deadline responses to some fundamental old military quandaries. In an official memorandum, within two months after the new Secretary took over, General Lyman L. Lemnitzer, then chairman of the Joint Chiefs, complained that the Chiefs had not been given a "full opportunity to study carefully" space weapons assignments, "which have far-reaching military implications."[6]

---

[6] *New York Times*, March 16, 1962. Full text of Lemnitzer memorandum to McNamara, dated March 2, 1961, follows:

I have studied the draft of the department of defense directive in Space Systems Development and what follows are my personal opinions:

Time precluded a development of a view by the Joint Chiefs of Staff. Although the service chiefs will undoubtedly have their views reflected in the comments of their respective service secretaries, I feel that in general the Joint Chiefs of Staff should be given a full opportunity to study carefully matters of this sort which have far-reaching military implications. In my opinion the new directive goes too far. It makes a change in basic policy whereas all that appears to me to be warranted at this time is an updating to meet those changes we can now foresee. I have reviewed carefully the existing directive, issued on 18 Sept. 1959 and believe that in the main, it continues to be a sound basis (on which to operate).

The current directive established the principle that under the overall direction of the department of defense, each service should develop those payloads in which it has a primary interest or special competence. Operating under this principle has in my opinion not resulted in waste, inefficiency, or lack of effectiveness. On the contrary, I believe it has contributed to a comprehensive, rapid and orderly development of the utilization of space for military purposes.

As Chief of Staff of the Army, I became intimately acquainted with the development of the communication satellite and in retrospect believe that the rather remarkable progress achieved could not have been possible if policy had not encouraged and permitted the army the degree of freedom it had.

I am quite sure this would apply equally to the Navy's development of the navigation satellite. . . .

(The new directive correctly recognizes that all

McNamara ordered four major studies in military policy and strategy. These were not assigned to the military, as in the past, but to the new civilian aides at the Pentagon. The basic study on nuclear war strategy, for example, was assigned to Charles J. Hitch, the Pentagon controller, a former official at RAND. The Defense Secretary delved into all details of operations instead of abiding by the military practice of giving out assignments, demanding results and leaving details to others. He seemed determined to disprove Forrestal's warning that one man could not do the job.

Lemnitzer, an experienced hand in Washington affairs, did not frontally counterattack the civilian assault on what had been regarded in the past as the military area of responsibility. A good soldier, he remained discreetly silent. But shortly before he was transferred from the Pentagon in the fall of 1962 to command the Allied forces in Europe, he expressed his feelings in a speech that received little notice in the press but must have been carefully read in the Secretary's office. Lemnitzer's subject was leadership and his audience the graduating class of the Command and General Staff College.

"We all recognize in the abstract," he said, "that it is simply a physical impos-

sibility for the leader of a higher organization to provide personal leadership at all places where it is simultaneously required. This is why such concepts as the chain of command and span of control have been devised. It is the foundation stone of our whole organizational system. This does not mean that you cannot impose your personality on your unit. Indeed, unless you do so—unless you make yourself the recognized symbol of command—your leadership will be ineffective. But to employ the chain of command concept and to make the organizational system work most effectively, an implicit requirement upon the higher commander is to delegate authority to his subordinates. This obvious requirement—with which everyone promptly agrees—is extremely difficult to achieve in practice. A battle group commander who occupies himself with the internal details of the operation of his companies may be showing how much he knows about being a company commander. But he is also showing how little he knows about commanding a battle group. He is doing an injustice to the ability and conscientiousness of his captains. He is failing to take advantage of the great asset they represent for carrying out the mission of the organization as a whole. Finally, he is displaying his own lack of confidence in his own ability to do his assigned job."

When McNamara assumed control of the Pentagon, much of the wartime glory of the military had receded. Whatever prestige the military incumbents of the Pentagon high comand had left was dealt a devastating blow in the Cuban invasion fiasco of 1961. In the immediate aftermath of the Bay of Pigs affair civilians of the Kennedy Administration sneeringly cast the blame for failure on the Chiefs. Newsmen were called into the White House and told that the Chiefs of Staff had selected the beaches for the invasion. A story, apparently inspired at the White House, appeared in the Washington *Post* hammering home the charge that the Chiefs were responsible for the failure in Cuba. On May 19, 1961, Senator Albert Gore, Democrat

military departments and the department of defense had substantial interests in space.)

However, the effect of these important concepts is lost, in my opinion, when they are relegated to the status of exceptions to rather than being within policy. I cannot demonstrate that maximum economy of defense resources might not be achieved by making a single service responsible for development of all space payloads, but I do feel strongly that such a move would result in our overall loss of effectiveness through failure to utilize to its full potential the initiative, background, experience, and brainpower available. We are just beginning to explore how to use space as a military working environment. We simply do not yet know what the full use of space will encompass and how the interests of the department of defense as a whole can best be served. Encouraging all services to develop space systems in which they have a primary interest or special competence is to me far the better way to use the resources we can allocate to this area.

I am confident that close department of defense supervision of expenditures can assure good economy and management.

of Tennessee, called for the removal of all the members of the Joint Chiefs of Staff after hearing secret testimony as a member of the Senate Foreign Relations Committee. The Senator called for "new, wiser and abler men."

Neither the President nor Secretary Mc-Namara spoke out for a week. The President, in fact, told a group of newsmen privately that he could have managed the military responsibilities of the Bay of Pigs affair better than his military experts. McNamara, when asked about the Senator's attack on the Chiefs, shrugged his shoulders and said he had decided against making a public comment, following consultation with General Lemnitzer. However, he telephoned some people on Capitol Hill to assure them of his confidence in the Chiefs. General Lemnitzer, as usual, kept his public silence. To a private visitor he said angrily that he had been on a tour in Southeast Asia when the seemingly high-placed insinuations of incompetence were being launched against him and his colleagues, "and I can assure you they did not help the United States very much."

Even when, at a news conference ten days afterward, McNamara ended the Administration's silence on the Chiefs, he did not deny the allegations against them. He finessed a question on the subject with a reply that he, as Secretary of Defense, was responsible for "the actions of all personnel in the department, both military and civilian" and that he accepted that responsibility. If any errors were committed, he said, they were his errors, and he looked forward to a "long and pleasant association" with the Chiefs.[7]

The chiefs at that time were Lemnitzer, General George H. Decker, of the Army; General Thomas D. White, of the Air Force; Admiral Arleigh A. Burke, Chief of Naval Operations; and General David M. Shoup, Commandant of the Marine Corps. Within a year, all but Shoup were gone. General Maxwell D. Taylor, who was brought out of retirement and given an office at the White House to review United States intel-

ligence, paramilitary and guerrilla warfare activities, as military representative of the President, eventually was named chairman of the Joint Chiefs of Staff. Lemnitzer was transferred to succeed General Lauris Norstad as commander of Allied forces in Europe. Admiral Burke, who had served an unprecedented series of three two-year terms, retired and was succeeded by Admiral George W. Anderson. General White retired and was succeeded by General Curtis E. LeMay, General Decker retired and was succeeded by General Earle G. Wheeler, General Shoup, appointed to a four-year term, retired January 1, 1964.

Admiral Anderson lasted two years, and his experience in the Cuban crisis of 1962 was perhaps the outstanding illustration of the low regard in which the Service Chiefs were held. First there was an incident on October 6. The Defense officials decided they wanted to send a squadron of Navy fighters from Oceana, Virginia, to Key West, Florida, and to put the squadron temporarily under Air Force control. Deputy Defense Secretary Gilpatric, without going through channels, ignored the Chief of Naval Operations, and called directly to Admiral Robert L. Dennison, the Commander in Chief, Atlantic, at Norfolk, Virginia, to give him the order. Admiral Anderson's bruised feelings, shared by many officers in the Pentagon, soon became well-known.

As the crisis grew worse, the United States undertook a naval quarantine of Cuba. Secretary McNamara began spending time in the Navy's Flag Plot, or operations center. This room, under Marine Guard, contains visual materials locating the position of every ship. It also has communications links with ship commanders. McNamara insisted upon making decisions on the spot. He wanted to call ship commanders directly on the voice-scrambling, single-side-band radios. Admiral Anderson tried to dissuade the civilian official. The Navy uses formal, stylized voice communications with coded names going through the chain of command. McNamara was inclined to ignore or belittle these techniques. He pointed to a symbol for one ship at sea and demanded of Admiral Anderson,

[7] *New York Times*, May 27, 1961.

"What's that ship doing there?" The Chief of Naval Operations replied, "I don't know, but I have faith in my officers."

Admiral Anderson, like General Lemnitzer, expressed his feelings on the subject of the exercise of authority when he spoke to the Navy League, May 3, 1963, at San Juan, Puerto Rico. "Without respect flowing both ways between juniors and seniors we have little hope of doing the jobs we will be called upon to do," he said. Three days later the White House announced that Admiral Anderson, who had testified against McNamara in the TFX dispute, had been dropped as Chief of Naval Operations, to be succeeded by Admiral David B. McDonald, a relative unknown. Anderson was named Ambassador to Portugal, apparently as a sop. After he left the Pentagon, Anderson made another speech, to the National Press Club, decrying the lack of "confidence and trust between the civilian and military echelons," but his post-mortem caused hardly a ripple.

During World War II and for many years after it, the Service Chiefs were well-known, heroic figures. They even participated in a variety of political and administrative roles. The chairmen of the Joint Chiefs of Staff in the postwar era, General Omar N. Bradley and Admiral Arthur S. Radford, operated in the continued glow of victory in war, but were impressive in their own right as well. Huntington described them as true "samurai," military statesmen rather than military experts. Their successors, General Nathan F. Twining, an Air Force officer who had risen from sergeant in the National Guard, and General Lemnitzer, who was caught in an administrative changing of the guard, had good war records but were bland, passive men in Washington. In the meantime, civilians came to the fore, especially during the Kennedy Administration. These civilians spread the notion that they had studied the military posture of the country and had found it wanting. "General," one young new Frontiersman was quoted as saying at Strategic Air Command headquarters, "you don't have a war plan. All you have is a sort of

horrible spasm."[8] McNamara himself made the charge, consistently denied during the Eisenhower Administration, that there were no unified strategic military plans at the Pentagon before he came along.[9]

As military heroes have receded from the public view, civilians have flourished. Theodore White, author of the classic *Making of the President*, noticed something about the Kennedy team at the Pentagon. They were, with few exceptions, an Ivy League team designed to be a direct descendant of the wartime Ivy League team of Lovett, McCloy, Patterson and Forrestal. "All through the Kennedy Administration runs the most intense, if unrecognized, desire to attach itself to the older traditions of American Government," White observed.[10]

McNamara's first Deputy Defense Secretary, Roswell L. Gilpatric, was a familiar headliner in the press. He had been an Under Secretary of the Air Force in the Truman Administration. Tall, nattily dressed, urbane, a New Yorker, he was considered a suave, tempering balance wheel for McNamara's reputed impolitic way with Congressmen as well as generals and admirals. But, like so many other high civilian officials, he "could not afford" to stay in government and returned to private life in January, 1964. Gilpatric's membership in a famous law firm, education at a good prep school—Hotchkiss—and scholastic honors at Yale made him a member of "The Establishment," that roster of distinguished public men to whom all Administrations turn for helpings of prestige.

Other Ivy Leaguers at the Pentagon are Cyrus R. Vance, of Kent School and Yale, Gilpatric's successor as Deputy Defense Secretary; Eugene M. Zuckert of Salisbury Prep and Yale, Secretary of the Air Force; Paul H. Nitze, of Hotchkiss and Princeton, Secretary of the Navy; Stephen Ailes, of Scarborough and Princeton, Secretary of the Army; and William P. Bundy, of Groton and Harvard, Assistant Secretary for International Security Affairs.

8 Stewart Alsop, *Saturday Evening Post*, November 27, 1962.
9 Speech, American Society of Newspaper Editors. April 20, 1963.
10 *Look Magazine*, April 23, 1963.

Despite the Ivy League coloration, the Pentagon is marked more by the "technipol" touch of another set of civilians, however, in which McNamara—although he had attended and taught at Harvard Business School—is a star figure. These are the "Whiz Kids," named after the McNamara outfit that gained fame at Ford; sneered at and resented by some of the military as downy-faced lads who seek pretentiously to ladle the fog of war with mathematically precise measuring cups. One star among the Pentagon "Whiz Kids," however, Charles J. Hitch, is by no means a kid, but a quiet-spoken former professor of economics, one of the few on the new team over fifty. He is the Pentagon controller. Others are Henry S. Rowen, a Deputy to Bundy; and Alain Enthoven, a tall, stringy, Seattle-born economist whose specialty is cost-efficiency techniques in strategic weapons systems. Hitch, Rowen, and Enthoven were colleagues at RAND.

High-ranking in the technipol hierarchy is Dr. Harold Brown, the Director of Research and Engineering. Another formidable civilian is Adam Yarmolinsky, whose father was a famous scholar in Russian literature, his mother a famous poet, and whose own bent appears to be political trouble-shooting. Yarmolinsky was one of the Kennedy talent scouts who put McNamara's name in the postelection hopper of government office holders. At the Pentagon he serves as McNamara's special assistant, and many believe that he is the "political man" in the building.

What irritates many of the military men at the Pentagon under McNamara is the implication that computer calculations, operational analysis and abstract theories somehow have greater weight in the decision-making process than the voices of experience and the recorded lessons of history. The picture of young smart-alecks invading the precincts of military responsibility was drawn by Retired Air Force Chief of Staff General Thomas D. White when he said that, *in common with other military men* I am profoundly apprehensive of the pipe-smoking, trees-full-of-owls type of so-called defense intellectuals who have been brought into this nation's capital."[11] Military men in the Pentagon argue, like General White, that civilian aides are making decisions without responsibility. That is, they safely and arrogantly propound various theories of strategy without having the responsibility of command.

And some of the high-ranking civilian officials, no less than the military brass, find McNamara a difficult boss. Many of the civilian officials, including but not limited to the career civil service, criticize the Secretary for delving into the details of management and making many minor decisions himself. In preparing the 1965 budget, he is said to have made more than 500 decisions.

Elvis J. Stahr, who was Secretary of the Army for a little over a year under McNamara, said after quitting to become president of the University of Indiana: "McNamara is certainly the ablest man I have ever been closely associated with. But he has a tendency to overreach in exercising control and intrude in small details of administration. The Defense Department is too big to be run by one man and there are just not enough McNamaras. The machinery of administration ought to be flexible. I, personally, favored most of the administration unification measures undertaken by the Defense Secretary, but I'm afraid there is a tendency to neglect the accumulated wisdom and responsible toughness of the career officers."[12]

President Kennedy was most emphatic in his support of McNamara, however. During one particularly virulent battle between the Secretary of Defense and the military, President Kennedy said: "We have a very good, effective Secretary of Defense, with a great deal of courage who is willing to make hard decisions and who doesn't mind when they are made that a good many people don't like it."[13] And President Johnson's endorsement has been no less

[11] General Thomas D. White, *Newsweek*, June, 1963.
[12] Author's interview with Mr. Stahr, July 7, 1962.
[13] President Kennedy's news conference, March 21, 1963.

emphatic. After his assumption of the Presidency placed him in a new, more intimate and more difficult relationship with the Defense Secretary, Johnson let it be known that he had found the "myth" of McNamara's excellence to be not a myth but "the truth."[14]

The resistance to "McNamara and his band" has been ineffectual. Even General Curtis E. LeMay, an early antagonist, faded into silence although he was reappointed Air Force Chief of Staff in 1963 for a single year instead of the customary two. LeMay had created the all-powerful Strategic Air Command, but the new strategic forces of computer-minded missiles had no place for a crushed-hat bomber pilot. LeMay's retirement in 1964 was inevitable.

One high officer has remained of the age of combat heroes. He is Maxwell Davenport Taylor, the vindicated author of *The Uncertain Trumpet*, whose strategic arguments—all rejected by the Eisenhower Administration—were adopted by Kennedy. Taylor is something special in American military history—a fighting hero, an acknowledged intellectual and a keenly political person with no apparent personal political ambitions. He runs counter to the prevailing image of professional soldiers as inarticulate men of narrow interests, men who are technicians and traditionalists with conceptions of patriotism drawn from textbooks. According to this image, they are fighting champions on the battlefield but helpless without plans of action off it. They are given to bellicose "habit of command" and unchallenging obedience to superior rank except when, like Billy Mitchell, they fight for a "cause" against higher authority.

J. P. Marquand once wrote that "Many generals appear to civilians like deceptively simple men. Most of them possess, from a civilian point of view, an unworldly character. . . . Debate, when protracted, makes [the professional officer] impatient." But General Taylor, who won his high school debating championship, does not fit this image. The son of a Keyesville, Mis-

souri, railroad lawyer, he finished high school at sixteen. He was fourth in his class at West Point in 1922. The class yearbook called him the "most learned" of the graduates. The pre-World War II years took him to China and Japan as a military attaché and to various European and Latin-American capitals on similar semidiplomatic assignments. As a paratroop commander in World War II and leader of the Eighth Army during the Korean War, he covered his tunic with combat laurels.

Fluent in several languages, he also received eight honorary engineering and law degrees from leading universities. Instead of the tough-talking bellicosity of the military stereotype, Taylor has been impressive for his soft-spoken suavity. During the Eisenhower Administration he did not immediately do battle for his "cause." Indeed, many Army officers felt that he had not pushed his ideas vigorously enough as Chief of Staff. When he finally did speak out, his retirement followed swiftly. Like General Matthew B. Ridgway before him, he could not persuade Eisenhower, a former Army Chief of Staff, that strategic air power, even with nuclear warheads, was a false god.

The return of Maxwell Taylor to the Pentagon is no mere personal drama, however. It has been significant also in terms of his administrative role. "A Secretary of Defense needs a strong chairman to direct the work of the chiefs, to keep their noses to the grindstone, and to extract from them timely advice and recommendations—preferably of a kind which can be accepted and approved without embarrassment," General Taylor wrote in his book criticizing the Eisenhower Administration.

Advice can be unpalatable and unwelcome, particularly if it runs afoul of political or economic considerations which the Administration holds in great store. A Secretary will look to the chairman to prevent this kind of advice and to bring forth harmonious views on appropriate subjects which can then be used in support of the Department's programs. If the chairman is to perform this function, obviously the Secretary must back him on the split issues. . . . Thus the chairman has come to be a

14 *New York Times*, January 2, 1964.

sort of party whip, charged with conveying the official line to the Chiefs in the hope and expectation that they will be guided thereby in their actions. . . . It is not an overstatement to say that the Chairman of the Joint Chiefs of Staff has come to assume much of the power of the dreaded single Chief of Staff who has been the bugbear of the Congress and of some elements of the public in past discussions of defense organization. This power is not bad in itself, but it is concealed power unaccompanied by public responsibility—which is bad.[15]

General Taylor wrote that as an Army Chief of Staff he had found himself repeatedly outweighed by Chairman Admiral Radford. To prevent continuance of this situation, he urged a drastic reorganization of the Joint Chiefs' setup. But when he returned as chairman, he did not press for reorganization. He silently proceeded to exercise the powers of the chairman that he recognized so clearly, as "a sort of party whip, charged with conveying the official line to the chiefs."

Taylor, true to his conception of his role, has proved a valuable adjutant to McNamara, although they differ on some fundamental issues. Together, without the legislation that was so often recommended, they have centralized the authority over the armed forces in the offices of the chairman of the Joint Chiefs and the Secretary of Defense, although many of their measures actually were proposed by predecessors. The transfer of authority over the unified and specified commands from the military departments of the Joint Chiefs of Staff was accomplished in the reorganization during the Eisenhower Administration. The creation of the new Strike Command, combining much of the Air Force's tactical aircraft with Army assault troops, was initiated in the Eisenhower Administration. Secretary of Defense Gates began the practice of sitting with the members of the Joint Chiefs to nip disputes in the bud. Gates ordered the formation of a single Defense Intelligence Agency in order to reduce conflicts in intelligence estimates.

[15] General Maxwell D. Taylor, *The Uncertain Trumpet*, pp. 109–11.

McNamara's predecessor also ordered the creation of a single defense communications to unify the long-distance networks that were operated separately by the services. Most important, perhaps, of all, Gates forced the services to adopt a single strategic targeting system. Each of these actions, however, although debated vigorously within the Pentagon, became sources of public friction when carried out in McNamara's uncompromising manner.

Much of the unification of the services—and thus centralization of authority—has been made inevitable by the technical changes in weaponry and the consequent changes in force structure. Indeed, General Eisenhower told West Point cadets in 1945 that if he had his way the Army, Navy and Air Force would "all be in the same uniform." That power has been centralized in the hands of a civilian Secretary rather than in a single "Prussian-style" Chief of Staff is due largely to the historical and legal barriers against military dominance that exist in the United States. But does that make one-man rule over so vast an establishment any less dangerous? The question has been asked repeatedly as McNamara realigns the administrative channels into a rather monolithic instrument of government. Critics of the centralization of authority fear that it silences the possible voices of dissent and reduces the arguments that must be offered and heard. In 1947 the defense establishment was created with a single Secretary of Defense who was regarded primarily as a coordinator, aided by three specialist assistants. Now, the civilian hierarchy directly under the Secretary of Defense includes a Deputy Secretary of Defense, a powerful Director of Research, seven Assistant Secretaries, a General Counsel, a Deputy General Counsel, two special Assistants and five Deputy Assistant Secretaries. The acknowledged excellence of a McNamara should not divert us from traditional precautions against centralized military authority outside the White House, whether exercised by a man in uniform or in civilian clothes. It is not the character of the man but the power he wields that should concern us.

CHAPTER 7

Methods of Defense Policymaking

In this second chapter on the management of force, we turn from the study of the organization of defense policymaking to a review of specific methods of defense policymaking. The following articles describe each method, explain their role in policymaking, and evaluate their utility.

The defense field has been in the forefront of the development of new management techniques. Many of these, particularly the economic ones, are proven, effective tools. Others, like game theory and gaming, are useful primarily for the insights they provide into the nature of war, policy, and policymaking. Many of these insights, while not explicitly used, are part of the general cultural knowledge of decisionmakers and implicitly influence the way they think about defense problems. For example, although game theory is not directly used in deciding policy, it has provided concepts such as tacit bargaining, compellence, and the art of commitment that permeate modern defense thinking. The student should be aware of the works of the scholars as well as those of the practitioners; he should also be aware of which methods are directly applicable and which are only ways of thinking about the management of force.

Burton Sapin defines and provides bases for evaluation of the traditional methods of defense policymaking: intelligence, planning, and policy analysis. While these three categories may not be the only ones that could be used they do permit discussion of the methods that are still basic even if they have been supplemented by more "systematic," "rational," and "scientific" techniques.

Harold Brown, Secretary of the Air Force and formerly Director of Defense Research and Engineering, writes as a practitioner about the planning of our increasingly more complex and technical military forces. He emphasizes the problems of uncertainty and how planners try to compensate for them by insuring that our forces are flexible.

Another practitioner, former Assistant Secretary of Defense (Comptroller) Charles Hitch writes about the Planning-Programming-Budgeting System (PPBS) that he introduced into the Department of Defense. This new programming system bridges the gap between the "inputs" (personnel, procurement, operations and maintenance, etc.) of the budget and the "outputs" (missions, weapons systems, forces, etc.) of planning. For the first time, the input costs can be measured in relationship to the output effectiveness at the national defense policy level. The program elements group the forces according to specific defense objectives, like strategic forces, general purpose forces, airlift and sealift. Thus, one can see all the related program elements and their resource costs for each major military mission.

Systems analysis provides the analytical foundation for making sound, objective choices among the alternative means of carrying out these program missions. Wesley Posvar presents an introduction to systems analysis, complete with a few examples of cost-effectiveness tests, marginal comparisons, and mixed-solution problems. Charles Hitch has stated that program budgeting and systems analysis are the tools the Secretary of Defense needed "to take the initiative in the planning and direction of the entire defense effort on a truly unified basis"—and without another major reorganization of the defense establishment.

Planning, programming and systems analysis are all methods that have direct application in American defense policymaking. Game theory and gaming are techniques that are not directly applicable, but they do provide insights into the nature of war and decisionmaking. Anatol Rapoport provides a taxonomy of games which suggests how to look for the best ways of playing them. He examines zero-sum games (those in which what one player wins, his opponent loses) for both dominating and mixed strategies. The real world is non-zero-sum, that is the players have both conflicting and coinciding interests. Rapoport uses the classic example of the non-zero-sum game, the Prisoner's Dilemma, to illustrate the logic of cooperative strategies.

Game theory and gaming are often confused. A simplified distinction might be that game theory emphasizes rationality, a minimum of detail, and its symbol would be a matrix. Gaming emphasizes simulation, a modicum of detail, and its symbol would be a sand table. Norman Dalkey introduces gaming in terms of its basics, some techniques and examples, and an evaluation. The editors are not as impressed as Dalkey with either the amount of use or the utility of gaming in defense policymaking. In teaching, however, we have found that gaming does appeal to students. They get involved even if there is some question as to how much they learn. We did not include in this volume the rules for a game, but here at the Air Force Academy we do play (and recommend to other schools) a brief war game.

INTELLIGENCE, PLANNING, AND POLICY ANALYSIS

BY BURTON M. SAPIN

The preceding chapters of this study have been primarily concerned with the organizational machinery and relationships through which foreign policy is developed and implemented and day-to-day problems met and resolved. Little has been said about what might be referred to as the analytical or intellectual dimension of foreign policy-making. This involves the characteristic processes of thought and analysis that take place within the foreign policy organization and their written embodiments in the form of policy papers, intelligence estimates, plans, programs, and the like. This chapter is an attempt to identify some of the intellectual requirements of foreign policy-making and their organizational implications. The focus is on the analytical and organizational underpinnings for the making of decisions, rather than on the actual processes of making final choices.

A few basic points should be made about the framework of policy that guides these activities. To start with a truism, societal values and fundamental national interests and purposes—particularly as these are translated into more specific goals and objectives—give direction, energy, and will to foreign policy. They set the fundamental courses of policy. At the same time, the most difficult decisions, often, are those of detailed implementation. There may be broad and solid consensus on values and objectives but strong disagreement on the programs most likely to accomplish them.

This suggests that the clarifying and specifying of goals and objectives are an important part of the policy-making process. Since objectives are likely to conflict as they are made more specific and since few are likely in any event to be fully achieved, it is necessary to be as clear as possible on the precise states of affairs that policies are designed to produce.

Reprinted by permission from *The Makings of United States Foreign Policy* (New York: Frederick A. Praeger, Inc., 1966), Chap. 10, pp. 287–314. Published for The Brookings Institution.

Mr. Sapin is Associate Professor of Political Science and Coordinator of International Programs at the University of Minnesota. He has served in the Department of State and is the co-author of *The Role of the Military in American Foreign Policy* (1954).

BASES FOR EVALUATION

There are many similarities between the pursuit of reliable knowledge by the foreign policy organization and by the academic scholar or university research group. Both are handicapped by the difficulty of obtaining important categories of relevant data—or their sheer inaccessibility, by the often subtle cultural presuppositions that even the best of observers bring to the scrutiny of societies other than their own, and by the relatively modest state of development that still characterizes the theories and research methods of the social science. Even more fundamentally, both are handicapped because many of the situations they would like to understand better, and make projections into the future about, are highly complex and not susceptible to simple causative explanation or prediction.

To calculate the behavior of the Russian or the Chinese Communist leadership; to understand the political dynamics of countries like Brazil, Turkey, Algeria, Burma, or France; to project major political and socioeconomic developments over the next five years, or even the next twelve months, in Africa south of the Sahara; to anticipate the broad political and military consequences of space exploration; or, perhaps even more difficult, to predict what the volatile leaders in some of the underdeveloped countries are going to do the day after tomorrow—these are intellectual tasks to challenge the best-trained and most highly skilled observers, whether in the bureaucracy or on the campus.

It might be added that each of these environments has its advantages. The government has or should have a superior capacity to gather data about most current international problems and situations while the presumably less hurried and harried atmosphere of the university should make for more deeply probing and systematic studies. This would seem to provide the basis for a natural division of labor between the two, although it does not always work out that way in practice.

There is at least one essential and significant difference between the scholar and the policy official: the policy official *must act* on the basis of what he knows or thinks he knows. In some instances, this means that he must act in full awareness that his knowledge is quite inadequate. This is not to imply that the scholar's knowledge is not useful or does not provide a basis for action. Sometimes, the scholar's knowledge is so relevant to the policy-maker's problem that the latter calls upon him for policy advice and recommendations. The point is that the policy-maker is *required* to act, that his approach to the knowledge available to him must be instrumental, and what he knows does serve as a direct basis for his actions.

INTELLECTUAL REQUIREMENTS

Whether the work of the foreign policy organization is viewed as problem solving or decision-making, whether the focus is policy formulation or its implementation, several broad categories of intellectual product and performance are called for. The terms commonly applied to them are *intelligence, policy analysis,* and *planning*. While there are sometimes separate organizational units designated to perform each of these functions, sometimes there are not. The distinction between the organizations and the intellectual functions is important and should be kept clearly in mind. Relevant skills and abilities exist throughout the foreign policy organization, and, therefore, useful intelligence and planning papers may well be produced by units other than the designated intelligence and planning staffs.

Intelligence. Within the framework of established policy objectives, the foreign policy official's first requirement is for the most accurate possible picture of the international environment in which he must pursue these objectives. This is far more easily said than done. Providing this "picture" is the special though not exclusive bailiwick of intelligence organizations. Some of what is needed falls in the category of straightforward factual data—biographic sketches of key foreign leaders, production and foreign trade statistics for other countries, or current military data like So-

viet monthly production of intercontinental ballistic missiles—although, as the
last example makes clear, these are not always easy to get.

The more important and difficult intelligence work, however, falls in the general category of selecting, analyzing, interpreting and attaching relevance to the
available data. This involves not only understanding and evaluating the present but,
more important and difficult, attempting in
some degree to predict or anticipate the
future. One aspect of such efforts, the
warning function, is particularly important in wartime. Learning the date of a
critical event, like a planned enemy attack,
and confusing the enemy about one's own
plans are of the utmost importance. Because this part of the intelligence job often
involves covert activities, it is the one most
frequently dramatized. There is probably
still too much of a tendency—kept alive
by wartime memory—to look at contemporary intelligence in terms of this
"detective-work" warning function. While
this is still very much a part of the contemporary intelligence responsibility, it
does not represent the major interpretive
effort for foreign policy purposes.

Foreign policy intelligence estimates are
concerned with much broader and more
complex sets of phenomena and problems:
political and economic trends in key developed and underdeveloped countries,
policy motivation and likely policy choices
of the leadership groups in these countries,
and likely developments in such world
trouble spots as Berlin, the Horn of Africa,
Yemen, the Near East, and Vietnam.

These estimates may vary from a quick
"reading" on the political orientation of a
military junta that has just taken power
in Latin America to a longer-term look
at the prospects for East Africa or Communist China. Whatever the urgency of
the request being responded to and the
time frame of the estimate itself, these are
predictions about the future. However
guarded or even hedged, they represent
challenging intellectual enterprises, difficult to do well, subject to strong differences
of view, only verifiable as events actually
unfold and, therefore, probably the most

easily ignored or rejected of intelligence
staff products.

Policy Analysis. The intellectual function
that has been labelled policy analysis is
performed by a relatively large number
of people in the foreign policy organization. In contrast to intelligence and planning, it is usually not carried on by a
specially designated organizational unit;
it is an important activity of many senior-
and middle-level officials in the operating
bureaus and policy staffs of the Department of State. The problems on which it is
brought to bear range from those with relatively narrow and modest implications to
the much smaller number that are of
momentous importance. The organizational levels at which policy analysis takes
place, and by whom, vary accordingly.

The policy analyst must attempt to define the external situation with which he
is dealing (with the help of intelligence
estimates, if he wishes), examine its implications for relevant U.S. policy objectives,
develop and evaluate alternative courses of
action for dealing with the situation,[1] and,
then, depending upon his location in the
hierarchy, either recommend or decide
upon that course of action that seems to
offer best net advantage to the interests
and objectives of the United States. In the
process, priorities must be established
among relevant objectives, possible short-
term consequences and longer-range implications weighed against one another, incomplete information discounted, and
significant differences in relevant intelligence analyses resolved. This is tough, demanding intellectual work, and the ability
to do it well must be spread rather widely
throughout the foreign policy organization.

To round out the picture, a choice final-

[1] Sometimes the facts are clearly established, and
what is called for is a new and imaginative way
of dealing with an old, familiar problem. W. W.
Rostow suggests that "one major form of intellectual contribution to public policy" is in the
redefining of problems, in expanding the range of
alternatives perceived to be open, and posing new
questions. He comments that "the definition of
alternatives in a rapidly changing field for action
is, in itself, a powerful creative act. . . ." See W. W.
Rostow, *The United States in the World Arena*
(Harper, 1960), pp. 490–98.

ly has to be made among the courses of action available. Even lack of choice and action represents a choice of sorts. Decisions will usually be followed in turn by actions of one kind of another, and, eventually, it can be assumed that feedback from these actions will produce new occasions for decision and perhaps even adjustment or major change in previous decisions.

This is a familiar formulation: clarification of objectives; definition of external situations; identification of problems; development and assessment of alternative courses of action; and, finally, the making of decisions. A number of points should be made about this formulation. First of all, this brief sketch is a highly simplified version of what is likely to be taking place, a model of rational decision-making rather than an exact replica of the policy-making world. That world is likely to be characterized as much by hurried analyses, snap decisions, and "crash" programs as by logical analysis and intellectual rigor.

At the same time, it is easy for one to forget, in setting forth in abstract terms the intellectual ingredients of decision-making, how much of a difference these elements can make in specific situations. The way a situation is defined, a problem formulated, a framework or theory for dealing with it conceptualized, can have significant policy consequences.

An obvious example is whether a native movement is conceived of as a group of "agrarian reformers" or "fervent nationalists" on the one hand, or as Moscow- or Peking-line Communists on the other. Somewhat less obviously, the theory of economic development that guides the policies and programs of the U.S. economic aid agency can make a great deal of difference in the likelihood of success or failure. To be more specific, a program of economic aid that ignores certain fundamental social and political characteristics and limitations may very well fall on its face.

Finally, it should be emphasized once again that while this discussion has been couched in terms of the individual analyst, these analytical processes are usually carried on collaboratively by a number, sometimes a considerable number, of officials representing a variety of bureaucratic interests and intellectual and policy perspectives.[2]

Planning. The term planning has been applied to a considerable range of activities and the organizations that carry them on. Common to all of them is an effort to look ahead in some systematic way, to anticipate future developments and problems, and then to prepare to deal with them, if necessary, by adjustments in present policies and programs.[3] This kind of activity is carried on both by separate planning staffs and by personnel elsewhere in the governmental structure.[4] It can be usefully differentiated from policy analysis to the extent that it is concerned with future rather than current problems.

Among the foreign policy and national security agencies, the military establishment without a doubt has a planning perspective and planning activities built most substantially into its normal functioning. Indeed, a standard military complaint about the civilian agencies, and particularly about the Department of State, is that they do not do enough planning and,

[2] Little systematic research attention has been directed to these processes of foreign policy analysis or "problem solving." For one such effort, focused on a geographic office in the Department of State, see Dean G. Pruitt, *Problem Solving in the Department of State* (The Social Science Foundation and Department of International Relations, University of Denver, Monograph Series in World Affairs, No. 2, 1964–65.

[3] Mr. Rostow, recent Chairman of the State Department's Policy Planning Council, comments: "The planner does not face a choice between long-run and short-run interests: he must combine them." See W. W. Rostow, "The Planning of Foreign Policy," in E. A. J. Johnson (ed.), *The Dimensions of Diplomacy* (Johns Hopkins Press, 1964), pp. 41–55.

[4] George Allen Morgan, a Foreign Service Officer with considerable planning experience, talks about planning in these terms: "Planning is thinking ahead with a view to action. It is thus an organic ingredient in the whole process of conducting foreign affairs, not the monopoly of a cloistered few. Indeed, most planning, and some of the weightiest, is neither so labelled nor done by planners so called." See his article, "Planning in Foreign Affairs: The State of the Art," *Foreign Affairs*, Vol. 39 (January 1961), p. 271. The article is a thoughtful, almost philosophical, essay on the subject.

furthermore, that this inadequacy is a handicap to the military establishment in its own planning efforts.

The nature of military responsibilities and functions makes planning of a quite detailed and precise nature both necessary and at the same time feasible. Even military operations of rather limited scope, like the dispatch of forces to Lebanon in July of 1958, may involve marshalling large numbers of men, weapons and other equipment, and supplying and supporting them in some remote corner of the globe for a perhaps indefinite period of time. Given the range and variety of military contingencies that may face the United States at any time in almost any part of the world, it is not possible to have either plans or capabilities to meet all of these contingencies, nor even to have plans in the files that will anticipate all the essential elements of situations as they actually arise.

Given the complex nature of military operations, something is better than nothing. To have planned in advance what specific forces one is prepared to commit to a particular situation and the detailed logistics of their support could make the difference between success and failure. The difficulties and uncertainties involved in contingency planning multiply as one broadens the scope of the planning effort.

The nation's military capabilities two, three, and five years in the future will rest to a considerable extent on present decisions about weapons systems development and procurement, the size and structure of the forces, their positioning at home and abroad, and the translation of these decisions into detailed programs and budgets. These decisions, in turn, presumably rest in part on projections into the future of present trends in world politics as well as in scientific and engineering research.

These complex burdens of the defense establishment have been discussed in more detail. What should be noted here is that while military planning has its share of uncertainties and dilemmas, it does have some "hard" empirical bases to work from in making its plans and projections and developing its programs: for example, the size, composition, and disposition of forces;

the nature and characteristics of weapons systems; the military capabilities of potential enemies and allies; the physical and socioeconomic geography of possible target or operating areas.

In comparison, the foreign policy planner is operating on a much more slippery, "softer" footing in making his own projections into the future. When it is also remembered that, at least traditionally, foreign affairs has had very little of an operational character about it, it is easy to understand why planning has tended to be a much less familiar and valued activity in the foreign policy organization than in the military. It seems fair to say that this situation is now in process of changing.

Planning was defined earlier as thinking ahead systematically and in depth about some problem or situation with a view to doing something about it in the present. It might be asked how far ahead the thinking has to be, and in how much depth, to rate as planning. Obviously, there is no magic point where the look into the future suddenly becomes planning. All policy analysis involves some projecting of present trends and circumstances into the future.

It is primarily a matter of posture and perspective, an assumption that detailed and systematic thinking ahead promises enough practical policy payoffs to warrant substantial investments of bureaucratic time and effort. There are differences of view about this basic point; there are also strong differences about how far ahead, in any event, it is worthwhile to project one's analysis. In practical organizational terms, the daily pressure of events on the line operating official leaves him relatively few moments for this kind of perspective. That is one of the reasons why separate planning units tend to get established.

Several kinds of foreign policy planning can be distinguished, and they parallel in a rough way the varieties of military planning. Foreign policy planners may find it useful to do some contingency planning. For example: what is likely to happen, and what courses of action would be open to the United States, if the key leader of some friendly foreign nation suddenly departs from the scene, or fighting flares again in the Near East between the Arabs and the Israelis, or an indigenous Communist-dominated political movement takes over a key country in Latin America?

As with the military, it is not possible to plan for all possible contingencies and, furthermore, even if one that has been anticipated does arise, it is bound to develop somewhat differently from what was anticipated. Even if it is a carbon copy of the scenario that is locked up in the planning staff's safe and the best course of action available to the U.S. government has been identified in advance, it still remains to be seen whether the unfolding of events will favor the interests of the United States.

Since contingency planning must be selective, it does involve some ability to identify possible future developments with particularly significant implications for U.S. interests, situations where advance planning may substantially improve this country's ability to respond effectively to the event and even exploit it to its own advantage. Since the best that is possible through such intellectual exercises is partial preparation for the future, it also becomes useful to recognize the rough limits beyond which anticipation of the future in detail can serve no useful policy purpose. The rising interest in and experimentation with gaming and simulating military and politico-military problems make available another set of techniques that may be helpful in contingency planning. In the process of "playing" through a particular contingency situation in advance of its occurrence, and perhaps doing so several times with differing sequences of events assumed, possible dimensions may be illuminated for the planner that would not otherwise have been.

The military establishment has the difficult job of translating national purposes and objectives into a national strategy and translating that strategy into forces-in-being ready to do a wide variety of jobs in a wide variety of places. In an era of far-reaching foreign policies backed by substantial and high varied foreign programs, the foreign policy organization has an almost equally difficult set of responsibilities. The cost and the numbers of people employed

here are considerably less than in the military, but the problems of operating in a hundred-odd foreign societies and attempting to influence in some degree events and decisions within them more than rival the complexities of weapons research and development. Thus, the foreign policy organization also has a requirement for what might be called program planning.

Franklin Lindsay defines it this way:

Program planning is the process by which policy objectives are translated into action programs of the scope, magnitude and timing required for their realization. Because today's policies require massive applications of manpower, money and facilities—and because it takes time to bring these assets into being—we must increasingly *anticipate* the needs posed by our objectives.[5]

This kind of planning has two major dimensions. It involves projecting into the future major political and socioeconomic developments in the foreign countries with which one is dealing. This is particularly relevant to development efforts in the underdeveloped nations and U.S. assistance to them. If the host country has its own development plan, the U.S. government must not only understand it in all its details but must also be able to assess it and estimate the likelihood of its accomplishment. Where the host government does not have a development plan, or perhaps even the capability to prepare one, the United States may have to provide one if its own development assistance is to accomplish any results.

Along with its concern for the program planning of other nations, as Mr. Lindsay indicates, the United States should be programming its own requirements in money, material, and personnel skills. The budgetary process makes some of this an absolute necessity, but critics like Mr. Lindsay feel that this is far from sufficient. The budgetary process in the federal government requires programming only a year, perhaps two, in advance. Furthermore, it does not assure that the agencies concerned are do-

5 Franklin A. Lindsay, "Program Planning: The Missing Element," *Foreign Affairs*, Vol. 39 (January 1961), p. 280. Italics in the original.

ing the personnel planning, and the in-depth analyses of other societies, which should underpin the program and project descriptions and the financial estimates required for budgeting purposes.

Program planning, in effect, is aimed at the more effective implementation of policy. What George Morgan calls "long-range planning" is designed to strengthen the formulation of policy. An underlying question about any such efforts is, as was suggested above, how far into the future one's analyses can be usefully projected. Again, this is essentially a matter of judgment rather than a fixed point rationally calculated. As Mr. Morgan reminds us, what the planner should be looking for is not a detailed blueprint of the future but insights that might prove helpful in coping more effectively with present and upcoming policy problems.

Morgan notes three general varieties of long-range planning. The first is plumbing the socio-political implications of significant developments in science and engineering, military technology, and in the economic structure and situation of societies. These provide some hard bases for the riskier social and political projections. One example is the question of the spread of nuclear technology and its possible military as well as peaceful implications. As with most other planning efforts, this is or should be a combination of the most difficult kind of intelligence estimate with the most sophisticated policy analysis.

The second general type of long-range planning is the analysis of present trends and forces that are likely to affect some important area of policy. The North Atlantic Treaty Organization and the role and purposes of the United States in it have been the subject of a number of such studies both inside and outside the government. The same can be said for the Alliance for Progress, the Common Market and its impact on world trading patterns, and the question of a strategic nuclear deterrent for Western Europe.

Finally, there is the grand strategy or overall policy framework that guides foreign and defense policies. During the last decade or so, the United States has had a basic national security policy document which presumably provides this kind of broad framework and guidance. It combines a statement of U.S. interests and objectives with a projection and analysis of major trends in world affairs and then sets forth a national strategy designed to maximize the accomplishment of U.S. purposes. This is truly planning on an ambitious scale, which perhaps explains why such an effort tends to be viewed skeptically by some.

If such a document is too specific and detailed, it is likely to go on endlessly, need almost continuing revision, stir almost continuing controversy within the government, and still not provide authoritative guidance on all the matters with which it deals. If it is general, it is likely to be dismissed as too vague to be meaningful. If this type of long-range planning is to be of any use at all, it must somehow steer a path between these two extremes.

It should be kept in mind that much of the benefit to be derived from the preparation of such a document comes from the very process of developing and drafting it, which includes the reconciliation of differences of view that emerge within as well as among the responsible government agencies. The clarification of problems and the identification of key policy issues for resolution that take place in the process are probably at least as important as their formal statement in the final document produced. At the same time, such a document can be quite useful in setting forth the official position on certain basic policy issues—for example, under what conditions nuclear weapons will be employed in support of certain U.S. policy interests.

The interrelations of foreign policy and military policy were previously suggested; these apply as much to planning as to current operations. Foreign policy objectives and assumptions about the international scene should be built into all military planning efforts, whether for the overall size and structure of the military establishment or for some specific contingency. Similarly, foreign policy planning should rest on reliable, detailed knowledge of what the military forces of the United States and any other nations that may be involved are capable of doing in any given situation. There is no point in the foreign policy planners projecting a show of force if the U.S. military establishment does not have the ability to send a force to the scene. On the other hand, there is no point in military planners either explicitly or implicitly making certain political assessments or assumptions if the experts of the foreign policy organization feel that these have no basis in current reality.

Two further points should be made about the intellectual or analytical aspects of foreign policy-making. First, it should not be assumed that these activities are always carried on with quite the self-consciousness implied in this discussion. Given the growing complexity of the problems to be dealt with and the number of individual and agency perspectives brought to bear upon them, the trend of events is nevertheless in this direction.

It should also be stressed once again that these intellectual operations can, at best, serve only to narrow and clarify the problems of choice faced by responsible policy officials, particularly when major policy decisions are involved.[6] The relevant intelligence will inevitably be incomplete, there will be conflicting interpretations of the present and estimates of the future, and there will be a variety of possibly relevant U.S. interests and objectives that must be sorted out and put in some sort of priority order. Experts may disagree, as may the heads of great government departments or important units within these departments. Domestic political considerations may have to be taken into account, including the views of a handful of extremely influential senators and congressmen.

In sum, the best efforts of the policy analysts, planners, and intelligence specialists can greatly facilitate the work of the high-level foreign policy-maker but cannot relieve him of the burden of painful choices and dilemmas. These tough decisions in the end are probably based as much on

[6] See the essay by Max Millikan, "Inquiry and Policy: The Relation of Knowledge to Action," in Daniel Lerner (ed.), *The Human Meaning of Social Sciences* (Meridian Books, 1959), pp. 158–80.

subtleties of judgment as on systematic research and rational analysis.

ORGANIZATIONAL IMPLICATIONS

While there are specifically designated organizational units carrying on at least two of the intellectual functions, namely, intelligence and planning, it must be kept in mind that both can be performed by any official in the policy-making structure. Thus, the Assistant Secretary heading one of the geographic bureaus in the State Department may rely on his own subordinates for intelligence estimates and completely ignore those of the Bureau of Intelligence and Research. If he wishes, the policy-maker can even be his own planning staff or his own interpreter of information. He may rely on his own personal reading of a situation. Since foreign policy planning is a much less well-defined and well-established function than intelligence, this is even more likely to be the case when a planning perspective and input are called for.

Given this lack of neat compartmentalization in the intellectual labors of the foreign policy organization, there is little point in trying to specify organizational arrangements and relationships in great detail. In the past, a good deal of discussion has revolved around the question of whether planning and intelligence units should be separately organized or be a part of operating line units. Starting with the reasonable premise that both intelligence and systematic "thinking ahead" are closely related to present actions and operations, it is possible to conclude that these functions should be performed within the same organizational unit as the latter.

On the other hand, it seems likely that the urgencies of current operations will sweep all available hands, including the intelligence analysts and the planners, into the business of the moment. In addition to the likelihood that the planning and intelligence types would get little time to perform their distinctive intellectual tasks, there is the further concern that intelligence estimates and planning studies, not necessarily by conscious direction but by the very nature of the close association, would tend to reflect and support present policies rather than provide an independent perspective and check on them.

Thus, the premise that intelligence and planning are closely related to current decision-making does not provide a clear-cut answer to the question of organizational arrangements. The fundamental problem is how to maintain the integrity of the intellectual function while at the same time assuring the necessary close link with the decision-making and problem-solving activities it is supposed to facilitate and support. It is likely to be difficult to maintain this integrity within an operating unit. On the other hand, it may be difficult to maintain it even when intelligence and planning are separately organized. Intelligence specialists and policy planners are far from immune to the lure of the immediate and the operational.

An organizational division of labor cannot guarantee effective intellectual performance. What may help is a widespread understanding within the foreign policy organization about the requirements of rational policy-making, a self-conscious and self-critical approach to the decision-making process and, ideally, some concern about how the various organizational units can best contribute to it.

On balance, there is something to be said for the separately organized intelligence unit, on the assumption that it is more likely to provide to responsible policy officials estimates of international situations independent of those developed by the line organizations dealing with those situations. Often the two estimates will coincide; sometimes, they will disagree. This is one way of building into the organization a check against any one set of interpretations of the state of the world remaining too long unchallenged by policy officials. It may be one of the major contributions of intelligence agencies to the foreign policy process.

Similarly, given the time pressures on operating officials, the best way of assuring that someone in the organization is looking ahead on a systematic basis is to make this his primary responsibility, and to reinforce

the distinction by establishing a separate organization to perform the function. The separate organization cannot guarantee this result; it just makes it somewhat more likely.

This is the way the actual organizational decisions have gone. The foreign policy and national security organizations are characterized by separate planning and intelligence units. The size and resources of the Central Intelligence Agency, symbolized by its massive new headquarters in Langley, Virginia, provides impressive evidence of the triumph of "separate and equal" in the intelligence field. The existence of Central Intelligence adds, in fact, another complication to this analysis. Not only are there separate intelligence units within most of the major national security agencies, but there is, in addition, a separate intelligence agency on a par with these other agencies. Effective working relationships between intelligence units and the policy-formulating and policy-implementing organizations that are their customers must develop across as well as within agency lines.

The fundamental organizational question remains the clarity with which organizational roles are defined and responsibilities divided and the extent to which these assignments are mutually agreed upon and understood. These in turn rest in good part on the conception of policy-making and its intellectual or analytical requirements held by both the top leadership of the foreign policy agencies and the substantial body of their career servants. There is no reason to assume a rigidly fixed state of affairs. For example, effective performance by intelligence or planning units may help change people's minds about the nature of relevant analytical needs and where in the organization these are likely to be satisfied.

DIFFERENCES IN BASIC INTELLECTUAL TRAINING AND ASSUMPTIONS

We return, then, to a number of basic themes. Organizational performance reflects the interaction of the formal organizational structure and the individuals who man it. How the latter define and interpret the structure, and operate within it, will determine its detailed functioning.

With regard to the intellectual capabilities of the organization, it is appropriate to ask whether particular attitudes, sets of assumptions, or views of the world dominate among its personnel and if they do, whether this in turn can be attributed to a common set of career experiences in the organization or to particular types of people recruited into the organization. Thus, for example, if an organization continues over time to recruit people with certain kinds of background and training to the exclusion of others, the intellectual performance of the organization may change very little even though its formal organizational arrangements have at the same time been radically altered. The first hypothesis is illustrated by the popular notion of a "military mind," or a "Foreign Service mind." Even if recruitment patterns do begin to change, it may take considerable time before previously dominant viewpoints are significantly altered. New recruits may continue to be provided with the organization's standard doctrine on the usefulness of planning, the intelligence-policy relationship, or how one goes about solving a policy problem.

However derived and maintained, such underlying attitudes, concepts, and views of the world have a considerable bearing on the intellectual performance of the foreign policy organization. While it may not strike others this way, this is somewhat reassuring to the outside researcher interested in the processes of contemporary foreign policy-making. The student of foreign policy-making must operate with at least one fundamental handicap: the intellectual materials of the foreign policy organization, the papers and documents that are the grist of the policy mill, are for the most part security-classified and thus normally not available to him. He is not in a position to judge for himself the intellectual quality of the foreign policy organization's work by direct examination of its present or recent intellectual products.

There are a number of ways, however, in which he can get at the intellectual skills,

attitudes, and frames of reference that help determine this quality. Memoirs and other writings by officials retired from public office or government service may be useful. Systematic interviewing of former officials is another possibility. Aside from the detailed documentation officially published twenty-five years after the event (as in the State Department's *Foreign Relations of the United States* series), certain critical or much debated policies sometimes call forth official White Papers or extensive congressional investigations which result in the availability of substantial bodies of official materials far sooner than the keepers of the archives would normally release them.

Former or present officials of the foreign policy organization can comment on intellectual skills and training without compromising classified data about substantive policy problems. Similarly, the outside scholar can himself probe attitudes and assumptions by interviewing operating officials in the various national security agencies. Interestingly enough, very little of this kind of research has been directed at the foreign policy organization. One of the exceptions is the study that Roger Hilsman did more than ten years ago on the prevalent doctrine among policy and intelligence officials regarding the role of intelligence in foreign policy-making.[7]

The study was based primarily on a series of interviews with intelligence and policy officials in the Executive Office of the President, the Central Intelligence Agency, and the Department of State. In brief summary, Hilsman found that for most of these officials, whether they were working in intelligence or policy, the realms of knowledge (that is, intelligence) and action (that is, policy) were essentially separate and could be kept separate: "facts were facts." The intelligence specialist gathered and organized the facts and presented them to the policy official, who then used them as he saw fit in making and carrying out decisions.

This may be a useful way of defending an organizational division of labor, but, as

[7] See Roger Hilsman, *Strategic Intelligence and National Decisions* (Free Press of Glencoe, 1956).

Hilsman suggested, it represents a rather crude and unsophisticated theory of knowledge. Without embarking on an elaborate philosophical discussion, it can be premised that it is impossible to describe the totality of a particular situation or event and that no analytical observer is in any case interested in so doing. Furthermore, facts do not "speak for themselves." They must be selected, related to other facts, interpreted, given meaning.

Put in terms of the foreign policy process, the inevitable selectivity of the intelligence analyst is useful to the policy official only to the extent that it is focused on problems of concern to the latter. Thus, the realms of intelligence analysis and policy-making are far from separate, intellectually speaking. They are intimately related, and this should be reflected in their organizational relationships.

It is not necessary to accept the specific organizational implications that Hilsman drew from his analysis. More relevant for present purposes is the fact that Hilsman's work was never followed up by other scholars. Thus, it is difficult to judge the applicability of his findings to present attitudes in the "intelligence community" and among those who are its clients. It seems reasonable to assume that Hilsman tried to implement his own philosophy during his tenure of approximately two years, from 1961 to 1963, as Director of Intelligence and Research in the State Department.

Reference was made above to the question of the kinds of intellectual skills typically recruited into the foreign policy and national security agencies, and the apparent consequences of such recruiting. This, too, has received relatively little systematic study. For example, the academic background and training of Foreign Service Officers typically have been and continue to be in history, political science, and law (with an increasing trend in recent years toward economics) rather than in the behavioral and the natural sciences. This pattern can probably be explained in terms of the kinds of interests that lead people into the Foreign Service and, also, the kinds of knowledge that make it possible to pass the Foreign Service Officer examinations.

What can be hypothesized about the consequences? For example, the behavioral sciences—psychology, sociology, anthropology—have been notably more oriented to explicit theory and conceptualization and to more precise and systematic research methods than history, law, and political science. If one assumes that, all other things being equal, such training will make for more rigor and depth of analysis and provide tools for the more systematic study and understanding of social and political behavior, it would have to be concluded that the relative scarcity in the Foreign Service of personnel so trained is unfortunate. It certainly means that the Department of State is not in a position to tap the knowledge and theories of these major fields of study directly through the backgrounds of its own personnel. The same general point can be made about the scarcity of people with considerable undergraduate and even graduate training in the natural sciences.[8]

There is amazingly little evidence on dominant intellectual orientations within the foreign policy organization and even less to explain how these may have developed and what their policy and organizational implications might be. These would seem to be data worth having.

ORGANIZATIONAL MACHINERY FOR INTELLIGENCE AND PLANNING

Since what has been defined as policy analysis has no separate and distinct organizational base, this section will be de-

[8] An experienced Foreign Service Officer, approaching this question of professional training from a somewhat different point of view, argues very strongly for cultural anthropology, the behavioral sciences (in which he does include political science), and the comparative study of value systems as part of the core curriculum for the "new diplomat." See Robert Rossow, "The Professionalization of the New Diplomacy," *World Politics*, Vol. 14 (July 1962), pp. 561–75. Rossow sees the "new diplomacy," defined as the facilitation of crosscultural communications and operations, as having a far wider area of application than the traditional field of government-to-government relations.

voted to a brief description of planning and intelligence units.

THE INTELLIGENCE COMMUNITY

The present U.S. organization for national security intelligence has been described at length elsewhere.[9] Some summary comments must suffice here. The key unit is the Central Intelligence Agency (CIA). Its size and its role have expanded greatly since its original establishment in the National Security Act of 1947. It is responsible for the overall coordination and integration of the efforts of the various departmental intelligence units working in the fields of national security and foreign policy. However, it does much more. It is assumed to have the primary responsibility for covert U.S. intelligence activities abroad as well as for certain covert U.S. operations. In the later category, published accounts of the preparation of Cuban exile forces for the Bay of Pigs landing in the spring of 1961 ascribe a key role to the Agency. The same is true for a more successful venture—the overthrow in 1954 of the Communist-oriented Arbenz regime in Guatemala.

It also carries on a great deal of independent intelligence research work. At one time, it may have been primarily a central coordinating, interpreting, and disseminating agency, with departmental intelligence units doing most of the substantive work. However, that time is past; the CIA does a great deal of its own research and analysis and has governmentwide responsibility for certain particularly sensitive and significant problem areas.

Substantial intelligence activities are carried on elsewhere in the government, and the various departmental intelligence units are still quite large and active. The functions of the Federal Bureau of Investigation are primarily domestic. There is the supersecret National Security Agency, a large and growing organization presumably responsible for worldwide communications,

including the important cryptographic function; this agency has apparently taken on in Washington some of the hush-hush atmosphere and reputation formerly the hallmark of CIA.

In the summer of 1961, a joint Defense Intelligence Agency (DIA) was established. It was designed to tie together more closely the separate intelligence efforts of the three services and to strengthen the capacity of the military establishment to provide overall military intelligence assessments. Each of the military services continues to carry on a wide range of intelligence activities through intelligence organizations in Washington and elsewhere and through the military attachés assigned as members of U.S. missions in countries around the world.

The Department of State, as already noted, has a large Bureau of Intelligence and Research, which went through a difficult transitional period as a result of the major personnel changes introduced by the Wriston reforms but now seems to be finding qualified Foreign Service Officers as well as civil servants to man its key positions.

All of these agencies taken together, plus the Atomic Energy Commission, are referred to as the "intelligence community." While this sounds suspiciously like an advertising label, it reflects the fact that the intelligence units of these agencies, in addition to carrying on their own intra-agency activities, work closely together in a number of important interdepartmental intelligence enterprises. In these activities, the Central Intelligence Agency is the unquestioned leader. In statutory terms, it is directly responsible to the National Security Council. Its Director sits as one of the statutory advisers on the Council and was a member of the Operations Coordinating Board during the latter's existence. The Director of Central Intelligence also sits as chairman of the U.S. Intelligence Board (USIB), formerly the Intelligence Advisory Committee, which is the highest-level interdepartmental intelligence unit in the government and has the final word on the important National Intelligence Estimates. These National Intelligence Estimates

---

[9] See Harry Howe Ransom, *Central Intelligence and National Security* (Harvard University Press, 1958). Also relevant is Ransom's *Can American Democracy Survive Cold War?* Chaps. VI and VII.

(or NIE's as they are called in the government) represent the intelligence community's agreed analysis and interpretation of the relevant facts and likely future developments with regard to some particular geographic area of functional problem, or some crisis situation that has suddenly arisen. These estimates may emerge from the usual periodic intelligence review of a question; on the other hand, they may be generated by the U.S. Intelligence Board or by the query of some high official (even the President or the National Security Council itself).

The estimates may be called for as part of an effort to reappraise U.S. policy in a particular country or area, to look ahead and anticipate likely future developments. In this case, it may take a number of months to produce the estimate. Some examples have been given earlier in the chapter. Others might be: Chinese Communist policy in Asia in light of the Sino-Soviet split; present and anticipated Soviet anti-missile missile development and capabilities; the present and likely future state of affairs in Indonesia, Algeria, or Japan, to name just a few. The estimates may also be called for in response to some immediate crisis: Suez in 1956; Lebanon in 1958; or the Chinese move into Korea in the winter of 1950–51. Under such circumstances, the estimates may be forthcoming in a matter of days or even hours.

The original draft for these estimates is usually prepared by an interdepartmental working group consisting primarily of representatives from the Department of State, the Defense Intelligence Agency, and the three military services, and chaired by a CIA representative. Presumably these are working-level officials expert in the particular problem or area under consideration. The key role in guiding these draft estimates through the working groups and then putting them into final shape for presentation to the U.S. Intelligence Board is played by the Board of National Estimates.

This little-known group within the Central Intelligence Agency is one of the most important in the entire intelligence field. The Board consists of fifteen to twenty experienced and senior intelligence officers

supported by a small professional staff; their function is the supervision, editing, and final preparation of the National Intelligence Estimates. Their work is highly regarded in many quarters, but it is obviously impossible for the outside observer to appraise it.

The National Intelligence Surveys represent another major product of the intelligence community. They are encyclopedic compendia dealing individually with most of the countries of the world and covering a broad range of topics, from political structure and processes and military capabilities to transportation and communcations networks and availability of natural resources. Different parts of the surveys are assigned to member agencies in terms of their special knowledge and skills, with Central Intelligence responsible for final editing and approval. These surveys are periodically reviewed and updated, sometimes every year; frequency of revision varies with the importance of the country and the pace of change within it.

Little has been said in this discussion about the overseas activities of the intelligence community. Brief comment on two major problem areas must suffice. First, the fact that many U.S. elements report on developments overseas produces a real need for coordinating their intelligence-gathering activities. The present division of labor represents neither a rational nor an economic use of intelligence resources.

It has been widely reported in published accounts that elements in the intelligence community are responsible for carrying on or supporting covert operations abroad designed to accomplish particular U.S. foreign policy objectives. These activities are said to go beyond espionage and to be of such a nature that knowledge of U.S. involvement would be damaging to its interests. For present purposes, it is enough to stress that any such operations as may take place require the same policy guidance and monitoring as the overt foreign affairs activities and programs of the U.S. government. The organizational means for implementing this requirement may be different, but the requirement itself is, in principle, the same.

PLANNING UNITS

It has already been made clear that planning, as defined, can be accomplished just about anywhere in the national security organization—and often is. Even when the initiative for a particular project comes from the planning staff, the contributions of line or operational units are likely to be sought. Requirements for providing such assistance may even be levied on them.

To generalize further, planning activities have expanded considerably in the last few years, and current operational problems are probably more commonly viewed from what might be called a planning perspective than would have been the case five years ago. A number of factors help explain this increasing orientation toward thinking ahead systematically with a view to present action.

The long-term character of the international situation that faces the United States suggests that *ad hoc* responses to crises and challenges are neither adequate nor reassuring. Such responses probably add to the cost of maintaining its national security, a factor not to be ignored; they become increasingly less acceptable as the United States grows more experienced in the business of international politics and more assured in the playing of its own role. Finally, they represent a mighty challenge to the scientific-rationalistic orientation of the American culture and character, which refuses to admit that even the complexities of contemporary international affairs cannot be more fully understood and anticipated and thus at least partially controlled and manipulated.

Perhaps this explanation is unnecessarily elaborate. Certainly it should not be implied that this change represents anything more than a developing trend. Particularly among the civilian foreign policy agencies, planning efforts are still very much at the experimental stage, with a variety of formats and techniques being explored. About many problems that concern the foreign policy-maker, the reliable knowledge and predictive power that can be contributed by the social sciences and others are relativity modest (although it should be added that even this modest body of knowledge has not been fully drawn on by the foreign policy agencies). Nevertheless, planning as a posture and as an activity is becoming increasingly important in the intellectual activities of national security agencies.

Under present arrangements, the President's national security affairs staff is not in a position to carry on policy planning of its own. Even under the more elaborate National Security Council structure and staffing of the Eisenhower Administration, the attached staffs were primarily concerned with the operation of the Security Council machinery. In both cases, the primary planning role of the presidential staffs and the National Security Council has been to focus and occasionally to prod the efforts of the line departments.

The National Security Council policy papers, as they were prepared before the Kennedy Administration, were an effort to anticipate future lines of development and set appropriate present courses of policy. The basic national security policy paper set forth the framework of guiding assumptions, objectives, and policies in terms of which more immediate decisions could presumably be taken. The operations plans prepared under the aegis of the Operations Coordination Board were a form of program planning—or at least a statement of present, ongoing programs, usually on a country basis. While the Kennedy Administration dropped almost all of these formats, it encouraged its own varieties of studies, planning exercises, and basic policy and program documents.

It should be noted that planning efforts directly or indirectly related to foreign policy are carried on or sponsored by other units within the Executive Office of the President. The Office of Science and Technology has a broad interest in the military and foreign policy implications of scientific research and development. Before its formal change in status in 1962, this presidential staff played a role in strengthening the scientific capabilities of the Defense and State Departments and in supporting the establishment of a strengthened Arms Control and Disarmament Agency. The Office of Science and Technology and the

President's Science Advisory Committee, together with its various subsidiary scientific advisory panels, continue to play an important role in drawing governmental attention to scientific fields being ignored or critical questions going unanswered.

The Office of Emergency Planning in the Executive Office, along with the Office of Civil Defense—now a part of the Defense Department—are the major responsible units attempting to plan, in terms of possible domestic consequences and requirements, for the variety of critical contingencies the nation may face, from a major natural disaster to the ultimate disaster of thermonuclear war.

The Bureau of the Budget, through its legislative clearance and budget preparation responsibilities, probably has the key role in coordinating program planning on a governmentwide basis. As budgetary problems mesh with broader considerations relating to the state of the economy, its concerns are closely related to those of the Council of Economic Advisers and, from a somewhat different perspective, those of the Treasury Department.

Most substantive planning continues to be done in the departments. Both the Kennedy and Johnson Administrations have strongly emphasized departmental planning responsibilities. Furthermore, certain major foreign policy documents, like the national policy papers, are now given final authoritative approval by the Secretary of State rather than the President.

After experimenting with a number of formats, the various foreign policy agencies, under the leadership of the State Department's Policy Planning Council, have been developing a series of "national policy papers" that embody U.S. policy toward particular foreign nations. These are distinguished from earlier efforts of this kind by the more detailed analysis of country situations and by the linking of U.S. objectives and policies with specific agency operations and programs in these countries.

The work of the Department of State's Policy Planning Council has been previously described in some detail. In addition to its own efforts, the Council and its members encourage and support planning efforts elsewhere in the Department and participate and sometimes provide leadership for a variety of interdepartmental planning efforts.

There is usually a designated point of contact with the Council within each of the operating bureaus in the State Department. Some of the Department's geographic and functional bureaus have relatively senior officers serving as "planning advisers." How much planning these officials actually engage in will vary from person to person and time to time. It is easy, and tempting, to use such a person—with no well-defined area of responsibility—as a kind of roving special assistant and added organizational resource. This may well leave little time for anything that could reasonably be labelled planning.

The present focus of the economic aid program on development of the underdeveloped countries suggests a considerable need for long-range planning, both within the recipient countries and within the U.S. government, as well as for the program planning necessary to translate long-term strategies into year-by-year U.S. assistance. In its current organizational setup, the Agency for International Development has an Office of Programming and Planning in each of its four geographic bureaus. The programming units are concerned with the detailed decisions and massive paperwork involved in translating foreign aid appropriations into approved country programs and projects. Their work is further complicated by the frequent readjustments and reprogramming called for as regional aid priorities are modified and funds reallocated for one reason or another.

The planning units are responsible for the longer-range view and projections. One effort now being pushed within the Agency for International Development is the formulation of a series of long-range country assistance studies. These are designed to put U.S. assistance on a more systematic basis, linked to an overall concept of a country's development and related strategic factors. Presumably, this is intended to minimize *ad hoc* responses to the political pressures of the moment and a resultant congeries of individual projects sometimes bearing little relation to one another and not reflecting any guiding development strategy.

There are obvious difficulties in the way of such an approach. Many of the countries being assisted do not have the indigenous planning and administrative capabilities that are an important if not essential counterpart of any U.S. planning efforts. Furthermore, there will continue to be significant uncertainties about the funds that Congress will appropriate for this purpose, and there will also continue to be situations where U.S. assistance will be provided to countries for reasons—often put in the broad category "political"— which have little to do with their economic needs, capabilities, or relationship to some overall concept or plan. Nevertheless, if long-term socioeconomic development is the guiding purpose of the economic aid program, and if the United States must provide a good deal of the planning in many of the countries being assisted, it seems quite appropriate for the Agency for International Development to be thinking in terms of long-range assistance strategies and to have organizational units charged with planning for their regions of responsibility.

Since the field of arms control and disarmament represents for the most part future possibilities and hopes, at least at present writing, much of the work of the Arms Control and Disarmament Agency is oriented to studies, research, and projections into the future. From its original establishment in 1961, its ranking officials have emphasized their interest in the assistance of outside scholars and research organizations and have contracted for a substantial number of outside studies. For a time, the Agency also had a special policy planning staff of three senior officials, the Disarmament Advisory Committee, which has now been abolished.

The range and variety of military planning activities were mentioned earlier. From the foreign policy viewpoint, the most important of these are carried on by the military staffs and the Office of the Secretary of Defense in Washington and by the

unified and specified commands in the field.

Two developments in military planning since World War II are particularly noteworthy. The first is the steadily increasing use of scientific theories and methods of analysis—borrowing particularly from the physical sciences and statistics—and the computers which so strikingly enhance the utility of these theories and methods. Perhaps an inevitable concomitant of the first has been the increasing role of civilian personnel in many of these analytical efforts of the military establishment, both directly on the government payroll and in the growing corps of satellite and independent research organizations, individual consultants, and public advisory panels that provide assistance to the Defense Department.

Secretary McNamara's distinctive contribution has been to put these massive intellectual resources to work on those problems he felt warranted priority attention and on which he planned to take action. To repeat a general point, Mr. McNamara's energy, keenness, and clear sense of direction have fashioned an effective organizational instrument from resources that were to a considerable extent already present. One important addition was the Directorate for Systems Analysis established in 1961 under the Defense Comptroller and headed by former RAND analyst Alain Enthoven. Also, the small Policy Planning Staff that had existed in the Office of International Security Affairs was expanded and another RAND alumnus, Henry Rowen, appointed as Deputy Assistant Secretary of Defense to head it.

It was pointed out above that there is in fact a U.S. "intelligence community" in the sense that departmental intelligence organizations do engage in joint enterprises and do produce estimates and surveys that represent their agreed views on particular subjects. If the intelligence community is the basis of comparison, there are only the modest beginnings of a U.S. "planning community," and much of it is a development of the last few years.

A good part of the explanation lies in the fact that the planning function is by no means as well-defined as intelligence and that what has been called planning here is carried out by a number of units within particular agencies to serve a wide variety of organizational purposes. Even where the substantive relationship between agency planning activities has been rather clear, it has not typically been reflected in organizational coordination. This is now beginning to change.

The State and Defense Departments do engage in some coordinated contingency planning. The Berlin situation provides one excellent example. Long-range planning for the Military Assistance Program involves the Agency for International Development as well as the State and Defense Departments. The State Department is be-

ginning to play a limited role with regard to military establishment budget and force planning.

The problems of social, economic, and political development in the less developed countries are also beginning to get the concerted attention of planners in the Agency for International Development and the United States Information Agency as well as in the State and Defense Departments. Whatever the specific results to date of these efforts at coordinated planning, it can be said with assurance that the desirability of such planning is gaining rapidly increasing recognition within the foreign policy organization.

PLANNING OUR MILITARY FORCES

BY HAROLD BROWN

Uncertainty is necessarily the lot of the planner, since he deals with the future. Uncertainty can never be completely removed. However, it can be compensated for, and to do so is a continuing responsibility of those who plan military forces. Primarily this can be done by insuring, in so far as we can, that future weapons and forces will be adaptable to the right range of defense needs or, as defense planners often put it, by insuring flexibility.

Modern weapons need not of themselves inexorably beget more sophisticated, expensive and destructive devices. It is true that pressures exist which, if unrestrained, would needlessly proliferate and duplicate weapon designs. There is a tendency to do what potential opponents are doing, or thought to be doing, or predicted to be able

to do. But restraint and direction *are* exercised. In acquiring the capability to defend the United States, direction is given and decisions are made at the highest level, by the President with the advice of the Secretaries of Defense and State. Assumptions, concepts, economic analyses, divergent estimates of potential danger to our national security—all periodically are translated into an explicit defense program for the United States. At least twice a year the Department of Defense updates this program and projects forces five years or more into the future. Specific decisions flow from a continuing interaction between perceptions of what is technologically and economically feasible, and defense policy—the broad guidelines for achieving national objectives by the direct or potential use of armed force. In

Reprinted by permission from *Foreign Affairs,* January 1967, pp. 277–290. Copyright by the Council on Foreign Relations, Inc., New York.

Mr. Brown is Secretary of the Air Force. Prior to this appointment, he served as Director of Defense Research and Engineering in the Department of Defense. He is a former Director of the University of California Lawrence Radiation Laboratory, and he has served as consultant and scientific adviser to a number of agencies.

turn, specific program decisions and their subsequent results condition both future weapons development and future defense policy.

To say that there is uncertainty in tomorrow or virtue in flexibility is hardly novel. Reconciling the two, however, is a job calling for much diverse information and refined analysis. To evaluate the process, we must examine further the uncertainty which surrounds weapon choices and consider how best to minimize it and live with it. Let us first consider some uses and limitations of intelligence estimates and then examine the interaction of strategy and technology. In the light of these two exercises, the timing of decisions leading to full-scale weapon development takes on special importance, because such decisions rough out critical boundaries of the capabilities of our future forces and the sensitivity of that capability to the actions of others. Finally, within these boundaries, we can attempt to indicate some general factors which enhance force flexibility and some examples of the sort of flexibility which may be demanded of weapons currently under development.

THE UTILITY OF INTELLIGENCE ESTIMATES

There are, of course, numerous broad areas where uncertainty complicates choices about the composition and overall magnitude of our forces. What, for example, are the prospects in fifteen or twenty years for widespread nuclear proliferation, for shifts in alliances, for a largely disarmed world, for increased or decreased Soviet or Communist Chinese militancy, for external aggression and subversion directed against developing nations, for a world realignment leading to conflict between the developed and the developing? Here the face of possible long-range political and strategic futures varies from perpetual peace to Armageddon. The temptation is strong to satisfy one's own policy predilections by immediately trying to leap over the ravine of short-range and mid-range uncertainty in order to program developments and deployments which meet (or encourage) one

or two of these long-range futures. But this ravine—the next five years—is far better lighted than the distant future. Within it the most pressing aspects of external military challenges appear. Here uncertainties about specific opposing deployments narrow; estimates of opposing capabilities in ballistic missile defenses, bombers, bomber defenses, submarines and advanced tactical aircraft become more precise. The pattern they present becomes extremely important in stimulating shifts in our own defense policy and development priorities.

By and large, our possible responses to five-year forecasts have to do with force procurement and deployment. At ten years, the forecasts are much less reliable, and our responses tend to become related more to questions of the development of particular weapons and systems. However, whether the forecast is for five or (less reliably) for ten years, intelligence gleaned across this wide range of subjects plays a critical role in determining what weapons and forces to proceed with part way, all the way or not at all, and in the timing of specific decisions.

Intelligence estimates provide no panacea, particularly if one insists on viewing policy-making as beginning with the "threat," a protean word whose meaning includes intent as well as capability, and embraces not only the number of ballistic missiles an opponent may have but the number of his targets that we want to be able to destroy. Because our planning is projected forward at least ten and sometimes fifteen years, intelligence estimates are made of what forces the other side will have far in the future. This may be a necessary exercise, but we sometimes tend to depend too much on the results. We may know with reasonable precision how many missiles the Soviets will have in their active force a year or two from now, because they must already have begun work on their deployment. We may have a fair idea how many they will have four or even five years from now, though a less precise idea of what kind of missiles and what their payloads will be. Yet in fact we know very little about how many or what kind of missiles the Russians will have ten years from now, because they probably have not reached a decision themselves. And even if they have, they might change their minds. Consequently, estimates beyond the immediate future enter, at best, a realm of educated extrapolation. They can readily pass beyond intelligence information, through telepathy—what others plan but have not done anything about—to clairvoyance—what they have not yet decided.

How many missiles the Soviets will have at the beginning of 1977 does not, of course, depend solely on their technical and productive capabilities—on what they *can* do. That is one kind of intelligence estimate often given—generally by people who want to "play it safe" by gearing our plans to the worst imaginable (even if not feasible) contingency. The development of Soviet forces will be influenced by the technical possibilities, of course, but even more strongly: (a) by Soviet military and foreign-policy goals; (b) by the Soviets' own fiscal requirements and allocations; and (c) by what the United States does, and the signals that we transmit, accurate or inaccurate, intentional or unintentional, about what we plan to do. When we try to look ahead ten to fifteen years, what we get are not intelligence estimates at all, but *planning* estimates. They should be treated as such. The "estimate" becomes more an examination of the question: "If countries A, B and C plan well (or poorly), what will they do in response to U.S. course of action X or Y?" This is the kind of question we ask ourselves frequently about military and political actions projected over the next year or two. We must learn to ask it (and try to give an answer) about developments and deployments other countries may make over a period of the next ten years. Our objective in military planning should be to provide ourselves with the capacity to take initiatives of our own, or to make timely responses to the force deployments of others at later times, as their actions inevitably become much clearer to us.

We are rightly concerned about the time that elapses between a decision to acquire a certain capability and the actual existence of that capability. This lead time may be as long as ten years. It can, of course, be compressed to some extent by giving a development program high priority. The urgency of a particular program often is based on intelligence information about an opponent's technical capabilities (or an imputation to him of our own present or future technical capabilities) and—always less certain—his intentions. But lead time cuts both ways. We often forget that our opponents also require substantial time between decision and the achievement of a particular military capability. We sometimes are tempted to act as though the Soviets have a capability in being as soon as our calculations indicate that a particular piece of hardware is technically feasible. In fact, to develop, produce, deploy and train is no mean task for any nation when large and complex new weapons systems are involved.

A good example of the two-edged nature of lead time and intelligence estimates is the intercontinental ballistic missile, which the Soviets were working on in the early 1950s. Knowledge that they were developing an ICBM was a major factor in the initiation of our own program in 1954–55. But the Soviets did not have a substantial ICBM capability until 1962, an elapsed time of about ten years. Starting two or three years later, we managed to finish about two years earlier than they—in addition to developing during the same period the solid-propellent Minuteman and an entirely separate ballistic-missile system, the submarine-launched Polaris. This is not to say that we can always make up a late start that well. Complacent contemplation of past achievements would be extremely dangerous. However, this example does show that the interval between our discovery that the other side is thinking about something (or our conjecture that they are thinking about something because we just thought of it) and the time they actually have a usable weapon generally will be long enough for us to take appropriate counteraction if our decisions are made expeditiously. Our counteraction need not always take the form of a parallel response. If we have been skillful in our evaluation of intelligence and wise in our choices of options, we may offset a particular challenge by making a quantitative rather than qualitative change in weaponry, by adaptation or minor improvements in existing weapons, or by producing a new weapon for which early development has already been done. On occasion we may also get good results by making a doctrinal change—that is, a change in how existing weapons are used.

INTERACTION OF STRATEGY AND TECHNOLOGY

Whether strategy or technology comes first is (perhaps fruitlessly) debatable, though flow charts frequently are drawn by operational or technological planners depicting one or the other as the fount of most really significant activity. There appears to be no foolproof cyclical pattern encompassing the two, nor any *ying-yang* replacement of one by the other. If, as some suggest, a pendulum swings between strategy and technology, its period has not been convincingly measured. At a given time when we ask what technologies should be developed, strategic aims must provide the direction. Yet, if we examine how our strategy got to be what it is, clearly technology had a big part in getting us there. Broad strategic direction must be given if there is to be coherence in and among development programs and the military forces which result. But the effect of technology on strategy also should be continuous. Technology provides opportunities which may or may not be recognized immediately; strategy, while usually dominant in terms of authority, must be informed by knowledge of these opportunities if it is to be fully effective.

At the onset of the cold war in the late 1940s, technical factors—our possession of the atomic bomb and aircraft which could deliver it—dominated our military strategy. The American monopoly or preponderance of nuclear power and its relatively low cost, combined with our abrupt demobilization of conventional forces, set in motion a strategy heavily committed to deterrence based on the Strategic Air Command's capability for nuclear retaliation. This strategy was, of course, a response to the evidence of Communist aggressiveness that accumulated

in the years immediately following World War II, and it lasted through the 1950s. After the Korean War, the Air Force consistently received just under half of the total defense budget, and the lion's share of its money went to strategic forces.

However, as the Soviet Union strengthened its own nuclear capability, the mutual devastation to be expected from a general nuclear exchange increased the likelihood of less dangerous forms of aggression. By 1961, strategy per se probably regained ascendancy over technology. Strategy would remain partially captive to nuclear technology; but in limited confrontations the end of extreme U.S. nuclear predominance had put a premium on uses of military force more believable than threatening the extinction of powers which, as they died, could cause the United States grave damage. Consequently, our ability to apply carefully measured, limited force increased in importance, though our ability to assure the destruction of any aggressor who might strike us retained first priority, as it does today. Development emphasis shifted to modernization of conventional forces, while long-range strategic nuclear capabilities were concurrently improved.

Since technology and strategy are so closely related and since so many fields of technology are growing increasingly complex and expensive, it is often assumed that lead time grows correspondingly and that there is unbearable danger in not having every technological bet covered. This assumption is too simplistic, and it would be impossible to pursue every promising idea to the point of producing hardware. Instead, we must seek innovation by providing adequate resources for basic research and exploratory development. We must hold open our option to adopt weapon systems which look promising, by developing those components which require long lead times. But we have no business buying insurance against every conceivable action by potential enemies, without regard for how likely or profitable that action may be.

Here the purposeful influence of strategy can be valuable, for it lends central direction and consistency to the commitment of technological resources. It determines whether a project should be pushed hard, placed on the back burner, or taken off the stove altogether. During the 1950s, for example, the Jupiter intermediate-range ballistic missile enjoyed a high priority as a feasible interim system until missiles of intercontinental range could be developed; hence, this radically new weapon took only three years to develop. On the other hand, in small-arms development, which during that period was given a low priority, the M–14 rifle was scheduled for eleven years in research and development and was to be followed by gradual replacement of the old M–1 rifle over a period of seven years.

An important part of the interaction between strategy and technology is a nation's total technological and productive capacity. In spite of current political evolution away from bipolarity, there remain two super-*technical* powers in the world: the United States and the Soviet Union. There is a good deal of merit in making clear to third powers that in the face of the capabilities of the two supertechnical powers the entry stakes into this technological competition are higher than the return in military capability and the political power it buys. This is a most important message to communicate, for the acquisition of weapons of mass destruction by additional powers, including some nations whose limited resources could be better used for their economic development, is likely to be far more destabilizing than acquisition of new weapons by the U.S. and U.S.S.R.

We have security today because deterrence has worked, and to the degree that deterrence remains assured we are more secure than in the past. But in another sense we are less secure, because the physical consequences of the "failure" of deterrence are worse. Technology has caused this. But since the Soviets detonated an atomic device in 1949, we have demonstrated that, with *two* principal nuclear powers involved, deterrence of general nuclear war can remain reasonably stable despite successive qualitative advances in weaponry, and despite asymmetry of purpose between the two great powers since World War II.

THE SIGNIFICANCE OF FULL-SCALE DEVELOPMENT

Considering the limitations of long-range intelligence and the complex interaction between strategy and technology, there is much to recommend a pragmatic approach to the development of major new weapons. The decision to proceed with full-scale development of a major new weapon system is an important event; almost without exception it indicates a large commitment of resources, and it defines, limits or expands the conditions under which future combat forces will be able to fight effectively. Normally the decision is made by the President or at the highest level in the Defense Department with Presidential concurrence.

The first important indication of full-scale development comes when the Secretary of Defense approves "contract definition" for a new weapon. It follows a period of "concept formulation," the thorough analysis of military need and concept of operation, studies of technical feasibility to determine "best" characteristics, cost and scheduling. The objective is to check earlier assumptions and to get a good contract, one which is unambiguous and is based on a fixed price or incentives which will properly motivate the contractor. The conditional decision to proceed with full-scale development can then be reviewed on the basis of firm costs, schedules and capabilities, and of any changes in conditions since the contract definition began.

Because the commitment of resources is large, decisions to undertake full-scale development or deployment must be made deliberately. Deliberation does not imply unwarranted delay, however.

The decision to go ahead at least a small part of the way may be made without irrevocable commitment to complete the project. Research and early development generally require 30 to 40 percent of the total time from conception to operational capability, and account for perhaps 5 to 20 percent of the development cost. The number of options that one can afford to take out in this way, while not unlimited, is none the less large. In sufficiently important cases we may have to go through full-scale development while reserving decision on deployment until the indications of need become apparent. An indication might be an opponent's deployment of a similar system, or more likely, of a related one which ours may be designed to neutralize. If we start after the other side has begun to deploy a new system, we may not have time for both development and production. Nike-X is an example of a system where development was pushed without a decision having been made as to deployment. However, it should be noted that a deployment decision on Nike-X depends on the nature and weight of the offensive forces we may expect to be used against us rather than on whether another country displays an anti-ballistic missile system. Unless the defense is much less expensive than the offense (informed analyses show it to be more expensive), the correct counter to an opponent's ABM deployment is an improved or increased offensive force.

Here again the directing and restraining influences of strategy deserve emphasis. If anything, strategy and the criterion of utility in support of national objectives merit increasing influence on development decisions. The development community argues too often for going ahead "because you can do it." This is a fine reason for mountain climbing, but not for multi-billion-dollar development programs. In building big systems, developers lacking explicit guidance tend to do the "best" job they can. A hazy operational concept encourages excessive performance requirements at the cost of utility, reliability, simplicity and early availability. Conversely, but less frequently, the same effect can result from too detailed an operational concept .or one which through ignorance makes excessive demands on available technology.

The health of our technological base directly supports our ability to move ahead rapidly with full-scale development. Contrary to the belief of some critics, there is no paucity of basic research and exploratory development money. The Department of Defense spends about $1.5 billion a year for these categories alone and $800 million more for advanced development short of

full systems development.[1] Though none of this is tied in detail to a specific military strategy, very little of it is largesse to be dispensed annually for the general advance of technology.

Development of technology represents one level of effort; development of big systems is an entirely different and far more costly effort. Costs rise dramatically as we leave research and exploratory and advanced development and move into engineering development and procurement in quantity of equipment for the field. The jump is likely to be from a level of tens or hundreds of millions for advanced development to a billion or even ten billion dollars for deployment of a major weapon system. Hopefully, by the time we have completed 5 or 10 percent—the development part—of the total cost of a large system, we can be confident of a project's high operational utility. But this magnitude of cost is a compelling reason for the Secretary of Defense to insist—as he does—on a convincing demonstration of operational utility within an overall national defense strategy before he will make decisions tantamount to full-scale development and procurement. This is precisely the problem faced by advocates of large anti-missile defenses or a follow-on bomber to replace the B–52 Gs and Hs.

The latter, for example, has required a massive study effort to determine its characteristics. Less than two years ago, few would have predicted that the B–52 would be delivering conventional bombs on the scale we have seen in Viet Nam. Yet we must attempt to predict whether this role will exist for the manned bomber 15 years from now. Bombing guerrilla supply areas with non-nuclear weapons requires a large payload, but high speed is not essential as long as enemy air defenses are absent or relatively primitive. On the other hand, in a nuclear role supplementing our strategic missiles, a bomber may need high speed to penetrate advanced defense sys-

[1] This is aside from perhaps another $2 billion in support of the equivalent categories of broadly applicable research and technology from other government agencies—the National Aeronautics and Space Administration, Atomic Energy Commission and others.

tems, but a very large payload may be less important. Is a satisfactory compromise feasible? Do we need two distinct types of manned bombers? Should we develop an optimum bomber for only one role? If so, which role? The questions whether to go ahead with *any* new bomber, if so what kind, and how far to commit it to development thus bring into focus a wide range of complex technological questions which must be squared with an even broader range of strategic and political issues.

Sometimes the divergence between the needs of strategy on the one hand and the use of technology to advance a poorly thought out concept of operation on the other leads to cancellation of a development project before commitment to, or before completion of, full-scale development. Invariably the result is traumatic for individuals who have invested years of talent and energy in the project. Nevertheless, in varying degrees a cancelled project leaves a heritage of improved technology. The XB–70 program has significantly advanced our knowledge of structures, engines and aerodynamics of large aircraft in supersonic flight. This knowledge cost us a billion and a half dollars. It is doubtful that the information was worth that price. But full-scale development and acquisition of the XB–70 truly would have been a waste, and of a different order of magnitude. It could easily have led to a $10 to $15 billion program, inadequately related to strategy. The same is true of many other programs.

PROSPECTS FOR FORCE FLEXIBILITY

If continued military strength is still necessary to achieve a more peaceful world, the single most important characteristic of future forces will probably be flexibility. The United States must be able to deter or combat aggression in such diverse forms as subversive insurgency or general nuclear war. The variety of contingencies which our military systems must be prepared to meet is very great, and the most efficient composition of *tactical* forces employed in future limited conflict can never be fully known long before the fact.

The development of tactical forces inevitably has called for choice and compromise. Our technical capabilities and the variety of the possible small-war situations we may face present us with far more options than our resources will allow us to take up. For example, to design one or more types of aircraft solely for each specific tactical air function—air superiority, interdiction, reconnaissance, close support—not only would reduce the flexibility of our tactical air force but would be prohibitively expensive. Also, we must make some compromise in meeting the vast numbers and kinds of contingencies that may occur in widely differing environments: from the arctic to the tropics, from Europe to Latin America. This is why our tactical aircraft have been designed or modified to provide a dual capability, nuclear and non-nuclear, and to perform outstandingly in one tactical function and creditably in one or more others—thus providing the *total* force with great flexibility at all levels of conflict. But against a capable enemy, all people and all units cannot do all jobs equally well—if they are to do anything well enough. To meet unique missions and fight in unique environments requires a high degree of specialization, and this in turn requires an ability to train or retrain skilled personnel rapidly; a modern, dynamic and rapidly expandable training capability is absolutely essential to force flexibility.

In the emphasis and publicity given to items of hardware, it is sometimes forgotten that the first necessity is for a highly qualified professional force-in-being capable of quick reaction and rapid doctrinal change. Adaptability and willing institutional support, as opposed to mere obedience, are important elements of a total capability. These are not achieved overnight, although the policy decision to effect change may have to come that quickly. The important requirement is that military doctrine be alive and responsive to shifts in national policy—whatever the individual frustration which may be caused by shifts in the prominence of particular types of weapons and military units.

Second, flexibility is improved by the existence of competent, well-equipped and readily available reserve forces. Whether or not they are activated in a given crisis, their availability provides greater leeway in the employment of active forces. As in the 1961 Berlin crisis, they also serve to reinforce the known U.S. strategy, lending credence to a position which it is most important for the opponent to comprehend fully.

Third, flexibility is enhanced by a broad research and industrial base. We cannot hope to equip our forces completely for every conceivable contingency. However, in particular combat situations, such as Viet Nam, the cost of achieving success can be reduced by a capacity to make swift innovations tailored to the immediate circumstances. In this respect the United States has a relative advantage because of our unequaled economic and technical strength.

These three factors, among others, greatly affect our ability to maintain flexibility in our armed forces. But current choices of specific weapons still under development will also set future boundaries within which policy initiatives can be taken. Acquisition of these weapons will generate new political problems and ease others. It may be instructive to consider a few of these developments and how they both derive from and influence defense policy.

Dramatic increases in range, payload and versatility for both our fighter and airlift forces come quickly to mind—specifically the versatility of the variable-wing F–111 fighter and the huge C–5 cargo aircraft. Both will soon be in our inventory. Ten C–5s could have handled the entire Berlin Airlift, which required more than 140 C–54s (the equivalent of a civilian DC 4). The range of these two aircraft, without refueling, will give us much wider choices as to how many troops and supplies need to be based overseas. For example, the "basic mission" of the C–5 calls for delivering a 100,000-pound payload a distance of 5,500 nautical miles. For shorter ranges of 2,500 miles, the payload increases to 265,000 pounds.

During Operation Big Lift in 1963, we airlifted 15,000 troops, a combat division, from Texas to Europe in 63 hours. This took 204 aircraft. Forty-two C–5s could do the same job in 13 hours. But while Big Lift was a great operational success, even with older aircraft, a number of Europeans expressed apprehension about American "neo-isolationism." While this concern was ill-founded, it is apparent that the broad political implications of our mushrooming airlift and fighter capability have to be continually reëxamined. The structure of our overseas bases will certainly be influenced by the increased capabilities of our troop and cargo carriers and fighters. It will also depend on many strategic factors, such as our estimate of how rapidly conflict might build up in specific locations. In some places, such as Europe, political and military considerations may require us both to have forces immediately available and to have others with which we can reinforce rapidly.

Still another area where current development is likely to affect future policy is our response to subversive insurgency. The Defense Department has given high priority to the development of weapons designed for the unique environment of Southeast Asia. Moreover, we are cutting lead times sharply. Thus far we have been quite successful in translating known technology into more effective non-nuclear ordnance and improved capability for aerial reconnaissance, finding targets, night and all-weather operations, and bombing accuracy. But our performance in these areas still leaves much to be desired; enormous changes for the better can be expected in the future. We are also seeking imaginative and effective ways to remove or transform incipient sources of insurgency wherever they may occur. For example, one of the most important tasks of Air Force Special Air Warfare Forces is to help the people in developing areas to better their economic and social environment. We would prefer to teach indigenous military forces how to use aircraft to fertilize crops rather than to drop bombs, to improve rather than interdict transportation. The problems of these and comparable American units, such as the Army's Special Forces, are as much political as military. Undoubtedly, their experience and success in Viet Nam will have a great bearing on their role in future programs.

Our greatest continuing concern must inevitably be in that area where we stand to lose the most, quickest: general nuclear war. Here we can afford no gaping holes either in our capacity to retaliate or in the technology to ensure that capability. Our most important current effort is the modernization of our strategic offensive forces through acquisition of Minuteman III and Poseidon missiles. This constitutes a forecast of our intention to deter general war by making it unprofitable for any potential enemy. It is important that enemies, allies and neutrals alike be spared misinterpretation. Even beginning development of a particular weapon system can have such an effect, since foreign perceptions are influenced before the weapon is translated into combat capability. By maintaining strategic deterrence, we gain considerable freedom at lesser levels to employ technology in support of strategies that will make limited aggression increasingly unprofitable.

Until greater congruity of purpose exists among nations, military forces will continue to be a foundation of policy. We must be wise enough to manage the interaction between weapons development and defense policy so that our weapons are always responsive to policy and our policy is based on a full consideration of the options made available by technology. This will remain a supreme challenge to policy-makers, who from a position of final responsibility must look at a partially obscure tomorrow and a distant future that seems opaque. They will find, almost invariably, that it is easier to produce military hardware than it is to know what policy to follow.

DEVELOPMENT AND SALIENT FEATURES OF THE PROGRAMMING SYSTEM

BY CHARLES J. HITCH

I have noted that although unification had been achieved in form with the passage of the National Security Act in 1947, it was not until 1961 that the full powers of the Secretary of Defense to run the Department on a unified basis—spelled out by various amendments in the intervening years—were actually used. And I suggested that this situation existed principally because earlier Secretaries of Defense lacked the necessary tools to do so.

. . . From a modest beginning, limited to the protection of our land frontiers against the Indians and our neighbors in Florida and Canada, our national security objectives have expanded to involve us in an interlocking system of free world military alliances with over forty sovereign nations. We now maintain for this purpose by far the largest peacetime establishment in our history. We have, today, a force of almost 2,700,000 military personnel on active duty, supported by about 900,000 civilians in the United States and about one-

Excerpts from the "H. Rowan Gaither Lectures in Systems Science" delivered at the University of California on 5–9 April 1965. Reprinted by permission from The Regents of the University of California, copyright owners, and published under the title *Decision-Making for Defense* (Berkeley and Los Angeles: University of California Press, 1965).

Mr. Hitch is President of the University of California. He previously served as Assistant Secretary of Defense (Comptroller) from 1961 to 1965. He was a Rhodes Scholar and don at Oxford University, and he worked as a senior staff economist at the RAND Corporation where he developed the systems analysis approach to military spending. He is the co-author of *The Economics of Defense in the Nuclear Age* (1960).

quarter of a million overseas, the latter mostly citizens of other countries. In addition, we have almost one million reserve personnel and about one-half million retired military personnel on our payrolls.

Pay alone accounts for more than $20 billion out of a total defense budget of $50 billion. The remaining $30 billion is used to procure a staggeringly large variety of goods and services from the private sector of the economy   aircraft, missiles, tanks, food, clothing, research and development, construction and utilities. We draw from virtually every segment of the American economy and utilize a very large share of the Nation's total research and development capacities. Because of the vast scope of our activities—on the land, on and under the seas, in the air and in space—and the great demands we make on our weapons and equipment, the Defense Department is vitally interested in virtually every field of scientific and technological knowledge. The value of our current inventory of equipment, weapons, and supplies is conservatively estimated at $135 billion. Our principal installations and facilities number in the thousands, and we control nearly 15,000 square miles of land. Our military operations extend around the world, and we spend almost $3 billion a year in other countries.

How, one might ask, can any one man or group of men ever hope to manage such a vast aggregation of men, equipment, installations, and activities spread all over the globe? And yet, . . . the defense effort, to be fully effective, must be managed on a unified basis, not only in the conduct of combat operations but also in the planning and execution of the programs. And, as President Eisenhower stressed in 1958: "It is . . . mandatory that the *initiative* for this planning and direction rest not with the separate services but directly with the Secretary of Defense and his operational advisors. . . ."[1]

---

[1] "Special Message to the Congress on Reorganization of the Defense Establishment, April 3, 1958," *Public Papers of the Presidents, Dwight D. Eisenhower,* 1958 (Washington: U.S. Government Printing Office, 1959), p. 278.

The revolution in military technology since the end of World War II, alone, would make necessary the central planning and direction of the military program. The great technical complexity of modern-day weapons, their lengthy period of development, their tremendous combat power and enormous cost have placed an extraordinary premium on sound choices of major weapon systems. These choices have become, for the top management of the Defense Department, the key decisions around which much else of the defense program revolves. They cannot be made properly by any subordinate echelon of the defense establishment. They must be directly related to our *national* security objectives, rather than simply to the tasks of just one of the military services.

The revolution in military technology has not only changed the character of our military program, it has also, to a significant degree, blurred the lines of demarcation among the various services. Is the missile an unmanned aircraft, as the Air Force likes to think, or extended-range artillery, which is the Army view? Most of our major military missions today require the participation of more than one of the military services. Therefore, our principal concern now must be centered on what is required by the defense establishment as a whole to perform a particular military mission—not on what is required of a particular service to perform its part of that mission. This is not only true with regard to the planning of our military forces and programs, but also with respect to the development of new major weapon systems.

BUDGETING BEFORE 1961

Because, prior to 1961, the Defense Secretaries lacked the tools to manage the overall effort on a truly unified basis, they had to resort (except in times of emergency, like Korea) to what might be described, generically, as the "budget ceiling" approach. The President would indicate the general level of defense expenditures which he felt was appropriate to the international situation and his overall economic and fis-

442   THE PROGRAMMING SYSTEM

cal policies.[2] The Secretary of Defense, by one means or another, would allocate this figure among the three military departments. Each military department would in turn prepare its basic budget submission, allocating its ceiling among its own functions, units, and activities, and present additional requests, which could not be accommodated within the ceiling, in what was variously called an "addendum" budget, "B" lists, etc. Then all the budget submissions were reviewed together by the Office of the Secretary of Defense in an attempt to achieve balance.

Let me make quite clear the fact that this was indeed the traditional way of preparing the defense budget. Frank Pace, then Director of the Bureau of the Budget, in testifying before a congressional committee in 1949 on how the defense budget was prepared in the Truman administration, described the process as follows:

We [the Bureau of the Budget] would provide him [the President] with certain factual information as to where certain policies would lead. From that the President sets a ceiling on the armed services, which was last year, I think, generally known as $15 billion.
However, I think it should be explained that under the ceiling process—and this is not solely for the armed forces but exists for every department of the Government—...
There is also the proviso that if within that limitation it is impossible to include certain programs which the Secretary of Defense considers of imperative importance to the national defense, they shall be included in . . . what is termed the 'B' list. . . . The 'B' list is what cannot be included under the ceiling.[3]

It was recognized long ago that this was a rather inefficient way to go about preparing the defense budget. Its consequences were precisely what could have been pre-

dicted. Each service tended to exercise its own priorities, favoring its own unique missions to the detriment of joint missions, striving to lay the groundwork for an increased share of the budget in future years by concentrating on alluring new weapon systems, and protecting the overall size of its own forces even at the cost of readiness. These decisions were made by patriotic generals and admirals, and by dedicated civilian leaders as well, who were convinced that they were acting in the best interests of the nation as well as their own service—but the end result was not balanced effective military forces.

The Air Force, for example, gave overriding priority to the strategic retaliatory bombers and missiles, starving the tactical air units needed to support the Army ground operations and the airlift units needed to move our limited war forces quickly to far-off trouble spots. The Navy gave over-riding priority to its own nuclear attack forces—notably the aircraft carriers —while its anti-submarine warfare capability was relatively neglected and its escort capability atrophied. The Army used its limited resources to preserve the number of its divisions, although this meant that they lacked equipment and supplies to fight for more than a few weeks.

Moreover, because attention was focused on only the next fiscal year, the services had every incentive to propose large numbers of "new starts," the full cost dimensions of which would only become apparent in subsequent years. This is the "foot in the door" or "thin edge of the wedge" technique which the one-year-at-a-time approach to defense budgeting greatly encouraged.

Another unsatisfactory aspect of this method of attempting to exercise control and direction of the defense effort through the annual budget was the almost complete separation between budgeting and military planning (I speak here of medium and long-range planning, including weapon systems planning—not the contingency planning for the use of existing forces to which I referred in my first lecture).

1. These critically important functions were performed by two different

2 For an interesting example of this technique, see "Memorandum for the Secretary of the Army," June 9, 1960, signed by the Special Assistant to the Secretary of Defense, Mr. O. M. Gale, which outlines the budget guidelines set forth by President Eisenhower at a Cabinet meeting on June 3, 1960. Reprinted in the Congressional Record, June 30, 1960, vol. 106, part 11, pp. 15100–15101.

3 Hearings on S. 1269 and S. 1843, U.S. Senate, Committee on Armed Services, 81st Cong., 1st Sess., April 6, 1949 (Washington: U.S. Government Printing Office, 1949), p. 79.

groups of people—the planning by the military planners and the budgeting by the civilian secretaries and the comptroller organizations.

2. Budget control was exercised by the Secretary of Defense but planning remained essentially in the services. It was not until 1955–56 that the first Joint Strategic Objective Plan (JSOP), projecting the requirements for major forces some four to five years into the future, was prepared by the Joint Chiefs of Staff organization, but the early JSOP was essentially a "pasting together" of unilaterally developed service plans.

3. Whereas the planning horizon extended four or more years into the future, the budget was projected only one year ahead, although it was clear to all involved that the lead time from the start of a weapon development to the equipping of the forces ranged from five to ten years, depending on the character of the particular development effort.

4. Planning was performed in terms of missions, weapon systems, and military units or forces—the "outputs" of the Defense Department; budgeting, on the other hand, was done in terms of such "inputs" or intermediate products as personnel, operation and maintenance, procurement, construction, etc.; and there was little or no machinery for translating one into the other.

5. Budgeting, however crudely, faced up to fiscal realities. The planning was fiscally unrealistic and, therefore, of little help to the decision-maker. The total implicit budget costs of the unilateral service plans or of the Joint Strategic Objectives Plan always far exceeded any budget that any Secretary of Defense or administration was willing to request of the Congress.

6. Military requirements tended to be stated in absolute terms, without reference to their costs. But the military effectiveness or military worth of any given weapon system cannot logically be considered in isolation. It must be considered in relation to its cost—and

in a world in which resources are limited, to the alternative uses to which the resources can be put. Military requirements are meaningful only in terms of benefits to be gained in relation to their cost. Accordingly, resource costs and military worth have to be scrutinized together.

As a consequence, the Secretary each year found himself in a position where he had, at least implicitly, to make major decisions on forces and programs without adequate information and all within the few weeks allocated to his budget review. Moreover, every year the plans and programs of each of the services had to be cut back severely to fit the budget ceiling, by program cancellations, stretch-outs, or postponements— but only for that year. Beyond the budget year, unrealistic plans continued to burgeon —perhaps next year the ceiling would be higher.

These deficiencies did not go unnoticed in the Congress. Representative George Mahon, then Chairman of the House Defense Appropriations Subcommittee and now also Chairman of the full Committee, addressed two letters to the Secretary of Defense in the summer of 1959 and fall of 1960. In his first letter he stressed the importance of looking at the defense program and budget in terms of major military missions, by grouping programs and their cost by mission.[4] In his second letter, he called "for more useful information and for a practical means of relating costs to missions."[5]

Many other students of the defense management problem had reached the same conclusion, including the group with which I had the honor to be associated at the RAND Corporation. Many of these conclusions found their way into a book, *The Economics of Defense in the Nuclear Age*[6]

[4] Letter from Representative George H. Mahon, Chairman of the House Subcommittee on Defense Appropriations, to Secretary of Defense Neil McElroy, August 18, 1959 (unpublished).

[5] Letter from Representative Mahon to Secretary of Defense Thomas S. Gates, September 6, 1960 (unpublished).

[6] Charles J. Hitch and Roland N. McKean, *The Economics of Defense in the Nuclear Age* (Cambridge, Mass.: Harvard University Press, 1960).

MILITARY PLANNING	BUDGETING
FY 60 $\longrightarrow$	FY 60

ARMY

- Infantry Divisions
- _____
- Armored Regiments
- Hawk Anti-Aircraft Bns.
- _____
- Engineer Combat Bns.
- Aviation Companies

NAVY

- Attack Carriers
- Attack Submarines
- _____
- Mine Warfare Vessels
- _____
- Marine Air Wings

AIR FORCE

- Heavy Bomber Wings
- _____
- Fighter Interceptor Sqds.
- Tactical Reconnaissance Sqds.
- Troop Carrier Sqds.
- _____

ARMY

- Military Personnel
- Operation & Maintenance
- Procurement
- Res., Dev., Test & Eval.
- Military Construction

NAVY

- Military Personnel
- Operation and Maintenance
- _____
- _____
- _____

AIR FORCE

- Military Personnel
- _____
- _____
- _____
- _____

which the RAND Corporation first published in March 1960, some ten months before I was called upon as Assistant Secretary of Defense (Comptroller) to help introduce them into the Defense Department.

BUDGETING AFTER 1961

The new Secretary of Defense, Robert S. McNamara, made it clear from the beginning that he intended to be the kind of Secretary that President Eisenhower had in mind in 1958 and take the initiative in the planning and direction of defense program. In a television interview, after having been in office less than one month, Secretary McNamara defined his managerial philosophy as follows:

I think that the role of public manager is very similar to the role of a private manager; in each case he has the option of following one of two major alternative courses of action. He can either act as a judge or a leader. In the former case, he sits and waits until subordinates bring to him problems for solution, or

alternatives for choice. In the latter case, he immerses himself in the operations of the business or the governmental activity, examines the problems, the objectives, the alternative courses of action, chooses among them, and leads the organization to their accomplishment. In the one case it's a passive role; in the other case, an active role. . . . I have always believed in and endeavored to follow the active leadership role as opposed to the passive judicial role.[7]

Furthermore, Secretary McNamara made it known that he wanted to manage the defense effort in terms of meaningful program entities—of "outputs" like the B–52 force, the POLARIS force, the Army Airborne Division force, etc., associating with each output all the inputs of equipment, personnel, supplies, facilities, and funds, regardless of the appropriation account in which financed. He wanted to know and, indeed, would have to know in order to optimize the allocation of resources, the

[7] Extract from the transcript of an interview with Secretary of Defense Robert S. McNamara on the National Broadcasting Company program, "Today," February 17, 1961.

cost of, for example, a B–52 wing—not only the cost of equipping the wing but also the cost of manning and operating it for its lifetime or at least for a reasonable period of years in the future. Only then would he be in a position to assess the cost and effectiveness of a B–52 wing as compared with other systems designed to perform the same or similar tasks.

Moreover, he wanted to know the total costs of the forces assigned to each of the major missions—the costs of the strategic offensive forces, the continental defense forces, the general purpose forces, etc. As General Maxwell Taylor had pointed out to a congressional committee in 1960:

. . . If we are called upon to fight, we will not be interested in the services as such. We will be interested rather in task forces, those combinations of Army, Navy, and Air Force which are functional in nature, such as the atomic retaliatory forces, overseas deployments, continental air defense forces, limited war expeditionary forces, and the like. But the point is that we do not keep our budget in these terms. Hence it is not an exaggeration to say that we do not know what kind and how much defense we are buying with any specific budget.[8]

These views closely coincided with my own. The Secretary and I both realized that the financial management system of the Defense Department must serve many purposes. It must produce a budget in a form acceptable to the Congress. It must account for the funds in the same manner in which they were appropriated. It must provide the managers at all levels in the defense establishment the financial information they need to do their particular jobs in an effective and economical manner. It must produce the financial information required by other agencies of the government—the Bureau of the Budget, the Treasury, and the General Accounting Office.

[8] Statement of Gen. Maxwell D. Taylor, *Hearings on Organizing for National Security*, Subcommittee on National Policy Machinery, Committee on Government Operations, U.S. Senate, 86th Cong., 2d Sess., June 14, 1960 (Washington: U.S. Government Printing Office, 1960), p. 769.

But we both were convinced that the financial management system must also provide the data needed by top defense management to make the really crucial decisions, particularly on the major forces and weapons systems needed to carry out the principal missions of the defense establishment. And we were well aware that the financial management system, as it had evolved over the years, could not directly produce the required data in the form desired. It was clear that a new function, which we call programming, would have to be incorporated in the financial management system. I had hoped that I would have at least a year to smooth the way for the introduction of this new function. I recall outlining the proposed programming system to Secretary McNamara in the spring of 1961 and recommending that we spend 18 months developing and installing it, beginning in the first year with a limited number of trial programs, with a view to expanding the system to include all programs during 1962. The Secretary approved the proposed system but shortened my timetable from eighteen months to six. Somehow we developed and installed it, department-wide, in time to use it as a basis for the FY 1963 defense budget. Submitted to Congress in January 1962, this was, of course, the first budget to be prepared wholly under the new administration.

Since the military planning function and the budget function were already well established, the role of programming was to provide a bridge between the two. It was, of course, theoretically possible to recast both the planning and budget structures in terms of major programs related to missions. In fact, the military planning operation was later adapted to the program structure, and I once thought that the budget structure should be similarly realigned. You will find on page 56 of *The Economics of Defense in the Nuclear Age* a format for such a program budget.

But the existing budget structure serves some very useful purposes. It is organized, essentially, in terms of resource categories: (1) Military Personnel; (2) Operation and Maintenance; (3) Procurement; (4) Research, Development, Test and Evaluation; and (5) Military Construction.

This type of structure lends itself ideally to the manner in which the Defense Department actually manages its resources. While military planning and the formulation of programs should logically be done in terms of missions and forces, the Department must be managed not only in those terms but also in terms of resources. For example, we have to manage the acquisition, training, and careers of military personnel; the operation of bases and facilities; the procurement of aircraft, missiles, ships, and tanks; the research and development program; and the construction of airfields, missile sites, quarters, and other additions to our existing physical plant. The present budget structure facilitates the estimation of resource costs as well as the execution of the resource programs.

This division of the budget by broad input or resource categories also provides needed flexibility for the adjustments in the program that are inevitably required in the course of the budget year. Program priorities and requirements always change in unanticipated ways even in the course of a single year as a result of international developments, technological breakthroughs (or disappointments), and all sorts of other events. It is important not to freeze programs in appropriation bills.

Finally, the Congress, and particularly the Appropriations Committees, prefer the existing arrangement of the defense budget.[9] They have been working with it for more than a decade and have established an historical basis for forming judgments on the validity of the budget requests. It is much easier for an Appropriations Committee, for example, to review a budget request of $4.3 billion for pay and allowances for 960,000 active duty Army personnel than, say, a request of $18 or $19 billion for the major program "General Purpose Forces," or even a request of $700 million for the program element "Army In-

fantry Divisions." Although the President, under the Budget and Accounting Act of 1921, can propose his budget in any form he pleases, it is the Congress that determines how the funds will be appropriated and this, in turn, determines how the funds will be accounted for. I now feel that the advantages of the existing budget structure far outweigh the disadvantages, which are principally mechanical, namely, the need to translate program categories into budget categories and vice versa. This is the sort of disadvantage that modern high speed computers are well designed to overcome.

Accordingly, we decided to leave the budget structure undisturbed and to span the gap between planning and budgeting with the new programming function. This resulted in a three phase operation: planning-programming-budgeting.

PLANNING PHASE

The first phase—military planning and requirements determination—we envisioned as a continuing year-around operation involving the participation of all appropriate elements of the Defense Department in their respective areas of responsibility. We anticipated that the Joint Chiefs of Staff organization and the planners in the military departments would play a particularly important role in this phase. What we were looking for here were not just requirement studies in the traditional sense, but military-economic studies which compared alternative ways of accomplishing national security objectives and which tried to determine the one that contributes the most for a given cost or achieves a given objective at the least cost. These are what we call "cost-effectiveness studies" or systems analyses, and are the subject of my third lecture.

I had originally thought that once an approved five-year program had been developed, the Joint Chiefs of Staff organization and the military planners in the departments would concentrate their attention on specific segments of the program which might require change, and that they would propose such changes whenever the need became apparent any time during the

9 For example, see House of Representatives Report No. 1607, 87th Cong., 2d Sess., (House Committee on Appropriations Report on the Department of Defense Budget for Fiscal Year 1963), April 13, 1962, pp. 4–7.

year. When these change proposals were approved, the five-year program would be modified accordingly, thereby providing an up-to-date long range plan at all times. But I had given too little weight to the need to review and analyze, at least once a year, the entire long range program in all of its interrelated parts, rather than in bits and pieces during the course of the entire year. I must confess that the Joint Chiefs of Staff saw this need more clearly than I did. They wanted to make a comprehensive program review each year to take account of the latest changes in military technology and in the international situation; so did each of the military departments; and so did the Secretary.

Accordingly, the planning-programming-budgeting process now starts with the Joint Strategic Objectives Plan prepared by the Joint Chiefs of Staff organization with the help of the military planners in the services. As I noted earlier, the format of this plan has been modified to bring it into harmony with the new program structure. Thus, the Joint Chiefs of Staff have the opportunity each year to recommend to the Secretary of Defense on a comprehensive basis the military forces and major programs which they believe should be supported over the next five to eight years. The Secretary of Defense in the spring of each year reviews these recommended forces and programs, makes preliminary decisions, and provides to the military departments what is called "tentative force guidance" to serve as a basis for the preparation of their formal change proposals to the official five-year program. The principal "cost-effectiveness" studies are scheduled for completion at about the same time in order to provide the Secretary and his principal advisors with information in depth on the most critical and difficult requirement problems.

I recall that the first list of these requirements projects was developed by Secretary McNamara and was known at the time as "McNamara's 100 trombones." These projects were assigned to the Joint Chiefs of Staff, the military departments, and various elements of the Office of the Secretary of Defense. One, for example, dealt with the question of how many strategic bombers and missiles we would need during the next decade to destroy priority targets. Another involved an examination of requirements for airlift and sealift to meet various contingency war plans and the most economical means of providing that lift. Still another dealt with the comparative advantages and cost of: (a) refurbishing existing items of ground equipment, (b) replacing them with new equipment off the assembly lines, and (c) expediting the development of still better equipment. The Secretary of Defense still originates many of these requirements studies. Others are originated by the Joint Chiefs of Staff, the military departments, and various elements of the Secretary's staff.

PROGRAMMING PHASE

The initial development of the programming system, the second phase, was an enormous undertaking, considering the short time allowed and the fact that we had to handle simultaneously three amendments to the fiscal year 1962 budget originally prepared by the preceding administration. The problem here was to sort out all of the myriad programs and activities of the defense establishment and regroup them into meaningful program elements, i.e., integrated combinations of men, equipment, and installations whose effectiveness could be related to our national security objectives. These are the basic building blocks as well as the decision-making levels of the programming process. As I noted earlier, the B–52 bomber force, together with all the supplies, weapons, and manpower needed to make it militarily effective, is one such program element. Other examples are Attack Carriers, F–4 Fighter Wings, the Manned Orbiting Laboratory development project, and Recruit Training. Wherever possible, program elements are measured in physical terms such as numbers of aircraft per wing, numbers of operational missiles on launchers, numbers of active ships, and so forth as well as in financial terms, thus including both "input" and "output"—costs and benefits. Of course, such program elements as research

COST CATEGORIES

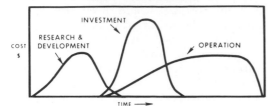

Research and Development: Development of a new capability to the point of introduction into operational use.

Investment: Costs required beyond the development phase to equip forces with new capability.

Operation: Recurring costs required to operate and maintain the capability.

---

projects can only be measured in terms of inputs.

Costs are measured in terms of what we call "total obligational authority"—the amount required to finance the program element in a given year, regardless of when the funds are appropriated by the Congress, obligated, placed on contract, or spent. Now, admittedly, this is something of a compromise.[10] It would be preferable to cost the program in terms of expenditures, or ideally in terms of resources consumed. However, the accounting difficulties appeared so great that we did not attempt that approach. Moreover, as long as the budget is in terms of obligational authority, the program must be, for the program has to be firmly anchored to the budget. We do not even find it necessary to cost individual program elements in terms of cash expenditures. We have a much better idea of the full cost of 100 MINUTEMAN missiles, for example, than of the phasing of the actual expenditures year by year. And from the point of view of planning and decision-making we are far more interested in the full cost of a program—in "cost to complete"—than in the precise phasing of the costs.

[10] For further discussion of program element costs as well as a description of the Defense programming system in 1962, see *Programming System for the Office of the Secretary of Defense, 25 June 1962* (Washington: U.S. Government Printing Office, 1963).

To tie in with the "branch points" at which critical decisions must be made, we subdivide program costs into three categories: development costs, investment costs, and operating costs. Because of the great expense involved in just developing a new weapon system to the point where it could be produced and deployed, a determination to go ahead with full-scale development is, in itself, a major decision. There are few major weapon system developments today that can be accomplished for less than $1 billion. For example, we will have spent $1.5 billion making two prototypes of the B–70. We have already spent $1.5 billion developing the NIKE-ZEUS antiballistic missile system and are now spending a comparable amount on the NIKE X. We spent $2.3 billion developing the ATLAS ICBM, $2.6 billion on TITAN, $2.5 billion on POLARIS, and $2.1 billion on MINUTEMAN I. Even the development of a new torpedo can cost as much as $75 million. Therefore, we need to know in advance the likely cost of completing any major weapon development.

Obviously, before we go ahead with the next phase, production and deployment, we need to know the investment cost of providing initial equipment for the proposed forces. And, finally, we need to know the cost of operating the proposed forces each year. In many cases, for example a B–52 wing, the five-year operating costs are about equal to the initial equipment costs, and in some few cases, for example an infantry division, the operating costs for just one year are actually greater than the initial investment costs.

To facilitate the conversion of program costs to the budget and vice versa, we also had to break down the costs of each program element by the various budget appropriation accounts in which it is financed. Operating costs typically are financed in the "Military Personnel" and "Operation and Maintenance" appropriations and, where operating spares are involved, in the "Procurement" accounts as well. Initial investment costs typically are financed in the "Procurement" and "Military Construction" appropriations.

ANNUAL PPBS CYCLE

PHASE	MAJOR DOCUMENT	PREPARED BY	APPROXIMATE DATE DONE
PLANNING	JSOP	JCS	MARCH
	TENTATIVE FORCE GUIDANCE	OSD	APR–MAY
PROGRAMMING	PCP'S *	SERVICES	APR–JUN
	5–YEAR PROGRAM	OSD	BY 31 AUG
BUDGETING	SERVICE BUDGET	SERVICES	OCT
	DOD BUDGET	OSD	DEC TO PRESIDENT
			JAN TO CONGRESS

* DRAFT PRESIDENTIAL MEMOS (DPM'S) ARE NOW USED FOR MAJOR–FORCE ORIENTED CHANGES.

Editors' Note: The above chart is not part of the Hitch article. It was prepared by the editors as a teaching aid.

We have nearly 1,000 program elements. Where military forces are involved, they are projected eight years ahead in order to provide the necessary lead time for the determination of the procurement programs. All other program data, both physical and financial, are projected five years ahead. For purposes of continuity, all program data are shown for each year beginning in fiscal year 1962; thus, our present Five-Year Force Structure and Financial Program extends from fiscal year 1962 through fiscal year 1970, with forces projected through fiscal year 1973. The entire program is subject to continual change and is, therefore, updated every other month. Whenever a change is made in the cost of a program element in the current fiscal year, it must also be reflected in the budget for the same year and vice versa. Considering the vast quantities of data involved in the planning-programming-budgeting system, the only practical solution was to computerize the entire operation. This we have now accomplished.

The next task was to relate the program elements to the major missions of the Defense Department. The objective here was to assemble related groups of program elements that, for decision purposes, should be considered together either because they supported one another or because they were close substitutes. The unifying principle underlying each major program is a common mission or set of purposes for the elements involved. We now have nine major programs—

    I. Strategic Retaliatory Forces.
    II. Continental Defense Forces.
    III. General Purpose Forces.
    IV. Airlift and Sealift.
    V. Reserve and Guard.
    VI. Research and Development.
    VII. General Support.
    VIII. Retired Pay.
    IX. Military Assistance.

The Strategic Retaliatory Forces program includes the manned bomber forces, the land-based missile forces, the sea-based missile forces, and related headquarters and command support activities. Within the aircraft forces are the B–52 long-range bombers together with their air-to-ground HOUND DOG missiles and QUAIL decoy missiles, the B–58 and B–47 medium bombers, and the refueling tankers. Within the missile forces are the ATLAS, TITAN, and MINUTEMAN ICBM's and the POLARIS submarine-launched missiles. Also included in the Strategic Retaliatory Forces are the SR–71 and other strategic reconnaissance air-

craft and the special communication links and control systems, such as the Post Attack Command and Control System aircraft, which are required for the effective direction of these forces.

The Continental Defense Forces, which might be called the strategic defensive forces, include the North American surveillance, warning, and control network, consisting of land-based, sea-based, and airborne radars and control centers; the manned interceptors; the surface-to-air missiles; the ballistic missile warning systems; the anti-satellite defense systems; and the civil defense program.

All of the forces in these two major programs would come into play in a general nuclear war. And, as a matter of interest, we have, during the last year, broadened our analyses to treat all of these forces simultaneously in the context of a general nuclear war. This is important because the strategic offensive forces also make a contribution to the "damage limiting" mission, which is the principal purpose of the Continental Defense Forces. A portion of our strategic offensive forces can be applied against an enemy's strategic offensive forces,

STRATEGIC RETALIATORY FORCES

AIRCRAFT FORCES

- B-47
- RB/B-47
- B-52
- B-58
- KC-97
- KC-135
- RC-135

MISSILE FORCES

LAND-BASED

- ATLAS
- TITAN
- MINUTEMAN

SEA-BASED

- FLEET BALLISTIC MISSILE SYSTEM (POLARIS)
- REGULUS MISSILE SYSTEM

COMMAND CONTROL, COMMUNICATION & SUPPORT

- SAC CONTROL SYSTEM
- POST-ATTACK COMMAND & COMMUNICATIONS SYSTEM
- BASE OPERATING SUPPORT
- ADVANCE FLYING AND MISSILE TRAINING
- HEADQUARTERS AND COMMAND SUPPORT

GENERAL PURPOSE FORCES ARMY
COMBATANT FORCES

DIVISIONS		Missile Commands
by type		

Brigades		S S Missile Battalions
by type		by type - Sep/Org.

Maneuver Battalions		Air Defense Batteries
by type - Sep/Org.		by type - Sep/Org.

Artillery Battalions		Aviation Companies
by type - Sep/Org.		Sep/Org.

Other Combat Battalions		Other Combat Forces
by type - Sep/Org.		

Special Forces Groups		Combat Support Units

Armored Cavalry Rgmnts.		Provisional Air Mobile Units

Command & Support Forces

Logistic and Support Forces   Support to Non-Army Agencies
Command and Admin. Forces   PACOM & EUCOM Elint. Centers
Base Support

thus reducing under certain circumstances the potential weight of his attack.

The third, and the largest, major program is that for the General Purpose Forces. These are the forces designed to fight local or limited wars and to engage in theater operations in general war. This major program is organized broadly along service lines. Within the service breakdowns, the basic identifiable combat units form the program elements. Army General Purpose Forces include almost all of the regular combat units and command support elements. They range from the four basic kinds of divisions—infantry, armor, mechanized, and airborne—through the missile commands to artillery battalions, air defense units for the field army, and aviation companies.

GENERAL PURPOSE FORCES—NAVY

Attack Carrier Strike Forces
Attack Carriers (By Type)
Attack Carrier Air Groups

Surv. & Ocean Control Forces
ASW Aircraft Carriers
Carrier ASW Air Groups
Submarines

Escort Ships
Small Patrol Ships
Patrol Aircraft (Sqdns)

Mine Warfare Forces

Amphibious Assault Forces

Multi-purpose Combat Forces
Cruisers
Frigates
Destroyers

Special Combat Support Forces

Logistic & Oper. Support Forces

Comd. Commun. & Comd. Support

Marine Corps Div. Wing Teams
Marine Divisions
Tank Battalions
Light Anti-Aircraft Msle. Bns.
Honest John Bns.
Amphib. Tractor Bns.
Other Combat Support Forces
Marine Air Wings
Air Sta. & Air Facil.
Hq. Fleet Marine Forces

Reserve Fleet Forces

Fleet Support Bases, Sta. & Activ.

The Navy's list is even longer, embracing all of the combatant ships and support vessels except for the strategic missile firing submarines, the radar warning picket ships, and the Military Sea Transportation Service ships. All of the fleet's various aircraft units are also included except, of course, those assigned to airborne early warning as part of the continental defense system. Components of Navy General Purpose Forces include the carrier task forces and anti-submarine warfare forces.

All Marine Corps units are listed under General Purpose Forces, including the Marine aircraft wings.

The Air Force General Purpose Forces consist principally of those units assigned to the Tactical Air Command in the United States and to the theater commands overseas. The tactical fighters and bombers, tactical reconnaissance aircraft, and the MACE missiles, and their associated command and control systems and headquarters, all fall within this category.

The fourth major program is that for Airlift and Sealift. The troop carrier wings of the Air Force, including theater airlift, the Military Air Transport Service aircraft, and the Military Sea Transportation Service ships, make up the essential components of this group.

The fifth major program is composed of the Reserve and National Guard Forces. The program elements are arranged by service and by the major mission each element or unit supports. Actually, Reserve and National Guard program elements are reviewed as parts of the appropriate mission packages—Continental Defense Forces, General Purpose Forces, Airlift and Sealift Forces, and so forth, as well as in the context of the reserve components themselves. This is a case where for decision purposes we want visibility both ways—as reserve components and as parts of mission forces.

The sixth major program, Research and Development, includes all of the R&D projects which are not directly associated with program elements in other major programs. The R&D program elements are grouped into several categories, ranging from pencil pushing to operational hardware—

1. Research—the effort directed toward the expansion of knowledge of natural phenomena and our environment and the solution of problems in the physical, biological, medical, behavioral, social, and engineering sciences.
2. Exploratory Developments—the effort directed toward the expansion of technological knowledge and the development of materials, components, devices, and sub-systems which it is hoped will have some useful application to new military weapons and equipment. Here the emphasis is on exploring the feasibility of new ideas, up to the point of demonstration with "breadboard" devices and prototype components and sub-systems.
3. Advanced Developments—the effort directed toward the development of experimental hardware for technical or operational testing of its suitability for military purposes, prior to the determination of whether the item should be designed or engineered for actual service use. Here is where we begin to identify each project with a specific

GENERAL PURPOSE FORCES—AIR FORCE

Tactical Aircraft Forces

F–84	B–57
F–100	B–66
F–101	RF–101
F–104	RF–4
F–105	RF–111
F–4C	RB–66
F–111	KB–50

Interceptor Aircraft Forces
F–102

Surface-to-surface Missile Forces
MACE

Counterinsurgency Forces

Command Control Comm. & Support
Air Weapon Control System
PACOM & EUCOM ELINT Centers
Other Communications
Base Operating Support
Advanced Flying Training
Hq. & Command Support

military application or technique, and we begin to question in depth its potential military utility. During this phase we also begin to explore the costs of the most likely applications in order to determine whether the potential operational benefit would be worth the cost of development, production, and deployment.

4. Engineering Developments—the effort directed toward the development of a particular system engineered for service use and for operational employment, but which has not as yet been approved for production and deployment. It is at this point that large commitments of resources must be made to single projects. Accordingly, before full-scale development is initiated, the specific operational requirements and the cost-effectiveness of the system must be confirmed, and goals, milestones, and time schedules must be established.

5. Operational Systems Developments—the effort directed toward the continued development, test, evaluation, and design improvement of projects which have already entered (or have been approved for) the production-deployment stage—are included in other major programs as integral parts of the appropriate program elements. For example, the continuing development of MINUTEMAN II is included in the program element "MINUTEMAN II" under the major program "Strategic Retaliatory Forces."*

The seventh major program, General Support, is the "all other" program containing all of the activities not readily allocable to mission forces or weapons systems. Some of its major subcategories are: individual training and education including recruit training, technical training, flight training, and service academies; communications between higher headquarters and

unified commands; most intelligence collection; medical services; support of higher headquarters; and so forth. In dollar value this is a large category accounting for almost 30% of the total defense budget. It is essentially the "overhead" of the Defense Department, although much of it, like training, is "variable" overhead.

The eighth major program, Retired Pay, has been separately identified because it represents costs beyond our direct control. The terms of retirement and the rates of pay are established by law. Expenditures for this purpose will amount to $1.5 billion in the next fiscal year and are increasing rapidly as World War II veterans join the retired ranks.

The last major program, Military Assistance, includes the military equipment and training being provided to some 59 foreign nations. For administrative purposes, we have found it best to retain this activity as a separate program."[11]

All of the program data, together with the description of the forces, their tasks and missions, procurement lists, facility lists and so forth, constitute, collectively, what we term "The Five-Year Force Structure and Financial Program." Since the data are machine processed, they can be summarized in different ways. For the use of top management in the Defense Department we prepare and update at regular intervals a special summary volume which displays in tabular form the forces, financial, manpower, and procurement programs. The Five-Year Force Structure and Financial Program is formally approved by the Secretary of Defense and is binding for programming purposes on all components of the Department.

We recognized from the beginning that the defense program is extremely dynamic and that changes would be required at various times during the year. Accordingly, we

---

* The Armed Services Procurement Regulation, Rev. 8, 1 Nov. 1964, also lists a sixth category, *Management and Support*. This category includes all effort directed toward support of installations or operations required for general research and development use.

[11] For another, fuller description of the Defense programming system, see presentation and testimony of Assistant Secretary Hitch, *Hearings on Systems Development and Management*, Subcommittee of the Committee on Government Operations, House of Representatives, 87th Cong., 2d Sess. (Washington: U.S. Government Printing Office, 1962), pp. 513–547.

established a formal program change control system. The basic elements of this system involve the submission of program change proposals by any major component of the Defense Department, their review by all interested components, the Secretary's decision on each proposal, and finally the assignment of responsibility for carrying out this particular decision to the appropriate military department or agency. Hundreds of program change proposals are submitted each year requesting changes involving billions of dollars.

BUDGETING PHASE

This brings us to the third phase of the planning-programming-budgeting process. It may be worth emphasizing at this point that the programming review is not intended as a substitute for the annual budget review. Rather, it is designed to provide a Defense Department-approved program to serve as a basis for the preparation of the annual budget as well as guidance for future planning. In the budget review we go into greater detail, for the next year of the Five-Year Program, on procurement lists, production schedules, lead times, prices, status of funds, and all the other facets involved in the preparation of an annual budget. And, as I pointed out earlier, we still manage our funds in terms of the appropriation accounts as well as in terms of the program structure. Essentially, the annual budget now represents a detailed analysis of the financial requirements of

the first annual increment of the approved Five-Year Program.

Thus, we have provided for the Secretary of Defense and his principal military and civilian advisors a system which brings together at one place and at one time all of the relevant information which they need to make sound decisions on the forward program and to control the execution of that program. And we have provided the necessary flexibility in the form of a program change control system. Now, for the first time the largest business in the world has a comprehensive Defense Department-wide plan that extends more than one year into the future. And it is a realistic and responsible one—programming not only the forces, but also the men, equipment, supplies, installations, and budget dollars required to support them. Budgets are in balance with programs, programs with force requirements, force requirements with military missions, and military missions with national security objectives. And the total budget dollars required by the plan for future years do not exceed the Secretary's responsible opinion of what is necessary and feasible.

With this management tool at his command, the Secretary of Defense is now in a position to carry out the responsibilities assigned to him by the National Security Act, namely, to exercise "direction, authority, and control over the Department of Defense"—and without another major reorganization of the defense establishment.

THE EASY MAGIC OF SYSTEMS ANALYSIS

BY WESLEY W. POSVAR

When I once discovered my first principles, everything I sought for appeared.—Montesquieu, Preface to The Spirit of the Laws.

The story is told about the high defense official, confident in the methods of systems analysis, and faced with a personal decision. He owned two self-winding watches (purchased in Hong Kong while returning from a quick trip to Vietnam) that had both become defective. The first lost four seconds every day; the second had stopped completely. So he called in his Chief Systems Analyst, and asked him to evaluate these two chronological "systems" and recommend what to do.

After study, the recommendation was clear: throw away the first watch and keep the second. Calculation showed that the first watch was correct only once every fifty-nine years, and the second was correct twice a day.

This is something more than a bad joke. It illustrates the fact that systems analysis, while it is a superb decisionmaking tool, operates in a broader setting that requires human judgment. Calculations may be precise, but the results of an analysis may be erroneous because it was too narrow in scope, or based on a wrong assumption, or addressed to the wrong question. An appreciation of systems analysis, therefore, calls for a balanced understanding of both its methods and its limitations in respect to the solution of policy questions. That balanced understanding is the purpose of the discussion that follows.

First, what is systems analysis? It is a term of many uses. It was previously referred to as an organizational arrangement and a multidisciplinary approach: a collectivity of experts from different fields, engaging in close intercourse, and producing studies in which the worth of the whole product wonderfully exceeds the sum of its individual inputs. In the context of administrative politics, especially now that there is an Assistant Secretary of Defense just for systems analysis, the term also becomes a focus of controversy. It evokes strong irritation in its critics and a missionary kind of enthusiasm in its practitioners and followers. In respect to its reliance upon scientific investigation and mathematics, systems analysis may be regarded as operations research expanded to the national level. Secretary McNamara calls it "quantitative common sense."

To define it fully, however, systems analysis must be viewed in an economic perspective. It contributes to defense decision-making in the economic dimension, where goods are scarce and are distributed among competing needs. More precisely, in the economic dimension it becomes necessary to evaluate a whole panoply of possible "systems," in the form of missions, programs, and weapons, according to their "cost-effectiveness." The resources for defense, consisting of funds, men, and materials, must then be distributed among these systems—more to some, less to others, nothing to yet others. So systems analysis for national defense may be defined as the study of major security programs, or "systems," in the total context of international conflict, in order to facilitate the allocation of resources among those systems.

Systems analysis has a powerful mystique. Hopefully, in the sections that follow the mystique will fade somewhat and systems analysis will be revealed more realistically as an extraordinarily useful procedure, yet built upon concepts that are basic and comprehensible. The Secretary of Defense refers to those concepts continually throughout his annual testimonies to Con-

Reprinted by permission of The Viking Press, Inc. The article is a chapter from a book manuscript to be published by The Viking Press, Inc.

gress.[1] He compares programs according to the "increments of effectiveness" that would be obtained by spending more on each of them. In evaluating different attack systems, he refers to their "marginal value." In discussing targeting concepts, he speaks of "diminishing returns" in the destruction obtainable beyond a limited number of enemy targets. He refers to the desirable "mix" of bombers and missiles and the "sensitivity" of the future effectiveness of U.S. forces to unexpected changes in Soviet defensive weapons.

It is true that complicated mathematical techniques, such as linear programming, are employed in systems analysis. Banks of computers assimilate acres of data and print out miles of digits. The technical aspects of analysis often require highly trained personnel, men who are at home in computer cubicles and whose talk with one another is beyond the ken of outsiders. The point to remember, though, is that the important judgments (as well as the great mistakes) of defense management can usually be explained in simple and nontechnical terms. This means that an intelligent discourse among those responsible for making or influencing the big program decisions is not only desirable but quite feasible.

MARGINAL COMPARISONS

The first analytical concept to consider is that of marginal comparison. For those in whom this phrase awakens dim memories of a basic course long ago in "Principles of Economics," there is here, at last, gratification that an academic principle can have practical applications of grave importance. The principle is a key device for judging all military functions and weapons, large and small. It helps determine how some $60 billion shall be distributed in meeting diverse and competitive defense needs each year. The principle serves as the arbitrator among these needs—the lever

by which huge programs are kept in balance with one another. It is probably the most valuable single analytical tool in the Secretary of Defense's kit for Gargantuan management.

The principle of marginal comparison is nonetheless easy to understand and apply. This can be illustrated by going, step by step, through an example. Consider the problem of determining the size of a new missile force.[2] For the sake of simplicity, suppose that the strategic planners decide that their force should be aimed at 100 different targets, in order to implement a modest strategy of deterrence. Suppose too that the operations research staff has computed that each missile will have a 30% probability of target destruction. (This simplified figure may be obtained, incidentally, by multiplying together other operational factors: the probability for each missile of being fired successfully, of detonating, and of destroying the target at the missile's average miss distance [known as the "circular error probable," or CEP].) How many missiles, then, are "required" in the missile force?

One further specification is needed—the overall level of target destruction to be attained. Since perfection is impossible, it seems reasonable to specify a level of destruction somewhere below 100%. A reasonable and safe figure seems to be 90%. By using the given data, it can be calculated that to destroy 90 targets, on the average, will require a force of 645 missiles. The calculation employs a relatively simple binomial equation that defines the relationships among the factors stated above.[3]

This seems to be a straightforward and scientific solution. All elements of the anal-

---

[1] For example, see the statement of Secretary of Defense Robert S. McNamara before the House Armed Services Committee on the Fiscal Year 1966–70 Defense Program and 1966 Defense Budget, February 18, 1965. Most of the phrases quoted are found on pp. 40–43.

[2] This example is similar to ones used by Alain C. Enthoven, "Systems Analysis and the Navy," *Naval Review 1965* (Annapolis, United States Naval Institute, 1964) and also by Charles J. Hitch, *Decision Making for Defense* (Berkeley: University of California Press, 1965), p. 51.

[3] The equation used is $D = T [1 - (1 - k)^{\frac{M}{T}}]$, where D is the number of targets destroyed, T is the number of targets attacked (given as 100), k is the probability of destruction of each target (given as 30%), and M is the number of missiles employed. When D is 90, the calculation requires the use of logarithms and M is solved to be 645.

ysis are clearly defined. Where assumptions are made regarding operational factors, those assumptions are exposed and made explicit.

In this respect, the example is representative of more complex computations that have often been employed to produce force requirements.[4] The early Pentagon plans for procurement of the B–52 bomber force, for instance, were supported by calculations of what force would be sufficient to destroy a given target system, with assumed rates of bomber aborts, losses to air defenses, target misses, duds, and so on.

However, there is still something missing in these computations. The economic environment of defense is one of scarcity. Buying 645 missiles may not, after all, be the best way to spend defense money. Other possibilities must be brought into the picture. By using the same calculations that produced the 645 missile requirement, it is possible to compute not a single solution but a whole range of missile forces with a different level of target destruction obtainable by each. The results are shown in the following schedule:

Number of missiles	Average number of targets destroyed
100	30
200	51
300	67
400	76
500	83
600	88
618	89
645	90
675	91
840	95
1290	99

This is actually a table of "cost" in the left column and "effectiveness" in the right. The figures are straightforward. Because of the 30% probability of individual large destruction assumed in this case, it is obvi-

ous that if one missile is programmed per target, 30 targets (30%) can be expected to be destroyed. As more missiles are added (and concentrated more heavily on each of the 100 targets), the increase in targets destroyed occurs at a diminishing rate, or tapers off. This happens to reflect the mathematical relationship of the factors involved (which, technically, is a binomial probability distribution). It also complies with the more general "law of diminishing returns," another hoary precept of economics, which holds that as an input, or resource, is added to a productive system, the output increases, after a point, in progressively smaller increments.

To make marginal comparisons requires examination of *marginal costs* in the left column and *marginal products* (the same as marginal effectiveness) in the right column. This means, in both columns, the *increment* is added with each step. So the marginal cost of moving from 89 to 90 targets destroyed is 27 missiles. At the same level, the marginal product of 27 missiles is one target (or, equivalently, the marginal product of 1 missile is 1/27 of a target).

Now a whole new vista is open for the decisionmaker. First of all, the table of figures helps avoid ill-advised decisions about program *changes*. With only the information that it takes 645 missiles to take out 90 targets, it would be natural to think in terms of the *average* cost per target destroyed. This is 645 divided by 90, or 7.2 missiles per target. But the *marginal* cost at that level is 27 missiles. Any sensible decision to add to or subtract from the target system must be made not in terms of the former, but the latter—the *true* effect of an incremental program change. Yet, in the absence of marginal costs, one of the commonest errors in justifying programs is to argue in terms of savings or expenditures in *average* costs. There is a homely parallel in evaluating federal income tax. A salary increase is not taxable at the average rate for the whole salary, say 10%, as its prospective recipient is tempted to think. It is taxable at the marginal rate, such as 30%, the rate that is applicable to the next higher income bracket. Salary increases, like extra missiles, are

---

[4] The example itself is artificial in that it does not reflect, among other things, the size and complexity of an actual target system, nor does it take account of the readiness posture and kind of early warning that might be provided in a realistic combat scenario. The example also assumes that the missiles are fired in salvo.

normally less rewarding than the averages make them appear.

The simple presentation of the figures in the table also provokes new questions. Why 90% as a goal of target destruction? Is it worth 27 extra missiles to increase the average number of targets destroyed from 89 to 90? For that matter, is it worth 245 missiles to increase the average number of targets destroyed from 76 to 90? The answer may well be yes, that the incremental cost is worth it. But—and this is the point—the answer cannot even be approached without considering alternative uses of resources, without thinking of other similar tables of performance for other available programs. It becomes necessary to make comparisons of different marginal products, or increments of output, at the same level of expenditure. Which is the better way to make that expenditure? Perhaps, for the same cost, it is possible to add to the strategic force an increment of manned bombers that would be more effective than the 27 missiles. Perhaps, for the same cost, electronic penetration aids for the missile force would be a better investment than adding 27 missiles. Perhaps, in terms of the state of international affairs at the time, it would even be acceptable to drop the level of desired target destruction below 90%. In the overall posture of deterrence, how important, really, is 90%? This is a question that could not be entertained without awareness of the full range of figures in the table.

So it is obvious that many important questions are raised by inspecting a single schedule of cost and effectiveness. To answer these questions requires careful consideration of alternative programs. More specifically, it requires comparison of the marginal products of all the alternative programs at the same level of expenditure, or, what amounts to the same thing (because of the inverse relationship of cost and effectiveness), comparison of the marginal costs at the same level of effectiveness.

Cost-Effectiveness Curves

The analyst therefore must consider a whole array of cost-effectiveness schedules for competing programs. Fortunately, to aid in the process of comparison, these schedules can be pictured in the form of plotted curves, which tend to have certain appearances in common.

If the figures of a typical schedule of cost and effectiveness are plotted with cost along the horizontal axis and effectiveness along the vertical axis, a curve emerges with the shape shown in Figure 1.[5] This characteristic shape is in accord with actual evidence and also with common sense. It shows what can be expected in most cases when resources are added progressively to a new weapon program. In the early stages, in the region of point A, considerable investment usually must be made in tests and manufacturing facilities, while effectiveness rises relatively slowly. This reflects the costs of "buying in" to the new program. When production is in full swing, effectiveness rises more steeply in the vicinity of point B. Subsequently, it is found that the desirability of buying more and more items falls off. The utility of each item diminishes as the demand is met and saturated. The curve flattens out in the area of point C. (Ultimately, in theory it will dip downward as the weapons overcrowd their own facilities.)

If one visualizes, instead of weapons production, the sending of existing aircraft against a target, the results are similar. To commit a small number of aircraft (cost) may result in few of them reaching the target system (effectiveness) because of heavy defenses. This situation is represented by point A in Figure 1. To commit more aircraft will be to breach the defenses, and so to produce a rapid improvement in results, as at point B. There always comes a stage, however, when the target system is virtually destroyed and additional aircraft have negligible effect, as at point C.

On the diagram, the *marginal* effectiveness is represented as an increment $\triangle e$ and the marginal cost as an increment $\triangle c$. The slope of the curve approximates the ratio

[5] In traditional economics, this is the familiar curve of total product (effectiveness) and variable service, or input (cost). See, for example, George J. Stigler, *The Theory of Price* (New York: Macmillan Co., 1947), pp. 123–25.

of the one to the other at any given point. The smaller the increment, the closer is the approximation. In the area of A, the slope is increasing (making the curve concave to the origin), and in the range from B to C it is decreasing (making the curve convex to the origin). This is in accordance with the law of "diminishing returns," previously referred to, which inexorably takes effect at some point like B in the cost-effectiveness schedule.

Marginal comparison, then, consists of comparing segments of different cost-effectiveness curves. To use another hypothetical example, suppose the combat airlift force is to be increased to provide an additional ton-mile capacity of "T" per month. There are three feasible alternatives: to procure the requisite quantity of the existing C-141, to procure the new and improved C-5 transport, or to procure a C-X vehicle which is in the early stages of development. Appropriate portions of their cost-effectiveness curves may be compared on the same scales, as in Figure 2. Here development and procurement dollars are regarded as "costs" and "T" ton-miles deliverable per month as "effectiveness."

In the illustration, the C-141 has already been procured in large quantity to a point well along its cost-effectiveness curve. The C-5 has a steeper curve, both because it is more efficient, and also because it is in an earlier stage of production. The ultraefficient C-X promises to have a very steep curve, but it is still in its primary and very costly investment phase, where the curve is flat. If the incremental effectiveness required, "T," is measured off vertically on each of these curves, the portions of the curves intersected will subtend, respectively, the incremental costs "X," "Y," and "Z." The C-5, with cost "Y," clearly wins the competition. The obsolescent C-141 does even better than the futuristic C-X, because the C-X is in a stage where it is penalized by heavy expenditures for development.

THE MODERNIZATION MUDDLE

Is this fair? Should a handsome new system be charged with such expenditures, when, for an older system, developmental

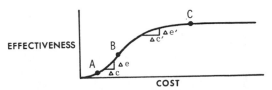

Figure 1. Typical cost-effectiveness curve.

expenditures are written off? This is a concern frequently expressed by advocates of technological modernization. The analyst's response is that it is not only fair, it is eminently sensible. Previously committed development expenditures on older systems are known as "sunk" costs. They need not be spent again. So far as present choices are concerned, such costs are quite irrelevant. The portions of curves to the left of the increments being considered are bygones —like puppy-dog tails, lost forever. To add them in is to distort the true nature of the choices presently available. It is to commit an error similar to the one, previously mentioned, of making comparisons on the basis of "average" rather than "marginal" costs. There can be no blinking the fact that if "T" effectiveness is to be obtained, the actual choices are between incurring "X," "Y," and "Z" costs.

However, systems analysts have some reassurances for the modernizers. In a complete analysis of the cost and effectiveness of new systems, these systems are found to enjoy certain advantages too. One is that if the full costing job is done properly, the costs counted will include not only heavy, immediate outlays for investment and procurement, but also projections of operating costs for the expected useful life of the items being procured. These operating costs may eventually become much lower for a more efficient new system like a C-X, provided a large enough number of items is built. The total cost picture of the new system is thus affected favorably.

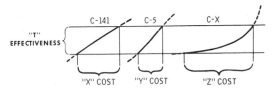

Figure 2. Comparative portions of cost-effectiveness curves.

Even more significant, proper analysis should also take account of any future growth in the system procured. At the end of the period of their specified use, to what extent might the procured items have improved their performance and hence increased their effectiveness? Also, proper analysis should take account of any terminal or "salvage" value.[6] What residual capabilities might the items then have for other missions, such as resale to airlines (in the case of air transports), and so on? Expected growths and residual values should either be *added* to the effectiveness of those systems under comparison or, what is equivalent, *subtracted* from the costs.

Therefore, it would seem that the advocates of modernization have less to fear than they might have thought. Their programs may be penalized by development costs, but they are benefited by accumulated future savings in operating costs, by salvage values, and by performance growths. Cost-effectiveness appears to be an impartial arbiter, after all.

Unfortunately, this is still not necessarily the case. The situation is badly muddled both by lack of foresight and wishful thinking. Future performance growths and salvage values are factors that are so difficult to envision that they are nearly always underestimated or ignored. This works *against* the advocates of modernization. In the classic example, how could the Douglas Aircraft Company's designer of the DC-3 in the 1930's have dreamed of its worldwide utilization still in the 1960's, even as an AC-47 combat attack plane in Vietnam? And not only airplanes, but submarines, trucks, and cannons often prove to be more versatile and stay in active service longer than their designers originally expected. On the other hand, there is a general tendency to underestimate future system costs, often by a factor of 2, 3, or even 20. This works *in favor* of the advocates of modernization. A decade ago, the new

ICBM was touted in military circles as a breakthrough in cheap weaponry, to cost only $1 or 2 million each; now we hear of "the missile's enormous unit cost—$40 million per ATLAS or TITAN on a launcher."[7] The combined effect of these favorable and unfavorable errors of estimation is confusion in deciding upon new weapons developments. Because of these errors, which are understandable in themselves, it must be acknowledged that really accurate cost-effectiveness analysis of new weapons developments can be a specious procedure. Precise answers are unavailable, and the judgment of the decisionmaker carries greater weight than it may seem.

Yet the general analytical concepts are valid, and they can still throw some light on the modernization muddle. The modernizers do embrace a fallacy if they argue that when a new system like a C-X is evaluated it should not be charged with its development costs. They should accept the fact of development costs and stress the need for better efforts to appraise the future —to improve the accuracy of estimating the costs, the utilities, and the salvage values of any new weapon system for which they are pressing. The systems analysts, on their part, should accept that future cost estimates are naturally vague and, at best, can serve as rough guides to judgment.

MARGINAL COMPARISONS OF ACTUAL PROGRAMS

Cases of marginal comparisons of actual defense programs fill the files and cover the desks of the Pentagon. Important examples are to be found in the Secretary of Defense's presentations to the Congress. In one of these he discusses the defensive posture of the United States for nuclear war. He compares the results of making additional investment on the one hand in active defenses, consisting principally of a new antimissile defense system, and on the other hand in passive defenses, consisting of a fallout shelter program for the entire U.S. population. The "product" is numbers of

---

[6] In Charles J. Hitch and Roland H. McKean, *The Economics of Defense in the Nuclear Age* (Cambridge: Harvard University Press, 1961), pp. 172–73, "sunk" costs and "salvage" values are discussed as part of a general treatment of analytical errors in the selection and use of criteria.

[7] Hitch, *op. cit.*, p. 49.

expected survivors. They were obtained from detailed calculations employing a model of nuclear war, with an assumed enemy force penetrating a balanced U.S. active defense system in the period of the early 1970's. The following figures represent corresponding portions of two performance schedules like the one in the earlier missile illustration. (They can also be visualized as representing corresponding segments of cost-effectiveness curves, like those in Figure 2). One schedule is for the active and the other for the passive defense programs:[8]

Cost: Additional investment	Effectiveness: Millions of U.S. survivors (of 210 million population) with:	
	Active defenses	Fallout shelters
$ 0 billion	61	61
5 billion	65	90

The difference between marginal products, 4 million additional survivors as opposed to 29 million, is most impressive indeed. The lesson is clear: however attractive new active defenses may be, it does not make sense to invest in them for the purpose of saving lives in the event of war unless the fallout shelter program is procured first. The marginal comparison makes this conclusion evident.

These figures serve as an official response to the vigorous proponents of the new antimissile defense system, known as the NIKE-X. The proponents have strong arguments. They insist that it is folly not to advance the technology of nuclear defense as rapidly as possible, even though it is expensive

to do so. They claim that the benefits of their favored system may prove to be greater than any economy-minded analyst can foresee. They point out that the Soviets are already reported to be building such defenses. The comparison, significantly, does *not* deny or refute these claims. By taking account of costs and by considering alternatives, it simply demonstrates that fallout shelters are initially more productive than antimissiles. In fact, the study presented by the Defense Secretary goes further to show that $10 billion spent on active defenses *besides* the $5 billion spent on fallout shelters could save 24 million more lives, beyond the 29 million already saved by the shelters.

The systems analysts cast their net of comparison over all perceptible alternatives. Often the alternatives, as in the air transport example of Figure 2, include the possibility of adding to existing programs as well as the prospect of buying new ones, with their higher performance and also their higher initial procurement costs. "We have examined," Mr. McNamara points out, "four alternative strategic offensive systems which could be available by the early 1970's." They are the existing MINUTEMAN and POLARIS missile systems, the existing B–52 armed with the new SRAM (a short-range air-to-ground missile), and, finally, a bomber proposed by the Air Force, AMSA (Advanced Manned Strategic Attack System), also armed with SRAM. He explains that each system was analyzed "in terms of its effectiveness against a given urban/industrial complex." He finds that in the early 1970's "any one of the four forces alone could, with a high degree of confidence, destroy this complex even after absorbing a surprise attack."

However, a comparison of the approximate incremental costs of the four alternative forces makes it clear that AMSA would be the most expensive way of accomplishing this particular task. Indeed, against improved defenses, which might be available by the 1970's, the cost of AMSA would be roughly four times the cost of MINUTEMAN, the least expensive of the four systems examined.[9]

---

[8] Statement, *op. cit.*, pp. 47–48. The statement itself was presented in a more elaborate form, showing different combinations of defense programs costing up to $25 billion. The results shown here assume that the enemy would initiate nuclear war with a simultaneous attack against military targets and cities. Other calculations were made on the assumption that the attack against cities would be delayed—that the cities would be "held hostage"—long enough to permit retaliation against the aggressor's military targets. The effect of this assumption was about 30 million additional lives saved.

[9] Statement; *op. cit.*, pp. 43–44.

Thus this official analysis actually consists of a comparison of portions of cost-effectiveness curves as in Figure 2. On the vertical axis the factor of effectiveness is given (the urban-industrial complex as a target system). On the horizontal axis, the cost of MINUTEMAN is revealed as the smallest of the four alternative programs.

MIXED SOLUTIONS

Thus far, the discussion has dealt with forthright comparisons between programs that are distinct alternatives, each with its own cost and effectiveness schedule. This kind of choice is a frequent one in defense decision-making, as the examples served to show. There is a more complicated kind of choice often required, however. It employs a somewhat greater degree of sophistication in the analytical process. It is the determination of a desirable *combination* of alternatives.

In analytical terms, this may be expressed more precisely as the determination of an efficient mixture of two or more inputs in order to obtain a given output. Marginal comparison, as explained in the examples, involved a single input (cost), whether that input was designated as missiles fired, bombers launched, or, simply, dollars spent, in order to produce the desired output (effectiveness), whether measured in number of targets destroyed, ton-miles delivered, and so on. Quite often, however, it is preferable for inputs like aircraft and missiles to be used in some combination in order to achieve a specified output such as a level of target destruction. What is the most efficient combination? The solution to this question is often referred to as a "balanced force." In short, the cost-effectiveness analogy of the seesaw, involving two elements of comparison, cost at one end and effectiveness at the other, must now be modified. For analysts, one end or the other had to be held steady. The seesaw is now three-cornered, one for effectiveness, and the other two for the costs of each of the inputs. If effectiveness is held steady, what are the preferred weights of the two inputs? The solution involves, simultaneously, the relationship

of each of the three corners to the other two.

It will be shown later that this case can be extended to more than two inputs by adding extra dimensions—more corners—and using more complex computations. Similarly, it is possible to reverse the order and to analyze, for a given input, two or more outputs. Yet all of these multiple comparisons involve a kind of analytical process that can be illustrated in a graphical presentation involving two inputs.

An example frequently used involves bomber airplanes and bombs as the two inputs.[10] The output is the expected number of targets destroyed. How many bombers and how many bombs are desired? In actual combat operations, many different combinations of numbers of bombs and bombers are possible; one bomb per bomber is only a special case. If the combination involves more bombers than bombs, the bombers not carrying bombs serve the tactical function of escorts, or decoys, aiding the armed bombers to get through by causing the enemy to expend some of his defenses uselessly. If there are more bombs than bombers, the bombers may be employed in attacking multiple targets, and thereby achieve greater effectiveness. (But why not, one may ask, *always* carry more bombs? Why not, indeed, load bombs on the escorts, too? This common-sense query neglects one essential fact: bombs are not free commodities. With a given budget, to buy more bombs means to buy fewer bombers.)

To begin with, suppose there are 30 bombers with 30 bombs. In Figure 3, these values are represented at the point P. The usual calculations are then made taking account of expected aborts, attrition from enemy defenses, navigation errors, weapon duds, and so on. Assume that in this case the resultant overall probability of target destruction turns out to be 50%. So the expected number of targets destroyed is 15 for the combination of bombs and bombers at point P. If there are only 20 bombs and 20 bombers, represented at point Q,

[10] Hitch and McKean, *op. cit.*, pp. 114–18; also Herman Kahn and Irwin Mann, *Techniques of Systems Analysis*, RM-1829 (Santa Monica, Calif.: The RAND Corporation, 1956), pp. 23–38.

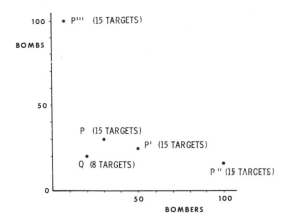

Figure 3. Substitution between bombs and bombers.

the attrition inflicted on this smaller force will naturally be higher, and the probability of target destruction lower, say 40%. So the expected target destruction at point Q is 8.

Carrying the computations further, many other points may be plotted in which the numbers and also the proportions of bombs and bombers are changed. When the whole chart is filled with figures, it is found that there are a series of points—different combinations of bombs and bombers—at which 15 targets can be expected to be destroyed. One of these points is shown at P', which happens to represent 50 bombers and 25 bombs. It is seen that this point lies a little below and much further to the right of point P. The reason for this location of P' is that bombers may be "substituted" for bombs at this stage only with declining advantage, due to the persistent law of diminishing marginal returns. The fewer bombs there are, the more bombers are required to compensate for the loss of another bomb.

Also, no matter how many bombers are added, it is obvious that at least 15 bombs will be required to destroy 15 targets, and this figure is a limit that is approached by points on the right side of the chart, such as P''. Likewise, when bombers are traded for bombs, there is also a diminishing rate of substitution, as shown at P'''. In this direction, too, there is a limit approached as more bombs are substituted for bombers; there must always be at least one

aircraft to do the job, no matter how many bombs it carries.

If all the points, P, P', P'', P''' that represent an expected target destruction of 15 are connected, they form a curve. It is shown in Figure 4. It is known as an "isoquant," because it represents the constant output of 15. It may also be called a "substitution curve," because it consists of the locus of points representing the values of inputs that can be substituted for one another to produce the constant output. The curve is convex to the origin, due to diminishing marginal returns. The curve converges gradually toward the limits (known as asymtotes) as described. Similarly, there can be plotted isoquants for other expected levels of target destruction, such as 8 targets and 25 targets. A whole family of other isoquants can be plotted, one for each possible level of target destruction, and none of them crossing the other.

The next step in searching for the mixed solution is to introduce the factor of cost. Suppose that the costs of bombs and bombers are constant, say in the ratio of one to three. This is known as a linear or "straight-line" relationship. Three bombs, therefore, can be exchanged for one bomber. Suppose, further, that the total budget is fixed at a level that will buy either 30 bombers, if it is all spent on bombers, or 90 bombs,

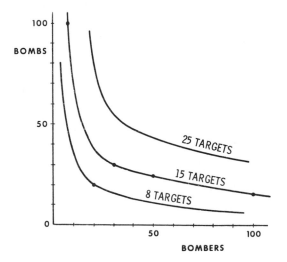

Figure 4. Substitution curves for bombs and bombers.

if it is all spent on bombs. These two points may then be plotted on the axes of the graph, at X and Y in Figure 5. A straight line connecting these two points represents all possible combinations of bombers and bombs that can be procured for the given budget. This is an "exchange" curve, as distinguished from the isoquant, or "substitution" curve. It is important to keep in mind that the one involves "exchanges" of inputs for a *constant budget* and other "substitutions" of inputs for a *constant output*, or level of effectiveness.

Now the payoff stage of analysis has been reached. Given this budget, what is the desired combination of bombs and bombers? The answer is easy. For the exchange curve shown, there can be found an isoquant, or substitution curve, that is precisely tangent to it, as shown at point O. At this point, both curves have a slope, or "steepness," that is exactly the same. (The slopes of these curves at any point are measures, respectively, of the "rate of exchange" and the "rate of substitution" at that point.) Point O represents the combination of bombers and bombs that, with the given budget, cannot be improved upon. In the example, this happens to be about 13 bombers and 49 bombs. In economic terminology, a solution that cannot be improved upon (moved to a higher output) by any change in allocation of inputs or use of

resources is known as *optimal*.[11] If a different combination of bombs and bombers were procured representing any other point on the exchange curve, such as at Z, that point would be a point on some other substitution curve that represents a lower output. Similarly, if any other point W were selected on the substitution curve, it would represent a combination of bombs and bombers that is not feasible in terms of the budget.

As in all economic comparisons, it is also possible to enter into this analytical procedure from the opposite direction by assuming not a given budget but a given level of target destruction. In such case the isoquant representing the specified level of target destruction is first identified (Figure 6). It happens that a whole family of possible exchange curves also exists for the inputs in question. The curves are parallel to one another (provided the exchange ratio of the two inputs remains the same) and they each represent a different-size budget. The particular exchange curve that is tangent to the isoquant is then selected. The point of tangency T represents the optimal solution: the desired allocation between two inputs, such that the specified output is obtained at minimum possible cost. Any other point on the exchange curve, like U, has a lower output. Any other point on the substitution curve, like V, is more expensive.

It should here be stressed that the relationships plotted on all these graphs and the solutions obtained from them are not just abstract theory. They are useful not only for illustration but also for practical application. They are representative of actual computations performed in reaching actual program decisions. The information re-

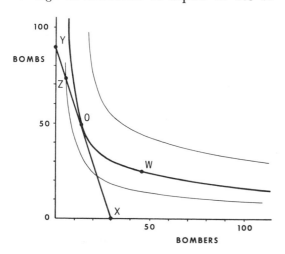

Figure 5. Budget given: An exchange curve tangent to a substitution curve.

[11] A more modest kind of solution is called "efficient." This is one in which waste has been eliminated. More precisely, it is a case in which it is not possible, with a given budget, to increase one output without decreasing another. Thus all points on the exchange curve shown are efficient; any point to the left of the exchange curve involves some waste of resources and is inefficient. For a rigorous discussion of economic efficiency, see Alain C. Enthoven's "The Simple Mathematics of Maximization," Appendix to Charles J. Hitch and Roland H. McKean, *op. cit.*

quired about weapons performance—"effectiveness"—is empirically available, either through actual measurement in weapons testing or combat operations, or as a result of deduction from mathematical models. Cost figures are obtainable from experience, from cost studies, and from projections of manufacturing schedules and operating expenses.[12]

A practical example of this kind of comparison is provided by a recent Department of Defense study of the desired mixture of aircraft carriers and the air wings that operate off those carriers. Heretofore, each ship had a single air wing assigned. The combination of ship and assigned aircraft was treated as a single package of offensive power, both for budgetary and operational purposes. Historically, this was probably a sound approach. The ship was the only expensive item, and its equipment was relatively cheap. The costs of aircraft, however, have increased greatly in recent years, so much so that aircraft now represent, almost surprisingly, the major single category of investment in the whole carrier force. Moreover, in respect to performance, aircraft are now so advanced that they can be deployed independently of particular mother ships. So a divorce seemed in order for purposes of analysis. It now made

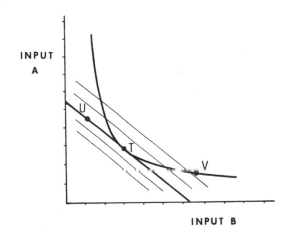

Figure 6.   Output given: An exchange curve tangent to a substitution curve.

sense to treat carriers and aircraft as separate inputs, and to prepare and analyze sets of substitution curves and exchange curves like those in the foregoing example.

The FY 1966–70 program had called for attack carrier forces of 13 ships and 13 air wings in the early 1970's. The new analysis of the desirable mix of ships and aircraft, however, suggested a new plan to McNamara:

Under the new plan, the number of ships would be held at 15 but the number of air wings would be reduced to 12, an increase of two ships and a reduction of one air wing compared with the previous plan. Significantly more useable combat power could be obtained from a force of 15 carriers and 12 air wings than from a force of 13 carriers and 13 air wings, and at no increase in cost.

Such a force structure would require some change in the present mode of operation. Carriers would normally deploy with less than the maximum complement of aircraft and additional aircraft would be flown to the carriers as needed. In effect, we would be treating the aircraft as the situation requires. It is this almost immediate operational availability which gives the attack carrier forces their unique importance.[13]

This analysis can be visualized in terms of Figure 5. The budget (exchange curve)

---

[12] Of course the graphs shown here are simplifications. For example, actual exchange curves for defense programs are not likely to be straight lines. This is due to the fact that defense programs are so large that they often dominate or monopolize the production capacities of the industries involved. Since there are few or no other customers for these industries, there are minimum levels of production below which it is not economical to procure weapons. For this reason, a true exchange curve would be truncated at those minimum levels for each input. Moreover, at lower ranges of production, weapons are far more costly than when they are produced in quantity. Therefore a true exchange curve for a given budget is likely to bow out and present a concave aspect to the origin of the graph, as follows:

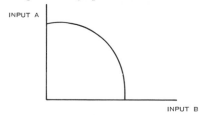

[13] *Statement of Secretary of Defense Robert S. McNamara Before the House Armed Services Committee on the Fiscal Year 1967–71 Defense Program and 1967 Defense Budget*, March 8, 1966.

is given, and it is found to produce a higher output at the point representing 15 carriers and 12 air wings than at the point representing 13 carriers and 13 air wings. In this manner the use of an analytical procedure, mechanical and arbitrary in itself, introduces the prospect of a whole new doctrine for carrier deployment and operations.

ADDING DIMENSIONS

Another sophistication of the analytical procedure for finding mixed solutions remains to be explained. Earlier, it was mentioned that two *or more* inputs could be analyzed. The graphical representation is limited to two inputs, quite obviously, because of its two dimensions. How can the analysis be extended to other dimensions? If there are three inputs the curves become three-dimensional surfaces. This kind of portrayal is feasible by use of solid, or three-dimensional, geometry. When there are many inputs, however, many-dimensional surfaces are required. Geometry is no longer helpful for dealing with n dimensions.

Fortunately, a device is available by which solutions can be sought for problems that involve more than three inputs. The device is the computer. Of course, it is not feasible here to elucidate the technical mysteries of computers. But it is possible to present a general impression of what they can accomplish in dealing with the n-dimensional problem.

Computer operations should first of all be regarded as a process of large-scale computation. The individual steps of computation are not complex in themselves. The service the computer provides is repetition of countless, laborious steps that are beyond human endurance or available physical resources to perform. In 1949, calculation of a missile trajectory took three persons using desk calculators six months to complete, at a cost of $5,000. The same task can be completed today by a computer in 1/200 second, at a cost of one cent, and at less than one trillionth the rate of er-

ror.[14] Obviously, whole new ranges of tedium, beyond human capacity, are opened by the use of computers. But the computer is still only an idiot who happens to have a phenomenal talent for speed and repetition. Like a virtuoso star of a television quiz show, the computer is lacking in intellectual depth.

A procedure by which the n-dimensional problem may be solved, employing computer calculation, is linear programming. This is a way of representing an activity or process by a number of linear equations. An example of a linear equation is the simple, straight-line exchange curve shown earlier in Figure 5, indicating that bombers are three times as expensive as bombs. A statement that C-X transports are four times as productive as C-141's is also a linear equation. Besides linear equations, a linear programming model involves the use of inequalities, or special limits. One such limit is the statement that a certain air transport can carry no more than 40 tons (i.e., a load equal to or less than 40 tons) and no more than 100 cubic meters of cargo if ranges are in excess of 3,000 miles. A single linear program may involve hundreds of such linear equations and associated inequality limitations. Obviously, a computer is required to store and employ such a mass of information as this.

To understand the use of a linear program, one may imagine a multidimensional problem pertaining to the whole overseas transport system for limited war. What is the desired mix of inputs when many of them are involved? The available air transports include not only C-141's and the projected C-X's, but also the new C-5's, obsolescent C-130's, smaller C-123's, and cargo helicopters for intratheater pickup. Also to be included are sea transports, including those employing a proposed concept of rapid "roll-on" of prestocked war supplies, immediate shipment, and rapid "roll-off" on the beaches at the overseas destination. All of these inputs have dif-

[14] Paul Armer, "The Use of Computers," in E. S. Quade (ed.), *An Appreciation of Analysis for Military Decisions* (Chicago: Rand McNally and Co., 1964), pp. 350–51.

ferent relationships (expressed by linear equations) of speed, range, payload, loading time, unloading time, and others. All are constrained by distances between bases, size of landing and docking facilities, and so on. The myriad linear equations and limitations that these factors represent are then fed into the computer.

The computer is instructed to make repeated substitutions of all the alternative transports under different conditions of use, over different routes, and with different constraints. If any comparison happens to improve effectiveness or to lower overall costs, it is repeated at high computer speed in conjunction with other contingencies. If not, it is rejected and another is tried.

In terms of the graphical analysis presented earlier, one may visualize a whole series of two-dimensional graphs like those in Figures 5 and 6. (Instead of smooth curves, however, the graphs contain segments of straight lines that approximate smooth curves, because linear equations are plotted as straight lines.) The series of graphs contains all possible combinations of the many inputs, input a with input b, input a with input c, b with c, d with a, b

with d, and so on. One graph is then solved for an optimal or near-optimal point, using the kind of data that were employed in the substitution and exchange curves. That solution is then compared with other solutions; the best is retained. It is in turn compared with others; the process is repeated again and again.

And thus, by massive calculation and tireless repetition, tentative solutions are prepared and tested repeatedly with all combinations of the inputs—a computerized system of "cut and try." A solution that is optimal with respect to *all* inputs is gradually approached and, for all practical purposes, is attained. An optimally mixed force of all the types of old and new aircraft and ships is indicated.

It must still be realized that "optimal" in such a case is not necessarily optimal in the real world, the actual scene of operations in which the mixed force will be employed. The data used in analysis are often inaccurate and projections of performance may be far off the mark. The benefit of such analysis is that the results are likely to be more nearly optimal than would be a purely intuitive decision about force composition.

THE OUTCOMES ARE PARTIALLY CONTROLLED BY ANOTHER

BY ANATOL RAPOPORT

When decisions are made under certainty, the decisionmaker has complete control of the outcome. Such situations are exceptional. Usually a choice of action can lead to a number of different outcomes. It is a matter of essential importance in decision

theory to know who, if anyone, selects the actual outcomes from among the possible ones associated with a given action. The crucial factor in such situations is whether the "other" has also assigned utilities to the outcomes and if so what these

Reprinted by permission of Harper & Row Publishers from pp. 31–57, *Strategy and Conscience*. Copyright © 1964 by Anatol Rapoport.

Mr. Rapoport is Professor of Mathematical Biology at the Mental Health Research Institute of the University of Michigan. In addition to his work in mathematical biology, he is a leading spokesman on game theory and is known for his original contributions to the study of semantics. He is the author of several books including *Fights, Games and Debates* (1960), and *Two-Person Game Theory: the Essential Ideas* (1966).

utilities are. If the nature of the other is unknown, or no utilities can be ascribed to him, the resulting situation is sometimes called a game against nature.

GAME AGAINST NATURE

As a simplest example of such a game, we can take the Commuter's chronic umbrella problem. Whether it is worthwhile to take an umbrella to work in the morning depends on what Nature is going to do. If Nature contemplates rain, it is definitely worthwhile; if not, not. Now the reason this game is called a game against Nature is not because rain is a natural phenomenon, but because rain, or whoever makes rain, does not care whether the Commuter takes his umbrella.

Games against Nature can be schematized by means of a notation fundamental in game theory, namely the game matrix. Our Commuter has two choices, namely to take or not to take the umbrella. Nature also has two choices: to "make it rain" or not. There are therefore four distinguishable outcomes in this game. It is these outcomes which are listed in the game matrix as shown in Matrix 1.

Commuter's choice	Nature's choice	
	Rain	Shine
Take umbrella	Stay dry in rain	Lug umbrella in fair weather
Leave it home	Get wet	Hands free in fair weather

Matrix 1. The entry in each box represents the outcome resulting from the corresponding pair of choices, one the Commuter's, one Nature's.

In order to have a decision problem, utilities must be assigned to each of the outcomes. Since Nature is a disinterested party, only the Commuter's utilities are relevant. Let us suppose the Commuter can assign numerical utilities to the outcomes, as shown in Matrix 2.

	Rain	Shine
Umbrella	−2	−1
No umbrella	−5	+3

Matrix 2.

The interpretation is as follows. If the umbrella is left at home, and the weather turns out fine, the Commuter finds himself in the best of all possible worlds. Hence his biggest payoff is in lower right. If he takes the umbrella, and the day is fine, he is somewhat irked but not very much, because he generally feels good on a sunny day (upper right). If it rains, he feels worse (upper left), but not as bad as when he leaves the umbrella and gets wet (lower left).

This game can be turned into a decision under risk if probabilities can be assigned to rain and shine. For example, if the chances are even, the man's expected utility is $0.5 \, (-2) + 0.5 \, (-1) = -1.5$, if he takes the umbrella. If he leaves it home, he expects $0.5 \, (-5) + 0.5 \, (3) = -1$. In this case it does not pay to take the umbrella. But if the chances of rain are, say, 0.75, then taking the umbrella gives him $0.75(-2) + 0.25 \, (-1) = -1.75$, while not taking it gives him $0.75 \, (-5) + 0.25(3) = -3.00$. In this case, it is prudent to take it.

Suppose, however, the man has no basis on which to assign probabilities to Nature's choices. When probabilities of the "states of nature" (as Nature's choices are called) are unknown, one cannot call the situation a decision under risk. Such situations are called decisions under uncertainty, and there is an extensive theory treating such problems. The discussion of that theory is beyond the scope of this book, but we shall need some of it to introduce the ideas of game theory.

Suppose our Commuter is a pessimist. He believes that whatever decision he makes will be the wrong decision. There is a decision principle that will be in complete harmony with his temperament. The pessimist scans the two "strategies" open to him and asks, "What is the worst thing that can happen to me if I take the umbrella?" The answer is, "A rainy day." The utility of this outcome is −2. Then he asks, "What is the worst thing that can happen to me if I don't take the umbrella?" The answer is, again, "A rainy day," but this time the utility of the outcome is −5. Clearly the first "worst" outcome is better than the second. The choice of the "best of the worsts" is called the Minimax Principle.

The Minimax Principle is not the only "rational" principle governing decision under uncertainty. There is no more reason for being a pessimist than for being an optimist. If our Commuter were an optimist, he would ask, "What is the best possible outcome if I take the umbrella or if I do not take it?" Clearly this man would always choose not to take it. There are also decision principles which are blends between the pessimistic and the optimistic outlooks, and still others. The interested reader will find in (99) [Savage, L. J., *Foundations of Statistics* (New York: John Wiley & Sons, 1954).] an excellent overview of the subject.

TWO-PERSON GAME

Let us now suppose that Nature is not neutral, that she behaves as the pessimist imagines. This would mean that Nature has an interest in the outcome and that her interests are diametrically opposed to those of the Commuter. Here we have the first genuine example of a two-person game. It turns out that the "solution" of this game is the same as the pessimist's solution of the decision problem, but this is not true of games in general. The kind of solution a game has (considered as a decision problem for two or more participants) and, indeed, whether a game has a "solution" at all depends on the kind of game it is. It turns out that the game theoretician classifies games in a way that would not immediately occur on intuitive grounds. It is essential to understand this method of classification in order to see how the theory of rational decisions extends to conflict situations and how far. Before we classify games, however, let us see what criteria must be met by a decision problem in order for it to be called a "game" at all in the technical sense of this term.

WHAT MAKES A GAME

We are now ready to define a game. We shall do so by listing certain features which a situation must exhibit in order to be described as a game.

1. *In a game we must have two or more "players" with at least partially conflicting interests.*

Note that this immediately excludes solitaires, in which there is only one player with an "interest." There is to be sure, another player, namely, Chance, whose role we shall soon discuss, but this player is disqualified as a bona fide player because she is indifferent to the outcome. Chance is only a dummy player.

2. *Each of the players has a range of choices called strategies.*

This requirement excludes playing a slot machine from the class of genuine games. To be sure, when a man plays a slot machine, there is a conflict of interests, because the slot machine represents the House or a gambling syndicate. Also the slot machine makes "choices." The fact that the choices are random does not matter. As we shall see, randomization of strategy choices is actually itself a rational strategy choice in many cases. So the slot machine is a bona fide player. But the man is not. He is the dummy, because he has no choices. He can do only one thing, namely, put a coin in the slot and pull the lever.

3. *A play of the game consists of a single simultaneous choice of a strategy by each of the players.*

This extremely important point requires elucidation. Ordinarily we think of games as *successions* of choices, for example, the moves which the players make, each move being a response to a move of the other. However, it is possible (in principle) to conceive of a decision which encompasses specific responses to all possible move sequences of the other player.

A simple example will serve to illustrate how moves are "collapsed" into strategies. Consider a game in which the first move is made by the first player, who has two choices. The second player, after learning the first player's choice, now also has two choices. Call the choices of each player 1 and 2. The first player has two strategies, each corresponding to a choice. The second player also has two choices, when his turn comes, but he has *four strategies*, namely:

1. Choose 1 regardless of what the other does.

2. Choose 1 if the other chooses 1; otherwise, choose 2.

3. Choose 2 if the other chooses 1; otherwise, choose 1.

4. Choose 2 regardless of what the other chooses.

Note that these strategies provide for all possible contingencies. Thus although an advance commitment to a *choice* by the second player does not give him all the flexibility that the situation allows, an advance commitment to a *strategy* does, since all contingencies which can arise are already included in the decision. The advantage of the concept of strategy is that it enables the game theoretician to lump everything that is known to the players into one category and everything that is unknown into another. What is known in any game is the complete set of all available strategies, one's own and the opponent's. What is unknown is the (single) choice of a particular strategy, which will constitute the player's "part" in the particular play of the game.

4. *When each of the players has chosen his strategy, the outcome of the game is determined.*

This is a direct consequence of the definition of strategy. The definition allows the two-person game to be represented as a matrix. The rows are the strategies open to one player; the columns are the strategies open to the other. When each has chosen a strategy, an outcome is determined. The outcomes are the "boxes" of the matrix. A game represented in this way is said to be "in normal form."

5. *Associated with each outcome is a set of payoffs, one to each player.*

The payoff sets are the entries in the strategy matrix, one payoff to each player. The payoffs are expressed in utiles. It is assumed that if the outcome of a game is not certain (e.g., when chance devices are used in the course of the play) the expected utility of the outcome can be computed by multiplying the utilities of the various outcomes by the respective probabilities of occurrence and adding the products. The resulting expected utility figures in strategic calculations just as any other utility.

These five requirements constitute the scope of situations which can in principle be represented as games. Let us now compare these requirements with those ordinarily ascribed to games in common parlance. We shall find that in many ways the technical requirements correspond to those commonly assumed. In other respects, however, there are important differences. Thus many situations ordinarily thought of as amenable to treatment by "game theory" (as it is popularly conceived) do not really meet the requirements, while other situations, on the contrary, commonly thought of as falling outside the scope of game theory, can be (in principle) included.

The most obvious feature of a game is a set of rules. In real games, rules are established by agreement among the players. Or one could say that when the players have agreed to play the game, they have implicitly agreed to abide by the rules. The games examined in game theory are, of course, also based on definite rules. Thus the denotation of the rule criterion is the same in game theory and in common parlance. Here, however, the difference between everyday language and the language of game theory becomes important. The meanings of the terms in purely formal language are strictly circumscribed. They carry no penumbras of connotation. In everyday language, on the contrary, connotations are unavoidable. Thus the term "rule," especially "rule of a game," reminds us ordinarily of voluntary agreements. Accordingly, if a situation is incompatible with such agreements, it may appear that such a situation does not fall within the scope of those subsumed under "games." One such situation comes readily to mind, namely, war. It is sometimes argued that game theory cannot be of assistance in the solution of strategic military problems because wars are not fought according to rules, or, in any case, are no longer fought this way. As we shall see, the applications of game theory to the conduct of wars are indeed extremely limited, but not primarily for the reason offered. For the term "rule of the game," as it is used in game theory, is free of all the connotations conferred upon it by everyday language. A rule of the game need not be an expression of any agreement, and the reliability of the rule need not depend on the good will or the honesty of the "players." The essential meaning of "rules of the game," as the phrase is used in game theory, resides in the circumstance that the totality of rules determines precisely all the situations that can occur in the course of a play of the game, and that the totality of the situations plus a termination rule determine, in turn, all the possible outcomes. Now when a game has been represented in normal form, the situations which can occur in the course of the play have already been abstracted out. Therefore the specific rules have become immaterial. The important things are the outcomes, or rather, the payoffs associated with the outcomes. Hence any situation can be represented as a game in normal form, provided only that:

1. The finite set of single choices (decisions) can be listed for each player; and
2. A pair of payoffs can be assigned to each pair of choices.

How these alternatives are put into effect, whether as explicitly stated complete strategies or in some other way, i.e., as a set of roughly specified courses of action, does not matter.

Moreover, the payoffs need not be associated with determinate results. They can well be expected utilities associated with a range of results, each characterized by a probability. Such situations sometimes occur in military or in business life. A commander may at some point in a campaign have at his disposal just so many "plans." And he may be aware of the range of plans available to the enemy. A business firm may at a given time have a choice of just so many policies and also information concerning the range of policies from which a rival firm must choose. The details of

carrying out the plan or the policy chosen may be irrelevant to the essential results. The essential results are the outcomes which obtain when the respective plans or policies are put into effect. Thus situations of this sort may be represented by games in normal form even if the detailed rules of the game are not specified or do not exist.

TAXONOMY OF GAMES

The principle achievement of game theory, as it was formulated by von Neumann and Morgenstern (124) [Von Neumann, J. and Morgenstern, O. *Theory of Games and Economic Behavior,* 2nd ed. (Princeton, N.J.: Princeton University Press, 1947).], was a profoundly discerning taxonomy of games, that is, of situations involving conflicts of interests.

To see the basis of this taxonomy, let us begin by examining the ordinary ways of classifying games which may occur to anyone. Asked to classify games, the proverbial man-in-the-street may, for example, start by dividing them into indoor games and outdoor games. Upon more careful reflection, if he is asked to concentrate on the essential elements of the game itself instead of on its recreational function, our man may abandon distinctions like indoor versus outdoor games in favor of, one, say, between games of chance and games of skill. Among the latter, he may distinguish card games from board games; he may place games like post office or charades in another class; he may create a category of "children's games," to include hopscotch, marbles, tic-tack-toe, etc.

After still more deliberation, he may admit that tic-tack-toe, simple as it is, is in a way more like chess than like hopscotch. He may recognize that chance is a frequent feature in some games of skill, e.g., bridge and poker; but he may not be sure to what extent skill enters such games of chance as craps. In this way, the attention of our man-in-the-street can be gradually focused on the "essentials" of games.

By the "essentials" of games we mean those features which remain after all the incidental features have been eliminated. These incidental features are the reasons for playing the games, social attitudes toward them, their effects on the characters of the players, the apparatus used, etc.

In game theory, even the specific rules of a game are usually removed from scrutiny. This is indeed climbing high on the ladder of abstraction, since the rules of the game are certainly thought of as essential features. But game theory, going still further in its abstracting process, has succeeded in reaching a vantage point from which the logic of strategy appears with dazzling clarity.

The mathematical theory of games distinguishes first of all between games involving two players and games involving more than two players. Our concern in this book will be only with two-person games.

Among the latter, there is a most important distinction between zero-sum games and non-zero-sum games. The name "zero-sum" derives from the fact that the sum of the payoffs accruing to the players is zero regardless of what the outcome of the game is. It follows that in two-person zero-sum games, what one player wins, the other necessarily loses. The same is essentially true in "constant-sum" games, where the sum of the payoffs is the same in all outcomes. Whether this sum is zero or not is irrelevant because the zero point of the utility scale on which the payoffs are determined is arbitrary anyway. In our discussion we shall be referring to both zero-sum and constant-sum games as zero-sum, since this term enjoys the broadest usage.[1]

Both zero-sum and non-zero-sum games can be further subdivided. We shall treat a selection of such subclasses which are relevant to the principal theme of this book. As in the case of the decision problems, we shall discuss the various classes of two-person games in the order of increasing complexity.

Here we must point out that we shall judge the "complexity" of a game by standards which may seem strange at first sight. "Complexity," in our way of speaking, will have next to nothing to do with the difficulty of mastering a game or with the range of its strategic potentialities. By ordinary standards, chess is an enormously complex game, while matching pennies is a ridiculously simple one. But according to game-theoretical taxonomy, chess is in the same class with tic-tac-toe, i.e., among the very simplest games, while matching pennies belongs to a "higher class." If this classification seems bizarre, this is largely due to the difficulty of discarding the notion that the theory of games is or ought to be concerned with the analysis of specific games (perhaps with a view of discovering how to play them cleverly). But game theory is not at all concerned with know-how. It is concerned with the logic which underlies the "know-how" of strategy. The difference between a game theorist and a game virtuoso (say, a chess master or a military genius) is, in a way, analogous to the difference between a physicist and an engineer. The physicist knows the principles on which the engineer's skills are based, but he may not be able to design an engine that will work. The difference between the linguist and the polyglot is of the same sort. The linguist knows the structure of many languages; yet he may not be able to speak any of them. The polyglot may speak a dozen languages fluently without being able to state correctly a single grammatical rule.

A taxonomy of games reveals not the way specific games should be played but how to *look* for the best ways of playing them and what to expect from the search. For example, game theory tells us that *there is* a way of playing chess which, if once found, will guarantee the best possible outcome to the player who plays that way, and moreover that the player need not ever vary this best strategy. But the situation in matching pennies is quite different. There is *no* pattern of choices that will always insure the best outcome to the player who makes them.[2] The best way of playing matching

[1] Indeed, the usage of this word has become so broad that its meaning is sometimes seriously perverted. Somewhere I read a statement characterizing a nuclear war as a "zero-sum game," because if it is fought, no one will have anything left. But this is just what makes the "game" non-zero-sum, if the choice is between fighting a nuclear war and not fighting it. In the first case, *both* parties lose; in the second case *both* win or, at any rate, do not lose.

[2] Matching pennies is defined here as follows. Players A and B place their pennies as they please. If they match, A wins; if they do not, B wins.

pennies is to randomize one's choices, preferably in such a way that the player himself does not know what choice he will make next. Thus the principles of playing chess and of playing matching pennies are entirely different. The former game requires the greatest possible awareness and discrimination; the latter game, on the contrary, is best played in complete ignorance of what one is doing!

Next we shall be concerned with the two principal types of zero-sum games, and then the problems associated with non-zero sum games.

ZERO-SUM GAMES

From the point of view of seeking an optimal strategy, there are just two classes of two-person zero-sum games: those with a saddle point and those without. (The meaning of a "saddle point" will be explained below.) The first class can be further subdivided into three subclasses:
1. Games in which both players have a dominating strategy.
2. Games in which only one player has a dominating strategy.
3. Games in which neither player has a dominating strategy.

These categories are listed in the order of increasing complexity of the reasoning which leads to the optimal strategy. Games without saddle points are the most complex. The following examples will make these distinctions clear.

BOTH PLAYERS HAVE A DOMINATING STRATEGY

Consider the game represented by Matrix 3.

	B_1	B_2	B_3
A_1	4, −4	−1, 1	3, −3
A_2	0, 0	−2, 2	2, −2
A_3	0, 0	−3, 3	1, −1

Matrix 3. The first payoff in each box is to the row chooser; the second to the column chooser.

Comparing the available strategies, A_1, A_2, and A_3, player A should see the perfect-

ly obvious choice, namely, A_1. No matter which strategy player B decides upon, A is at least as well off and sometimes better off with A_1 than with either of the other strategies. Player B is in the same position. No matter which strategy is chosen by A, B is better off with B_2. Note that in the decision problem, each player can arrive at this decision *without taking account of the character of the adversary*. If instead of player B, Nature chose among the columns, A's best choice would still be A_1. Also it does not matter to A whether B is clever or stupid. B's choice need not be taken into account by A, since A_1 is best for A regardless of how B chooses. The situation is the same from B's point of view.

A strategy which is best (or at least as good as any) regardless of what happens is called a *dominating* strategy. In general, one strategy will be said to dominate another if all of its outcomes are better than or at least as good as the *corresponding* outcomes of the other strategy (i.e., no matter what happens). The choice of a dominating strategy is sometimes referred to as an application of the "sure-thing principle."[3]

ONLY ONE HAS A DOMINATING STRATEGY

Let us now introduce a minor change in the matrix and obtain the following game (Matrix 4):

	B_1	B_2	B_3
A_1	4, −4	−1, 1	3, −3
A_2	−3, 3	−2, 2	2, −2
A_3	0, 0	−3, 3	1, −1

Matrix 4.

We see that A_1 still dominates A_2 and A_3. But B_2 no longer dominates B_1. For should A choose A_2, B would be better off with B_1. Thus, although A can still act as promptly as in the preceding case, B has to go one step further in his reasoning. He can no longer say, "B_2 is best for me no matter what A does." All he can say now is, "B_2 is

[3] Savage, L. J. *Foundations of Statistics* (New York: John Wiley & Sons, 1954), p. 21.

best for me unless A choses A_2." Then he must inquire whether there is a chance that A may, in fact, choose A_2. Thus B, in contrast to A, must now take into account what the other player *may* do. Accordingly, he looks the matrix over and decides that A will *not* choose A_2 since there is no inducement whatever for him to do so. In coming to this decision, player B need not ascribe to A any "reasoning power"—only the ability to discriminate payoffs and to act on the sure thing principle. Certainly this is the minimal assumption one can make about the rationality of the other. In short, when one of the players has a dominating strategy, while the other does not, the former can still act without assuming anything about the other's rationality, but the latter must make the *minimal* assumption about the former's rationality, namely, that the former knows enough to choose according to the sure thing principle.

NEITHER HAS A DOMINATING STRATEGY

Our next step, which the reader may already have anticipated, is to deprive both players of the dominating strategy and so of the sure thing principle. This has been done in Matrix 5.

	B_1	B_2	B_3
A_1	5, −5	−1, 1	4, −4
A_2	−3, 3	−2, 2	5, −5
A_3	10, −10	−3, 3	−20, 20

Matrix 5.

Here neither player has a dominating strategy. A_1 fails to dominate A_2, and vice versa, because A_1 is better in the first column but worse in the third; A_1 does not dominate A_3, nor is dominated by it, because A_1 is better in the third column but worse in the first. A_2 fails to dominate A_3 because A_3 is better in the first column; but neither is A_2 dominated by A_3, because A_2 is better in the second column. Similar comparisons will establish the fact that none of the column strategies dominates any other.

In a game of this type it is not possible for either player to arrive at a rational de-

cision without taking into account the other player's decision process. Moreover, the "taking into account of the other player's decision process" means in this case not only taking into account the other's choice preferences but also taking into account the other's taking into account one's own choice preferences, as well as one's own taking into account of the other's taking into account, etc., ad infinitum.

Although this reasoning goes on ad infinitum, it leads to a perfectly definite conclusion, provided the game has a saddle point. A saddle point is an outcome in which the payoffs to both players are the "best of the worst." We see that in Matrix 5 the outcome in the first row, second column, is of this sort. The row player's payoff, −1, is the worst in that row, but it is better than the other two worst payoffs, namely, −3 (in row 2) and −20 (in row 3). B's payoff, +1, is the worst in that column, but it is better than either of the other two worst outcomes. A saddle point is also known as a minimax. The meaning of minimax is the same here as in the game against Nature, discussed previously.

We shall now show that in a game with a saddle point, both players should choose strategies containing a saddle point. The outcome of such a game will be the minimax payoff to each player.

Suppose A decides to choose the row containing the minimax (row 1 in Matrix 5) as the "safest" choice. He asks himself, "If B knew that I chose this row, which column would he choose?" The answer is, obviously, the column containing the minimax (column 2), for that is B's best reply to A's choice. "Now knowing that B will choose column 2 (since he assumes I will choose row 1) can I improve the outcome for myself?" asks A. The answer is no. "Can B improve his outcome, knowing that I will choose row 1?" Again no. Therefore the minimax outcome is a sort of stable equilibrium. Neither player can get more than it gives unless the other acts foolishly, and a rational player does not expect another rational player to act foolishly.

Examining the simpler games with dominating strategies (Matrices 3 and 4), we see that they too have saddle points. In fact, the Commuter's game against Nature (Matrix 2) turns out to be of the type in which only one player has a dominating strategy (in this case Nature). We see also that the pessimistic Commuter chooses the strategy with the saddle point. We would expect this, because pessimism in this context is tantamount to attributing malevolent intentions (opposite interests) to Nature.

Now let us change the Commuter's personality somewhat. Assume that he is not very adversely affected by rainy weather as such (although he still dislikes getting wet). Let this upper-left payoff be +2. Assume also that Nature is indeed malevolent, so that the decision problem is a genuine two-person zero-sum game. Now Nature's payoffs are those of the Commuter with opposite signs, and we need to show only the Commuter's payoffs. The resulting game is shown in Matrix 6.

	Rain	Shine
Take umbrella	+2	−1
Leave it	−5	+3

Matrix 6.

Observe that this game has no saddle point. For the Commuter's minimax is −1, at upper right, while Nature's minimax, −2, is at upper left. Let us see where the Commuter's reasoning now gets him if he tries to figure out what (malevolent) Nature is likely to do. Beginning with his own minimax, he tentatively decides to take the umbrella. If Nature "knows" of this decision, the weather will be fine (so as to give the Commuter −1, not 2). But if Nature decides to shine, clearly the Commuter should leave the umbrella home and take advantage of +3 at lower right. But Nature, being intelligent as well as malevolent, is expected to be aware of *this* decision of the Commuter. Therefore, concludes the Commuter, it will rain. But if it rains, he should take the umbrella. But Nature is up to *that* too. . . . We see that the ad infinitum reasoning process has here a literal meaning. And if instead of Nature, we had a real opponent, he, too, would be going around in circles.

The principal result in the theory of the two-person zero-sum game shows a way out of this impasse. The Commuter can *randomize* his choices in such a way as to guarantee for himself the maximum *expected* payoff, regardless of what Nature does. This will happen if the Commuter takes the umbrella on eight days out of eleven. His expected payoff will be $+\frac{1}{11}$ utiles. Nature, as the opponent, can make sure that the Commuter gets *no more* than $+\frac{1}{11}$ by making rain on 4 days out of 11 and fair weather on 7.[4]

To be absolutely sure of these results, each player must completely randomize his choices. That is, he must leave the choice on any particular play of the game to some chance device appropriately constructed so that each alternative results with the assigned probability. Such a choice is called a mixed strategy. The game-theoretical result mentioned above proves that every two-person zero-sum game representable in normal form has a solution, i.e., a prescribed mixed strategy to each player. That is to say, each player computes a certain optimal probability with which to choose his own available strategies. (Some of the probabilities may be zero, that is to say, the corresponding strategies are never to be chosen. In case the game has a saddle point, probability 1 is assigned to the strategy which contains it.)[5]

The spirit of the mathematical theory of games can be clearly appreciated from the implications of this result. We are not told how to play any specific game. But we are told what an "optimal strategy" *means* in

[4] A very simple way of calculating both the optimal randomization mixtures and the resulting expected utilities is explained in [Williams, J. D., *The Compleat Strategyst* (New York: McGraw-Hill, 1954), p. 62]. Unfortunately, this method does not work when more than two strategies are available to each player. For a general method of calculating mixed strategies, the interested reader is referred to, [Von Neumann, J., "A numerical method to determine optimum strategy," *Naval Research Logistics Quarterly*, 1 (1954), pp. 109–115].

[5] The mixed strategy so determined is *defined* as the optimal strategy in the formal theory. This is not to say that it can necessarily be justified as optimal in the practical sense. The same problems arise here with respect to optimality as in decisions under risk.

the two main classes of zero-sum games. In games with saddle points, there is *a* best strategy for each player (there may be several, but they all lead to the same payoffs). Once such a strategy is found, it can *always* be used. There is no point in keeping such a strategy secret (assuming of course, that the other player is also rational, that is, that he too can figure out both optimal strategies). In fact, there is no point in playing such a game at all, once it has been solved, because the outcome is known in advance. Tic-tack-toe has been solved, and that is why adults do not play this game. Chess is also known to be a game with a saddle point, but this game has not been solved. That is why the victory goes sometimes to White, sometimes to Black, and sometimes to neither. If the game were solved, the results of all chess games would be the same.

With games without saddle points, it is a somewhat different matter. Optimal strategies in these games are mixed strategies, and so the results of each play of the game may be different even if the players are rational. But the long-term results (if the payoffs can be added or averaged) will be the same. Poker is a game without a saddle point. Like chess, it has never been solved [although some simplified forms of poker are solved in von Neumann and Morgenstern's treatise].[6]

The notion of mixed strategy was known, of course, to players of games long before the advent of game theory. In poker, mixed strategy is involved in bluffing and in raising. The experienced poker player does not bet in accordance with the strength of his hand, since this would give away his hand. Occasionally he raises by a large amount when his hand is weak (bluffs), and occasionally raises only by small amounts when his hand is quite strong (in order not to scare away the other players). If someone took the trouble to solve poker, each player would know just how to *randomize* his bets, depending on his hand. No player could do better (in the long run) than with this optimal strategy. The results of each play would still be different, but in the long run each player would come out with-

out gains or losses, since poker is a game in which each player's expected gain is zero.

Mixed strategies can, in principle, be applied in military tactics provided a situation can be depicted as a zero-sum game. The commander of each side lets *chance* decide for him which of the available plans to choose (assuming that the opponent is aware of all the possibilities). The commander only fixes the probabilities with which the various plans are to be chosen. These *probabilities* need not, in fact cannot be, kept secret from a rational enemy even though the particular plan chosen on a specific occasion must be kept secret.

Thus there is a definitive procedure recommended by game theory for every solved two-person zero-sum game. It is in this sense that the theory of such games is called complete, and it is in this sense that it can be called normative.

PRISONER'S DILEMMA

Prisoner's dilemma is the best known example of a non-zero-sum game which illustrates the dramatic failure of zero-sum methods in the new context. The name of the game derives from an anecdote which was originally used to illustrate it.[7] We shall use another illustration closer to the main theme of this book.

The players are two nations, A and B. Each has a range of defense policies, i.e., levels of armaments, deployment of weapon systems, etc. For simplicity we shall assume that only two policies are under

---

[6] Von Neumann, J. and Morgenstern, O., *Theory of Games and Economic Behavior* (2nd ed.) (Princeton, N.J.: Princeton University Press, 1947).

[7] Two prisoners charged with the same crime are held incommunicado. If both confess, both can be convicted. If neither confesses, neither can be convicted. But if one confesses but the other holds out, the first not only goes scot free but gets a reward to boot, while the second gets a more severe punishment than he would have got if both confessed. Should a rational prisoner confess or hold out under these circumstances?

The story illustrating the game is attributed to A. W. Tucker. The essentials of the game have appeared in the early experiments of M. M. Flood [Flood, M. M., "Game-learning theory and some decision making experiments," *in* Thrall, R. M., Coombs, C. H., and Davis, R. L., eds., *Decision Processes* (New York: John Wiley & Sons, 1954), and Flood, M. M., "Some experimental games," *Research Memorandum* RM-789, (Santa Monica, Calif.: RAND Corporation, 1952)].

consideration by each government, namely, Policy C: total disarmament; and Policy D: high level of armaments. To continue to keep the problem simple, we shall also assume that A and B are the only nations whose military potential needs to be considered, and that when both are fully armed, a "balance of power" obtains, that is, each nation has reasonable assurance that the other will not attack it. When both countries are disarmed, we shall assume that each is likewise secure from attack. However, *unilateral* disarmament (we shall suppose) is highly disadvantageous to the disarmed nation, and advantageous to the nation that has remained armed (or, say, has rearmed while the other has remained disarmed).

Besides safety there are also costs to take into account. High levels of armament, it is generally conceded, are more costly than low levels. Thus, the degrees of safety in both the bilaterally armed and the bilaterally disarmed state being the same, we must assign a lower utility to the bilaterally armed than to the bilaterally disarmed state. Let us assign that value +5 to the latter state and the value of −5 to the former. Since being disarmed alone is worse than being armed (even if the other is) we shall assign −10 to this state. Similarly, the advantage of being the only armed nation shall be represented by +10. The resulting game is represented by Matrix 7.

	C	D
C	5, 5	−10, 10
D	10, −10	−5, −5

Matrix 7.

Now the principal feature of this game is that strategy D dominates strategy C for both players. On the face of it, therefore, we seem to be confronted with the simplest type of two-person game, namely, one in which each player has a clearly dominating strategy, one that is sure to be better than the other no matter what the other player does. In fact, if B is armed, this is the strongest of reasons for A to remain armed. If B disarms, A is still better off armed, because it is then the only armed one. In the case of the zero-sum game, the choice of a dominating strategy, if such exists, is the only rational choice. Observe, however, that in the game now before us, this is no longer the case. If both players choose the dominating strategy (remain armed), they both do worse than they would have done if they had both chosen the dominated strategy (to disarm).

An obvious way out of the dilemma is for the players to get together and to agree to disarm. But this raises a host of questions. For example, what does it mean to "agree"? The concept has not been used heretofore except in the context of agreeing to abide by the rules of the game. But here the meaning of "to agree" is clearly different. Agreement refers here not to something that occurs before the game (and so need not be considered again) but to something that takes place *during* the game. Is agreement a "move"? But games schematized in matrix form do not have "moves." Is an agreement a new rule set up while the game is progressing? Whatever the nature of this "agreement," the following question is interesting in its own right. What if the rules of the game explicitly prohibit communication (or the nature of the situation makes it impossible)? Can one speak of "agreement" in that case?

CAN THE COOPERATIVE CHOICE BE RATIONALIZED?

The dilemma results from a bifurcation of the idea of rationality. If one asks, "With which strategy am I better off?" the answer is unequivocally, "With strategy D." The choice of strategy C is dictated by collective interest. If one asks, "Where are we both better off?" the answer is, "With strategy C." Thus, strategy D is dictated by self-interest while strategy C is dictated by collective interest. Nevertheless the choice between C and D is not quite a choice between altruism and selfishness. In choosing C, a player does not necessarily serve collective interest *at the expense* of his self-interest as does, say, a man who suffers discomforts or faces danger to promote the welfare of others. The motivation for choosing C is cooperation, not self-sacrifice. But the player who chooses C does not control the outcome by himself. The outcome depends on what the other player does. If the other chooses D, the attempt to induce cooperation fails. The defector benefits at the cooperator's expense, but it was not intended this way. The cooperator assumed that the other would cooperate, not defect. If he had cooperated, *both* would have benefited. Therefore the choice of C is not an act of self-sacrifice but rather an act of trust. But trust is not enough, because even convincing evidence that the other will choose C need not induce C.[8] Not only must one be trusting; one must also be trustworthy; that is, one must resist the temptation to betray the other's trust.

Is it "rational" to be trusting and trustworthy? Here the common usage of the term "rational" sometimes intrudes and beclouds the issue. The usual sense of this question is, "Is it safe to trust people?" But put in this way, the question is clearly an empirical one, to be answered by examining the behavior of a given sample of people in given circumstances. It is not the justification of a policy on the basis of empirical evidence that makes the policy rational but rather the consistency of the policy with certain axiomatically stated principles. Clearly to be "trusting" in a prisoner's dilemma game means to assume that the other will not choose a dominating strategy, i.e., to deny "rationality" to the other. On the other hand to be "trustworthy" means to discard the dominating strategy in favor of a dominated one, which is not "rational."

To be sure, one could defend trustworthiness, at least in response to the other's trust, on the basis of insuring the other's trust the *next* time. This is clearly advantageous and is reflected in the business dictum "Honesty is the best policy." However, such pragmatic arguments do not apply if there is no next time, if the game is played only once. In this case, there is only one good reason to choose C, namely, in order to remain at peace with one's conscience.

It appears that we have now brought in a concept totally alien to the notion of rational decision. The notion of conscience is

sometimes gotten around by invoking the idea of "hidden utility." The man who chooses C, it is argued, must assign greater utilities to the associated outcomes than are indicated in the game matrix. (In other words, if we observe that someone chooses C, we conclude that the game he is playing is not prisoner's dilemma.) Such an argument cannot be refuted, because it reduces the question of motivation to a tautology. Whatever is chosen guarantees *ipso facto* the greater utility. But we have seen how such a reduction makes trivial the very notion of utility and with it of motivation. We learn nothing if we always redefine utilities in such a way that the choices come out "right." But we may learn a great deal if we observe how people choose when the motivations dictating the choices conflict, e.g., when desire for gain indicates one choice while other considerations prescribe another.

Whatever "conscience" is, considerations having to do with it are not instrumental. One does not obey one's conscience in order to gain some other end, but simply in order to appease it. In other words, obeying one's conscience is an end in itself like escaping from pain.

Actually we encounter situations of this sort already in those decisions under risk where one must gamble on unique events. Suppose the decisionmaker must choose between two acts, each involving a risky outcome, knowing that the situation will never recur. The prevailing opinion is that he should choose the risk with the greater expected gain. But why? If the situation were to be repeated many times, the choice could be rationalized on the grounds that the expected gains will in the long run become *actual* gains, so that the gambler will be simply choosing a larger gain over a smaller one (supposing that the utilities accruing successively can be added). But clearly this argument does not hold for the single case.

There is no getting around the fact that the decisionmaker who chooses the gamble with the greater "expected value" cannot rationalize his choice on the basis of comparing the actual returns. What he compares are *expectations*, i.e., his own states

8 For an experimental demonstration of what can be expected in response to a trusting act, *see* Deutsch, M., "Trust and suspicion," *Journal of Conflict Resolution*, 2 (1958), pp. 265–279.

of mind associated with each of the choices. If there is no long run, the expectation remains an expectation, that is, only a mental state like conscience. In the last analysis, one chooses the gamble with the greater expectation simply because "it is the right thing to do."

If the choice of strategy C in a *single* play of prisoner's dilemma can be rationalized at all, it must be rationalized on similar grounds. The player who chooses C does so because he feels it is the proper thing to do. He feels that he ought to behave as he would like the other to behave. He knows that if they both behave as he expects, both will benefit. I submit that these are pretty compelling reasons for choosing C. However, they are not strategic reasons. Indeed they contradict the "rational" strategic principle, which dictates D unconditionally.

The strategic superiority of D ceases to be unconditional if the game is repeated. We shall analyze this situation by representing a repeated prisoner's dilemma as a supergame, in which the successive plays become the moves. The supergame too can be collapsed into normal form. We shall do this and then examine the properties of the resulting matrix.

Since the number of available strategies grows very rapidly with the number of moves, it will be impractical to consider even a moderately large number of repeat-ed plays. Fortunately, the principle we wish to illustrate comes out clearly, even in a two-move supergame.

PRISONER'S DILEMMA PLAYED TWICE

Imagine a game with two moves. Each of the moves, made by the players simultaneously, is a play of an ordinary prisoner's dilemma game (cf. Matrix 7). The result of the first move is announced to the players before they make the second (final) move.

In this game, each player has eight strategies (compared with two in the simple game). A's strategies are shown in Table 1.

Table 1

Strategy	On first move play	If B played C on first move, on second move play	If B played D on first move, on second move play
1	C	C	C
2	C	C	D
3	C	D	C
4	C	D	D
5	D	C	C
6	D	C	D
7	D	D	C
8	D	D	D

B's strategies are, of course, entirely analogous. In normal form, this game is represented by Matrix 8.

	B₁	B₂	B₃	B₄	B₅	B₆	B₇	B₈
A₁	10, 10	10, 10	−5, 15	−5, 15	−5, 15	−5, 15	−20, 20	−20, 20
A₂	10, 10	10, 10	−5, 15	−5, 15	0, 0	0, 0	−15, 5	−15, 5
A₃	15, −5	0, 0	0, 0	0, 0	−5, 15	−5, 15	−20, 20	−20, 20
A₄	15, −5	15, −5	0, 0	0, 0	0, 0	0, 0	−15, 5	−15, 5
A₅	15, −5	0, 0	15, −5	0, 0	0, 0	−15, 5	0, 0	−15, 5
A₆	15, −5	0, 0	15, −5	0, 0	15, −5	−10, −10	15, −5	−10, −10
A₇	20, −20	5, −15	20, −20	5, −15	0, 0	−15, 5	0, 0	−15, 5
A₈	20, −20	5, −15	20, −20	5, −15	5, −15	10, −10	5, −15	−10, −10

Matrix 8.

We shall henceforth refer to the ordinary prisoner's dilemma game as PD and to the two-move game as PD^2. From the matrix we learn that strategy 8, the totally uncooperative strategy, analogous to strategy D in the simple game, is still an *equilibrium* (minimax) strategy for each player. If one of the players holds on to this strategy, the other must also, since none of the other strategies are better against it, and all but one are actually worse. In this sense the new two-move game is no different from the simple game. However, in PD^2 it is no longer true that strategy 8, the totally uncooperative strategy *dominates* every other (the way strategy D dominates strategy C in PD). For instance, we see from Matrix 8 that against B's strategy 2, A's strategy 4 is better than strategy 8.

Therefore, we can no longer say that it is to each player's *unconditional* advantage (even strategically speaking) to choose the totally uncooperative strategy 8. It is still true, however, that neither player has any reason to suppose that the other will play anything but the totally uncooperative strategy. This strategy (being the minimax) remains "the most prudent," just as strategy D had been in PD. However, while the knowledge of what the other was going to do was irrelevant in PD (cf. page 49) it is no longer irrelevant in PD^2. Hence the reasons for choosing strategy 8 are not as *compelling* as the reasons for choosing strategy D had been in the simple prisoner's dilemma game. To rationalize strategy 8 it is no longer enough to point out that it is obviously superior against *any* opponent, friendly or hostile. The rationalization now requires an argument based on the assumed nature of the opponent, namely, that he is a "prudent man" rather than a "just man with an initial reservoir of good will," for the latter is what we might call a player who chooses strategy 2 in PD^2, as we shall see in a moment.

Strategy 2 could properly be called an "initially trusting tit-for-tat strategy." Stated in words, the strategy says: "I shall play cooperatively on the first move; on the second move, I shall play the way the other has played on the first." Against this strategy, the other player will do better to cooperate, at least on the first move. Even if he cooperates on both moves, he does better than with the totally uncooperative strategy 8. However, his "best" answer (from the point of view of self-interest) is to cooperate on the first play and to defect on the second, which is strategy 4.

But in order to be safe in playing strategy 4, B needs to be assured that A will indeed play strategy 2, rather than strategy 8. To be sure, it is to A's advantage to play strategy 2 (against which B will play strategy 4 if he is rational), but this will happen only if B *knows* that A has chosen strategy 2 (rather than, say, 8). Now in the game under consideration, there is no way for A to communicate to B that he is in fact choosing strategy 2 (which is of advantage to both). This may seem like an artificial restriction. If a real life situation resembles PD^2, why should not one player inform the other that he will use strategy 2, which is of advantage to both? In our formalized game, the rules do not allow it (as for example, the rules of bridge do not allow communication between partners which would be of advantage to both). But in real life cannot one of the parties take things into his own hands?

To this there are at least three answers.

One answer is on the basis of an assumption that there are rules governing communication, for example, a rule that states who communicates first. Note that this does not contradict the assumption that a player "takes matters into his own hands." If he is in a *position* to do this, this means that the situation makes this possible. Recall that the source of the rules is not specified in game theory. The rules need not be agreements; they may be in the nature of the situation itself. If this is so, then the choices of acts under the constraints of the rules, in particular choices of communicative acts *which are not simultaneous*, constitute *moves* (not strategies) in a still larger supergame. It is that game which we must now represent in normal form. Once we have done this, we are again faced with a situation where strategies are chosen simultaneously and only one choice (by both players) determines the outcome.

The second answer is on the basis of the

assumption that there are no rules. That is, the constraints are not known. If so, a player can make no "plans" as to what he will communicate. The timing of the communication may be an essential element in its effect. This is especially true in pre-empted communications like irreversible threats, of which we shall have more to say in later chapters. An irreversible threat is effective only if it arrives before the opponent has sent *his* irreversible threat. If there are no rules one cannot be sure that one can beat the other to the punch. If the irreversible threats arrive simultaneously, the effect of "taking things into one's own hands" may be not at all the intended one.

The third answer is also on the assumption that there are no rules. If so, there is no rule governing the credibility of the communication. In fact "to believe or not to believe" is a choice open to the receiver of communication and can itself be considered a move of a game.

Formally speaking, a "game" can in principle be constructed from any of these situations, if we allow for indeterminate outcomes, for example, if the question of whose communication arrives first is a matter of chance (in case there are no rules governing the sequence of communications). But this is *another* game and must be analyzed in its own context. Whatever the game is, we arrive at the same sort of situation when we have reduced it to normal form. If the game in normal form has a dilemma in it, one does not resolve the dilemma of *that game* by introducing communication moves. If one does this, one is considering another game.

THE DILEMMA HAS NOT BEEN RESOLVED

It appears we have again arrived at an obstacle, the same obstacle we faced every time when a definition of "rational deci-sion," which had been sufficient to provide optimal choices in previous decision problems, ceased to be sufficient in a new problem. Previously, when faced with such situations, we extended the range of concepts needed to define rational decision, successively adding utility, probability, awareness of others' interests, mixed strategy, etc.

In the original formulation of game theory,[9] the decision problem generated by the non-zero-sum game is solved in the extended context of *enforceable agreement* between the players. Such agreements were not assumed as a factor in the zero-sum game; and indeed there is no point to such agreements, since in those games the interests of the players are diametrically opposed. In the context of the non-zero-sum game, an enforceable agreement can be a crucial factor. This can be seen immediately if we assume that the two players of prisoner's dilemma can make a pact (collusion, coalition) to effect the mutually advantageous outcome (CC). But a pact implies concepts not considered hitherto. The prospective partners must have a common language. They must also either profess allegiance or render obedience to a common authority, either coercive, like a police force, or internalized, like conscience. That is to say, pacts must be enforceable. Observe that if a non-enforceable agreement to choose C is made by the two players of PD, the question "Should I *keep* the pact?" induces another game exactly like PD: of the two available strategies, namely C' (to keep the pact) and D' (to break the pact), D' is the dominating strategy. (It is more advantageous to break the pact regardless of whether the other keeps his.) The assumption that agreements are enforceable is therefore vital if coalitions and collusions are to be included as factors in rational decisions.

[9] Von Neumann, J. and Morgenstern, O. *Theory of Games and Economic Behavior* (2nd ed.) (Princeton, N.J.: Princeton University Press, 1947).

SIMULATION

BY NORMAN C. DALKEY

Simulation is a technique for studying complex military processes. It consists of an abstract representation of the more important features of the situation to be studied, designed to be played through in time either by hand or by computer. The basic advantages of simulation are that hypothetical future conflicts can be investigated in terms of elementary events, and precise, reproducible models can be constructed of processes for which there are no general theories or analytical descriptions. The major disadvantages are that simulation is slow and expensive and the range of cases that can be treated is highly limited. New developments in computers, simulation languages, and model structures will extend the utility of simulation for the military analyst.

INTRODUCTION

Simulation is one of the more extensively used of the tools available to the military analyst. The primary reason is that military conflict involves a complex interaction of of numerous elements—kinds of weapons, patterns of deployment and employment, rapid changes over time. In many instances, simulation is the only technique by which this intricate interplay of factors can be studied in a precise and reproducible fashion.

The word "simulation," a distant relative of the term "similar," refers to a construct which resembles the process or system to be studied but which is easier to manipulate or investigate. Examples might be a model aircraft in a wind tunnel, an army field exercise, a group of subjects in a psychological laboratory where the individuals play the role of major military commands, a computer routine which describes the minute-by-minute activity of aircraft and missiles in a nuclear exchange. In these cases, the real object of interests, because of its size, expense, uncontrollability, or danger to national security, is difficult or impossible to study. A representation of the object which is similar to it in essential properties is investigated instead.

If we include all the kinds of investigative aids mentioned above, we wind up with a very diverse set of things to talk about. For the purposes of this book, it is convenient to focus on a limited few. Accordingly, study objects which physically resemble the phenomena of interest, such as the wind-tunnel model or the field exercise, will not be discussed. Constructs where human subjects play the analogue role or where human judgment and decisions influence the course of the exercise will—rather arbitrarily—be assigned to gaming.[1] There remains the case where the construct or representation is a logical or mathematical model and where the course of a play or run of the simulation is determined by a set of formulated rules.

There is no sharp distinction between simulation and analytic models of the sort previously discussed. What difference exists lies primarily in degree of generality or abstractness, and in the way in which the models are manipulated.

---

[1] This limitation is arbitrary in the sense that the term "simulation" is frequently applied to laboratory exercises involving human subjects as representations of suborganizations.

Reprinted by permission from *Systems Analysis and Policy Planning: Applications in Defense* (New York: American Elsevier Publishing Company, Inc., 1968), Chap. 12, pp. 241–254.

Mr. Dalkey has been a mathematician with the RAND Corporation since 1948, and he has served in the Office of Operations Analysis, Headquarters, USAF. He is a specialist in mathematical logic and the application of computers to complex decision-making.

The analytic model is likely to be quite abstract and deal with aggregated entities, such as number of weapons and number of targets, whereas the simulation is likely to refer to a list of specific weapons or individually named targets. The analytic model is likely to be expressed by a set of equations, whereas the simulation may be expressed by a set of rules determining what "happens" under various circumstances. Finally, the analytic model is likely to be formulated primarily for the purpose of finding a "solution" to the equations—for example, an optimal strategy, a least expensive combination of weapons, a best mix of warheads and decoys in a missile payload. The simulation, however, will be used to investigate a specific case, such as the outcome of a duel between a given type of fighter and a given type of bomber when the fighter undertakes a tail chase from a given position relative to the bomber; the relative damage to each side in a central nuclear war if each uses a specific allocation of weapons to targets; and so on. In short, the simulation is likely to be used in an experimental fashion, to generate specific case studies or instances; the analytic model will be used to compute some over-all quantity or strategy. Simulation can be used in a laboratory fashion to generate data to suggest or test hypotheses. If systems analysis is viewed as a scientific endeavor, the experimental role of simulation is probably the preferred employment. However, in many studies this process is shortened—because of exigencies of time, cost, or the simple failure of the results to suggest a useful theory—and specific results are presented for the edification of the decisionmaker.

Although a simulation can be carried through manually, using more or less traditional map exercise and hand accounting methods, the high-speed computer is ideally suited for keeping track of the many items and performing the large number of separate computations that determine the changing status of the elements. In the case of more extensive simulations, manual computation is only a theoretical possibility. Literally millions of man-hours would be required to perform the exercise.

SIMULATION BASICS

Most military simulations exhibit a common structure which can be expressed in terms of

1. Elements,
2. Attributes,
3. Activities,
4. Plans,
5. Time.

"Elements" are all the items involved in the interaction—missiles, aircraft, missile sites, airfields, support targets, and the like. "Attributes" are the properties of the elements—location, type, speed, status (surviving or destroyed), and so on. Some of the attributes such as CEP, weapon load, or kill probability, may be designated as *parameters* on the ground that these are the factors likely to be varied during a study. "Activities" are rules prescribing what will occur under various circumstances—such as radar detection, fighter-bomber duel, bomb drop, missile interception, and so on. "Plans" are the prescriptions of how weapons are to be employed (strategy, tactics, doctrine). In many instances where plans are reducible to a simply formulated doctrine—as, for example, a simple x to 1 allocation of fighters to bombers in an air-defense model—they may be included as an aspect of "activities," but in other cases they may require elaborate instructions that indicate how each individual weapon is to be employed. In such cases, a large part of the input may consist of the plans for each side.

The role of time in a military simulation is of basic importance. Military conflict is not a static balance of forces; it is a dynamic interaction of destructive events, where the relative time of an occurrence can be crucial. A large measure of the complexity in military matters stems from the intricacies of temporal change. One of the fundamental values of simulation is that it can display a complex pattern of events in time.

There are two ways of handling time in a simulation: the *interval* and the *event* technique. In the interval technique, time is divided into a number of sections, usually equal. The conflict is examined interval by interval and, except for the order in which activities are taken up, the occurrences during a time interval are considered as simultaneous.

In the event type of model, a list of potential occurrences is compiled on the basis of planned actions and the events these can produce. This list must be edited frequently, some events being cancelled and new events added. For example, the planned arrival of a bomber over target must be cancelled if, prior to arrival, it is shot down by air defenses. This event may, on the other hand, give rise to a new one, namely, the unplanned detonation of weapons during the crash. Otherwise, the events list is processed by taking up each event at the time it is scheduled to occur and applying the appropriate activity. Theoretically, the event type of model allows as fine a division of time as might be wished; practically, the fineness of division is limited by the number of events that can be managed.

Event-type models have become more popular than interval types because of their greater freedom in dealing with highly time-dependent interactions. However, this advantage is compensated for by the need for storing and updating a large list of events. In some models, both methods of handling time are used, where event processing is resorted to only for critical interactions.

Another basic consideration relates to the treatment of chance, or probabilistic events. Most events of military interest are partially determined by chance. Abort probability, target damage probability, kill probability, CEP, and so on represent instances of basic planning factors in military analysis that are by and large statistical rather than exact. As in the case of time, there are two major techniques for handling chance events, though combinations are also possible. The two are *expected-value* and *Monte Carlo*. In an expected-value model, when a chance event arises, the expected result of that event is assumed to occur. For example, if a group of 10 aircraft is flying over a defended area, and the probability of a plane being shot down

is 30 per cent, the model presumes that 3 are shot down and 7 survive. In a Monte Carlo model, on the other hand, the outcome of probabilistic events is determined by chance. In the example just given, a random number between one and a hundred might be generated for each aircraft. This random number would be compared with, say, 30. If it is greater than 30, the aircraft is assumed to survive; if less, the aircraft is presumed to be shot down. Although, in a large number of such events, the average number surviving will be 7, in any particular case the number might be larger or smaller.

In a Monte Carlo model, a single run is one sample out of a very large number of possible cases. In order to discover what the expected or average outcome of the conflict would be, it may be necessary to run many cases—take a large sample—varying only the random numbers selected. This is a drawback of the Monte Carlo method of handling chance events in large models. On the other hand, the expected-value model says nothing about the variance—how widely outcomes can differ from the average result. The Monte Carlo technique can, with sufficient cases, give some indication of how far away from the average outcomes may be.

Both types of models have their value. The Monte Carlo type appears to have greater favor at the moment because of the advantages mentioned, but also because it lends an air of realism to a simulation, and because it allows chance to be applied to single events. If a lone aircraft is examined flying over a defense, and the probability of its being shot down is, say, 45 per cent, there is something repellent about saying that 45 per cent of the plane is shot down and 55 per cent continues on to bomb a target.[2] But while the language of the expected-value model is perhaps strange, it is not necessarily wrong. With the Monte Carlo technique the plane is either shot down or it is not, depending on the random number drawn.

[2] I have had an Air Force officer challenge me by asking, "If you were 65 per cent of a fighter pilot, how would you attack 15 per cent of a bomber?"

Another basic consideration in constructing a simulation is level of detail. Air forces can be described in terms of individual aircraft flying separate routes to specific bomb release points, or in terms of groups of aircraft of varying size attacking groups of targets. Local defenses can be expressed in terms of individual missile launchers, missile complexes, or simply the level of local defense for a set of targets. Time can be divided into seconds, minutes, or hours. In general, there is no "right" level—the level of detail that is selected should depend on the problem being posed and the resources of the analysis team. However, it rarely is worth creating a detailed simulation for a single study unless the study is very extensive. The reason is that building a simulation is expensive in time and effort, and an extensive use of the model is necessary to make the cost worthwhile. The statement is made more than once in this book that there are no general-purpose models, that the model should be tailored to the problem.[3] This is correct, but in the case of large-scale simulations an attempt is usually made to introduce some general-purpose features—to make the model sufficiently flexible, so that a variety of problems can be dealt with. This can be done to some extent by allowing a fairly large number of parameters that can be easily changed to define new weapons characteristics, changed force structures, or different modes of employment. As a result, simulations are commonly constructed with more detail than a particular problem requires.

Finally, a basic question concerning simulation is the computation technique selected. It has already been pointed out that high-speed computers are ideally suited for the type of data manipulation involved in most simulations. For some elaborate simulations, it would be completely impractical to conduct the exercise without a high-speed computer. In other cases, however, different methods have been useful. One technique, the map exercise, has proved of continuing value, especially for simulations involving ground forces. Variants of the map exercise, in which forces

[3] Note especially chapters 3 and 10.

are represented by poker chips, have been useful in exercises on a smaller scale. The chips are convenient for bookkeeping purposes. Furthermore, the graphic "picture" of the course of the war afforded by the map is often valuable to the analyst in furthering his understanding of what is going on.

CHOICE OF SIMULATION TECHNIQUES

The preceding remarks lead naturally to the question, When is it reasonable to use a simulation, and how does the analyst go about setting one up? The principal reason for resorting to simulation, as was indicated in the introduction, is that the phenomena to be studied are too complex to be manageable in any other way. It is fair to say that simulation is often used because of ignorance—the analyst does not know how military events proceed in the large, and hence cannot formulate a simple, general model of the conflict. On the other hand, he can express the situation in terms of elementary events because he understands them or, equivalently, he may have data only on elementary events and not on global interactions. There have been too few modern wars to derive general relationships from direct experience. War is especially difficult in this regard, because of the two-sidedness of the conflict. Many wars would have to occur to give some indication of the effect of different war plans. Elementary events, on the other hand, are more closely related to peacetime activities. Many are subject to peacetime exercise and test. By formulating the simulation in terms of elementary events, complex interactions can be synthesized.

A problem can be complex in ways other than involving a large number of elements or intricate interactions. In general, the formulation of a simple model of a military situation requires that a simple expression for the payoff or the criterion must be available. But in many cases it is not possible to express a simple payoff. For example, in a nuclear exchange we would be interested in the damage to civilian targets on each side, in the forces remaining, in the fallout contamination, in effects on allied nations, and so on. But there is no simple trade-off among these effects that will allow us to produce a single index, and, above all, there is no simple criterion for determining which mode of attack is preferable. This is so because—among other reasons—nuclear conflict is nonzero-sum. Both sides can lose catastrophically, depending upon the modes of attack selected.

In a case where the payoff and the criterion are unclear or complex, it frequently happens that the only useful method of proceeding is to exhibit the outcomes of several cases, and let the decisionmaker "make up his feelings" about them.

A third kind of complexity is related to uncertainty. There may be many factors in the situation about which—even in elementary form—we do not have sufficient information. This is particularly true if we are examining proposed weapon systems or conflicts several years from now. One popular mode of procedure in this kind of situation is to express in the formal analysis just that part of the situation that we do have solid information about and leave the uncertainties to an informal, judgmental "discussion." For many types of problems this is a reasonable way to proceed. But for many others it is desirable to include the uncertain elements in the formal analysis. There are several ways in which this can be done. Separate cases can be run for a range of values of the uncertain items; or the cases can be examined closely to see at what stage—if at all—the uncertain items are crucial; or a set of extreme values can be tried to see what the total effect of the uncertain factors might be. None of these procedures is a completely satisfactory answer to the problem of uncertainty because it is rarely possible to do a thorough job—the number of cases required is generally prohibitive. But they are frequently more informative than the less formal exercise of judgment.

When it comes to the specifics of laying out a simulation, the familiar caveat that we are concerned with an art and not a science holds. In general, the form of the simulation and the level of detail will be determined by the problem to be tackled and by the resources at the analyst's com-mand. Other factors will be influential—the kind of data available, deadlines, and so on.

It should be reiterated that a simulation is generally only a part of the over-all systems analysis. Usually, simulation will be concerned with the effectiveness computation. The simulation model needs to be supplemented by a cost model and an evaluation technique. This last is frequently referred to as "analysis of results," but a great deal more is involved than mere tabulation.

In setting up a simulation it is generally a good practice to formulate first a small, possibly aggregated example and play this simulation by hand. The small model provides a way of checking whether or not the simulation has a complete structure and adequately contains the factors of primary interest. Several attempts to develop simulation of ground warfare have failed at this stage. There is no problem in defining the elements, attributes, activities, and time scale for ground warfare, but the representation of *plans*—that is, the simulation of the complex decision process for ground forces—has not been satisfactorily solved. The small model also provides a way of obtaining gross estimates of the significance of various factors. Some items can be left out of, or aggregated in, the production model if the exploratory model indicates they are not critical.

After the exploratory phase there are several directions in which one can proceed. The basic model must be translated into a detailed program and this in turn must be checked by trial runs. If the program is to be run on a computer, additional coding and debugging are involved. A large proportion of the study effort is usually absorbed by the collection of data and transformation of those data to a form suitable for the model. After the runs or exercises, analyzing the voluminous information generated is normally a major task.

EXAMPLES OF THE USE OF SIMULATION

Some examples may give a feeling for the wide range of military situations which have been dealt with by simulations and some feeling for the variety of model structures that have been employed.

Perhaps the archetype of the large-scale military simulation is the global air war model, STAGE, used in the U.S. Air Force by the Office of the Assistant Chief of Staff for Studies and Analysis. This model, which has gone through a number of versions (it was known as the Strategic Operations Model when initiated at RAND and later as the Air Battle Model), provides a highly detailed play of a world-wide nuclear exchange. It follows the movement of individual aircraft and missiles as they leave their airfields or sites, as they travel through air or space, and as they pass through surveillance radar coverage and defenses; it computes how many are lost to enemy interception; and it determines the damage that the surviving weapons inflict on military and civilian targets. For bombers, the activity of supporting tankers is followed, and, for missiles, decoys and other penetration aids can be programmed in.

The air battle is scrutinized every few minutes of simulated time, allowing a rich interplay of operational constraints, relative timing of penetration and attacks on defenses, and so on. Because of its large size, STAGE requires several hours on an IBM 7090 computer for a single Monte Carlo run, in which many thousands of chance events are evaluated. It also requires the investment of hundreds of man-days in the preparation of inputs. STAGE is admirably suited for the detailed evaluation of war plans and for testing the effect of operational constraints on the execution of a war plan during enemy attack.

On the opposite extreme is a model called FLIOP, which was designed at RAND as an aid in strategic planning. FLIOP checks the feasibility of a single bomber mission. The input is a detailed profile, including potential refueling points, of a bomber mission from its beginning at the take-off base, through its flight over enemy territory (visiting one or more targets), to its ending at a recovery base. FLIOP is also coded for high-speed computer. It operates by "flying the bomber backwards," that is, by starting at the landing base and accumulating fuel and the weight of bombs as it backs up. Missions are judged infeasi-

ble if the fuel required exceeds the capacity of the bomber or if the over-all weight exceeds the maximum flying weight before a refueling point is reached. If these restraints do not operate, a tanker can, as it were, remove the excess fuel at refueling and the bomber can accumulate more weight on its way back to the take-off base. The routine computes the required off-load and also determines the feasibility of the tanker mission. The routine takes only a few minutes on the computer, allowing the computation of hundreds of flight plans in a day. As an aside, we might note that the peculiarity that the simulation operates in reverse has been modified in practice. It is clearly more intuitive to have the aircraft fly forward, even in a computer!

Several models exist which evaluate an anti-ballistic missile defense against combinations of incoming warheads and penetration aids. Because time is critical in ballistic missile interception, these models break time down into very fine-grained intervals. They are examples of a rather rare sort of simulation using high speed computers. It may take several hours to compute an interaction that in reality would involve only seconds.

The models follow the trajectories of incoming warheads, decoys, and other penetration aids, assess the probability of detection at various stages, schedule interceptors according to input doctrines, and assess kill probabilities. A variety of interceptor characteristics, payloads of ICBMs, and firing doctrines can be examined.

Similar models exist for evaluating a duel between a fighter plane and a bomber. An initial relative position and heading for the fighter and the bomber are selected, and the model simulates the chase, taking into account the constraints on speed and turning radius of the fighter and the effects the bomber can produce on the fighter's radar by using electronic countermeasures. The fighter's armament will be activated if it is successful in achieving a firing position (as defined by a preassigned doctrine). By running a large number of initial positions and headings, we can estimate an average kill probability for a specific fighter configuration against a given bomber type.

It should be pointed out that simulations, in the sense in which the term has been used here, can be submodels in a larger, less formal exercise. Thus, the activities of a depot can be simulated as an element in a larger logistics exercise. Attrition models, or damage models, have been used as parts of a theatre war game where much of the play is determined by the decisions of teams of players or of umpire teams, or both.

The preceding examples are only a few of the hundreds of simulations that have been developed in the last few years for military analysis. Simulation routines have been developed for evaluating damage to communications in a nuclear war, evaluating the effects of conventional bombing on troops and equipment in a non-nuclear attack, assessing the effects of terrain on the coverage of defensive radars, computing the rapidity with which a task force can deploy from the United States to a foreign theatre. There are very few areas of interest to the Air Force that have not been made the subject of a simulation.

PROS AND CONS

Because of the widespread use of simulation for military analyses, it is important to achieve a perspective on its good and bad features. On the positive side, and preeminently, a simulation may be the only feasible way to analyze a highly complex system or process. By reducing the complex process to more elementary activities, simulation provides data from peacetime experience or tests that can be used for analyzing hypothetical conflicts. In addition, by breaking a complicated situation down into a series of simple interactions, a simulation can make the evaluation of plans or weapons effectiveness more understandable to military decisionmakers. The language of a simulation is usually much closer to the language of the military officer than the language of a mathematical analysis. This aspect of simulations has a number of ramifications. Since the simulation is a completely formulated model, all

concepts employed in it must be completely and sharply defined. This is especially true if the simulation is programmed for a computer. Hence, the simulation furnishes a common and precise language for a team of specialists working with it. It also can provide a common language for the specialists and the decisionmaker. The fact that the assumptions of the model are explicit and the results can be duplicated is extremely important when a sizable community with differing interests (for example, the various agencies of the Department of Defense) is interacting on a problem.

The model also furnishes a logical structure or framework for the data involved. Frequently the simulation is itself a check on the consistency and completeness of the data. Some of the most useful data files in the Pentagon are those developed for simulation exercises.

More generally, even in those areas where solid data are lacking and the analyst must proceed by assumption, judgment, or guesstimate, a formulated model requires that the assumptions be clearly spelled out. The simulation can check the consistency of assumptions. Most important of all, the simulation can derive the consequences of assumptions in an impersonal, objective fashion. These properties, of course, are common to all completely formulated models.

On the negative side, simulation has a number of shortcomings from the point of view of an analyst conducting studies for military decisions. Above all, simulation is likely to be a slow and cumbersome method of attacking a problem. This is especially true if the simulation is coded for a computer. Despite advances in the programming art, a sizable effort is required to formulate and code a simulation of even moderate size. Furthermore, a large computer routine is difficult to modify. If some assumptions turn out to be inappropriate after the first few runs, a major reprogramming may be required. In many cases, this fact leads the analyst to build in general-purpose features ("flexibility") which overly complicate the model and extend programming time. Almost by definition, simulations pose difficulties in predicting which features will turn out to be inappropriate, or be outrun by technology.

A simulation is likely to be restrictive with respect to the range of cases that can be examined. In most situations of military interest, the number of possibilities worth looking at is enormous. There will be a range of possible weapons, a variety of possible employments, and large areas governed by chance. And these possibilities are inflated by applying to both contestants. For most simulations, the best the analyst can do is select a very few cases out of this vast spectrum of possibilities for examination.

Some of the values of simulation can easily be overplayed and turned into liabilities. The fact that simulations are couched in a language close to that of the military can give a false air of reality to the results. The fact that activities are examined in minute detail and at electronic speed can lend an air of glamour to an exercise that can turn the head of a decisionmaker who is not fully aware of the guesses and approximations that went into the study. Because simulations can be set up in a fairly direct fashion, by stringing elementary processes together, it is all too frequently the lazy way out of a problem. In many instances, simulation is not the best approach, but it is the easiest.

One of the more insidious drawbacks of large simulations is that—although the elementary events are perspicuous and easy to understand—the sheer volume of occurrences is so great that the model will be treated as a black box into which data are shoveled and out of which neatly packaged results are delivered. I once sat in on a briefing on a large military model in which one "explanatory" chart showed precisely this analogy, complete with hopper and conveyor belts.

The question inevitably arises, "How do you know that a simulation actually represents what it is supposed to?" This question is usually accompanied by the query, "Why don't you try your simulation on some historical war or battle and see if it can predict the outcome?" This issue is common, of course, to all military systems analysis, but it arises more naturally with regard to simulation because of the greater air of authenticity which surrounds it.

The answer is that in most cases we can't determine how good the simulation is. The ultimate test might appear to be a war of the type being simulated. But even if such a war should occur, the outcome might look quite different from the outcome of the simulation, and yet the simulation might not be wrong. Chance, accidental features not in the model, on the spot decisions of commanders, and so on may strongly affect the outcome. This, in effect, is the answer to those who ask why we do not try to simulate a specific historical battle. One of the major determinants of historical battles is the specific decisions made by commanders. To be candid, we do not have a good way to simulate such decisions. In a simulation, the course of the exercise is determined by a set of decisions—plans or doctrine—usually devised by the analyst. The plans and the doctrine may be very good, but they may not represent the decisions of any real commander in the thick of battle—both may be right, but very different.

Why not limit simulation to those situations or those problem areas where there is good solid information? A rather good case can be made for the presumption that simulation has been applied where not enough is known to justify the elaboration of ignorance. On this question, the good sense of the analyst generally provides the only guide. Limiting simulation to problem areas where impeccable data exist would exclude the technique from most systems analyses. Frequently, the attempt to build a simulation in a shadowy area uncovers significant features of the problem that were overlooked or hidden in qualitative discussions. The simulation then serves to define the needed information in a sharp fashion, and to point up its importance.

NEW DEVELOPMENTS

Some of the drawbacks of simulation can be ameliorated, and several developments are under way that promise to increase its practicality and power.

This chapter is not the place to discuss at

any length the impact of increasing computer capabilities, but it should be pointed out that developments in faster, more capacious machines, with the capability, for example, of parallel rather than purely serial computation, will make some of the larger types of simulation easier to manage. Improvements in data handling—for example, more direct access by the machine to data files—will simplify generating inputs. The major transformation that is now under way toward maintaining military information in machine accessible form will undoubtedly make the task of simulation-building easier. Conversely, the construction of more extensive simulations will improve the structure of data files.

Of more direct interest is the rapidly expanding number of simulation languages being developed for high-speed computers. These languages, which bear interesting names like GASP, SOL, Militran, Simscript, and SOS, are an attempt to furnish the analyst with a certain basic skeleton of a simulation: list-processing structures to simplify the defining of elements and attributes and the handling of internal data; an event processor for automatically scheduling and computing events according to activities specified by the analyst; output techniques for more or less automatically generating the information the analyst wishes from his simulation. These meta-simulations save the analyst the time required to reproduce those elements which are common to a large number of simulation routines. They have proved highly useful in a number of studies in reducing the time required to set up a simulation and also in simplifying modifications in a routine after its initial formulation. Although not applicable to all types of simulation, and probably not yet of great value for the larger models, these efforts are expanding rapidly and promise to remove much of the repetitive, housekeeping part of the job of constructing simulations.

One other development we might note is the marriage of simulation with other techniques. Outstanding among the serious handicaps of simulation is its case-study quality. On the other hand, one of its strong points is its ability to deal with a richly detailed problem area. It is feasible to construct not a single model, but a family of models, at different levels of generality or aggregation. By covering the same problem at several levels, it would be possible to employ the tools of mathematical analysis—optimization, sensitivity analysis, trade-off analysis, and so on—at the higher levels of generality and then check the accuracy and feasibility of the solution against more detailed models of the simulation type. This prospect appears most inviting in the area of complex planning—for example, in strategic attack planning or in logistics planning for a large deployment—where it is desirable to survey a large number of possible plans before deciding on a preferred one, but where, at the same time, the operational feasibility of the plan is a significant criterion.

In the area of strategic attack planning, RAND has developed experimentally such a family of models. It consists of a highly aggregated, two-sided war game which plays a single nuclear exchange in a hundredth of a second, an intermediate-level simulation of a two-sided air war which computes the result of implementing a pair of plans in a matter of minutes, and finally a planning routine which takes the intermediate-level plan and unpacks it in great detail, including tanker support for bombers, relative timing of penetration, and specific geography for launch sites and targets. The smallest model can be employed to survey thousands of cases in a hasty or—so to speak—back-of-the-envelope fashion. The lower-level models can then be used to spell out the details and check the reasonableness of the outcome of the upper-level survey.[4]

This type of hierarchy of models can be used to compensate for the cumbersomeness of the simulation, and to relieve the abstractness of more analytic techniques.

[4] For a fuller description, *see* N. C. Dalkey, *Families of Models*, The RAND Corporation, P-3198, August, 1965.

PART III

ARMS AND MORALITY: THE PARADOXICAL EFFECTS OF FORCE

We have suggested that force is the distinguishing feature of defense policy. In the earlier parts of this volume we considered the *employment* of force and then the *management* of force. In this concluding part we turn to the *effects* of force. This latter, we think, is a more elusive topic. While a fairly voluminous literature exists on the ethical problems of war and peace, the appearance of thermonuclear weapons has added a new dimension and the problems have become even more complicated and controversial.

There is a grave and growing concern expressed about the effects of force, not only in terms of the international environment but also in terms of our own national environment. There seems to be, for example, an increasing awareness of the insufficiency of threats to use force as a basis for international order. Conflicts have been kept limited. Since World War II nuclear weapons have not been used, but there are no guarantees for the future. Nuclear war may occur. There could be a deliberate thermonuclear attack by one nation against another. Small-scale, limited wars can escalate to nuclear conflict. And, there is ever the danger of accident, error, miscalculation, or folly.

Indeed, we are living in the shadows of a third world war, a war that may be fought with nuclear weapons, a war that will leave no victors, only the vanquished. We have already suggested that one of the more startling characteristics of the nineteen-sixties is that there are two nations mutually able to annihilate each other. Moreover, this number may increase in the next decade. While none of the new members of "the Nuclear Club" has shown a lack of respect for the inherent danger of mass destruction weapons, the future is considerably less certain.

We feel that one of the great paradoxes of modern warfare is that armed forces and arms, even by their very existence, to say nothing of their use, destroy that which they are created to protect and preserve. In the international environment, it seems paradoxical that the nuclear superpowers prepare for a war that neither wants to fight, a war which, in reality, neither can win, a war for which there is no effective military defense. Yet, as these nations try to avoid a cataclysmic all-out thermonuclear exchange, their preparation for "avoiding" such terror may make that terror more likely. This effect of force is certainly unintended, for the deterrence of general nuclear war is the basic rationale for the existence of nuclear weapons.

Internally, too, nations exhibit increasing concern about the bankruptcy of force and this seems particularly true in the United States. Our defense posture, which calls for our capability to deter, and if need be fight, at any level of conflict—from insurgencies, to limited regional wars, to general nuclear war—is incredibly expensive. It is expensive not only in terms of dollar costs, but also in terms of other values since the defense budget itself represents competition for resources which might be applied to education, urban development, transportation, and other domestic programs. Again, there are logical reasons for our buildup and maintenance of a huge defense establishment. And, again, these consequences of our defense policies are unintended. Policymakers and thoughtful citizens alike worry about whether or not we may be sacrificing national values for national defense, when the rationale of forces and arms should be, instead, that they exist to protect and promote national values.

The above frustrating, unintended effects of force are the major focus of the next three chapters. We believe they are compelling issues which must be discussed. What are the moral aspects of the existence and use of forces and arms? When is it "just" to use force, especially in the mod-

ern cases of intervention? What is the role of the military profession in American society? What is the impact of a large defense establishment on our basic institutions of government? Are there practical political alternatives to force in a nuclear world?

The purpose of Part III is to raise these important questions and to provide a representative sample of the more thoughtful answers to them. If there is a common thread among the articles it is that each author is deeply concerned about the adverse effects of force.

CHAPTER 8

The Just Use of Force: Nuclear Deterrence and Limited Intervention

Nuclear deterrence has worked for nearly two decades. Nation-states possessing nuclear weapons, particularly the nuclear superpowers, have calculatedly tried to avoid direct confrontations in which their nation's interests could be considered immediately at stake—where the threat of use or the actual use of nuclear weapons might be considered strategically necessary. Paradoxically, of course, the major powers maintain nuclear forces which are useful only if they are not used. But within the context of unlimited nuclear war, limited wars, especially limited interventions, have become the pattern of conflict in the post-World War II period, with more than a dozen limited conflicts occurring.

We have indicated that we believe that limited war represents the pattern of future conflict. Hopefully, nuclear war will continue to be deterred. However, the risks continue to be extremely high at any level of conflict. There is always the frightening danger that lesser conflicts might escalate to become nuclear. And many persons believe that this danger becomes more likely as nuclear-owning nations proliferate. This situation leads to rather fundamental questions regarding the use of American armed forces: Can we justify the use of force? When should force be used? Are interventions ever justified?

In his short, thoughtful essay, Alain Enthoven presents his reconciliation of the Christian doctrine and the use of force in the nuclear era. He sets up certain criteria for using force in the suppression of evil. He believes that United States force basically exists to make conflict less likely, and he worries about "whether we have a better alternative."

Hans Morgenthau, in the second article, suggests that in the foreseeable future the nuclear superpowers will continue to avoid direct confrontation and instead, will continue to intervene either directly or indirectly in the political affairs of smaller nations, most often in the newer, developing nations. He believes that the United States has intervened too often with the rationale of combatting communism and suggests that the United States is justified in intervening only when our national interests require it and when our intervention has a good chance of succeeding.

MORAL ASPECTS

BY ALAIN C. ENTHOVEN

I am sure that you are all concerned, as I am, about the moral problems raised by our military preparations. Is it right or wrong for us to be buying hundreds of inter-continental ballistic missiles, fighter-bomber aircraft, and equipment for many Army divisions? Can we justify weapon systems and war plans that would enable us, if a nuclear war were thrust upon us, to fight back even though doing so might lead to the deaths of many millions of people?

These are extremely complex and difficult problems that we can neither escape nor hope to understand fully. Their moral solution cannot come from artificial simplification. Tonight what I would like to do is offer you some questions and some reflections that may illuminate some of the issues. A proper appreciation of the moral aspects of defense policy requires an understanding of theology as well as the alternative strategies and their implications. A dialogue is required, and I offer the following remarks in that spirit.

According to traditional Christian doctrine, the use of force to repress evil can be justifiable under certain conditions including the following: First, the use of force must have a reasonable chance of success. Second, if successful, it must offer a better situation than the one that would prevail in the absence of the use of force. Third, the force that is used must be proportional to the objectives being sought (or the evil being repressed). For this to be satisfied, peaceful means of redress must have failed. Fourth, the force must be used with the intention of sparing non-combatants and with a reasonable prospect of actually doing so.

It is interesting to observe that the potentially catastrophic character of thermonuclear war has forced practical decision-makers, reasoning in a secular context, to adopt a set of criteria very much like those of the traditional Christian doctrine and to apply them to the design of the military posture of the United States. Now, much more than in the recent past, our use of force is being carefully proportioned to the objectives being sought, and the objectives are being carefully limited to those which at the same time are necessary for our security and which do not pose the kind of unlimited threat to our opponents in the cold war that would drive them to unleash nuclear war. In the past, before nuclear weapons, deliberate limitations in the use of force did not present much of a practical problem because of the limited destructive power of non-nuclear weapons. Nuclear weapons have now given such contraints great practical importance.

Within the broad policy of armed resistance to aggression, which is one of the alternatives open to us, and in terms of the moral criteria of the traditional Christian doctrine, I think it is fair to say that we have made considerable progress. This is not to say that we have gone as far as we can go. But it does suggest that all the moral questions are not concerned with whether or not armed resistance can be justifiable.

During the past fifteen years, a number of commentators, theologians and others, have taken the position that although in former times the traditional doctrine was valid and, under appropriate conditions the use of armed force could be justified, now,

Reprinted by permission. Excerpts from an address before the Loyola University Forum for National Affairs, Los Angeles, California, February 10, 1963 and before Students, Faculty, and Friends of Seattle University, Seattle, Washington, February 11, 1963. The address appears in Samuel A. Tucker (ed.), *A Modern Design for Defense Decision: A McNamara-Hitch-Enthoven Anthology* (Washington, D.C.: Industrial College of the Armed Forces, 1966), pp. 210–212.

Mr. Enthoven is Assistant Secretary of Defense (Systems Analysis). He is a Rhodes Scholar and was on the economics staff of the RAND Corporation prior to joining the Department of Defense.

in the atomic age, there can be no justifiable war. The argument has been made that nuclear war does not and cannot offer a reasonable chance of bringing about a better situation than that which would have prevailed in the absence of the use of force; that the thermonuclear force, being essentially unlimited in its destructive effects, cannot be proportioned to reasonable objectives; and that with it the non-combatants cannot be spared. Therefore, many argue that the traditional doctrine is obsolete and that a new doctrine must be found. Some argue that the only morally acceptable course is to renounce nuclear weapons; others believe that we must renounce the use of force altogether.

I would not want to suggest that this line of thought is not based on good and compelling reasons, even though I have not found it convincing myself. It may prove to be the case that the danger of escalation is so great that future limited non-nuclear wars will bring with them an intolerable risk of massive thermonuclear destruction. However, experience in the past fifteen years has shown that non-nuclear wars can be kept limited and that freedom can be defended from Communist aggression without massive destruction.

A question to consider in one's critical thought on this problem is whether the view that the traditional doctrine is obsolete is based on an overemphasis on unlimited nuclear war, perhaps an identification of all armed conflict with it. An unlimited nuclear war is an extreme on a broad spectrum of possible armed conflicts. Of course, it is a very important extreme because of its disastrous consequences, but it is not the whole spectrum. In fact, it is only one among many possible kinds of thermonuclear war. It can be a mistake to apply reasoning based on this extreme to all kinds of armed resistance to aggression and injustice. I think it is important to recognize this, for if our thinking is unclear

on this point, and if we identify any use of armed force with unlimited destruction, we are likely unnecessarily to disarm ourselves and leave ourselves victims of Communist aggression.

It is clear that we have elected to retain the threat of use of nuclear weapons in our own defense and that of our allies. We thereby consciously accept the risk that we will have to use them. Some people believe that we should reject the use of nuclear weapons. Before accepting such a judgment, one should consider carefully the full implications of such a decision. We do have worldwide responsibilities. Many millions of people depend for their lives and freedom on our military strength. In this respect, the United States is in a very different position from any other country in the free world.

The question I would like to leave with you . . . is whether current U.S. defense policy, which emphasizes deterrence, control, and the use of the appropriately limited amount of force, represents a good reconciliation of the traditional doctrine with the facts of life in the nuclear age. We have achieved some success with the controlled use of force. We are still alive and free today, and the missiles are out of Cuba. We are running great risks, to be sure, but would the risks be ameliorated by laying down our arms? It is tragic that nations must at times resort to armed force to resolve their differences. War is destructive and it has evil consequences. But our defense posture is being designed to make war less likely and less destructive. I am not suggesting that we can make war and violence desirable. The question is whether we have a better alternative.

. . . I have defended our policies on the grounds that they make sense. Can they also be defended on the grounds that they are moral? Viewed with perspective, the two should be the same.

TO INTERVENE OR NOT TO INTERVENE

BY HANS J. MORGENTHAU

I.

Intervention is as ancient and well-established an instrument of foreign policy as are diplomatic pressure, negotiations and war. From the time of the ancient Greeks to this day, some states have found it advantageous to intervene in the affairs of other states on behalf of their own interest and against the latters' will. Other states, in view of their interests, have opposed such interventions and have intervened on behalf of theirs.

It is only since the French Revolution of 1789 and the rise of the nation-state that the legitimacy of intervention has been questioned. Article 119 of the French Constitution of 1793 declared that the French people "do not interfere in the domestic affairs of other nations and will not tolerate interference by other nations in their affairs." This declaration ushered in a period of interventions by all concerned on the largest possible scale. For a century and a half afterwards, statesmen, lawyers and political writers tried in vain to formulate objective criteria by which to distinguish between legitimate and illegitimate intervention. The principle of nonintervention was incorporated into the textbooks of international law, and statesmen have never ceased to pay lip service to it. In December, 1965, the United Nations General Assembly adopted a "Declaration on the Inadmissibility of Intervention in the Domestic Affairs of States and the Protection of their Independence and Sovereignty," according to which "no state has the right to intervene, directly or indirectly, for any reason whatever, in the internal or external affairs of any other state . . ." and "no state shall organize, assist, foment, finance, incite or tolerate subversive, terrorist or armed activities directed toward the violent overthrow of another state, or interfere in civil strife in another state." Yet again we are witnessing throughout the world activities violating all the rules laid down in this Declaration.

Both the legal commitments against intervention and the practice of intervention serve the political purposes of particular nations. The former serve to discredit the intervention of the other side and to justify one's own. Thus the principle of nonintervention, as formulated at the beginning of the nineteenth century, sought to protect the new nation-states from interference by the traditional monarchies of Europe. For the main instrument of the Holy Alliance, openly proclaimed in the treaty establishing it, was intervention. Thus, to give only two examples among many, Russia tried to intervene in Spain in 1820, and actually intervened in Hungary in 1848, in order to defeat liberal revolutions. Great Britain opposed these interventions because it was opposed to the expansion of Russian power. Yet it intervened on behalf of nationalism in Greece and on behalf of the conservative status quo in Portugal because its interests seemed to require it.

What we have witnessed since the end of the Second World War thus appears as a mere continuation of a tradition which was well established in the nineteenth century. There is nothing new either in the contemporary doctrine opposing intervention or in the pragmatic use of intervention on behalf of the interests of indi-

Reprinted by permission from *Foreign Affairs*, April, 1967, pp. 425–436. Copyright by The Council on Foreign Relations, Inc., New York.

Mr. Morgenthau is Professor of Political Science and Modern History and Director of the Center for the Study of American Foreign Policy at the University of Chicago. He has served as Visiting Senior Fellow on the Council of Foreign Relations and as a consultant to the Departments of State and Defense. He is the author of *Politics Among Nations* (4th ed., 1967), *Vietnam and the United States* (1965), and many other books and articles.

vidual nations. What Great Britain and Russia were doing in the nineteenth century, the United States and the Soviet Union seem to be doing today. Thus, to cite again two spectacular examples among many, the Soviet Union intervened in Hungary in 1956 as Russia had done in 1848, and the United States intervened in Cuba at the beginning of the sixties as it had done in the first decades of the century. Yet there are fundamental differences between the interventions of the past and those of the present. Five such differences have significantly altered the techniques of contemporary intervention, have drastically reduced the traditional legal significance of the consent of the state intervened against, and have affected in a general way the peace and order of the world.

First, the process of decolonization, which started after the Second World War and is now almost completed, has more than doubled the number of sovereign nations. Many if not most of these new nations are not viable political, military and economic entities; they are lacking in some if not all of the prerequisites of nationhood. Their governments need regular outside support. Thus France subsidizes its former colonies in Africa; all the major industrial nations extend economic and financial aid to the new ones, and the United States, the Soviet Union and China do so on a competitive basis.

What makes this aid a lever for intervention is the fact that in most cases it is not just an advantage which the new nations can afford to take or leave, but a condition for their survival. The Indian economy, for example, would collapse without outside support, and in consequence the Indian state itself would probably distintegrate. Large masses of Egyptians would starve without the outside supply of food. What is true of these two ancient and relatively well developed nations is of course true of most of the new nations which are nations within their present boundaries only by virtue of the accidents of colonial policy: the supplier of foreign aid holds the power of life and death over them. If a foreign nation supplies aid it intervenes; if it does not supply

aid it also intervenes. In the measure that the government must depend on foreign aid for its own and its nation's survival it is inevitably exposed to political pressures from the supplying government. Many of the recipient governments have been able to minimize or even neutralize these political pressures by keeping open alternative sources of foreign aid and by playing one supplying government against the other. Some nations, such as Egypt, have developed this technique into a fine and highly successful art.

Second, our age resembles the period of history after the Napoleonic Wars, when the theory of nonintervention and the practice of intervention flourished, in that it is a revolutionary age. Many nations, new and old, are threatened by revolution, or are at one time or another in the throes of it. A successful revolution frequently portends a new orientation in the country's foreign policy, as it did in the Congo, Cuba, and Indonesia. Thus the great powers, expecting gains or fearing disadvantages from the revolution, are tempted to intervene on the side of the faction favoring them. This is particularly so when the revolution is committed to a communist or anti-communist position. Thus China has almost indiscriminately intervened throughout the world on behalf of subversive movements, very much in the manner in which the Bolshevist government under Lenin and Trotsky tried to promote world revolution. In many nations, the United States and the Soviet Union oppose each other surreptitiously through the intermediary of governments and political movements. It is at this point that the third new factor comes into play.

Of all the revolutionary changes that have occurred in world politics since the end of the Second World War, none has exerted a greater influence upon the conduct of foreign policy than the recognition on the part of the two superpowers, armed with a large arsenal of nuclear weapons, that a direct confrontation between them would entail unacceptable risks; for it could lead to their mutual destruction. Both have recognized that a nuclear war fought against each other would be a suicidal absurdity. Thus they have decided that they must avoid a direct confrontation. This is the real political and military meaning of the slogan of "peaceful coexistence."

Instead of confronting each other openly and directly, the United States and the Soviet Union have chosen to oppose and compete with each other surreptitiously through the intermediary of third parties. The internal weakness of most new and emerging nations requiring foreign support and the revolutionary situation in many of them give the great powers the opportunity of doing so. Thus, aside from competing for influence upon a particular government in the traditional ways, the United States and the Soviet Union have interjected their power into the domestic conflicts of weak nations, supporting the government or the opposition as the case may be. While one might think that on ideological grounds the United States would always intervene on the side of the government and the Soviet Union on the side of the opposition, it is characteristic of the interplay between ideology and power politics, to which we shall turn in a moment, that this has not always been so. Thus the Soviet Union intervened in Hungary in 1956 on the side of the government, and the United States has been intervening in Cuba on the side of the opposition. The Soviet slogan of support for "wars of national liberation" is in truth an ideological justification of Soviet support for that side in a civil conflict in which the Soviet Union happens to have an interest. In the Congo, the United States and the Soviet Union have switched their support from the government to the opposition and back again according to the fortunes of a succession of civil wars.

While contemporary interventions serving national power interests have sometimes been masked by the ideologies of communism and anti-communism, these ideologies have been an independent motivating force. This is the fourth factor which we must consider. The United States and the Soviet Union face each other not only as two great powers which in the traditional ways compete for advantage. They also face each other as the fountainheads of two hostile and incompatible ideologies,

systems of government and ways of life, each trying to expand the reach of its respective political values and institutions and to prevent the expansion of the other. Thus the cold war has not only been a conflict between two world powers but also a contest between two secular religions. And like the religious wars of the seventeenth century, the war between communism and democracy does not respect national boundaries. It finds enemies and allies in all countries, opposing the one and supporting the other regardless of the niceties of international law. Here is the dynamic force which has led the two superpowers to intervene all over the globe, sometimes surreptitiously, sometimes openly, sometimes with the accepted methods of diplomatic pressure and propaganda, sometimes with the frowned-upon instruments of covert subversion and open force.

These four factors favoring intervention in our time are counteracted by a fifth one, which in a sense compensates for the weakness of the nations intervened in. Having just emerged from a colonial status or struggling to emerge from a semicolonial one, these nations react to their dependence on outside support with a fierce resistance to the threat of "neo-colonialism." While they cannot exist without support from stronger nations, they refuse to exchange their newly won independence for a new dependency. Hence their ambivalent reaction to outside intervention. They need it and they resent it. This ambivalence compels them to choose among several different courses of action. They can seek support from multiple outside sources, thereby canceling out dependence on one by dependence on the other. They can alternate among different sources of support, at one time relying on one, and at another time relying on another. Finally, they can choose between complete dependence and complete independence, either by becoming a client of one of the major powers or by forswearing outside support altogether.

This ambivalence of the weak nations imposes new techniques upon the intervening ones. Intervention must either be brutally direct in order to overcome resistance or it must be surreptitious in order to be acceptable, or the two extremes may be combined. Thus the United States intervened in Cuba in 1961 through the proxy of a refugee force, and the Soviet Union intervened in Hungary in 1956 by appointing a government which asked for its intervention.

II.

What follows from this condition of intervention in our time for the foreign policies of the United States? Four basic conclusions can be drawn: the futility of the search for abstract principles, the error of anti-communist intervention per se, the self-defeating character of anti-revolutionary intervention per se, and the requirement of prudence.

First, it is futile to search for an abstract principle which would allow us to distinguish in a concrete case between legitimate and illegitimate intervention. This was so even in the nineteenth century when intervention for the purpose of colonial expansion was generally regarded to be legitimate and when the active players on the political stage were relatively self-sufficient nation-states, which not only were not in need of intervention but actually were opposed to it as a threat to their existence. If this was so then, it stands to reason that in an age where large segments of whole continents must choose between anarchy and intervention, intervention cannot be limited by abstract principles, let alone effectively outlawed by a United Nations resolution.

Let us suppose that nation *A* intervenes on behalf of the government of nation *B* by giving it military, economic and technical aid on the latter's request, and that the government of *B* becomes so completely dependent upon *A* as to act as the latter's satellite. Let us further suppose that the local opposition calls upon country *C* for support against the agents of a foreign oppressor and that *C* heeds that call. Which one of these interventions is legitimate? Country *A* will of course say that its own is and *C*'s is not, and vice versa, and the ideologues on both sides will be kept busy justifying the one and damning the

other. This ideological shadowboxing cannot affect the incidence of interventions. All nations will continue to be guided in their decisions to intervene and their choice of the means of intervention by what they regard as their respective national interests. There is indeed an urgent need for the governments of the great powers to abide by certain rules according to which the game of intervention is to be played. But these rules must be deduced not from abstract principles which are incapable of controlling the actions of governments, but from the interests of the nations concerned and from their practice of foreign policy reflecting those interests.

The failure to understand this distinction between abstract principles and national interests as guidance for a policy of intervention was in good measure responsible for the fiasco of the Bay of Pigs in 1961. The United States was resolved to intervene on behalf of its interests, but it was also resolved to intervene in such a way as not openly to violate the principle of nonintervention. Both resolutions were legitimate in terms of American interests. The United States had an interest in eliminating the political and military power of the Soviet Union, which used Cuba as a base from which to threaten the security interests of the United States in the Western Hemisphere. The United States also had an interest in avoiding whatever would jeopardize its standing in the new and emerging nations. The United States failed to assign priorities to these two interests. In order to minimize the loss of prestige, the United States jeopardized the success of the intervention. Instead of using concern for prestige as a datum among others in the political equation—that is, as an interest among others—it submitted to it as though it were an abstract principle imposing absolute limits upon the actions necessary to achieve success. In consequence, the United States failed thrice. The intervention did not succeed; in the attempt we suffered the temporary impairment of our standing among the new and emerging nations; and we lost much prestige as a great nation able to use its power successfully on behalf of its interests.

Had the United States approached the problem of intervening in Cuba in a rational fashion, it would have asked itself which was more important: to succeed in the intervention or to prevent a temporary loss of prestige among the new and emerging nations. Had it settled upon the latter alternative, it would have refrained from intervening altogether; had it chosen the former alternative, it would have taken all the measures necessary to make the intervention a success, regardless of unfavorable reactions in the rest of the world. Instead, it sought the best of both worlds and got the worst.

The Soviet Union's intervention in Hungary in 1956 is instructive in this respect. The Soviet Union put the success of the intervention above all other considerations, and succeeded. Its prestige throughout the world suffered drastically in consequence. But Hungary is today a communist state within the orbit of the Soviet Union, and Soviet prestige recovered quickly from the damage it suffered in 1956.

The interventions of the United States in Cuba, the Dominican Republic and Viet Nam, as well as others less spectacular, have been justified as reactions to communist intervention. This argument derives from the assumption that communism everywhere in the world is not only morally unacceptable and philosophically hostile to the United States, but is also detrimental to the national interests of the United States and must therefore be opposed on political as well as moral and philosophic grounds. I shall assume for the purposes of this discussion that, as a matter of fact, communist intervention actually preceded ours in all these instances, and shall raise the question as to whether our national interest required our counter-intervention.

Ten or twenty years ago, this question could have been answered in the positive without further examination. For then communism anywhere in the world was a mere extension of Soviet power, controlled and used for the purposes of that power. Since we were committed to the containment of the Soviet Union, we were also committed to the containment of communism anywhere in the world. However, today we are faced not with one monolithic communist bloc controlled and used by the Soviet Union, but with a variety of communisms, whose relations with the Soviet Union and China change from country to country and from time to time and whose bearing upon the interests of the United States requires empirical examination in each concrete instance. Communism has become polycentric, that is to say, each communist government and movement, to a greater or lesser extent, pursues its own national interests within the common framework of communist ideology and institutions. The bearing which the pursuit of those interests has upon the interests of the United States must be determined in terms not of communist ideology but of the compatibility of those interests with the interests of the United States.

Subjecting our interventions in Cuba, the Dominican Republic and Viet Nam to this empirical test, one realizes the inadequacy of the simple slogan "stop communism" as the rationale of our interventions. While this slogan is popular at home and makes but minimal demands upon discriminating judgment, it inspires policies which do either too much or too little in opposing communism and can provide no yardstick for a policy which measures the degree of its opposition by the degree of the communist threat. Thus on the one hand, as part of the settlement of the missile crisis of 1962, we pledged ourselves not to intervene in Cuba, which is today a military and political outpost of the Soviet Union and the fountainhead of subversion and military intervention in the Western Hemisphere, and as such directly affects the interests of the United States. On the other hand, we have intervened massively in Viet Nam, even at the risk of a major war, although the communist threat to American interests from Viet Nam is at best remote and in any event is infinitely more remote than the communist threat emanating from Cuba.

As concerns the intervention in the Dominican Republic, even if one takes at face value the official assessment that the revolution of April 1965 was controlled by Cuban communists, it appears incongruous that we intervened massively in the Dominican Republic, whose revolution was, according to our government's assessment of the facts, a mere symptom of the disease, while the disease itself—that is, Cuban communism—is exempt from effective intervention altogether.

This type of intervention against communism per se naturally tends to blend into intervention against revolution per se. Thus we tend to intervene against all radical revolutionary movements because we are afraid lest they be taken over by communists, and conversely we tend to intervene on behalf of all governments and movements which are opposed to radical revolution, because they are also opposed to communism. Such a policy of intervention is unsound on intellectual grounds for the reasons mentioned in our discussion of contemporary communism; it is also bound to fail in practice.

Many nations of Asia, Africa and Latin America are today in a pre-revolutionary stage, and it is likely to be only a matter of time until actual revolution will break out in one or another of these nations. The revolutionary movements which will then come to the fore are bound to have, to a greater or lesser degree, a communist component; that is, they risk being taken over by communism. Nothing is simpler, both in terms of intellectual effort and, at least initially, practical execution, than to trace all these revolutions to a common conspiratorial source, to equate all revolutionary movements with world communism, and to oppose them with indiscriminate fervor as uniformly hostile to our interests. The United States would then be forced to intervene against revolutions throughout the world because of the ever-present threat of a communist take-over, and would transform itself, in spite of its better insight and intentions, into an anti-revolutionary power per se.

Such a policy of intervention might succeed if it had to deal with nothing more than isolated revolutionary movements which could be smothered by force of arms. But it cannot succeed, since it is faced with revolutionary situations all over the world; for even the militarily most powerful nation does not have sufficient usable resources to deal simultaneously with a number of acute revolutions. Such a policy of indiscriminate intervention against revolution is bound to fail not only with regard to the individual revolution to which it is applied but also in terms of its own indiscriminate anti-communism. For the very logic which would make us appear as the anti-revolutionary power per se would surrender to communism the sponsorship of revolution everywhere. Thus anti-communist intervention achieves what it aims to prevent: the exploitation of the revolutions of the age by communism.

In truth, the choice before us is not between the status quo and revolution or even between communist and non-communist revolution, but between a revolution hostile to the interests of the United States and a revolution which is not hostile to these interests. The United States, far from intervening against revolutions per se, has therefore to intervene in competition with the main instigators of revolution—the Soviet Union, Communist China, and Cuba—on behalf of revolution. This intervention should serve two alternative aims: first, to protect the revolution from a communist take-over, and second, if we should fail in this, to prevent such a communist revolution from turning against the interest of the United States. Such a policy, substituting the yardstick of the American national interest for that of anti-communism, would obviously form a complete reversal of the positions which we have taken in recent years and of which our interventions in Viet Nam and the Dominican Republic are the recent prime examples.

If this analysis of our policy of intervention is correct, then we have intervened not wisely but too well. Our policy of intervention has been under the ideological spell of our opposition to communism and potentially communist-led revolutions. Yet while this ideological orientation has continued to determine our policy of intervention, the Soviet Union has continued to pay lip service to support for "wars of national liberation" but has in practice relegated these wars to a secondary place in the struggle for the world. This softening of the Soviet ideological position has become one of the points of contention in the ideological dispute between the Soviet Union and China.

In a statement of June 14, 1963, the Chinese Communist Party declared that "the whole cause of the international proletarian revolution hinges on the outcome of revolutionary struggles" in the "vast areas of Asia, Africa and Latin America" that are today the "storm centers of world revolution dealing direct blows at imperialism." In their reply of July 14 of the same year, Soviet leaders opposed the "'new theory' according to which the decisive force in the struggle against imperialism . . . is not the world system of socialism, not the struggle of the international working class, but . . . the national liberation movement." The Soviet Union's recent practice of restraint in fomenting and supporting revolution has matched this theoretical position. This ideological "revisionism" has of course not prevented the Soviet Union from intervening, as in Syria and Somalia, when its national interest appeared to require intervention.

One factor which cannot have failed to influence the Soviet Union in toning down its ideological commitment to intervention has been the relative failure of ideological intervention. The United States, China and Cuba have joined the Soviet Union in the experience of that failure. The new and emerging nations have been eager to reap the benefits of intervention, but have also been very anxious not to be tied with ideological strings to the intervening nation. After making great efforts, expending considerable resources and running serious risks, the participants in this worldwide ideological competition are still approximately at the point from which they started: measured against their ambitions and expectations, the uncommitted third of the world is still by and large an ideological no-man's-land.

This experience of failure is particularly painful, and ought to be particularly instructive, for the United States. For we have intervened in the political, military and economic affairs of other countries to the tune of far in excess of $100 billion, and we are at present involved in a costly and risky war in order to build a nation in South Viet Nam. Only the enemies of the United States will question the generosity of these efforts, which have no parallel in history. But have these efforts been wise? Have the commitments made and risks taken been commensurate with the results to be expected and actually achieved? The answer must be in the negative. Our economic aid has been successful in supporting economies which are already in the process of development; it has been by and large unsuccessful in creating economic development where none existed before, largely because the moral and rational preconditions for such development were lacking. Learning from this failure, we have established the theoretical principle of concentrating aid upon the few nations which can use it rather than giving it to the many who need it. While this principle of selectivity is sound in theory, its consistent practical application has been thwarted by the harsh political and military realities which may require economic aid which is economically not justified, as well as by political and military considerations derived from the ideological concerns discussed above.

This principle of selectivity must be extended to the political and military sphere as well. We have come to overrate enormously what a nation can do for another nation by intervening in its affairs—even with the latter's consent. This overestimation of our power to intervene is a corollary of our ideological commitment, which by its very nature has no limit. Committed to intervening against communist aggression and subversion anywhere, we have come to assume that we have the power to do so successfully. But in truth, both the need for intervention and the chances for successful intervention are much more limited than we have been led to believe. Intervene we must where our national interest requires it and where our power gives us a chance to succeed. The choice of these occasions will be determined not by sweeping ideological commitments nor by blind reliance upon American power but by a careful calculation of the interests involved and the power available. If the United States applies this standard, it will intervene less and succeed more.

CHAPTER 9

The Effects of Force: The Warfare State and American Democracy

One of the fundamental reasons for the existence of American military force is that it serves as perhaps the ultimate instrument of statecraft to protect our vital interests and values. At the same time, the basic paradox is that even when force is not used its very existence may be destructive of those things which serve as its *raison d'être*. There are several examples: (1) We maintain large military forces to preserve world peace, yet our production of arms may provoke increased production of arms by our adversaries, which in turn may make war both more likely and more dangerous. Thus armaments themselves may be considered a source of insecurity as well as a source of security and peace. (2) The basic purpose of maintaining military forces is to protect our basic liberal democratic values, our individual liberties. Yet drafting men, training them in violence, and maintaining large, standing armies, the concomitant secrecy, loyalty oaths, and investigations, and the inuring of men to killing that takes place in limited wars, all eat away at our fundamental values. (3) Force exists to preserve our constitutional system of government, yet the maintenance of a large military complex may lead to a reversal of roles for our basic governmental institutions. It is often alleged that policymaking has become too centralized in the executive branch with the legislative branch becoming only the approving or amending agency, which is antithetical to the concept of a representative democracy. (4) Force exists as only one of the instruments of American policy, yet there is the fear that it will become the dominant instrument. (5) Overarching, perhaps, there is the specter of the "military-industrial" complex which no one seems to understand fully, and to which very few commentators have been able to apply explicit criticism. While there are still other examples, perhaps these suffice. All add fuel to the fire of fear that the United States's maintenance of the arms necessary to deter or to fight an adversary leads to the creation of a warfare state in which basic national values may be sacrificed in the name of national security.

Samuel Huntington's book on *The Soldier and the State* is referred to as "a searching analysis of the tensions in American society caused by military professionalism and the demands of national security." In the excerpt used in our Chapter 9, the Lasswellian concept of the "Garrison State" is explained and refuted, and there is an incisive commentary on the role and influence of the American military profession since World War II.

Harry Ransom poses the critical dilemma of whether the United States can provide the necessary defense and at the same time protect democratic values and institutions. He states that "the basic problem is not whether the American system can continue to provide both defense and democracy, but whether it can provide either."

CIVIL-MILITARY RELATIONS IN THE POSTWAR DECADE

BY SAMUEL P. HUNTINGTON

THE ALTERNATIVES OF CIVIL-MILITARY RELATIONS

The outstanding aspect of civil-military relations in the decade after World War II was the heightened and persistent peacetime tension between military imperatives and American liberal society. This tension was the product of the continued dominance of liberalism in the American mind and the continued acceptance of the liberal approach to civil-military relations, on the one hand, and, on the other, the intensified threats to American military security, which increased the need for military requirements and the relevance of the military ethic to national policy. The Cold War shifted the emphasis in foreign policy from diplomacy and maneuver to construction and operation. Under the old pattern of international politics with a number of major powers, the static element tended to be the relative power of the various states. The dynamic element was the shifts in coalitions and alignments among the states. After World War II, however, the diplomatic element was relatively static—countries were generally on one side or the other in the Cold War—and the dynamic element was the relative military and economic strength of the two coalitions. The changes of China and Yugoslavia from one side to the other in the Cold War altered the balance of power, but their significance paled before the relative progress of the Soviet Union and the United States in developing thermonuclear capabilities. Military requirements thus became a fundamental ingredient of foreign policy, and

military men and institutions acquired authority and influence far surpassing that ever previously possessed by military professionals on the American scene.

The basic issue raised was: how can a liberal society provide for its military security when this requires the maintenance of professional military forces and institutions fundamentally at odds with liberalism? Theoretically, three answers were possible. The tension could be relieved by returning to the pre-1940 pattern of civil-military relations: cutting military forces to the bone, isolating military institutions from society, and reducing military influence to negligible proportions. American society would remain true to its liberalism, and the American military would return within the shell of professional conservatism. Pursuit of this policy, however, would realize these values at the expense of the nation's military security. A second solution was to accept increased military authority and influence but to insist that military leaders abandon their professional outlook and that military institutions be reformed along liberal lines. While sacrificing traditional military conservatism, this would assure the continuance of liberalism in American society and would provide, at least temporarily, for the military security of the nation. But, as happened in World War II, it might accomplish these ends at the expense of long-range goals and at the ultimate loss of military effectiveness. Finally, the tension between the military and society could be lessened if society adopted a more sympathetic understanding and appreciation of the military viewpoint

Mr. Huntington is Chairman of the Department of Government and a member of the Center for International Affairs at Harvard University. He has written extensively in the areas of national security policy and civil-military relations. He is the author of many books including *The Common Defense: Strategic Problems in National Politics* (1961). He is currently specializing in the study of political development.

and military needs. This would involve a drastic change in the basic American liberal ethic. The most difficult, it would also be the most permanent solution of the problem. In actual practice, American civil-military relations in the decade after World War II followed no one of these paths exclusively. The tension between conservative military outlook, liberal social values, and increased military power largely went unresolved. The dominant tendencies in policy and practice, however, tended toward the first and second solutions: the traditional liberal approaches of the extirpation or transmutation of military values and institutions.

POSTWAR PERSPECTIVES ON CIVIL-MILITARY RELATIONS

The Garrison-State Hypothesis. The postwar decade saw the appearance on the American scene of the first conscious, systematic, and sophisticated theory of civil-military relations since the business pacifism of Spencer, Sumner, and Carnegie. This was the concept of the garrison state. Originally stated by Harold Lasswell in 1937 as an interpretation of the Sino-Japanese War, the garrison-state idea was not fully elaborated and popularized by its creator until World War II and later.[1]

[1] "Sino-Japanese Crisis: The Garrison State versus the Civilian State," *China Quarterly*, II (Fall 1937), 643–649; "The Garrison State and Specialists on Violence," *Amer. Jour. of Sociology*, XLVI (January 1941), 455–468, reprinted in *The Analysis of Political Behavior* (New York, 1947); "The Interrelations of World Organization and Society," *Yale Law Journal*, LV (August 1946), 889–909; "The Prospects of Cooperation in a Bipolar World," *Univ. of Chicago Law Rev.*, XV (Summer 1948), 877–901; " 'Inevitable' War: A Problem in the Control of Long-Range Expectations," *World Politics*, II (October 1949), 1–39; "The Threat Inherent in the Garrison-Police State," in *National Security and Individual Freedom* (New York), 1950, pp. 23–49; "The Universal Peril: Perpetual Crisis and the Garrison-Prison State," in Lyman Bryson, Louis Finkelstein, and R. M. MacIver (eds.), *Perspectives on a Troubled Decade: Science, Philosophy, and Religion, 1939–1949* (New York, 1950), pp. 323–328; "Does the Garrison State Threaten Civil Rights?" *Annals* of the American Academy, CCLXXV (May 1951), 111–116; "The Threat to Privacy," in Robert M. MacIver, (ed.), *Conflict of Loyalties* (New York, 1952), pp. 121–140; "The

It then became a dominant theory of civil-military relations, adhered to by intellectuals and alluded to by mass media. The significance of Lasswell's concept derived from its attempt to apply the traditional assumptions and values of American liberalism to the apparent reality of continuing military crisis. It combined three elements: an analysis of twentieth-century international conflicts; a prediction that the result of permanent warfare would be the general emergence of a particular form of social organization, the garrison state; and a statement of preference for a world commonwealth as the only possible alternative to the garrison state.

Lasswell's analysis began where Herbert Spencer left off. The natural course of history is progressive and upward from bellicose, militaristic caste society to pacific, bourgeois, democratic society. The polar opposite of the war state or garrison state is the business state, which in the nineteenth century was becoming increasingly dominant. The goals of society at that time were economic—"the peaceable pursuit of prosperity"—and the rise of complex commercial relations "seemed to create a world market which would furnish the material basis for a limited world order." Beginning about the time of World War I, however, history went off the track. The trend was reversed "*from* progress toward a world commonwealth of free men, *toward* a world order in which the garrison-prison state reintroduces caste bound social systems." As a result of this interruption or deflection of history, the tendency "of our time is away from the dominance of the business man, and toward the supremacy of the soldier." War hastens this tendency, but even the "continuing threat of war can bring about a reversal in the direction of history." Lasswell was vague as to the causes of war, crisis, and insecurity. Looking out on the mid-twentieth-century world, he accepted the fact of their existence. Starting from the liberal theory of progress, however, he had no real ex-

World Revolutionary Situation," in Carl J. Friedrich (ed.), *Totalitarianism* (Cambridge, Mass., 1954), pp. 360–380.

planation of why they did exist. They were apparently linked to the "world revolutionary pattern of our times" which began with the Communist seizure of power in Russia in 1917. This caused continuing tension between the universal ideas of communism and the particular needs and institutions of the Russian state. The garrison state is either the logical product of the world revolution or a reaction against it. In his earlier writings Lasswell appeared to assume the latter; in his subsequent ones the former. Once one state adopts the garrison state form of social organization, the pattern tends to be universalized. In both the United States and the Soviet Union, the garrison state will be the necessary product of the prolonged continuation of the Cold War.

Inherent in Lasswell's prediction as to the nature of the garrison state were many misconceptions with respect to the content of military values, the possibility of militarization in a liberal society, and the relation between patterns of civil-military relations and forms of the state. Basic to the garrison state, in his view, was the subordination of all other purposes and activities to war and the preparation for war. The preeminence of bellicose intentions and values is reflected in the dominant role which the military play in the state. Lasswell here made the traditional liberal identification of the military with war and violence. Holding to the erroneous view that the military have a greater preference for war than do civilians, he easily arrived at a magnified estimate of their strength in modern society, concluding that the militarization of belief systems would be relatively easy under the threat of war. In his earlier formulations, he stressed the predominant role of the military skill group in the direction of the garrison state. In subsequent essays, he broadened his view of the ruling elite to include the police as well as the military; the specialists in violence, foreign and domestic, were now the top group. Coincidentally, he spoke more of the "garrison-police" state or "garrison-prison" state than just simply the garrison state. Lasswell continued the liberal pattern of linking the military with the enemy, identifying them here with the totalitarian police. He also tended, more specifically, to identify the garrison state with the immediate threat of the moment. In 1937, Japan was its closest approximation; after the beginning of the Cold War, Soviet Russia most fully manifested garrison-state tendencies.

The garrison state requires the centralization of power in the hands of the few. The executive and the military gain power at the expense of the legislature and civilian politicians. Democratic institutions are abolished or become purely ceremonial. "Authority flows downward from commanders at the top; initiative from the bottom can hardly be endured." Lasswell assumed that military control is incompatible with democracy, identifying a form of civil-military relations with a form of government. With the garrison state, the scope of the government eventually expands and becomes practically coextensive with society. Technology, industry, science, and labor are all regimented for the purposes of war. This utilization of the resources of society for military defense is essentially unproductive. The garrison state differs from both capitalism and socialism where production is for use: indeed, at one point Lasswell defined the "dominant crisis of our time" as "socialism *and* capitalism *versus* the garrison-prison state." The garrison state has an egalitarian aspect but it is the egalitarianism of the camp: an equality of short rations and much danger. The garrison state is, in short, Ludendorff's nation at war, Spencer's militant society plus modern technology. In its ultimate form it is indistinguishable from modern totalitarianism.

Lasswell variously rated the emergence of a garrison state as "probable," "likely," or "what might happen." The only admissible alternative to the garrison state, the "triumph of human felicity" in a world commonwealth is, however, "at least not out of the question." Modern science and technology bind the world together. The fundamental aspirations of mankind are the same the world over. Even Russian and American cultures share many points of similarity. The self-interest of the ruling elites in raising the standard of living and the level of scientific knowledge will lead them to reduce the likelihood of war. If war can be deferred, the factors of "common consciousness and enlightenment" will permit the "steady resumption of co-operation." Once this begins, the "meagre trickle of pacific contact between the two polar camps will swell into an enlarging stream, inaugurating a new era of peaceful association in which the world community makes direct progress toward a more perfect community of free men." The end result will be "a homogeneous world culture combining science and democracy," a "global correlation of power," and an "eventual integration of humanity." Lasswell combined a variety of liberal approaches in his stress on the formative influences of science, culture, reason, psychiatry, economics, and technology.

World unity should be the end of American policy. "Our goals are, in fact, positive and world-embracing." Just as the maintenance of liberal institutions and military institutions is impossible within the same society, so also is the continuance of two conflicting social systems in the same world. Either there is peaceful unity or there is the continued development of garrison states eventually coming into mortal conflict. This conflict can only mean the "near-total annihilation of humanity." It will produce not one Rome but two Carthages. By that time, however, destruction will be preferable to continued life in a militarized society. The undermining of free institutions by war preparation is a "more insidious menace" than a third world war even though this would "devastate man and his works on a scale without precedent." The "final fact of war is likely to be less perilous than perpetual preparation for war."

Lasswell held that there must be either total peace in a world commonwealth or total war and destruction. He ruled out the possibility of continuing strife and adjustment. In this he reflected the liberal refusal to tolerate the prospect of continuous friction among social units. History must come to a stop in one way or another. At the root of this outlook is the psychological intolerance of difference and the psychological craving for universality and harmony. The alternatives are world oneness or world war: the unattainable or the unbearable. Lasswell's theory was a measure of the pessimism and, indeed, desperation to which the liberal was driven in contemplating the post-World War II scene. His was the voice of despair and hopelessness, the anguished recognition of the extent to which liberal illusions had been shattered by the stubborn grimness of the human situation.

Political-Military Fusion. The theory of the garrison state was an effort to adjust to the fact of protracted military crisis. The theory of political-military fusion was an effort to adjust to the fact of enhanced military power. While the garrison-state hypothesis was a passive expression of helplessness in the face of world-wide conditions, the demand for fusion was a positive attempt to solve one aspect of the problem by denying the possibility of functional specialization. This theory started from the undeniable fact that military policy and political policy were much more closely interrelated in the postwar world than they had been previously. It went on, however, to assert that it had become impossible to maintain the distinction between political and military functions at the highest level of government. Over and over again it was argued that new developments had rendered the old categories of "political" and "military" sterile, obsolete, and meaningless. Fusionist theory dominated civilian thinking on the administrative problems of civil-military relations in the postwar period.[2] In the specific forms in which it was applied to the analysis of governmental institutions, this demand for the merger of political-military functions was itself a new element in the American approach to the military. In part it reflected the inherent constitutional diffi-

[2] See, for example, Townsend Hoopes, "Civilian-Military Balance," *Yale Review,* XLIII (Winter 1954), 221–222; *Report* of the Rockefeller Committee on Department of Defense Organization, April 11, 1953, pp. 3–4; H. Struve Hensel, "Changes Inside the Pentagon," *Harvard Business Review,* XXXII (January-February 1954), 102–103.

culties of maintaining a clearcut delimitation of military responsibilities, and in part
it derived from the feeling that because
war had become total, so also had the
sphere of military affairs. To a greater
extent, however, it simply reflected liberal
fear that the increased power of military
leadership would mean increased acceptance of the professional military viewpoint.
Consequently, it attempted to weaken and
subordinate the professional military approach and to reconcile increased military
power with liberal values by positing the
inevitable transmutation of military leadership. In effect, the fusionist theory attempted to solve the postwar problem of civil-
military relations by denying its existence.

Fusionist theory manifested itself in two
forms. One demand was that military leaders incorporate political, economic, and social factors into their thinking. This school
of thought answered the recurring question "Should military men have military
minds?" by replying: "No, they should not
and cannot have military minds, at least
at the highest levels of military authority."
It condemned narrow-minded "military
mechanics" and praised broad-minded
"military statesmen" whose perspectives
transcended the purely military. It argued
that the only means whereby administrative coordination could be secured among
the Joint Chiefs of Staff, the State Department, and other agencies was for them to
share a common national outlook. Every
decision on national policy, it was held,
contained both military and nonmilitary
elements which could not be segregated.
"There is no such thing as a purely military decision," chorused the fusionists,
thereby begging the issue of what were the
proper civil-military administrative arrangements. Of course, there is no "purely
military decision" at the level of the Joint
Chiefs of Staff. This is the exact reason
why the Joint Chiefs are legally constituted
as an advisory body rather than a decision-
making body. There is very definitely, however, a military viewpoint on national policy which stresses the importance of military
security considerations. Any decision on
national policy involves choices among
competing values. The job of the military

is to insure that military security is not
neglected by the political decision-maker
who must balance the desirability of maximizing military security against its costs in
other values. The fusionist call for broad-
minded military statesmen was a demand
that the military leaders deny themselves
in order to play a higher role. As such, it
was the most subtle and most persuasive
form which liberal antimilitarism could assume. Fusionist theory extended the undeniable fact that every military policy recommendation must rest upon certain political and economic assumptions to mean
that the military should furnish themselves
with those assumptions. Supporters of this
position pointed to the extent to which
at interdepartmental conferences State Department representatives brought up military arguments while the Joint Chiefs
defended the importance of political considerations. They also praised the establishment of institutions such as the National
War College, not just because they would
enable military officers to appreciate the
complexities of national policy, but because they would also enable military officers to arrive at their own conclusions concerning political and economic issues. The
one point on which exponents of this theory remained vague was the substantive
content of the political thinking they wished to see the officers engage in. To what,
or, more significantly, to whose political
ideas were the officers to adhere? This
question the fusionists never answered specifically. If they had grappled with it, the
almost unanimous civilian opinion that
the military leaders should integrate non-
military elements into their thinking inevitably would have dissolved into the bitter controversy of one civilian against
another.

A second manifestation of fusionist theory
was the demand that military leaders assume nonmilitary responsibilities. The
argument for nonmilitary thinking on the
part of military leaders implicitly rejected
functional specialization and objective civilian control. This second demand explicitly preferred subjective civilian control.
It was impossible, it was argued, to rely
upon the political neutrality of military

leaders and their simple obedience to state institutions. Instead, as Lasswell put it, minimizing the possibility of military professionalism, "the perpetuation of civilian supremacy would appear to depend not upon maintaining a specific set of governmental forms but upon ensuring the vitality of the value goals of the free society among all members of society, in or out of uniform."[3] Just as "military mechanics" who restricted their thinking to military considerations had been rejected, so also were "military technicians" who narrowly defined the scope of their responsibilities. One most notable manifestation of fusionist theory was the argument that the German generals shared in the moral and political guilt of Hitlerism by not openly and energetically opposing the domestic and foreign programs of the Nazi regime. Some supporters of this critique rather brazenly defied logic by supplementing their denunciation of von Rundstedt in 1945 with an equally vehement attack on MacArthur in 1951. Other critics, such as Telford Taylor, understood the dilemma and attempted to deal with the implications of their criticism for the American scene.[4] American military officers themselves in the postwar decade did not miss the relevance of the Nuremberg "higher loyalty" philosophy to their own behavior. General MacArthur echoed many of the American civilian critics of the German generals when he denounced the "new and heretofore unknown and dangerous concept that the members of our armed forces owe primary allegiance and loyalty to those who temporarily exercise the authority of the executive branch of government rather than to the country and its Constitution which they are sworn to defend."[5] More explicitly, another American officer defended what he agreed was the "insubordina-

tion" of Captain Crommelin in the 1949 B-36 controversy on the grounds that:

The decisions of the Nuremberg International Military Tribunal were in large part based on the tenet that the professional military defendants should have followed their consciences and not the orders of Hitler. There are, then, occasions when the refusal of a military man to comply is not insubordinate, but is positively his duty.[6]

In cutting loose from the safe grounds of objective civilian control, the advocates of fusion brought out a weapon which could be turned to a variety of uses.

MILITARY INFLUENCE IN AMERICAN SOCIETY

The influence of military professionals in American society between 1946 and 1955 was significantly less than it had been during World War II. Nonetheless, it was still at an unprecedented level in the absence of total war. The extent to which professional military officers assumed nonmilitary roles in government, industry, and politics, and developed affiliations with nonmilitary groups was a new phenomenon in American history. Military officers wielded far greater power in the United States during this period than they did in any other major country. Three of the most significant manifestations of their influence were: (1) the influx of military officers into governmental positions normally occupied by civilians; (2) the close ties which developed between military leaders and business leadership; and (3) the widespread popularity and prestige of individual military figures.

In analyzing these postwar military roles, two issues are of peculiar importance. First, was the increased influence of the military due fundamentally to factors associated with World War II, and, consequently, a temporary phenomenon? Or did it arise from causes associated with the Cold War and, consequently, something which might

[3] *National Security and Individual Freedom*, pp. 186–187.

[4] *Sword and Swastika* (New York, 1952), pp. 368–370. One of the most acute critical analyses by an American of the responsibility of the German generals is G. A. Craig, "Army and National Socialism 1933–1945: The Responsibility of the Generals," *World Politics*, II (April 1950), 426–438.

[5] Speech to the Massachusetts legislature, July 25, 1951, *New York Times*, July 26, 1951, p. 12.

[6] Lawrence J. Legere, Jr., "Unification of the Armed Forces" (Ph.D. Thesis, Harvard Univ., 1951), p. 406. Quoted by permission of the author. See also Crommelin's statement, *New York Times*, Nov. 9, 1949, p. 33.

continue indefinitely into the future? Unquestionably, the increased military imperatives stemming from America's involvement in world politics contributed to a much higher level of military influence than ever existed prior to 1940. Nonetheless, military influence during the first postwar decade was also in many respects an aftermath of World War II, a carry-over into peacetime both of the prestige and influence which the military acquired between 1940 and 1945 and of the weakness of civilian institutions and leadership during those years.

Second, was increased military influence accompanied by more widespread acceptance of the professional military viewpoint? In general, the inverse relationship between these two factors which had prevailed earlier in American society continued throughout the 1946–1955 period. A significant gap existed between the rapid and extensive rise of military influence and the considerably less success of military demands and military requirements. Those military elements which acquired the greatest political influence went farthest in abandoning the professional ethic, and their diversified roles made it easier for civilians to reject the postulates of professional military thinking. On issues where there was a clear-cut distinction between the professional military viewpoint and the traditional American civilian attitudes, such as universal military service and the size of the military budget, the latter usually triumphed. Indeed, American military policy throughout these years was in many ways a series of continuing efforts to escape from the professional military conclusion that the best means of achieving military security is through the maintenance of substantial forces in being.

Participation in Civil Government. The penetration of professional officers into governmental positions not requiring solely military skills took two forms: military occupancy of conjoint positions combining military and political functions, and military occupancy of civilian positions with exclusively nonmilitary functions. The most notable examples of conjoint positions were: (1) the military governorships of occupied territories such as existed in Germany until 1949 and in Japan until 1952; (2) international military commands such as the North Atlantic Treaty Organization's SHAPE and the United Nations Korean Command; and (3) military advisory and training groups in nations receiving American aid. The conjoint positions reflected the failure of governmental organization to adjust rapidly enough to increased functional specialization. They were one area where fusionist theory was manifested in reality. In the absence of appropriate institutional mechanisms for the separate performance of the military and political responsibilities, the occupants of the conjoint positions discharged both duties. The occupation governorships were a temporary phenomenon developing out of World War II. While hostilities were still in progress and immediately after their termination, the separation of political and military functions was virtually impossible. Military government and civil affairs were naturally handled through the military command organization. After the end of the war, however, the military security function in the occupied territory declined in importance; the immediate problems were economic, social, political, and constitutional. Theoretically, military control should at this point have given way to civilian direction, and in the French, British, and Russian zones of Germany, civilian control did replace military control. The national popularity and political support of General MacArthur, however, made it impossible to reduce him to the status of a military subordinate to a civilian occupation governor. In Germany, the reluctance of the State Department to undertake the responsibility for occupation rule prolonged military control until 1949. In the Far East and in Germany large staffs, devoted purely to political and civil affairs, developed to assist the military governor in the discharge of his political responsibilities. In one form or another, these staffs, largely civilian in composition, were subsumed under or attached to the military command organization.

The international military commands were a reaction to military security threats stemming from the Cold War. Consequently, as a type they were a more permanent manifestation of conjoint office. The Commanders in Chief of SHAPE and of the United Nations Command in the Far East both had to devote substantial portions of their time to the discharge of political and diplomatic duties. The more *ad hoc* nature of the UN Command precluded any effort to develop means of segregating political and military responsibilities. In Europe, on the other hand, the initial creation of the SHAPE military organization and the piloting of it through its first tests required a unique combination of military, political, and diplomatic skills. Once the structure was established, however, a degree of segregation of function became possible. The more thoroughly military approaches of Ridgway and Gruenther to their job and the emergence of the civilian organization under Lord Ismay both reflected an effort to disassociate military and civilian activities in NATO. The complete segregation of the two functions, however, required the development of new forms of international political institutions which were probably impractical. Consequently, under a military guise and through military mechanisms, the commanders and staffs of NATO continued to perform political functions which the exigencies of politics did not permit to be performed more openly.[7]

The military advisory groups to nations receiving American military assistance combined diplomatic and military responsibilities. By virtue of their control over the most significant form of American assistance, the advisory group and its chief at times tended to absorb duties and influence which properly belonged to the ambassador and the State Department. While the problem of the organizing of civil and military representation in foreign countries on such a scale was relatively new to the

United States, it had in the past been effectively dealt with by other nations. American military assistance and advisory groups will undoubtedly continue as a relatively permanent fixture in the conduct of American foreign affairs, and the eventual delimitation of responsibilities and duties between military and civil missions abroad should not present insoluble difficulties.

Prior to World War II professional military officers occasionally held civilian positions in the national government. However, the scope of military penetration into the civilian hierarchy after World War II was completely without precedent in American history. In 1948 it was estimated that one hundred and fifty military men occupied important policy-making posts in civilian government.[8] Many of the most significant appointive positions in the government were at one time or another occupied by military officers. The reasons behind this influx of officers into civil posts were complex: some represented factors which had long been present in the American scene; some were the result of World War II; some derived from the new and continuing demands of the Cold War.

(1) Traditional appointments had been continuingly characteristic of American civil-military relations. In some areas of the federal government a tradition of military appointments antedated World War II. Officers were appointed to these positions either upon detached duty from their services or after retirement. The most significant areas of traditional appointments were closely associated with the technical specialties of the two services. Naval officers were frequently selected for federal posts connected with maritime affairs. Between 1937 and 1949, for instance, the United States Maritime Commission always had one to three officers among its five members, and throughout much of its life it was headed by an admiral. From an early period, Army engineering officers had been often appointed to civilian public works positions. In the thirties the New Deal utilized the services of a number of

[7] Compare General Ridgway's comments in *Soldier: The Memoirs of Matthew B. Ridgway* (New York, 1956), pp. 239–240. On this problem generally, see William Yandell Elliott and associates, *United States Foreign Policy: Its Organization and Control* (New York, 1952), pp. 168–172, and G. C. Reinhardt and W. R. Kintner, "The Need for a National Staff," U.S. Naval Inst. *Proceedings,* LXXVII (July 1952), 721–727.

[8] Richard C. Snyder and H. Hubert Wilson, *The Roots of Political Behavior* (New York, 1949), p. 557.

officers in the WPA and similar agencies, and their employment in comparable positions was continued by the Truman and Eisenhower administrations.* In another area, the directorship of veterans affairs to which General Bradley was appointed in 1945 had been occupied by another general since 1923. Although Bradley was succeeded by a civilian, it seems legitimate to conclude that a tradition of military occupancy also inheres in this post. The traditional appointments reflected civilian desire to capitalize upon special types of nonmilitary expertise possessed by certain classes of professional officers. They appeared to be a continuing and relatively constant phenomenon in American government.

(2) Honorific and political appointments were peculiarly characteristic of the years immediately following World War II. After World War II many military appointments were designed primarily to honor or reward military commanders who had distinguished themselves in the war. The selection of leading generals and admirals to serve on the American Battle Monuments Commission, the appointment of various military figures to *ad hoc* commissions, and some appointments of military men as ambassadors fell into this category. Honorific appointments were more frequent under Truman's administration than under Eisenhower's. Many of the military appointments between 1945 and 1953 also undoubtedly reflected the desire of the Truman Administration to utilize the political popularity of the top World War II commanders to carry the burden of its foreign policies. Probably the most notable instance where this motivation was present was the employment of General Marshall as presidential envoy to China, Secretary of State, and Secretary of Defense. Honorific and

political appointments were both temporary phenomena. No subsequent administration was likely to have quite the peculiar need for such political support that the Truman Administration did, and nothing short of total war was likely to produce popular military heroes of sufficient stature to furnish such support or to be eligible for honorary posts.

(3) Administrative appointments reflected the new but continuing demands of the Cold War. The great bulk of the military appointments to civil positions in the postwar decade occurred in the foreign affairs and defense agencies and may be termed "administrative" in nature. They derived from new imperatives likely to remain in existence for an indefinite length of time. Before 1933 the personnel requirements of the federal government were fairly small. The expansion of the domestic agencies during the New Deal period was handled by the movement to Washington of program-oriented professional workers, academicians, lawyers, and others. To perform its wartime activities the government attracted business and professional men through the double appeal of the temporary nature of its employment and the patriotic duty of government service. The staffing of those significant foreign affairs and defense activities which continued after 1945, however, presented a difficult problem. The temporary war employees dispersed homeward; the New Dealers were generally uninterested in foreign affairs; and the businessmen were generally unwilling to work for the Democratic administration. No ready source of civilians with administrative and diplomatic skills was available. Consequently, the military were called upon to fill the vacuum. The officers were willing to serve, used to public employment, accustomed to low salaries, untainted by leftist affiliations, and divorced from ties with special interest groups. While military skills were not prerequisite for the positions to which they were appointed, their military background furnished them with certain types of experience and training not possessed by any significant groups of available citizens. The State Department, in particular among civilian

---

* Maj. Gen. Philip Fleming, for instance, was executive officer and deputy administrator of the P.W.A., 1933–35, and Federal Works Administrator, 1941–49. Maj. Gen. Edmond H. Leavy was deputy administrator of the W.P.A. in New York City, 1936–40, and assistant commissioner of the W.P.A. in 1940. The Eisenhower Administration appointed Brig. Gen. Herbert D. Vogel chairman of the T.V.A. and Brig. Gen. John S. Bragdon public works coordinator.

agencies, required experienced, competent personnel in the immediate postwar years and utilized the services of professional officers.* The proportion of officers in civilian foreign affairs and defense posts tended to decline after 1946 and 1947, and the Eisenhower Administration to some extent replaced professional officers with recruits from business. The complete elimination of military administrative appointments, however, depended upon the development of a continuing source of high-level civilian administrators with education and experience in this field superior to those of the military.

The influx of military men into civilian posts aroused considerable criticism, particularly in the years from 1946 through 1948. The military appointments were held to be a sign of the militarization of the government, the abandonment of civilian control, and the imminency of the garrison state. Congress refused to approve three of President Truman's military appointments.†

The selection of General Marshall as Secretary of Defense in 1950 stimulated renewed debate of the issue. Some of the Eisenhower Administration's military appointees met vigorous congressional opposition.[9] Virtually all the criticism of the military influx was couched in terms of abstract constitutional and political principles and generalized dangers to civil government. With a few exceptions, it was impossible to demonstrate that the actions of any particular military officer reflected the inherently dangerous qualities of the military mind. It was all very well to cite the general influx of military men as evidence of a trend toward the garrison state. But, when one got down to the specifics of Bradley as Veterans Administrator or Marshall as Secretary of State, the threat of militarization rapidly evaporated. The professional officers blended into their new civilian milieu, serving nonmilitary ends, motivated by nonmilitary considerations, and performing their jobs little differently from their civilian predecessors and successors. Undoubtedly the officers who moved into the State Department in 1946 and 1947 did contribute to the more conservative outlook which developed in that department during those

---

* These included: Gen. of the Army George C. Marshall, Special Representative to China, 1946, Secretary of State, 1947–49; Brig. Gen. Henry C. Byroade, Dir., Bur. of German Affairs, 1949–52, Asst. Sec. of State, 1952–55, Amb. to Egypt, 1955—; Maj. Gen. John H. Hilldring, Asst. Sec. of State, 1946–47; Lt. Gen. Walter Bedell Smith, Amb. to U.S.S.R., 1946–49, Under Sec. of State, 1953–55; Rear Adm. John W. Bays, Chief, Div. of Forgn. Service Adm., 1947–49; Capt. Lee W. Park, USN, Chief Div. of Cartography, 1944—; Maj. Gen. Thomas Holcomb, USMC, Min. to South Africa, 1944–48; Lt. Gen. Albert C. Wedemeyer, Special Representative to China and Korea, 1947; Adm. Alan G. Kirk, Amb. to Belgium, 1946–49, Amb. to U.S.S.R., 1949–52; Maj. Gen. Philip Fleming, Amb. to Costa Rica, 1951–53; Adm. Raymond A. Spruance, Amb. to Philippines, 1952–53; Brig. Gen. Frank T. Hines, Amb. to Panama, 1945–48; Rear Adm. Arthur A. Ageton, Amb. to Paraguay, 1955—. Other significant military appointments included: Maj. Gen. Kenneth D. Nichols, Genl. Manager, A.E.C., 1953—; Maj. Gen. Edmund B. Gregory, Admistr., War Assets Adm., 1946; Maj. Gen. Robert M. Littlejohn, Admistr., War Assets Adm., 1946–47; Lt. Gen. William E. Riley, USMC, Dep. Dir., F.O.A., 1953—; Vice Adm. Walter S. DeLaney, Dep. Dir., F.O.A., 1953—; Maj. Gen. Glen E. Edgerton, Mnging. Dir. & Chrman. Bd. of Dirs., Export-Import Bank, 1953—.

† Maj. Gen. Lawrence S. Kuter to be Chrmn. of the C.A.B., Gen. Mark Clark to be Ambassador to the Vatican, Flt. Adm. Chester W. Nimitz to be Chrmn. of the President's Commission on Internal Security and Individual Rights. All three cases in-

volved controversial issues other than the military background of the nominees. President Truman reportedly offered the C.A.B. chairmanship to six civilians, all of whom declined the job, before selecting Gen. Kuter.

[9] For civilian criticism, see Hanson Baldwin, "The Military Move In," *Harper's*, CXCV (December, 1947), 481–489; J. F. Dobie, "Samples of the Army Mind," *ibid.*, CXCIII (December 1946), 529–536; L. B. Wheildon, "Militarization," *Editorial Research Reports* (May 12, 1948), pp. 301–310; William R. Tansill, *The Concept of Civil Supremacy over the Military in the United States* (Library of Congress, Legislative Reference Service, Public Affairs Bulletin No. 94, Washington, 1951), pp. 38–59; *Cong. Record* (Daily ed.), CI (May 17, 1955), 5518 (July 14, 1955), 9069–9071 (Aug. 1, 1955), 11024–11026, CII (Mar. 20, 1956), 4595–4597 (Mar. 21, 1956), 4691–4706. For the military defense, see *Inf. Jour.*, LX (April 1947), 71, CXII (January 1948), 76–77; J. W. Stryker, "Are the Military Moving In?", U.S. Naval Inst. *Proceedings*, LXXV (March 1949), 295–301; L. B. Blair, "Dogs and Sailors Keep Off," *ibid.*, LXXVI (October 1950), 1102.

years. Yet even this was largely an adjustment to the civilian environment, for the new approach to foreign policy which became dominant in the Department in 1947 and 1948 had deep roots in the Department's own professional staff. The general ease with which the officers adjusted to their civilian roles and outlook forced their critics to shift to the argument that, although the particular officers appointed were harmless exceptions to the desirable rule, dangerous precedents were being set for the future. This, too, was unconvincing. The "civilianizing" of the officers was not the exception. It was instead the only rule which American liberalism would permit.

The Military-Business Rapprochement. Few developments more dramatically symbolized the new status of the military in the postwar decade than the close associations which they developed with the business elite of American society. Prior to World War II, the professional officers and the capitalists in spirit and in fact had been poles apart. The American business community had little use for military needs, little appreciation of the military outlook, and little respect for military men. The military reciprocated in kind. After World War II, an abrupt change took place in this relationship. Professional officers and businessmen revealed a new mutual respect. Retired generals and admirals in unprecedented numbers moved into the executive staffs of American corporations; new organizations arose bridging the gap between corporate management and military leadership. For the military officers, business represented the epitome of the American way of life. Association with business was positive proof and assurance that they had abandoned their outcaste status and had become respected members of the American community. Financially and psychologically, the military men who moved from the officers corps to the corporation gained in security, acceptance, and well-being. The business firms, on the other hand, capitalized upon the prestige of well-known commanders, the special skills and expertise of their officers in nonmilitary technical fields, the general administrative and organizing abilities, and their as-

sistance in doing business with the Department of Defense. The ties that bound the two groups together in the postwar decade were apparently many and strong. In actuality, they rested upon two quite different foundations: one broad in scope but temporary in duration; the other more restricted but also more permanent.

The more ephemeral basis of the military-business alliance was the prestige of the military from World War II. Big business was eager to employ famous battle commanders: MacArthur went to Remington Rand, Bedell Smith to American Machine and Foundry, Bradley to Bulova, Halsey to International Standard Electric. This type of appointment was necessarily a temporary phenomenon, the Cold War producing few military figures of sufficient prestige to be of interest to business. The businesses which appointed these officers were usually large manufacturing corporations, holding sizable defense contracts, but so large and diversified as to be in most cases neither exclusively nor even primarily dependent upon government business. The military heroes came in at the top of the corporate structure, assuming posts as president, vice president, board chairman, or director. Although a few had occurred after World War I, prestige appointments on this scale were quite unprecedented in the United States. They were the American equivalent of the British practice of rewarding successful generals with peerages, a commercial society substituting corporation presidencies and board chairmanships for earldoms and viscountcies. The military heroes, on the other hand, brought glamour and public attention to the businesses.* The corporations were honored

* The pros and cons of adding General Marshall to the General Motors board of directors were debated among corporation officials in 1945, President Sloan suggesting that: "General Marshall might do us some good, when he retires, following his present assignment—assuming he continues to live in Washington; recognizing the position he holds in the community and among the government people and the acquaintance he has—and [if] he became familiar with our thinking and what we are trying to do, it might offset the general negative attitude toward big business, of which we are a symbol and a profitable business, as well." Lammot du Pont, on the other hand, secured

and so were the generals. The large industrial concerns which hired the military men, however, had been the principal locus of opposition to a large military establishment. They were the major institutional base of business liberalism and the dominating element in the National Association of Manufacturers, which consistently demanded the reduction of military expenditures. There is little evidence that their employment of the military officers signalized any fundamental change in what Walter H. McLaughlin, Jr., has described as their "indifferent attitude" toward military affairs. Nor, apparently, were the officers able to work any change in the business political outlook. The corporations accepted the officers and utilized their talents and reputations, but they did not accept the professional military viewpoint. Insofar as there was a rapprochement in thinking between the military heroes and their business colleagues, it was the military men who made the concessions, adjusting to their new environment by surrendering their professional outlook.

A more restricted but more lasting tie developed between the military leadership and those businesses supplying goods to the Department of Defense. Prior to 1940, the Army and Navy offered little in the way of markets to American industry. In World War I industry had accepted large defense contracts only to suffer dislocation and hardship when they were abruptly canceled at the end of hostilities. As a result, business was most reluctant to take on military orders again in 1939 and 1940. Once the United States entered the war, of course, industry cooperated wholeheartedly in the production of military goods and equipment, and hundreds of businessmen went to Washington to work in the War and Navy Departments. The rapid demobilization in 1945 and 1946 first seemed to indicate a repetition of the post-World War I pattern. In due course, however, and particularly after the outbreak of the Korean War, it became obvious that the Cold War military demand was going to be substantial and relatively stable. The dollar volume of military orders and the complex technological requirements of the modern armed forces brought a significant permanent defense industry into existence for the first time in the United States. The defense suppliers were composed in part of large general manufacturing corporations, such as those in the automobile industry, which furnished military items while at the same time catering to the civilian market.* On the other hand, some industries, such as the aircraft manufacturers and sections of the electronics industry, were almost totally dependent upon military orders.

The economic nexus which joined the defense producers to the military was reflected both in the large numbers of former

---

the rejection of Marshall on the grounds of, "First, his age; second, his lack of stockholdings, and, third, his lack of experience in industrial business affairs." *New York Times*, Jan. 7, 1953, pp. 33, 35. Owen D. Young, after World War I, defined the qualifications he wanted in the president of the Radio Corporation of America in the following words, and concluded that they could best be filled by a military man, General James G. Harbord, Pershing's Chief of Staff in France:

"1st. He should be well known both nationally and internationally and he should have made such a place for himself as would enable him to speak with authority either to foreign Governments or to our own Government.

"2nd. He should not have been previously identified with politics because that would mean party alignment and partisan reaction.

"3rd. He should not have been identified with Wall Street or the money interests because it is important that the American people should accept the Radio Corporation as an organization for service to American interests both at home and abroad rather than as an organization primarily to make a profit for Wall Street interests.

"4th. He should have had administrative experience and if possible business experience.

"5th. He should be well known in Washington and in a position to appear before Committees of Congress and before the Departments and have his statements of facts accepted without question. It is particularly important in this connection that no one should be able to question his Americanism, such as they have done in several instances in the case of our international bankers.

"6th. He should be a man of public position whom to attack would be bad politics rather than good politics."
Quoted in Gleason L. Archer, *The History of Radio to 1926* (New York, 1938), pp. 246–247.

* General Motors was the largest producer of defense goods, yet only 19.3 per cent of its 1951 sales were to the military. *New York Times*, Mar. 11, 1952, p. 42.

officers who entered the management of these companies and in the various organizations which developed to cement the military-business tie. The officers hired by the defense producers were not normally well-known public figures, but rather younger men who entered the corporations in operational rather than honorific positions. Most of the officers were technical experts in some specialized scientific field and many had held high positions in the Army's technical services and in the Navy's bureaus. Some of them resigned from the service to pursue their careers in business. The technical specialists employed by defense industries constituted the largest single group of general and flag officers hired by private business in the postwar decade. The aircraft companies and their associated industries alone accounted for a significant portion of them. Unlike the prestige appointments, this type of business-military arrangement appeared to increase rather than decrease during the course of the postwar decade.[10]

The professionalization of the military in the 1880's and 1890's and their withdrawal from society had been reflected in the organization of numerous military associations designed for officers only. The return of the military to society and their close links with the Cold War defense industries were marked by the formation of a different type of organization open both to officers and to civilians and business firms. Probably most significant among these groups was the National Security Industrial Association organized by James Forrestal in 1944 to insure that "American business will remain close to the services." The Association in 1954 was composed of six hundred industrial firms, virtually all of whom had significant defense contracts. Many officers of the Association were former generals or admirals. The Association was principally active in helping its

member firms and the Department of Defense resolve problems of production techniques, procurement, and patents. The Armed Forces Chemical Association and the Armed Forces Communications Association came into existence in the immediate postwar years to bridge the gap between the interested segments of the military and of business. The previously existing Quartermaster Association, formed in 1920 as an organization of military officers only, was broadened to admit civilians to active membership and to provide for company membership. The Army Ordnance Association, founded in 1919, was reorganized as the American Ordnance Association, covering all three services. While its staff was composed largely of retired military officers, the thirty-five thousand members of AOA were mostly representatives of ordnance manufacturers.[11] Both the Aircraft Industries Association and the Air Force Association provided links between the aviation industries and the military.*

In general, the defense businesses supported for economic reasons the same military policies which the officers supported for professional reasons. Exceptions to this existed, of course, in the case of businesses interested in producing or continuing to produce weapons or equipment not believed essential by professional judgment. But on the whole a coincidence of viewpoint existed which permitted the officers an easier association with defense industry than with those businesses which had more diversified customers. Corporation officials

---

[10] The activities of former officers are reported weekly in the "Retired Service Notes" in the *Army Navy, Air Force Journal*. For lists of some of the more notable business appointments, see "The Military Businessmen," *Fortune*, XLVI (September 1952), 128ff.; *Cong. Record*, CI (July 14, 1955, daily ed.), 9070–9071; *U. S. News and World Report*, XL (Apr. 27, 1956), 55–56.

[11] Walter H. McLaughlin, Jr., "Business Attitudes Towards Defense Policy During the Cold War" (Honors Thesis, Harvard Univ., 1955), pp. 36–59; U.S. Dept. of the Army, *The Army Almanac* (Washington, 1950), pp. 883–908.

*The new military-business relationship was illustrated by the career lines of Maj. Gen. Harry C. Ingles—Chief Signal Officer in World War II, organizer of the Armed Forces Communications Assoc. in 1946 and 1947, president of R.C.A. Communications in 1948—and Lt. Gen. Levin H. Campbell—World War II Chief of Ordnance, later exec. vice pres. of International Harvester and president of the Amer. Ordnance Association, author of *The Industry-Ordnance Team* (New York, 1946) which expresses the philosophy of military-business cooperation.

and military officials shared a common interest in technological development, and the defense industries for the first time in American history furnished the military program with a significant base of economic support. In other respects, however, association with the defense industries did not aid military professionalism. Inevitably, the businesses thought of themselves first and attracted to their staffs many younger officers who still had many years of useful service to offer their country. In the middle 1950's over two thousand regular officers each year were leaving the services for the more lucrative positions in business. In addition, there was the likelihood that the ability to move from one of the technical branches of the armed forces into a well-paying industry job would enhance the popularity and attractiveness of the technical staffs as against the line. A very small proportion of the business appointments in the postwar decade went to military commanders who were neither famous public figures nor technical specialists, but simply regular line officers with backgrounds in military command. The businesses who hired these officers seemed to assume that any general or flag officer must necessarily be a good administrator. Their relatively small numbers, however, were indicative of the gap which still remained between even defense business and the more strictly professional military elements of the services. A major general whose principal experience was in commanding regiments and divisions had little to offer the manufacturing corporation.

The Macs and the Ikes: Return of the Samurai. In an engaging article, T. Harry Williams argues that the United States has two military traditions.[12] One is represented by the friendly, folksy, easygoing soldier who reflects the ideals of a democratic and industrial civilization and who cooperates easily with his civilian superiors. This "Ike" tradition is exemplified by Zachary Taylor, U.S. Grant, and Dwight D. Eisenhower. Opposing this is the "Mac" tradi-

tion, embodied in Winfield Scott, George B. McClellan, and Douglas MacArthur—brilliant, imperious, cold, dramatic officers deriving their values and behavior from an older, aristocratic heritage and finding it difficult to subordinate themselves to civilian authorities. Williams' dichotomy is obviously real and significant; yet, in a sense, it is restricted in scope, failing to encompass important elements of the American military tradition which fall into neither the "Ike" nor the "Mac" category. Essentially, the Ikes and the Macs represent two aspects of the same strand of American militarism: the tradition of political involvement. The true opposition is not between the Taylor-Grant-Eisenhower line and the Scott-McClellan-MacArthur line, but rather between both of these, on the one hand, and the professional strand of American militarism (which might be described as the Sherman-Pershing-Ridgway line), on the other. The basic distinction is not between the Ikes and the Macs, but between the "Ike-Macs" and the "Uncle Billies" or "Black Jacks." The differences between the Ike type and the Mac type are the differences between two kinds of politicians: the charismatic, inspirational, unbending political leader who leads because he is superior to his followers, and the flexible, earthy, unpretentious political leader who leads because he is representative of his followers. That the Ikes generally have been more successful than the Macs in their political pursuits indicates only that the American environment generally is more favorable to the Ike type, irrespective of whether he is civilian or military. The difference between the Ikes and the Macs is simply the difference between Jackson and Calhoun, Theodore Roosevelt and LaFollette, Wendell Willkie and Robert A. Taft.

Significantly, Williams mentioned no representative of either the Ike or the Mac traditions between the Civil War heroes and the post-World War II figures. During the intervening years both elements of the political strand of the American tradition were subordinated to the prevailing professionalism. Only with the return of the military to society after World War II did

12 "The Macs and the Ikes: America's Two Military Traditions," *American Mercury,* LXXV (October 1952), 32–39.

the political tradition which had wilted in the 1870's and 1880's reemerge as a major theme of American militarism. For the first time in American history in the postwar decade, professional officers not only became popular public figures but also became deeply involved in the domestic politics of candidates and elections, political movements and political parties. The most obvious figures were, of course, Eisenhower and MacArthur. But other officers, although not numerous, also assumed conspicuous roles in popular politics. The causes of this political involvement essentially had little relation to the continuing issues and policies of the Cold War. While the officers disputed many points of national policy, their entrance into the partisan political arena does not appear to have been motivated primarily by ideological or policy considerations. Instead, their participation was fundamentally the result of the popularity of Eisenhower and MacArthur and the rivalry between these two great military figures. The conflict between the Macs and Ikes in the postwar decade was real, but it was a conflict of personalities not of traditions. Its roots lay in the confused events of World War I and in the inner tensions and feuds, obscured from public view, of the Regular Army of the 1920's and 1930's. At an early date MacArthur and George C. Marshall became identified with opposing groups within the Army. During and after World War I a rivalry, fed by a series of incidents and misunderstandings, developed between them. Eisenhower was an aide to MacArthur while the latter was Chief of Staff from 1930 to 1935 and military advisor to the Philippine government thereafter. Eventually, however, Eisenhower, too, broke with MacArthur, returning to the United States in 1939. In due course, he came to the attention of Marshall, now himself Chief of Staff, and was rapidly advanced on the career which eventually led to his appointment as Supreme Commander of the European invasion. In this process Eisenhower became completely identified with the Marshall group. His rapid promotion and the priority given to the European theater over the Pacific necessarily drew the ire of the MacArthur supporters.

The emergence of Eisenhower and MacArthur as the two popular military heroes of the war projected the essentially intramilitary feud upon the larger framework of national politics. The personal rivalry was enhanced by the identification of the contests with Europe-oriented and Asia-oriented strategies. Virtually all the significant participation of individual military officers in postwar partisan controversy was a function of the rivalry between these two personalities. On the one hand, there was the Marshall-Eisenhower, Europe, SHAEF-SHAPE, Pentagon group; on the other hand stood the MacArthur, Asia, SCAPE, "Bataan" group. Retired officers played active roles on behalf of one or the other generals: MacArthur had his Wedemeyer and Bonner Fellers, Eisenhower his Clay and Bedell Smith. Other officers essayed a neutral role or made a difficult choice between the two.[13] The impact of this controversy continued for some while after the war, but the passing of the World War II generation of military leaders and the rise of a new crop of generals removed from its animosities will undoubtedly diminish military political participation.

The political involvement of Eisenhower and MacArthur affected not only the officer corps but the men themselves. Neither was able to adhere to the fundamentals of the professional military ethic. In due course, both emerged as "unmilitary" military men, deviants from the professional standard, heroic and symbolic figures for millions of Americans. MacArthur's involvement in political roles long antedated that of Eisenhower as did also his deviation from the professional military ethic. From the start, MacArthur had been

[13] For aspects of the MacArthur versus Marshall and Eisenhower feud, see Clark Lee and Richard Henschel, *Douglas MacArthur* (New York, 1952), pp. 98–102, 115–131; Richard H. Rovere and Arthur Schlesinger, Jr., *The General and the President* (New York, 1951), pp. 70–71; Robert E. Sherwood, *Roosevelt and Hopkins* (New York, 1948), p. 759, and "The Feud between Ike and Mac," *Look*, XVI (July 1, 1952), 17ff.; Marquis Childs, "Soldiers and 1952 Politics," *Washington Post*, July 8, 1952, p. 12; Frazier Hunt, *The Untold Story of Douglas MacArthur* (New York, 1954), *passim*; Robert Payne, *The Marshall Story* (New York, 1951), pp. 108–110; James K. Eyre, Jr., *The Roosevelt-MacArthur Conflict* (Chambersburg, Pa., 1950), *passim*.

a brilliant soldier but always something more than a soldier: a controversial, ambitious, transcendent figure, too able, too assured, too talented to be confined within the limits of professional function and responsibility. As early as 1929 his name was mentioned in connection with the Presidency, and in 1944, 1948, and 1952 he was on the fringes of the presidential political arena. The MacArthur ideology which evolved in the 1920's and 1930's was essentially religious, mystical, and emotional, contrasted with the normally practical, realistic, and materialistic approach of the professional soldier. To an even greater extent than Mahan, MacArthur's attitudes appeared to reflect a deeply felt and profoundly personalized version of Christianity. In contrast to the professional stress on military force in being, he emphasized the moral and spiritual aspects of war and the importance of the citizen-soldier. In contrast to the bulk of the officer corps, MacArthur viewed the threats to the United States as arising from insidious political philosophies rather than from other nation-states of equal or superior material strength. His sense of mission and dedication gave rise to a sustained and unbridled optimism which contrasted with the normal professional pessimism. The professional officer exists in a world of grays. MacArthur's universe was one of blacks and whites and loud and clashing colors. His articulate and varying views reflected a continuing quest for beliefs and policies which would satisfy his own ideological inclinations and at the same time inspire favorable popular response.

In contrast to MacArthur, Eisenhower was still an unknown lieutenant colonel as the nation moved toward involvement in World War II. While MacArthur had specialized in being different, Eisenhower specialized in adjusting to and reflecting his environment, absorbing the attitudes and behavior patterns of those about him. During the 1920's and 1930's, immersed in a professional milieu, he was the typical professional officer. When he catapulted to the heights of rank and fame, Eisenhower rapidly adjusted to his successive new environments, easily emerging as distinctly "civilian minded." Speaking less and smil-

ing more than MacArthur, he appeared the embodiment of consensus rather than controversy. MacArthur was a beacon, Eisenhowerhower a mirror. While the former attempted to build a variety of bridges to the American consciousness, the latter waited and let the bridges be constructed under him. With few pretensions to philosophy and creative originality, Eisenhower had little need to commit himself on public issues or to identify himself with any except the most widely held American values. The Eisenhower ideology was elusive because it was so familiar and acceptable. Substituted for it was a warm, sympathetic, but noncommittal, understanding.

The full measure of the extent to which both MacArthur and Eisenhower by their different paths departed from the professional code was dramatically indicated in the early 1950's. MacArthur became the leading advocate of the abolition of war. Eisenhower emerged as the most effective instrument in the reduction of the armed forces. Both roles reflected the influence of the civilian environments in which the soldiers had become immersed. By 1956 even Henry Wallace was endorsing the views of the two old soldiers on peace and war.

From an early period MacArthur's attitude toward war embodied the dominant ideas of the American liberal tradition. During the 1920's and 1930's he had justified war on moral and religious grounds, and surrounded the warrior's art with a sentimental romanticism. Unlike Dennis Hart Mahan, but similar to Mahan's Jacksonian opponents, MacArthur preferred the warlike spirit to the military spirit.[14] Some observers detected irony many years later in 1951 and 1952, when MacArthur denounced the dangers of the "military mind." But the general was on firm ground. A vast gulf existed between his thinking and that of the professional officer. After World War II he adopted the pacifist ideas which he had castigated in the 1920's and 1930's, urging in Kellogg-Briand terms that war must be "outlawed from the world." Sel-

[14] "The Necessity for Military Forces," *Inf. Jour.*, XXX (March 1927), 330; Speech to the Rainbow Division, July 14, 1935, in Frank C. Waldrop (ed.), *MacArthur on War* (New York, 1942), pp. 31ff.

dom has a professionally trained military man more completely departed from the cardinal tenet of military doctrine that war is ultimately inevitable and beyond the power of humans to prevent. MacArthur had the ban on the maintenance of armed forces written into the constitution of Japan. He urged his own nation to "proclaim our readiness to abolish war in concert with the great powers of the world." MacArthur's demand for the total abolition of war reflected his unwillingness to accept the frustrations, embarrassment, and burdens of continued international friction. In Lasswellian phrases he declared that "in final analysis the mounting cost of preparation for war is in many ways as materially destructive as war itself." Instead he turned to the abolition of war as the panacea of the world's ills, "the one issue, which, if settled, might settle all others."[15] Despite their differences, an underlying consistency existed between MacArthur's earlier and later views on war. War was always a total, cataclysmic act. In his earlier years he stressed the heroic self-sacrifice and glory involved in this act. In his later years he saw the destruction and calamity it entailed. But his reactions to war were always extreme. "You cannot control war; you can only abolish it," he declared, rejecting vigorously the concept that "when you use force, you can limit that force." Adherence to the total war-total peace dichotomy necessarily led MacArthur to a theory of civil-military relations closer to Ludendorff than to Clausewitz. War represented the utter bankruptcy of politics, not simply the extension of politics. Consequently, in war full control, "politically, economically, militarily," must be in the hands of the military commanders, and the nation must concentrate its complete trust in the military leadership.[16]

While MacArthur emerged as the nation's most eloquent advocate of the abolition of war, Eisenhower became its most effective instrument in the reduction of American military strength. In this again Eisenhower demonstrated his responsiveness to the forces about him, performing a double service for the Republican Party. As a popular military hero candidate, he helped the minority party secure control of the national government for the first time in two decades. Once in office, his military prestige aided the dominant elements in that party toward a realization of their goals of reducing expenditures, lowering taxes, and balancing the budget. The first three military budgets submitted by his administration all cut back the size of the armed forces, all encountered resistance in Congress, and all were approved on the personal assurance of the President that they would provide adequately for the national defense. When in 1953, for instance, congressional supporters of air power threatened to upset Administration plans to reduce Air Force appropriations by $5 billion, the President intervened and saved the budget, assuring Congress that the cuts had his "personal endorsement in all major particulars." As Senator Ferguson accurately predicted: "I believe . . . most of the Senators will go along with the President on this because he is a military expert and his judgment must be trusted."[17] He was the indispensable instrument of the arms cuts. Neither Adlai Stevenson nor Robert A. Taft could have carried out the reductions with so little resistance. The opposition was disarmed from the start. As one Democrat sadly remarked, "How in the devil can a mere Senator argue about military matters with General Ike Eisenhower?"[18] The result was a rift between the President and his erstwhile professional colleagues, and the identification of America's most popular military officer with its most antimilitary philosophy of business liberalism.

[15] Address, Los Angeles, Jan. 26, 1955, *U.S. News and World Report*, XXXVIII (Feb. 4, 1955), 86–88; Douglas MacArthur, *Revitalizing a Nation* (Chicago, John M. Pratt, ed., 1952), p. 16.

[16] *New York Times*, July 26, 1951, p. 12; *Hearings before the Senate Committee on the Armed Services and the Committee on Foreign Relations on the Military Situation in the Far East*, 82d Cong., 1st Sess., pp. 39–40, 44–45, 114–115 (1951).

[17] *New York Times*, May 24, 1953, p. 34, July 2, 1953, p. 1.

[18] Quoted by Stewart Alsop, *New York Herald Tribune*, Apr. 24, 1955, Sec. 2, p. 1.

DEFENSE AND DEMOCRACY

BY HARRY HOWE RANSOM

Primo vivere deinde philosophari is an enduring rule for all societies: think first about survival, then about other things.

Survival is a categorical imperative for any government. The writing of this book has been stimulated, however, by my strong preference to think concurrently about national survival and the survival of American democratic values and institutions, both of which are gravely challenged by the contemporary world political environment.

I believe that America's defense and democracy are threatened partly because we may fail to recognize and to cope adequately with what I shall call the problem of organizational lead-time. Our governmental system resists rapid structural change. My greatest concern is that in periods of obsessive fear or true national emergency, radical changes will occur in our institutions—in the name of national security—that will severely damage the democratic framework. My thesis is that this can be avoided by organizational foresight.

Communist imperialism and subversion around the world constitute one major threat we face. Reacting to this, the United States has undertaken enormous commitments to preserve the security and promote the democratic development of the non-Communist world. But even without world communism, the innovations of this century—an accelerating technology which has vastly magnified military power; the "revolution of rising expectations" among three-score new nations; and other revolutionary features of the great transformations in international politics in the mid-twentieth century—would challenge American sovereignty, security, and way of life.

Americans seem inclined to regard such agencies as the National Security Council, the Department of Defense, the Central Intelligence Agency, and other sectors of the national security aparatus as bulwarks of the common defense. But how these complex, partially secret bureaucracies impinge upon the ideals of democratic government *or*, conversely, how the American democratic system impinges upon the efficient functioning of these agencies in the performance of their mission of providing for the common defense, are questions inadequately discussed.

The basic paradox is this: an efficient strategy for survival and security in the years ahead may be dangerously threatened by the forms and processes of American constitutional democracy. At the same time, the requirements and values of American democracy are themselves threatened by the organizational and policy responses already made to Cold War.

The compatibility of the requirements of defense and democracy is an old question that has assumed a new urgency. Alexis de Tocqueville, observing American democracy in the 1830s, concluded that in the conduct of foreign relations democracies are "decidedly inferior to other governments." Democracy, he wrote, was better adapted to peace than to war or to prolonged crisis. In a world radically different from Tocqueville's, the United States maintains virtually the same constitutional structure that the perceptive Frenchman found so deficient.

A democracy, Tocqueville wrote,

. . . can only with great difficulty regulate the details of an important undertaking, persevere in a fixed design, and work out its execution in spite of serious obstacles. It cannot combine its measures with secrecy or await their consequences with patience.[1]

[1] *Democracy in America*, ed., Phillips Bradley (New York: Knopf, 1945), Vol. I, pp. 234–35.

America's incipient crisis involves the confidence of Americans in both themselves and their governmental system. President Kennedy's assertion in his first State of the Union message that "we shall have to test anew whether a nation organized and governed such as ours can endure," suggests that the confidence is uncertain. There is also the more objective question whether our open, democratic system can produce the required security and compete effectively in protracted cold warfare with a closed Communist society.

The Communist leaders have the advantage of being able to pursue their world-wide objectives with an intense ideological purpose and a refined doctrine implemented by a disciplined, centralized regime. There is no free press within the U.S.S.R. or China to disclose prematurely details of secret operations; and despite internecine party strife, no opposition parties exist outside the Communist Party to question the wisdom of policies or the competence of operations. No autonomous legislature reviews policy recommendations or investigates failures. The people learn only what their government wants them to know.

Against such a competitor, the basic problem is not whether the American system can continue to provide both defense and democracy, but whether it can provide either.

Alexander Hamilton, writing in *The Federalist*, No. 8, early foresaw the dilemma:

Safety from external danger is the most powerful director of national conduct. Even the ardent love of liberty will after a time, give way to its dictates. . . . To be more safe . . . [nations] at length become willing to run the risk of being less free.

Abraham Lincoln also grasped the critical question in a later national crisis when he rhetorically asked Congress, on July 4, 1861: "Must a government of necessity be too strong for the liberties of its own people, or too weak to maintain its own existence?"

The American people emerged from the crises of 1776–87 and 1860–64 with their democracy expanded and more secure, but also with greater authority and power in the national government. As we approach the end of the Republic's second century, we find the nation involved in a more tenuous, long-term crisis, a crisis in which Lincoln's question remains relevant and urgent.

Surely a government that is insecure, or believes itself to be insecure against external (or internal) enemies will be currently unwilling and ultimately unable to dispense the "Blessings of Liberty" to its citizens. Conversely, unrestrained individualism and rampant pluralism can prevent a government from responding adequately to either common dangers or great opportunities.

The American system is designed to preserve a delicate balance between authority and freedom. In exploring the current security-liberty dilemma, this book focuses upon the organization, procedures, and major features of the national security bureaucracies spawned by contemporary world-affairs crises. It does not attempt to encompass all the dimensions of the problem of preserving American democracy in the modern world, neither is it a survey of all of the departments and agencies concerned with, nor of all of the ramifications of, national security policies. American democracy is profoundly threatened in many ways by the new role of scientists, technologists, and managers of the Cold War apparatus in a world we cannot fully understand. This book considers but one slice of a much larger problem: the structure and process developed for defense policymaking, particularly in the period since World War II.

To understand and describe this process, and the impact of the Cold War upon it, is a formidable task. It is particularly challenging in the national defense field, not only because of the increasing complexity and dynamism of policymaking, but because most of the crucial institutions and processes are shrouded by at least partial secrecy. By examining in the following chapters the American system for coordinating defense policy, the defense organization, the defense budget, problems of secret intelligence organization, policy and control, and the more general policies of government secrecy and disclosure, I hope to illuminate some of the significant sectors of a vast new gray zone of government.

The purpose throughout is not to give final answers to the perplexing and significant questions that arise, or to solve the central problems they represent, but rather to define some of the major issues facing the American Constitutional system as it attempts to sustain defense and democracy during an indefinite period of neither war nor peace.

The success of democracy depends ultimately upon the personal initiative of its citizenry and the application of intelligence and will power. My bias is toward a voluntaristic rather than fatalistic theory of man and society. We can survive with our democratic values essentially intact if we have the will to do so. Greater public awareness and understanding of the defense-democracy dilemmas are the first steps toward a proper perspective for arriving at a national consensus on the adjustments that are required for the survival of the American system.

As this is written there is no national consensus on the requirements of defense, or the prerequisites of democracy, or, indeed, on the ways in which defense and democracy are threatened. Only posterity can judge the success with which the United States manages to balance security with liberty, or whether the nation's survival, or demise, will be attributable to too much or too little democracy. The plausibility of the democratic ideal is always on trial. Democracy's premise is that the people shape their own instruments of governance. Therefore it is essential to keep an information spotlight on government institutions, to watch the nature and direction of their growth, and to attempt to judge their impact upon the viability of the democratic ideal. It may not be an exaggeration to suggest that the fate of mankind rests upon the success of the United States in uniting purpose, policy, and organization.

In the early days of the Republic, James Madison, writing in 1798 to Thomas Jefferson about foreign affairs, remarked that "Perhaps it is a universal truth that the loss of liberty at home is to be charged to the provisions against dangers, real or pretended, from abroad." Our contemporary dangers are not imaginary, and the efforts to meet them are endangering liberty at home. Yet faith in the power of the democratic idea inspires the belief that liberty need not be lost and a relatively high degree of national security need not remain beyond reach, if the citizenry make an effort to understand and help to solve the modern version of the old problem of balancing security and freedom.

CHAPTER 10

Critiques of Deterrence:
Alternatives to Force

As war becomes more unfightable and, paradoxically, peace becomes less assured, man searches for alternatives to the existence and use of force to settle disputes among nation states. The deeply felt fears of a thermonuclear war are simply not assuaged by the old assurances of an Edward Teller, a Herman Kahn, or an Ernest Lefever that America can survive a general nuclear attack with enough men and resources to recover fully in twenty to twenty-five years. And, technology is not static. Therefore, the prospects for even more destructive doomsday weapons cast a darker gloom. Nations, including our own, have the capability for almost total destruction at their command, but this destructive power has not brought with it the security which is its basic rationale for existence. Nuclear deterrence has been a reality, but the increased number and destructive power of nuclear weapons and the relatively large number of limited conflicts have continued, thus there is extensive anxiety regarding the future of modern man.

Many solutions to the problem of war have been suggested, ranging from pacifism to world government and including unilateral disarmament, negotiated total disarmament, and arms control. Unfortunately, none of these proposals has gained broad acceptance. But the search for a political equivalent of war—some alternative to force—continues, and the purpose of this chapter is to present recent examples of serious thought devoted to this pressing problem.

In the first article in this chapter, Gene Sharp presents a fascinating proposal for the use of nonviolent action as an alternative to military action. He defines nonviolent action as "those methods of protest, resistance, and intervention without physical violence in which the members of the nonviolent group do, or refuse to do, certain things." To be successful, the opponent's military action must be met with widespread noncooperation and disobedience. Nonviolent action may include a number of techniques such as strikes, boycotts, parades, defiance, and mass disobedience. In a sense, then, military defense policy is replaced by civilian defense policy.

The final article in this volume is a brilliant essay by Kenneth Boulding of the dilemma of conflict and defense. He feels that in an era of nuclear armed intercontinental ballistic missiles when all nations are vulnerable to attack, the system of unilateral national defense is no longer appropriate. In fact, he says that "unless we abandon it . . . we are doomed." He carefully points out, however, that the defense dilemma is not easily solved. He rejects the peace movement as an adequate solution; he endorses world government but does not feel that we will attain it; he considers nonviolent resistance as an "upward path" but thinks there is a possibility that it may have "unexpected and unwanted consequences"; he believes arms control measures are a "sign of hope"; and he worries that limited war may not continue to work because of the lack of institutions for limiting war. He even questions whether we would want peace if we were able to attain it, but stresses that because technology may lead us to annihilation, "peace is a necessity." An alternative to force must somehow be found. Boulding completes his epilogue by expressing his faith in man to "carry us not to destruction but to that great goal for which the world was made."

CONTROL OF POLITICAL POWER AND CONDUCT OF OPEN STRUGGLE

BY GENE SHARP

The assumption that only military action can be effective in resisting an opponent using military action is belied by evidence of non-military types of resistance. These have proved so powerful and effective that the will of the military-supported opponent has been thwarted, and significant concessions on major objectives have been won. Too little study has been devoted to these cases and to the means of struggle employed. Not only is our knowledge unduly limited, but, in addition, there exists serious misunderstanding about these non-military means of struggle.

INDIRECT STRATEGY

A frequent reaction to the idea that resistance without military arms could be effective against an enemy able to use military power is to dismiss the idea. It is generally assumed that resistance to a military attack must be made frontally by the same means, at the same time, and at the same place. Since non-military resistance cannot do this, the whole idea is deemed unworthy of consideration. A closer look at strategic problems of resistance, within the narrow context of military struggle, shows that it is not necessarily true that the wisest course is to resist an enemy's attack head-on, precisely because that is where he has concentrated his strength. Napoleon, for example, laid down as a basic principle that one should never "attack a position in front which you can gain by turning."[1] Similarly, B. H. Liddell Hart argues that

throughout the ages, effective results in war have rarely been attained unless the approach has had such indirectness as to ensure the opponent's unreadiness to meet it.[2]

If even in military conflict it is not always the wisest strategy to resist and attack where the enemy has concentrated his combat strength, there is no reason to dismiss lightly another kind of indirection that would attack the enemy's power, including his military capacity, by means other than a direct matching of forces of the same type. It is very possible that if the basic principle in that indirect strategy were further developed and extended, even to a point where a nation might decide to fight not with the weapons chosen by the opponent but by different means entirely, the result of such action might be a significant increase in combat effectiveness over that possible by reliance on military weapons.

There is a need, therefore, to explore the possibility of a defense policy in which the opponent's means of military action are always confronted indirectly by quite different means of resistance and intervention; in which his power of repression is used against his own power position in a kind of political *jiu jitsu*; and in which the very sources of his power are reduced or removed, with the inevitable result that his political and military position is significantly weakened or destroyed.

The opponent's power is often assumed to be a relatively fixed entity, a kind of monolith, a "given" factor in the situation that, by and large, can only be controlled or destroyed by the threat or use of over-

[1] Napoleon's *Maxims of War* (New York: James G. Gregory, 1861), Maxim XVI.

[2] *Strategy* (New York: Frederick A. Praeger, 1955), p. 25.

Reprinted with permission from the Carnegie Endowment for International Peace. Excerpt from *The Political Equivalent of War*, International Conciliation, November, 1965, No. 555, pp. 20–33.

Mr. Sharp is a Research Fellow at the Center for International Affairs at Harvard University, and a Visiting Lecturer at the University of Massachusetts. He is the editor of *Defense Without War* (1967) and a contributor to *Civilian Resistance As a National Defense* (1968).

whelming physical might. Faced with the potential destruction of men, weapons, cities, industries, communications, and so forth, the enemy is forced to agree to an acceptable settlement. But this view of a ruler's power as a kind of stone block that can only be reduced or destroyed by blasts of explosives is extremely crude and ignores the nature of the power at the disposal of any ruler or regime.

For an intelligent study of how to control political power, it is necessary to examine the nature and roots of the phenomenon to determine whether it can be attacked at the source instead of trying merely to deal with its manifestations. The enemy's capacity to wage war must be viewed, therefore, within the context of his over-all political power, and that political power must be seen in the context of the society as a whole, with regard to the sources of that power.[3] "The notion that force is the creator of government is one of those part-truths that beget total errors."[4] It is a simple truth of fundamental political significance that power wielded by any ruler comes from sources external to the power-holder. The wielding of political power by a ruler involves the ability to direct the behavior of other people, to draw on large resources (human and material), to wield an aparatus of coercion, and to direct a bureaucracy to administer his policies. These capacities have their origin in the society itself.[5]

Political power appears to emerge from the interaction of all or several of the following sources.

1) *Authority*: the extent of the ruler's authority among the subjects, i.e., "the quality which leads some men's judgements, decisions, and recommendations to be accepted voluntarily as right and to be implemented by others through obedience or assistance in achieving certain objectives."[6]

2) *Human resources*: the number of persons who accept the ruler's authority, obey and cooperate with him, or offer special assistance, and the proportion of these persons among the general population.

3) *Skills and knowledge*: the types of skills, knowledge, abilities, and similar qualities possessed by the persons accepting the ruler's authority, and the relation of these to his needs.

4) *Intangible factors*: the psychological and ideological factors, such as habits and attitudes toward obedience and submission, presence or absence of a common faith and ideology, a sense of mission, and similar factors.

5) *Material resources*: the degree to which property, natural resources, financial resources, the economic and industrial system, and the means of communication and transportation are under the control and at the disposal of the ruler.

6) *Sanctions*: the type and extent of sanctions at the ruler's disposal, both for use against his own subjects and in conflicts with other rulers.

The degree to which these factors are present varies, but they are seldom, if ever, completely present or completely absent. Variations induce an increase or a decrease in the ruler's power.[7] A closer examination of the mainsprings of a ruler's power indicates how intimately they depend upon the obedience and cooperation of the subjects. This is true even in the case of sanctions. The very ability to inflict sanctions depends upon the obedience and cooperation of the subjects. In turn, the effectiveness of sanctions depends upon the subjects' particular pattern of submission, and whether or not their fear of sanctions is greater than their determination to re-

[3] See Auguste Comte, *The Positive Philosophy of Auguste Comte*, trans. Harriet Martineau (London: John Chapman, 1896), Vol. II, pp. 223–225; see also Thomas H. Green, *Lectures on the Principles of Political Obligation* (London: Longmans, Green and Co., 1895), pp. 121–141.

[4] Robert M. MacIver, *The Web of Government* (New York: The Macmillan Co., 1947), p. 15.

[5] See Comte, *op. cit.*, pp. 223–225; MacIver, *op. cit.*, pp. 107–188; and Harold D. Lasswell, *Power and Personality* (New York: W. W. Norton and Co., 1948), p. 10.

[6] For a fuller definition, *see* Sharp *in* Adam Robert, *et al.*, *Civilian Defence* (London: *Peace News*, 1964), Appendix II.

[7] See Introduction by Arthur Livingstone *in* Gaetano Mosca, *The Ruling Class* (New York: McGraw-Hill Book Co., 1939), p. xix.

sist.[8] The ruler's power is thus not a "given" static factor but varies with the degree of acquiescence and consensus of the governed.[9] "If the state is to exist, the dominated must obey the authority claimed by the powers that be."[10] In this "two-sided relationship," it can be assumed that the necessary degree of obedience and cooperation will occur automatically.[11] Any government's power, both domestic and international, therefore, "is in proportion to its ability to make itself obeyed and win from that obedience the means of action. It all turns on that obedience."[12] Prominent cases of mass disobedience, defiance, and non-cooperation are simply the more dramatic evidences of this general truth. Since the reasons for obedience are not constant and the degree of obedience varies, there is a possibility of controlling or destroying the ruler's power by deliberately withholding the necessary obedience, cooperation, and submission.

In order to achieve this, non-cooperation and disobedience must be made sufficiently widespread to achieve and maintain an effective impact, despite repression inflicted by the ruler in an effort to force resumption of the previous submission and cooperation. Once there is a willingness to accept the sanctions as the cost of dis-

obedience for righting political wrongs, disobedience and non-cooperation are possible on a large scale. Such action then becomes politically relevant, and the ruler's will is thwarted in proportion to the number of disobedient subjects and the degree of his dependence on them.

POLITICAL POTENTIALITIES

One of the most vivid expositions of the theory that tyrants can be controlled and freedom restored if only the citizens will refuse to give them the necessary sources of power was written in the sixteenth century by the French writer Etienne de la Boetie. If tyrants

are given nothing, if they are not obeyed, without fighting, without striking a blow, they remain naked and undone, and do nothing further, just as the root, having no soil or food, the branch withers and dies. . . . Only be resolute not to be servile and there you are free. I don't want you to push him or shake him, but just don't support him, and you will see him like a great colossus whose base has been stolen, of his own weight sink to the ground and shatter.[13]

Machiavelli, similarly, noted the dangers for a prince of disobedience by both his agents and his ordinary subjects, especially in times of transition from a civil to an absolutist order of government. The prince must then depend on the uncertain goodwill of his agents (magistrates), who may refuse to assist him, or of his subjects, who may not be "of a mind to obey him amid these confusions."[14]

In the face of non-cooperation and disobedience from anything less than the total population, the ruler would inflict severe sanctions through those agents remaining faithful. The repression *may* force a resumption of submission, but not necessarily.

If the bulk of the community were fully determined to destroy it (the government), and to brave and endure the evils through which they must pass to their object, the might of the

---

[8] See Austin, *op. cit.*, pp. 302–306 and 457–458; Wolff, *op. cit.*, pp. 183 and 250; and de Jouvenel, *Sovereignty: An Inquiry into the Political Good* (Chicago: Univ. of Chicago Press, 1957), pp. 32–33.

[9] See Jeremy Bentham, *A Fragment on Government and An Introduction to the Principles of Morals and Legislation* (Oxford: Basil Blackwell, 1948), pp. 84–103; Bertrand de Jouvenel, *On Power: Its Nature and the History of its Growth* (New York: Viking Press, 1949), pp. 27–28; Lasswell, *op. cit.*, pp. 10–12 and 16; and Kurt H. Wolff, *The Sociology of Georg Simmel* (Glencoe, Ill.: The Free Press, 1950), pp. 183–186 and 250.

[10] "Politics as a Vocation," *From Max Weber: Essays in Sociology*, trans. and ed. H. H. Gerth and C. Wright Mills (New York: Oxford Univ. Press, 1946), p. 78.

[11] See Franz Neumann, "Approaches to the Study of Political Power," *Political Science Quarterly*, Vol. LXV, No. 2 (June 1950), p. 162. "No conceivable motive will *certainly* determine to compliance, or no conceivable motive will render obedience inevitable," John Austin, *Lectures on Jurisprudence or the Philosophy of Positive Law* (4th ed.; London: John Murray, 1873), Vol. I, p. 92.

[12] De Jouvenel, *op. cit.*, p. 27.

[13] *Discours de la Servitude Volontaire Suivi du Memoire* (Paris: Editions Bosard, 1922), pp. 57 and 60.

[14] Niccolo Machiavelli, *The Prince* (London: J. M. Dent & Sons, 1944), p. 77.

government itself, with the might of the minority attached to it, would scarcely suffice to preserve it, or even to retard its subversion. And though it were aided by foreign governments, and therefore were more than a match for the disaffected and rebellious people, it hardly could reduce them to subjection, or constrain them to permanent obedience, in case they hated it mortally, and were prepared to resist it to the death.[15]

Machiavelli even argued that the prince "who has the public as a whole for his enemy can never make himself secure; and the greater his cruelty, the weaker does his regime become."[16] As Rousseau has observed, "it is easier to conquer than to reign."[17]

There is historical evidence that these theoretical insights are valid and that massive non-cooperation can be effective, at least in certain circumstances, in controlling rulers' political power. Jawaharlal Nehru's experiences in the Indian struggle for independence led him to the opinion that "nothing is more irritating and, in the final analysis, harmful to a Government than to have to deal with people who will not bend to its will, whatever the consequences."

It is perhaps more instructive, however, to consider the conclusions of occupation officials themselves on the need to obtain and maintain the support of the populace, and the dangers posed by the withholding of that cooperation with or without violent resistance. In the midst of the 1930–31 civil disobedience movement in India, the British Viceroy, Lord Irwin, warned of the political power of such means of resistance.

In my judgement and that of my Government it is a deliberate attempt to coerce established authority by mass action, and for this reason, as also because of its nature and inevitable developments, it must be regarded as unconstitutional and dangerously subversive. Mass action, even if it is intended by its promoters to

be nonviolent, is nothing but the application of force under another form, and, when it has as its avowed objective the making of Government impossible, a Government is bound either to resist or abdicate. . . . So long as the Civil Disobedience Movement persists, we must fight it with all our strength.[18]

The German occupation of major sections of the Soviet Union during World War II, which was vastly different from the circumstances prevailing in India, also led certain officials and officers with the Nazi army and agencies to an appreciation of the necessity of cooperation and obedience for the maintenance of the occupation regime. Reviewing the history of the occupation, Alexander Dallin wrote:

While the whip continued to be the rather universal attribute of German rule, there slowly matured an elementary realization that the active co-operation of the people was needed for maximum security and optimum performance. A pragmatic imperative, perceived primarily in the field, dictated a departure from the practice, if not the theory of Nazi-style colonialism.[19]

In 1942, for example, Kube, the Reich Kommissar in Byelorussia, became persuaded that "German forces could not exercise effective control without enlisting the population."[20] A memorandum of the Propaganda Ministry in Berlin, on the basis of dispatches from Minsk, stated:

Once one gets to the point where our awkward policy uproots the huge and heavy mass of neutrals who want to risk nothing, then one gets a popular movement that cannot be suppressed unless one has an overpowering police machine, and such a machine Germany does not possess.[21]

Lecturing in a General Staff training course, Captain Wilfried Strik-Strikfeldt concluded that "Germany . . . faced the choice of proceeding with or without the people: it could not succeed without them if only

[15] Austin, *op. cit.*, p. 302.
[16] *The Discourses of Niccolo Machiavelli* (New Haven: Yale Univ. Press, 1950), Vol. I, p. 254.
[17] *Rousseau: Political Writings*, trans. and ed. Frederick Watkins (London: Thomas Nelson & Sons, 1952), p. 79.

[18] *India in 1930–1931* (Calcutta: Government of India, 1932), pp. 80–81.
[19] *German Rule in Russia, 1941–1945* (London: Macmillan and Co., 1957), p. 663. Reprinted by permission of the Macmillan Co. of Canada, Ltd.
[20] As quoted in *ibid.*, p. 218.
[21] As quoted in *ibid.*, p. 220.

because such a course required a measure of force which it was incapable of marshalling."[22] In May, 1943, General Harteneck wrote: "We can master the wide Russian expanse which we have conquered only with the Russians and Ukrainians who live in it, never against their will."[23] This change of views is all the more significant because it was diametrically opposite to the Nazi ideological position concerning the East Europeans, regarded as *untermenschen*, and to the earlier plans for annihilating the population in major areas of the occupied territory. Hitler's staunch supporter in Nazi-occupied Norway, Vidkun Quisling, who by this time had considerable experience in the difficulties of dealing with a defiant non-cooperating population, submitted a long report to Hitler in early 1944 which also contained the thesis that Russia could not be held without the support of the population.

Remarkably, Hitler himself admitted that "force" alone is inadequate in ruling conquered peoples. In July, 1943, he noted that German policy had to be so tough in the occupied East that it would numb the population's political consciousness. However, he continued:

Ruling the people in the conquered regions is, I might say, of course a psychological problem. One cannot rule by force alone. True, force is decisive, but it is equally important to have this psychological something which the animal trainer also needs to be master of his beast. They must be convinced that we are the victors.[24]

What happens if the subjects, despite occupation, refuse to be convinced that they are beaten? Hitler might possibly have been better prepared for this difficulty if he had paid a little attention to a rather different political leader, M. K. Gandhi, who stated nearly four and a half years earlier that

At the back of the policy of terrorism is the assumption that terrorism if applied in a sufficient measure will produce the desired result, namely, bend the adversary to the tyrant's will.

22 As quoted in *ibid.*, p. 516.
23 As quoted in *ibid.*, p. 550.
24 As quoted in *ibid.*, p. 498.

But supposing a people make up their mind that they will never do the tyrant's will. . . .[25]

Thus even totalitarian regimes cannot free themselves from dependency upon their subjects.

Compliance and enforcement are interdependent; they reinforce each other, and the varying proportions in which they do so, form as it were a continuous spectrum. . . . Totalitarian power is strong only if it does not have to be used too often. If totalitarian power must be used at all times against the entire population, it is unlikely to remain powerful for long. Since totalitarian regimes require more power for dealing with their subjects than do other types of government, such regimes stand in greater need of widespread and dependable compliance habits among their people; more than that, they need to be able to count on the active support of at least significant parts of the population in case of need.[26]

This interdependence of enforcement and obedience in totalitarian systems is but one possible illustration that they are not necessarily as monolithic and omnipotent as the totalitarians themselves would like potential opponents to believe. There exist in these systems various weaknesses that reduce their efficiency, totality of control, and permanence. While further investigation is necessary before a comprehensive list can be drawn up, some of these weaknesses can be suggested.

The totalitarian ideology, if maintained in a relatively "pure" form, may interfere with political judgment and adaptability. If it adapts to new knowledge and new political events, it is likely with the passage of time to become eroded or modified. Pressures for regular allocation of resources may limit the regime's maneuverability and contribute to tendencies toward a more regular and traditional system. Subjects may cease to be enthusiastic and become apathetic or resentful, thereby altering the psychological situation within which the

25 For text, see M. K. Gandhi, *Non-violence in Peace and War* (Ahmedabad: Navajivan Publishing House, 1948), Vol. I, p. 147.
26 Karl W. Deutsch, "Cracks in the Monolith: Possibilities and Patterns of Disintegration in Totalitarian Systems," in *Totalitarianism*, ed. Carl J. Friedrich (Cambridge: Harvard Univ. Press, 1954), pp. 313–315.

regime operates. The concentration of decision-making power in fewer hands, combined with the multiplication of decisions because of greater control over society may lead either to a greater risk of errors or to the devolution of decision-making from the center. Intermediate layers of command may gain increasingly independent power and the capacity for collusion against the top ruling group. Inaccurate or incomplete information passed up the hierarchy to the center may lead to decisions harmful to the regime. Inefficiency or inaccuracy in the relay and interpretation of central decisions and orders to subordinate agents and to the general population may hamper their implementation. Economic problems may lead to or aggravate political difficulties. Despite outward appearances of unity, deep conflicts may exist within the regime, party, and even the top hierarchy, which may reduce efficiency and capacity for concerted action and facilitate the modification or disintegration of the system. Subordinate officials, agencies, soldiers, and the police may carry out instructions with less than complete accuracy and efficiency.

Many of these possible weaknesses are related to the general requirement of obtaining the cooperation, obedience, and assistance of the subjects. If these or similar weaknesses exist in a totalitarian system and tend in the long run to a liberalization or disintegration of the system,[27] is it possible to produce deliberately conditions in which this tendency is accentuated? Might certain types of resistance aggravate the weaknesses? Putting it a different way, can there be a means of defense against an aggressive tyrannical system, which, instead of reinforcing the system and attacking at its strongest points, strikes at the weak points and stimulates or facilitates the operation of forces, thus helping to alter the system itself? Obviously, even if such means of defense were developed, severe problems of implementation in any given crisis situation would still remain. This would not provide an easy way—without dangers and suffering—to solve the problem of war.

But that is no reason for not considering such a policy.

TECHNIQUE OF NONVIOLENT ACTION

The technique of nonviolent action, while still relatively undeveloped in comparison with other political techniques, such as parliamentary democracy, guerrilla war, and conventional war, is rooted in both current theory and practice. Based on the theory that rulers are dependent on those they rule, and that persistent withholding of the necessary cooperation, obedience, and submission means an inevitable weakening and possible collapse of the regime, this technique offers the possibility of implementing the "withdrawal by the sovereign people of power from . . . legislative or executive representatives."[28] Moreover, it applies, perhaps most importantly, not only to potential domestic tyrants but also to foreign aggressors.

In his classic study of the strike, E. T. Hiller states that "co-operation produces dependence, and withholding co-operation provides each party with a means of coercion and of opposition against the other." The strike "is conflict in the form of a corporate refusal to participate." He goes on to discuss the wider characteristics of political noncooperation, which most frequently takes the form of a "refusal to share in the prescribed institutional activities or to participate in political affairs."[29]

This is the broad technique of nonviolent action, which includes types of behavior known as nonviolent resistance, passive resistance, Satyagraha, nonviolent direct action, and a large variety of specific methods. Because there is widespread misapprehension of the nature of this technique, a detailed definition may be useful.

Nonviolent action refers to those methods of protest, resistance, and intervention without physical violence in which the members of the nonviolent group do, or refuse to do, certain things. They may com-

---

[27] For a discussion, see *ibid.*, pp. 309–331. Some of the internal conflicts within the Nazi regime are documented by Dallin, *op. cit.*

[28] Green, *op. cit.*, p. 77.

[29] *The Strike: A Study in Collective Action* (Chicago: Univ. of Chicago Press, 1928), pp. 125 and 234.

mit acts of *omission*—refuse to perform acts which they usually perform, are expected by custom to perform, or are required by law or regulation to perform; or acts of *commission*—perform acts which they usually do not perform, are not expected by custom to perform, or are forbidden by law or regulation from performing; or a combination of both.

The technique has three main categories of methods. Where the group acts largely by symbolic acts of disapproval, its behavior may be called "nonviolent protest." Included in this category are demonstrations of protest and moral condemnation, such as marches, parades, and vigils. Where the group acts largely by non-cooperation its behavior may be described as "nonviolent resistance," for it is in a sense reacting to the policy and initiative of the opponent group. The many types of strikes and economic boycotts, the social boycott, and a considerable number of forms of political non-cooperation, including, for example, boycotts of political institutions, civil disobedience of "immoral" laws, and mutiny, may be grouped under this heading. Where the group acts largely by directly intervening in the situation, its action may be referred to as "nonviolent intervention." Examples of this category are sit-ins, nonviolent obstruction, nonviolent invasion, and parallel government.

Nonviolent action embraces the rejection of violence because of religious, ethical, or moral reasons, considerations of expediency or practicality, and mixed motivations of various types. The technique is *not* synonymous with pacifism.[30] The rather exaggerated claim sometimes pressed by pacifists that only they can practice nonviolent action is simply not true; in probably an overwhelming number of cases of nonviolent action, both the participants and the leadership have not been pacifists,[31] although the groups have often cooperated. This technique has nothing to do with passivity, submissiveness, and cowardice. By no means is it to be equated with verbal

or purely psychological persuasion; it is a sanction and technique of struggle that involves power; it is not dependent on the assumption that man is inherently "good." As repeatedly stated, the major justification here for nonviolent action is pragmatic.

Although the opponent is usually well equipped to apply violent means of struggle, the actionists, by using nonviolent techniques, fight with quite different weapons. They use weapons with which the enemy is least equipped to cope, and which tend to maximize the actionists' own strength while disrupting and weakening the opponent's power position. Nonviolent action has been successfully practiced by "ordinary" people. Its success does not require—though it is, of course, helped by— shared standards and principles, a high degree of community interests, or a high degree of psychological closeness between the contending groups. Nonviolent action has been used with effectiveness against opponents with radically different outlooks and objectives from the actionists. It is as much a Western phenomenon as an Eastern one.[32]

Nonviolent action may be used to change, modify, or abolish; to defend against efforts to change, modify, or abolish established outlooks, attitudes, social patterns, customs, laws, policies, programs, or social and political structures; or for a combination of these purposes. Attitudes toward the opponent and the conflict may vary widely, ranging from a desire to change the opponent's attitudes and beliefs and a determination not to allow time to change the resisters' outlook, to a determination to thwart attempts to change policies and other factors whether or not the opponent changes his views. Moreover, "conversion" and "nonviolent coercion" may be attempted simultaneously.

There is no assumption that the opponent will not resort to violence as an irrational reaction to the challenge or as a deliberately chosen means of repression against the nonviolent actionists. Whereas it is possible for both sides to rely on non-

[30] Pacifists may support or oppose the use of nonviolent action.

[31] See study by Sharp, *in* Roberts *et al., op. cit.*, Appendix I.

[32] See *ibid.*

violent action, the technique has primarily developed as one that could be practiced against an opponent willing and able to use his police and military power to maintain or extend his position and to carry out his objectives.

There are a multitude of socially and politically significant instances of nonviolent action, some successes, some failures, and some with mixed results, but they could, if carefully studied and analyzed, shed important light on the political potentialities of nonviolent action. In many cases the nonviolent technique has been accompanied by varying amounts of violence; in others violence has been largely excluded. But they are all relevant.

In studies of war, one can learn from lost battles and unsuccessful campaigns how to avoid similar mistakes and how to increase combat effectiveness in the future. Similar studies should also be useful in this type of struggle. An overwhelming number of past instances of nonviolent action have occurred without advance preparations. Until recently, there has been almost no serious thought or study about the operation of the technique, and relatively little in the way of experience and insight has been passed on from past struggles to present and future practitioners. Even under such unfavorable circumstances, and even in a world based on the assumption of the necessity of violent struggle, nonviolent action has won significant victories and forced concessions from harsh occupation regimes and tyrants. It is reasonable, therefore, to explore whether its political applicability might be expanded.

The following list of examples illustrates the wide variation in political, cultural, and geographic conditions under which nonviolent action has occurred:

American colonies, economic boycotts and tax refusal, 1763–76;
Hungarian passive resistance to Austria, 1850–67;
Belgian general strikes for broader suffrage, 1893, 1902, and 1913;
Finnish resistance to Russian rule, major aspects, 1898–1905;
Russian revolution, major aspects, 1905;

Chinese anti-Japanese boycotts, 1906, 1908, 1915, and 1919;
South Africa, Indian campaigns, 1906–14 and 1946;
Samoan resistance to New Zealand rule, 1919–36;
Germany, general strike and non-cooperation to Kapp *putsch*, 1920;
Ruhr, government-sponsored passive resistance to French occupation, 1923–25,
Indian independence movement, various campaigns;
Danish resistance, major aspects, including 1944 Copenhagen general strike, 1940–45;
Norwegian resistance, major aspects, 1940–45;
Dutch resistance, major aspects, including various large strikes, 1940–45;
South Africa, non-whites' struggles, 1952 and 1959;
Soviet Union, political prisoners' camps, various strikes, especially in 1953 (particularly at Vorkuta);
East German uprising, major aspects, June 1953;
United States civil rights movements, various campaigns and demonstrations;
Hungarian revolution, major aspects, 1956;
Johannesburg, Pretoria, Port Elizabeth, and Bloemfontein, African bus boycotts, 1957;
Kerala State, nonviolent resistance to elected Communist government's education policy, 1959;
Belgian general strike, 1960–61; and South Vietnam, Buddhist campaign against Ngo regime, 1963.

POLITICAL *JIU JITSU*

Because of the variety of methods, issues, attitudes, objectives, types of action groups, and so forth, it is impossible to say that nonviolent action always "works" in one precise way. Within the technique various influences and forces may produce change by one of three broad mechanisms. The relative strength and power of the contending groups in such a struggle are always subject to continuous and wide variation, depending on the course of the conflict.

The methods of nonviolent protest described above, such as marches and vigils, operate largely as extensions of verbal persuasion and protest into the field of social action. Unless the opponent is so authoritarian that he prohibits demonstrations of dissent (and the use of such methods then becomes a direct challenge to his position), the impact is likely to be limited to the level of changes in attitudes and ideas. However, when the methods of non-cooperation or nonviolent resistance are utilized, the picture changes. They may contribute to changes in attitudes and ideas, but they are primarily methods of exerting pressure and wielding power. Directed toward the attainment of certain objectives, they effect the deliberate withholding of various types of cooperation which the opponent expects or demands. Whether the non-cooperation takes the form of a bus boycott, an industrial strike, a general strike, a civil disobedience campaign, or the open mutiny of soldiers, the action has the potential of seriously disrupting the social or political system, depending, of course, on the numbers involved, the importance of the withheld cooperation, and the duration of the resistance.

Two examples may serve as illustrations. The first is the Negro bus boycott in Montgomery, Alabama, in 1955. A Negro woman refused to give up her seat to a newly boarded white man and was arrested. This unleashed a general protest boycott that was nearly 100 per cent effective.

Negroes walked, took taxis and shared rides, but stayed off the buses. . . . Negotiations failed to produce a satisfactory settlement. The use of taxis at reduced fares was prohibited. A car pool of 300 vehicles was organized. Money began to pour in, and a fleet of over 15 new station wagons was added . . . Negro drivers were arrested for minor, often imaginary, traffic violations. Police intimidation became common. (Houses were bombed.) A suit was filed by the Negroes in the Federal District Court, which declared the city bus segregation laws unconstitutional. The city appealed to the U.S. Supreme Court.
Meanwhile the bus protest continued, asking now an end to bus segregation. Insurance poli-

cies on the station wagons were cancelled; they were transferred to a London firm. City officials declared the car pool illegal. The same day the U.S. Supreme Court affirmed the unconstitutionality of the bus segregation laws. . . .
The Court's bus integration order finally reached Montgomery on December 20th. On the first day of integration there were no major incidents.
Then the white extremists began a reign of terror. Shots were fired at buses. A teenage girl was beaten. A pregnant Negro woman was shot in the leg. The Klan paraded again. But the Negroes' fear of them had gone. A small Negro boy warmed his hands at one of the burning crosses.
Then the homes of more leaders and several Negro churches were bombed. This turned the tide against the white supremacists. The local newspaper, several white ministers and the businessmen's association denounced the bombings.
The Negroes adhered to non-violence. More bombs exploded. Arrested whites were quickly found not guilty, but the disturbances abruptly ceased. The de-segregation proceeded smoothly, and in a few weeks transport was back to normal, with Negroes and whites sitting where they pleased on integrated buses—a compliance with the court order that would have been virtually inconceivable, without the forces set in operation by the Negroes' non-violent action.

The second example is a situation in 1953 when political prisoners in the coal mining camps at Vorkuta established strike committees.

The central leadership was arrested and removed to Moscow; a new committee was elected . . . many prisoners remained in their barracks, refusing to work. They insisted on presenting their demands only to the commandant of all the Vorkuta camps, which they did two days later when 30,000 had joined the strike. Then the General made a long speech containing vague promises and specific threats.
A week passed without decisive action; no clear orders came from Moscow. Food would continue only while existing provisions lasted, it was announced. A strike leaflet appeared in thousands of copies urging self-reliance to gain freedom, and the strike as the only possible means of action. Sympathetic soldiers helped to spread these and to maintain contacts between the camps. Twenty big pits were shut down.
Russian-speaking troops were then withdrawn and replaced by soldiers from the Far East

tribes. With the strike at its peak in early August, the State Prosecutor arrived with several generals from Moscow, offering minor concessions: two letters home a month (instead of a year), one visit a year, removal of identification numbers from clothes and of iron bars from barracks windows.

In an open letter, the strike leadership rejected these. The Prosecutor spoke at the camps, promising better food, higher pay, shorter shifts. Only a few wavered. The Strike Committee leaders went to an interview with the General but never returned. (Some strikers were shot.)

After holding out for over three months the strike finally ended in face of food and fuel shortages. Considerable material improvements were made, and a spokesman of the International Commission on Concentration Camp Practices considered the strike action in this and other camps to have been one of the most important factors in the improvement in the lot of the political prisoners.[33]

Methods of nonviolent intervention, such as sit-ins, nonviolent raids to demand possession of certain objects or places, nonviolent occupation of specific places by multitudes of people, or parallel government operating in rivalry to the opponent's regime, are all methods that go beyond the withholding of desired or expected cooperation. They challenge the opponent's authority and capacity to rule. Although undoubtedly of more limited applicability than the methods of non-cooperation, in particular circumstances they may be used advantageously to the detriment of the opponent's authority and capacity to maintain his system. The choice of methods determines to a considerable degree how the technique will work in a given situation.

This, however, is not the only factor. It is assumed in the following discussion that while methods of nonviolent protest may be used, the bulk of the action is conducted by non-cooperation with a limited use of nonviolent intervention. If the nonviolent action is then applied at vulnerable points with appropriate numbers and maintained over an adequate period of time (these will vary with the case), the result is likely to

be a challenge to the opponent's position, policy, or power, which he may not be able to ignore as was evident, for example, in Berlin in 1943. The Gestapo carried out a massive raid, arresting every Jew in Germany. Those with "Aryan kin" were placed in a separate prison. The following day wives of the Aryan-related prisoners turned up en masse at the gate of the detention center.

In vain the security police tried to turn away the demonstrators, some 6,000 of them, and to disperse them. Again and again they massed together, advanced, called for their husbands, who despite strict instructions to the contrary, showed themselves at the windows, and demanded their release.

For a few hours the routine of a working day interrupted the demonstration, but in the afternoon the square was again crammed with people, and the demanding, accusing cries of the women rose above the noise of the traffic like passionate avowals of a love strengthened by the bitterness of life.

Gestapo headquarters was situated in the Burgstrasse, not far from the square where the demonstration was taking place. A few salvoes from a machine gun could have wiped the women off the square, but the SS did not fire, not this time. Scared by an incident which had no equal in the history of the Third Reich, headquarters consented to negotiate. They spoke soothingly, gave assurances, and finally released the prisoners.[34]

The opponent may find that, if he is not to give in readily to the demands of the nonviolent actionists, he must apply sanctions against them in an effort to halt their action and obtain cooperation and submission. Exactly how severe his sanctions may be will vary with the seriousness of the nonviolent challenge, the importance of the issue at stake, the political situation, and the nature of the opponent.

Repression or other countermeasures are to be expected in most situations. This repression would probably involve the threat or use of physical violence, including imprisonment, beatings, shootings, and perhaps executions. But these means do not necessarily produce submission; nonviolent

[33] For text of both examples, *see* Sharp, *Creative Conflict in Politics* (London: Housmans, 1962), pp. 5–6.

[34] Heinz Ullstein translation reproduced *in* Theodor Ebert, "Effects of repression by the invader," *Peace News* (London), 19 Mar. 1965.

536 POLITICAL POWER AND OPEN STRUGGLE
536 POLITICAL POWER AND OPEN STRUGGLE

action is a technique designed to operate against opponents with the capacity for, and the willingness to, apply violence to attain their objectives. For sanctions to be effective, they must operate on the minds of the subjects and produce fear and the consequent willingness to obey. In nonviolent action, danger of injury or death does not necessarily cause the combatants to withdraw any more than it does on the battlefield. If the nonviolent actionists are willing to pay the price of resistance, the repression may not produce the desired submission. Arrests and selected reprisals may increase the spirit of resistance as they did in Nazi-occupied Norway. This, for example, was evident in the attempt to put all the teachers into a "corporation" under the head of the Norwegian Gestapo.

The underground called on the teachers to resist by writing to Quisling's Education Department, stating they could not assist in promoting fascist education of the children nor regard themselves members of the new teachers' organization.
Between 8,000 and 10,000 of the country's 12,000 teachers wrote such letters, each signing their names and addresses to the prescribed wording.
After threatening dismissal, the (Quisling) Government closed all schools for a month. The teachers then held classes in private homes. Despite censorship, news of the resistance spread. Tens of thousands of letters of protest poured into the Government office from parents.
After the deadline for compliance had passed, about 1,000 teachers were arrested and sent to concentration camps. As their cattle trucks passed through, children sang at the railway stations.
In the camps, the Gestapo imposed an atmosphere of terror. On starvation rations, the teachers were put through "torture gymnastics" in deep snow. Only a very few gave in. When the spirit of resistance remained unaffected, the "treatment" continued.
When the schools were re-opened, the remaining teachers told their pupils they repudiated membership in the new organization and spoke of a duty to conscience.
Rumors were spread that if the teachers at their jobs did not give in, some or all of those arrested would meet death in one way or another. (The) teachers stood firm.
Then, by cattle truck trains and overcrowded steamers, the arrested teachers were shipped to a camp near Kirkenes, in the Far North. . . . Their suffering strengthened the home front morale, while it posed several problems to Quisling and his followers. On one occasion, Quisling raged at the teachers of a school near Oslo, ending: "You teachers have destroyed everything for me!"
Fearful of alienating the Norwegians still further from his regime, Quisling finally ordered the teachers' release. Eight months after the arrests, the last of the teachers returned home to triumphal receptions.[35]

There is a fairly common assumption that victory inevitably comes to him who wields the greatest military power. It seems incredible that citizens without military weapons can thwart an enemy willing and able to use violence to achieve his goals. The military or paramilitary, it can be argued, are a highly professional group, responding not to their own self-imposed drives but to commands and trained reflexes. How can any citizenry turn itself, of its own volition, into a "sitting duck"? The answer is that this has happened in the past—the struggle of the Buddhist priests in South Vietnam is one of the most dramatic recent examples—and there is no reason that it cannot and will not happen again. In fact, the opponent may find that nonviolent action is more intangible and difficult to overcome than overt violence. Not only is it difficult to justify repressive violence against nonviolent people, but such violence, instead of strengthening the opponent's position and weakening the nonviolent actionists, may achieve the reverse. In short, the nonviolent technique applied against a violent opponent uses the opponent's "strength," as in *jiu jitsu*, to upset his balance and contribute to his own defeat. This is not simply because of the novelty of nonviolent action, which with the spread of the technique is already wearing off, but because of the inherent nature of the technique itself.
Violence against nonviolent citizens may also alienate the general populace from the opponent's regime. Repression may rally public opinion to the support of the nonviolent actionists (though its effectiveness varies), which may lead to supporting action. Repression may even alienate the op-

[35] Sharp, *Creative Conflict in Politics*, op. cit., p. 3.

ponent's own subjects, usual supporters, and agents; initial uneasiness may lead to internal opposition and, at times, to non-co-operation and disobedience. If the repression does lead to a significant increase in the number of nonviolent actionists, and conceivably also to action such as strikes, disobedience, and troop mutiny among the opponent's own supporters, the repression clearly will have rebounded against the regime.

Furthermore, apart from this *jiu jitsu* effect, the repression may be highly ineffective in bending the actionists to the opponent's will. The arrest of the leadership may simply lead to the movement developing in such a way as to enable it to carry on, first, with secondary lines of leaders (either preselected or who have emerged from the ranks) and, possibly later, even without a recognizable leadership. The opponent may make new acts illegal only to find that he has opened up new opportunities for defiance. While he attempts to repress defiance at certain points, the nonviolent actionists may develop sufficient strength to broaden their attack on other fronts and challenge his very ability to rule. Instead of mass repression forcing cooperation and obedience, the opponent may discover that the repression is constantly being met with refusal to submit or flee. In extreme cases, the very agencies of repression may be immobilized by the massive defiance. Physically incapable of enforcing the opponent's will, the police may abandon the struggle, officials resign, and troops mutiny. This situation, it is emphasized, cannot be produced except when the aims of the nonviolent actionists have the overwhelming support of the populace and when the activists and the population are willing to pay the price. There have been situations in the past when mass defiance by the populace has made a government powerless. One vivid illustration of this is the 1920 military coup which failed to overthrow the young Weimar Republic. On 10 March, a year after the Republic had been established, the government was presented with a virtual ultimatum by General von Luttwitz on behalf of a right-wing pro-monarchist group led by Luttwitz and a German politician, Wolfgang Kapp. The group's demands included new elections, a cabinet of "experts," and a halt to the disbandment of the armed forces (in accordance with provisions of the Versailles Treaty). The ultimatum was rejected, and the same day the Kappists began their march on Berlin. Police officers sided with the conspirators, and the government troops could not be trusted to oppose them.

President Friedrich Ebert and his government abandoned Berlin without a fight, retreating first to Dresden and then to Stuttgart. Berlin was occupied on 13 March, and Kapp proclaimed himself Chancellor of the Reich. The Ebert Cabinet and the Executive Committee of the Social Democratic Party retaliated by calling for a general strike: "There is but one means to prevent the return of Wilhelm II; the paralysis of all economic life. Not a hand must stir, not a worker give aid to the military dictatorship." Thousands had already initiated a spontaneous strike in Berlin, so that by 14 March the general strike, supported by workers of all political and religious groups, was in full swing. No "essential services" were exempted. Seizure of two pro-Ebert newspapers in Berlin led to a printers' strike. The Kappist regime lacked money, and civil servants struck or refused to head ministries under Kapp.

On 15 March, the Ebert government rejected proposals for a compromise. Leaflets titled "The Collapse of the Military Dictatorship" were showered by plane on Berlin. Some *Reichswehr* commanders defected from the Kappist regime. The strike continued to spread despite severe threats and the shooting of some strikers. On the morning of 17 March, the Berlin Security Police changed its attitude and demanded Kapp's resignation. Later that day Kapp resigned and fled to Sweden. Bloody clashes took place in many towns, but by evening most of the conspirators had left Berlin and Luttwitz had resigned. The leaders of the coup had been defeated, and the Weimar Republic was preserved.[36]

[36] For more details, *see* Wilfrid Harris Crook, *The General Strike: A Study of Labor's Tragic Weapon in Theory and Practice* (Chapel Hill: Univ. of North Carolina Press, 1931), pp. 496–527; and D. J. Goodspeed, *The Conspirators: A Study of the Coup d'Etat* (New York: Viking Press, 1962), pp. 108–143 and 211–213.

EPILOGUE: THE PRESENT CRISIS OF CONFLICT AND DEFENSE

BY KENNETH E. BOULDING

The last chapter concluded the formal part of this volume. This is a work in abstract social theory. It purports simply to identify and build theoretical models of a set of social processes related to the phenomenon of conflict. Its theory is ethically neutral; in so far as it is useful to anybody, it may be equally useful to the nationalist as to the internationalist, to the militarist as to the pacifist, and to the communist as to the democrat. Even the previous chapter, which comes closest to the ethical judgment, treats this judgment as an abstract process, capable of producing many different ethical positions.

In this epilogue, I wish to go further and commit myself to what seem to me the implications of the theory I have developed, in the light of my own values. The reader is warned that his possibly different values may produce different conclusions. Nevertheless, this is not merely a matter of taste. Values must constantly be restructured by one's image of the world of fact and relationship. The theory of this volume represents a view of social reality that is different from what I must call, without intent of being insulting, the naïve view. The naïve view of the universe is egocentric and ethnocentric; for the naïve man, the sun goes round the earth, and society revolves around himself and his own group and culture. It is one of the first tasks of science, both natural and social, to destroy this naïveté and to exhibit man as part of a system the perception of which is liberated from perspective. The astronomer knows that the bright stars in our sky are merely near and that intrinsic brightness bears

little relation to apparent brightness. Similarly, the student of social systems, by his very abstraction, develops a view of society that is, in theory, free from the perspective of his own person, culture, and nation. This Copernican revolution by which the illusion of perspective is perceived always represents the transition from the naïve to the scientific or even to the religious view of the universe.

This perspective revolution in the view of the universe, however, always produces a profound disturbance of the value system of the individual. This is true even in the physical sciences, and it is even more true in the social sciences. Values of rigidity, of combativeness, and even of loyalty that are quite consistent with the egocentric view of the universe are seen to be inconsistent with a scientific view. It will not be surprising, therefore, if the view of the social universe that is found in this volume will be associated with some transformation in basic values: it will be seen as a threat by those who hold egocentric values and as a reinforcement by those whose values have adapted themselves to the perspective revolution. The perspective revolution does not, of course, destroy either perspective itself or egocentric values. In the sight of God and in the light of social science, the child in a remote corner of Tibet is just as valuable as one of my own children. I must confess, however, that, even though I know the brilliance with which my own children shine in the sky of my attention is only an illusion of perspective, my personal concern and activity are heavily weighted in the direction of the near and dear. Brightness may be an

Reprinted by permission of Harper & Row Publishers, from pp. 329–343, *Conflict and Defense: A General Theory.* Copyright © 1962 by Kenneth E. Boulding.

Mr. Boulding was formerly Professor of Economics at the University of Michigan, and he is now Professor of Economics at the University of Colorado. He is the author of numerous books, including *The Meaning of the Twentieth Century: The Great Transition* (1964), *The Impact of the Social Sciences* (1966) and *Economic Analysis* (4th ed., 1966), and he is the co-editor of *Disarmament and the Economy* (1963).

illusion of perspective, but nearness is not; and it is quite compatible with the most universalistic of ethics to concentrate on the matters that are close at hand. Indeed, this is required; an ethical system that was so universalistic as to persuade a man to neglect his own children in the interest of spreading his attention over the whole wide world would be subject to severe criticism. The allocation of responsibility is an important task of any ethical system, and the allocation by nearness is the simplest and most workable, provided it does not lead us actually to believe the illusion of perspective.

We are still left, however, with a serious ethical dilemma that has become overwhelmingly acute in the modern world— that of reconciling the universal ethic that both science and high religion imply with the particularist loyalty to existing institutions and responsibilities. What we face in the modern world is a fundamental breakdown in the concept of defense as a social system, largely, as I have tried to show, as a result of the constant decline in the LSG[1] affecting almost all institutions as a result both of physical and social invention. The concept of defense has always been somewhat naïve, as I defined it, in the sense that it has rested on an egocentric and ethnocentric view of the universe that takes the defended person or institution as given, known, and valued and the outside enemy as also given but unknown and negatively valued and regards the problem of virtue as that of the preservation of a little island of defended goodness in the middle of the howling chaos of the hostile world. There are times and places where this naïve view is not unrealistic, as when, for instance, Robinson Crusoe builds his stockade against unknown marauders. Unilateral defense against the vast unknown, however, soon passes over into a system of unilateral de-

fense, in which two or more parties try unilaterally to defend themselves against each other. Once this happens, the naïve view no longer expresses the social reality; unilateral defense turns into a conflict system, the dynamics of which is not in the control of any one party but emerges as a result of the unconsciously coordinated decisions of all. Once this happens, the record of unilateral defense as a system is dismal. When individuals rely on it, we get a Hobbesian society, constantly re-enacted in gangsterdom, in which the life of a man is indeed nasty, brutish, and short and, to get away from it, men build political structures, enter into social contracts, and even submit to tyranny. This is because, even with quite primitive means of violence, no two men are unconditionally viable with regard to each other. We must, therefore, as persons learn to live with conditional viability. This is why unilateral defense for persons has always proved to be unstable, even though new weapons and social situations may revive it from time to time, as in the cowboy era of the wild West.

Now, however, we face the same problem of the breakdown of unconditional viability in the relations of national states. Unilateral national defense has created an enormous amount of human misery through history, but, up to the present century, it has been a workable system, in the sense that it has provided occasional protected heartlands of peace in which civilization and the arts could flourish even though surrounded by a periphery of war. Now it is no longer workable; the decline in the LSG, coupled with the increasing range of the missile to more than half of the earth's circumference makes all heartlands hopelessly vulnerable. A beautiful example of this is provided by a Report on a Study of Non-Military Defense by the RAND Corporation.[2] The RAND Corporation is financed mainly by the United States Air Force, so that its studies must be accepted with the same kind of reserve that, shall we say, we might greet a study of the Reformation by Jesuits based on unpublished and secret documents in the Vatican; there is the same

[1] Loss-of-strength gradient (LSG). This concept is taken from Professor Boulding's basic model of international conflict which is fully explained in Chapter 12 of his book. A brief explanation of LSG is, in the author's words, "that each party can be supposed to be at his maximum power at home . . . but that his competitive power, in the sense of his ability to dominate another [party], declines the farther from home he operates." See pp. 78–79 and 230.

[2] Report R.322.RC, July 1, 1958.

combination of honesty in the value system and bias in the commitment. By making what seem to me fantastically optimistic assumptions, this report concludes that, by taking adequate precautions, the United States might lose not more than from 5 to 85 million people, and the economy would recover almost to previous levels, assuming a gigantic effort, in twenty-five years. What the report does not say is that the purpose of all this misery and sacrifice is so that the next generation can go through it all again; that is, the purpose of national defense is to re-establish the system that gave rise to the catastrophe. Under these circumstances, unilateral national defense seems to me to be sheer lunacy; it can only persist as an ideology because of the smallness of men's imaginations and their refusal to let go of an outworn concept that has served them in good stead in the past. The abandonment of the ideology of unilateral national defense is particularly hard for Americans, who for 200 years have been served well by it, because of the accident of geography and history. Unless we abandon it, however, I believe we are doomed.

In this dreadful dilemma, where the ideas and values with which we have mostly been brought up have turned to poison in our hands, to what can we turn? The peace movement, one fears, is not adequate to meet this challenge. The history of the peace movement still remains to be written, and the movement is in great need of study and research. It can be traced back in Western history to mainly Christian origins. The early Christian church was pacifist in doctrine until it was taken over by Constantine. The monastic movement represents a pacifist withdrawal from the world, though not a direct criticism of it. From the time of the Reformation, each century has seen the rise of a peace church—the Mennonites in the sixteenth, the Quakers in the seventeenth, the Brethren in the eighteenth, and, more doubtfully perhaps, the Adventists in the nineteenth and Jehovah's Witnesses in the twentieth century. There were peace-movement elements in early socialism; the War Resisters International represents a very small secular pacifist movement. In the 1930s in Britain, the Peace Pledge Union

showed signs of becoming an incipient mass movement. On the whole, however, the peace movement has been small in numbers and sectarian in outlook. It has kept alive the hope of peace, and it has provided a constant challenge to a blind acceptance of war as an institution. It has not, however, made much contribution to developing the institutions of peace, and it has not had much impact on the course of world events.

The invention of military conscription has forced the peace movement to channel its energies mainly into the defense of its individual adherents against the governments of their own countries. This is a very important conflict, but it does not have much to do with world peace. The struggle for the rights of conscientious objectors is part of the whole movement of defense of the individual against the power of large organizations. In so far as this struggle is successful, it is a tribute to the bargaining power of the inflexible; a man or group that will die or go to prison rather than be coerced cannot be coerced. If society is convinced that a group cannot be coerced, they may be able to strike a successful bargain with society, simply because, in spite of their intransigence, they may be of more use to the society alive and free than dead or in prison. The inflexibly conscientious, therefore, are important defenders of the rights of all individuals against the pressures of society, and the bargains they strike frequently benefit those of less determination and are an important check on the power of organized society. Thus, while the lone pacifist is an important bargainer with society and helps to keep it from sinking into tyranny, he makes little contribution to the organization of society. He takes liberty, for liberty is something that people have to take: in a sense, it can neither be given to people nor organized by them; otherwise, it is not liberty. He does not, however, organize liberty; this is a political task for the compromisers and the bargainers, and, in a sense also, liberty has to be organized as well as taken.

Just as war is too important to leave to the generals, so peace is too important to leave to the pacifists. It is not enough to condemn violence, to abstain from it, or to withdraw from it. There must be organization against it; in other words, institutions of conflict control or, in still other words, government. The case for world government to police total disarmament as put forward for instance by Clark and Sohn seems to me absolutely unshakeable,[3] in spite of the fact that the march of technology has made some of their specific proposals obsolete. In general, we know the main lines of the kind of world organization that can eliminate the present dangers and give us permanent peace. What we do not know is how to get to it. The problem essentially is how do we bargain with each other, and especially how now do the nations of the world bargain with each other, to create a social contract and a machinery that will give the social contract stability. The world dilemma is illustrated admirably by the game matrix of Fig. 3.5, p. 50. We reproduce it below (Fig. 1) in terms of the social contract. If both parties keep the contract at N, all are better off; with the kind of payoff matrix shown, however, there is a payoff to either party in breaking the contract if the other party does not. If one party breaks it, however, the other must follow suit, and we end up in the Hobbesian state of unilateral defense and natural misery as S. The state we now seem to be in, however, is illustrated by Fig. 2. Here, the situation at S is worse than it is in Fig. 1, and if it becomes bad enough, it alters the whole character of the game, as we see from the arrows. Now, even if one party breaks the

[3] Grenville Clark and Louis B. Sohn, *World Peace Through World Law* (2d ed.; Cambridge: Harvard University Press, 1960).

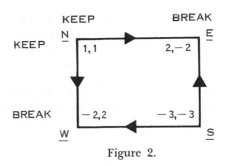

Figure 2.

contract, it still does not pay the other to do so; the game as it stands will end up either at E or at W, depending on which party moves first. Figure 1 is the traditional position of unilateral defense; this has been the state of the world for many thousands of years. Now, the question arises, "Have we moved internationally into the condition of Fig. 2?" This might be called the pattern of unilateral virtue. It is a commoner pattern in human life than might be imagined. It is the pattern of long suffering. The peasant, the slave, the woman, and the underdog in innumerable societies have sat for generations at positions like E or W, unable to bargain to N and unwilling to fight to S. This, indeed, has been the characteristic feature of the internal relations of most human societies, just as Fig. 1 has characterized their external relations. For the heirs of the Enlightenment, however, this is not good enough. Responsible government is an attempt and, by and large, a fairly successful attempt to devise institutions that will keep us at the optimum at N in the internal relations of society. By devising orderly institutions for removing politicians from power and by devising constitutional checks through the courts, we make it more and more difficult for the powerful to break the social contract, and the Communist and democratic world alike share the ultimate ideal, as yet unrealized anywhere, of a society without aliens, without any excluded class or group, a society from which nobody shall be alienated. Now, the great problem before mankind is how to build responsible government at the world level. This is no longer a dream but a necessity, simply because the breakdown of the system of national

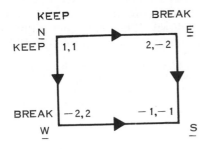

Figure 1.

defense makes it impossible any more to build defended islands of responsible government and peace in the midst of the Hobbesian wilderness of the warring world.

It is not too hard to see where we have to go; the difficulty is that no road leads there. Perhaps we should say more hopefully that the road to life, to government, and to organization always leads uphill. The easy roads, the intrinsic dynamics, always lead downhill to ultimate destruction. Both life and government are unstable castles of order in the midst of a universe of increasing entropy and chaos. They can be built, however, because of the learning process, because the gene can teach patterns to unorganized matter, and because the human organism can learn from its imagination, from its experience, and from others. Our hope for the future of mankind, therefore, lies first in the human imagination, which can create the forms of things unknown and so create the image of possible futures that have not been previously imagined. Secondly, hope lies in the learning process; man can take the images of possible futures and test them, partly in the imagination itself, partly in experience, and partly by trusting the word of the teachers who have tested the images.

Where, then, are the new ideas and the new images of the future that look like upward paths? One is clearly the idea of nonviolent resistance associated with the name of Gandhi. This is a powerful method of bargaining for a social contract. It is more sophisticated in its psychology than in military defense, and it fits well into the Schelling type of bargaining theory. It assumes that the enemy is not merely another, to be crushed or excluded from the society, but it is part of the same social system as the defender. It is unfortunate that, in English, we have no word that expresses the positive aspect of *ahimsa*, or nonviolence. It is something, however, that we experience constantly in daily life, especially in the family: it is the characteristic activity of what I called in the previous chapter the reconciling personality. What was remarkable about Gandhi was that he was able to organize a large number of

people into the political movement of *Satyagraha* (truth seeking) aimed at the establishment of a new social contract in the form of *swaraj*, or independence. This is perhaps the most important political idea of the twentieth century. We see it in operation at the moment, for instance, in the nonviolent campaign of Negroes in the United States for civil rights, full citizenship, and integration into American society.

There is great need for research into the dynamic processes of political movements of this kind and into the problem of the limiting conditions within which they are most likely to be successful.[4] The method is dismissed too easily by the militarists, who are committed to a less sophisticated and more primitive method of defense. It is perhaps welcomed too uncritically by the pacifists, who tend to assume its universal applicability. As with any powerful movement in human affairs, nonviolent resistance movements operate in the midst of a complex social system the course of which through time is the result of many interacting decisions and movements. Thus, like military defense, nonviolent resistance may turn out to have unexpected and unwanted consequences. Even in India, for instance, the Gandhian movement led to the tragedy of partition and to one of the major human catastrophes of the twentieth century.

Another sign of hope is the interest in arms control that is now spreading even to the military. It may be that the institutions of peace will have to be worked out by conscientious military men, simply because they control the organizations that must be transformed if peace is to be organized. There is, I think, a largely subconscious feeling among military men who take their responsibility for national defense seriously that they are facing an unprecedented system breakdown. They may not think in quite the terms of this volume, and they

[4] The classic study by Richard B. Gregg, *The Power of Non-Violence* (Philadelphia: Lippincott, 1936), is still the best descriptive and analytic work in the field, in spite of, or perhaps because of, a certain amateur quality. The phenomenon has never been adequately studied by professional social scientists. *The Conquest of Violence*, By Joan V. Bondurant (Princeton, N.J.: Princeton University Press, 1958) is a good recent work.

will not have the prejudices of the author; but they are deeply worried about their inability, in the last analysis, to perform their traditional function of protecting the heartland from disruption and disorganization.

The interest in limited war is one straw in the wind. There is a nostalgia among the military and their academic friends for the good, old pretechnical days, when wars could be fought without the dangers of mass annihilation, and even for the good old eighteenth century, when war was still largely a professional business. Napoleon destroyed this idyll, and the democratization of war may well prove its ultimate undoing. The difficulty with limited war, however, is that there are no institutions for limiting it; its limitation depends on a tacit social contract between the opposing parties, and even though, as Schelling has shown, these tacit contracts may be of great importance and may be necessary to the formation of more explicit contracts, they do not seem adequate to carry the burden of the world's frightful danger. Furthermore, the simplest tacit contract and most obvious place to strike a bargain is at no war at all; the great weakness of limited war is that there is no salient configuration of the social system that limits it, whereas no war is a highly salient position around which a bargaining solution may cluster.

Arms control goes a little further than tacit contract. It may be defined as military cooperation with potential enemies in the interest of mutual security; its military object is presumably to restore unconditional viability and permit the re-establishment of the game of diplomacy without the constant threat of total disaster. Arms control unquestionably offers some real hope. It is the disunion of the military organizations of the world that threatens us with disaster, and the more organizational ligaments can be built between them, the better off we may be. A suggestive analogy is the elimination of religious war, though not by any means of religious conflict, by what now seems to us the very simple device of the separation of church and state. The idea that religion could be left to the personal preference of the individual and that, indeed, this would probably strengthen religious organizations rather than weaken them is something that would never have occurred to the man of the seventeenth century. This simple idea, however, has largely eliminated religion as a major source of violence, after centuries of devastation in its name. One wonders whether we may not now proceed to the separation of the armed forces from the state. The myth of the modern national state is that its armed forces are its servants, to protect it from having to submit to the will of other states or to enable it to impose its will upon others. What, in fact, seems to be the case is that the armed forces of the world form a social system of their own, almost independent of the states which support them and which they are supposed to defend. This paradoxical situation arises because what an armed force is organized for is to fight another armed force; hence, the existence of the national armed forces is completely self-justifying: each armed force justifies the existence of its potential enemy and has practically no other justification for its existence. In this, the military forces differ strongly from the police force, which is not organized against other police forces but against individual violaters of the law and which does not theoretically have a punitive but only an apprehending function. The business of the police, that is, is to bring the offender before the apparatus of the law to be tried, and if found guilty, punished; it is the courts, however, not the police, who are supposed to do the trial and punishment. This division of labor is not always strictly observed, but it represents the fundamental differences between a legal, responsible police force on the one hand and banditry, secret political police, and armed forces on the other.

One wonders, therefore, whether the path to national security does not lie through detaching and weakening the organizational and hierarchical bonds that bind the armed forces to the civilian state and through a corresponding strengthening of the bonds that connect the various armed forces of the world with one another. It may be more important to exchange generals with other countries, and especially with potential enemies, than to exchange professors and concert artists. The open-skies and open-spies proposals that have been in the air in recent years are again straws in a very strange wind of change. Once we realize that the object of a disarmament conference is not necessarily to agree to disarm but to build an organization that unites the various national armed forces, the road to disarmament, which has seemed so hopeless, may be opened up. Once the armed forces of the world are united into a single organization, their functions obviously will cease, and, like the ideal Marxian state, they will wither away or, perhaps, one should say, fade.

Suppose now we get peace, real peace; what then? Our troubles are, of course, far from over. Mankind has very rarely had peace and is inexperienced in it. The few civilizations that have not had the institution of war, like that of Mohenjo-Daro and of the Mayans, are not wholly inspiring to contemplate; they seem to have been static, indeed stagnant societies endlessly repeating a ritualized and stylized form of life without change, adventure, discovery, or excitement beyond what ritual can offer. Both these examples probably came to an end through overpopulation, soil erosion, and a gradual worsening of conditions until a revolution of the proletarian cultivators destroyed the whole society. The warrior civilizations destroyed themselves too, of course, and the record of cruelty, destructiveness, and tyranny that these offer is no more pleasant to contemplate than the dullness of the unchallenged.

In my personal life, I see war only as a threat, with no virtues whatever. I lead a full and interesting life in peacetime, and I see nothing coming from war but misery and deprivation. I must recognize, however, that this is not true of all men and that, in the past at any rate, war has given color and excitement to otherwise drab lives, especially where it can be enjoyed by proxy. There is, therefore, an important problem facing mankind, failing its destruction, by the adjustment to permanent peace and the abolition of war as a social institution. We want peace, just as we want utopia, just as long as we are pretty sure of not getting it. When the choice is placed before us, however, as it seems to be in the modern world, between utopia or, at least, peace, which is something less, or annihilation, our embarrassment may become so acute that we choose annihilation. One sees this in the conventional cartoon image of peace as a wispy and rather bedraggled female in a bedsheet holding a wan olive branch as a corsage. She is not a girl that any red-blooded American or Russian would particularly want to go out with, much less make love to. Still, she haunts us. It is a specter even more frightening, perhaps, than that which Karl Marx invoked in 1848, because we have always thought in terms of war as a last resort. Now there may be no last resort, except doomsday, which is no resort at all. There is no defense, no isolation, no protection from the awful task of living together with monstrously strange bedfellows. As long as we had defense, we could simplify the task of living together by only loving the like and the lovable and by keeping away the unlike and the unlovable. Now we find ourselves all cooped up together on this little ball of a spaceship and forced to live together in peace for fear of wrecking it.

The problem is part of a still larger one, and we may have to think about the larger one before we can solve the smaller. The technical revolution in warfare that has made peace a necessity is part of a larger change in the knowledge, skills, and abilities of mankind through which we are now passing, which began to get noticeably under way in the seventeenth century and has been accelerating ever since. It is carrying mankind to a state of affairs so different from that of the civilized societies out of which it developed that it has been called postcivilization. We are still in the era of rapid transition and are not within sight of the final equilibrium state. An equilibrium state there must be, however, or at least a state that is not merely transition, for every transition must lead toward something. We only see very dimly what this high-level equilibrium might be like. It must clearly involve population control by means other than high infant mortality, which implies a revolution in family life and in sexual behavior that we have not even begun to accomplish as yet. If the expectation of life is going to be seventy years, then, in an equilibrium population, birth and death rates must be about fourteen, and the two-child family must be standard. It must likewise involve conflict control, so that the enormous powers that the new technology places in the hands of man are not used for his destruction. It will likewise involve boredom control, to prevent man from simply committing suicide from inanition in a utopian society. Of course it involves control of disease, ignorance, poverty, depressions, and tyranny, and it must involve some sense of high purpose for the human race, whether in the physical conquest of the universe, the conquest of man's own depravity, or in reaching out toward the divine. These are dreams, but they are dreams that we must dream, and dream well, if the vast dynamic process of change in which we are all caught up is not to take us to irretrievable disaster of one kind or another. There is no way back to Eden, to innocence or to ignorance; having eaten of the fruit of the tree of knowledge, it is Zion or nothing.

I was recently sitting in an airplane waiting to take off. It was spring, and a little bird was trying to build her nest in a little hole at the end of the wing. She flew busily in and out carrying bits of straw and twigs as the plane sat on the ground waiting for the signal to take off, and then the plane roared away and left her far behind. I could not help seeing in this a parable of our day. We are all going about our various tasks, each trying to build for himself a little shelter from the inclement world, a little defense against want or hardship or loneliness, and we are all building on the wing of a great sweeping process of change that may soon roar away with our little efforts, we know not where nor how. There were men in the cockpit, however, and we are men and not sparrows. We do have the gift of understanding, even of the systems that we create ourselves. It is not too much to hope, therefore, that man can learn to fly the great engine of change that he has made and that it may carry us not to destruction but to that great goal for which the world was made.

INDEX

THE JOHNS HOPKINS PRESS
Designed by Gerard A. Valerio
Composed in Baskerville by Monotype Composition Company
Printed offset by Universal Lithographers, Inc.
on 50# Warren 1854
Bound by L. H. Jenkins, Inc.